Question Help consists of homework and practice questions to give students unlimited opportunities to master concepts. **Learning aids** walk students through the problem—giving them assistance when they need it most.

"I love the 'Help Me Solve This' feature. It really helped me figure out what I was doing wrong and how to fix a problem rather than just saying 'wrong' or 'right'."

— Student, Illinois State University

91%	90%	90%
eText	Study Plan	Dynamic Study Modules

Dynamic Study Modules use the latest developments in cognitive science and help students study chapter topics by adapting to their performance in real time.

% of students who found learning aids helpful

Pearson eText enhances student learning. Worked examples, videos, and interactive tutorials bring learning to life, while algorithmic practice and self-assessment opportunities test students' understanding of the material.

The **Gradebook** offers an easy way for you and your students to see their performance in your course.

89%

of students would tell their instructor to keep using MyLab Economics

For additional details visit: www.pearson.com/mylab/economics

Featured Applications in This Book

MICROECONOMICS

THEORY AND APPLICATIONS WITH CALCULUS

FIFTH EDITION

MICROECONOMICS

THEORY AND APPLICATIONS WITH CALCULUS

FIFTH EDITION

JEFFREY M. PERLOFF

University of California, Berkeley

Pearson

FOR LISA

Vice President, Business, Economics, and UK Courseware: Donna Battista

Director of Portfolio Management: Adrienne D'Ambrosio

Specialist Portfolio Manager: Christopher DeJohn

Editorial Assistant: Aly Grindall

Vice President, Product Marketing: Roxanne McCarley

Senior Product Marketer: Carlie Marvel

Product Marketing Assistant: Marianela Silvestri

Manager of Field Marketing, Business Publishing: Adam Goldstein

Field Marketing Manager: Ashley Bryan

Vice President, Production and Digital Studio, Arts and Business: Etain O'Dea

Director, Production and Digital Studio, Business and Economics: Ashley Santora

Managing Producer, Business: Alison Kalil

Content Producer: Carolyn Philips

Operations Specialist: Carol Melville

Design Lead: Kathryn Foot

Manager, Learning Tools: Brian Surette

Senior Learning Tools Strategist: Emily Biberger

Managing Producer, Digital Studio and GLP: James Bateman

Managing Producer, Digital Studio: Diane Lombardo

Digital Studio Producer: Melissa Honig

Digital Studio Producer: Alana Coles

Digital Content Team Lead: Noel Lotz

Digital Content Project Lead: Courtney Kamaouf

Full Service Project Management: Pearson CSC, Nicole Suddeth and Kathy Smith

Interior Design: Pearson CSC

Cover Design: Pearson CSC

Cover Art: Simon Gribkov/EyeEm, GettyImages

Printer/Binder: LSC Communications

Cover Printer: LSC Communications

ISBN 10: 0-13-518377-4

ISBN 13: 978-0-13-518377-9

Brief Contents

Contents

Preface

This book is a new type of intermediate microeconomics textbook. Previously, the choice was between books that use calculus to present formal theory dryly and with few, if any, applications to the real world and books that include applications but present theory using algebra and graphs only. This book uses calculus, algebra, and graphs to present microeconomic theory based on actual examples and then uses the theory to analyze real-world problems. My purpose is to show that economic theory has practical, problem-solving uses and is not an empty academic exercise.

This book shows how individuals, policymakers, and firms use microeconomic tools to analyze and resolve problems. For example, students learn that:

- individuals can draw on microeconomic theories when deciding whether to invest and whether to sign a contract that pegs prices to the government's measure of inflation;
- policymakers (and voters) can employ microeconomics to predict the impact of taxes, regulations, and other measures before they are enacted;
- lawyers and judges use microeconomics in antitrust, discrimination, and contract cases; and
- firms apply microeconomic principles to produce at least cost and maximize profit, select strategies, decide whether to buy from a market or to produce internally, and write contracts to provide optimal incentives for employees.

My experience in teaching microeconomics for the departments of economics at the Massachusetts Institute of Technology; the University of Pennsylvania; the University of California, Berkeley; the Department of Agricultural and Resource Economics at Berkeley; and the Wharton Business School has convinced me that students prefer this emphasis on real-world issues.

Changes in the Fifth Edition

This edition is substantially revised:

- It added an extensive Appendix on basic calculus (which was available only online in the previous edition).
- It includes two new features: Common Confusions and Unintended Consequences. Common Confusions describe a widely held belief that economic theory or evidence rejects. Unintended Consequences describe how some policies and other actions have potent side-effects beyond the intended ones.
- All the chapters are moderately to substantially revised and updated, including the many examples embedded in the chapters, Solved Problems, end-of-chapter problems, and other features.

- Of this edition's 128 Applications, 81% are new (26%) or revised (55%). Sixty percent of the Applications are international or concern countries other than the United States. In addition, we've added 23 Applications to MyLab Economics, bringing the total number of additional Applications online to 238.
- Compared to the previous edition, this edition has 7 additional figures (215 total), 2 more photos (52), and 4 new cartoons (22), which I claim illustrate important economic concepts.

Revised Chapters

Some of the major changes in the presentation of theories in the chapters include:

Supply and Demand. Chapter 2 was generally rewritten and has a revised section on taxes.

Consumer Theory. The most important changes to Chapters 3–5 include a major revision to the consumer surplus section, an embedded example based on UberX, more details about federal marginal tax rates, and a new Solved Problem.

Production and Costs. Chapter 6 has a new discussion of kinked isoquants based on self-driving trucks and a revised discussion of efficiency and a revised Challenge Solution. Chapter 7 also has a revised discussion of efficiency and a revised Challenge Solution.

Competition. Chapters 8 and 9 have revised Challenge Solutions and a Solved Problem, a new Solved Problem, a revised section comparing tariffs to quotas, a revised discussion of efficiency and market failures including adding a discussion of allocative inefficiency. This edition now systematically defines deadweight loss as a positive number in this chapter and in subsequent chapters.

General Equilibrium and Economic Welfare. Chapter 10 has a revised Solved Problem.

Monopoly. Chapter 11 has many changes. The previous section on Network Externalities was replaced with a new section, Internet Monopolies: Network Externalities, Behavioral Economics, and Natural Monopoly, which emphasizes new economic challenges in internet industries. Subsections include new discussions of two-sided markets and disruptive technologies. It includes a revised and a new Solved Problem.

Pricing and Advertising. Chapter 12 has many new examples. The key price discrimination analysis now uses Tesla car sales in the United States and in Europe (based on actual data, as always). Its discussions on identifying groups, two-part pricing, the mathematical parts of the Challenge Solution, and several figures are revised. One of the Solved Problems is new.

Game Theory and Oligopoly. Chapter 13 on game theory has two new Solved Problems. It uses new examples to illustrate the theory. It has a new two-sided market section. Its section on Dynamic Games is revised. It has new material on limit pricing and double auctions. Chapter 14 has revised discussions of strategic trade and differentiated products and new figures and a table.

Factor Markets. Chapter 15 includes a new discussion on the frequency of compounding. The Challenge Solution is revised.

Uncertainty. Chapter 16 has a revised section on the risk premium and now formally defines certainty equivalence.

Externalities and Public Goods. Chapter 17 has a new Solved Problem. The section on public goods is completely revised including the figure.

Asymmetric Information. Chapter 18 has revisions to the sections on Products of Unknown Quality and Universal Coverage. It includes a new section on noisy monopoly.

Challenges, Solved Problems, and End-of-Chapter Exercises

The Solved Problems (which show students how to answer problems using a step-by-step approach) and Challenges (which combine an Application with a Solved Problem) are very popular with students, so this edition increases the number by 6 to 116. After Chapter 1, each chapter starts with a Challenge (a problem based on an Application) and ends with its solution. In addition, many of the Solved Problems are linked to Applications. Each Solved Problem has at least one similar end-of-chapter exercise, which allows students to demonstrate that they've mastered the concept in the Solved Problem.

This edition has 809 end-of-chapter exercises, which is over 8% more than in the last edition. Of the total, 12% are new or revised and updated. Every end-of-chapter exercise is available in MyLab Economics. Students can click on the end-of-chapter exercise in the eText to go to MyLab Economics to complete the exercise online, get tutorial help, and receive instant feedback.

How This Book Differs from Others

Microeconomics: Theory and Applications with Calculus differs from most other microeconomics texts in four main ways, all of which help professors teach and students learn. First, it uses a mixture of calculus, algebra, and graphs to define economic theory. Second, it integrates estimated, real-world examples throughout the exposition, in addition to offering extended Applications. Third, it places greater emphasis on modern theories—such as industrial organization theories, game theory, transaction cost theory, information theory, contract theory, and behavioral economics—that are useful in analyzing actual markets. Fourth, it employs a step-by-step approach that demonstrates how to use microeconomic theory to solve problems and analyze policy issues.

To improve student results, I recommend pairing the text content with MyLab Economics, which is the teaching and learning platform that empowers you to reach every student. By combining trusted author content with digital tools and a flexible platform, MyLab personalizes the learning experience and will help your students learn and retain key course concepts while developing skills that future employers are seeking in their candidates. MyLab Economics allows professors increased flexibility in designing and teaching their courses. Learn more at www.pearson.com/mylab/economics.

Solving Teaching and Learning Challenges

In the features of the book and MyLab Economics, I show how to apply theory and analysis learned in the classroom to solving problems and understanding real-world market issues outside of class.

Using Calculus to Make Theory Clear to Students

Microeconomic theory is primarily the study of maximizing behavior. Calculus is particularly helpful in solving maximization problems, while graphs help illustrate how to maximize. This book combines calculus, algebra, graphs, and verbal arguments to make the theory as clear as possible.

Real-World Examples and Applications

To convince students that economics is practical and useful—not just a textbook exercise—this book presents theories using examples of real people and real firms based on actual market data rather than artificial examples. These real economic stories are integrated into the formal presentation of many economic theories, discussed in Applications, and analyzed in what-if policy discussions.

Integrated Real-World Examples. This book uses real-world examples throughout the narrative to illustrate many basic theories of microeconomics. Students learn the basic model of supply and demand using estimated supply-and-demand curves for corn and coffee. They analyze consumer choice by employing estimated indifference curves between live music and music tracks. They see estimates of the consumer welfare from UberX. They learn about production and cost functions using estimates from a wide variety of firms. Students see monopoly theory applied to a patented pharmaceutical, Botox. They use oligopoly theories to analyze the rivalry between United Airlines and American Airlines on the Chicago–Los Angeles route, and between Coke and Pepsi in the cola industry. They see Apple's monopoly pricing of iPads and learn about multimarket price discrimination through the use of data on how Tesla sets prices across countries.

Applications. The text includes many Applications at the end of sections that illustrate the versatility of microeconomic theory. The Applications focus on such diverse topics as:

- the derivation of an isoquant for semiconductors, using actual data;
- how 3D printing affects firms' decisions about scale and its flexibility over time and is undermining movie studios;
- the amount by which recipients value Christmas presents relative to the cost to gift givers;
- why oil companies that use fracking are more likely to shut down;
- whether buying flight insurance makes sense;
- whether going to college pays.

APPLICATION	Technological advances have made hydraulic fracturing—fracking—a practical
Welfare Effects of Allowing Fracking	means to extract natural gas as well as oil from shale formations that previously could not be exploited (see the Application "Fracking and Shutdowns" in Chapter 8). Opponents of fracking fear that it pollutes air and water and triggers earthquakes. Due to their opposition, governments limit or prohibit fracking in parts of the United States and Europe.

Hausman and Kellogg (2015) used estimated natural gas supply and demand curves to calculate the welfare effects of permitting fracking firms to enter the gas market. They found that the rightward shift of the supply curve reduced the U.S. natural gas price by 47% in 2013. As a result, consumer surplus increased substantially, particularly in the south central and midwestern United States, where the industrial and electric power industries use large quantities of gas. This drop in price was sufficient to reduce producer surplus. Hausman and Kellogg concluded that the total surplus increased by $48 billion, but noted that this calculation ignores any possible harmful environmental effects.

What-If Policy Analysis. This book uses economic models to probe the likely outcomes of changes in public policies. Students learn how to conduct what-if analyses of policies such as taxes, subsidies, barriers to entry, price floors and ceilings, quotas and tariffs, zoning, pollution controls, and licensing laws. The text analyzes the effects of taxes on virtually every type of market. The book also reveals the limits of economic theory for policy analysis. For example, to illustrate why attention to actual institutions is important, the text uses three different models to show how the effects of minimum wages vary across types of markets and institutions. Similarly, the text illustrates that a minimum wage law that is harmful in a competitive market may be desirable in certain noncompetitive markets.

Modern Theories

The first half of the book (Chapters 2–10) examines competitive markets and shows that competition has very desirable properties. The rest of the book (Chapters 11–19) concentrates on imperfectly competitive markets—in which firms have market power (the ability to profitably set price above the unit cost of production), firms and consumers are uncertain about the future and have limited information, a market has an externality, or a market fails to provide a public good. This book goes beyond basic microeconomic theory and looks at theories and applications from many important contemporary fields of economics. It extensively covers problems from resource economics, labor economics, international trade, public finance, and industrial organization. The book uses behavioral economics to discuss consumer choice, bandwagon effects on monopoly pricing over time, and the importance of time-varying discounting in explaining procrastination and in avoiding environmental disasters. This book differs from other microeconomics texts by using game theory throughout the second half rather than isolating the topic in a single chapter. The book introduces game theory in Chapter 13, analyzing both static games (such as the prisoners' dilemma) and multi-period games (such as collusion and preventing entry). Special attention is paid to auction strategies. Chapters 14, 16, 17, 18, and 19 employ game theory to analyze oligopoly behavior and many other topics. Unlike most texts, this book covers pure and mixed strategies and analyzes both normal-form and extensive-form games. The last two chapters draw from modern contract theory to extensively analyze adverse selection and moral hazard, unlike other texts that mention these topics only in passing, if at all. The text covers lemons markets, signaling, shirking prevention, and revealing information (including through contract choice).

Step-by-Step Problem Solving

Many instructors report that their biggest challenge in teaching microeconomics is helping students learn to solve new problems. This book is based on the belief that the best way to teach this important skill is to demonstrate problem solving repeatedly and then to give students exercises to do on their own. Each chapter (after Chapter 1) provides several Solved Problems that show students how to answer qualitative and quantitative problems using a step-by-step approach. Rather than empty arithmetic exercises demanding no more of students than employing algebra or a memorized mathematical formula, the Solved Problems focus on important economic issues such as analyzing government policies and determining firms' optimal strategies.

One Solved Problem uses game theory to examine why Intel and AMD use different advertising strategies in the central processing unit (CPU) market. Another shows how a monopolistically competitive airline equilibrium would change if fixed costs (such as fees for landing slots) rise. Others examine why firms charge different prices at factory stores than elsewhere and when markets for lemons exist, among many other topics.

The Solved Problems illustrate how to approach the formal end-of-chapter exercises. Students can solve some of the exercises using graphs or verbal arguments, while others require math.

SOLVED PROBLEM 18.1

MyLab Economics Solved Problem

Suppose that everyone in our used-car example is risk neutral; potential car buyers value lemons at $4,000 and good used cars at $8,000; the reservation price of lemon owners is $3,000; and the reservation price of owners of high-quality used cars is $7,000. The share of current owners who have lemons is θ. (In our previous example, the share was $\theta = \frac{1}{2} = 1,000/[1,000 + 1,000]$). For what values of θ do all the potential sellers sell their used cars? Describe the equilibrium.

Answer

1. *Determine how much buyers are willing to pay if all cars are sold.* Because buyers are risk neutral, if they believe that the probability of getting a lemon is θ, the most they are willing to pay for a car of unknown quality is

$$p = [\$8,000 \times (1 - \theta)] + (\$4,000 \times \theta) = \$8,000 - (\$4,000 \times \theta). \quad (18.1)$$

For example, $p = \$6,000$ if $\theta = \frac{1}{2}$ and $p = \$7,000$ if $\theta = \frac{1}{4}$.

2. *Solve for the values of θ such that all the cars are sold, and describe the equilibrium.* All owners will sell if the market price equals or exceeds their reservation price, $7,000. Using Equation 18.1, we know that the market (equilibrium) price is $7,000 or more if a quarter or fewer of the used cars are lemons, $\theta \leq \frac{1}{4}$. Thus, for $\theta \leq \frac{1}{4}$, all the cars are sold at the price given in Equation 18.1.

MyLab Economics Videos

Today's students learn best when they analyze and discuss topics in the text outside of class. To further students' understanding of what they are reading and discussing in the classroom, we provide a set of videos in MyLab Economics. In these videos, Tony Lima presents key figures, tables, and concepts in step-by-step animations with audio explanations that discuss the economics behind each step.

Developing Career Skills

This book helps you develop valuable career skills. Whether you want to work in business, government, academia, or in other areas, a solid knowledge of economics is invaluable. Employers know that you need economic skills to perform well. They also know that the more rigorous and mathematically based your training, the better you will be at logical thinking.

- Studies show that job seekers with an undergraduate degree who have economics and math training generally receive higher salaries than those with degrees in most other fields. Law schools and MBA programs are more likely to admit students with economics and math training than others, because they know how useful these skills are as well as the training in logic thinking. This training also increases your chances of getting into top graduate programs in economics, agricultural and resource economics, public policy, urban planning, and other similar fields, which is a necessary step for many careers in academia, government, and consulting.
- This book starts by illustrating how to use economic reasoning to analyze and solve a variety of problems. It trains you to use logical analysis based on empirical evidence. You will learn how to apply a variety of verbal, graphical, and mathematical techniques to solve the types of problems that governments, firms, and other potential employers face on a daily basis. In addition to training you in traditional economic analysis, this book shows you how to use game theory, behavioral economics, and other cutting-edge theories to confront modern-day challenges. For example, you'll see how firms develop contracts to motivate workers and executives to perform well, analyze how oligopolistic firms develop strategies; why online platforms (two-sided markets) that bring buyers and sellers together, such as eBay, are highly concentrated; and how disruptive innovations such as 3D printing affect markets.

Alternative Organizations

Because instructors cover material in many different orders, the text permits maximum flexibility. The most common approach to teaching microeconomics is to cover some or all of the chapters in their given sequence. Common variants include:

- presenting uncertainty (Sections 16.1 through 16.3) immediately after consumer theory;
- covering competitive factor markets (Section 15.1) immediately after competition (Chapters 8 and 9);
- introducing game theory (Chapter 13) early in the course; and
- covering general equilibrium and welfare issues (Chapter 10) at the end of the course instead of immediately after the competitive model.

Instructors can present the material in Chapters 13–19 in various orders, although Section 16.4 should follow Chapter 15, and Chapter 19 should follow Chapter 18 if both are covered.

Many business school courses skip consumer theory (and possibly some aspects of supply and demand) to allow more time for the topics covered in the second half of the book. Business school faculty may want to place particular emphasis on game theory, strategies, oligopoly, and monopolistic competition (Chapters 13 and 14); capital markets (Chapter 15); uncertainty (Chapter 16); and modern contract theory (Chapters 18 and 19).

Instructor Teaching Resources

This book has a full range of supplementary materials that support teaching and learning. This program comes with the following teaching resources:

Supplements available to instructors at www.pearsonhighered.com	Features of the Supplement
Instructor's Manual Authored by Leonie Stone of SUNY Geneseo	• *Chapter Outlines* include key terminology, teaching notes, and lecture suggestions. • *Teaching Tips* and *Additional Applications* provide tips for alternative ways to cover the material and brief reminders on additional help to provide students. • *Solutions* are provided for all problems in the book.
Test Bank Authored by Xin Fang of Hawaii Pacific University	• Multiple-choice problems of varying levels of complexity, suitable for homework assignments and exams • Many of these draw on current news and events
Computerized TestGen	TestGen allows instructors to: • Customize, save, and generate classroom tests • Edit, add, or delete questions from the Test Item Files • Analyze test results • Organize a database of tests and student results.

PowerPoints Authored by James Dearden of Lehigh University	• Slides include all the graphs, tables, and equations in the textbook, as well as lecture notes.
	• PowerPoints meet accessibility standards for students with disabilities. Features include, but are not limited to:
	  • Keyboard and Screen Reader access
	  • Alternative text for images
	  • High color contrast between background and foreground colors

Acknowledgments

This book evolved from my earlier, less-mathematical, intermediate microeconomics textbook. I thank the many faculty members and students who helped me produce both books, as well as Jane Tufts, who provided invaluable editorial help on my earlier text. I was very lucky that Sylvia Mallory, who worked on the earlier book, was my development editor on the first edition of this book as well. Sylvia worked valiantly to improve my writing style and helped to shape and improve every aspect of the book's contents and appearance.

Denise Clinton, Digital Editor, and Adrienne D'Ambrosio, my outstanding Executive Acquisitions Editor, worked closely with Sylvia and me in planning the book and were instrumental in every phase of the project. In this edition, Chris DeJohn, Executive Portfolio Manager, and Carolyn Philips, Content Producer, were involved in each step of this revision and provided invaluable help with the online resources.

I have an enormous debt of gratitude to my students at MIT; the University of Pennsylvania; and the University of California, Berkeley, who dealt patiently with my various approaches to teaching them microeconomics and made useful (and generally polite) suggestions. Peter Berck, Ethan Ligon, and Larry Karp, my colleagues at the University of California, Berkeley, made many useful suggestions. Guojun He, Yann Panassie, and Hugo Salgado were incredibly helpful in producing figures, researching many of the Applications, or making constructive comments on chapter drafts.

Many people were very generous in providing me with data, models, and examples for the various Applications and Solved Problems in various editions of this book, including among others: Thomas Bauer (University of Bochum); Peter Berck (deceased); James Brander (University of British Columbia); Alex Chun (Business Intelligence Manager at Sungevity); Leemore Dafny (Northwestern University); Lucas Davis (University of California, Berkeley); James Dearden (Lehigh University); Farid Gasmi (Université des Sciences Sociales); Avi Goldfarb (University of Toronto); Claudia Goldin (Harvard University); Rachel Goodhue (University of California, Davis); William Greene (New York University); Nile Hatch (University of Illinois); Larry Karp (University of California, Berkeley); Ryan Kellogg (University of Michigan); Arthur Kennickell (Federal Reserve, Washington); Fahad Khalil (University of Washington); Lutz Killian (University of Michigan); J. Paul Leigh (University of California, Davis); Christopher Knittel (Massachusetts Institute of Technology); Jean-Jacques Laffont (deceased); Ulrike Malmendier (University of California, Berkeley); Karl D. Meilke (University of Guelph); Eric Muehlegger (Harvard University); Giancarlo Moschini (Iowa State University); Michael Roberts (North Carolina State University); Junichi Suzuki (University of Toronto); Catherine Tucker (MIT); Harald Uhlig (University of Chicago); Quang Vuong (Université des Sciences Sociales, Toulouse, and University of Southern California); and Joel Waldfogel (University of Minnesota).

I am grateful to the many teachers of microeconomics who spent untold hours reading and commenting on chapter drafts. Many of the best ideas in this book are due to the following individuals who provided valuable comments at various stages:

R. K. Anderson, *Texas A&M*
Fernando Aragon, *Simon Fraser University*
Richard Beil, *Auburn University*
Kenny Bell, *University of California, Berkeley*
Robert A. Berman, *American University*
Douglas Blair, *Rutgers University*
James Brander, *University of British Columbia*
Jurgen Brauer, *Augusta State University*

Margaret Bray, *London School of Economics*
Helle Bunzel, *Iowa State University*
Paul Calcott, *Victoria University of Wellington*
Lauren Calimeris, *University of Colorado at Boulder*
Anoshua Chaudhuri, *San Francisco State University*
Finn Christensen, *Towson University*
Anthony Davies, *Duquesne University*
James Dearden, *Lehigh University*

Stephen Devadoss, *Texas Tech University*

Wayne Edwards, *University of Alaska, Anchorage*

Steven Elliot, *University of Miami*

Susan Elmes, *Columbia University*

Patrick M. Emerson, *Oregon State University*

Eduardo Faingold, *Yale University*

Rachael Goodhue, *University of California, Davis*

Ron Goettler, *Carnegie Mellon University, Doha, Qatar*

Thomas Gresik, *University of Notre Dame*

Barnali Gupta, *Miami University*

Per Svejstrup Hansen, *University of Southern Denmark*

Joannes Jacobsen, *University of the Faroe Islands*

Byoung Heon Jun, *Korea University*

Rebecca Judge, *St. Olaf College*

Johnson Kakeu, *Georgia Institute of Technology*

Süleyman Keçeli, *Pamukkale University*

Vijay Krishna, *University of North Carolina, Chapel Hill*

Alberto Lamadrid, *Lehigh University*

Stephen Lauermann, *University of Michigan*

Gordon Lenjosek, *University of Ottawa*

Tony Lima, *Cal State East Bay*

Holly Liu, *UC Davis*

Urzo Luttmer, *Dartmouth University*

Vikram Manjunath, *Texas A&M University*

Carrie A. Meyer, *George Mason University*

Joshua B. Miller, *University of Minnesota, Twin Cities*

Laurie Miller, *University of Nebraska Lincoln*

Stephen M. Miller, *University of Nevada, Las Vegas*

Olivia Mitchell, *University of Pennsylvania*

Jeffery Miron, *Harvard University*

Shalah Mostashari, *Texas A&M University*

Felix Naschold, *University of Wyoming*

Orgul Ozturk, *University of Southern Carolina*

Alexandre Padilla, *Metropolitan State College of Denver*

Michael R. Ransom, *Brigham Young University*

Alfonso Sánchez-Peñalver, *University of Massachusetts, Boston*

Riccardo Scarpa, *University of Waikato, New Zealand*

Burkhard C. Schipper, *University of California, Davis*

Riccardo Scarpa, *University of Waikato*

Galina A. Schwartz, *University of California, Berkeley*

Kevin Shaver, *University of Pittsburgh*

Steven Snyder, *Lehigh University*

Barry Sopher, *Rutgers University*

Ilya Sorvachev, *New Economic School, Russia*

Stephen Snyder, *University of Pittsburgh*

Scott Templeton, *Clemson University*

Etku Unver, *Boston College*

Ruth Uwaifo, *Georgia Institute of Technology*

Rodrigo Velez, *Texas A&M University*

Ron S. Warren, Jr., *University of Georgia*

Ryan Blake Williams, *TexasTech University*

Christopher Wright, *Montana State University*

Bruce Wydick, *University of California, San Francisco*

Albert Zeveley, *Wharton School, University of Pennsylvania*

I am particularly grateful to Jim Brander of the University of British Columbia who has given me many deep and insightful comments on this book. One of my biggest debts is to Jim Dearden, who not only provided incisive comments on every aspect of my earlier textbook, but also wrote a number of the end-of-chapter exercises. I am very grateful to Ethan Ligon for co-authoring the Calculus Appendix.

For this edition, my biggest debts are to Tony Lima and Gordon Lenjosek. Tony prepared the many excellent MyLab Economics Videos. Gordon extremely carefully checked for typographic and other errors in the previous edition and suggested better ways to present many topics.

In addition, I thank Bob Solow, the world's finest economics teacher, who showed me how to simplify models without losing their essence. I've also learned a great deal over the years about economics and writing from my co-authors on other projects, especially Dennis Carlton (my co-author on *Modern Industrial Organization*), Jackie Persons, Steve Salop, Michael Wachter, Larry Karp, Peter Berck, Amos Golan, George Judge, Ximing Wu, and Dan Rubinfeld (whom I thank for still talking to me despite my decision to write microeconomics textbooks).

It was a pleasure to work with the good people at Pearson CSC, who were incredibly helpful in producing this book. Kathy Smith and Nicole Suddeth did a superlative job of supervising the production process and assembling the extended publishing team. I also want to acknowledge, with gratitude, the efforts of Melissa Honig in developing the MyLab Economics course, along with Noel Lotz and Courtney Kamauf.

Finally, I thank my family, Jackie Persons and Lisa Perloff, for their great patience and support during the nearly endless writing process. And I apologize for misusing their names—and those of my other relatives and friends—in this book!

J.M.P.

Introduction

1

An Economist's Theory of Reincarnation: If you're good, you come back on a higher level. Cats come back as dogs, dogs come back as horses, and people—if they've been really good like George Washington—come back as money.

If each of us could get all the food, clothing, and toys we want without working, no one would study economics. Unfortunately, most of the good things in life are scarce—we can't all have as much as we want. Thus, scarcity is the mother of economics.

Microeconomics is the study of how individuals and firms make themselves as well off as possible in a world of scarcity, and the consequences of those individual decisions for markets and the entire economy. In studying microeconomics, we examine how individual consumers and firms make decisions and how the interaction of many individual decisions affects markets.

Microeconomics is often called *price theory* to emphasize the important role that prices play in determining market outcomes. Microeconomics explains how the actions of all buyers and sellers determine prices, and how prices influence the decisions and actions of individual buyers and sellers.

In this chapter, we discuss three main topics	1. **Microeconomics: The Allocation of Scarce Resources.** Microeconomics is the study of the allocation of scarce resources.
	2. **Models.** Economists use models to make testable predictions.
	3. **Uses of Microeconomic Models in Your Life and Career.** Individuals, governments, and firms use microeconomic models and predictions in decision making.

1.1 Microeconomics: The Allocation of Scarce Resources

Individuals and firms allocate their limited resources to make themselves as well off as possible. Consumers select the mix of goods and services that makes them as happy as possible given their limited wealth. Firms decide which goods to produce, where to produce them, how much to produce to maximize their profits, and how to produce those levels of output at the lowest cost by using more or less of various inputs such as labor, capital, materials, and energy. The owners of a depletable natural resource such as oil decide when to use it. Government decision makers decide which goods and services the government will produce and whether to subsidize, tax, or regulate industries and consumers to benefit consumers, firms, or government employees.

Trade-Offs

People make trade-offs because they can't have everything. A society faces three key trade-offs:

1. **Which goods and services to produce.** If a society produces more cars, it must produce fewer of other goods and services, because it has only a limited amount of *resources*—workers, raw materials, capital, and energy—available to produce goods.
2. **How to produce.** To produce a given level of output, a firm must use more of one input if it uses less of another input. For example, cracker and cookie manufacturers switch between palm oil and coconut oil, depending on which is less expensive.
3. **Who gets the goods and services.** The more of society's goods and services you get, the less someone else gets.

Who Makes the Decisions

The government may make these three allocation decisions explicitly, or the final decisions may reflect the interaction of independent decisions by many individual consumers and firms. In the former Soviet Union, the government told manufacturers how many cars of each type to make and which inputs to use to make them. The government also decided which consumers would get cars.

In most other countries, how many cars of each type are produced and who gets them are determined by how much it costs to make cars of a particular quality in the least expensive way and how much consumers are willing to pay for them. More consumers would own a handcrafted Rolls-Royce and fewer would buy a mass-produced Toyota Camry if a Rolls were not 14 times more expensive than a Camry.

How Prices Determine Allocations

Prices link the decisions about *which goods and services to produce, how to produce them*, and *who gets them*. Prices influence the decisions of individual consumers and firms, and the interactions of these decisions by consumers, firms, and the government determine price.

Interactions between consumers and firms take place in a **market**, which is an exchange mechanism that allows buyers to trade with sellers. A market may be a town square where people go to trade food and clothing, or it may be an international telecommunications network over which people buy and sell financial securities. Typically, when we talk about a single market, we are referring to trade in a single good or a group of goods that are closely related, such as soft drinks, movies, novels, or automobiles.

Most of this book concerns how prices are determined within a market. We show that the organization of the market, especially the number of buyers and sellers in the market and the amount of information they have, helps determine whether the price equals the cost of production. We also show that in the absence of a market (and market price), serious problems, such as high pollution levels, result.

APPLICATION

Twinkie Tax

Many government actions affect prices and hence the allocation decisions.

Many U.S., Australian, British, Canadian, New Zealand, and Taiwanese jurisdictions have or are considering imposing a *Twinkie tax* on unhealthful fatty and sweet foods or a tax on sugary soft drinks to reduce obesity and cholesterol problems, particularly among children. A 2017 poll found that 57% of the U.S. public supports "taxing soda and other sugary drinks to raise money for pre-school and children's health programs and help address the problem of obesity."

In recent years, many communities around the world debated and some passed new taxes on sugar-sweetened soft drinks. New beverage taxes went into effect in Mexico in 2014; Cook County, Illinois, in 2016; United Kingdom in 2018; and San Francisco, California, in 2018. At least 34 states differentially tax soft drinks, candy, chewing gum, and snack foods such as potato chips. These taxes affect prices and decisions people make. In addition, many U.S. school districts ban soft drink vending machines. These bans discourage consumption, as would an extremely high tax.

Taxes and bans affect *which foods are produced*, as firms offer new low-fat and low-sugar products, and *how fast-foods are produced*, as manufacturers reformulate their products to lower their tax burden. These taxes also influence *who gets these goods* as consumers, especially children, replace them with relatively less expensive, untaxed products.[1]

1.2 Models

Everything should be made as simple as possible, but not simpler. —Albert Einstein

To *explain* how individuals and firms allocate resources and how market prices are determined, economists use a **model**: a description of the relationship between two or more variables. Economists also use models to *predict* how a change in one variable will affect another variable.

APPLICATION

Income Threshold Model and China

According to an *income threshold model*, people whose incomes are below a threshold do not buy a particular consumer durable, while many people whose income exceeds that threshold buy it.

If this theory is correct, we predict that, as most people's incomes rise above the threshold in lower-income countries, consumer durable purchases will increase from near zero to large numbers virtually overnight. This prediction is consistent with evidence from Malaysia, where the income threshold for buying a car is about $4,000.

In China, incomes have risen rapidly and now exceed the threshold levels for many types of durable goods. In response to higher incomes, Chinese car purchases have taken off. For example, Li Rifu, a 46-year-old Chinese farmer and watch

---

[1]The sources for Applications are available at the back of this book.

repairman, thought that buying a car would improve the odds that his 22- and 24-year-old sons would find girlfriends, marry, and produce grandchildren. Soon after Mr. Li purchased his Geely King Kong for the equivalent of $9,000, both sons met girlfriends, and his older son got married.

Given the rapid increase in Chinese incomes in the past couple of decades, four-fifths of all new cars sold in China are bought by first-time customers. An influx of first-time buyers was responsible for Chinese car sales increasing by a factor of nearly 18 between 2000 and 2017. In 2005, China produced fewer than half as many cars as the United States. In 2017, China was by far the largest producer of cars in the world, producing one out of every three cars in the world. It produced nearly three times as many cars as the United States—the second largest producer—as well as 39% more than the entire European Union. One out of every three cars is produced in China.

Simplifications by Assumption

We stated the income threshold model verbally, but we could have presented it graphically or mathematically. Regardless of how the model is described, an economic model is a simplification of reality that contains only reality's most important features. Without simplifications, it is difficult to make predictions because the real world is too complex to analyze fully.

By analogy, if the owner's manual accompanying a new DVD recorder had a diagram showing the relationships among all the parts in the recorder, the diagram would be overwhelming and useless. But a diagram that includes a photo of the buttons on the front of the machine, with labels describing the purpose of each, is useful and informative.

Economists make many *assumptions* to simplify their models.[2] When using the income threshold model to explain car-purchasing behavior in China, we assume that factors other than income, such as the vehicles' color choices, are irrelevant to the decision to buy cars. Therefore, we ignore the color of cars that are sold in China when we describe the relationship between average income and the number of cars that consumers want. If our assumption is correct, we make our auto market analysis simpler without losing important details by ignoring color. If we're wrong and these ignored issues are important, our predictions may be inaccurate.

Throughout this book, we start with strong assumptions to simplify our models. Later, we add complexities. For example, in most of the book, we assume that consumers know each firm's price for a product. In many markets, such as the New York Stock Exchange, this assumption is realistic. However, it is not realistic in other markets, such as the market for used automobiles, in which consumers do not know the prices that each firm charges. To devise an accurate model for markets in which consumers have limited information, in Chapter 16, we add consumer uncertainty about price into the model.

---

[2]An engineer, an economist, and a physicist are stranded on a deserted island with a can of beans but no can opener. How should they open the can? The engineer proposes hitting the can with a rock. The physicist suggests building a fire under the can to increase pressure and burst it open. The economist thinks for a while and then says, "Assume that we have a can opener. . . ."

An alternative theory.

Testing Theories

Blore's Razor: Given a choice between two theories, take the one which is funnier.

Economic *theory* is the development and use of a model to formulate *hypotheses*, which are predictions about cause and effect. We are interested in models that make clear, testable predictions, such as "If the price rises, the quantity demanded falls." A theory stating that "People's behaviors depend on their tastes, and their tastes change randomly at random intervals" is not very useful because it does not lead to testable predictions.

Economists test theories by checking whether predictions are correct. If a prediction does not come true, economists may reject the theory.[3] Economists use a model until it is refuted by evidence or until a better model is developed.

A good model makes sharp, clear predictions that are consistent with reality. Some very simple models make sharp predictions that are incorrect, and other, more complex models make ambiguous predictions—in which any outcome is possible—that are untestable. The skill in model building is to chart a middle ground.

The purpose of this book is to teach you how to think like an economist, in the sense that you can build testable theories using economic models or apply existing models to new situations. Although economists think alike, in that they develop and use testable models, they often disagree. One may present a logically consistent argument that prices will go up in the next quarter. Another economist, using a different but equally logical theory, may contend that prices will fall in that quarter. If the economists are reasonable, they agree that pure logic alone cannot resolve their dispute. Indeed, they agree that they'll have to use empirical evidence—facts about the real world—to determine which prediction is correct.

Maximizing Subject to Constraints

Although one economist's model may differ from another's, a key assumption in most microeconomic models is that individuals allocate their scarce resources to make themselves as well off as possible. Of all the affordable combinations of goods,

---

[3]We can use evidence of whether a theory's predictions are correct to refute the theory but not to prove it. If a model's prediction is inconsistent with what actually happened, the model must be wrong, so we reject it. Even if the model's prediction is consistent with reality, however, the model's prediction may be correct for the wrong reason. Hence, we cannot prove that the model is correct—we can only fail to reject it.

consumers pick the bundle of goods that gives them the most possible enjoyment. Firms try to maximize their profits given limited resources and existing technology. That resources are limited plays a crucial role in these models. Were it not for scarcity, people could consume unlimited amounts of goods and services, and sellers could become rich beyond limit.

As we show throughout this book, the maximizing behavior of individuals and firms determines society's three main allocation decisions: which goods are produced, how they are produced, and who gets them. For example, diamond-studded pocket combs will be sold only if firms find it profitable to sell them. The firms will make and sell these combs only if consumers value the combs at least as much as it costs the firm to produce them. Consumers will buy the combs only if they get more pleasure from the combs than they would from other goods they could buy with the same resources.

Many of the models that we examine are based on maximizing an objective that is subject to a constraint. Consumers maximize their well-being subject to a budget constraint, which says that their resources limit how many goods they can buy. Firms maximize profits subject to technological and other constraints. Governments may try to maximize the welfare of consumers or firms subject to constraints imposed by limited resources and the behavior of consumers and firms. We cover the formal economic analysis of maximizing behavior in Chapters 2 through 19 and review the underlying mathematics in the Calculus Appendix at the end of the book.

Positive Versus Normative

Those are my principles. If you don't like them I have others. —Groucho Marx

Using models of maximizing behavior sometimes leads to predictions that seem harsh or heartless. For instance, a World Bank economist predicted that if an African government used price controls to keep the price of food low during a drought, food shortages would occur and people would starve. The predicted outcome is awful, but the economist was not heartless. The economist was only making a scientific prediction about the relationship between cause and effect: Price controls (cause) lead to food shortages and starvation (effect).

Such a scientific prediction is known as a **positive statement**: a testable hypothesis about matters of fact such as cause-and-effect relations. *Positive* does not mean that we are certain about the truth of our statement; it indicates only that we can test whether it is true.

If the World Bank economist is correct, should the government control prices? If government policymakers believe the economist's predictions, they know that the low prices will help consumers who are able to buy as much food as they want, and hurt both the food sellers and those who are unable to buy as much food as they want, some of whom may die from malnutrition. As a result, the government's decision of whether to use price controls turns on whether the government cares more about the winners or the losers. In other words, to decide on its policy, the government makes a value judgment.

Instead of making a prediction and testing it and then making a value judgment to decide whether to use price controls, government policymakers could make a value judgment directly. The value judgment could be based on the belief that "because people *should* have prepared for the drought, the government should not try to help them by keeping food prices low" or "people should be protected against price gouging during a drought, so the government should use price controls."

These two statements are *not* scientific predictions. Each is a value judgment, or **normative statement**: a conclusion as to whether something is good or bad. A normative statement cannot be tested because a value judgment cannot be refuted by evidence.

It is a prescription rather than a prediction. A normative statement concerns what somebody believes should happen; a positive statement concerns what will happen.

Although a normative conclusion can be drawn without first conducting a positive analysis, a policy debate will be more informed if positive analyses are conducted first.[4] Suppose your normative belief is that the government should help the poor. Should you vote for a candidate who advocates a higher minimum wage (a law that requires firms to pay wages at or above a specified level); a European-style welfare system (guaranteeing health care, housing, and other basic goods and services); an end to our current welfare system; a negative income tax (the less income a person receives, the more that person receives from the government); or job training programs? Positive economic analysis can be used to predict whether these programs will benefit poor people but *not* whether these programs are good or bad. Using these predictions and your value judgment, you decide for whom to vote.

Economists' emphasis on positive analysis has implications for what they study and even their use of language. For example, many economists stress that they study people's *wants* rather than their needs. Although people need certain minimum levels of food, shelter, and clothing to survive, most people in developed economies have enough money to buy goods well in excess of the minimum levels necessary to maintain life. Consequently, calling something a *need* in a wealthy country is often a value judgment. You almost certainly have been told by an elder that "you *need* a college education." That person was probably making a value judgment—"you *should* go to college"—rather than a scientific prediction that you will suffer terrible economic deprivation if you don't go to college. We can't test such value judgments, but we can test hypotheses such as "people with a college education earn substantially more than comparable people with only a high school education."

New Theories

One of the strengths of economics is that it is continually evolving, for two reasons. First, economists—like physicists, biologists, and other scientists—are always trying to improve their understanding of the world around them.

For example, traditional managerial textbooks presented theories based on the assumptions that decision makers always optimize: They do the best they can with their limited resources. While we cover these traditional theories, we also present another recently developed approach referred to as *behavioral economics*, which is the study of how psychological biases and cognitive limits can prevent managers and others from optimizing.

Second, economic theory evolves out of necessity. Unlike those who work in the physical and biological sciences, economists and managers also have to develop new ways to think about *disruptive innovations*. Although most innovations are incremental, some are sufficiently disruptive to dramatically change the way an industry is structured—or even to create new industries and destroy old ones.

The internet is an example of a disruptive innovation, which led to other disruptions. Online retailing has displaced much traditional brick-and-mortar retailing, online payment systems have largely replaced cash and checks, and online media, especially social media, have changed the way most people acquire and transmit information.

To analyze the economic effects of the internet and other disruptive innovations, economists have extended established theories and developed new ones. For example,

---

[4]Some economists draw the normative conclusion that, as social scientists, we economists should restrict ourselves to positive analyses. Others argue that we shouldn't give up our right to make value judgments just like the next person (who happens to be biased, prejudiced, and pigheaded, unlike us).

the internet has given rise to many services that allow two groups of users to interact—such as auction services, dating sites, job matching services, and payment services. In response, economists have developed the theory of such *two-sided* markets, which has influenced court decisions and government policy toward such markets. This book describes economic theories of the internet and of two-sided markets, along with other recent developments in economics.

1.3   Uses of Microeconomic Models in Your Life and Career

Have you ever imagined a world without hypothetical situations?

Because microeconomic models *explain* why economic decisions are made and allow us to make *predictions*, they can be very useful for individuals, governments, and firms in making decisions. Throughout this book, we consider examples of how microeconomics aids in actual decision making. Here, we briefly look at some uses by individuals and governments.

Individuals use microeconomics to make purchasing and other decisions. Examples include considering inflation when choosing whether to rent an apartment (Chapter 4); determining whether going to college is a good investment (Chapter 15); deciding whether to invest in stocks or bonds (Chapter 16); determining whether to buy insurance (Chapter 16); and knowing whether you should pay a lawyer by the hour or a percentage of any award (Chapter 19).

Microeconomics can help citizens make voting decisions based on candidates' views on economic issues. Elected and appointed government officials use economic models in many ways. Recent administrations have placed increased emphasis on economic analysis. Economic and environmental impact studies are required before many projects can commence. The President's Council of Economic Advisers and other federal economists analyze and advise national government agencies on the likely economic effects of all major policies.

Indeed, often governments use microeconomic models to predict the probable impact of a policy. We show how to predict the likely impact of a tax on the tax revenues raised (Chapter 2), the effects of trade policies such as tariffs and quotas on markets (Chapter 9), and the effects on collusion of governments posting the results of bidding (Chapter 14). Governments also use economics to decide how best to prevent pollution and global warming (Chapter 17).

Decisions by firms reflect microeconomic analysis. Firms price discriminate (charge individuals different prices) or bundle goods to increase their profits (Chapter 12). Strategic decisions concerning pricing, setting quantities, advertising, or entering into a market can be predicted using game theory (Chapter 13). An example in an oligopolistic market is the competition between American Airlines and United Airlines on the Chicago–Los Angeles route (Chapter 14). When a mining company should extract ore depends on interest rates (Chapter 15). A firm decides whether to offer employees deferred payments to ensure they work hard (Chapter 19).

Thus, this book will help you develop skills in economic analysis that are crucial in careers such as those in economics, business, law, and many others. Some of you will get jobs that use economic analysis intensively, such as working as an economist or setting prices or assessing financial investment options for firms. Others will use your knowledge of economics in both your work to analyze the likely outcomes from government actions and other events.

SUMMARY

1. **Microeconomics: The Allocation of Scarce Resources.**
Microeconomics is the study of the allocation of scarce resources. Consumers, firms, and governments must make allocation decisions. A society faces three key trade-offs: which goods and services to produce, how to produce them, and who gets them. These decisions are interrelated and depend on the prices that consumers and firms face and on government actions. Market prices affect the decisions of individual consumers and firms, and the interaction of the decisions of individual consumers and firms determines market prices. The organization of the market, especially the number of firms in the market and the information consumers and firms have, plays an important role in determining whether the market price is equal to or higher than the cost of producing an additional unit of output.

2. **Models.** Models based on economic theories are used to answer questions about how some change, such as a tax increase, will affect various sectors of the economy in the future. A good theory is simple to use and makes clear, testable predictions that are not refuted by evidence. Most microeconomic models are based on maximizing behavior. Economists use models to construct *positive* hypotheses concerning how a cause leads to an effect. These positive questions can be tested. In contrast, *normative* statements, which are value judgments, cannot be tested.

3. **Uses of Microeconomic Models in Your Life and Career.** Individuals, governments, and firms use microeconomic models and predictions to make decisions. For example, to maximize its profits, a firm needs to know consumers' decision-making criteria, the trade-offs between various ways of producing and marketing its product, government regulations, and other factors. You can use economic analysis in many different careers, particularly in economics and business.

2 Supply and Demand

Talk is cheap because supply exceeds demand.

CHALLENGE

Quantities and Prices of Genetically Modified Foods

Countries around the globe are debating whether to permit firms to grow or sell genetically modified (GM) foods, which have their DNA altered through genetic engineering rather than through conventional breeding.[1] The introduction of GM techniques can affect both the quantity of a crop farmer's supply and whether consumers want to buy that crop. Using GM techniques, farmers can produce more output at a given cost. Common GM crops include canola, corn, cotton, rice, soybean, and sugar beet.

At least 29 countries grow GM food crops, which are mostly herbicide-resistant varieties of corn (maize), soybean, and canola (oilseed rape). Developing countries grow more GM crops than developed countries, though the United States plants 40% of worldwide GM acreage. The largest GM-producing country is the United States, followed by Brazil, Argentina, India, Canada, and China.

According to some polls, 70% of consumers in Europe object to GM foods. Fears cause some consumers to refuse to buy a GM crop. Consumers in other countries, such as the United States, are less concerned about GM foods. Only about one in six Americans care "a great deal" about GM foods. However, even in the United States, a 2017 ABC poll found that 52% of U.S. consumers believe that GM foods are generally unsafe to eat. The U.S. National Academy of Science reported that it could find no evidence to support claims that genetically modified organisms are dangerous for either the environment or human health. A letter signed by 131 Nobel Prize winners concludes that these fears are unjustified.

Nonetheless, as of 2018, 64 nations require labeling of GM foods, including European Union countries, Japan, Australia, Brazil, Russia, China, and the United States. Consumers are unlikely to avoid GM crops if products are unlabeled.

Will the use of GM seeds lead to lower prices and more food sold? What happens to prices and quantities sold if many consumers refuse to buy GM crops? We will use the models in this chapter to answer these questions at the end of the chapter.

To analyze questions concerning the price and quantity responses from introducing new products or technologies, imposing government regulations or taxes, or other events, economists may use the *supply-and-demand model*. When asked, "What is the most important

---

[1]Sources for Applications and Challenges appear at the back of the book.

thing you know about economics?" many people reply, "Supply equals demand." This statement is shorthand for one of the simplest yet most powerful models of economics. The supply-and-demand model describes how consumers and suppliers interact to determine the price and the quantity of a good or service. To use the model, you need to determine three things: buyers' behavior, sellers' behavior, and their interaction.

After reading that grandiose claim, you might ask, "Is that all there is to economics? Can I become an expert economist that fast?" The answer to both questions, of course, is no. In addition, you need to learn the limits of this model and which other models to use when this one does not apply. (You must also learn the economists' secret handshake.)

Even with its limitations, the supply-and-demand model is the most widely used economic model. It provides a good description of how markets function, and it works particularly well in markets that have many buyers and sellers, such as most agricultural and labor markets. Like all good theories, the supply-and-demand model can be tested—and possibly proven false. But in markets where it is applicable, it allows us to make accurate predictions easily.

In this chapter, we examine eight main topics

1. **Demand.** The quantity of a good or service that consumers demand depends on price and other factors such as consumers' incomes and the prices of related goods.

2. **Supply.** The quantity of a good or service that firms supply depends on price and other factors such as the cost of inputs that firms use to produce the good or service.

3. **Market Equilibrium.** The interaction between the consumers' demand curve and the firms' supply curve determines the market price and quantity of a good or service that is bought and sold.

4. **Shocking the Equilibrium: Comparative Statics.** Changes in a factor that affect demand (such as consumers' incomes), supply (such as a rise in the price of inputs), or a new government policy (such as a new tax) alter the market or *equilibrium* price and quantity of a good.

5. **Elasticities.** Given estimates of summary statistics called *elasticities*, economists can forecast the effects of changes in taxes and other factors on market price and quantity.

6. **Effects of a Sales Tax.** How a sales tax increase affects the price and quantity of a good, and whether the tax falls more heavily on consumers or on suppliers, depend on the supply and demand curves.

7. **Quantity Supplied Need Not Equal Quantity Demanded.** If the government regulates the prices in a market, the quantity supplied might not equal the quantity demanded.

8. **When to Use the Supply-and-Demand Model.** The supply-and-demand model applies to competitive markets only.

2.1 Demand

The **quantity demanded** is the amount of a good that consumers are *willing* to buy at a given price during a specified period (such as a day or a year), holding constant the other factors that influence purchases. The quantity demanded of a good or service can exceed the quantity actually sold. For example, as a promotion, a local store might sell Lindt Excellence Dark Chocolate Bar with A Touch of Sea Salt for $1 each today only. At that low price, you might want to buy 10 bars, but because the store has only

5 remaining, you can buy at most 5 bars. The quantity you demand is 10 bars—it's the amount you want—even though the amount you actually buy is 5.

Potential consumers decide how much of a good or service to buy based on its price, which is expressed as an amount of money per unit of the good (for example, dollars per pound), and many other factors, including consumers' tastes, information, and income; prices of other goods; and government actions. Before concentrating on the role price plays in determining demand, let's look briefly at some of the other factors.

Consumers make purchases based on their *tastes*. Consumers do not purchase foods they dislike, works of art they don't appreciate, or clothes they think are unfashionable or uncomfortable. However, advertising can influence people's tastes.

Similarly, *information* (or misinformation) about the uses of a good affects consumers' decisions. A few years ago, when many consumers were convinced that oatmeal could lower their cholesterol level, they rushed to grocery stores and bought large quantities of oatmeal. (They even ate it until they remembered that they disliked the taste.)

The *prices of other goods* also affect consumers' purchase decisions. Before deciding to buy a pair of Levi's jeans, you might check the prices of other brands. If the price of a close *substitute*—a product that you think is similar or identical to the jeans you are considering purchasing—is much lower than the price of the Levi's, you might buy that other brand instead. Similarly, the price of a *complement*—a good that you like to consume at the same time as the product you are considering buying—could affect your decision. If you only eat pie with ice cream, the higher the price of ice cream, the less likely you are to buy pie.

People's incomes play a major role in determining what and how much of a good or service they purchase. A person who suddenly inherits great wealth might purchase a Mercedes and other luxury items, and may be less likely to buy do-it-yourself repair kits.

Government rules and regulations affect people's purchase decisions. Sales taxes increase the price that a consumer must spend on a good, and government-imposed limits on the use of a good can affect demand. For example, if a city government bans the use of skateboards on its streets, skateboard sales fall.[2]

Other factors can also affect the demand for specific goods. Some people are more likely to buy a pair of $200 shoes if their friends do. The demand for small, dying evergreen trees is substantially higher in December than in other months.

Although many factors influence demand, economists usually concentrate on how a product's price affects the quantity demanded. To determine how a change in price affects the quantity demanded, economists must hold constant other factors, such as income and tastes, which affect the quantity demanded.

The Demand Function

The **demand function** shows the correspondence between the quantity demanded, price, and other factors that influence purchases. Some other factors that may influence the quantity demanded include income, substitutes, and complements. A **substitute** is a good or service that may be consumed instead of another good or service. For many people, tea is a substitute for coffee. A **complement** is a good or service that is jointly consumed with another good or service. For example, many people drink coffee with sugar.

---

[2]When a Mississippi woman attempted to sell her granddaughter for $2,000 and a car, state legislators were horrified to discover that they had no law on the books prohibiting the sale of children and quickly passed such a law. (Mac Gordon, "Legislators Make Child-Selling Illegal," *Jackson Free Press*, March 16, 2009.)

Let's examine the demand function for coffee. The quantity of coffee demanded, Q, varies with the price of coffee, p, the price of sugar, p_s, and consumers' income, Y, so the coffee demand function, D, is

$$Q = D(p, p_s, Y). \tag{2.1}$$

We assume that any other factors that are not explicitly listed in the demand function are irrelevant (such as the price of llamas in Peru) or constant (such as the prices of substitutes and complements, tastes, and consumer information).

Equation 2.1 is a general functional form—it does not specify exactly how Q varies with the explanatory variables, p, p_s, and Y. An estimated world demand function for green (unroasted) coffee beans is[3]

$$Q = 8.56 - p - 0.3p_s + 0.1Y, \tag{2.2}$$

where Q is the quantity of coffee in millions of tons per year, p is the price of coffee in dollars per pound (lb), p_s is the price of sugar in dollars per lb, and Y is the average annual household income in high-income countries in thousands of dollars.

Usually, we're primarily interested in the relationship between the quantity demanded and the price of the good. That is, we want to know the relationship between the quantity demanded and price, holding all other factors constant. For example, given that the price of sugar, p_s, is $0.20 per lb and the average income, Y, is $35 thousand per year, we can substitute those values into Equation 2.2 and write the quantity demanded as a function of only the price of coffee:

$$Q = 8.56 - p - 0.3p_s + 0.1Y$$
$$= 8.56 - p - (0.3 \times 0.2) + (0.1 \times 35)$$
$$= 12 - p. \tag{2.3}$$

We can graphically show this relationship, $Q = D(p) = 12 - p$, between the quantity demanded and price. A **demand curve** is a plot of the demand function that shows the quantity demanded at each possible price, holding constant the other factors that influence purchases. Figure 2.1 shows the estimated demand curve, D, for coffee. (Although this estimated demand curve is a straight line, demand curves can be smooth curves or wavy lines.) By convention, the vertical axis of the graph measures the price, p, per unit of the good, which in our coffee example is dollars per lb. The horizontal axis measures the quantity, Q, of the good, per physical measure of the good per period, which in this case is million tons per year.[4]

---

[3]Because prices, quantities, and other factors change simultaneously over time, economists use statistical techniques to hold the effects of factors other than the price of the good constant so that they can determine how price affects the quantity demanded (see Regression Appendix at the back of the book). As with any estimate, the demand curve estimates are probably more accurate in the observed range of prices than at very high or very low prices. I estimated this model using data from the Food and Agriculture Organization, *Commodity Review and Outlook*; International Coffee Organization, **www.ico.org/new_historical.asp**; International Cocoa Organization, *The World Cocoa Economy: Past and Present* (July 2012); and World Bank, *World Development Indicators*.

[4]Economists typically do not state the relevant physical and period measures unless these measures are particularly useful in context. I'll generally follow this convention and refer to the price as, say, $2 (with the "per lb" understood) and the quantity as 10 (with the "million tons per year" understood).

Figure 2.1 A Coffee Demand Curve

The estimated global demand curve, *D*, for coffee shows the relationship between the quantity demanded per year and the price per lb. The downward slope of the demand curve shows that, holding other factors that influence demand constant, consumers demand a smaller quantity of a good when its price is high and a larger quantity when the price is low. A change in price causes a *movement along the demand curve*. For example, an increase in the price of coffee causes consumers to demand a smaller quantity of coffee.

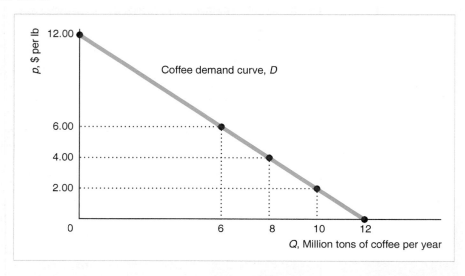

If we set the quantity equal to zero in Equation 2.3, $Q = 12 - p = 0$, we find that $p = \$12$. That is, the demand curve, *D*, hits the price (vertical) axis at $12, indicating that no quantity is demanded when the price is $12 per lb or higher. If we set the price equal to zero in Equation 2.3, $Q = 12 - 0 = 12$, we learn that the demand curve hits the horizontal quantity axis at 12 million tons. That is the amount of coffee that people would consume if coffee were free.

By plugging any particular value for *p* into the demand equation, we can determine the corresponding quantities. For example, if $p = \$2$, then $Q = 12 - 2 = 10$, as Figure 2.1 shows.

A Change in a Product's Price Causes a Movement Along the Demand Curve. The demand curve in Figure 2.1 shows that if the price decreases from $6 to $4 per lb, the quantity consumers demand increases by 2 units (million tons), from 6 to 8. These changes in the quantity demanded in response to changes in price are *movements along the demand curve*. The demand curve is a concise summary of the answers to the question "What happens to the quantity demanded as the price changes, when all other factors are held constant?"

One of the most important empirical findings in economics is the **Law of Demand**: Consumers demand more of a good the lower its price, holding constant tastes, the prices of other goods, and other factors that influence the amount they consume.[5] One way to state the Law of Demand is that the demand curve slopes downward, as in Figure 2.1.

Because the derivative of the demand function with respect to price shows the *movement along the demand curve as we vary price*, another way to state the Law of Demand is that this derivative is negative: A higher price results in a lower quantity demanded. If the demand function is $Q = D(p)$, then the Law of Demand says that $dQ/dp < 0$, where dQ/dp is the derivative of the *D* function with respect to *p*. (Unless we state otherwise, we assume that all demand and other functions are

---

[5]In Chapter 4, we show that theory does not require that the Law of Demand holds; however, available empirical evidence strongly supports the Law of Demand.

continuous and differentiable everywhere.) The derivative of the quantity of coffee demanded with respect to its price in Equation 2.3 is

$$\frac{dQ}{dp} = -1,$$

which is negative, so the Law of Demand holds. Given $dQ/dp = -1$, a small change in the price (measured in dollars per lb) causes an equal unit decrease in the quantity demanded (measured in million tons per year).

This derivative gives the change in the quantity demanded in response to an infinitesimal change in the price. In general, if we look at a discrete, relatively large increase in the price, the change in the quantity might not be proportional to the change for a small increase in the price. However, here the derivative is a constant that does not vary with the price, so the same derivative holds for large and small price changes.

For example, let the price increase from $p_1 = \$2$ to $p_2 = \$4$. That is, the change in the price $\Delta p = p_2 - p_1 = \$4 - \$2 = \$2$. (The Δ symbol, the Greek letter capital delta, means "change in" the following variable, so Δp means "change in price.") As Figure 2.1 shows, the corresponding quantities are $Q_1 = 10$ and $Q_2 = 8$. Thus, if $\Delta p = \$2$, then the change in the quantity demanded is $\Delta Q = Q_2 - Q_1 = 8 - 10 = -2$.

Because we put price on the vertical axis and quantity on the horizontal axis, the slope of the demand curve is the reciprocal of the derivative of the demand function: slope $= dp/dQ = 1/(dQ/dp)$. In our example, the slope of demand curve D in Figure 2.1 is $dp/dQ = 1/(dQ/dp) = 1/(-1) = -1$. We can also calculate the slope in Figure 2.1 using the rise-over-run formula and the numbers we just calculated (because the slope is the same for small and for large changes):

$$\text{slope} = \frac{\text{rise}}{\text{run}} = \frac{\Delta p}{\Delta Q} = \frac{\$1 \text{ per lb}}{-1 \text{ million tons per year}} = -\$1 \text{ per million tons per year.}$$

This slope tells us that to sell one more unit (a million tons per year) of coffee, the price (per lb) must fall by $1.

A Change in Another Factor Causes the Demand Curve to Shift. If a demand curve shows how a price change affects the quantity demanded, holding all other factors that affect demand constant, how can we use demand curves to show the effects of a change in one of these other factors, such as the income? One solution is to draw the demand curve in a three-dimensional diagram with the price of coffee on one axis, the income on a second axis, and the quantity of coffee on the third axis. But just thinking about drawing such a diagram probably makes your head hurt.

Economists use a simpler approach to show how a change in a factor other than the price of a good affects its demand. A change in any factor except the price of the good itself causes a *shift of the demand curve* rather than a *movement along the demand curve*.

If the average income rises and the price of coffee remains constant, people buy more coffee. Suppose that the average income rises from $35,000 per year to $50,000, an increase of $15,000. Using the demand function in Equation 2.2, we can calculate the new coffee demand function relating the quantity demanded to only its price:[6]

$$Q = 13.5 - p. \tag{2.4}$$

Figure 2.2 shows that the higher income causes the coffee demand curve to shift 1.5 units to the right from D^1 (corresponding to the demand function in Equation 2.3) to D^2 (corresponding to the demand function in Equation 2.4).

---

[6]Substituting $Y = 50$ and $p_s = 0.2$ into Equation 2.2, we find that $Q = 8.56 - p - (0.3 \times 0.2) + (0.1 \times 50) = 13.5 - p$.

Figure 2.2 A Shift of the Demand Curve

The global demand curve for coffee shifts to the right from D^1 to D^2 as average annual household income in high-income countries rises by $15,000, from $35,000 to $50,000. At the higher income, more coffee is demanded at any given price.

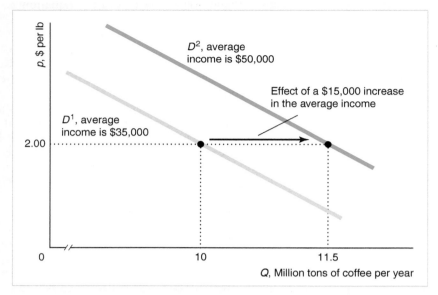

Why does the demand function shift by 1.5 units (million tons per year)? Using the demand function Equation 2.2, we find that the partial derivative of the quantity of coffee demanded with respect to the income is $\partial Q/\partial Y = 0.1$. Thus, if the income increases by $15 thousand, the quantity of coffee demanded rises by $0.1 \times 15 = 1.5$ units, holding all other factors constant.

To properly analyze the effects of a change in some variable on the quantity demanded, we must distinguish between a *movement along a demand curve* and a *shift of a demand curve*. A change in the *price of a good* causes a *movement along its demand curve*. A change in *any other factor besides the price of the good* causes a *shift of the demand curve*.

Summing Demand Functions

If we know the demand curve for each of two consumers, how do we determine the total or aggregate demand for the two consumers combined? The total quantity demanded at a given price is the sum of the quantity each consumer demands at that price.

We can use the demand functions to determine the total demand of several consumers. Suppose the demand function for Consumer 1 is $Q_1 = D^1(p)$, and the demand function for Consumer 2 is $Q_2 = D^2(p)$. At price p, Consumer 1 demands Q_1 units, Consumer 2 demands Q_2 units, and the total demand of both consumers is the sum of the quantities each demands separately:

$$Q = Q_1 + Q_2 = D^1(p) + D^2(p).$$

We can generalize this approach to look at the total demand for three or more consumers.

APPLICATION

Aggregating Corn
Demand Curves

We illustrate how to sum individual demand curves to get an aggregate demand curve graphically using estimated demand curves for corn (McPhail and Babcock, 2012). The figure shows the U.S. feed demand (the use of corn to feed animals) curve, the U.S. food demand curve, and the aggregate demand curve from these two sources.[7]

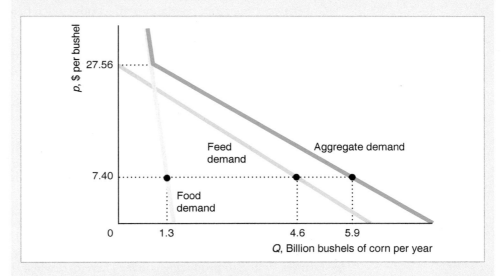

To derive the sum of the quantity demanded for these two uses at a given price, we add the quantities from the individual demand curves at that price. That is, we add the demand curves horizontally. At the 2012 average price for corn, $7.40, the quantity demanded for food is 1.3 billion bushels per year and the quantity demanded for feed is 4.6 billion bushels. Thus, the total quantity demanded at that price is $Q = 1.3 + 4.6 = 5.9$ billion bushels.

When the price of corn exceeds $27.56 per bushel, farmers stop using corn for animal feed, so the quantity demanded for this use equals zero. As a result, the total demand curve is the same as the food demand curve at prices above $27.56.

2.2 Supply

To determine the market price and quantity sold of a product, knowing how much consumers want is not enough. We also need to know how much firms want to supply at any given price.

The **quantity supplied** is the amount of a good that firms *want* to sell during a given period at a given price, holding constant other factors that influence firms' supply decisions, such as costs and government actions. Firms determine how much of a good to supply based on its price and other factors, including the costs of production and government rules and regulations. Usually, we expect firms to supply more at a higher price. Before concentrating on the role price plays in determining supply, we'll briefly consider the role of some other factors.

---

[7]For graphical simplicity, we do not show the other major U.S. demand curves for export, storage, and use in biofuels (ethanol). Thus, this aggregate demand curve is not the total demand curve for corn.

Production cost affects how much of a good a firm wants to sell. As a firm's cost rises, it is willing to supply less of the good, all else the same. In the extreme case where the firm's cost exceeds what it can earn from selling the good, the firm sells nothing. Thus, factors that affect cost also affect supply. For example, a technological advance that allows a firm to produce a good at a lower cost causes the firm to supply more of that good, all else the same.

Government rules and regulations affect how much firms want to sell or may sell. Taxes and many government regulations—such as those covering pollution, sanitation, and health insurance—alter the costs of production. Other regulations affect when and how firms may sell the product. For instance, most Western governments prohibit the sale of cigarettes and liquor to children. Also, most major cities around the world restrict the number of taxicabs.

The Supply Function

The **supply function** shows the correspondence between the quantity supplied, price, and other factors that influence the number of units offered for sale. Written generally (without specifying the functional form), the coffee supply function is

$$Q = S(p, p_c), \tag{2.5}$$

where Q is the quantity of coffee supplied, p is the price of coffee, and p_c is the price of cocoa (which is a key input in making chocolate). The land on which coffee is grown is also suitable for growing cocoa. When the price of cocoa rises, many coffee farmers switch to producing cocoa. Therefore, when the price of cocoa rises, the amount of coffee produced at any given price falls. The supply function, Equation 2.5, might also incorporate other factors such as wages, transportation costs, and the state of technology, but by leaving them out, we are implicitly holding them constant.

Our estimate of the supply function for coffee is

$$Q = 9.6 + 0.5p - 0.2p_c, \tag{2.6}$$

where Q is the quantity of coffee in millions of tons per year, p is the price of coffee in dollars per lb, and p_c is the price of cocoa in dollars per lb.

If we fix the cocoa price at \$3 per lb, we can rewrite the supply function in Equation 2.6 as solely a function of the coffee price. Substituting $p_c = \$3$ into Equation 2.5, we find that

$$Q = 9.6 + 0.5p - (0.2 \times 3) = 9 + 0.5p. \tag{2.7}$$

Because we hold fixed other variables that may affect the quantity supplied, such as costs and government rules, this supply function concisely answers the question "What happens to the quantity supplied as the price changes, holding all other factors constant?"

Corresponding to the supply function is a **supply curve**, which shows the quantity supplied at each possible price, holding constant the other factors that influence firms' supply decisions. Figure 2.3 shows the coffee supply curve, S, that corresponds to the supply function Equation 2.7. Because the supply function is linear, the corresponding supply curve is a straight line.

A Change in a Product's Price Causes a Movement Along the Supply Curve. As the price of coffee increases from \$2 to \$4 in Figure 2.3, holding other factors (the price of cocoa) constant, the quantity of coffee supplied increases from 10 to 11 million tons per year, which is a *movement along the supply curve.*

Figure 2.3 A Coffee Supply Curve

The estimated global supply curve, S, for coffee shows the relationship between the quantity supplied per year and the price per lb, holding constant cost and other factors that influence supply. The upward slope of this supply curve indicates that firms supply more coffee when its price is high and less when the price is low. An increase in the price of coffee causes firms to supply a larger quantity of coffee; any change in price results in a *movement along the supply curve*.

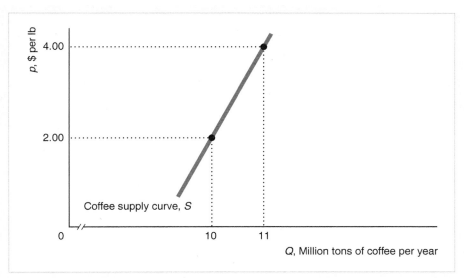

How much does an increase in the price affect the quantity supplied? Differentiating the supply function, Equation 2.7, with respect to price, we find that $dQ/dp = 0.5$. As this derivative is not a function of p, it holds for all price changes, both small and large. It shows that the quantity supplied increases by 0.5 units for each $1 increase in price.

Because the derivative is positive, the supply curve S slopes upward in Figure 2.3. Although the Law of Demand states that the demand curve slope downward, we have *no* "Law of Supply" that requires the market supply curve to have a particular slope. The market supply curve can be upward sloping, vertical, horizontal, or downward sloping.

A Change in Another Factor Causes the Supply Curve to Shift. A change in a factor other than a product's price causes a *shift of the supply curve*. If the price of cocoa increases by $3 from $3 to $6 per lb, the supply function for coffee becomes

$$Q = 9.6 + 0.5p - (0.2 \times 6) = 8.4 + 0.5p. \qquad (2.8)$$

By comparing this supply function to the original one in Equation 2.7, $Q = 9 + 0.5p$, we see that the original supply curve, S^1, shifts 0.6 units to the left, to S^2 in Figure 2.4.

Alternatively, we can determine how far the supply curve shifts by partially differentiating the supply function Equation 2.6 with respect to the price of cocoa: $\partial Q/\partial p_c = -0.2$. This partial derivative holds for all values of p_c and hence for both small and large changes in p_c. Thus, a $3 increase in the price of cocoa causes a $-0.2 \times 3 = -0.6$ units change in the quantity of coffee supplied at any price of coffee.

Again, it is important to distinguish between a *movement along a supply curve* and a *shift of the supply curve*. When the coffee price changes, the change in the quantity supplied reflects a *movement along the supply curve*. When costs, government rules, or other variables that affect supply change, the entire *supply curve shifts*.

Figure 2.4 A Shift of a Supply Curve

A $3 per lb increase in the price of cocoa, which farmers can grow instead of coffee, causes the supply curve for coffee to shift left from S^1 to S^2. At the price of coffee of $2 per lb, the quantity supplied falls from 10 million tons on S^1 to 9.4 million tons on S^2.

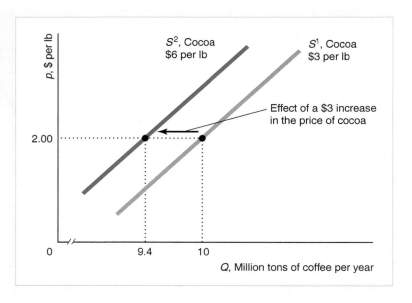

Summing Supply Functions

The total supply curve shows the total quantity of a product produced by all suppliers at each possible price. For example, the total supply curve of rice in Japan is the sum of the domestic and the foreign supply curves of rice.

Figure 2.5 shows the domestic supply curve, panel a, and foreign supply curve, panel b, of rice in Japan. The total supply curve, S in panel c, is the horizontal sum of the Japanese *domestic* supply curve, S^d, and the *foreign* supply curve, S^f. In the figure, the Japanese and foreign supplies are zero at any price equal to or less than $\underline{p}$, so the total supply is zero. At prices greater than $\underline{p}$, the Japanese and foreign supplies are positive, so the total supply is positive. For example, when the price is p^*, the quantity supplied by Japanese firms is Q_d^*, panel a, the quantity supplied by foreign firms is Q_f^*, panel b, and the total quantity supplied is $Q^* = Q_d^* + Q_f^*$, panel c. Because the total supply curve is the horizontal sum of the domestic and foreign supply curves, the total supply curve is flatter than each of the other two supply curves.

How Government Import Policies Affect Supply Curves

We can use this approach for deriving the total supply curve to analyze the effect of government policies on the total supply curve. Traditionally, the Japanese government has banned the importation of foreign rice. We want to determine how much less rice is supplied at any given price to the Japanese market because of this ban.

Without a ban, the foreign supply curve is S^f in panel b of Figure 2.5. A ban on imports eliminates the foreign supply, so the foreign supply curve after the ban is imposed, $\overline{S}^f$, is a vertical line at $Q_f = 0$. The import ban has no effect on the domestic supply curve, S^d, so the supply curve is the same as in panel a.

Figure 2.5 Total Supply: The Sum of Domestic and Foreign Supply

If foreigners are allowed to sell their rice in Japan, the total Japanese supply of rice, S, is the horizontal sum of the domestic Japanese supply, S^d, and the imported foreign supply, S^f. With a ban on foreign imports, the foreign supply curve, $\overline{S}^f$, is zero at every price, so the total supply curve, $\overline{S}$, is the same as the domestic supply curve, S^d.

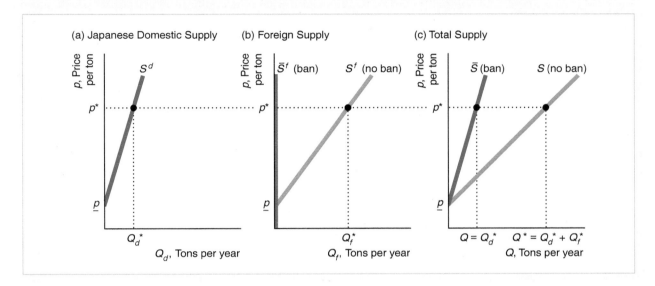

Because the foreign supply with a ban, $\overline{S}^f$ in panel b, is zero at every price, the total supply with a ban, $\overline{S}$ in panel c, is the same as the Japanese domestic supply, S^d, at any given price. The total supply curve under the ban lies to the left of the total supply curve without a ban, S. Thus, the effect of the import ban is to rotate the total supply curve toward the vertical axis.

A limit that a government sets on the quantity of a foreign-produced good that may be imported is a **quota**. By absolutely banning the importation of rice, the Japanese government sets a quota of zero on rice imports. Sometimes governments set positive quotas, $\overline{Q} > 0$. The foreign firms may supply as much as they want, Q_f, as long as they supply no more than the quota: $Q_f \leq \overline{Q}$.

2.3 Market Equilibrium

The supply and demand curves jointly determine the price and quantity at which goods and services are bought and sold. The demand curve shows the quantities that consumers want to buy at various prices, and the supply curve shows the quantities that firms want to sell at various prices. Unless the price is set so that consumers want to buy exactly the same amount that suppliers want to sell, either some buyers cannot buy as much as they want or some sellers cannot sell as much as they want.

When all traders are able to buy or sell as much as they want, we say that the market is in **equilibrium**: a situation in which no participant wants to change its behavior. At the *equilibrium price*, consumers want to buy the same quantity that firms want to sell. The quantity that consumers buy and firms sell at the equilibrium price is the *equilibrium quantity*.

Finding the Market Equilibrium

To illustrate how supply and demand curves determine the equilibrium price and quantity, we use our old friend, the coffee example. Figure 2.6 shows the supply, S, and the demand, D, curves for coffee. The supply and demand curves intersect at point e, the market equilibrium, where the equilibrium price is $2 per lb and the equilibrium quantity is 10 million tons per year, which is the quantity that firms want to sell and the quantity that consumers want to buy at the equilibrium price.

We can determine the market equilibrium for coffee mathematically using the demand and supply functions, Equations 2.3 and 2.7. We use these two functions to solve for the equilibrium price at which the quantity demanded equals the quantity supplied (the equilibrium quantity).

The demand function in Equation 2.3 shows the relationship between the quantity demanded, Q_d, and the price:

$$Q_d = 12 - p.$$

The supply curve, Equation 2.7, tells us the relationship between the quantity supplied, Q_s, and the price:

$$Q_s = 9 + 0.5p.$$

We want to find the price at which $Q_d = Q_s = Q$, the equilibrium quantity. Because the left sides of the two equations are the same in equilibrium, $Q_s = Q_d$, the right sides of the two equations must be equal as well:

$$9 + 0.5p = 12 - p.$$

Adding p to both sides of this expression and subtracting 9 from both sides, we find that $1.5p = 3$. Dividing both sides of this last expression by 1.5, we learn that the equilibrium price is $p = 2.

Figure 2.6 Market Equilibrium

The intersection of the supply curve, S, and the demand curve, D, for coffee determines the market equilibrium point, e, where $p = 2 per lb and $Q = 10$ million tons per year. At the lower price of $p = 1, the quantity demanded is 11, but the quantity supplied is only 9.5, so the excess demand is 1.5. At $p = 3, the price exceeds the equilibrium price. As a result, the market has an excess supply of 1.5 because the quantity demanded, 9, is less than the quantity supplied, 10.5. With either excess demand or excess supply, market forces drive the price back to the equilibrium price of $2.

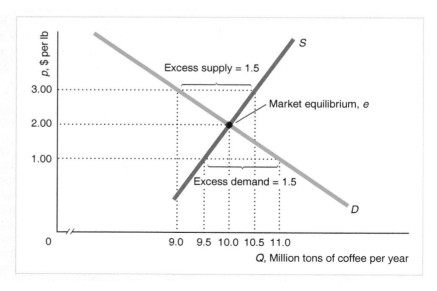

We can determine the equilibrium quantity by substituting this equilibrium price, $p = \$2$, into either the supply or the demand equation:

$$Q_d = Q_s$$
$$12 - 2 = 9 + (0.5 \times 2)$$
$$10 = 10.$$

Thus, the equilibrium quantity is 10 million tons per year.

Forces That Drive a Market to Equilibrium

A market equilibrium is not just an abstract concept or a theoretical possibility.[8] We observe markets in equilibrium. The ability to buy as much as you want of a good at the market price is indirect evidence that a market is in equilibrium. You can usually buy as much as you want of milk, ballpoint pens, and many other goods.

Amazingly, a market equilibrium occurs without any explicit coordination between consumers and firms. In a competitive market such as that for agricultural goods, millions of consumers and thousands of firms make their buying and selling decisions independently. Yet, each firm can sell as much as it wants, and each consumer can buy as much as he or she wants. It is as though an unseen market force, like an *invisible hand*, directs people to coordinate their activities to achieve market equilibrium.

What really causes the market to be in equilibrium? If the price were not at the equilibrium level, consumers or firms would have an incentive to change their behavior in a way that would drive the price to the equilibrium level.[9]

If the price were initially lower than the equilibrium price, consumers would want to buy more than suppliers would want to sell. If the price of coffee were $1 in Figure 2.6, consumers would demand $12 - 1 = 11$ million tons per year, but firms would be willing to supply only $9 + (0.5 \times 1) = 9.5$ million tons. At this price, the market would be in *disequilibrium*, meaning that the quantity demanded would not equal the quantity supplied. The market would have **excess demand**—the amount by which the quantity demanded exceeds the quantity supplied at a specified price—of $11 - 9.5 = 1.5$ million tons per year at a price of $1 per lb.

Some consumers would be lucky enough to be able to buy coffee at $1. Other consumers would not find anyone willing to sell them coffee at that price. What could they do? Some frustrated consumers might offer to pay suppliers more than $1. Alternatively, suppliers, noticing these disappointed consumers, might raise their prices. Such actions by consumers and producers would cause the market price to rise. At higher prices, the quantity that firms want to supply increases and the quantity that consumers want to buy decreases. The upward pressure on the price would continue until it reached the equilibrium price, $2, where the market has no excess demand.

If, instead, the price were initially above the equilibrium level, suppliers would want to sell more than consumers would want to buy. For example, at a price of coffee of $3, suppliers would want to sell 10.5 million tons per year but consumers

---

[8]**MyLab Economics** has games (called *experiments*) for your course. These online games allow you to play against the computer. The *Market Experiment* illustrates the operation of the supply-and-demand model, allowing you to participate in a simulated market. To play, go to **MyLab Economics** Multimedia Library, Single Player Experiment, and set the Chapter field to "All Chapters."

[9]Our model of competitive market equilibrium, which occurs at a point in time, does not formally explain how dynamic adjustments occur. The following explanation, though plausible, is just one of a number of possible dynamic adjustment stories that economists have modeled.

would want to buy only 9 million, as the figure shows. Thus, at a price of $3, the market would be in disequilibrium. The market would have **excess supply**—the amount by which the quantity supplied is greater than the quantity demanded at a specified price—of $10.5 - 9 = 1.5$ million tons at a price of $3. Not all firms could sell as much as they wanted. Rather than incur storage costs (and possibly have their unsold coffee spoil), firms would lower the price to attract additional customers. As long as the price remained above the equilibrium price, some firms would have unsold coffee and would want to lower the price further. The price would fall until it reached the equilibrium level, $2, without excess supply and hence no pressure to lower the price further.[10]

In summary, at any price other than the equilibrium price, either consumers or suppliers would be unable to trade as much as they want. These disappointed people would act to change the price, driving the price to the equilibrium level. The equilibrium price is called the *market clearing price* because it removes from the market all frustrated buyers and sellers: The market has no excess demand or excess supply at the market clearing price.

2.4 Shocking the Equilibrium: Comparative Statics

If the variables we hold constant in the demand and supply functions do not change, an equilibrium would persist indefinitely because none of the participants in the market would apply pressure to change the price. However, the equilibrium changes if a shock occurs so that one of the variables we were holding constant changes, causing a shift in either the demand curve or the supply curve.

Comparative statics is the method economists use to analyze how variables controlled by consumers and firms—here, price and quantity—react to a change in *environmental variables* (also called *exogenous variables*) that they do not control. Such environmental variables include the prices of substitutes, the prices of complements, the income level of consumers, and the prices of inputs. The term *comparative statics* literally refers to comparing a *static* equilibrium—an equilibrium at a point in time from before the change—to a static equilibrium after the change. (In contrast, economists may examine a dynamic model, in which the dynamic equilibrium adjusts over time.)

Well, there goes the price of lobsters!

---

[10]Not all markets reach equilibrium through the independent actions of many buyers or sellers. In institutionalized or formal markets, such as the Chicago Mercantile Exchange—where agricultural commodities, financial instruments, energy, and metals are traded—buyers and sellers meet at a single location (or on a single website). In these markets, certain individuals or firms, sometimes referred to as *market makers*, act to adjust the price and bring the market into equilibrium very quickly.

Comparative Statics with Discrete (Large) Changes

We can determine the comparative statics properties of an equilibrium by examining the effects of a discrete (relatively large) change in one environmental variable. We can do so by solving for the before- and after-equilibria and comparing them using mathematics or a graph. We illustrate this approach using our beloved coffee example. Suppose all the environmental variables remain constant except the price of cocoa, which increases by $3 per lb.

Because the price of cocoa is not an environmental variable in the demand function, the demand curve does not shift. However, as we saw in Figure 2.4, the increase in the price of cocoa causes the coffee supply curve to shift 0.6 units to the left from S^1 to S^2 at every possible price of coffee.

Figure 2.7 reproduces this shift of the supply curve and adds the original demand curve. At the original equilibrium price of coffee, $2, consumers still want to buy 10 million tons, but suppliers are now willing to supply only 9.4 million tons at that price, so the market has an excess demand of $10 - 9.4 = 0.6$. Market pressure forces the coffee price upward until it reaches the new equilibrium, e_2.

At e_2, the new equilibrium price is $2.40, and the new equilibrium quantity is 9.6 million tons. Thus, the increase in the price of cocoa causes the equilibrium price of coffee to rise by 40¢ per lb, and the equilibrium quantity to fall by 0.4 million tons. Here the increase in the price of cocoa causes a *shift of the supply curve* and a *movement along the demand curve*.

We can derive the same result by using equations to solve for the equilibrium before and after the discrete change in the price of cocoa and by comparing the two equations. We have already solved for the original equilibrium, e_1, by setting the quantity in the demand function Equation 2.3 equal to the quantity in the supply function Equation 2.7.

Figure 2.7 The Equilibrium Effect of a Shift of the Supply Curve

A $3 per lb increase in the price of cocoa causes some producers to shift from coffee production to cocoa production, reducing the quantity of coffee supplied at every price. The supply curve shifts to the left from S^1 to S^2, driving the market equilibrium from e_1 to e_2, where the new equilibrium price is $2.40.

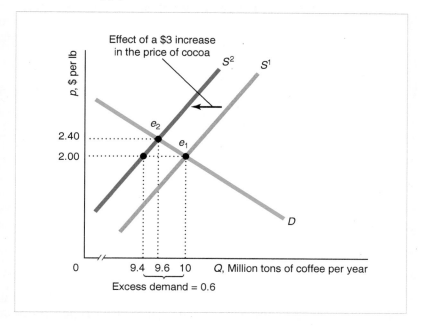

We obtain the new equilibrium, e_2, by equating the quantity in the demand function Equation 2.3 to that of the new supply function, with the $3 higher cocoa price, Equation 2.8:

$$12 - p = 8.4 + 0.5p.$$

Solving this expression, we find that the new equilibrium price is $p_2 = \$2.40$. Substituting that price into either the demand or the supply function, we learn that the new equilibrium quantity is $Q_2 = 9.6$, as Figure 2.7 shows. Thus, both methods show that an increase in the price of cocoa causes the equilibrium price to rise and the equilibrium quantity to fall.

APPLICATION The Opioid Epidemic's Labor Market Effects	Opioids are drugs that act on the nervous system to relieve pain. They include heroin, fentanyl, and pain relievers that are available legally by prescription, such as oxycodone (OxyContin), hydrocodone (Vicodin), codeine, and morphine. Although patients can safely use opioid pain relievers for a short period, many patients continue to use them for longer periods because these drugs produce euphoria in addition to pain relief. Unfortunately, continued use can cause dependence, and excessive use can cause death. Every day, 90 Americans die from opioid overdoses. Opioid prescriptions per capita rose 350% nationwide between 1999 and 2015. The use and abuse of opioids are responsible for fewer people working due to premature deaths, an inability to pass a job drug test, or an unwillingness to work due to sedation and other effects of the drug. Labor-force participation rate of men—the ratio of employed working-age men to all working-age men—was 3.2 percentage points lower during 2014–2016 than during 1999–2001. According to Krueger (2017), labor-force participation fell more in areas where doctors prescribe relatively more opioid pain medication. He calculated that 0.6 percentage points of the decline for men, a fifth of the total, was due to opioid prescriptions. Similarly, the study estimated that about one-quarter of the decline in women's labor-force participation was due to the growth in opioid prescriptions. Thus, the opioid epidemic caused the labor supply curve to shift to the left, similar to Figure 2.7. As a result, the equilibrium quantity of labor fell and the equilibrium wage rose.

Comparative Statics with Small Changes

Alternatively, we can use calculus to determine the effect of a small change (as opposed to the discrete change we just used) in one environmental variable, holding the other such variables constant. Until now, we have used calculus to examine how an argument of a demand function affects the quantity demanded or how an argument of a supply function affects the quantity supplied. Now, however, we want to know how an environmental variable affects the equilibrium price and quantity that are determined by the intersection of the supply and demand curves.

Our first step is to characterize the equilibrium values as functions of the relevant environmental variables. Suppose that we hold constant all the environmental variables that affect demand so that the demand function is

$$Q = D(p). \tag{2.9}$$

One environmental variable, a, in the supply function changes, which causes the supply curve to shift. We write the supply function as

$$Q = S(p, a). \tag{2.10}$$

As before, we determine the equilibrium price by equating the quantities, Q, in Equations 2.9 and 2.10:

$$D(p) = S(p, a). \qquad (2.11)$$

Equation 2.11 is an example of an *identity*. As a changes, p changes, so that this equation continues to hold—the market remains in equilibrium. Thus, based on this equation, we can write the equilibrium price as an implicit function of the environmental variable: $p = p(a)$. That is, we can write the equilibrium condition in Equation 2.11 as

$$D(p(a)) = S(p(a), a). \qquad (2.12)$$

We can characterize how the equilibrium price changes with a by differentiating the equilibrium condition Equation 2.12 with respect to a using the chain rule at the original equilibrium,[11]

$$\frac{dD(p(a))}{dp}\frac{dp}{da} = \frac{\partial S(p(a), a)}{\partial p}\frac{dp}{da} + \frac{\partial S(p(a), a)}{\partial a}. \qquad (2.13)$$

Using algebra, we can rearrange Equation 2.13 as

$$\frac{dp}{da} = \frac{\dfrac{\partial S}{\partial a}}{\dfrac{dD}{dp} - \dfrac{\partial S}{\partial p}}, \qquad (2.14)$$

where we suppress the arguments of the functions for notational simplicity. Equation 2.14 shows the derivative of $p(a)$ with respect to a.

We know that $dD/dp < 0$ because of the Law of Demand. If the supply curve is upward sloping, then $\partial S/\partial p$ is positive, so the denominator of Equation 2.14, $dD/dp - \partial S/\partial p$, is negative. Thus, dp/da has the opposite sign as the numerator of Equation 2.14. If $\partial S/\partial a$ is negative, then dp/da is positive: As a increases, the equilibrium price rises. If $\partial S/\partial a$ is positive, an increase in a causes the equilibrium price to fall.

By using either the demand function or the supply function, we can use this result concerning the effect of a on the equilibrium price to determine the effect of a on the equilibrium quantity. For example, we can rewrite the demand function Equation 2.9 as

$$Q = D(p(a)). \qquad (2.15)$$

Differentiating the demand function Equation 2.15 with respect to a using the chain rule, we find that

$$\frac{dQ}{da} = \frac{dD}{dp}\frac{dp}{da}. \qquad (2.16)$$

Because $dD/dp < 0$ by the Law of Demand, the sign of dQ/da is the opposite of that of dp/da. That is, as a increases, the equilibrium price moves in the opposite direction of the equilibrium quantity. In Solved Problem 2.1, we use the coffee example to illustrate this type of analysis.

---

[11]The chain rule is a formula for the derivative of the composite of two functions, such as $f(g(x))$. According to this rule, $df/dx = (df/dg)(dg/dx)$. See the Calculus Appendix at the end of the book.

**SOLVED PROBLEM
2.1**

**MyLab Economics
Solved Problem**

How do the equilibrium price and quantity of coffee vary as the price of cocoa changes, holding the variables that affect demand constant at their typical values? Answer this comparative statics question using calculus. (*Hint*: This problem has the same form as the more general one we just analyzed. In the cocoa market, the environmental variable that shifts supply, a, is p_c.)

Answer

1. *Solve for the equilibrium coffee price in terms of the cocoa price.* To obtain an expression for the equilibrium similar to Equation 2.14, we equate the right sides of the demand function in Equation 2.3 and the supply function Equation 2.6 to obtain

$$12 - p = 9.6 + 0.5p - 0.2p_c, \text{ or}$$

$$p = (2.4/1.5) + (0.2/1.5)p_c = 1.6 + 0.133\dot{3}p_c. \tag{2.17}$$

(As a check, when p_c equals its original value, $3, in Equation 2.17, the equilibrium coffee price is $p = \$2$, which is consistent with our earlier calculations.)

2. *Use this equilibrium price equation to show how the equilibrium price changes as the price of cocoa changes.* Differentiating the equilibrium price Equation 2.17 with respect to p_c gives an expression of the form of Equation 2.16:

$$\frac{dp}{dp_c} = 0.133\dot{3}. \tag{2.18}$$

Because this condition holds for any value of p_c (the derivative does not vary with p_c), it also holds for large changes in the price of cocoa. For example, as the cocoa price increases by $3, the equilibrium cocoa price increases by $0.133\dot{3} \times \$3 = \$0.40$, as Figure 2.7 shows.

3. *Write the coffee demand function as in Equation 2.15, and then differentiate it with respect to the cocoa price to show how the equilibrium quantity of coffee varies with the cocoa price.* From the coffee demand function, Equation 2.3, we can write the quantity demanded as

$$Q = D(p(p_c)) = 12 - p(p_c),$$

where $p(p_c)$ is given by Equation 2.17. That is,

$$Q = D(p(p_c)) = 12 - (1.6 + 0.133\dot{3}p_c) = 10.4 - 0.133\dot{3}p_c.$$

Differentiating this expression with respect to p_c using the chain rule, we obtain

$$\frac{dQ}{dp_c} = \frac{dD}{dp}\frac{dp}{dp_c} = -1 \times 0.133\dot{3} = -0.133\dot{3}, \tag{2.19}$$

where dp/dp_c is given by Equation 2.18. That is, as the price of cocoa increases by $1, the equilibrium quantity of coffee falls by $0.133\dot{3}$ tons per year. Because the derivative in Equation 2.19 does not vary with p_c, it holds for large changes. Thus, if the price of cocoa increases by $3, then the equilibrium quantity falls by $0.133\dot{3} \times 3 = 0.4$ million tons per year, as Figure 2.7 shows.

Why the Shapes of Demand and Supply Curves Matter

The shapes and positions of the demand and supply curves determine how much a shock affects the equilibrium price and quantity. We illustrate the importance of the shape of the demand curve using the estimated avocado demand and supply curves.[12] We start by determining what happens if the price of fertilizer (an input to the production of avocados) increases by 55¢ per lb, which causes the avocado supply curve to shift to the left from S^1 to S^2 in panel a of Figure 2.8. The *shift of the supply curve* causes a *movement along the estimated demand curve, D^1.* The equilibrium quantity falls from 80 to 72 million lb per month, and the equilibrium price rises 20¢ from $2.00 to $2.20 per lb, hurting consumers.

A supply shock would have different effects if the demand curve had a different shape. Suppose that the quantity demanded were not sensitive to a change in the price, so that a change in the price does not affect the amount demanded, as the vertical demand curve D^2 in panel b shows. A 55¢ increase in the fertilizer price again shifts the supply curve from S^1 to S^2. However, with the vertical demand curve, the equilibrium quantity does not change, but the price consumers pay rises by more, going from $2 to $2.73. Thus, the amount consumers spend rises by more when the demand curve is vertical instead of downward sloping.

Now suppose that consumers are extremely sensitive to price changes, as the horizontal demand curve, D^3, in panel c shows. Consumers will buy virtually

Figure 2.8 The Effects of a Shift of the Supply Curve Depend on the Shape of the Demand Curve

A 55¢ increase in the price of fertilizer shifts the avocado supply curve to the left from S^1 to S^2. (a) Given the actual, estimated downward-sloping linear demand curve, D^1, the equilibrium price rises from $2.00 to $2.20 and the equilibrium quantity falls from 80 to 72. (b) If the demand curve were vertical, D^2, the supply shock would cause price to rise to $2.73 while quantity would remain unchanged. (c) If the demand curve were horizontal, D^3, the supply shock would not affect price but would cause quantity to fall to 69.

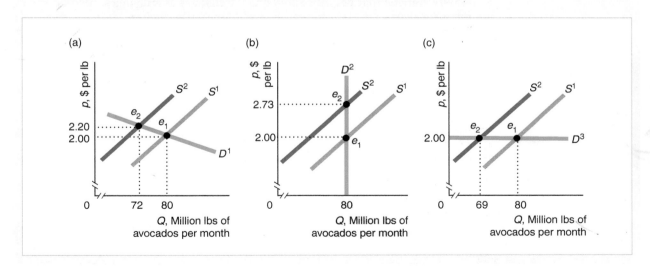

---

[12]The supply and demand curves are based on estimates from Carman (2006), which we updated with more recent data from the California Avocado Commission and supplemented with information from other sources.

unlimited quantities of avocados at $2 per lb (or less). However, if the price rises even slightly, they stop buying avocados altogether. With a horizontal demand curve, an increase in the price of avocados has *no* effect on the price consumers pay; however, the equilibrium quantity drops substantially from 80 to 69 million lb per month. Thus, how much the equilibrium quantity falls and how much the equilibrium price of avocados rises when the fertilizer price increases depend on the shape of the demand curve.

2.5 Elasticities

It is convenient to be able to summarize the responsiveness of one variable to a change in another variable using a summary statistic. In our last example, we wanted to know whether an increase in the price of a product causes a large or a small change in the quantity demanded (that is, whether the demand curve is relatively vertical or relatively horizontal at the current price). We can use summary statistics of the responsiveness of the quantity demanded and the quantity supplied to determine comparative statics properties of the equilibrium. Often, we have reasonable estimates of these summary statistics and can use them to predict what will happen to the equilibrium in a market—that is, to make comparative statics predictions. Later in this chapter, we will examine how the government can use these summary measures to predict how a tax on a product will affect the equilibrium price and quantity, and hence firms' revenues and the government's tax receipts.

Suppose that a variable z (for example, the quantity demanded or the quantity supplied) is a function of a variable x (say, the price of z) and possibly other variables such as y. We write this function as $z = f(x, y)$. For example, f could be the demand function, where z is the quantity demanded, x is the price, and y is income. We want a summary statistic that describes how much z changes as x changes, holding y constant. An **elasticity** is the percentage change in one variable (here, z) in response to a given percentage change in another variable (here, x), holding other relevant variables (here, y) constant. The elasticity, E, of z with respect to x is

$$E = \frac{\text{percentage change in } z}{\text{percentage change in } x} = \frac{\Delta z/z}{\Delta x/x} = \frac{\partial z}{\partial x} \frac{x}{z}, \tag{2.20}$$

where Δz is the change in z, so $\Delta z/z$ is the percentage change in z. If z changes by 3% when x changes by 1%, then the elasticity E is 3. Thus, the elasticity is a pure number (it has no units of measure).[13] As Δx goes to zero, $\Delta z/\Delta x$ goes to the partial derivative $\partial z/\partial x$. Economists usually calculate elasticities at this limit—that is, for infinitesimal changes in x.

Demand Elasticity

The **price elasticity of demand** (or simply the *demand elasticity* or *elasticity of demand*) is the percentage change in the quantity demanded, Q, in response to a given percentage change in the price, p, at a particular point on the demand curve.

---

[13]Economists use the elasticity rather than the slope, $\partial z/\partial x$, as a summary statistic because the elasticity is a pure number, whereas the slope depends on the units of measurement. For example, if x is a price measured in pennies and we switch to measuring price using dollars, the slope changes, but the elasticity remains unchanged.

The price elasticity of demand (represented by ε, the Greek letter epsilon), a special case of Equation 2.20, is

$$\varepsilon = \frac{\text{percentage change in quantity demanded}}{\text{percentage change in price}} = \frac{\Delta Q/Q}{\Delta p/p} = \frac{\partial Q}{\partial p} \frac{p}{Q}, \qquad (2.21)$$

where $\partial Q/\partial p$ is the partial derivative of the demand function with respect to p (that is, holding constant other variables that affect the quantity demanded).

The elasticity of demand concisely answers the question "How much does the quantity demanded of a product fall in response to a 1% increase in its price?" A 1% increase in price leads to an ε% change in the quantity demanded. For example, Roberts and Schlenker (2013) estimated that the elasticity of corn is -0.3. A 1% increase in the price of corn leads to a -0.3% fall in the quantity of corn demanded. Thus, a price increase causes a less than proportionate fall in the quantity of corn demanded.

We can use Equation 2.21 to calculate the elasticity of demand for a linear demand function that holds fixed other variables that affect demand:

$$Q = a - bp,$$

where a is the quantity demanded when the price is zero, $Q = a - (b \times 0) = a$, and $-b$ is the ratio of the fall in the quantity relative to the rise in price: the derivative dQ/dp. The elasticity of demand is

$$\varepsilon = \frac{dQ}{dp} \frac{p}{Q} = -b \frac{p}{Q}. \qquad (2.22)$$

SOLVED PROBLEM 2.2

MyLab Economics Solved Problem

The estimated U.S. linear corn demand function is

$$Q = 15.6 - 0.5p, \qquad (2.23)$$

where p is the price in dollars per bushel and Q is the quantity demanded in billion bushels per year.[14] What is the elasticity of demand at the point on the demand curve where the price is $p = \$7.20$ per bushel?

Answer

Substitute the slope coefficient b, the price, and the quantity in Equation 2.22.
Equation 2.23 is a special case of the general linear demand function $Q = a - bp$, where $a = 15.6$ and $b = 0.5$. Evaluating Equation 2.23 at $p = \$7.20$, we find that the quantity demanded is $Q = 15.6 - (0.5 \times 7.20) = 12$ billion bushels per year. Substituting $b = 0.5$, $p = \$7.20$, and $Q = 12$ into Equation 2.22, we learn that the elasticity of demand at this point on the demand curve is

$$\varepsilon = -b \frac{p}{Q} = -0.5 \times \frac{7.20}{12} = -0.3.$$

The negative sign on the corn elasticity of demand illustrates the Law of Demand: Less quantity is demanded as the price rises.

---

[14]This demand curve is a linearized version of the estimated demand curve in Roberts and Schlenker (2013). I have rounded their estimated elasticities slightly for algebraic simplicity.

APPLICATION

The Demand
Elasticities for Google
Play and Apple Apps

As of the first quarter of 2018, the Apple App Store (iOS) had about 2.0 million apps (mobile applications for smartphones and tablets) and Google Play (Android) had 3.8 million. How price sensitive are consumers of apps? Are Apple aficionados more or less price sensitive than people who use Android devices?

Ghose and Han (2014) estimated the demand for an app in the Apple App Store is −2.0. That is, a 1% increase in price causes a 2% drop in the

demand for an Apple app. Thus, demand is elastic in the Apple App Store.

The estimated demand elasticity for an app in Google Play is −3.7, which means an Android app has a nearly twice as elastic demand as does an Apple app. Therefore, Google Play consumers are more price sensitive than are Apple App consumers.

Elasticities Along the Demand Curve. The elasticity of demand varies along most demand curves. On downward-sloping linear demand curves (lines that are neither vertical nor horizontal), the higher the price, the more negative the elasticity of demand. Consequently, even though the slope of the linear demand curve is constant, the elasticity varies along the curve. A 1% increase in the price causes a larger percentage fall in the quantity demanded near the top (left) of the demand curve than near the bottom (right).

Where a linear demand curve hits the quantity axis ($p = 0$ and $Q = a$), the elasticity of demand is $\varepsilon = -b \times (0/a) = 0$, according to Equation 2.22. The linear coffee demand curve in Figure 2.9 illustrates this pattern. Where the price is zero, a 1% increase in price does not raise the price, so quantity demanded does not change. At a point where the elasticity of demand is zero, the demand curve is said to be *perfectly inelastic*. As a physical analogy, if you try to stretch an inelastic steel rod, the length does not change. The change in the price is the force pulling at demand; if the quantity demanded does not change in response to this force, the demand curve is perfectly inelastic.

For quantities between the midpoint of the linear demand curve and the lower end, where $Q = a$, the demand elasticity lies between 0 and −1: $0 > \varepsilon > -1$. A point along the demand curve where the elasticity is between 0 and −1 is *inelastic* (but not perfectly inelastic): A 1% increase in price leads to a fall in quantity of less than 1%. For example, at $p = \$3$ and $Q = 9$, $\varepsilon = -\frac{1}{3}$, so a one percent increase in price causes quantity to fall by one-third of a percent. A physical analogy is a piece of rope that does not stretch much—is inelastic—when you pull on it: Changing price has relatively little effect on quantity.

At the midpoint of any linear demand curve, $p = a/(2b)$ and $Q = a/2$, so $\varepsilon = -bp/Q = -b[a/(2b)]/(a/2) = -1$.[15] Such an elasticity of demand is called a *unitary elasticity*.

---

[15]The linear demand curve hits the price axis at $p = a/b$ and the quantity axis at $p = 0$. The midpoint occurs at $p = (a/b - 0)/2 = a/(2b)$, where the quantity is $Q = a - b[a/(2b)] = a/2$.

Figure 2.9 The Elasticity of Demand Varies Along the Linear Coffee Demand Curve

With a linear demand curve, such as the coffee demand curve, the higher the price, the more elastic the demand curve (ε is larger in absolute value: It becomes a more negative number as we move up the demand curve). The demand curve is perfectly inelastic ($\varepsilon = 0$) where the demand curve hits the horizontal axis, is perfectly elastic where the demand curve hits the vertical axis, and has unitary elasticity at the midpoint of the demand curve.

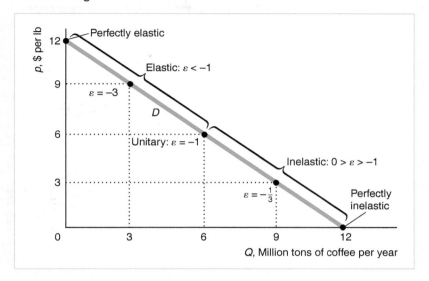

At prices higher than at the midpoint of the demand curve, the elasticity of demand is less than negative one, $\varepsilon < -1$. In this range, the demand curve is called *elastic*: A 1% increase in price causes more than a 1% fall in quantity. A physical analogy is a rubber band that stretches substantially when you pull on it. Figure 2.9 shows that the coffee demand elasticity is -3 where $p = \$9$ and $Q = 3$: A 1% increase in price causes a 3% drop in the quantity demanded.

As the price rises, the elasticity gets more and more negative, approaching negative infinity.[16] Where the demand curve hits the price axis, it is *perfectly elastic*. At the price a/b where $Q = 0$, a 1% decrease in p causes the quantity demanded to become positive, which is an infinite increase in quantity.

The elasticity of demand varies along most demand curves, not just downward-sloping linear ones. However, along a special type of demand curve, called a *constant-elasticity demand curve*, the elasticity is the same at every point along the curve. Constant-elasticity demand curves all have the exponential form

$$Q = Ap^\varepsilon, \tag{2.24}$$

where A is a positive constant and ε, a negative constant, is the elasticity at every point along this demand curve. By taking natural logarithms of both sides of Equation 2.24, we can rewrite this exponential demand curve as a log-linear demand curve:

$$\ln Q = \ln A + \varepsilon \ln p. \tag{2.25}$$

For example, given the information in the Application "The Demand Elasticities for Google Play and Apple Apps," the estimated demand function for Apple apps

---

[16]The linear demand curve hits the price axis at $p = a/b$ and $Q = 0$, so the elasticity of demand is $-bp/0$. As the price approaches a/b, the elasticity approaches negative infinity, $-\infty$. An intuition for this result is provided by looking at a sequence where -1 divided by 0.1 is -10, -1 divided by 0.01 is -100, and so on. The smaller the number we divide by, the more negative the result, which goes to $-\infty$ in the limit.

(mobile applications) is $Q = 1.4p^{-2}$, where the quantity is in millions of apps. Here, $A = 1.4$, and $\varepsilon = -2$ is the constant-elasticity of demand. That is, the demand for Apple apps is elastic: $\varepsilon < -1$. We can equivalently write this demand function as $\ln Q = \ln 1.4 - 2 \ln p$.

Figure 2.10 shows several constant-elasticity demand curves with different elasticities. Except for the vertical and the horizontal demand curves, the curves are convex to the origin (bend away from the origin). The two extreme cases of these constant-elasticity demand curves are the vertical and the horizontal demand curves. Along the demand curve that is horizontal at p^* in Figure 2.10, the elasticity is infinite everywhere. It is also a special case of a linear demand curve with a zero slope ($b = 0$). Along this demand curve, people are willing to buy as much as firms sell at any price less than or equal to p^*. If the price increases even slightly above p^*, however, demand falls to zero. Thus, a small increase in price causes an infinite drop in the quantity demanded, which means that the demand curve is perfectly elastic.

Why would a demand curve be horizontal? One reason is that consumers view one good as identical to another good and do not care which one they buy. Suppose that consumers view Washington State apples and Oregon apples as identical. They won't buy Washington apples if these apples sell for more than Oregon apples. Similarly, they won't buy Oregon apples if their price is higher than that of Washington apples. If the two prices are equal, consumers do not care which type of apple they buy. Thus, the demand curve for Oregon apples is horizontal at the price of Washington apples.

The other extreme case is the vertical demand curve, which is perfectly inelastic everywhere. Such a demand curve is also an extreme case of the linear demand curve with an infinite (vertical) slope. If the price goes up, the quantity demanded is unchanged, $dQ/dp = 0$, so the elasticity of demand must be zero: $\varepsilon = (dQ/dp)(p/Q) = 0 \times (p/Q) = 0$.

A demand curve is vertical for *essential goods*—goods that people feel they must have and will pay anything to get. Because Sydney has diabetes, her demand curve for insulin could be vertical at a day's dose, Q^*.[17]

Figure 2.10 Constant-Elasticity Demand Curves

These constant-elasticity demand curves, $Q = Ap$, vary with respect to their elasticities. Curves with negative, finite elasticities are convex to the origin. The vertical, constant-elasticity demand curve is perfectly inelastic, while the horizontal curve is perfectly elastic.

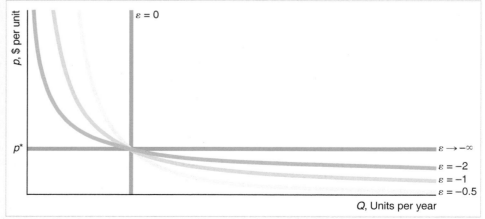

---

[17]More realistically, she may have a maximum price, p^*, that she can afford to pay. Thus, her demand curve is vertical at Q^* up to p^* and horizontal at p^* to the left of Q^*.

SOLVED PROBLEM 2.3

Show that the price elasticity of demand is a constant ε if the demand function is exponential, $Q = Ap^\varepsilon$, or, equivalently, log-linear, $\ln Q = \ln A + \varepsilon \ln p$.

Answer

1. *Differentiate the exponential demand curve with respect to price to determine dQ/dp, and substitute that expression into the definition of the elasticity of demand.* Differentiating the demand curve $Q = Ap^\varepsilon$, we find that $dQ/dp = \varepsilon Ap^{\varepsilon-1}$. Substituting that expression into the elasticity definition, we learn that the elasticity is

$$\frac{dQ}{dp}\frac{p}{Q} = \varepsilon Ap^{\varepsilon-1}\frac{p}{Q} = \varepsilon Ap^{\varepsilon-1}\frac{p}{Ap^\varepsilon} = \varepsilon.$$

Because the elasticity is a constant that does not depend on the particular value of p, it is the same at every point along the demand curve.

2. *Differentiate the log-linear demand curve to determine dQ/dp, and substitute that expression into the definition of the elasticity of demand.* Differentiating the log-linear demand curve, $\ln Q = \ln A + \varepsilon \ln p$, with respect to p, we find that $d(\ln Q)/dp = (dQ/dp)/Q = \varepsilon/p$. Multiplying this Equation by p, we again discover that the elasticity is constant:

$$\frac{dQ}{dp}\frac{p}{Q} = \varepsilon\frac{Q}{p}\frac{p}{Q} = \varepsilon.$$

Other Types of Demand Elasticities. We refer to the price elasticity of demand as *the* elasticity of demand. However, other types of demand elasticities show how the quantity demanded changes in response to changes in variables other than price that affect the quantity demanded. Two such demand elasticities are the income elasticity of demand and the cross-price elasticity of demand.

As people's incomes increase, their demand curves for products shift. If a demand curve shifts to the right, consumers demand a larger quantity at any given price. If instead the demand curve shifts to the left, consumers demand a smaller quantity at any given price.

We can measure how sensitive the quantity demanded at a given price is to income by using the **income elasticity of demand** (or *income elasticity*), which is the percentage change in the quantity demanded in response to a given percentage change in income, Y. The income elasticity of demand is

$$\xi = \frac{\text{percentage change in quantity demanded}}{\text{percentage change in income}} = \frac{\Delta Q/Q}{\Delta Y/Y} = \frac{\partial Q}{\partial Y}\frac{Y}{Q},$$

where ξ is the Greek letter xi. If the quantity demanded increases as income rises, the income elasticity of demand is positive. If the quantity demanded does not change as income rises, the income elasticity is zero. Finally, if the quantity demanded falls as income rises, the income elasticity is negative.

By partially differentiating the coffee demand function, Equation 2.2, $Q = 8.5 - p - 0.3p_s + 0.1Y$, with respect to Y, we find that $\partial Q/\partial Y = 0.1$, so the coffee income elasticity of demand is $\xi = 0.1Y/Q$. At our original equilibrium, quantity is $Q = 10$ and income is $Y = 35$ ($\$35,000$), so the income elasticity is $\xi = 0.1 \times (35/10) = 0.35$. The positive income elasticity shows that an increase in income causes the coffee demand curve to shift to the right. Holding the price of coffee constant at \$2 per lb, a 1% increase in income causes the demand curve for coffee to shift to the right by 0.35%.

Income elasticities play an important role in our analysis of consumer behavior in Chapter 5. Typically, goods that consumers view as necessities, such as food, have income elasticities near zero. The estimated income elasticity for wireless access is 0.42 (Kridel, 2014). Goods that they consider luxuries generally have income elasticities greater than one.

The **cross-price elasticity of demand** is the percentage change in the quantity demanded in response to a given percentage change in the price of another good, p_o. The cross-price elasticity is

$$\frac{\text{percentage change in quantity demanded}}{\text{percentage change in price of another good}} = \frac{\Delta Q/Q}{\Delta p_o/p_o} = \frac{\partial Q}{\partial p_o}\frac{p_o}{Q}.$$

If the cross-price elasticity is positive, the goods are *substitutes*. As the price of the second good increases, the demand curve for the first good shifts to the right, so people buy more of the first good at any given price.

If the cross-price elasticity is negative, the goods are *complements*.[18] An increase in the price of the second good causes the demand curve for the first good to shift leftward, so people buy less of the first good at any given price.

For example, coffee and sugar are complements: Many people put sugar in their coffee. By partially differentiating the coffee demand function, Equation 2.2, $Q = 8.5 - p - 0.3p_s + 0.1Y$, with respect to the price of sugar, p_s, we find that $\partial Q/\partial p_s = -0.3$. That is, an increase in the price of sugar causes the quantity demanded of coffee to fall, holding the price of coffee and income constant. The cross-price elasticity between the price of sugar and the quantity demanded of coffee is $(\partial Q/\partial p_s)(p_s/Q) = -0.3p_s/Q$. At the original equilibrium, where $Q = 10$ million tons per year and $p_s = \$0.20$ per lb, the cross-price elasticity is $-0.3 \times (0.20/10) = -0.006$. As the price of sugar rises by 1%, the quantity of coffee demanded falls by only 0.006%.

Taking account of cross-price elasticities is important in making business and policy decisions. For example, General Motors wants to know how much a change in the price of a Toyota affects the demand for its Chevy. Society wants to know if taxing soft drinks will substantially increase the demand for milk.

Supply Elasticity

Just as we can use the elasticity of demand to summarize information about the responsiveness of the quantity demanded to price or other variables, we can use the elasticity of supply to summarize how responsive the quantity supplied of a product is to price changes or other variables. The **price elasticity of supply** (or *supply elasticity*) is the percentage change in the quantity supplied in response to a given percentage change in the price. The price elasticity of supply (η, the Greek letter eta) is

$$\eta = \frac{\text{percentage change in quantity supplied}}{\text{percentage change in price}} = \frac{\Delta Q/Q}{\Delta p/p} = \frac{\partial Q}{\partial p}\frac{p}{Q}, \qquad (2.26)$$

where Q is the *quantity supplied*. If $\eta = 2$, a 1% increase in price leads to a 2% increase in the quantity supplied.

The definition of the price elasticity of supply, Equation 2.26, is very similar to the definition of the price elasticity of demand, Equation 2.21. The key distinction is

---

[18]*Jargon alert*: Graduate-level textbooks generally call these goods *gross complements* and the goods in the previous example *gross substitutes*.

that the elasticity of supply describes the movement along the *supply* curve as price changes, whereas the elasticity of demand describes the movement along the *demand* curve as price changes. That is, in the numerator, supply elasticity depends on the percentage change in the *quantity supplied*, whereas demand elasticity depends on the percentage change in the *quantity demanded*.

If the supply curve is upward sloping, $\partial p/\partial Q > 0$, the supply elasticity is positive: $\eta > 0$. If the supply curve slopes downward, the supply elasticity is negative: $\eta < 0$.

At a point on a supply curve where the elasticity of supply is $\eta = 0$, we say that the supply curve is *perfectly inelastic*: The supply does not change as the price rises. If $0 < \eta < 1$, the supply curve is *inelastic* (but not perfectly inelastic): A 1% increase in the price causes a less than 1% rise in the quantity supplied. If $\eta = 1$, the supply curve is *unitary elastic*. If $\eta > 1$, the supply curve is *elastic*. If η is infinite, the supply curve is *perfectly elastic*.

To illustrate the supply elasticity, we use the estimated linear U.S. corn supply function (based on Roberts and Schlenker, 2013)

$$Q = 10.2 + 0.25p, \qquad (2.27)$$

where Q is the quantity of corn supplied in billion bushels per year and p is the price of corn in dollars per bushel. Differentiating Equation 2.27, we find that $dQ/dp = 0.25$. At the point on the supply curve where $p = \$7.20$ and $Q = 12$, the elasticity of supply is

$$\eta = \frac{dQ}{dp}\frac{p}{Q} = 0.25 \times \frac{7.20}{12} = 0.15.$$

At this point on the supply curve, a 1% increase in the price of corn leads to a 0.15% rise in the quantity of corn supplied. That is, the supply curve is inelastic at this point.

The elasticity of supply may vary along a supply curve. For example, because the corn elasticity of supply is $\eta = 0.25p/Q$, as the ratio p/Q rises, the supply elasticity rises.

The supply elasticity does not vary along constant-elasticity supply functions, which are exponential or (equivalently) log-linear: $Q = Bp^{\eta}$ or $\ln Q = \ln B + \eta \ln p$. If η is a positive, finite number, the constant-elasticity supply curve starts at the origin, as Figure 2.11 shows. Two extreme examples of both constant-elasticity of supply curves and linear supply curves are the vertical supply curve and the horizontal supply curve.

Figure 2.11 Constant-Elasticity Supply Curves

Constant-elasticity supply curves, $Q = Bp^{\eta}$, with positive, finite elasticities, start at the origin. They are concave to the horizontal axis if $1 < \eta < \infty$ and convex if $0 < \eta < 1$. The unitary-elasticity supply curve is a straight line through the origin. The vertical constant-elasticity supply curve is perfectly inelastic, while the horizontal curve is perfectly elastic.

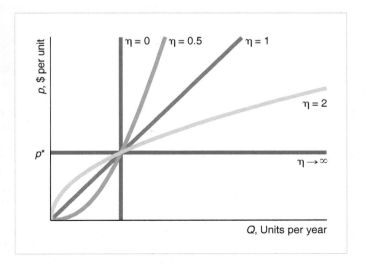

A supply curve that is vertical at a quantity, Q^*, is perfectly inelastic. No matter what the price is, firms supply Q^*. An example of inelastic supply is a perishable item such as already-picked fresh fruit. Unsold perishable goods quickly become worthless. Thus, the seller will accept any market price for the good.

A supply curve that is horizontal at a price, p^*, is perfectly elastic. Firms supply as much as the market wants—a potentially unlimited amount—if the price is p^* or above. Firms supply nothing at a price below p^*, which does not cover their cost of production.

SOLVED PROBLEM 2.4

MyLab Economics
Solved Problem

Show that the price elasticity of supply is 1 for a linear supply curve that starts at the origin.

Answer

1. *Write the formula for a linear supply curve that starts at the origin.* In general, a linear supply function is $Q = A + Bp$. If $p = 0$, then $Q = A$. For a linear supply curve to start at the origin ($p = 0$, $Q = 0$), A must be zero. Thus, the supply function is $Q = Bp$. For firms to supply positive quantities at a positive price, we need $B > 0$.

2. *Calculate the supply elasticity based on this linear function by using the definition.* The supply elasticity is $\eta = (dQ/dp)(p/Q) = B(p/Q) = B(p/[Bp]) = 1$, regardless of the slope of the line, B.

Comment: This supply function is a special case of the constant-elasticity supply function where $Q = Bp^{\eta} = Bp^1$, so $\eta = 1$.

Long Run Versus Short Run

Typically, short-run demand or supply elasticities differ substantially from long-run elasticities. The duration of the short run depends on the planning horizon—how long it takes consumers or firms to adjust for a particular good.

Demand Elasticities over Time. Two factors that determine whether short-run demand elasticities are larger or smaller than long-run elasticities are the ease of substitution and storage opportunities. Often one can substitute between products in the long run but not in the short run.

The shape of a demand curve depends on the period under consideration. Often consumers substitute between products in the long run but not in the short run. The price of U.S. gasoline in May 2018 was nearly one-third higher than in the previous year. However, most consumers did not change their consumption demand very much in the short run. Someone who drives 27 miles to and from work every day in a Ford Explorer did not suddenly start using less gasoline. However, if gas prices were to remain high in the long run, people would reduce their consumption of gasoline. Many people would buy smaller, more fuel-efficient cars, some people would take jobs closer to home, and some would even move closer to their work or closer to convenient public transportation.

Liddle (2012) estimated the gasoline demand elasticities across many countries and found that the short-run elasticity for gasoline was −0.16 and the long-run elasticity was −0.43. Thus, a 1% increase in price lowers the quantity demanded by only 0.16% in the short run but by more than twice as much, 0.43%, in the long run.

In contrast, the short-run demand elasticity for goods that can be stored easily may be more elastic than the long-run ones. Prince (2008) found that the demand for computers was more elastic in the short run (−2.74) than in the long run (−2.17). His explanation was that consumers worry about being locked-in with an older technology in the short run so that they were more sensitive to price in the short run.

Supply Elasticities over Time. Short-run supply curve elasticities may differ from long-run elasticities. If a manufacturing firm wants to increase production in the short run, it can do so by hiring workers to use its machines around the clock. However, the fixed size of its manufacturing plant and fixed number of machines in the plant limit how much it can expand its output.

In the long run, however, the firm can build another plant and buy or build more equipment. Thus, we would expect a firm's long-run supply elasticity to be greater than it is in the short run.

Similarly, the market supply elasticity may be greater in the long run than in the short run. For example, Clemens and Gottlieb (2014) estimated that the health care supply elasticity is twice as elastic in the long run (1.4) as in the short run (0.7).

APPLICATION

Oil Drilling in the Arctic National Wildlife Refuge

We can use information about supply and demand elasticities to answer an important public policy question: Would selling oil from the Arctic National Wildlife Refuge (ANWR) substantially affect the price of oil? ANWR, established in 1960, is the largest of Alaska's 16 national wildlife refuges, covers 20 million acres, and is believed to contain large deposits of petroleum (about the amount consumed in the United States in a year). For decades, a debate has raged over whether U.S. citizens, who own the refuge, should keep it pristine or permit oil drilling.[19]

The Obama administration sided with environmentalists who stress that drilling would harm the wildlife refuge and pollute the environment. On the other side, the Trump administration and drilling proponents argue that extracting this oil would substantially reduce the price of petroleum as well as decrease U.S. dependence on foreign oil. Recent large fluctuations in the price of gasoline and unrest in the Middle East have heightened this intense debate.

The effect of selling ANWR oil on the world price of oil is a key element of this dispute. We can combine oil production information with supply and demand elasticities to make a "back of the envelope" estimate of the price effects. Baumeister and Peersman (2013) estimated that the short-run elasticity of demand, ε, for oil is about -0.25 and the long-run supply elasticity, η, is about 0.25.

Analysts dispute how much ANWR oil could be produced. The U.S. Department of Energy's Energy Information Service predicts that production from ANWR would average about 800,000 barrels per day. That production would be less than 1% of the worldwide oil production, which is predicted to be about 100 million barrels per day in 2018.

A report by the Department of Energy predicted that drilling in the refuge could lower the price of oil by about 1%. In Solved Problem 2.5, we make our own calculation of the price effect of drilling in ANWR. Here and in many of the solved problems, you are asked to determine how a change in a variable or policy (such as permitting ANWR drilling) affects one or more variables (such as the world equilibrium price of oil).

---

[19]I am grateful to Robert Whaples, who wrote an earlier version of this analysis. In the following discussion, we assume for simplicity that the oil market is competitive, and use current values of price and quantities even though drilling in the Arctic National Wildlife Refuge could not take place for at least a decade from when the decision to drill occurs.

SOLVED PROBLEM 2.5

MyLab Economics
Solved Problem

What would be the effect of ANWR production on the world equilibrium price of oil given that $\varepsilon = -0.25$, $\eta = 0.25$, the pre-ANWR daily world production of oil is $Q_1 = 100$ million barrels per day, the pre-ANWR world price is $p_1 = \$70$ per barrel, and daily ANWR production is 0.8 million barrels per day?[20] We assume that the supply and demand curves are linear and that the introduction of ANWR oil would cause a parallel shift in the world supply curve to the right by 0.8 million barrels per day.

Answer

1. *Determine the long-run linear demand function that is consistent with pre-ANWR world output and price.* The general formula for a linear demand curve is $Q = a - bp$, where a is the quantity when $p = 0$ (where the demand curve hits the horizontal axis) and $b = dQ/dp$. At the original equilibrium, e_1 in the figure, $p_1 = \$70$ and $Q_1 = 100$ million barrels per day, so the elasticity of demand is $\varepsilon = (dQ/dp)(p_1/Q_1) = -b(70/100) = -0.25$. Using algebra, we find that $b = 0.25(100/70) \approx 0.357$, so the demand function is $Q = a - 0.357p$. At e_1, the quantity demanded is $Q = 100 = a - (0.357 \times 70)$. Using algebra, we find that $a = 100 + (0.357 \times 70) = 125$. Thus, the demand function is $Q = 125 - 0.357p$.

2. *Determine the long-run linear supply function that is consistent with pre-ANWR world output and price.* The general formula for a linear supply curve is $Q = c + dp$, where c is the quantity at $p = 0$, and $d = dQ/dp$. Where S^1 intercepts D at the original equilibrium, e_1, the elasticity of supply is $\eta = (dQ/dp)(p_1/Q_1) = d(70/100) = 0.25$. Solving this equation, we find that $d = 0.25(100/70) \approx 0.357$, so the supply function is $Q = c + 0.357p$. Evaluating this Equation at e_1, $Q = 100 = c + (0.357 \times 70)$. Solving for c, we find that $c = 100 - (0.357 \times 70) = 75$. Thus, the supply function is $Q = 75 + 0.357p$.

3. *Determine the post-ANWR linear supply function.* The oil pumped from the refuge would cause a parallel shift in the supply curve, moving S^1 to the right by 0.8 to S^2. That is, the slope remains the same, but the intercept on the quantity axis increases by 0.8. Thus, the supply function for S^2 is $Q = 75.8 + 0.357p$.

4. *Use the demand curve and the post-ANWR supply function to calculate the new equilibrium price and quantity.* The new equilibrium, e_2, occurs where S^2 intersects D. Setting the right side of the demand function equal to the right side of the post-ANWR supply function, we obtain an expression for the post-Arctic National Wildlife Refuge price, p_2:

$$125 - 0.357p_2 = 75.8 + 0.357p_2.$$

We can solve this expression for the new equilibrium price: $p_2 \approx \$68.91$. That is, the price drops about $1.09, or 1.6%. If we substitute this new price into either the demand curve or the post-ANWR supply curve, we find that the new equilibrium quantity is 100.4 million barrels per day. That is, equilibrium output rises by 0.4 million barrels per day (0.4%), which is only a little more than half of the predicted daily refuge supply, because other suppliers will decrease their output slightly in response to the lower price.

---

[20]This price is for June 2018. From 2007 through 2018, the price of a barrel of oil fluctuated between about $30 and $140. The calculated percentage change in the price in Solved Problem 2.5 is not sensitive to the choice of the initial price of oil.

Comment: Our estimate that selling ANWR oil would cause only a small drop in the world oil price would not change substantially if our estimates of the elasticities of supply and demand were moderately larger or smaller or if the equilibrium price of oil were higher or lower. The main reason for this result is that the refuge output would be a very small portion of worldwide supply—the new supply curve would lie only slightly to the right of the initial supply curve. Thus, drilling in ANWR alone cannot insulate the U.S. market from international events that roil the oil market.

In contrast, a new war in the Persian Gulf could shift the worldwide supply curve to the left by up to 24 million barrels per day (the amount of oil produced in the Persian Gulf), or 30 times the ANWR's potential production. Such a shock would cause the price of oil to soar whether we drill in the ANWR or not.

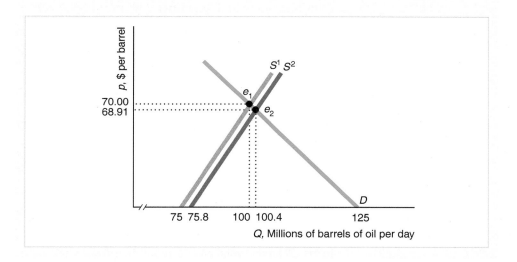

2.6 Effects of a Sales Tax

New Jersey's decision to eliminate the tax on Botox has users elated. At least I think they're elated—I can't really tell.

Before voting for a new sales tax, legislators want to predict the effect of the tax on prices, quantities, and tax revenues. If the new tax will produce a large price increase, legislators who vote for the tax may lose their jobs in the next election. Voters' ire is likely to be even greater if the tax fails to raise significant tax revenues.

Governments use two types of sales taxes: ad valorem and specific taxes. Economists call the most common sales tax an *ad valorem* tax, while real people call it *the* sales tax. For every dollar the consumer spends, the government keeps a fraction, v, which is the ad valorem tax rate. For example, Japan's national ad valorem sales tax is 8%. If a Japanese consumer buys a Nintendo Wii for ¥40,000,[21] the government

---

[21]The symbol for Japan's currency, the yen, is ¥. Roughly, ¥111 = $1.

collects $v \times ¥40{,}000 = 8\% \times ¥40{,}000 = ¥3{,}200$ in taxes, and the seller receives $(1 - v) \times ¥40{,}000 = 92\% \times ¥40{,}000 = ¥36{,}800$.[22]

The other type of sales tax is a *specific* or *unit* tax: The government collects a specified dollar amount, t, per unit of output. For example, the federal government collects $t = 18.4¢$ on each gallon of gas sold in the United States.

In this section, we examine four questions about the effects of sales taxes:

1. What effect does a specific sales tax have on the equilibrium price, the equilibrium quantity, and tax revenue?
2. Are the equilibrium price and quantity dependent on whether the government collects the specific tax from suppliers or their customers?
3. Is it true, as many people claim, that producers *pass along* to consumers any taxes collected from producers? That is, do consumers pay the entire tax?
4. Do comparable ad valorem and specific taxes have equivalent effects on equilibrium prices and quantities and on tax revenue?

The shapes of the supply and demand curves determine how much a tax affects the equilibrium price and quantity and how much of the tax consumers pay. Knowing only the elasticities of supply and demand, which summarize the shapes of these curves, we can make accurate predictions about the effects of a new tax and determine how much of the tax is paid by consumers.

Effects of a Specific Tax on the Equilibrium

We use our estimated corn supply and demand curves to illustrate the answer to our first question: What effect does a specific sales tax have on the equilibrium price, the equilibrium quantity, and tax revenue?[23]

Panel a of Figure 2.12 shows that in the before-tax equilibrium, e_1, where S^1 and D^1 intersect, the equilibrium price is $p_1 = \$7.20$ and the equilibrium quantity is $Q_1 = 12$ billion bushels of corn.

Suppose the government imposes a specific tax of $t = \$2.40$ per bushel of corn on firms. If a customer pays a price of p to a firm, the government takes t, so the firm keeps $p - t$. Thus, at every possible price paid by customers, firms are willing to supply less than when they received the full amount that customers paid. Before the tax, firms were willing to supply 11.6 billion bushels of corn per year at a price of \$5.60 per bushel, as the pre-tax supply curve S^1 in panel a shows. After the tax, if customers pay \$5.60, firms receive only \$3.20 (= \$5.60 − \$2.40), so they are not willing to supply 11.6 billion bushels. For firms to be willing to supply that quantity, customers must pay \$8.00 so that firms receive \$5.60 (= \$8.00 − \$2.40) after paying the tax. By this reasoning, the after-tax supply curve, S^2, is $t = \$2.40$ above the original supply curve S^1 at every quantity, as the figure shows.

The after-tax supply curve S^2 intersects the demand curve D^1 at e_2. In the after-tax equilibrium, consumers pay $p_2 = \$8$ and buy $Q_2 = 11.6$ billion bushels. At that quantity, firms receive the price corresponding to e_3 on the original supply curve, $p_2 - t = \$5.60$. Thus, the tax causes the equilibrium price that customers pay to

---

[22]For specificity, we assume that the price firms receive is $p = (1 - v)p^*$, where p^* is the price consumers pay and v is the ad valorem tax rate on the price consumers pay. However, many governments set the ad valorem sales tax, V, as an amount added to the price sellers charge, so consumers pay $p^* = (1 + V)p$. By setting v and V appropriately, the taxes are equivalent. Here $p = p^*/(1 + V)$, so $(1 - v) = 1/(1 + V)$. For example, if $V = \frac{1}{3}$, then $v = \frac{1}{4}$.

[23]MyLab Economics has a *Taxes Experiment* that illustrates the effect of sales taxes. To participate, go to the MyLab Economics Multimedia Library, Single Player Experiment, and set the Chapter field to "All Chapters."

Figure 2.12 The Equilibrium Effects of a Specific Tax

(a) The specific tax of $t = \$2.40$ per bushel of corn collected from producers shifts the pre-tax corn supply curve, S^1, up to the post-tax supply curve, S^2. The tax causes the equilibrium to shift from e_1 (determined by the intersection of S^1 and D^1) to e_2 (intersection of S^2 with D^1). The equilibrium price—the price consumers pay—increases from $p_1 = \$7.20$ to $p_2 = \$8.00$. The government collects tax revenues of $T = tQ_2 = \$27.84$ billion per year. (b) The specific tax collected from customers shifts the demand curve down by $t = \$2.40$ from D^1 to D^2. The intersection of D^2 and S^1 determines the new price that firms receive, $p_2 - t = \$5.60$, at e_3. Corresponding to this point is e_2 on D^1, which shows the equilibrium price that consumers pay, $p_2 = \$8.00$, is the same as when the tax is applied to suppliers in panel a.

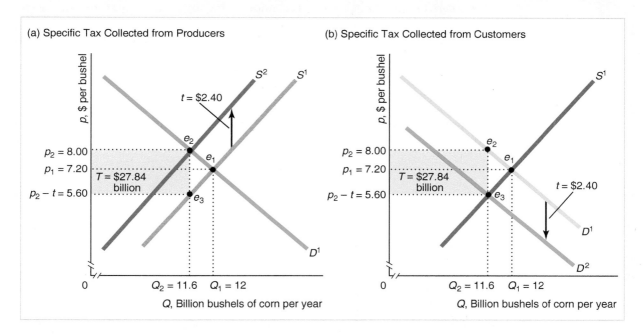

(a) Specific Tax Collected from Producers

(b) Specific Tax Collected from Customers

increase ($\Delta p = p_2 - p_1 = \$8 - \$7.20 = 80¢$) and the equilibrium quantity to fall ($\Delta Q = Q_2 - Q_1 = 11.6 - 12 = -0.4$).

Although the customers and producers are worse off because of the tax, the government acquires tax revenue of $T = tQ = \$2.40$ per bushel $\times$ 11.6 billion bushels per year = \$27.84 billion per year. The length of the shaded rectangle in Figure 2.12 panel a is $Q_2 = 11.6$ billion per year, and its height is $t = \$2.40$ per bushel, so the area of the rectangle equals the tax revenue.

Thus, the answer to our first question is that a specific tax causes the equilibrium price customers pay to rise, the price that firms receive to fall, the equilibrium quantity to fall, and tax revenue to rise. Usually, a government imposes a tax to obtain tax revenue, which is a desired intended consequence of the tax. However, it views the other effects as predictable, but unfortunate:

Unintended Consequences A sales tax usually causes the price to consumers to rise, the price received by firms to fall, and the quantity sold to drop.

Of course, a government may tax "sin" goods—such as alcohol, marijuana, and soda—to discourage consumption, in which case these price and quantity effects are intended and desired.

The Same Equilibrium No Matter Who Is Taxed

Our second question is, "Are the equilibrium price and quantity dependent on whether the specific tax is collected from suppliers or their customers?" We can use our supply-and-demand model to answer this question, showing that the equilibrium is the same regardless of whether the government collects the tax from suppliers or their customers.

If a customer pays a firm p for a bushel of corn, and the government collects a specific tax t from the customer, the total the customer pays is $p + t$. Suppose that customers bought a quantity Q at a price p^* before the tax. After the tax, they are willing to continue to buy Q only if the price falls to $p^* - t$, so that the after-tax price, $p^* - t + t$, remains at p^*. Consequently, the demand curve, from the perspective of firms, shifts down by $t = \$2.40$ from D^1 to D^2 in panel b of Figure 2.12.

The intersection of D^2 and the supply curve S^1 determines e_3. At e_3, the price received by producers is $p_2 - t = \$5.60$ and the quantity is $Q_2 = 11.6$ billion bushels. At this after-tax quantity on D^1 is e_2, where the price consumers pay is $p_2 = \$8$. The tax revenue that the government collects is $T = \$27.84$ billion.

Comparing the two panels in Figure 2.12, we see that the after-tax equilibrium prices, quantities, and tax revenue are the same regardless of whether the government imposes the tax on consumers or sellers. Consequently, regardless of whether sellers or buyers pay the tax to the government, you can solve tax problems by shifting the supply curve or by shifting the demand curve.

Firms and Customers Share the Burden of the Tax

Our third question concerns whether customers bear the entire burden of a tax, as many politicians and news stories assert.

> **Common Confusion** Businesses pass any sales tax along to consumers, so that the entire burden of the tax falls on consumers.

This claim is not generally true, as we now demonstrate. We start by determining the share of the tax that consumers bear and then show how that share depends on the elasticities of supply and demand.

Tax Incidence. The **incidence of a tax on consumers** is the share of the tax that consumers pay. We start by illustrating this concept in our corn example for a discrete change in the tax. If the government sets a new specific tax of t, the change in the tax from 0 to t is $\Delta t = t - 0 = t$. The incidence of the tax on consumers is the amount by which the price consumers pay rises as a fraction of the amount the tax increases: $\Delta p / \Delta t$.

In the corn example, as both panels of Figure 2.12 show, a $\Delta t = \$2.40$ increase in the specific tax causes customers to pay $\Delta p = 80¢$ more per bushel than before the tax. Thus, customers bear one-third of the incidence of the corn tax: $\Delta p / \Delta t = \$0.80 / \$2.40 = \frac{1}{3}$.

The change in the price that firms receive is $(p_2 - t) - p_1 = (\$8 - \$2.40) - \$7.20 = \$5.60 - \$7.20 = -\$1.60$. That is, they receive $\$1.60$ less per bushel than they would in the absence of the tax. Thus, the incidence of the tax on firms—the amount by which the price firms receives falls, divided by the tax—is $\$1.60 / \$2.40 = \frac{2}{3}$.

The sum of the share of the tax on customers, $\frac{1}{3}$, and that on firms, $\frac{2}{3}$, equals the entire tax effect, 1. Equivalently, the price increase to customers minus the price decrease to farmers equals the tax: $\$0.80 - (-\$1.60) = \$2.40 = t$.

The Incidence Depends on Elasticities. The tax incidence on customers depends on the elasticities of supply and demand, as we illustrate for small changes in the unit tax, t. If the government collects t from sellers, sellers receive $p - t$ when consumers pay p. We can use this information to determine the effect of the tax on the equilibrium. In the new equilibrium, the price that consumers pay is determined by the equality between the demand function and the after-tax supply function, $D(p) = S(p - t)$. As a result, the equilibrium price varies with t, so we can write the equilibrium price as an implicit function of the tax: $p = p(t)$. Consequently, the equilibrium condition is

$$D(p(t)) = S(p(t) - t). \tag{2.28}$$

We determine the effect a small change in the tax has on the price by differentiating Equation 2.28 with respect to t:

$$\frac{dD}{dp}\frac{dp}{dt} = \frac{dS}{dp}\frac{d(p(t) - t)}{dt} = \frac{dS}{dp}\left(\frac{dp}{dt} - 1\right).$$

By rearranging these terms, we discover that the change in the price that consumers pay with respect to the change in the tax is

$$\frac{dp}{dt} = \frac{\dfrac{dS}{dp}}{\dfrac{dS}{dp} - \dfrac{dD}{dp}}. \tag{2.29}$$

We know that $dD/dp < 0$ from the Law of Demand. If the supply curve slopes upward (as in Figure 2.12), $dS/dp > 0$, so $dp/dt > 0$. The higher the tax, the greater the price consumers pay. If $dS/dp < 0$, the direction of change is ambiguous: It depends on the relative slopes of the supply and demand curves (the denominator).

By multiplying both the numerator and denominator of the right side of Equation 2.29 by p/Q, we can express this derivative in terms of elasticities,

$$\frac{dp}{dt} = \frac{\dfrac{dS}{dp}\dfrac{p}{Q}}{\dfrac{dS}{dp}\dfrac{p}{Q} - \dfrac{dD}{dp}\dfrac{p}{Q}} = \frac{\eta}{\eta - \varepsilon}, \tag{2.30}$$

where the last equality follows because dS/dp and dD/dp are the changes in the quantities supplied and demanded as price changes, and the consumer and producer prices are identical when $t = 0$.[24] This expression holds for any size change in t if both the demand and supply curves are linear. For most other shaped curves, the expression holds only for small changes.

At the corn equilibrium, $\varepsilon = -0.3$ and $\eta = 0.15$, so the incidence of a specific tax on consumers is $dp/dt = \eta/(\eta - \varepsilon) = 0.15/[0.15 - (-0.3)] = 0.15/0.45 = \frac{1}{3}$, and the incidence of the tax on firms is $1 - \frac{1}{3} = \frac{2}{3}$.

Equation 2.30 shows that, for a given supply elasticity, the more elastic the demand curve at the equilibrium, the less the equilibrium price rises when a tax is imposed.

---

[24]To determine the effect on quantity, we can combine the price result from Equation 2.29 with information from either the demand or the supply function. For example, differentiating the demand function with respect to t, we know that $\dfrac{dD}{dp}\dfrac{dp}{dt} = \dfrac{dD}{dp}\dfrac{\eta}{\eta - \varepsilon}$, which is negative if the supply curve is upward sloping, so $\eta > 0$.

Similarly, for a given demand elasticity, the smaller the supply elasticity, the smaller the increase in the equilibrium price that consumers pay in response to a tax. In the corn example, if the supply elasticity changed to $\eta = 0$ (a perfectly inelastic vertical supply curve) and ε remained -0.3, then $dp/dt = 0/[0 - (-0.3)] = 0$. Here, none of the incidence of the tax falls on consumers, so the entire incidence of the tax falls on firms.

SOLVED PROBLEM 2.6

MyLab Economics Solved Problem

If the supply curve is perfectly elastic and the demand curve is linear and downward sloping, what is the effect of a $1 specific tax collected from producers on equilibrium price and quantity, and what is the incidence on consumers? Why?

Answer

1. *Determine the equilibrium in the absence of a tax.* Before the tax, the perfectly elastic supply curve, S^1 in the graph, is horizontal at p_1. The downward-sloping linear demand curve, D, intersects S^1 at the pre-tax equilibrium, e_1, where the price is p_1 and the quantity is Q_1.

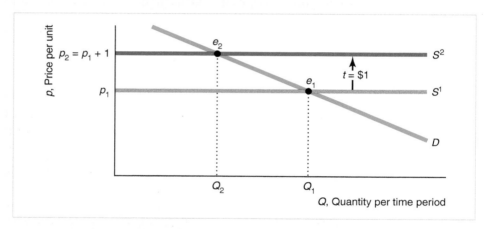

2. *Show how the tax shifts the supply curve and determine the new equilibrium.* A specific tax of $1 shifts the pre-tax supply curve, S^1, upward by $1 to S^2, which is horizontal at $p_1 + 1$. The intersection of D and S^2 determines the after-tax equilibrium, e_2, where the price consumers pay is $p_2 = p_1 + 1$, the price firms receive is $p_2 - 1 = p_1$, and the quantity is Q_2.

3. *Compare the before- and after-tax equilibria.* The specific tax causes the equilibrium quantity to fall from Q_1 to Q_2, the price firms receive to remain at p_1, and the equilibrium price consumers pay to rise from p_1 to $p_2 = p_1 + 1$. The entire incidence of the tax falls on consumers:

$$\frac{\Delta p}{\Delta t} = \frac{p_2 - p_1}{\Delta t} = \frac{\$1}{\$1} = 1.$$

(We can use Equation 2.30 to draw the same conclusion.)

4. *Explain why.* The reason consumers must absorb the entire tax is that firms will not supply the good at a price that is any lower than they received before the tax, p_1. Thus, the price must rise enough that the price suppliers receive after tax is unchanged. As consumers do not want to consume as much at a higher price, the equilibrium quantity falls.

APPLICATION
 	
Subsidizing Ethanol
	For 30 years, the U.S. government subsidized ethanol directly and indirectly with the goal of replacing 15% of U.S. gasoline consumption with this biofuel. The explicit ethanol subsidy was eliminated in 2012.[25] However, as of 2018, the government continues to subsidize corn, the main input, and requires that gas stations sell a gasoline-ethanol mix, which greatly increases the demand for ethanol.
	
	    What was the subsidy's incidence on consumers? That is, how much of the subsidy went to purchasers of ethanol? Because a subsidy is a negative tax, we need to change the sign of the consumer incidence formula, Equation 2.30, when using it for a subsidy, s, rather than for a tax. That is, the consumer incidence is $dp/ds = \eta/(\varepsilon - \eta)$.
	
	    According to McPhail and Babcock (2012), the supply elasticity of ethanol, η, is about 0.13, and the demand elasticity is about -2.1. Thus, at the equilibrium, the supply curve is relatively inelastic (nearly the opposite of the situation in Solved Problem 2.6, where the supply curve was perfectly elastic), and the demand curve is relatively elastic. Using Equation 2.30, the consumer incidence was $\eta/(\eta - \varepsilon) = 0.13/(-2.1 - 0.13) \approx -0.06$. Thus, consumers received virtually none (6%) of the subsidy, so producers captured almost the entire subsidy. A detailed empirical study by Bielen, Newell, and Pizer (2018) confirmed these results: Consumers and corn farmers received a negligible amount of the benefits from the ethanol subsidy, with virtually all of the benefits going to ethanol producers and gasoline blenders.

The Similar Effects of Ad Valorem and Specific Taxes

Our fourth question concerns whether comparable ad valorem and specific taxes have the same equilibrium and revenue effects. Unlike specific sales taxes, which are applied to relatively few goods, governments levy ad valorem taxes on a wide variety of goods. Most states apply ad valorem sales taxes to most goods and services, exempting only a few staples such as food and medicine.

    Suppose the government imposes an ad valorem tax of v, instead of a specific tax, on the price that consumers pay for corn. We already know that the equilibrium price of corn is $8.00 with a specific tax of $2.40 per bushel. At that price, an ad valorem tax of $v = \$2.40/\$8 = 30\%$ raises the same amount of tax per unit as a $2.40 specific tax.

    It is usually easiest to analyze the effects of an ad valorem tax by shifting the demand curve. Figure 2.13 shows how a specific tax and an ad valorem tax shift the corn demand curve. The specific tax shifts the original, pre-tax demand curve, D, down to D^s, which is parallel to the original curve. The ad valorem tax rotates the demand curve to D^a. At any given price p, the gap between D and D^a is vp, which is greater at high prices than at low prices. The gap is $2.40 ($= 0.3 \times \$8$) per unit when the price is $8, and $1.20 when the price is $4.

    If the government imposes the ad valorem tax, D^a intersects S at e_3. The equilibrium quantity falls from 12 billion bushels to 11.6 billion bushels at e_1. The after-tax price, $p_2 = \$8$, at e_2 is higher than the original price, $p_1 = \$7.20$, at e_1. The tax collected per unit of output is $t = vp_2 = \$2.40$. The incidence of the tax that falls on consumers is the change in price, $\Delta p = p_2 - p_1 = \$0.80$, divided by the change in the per-unit tax, $\Delta t = vp_2 - 0 = \$2.40$, that is collected, $\Delta p/(vp_2) = \$0.80/\$2.40 = \frac{1}{3}$.

---

[25] In 2011, the last year of the ethanol subsidy, the subsidy cost the government $6 billion. According to a 2010 Rice University study, in 2008, ethanol replaced about 2% of the U.S. gasoline supply, at a cost of about $1.95 per gallon on top of the gasoline retail price. The combined ethanol and corn subsidies amounted to about $2.59 per gallon of ethanol.

Figure 2.13 The Effects of a Specific Tax and an Ad Valorem Tax on Consumers

Without a tax, the demand curve is D and the supply curve is S. An ad valorem tax of $v = 30\%$ shifts the demand curve facing firms to D^a. The gap between D and D^a, the per-unit tax, is larger at higher prices. In contrast, the demand curve facing firms given a specific tax of $2.40 per bushel, D^s, is parallel to D. The after-tax equilibrium, e_2, and the tax revenue, T, are the same with both of these taxes.

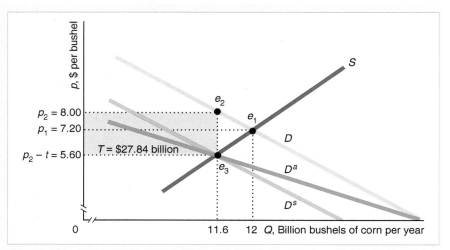

The incidence of an ad valorem tax is generally shared between consumers and producers. Because the ad valorem tax of $v = 30\%$ has exactly the same impact on the equilibrium corn price and raises the same amount of tax per unit as the $t = \$2.40$ specific tax, the incidence is the same for both types of taxes. (As with specific taxes, the incidence of the ad valorem tax depends on the elasticities of supply and demand, but we'll spare you from having to go through that in detail.)

2.7 Quantity Supplied Need Not Equal Quantity Demanded

In a supply-and-demand model, the quantity supplied does not necessarily equal the quantity demanded because of the way we defined these two concepts. We defined the quantity supplied as the amount firms want to sell at a given price, holding constant other factors that affect supply, such as the price of inputs. We defined the quantity demanded as the quantity that consumers want to buy at a given price, if other factors that affect demand are held constant. The quantity that firms want to sell and the quantity that consumers want to buy at a given price need not equal the quantity that is bought and sold.

We could have defined the quantity supplied and the quantity demanded so that they must be equal. Had we defined the quantity supplied as the amount firms *actually* sell at a given price and the quantity demanded as the amount consumers *actually* buy, supply would have to equal demand in all markets because we *defined* the quantity demanded and the quantity supplied as the same quantity.

It is worth emphasizing this distinction because politicians, pundits, and the press are so often confused on this point. Someone who insists "demand *must* equal supply" must be defining demand and supply as the *actual* quantities sold. Because we define the quantities supplied and demanded in terms of people's *wants* and not *actual* quantities bought and sold, the statement that "supply equals demand" is a theory, not merely a definition.

According to our theory, the quantity supplied equals the quantity demanded at the intersection of the supply and demand curves if the government does not intervene. However, not all government interventions prevent markets from *clearing*: equilibrating the quantity supplied and the quantity demanded. For example, as we've seen, a government tax affects the equilibrium by shifting the supply curve or demand curve of a good but does not cause a gap between the quantity demanded and the quantity supplied. However, some government policies do more than merely shift the supply curve or demand curve.

For example, governments may directly control the prices of some products. New York City, for instance, limits the price or rent that property owners can charge for an apartment. If the price a government sets for a product differs from its market clearing price, either excess supply or excess demand results. We illustrate this result with two types of price control programs. The government may set a *price ceiling* at $\bar{p}$ so that the price at which goods are sold may be no higher than $\bar{p}$. When the government sets a *price floor* at $\underline{p}$, the price at which goods are sold may not fall below $\underline{p}$.[26]

We can study the effects of such regulations using the supply-and-demand model. Despite the lack of equality between the quantity supplied and the quantity demanded, the supply-and-demand model is useful for analyzing price controls because it predicts the excess demand or excess supply that is observed.

Price Ceiling

A price ceiling legally limits the amount that a firm can charge for a product. The ceiling does not affect market outcomes if it is set above the equilibrium price that would be charged in the absence of the price control. For example, if the government

says firms can charge no more than $\bar{p} = \$5$ per gallon of gas and firms are actually charging $p = \$3$, the government's price control policy is irrelevant. However, if the equilibrium price had been $6 per gallon, the price ceiling would limit the price in that market to only $5.

Currently, Canada and many European countries set price ceilings on pharmaceuticals. The United States used price ceilings during both world wars, the Korean War, and in 1971–1973 during the Nixon administration, among other times. Many states impose price controls during a declared state of emergency.

The U.S. government imposed price controls on gasoline several times. In the 1970s, the Organization of Petroleum Exporting Countries (OPEC) reduced supplies of oil—which is converted into gasoline—to Western countries. As a result, the total supply curve for gasoline in the United States—the horizontal sum of domestic and OPEC supply curves—shifted to the left from S^1 to S^2 in Figure 2.14. Because of this shift, the equilibrium price of gasoline would have risen substantially, from p_1 to p_2. In an attempt to protect consumers by keeping gasoline prices from rising, the U.S. government set price ceilings on gasoline in 1973 and 1979.

The government told gas stations that they could charge no more than $p_1 = \bar{p}$. Figure 2.14 shows the price ceiling as a solid horizontal line extending from the price axis at $\bar{p}$. The price control is binding because $p_2 > \bar{p}$. The observed price is the price ceiling. At $\bar{p}$, consumers *want* to buy $Q_d = Q_1$ gallons of gasoline, which is the equilibrium quantity they bought before OPEC acted. However, because of the

---

[26]MyLab Economics has a *Price Ceilings Experiment* and a *Price Floors Experiment* that illustrate the operation of price controls. To participate, go to the MyLab Economics Multimedia Library, Single Player Experiment, and set the Chapter field to "All Chapters."

Figure 2.14 The Effects of a Gasoline Price Ceiling

Supply shifts from S^1 to S^2. Under the government's price control program, gasoline stations may not charge a price above the price ceiling $\bar{p} = p_1$. At that price, producers are willing to supply only Q_s, which is less than the amount $Q_1 = Q_d$ that consumers want to buy. The result is excessive demand, or a shortage of $Q_d - Q_s$.

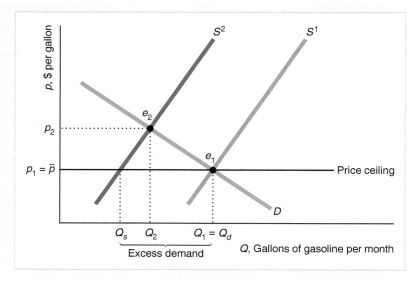

price control, firms are willing to supply only Q_s, which is determined by the intersection of the price control line with S^2. As a result, a binding price control causes excess demand of $Q_d - Q_s$.

Were it not for the price controls, market forces would drive up the market price to p_2, where the excess demand would be eliminated. The government's price ceiling prevents this adjustment from occurring, which causes a **shortage**, or persistent excess demand.

Unintended Consequence A price control causes shortages.

At the time the controls were implemented, some government officials falsely contended that the shortages were the result of OPEC's cutting off its supply of oil to the United States, but that's not true. Without the price controls, the new equilibrium would be e_2, where the equilibrium price, p_2, is greater than p_1, and the equilibrium, Q_2, is greater than the quantity sold under the control program, Q_s. Allowing the price to rise to p_2 would have prevented a shortage.

The supply-and-demand model predicts that a binding price control results in equilibrium *with a shortage*. In this equilibrium, the quantity demanded does not equal the quantity supplied. The reason that we call this situation an equilibrium even though a shortage exists is that no consumers or firms want to act differently, *given the law*. Without a price control, consumers facing a shortage would try to get more output by offering to pay more, or firms would raise their prices. With an enforced price control, consumers know that they can't drive up the price, so they live with the shortage.

So what happens when a shortage occurs? Lucky consumers get to buy Q_s units at the low price of $\bar{p}$. Other potential customers are disappointed: They would like to buy at that price, but they cannot find anyone willing to sell gas to them. With enforced price controls, sellers use criteria other than price to allocate the scarce commodity. They may supply the commodity to their friends; long-term customers;

or people of a certain race, gender, age, or religion. They may sell their goods on a first-come, first-served basis. Or they may limit everyone to only a few gallons.

Another possibility is for firms and customers to evade the price controls. A consumer could go to a gas station owner and say, "Let's not tell anyone, but I'll pay you twice the price the government sets if you'll sell me as much gas as I want." If enough customers and gas station owners behaved that way, no shortage would occur. A study of 92 major U.S. cities during the 1973 gasoline price control found no gasoline lines in 52 of the cities, where apparently the law was not enforced. However, in cities where the law was effective, such as Chicago, Hartford, New York, Portland, and Tucson, potential customers waited in line at the pump for an hour or more. Deacon and Sonstelie (1989) calculated that for every dollar consumers saved during the 1980 gasoline price controls, they lost $1.16 in waiting time and other factors.

APPLICATION

Venezuelan Price Ceilings and Shortages

Venezuela is one of the richest countries in Latin America. It is a leading oil producer, and it has many other agricultural and nonagricultural industries.

So, why do people start lining up to buy groceries in Venezuela at 4 a.m., when shops open at 8 a.m.? Strict price ceilings on food and other goods create shortages throughout the country.

According to a university study in 2018, one-quarter of Venezuelans eat two or fewer meals a day, 60% reported waking up hungry, and people reported losing 24 lb of weight, on average, during the previous year. Venezuelans also suffer from condom, birth control pill, and toilet paper shortages.

One would think that Venezuela should be able to supply its citizens with coffee, which it has been producing in abundance for centuries. Indeed, Venezuela exported coffee until 2009. However, since then, it has been importing large amounts of coffee to compensate for a drop in production. Why have farmers and coffee roasters cut production? Due to low retail price ceilings, they would have to produce at a loss.

Because Venezuela regulates the prices of many goods such as gasoline and corn flour, while Colombia, its direct neighbor to the west, does not, smuggling occurs. Given that gasoline sold in 2015 for 4¢ a gallon in Venezuela, and the price was 72¢ a gallon in most of Colombia, the temptation to smuggle is great. Venezuela's Táchira state is adjacent to the Colombian border. Its government says that as much as 40% of the food sent to Táchira is smuggled into Colombia. Why sell corn flour at an artificially low price in Venezuela if you can sell it at a higher, market price in Colombia?

Venezuela's populist President Hugo Chávez and his hand-picked successor, Nicolás Maduro, imposed strict price ceilings purportedly to rein in inflation and make the goods more affordable for the poor. Do the ceilings help the poor?

For many Venezuelans, the answer is "No!" As Nery Reyes, a restaurant worker, said, "Venezuela is too rich a country to have this. I'm wasting my day here standing in line to buy one chicken and some rice."

Demonstrators have taken to the streets to protest persistent economic and social problems, including shortages. Many have died in these violent clashes with the National Guard. Hundreds of thousands of people have left Venezuela, and more than half of those between the ages of 15 and 29 say they want to leave the country.

The ultimate irony was that President Nicolás Maduro advised Venezuelans to consume less to alleviate the shortages.

Price Floor

Governments also commonly impose price floors. One of the most important examples of a price floor is the minimum wage in labor markets.

Minimum wage laws date from 1894 in New Zealand, 1909 in the United Kingdom, and 1912 in Massachusetts. The Fair Labor Standards Act of 1938 set a federal U.S. minimum wage of 25¢ per hour. The U.S. federal minimum hourly wage rose to $7.25 in 2009 and remained at that level through early 2018, but 29 states and a number of cities set higher minimum wages.[27] As of 2018, the highest minimum wage is in Washington D.C. ($12.50), followed by Washington State ($11.50), California ($11.00), and Massachusetts ($11.00).

The minimum wage in Canada differs across provinces, ranging from C$14.00 to C$10.96 (where C$ stands for Canadian dollars) in 2018. In 2018, the United Kingdom's minimum hourly wage is £7.83 for adult workers.

If the minimum wage binds—exceeds the equilibrium wage, w^*—the minimum wage causes *unemployment*, which is a persistent excess supply of labor. For simplicity, we examine a labor market in which everyone receives the same wage.[28] Figure 2.15 shows the supply and demand curves for labor services (hours worked). Firms buy hours of labor service—they hire workers. The quantity measure on the horizontal axis is hours worked per year, and the price measure on the vertical axis is the wage per hour.

Figure 2.15 The Effects of a Minimum Wage

In the absence of a minimum wage, the equilibrium wage is w^*, and the equilibrium number of hours worked is L^*. A minimum wage, $\underline{w}$, set above w^*, leads to unemployment—persistent excess supply—because the quantity demanded, L_d, is less than the quantity supplied, L_s.

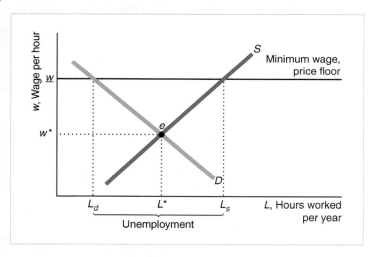

[27]See **www.dol.gov** for U.S. state and federal minimum wages. See **www.fedee.com/pay-job-evaluation/minimum-wage-rates/** for minimum wages in European countries.

[28]Where the minimum wage applies to only some labor markets (Chapter 10) or where only a single firm hires all the workers in a market (Chapter 11), a minimum wage might not cause unemployment. Card and Krueger (1995) argued, based on alternatives to the simple supply-and-demand model, that minimum wage laws raise wages in some markets (such as fast foods) without significantly reducing employment. In contrast, Neumark, Salas, and Wascher (2014) concluded, based on an extensive review of minimum wage research, that increases in the minimum wage often have negative effects on employment.

With no government intervention, the market equilibrium is e, where the wage is w^* and the number of hours worked is L^*. The minimum wage creates a price floor, a horizontal line, at $\underline{w}$. At that wage, the quantity demanded falls to L_d and the quantity supplied rises to L_s. The result is an excess supply or unemployment of $L_s - L_d$. The minimum wage prevents market forces from eliminating the excess supply, so it leads to an equilibrium with unemployment. The original 1938 U.S. minimum wage law caused massive unemployment in the U.S. territory of Puerto Rico.

It is ironic that a law designed to help workers by raising their wages may harm some workers.

Unintended Consequence If a minimum wage applies to all workers in a competitive market, it may cause some workers to become unemployed.

Thus, minimum wage laws benefit only people who manage to remain employed.

2.8 When to Use the Supply-and-Demand Model

As we've seen, the supply-and-demand model can help us understand and predict real-world events in many markets. Through Chapter 10, we discuss *perfectly competitive* markets, in which the supply-and-demand model is a powerful tool for predicting what will happen to market equilibrium if underlying conditions—tastes, incomes, and prices of inputs—change. A perfectly competitive market (Chapter 8) is one in which all firms and consumers are *price takers*: No market participant can affect the market price.

Perfectly competitive markets have five characteristics that result in price-taking behavior:

1. The market has many small buyers and sellers.
2. All firms produce identical products.
3. All market participants have full information about prices and product characteristics.
4. Transaction costs are negligible.
5. Firms can easily enter and exit the market.

In a market with many firms and consumers, no single firm or consumer is a large enough part of the market to affect the price. If you stop buying bread or if one of the many thousands of wheat farmers stops selling the wheat used to make the bread, the price of bread will not change.

In contrast, if a market has only one seller of a good or service—a *monopoly* (Chapter 11)—that seller is a *price setter* and can affect the market price. Because demand curves slope downward, a monopoly can increase the price it receives by reducing the amount of a good it supplies. Firms are also price setters in an *oligopoly*— a market with only a small number of firms—or in markets in which they sell differentiated products and consumers prefer one product to another (Chapter 14), such as the automobile market. In markets with price setters, the market price is usually higher than that predicted by the supply-and-demand model. That doesn't make the supply-and-demand model generally wrong. It means only that the supply-and-demand model does not apply to those markets.

If consumers believe all firms produce identical products, consumers do not prefer one firm's good to another's. Thus, if one firm raises its price, consumers buy from the other firm. In contrast, if some consumers prefer Coke to Pepsi, Coke can charge more than Pepsi and not lose all its customers.

If consumers know the prices all firms charge and one firm raises its price, that firm's customers will buy from other firms. If consumers have less information about a product's quality than the firm that produces it, the firm can take advantage of consumers by selling them inferior-quality goods or by charging a higher price than other firms charge. In such a market, the observed price may be higher than that predicted by the supply-and-demand model, the market may not exist at all (consumers and firms cannot reach agreements), or different firms may charge different prices for the same good (Chapter 18).

If it is cheap and easy for a buyer to find a seller and make a trade, and if one firm raises its price, consumers can easily arrange to buy from another firm. That is, perfectly competitive markets typically have very low **transaction costs**: the expenses, over and above the price of the product, of finding a trading partner and making a trade for the product. These costs include the time and money spent gathering information about a product's quality and finding someone with whom to trade. Other transaction costs include the costs of writing and enforcing a contract, such as the cost of a lawyer's time. If transaction costs are very high, no trades at all might occur. In less extreme cases, individual trades may occur, but at a variety of prices.

The ability of firms to enter and exit a market freely leads to a large number of firms in a market and promotes price taking. Suppose a firm could raise its price and make a higher profit. If other firms could not enter the market, this firm would not be a price taker. However, if other firms can quickly and easily enter the market, the higher profit will encourage entry until the price is driven back to its original level.

Thus, the supply-and-demand model is not appropriate in markets that have

- only one or a few sellers, such as the market for local water and sewage services,
- firms producing differentiated products, such as music CDs,
- consumers who know less than sellers about the quality of products or their prices, such as used cars,
- consumers incurring high transaction costs, such as nuclear turbine engines, or
- firms facing high entry or exit costs, such as aircraft manufacturing.

Markets in which the supply-and-demand model has proved useful—markets with many firms and consumers and in which firms sell identical products—include agriculture, finance, labor, construction, services, wholesale, and retail.

CHALLENGE SOLUTION

Quantities and Prices of Genetically Modified Foods

We conclude this chapter by returning to the Challenge posed at the beginning of the chapter, where we asked about the effects on the price and quantity of a crop, such as corn, from the introduction of GM seeds. The supply curve shifts to the right because GM seeds produce more output than traditional seeds, holding all else constant. If consumers fear GM products, the demand curve for corn shifts to the left. We want to determine how the after-GM equilibrium compares to the before-GM equilibrium. When an event shifts both curves, the qualitative effect on the equilibrium price and quantity may be difficult to predict, even if we know the direction in which each curve shifts. Changes in the equilibrium price and quantity depend on exactly how much the curves shift. In our analysis, we consider the possibility that the demand curve may shift only slightly in some countries where consumers don't mind GM products but substantially in others where many consumers fear GM products.

In the figure, the original, before-GM equilibrium, e_1, is determined by the intersection of the before-GM supply curve, S^1, and the before-GM demand curve, D^1, at price p_1 and quantity Q_1. Both panels a and b of the figure show this same equilibrium.

When GM seeds are introduced, the new supply curve, S^2, lies to the right of S^1. In panel a, the new demand curve, D^2, lies only slightly under D^1, while in panel b, D^3 lies substantially below D^1. In panel a, the new equilibrium e_2 is determined by the intersection of S^2 and D^2. In panel b, the new equilibrium e_3 reflects the intersection of S^2 and D^3.

The equilibrium price falls from p_1 to p_2 in panel a and to p_3 in panel b. However, the equilibrium quantity rises from Q_1 to Q_2 in panel a, but falls from Q_1 to Q_3 in panel b. Thus, when both curves shift, we can predict the direction of change of the equilibrium price, but cannot predict the change in the equilibrium quantity without knowing how much each curve shifts. Whether growers in a country decide to adopt GM seeds turns crucially on how resistant consumers are to these new products.

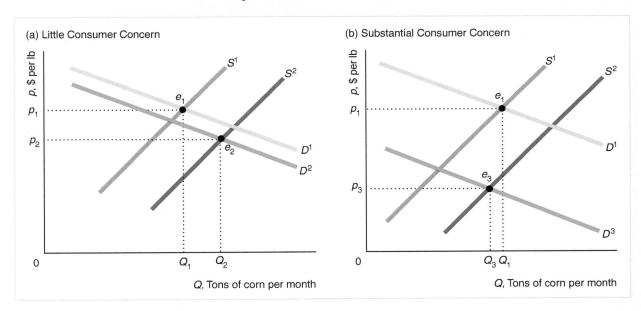

SUMMARY

1. Demand. The quantity of a good or service demanded by consumers depends on their tastes, the price of a good, the price of goods that are substitutes and complements, consumers' income, information, government regulations, and other factors. The *Law of Demand*—which is based on observation—says that *demand curves slope downward*. The higher the price, the less quantity is demanded, holding constant other factors that affect demand. A change in price causes a *movement along the demand curve*. A change in income, tastes, or another factor that affects demand other than price causes a *shift of the demand curve*. To derive a total demand curve, we horizontally sum the demand curves of individuals or types of consumers or countries. That is, we add quantities demanded by each individual at a given price to determine the total quantity demanded.

2. **Supply.** The quantity of a good or service supplied by firms depends on the price, the firm's costs, government regulations, and other factors. The market supply curve need not slope upward but it usually does. A change in price causes a *movement along the supply curve*. A change in the price of an input or government regulation causes a *shift of the supply curve*. The total supply curve is the horizontal sum of the supply curves for individual firms.

3. **Market Equilibrium.** The intersection of the demand curve and the supply curve determines the equilibrium price and quantity in a market. Market forces—actions of consumers and firms—drive the price and quantity to the equilibrium levels if they are initially too low or too high.

4. **Shocking the Equilibrium: Comparative Statics.** A change in an underlying factor other than price causes a shift of the supply curve or the demand curve, which alters the equilibrium. Comparative statics is the method that economists use to analyze how variables controlled by consumers and firms—such as price and quantity—react to a change in *environmental variables*, such as prices of substitutes and complements, income, and prices of inputs.

5. **Elasticities.** An elasticity is the percentage change in a variable in response to a given percentage change in another variable, holding all other relevant variables constant. The price elasticity of demand, ε, is the percentage change in the quantity demanded in response to a given percentage change in price: A 1% increase in price causes the quantity demanded to fall by ε%. Because demand curves slope downward according to the Law of Demand, the elasticity of demand is always negative. The price elasticity of supply, η, is the percentage change in the quantity supplied in response to a given percentage change in price. Given estimated

elasticities, we can forecast the comparative statics effects of a change in taxes or other variables that affect the equilibrium.

6. **Effects of a Sales Tax.** The two common types of sales taxes are ad valorem taxes, by which the government collects a fixed percentage of the price paid per unit, and specific taxes, by which the government collects a fixed amount of money per unit sold. Both types of sales taxes typically raise the equilibrium price and lower the equilibrium quantity. Also, both usually raise the price consumers pay and lower the price suppliers receive, so consumers do not bear the full burden or incidence of the tax. The effects on quantity, price, and the incidence of the tax that falls on consumers depend on the demand and supply elasticities. In competitive markets, the impact of a tax on equilibrium quantities, prices, and the incidence of the tax is unaffected by whether the tax is collected from consumers or producers.

7. **Quantity Supplied Need Not Equal Quantity Demanded.** The quantity supplied equals the quantity demanded in a competitive market if the government does not intervene. However, some government policies—such as price floors or ceilings—cause the quantity supplied to be greater or less than the quantity demanded, leading to persistent excesses or shortages.

8. **When to Use the Supply-and-Demand Model.** The supply-and-demand model is a powerful tool to explain what happens in a market or to make predictions about what will happen if an underlying factor in a market changes. However, this model is applicable only in competitive markets—markets with many buyers and sellers, in which firms sell identical goods, participants have full information, transaction costs are low, and firms can easily enter and exit.

EXERCISES

If you ask me anything I don't know, I'm not going to answer. —Yogi Berra

All exercises are available on **MyLab Economics** * *= answer appears at the back of this book;* **M** *= mathematical problem.*

1. Demand

*1.1 The estimated demand function (Moschini and Meilke, 1992) for Canadian processed pork is $Q = 171 - 20p + 20p_b + 3p_c + 2Y$, where Q is the quantity in million kilograms (kg) of pork per year, p is the dollar price per kg, p_b is the price of beef per kg, p_c is the price of chicken in dollars per kg, and Y is average income in thousands of dollars. What is the demand function if we hold p_b, p_c, and

Y at their typical values during the period studied: $p_b = 4$, $p_c = 3\frac{1}{3}$, and $Y = 12.5$? **M**

*1.2 Using the estimated demand function for processed pork from Exercise 1.1, show how the quantity demanded at a given price changes as per capita income, Y, increases by $100 a year. **M**

1.3 Given an estimated demand function for avocados of $Q = 104 - 40p + 20p_t + 0.01Y$, show how the demand curve shifts as per capita income, Y, increases from \$4,000 to \$5,000 per month. (*Note:* The price of tomatoes, p_t, is \$0.80.) Illustrate this shift in a diagram. **M**

*1.4 Suppose that the demand function for movies is $Q_1 = 120 - p$ for college students and $Q_2 = 60 - 0.5p$ for other town residents. What is the town's total demand function ($Q = Q_1 + Q_2$ as a function of p)? Carefully draw a figure to illustrate your answer. **M**

1.5 The food and feed demand curves used in the Application "Aggregating Corn Demand Curves" were estimated by McPhail and Babcock (2012) to be $Q_{food} = 1,487 - 22.1p$ and $Q_{feed} = 6,247.5 - 226.7p$, respectively. Mathematically derive the total demand curve, which the Application's figure illustrates. (*Hint:* Remember that the demand curve for feed is zero at prices above \$27.56, so be careful when writing the Equation for the aggregate demand function.) **M**

1.6 Based on information in the Application "The Demand Elasticities for Google Play and Apple Apps," the demand function for mobile applications at the Apple App Store is $Q_A = 1.4p^{-2}$ and the demand function at Google Play is $1.4p^{-3.7}$, where the quantity is in millions of apps. What is the total demand function for both firms? If the price for an app is \$1, what is the equilibrium quantity demanded by Apple customers, Google customers, and all customers? (*Hint:* Look at the Application "Aggregating Corn Demand Curves.") **M**

2. Supply

2.1 The estimated supply function (Moschini and Meilke, 1992) for processed pork in Canada is $Q = 178 + 40p - 60p_h$, where quantity is in millions of kg per year and the prices are in Canadian dollars per kg. How does the supply function change if the price of hogs doubles from \$1.50 to \$3 per kg? **M**

2.2 Given an estimated supply function for avocados of $Q = 58 + 15p - 20p_f$, determine how much the supply curve for avocados shifts if the price of fertilizer rises from \$0.40 to \$1.50 per lb. Illustrate this shift in a diagram. **M**

2.3 If the U.S. supply function for corn is $Q_a = 10 + 10p$ and the supply function of the rest of the world for corn is $Q_r = 5 + 20p$, what is the world supply function? **M**

*2.4 Between 1971 and 2006, the United States from time to time imposed quotas or other restrictions on importing steel. A quota says that no more than $\overline{Q} > 0$ units of steel can be imported into the country. Suppose both the domestic supply curve of steel,

S^d, and the foreign supply curve of steel for sale in the United States, S^f, are upward-sloping straight lines. How did a quota set by the United States on foreign steel imports of $\overline{Q}$ affect the total U.S. supply curve for steel (domestic and foreign supply combined)?

2.5 A cartoon in this chapter shows two people in front of a swimming pool discussing whether they want to go swimming. How does colder weather in the winter affect the desire of people to go swimming? Does it cause a movement along the demand curve or a shift of the demand curve? Use a figure to illustrate your answer.

3. Market Equilibrium

*3.1 Use a supply-and-demand diagram to explain the statement "Talk is cheap because supply exceeds demand." At what price is this comparison being made?

3.2 If the demand function is $Q = 110 - 20p$, and the supply function is $Q = 20 + 10p$, what are the equilibrium price and quantity? **M**

*3.3 Green, Howitt, and Russo (2005) estimated the supply and demand curves for California processing tomatoes. The supply function is $\ln Q = 0.2 + 0.55 \ln p$, where Q is the quantity of processing tomatoes in millions of tons per year and p is the price in dollars per ton. The demand function is $\ln Q = 2.6 - 0.2 \ln p + 0.15 \ln p_t$, where p_t is the price of tomato paste (which is what processing tomatoes are used to produce) in dollars per ton. In 2002, $p_t = 110$. What is the demand function for processing tomatoes, where the quantity is solely a function of the price of processing tomatoes? Solve for the equilibrium price and the quantity of processing tomatoes (rounded to two digits after the decimal point). Draw the supply and demand curves (note that they are not straight lines), and label the equilibrium and axes appropriately. **M**

3.4 The estimated Canadian processed pork demand function (Moschini and Meilke, 1992) is $Q = 171 - 20p + 20p_b + 3p_c + 2Y$ (see Exercise 1.1), and the supply function is $Q = 178 + 40p - 60p_h$ (see Exercise 2.1). Solve for the equilibrium price and quantity in terms of the price of hogs, p_h; the price of beef, p_b; the price of chicken, p_c; and income, Y. If $p_h = 1.5$ (dollars per kg), $p_b = 4$ (dollars per kg), $p_c = 3\frac{1}{3}$ (dollars per kg), and $Y = 12.5$ (thousands of dollars), what are the equilibrium price and quantity? **M**

3.5 The demand function for a good is $Q = a - bp$, and the supply function is $Q = c + ep$, where a, b, c, and e are positive constants. Solve for the equilibrium price and quantity in terms of these four constants.

4. Shocking the Equilibrium: Comparative Statics

*4.1 Use a figure to explain the fisher's comment about the effect of a large catch on the market price in the cartoon about catching lobsters in this chapter. What is the supply shock?

4.2 The 9/11 terrorist attacks caused the U.S. airline travel demand curve to shift left by an estimated 30% (Ito and Lee, 2005). Use a supply-and-demand diagram to show the likely effect on price and quantity (assuming that the market is competitive). Indicate the magnitude of the likely equilibrium price and quantity effects—for example, would you expect equilibrium quantity to change by about 30%? Show how the answer depends on the shape and location of the supply and demand curves.

4.3 Production of ethanol, a fuel made from corn, increased more than 8.5 times from 1.63 billion gallons in 2000 to 15.8 billion gallons in 2017 (**www.ethanolrfa.org/pages/statistics**). Use a supply-and-demand diagram to show the effect of this increased use of corn for producing ethanol on the price of corn and the consumption of corn as food. (*Hint:* See the Application "Subsidizing Ethanol.")

*4.4 The demand function is $Q = 220 - 2p$, and the supply function is $Q = 20 + 3p - 20r$, where r is the rental cost of capital. How do the equilibrium price and quantity vary with r? (*Hint:* See Solved Problem 2.1.) **M**

4.5 Due to a recession that lowered incomes, the market prices for last-minute rentals of U.S. beachfront properties were lower than usual. Suppose that the demand function for renting a beachfront property in Ocean City, New Jersey, during the first week of August is $Q = 1,000 - p + Y/20$, where Y is the median annual income of the people involved in this market, Q is quantity, and p is the rental price. The supply function is $Q = 2p - Y/20$.

   a. Derive the equilibrium price, p, and quantity, Q, in terms of Y.

   b. Use a supply-and-demand analysis to show the effect of decreased income on the equilibrium price of rental homes. That is, find dp/dY. Does a decrease in median income lead to a decrease in the equilibrium rental price? (*Hint:* See Solved Problem 2.1.) **M**

4.6 DeCicca and Kenkel (2015) report that the price elasticity of demand for cigarettes is -0.4. Suppose that the daily market demand for cigarettes in New York City is $Q = 20,000p^{-0.4}$ and that the market supply curve of cigarettes in the city is a horizontal line at a price, p, which equals $1.5p_w$, where p_w is the wholesale price of cigarettes. (That is, retailers sell cigarettes if they receive a price that is 50% higher than what they pay for the cigarettes to cover their other costs.)

   a. Assume that the New York retail market for cigarettes is competitive. Calculate the equilibrium price and quantity of cigarettes as a function of the wholesale price. Let Q^* represent the equilibrium quantity. Find dQ^*/dp_w.

   b. New York retailers pay a specific tax on each pack of cigarettes of $1.50 to New York City and $4.35 to New York State for a total of $5.85 per pack. Using both math and a graph, show how the introduction of the tax shifts the market supply curve. How does the introduction of the tax affect the equilibrium retail price and quantity of cigarettes?

   c. Given the specific tax, calculate the equilibrium price and quantity of cigarettes as a function of wholesale price. How does the presence of the tax affect dQ^*/dp_w? **M**

*4.7 Given the answer to Exercise 2.4, what effect does a U.S. quota on steel of $\overline{Q} > 0$ have on the equilibrium in the U.S. steel market? (*Hint:* The answer depends on whether the quota *binds*: that is, is low enough to affect the equilibrium.)

4.8 Suppose the demand function for carpenters is $Q = 100 - w$, and the supply curve is $Q = 10 + 2w - T$, where Q is the number of carpenters, w is the wage, and T is the test score required to pass the licensing exam (which one must do to be able to work as a carpenter). By how much do the equilibrium quantity and wage vary as T increases? **M**

4.9 Use a figure to illustrate the wage (price) and quantity effects of the opioid as described in the Application "The Opioid Epidemic's Labor Market Effects."

4.10 Use calculus to illustrate how increased use of opioids, O, affects the equilibrium quantity of labor, L, as described in the Application "The Opioid Epidemic's Labor Market Effects," dL/dO. The labor demand function is $L = D(w)$, where L is the hours of work demanded and w is the wage. The labor supply function is $L = S(w, O)$, where L is the hours of work supplied. **M**

4.11 The Aguiar et al. (2017) study concluded that a revolution in the video game market—better games at a lower price—dramatically increased the amount of time young men spend playing video games and shifted their labor supply curve. In 2015, young men played video games for 3.4 hours per week on average. From 2000 through 2015, average annual hours of work for men aged 21–30, excluding full-time students, dropped by 12%. Suppose the labor demand function is $L = 200 - w$, and the supply curve is $L = 40 + w - 2V$, where L is the hours worked, w is the wage, and V is a measure of the quality of video games. By how much do the equilibrium hours and wage vary as V increases? **M**

4.12 Bentonite clay, which consists of ancient volcanic ash, is used in kitty litter, to clarify wine, and for many other uses. One of the major uses is for drilling mud, a material pumped down oil and gas wells during drilling to keep the drilling bit cool. When oil drilling decreases, less bentonite is demanded at any given price. The price of crude oil was about $50 a barrel in 2016–2017. However, by 2018, it was over $70, causing drilling to increase. Use a supply-and-demand diagram to show the effect on the bentonite market and explain in words what happened.

5. Elasticities

5.1 The U.S. Tobacco Settlement Agreement between the major tobacco companies and 46 states caused the price of cigarettes to jump 45¢ (21%) in November 1998. Levy and Meara (2006) found only a 2.65% drop in prenatal smoking 15 months later. What is the elasticity of demand for prenatal smokers? **M**

5.2 Calculate the elasticity of demand, if the demand function is

a. $Q = 120 - 2p + 4Y$, at the point where $p = 10$, $Q = 20$. (*Hint*: See Solved Problem 2.2.)

b. $Q = 10p^{-2}$. (*Hint*: See Solved Problem 2.3.) **M**

5.3 Based on information in the Application "The Demand Elasticities for Google Play and Apple Apps," the demand function for mobile applications at the Apple App Store is $Q_A = 1.4p^{-2}$ and the demand function at Google Play is $1.4p^{-3.7}$, where the quantity is in millions of apps. These demand functions are equal (cross) at one price. Which one? What are the elasticities of demand on each demand curve where they cross? Explain. (*Hint*: You can answer the last problem without doing any calculations. See Solved Problem 2.3.) **M**

5.4 When the U.S. government announced that a domestic mad cow was found in December 2003, analysts estimated that domestic supplies would increase in the short run by 10.4% as many other countries barred U.S. beef. An estimate of the price elasticity of beef demand is −0.626 (Henderson, 2003). Assuming that only the domestic supply curve shifted, how much would you expect the price to change? (*Note*: The U.S. price fell by about 15% in the first month, but that probably reflected shifts in both supply and demand curves.) **M**

5.5 According to Borjas (2003), immigration to the United States increased the labor supply of working men by 11.0% from 1980 to 2000, and reduced the wage of the average native worker by 3.2%. From these results, can we make any inferences about the elasticity of supply or demand? Which curve (or curves) changed, and why? Draw a supply-and-demand diagram and label the axes to illustrate what happened.

5.6 Keeler et al. (2004) estimated that the U.S. Tobacco Settlement between major tobacco companies and 46 states caused the price of cigarettes to jump by 45¢ per pack (21%) and overall per capita cigarette consumption to fall by 8.3%. What is the elasticity of demand for cigarettes? Is cigarette demand elastic or inelastic? **M**

5.7 In a commentary piece on the rising cost of health insurance ("Healthy, Wealthy, and Wise," *Wall Street Journal*, May 4, 2004, A20), economists John Cogan, Glenn Hubbard, and Daniel Kessler stated, "Each percentage-point rise in health-insurance costs increases the number of uninsured by 300,000 people." (This analysis refers to a period before the Affordable Care Act.) Assuming that their claim is correct, demonstrate that the price elasticity of demand for health insurance depends on the number of people who are insured. What is the price elasticity if 200 million people are insured? What is the price elasticity if 220 million people are insured? **M**

*5.8 Calculate the price and cross-price elasticities of demand for coconut oil. The coconut oil demand function (Buschena and Perloff, 1991) is $Q = 1,200 - 9.5p + 16.2p_p + 0.2Y$, where Q is the quantity of coconut oil demanded in thousands of metric tons per year, p is the price of coconut oil in cents per lb, p_p is the price of palm oil in cents per lb, and Y is the income of consumers. Assume that p is initially 45¢ per lb, p_p is 31¢ per lb, and Q is 1,275 thousand metric tons per year. **M**

5.9 Show that the supply elasticity of a linear supply curve that cuts the price axis is greater than 1 (elastic), and the coefficient of elasticity of any linear supply curve that cuts the quantity axis is less than 1 (inelastic). (*Hint*: See Solved Problem 2.4.) **M**

5.10 Solved Problem 2.5 claims that a new war in the Persian Gulf could shift the world oil supply curve to the left by 24 million barrels a day or more, causing the world price of oil to soar regardless of whether we drill in the Arctic National Wildlife Refuge (ANWR). How accurate is this claim? Use the same type of analysis as in the Solved Problem to calculate how much such a shock would cause the price to rise with and without the refuge production. **M**

5.11 In 2018, President Trump proposed opening nearly all offshore water to oil and gas drilling. The Bureau of Ocean Energy Management, which oversees government offshore leasing, estimated that President Trump's plan could eventually result in 21 billion barrels being economically recoverable.

6. Effects of a Sales Tax

6.1 What effect does a $1 specific tax have on equilibrium price and quantity, and what is the incidence on consumers, if the following is true:

   a. The demand curve is perfectly inelastic.

   b. The demand curve is perfectly elastic.

   c. The supply curve is perfectly inelastic.

   d. The supply curve is perfectly elastic.

   e. The demand curve is perfectly elastic and the supply curve is perfectly inelastic.

   Use graphs and math to explain your answers. (*Hint*: See Solved Problem 2.6.) **M**

6.2 On July 1, 1965, the federal ad valorem taxes on many goods and services were eliminated. Comparing prices before and after this change, we can determine how much the price fell in response to the tax's elimination. Given an ad valorem tax of v, the tax collected on a good that sold for p was vp. If the price fell by vp when the tax was eliminated, consumers must have been bearing the full incidence of the tax. Consequently, consumers got the full benefit of removing the tax from those goods. The entire amount of the tax cut was passed on to consumers for all commodities and services that were studied for which the taxes were collected at the retail level (except admissions and club dues) and for most commodities for which excise taxes were imposed at the manufacturer level, including face powder, sterling silverware, wristwatches, and handbags (Brownlee and Perry, 1967). List the conditions (in terms of the elasticities or shapes of supply or demand curves) that are consistent with 100% pass-through of the taxes. Use graphs to illustrate your answer.

6.3 Essentially none of the savings from removing the federal ad valorem tax were passed on to consumers for motion picture admissions and club dues (Brownlee and Perry, 1967; see Exercise 6.2). List the conditions (in terms of the elasticities or shapes of supply or demand curves) that are consistent with 0% pass-through of the taxes. Use graphs to illustrate your answer. **M**

*6.4 Do you care whether a 15¢ tax per gallon of milk is collected from milk producers or from consumers at the store? Why or why not?

6.5 Green, Howitt, and Russo (2005) estimated that for almonds, the demand elasticity was −0.47 and the long-run supply elasticity was 12.0. The corresponding elasticities were −0.68 and 0.73 for cotton and −0.26 and 0.64 for processing tomatoes. If the government were to apply a specific tax to each of these commodities, what would be the consumer tax incidence for each of these commodities? **M**

6.6 A subsidy is a negative tax through which the government gives people money instead of taking it from them. If the government applied a $1.05 specific subsidy instead of a specific tax in Figure 2.12, what would happen to the equilibrium price and quantity? Use the demand function and the after-subsidy supply function to solve for the new equilibrium values. What is the incidence of the subsidy on consumers? (*Hint*: See the Application "Subsidizing Ethanol.") **M**

6.7 Canada provided a 35% subsidy of the wage of video game manufacturers' employees in 2011.

   a. What is the effect of a wage subsidy on the equilibrium wage and quantity of workers?

   b. What happens when the wage subsidy rate falls?

   c. What is the incidence of the subsidy?

*6.8 Use calculus to show that the less elastic the demand curve, an increase in a specific sales tax t reduces quantity less and tax revenue more. (*Hint*: The quantity demanded depends on its price, which in turn depends on the specific tax, $Q(p(t))$, and tax revenue is $R = p(t)Q(p(t))$.) **M**

6.9 The United Kingdom had a drinking problem. British per capita consumption of alcohol rose 19% between 1980 and 2007, compared with a 13% decline in other developed countries. Worried about excessive drinking among young people, the British government increased the tax on beer by 42% from 2008 to 2012. Under what conditions will this specific tax substantially reduce the equilibrium quantity of alcohol? Answer in terms of the elasticities of the demand and supply curves.

6.10 The estimated demand function for coffee is $Q = 12 - p$ (Equation 2.3), and the estimated supply function is $Q = 9 + 0.5p$ (Equation 2.7).

   a. Write equations for the equilibrium price and quantity as a function of a specific tax t.

   b. What are the equilibrium price and quantity and the tax incidence on consumers if $t = \$0.75$? **M**

7. Quantity Supplied Need Not Equal Quantity Demanded

7.1 After Hurricane Katrina damaged a substantial portion of the nation's oil-refining capacity in 2005, the price of gasoline shot up around the country. In 2006, many state and federal elected officials called for price controls. Had they been imposed, what effect would price controls have had? Who would have benefited, and who would have been harmed by the controls? Use a supply-and-demand diagram to illustrate your answers. (*Hint*: See the discussion in the Application "Venezuelan Price Ceilings and Shortages.")

7.2 The Thai government actively intervenes in markets (Nophakhun Limsamarnphun, "Govt Imposes Price Controls in Response to Complaints," *The Nation*, May 12, 2012).

   a. The government increased the daily minimum wage by 40% to Bt 300 ($9.63). Show the effect of a higher minimum wage on the number of workers demanded, the supply of workers, and unemployment if the law is applied to the entire labor market.

   b. Show how the increase in the minimum wage and higher rental fees at major shopping malls and retail outlets affected the supply curve of ready-to-eat meals. Explain why the equilibrium price of a meal rose to Bt 40 from Bt 30.

   c. In response to complaints from citizens about higher prices of meals, the government imposed price controls on 10 popular meals. Show the effect of these price controls in the market for meals.

   d. What is the likely effect on the labor market of the price controls on meals?

*7.3 Usury laws place a ceiling on interest rates that lenders such as banks can charge borrowers. Low-income households in states with usury laws have significantly lower levels of consumer credit (loans) than comparable households in states without usury laws (Villegas, 1989). Why? (*Hint*: The interest rate is the price of a loan, and the amount of the loan is the quantity.)

*7.4 An increase in the minimum wage could raise the total wage payment, $W = wL(w)$, where w is the minimum wage and $L(w)$ is the demand function for labor, despite the fall in demand for labor services. Show that whether the wage payments rise or fall depends on the elasticity of demand of labor. **M**

8. When to Use the Supply-and-Demand Model

8.1 Are predictions using the supply-and-demand model likely to be reliable in each of the following markets? Why or why not?

   a. Apples

   b. Convenience stores

   c. Electronic games (a market dominated by three firms)

   d. Used cars

9. Challenge

9.1 In the Challenge Solution, we could predict the change in the equilibrium price of crops but not the quantity when firms start selling GM seeds. For what shape supply and demand curves (or for which elasticities) could we predict the effect on quantity?

*9.2 Soon after the United States revealed the discovery of a single case of mad cow disease in December 2003, more than 40 countries slapped an embargo on U.S. beef. In addition, some U.S. consumers stopped eating beef. In the three weeks after the discovery, the quantity sold increased by 43% during the last week of October 2003, and the U.S. price in January 2004 fell by about 15%. Use supply-and-demand diagrams to explain why these events occurred.

3 A Consumer's Constrained Choice

If this is coffee, please bring me some tea; but if this is tea, please bring me some coffee.

CHALLENGE

Why Americans Buy E-Books and Germans Do Not

Are you reading this text electronically? E-books are appearing everywhere in the English-speaking world. Thanks to the popularity of the Kindle, iPad, and other e-book readers, e-books accounted for about 11.5% of the U.K. and close to 20% of the U.S. markets, but only about 4.5% of the German market in 2017.

Why are e-books more successful in the United States than in Germany? Jürgen Harth of the German Publishers and Booksellers Association attributed the difference to tastes or what he called a "cultural issue." More than others, Germans love printed books. After all, a German invented printing. As Harth said, "On just about every corner there's a bookshop. That's the big difference between Germany and the United States."

An alternative explanation concerns government regulations and taxes that affect prices in Germany. Even if Germans and Americans have the same tastes, Americans are more likely to buy e-books because they are less expensive than printed books in the United States. However, e-books are more expensive than printed books in Germany. Unlike in the United States, where publishers and booksellers are free to set prices, Germany regulates book prices. To protect small booksellers, Germany's fixed-price system requires all booksellers to charge the same price for new printed books and e-books. However, as of 2018, the tax on e-books is 19%, while the tax on print books is only 7%. Thus, the German after-tax price of an e-book is higher than for a print book. Is the only reason why U.S. consumers buy relatively more e-books than Germans do is that their tastes differ, or can different relative prices in the two countries explain this phenomenon?

Microeconomics provides powerful insights into the myriad questions and choices facing consumers. In addition to the e-book question, we can address questions such as the following: How can we use information about consumers' allocations of their budgets across various goods in the past to predict how a price change will affect their demands for goods today? Are consumers better off receiving cash or a comparable amount in food stamps? Why do young people buy relatively more alcohol and less marijuana when they turn 21?

To answer these and other questions about how consumers allocate their income over many goods, we use a model that lets us look at an individual's decision making when faced with limited income and market-determined prices. This model allows us to derive the market demand curve that we used in our supply-and-demand model and to make a variety of predictions about consumers' responses to changes in prices and income.

We base our model of consumer behavior on three premises:

1. Individual *tastes* or *preferences* determine the amount of pleasure people derive from the goods and services they consume.
2. Consumers face *constraints*, or limits, on their choices.
3. Consumers *maximize* their well-being or pleasure from consumption subject to the budget and other constraints they face.

Consumers spend their money on the bundle of products that gives them the most pleasure. If you love music and don't have much of a sweet tooth, you probably spend a lot of your money on concerts and music downloads and relatively little on candy.[1] By contrast, your chocoholic friend with the tin ear might spend a great deal of money on Hershey's Kisses and very little on music downloads.

All consumers must choose which goods to buy because their limited incomes prevent them from buying everything that catches their fancy. In addition, government rules restrict what they can buy: Young consumers cannot buy alcohol or cigarettes legally, and laws prohibit people of all ages from buying crack cocaine and some other recreational drugs (although, of course, enforcement is imperfect). Therefore, consumers buy the goods that give them the most pleasure, subject to the constraints that they cannot spend more money than they have nor can they spend it in ways forbidden by the government.

When conducting *positive* economic analyses (Chapter 1) designed to explain behavior rather than to judge it (*normative* statements), economists assume that *the consumer is the boss*. If your brother gets pleasure from smoking, economists wouldn't argue with him that it's bad for him any more than they'd tell your sister, who likes reading Stephen King novels, that she should read Adam Smith's *Wealth of Nations* instead.[2] Accepting each consumer's tastes is not the same as condoning how people behave. Economists want to predict behavior. They want to know, for example, whether your brother will smoke more next year if the price of cigarettes decreases 10%. The following prediction is unlikely to be correct: "He shouldn't smoke; therefore, we predict he'll stop smoking next year." A prediction based on your brother's actual tastes is more likely to be correct: "Given that he likes cigarettes, he is likely to smoke more of them next year if the price falls."

In this chapter, we examine five main topics	1. **Preferences.** We use five properties of preferences to predict which combinations, or bundle, of goods an individual prefers to other combinations.
	2. **Utility.** Economists summarize a consumer's preferences using a utility function, which assigns a numerical value to each possible bundle of goods, reflecting the consumer's relative ranking of the bundles.
	3. **Budget Constraint.** Prices, income, and government restrictions limit a consumer's ability to make purchases by determining the rate at which a consumer can trade one good for another.
	4. **Constrained Consumer Choice.** Consumers maximize their pleasure from consuming various possible bundles of goods given their income, which limits the amount of goods they can purchase.
	5. **Behavioral Economics.** Experiments indicate that people sometimes deviate from rational, utility-maximizing behavior.

---

[1]Microeconomics is the study of trade-offs: Should you save your money or buy that Superman *Action Comics* Number 1 you always wanted? Indeed, an anagram for *microeconomics* is *income or comics*.

[2]As the ancient Romans phrased it, "De gustibus non est disputandum"—there is no disputing about (accounting for) tastes. Or, as it was put in the movie *Grand Hotel* (1932), "Have caviar if you like, but it tastes like herring to me."

3.1 Preferences

Do not do unto others as you would that they would do unto you. Their tastes may not be the same. —George Bernard Shaw

We start our analysis of consumer behavior by examining consumer preferences. Using three assumptions, we can make many predictions about people's preferences. Once we know about consumers' preferences, we can add information about the constraints that consumers face so that we can answer many questions, such as the ones posed at the beginning of the chapter, or derive demand curves, as we do in Chapter 4.

As a consumer, you choose among many goods. Should you have ice cream or cake for dessert? Should you spend most of your money on a large apartment or rent a single room and use the money you save to pay for trips and concerts? In short, you must allocate your money to buy a *bundle* of goods (*market basket*, or combination of goods).

How do consumers choose the bundle of goods they buy? One possibility is that consumers behave randomly and blindly choose one good or another without any thought. However, consumers appear to make systematic choices. For example, you probably buy the same specific items, more or less, each time you go to the grocery store.

To explain consumer behavior, economists *assume* that consumers have a set of tastes or preferences that they use to guide them in choosing between goods. These tastes differ substantially among individuals.[3] Let's start by specifying the underlying assumptions in the economist's model of consumer behavior.

Properties of Consumer Preferences

I have forced myself to contradict myself in order to avoid conforming to my own taste. —Marcel Duchamp, Dada artist

A consumer chooses between bundles of goods by ranking them as to the pleasure the consumer gets from consuming each. We summarize a consumer's ranking with *preference relation* symbols: weakly prefers, $\succsim$, strictly prefers, $>$, and indifferent between, $\sim$. If the consumer likes Bundle a at least as much as Bundle b, we say that the consumer *weakly prefers* a to b, which we write as $a \succsim b$.

Given this weak preference relation, we can derive two other relations. If the consumer weakly prefers Bundle a to b, $a \succsim b$, but the consumer does not weakly prefer b to a, then we say that the consumer *strictly prefers* a to b—would definitely choose a rather than b if given a choice—which we write as $a > b$.

Suppose a consumer weakly prefers a to b and weakly prefers b to a, so that $a \succsim b$ and $b \succsim a$. This consumer is *indifferent* between the bundles, or likes the two bundles equally, which we write as $a \sim b$.

We make three assumptions about the properties of consumers' preferences. For brevity, we refer to these properties as *completeness*, *transitivity*, and *more is better*.

Completeness. The completeness property holds that, when facing a choice between any two bundles of goods, Bundles a and b, a consumer can rank them so that one and only one of the following relationships is true: $a \succsim b$, $b \succsim a$, or both relationships hold so that $a \sim b$. The completeness property rules out the possibility that the consumer cannot rank the bundles.

---

[3]Of Americans younger than 35, half the women but only a quarter of the men have tattoos. *Harper's Index*, *Harper's Magazine*, August 2014. A 2018 study, **www.nature.com/articles/s41467-018-04923-0**, found that higher testosterone levels in men result in stronger preference for luxury or status symbol goods.

Transitivity. It would be very difficult to predict behavior if consumers' rankings of bundles were not logically consistent. The transitivity property eliminates the possibility of certain types of illogical behavior. According to this property, a consumer's preferences over bundles is consistent in the sense that, if the consumer *weakly prefers* a to b, $a \succsim b$, and weakly prefers b to c, $b \succsim c$, then the consumer also weakly prefers a to c, $a \succsim c$.

If your sister told you that she preferred a scoop of ice cream to a piece of cake, a piece of cake to a candy bar, and a candy bar to a scoop of ice cream, you'd probably think she'd lost her mind. At the very least, you wouldn't know which dessert to serve her.

If completeness and transitivity hold, then the preference relation $\succsim$ is said to be *rational*. That is, the consumer has well-defined preferences between any pair of alternatives.

More Is Better. *If they could afford it, 23% of U.S. adults would have plastic surgery.* —2012 poll

The more-is-better (nonsatiation) property states that, all else the same, more of a commodity is better than less of it. Indeed, economists define a **good** as a commodity for which more is preferred to less, at least at some levels of consumption. In contrast, a **bad** is something for which less is preferred to more, such as pollution. Other than in Chapter 17, we concentrate on goods.

Although the completeness and transitivity properties are crucial to the analysis that follows, the more-is-better property is included to simplify the analysis; our most important results would follow even without this property.

So why do economists assume that the more-is-better property holds? The most compelling reason is that it appears to be true

Mackenzie and Chase are Civilization's greatest threat.

APPLICATION

You Can't Have Too Much Money

Having more money doesn't make you happier. I have 50 million dollars but I was just as happy as when I had 48 million. —Arnold Schwarzenegger

Not surprisingly, studies based on data from many nations find that richer people are happier on average than poorer people (Gere and Schimmack, 2017). But, do people become satiated? Can people be so rich that they can buy everything they want so that additional income does not increase their feelings of well-being? Using data from many countries, Stevenson and Wolfers (2013) found no evidence of a satiation point beyond which wealthier countries or wealthier individuals have no further increases in subjective well-being. Moreover, they found a clear positive relationship between average levels of self-reported feelings of happiness or satisfaction and income per capita within and across countries, although this effect is small at very high income levels.

Lindqvist, Östling, and Cesarini (2018) found that Swedish large-prize lottery winners have sustained increases in overall life satisfaction when compared to similar non-winners.

Less scientific, but perhaps more compelling, is a survey of wealthy U.S. citizens who were asked, "How much wealth do you need to live comfortably?" On average, those with a net worth of over $1 million said that they needed $2.4 million to live comfortably, those with at least $5 million in net worth said that they needed $10.4 million, and those with at least $10 million wanted $18.1 million. Apparently, most people never have enough.

for most people. Another reason is that if consumers can freely dispose of excess goods, consumers can be no worse off with extra goods. (We examine a third reason later in the chapter: We observe consumers buying goods only when this condition is met.)

Preference Maps

Surprisingly, with just the completeness, transitivity, and more-is-better properties, we can tell a lot about a consumer's preferences. One of the simplest ways to summarize information about a consumer's preferences is to create a graphical interpretation—a map—of them. For simplicity, we concentrate on choices between only two goods, but the model can be generalized to handle any number of goods.

Each semester, Lisa, who lives for fast food, decides how many pizzas and burritos to eat. The various bundles of pizzas and burritos she might consume are shown in panel a of Figure 3.1, with (individual-size) pizzas per semester, q_1, on the horizontal axis and burritos per semester, q_2, on the vertical axis.

At Bundle e, for example, Lisa consumes 25 pizzas and 15 burritos per semester. According to the more-is-better property, all the bundles that lie above and to the right (area A) are preferred to Bundle e because they contain at least as much of both pizzas and burritos as Bundle e. Thus, Bundle f (30 pizzas and 20 burritos) in that region is preferred to e. By the same reasoning, Lisa prefers e to all the bundles that lie in area B, below and to the left of e, such as Bundle d (15 pizzas and 10 burritos).

From panel a, we do not know whether Lisa prefers Bundle e to bundles such as b (30 pizzas and 10 burritos) in area D, which is the region below and to the right of e, or c (15 pizzas and 25 burritos) in area C, which is the region above and to the left of Bundle e. We can't use the more-is-better property to determine which bundle she prefers because each of these bundles contains more of one good and less of the other than e does. To be able to state with certainty whether Lisa prefers particular

Figure 3.1 Bundles of Pizzas and Burritos Lisa Might Consume

(a) Lisa prefers more to less, so she prefers Bundle e to any bundle in area B, including d. Similarly, she prefers any bundle in area A, such as f, to e. (b) The indifference curve, I^1, shows a set of bundles (including c, e, and a) among which she is indifferent. (c) The three indifference curves, I^1, I^2, and I^3, are part of Lisa's preference map, which summarizes her preferences.

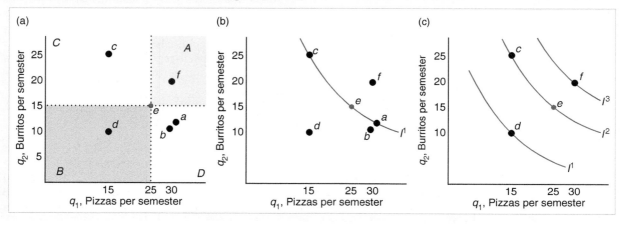

bundles in areas *C* or *D* to Bundle *e*, we have to know more about her tastes for pizza and burritos.

Indifference Curves

Suppose we asked Lisa to identify all the bundles that give her the same amount of pleasure as consuming Bundle *e*.[4] In panel b of Figure 3.1, we use her answers to draw curve I^1 through all bundles she likes as much as she likes *e*. Curve I^1 is an **indifference curve**: the set of all bundles of goods that a consumer views as being equally desirable.

Indifference curve I^1 includes Bundles *c*, *e*, and *a*, so Lisa is indifferent about consuming Bundles *c*, *e*, and *a*. From this indifference curve, we also know that Lisa prefers *e* (25 pizzas and 15 burritos) to *b* (30 pizzas and 10 burritos). How do we know that? Bundle *b* lies below and to the left of Bundle *a*, so Bundle *a* is preferred to Bundle *b* according to the more-is-better property. Both Bundles *a* and *e* are on indifference curve I^1, so Lisa likes Bundle *e* as much as Bundle *a*. Because Lisa is indifferent between *e* and *a*, and she prefers *a* to *b*, she must prefer *e* to *b* by transitivity.

If we asked Lisa many, many questions, we could, in principle, draw an entire set of indifference curves through every possible bundle of burritos and pizzas. Lisa's preferences can be summarized in an **indifference map**, or *preference map*, which is a complete set of indifference curves that summarize a consumer's tastes. We call it a *map* because it uses the same principle as a topographical or contour map, in which each line shows all points with the same height or elevation. Each indifference curve in an indifference map consists of bundles of goods that provide the same utility or well-being for a consumer, but the level of well-being differs from one curve to another. Panel c of Figure 3.1 shows three of Lisa's indifference curves: I^1, I^2, and I^3. The indifference curves are parallel in the figure, but they need not be.

Given our assumptions, all indifference curve maps must have five important properties:

1. Bundles on indifference curves farther from the origin are preferred to those on indifference curves closer to the origin.
2. Every bundle lies on an indifference curve.
3. Indifference curves cannot cross.
4. Indifference curves slope downward.
5. Indifference curves cannot be thick.

First, we show that bundles on indifference curves farther from the origin are preferred to those on indifference curves closer to the origin. Because of the more-is-better property, Lisa prefers Bundle *f* to Bundle *e* in panel c of Figure 3.1. She is indifferent among all the bundles on indifference curve I^3 and Bundle *f*, just as she is indifferent among all the bundles on indifference curve I^2, such as between Bundle *c* and Bundle *e*. By the transitivity property, she prefers Bundle *f* to Bundle *e*, which she likes as much as Bundle *c*, so she prefers Bundle *f* to Bundle *c*. Using this type of reasoning, she prefers all bundles on I^3 to all bundles on I^2.

---

[4]For example, by questioning people about which goods they would choose, Rousseas and Hart (1951) constructed indifference curves for eggs and bacon, and MacCrimmon and Toda (1969) constructed indifference curves for French pastries and money (which can be used to buy all other goods).

Second, we show that every bundle lies on an indifference curve because of the completeness property: The consumer can compare any bundle to another bundle. Compared to a given bundle, some bundles are preferred, some are enjoyed equally, and some are inferior. Connecting the bundles that give the same pleasure produces an indifference curve that includes the given bundle.

Third, we show that indifference curves cannot cross. If two indifference curves did cross, the bundle at the point of intersection would be on both indifference curves. However, a given bundle cannot be on two indifference curves. Suppose that two indifference curves crossed at Bundle e in panel a of Figure 3.2. Because Bundles e and a lie on the same indifference curve I^1, Lisa is indifferent between e and a. Similarly, she is indifferent between e and b because both are on I^2. By transitivity, if Lisa is indifferent between e and a, and she is indifferent between e and b, she must be indifferent between a and b. But that's impossible! Bundle b is on a different indifference curve than Bundle a, so Lisa *must* prefer one bundle to the other. By the more-is-better property, she prefers b to a, because b is above and to the right of a, so it contains more of both goods. Thus, because preferences are transitive, indifference curves cannot cross.

Fourth, we show that indifference curves must be downward sloping. Suppose, to the contrary, that an indifference curve sloped upward, as in panel b of Figure 3.2. The consumer is indifferent between Bundles a and b because both lie on the same indifference curve, I. But the consumer prefers b to a by the more-is-better property: Bundle a lies strictly below and to the left of Bundle b. Because of this contradiction—the

Figure 3.2 Impossible Indifference Curves

(a) Suppose that the indifference curves cross at Bundle e. Lisa is indifferent between Bundles e and a on indifference curve I^0 and between e and b on I^1. If Lisa is indifferent between e and a, and she is indifferent between e and b, she must be indifferent between a and b due to transitivity. But b has more of both pizzas and burritos than a, so she *must* prefer b to a. Because of this contradiction, indifference curves cannot cross. (b) Suppose that indifference curve I slopes upward. The consumer is indifferent between b and a because they lie on I, but prefers b to a by the more-is-better assumption. Because of this contradiction, indifference curves cannot be upward sloping. (c) Suppose that indifference curve I is thick enough to contain both a and b. The consumer is indifferent between a and b because both are on I. However, the consumer prefers b to a by the more-is-better assumption because b lies above and to the right of a. Because of this contradiction, indifference curves cannot be thick.

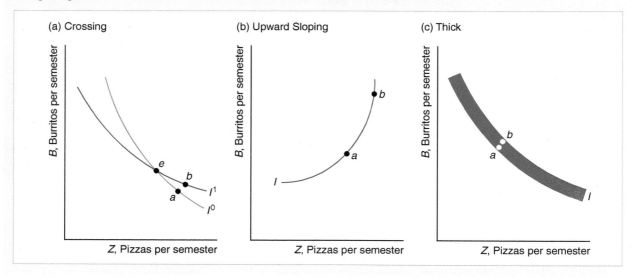

(a) Crossing   (b) Upward Sloping   (c) Thick

consumer cannot be indifferent between *a* and *b* *and* strictly prefer *b* to *a*—indifference curves cannot be upward sloping. For example, if Lisa views pizza and burritos as goods, she cannot be indifferent between a bundle of one pizza and one burrito and another bundle with two of each.

We show the fifth property in Solved Problem 3.1.

SOLVED PROBLEM 3.1

MyLab Economics Solved Problem

Can indifference curves be thick?

Answer

Draw an indifference curve that is at least two bundles thick, and show that a preference property is violated. Panel c of Figure 3.2 shows a thick indifference curve, *I*, with two bundles, *a* and *b*, identified. Bundle *b* lies above and to the right of *a*: Bundle *b* has more of both burritos and pizzas. Thus, because of the more-is-better property, Bundle *b* must be strictly preferred to Bundle *a*. But the consumer must be indifferent between *a* and *b* because both bundles are on the same indifference curve. Both these relationships between *a* and *b* cannot be true, so we have a contradiction. Consequently, indifference curves cannot be thick. (We illustrate this point by drawing indifference curves with very thin lines in our figures.)

3.2 Utility

Underlying our model of consumer behavior is the belief that consumers can compare various bundles of goods and decide which bundle gives them the greatest pleasure. We can summarize a consumer's preferences by assigning a numerical value to each possible bundle to reflect the consumer's relative ranking of these bundles.

Following the terminology of Jeremy Bentham, John Stuart Mill, and other nineteenth-century British utilitarian economist-philosophers, economists apply the term **utility** to this set of numerical values that reflect the relative rankings of various bundles of goods.

Utility Function

The **utility function** is the relationship between utility measures and every possible bundle of goods. We can summarize the information in indifference maps succinctly in a utility function. A utility function $U(x)$ assigns a numerical value to the Bundle *x*, which might consist of certain numbers of pizzas and burritos. The statement that "Bonnie weakly prefers Bundle *x* to Bundle *y*," $x \succsim y$, is equivalent to the statement that "Consuming Bundle *x* gives Bonnie at least as much utility as consuming Bundle *y*," $U(x) \geq U(y)$.[5] Bonnie prefers *x* to *y* if Bundle *x* gives Bonnie 10 *utils*—units of utility—and Bundle *y* gives her 8 utils.

---

[5]A utility function represents a preference relation $\succsim$ only if the preference relation is rational (which we have assumed)—that is, it is complete and transitive. A proof is based on the idea that, because the utility function over real numbers includes any possible bundle and is transitive, the preference relation must also be complete and transitive.

One commonly used utility function is called a *Cobb-Douglas* utility function:[6]

$$U = q_1^a q_2^{1-a}, \tag{3.1}$$

where U is the number of utils that the consumer receives from consuming q_1 and q_2, and $0 < a < 1$. Suppose that Lisa's utility function is a Cobb-Douglas with $a = 0.5$. Then the amount of utility that she gets from consuming pizzas and burritos is

$$U = q_1^{0.5} q_2^{0.5} = \sqrt{q_1 q_2}.$$

From this function, we know that the more Lisa consumes of either good, the greater her utility. Using this function, we can determine whether she would be happier if she had Bundle x with 16 pizzas and 9 burritos or Bundle y with 13 of each. The utility she gets from x is $U(x) = 12 (= \sqrt{16 \times 9})$ utils. The utility she gets from y is $U(y) = 13 (= \sqrt{13 \times 13})$ utils. Therefore, she prefers y to x.

The utility function is a concept that economists use to help them think about consumer behavior; utility functions do not exist in any fundamental sense. For example, if you asked your mother, who is trying to decide whether to go to a movie or a play, what her utility function is, she would be puzzled—unless, of course, she is an economist. But if you asked her enough questions about which goods she would choose under various circumstances, you could construct a function that accurately summarizes her preferences.

Ordinal Preferences. Typically, consumers can easily answer questions about whether they prefer one bundle to another, such as "Do you prefer a bundle with one scoop of ice cream and two pieces of cake to a bundle with two scoops of ice cream and one piece of cake?" However, they have difficulty answering questions about how much more they prefer one bundle to another because they don't have a measure to describe how their pleasure from two goods or bundles differs. Therefore, we may know a consumer's rank ordering of bundles, but we are unlikely to know by how much more that consumer prefers one bundle to another.

If we know only consumers' relative rankings of bundles but not how much more they prefer one bundle to another, our measure of pleasure is an *ordinal* measure rather than a *cardinal* measure. An ordinal measure is one that tells us the relative ranking of two things but does not tell us by how much more one is valued than the other. If a professor assigns letter grades only to an exam, we know that a student who receives a grade of A did better than a student who receives a B, but we can't say how much better from that ordinal scale. Nor can we tell whether the difference in performance between an A student and a B student is greater or less than the difference between a B student and a C student.

A cardinal measure is one by which absolute comparisons between ranks may be made. Money is a cardinal measure. If you have $100 and your brother has $50, we know not only that you have more money than your brother but also that you have exactly twice as much money as he does.

In most of the book, we consider only ordinal utility. However, we use cardinal utility in our analysis of uncertainty in Chapter 16, and in a couple of other cases. If we use an ordinal utility measure, we should not put any weight on the absolute differences between the utility number associated with one bundle and that associated with another. We care only about the relative utility or ranking of the two bundles.

Because preference rankings are ordinal and not cardinal, many utility functions can correspond to a particular preference map. Suppose we know that Bill

---

[6]This functional form is named after Charles W. Cobb, a mathematician, and Paul H. Douglas, an economist and U.S. senator, who popularized it.

prefers Bundle x to Bundle y. A utility function that assigned 6 to x and 5 to y would be consistent with Bill's preference ranking. If we double all the numbers in this utility function, we would obtain a different utility function that assigned 12 to x and 10 to y, but both of these utility functions are consistent with Bill's preference ordering.

In general, given a utility function that is consistent with a consumer's preference ranking, we can transform that utility function into an unlimited number of other utility functions that are consistent with that ordering. Let $U(q_1, q_2)$ be the original utility function that assigns numerical values corresponding to any given combination of q_1 and q_2. Let F be an *increasing function* (in jargon, a *positive monotonic transformation*) such that if $x > y$, then $F(x) > F(y)$. By applying this transformation to the original utility function, we obtain a new function, $V(q_1, q_2) = F(U(q_1, q_2))$, which is a utility function with the same ordinal-ranking properties as $U(q_1, q_2)$. As an example, suppose that the transformation is linear: $F(x) = a + bx$, where $b > 0$. Then, $V(q_1, q_2) = a + bU(q_1, q_2)$. The rank ordering is the same for these utility functions because $V(q_1, q_2) = a + bU(q_1, q_2) > V(q_1^*, q_2^*) = a + bU(q_1^*, q_2^*)$ if and only if $U(q_1, q_2) > U(q_1^*, q_2^*)$.

Thus, when we talk about utility numbers, we need to remember that these numbers are not unique and that we assign little meaning to the absolute numbers. We care only whether one bundle's utility value is greater than that of another.[7]

Utility and Indifference Curves. An indifference curve consists of all those bundles that correspond to a particular utility measure. If a consumer's utility function is $U(q_1, q_2)$, then the expression for one of the corresponding indifference curves is

$$\overline{U} = U(q_1, q_2). \tag{3.2}$$

This expression determines all those bundles of q_1 and q_2 that give the consumer $\overline{U}$ utils of pleasure.

For example, if Lisa's utility function is $U = \sqrt{q_1 q_2}$, then her indifference curve $4 = \overline{U} = \sqrt{q_1 q_2}$ includes any (q_1, q_2) bundles such that $q_1 q_2 = 16$, including the bundles (4, 4), (2, 8), (8, 2), (1, 16), and (16, 1).

A three-dimensional diagram, Figure 3.3, shows how Lisa's utility varies with the amounts of pizza, q_1, and burritos, q_2, that she consumes. Panel a shows this relationship from a frontal view, while panel b shows the same relationship looking at it from one side. The figure measures q_1 on one axis on the "floor" of the diagram, q_2 on the other axis on the floor of the diagram, and $U(q_1, q_2)$ on the vertical axis. For example, in the figure, Bundle a lies on the floor of the diagram and contains two pizzas and two burritos. Directly above it on the utility surface or *hill of happiness* is a point labeled $U(2, 2)$. The vertical height of this point shows how much utility Lisa gets from consuming Bundle a. In the figure, $U(q_1, q_2) = \sqrt{q_1 q_2}$, so this height is $U(2, 2) = \sqrt{2 \times 2} = 2$. Because she prefers more to less, her utility rises as q_1 increases, q_2 increases, or both goods increase. That is, Lisa's hill of happiness rises as she consumes more of either or both goods.

What is the relationship between Lisa's utility function and one of her indifference curves—those combinations of q_1 and q_2 that give Lisa a particular level of utility? Imagine that the hill of happiness is made of clay. If you cut the hill at a particular level of utility, the height corresponding to Bundle a, $U(2, 2) = 2$, you get a smaller hill above the cut. The bottom edge of this hill—the edge where you cut—is the

---

[7]The Cobb-Douglas utility function can be written generally as $U = Aq_1^c q_2^d$. However, we can always transform that utility function into the simpler one in Equation 3.1 through a positive monotonic transformation: $q_1^a q_2^{1-a} = F(Aq_1^c q_2^d)$, where $F(x) = x^{1/(c+d)}/A$, so that $a = c/(c + d)$.

Figure 3.3 The Relationship Between the Utility Function and Indifference Curves

Both panels a and b show Lisa's utility, $U(q_1, q_2)$, as a function of the amount of pizza, q_1, and burritos, q_2, that she consumes. The figure measures q_1 along one axis on the floor of the diagram, and q_2 along the other axis on the floor. Utility is measured on the vertical axis. As q_1, q_2, or both increase, she has more utility: She is on a higher point on the diagram. If we take all the points, the curve I^*, that are at a given height—given level of utility—on the utility surface and project those points down onto the floor of the diagram, we obtain the indifference curve I.

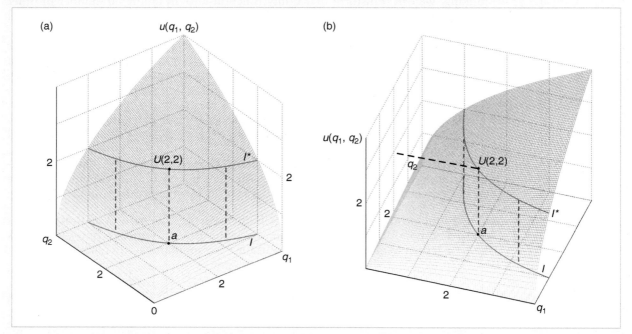

curve I^*. Now, suppose that you lower that smaller hill straight down onto the floor and trace the outside edge of this smaller hill. The outer edge of the hill on the two-dimensional floor is indifference curve I. Making other parallel cuts in the hill of happiness, placing the smaller hills on the floor, and tracing their outside edges, you can obtain a map of indifference curves on which each indifference curve reflects a different level of utility.

Willingness to Substitute Between Goods

How willing a consumer is to trade one good for another depends on the slope of the consumer's indifference curve, dq_2/dq_1, at the consumer's initial bundle of goods. Economists call the slope at a point on an indifference curve the **marginal rate of substitution** (*MRS*), because it is the maximum amount of one good that a consumer will sacrifice (trade) to obtain one more unit of another good.[8]

---

[8]Sometimes it is difficult to guess whether other people think certain goods are close substitutes. For example, according to *Harper's Index*, 1994, flowers, perfume, and fire extinguishers rank 1, 2, and 3 among Mother's Day gifts that Americans consider "very appropriate."

We are out of tickets for Swan Lake. Do you want tickets for Wrestlemania?

Lisa's *MRS* at Bundle *e* in Figure 3.4 is equal to the slope of the dashed line that is tangent to her indifference curve *I* at *e*. Because her indifference curve has a downward slope (and hence so does the line tangent to the indifference curve), her *MRS* at *e* is a negative number. The negative sign tells us that Lisa is willing to give up some pizza for more burritos and vice versa.

Although the *MRS* is defined as the slope at a particular bundle, we can illustrate the idea with a discrete change. If Lisa's *MRS* = −2, then she is indifferent between her current bundle and another bundle in which she gives up one unit of q_1 in exchange for two more units of q_2 (or gives up two units of q_2 for one more unit of q_1). For example, if Lisa's original Bundle *e* has nine pizzas, q_1, and three burritos, q_2, she would be indifferent between that bundle and one in which she had eight (one fewer) pizzas and five (two additional) burritos.

The Relationship Between the Marginal Rate of Substitution and Marginal Utility. We can use calculus to determine the *MRS* at a point on Lisa's indifference curve in Equation 3.2. We show that the *MRS* depends on how much extra utility Lisa gets from a little more of each good. We call the extra utility that a consumer gets from consuming the last unit of a good the **marginal utility**. Given that Lisa's utility function is $U(q_1, q_2)$, the marginal utility she gets from a little more pizza, holding the quantity of burritos fixed, is

$$\text{marginal utility of pizza} = \frac{\partial U}{\partial q_1} = U_1.$$

Figure 3.4 Marginal Rate of Substitution

Lisa's marginal rate of substitution, $MRS = dq_2/dq_1$, at her initial bundle *e* is the slope of indifference curve *I* at that point. The marginal rate of substitution at *e* is the same as the slope of the line that is tangent to *I* at *e*. This indifference curve illustrates a diminishing marginal rate of substitution: The slope of the indifference curve becomes flatter as we move down and to the right along the curve (from Bundle *f* to *e* to *g*).

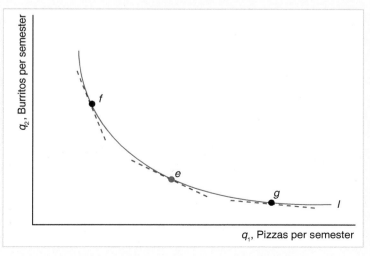

Similarly, the marginal utility from more burritos is $U_2 = \partial U/\partial q_2$, where we hold the amount of pizza constant.

We can determine the *MRS* along an indifference curve by ascertaining the changes in q_1 and q_2 that leave her utility unchanged, keeping her on her original indifference curve, $\overline{U} = U(q_1, q_2)$. Let $q_2(q_1)$ be the implicit function that shows how much q_2 it takes to keep Lisa's utility at $\overline{U}$, given that she consumes q_1. We want to know how much q_2 must change if we increase q_1, dq_2/dq_1, given that we require her utility to remain constant. To answer this question, we use the chain rule to differentiate $\overline{U} = U(q_1, q_2(q_1))$ with respect to q_1, noting that because $\overline{U}$ is a constant, $d\overline{U}/dq_1 = 0$:

$$\frac{d\overline{U}}{dq_1} = 0 = \frac{\partial U(q_1, q_2(q_1))}{\partial q_1} + \frac{\partial U(q_1, q_2(q_1))}{\partial q_2}\frac{dq_2}{dq_1} = U_1 + U_2\frac{dq_2}{dq_1}. \tag{3.3}$$

The intuition behind Equation 3.3 is that as we move down and to the right along the indifference curve in Figure 3.4, we increase the amount of q_1 slightly, which increases Lisa's utility by U_1, so we must decrease her consumption of q_2 to hold her utility constant and keep her on the $\overline{U}$ indifference curve. Her decrease in utility from reducing q_2 in response to the increase in q_1 is $U_2(dq_2/dq_1)$, which is negative because dq_2/dq_1 is negative.

Rearranging the terms in Equation 3.3, we find that her marginal rate of substitution is

$$MRS = \frac{dq_2}{dq_1} = -\frac{\partial U/\partial q_1}{\partial U/\partial q_2} = -\frac{U_1}{U_2}. \tag{3.4}$$

Thus, the slope of her indifference curve is the negative of the ratio of her marginal utilities.

SOLVED PROBLEM 3.2

MyLab Economics Solved Problem

Jackie has a Cobb-Douglas utility function, $U = q_1^a q_2^{1-a}$, where q_1 is the number of tracks of recorded music she buys a year, and q_2 is the number of live music events she attends. What is her marginal rate of substitution?

Answer

1. *Determine the marginal utility Jackie gets from extra music tracks and the marginal utility she derives from more live music.* Her marginal utility from extra tracks is

$$U_1 = \frac{\partial U}{\partial q_1} = a q_1^{a-1} q_2^{1-a} = a\frac{U(q_1, q_2)}{q_1},$$

and her marginal utility from extra live music is

$$U_2 = (1-a)q_1^a q_2^{-a} = (1-a)\frac{U(q_1, q_2)}{q_2}.$$

2. *Express her marginal rate of substitution in terms of her marginal utilities.* Using Equation 3.4, we find that her marginal rate of substitution is

$$MRS = \frac{dq_2}{dq_1} = -\frac{U_1}{U_2} = -\frac{aU/q_1}{(1-a)U/q_2} = -\frac{a}{1-a}\frac{q_2}{q_1}. \tag{3.5}$$

For example, $MRS = -q_2/q_1$ if $a = 0.5$, and $MRS = -3q_2/q_1$ if $a = 0.75$.

APPLICATION

MRS Between
Recorded Tracks
and Live Music

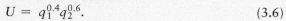

In 2008, a typical 14- to 24-year-old British consumer bought 24 music tracks, q_1, per quarter and consumed 18 units of live music, q_2, per quarter.[9] We estimate this average consumer's Cobb-Douglas utility function as

$$U = q_1^{0.4} q_2^{0.6}. \tag{3.6}$$

That is, in the Cobb-Douglas utility function Equation 3.1, $a = 0.4$.

Given that Jackie's Cobb-Douglas utility function is Equation 3.6, we can use our analysis in Solved Problem 3.2 to determine her marginal rate of substitution by substituting $q_1 = 24$, $q_2 = 18$, and $a = 0.4$ into Equation 3.5:

$$MRS = -\frac{a}{1-a}\frac{q_2}{q_1} = -\frac{0.4}{0.6}\frac{18}{24} = -0.5.$$

Diminishing Marginal Rate of Substitution. The marginal rate of substitution varies along a typical indifference curve that is convex to the origin, as is Lisa's indifference curve in Figure 3.4. As we move down and to the right along this indifference curve, the slope or *MRS* of the indifference curve becomes smaller in absolute value: Lisa will give up fewer burritos to obtain one pizza. This willingness to trade fewer burritos for one more pizza as we move down and to the right along the indifference curve reflects a *diminishing marginal rate of substitution*: The *MRS* approaches zero—becomes flatter or less sloped—as we move from Bundle *f* to *e* and then to *g* in the figure.

We can illustrate the diminishing marginal rate of substitution given that Lisa's has a Cobb-Douglas utility function where $a = 0.5$: $U = q_1^{0.5} q_2^{0.5}$. We know that this utility function has an $MRS = -q_2/q_1$ by setting $a = 0.5$ in Equation 3.5. On the indifference curve $4 = \overline{U} = q_1^{0.5} q_2^{0.5}$, two of the (q_1, q_2) bundles are $(2, 8)$ and $(4, 4)$. The *MRS* is $-8/2 = -4$ at $(2, 8)$ and $-4/4 = -1$ at $(4, 4)$. Thus, at $(2, 8)$, where Lisa has a relatively large amount of q_2 compared to q_1, Lisa is willing to give up four units of q_2 to get one more unit of q_1. However at $(4, 4)$, where Lisa has relatively less q_2, she is only willing to trade a unit of q_2 for a unit of q_1.

Curvature of Indifference Curves

The marginal rate of substitution varies along our typical convex indifference curve. How the marginal rate of substitution varies along an indifference curve depends on the underlying utility function. Table 3.1 uses Equation 3.4 to determine the *MRS* for five types of utility functions.

---

[9]A unit of live music is the amount that £1 purchases (that is, it does not correspond to a full concert or a performance in a pub).

Table 3.1 The Marginal Rate of Substitution (*MRS*) for Five Utility Functions

Utility Function	$U(q_1, q_2)$	$U_1 = \dfrac{\partial U(q_1, q_2)}{\partial q_1}$	$U_2 = \dfrac{\partial U(q_1, q_2)}{\partial q_2}$	$MRS = -\dfrac{U_1}{U_2}$
Perfect substitutes	$iq_1 + jq_2$	i	j	$-\dfrac{i}{j}$
Perfect complements	$\min(iq_1, jq_2)$	0	0	0
Cobb-Douglas	$q_1^a q_2^{1-a}$	$a\dfrac{U(q_1, q_2)}{q_1}$	$(1-a)\dfrac{U(q_1, q_2)}{q_2}$	$-\dfrac{a}{1-a}\dfrac{q_2}{q_1}$
Constant Elasticity of Substitution (CES)	$(q_1^\rho + q_2^\rho)^{1/\rho}$	$(q_1^\rho + q_2^\rho)^{(1-\rho)/\rho} q_1^{\rho-1}$	$(q_1^\rho + q_2^\rho)^{(1-\rho)/\rho} q_2^{\rho-1}$	$-\left(\dfrac{q_1}{q_2}\right)^{\rho-1}$
Quasilinear	$u(q_1) + q_2$	$\dfrac{du(q_1)}{dq_1}$	1	$-\dfrac{du(q_1)}{dq_1}$

Notes: $i > 0, j > 0, 0 < a < 1, \rho \neq 0$, and $\rho < 1$. We are evaluating the perfect complements' indifference curve at its right-angle corner, where it is not differentiable; hence the formula $MRS = -U_1/U_2$ is not well defined. We arbitrarily say that the $MRS = 0$ because no substitution is possible.

The indifference curves corresponding to these utility functions range between straight lines, where the *MRS* is a constant, to right-angle indifference curves, where no substitution is possible. Convex indifference curves lie between these extremes.[10]

Straight-Line Indifference Curve. One extreme case of an indifference curve is a straight line, which occurs when two goods are **perfect substitutes**: goods that a consumer is completely indifferent as to which to consume. Because Ben cannot taste any difference between Coca-Cola and Pepsi-Cola, he views them as perfect substitutes: He is indifferent between having one additional can of Coke and one additional can of Pepsi. His indifference curves for these two goods are straight, parallel lines with a slope of -1 everywhere along the curve, as in panel a of Figure 3.5, so his *MRS* is -1 at every point along these indifference curves. We can draw the same conclusion by noting that Ben's marginal utility from each good is identical, so his $MRS = -U_1/U_2 = -1$.

The slope of indifference curves of perfect substitutes need not always be -1; it can be any constant rate. For example, Amos knows from reading the labels that Clorox bleach is twice as strong as a generic brand. As a result, Amos is indifferent between one cup of Clorox and two cups of the generic bleach. His utility function over Clorox, q_1, and the generic bleach, q_2, is

$$U(q_1, q_2) = iq_1 + jq_2, \tag{3.7}$$

where both goods are measured in cups, $i = 2$, and $j = 1$. His indifference curves are straight lines. Because $U_1 = i$ and $U_2 = j$, his marginal rate of substitution is the same everywhere along this indifference curve: $MRS = -U_1/U_2 = -i/j = -2$.

---

[10]It is difficult to imagine that Lisa's indifference curves are *concave* to the origin. If her indifference curve were strictly concave, Lisa would be willing to give up more burritos to get one more pizza, the fewer the burritos she has.

Figure 3.5 Perfect Substitutes, Perfect Complements, Imperfect Substitutes

(a) Ben views Coke and Pepsi as perfect substitutes. His indifference curves are straight, parallel lines with a marginal rate of substitution (slope) of −1. Ben is willing to exchange one can of Coke for one can of Pepsi. (b) Maureen likes pie à la mode but does not like pie or ice cream by itself: She views ice cream and pie as perfect complements. She will not substitute between the two; she consumes them only in equal quantities. (c) Lisa views burritos and pizza as imperfect substitutes. Her indifference curve lies between the extreme cases of perfect substitutes and perfect complements.

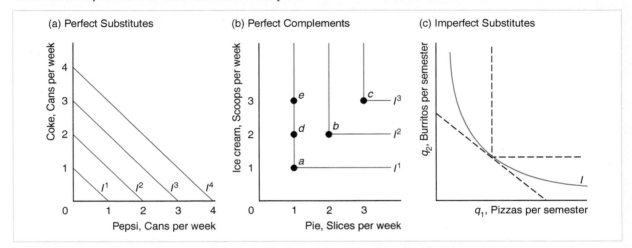

Right-Angle Indifference Curve. The other extreme case of an indifference curve occurs when two goods are **perfect complements**: goods that a consumer is interested in consuming only in fixed proportions. Maureen doesn't like apple pie, q_1, by itself or vanilla ice cream, q_2, by itself but she loves apple pie à la mode, a slice of pie with a scoop of vanilla ice cream on top. Her utility function is

$$U(q_1, q_2) = \min (iq_1, jq_2), \tag{3.8}$$

where $i = j = 1$ and the *min* function says that the utility equals the smaller of the two arguments, iq_1 or jq_2.

Her indifference curves have right angles in panel b of Figure 3.5. If she has only one piece of pie, she gets as much pleasure from it and one scoop of ice cream, Bundle a, as from one piece and two scoops, Bundle d, or one piece and three scoops, Bundle e. The marginal utility is zero for each good, because increasing that good while holding the other one constant does not increase Maureen's utility. If she were at b, she would be unwilling to give up an extra slice of pie to get, say, two extra scoops of ice cream, as at point e. She wouldn't eat the extra scoops because she would not have pieces of pie to go with the ice cream. The only condition in which she doesn't have an excess of either good is when $iq_1 = jq_2$, or $q_2/q_1 = i/j$. She only consumes bundles like a, b, and c, where pie and ice cream are in equal proportions.

We cannot use Equation 3.4 to calculate her *MRS* because her utility function is nondifferentiable. We arbitrarily say that her *MRS* = 0 because she is unwilling to substitute more of one good for less of another.

Convex Indifference Curve. The standard-shaped, convex indifference curve in panel c of Figure 3.5 lies between these two extreme examples. Convex indifference curves show that a consumer views two goods as imperfect substitutes. A consumer with a Cobb-Douglas utility function, Equation 3.1, has convex indifference curves similar to that in panel c. That curve approaches the axes but does not hit them.

Another utility function that has convex indifference curves is the *constant elasticity of substitution* (CES) utility function

$$U(q_1, q_2) = (q_1^\rho + q_2^\rho)^{1/\rho},$$

where $\rho \neq 0$ and $\rho < 1$. [If $\rho = 1$, then this utility function is a perfect substitutes utility function $U(q_1, q_2) = q_1 + q_2$.]

The marginal utility from q_i is $U_i = (q_1^\rho + q_2^\rho)^{(1-\rho)/\rho} q_i^{\rho-1}$, so the MRS $= -U_1/U_2 = -(q_1/q_2)^{\rho-1}$. For example, if $\rho = 0.5$, then the MRS $= -(q_1/q_2)^{-0.5} = -(q_2/q_1)^{0.5}$.

Another utility function that has convex indifference curves is the *quasilinear utility function,*

$$U(q_1, q_2) = u(q_1) + q_2, \tag{3.9}$$

where $u(q_1)$ is an increasing function of q_1, $du(q_1)/dq_1 > 0$, and $d^2u(q_1)/dq_1^2 \leq 0$. This utility function is called *quasilinear* because it is linear in one argument, q_2, but not necessarily in the other, q_1. [If $u(q_1) = q_1$, so both terms are linear, then this special case of the quasilinear utility function is the perfect substitutes utility function, $U(q_1, q_2) = q_1 + q_2$.]

An example is $u(q_1) = 4q_1^{0.5}$, which has the properties that $du(q_1)/dq_1 = 2q_1^{-0.5} > 0$, and $d^2u(q_1)/dq_1^2 = -q_1^{-1.5} < 0$. Figure 3.6 shows two indifference curves for the quasilinear utility function $U(q_1, q_2) = 4q_1^{0.5} + q_2$. Along an indifference curve in which utility is held constant at $\overline{U}$, the indifference curve is $\overline{U} = 4q_1^{0.5} + q_2$. Thus, this indifference curve hits the q_2-axis at $q_2 = \overline{U}$ because $q_1 = q_1^{0.5} = 0$ at the q_2-axis. Similarly, it hits the q_1-axis at $q_1 = (\overline{U}/4)^2$.

Figure 3.6 Quasilinear Preferences

The indifference curves I^1 and I^2 corresponding to the quasilinear utility function $U(q_1, q_2) = 4q_1^{0.5} + q_2$ are parallel. Each indifference curve has the same slope at a given q_1.

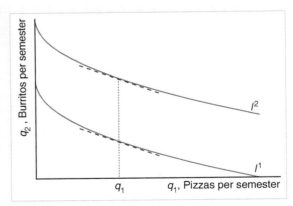

_____

SOLVED PROBLEM 3.3

A consumer has a quasilinear utility function, Equation 3.9, $U = u(q_1) + q_2$, where $du(q_1)/dq_1 > 0$ and $d^2u(q_1)/dq_1^2 < 0$. Show that the consumer's indifference curves are parallel and convex.

MyLab Economics
Solved Problem

Answer

1. *Use the formula for an indifference curve to show that the slope at any q_1 is the same for all indifference curves, and thus the indifference curves must be parallel.* At every point on an indifference curve, $\overline{U} = u(q_1) + q_2$. By rearranging this indifference curve equation, we find that the height of this

indifference curve at a given q_1 is $q_2 = \overline{U} - u(q_1)$. By differentiating this expression with respect to q_1, we find that the slope of this indifference curve is $dq_2/dq_1 = d[\overline{U} - u(q_1)]/dq_1 = -du(q_1)/dq_1$. Because this expression is not a function of q_2, the slope for a given q_1 is independent of q_2 (the height of the indifference curve). Thus, the slope at q_1 must be the same on both the indifference curves in Figure 3.6. Because the indifference curves have the same slopes for each given q_1 and differ only in where they hit the q_2-axis, the indifference curves are parallel.

2. *Show that the indifference curves are convex by demonstrating that the derivative of the slope of the indifference curve with respect to q_1 is positive.* We just determined that the slope of the indifference curve is $dq_2/dq_1 = -du(q_1)/dq_1$. If we differentiate it again with respect to q_1, we find that the change in the slope of the indifference curve as q_1 increases is $d^2q_2/dq_1^2 = -d^2u(q_1)/dq_1^2$. Because $d^2u(q_1)/dq_1^2 < 0$, we know that $d^2q_2/dq_1^2 > 0$. The negative slope of an indifference curve becomes flatter as q_1 increases, which shows that the indifference curve is convex: It bends away from the origin. That is, the indifference curve has a diminishing marginal rate of substitution.

APPLICATION

Indifference Curves Between Food and Clothing

The figure shows estimated indifference curves of the average U.S. consumer between food consumed at home and clothing. The food and clothing measures are weighted averages of various goods. At relatively low quantities of food and clothing, the indifference curves, such as I^1, are nearly right angles: perfect complements. As we move away from the origin, the indifference curves become flatter—closer to perfect substitutes.

One interpretation of these indifference curves is that people need minimum levels of food and clothing to support life. The consumer cannot trade one good for the other if it means having less than the critical level. As the consumer obtains more of both goods, however, the consumer is increasingly willing to trade between the two goods. According to these estimates, food and clothing are perfect complements when the consumer has little of either good, and perfect substitutes when the consumer has large quantities of both goods.

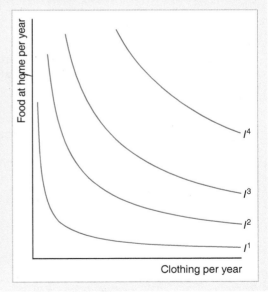

3.3 Budget Constraint

Knowing an individual's preferences is only the first step in analyzing that person's consumption behavior. Consumers maximize their well-being subject to constraints. The most important constraint most of us face in deciding what to consume is our personal budget constraint.

If we cannot save and borrow, our budget is the income we receive in a given period. If we can save and borrow, we can save money early in life to consume later, such as when we retire; or we can borrow money when we are young and repay those sums later. Savings is, in effect, a good that consumers can buy. For simplicity, we assume that each consumer has a fixed amount of money to spend now, so we can use the terms *budget* and *income* interchangeably.

For graphical simplicity, we assume that consumers spend their money on only two goods. If Lisa spends all her budget, Y, on pizza and burritos, then

$$p_1 q_1 + p_2 q_2 = Y, \tag{3.10}$$

where $p_1 q_1$ is the amount she spends on pizza and $p_2 q_2$ is the amount she spends on burritos. Equation 3.10 is her **budget line**, or *budget constraint*: the bundles of goods that can be bought if a consumer's entire budget is spent on those goods at given prices. In Figure 3.7, we plot Lisa's budget line in pizza-burrito space, just as we did with her indifference curves. How many burritos can Lisa buy? Using algebra, we can rewrite her budget constraint, Equation 3.10, as

$$q_2 = \frac{Y - p_1 q_1}{p_2}. \tag{3.11}$$

According to Equation 3.11, she can buy more burritos, q_2, if she has a higher income ($dq_2/dY = 1/p_2 > 0$), she purchases fewer pizzas ($dq_2/dq_1 = -p_1/p_2 < 0$), or the price of burritos or pizzas fall [$dq_2/dp_2 = -(Y - p_1 q_1)/p_2^2 = -q_2/p_2 < 0, dq_2/dp_1 = -q_1/p_2 < 0$]. For example, if she has $1 more of income (Y), she can buy $1/p_2$ more burritos.

If $p_1 = \$1, p_2 = \$2$, and $Y = \$50$, Equation 3.11 is

$$q_2 = \frac{\$50 - (\$1 \times q_1)}{\$2} = 25 - \frac{1}{2} q_1.$$

This equation is plotted in Figure 3.7. The budget line in the figure shows the combinations of burritos and pizzas that Lisa can buy if she spends all of her $50 on these two goods. As this equation shows, every two pizzas cost Lisa one burrito. How many burritos can she buy if she spends all her money on burritos? By setting $q_1 = 0$ in Equation 3.11, we find that $q_2 = Y/p_2 = \$50/\$2 = 25$. Similarly, if she spends all her money on pizzas, $q_2 = 0$ and $q_1 = Y/p_1 = \$50/\$1 = 50$.

Figure 3.7 Budget Constraint and Opportunity Set

If $Y = \$50, p_1 = \$1$, and $p_2 = \$2$, Lisa can buy any bundle in the opportunity set—the shaded area—including points on the *budget line L*, which has a slope of $-\frac{1}{2}$.

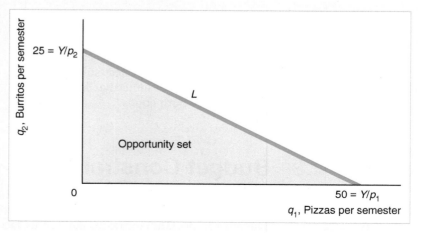

The budget constraint in Figure 3.7 is a smooth, continuous line. The continuous line shows that Lisa can buy fractional numbers of burritos and pizzas. Is that true? Do you know of a restaurant that will sell you a quarter of a burrito? Probably not. Why, then, don't we draw the opportunity set and the budget constraint as points (bundles) of whole numbers of burritos and pizzas? The reason is that Lisa can buy a burrito at a *rate* of one-half per period. If Lisa buys one burrito every other week, she buys an average of one-half burrito every week. Thus, it is plausible that she could purchase fractional amounts over time, and this diagram reflects her behavior over a semester.

Lisa could, of course, buy any bundle that costs less than $50. An **opportunity set** consists of all the bundles a consumer can buy, including all the bundles inside the budget constraint and on the budget constraint (all those bundles of positive q_1 and q_2 such that $p_1q_1 + p_2q_2 \leq Y$). Lisa's opportunity set is the shaded area in the figure. For example, she could buy 10 burritos and 15 pizzas for $35, which falls inside her budget constraint. However, she can obtain more of the two foods by spending all of her budget and picking a bundle on the budget line rather than a bundle below the line.

We call the slope of the budget line the **marginal rate of transformation** (*MRT*): the trade-off the market imposes on the consumer in terms of the amount of one good the consumer must give up to obtain more of the other good. The marginal rate of *transformation* is the rate at which Lisa is able to trade burritos for pizzas in the marketplace when the prices she pays and her income are fixed. In contrast, the marginal rate of *substitution* is the trade-off Lisa would *want* to make regardless of her income.

Holding prices and income constant and differentiating Equation 3.11 with respect to q_1, we find that the slope of the budget constraint, or the marginal rate of transformation, is

$$MRT = \frac{dq_2}{dq_1} = -\frac{p_1}{p_2}. \tag{3.12}$$

Because the price of a pizza is half that of a burrito ($p_1 = \$1$ and $p_2 = \$2$), the marginal rate of transformation that Lisa faces is

$$MRT = -\frac{p_1}{p_2} = -\frac{\$1}{\$2} = -\frac{1}{2}.$$

An extra pizza costs her half an extra burrito—or, equivalently, an extra burrito costs her two pizzas.

3.4 Constrained Consumer Choice

My problem lies in reconciling my gross habits with my net income. —Errol Flynn

Were it not for budget constraints, consumers who prefer more to less would consume unlimited amounts of at least some goods. Well, they can't have it all! Instead, consumers maximize their well-being subject to their budget constraints. To complete our analysis of consumer behavior, we have to determine the bundle of goods that maximizes an individual's well-being subject to the person's budget constraint.

Because Lisa enjoys consuming two goods only, she spends her entire budget on them.[11] That is, she chooses a bundle on the budget constraint rather than inside her opportunity set, where she would have money left over after buying the two goods. To spend her entire budget on these two goods, she must buy a positive amount of one or both of the goods.

An optimal bundle that has positive quantities of both goods so that it lies between the ends of the budget line is called an *interior solution*. If the consumer only buys one of the goods, the optimal bundle is at one end of the budget line, where the budget line forms a corner with one of the axes, so it is called a *corner solution*. We start our analysis by finding interior solutions using graphical and calculus methods. Then we address corner solutions.

Finding an Interior Solution Using Graphs

Veni, vidi, Visa. (We came, we saw, we went shopping.)

First, we use graphical methods to demonstrate that Lisa's optimal bundle must be on the budget line. Then, we show how to find the optimal bundle.

Figure 3.8 illustrates that Lisa's optimal bundle must be on the budget line. Bundles that lie on indifference curves above the constraint, such as those on I^3, are not in her opportunity set (area $A + B$). Although Lisa prefers Bundle f on indifference curve I^3 to Bundle e on I^2, she cannot afford to purchase f. Even though Lisa could buy a bundle inside the budget line L, she does not want to, because more is better than less: For any bundle inside the constraint (such as d on I^1), she prefers another bundle on the constraint with more of at least one of the two goods. Therefore, the optimal bundle must lie on the budget line.[12]

Bundles that lie on indifference curves that cross the budget line—such as I^1, which crosses the constraint at a and c—are less desirable than certain other bundles on the constraint. Only some of the bundles on indifference curve I^1 lie within the opportunity set: Lisa can afford to purchase Bundles a and c and all the points on I^1 between them, such as d. Because I^1 crosses the budget line, the bundles between a and c on I^1 lie strictly inside the constraint, so the affordable bundles in area B are preferable to a and c because they contain more of one or both goods. In particular, Lisa prefers Bundle e to d because e has more of both pizza and burritos than d. Because of transitivity, e is preferred to a, c, and all the other bundles on I^1—even those, like g, that Lisa can't afford. Thus, the optimal bundle—the *consumer's optimum*—must lie on the budget line and be on an indifference curve that does not cross it. If Lisa is consuming this bundle, she has no incentive to change her behavior by substituting one good for another.

---

[11]We examine the two-goods case for graphic simplicity. Although it is difficult to use graphs to analyze behavior if consumers derive positive marginal utility from more than two goods, it is straightforward to do so using calculus.

[12]Given that Lisa consumes positive quantities of both goods and their prices are positive, more of either good must be preferred to less at her optimal bundle. Suppose that the opposite were true, and that Lisa prefers fewer burritos to more. Because burritos cost her money, she could increase her well-being by reducing the quantity of burritos she consumes (and increasing her consumption of pizza) until she consumes no burritos—a scenario that violates our assumption that she consumes positive quantities of both goods.

Figure 3.8 Interior Solution

Lisa's optimal bundle is *e* (10 burritos and 30 pizzas) on indifference curve I^2. Indifference curve I^2 is tangent to her budget line *L* at *e*. Bundle *e* is the bundle on the highest indifference curve (highest utility) that she can afford. Any bundle that she prefers to *e* (such as points on indifference curve I^3) lies outside her opportunity set, so she cannot afford them. Bundles inside the opportunity set, such as *d*, are less desirable than *e* because they represent less of one or both goods.

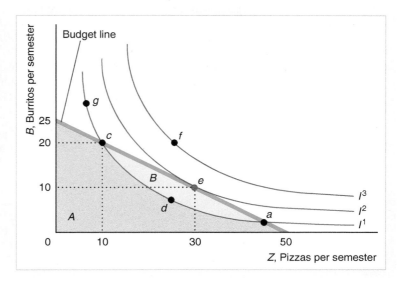

Bundle *e* on indifference curve I^2 is the optimum bundle. *The optimal bundle is on the highest indifference curve that touches the budget line,* so it is the bundle that gives Lisa the highest utility subject to her budget constraint.

In this figure, the optimal bundle lies in the interior of the budget line away from the corners. Lisa prefers consuming a balanced diet, *e*, of 10 burritos and 30 pizzas, to eating only one type of food.

For the indifference curve I^2 to touch the budget constraint but not cross it, it must be *tangent* to the budget constraint. Thus, the budget constraint and the indifference curve have the same slope at the point *e* where they touch. The slope of the indifference curve is the marginal rate of substitution. It measures the rate at which Lisa is *willing* to trade burritos for pizzas: $MRS = -U_1/U_2$ (Equation 3.4). The slope of the budget line is the marginal rate of transformation. It measures the rate at which Lisa *can* trade her money for burritos or pizza in the market: $MRT = -p_1/p_2$ (Equation 3.12). Thus, Lisa's utility is maximized at the bundle where the rate at which she is willing to trade burritos for pizzas equals the rate at which she can trade in the market:

$$MRS = -\frac{U_1}{U_2} = -\frac{p_1}{p_2} = MRT. \tag{3.13}$$

We can rearrange Equation 3.13 to obtain

$$\frac{U_1}{U_2} = \frac{p_1}{p_2}. \tag{3.14}$$

Equation 3.14 says that U_1/p_1, the marginal utility of pizzas divided by the price of a pizza—the amount of extra utility from pizza per dollar spent on pizza—equals U_2/p_2, the extra utility from burritos per dollar spent on burritos. Thus, Lisa's utility is maximized if the last dollar she spends on pizzas gets her as much extra utility as the last dollar she spends on burritos. If the last dollar spent on pizzas gave Lisa more extra utility than the last dollar spent on burritos, Lisa could increase her happiness by spending more on pizzas and less on burritos.

Thus, to find the interior solution in Figure 3.8, we can use either of two equivalent conditions:

1. *Highest indifference curve rule:* The optimal bundle is on the highest indifference curve that touches the constraint.
2. *Tangency rule:* The optimal bundle is the point where an indifference curve is tangent to the budget line. Equivalently, $MRS = MRT$ (Equation 3.13) and $U_1/p_1 = U_2/p_2$ (Equation 3.14).

The highest indifference curve rule can always be used to find either interior or corner solutions. The tangency rule only applies for interior solutions where the indifference curve has the usual shape: It is a downward sloping, smooth curve that is convex to the origin.

SOLVED PROBLEM 3.4

MyLab Economics Solved Problem

Maureen loves apple pie à la mode but she doesn't like apple pie, q_1, by itself or vanilla ice cream, q_2, by itself. That is, she views apple pie and ice cream as perfect complements. Show that the highest indifference curve rule can be used to find Maureen's optimal bundle, but that the tangency rule does not work. How many slices of pie and ice cream does she buy given that her income is Y?

Answer

1. *Use the highest indifference curve rule to find her optimal bundle in the figure.* Given budget line L^1, Maureen's optimal bundle is b because it is on the highest indifference curve that touches the budget line. Maureen can afford to buy Bundles a and b, but not c. She prefers b to a, because b contains more slices of apple pie à la mode.

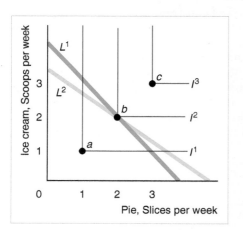

2. *Show that the indifference curve is not tangent to the budget line at the optimal bundle.* At the optimal bundle, the budget line L^1 has a negative slope (its MRT is negative). Because the budget line hits the indifference curve at its right-angle corner—where no substitution is possible and the slope is not well-defined—the budget line cannot be tangent to the indifference curve. Indeed, if the budget line were L^2, b would remain Maureen's optimal bundle, even though L^2 has a different slope than L^1.

3. *Derive her optimal bundle using her budget constraint.* She buys q slices of apple pie à la mode by buying $q_1 = q$ slices of apple pie and $q_2 = q$ scoops of ice cream. The cost of one unit of apple pie à la mode is the sum of the price of a slice of apple pie, p_1, and the price of a scoop of ice cream, p_2. Thus, given that she spends all her income on apple pie à la mode, she buys $q = q_1 = q_2 = Y/(p_1 + p_2)$ units of each.

Finding an Interior Solution Using Calculus

The individual choice of garnishment of a burger can be an important point to the consumer in this day when individualism is an increasingly important thing to people. —Donald N. Smith, president of Burger King

We have just shown how to use a graphical approach to determine which affordable bundle gives a consumer the highest possible level of utility. We now express this choice problem mathematically, and use calculus to find the optimal bundle.

Lisa's objective is to maximize her utility, $U(q_1, q_2)$, subject to (s.t.) her budget constraint:

$$\max_{q_1, q_2} U(q_1, q_2) \tag{3.15}$$

$$\text{s.t. } Y = p_1 q_1 + p_2 q_2.$$

In this mathematical formulation, Problem 3.15, the "max" term instructs us to maximize her utility function by choice of her *control variables*—those variables that she chooses—q_1 and q_2, which appear under the max term. We assume that Lisa has no control over the prices she faces, p_1 and p_2, or her income, Y.

Because this problem is a constrained maximization—contains the "subject to" provision—we cannot use the standard unconstrained maximization calculus approach. However, we can transform this problem into an unconstrained problem that we know how to solve. If we know that Lisa buys both goods, we can use the substitution method, the Lagrangian method, or a short-cut method.

Substitution Method. First, we can substitute the budget constraint into the utility function. Using algebra, we can rewrite the budget constraint as $q_1 = (Y - p_2 q_2)/p_1$. If we substitute this expression for q_1 in the utility function, $U(q_1, q_2)$, we can rewrite Lisa's problem as

$$\max_{q_2} U\left(\frac{Y - p_2 q_2}{p_1}, q_2\right). \tag{3.16}$$

Problem 3.16 is an unconstrained problem, so we can use standard maximization techniques to solve it. The first-order condition is obtained by setting the derivative of the utility function with respect to the only remaining control variable, q_2, equal to zero:

$$\frac{dU}{dq_2} = \frac{\partial U}{\partial q_1}\frac{dq_1}{dq_2} + \frac{\partial U}{\partial q_2} = \left(-\frac{p_2}{p_1}\right)\frac{\partial U}{\partial q_1} + \frac{\partial U}{\partial q_2} = \left(-\frac{p_2}{p_1}\right)U_1 + U_2 = 0, \tag{3.17}$$

where $\partial U/\partial q_1 = U_1$ is the partial derivative of the utility function with respect to q_1 (the first argument) and dq_1/dq_2 is the derivative of $q_1 = (Y - p_2 q_2)/p_1$ with respect to q_2.

To be sure that we have a maximum, we need to check that the second-order condition holds (see the Calculus Appendix at the end of the book). This condition holds if the utility function is quasiconcave, which implies that the indifference curves are convex to the origin: The *MRS* is diminishing as we move down and to the right along the curve.

By rearranging these terms in Equation 3.17, we get the same condition for an optimum that we obtained using a graphical approach, Equation 3.13, which is that the marginal rate of substitution equals the marginal rate of transformation:[13]

$$MRS = -\frac{U_1}{U_2} = -\frac{p_1}{p_2} = MRT.$$

By rearranging these terms, we obtain the same expression as in Equation 3.14: $U_1/p_1 = U_2/p_2$.

If we combine the $MRS = MRT$ condition with the budget constraint, we have two equations in two unknowns, q_1 and q_2, so we can solve for the optimal q_1 and q_2 as functions of prices, p_1 and p_2, and income, Y.

---

[13]Had we substituted for q_2 instead of for q_1 (which you should do to make sure that you understand how to solve this type of problem), we would have obtained the same condition.

SOLVED PROBLEM 3.5

MyLab Economics
Solved Problem

Michael has a constant elasticity of substitution (CES) utility function, $U(q_1, q_2) = (q_1^\rho + q_2^\rho)^{\frac{1}{\rho}}$, where $\rho \neq 0$ and $\rho \leq 1$.[14] Given that Michael's $\rho < 1$, what are his optimal values of q_1 and q_2 in terms of his income and the prices of the two goods?

Answer

1. *Substitute the income constraint into Michael's utility function to eliminate one control variable.* Michael's constrained utility maximization problem is

$$\max_{q_1, q_2} U(q_1, q_2) = (q_1^\rho + q_2^\rho)^{\frac{1}{\rho}}$$
$$\text{s.t. } Y = p_1 q_1 + p_2 q_2.$$

We can rewrite Michael's budget constraint as $q_2 = (Y - p_1 q_1)/p_2$. Substituting this expression into his utility function, we can express Michael's utility maximization problem as:

$$\max_{q_1} U\left(q_1, \frac{Y - p_1 q_1}{p_2}\right) = \left(q_1^\rho + \left[\frac{Y - p_1 q_1}{p_2}\right]^\rho\right)^{1/\rho}.$$

By making this substitution, we have converted a constrained maximization problem with two control variables into an unconstrained problem with one control variable, q_1.

2. *Use the standard, unconstrained maximization approach to determine the optimal value for q_1.* To obtain the first-order condition, we use the chain rule and set the derivative of the utility function with respect to q_1 equal to zero:

$$\frac{1}{\rho}\left(q_1^\rho + \left[\frac{Y - p_1 q_1}{p_2}\right]^\rho\right)^{\frac{1-\rho}{\rho}}\left(\rho q_1^{\rho-1} + \rho\left[\frac{Y - p_1 q_1}{p_2}\right]^{\rho-1}\left[-\frac{p_1}{p_2}\right]\right) = 0.$$

Using algebra, we can solve this equation for Michael's optimal q_1 as a function of his income and the prices:[15]

$$q_1 = \frac{Y p_1^{-\sigma}}{p_1^{1-\sigma} + p_2^{1-\sigma}}, \tag{3.18}$$

where $\sigma = 1/[1 - \rho]$. By repeating this analysis, substituting for q_1 instead of for q_2, we derive a similar expression for his optimal q_2:

$$q_2 = \frac{Y p_2^{-\sigma}}{p_1^{1-\sigma} + p_2^{1-\sigma}}. \tag{3.19}$$

Thus, the utility-maximizing q_1 and q_2 are functions of his income and the prices.

---

[14]In Chapter 6, we discuss why this functional form has this name and that the Cobb-Douglas, perfect substitutes, and perfect complements functional forms are special cases of the CES.

[15]The term at the beginning of the first-order condition, $(1/\rho)(q_1^\rho + ([Y - p_1 q_1]/p_2)^\rho)^{(1-\rho)/\rho}$, is strictly positive because Michael buys a nonnegative amount of both goods, $q_1 \geq 0$ and $q_2 = [Y - p_1 q_1]/p_2 \geq 0$, and a positive amount of at least one of them. Thus, we can divide both sides of the equation by this term. We are left with $\rho q_1^{\rho-1} + \rho[(Y - p_1 q_1)/p_2]^{\rho-1}[-p_1/p_2] = 0$. Divide both sides of this equation by $\rho[(Y - p_1 q_1)/p_2]^{\rho-1}$ and move the second term to the right side of the equation: $(p_2 q_1/[Y - p_1 q_1])^{\rho-1} = p_1/p_2$. Exponentiate both sides by $1/[\rho - 1]$ and multiply both sides by $[Y - p_1 q_1]/p_2$ to obtain $q_1 = [Y - p_1 q_1](p_1/p_2)^{1/(\rho-1)}/p_2$. Use algebra to combine the q_1 terms: $q_1(1 + (p_1/p_2)^{\rho/(\rho-1)}) = Y(p_1/p_2)^{1/(\rho-1)}/p_2$. Multiply both sides by $p_2^{\rho/(\rho-1)}$: $q_1(p_2^{\rho/(\rho-1)} + p_1^{\rho/(\rho-1)}) = Y(p_1/p_2)^{1/(\rho-1)}p_2^{\rho/(\rho-1)} = Yp_1^{1/(\rho-1)}$. Divide both sides by the term in first parentheses: $q_1 = Yp_1^{1/(\rho-1)}/(p_2^{\rho/(\rho-1)} + p_1^{\rho/(\rho-1)})$. Defining $\sigma = 1/[1 - \rho]$, we obtain Equation 3.18.

Lagrangian Method. Another way to solve this constrained maximization problem is to use the Lagrangian method. The Lagrangian expression that corresponds to Problem 3.16 is

$$\mathcal{L} = U(q_1, q_2) + \lambda(Y - p_1q_1 - p_2q_2), \tag{3.20}$$

where λ (the Greek letter lambda) is the Lagrange multiplier. For values of q_1 and q_2 such that the constraint holds, $Y - p_1q_1 - p_2q_2 = 0$, so the functions $\mathcal{L}$ and U have the same values. Thus, if we look only at values of q_1 and q_2 for which the constraint holds, finding the constrained maximum value of U is the same as finding the critical value of $\mathcal{L}$.

Equations 3.21, 3.22, and 3.23 are the first-order conditions that determine the critical values q_1, q_2, and λ for an interior maximization:

$$\frac{\partial \mathcal{L}}{\partial q_1} = \frac{\partial U}{\partial q_1} - \lambda p_1 = U_1 - \lambda p_1 = 0, \tag{3.21}$$

$$\frac{\partial \mathcal{L}}{\partial q_2} = U_2 - \lambda p_2 = 0, \tag{3.22}$$

$$\frac{\partial \mathcal{L}}{\partial \lambda} = Y - p_1q_1 - p_2q_2 = 0. \tag{3.23}$$

At the optimal levels of q_1, q_2, and λ, Equation 3.21 shows that the marginal utility of pizza, $U_1 = \partial U/\partial q_1$, equals its price times λ. Equation 3.22 provides an analogous condition for burritos. Equation 3.23 restates the budget constraint.

These three first-order conditions can be solved for the optimal values of q_1, q_2, and λ. Again, we should check that we have a maximum (see the Calculus Appendix).

What is λ? If we solve both Equations 3.21 and 3.22 for λ and then equate these expressions, we find that

$$\lambda = \frac{U_1}{p_1} = \frac{U_2}{p_2}. \tag{3.24}$$

That is, the optimal value of the Lagrangian multiplier, λ, equals the marginal utility of each good divided by its price, U_i/p_i, which is the extra utility one gets from the last dollar spent on that good.[16] Equation 3.24 is the same as Equation 3.14 (and Equation 3.13), which we derived using a graphical argument.

**SOLVED PROBLEM
3.6**

**MyLab Economics
Solved Problem**

Julia has a Cobb-Douglas utility function, $U(q_1, q_2) = q_1^a q_2^{1-a}$. Use the Lagrangian method to find her optimal values of q_1 and q_2 in terms of her income and the prices.

Answer

1. *Show Julia's Lagrangian function and her first-order conditions.* Julia's Lagrangian function is $\mathcal{L} = q_1^a q_2^{1-a} + \lambda(Y - p_1q_1 - p_2q_2)$. The first-order conditions for her to maximize her utility subject to the constraint are

$$\frac{\partial \mathcal{L}}{\partial q_1} = U_1 - \lambda p_1 = aq_1^{a-1}q_2^{1-a} - \lambda p_1 = a\frac{U}{q_1} - \lambda p_1 = 0, \tag{3.25}$$

---

[16]Economists often call the Lagrangian multiplier a *shadow value* because it reflects the marginal rate of change in the objective function as the constraint is relaxed (see the Calculus Appendix).

$$\frac{\partial \mathscr{L}}{\partial q_2} = U_2 - \lambda p_2 = (1 - a)q_1^a q_2^{-a} - \lambda p_2 = (1 - a)\frac{U}{q_2} - \lambda p_2 = 0, \quad (3.26)$$

$$\frac{\partial \mathscr{L}}{\partial \lambda} = Y - p_1 q_1 - p_2 q_2 = 0. \quad (3.27)$$

2. *Solve these three first-order equations for q_1 and q_2.* By solving the right sides of the first two conditions for λ and equating the results, we obtain an equation that depends on q_1 and q_2 but not on λ:

$$(1 - a)p_1 q_1 = ap_2 q_2. \quad (3.28)$$

The budget constraint, Equation 3.27, and the optimality condition, Equation 3.28, are two equations in q_1 and q_2. Rearranging the budget constraint, we know that $p_2 q_2 = Y - p_1 q_1$. By substituting this expression for $p_2 q_2$ into Equation 3.28, we can rewrite this expression as $(1 - a)p_1 q_1 = a(Y - p_1 q_1)$. By rearranging terms, we find that

$$q_1 = a\frac{Y}{p_1}. \quad (3.29)$$

Similarly, by substituting $p_1 q_1 = Y - p_2 q_2$ into Equation 3.26 and rearranging, we find that

$$q_2 = (1 - a)\frac{Y}{p_2}. \quad (3.30)$$

Thus, we can use our knowledge of the form of the utility function to solve the expression for the q_1 and q_2 that maximize utility in terms of income, prices, and the utility function parameter a.

Finding an Interior Solution Using a Short Cut. The graphical, substitution, and Lagrangian methods all show that we need two equations to determine the two equilibrium quantities in our two-goods, constrained maximization problem. In the graphic approach, we combine a tangency condition (the slope of the highest indifference curve equals the slope of the budget line), $MRS = -U_1/U_2 = -p_1/p_2 = MRT$, Equation 3.13, and the budget constraint, $p_1 q_1 + p_2 q_2 = Y$, Equation 3.10.

In the substitution approach, we substitute the budget constraint into the utility function to derive the tangency condition, Equation 3.13. The Lagrangian approach produces three equilibrium conditions. We can combine the first two conditions, Equations 3.21 and 3.22, to derive the tangency condition, Equation 3.13. The third condition, Equation 3.23, is the budget constraint.

Rather than laboriously deriving these conditions using the substitution or Lagrangian method, we can use the tangency and budget line equations to solve for the equilibrium quantities directly. We illustrated this approach for the Cobb-Douglas utility ($U = q_1^a q_2^{1-a}$) in Solved Problem 3.6. Using the Cobb-Douglas MRS from Table 3.1, the $MRS = -(a/[1 - a])(q_2/q_1) = -p_1/p_2 = MRT$. This expression is equivalent to Equation 3.28, $(1 - a)p_1 q_1 = ap_2 q_2$. As Solved Problem 3.6 shows, if we combine this equation with the budget constraint, we obtain the Cobb-Douglas equilibrium quantities, Equations 3.29 and 3.30.

SOLVED PROBLEM 3.7

MyLab Economics
Solved Problem

Given that Julia has a Cobb-Douglas utility function $U = q_1^a q_2^{1-a}$, what share of her budget does she spend on q_1 and q_2 in terms of her income, prices, and the positive constant a?

Answer

Use Equations 3.29 and 3.30 to determine her budget shares. The share of her budget that Julia spends on pizza, s_1, is her expenditure on pizza, $p_1 q_1$, divided by her budget, Y, or $s_1 = p_1 q_1 / Y$. By multiplying both sides of Equation 3.29, $q_1 = aY/p_1$, by p_1, we find that $p_1 q_1 = aY$, so $s_1 = p_1 q_1 / Y = a$. Thus, a is both her budget share of pizza and the exponent on the units of pizza in her utility function. Similarly, from Equation 3.30, we find that her budget share of burritos is $s_2 = p_2 q_2 / Y = 1 - a$.

Comment: The Cobb-Douglas functional form was constructed to have constant budget shares equal to the exponents a and $1 - a$. If an individual has a Cobb-Douglas utility function, we can estimate a solely from information about the individual's budget shares. That is how we obtained our estimate of Jackie's Cobb-Douglas utility function for recorded tracks and live music in the Application "*MRS* Between Recorded Tracks and Live Music."

APPLICATION

Utility Maximization for Recorded Tracks and Live Music

We return to our typical consumer, Jackie, who has an estimated Cobb-Douglas utility function of $U = q_1^{0.4} q_2^{0.6}$ for music tracks, q_1, and live music, q_2. The average price of a track from iTunes, Amazon, Rhapsody, and other vendors was about $p_1 = £0.5$ in 2008, and we arbitrarily set the price of live music, p_2, at £1 per unit (so the units do not correspond to a concert or a club visit). Jackie's budget constraint for purchasing these entertainment goods is

$$p_1 q_1 + p_2 q_2 = 0.5 q_1 + q_2 = 30 = Y,$$

given that Jackie, like the average 14- to 24-year-old British consumer, spends £30 on music per quarter.

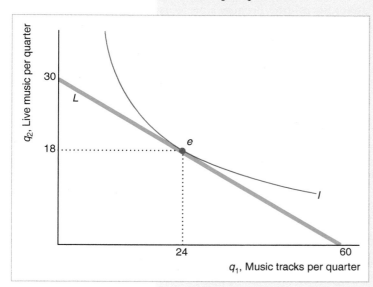

q_2, Live music per quarter

q_1, Music tracks per quarter

Using Equations 3.29 and 3.30 from Solved Problem 3.6, we can solve for Jackie's optimal numbers of tracks and units of live music:

$$q_1 = 0.4 \frac{Y}{p_1} = 0.4 \times \frac{30}{0.5} = 24,$$

$$q_2 = 0.6 \frac{Y}{p_2} = 0.6 \times \frac{30}{1} = 18.$$

These quantities are the average quarterly purchases for a British youth in 2008. The figure shows that the optimal bundle is e where the indifference curve I is tangent to the budget line L.

We can use the result in Solved Problem 3.7 to confirm that the budget shares equal the exponents in Jackie's utility function.

The share of Jackie's budget devoted to tracks is $p_1 q_1/Y = (0.5 \times 24)/30 = 0.4$, which is the exponent on recorded tracks in her utility function. Similarly, the budget share she allocates to live music is $p_2 q_2/Y = (1 \times 18)/30 = 0.6$, which is the live music exponent.

Finding Corner Solutions

So far, we have concentrated on utility functions for which only an interior solution is possible. However, for some utility functions, we may have either a corner or an interior solution.

If a utility function's indifference curves do not hit the axes, a consumer's optimal bundle must be in the interior of the budget constraint. If a consumer has a perfect complements utility function or Cobb-Douglas utility function, the indifference curves do not hit the axes, so the optimal bundle lies in the interior, as Table 3.2 shows. Similarly, the indifference curves have this property if the consumer has a constant elasticity of substitution (CES) utility function, $U(q_1, q_2) = (q_1^\rho + q_2^\rho)^{\frac{1}{\rho}}$, where $\rho < 1$. However, if $\rho = 1$ in the CES utility function, then the utility function is $U(q_1, q_2) = q_1 + q_2$, which is a perfect substitutes utility function.

Table 3.2 Type of Solution for Five Utility Functions

Utility Function	$U(q_1, q_2)$	Type of Solution
Perfect complements	$\min(iq_1, jq_2)$	interior
Cobb-Douglas	$q_1^a q_2^{1-a}$	interior
Constant Elasticity of Substitution	$(q_1^\rho + q_2^\rho)^{1/\rho}$	interior
Perfect substitutes	$iq_1 + jq_2$	interior or corner
Quasilinear	$u(q_1) + q_2$	interior or corner

Notes: $i > 0, j > 0, 0 < a < 1, \rho \neq 0$, and $\rho < 1$.

Perfect Substitutes Utility Function. Because a perfect substitutes utility function has straight-line indifference curves that hit the axes, the optimal bundle may be at a corner or in the interior of the budget line. To illustrate why, we consider Ben's choice. Ben views Coca-Cola, q_1, and Pepsi-Cola, q_2, as perfect substitutes, so his utility function is $U(q_1, q_2) = q_1 + q_2$. Figure 3.9 shows three straight-line indifference curves that correspond to this utility function.

The price of a 12-ounce can of Coke is p_1, and the price of a 12-ounce can of Pepsi is p_2. If $p_1 < p_2$, Ben gets more extra utility from the last dollar spent on Coke, $U_1/p_1 = 1/p_1$, than he gets from Pepsi, $U_2/p_2 = 1/p_2$, so he spends his entire income on Coke, $q_1 = Y/p_1$, and buys no Pepsi, $q_2 = 0$.

Figure 3.9 illustrates Ben's decision. Because Coke is less expensive than Pepsi, his budget line, L, is flatter than his indifference curves, I^1, I^2, and I^3. He can afford to buy Bundle a on indifference curve I^1 or Bundle b on indifference curve I^2, but he cannot afford any bundle on I^3 because it is above his budget constraint everywhere. We can find Ben's optimal bundle using the highest indifference curve rule: Ben's optimal bundle is b because it is on the highest indifference curve, I^2, that touches the budget constraint.

At the optimal Bundle b, the slope of the indifference curve, $MRS = -1$, does not equal the slope of the budget line, $MRT = -p_1/p_2 > -1$. Thus, we cannot find the optimal bundle at a corner using the tangency rule.

Figure 3.9 Corner Solution with Perfect Substitutes Utility Function

Ben views Coke and Pepsi as perfect substitutes, so his indifference curves are straight lines with a slope of -1. Because Coke is less expensive than Pepsi, his budget line, L, is flatter than his indifference curves. Although he can afford to buy bundle a on indifference curve I^1, his optimal bundle is b, because it is on the highest indifference curve, I^2, that touches the budget constraint.

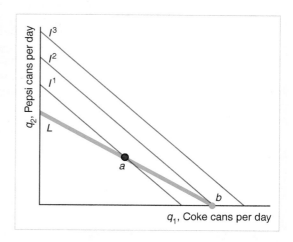

By symmetry, if $p_1 > p_2$, Ben chooses $q_1 = 0$ and $q_2 = Y/p_2$. If the prices are identical, $p_1 = p_2 = p$, he is indifferent as to which good to buy. Both his budget line and his indifference curves have the same slope, -1, so one of his indifference curves lies on top of the budget line. He is willing to buy any bundle on that budget line, in the interior or at either corner. All we know is that $q_1 + q_2 = Y/p$.

Quasilinear Utility Function. Similarly, if a consumer has a quasilinear utility function, the indifference curves hit the axes, so either an interior or a corner solution is possible. For example, Spenser has a quasilinear utility function $U(q_1, q_2) = 4q_1^{0.5} + q_2$.

We use a two-step procedure to determine the optimal bundle.[17] We first check for an interior solution using the tangency condition and the budget constraint. If we find that these conditions imply that he wants to buy positive quantities of both goods, we have found an interior solution. Otherwise, we have to determine a corner solution as a second step.

At an interior solution, such as panel a of Figure 3.10 shows, his indifference curve I is tangent to his budget line L at Bundle e, so that the $MRS = MRT = -p_1/p_2$. We can use the short-cut method to derive an interior solution.

His marginal utility of q_1 is $U_1 = 2q_1^{-0.5}$ and his marginal utility of $q_2 = 1$, so his $MRS = -U_1/U_2 = -2q_1^{-0.5}$. Thus, his tangency condition, Equation 3.13, is $MRS - 2q_1^{-0.5} = -p_1/p_2 = MRT$. Rearranging this equation, we learn that $q_1 = 4(p_2/p_1)^2$. Because q_1 does not depend on Y, Spenser buys the same quantity of q_1 regardless of his income, given that we have an interior solution where the tangency condition holds.[18]

By substituting this value of q_1 into the budget constraint, we can solve for q_2. We can rearrange his budget constraint as $q_2 = Y/p_2 - (p_1q_1)/p_2$, so $q_2 = Y/p_2 - (p_1 \times [4(p_2/p_1)^2])/p_2 = Y/p_2 - 4(p_2/p_1)$.

---

[17]A more direct approach to solving the consumer-maximization problem allowing for a corner solution is to use a Kuhn-Tucker analysis, which is discussed in the Calculus Appendix.

[18]Solved Problem 3.3 provides the intuition for this result. At any given q_1, the slope of the quasilinear utility's indifference curve is the same. Thus, if we have a tangency with a low Y at a given q_1, we must have a tangency with a higher Y at that same quantity.

Figure 3.10 Interior or Corner Solution with Quasilinear Utility

Spenser has a quasilinear utility function $U(q_1, q_2) = 4q_1^{0.5} + q_2$. (a) When his income is greater than 4, he has an interior solution at e, where q_1 and q_2 are positive. His indifference curve I is tangent to his budget line L, so that his $MRS = MRT$. (b) At a lower income, he has a corner solution at point b, where he spends all his income on q_1. The only possible point of tangency, point a, involves a negative quantity of q_2, which is not plausible. Spenser always buys q_1 and buys q_2 only if his income exceeds a threshold.

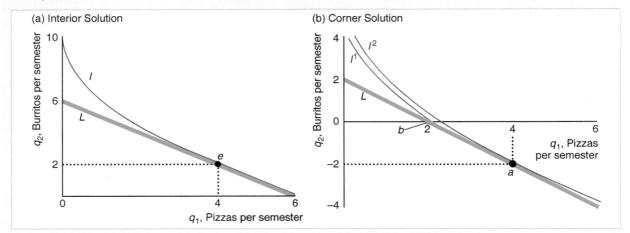

If the prices are $p_1 = p_2 = 1$, the tangency condition is $q_1 = 4(p_2/p_1)^2 = 4 \times (1/1)^2 = 4$. Substituting this value into the budget constraint, $q_2 = Y/p_2 - 4(p_2/p_1) = Y - 4$. Thus, if $Y > 4$, we have an interior solution where both quantities are positive. Panel a of Figure 3.10 shows an interior solution where Spenser's income is $Y = 6$. At the optimal Bundle e, where his indifference curve I is tangent to his budget line L, he buys $q_1 = 4$, and $q_2 = 6 - 4 = 2$.

At incomes below $Y = 4$, we do not have an interior solution—a tangency at positive levels of q_1 and q_2—as we illustrate in panel b of Figure 3.10. We first show that the only possible point of tangency involves a negative quantity of one good. Then we determine the corner solution.

For example, if $Y = 2$, the formula we derived, assuming that we were at a point of tangency, tells us that $q_2 = 2 - 4 = -2$, which is not plausible. We illustrate this result in panel b, where we show two indifference curves. We draw I^1 for only non-negative quantities of the two goods. However, we use the indifference curve formula to extend I^2 to show what it would look like at negative values of q_2. By extending the indifference curve I^2 and the budget line L into the area below the horizontal axis where q_2 is negative, we show that the point of tangency a occurs at $q_1 = 4$ and $q_2 = -2$, which is implausible.

If we don't have an interior solution, we must have a corner solution. How do we know which good he buys? We know that if we are not at an interior (tangency) solution, then the marginal utility from the last dollar spent on each of the two goods are not equal: $U_1/p_1 \neq U_2/p_2$. Spenser prefers to buy only q_1 if $U_1/p_1 > U_2/p_2$. Given that both prices equal one, this condition holds if $U_1 = 2q_1^{-0.5} > U_2 = 1$. When $q_1 < 4$, $U_1 > U_2$. For example, when $q_1 = 2$, $U_1 \approx 1.41$, which is greater than $U_2 = 1$. Because the marginal utility of q_1 exceeds that of q_2 at low levels of q_1, if Spenser is going to have to give up one of the goods due to a lack of money, he'll give up q_2 and spend all his money on q_1. Thus, $q_1 = Y/p_1 = 2/1 = 2$, and $q_2 = 0$, which is the corner point b on indifference curve I^1 in panel b.

To summarize, if his income is low, Spenser spends all his money on q_1, buying $q_1 = Y/p_1 = Y$, which is a corner solution. If he has enough income for an interior solution, he buys a fixed amount of $q_1 = 4(p_2/p_1)^2 = 4$ and spends all his extra money on q_2 as his income rises.

Optimal Bundles on Convex Sections of Indifference Curves. Earlier, based on introspection, we argued that most indifference curves are convex to the origin. Now that we know how to determine a consumer's optimal bundle, we can give a more compelling explanation about why we assume that indifference curves are convex. We can show that if indifference curves are smooth, optimal bundles lie either on convex sections of indifference curves or at the point where the budget constraint hits an axis.

Suppose that indifference curves were strictly concave to the origin as in panel a of Figure 3.11. Indifference curve I^1 is tangent to the budget line L at d, but Bundle d is not optimal. Bundle e on the corner between the budget constraint L and the burrito axis is on a higher indifference curve, I^2, than d. If a consumer had strictly concave indifference curves, the consumer would buy only one good—here, burritos. Thus, if consumers are to buy more than a single good, indifference curves must have convex sections.

If indifference curves have both concave and convex sections, as in panel b of Figure 3.11, the optimal bundle lies in a convex section or at a corner. Bundle d, where a concave section of indifference curve I^1 is tangent to the budget line L,

Figure 3.11 Optimal Bundles on Convex Sections of Indifference Curves

(a) If indifference curves are strictly concave to the origin, the optimal bundle is at a corner (on one of the axes, where the consumer buys only one good). Indifference curve I^1 is tangent to the budget line L at Bundle d, but Bundle e is superior because it lies on a higher indifference curve, I^2. (b) If indifference curves have both concave and convex sections, a bundle such as d, which is tangent to the budget line L in the concave portion of indifference curve I^1, cannot be an optimal bundle because Bundle e, in the convex portion of a higher indifference curve I^2, is preferred and affordable.

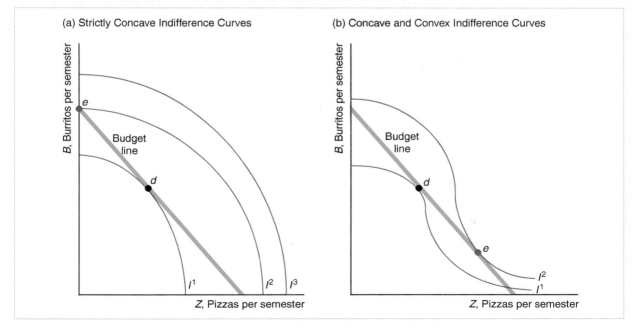

cannot be an optimal bundle. Here, e is the optimal bundle. It is tangent to the budget constraint in the convex portion of the higher indifference curve, I^2. Thus, if a consumer buys positive quantities of two goods, the indifference curve is convex and tangent to the budget line at the optimal bundle.

Minimizing Expenditure

Earlier, we showed how Lisa chooses quantities of goods to maximize her utility subject to a budget constraint. In a related or *dual* constrained minimization problem, Lisa wants to find that combination of goods that achieves a particular level of utility for the least expenditure.[19]

In Figure 3.8, we showed that, given the budget constraint that she faced, Lisa maximized her utility by picking a bundle of $q_1 = 30$ and $q_2 = 10$. She did that by choosing the highest indifference curve, I^2, that touched the budget constraint so that the indifference curve was tangent to the budget line.

Now, let's consider the alternative problem in which we ask how Lisa can make the lowest possible expenditure to maintain her utility at a particular level, $\overline{U}$, which corresponds to indifference curve I. Figure 3.12 shows three possible budget lines corresponding to budgets or expenditures of E_1, E_2, and E_3. The lowest of these budget lines with expenditure E_1 lies below I, so Lisa cannot achieve the level of utility on I for such a small expenditure. Both the other budget lines cross I; however, the budget line with expenditure E_2 is the least expensive way for her to stay on I. The rule for minimizing expenditure while achieving a given level of utility is to choose the lowest expenditure such that the budget line touches—is tangent to—the relevant indifference curve.

The slope of all the expenditure or budget lines is $-p_1/p_2$ (see Equation 3.12), which depends only on the market prices and not on income or expenditure. Thus, the point of tangency in Figure 3.12 is the same as in Figure 3.8. Lisa purchases

Figure 3.12 Minimizing the Expenditure

The lowest expenditure that Lisa can make that will keep her on indifference curve I is E_2. She buys 30 pizzas and 10 burritos.

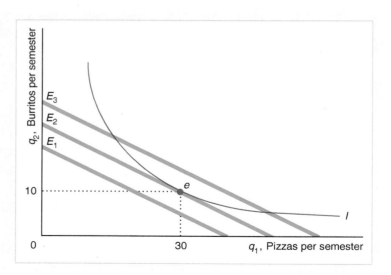

---

[19]For a formal calculus presentation, see "Duality" in MyLab Economics, Chapter Resources, Calculus Appendix.

$q_1 = 30$ and $q_2 = 10$ because that is the bundle that minimizes her expenditure conditional on staying on I.

Thus, solving either of the two problems—maximizing utility subject to a budget constraint or minimizing the expenditure subject to maintaining a given level of utility—yields the same optimal values for this problem. It is sometimes more useful to use the expenditure-minimizing approach because expenditures are observable and utility levels are not.

We can use calculus to solve the expenditure-minimizing problem. Lisa's objective is to minimize her expenditure, E, subject to the constraint that she hold her utility constant at $\overline{U} = U(q_1, q_2)$:

$$\min_{q_1, q_2} E = p_1 q_1 + p_2 q_2$$
$$\text{s. t. } \overline{U} = U(q_1, q_2). \tag{3.31}$$

The solution of this problem is an expression of the minimum expenditure as a function of the prices and the specified utility level:

$$E = E(p_1, p_2, \overline{U}). \tag{3.32}$$

We call this expression the **expenditure function**: the relationship showing the minimal expenditures necessary to achieve a specific utility level for a given set of prices.

SOLVED PROBLEM 3.8

Given that Julia has a Cobb-Douglas utility function $U = q_1^a q_2^{1-a}$, what is her expenditure function?

Answer

1. *Show Julia's Lagrangian function and derive her first-order conditions.* Julia's Lagrangian function is $\mathcal{L} = p_1 q_1 + p_2 q_2 + \lambda(\overline{U} - q_1^a q_2^{1-a})$. The first-order conditions for her to minimize her expenditure subject to remaining on a given indifference curve are obtained by differentiating the Lagrangian function with respect to q_1, q_2, and λ, and setting each derivative equal to zero:

$$\frac{\partial \mathcal{L}}{\partial q_1} = p_1 - \lambda a q_1^{a-1} q_2^{1-a} = p_1 - \lambda a \frac{U}{q_1} = 0, \tag{3.33}$$

$$\frac{\partial \mathcal{L}}{\partial q_2} = p_2 - \lambda(1-a) q_1^a q_2^{-a} = p_2 - \lambda(1-a) \frac{U}{q_2} = 0, \tag{3.34}$$

$$\frac{\partial \mathcal{L}}{\partial \lambda} = \overline{U} - q_1^a q_2^{1-a} = 0. \tag{3.35}$$

2. *Solve these three first-order equations for q_1 and q_2.* By solving the right sides of the first two conditions for λ and equating the results, we obtain an equation that depends on q_1 and q_2, but not on λ:

$$p_1 q_1 / (aU) = p_2 q_2 / [(1-a)U], \text{ or}$$
$$(1-a) p_1 q_1 = a p_2 q_2. \tag{3.36}$$

This condition is the same as Equation 3.28, which we derived in Solved Problem 3.6 when we maximized Julia's utility subject to the budget constraint.

Rearranging Equation 3.36, we learn that $p_2q_2 = p_1q_1(1 - a)/a$. By substituting this expression into the expenditure definition, we find that

$$E = p_1q_1 + p_2q_2 = p_1q_1 + p_1q_1(1 - a)/a = p_1q_1/a.$$

Rearranging these terms, we find that

$$q_1 = a\frac{E}{p_1}. \tag{3.37}$$

Similarly, by rearranging Equation 3.36 to obtain $p_1q_1 = p_2q_2a/(1 - a)$, substituting that expression into the expenditure definition, and rearranging terms, we learn that

$$q_2 = (1 - a)\frac{E}{p_2}. \tag{3.38}$$

By substituting the expressions in Equations 3.37 and 3.38 into the indifference curve expression, Equation 3.35, we observe that

$$\overline{U} = q_1^a q_2^{1-a} = \left(a\frac{E}{p_1}\right)^a\left([1 - a]\frac{E}{p_2}\right)^{1-a} = E\left(\frac{a}{p_1}\right)^a\left(\frac{1 - a}{p_2}\right)^{1-a}. \tag{3.39}$$

Solving this expression for E, we can write the expenditure function as

$$E = \overline{U}\left(\frac{p_1}{a}\right)^a\left(\frac{p_2}{1 - a}\right)^{1-a}. \tag{3.40}$$

3. Equation 3.40 shows the minimum expenditure necessary to achieve utility level $\overline{U}$ given the prices p_1 and p_2. For example, if $a = 1 - a = 0.5$, then

$$E = \overline{U}(p_1/0.5)^{0.5}(p_2/0.5)^{0.5} = 2\overline{U}(p_1p_2)^{0.5}.$$

3.5 Behavioral Economics

He who has choice has trouble. —Dutch proverb

So far, we have assumed that consumers are rational, maximizing individuals. A recent field of study, **behavioral economics**, adds insights from psychology and empirical research on human cognition and emotional biases to the rational economic model to better predict economic decision making.[20] We discuss three applications of behavioral economics in this section: tests of transitivity, the endowment effect, and salience. Later in the book, we examine whether a consumer is influenced by the purchasing behavior of others (Chapter 11), whether individuals bid optimally in auctions (Chapter 13), why many people lack self-control (Chapter 16), and the psychology of decision making under uncertainty (Chapter 17).

---

[20]The introductory chapter of Camerer, Loewenstein, and Rabin (2004) and DellaVigna (2009) are excellent surveys of the major papers in this field and heavily influenced the following discussion.

Tests of Transitivity

In our presentation of the basic consumer choice model at the beginning of this chapter, we assumed that consumers make transitive choices. But do consumers actually make transitive choices?

A number of studies of animals and humans show that preferences usually are transitive. Monteiro, Vasconcelos, and Kacelnik (2013) report that starlings (birds) have transitive preferences.

Weinstein (1968) used an experiment to determine how frequently people give intransitive responses. Subjects were given choices between 10 goods, offered in pairs, in every possible combination. To ensure that the monetary value of the items would not affect people's calculations, they were told that all of the goods had a value of $3. (None of the subjects knew the purpose of the experiment.) Weinstein found that 93.5% of the responses of adults—people over 18 years old—were transitive. However, only 79.2% of children ages 9 through 12 gave transitive responses.

Psychologists have also tested for transitivity using preferences for colors, photos of faces, and so forth. Bradbury and Ross (1990) found that, given a choice of three colors, nearly half of 4- to 5-year-olds gave intransitive responses, compared to 15% of 11- to 13-year-olds, and 5% of adults. Bradbury and Ross showed that novelty (a preference for a new color) is responsible for most intransitive responses, and that this effect is especially strong in children.

Based on these results, one might conclude that it is appropriate to assume that birds and most adults have transitive preferences for most economic decisions, but many children do not have such preferences. Economists normally argue that rational people should be allowed to make their own consumption choices to maximize their well-being. However, some people argue that children's lack of transitivity or rationality provides a justification for political and economic restrictions and protections placed on young people. For example, many governments effectively prevent youths from drinking.[21]

Endowment Effect

Experiments show that people have a tendency to stick with the bundle of goods that they currently possess. One important reason for this tendency is called the **endowment effect**, which occurs when people place a higher value on a good if they own it than if they are considering buying it.

Normally we assume that an individual can buy or sell goods at the market price. Rather than rely on income to buy some mix of two goods, an individual who was *endowed* with several units of one good could sell some of them and use that money to buy units of another good.

We assume that a consumer's endowment does not affect the indifference map. In a classic buying and selling experiment, Kahneman, Knetsch, and Thaler (1990) challenged this assumption. In an undergraduate law and economics class at Cornell University, 44 students were divided randomly into two groups. Members of one group were each given a coffee mug, which was available for sale at the student store for $6. Those students *endowed* with a mug were told that they could sell it and were asked the minimum price that they would accept for it. The subjects in

---

[21]U.S. federal law prevents drinking before the age of 21, but most other countries set the minimum drinking age between 16 and 18. It is 16 in Belgium, Denmark, and France; 18 in Australia, Sweden, and the United Kingdom; and 18 or 19 in Canada. A justification for limiting drinking is given by Carpenter and Dobkin (2009). They find that when U.S. youths may start drinking alcohol legally at age 21, the number of days on which they drink increases by 21%, which results in a 9% increase in their mortality rate.

the other group, who did not receive a mug, were asked how much they would pay to buy the mug. Given the standard assumptions of our model and that the subjects were chosen randomly, we would expect no difference between the selling and buying prices. However, the median selling price was $5.75 and the median buying price was $2.25, so sellers wanted more than twice what buyers would pay. This type of experiment has been repeated with many variations and typically an endowment effect is found.

However, some economists believe that this result has to do with how the experiment is designed. Plott and Zeiler (2005) argued that if you take adequate care to train the subjects in the procedures and make sure they understand them, the result didn't hold. List (2003) examined the actual behavior of sports memorabilia collectors and found that amateurs who do not trade frequently exhibited an endowment effect, unlike professionals and amateurs who traded extensively. Thus, experience may minimize or eliminate the endowment effect, and people who buy goods for resale may be less likely to become attached to these goods.

Others accept the results and have considered how to modify the standard model to reflect the endowment effect (Knetsch, 1992). One implication of these experimental results is that people will only trade away from their endowments if prices change substantially. This resistance to trade could be captured by having a kink in the indifference curve at the endowment bundle. (We showed indifference curves with a kink at a 90° angle in panel b of Figure 3.5.) A kinked indifference curve could have an angle greater than 90° and be curved at points other than at the kink. If the indifference curve has a kink, the consumer does not shift to a new bundle in response to a small price change but does shift if the price change is large.

One practical implication of the endowment effect is that consumers' behavior may differ depending on how a choice is posed. However, that's not the common belief.

Common Confusion People respond the same way regardless of how you pose a question.

The following Application shows that this belief is false.

APPLICATION How You Ask a Question Matters	Traditionally, electricity customers in Sacramento, California, paid a single price for each kilowatt of electricity all day. However, the cost of producing electricity is greatest when daily demand peaks during certain hours. Thus, the power company considered charging a higher than traditional price during those hours and a lower rate during the rest of the day. By doing so, they hoped to encourage households to run dishwashers and other appliances during low-production-cost periods. To find out whether customers would voluntarily agree to switch to time-based pricing, the electric utility ran an experiment. One group of electricity customers was invited to sign up for (*opt in*) a new time-based pricing structure. Another group was told that they would be put into the new pricing program unless they *opt out*. Fowlie et al. (2017) reported that only 20% of the first group chose to switch to time-based pricing. However, 90% of the second group stuck with default choice of time-based pricing. This difference in response demonstrates the power of the endowment effect.

Salience

Except in the last two chapters of this book, we examine economic theories that are based on the assumption that decision makers are aware of all relevant information. Historically, economists have generally assumed that consumers know their own income or endowment, the relevant prices, and their own tastes, and hence they make informed decisions. However, behavioral economists and psychologists have demonstrated that people are more likely to consider information if it is presented in a way that grabs their attention or if it takes relatively little thought or calculation to understand. Economists use the term *salience*, in the sense of *striking* or *obvious*, to describe this idea.

For example, *tax salience* is the awareness of a tax. If a store's posted price includes the sales tax, consumers observe a change in the price as the tax rises. On the other hand, if a store posts the pre-tax price and collects the tax at the cash register, consumers are less likely to be aware that the post-tax price increases when the tax rate increases. Chetty, Looney, and Kroft (2009) compared consumers' response to a rise in an ad valorem sales tax on beer that is included in the posted price to an increase in a general ad valorem sales tax that is collected at the cash register but not reflected in the posted beer price. Both means of collecting the tax have the same effect on the final price, so both should have the same effect on purchases if consumers pay attention.[22] However, a 10% increase in the posted price, which includes the sales tax, reduces beer consumption by 9%, whereas a 10% increase in the price due to an increased sales tax that is collected at the register reduces consumption by only 2%. Chetty et al. also conducted an experiment in which they posted tax-inclusive prices for 750 products in a grocery store and found that demand for these products fell by about 8% relative to control products in the store and comparable products at nearby stores.

One explanation for why a tax has no effect on consumer behavior is consumer ignorance. For example, Furnham (2005) found that even by the age of 14 or 15, British youths do not fully understand the nature and purpose of taxes. Similarly, unless the tax-inclusive price is posted, many consumers ignore or are unaware of taxes.

An alternative explanation for ignoring taxes is **bounded rationality**: People have a limited capacity to anticipate, solve complex problems, or enumerate all options. To avoid having to perform hundreds of calculations when making purchasing decisions at a grocery store, many people choose not to calculate the tax-inclusive price. However, when post-tax price information is easily available to them, consumers use it. One way to modify the standard model is to assume that people incur a cost to making calculations—such as the time taken or the mental strain—and that deciding whether to incur this cost is part of their rational decision-making process.

People incur this calculation cost only if they think the gain from a better choice of goods exceeds the cost. More people pay attention to a tax when the tax rate is high or when their demand for the good is elastic (sensitive to price changes). Similarly, some people are more likely to pay attention to taxes when making large, one-time purchases—such as buying a computer or car—rather than small, repeated purchases—such as soap or batteries.

Tax salience has important implications for tax policy. In Chapter 2, we showed that if everyone is aware of a tax, the tax incidence on consumers (the share of the tax that consumers pay) is the same regardless of whether the tax is collected from consumers or sellers. However, if consumers are inattentive to taxes, they're more likely to bear the tax burden. If a tax on consumers rises and consumers don't notice, their demand for the good is relatively inelastic, causing consumers to bear more of the tax incidence (see Equation 2.30). In contrast, if the tax is placed on sellers, and sellers pass on at least some of the tax to consumers, consumers observe the higher prices.

---

[22]The final price consumers pay is $p^* = p(1 + V)(1 + v)$, where p is the pre-tax price, v is the general ad valorem sales tax, and V is the excise tax on beer.

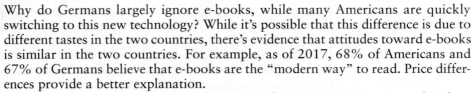

CHALLENGE SOLUTION

Why Americans Buy E-Books and Germans Do Not

Why do Germans largely ignore e-books, while many Americans are quickly switching to this new technology? While it's possible that this difference is due to different tastes in the two countries, there's evidence that attitudes toward e-books is similar in the two countries. For example, as of 2017, 68% of Americans and 67% of Germans believe that e-books are the "modern way" to read. Price differences provide a better explanation.

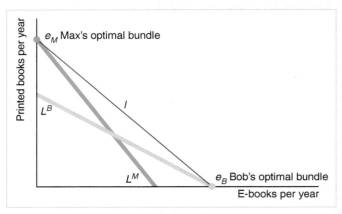

Suppose that Max, a German, and Bob, a Yank, are avid readers with identical incomes and tastes. Each is indifferent between reading a novel in a printed book or on an e-reader, so their indifference curves have a slope of -1, as the red line in the figure illustrates. We can use an indifference curve–budget line analysis to explain why Max buys printed books while Bob chooses electronic ones.

In the United States, the after-tax price of e-books is lower than that of print books, so Bob's budget line, L^B, is flatter than his indifference curve. In contrast in Germany, the after-tax price of e-books is higher than for print books, so Max's budget line, L^M, is steeper than his indifference curve. Thus, as the figure shows, Bob maximizes his utility by spending his entire book budget on e-books. He chooses the Bundle e_B where his indifference curve I hits his budget line, L^B, on the e-book axis. In contrast, Max spends his entire book budget on printed books, at point e_M.

If Bob and Max viewed the two types of books as imperfect substitutes and had the usual convex indifference curves, they would each buy a mix of e-books and printed books. However, because of the relatively lower price of e-books in the United States, Bob would buy relatively more e-books.

SUMMARY

Consumers maximize their utility (well-being) subject to constraints based on their incomes and the prices of goods.

1. **Preferences.** To predict consumers' responses to changes in these constraints, economists use a theory about individuals' preferences. One way of summarizing consumer preferences is with an indifference map. An indifference curve consists of all bundles of goods that give the consumer a particular level of utility. Based on observations of consumer behavior, economists assume that consumers' preferences have three properties: completeness, transitivity, and more-is-better. Given these three assumptions, indifference curves have the following properties:

   • Consumers get more pleasure from bundles on indifference curves the farther the curves are from the origin.

   • Indifference curves cannot cross.
   • Every bundle lies on an indifference curve.
   • Indifference curves cannot be thick.
   • Indifference curves slope downward.

   We also assume that consumers' preferences are continuous, and we use this assumption in our utility function analysis.

2. **Utility.** *Utility* is the set of numerical values that reflect the relative rankings of bundles of goods. Utility is an ordinal measure: By comparing the utility a consumer gets from each of two bundles, we know that the consumer prefers the bundle with the higher utility, but we can't tell by how much more the consumer prefers that bundle. The utility function is unique only up to a positive monotonic

transformation. The marginal utility from a good is the extra utility a person gets from consuming one more unit of it, holding the consumption of all other goods constant. The rate at which a consumer is willing to substitute one good for another, the marginal rate of substitution (*MRS*), depends on the relative amounts of marginal utility the consumer gets from each of the two goods.

3. **Budget Constraint.** The amount of goods consumers can buy at given prices is limited by their incomes. The greater their incomes and the lower the prices of goods, the better off consumers are. The rate at which they can exchange one good for another in the market, the marginal rate of transformation (*MRT*), depends on the relative prices of the two goods.

4. **Constrained Consumer Choice.** Consumers pick an affordable bundle of goods to buy to maximize their pleasure. If an individual consumes both Good 1 and Good 2 (an interior solution) and has the usual shape indifference curves, the individual's utility is maximized when the following equivalent conditions hold:

   - The consumer buys the bundle of goods that is on the highest obtainable indifference curve.
   - The indifference curve between the two goods is tangent to the budget constraint.
   - The consumer's marginal rate of substitution (the slope of the indifference curve) equals the marginal rate of transformation (the slope of the budget line).

   - The last dollar spent on Good 1 gives the consumer as much extra utility as the last dollar spent on Good 2.

   However, consumers do not buy some of all possible goods, so their optimal bundles are corner solutions. At a corner, the last dollar spent on a good that is actually purchased gives a consumer more extra utility than would a dollar's worth of a good the consumer chose not to buy.

   We can use our model in which a consumer maximizes a utility subject to a budget constraint to predict the consumer's optimal choice of goods as a function of the individual's income and market prices.

5. **Behavioral Economics.** Using insights from psychology and empirical research on human cognition and emotional biases, economists are modifying the rational economic model to better predict economic decision making. While adults tend to make transitive choices, children are less likely to do so, especially when novelty is involved. Consequently, some people would argue that the ability of children to make economic choices should be limited. Consumers exhibit an endowment effect if they place a higher value on a good that they own than on the same good if they are considering buying it. Such consumers are less sensitive to price changes and hence less likely to trade goods, as predicted by the standard consumer choice model. Many consumers fail to pay attention to sales taxes unless they are included in the product's final price, and thus ignore them when making purchasing decisions.

EXERCISES

All exercises are available on **MyLab Economics;** * = *answer appears at the back of this book;* **M** = *mathematical problem.*

1. Preferences

1.1 Explain why economists assume that the more-is-better property holds and describe how these explanations relate to the results in the Application "You Can't Have Too Much Money."

1.2 Can an indifference curve be downward sloping in one section, but then bend backward so that it forms a "hook" at the end of the indifference curve? (*Hint*: Look at Solved Problem 3.1.)

1.3 Give as many reasons as you can why we believe that indifference curves are convex and explain.

1.4 Don is altruistic. Show the possible shape of his indifference curves between charitable contributions and all other goods. Does this indifference curve violate any of our assumptions? Why or why not?

*1.5 Arthur spends his income on bread and chocolate. He views chocolate as a good but is neutral about bread, in that he doesn't care if he consumes it or not. Draw his indifference map.

2. Utility

2.1 Miguel considers tickets to the Houston Grand Opera and to Houston Astros baseball games to be perfect substitutes. Show his preference map. What is his utility function?

*2.2 Sofia will consume hot dogs only with whipped cream. Show her preference map. What is her utility function?

2.3 Fiona requires a minimum level of consumption, a *threshold*, to derive additional utility: $U(X, Z)$

is 0 if $X + Z \le 5$ and is $X + Z$ otherwise. Draw Fiona's indifference curves. Which of our preference assumptions does this example violate?

*2.4 Tiffany's constant elasticity of substitution (CES) utility function is $U(q_1, q_2) = (q_1^\rho + q_2^\rho)^{1/\rho}$. What is the positive monotonic transformation such that Tiffany's utility function is equivalent to (has the same preference ordering) the utility function $U(q_1, q_2) = q_1^\rho + q_2^\rho$? **M**

*2.5 Suppose we calculate the *MRS* at a particular bundle for a consumer whose utility function is $U(q_1, q_2)$. If we use a positive monotonic transformation, F, to obtain a new utility function, $V(q_1, q_2) = F(U(q_1, q_2))$, then this new utility function contains the same information about the consumer's rankings of bundles. Prove that the *MRS* is the same as with the original utility function. **M**

*2.6 What is the *MRS* for the CES utility function (which is slightly different from the one in the text) $U(q_1, q_2) = (aq_1^\rho + [1 - a]q_2^\rho)^{1/\rho}$? (*Hint*: Look at Solved Problem 3.2.) **M**

2.7 If José Maria's utility function is $U(q_1, q_2) = q_1 + Aq_1^a q_2^b + q_2$, what is his marginal utility from q_2? What is his marginal rate of substitution between these two goods? (*Hint*: Look at Solved Problem 3.2.) **M**

2.8 Phil's quasilinear utility function is $U(q_1, q_2) = \ln q_1 + q_2$. Show that his *MRS* is the same on all of his indifference curves at a given q_1. (*Hint*: Look at Solved Problem 3.3.) **M**

2.9 Sanghoon has a utility function over audiobooks, A, and movie downloads, M, given by $U = \sqrt{BM}$. Linh has a utility function given by $U = BM$. Explain why Sanghoon and Linh have the same ordering over any two bundles and therefore have the same ordinal preferences. **M**

3. Budget Constraint

*3.1 What is the effect of a 50% income tax on Dale's budget line and opportunity set?

3.2 What happens to a consumer's optimal choice of goods if all prices and the consumer's income double? (*Hint*: What happens to the intercepts of the budget constraint?)

*3.3 Governments frequently limit how much of a good a consumer can buy. During emergencies, governments may ration "essential" goods such as water, food, and gasoline rather than let their prices rise. Suppose that the government rations water, setting quotas on how much a consumer can purchase. If a consumer can afford to buy 12,000 gallons a month but the government restricts purchases to no more than 10,000 gallons a month, how do the consumer's budget line and opportunity set change?

3.4 What happens to the budget line if the government applies a specific tax of $1 per gallon on gasoline but does not tax other goods? What happens to the budget line if the tax applies only to purchases of gasoline in excess of 10 gallons per week?

4. Constrained Consumer Choice

4.1 Suppose that Boston consumers pay twice as much for avocados as they pay for tangerines, whereas San Diego consumers pay half as much for avocados as they pay for tangerines. Assuming that consumers maximize their utility, which city's consumers have a higher marginal rate of substitution of avocados for tangerines if tangerines are on the horizontal axis? Explain your answer.

4.2 Elise consumes cans of anchovies, q_1, and boxes of biscuits, q_2. Each of her indifference curves reflects strictly diminishing marginal rates of substitution. Where $q_1 = 2$ and $q_2 = 2$, her marginal rate of substitution between cans of anchovies and boxes of biscuits equals -1. Will she prefer a bundle with three cans of anchovies and a box of biscuits to a bundle with two of each? Why? **M**

*4.3 Andy purchases only two goods, apples (q_1) and kumquats (q_2). He has an income of $40 and can buy apples at $2 per pound and kumquats at $4 per pound. His utility function is $U(q_1, q_2) = 3q_1 + 5q_2$. What is his marginal utility for apples, and what is his marginal utility for kumquats? What bundle of apples and kumquats should he purchase to maximize his utility? Why? **M**

4.4 Mark consumes only cookies and books. At his current consumption bundle, his marginal utility from books is 10 and from cookies is 5. Each book costs $10, and each cookie costs $2. Is he maximizing his utility? Explain. If he is not, how can he increase his utility while keeping his total expenditure constant? **M**

4.5 Some of the largest import tariffs, the tax on imported goods, are on shoes. Strangely, the cheaper the shoes, the higher the tariff. The highest U.S. tariff, 67%, is on a pair of $3 canvas sneakers, while the tariff on $12 sneakers is 37%, and that on $300 Italian leather imports is 12% (Blake W. Krueger, "A Shoe Tariff with a Big Footprint," *Wall Street Journal*, November 22, 2012). Laura buys either inexpensive, canvas sneakers ($3 before the tariff) or more expensive gym shoes ($12 before the tariff) for her many children. Use an indifference curve–budget line analysis to show how imposing these unequal tariffs affects the bundle of shoes that she buys compared to what she would have bought in the absence of tariffs. Can you confidently predict whether she'll buy relatively more expensive gym shoes after the tariff? Why or why not?

4.6 Helen views raspberries and blackberries as perfect complements. Initially, she buys five pints of each this month. Suppose that the price of raspberries falls while the price of blackberries rises such that the bundle of five pints of each lies on her budget line. Does her optimal bundle change? Explain. (*Hint*: See Solved Problem 3.4.)

4.7 Use indifference curve–budget line diagrams to illustrate the results in Table 3.2 for each of these utility functions.

4.8 For the utility function $U(q_1, q_2) = q_1^\rho + q_2^\rho$, solve for the optimal q_1 and q_2 as functions of the prices, p_1 and p_2, and income, Y. (*Hint*: See Solved Problem 3.5.) **M**

4.9 The Application "Indifference Curves Between Food and Clothing" postulates that minimum levels of food and clothing are necessary to support life. Suppose that the amount of food one has is F, the minimum level to sustain life is $\underline{F}$, the amount of clothing one has is C, and the minimum necessary is $\underline{C}$. We can then modify the Cobb-Douglas utility function to reflect these minimum levels: $U(C, F) = (C - \underline{C})^a (F - \underline{F})^{1-a}$, where $C \geq \underline{C}$ and $F \geq \underline{F}$. Using the approach similar to that in Solved Problem 3.6, derive the optimal amounts of food and clothing as a function of prices and a person's income. To do so, introduce the idea of *extra income*, Y^*, which is the income remaining after paying for the minimum levels of food and clothing: $Y^* = Y - p_C \underline{C} - p_F \underline{F}$. Show that the optimal quantity of clothing is $C = \underline{C} + aY^*/p_C$ and that the optimal quantity of food is $F = \underline{F} + (1 - a)Y^*/p_F$. Derive formulas for the share of income devoted to each good. **M**

4.10 A function $f(X, Y)$ is homogeneous of degree g if, when we multiply each argument by a constant a, $f(aX, aY) = a^g f(X, Y)$. Thus, if a function is homogeneous of degree zero ($g = 0$), $f(aX, aY) = a^0 f(X, Y) = f(X, Y)$, because $a^0 = 1$. Show that the optimality conditions for the Cobb-Douglas utility function in Solved Problem 3.6 are homogeneous of degree zero. Explain why that result is consistent with the intuition that if we double all prices and income the optimal bundle does not change. **M**

4.11 Diogo's utility function is $U(q_1, q_2) = q_1^{0.75} q_2^{0.25}$, where q_1 is chocolate candy and q_2 is slices of pie. If the price of a chocolate bar, p_1, is \$1, the price of a slice of pie, p_2, is \$2, and Y is \$80, what is Diogo's optimal bundle? (*Hint*: See Solved Problem 3.6.) **M**

4.12 In 2005, Americans bought 9.1 million home radios for \$202 million and 3.8 million home-theater-in-a-box units for \$730 million (*TWICE*, March 27, 2006). Suppose the average consumer has a Cobb-Douglas utility function and buys these two goods only. Given the results in Solved Problem 3.7, estimate a plausible Cobb-Douglas utility function such that the consumer would allocate income in the proportions actually observed. **M**

4.13 According to the U.S. Bureau of Labor Statistics, in 2018, average annual consumer expenditures were \$1,329 on education, \$4,612 on health care, and \$2,913 on entertainment. Given that a person buys only these three goods, estimate the person's Cobb-Douglas utility function for these three goods. (*Hint*: See Solved Problem 3.7.) **M**

*4.14 David's utility function is $U = q_1 + 2q_2$. Describe his optimal bundle in terms of the prices of q_1 and q_2. **M**

*4.15 Vasco likes spare ribs, q_1, and fried chicken, q_2. His utility function is $U = 10q_1^2 q_2$. His weekly income is \$90, which he spends on ribs and chicken only.

a. If he pays \$10 for a slab of ribs and \$5 for a chicken, what is his optimal consumption bundle? Show his budget line, indifference curve, and optimal bundle, e_1, in a diagram.

b. Suppose the price of chicken doubles to \$10. How does his optimal consumption of chicken and ribs change? Show his new budget line and optimal bundle, e_2, in your diagram. **M**

4.16 Ann's utility function is $U = q_1 q_2/(q_1 + q_2)$. Solve for her optimal values of q_1 and q_2 as a function of p_1, p_2, and Y. **M**

4.17 Wolf's utility function is $U = aq_1^{0.5} + q_2$. For given prices and income, show how whether he has an interior or corner solution depends on a. **M**

4.18 Given that Kip's utility function is $U(q_c, q_m) = q_c^{0.5} + q_m^{0.5}$, what is his expenditure function? (*Hint*: See Solved Problem 3.8.) **M**

4.19 Ajay and Florencia each have a budget of \$80 per month to spend on downloaded music tracks and live concert tickets. At the initial prices, Ajay consumes both goods but Florencia buys only downloaded music and does not go to live concerts. Now the price of live concerts falls. Show that Ajay's utility must increase and that Florencia's utility may increase or stay the same but cannot fall.

5. Behavioral Economics

5.1 Illustrate the logic of the endowment effect using a kinked indifference curve. Let the angle be greater than 90°. Suppose that the prices change, so the slope of the budget line through the endowment changes.

a. Use the diagram to explain why an individual whose endowment point is at the kink will only trade from the endowment point if the price change is substantial.

b. What rules can we use to determine the optimal bundle? Can we use all the conditions that we derived for determining an interior solution?

*5.2 Why would a consumer's demand for a supermarket product change when the product price is quoted inclusive of taxes rather than before tax? Is the same effect as likely for people buying a car?

6. Challenge

6.1 Suppose the Challenge Solution were changed so that Max and Bob still have identical tastes, but have the usual-shaped indifference curves. Use a figure to discuss how the different slopes of their budget lines affect the bundles of printed books and e-books that each chooses. Can you make any unambiguous statements about how their bundles differ? Can you make an unambiguous statement if you know that Bob's budget line goes through Max's optimal bundle?

*6.2 West Virginians who live near the border with other states can shop on either side of the border. When a 6% food tax was imposed in West Virginia, if West Virginians bought food in West Virginia, their total cost was the price of the food plus the tax. If they bought across the border in states that do not tax food, the total cost was the price plus the cost due to the extra travel. Tosun and Skidmore (2007) found that West Virginian food sales dropped 8% in border counties when a 6% sales tax on food was imposed. Explain why. West Virginia eliminated the tax in 2013. (*Hint*: See the Challenge Solution.)

6.3 Einav et al. (2012) found that people who live in high sales tax locations are much more likely than other consumers to purchase goods over the internet because internet purchases are generally exempt from the sales tax if the firm is located in another state. They found that a 1% increase in a state's sales tax increases online purchases by that state's residents by just under 2%. Is the explanation for this result similar to that in the Challenge Solution? Why or why not?

6.4 Salvo and Huse (2013) found that roughly one-fifth of owners of flexible-fuel cars (cars that can run on a mix of ethanol and gasoline) choose gasoline when the price of gas is 20% above that of ethanol (in energy-adjusted terms) and, similarly, one-fifth of motorists choose ethanol when ethanol is 20% more expensive than gasoline. What can you say about these people's tastes? Do they view ethanol and gasoline as perfect substitutes?

6.5 Until 2012, California, Pennsylvania, and Texas required firms to collect sales taxes for online sales only if the chain had a physical presence (a "brick" store as opposed to a "click" store) in those states. Thus, those states collected taxes on Best Buy's online sales, because it had stores in each of those states, but they did not collect taxes from Amazon.com because it did not have physical locations in those states. Starting in 2012, Amazon had to pay taxes in these states. According to Baugh, Ben-David, and Park (2015), consumers living in states that collected sales tax during checkout reduced Amazon purchases by 11%. After the tax was imposed on Amazon, Best Buy had a 4% to 6% increase in its online sales in those states relative to the rest of the chain (**www.bizjournals.com/twincities/news/2013/01/11/best-buys-online-sales-up-in-states.html**). Use an indifference curve–budget line diagram to show why Best Buy's sales rose after taxes were imposed on Amazon. (*Hint*: Start by drawing a typical consumer's indifference curve between buying a good from Amazon or buying it from Best Buy.)

Demand

4

I have modest demands—they hardly exceed my income.

When Google wants to transfer an employee from its Washington, D.C., office to its London branch, it must decide how much compensation to offer the worker to move. International firms are increasingly relocating workers throughout their home countries and internationally.

According to Atlas World Group's 2018 international survey of corporations, roughly 40% of corporations expect an increase in relocations and 50% expect relocation volumes to stay constant.

As you might expect, workers are not always enthusiastic about relocating. In the Atlas survey, 60% of firms had employees who declined to relocate. Of these, 34% said they declined because of the high cost of living in the new location.

One possible approach to enticing employees to relocate is for the firm to assess the goods and services consumed by employees in the original location and then pay those employees enough to allow them to consume essentially the same items in the new location. According to a Mercer survey, 72% of firms in the Americas reported that they provided their workers with enough income abroad to maintain their home lifestyle.

At the end of the chapter, you will be asked: Do firms' standard compensation packages overcompensate workers by paying them more than is necessary to induce them to relocate? To answer that question, you will need to determine the firm's optimal compensation.

In Chapter 3, we introduced consumer theory, which explains how consumers make choices when faced with constraints. We begin this chapter by using consumer theory to determine the shape of a demand curve for a good by varying the good's price, holding other prices and income constant. Firms use information about the shape of demand curves when setting prices: How much can Apple profitably raise its price for the iPhone above its cost of producing it? Governments also use this information to predict the impact of policies such as taxes and price controls: If the government cuts the income tax rate, will tax revenues rise or fall?

Then, we apply consumer theory to show how an increase in people's incomes causes a demand curve to shift. Firms use information about the relationship between income and demand to predict which less developed countries will substantially increase their demand for the firms' products when incomes rise.

Next, we discover that an increase in the price of a good has two effects on demand. First, consumers buy less of the now relatively more expensive good even if they are compensated with cash for the price increase. Second, holding consumers' incomes constant, an increase in price forces them to buy less of at least some goods.

We use the analysis of these two demand effects of a price increase to show why the government's measure of inflation, the Consumer Price Index (CPI), overestimates the amount of inflation. If you signed a long-term lease for an apartment in which your rent payments increase over time in proportion to the change in the CPI, you lose and your landlord gains from the bias.

Finally, having determined that we can infer how a consumer will behave based on personal preferences, we use a *revealed preference* approach to show the opposite: that we can infer what a consumer's preferences are if we know the consumer's behavior. Using revealed preference, we can demonstrate that consumers substitute away from a good when its price rises.

In this chapter, we examine five main topics

1. **Deriving Demand Curves.** We use consumer theory to derive demand curves, showing how a change in a product's price causes a movement along its demand curve.

2. **Effects of an Increase in Income.** We use consumer theory to determine how an increase in consumers' incomes results in their buying more of some or all goods.

3. **Effects of a Price Increase.** A change in price has two effects on demand, one relating to a change in relative prices and the other concerning a change in consumers' opportunities.

4. **Cost-of-Living Adjustment.** Using the analysis of the two effects of price changes, we show that the CPI overestimates the rate of inflation.

5. **Revealed Preference.** Observing a consumer's choice at various prices allows us to infer what the consumer's preferences are and show that the consumer substitutes away from a good when its price increases.

4.1 Deriving Demand Curves

Holding people's tastes, their incomes, and the prices of other goods constant, an increase in the price of a good causes a *movement along the demand curve* for the good (Chapter 2). We use consumer theory to show how a consumer's choice changes as the price changes, thereby tracing out the demand curve.

System of Demand Functions

In Chapter 3, we used calculus to maximize a consumer's utility subject to a budget constraint. We solved for the optimal quantities of sets of goods that the consumer chooses as functions of prices and the consumer's income. In doing so, we derived the consumer's system of demand functions for the goods.

For example, Lisa chooses between pizzas, q_1, and burritos, q_2, so her demand functions for pizza, q_1, and burritos, q_2, are of the form

$$q_1 = D_1(p_1, p_2, Y),$$
$$q_2 = D_2(p_1, p_2, Y),$$

where p_1 is the price of pizza, p_2 is the price of burritos, and Y is her income. We can trace out the demand function for one good by varying its price while holding other prices and income constant.

In Chapter 3, we illustrated this approach with five utility functions whereby a consumer chooses between two goods. Table 4.1 summarizes what we know about their demand functions. For the first three utility functions in the table—perfect complements, constant elasticity of substitution (CES, where $\rho < 1$), and Cobb-Douglas—we have an interior solution where the consumer buys both goods. Here, the quantities demanded of both goods are strictly positive. The other two utility functions—perfect substitutes and quasilinear—may have either an interior solution or a corner solution, where the consumer buys only one of the goods.

Table 4.1 Demand Functions for Five Utility Functions

Utility Function	$U(q_1, q_2)$	Solution	Demand Functions q_1	q_2
Perfect complements	$\min(q_1, q_2)$	interior	$Y/(p_1 + p_2)$	$Y/(p_1 + p_2)$
CES, $\rho \neq 0, \rho < 1, \sigma = 1/(1 - \rho)$	$(q_1^\rho + q_2^\rho)^{\frac{1}{\rho}}$	interior	$\dfrac{Yp_1^{-\sigma}}{p_1^{1-\sigma} + p_2^{1-\sigma}}$	$\dfrac{Yp_2^{-\sigma}}{p_1^{1-\sigma} + p_2^{1-\sigma}}$
Cobb-Douglas	$q_1^a q_2^{1-a}$	interior	aY/p_1	$(1 - a)Y/p_2$
Perfect substitutes	$q_1 + q_2$			
$\quad p_1 = p_2 = p$		interior	$q_1 + q_2 = Y/p$	
$\quad p_1 < p_2$		corner	Y/p_1	0
$\quad p_1 > p_2$		corner	0	Y/p_2
Quasilinear,	$aq_1^{0.5} + q_2$			
$\quad Y > a^2 p_2^2/[4p_1]$		interior	$\left(\dfrac{a}{2}\dfrac{p_2}{p_1}\right)^2$	$\dfrac{Y}{p_2} - \dfrac{a^2}{4}\dfrac{p_2}{p_1}$
$\quad Y \leq a^2 p_2^2/[4p_1]$		corner	Y/p_1	0

We solved for the demand functions for the perfect complements utility function, $U(q_1, q_2) = \min(q_1, q_2)$, in Solved Problem 3.4 and for the constant elasticity of substitution (CES) utility function, $U(q_1, q_2) = (q_1^\rho + q_2^\rho)^{\frac{1}{\rho}}$, in Solved Problem 3.5. For both these utility functions, the demand functions for q_1 and q_2 depend on both prices and income, as Table 4.1 shows.

In contrast, for the Cobb-Douglas utility function, $U(q_1, q_2) = q_1^a q_2^{1-a}$, the demand functions depend on the consumer's income and each good's own price, but not on the price of the other good. In Solved Problem 3.6, we derived the Cobb-Douglas demand functions, Equations 3.29 and 3.30, $q_1 = aY/p_1$ and $q_2 = (1 - a)Y/p_2$. Panel a of Figure 4.1 shows the demand curve for q_1, which we plot by holding Y fixed and varying p_1. The demand curve asymptotically approaches the quantity axis.

The demand curves for the perfect substitutes utility function, $U(q_1, q_2) = q_1 + q_2$, which has straight-line indifference curves, do not change smoothly with a good's price. Suppose Ben chooses between Coke and Pepsi, which he views as perfect substitutes. If the price of Coke, p_1, is above that of Pepsi, p_2, the demand for Coke is zero (corner solution), as panel b of Figure 4.1 shows. If the two prices are equal, $p_1 = p_2 = p$, then Ben buys Y/p cans of either Coke or Pepsi (interior solution), so the demand curve is horizontal and ranges between 0 and Y/p cans. Finally, if $p_1 < p_2$, Ben spends all his income on Coke, buying $q_1 = Y/p_1$ cans. Thus, in the corner solution where Coke is relatively cheap, the Coke demand curve has the same shape as the Cobb-Douglas demand curve.

A quasilinear utility function, $U(q_1, q_2) = u(q_1) + q_2$, can also have an interior or corner solution. In Chapter 3, we considered a particular example, $4q_1^{0.5} + q_2$. In Table 4.1, we slightly generalize this example to $aq_1^{0.5} + q_2$. If the consumer's income is low, $Y \leq a^2 p_2^2/[4p_1]$, the consumer buys none of q_2 (corner solution) and $q_1 = Y/p_1$. At higher incomes, the consumer buys a fixed amount of $q_1 = [(a/2)(p_2/p_1)]^2$, which is independent of Y, and spends the rest on $q_2 = Y/p_2 - (a^2/4)(p_2/p_1)$.

Graphical Interpretation

We can derive demand curves graphically. An individual chooses an optimal bundle of goods by picking the point on the highest indifference curve that touches the budget line. A change in a price causes the budget line to rotate, so that the consumer

Figure 4.1 Cobb-Douglas and Perfect Substitute Demand Curves

(a) The Cobb-Douglas demand curve for $q_1 = aY/p_1$ is a smooth curve that approaches the horizontal, q_1-axis as p_1 becomes smaller. (b) Ben demands no cans of Coca-Cola when the price of Coke, p_1, is greater than the price of Pepsi, p_2. When the two prices are equal, he wants a total number of cans equal to $Y/p_1 = Y/p_2$, but he is indifferent as to how many are Coke and how many are Pepsi. If $p_1 < p_2$, he only buys Coke, and his demand curve is $q_1 = Y/p_1$.

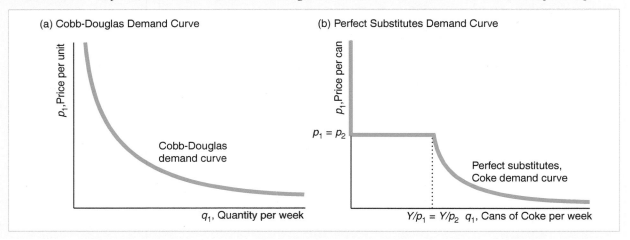

(a) Cobb-Douglas Demand Curve

p_1, Price per unit

Cobb-Douglas demand curve

q_1, Quantity per week

(b) Perfect Substitutes Demand Curve

p_1, Price per can

$p_1 = p_2$

Perfect substitutes, Coke demand curve

$Y/p_1 = Y/p_2$ q_1, Cans of Coke per week

chooses a new optimal bundle. By varying one price and holding other prices and income constant, we determine how the quantity demanded changes as the price changes, which is the information we need to draw the demand curve.

We start by estimating a utility function between wine and beer, using data for U.S. consumers.[1] Panel a of Figure 4.2 shows three of the corresponding estimated indifference curves for the average U.S. consumer, whom we call Mimi.[2] These indifference curves are convex to the origin because Mimi views beer and wine as imperfect substitutes (Chapter 3).

The vertical axis in panel a measures the number of gallons of wine Mimi consumes each year, and the horizontal axis measures the number of gallons of beer she drinks each year. Mimi spends $Y = \$419$ per year on beer and wine. The price of beer, p_b, is \$12 per unit, and the price of wine, p_w, is \$35 per unit. The slope of her budget line, L^1, is $-p_b/p_w = -12/35 \approx \frac{1}{3}$. At those prices, Mimi consumes Bundle e_1, 26.7 gallons of beer per year and 2.8 gallons of wine per year, a combination that is determined by the tangency of indifference curve I^1 and budget line L^1.[3]

---

[1]We estimated the utility function that underlies Figure 4.2 using an almost ideal demand system, which is a more flexible functional form than the Cobb-Douglas, and which includes the Cobb-Douglas as a special case.

[2]My mother, Mimi, wanted the most degenerate character in the book named after her. I hope that you do not consume as much beer or wine as the typical American in this example. ("One reason I don't drink is that I want to know when I am having a good time."—Nancy, Lady Astor)

[3]These figures are the U.S. average annual per capita consumption of wine and beer. These numbers are surprisingly high given that they reflect an average of teetotalers and (apparently very heavy) drinkers. According to the World Health Organization statistics for 2015, the consumption of liters of pure alcohol per capita by people 15 years and older was 9.0 in the United States compared to 0.2 in Saudi Arabia, 3.1 in Israel, 6.1 in Italy, 7.6 in China, 7.5 in Japan, 9.6 in the Netherlands, 10.3 in Canada, 10.6 in Germany, 10.9 in Ireland, 11.2 in New Zealand, 11.6 in France, 12.0 in the United Kingdom, 12.6 in Australia, and 17.4 in Moldova.

Figure 4.2 Deriving Mimi's Demand Curve

If the price of beer falls, holding the price of wine, the budget, and tastes constant, the typical American consumer, Mimi, buys more beer, according to our estimates. (a) At the actual budget line, L^1, where the price of beer is $12 per unit and the price of wine is $35 per unit, the average consumer's indifference curve I^1 is tangent at Bundle e_1, 26.7 gallons of beer per year and 2.8 gallons of wine per year. If the price of beer falls to $6 per unit, the new budget constraint is L^2, and the average consumer buys 44.5 gallons of beer per year and 4.3 gallons of wine per year. (b) By varying the price of beer, we trace out Mimi's demand curve for beer. The beer price-quantity combinations E_1, E_2, and E_3 on the demand curve for beer in panel b correspond to optimal bundles e_1, e_2, and e_3 in panel a.

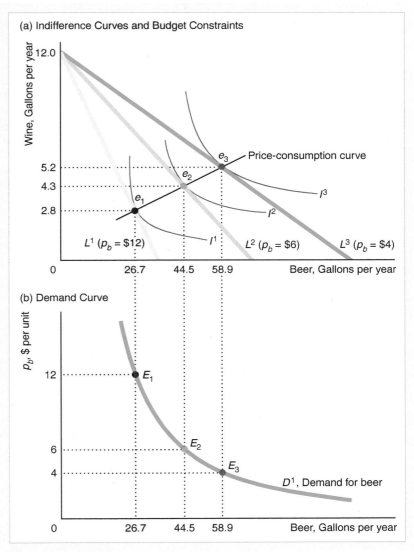

If the price of beer falls by half to $6 per unit and the price of wine and her budget remain constant, Mimi's budget line rotates outward to L^2. If she were to spend all her money on wine, she could buy the same 12 ($\approx$ 419/35) gallons of wine per year as before, so the intercept on the vertical axis of L^2 is the same as for L^1. However, if she were to spend all her money on beer, she could buy twice as much as before (70 instead of 35 gallons of beer), so L^2 hits the horizontal axis twice as far from the origin as L^1. As a result, L^2 has a flatter slope than L^1, about $-\frac{1}{6}$ ($\approx$ $-6/35$).

Because beer is now relatively less expensive, Mimi drinks relatively more beer. She chooses Bundle e_2, 44.5 gallons of beer per year and 4.3 gallons of wine per year, where her indifference curve I^2 is tangent to L^2. If the price of beer falls to $4 per unit, Mimi consumes Bundle e_3, 58.9 gallons of beer per year and 5.2 gallons of wine per year. The lower the price of beer, the happier Mimi is because she can consume more on the same budget: She is on a higher indifference curve (or perhaps just higher).

Panel a also shows the *price-consumption curve*, which is the line through the optimal bundles, such as e_1, e_2, and e_3, that Mimi would consume at each price of beer, when the price of wine and Mimi's budget are held constant. Because the price-consumption curve is upward sloping, we know that Mimi's consumption of both beer and wine increases as the price of beer falls.

We can use the same information in the price-consumption curve to draw Mimi's demand curve, D^1, for beer in panel b. For each possible price of beer on the vertical axis of panel b, we record on the horizontal axis the quantity of beer demanded by Mimi from the price-consumption curve in panel a.

Points E_1, E_2, and E_3 on the demand curve in panel b correspond to Bundles e_1, e_2, and e_3 on the price-consumption curve in panel a. Both e_1 and E_1 show that when the price of beer is $12, Mimi demands 26.7 gallons of beer per year. When the price falls to $6 per unit, Mimi increases her consumption to 44.5 gallons of beer, point E_2. The demand curve for beer is downward sloping, as the Law of Demand predicts.

We can use the relationship between the points in panels a and b to show that Mimi's utility is lower at point E_1 on D^1 than at point E_2. Point E_1 corresponds to Bundle e_1 on indifference curve I^1, whereas E_2 corresponds to Bundle e_2 on indifference curve I^2, which is farther from the origin than I^1, so Mimi's utility is higher at E_2 than at E_1. Mimi is better off at E_2 than at E_1 because the price of beer is lower at E_2, so she can buy more goods with the same budget.

APPLICATION

Cigarettes Versus E-Cigarettes

Tobacco use, one of the biggest public health threats the world has ever faced, killed 100 million people in the twentieth century. In 2018, the U.S. Centers for Disease Control and Prevention (CDC) reported that cigarette smoking and secondhand smoke are responsible for about half a million deaths each year in the United States—approximately 1,370 deaths every day. Half of all smokers die of tobacco-related causes. Worldwide, tobacco kills 6 million people a year.

Tobacco use generally starts during early adolescence. According to the CDC, 9 out of 10 cigarette smokers tried smoking before they turned 18. Although fewer youths now smoke cigarettes, they are increasingly using e-cigarettes.

In 2018, the American Cancer Society concluded that e-cigarettes are less harmful than cigarettes. How do price changes in e-cigarettes affect the consumption of e-cigarettes and cigarettes?

Pesko and Warman (2017) found that changes in the prices of e-cigarettes affect its use and that of combustible cigarettes among U.S. youths. Increasing the price of e-cigarettes reduces the consumption of e-cigarettes. However, it also increases the consumption of combustible cigarettes: The price-consumption curve for cigarettes and e-cigarettes is upward sloping. They estimated that the price elasticity of e-cigarettes is −1.8, so that a 10% increase in the price of e-cigarettes reduces current e-cigarette use by 18%. But the cross-price elasticity between e-cigarettes and cigarettes is 2.9: A 10% increase in the price of e-cigarettes increases cigarette consumption by 29%.

4.2   Effects of an Increase in Income

It is better to be nouveau riche than never to have been riche at all.

An increase in an individual's income, holding tastes and prices constant, causes a *shift of the demand curve*. An increase in income causes a parallel shift of the budget constraint away from the origin, prompting a consumer to choose a new optimal bundle with more of some or all of the goods.

How Income Changes Shift Demand Curves

We illustrate the relationship between the quantity demanded and income by examining how Mimi's behavior changes when her income rises while the prices of beer and wine remain constant. Figure 4.3 shows three ways of looking at the relationship

Figure 4.3 Effect of a Budget Increase

As the annual budget for wine and beer, Y, increases from \$419 to \$628 and then to \$837, holding prices constant, the typical consumer buys more of both products, as the upward slope of the income-consumption curve illustrates (a). Because Mimi, the typical consumer, buys more beer as her income increases, her demand curve for beer shifts rightward (b) and her Engel curve for beer slopes upward (c).

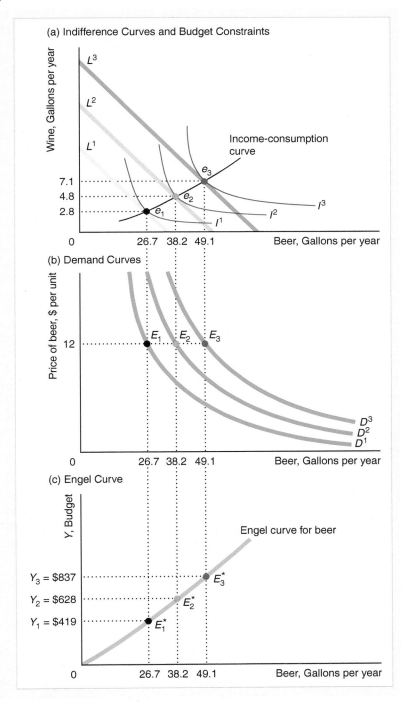

between income and the quantity demanded. All three diagrams have the same horizontal axis: the quantity of beer consumed per year. In the consumer theory diagram, panel a, the vertical axis is the quantity of wine consumed per year. In the demand curve diagram, panel b, the vertical axis is the price of beer per unit. In panel c, which directly shows the relationship between income and the quantity of beer demanded, the vertical axis is Mimi's budget, Y.

A rise in Mimi's income causes a parallel shift out of the budget constraint in panel a, which increases Mimi's opportunity set. Her budget constraint L^1 at her original income, $Y = \$419$, is tangent to her indifference curve I^1 at e_1.

As before, Mimi's demand curve for beer is D^1 in panel b. Point E_1 on D^1, which corresponds to point e_1 in panel a, shows how much beer, 26.7 gallons per year, Mimi consumes when the price of beer is $12 per unit and the price of wine is $35 per unit.

Now suppose that Mimi's beer and wine budget, Y, increases by roughly 50% to $628 per year. Her new budget line, L^2 in panel a, is farther from the origin but parallel to her original budget constraint, L^1, because the prices of beer and wine are unchanged. Given this larger budget, Mimi chooses Bundle e_2. The increase in her income causes her demand curve to shift to D^2 in panel b. Holding Y at $628, we can derive D^2 by varying the price of beer. When the price of beer is $12 per unit, she buys 38.2 gallons of beer per year, E_2 on D^2. Similarly, if Mimi's income increases to $837 per year, her demand curve shifts to D^3.

The *income-consumption curve* (or *income-expansion path*) through Bundles e_1, e_2, and e_3 in panel a shows how Mimi's consumption of beer and wine increases as her income rises. As Mimi's income goes up, her consumption of both wine and beer increases.

We can show the relationship between the quantity demanded and income directly rather than by shifting demand curves to illustrate the effect. In panel c, we plot an **Engel curve**, which shows the relationship between the quantity demanded of a single good and income, holding prices constant. Income is on the vertical axis, and the quantity of beer demanded is on the horizontal axis. On Mimi's Engel curve for beer, points E_1^*, E_2^*, and E_3^* correspond to points E_1, E_2, and E_3 in panel b and to e_1, e_2, and e_3 in panel a.

SOLVED PROBLEM 4.1

MyLab Education
Solved Problem

Mahdu views Coke and Pepsi as perfect substitutes: He is indifferent as to which one he drinks. The price of a 12-ounce can of Coke, p, is less than the price of a 12-ounce can of Pepsi, p^*. What does Mahdu's Engel curve for Coke look like? How much does his weekly cola budget have to rise for Mahdu to buy one more can of Coke per week?

Answer

1. *Use indifference curves to derive Mahdu's optimal choice.* Because Mahdu views the two drinks as perfect substitutes, his indifference curves, such as I^1 and I^2 in panel a of the graph, are straight lines with a slope of -1 (see Chapter 3). When his income is Y_1, his budget line hits the Pepsi axis at Y_1/p^* and the Coke axis at Y_1/p. Mahdu maximizes his utility by consuming Y_1/p cans of the less expensive Coke and no Pepsi (a corner solution). As his income rises, say, to Y_2, his budget line shifts outward and is parallel to the original one, with the same slope of $-p/p^*$. Thus, at each income level, his budget lines are flatter than his indifference curves, so his equilibria lie along the Coke axis.

2. *Use the result from panel a to derive his Engel function.* We saw in panel a that because his entire budget, Y, goes to buying Coke, Mahdu buys $q = Y/p$ cans of Coke. This expression, which shows the relationship between his income and the quantity of Coke he buys, is Mahdu's Engel curve for Coke. The points E_1 and E_2 on the Engel curve in panel b correspond to e_1 and e_2 in panel a. We can rewrite this expression for his Engel curve as $Y = pq$. Panel b shows that

the Engel curve is a straight line, with a slope of $dY/dq = p$. Because his entire drink budget goes to buy Coke, his income needs to rise by p for him to buy one more can of Coke per week.

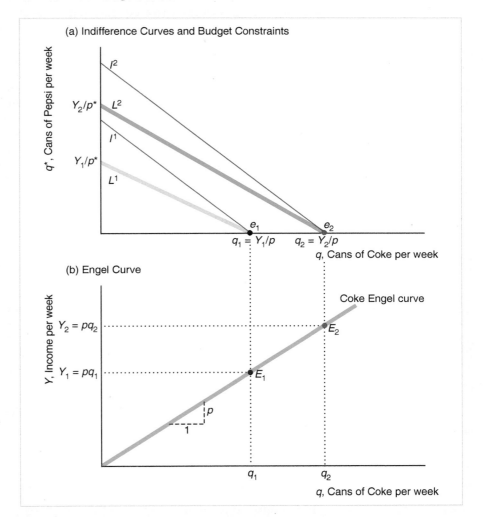

Consumer Theory and Income Elasticities

Income elasticities tell us how much the quantity demanded of a product changes as income increases. We can use income elasticities to summarize the shape of the Engel curve or the shape of the income-consumption curve. Such knowledge is useful. For example, firms use income elasticities to predict the impact that a change in the income tax will have on the demand for their goods.

Income Elasticity. The *income elasticity of demand* (or *income elasticity*) is the percentage change in the quantity demanded of a product in response to a given percentage change in income, Y (Chapter 2):

$$\xi = \frac{\text{percentage change in quantity demanded}}{\text{percentage change in income}} = \frac{\Delta Q/Q}{\Delta Y/Y} = \frac{\partial Q}{\partial Y}\frac{Y}{Q},$$

where ξ is the Greek letter xi.

Mimi's income elasticity for beer, ξ_b, is 0.88 and that for wine, ξ_w, is 1.38 (based on our estimates for the average American consumer). When her income goes up by 1%, she consumes 0.88% more beer and 1.38% more wine. Similarly, as her income falls by 1%, she reduces her consumption of beer by 0.88% and wine by 1.38%. Contrary to frequent (and unsubstantiated) claims in the media, during a recession, average Americans do not drink more as their incomes fall—they drink less.

Some goods have negative income elasticities: $\xi < 0$. A good is called an **inferior good** if less of it is demanded as income rises. No value judgment is intended by the use of the term *inferior*. An inferior good need not be defective or of low quality. Some of the better-known examples of inferior goods are starchy foods such as potatoes and cassava, which very poor people eat in large quantities because they cannot afford meats or other foods. Some economists—apparently seriously—claim that human meat is an inferior good: Only when the price of other foods is very high and people are starving will they turn to cannibalism. Bezmen and Depken (2006) estimated that pirated goods are inferior: A 1% increase in per capita income leads to a 0.25% reduction in piracy.

Another strange example concerns treating children as a consumption good. Even though people can't buy children in a market, people can decide how many children to have. Guinnane (2011) surveyed the literature and reported that most studies find that the income elasticity for the number of children in a family is negative but close to zero. Thus, the number of children demanded is not very sensitive to income.

A **normal good** is a commodity for which more is demanded as income rises. A good is a normal good if its income elasticity is greater than or equal to zero: $\xi \geq 0$. Most goods, including beer and wine, have positive income elasticities and thus are normal goods.

If the quantity demanded of a normal good rises more than in proportion to a person's income, $\xi > 1$, we say it is a *luxury good* (as well as being a normal good). On the other hand, if the quantity demanded rises less than or in proportion to the person's income ($0 \leq \xi \leq 1$), we say it is a *necessity*. Because Mimi's income elasticities are 0.88 for beer but 1.38 for wine at her optimum, Mimi views beer as a necessity and wine as a luxury according to this terminology.

SOLVED PROBLEM 4.2

For a Cobb-Douglas utility function, $U = q_1^a q_2^{1-a}$, show that the income elasticity ξ_1 for q_1 equals one for all values of a and Y.

MyLab Economics Solved Problem

Answer

1. *Derive the income elasticity by differentiating the Cobb-Douglas demand function and multiplying by Y/q_1.* According to Table 4.1, the Cobb-Douglas demand function is $q_1 = aY/p_1$. Partially differentiating with respect to Y, we find that $\partial q_1/\partial Y = a/p_1$. Thus, the income elasticity is $\xi_1 = (\partial q_1/\partial Y)(Y/q_1) = (a/p_1)(Y/q_1) = aY/(p_1 q_1)$.

2. *Show that the income elasticity equals one in general.* By multiplying both sides of the demand function for the first good, $q_1 = aY/p_1$, by p_1, we find that $p_1 q_1 = aY$. Using this expression to substitute for aY in the income elasticity formula, we find that $\xi_1 = 1$.

Comment: By a similar argument, the income elasticity for q_2 is one.

Figure 4.4 Income-Consumption Curves and Income Elasticities

At the initial income, the budget constraint is L^1 and the optimal bundle is e. After income rises, the new constraint is L^2. With an upward-sloping income-consumption curve such as ICC^2, both goods are normal. With an income-consumption curve such as ICC^1, which goes through the upper-left section of L^2 (to the left of the vertical dotted line through e), housing is normal and food is inferior. With an income-consumption curve such as ICC^3, which cuts L^2 in the lower-right section (below the horizontal dotted line through e), food is normal and housing is inferior.

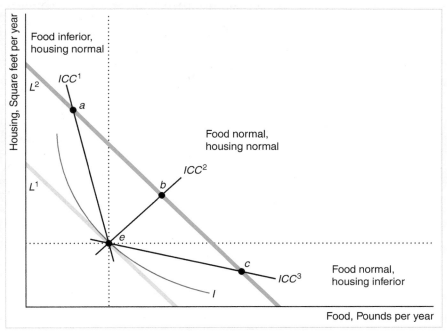

Income-Consumption Curves and Income Elasticities. The shape of the income-consumption curve for two goods tells us the sign of their income elasticities: whether the income elasticities for those goods are positive or negative. To illustrate the relationship between the slope of the income-consumption curve and the sign of income elasticities, we examine Peter's choices of food and housing. Peter purchases Bundle e in Figure 4.4 when his budget constraint is L^1. When his income increases so that his budget constraint is L^2, he selects a bundle on L^2. Which bundle he buys depends on his tastes—his indifference curves.

The horizontal and vertical dotted lines through e divide the new budget line, L^2, into three sections. The section where the new optimal bundle is located determines Peter's income elasticities of food and housing.

Suppose that Peter's indifference curve is tangent to L^2 at a point in the upper-left section of L^2 (to the left of the vertical dotted line that goes through e), such as a. If Peter's income-consumption curve is ICC^1, which goes from e through a, he buys more housing and less food as his income rises, so housing is a normal good for Peter and food is an inferior good. (Although we draw these possible ICC curves as straight lines for simplicity, they could be curves.)

If instead the new optimal bundle is located in the middle section of L^2 (above the horizontal dotted line and to the right of the vertical dotted line), such as at b, his income-consumption curve ICC^2 through e and b is upward sloping. He buys more of both goods as his income rises, so both food and housing are normal goods.

Finally, suppose that his new optimal bundle is in the bottom-right segment of L^2 (below the horizontal dotted line). If his new optimal bundle is c, his income-consumption curve ICC^3 slopes downward from e through c. As his income rises, Peter consumes more food and less housing, so food is a normal good and housing is an inferior good.

APPLICATION

Fast-Food Engel Curve

Is a meal at a fast-food restaurant a normal or inferior good? This question is important because, as incomes have risen over time, Americans have spent a larger share of their income on fast food, which many nutritionists blame for increasing obesity rates. However, a number of studies find that obesity falls with income, which suggests that a fast-food meal may be an inferior good, at least at high incomes.

Kim and Leigh (2011) estimated the demand for fast-food restaurant visits as a function of prices, income, and various socioeconomic variables such as age, family size, and whether the family received food stamps (which lowers the price of supermarket food relative to restaurant food). They found that fast-food restaurant visits increase with income up to $60,000, and then decrease as income rises more.[4]

The figure derives the Engel curve for Gail, a typical consumer, based on their estimates. Panel a shows that Gail spends her money on fast-food meals (horizontal axis, where Y is measured in thousands) and all other goods (vertical axis). As Gail's income increases from $30,000 to $60,000, her budget line shifts outward, from L^1 to L^2.

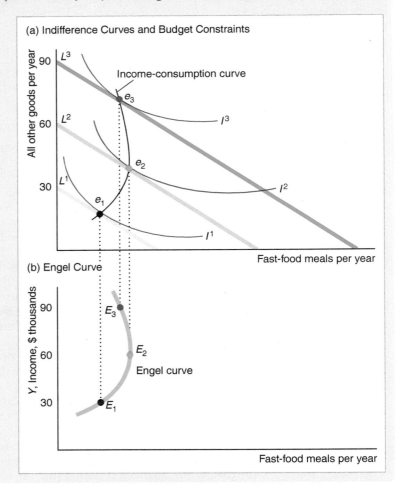

---

[4]In contrast, they found that full-service restaurant visits increase with income at least up to $95,000.

As a result, she eats more restaurant meals: Her new optimal bundle e_2 lies to the right of e_1. Thus, a fast-food meal is a normal good in this range.

As her income increases further to $90,000, her budget line shifts outward to L^3, and she reduces her consumption of fast food: Bundle e_3 lies to the left of e_2. Thus, at higher incomes, Gail views a fast-food meal as an inferior good.

Panel b shows her corresponding Engel curve for fast food. As her income rises from $30,000 to $60,000, she moves up and to the right from E_1 (which corresponds to e_1 in panel a) to E_2. Her Engel curve is upward sloping in this range, indicating that she buys more fast-food meals as her income rises. As her income rises further, her Engel curve is backward bending.

Some Goods Must Be Normal. It is impossible for all goods to be inferior, as Figure 4.4 illustrates. At his original income, Peter faces budget constraint L^1 and buys the combination of food and housing e. When his income goes up, his budget constraint shifts outward to L^2. Depending on his tastes (the shape of his indifference curves), he may buy more housing and less food, such as Bundle a; more of both, such as b; or more food and less housing, such as c. Therefore, either both goods are normal or one good is normal and the other is inferior.

If both goods were inferior, Peter would buy less of both goods as his income rises—which makes no sense. Were he to buy less of both, he would be buying a bundle that lies inside his original budget constraint, L^1. Even at his original, relatively low income, he could have purchased that bundle but chose not to, buying e instead.[5]

Weighted Income Elasticities. We just argued using graphical and verbal reasoning that a consumer cannot view all goods as inferior. We can derive a stronger result: The weighted sum of a consumer's income elasticities equals one. Firms and governments use this result to make predictions about income effects.

We start with the consumer's budget constraint for n goods, where p_i is the price and q_i is the quantity for Good i:

$$p_1 q_1 + p_2 q_2 + \cdots + p_n q_n = Y.$$

By differentiating this equation with respect to income, we obtain

$$p_1 \frac{dq_1}{dY} + p_2 \frac{dq_2}{dY} + \cdots + p_n \frac{dq_n}{dY} = 1.$$

Multiplying and dividing each term by $q_i Y$, we can rewrite this equation as

$$\frac{p_1 q_1}{Y} \frac{dq_1}{dY} \frac{Y}{q_1} + \frac{p_2 q_2}{Y} \frac{dq_2}{dY} \frac{Y}{q_2} + \cdots + \frac{p_n q_n}{Y} \frac{dq_n}{dY} \frac{Y}{q_n} = 1.$$

If we define the budget share of Good i as $\theta_i = p_i q_i / Y$ and note that the income elasticities are $\xi_i = (dq_i/dY)(Y/q_i)$, we can rewrite this expression to show that the weighted sum of the income elasticities equals one:

$$\theta_1 \xi_1 + \theta_2 \xi_2 + \cdots + \theta_n \xi_n = 1. \tag{4.1}$$

We can use this formula to make predictions about income elasticities. If we know the budget share of a good and a little bit about the income elasticities of

---

[5]Even if an individual does not buy more of the usual goods and services, that person may put the extra money into savings. We can use the consumer theory model to treat savings as a good if we allow for multiple periods. Empirical studies find that savings is a normal good.

some goods, we can calculate bounds on other, unknown income elasticities. Being able to obtain bounds on income elasticities is very useful to governments and firms. For example, over the past couple of decades, many Western manufacturing firms, learning that Chinese incomes were rising rapidly, have tried to estimate the income elasticities for their products among Chinese consumers to decide whether to enter the Chinese market.

SOLVED PROBLEM 4.3

MyLab Economics Solved Problem

A firm is considering building a plant in a developing country to sell manufactured goods in that country. The firm expects incomes to start rising soon and wants to know the income elasticity for goods other than food. The firm knows that the budget share spent on food is θ and that food is a necessity (its income elasticity, ξ_f, is between 0 and 1). The firm wants to know "How large could the income elasticity of all other goods, ξ_o, be? How small could it be?" What were the bounds on ξ_o for Chinese urban consumers whose θ was 60% in 1983? What are the bounds today when θ is 29%?[6]

Answer

1. *Write Equation 4.1 in terms of ξ_f, ξ_o, and θ, and then use algebra to rewrite this expression with the income elasticity of other goods on the left side.* By substituting ξ_f, ξ_o, and θ into Equation 4.1, we find that $\theta\xi_f + (1 - \theta)\xi_o = 1$. We can rewrite this expression with the income elasticity of other goods—the number we want to estimate—on the left side:

$$\xi_o = \frac{1 - \theta\xi_f}{1 - \theta}. \tag{4.2}$$

2. *Use Equation 4.2 and the bounds on ξ_f to derive bounds on ξ_o.* Because $\xi_o = (1 - \theta\xi_f)/(1 - \theta)$, ξ_o is smaller the larger ξ_f is. Given that food is a necessity, the largest ξ_o can be is $1/(1 - \theta)$, where $\xi_f = 0$. The smallest it can be is $\xi_o = 1$, which occurs if $\xi_f = 1$. [*Note:* If ξ_f equals one, $\xi_o = (1 - \theta)/(1 - \theta) = 1$ regardless of food's budget share, θ.]

3. *Substitute for the two Chinese values of θ to determine the upper bounds.* The upper bound for ξ_o was $1/(1 - \theta) = 1/0.4 = 2.5$ in 1983 and $1/0.71 \approx 1.41$ now.[7]

4.3 Effects of a Price Increase

Holding tastes, other prices, and income constant, an increase in the price of a good has two effects on an individual's demand. One is the **substitution effect**: the change in the quantity of a good that a consumer demands when the good's price rises, holding other prices and the consumer's utility constant. If the consumer's utility is held

---

[6]State Statistical Bureau, *Statistical Yearbook of China,* State Statistical Bureau Publishing House, Beijing, China, 2017.

[7]The upper bound on the income elasticity of nonfood goods in the United States is lower than in China because the share of consumption of food in the United States is smaller. The U.S. share of expenditures on food, θ, was 15% for poorest fifth of households and 11% for the top fifth in 2017 according to the U.S. Bureau of Labor Statistics. Thus, the upper bound on ξ_o was about 1.18 for the poorest households and 1.12 for richest.

constant as the price of the good increases, the consumer *substitutes* other goods that are now relatively cheaper for this now more expensive good.

The other effect is the **income effect**: the change in the quantity of a good a consumer demands because of a change in income, holding prices constant. An increase in price reduces a consumer's buying power, effectively reducing the consumer's *income* or opportunity set and causing the consumer to buy less of at least some goods. A doubling of the price of all the goods the consumer buys is equivalent to a drop in the consumer's income to half its original level. Even a rise in the price of only one good reduces a consumer's ability to buy the same amount of all goods previously purchased. For example, when the price of food increases in a poor country in which half or more of the population's income is spent on food, the effective purchasing power of the population falls substantially.

When the price of a product rises, the total change in the quantity purchased is the sum of the substitution effect and the income effect. When economists estimate the effect of a product's price change on the quantity an individual demands, they decompose the combined effect into the two separate components. By doing so, they gain extra information they can use to answer questions about whether inflation measures are accurate, whether an increase in tax rates will raise tax revenue, and what the effects are of government policies that compensate some consumers. For example, President Jimmy Carter, when advocating a tax on gasoline, and President Bill Clinton, when calling for an energy tax, proposed compensating poor consumers to offset the harms from the tax. We can use our knowledge of the substitution and income effects from energy price changes to evaluate the effect of these policies.

Income and Substitution Effects with a Normal Good

To illustrate the substitution and income effects, we return to Jackie's choice between music tracks and live music based on our estimate of the average young British person's Cobb-Douglas utility function, $U = q_1^{0.4} q_2^{0.6}$ (see the Application "*MRS Between Recorded Tracks and Live Music*" in Chapter 3). The price of a unit of live music is $p_2 = £1$, and the price of downloading a music track is $p_1 = £0.5$. Now, suppose that the price of music tracks rises to £1, causing Jackie's budget constraint to rotate inward from L^1 to L^2 in Figure 4.5. The new budget constraint, L^2, is twice as steep $(-p_1/p_2 = -1/1 = -1)$ as L^1 $(-0.5/1 = -0.5)$.

Because of the price increase, Jackie's opportunity set is smaller, so she must choose between fewer bundles of music tracks and live music than she could at the lower price. The area between the two budget constraints reflects the decrease in her opportunity set owing to the increase in the price of music tracks.

Substituting into the general Cobb-Douglas formula in Table 4.1, we learn that Jackie's demand functions for music tracks (songs), q_1, and live music, q_2, are

$$q_1 = 0.4Y/p_1, \tag{4.3}$$

$$q_2 = 0.6Y/p_2. \tag{4.4}$$

At the original price of tracks and with an entertainment budget of £30 per quarter, Jackie chooses Bundle e_1, $q_1 = 0.4 \times 30/0.5 = 24$ tracks and $q_2 = 0.6 \times 30/1 = 18$ units of live music per quarter, where her indifference curve I^1 is tangent to her budget constraint L^1. When the price of tracks rises, Jackie's new optimal bundle is e_2 (where she buys $q_1 = 0.4 \times 30/1 = 12$ tracks), which occurs where her indifference curve I^2 is tangent to L^2.

The decrease in the q_1 that she consumes as she moves from e_1 to e_2 is the *total effect* from the rise in the price: She buys 12 (= 24 − 12) fewer tracks per quarter. In

Figure 4.5 Substitution and Income Effects with Normal Goods

An increase in the price of music tracks from £0.5 to £1 causes Jackie's budget line to rotate from L^1 to L^2. The imaginary budget line, L^*, has the same slope as L^2 and is tangent to indifference curve I^1. The shift of the optimal bundle from e_1 to e_2 is the *total effect* of the price change. The total effect can be decomposed into the *substitution effect*—the movement from e_1 to e^*—and the *income effect*—the movement from e^* to e_2.

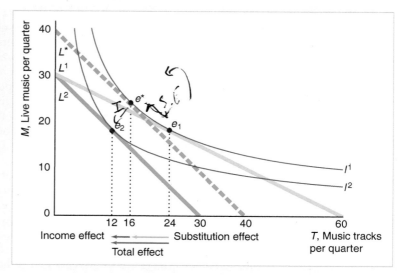

the figure, the red arrow pointing to the left labeled *Total effect* shows this decrease. We can break the total effect into a substitution effect and an income effect.

As the price increases, Jackie's opportunity set shrinks even though her income is unchanged. If, as a thought experiment, we compensate her for this loss by giving her extra income, we can determine her substitution effect. The substitution effect is the change in the quantity demanded from a *compensated change in the price* of music tracks, which occurs when we increase Jackie's income by enough to offset the rise in price so that her utility stays constant.[8] To determine the substitution effect, we draw an imaginary budget constraint, L^*, that is parallel to L^2 and tangent to Jackie's original indifference curve, I^1. This imaginary budget constraint, L^*, has the same slope, -1, as L^2 because both curves are based on the new, higher price of tracks. For L^* to be tangent to I^1, we need to increase Jackie's budget from £30 to £40 to offset the harm from the higher price of music tracks. If Jackie's budget constraint were L^*, she would choose Bundle e^*, where she buys $q_1 = 0.4 \times 40/1 = 16$ tracks.

Thus, if the price of tracks rises relative to that of live music *and* we hold Jackie's utility constant by raising her income to compensate her, Jackie's optimal bundle shifts from e_1 to e^*. The corresponding change in q_1 is the *substitution effect*. She buys 8 ($= 24 - 16$) fewer tracks per quarter, as the green arrow pointing to the left labeled *Substitution effect* illustrates.

Jackie also faces an income effect because the increase in the price of tracks shrinks her opportunity set, so that she must buy a bundle on a lower indifference curve. As a thought experiment, we can ask how much we would have to lower her income while holding prices constant at the new level for her to choose a bundle on this new, lower indifference curve. The *income effect* is the change in the quantity of a good

---

[8]Economists call this type of compensation that offsets the price change to hold her utility constant at the original level a *compensating variation*. In Chapter 5, we compare this approach to the alternative approach, an *equivalent variation*, where the income adjustment harms the consumer by the same amount as does the price change.

a consumer demands because of a change in income, holding prices constant. The parallel shift of the budget constraint from L^* to L^2 captures this effective decrease in income. The change in q_1 due to the movement from e^* to e_2 is the *income effect*, as the brown arrow pointing to the left labeled *Income effect* shows. Holding prices constant, as her budget decreases from £40 to £30, Jackie consumes 4 (= 16 − 12) fewer tracks per quarter.

The *total effect* from the price change is the *sum of the substitution and income effects*, as the arrows show. Jackie's total effect (in tracks per quarter) from a rise in the price of tracks is

$$\text{total effect} = \text{substitution effect} + \text{income effect}$$
$$-12 \quad = \quad -8 \quad + \quad (-4).$$

Because indifference curves are convex to the origin, *the substitution effect is unambiguous*: Less of a good is consumed when its price rises given that the consumer is compensated so that she remains on the original indifference curve. The substitution effect causes a *movement along an indifference curve*.

The income effect causes a shift to another indifference curve due to a change in the consumer's opportunity set. The direction of the income effect depends on the income elasticity. Because a music track is a normal good for Jackie, her income effect is negative as her income drops. Thus, both Jackie's substitution effect and her income effect move in the same direction, so the total effect of the price rise must be negative.

SOLVED PROBLEM 4.4

**MyLab Economics
Solved Problem**

Kathy loves apple pie à la mode (a slice of pie with a scoop of vanilla ice cream on top), but she doesn't like apple pie by itself or vanilla ice cream by itself. That is, she views apple pie and vanilla ice cream as perfect complements. At the initial prices, she consumed two pieces of pie per week. After the price of pie rises, she chooses to consume only one piece of pie. In a graph similar to Figure 4.5, show the substitution, income, and total effects of the price change.

Answer

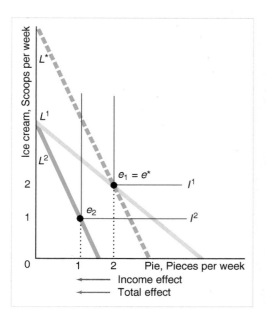

Income effect
Total effect

1. *Show that the price increase causes the budget line to rotate at the intersection on the ice cream axis and that her optimal bundle shifts from two units of pie and ice cream to one unit.* In the figure, her initial budget line is L^1 and her optimal bundle is e_1, where her indifference curve I^1 touches L^1. When the price of pie increases, her new budget line is L^2 and her new optimal bundle is e_2.

2. *Draw a line, L^*, that is parallel to L^2 and that touches her original indifference curve, I^1, and show the relationship between the new tangency point, e^*, and her original one, e^1.* The indifference curve I^1 touches L^* at e^*, which is the same point as e_1.

3. *Discuss the substitution, income, and total effects.* No substitution effect occurs because Kathy is unwilling to substitute between pie and ice cream. The brown arrow shows the income effect of the price increase is a decrease from two pieces of pie per week to one. The red arrow shows that the total effect is identical to the income effect.

APPLICATION

Substituting Marijuana for Alcohol

Because alcohol and marijuana are commonly abused, governments want to know how their uses are linked, especially among young people. Baggio, Chong, and Kwon (2017) compared alcoholic beverage purchases in U.S. counties that legalized medical marijuana to other counties. They found that alcohol consumption fell by 13% in counties where medical marijuana was legal compared to other counties.

Similarly, Crost and Guerrero (2012) found that when young people turn 21 and can legally drink, so that their cost of buying alcohol drops substantially (taking into account their time and the risk of being caught buying it illegally), they drink more alcohol and sharply decrease their consumption of marijuana. This uncompensated substitution effect is stronger for women, whose consumption of marijuana falls by 17%, than for men, whose consumption drops by 6%.

Unintended Consequence Barring teenagers from legally drinking raises the likelihood that they consume marijuana.

SOLVED PROBLEM 4.5

MyLab Economics
Solved Problem

Next to its plant, a manufacturer of dinner plates has an outlet store that sells first-quality plates (perfect plates) and second-quality plates (slightly blemished plates). The outlet store sells a relatively large share of second-quality plates (or seconds). At its regular retail stores elsewhere, the firm sells many more first-quality plates than second-quality plates. Why? (Assume that consumers' tastes with respect to plates are the same everywhere, the income effects are very small, and the cost of shipping each plate from the factory to the firm's other stores is s.)

Answer

1. *Determine how the relative prices of plates differ between the two types of stores.* The slope of the budget line that consumers face at the factory outlet store is $-p_1/p_2$, where p_1 is the price of first-quality plates (on the horizontal axis), and p_2 is the price of seconds. It costs the same, s, to ship a first-quality plate as a second because they weigh the same and need the same amount of packing. At its retail stores elsewhere, the firm adds the cost of shipping to the price it charges at its factory outlet store, so the price of a first-quality plate is $p_1 + s$ and the price of a second is $p_2 + s$. As a result, the slope of the budget line that consumers face at the retail stores is $-(p_1 + s)/(p_2 + s)$. The seconds are relatively less expensive at the factory outlet than they are at the other stores. For example, if $p_1 = \$2$, $p_2 = \$1$, and $s = \$1$ per plate, the slope of the budget line is -2 at the outlet store and $-3/2$ elsewhere. Thus, a first-quality plate costs twice as much as a second at the outlet store but only 1.5 times as much elsewhere.

2. *Use the relative price difference to explain why relatively more seconds are bought at the factory outlet.* Holding a consumer's income and tastes fixed, if the price of seconds rises relative to that of firsts (as we go from the factory

outlet to the other retail shops), most consumers will buy relatively more firsts. The substitution effect is unambiguous: Were they compensated so that their utilities were held constant, consumers would unambiguously substitute firsts for seconds. It is possible that the income effect could go in the other direction (if plates are an inferior good); however, as most consumers spend relatively little of their total budgets on plates, the income effect is presumably small relative to the substitution effect. Thus, we expect the retail stores to sell relatively fewer seconds than the factory outlet.

Income and Substitution Effects with an Inferior Good

If a good is inferior, the income effect and the substitution effect cause its output to move in opposite directions. For most inferior goods, the income effect is smaller than the substitution effect. As a result, the total effect moves in the same direction as the substitution effect, but the total effect is smaller. However, for a **Giffen good**, a decrease in its price causes the quantity demanded to fall because the income effect more than offsets the substitution effect.[9]

Jensen and Miller (2008) found that rice is a Giffen good in Hunan, China. Because rice is a Giffen good for Ximing, a fall in the rice price saves him money that he spends on other goods. Indeed, he decides to increase his spending on other goods even further by buying less rice. Thus, his demand curve for this Giffen good has an *upward* slope.

However, in Chapter 2, I claimed that, according to the Law of Demand, demand curves slope downward: Quantity demanded falls as the price rises. You're no doubt wondering how I'm going to worm my way out of this contradiction. I have two explanations. The first is that, as I noted in Chapter 2, the Law of Demand is an empirical regularity, not a theoretical necessity. Although it's theoretically possible for a demand curve to slope upward, other than the Hunan rice example, economists have found few, if any, real-world Giffen goods.[10] My second explanation is that the Law of Demand must hold theoretically for compensated demand curves, as we show in the next section.

SOLVED PROBLEM 4.6

Ximing spends his money on rice, a Giffen good, and all other goods. Show that when the price of rice falls, Ximing buys less rice. Decompose this total effect of a price change on his rice consumption into a substitution effect and an income effect.

MyLab Economics Solved Problem

Answer

1. *Determine Ximing's original optimal bundle e_1, using the tangency between his original budget line and one of his indifference curves.* In the figure, his original budget line L^1 is tangent to his indifference curve I^1 at e_1.

---

[9]Robert Giffen, a nineteenth-century British economist, argued that poor people in Ireland increased their consumption of potatoes when the price rose because of a potato blight. However, more recent studies of the Irish potato famine dispute this observation.

[10]However, Battalio, Kagel, and Kogut (1991) showed in an experiment that quinine water is a Giffen good for lab rats.

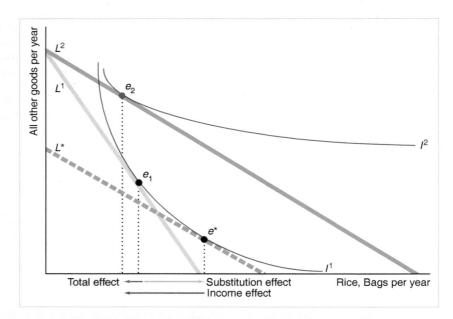

2. *Show how the optimal bundle changes from a drop in the price of rice.* As the price of rice drops, his new budget line L^2 becomes flatter, rotating around the original budget line's intercept on the vertical axis. The tangency between L^2 and indifference curve I^2 occurs at e_2, where Ximing consumes less rice than before because rice is a Giffen good.

3. *Draw a new, hypothetical budget line L* based on the new price but that keeps Ximing on the original indifference curve.* Ximing's opportunity set grows when the rice price falls. To keep him on his original indifference curve, his income would have to fall by enough so that his new budget line L^2 shifts down to L^*, which is tangent to his original indifference curve I^1 at e^*.

4. *Identify the substitution and income effects.* The substitution effect is the change in q_1 from the movement from e_1 to e^*: Ximing buys more rice when the price of rice drops but he remains on his original indifference curve. The movement from e^* to e_2 determines the income effect: Ximing buys less rice as his income increases holding prices constant. The total effect, the movement from e_1 to e_2, is the sum of the substitution effect, which causes the output to rise, and the income effect, which causes output to fall. Ximing buys less rice because the income effect is larger than the substitution effect.

Compensated Demand Curve

So far, the demand curves that we have derived graphically and mathematically allow a consumer's utility to vary as the price of the good increases. For example, a consumer's utility falls if the price of one of the goods rises. Consequently, the consumer's demand curve reflects both the substitution and income effects as the price of the product changes.

As panel a of **Figure 4.2** illustrates, Mimi chooses a bundle on a lower indifference curve as the price of beer rises, so her utility level falls. Along her demand curve for beer, we hold other prices, income, and her tastes constant, while allowing her utility to vary. We can observe this type of demand curve by seeing how the purchases of a product change as its price increases. It is called *the* demand curve, the Marshallian demand curve (after Alfred Marshall, who popularized this approach), or the *uncompensated demand curve*. (Unless otherwise noted, when we talk about a demand curve, we mean the uncompensated demand curve.)

Alternatively, we could derive a *compensated demand curve*, which shows how the quantity demanded changes as the price rises, holding utility constant, so that the change in the quantity demanded reflects only the pure substitution effect from a price change. It is called the compensated demand curve because we would have to compensate an individual—give the individual extra income—as the price rises to hold the individual's utility constant. A common name for the compensated demand curve is the *Hicksian demand curve*, after John Hicks, who introduced the idea.

The compensated demand function for the first good is

$$q_1 = H(p_1, p_2, \overline{U}), \tag{4.5}$$

where we hold utility constant at $\overline{U}$. We cannot observe the compensated demand curve directly because we do not observe utility levels. Because the compensated demand curve reflects only substitution effects, the Law of Demand must hold: A price increase causes the compensated demand for a good to fall.

In Figure 4.6, we derive Jackie's compensated demand function, H, evaluated at her initial indifference curve, I, where her utility is $\overline{U}$. In 2008, the price of music tracks was $p_1 = £0.5$ and the price per unit of live music was $p_2 = £1$. At those prices, Jackie's budget line, L, has a slope of $-p_1/p_2 = -0.5/1 = -\frac{1}{2}$ and is tangent to I at e_2 in panel a. At this optimal bundle, she buys 24 tracks. The corresponding point E_2 on her compensated demand curve in panel b shows that she buys 24 tracks when they cost £0.5 each.

The two thin blue line segments in panel a show portions of other budget lines where we change p_1 and adjust Jackie's income to keep her on indifference curve I. At the budget line segment in the upper left, the price of tracks is £1, so Jackie's budget line has a slope of -1. We increase her budget just enough that her new budget line is tangent to the original indifference curve, I, at e_1. This optimal bundle corresponds to E_1 on her compensated demand curve in panel b. Similarly, when p_1 is £0.25, we decrease her budget so that this budget line is tangent to her original indifference curve at e_3, which corresponds to E_3 on her compensated demand curve.

Panel b also shows Jackie's uncompensated demand curve: Equation 4.3, $q_1 = 0.4Y/p_1$. Her compensated and uncompensated demand curves *must* cross at the original price, $p_1 = £0.5$, where the original budget line, L, is tangent to I along which utility is $\overline{U}$. At that price, and only at that price, both demand curves correspond to a tangency on the same budget line. The compensated demand curve is steeper than the uncompensated curve around this common point. The compensated demand curve is relatively steep because it reflects only the substitution effect. The uncompensated demand curve is flatter because the (normal good) income effect reinforces the substitution effect.

One way to derive the compensated demand curve is to use the expenditure function (Equation 3.32),

$$E = E(p_1, p_2, \overline{U}),$$

where E is the smallest expenditure that allows the consumer to achieve utility level $\overline{U}$, given market prices. If we differentiate the expenditure function with

Figure 4.6 Deriving Jackie's Compensated Demand Curve

Initially, Jackie's optimal bundle is determined by the tangency of budget line L and indifference curve I in panel a. If we vary the price of music tracks but change her budget so that the new line (segments) are tangent to the same indifference curve, we can determine how the quantity that she demands varies with price, holding her utility constant. Hence, the corresponding quantities in panel b on her compensated demand curve reflect the pure substitution effect of a price change.

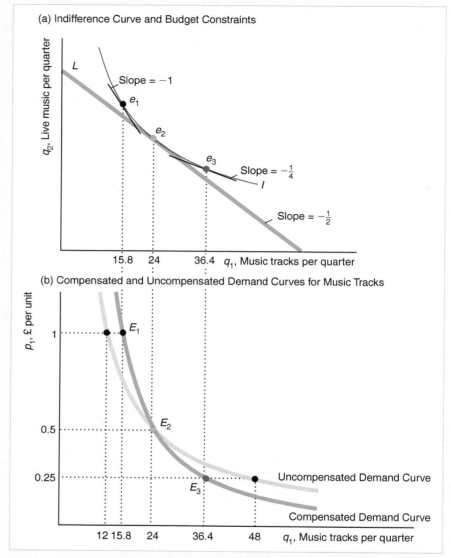

(a) Indifference Curve and Budget Constraints

q_2, Live music per quarter

L

Slope = −1

e_1

e_2

e_3

Slope = $-\frac{1}{4}$

I

Slope = $-\frac{1}{2}$

15.8   24   36.4 q_1, Music tracks per quarter

(b) Compensated and Uncompensated Demand Curves for Music Tracks

p_1, £ per unit

1   E_1

0.5 E_2

0.25

E_3

Uncompensated Demand Curve

Compensated Demand Curve

12 15.8   24   36.4   48 q_1, Music tracks per quarter

respect to the price of the first good, we obtain the compensated demand function for that good:[11]

$$\frac{\partial E}{\partial p_1} = H(p_1, p_2, \overline{U}) = q_1. \tag{4.6}$$

---

[11]This result is called Shephard's lemma. As we showed in Solved Problem 3.8, we can use the Lagrangian method to derive the expenditure function, where we want to minimize $E = p_1 q_1 + p_2 q_2$ subject to $\overline{U} = U(q_1, q_2)$. The Lagrangian equation is $\mathcal{L} = p_1 q_1 + p_2 q_2 + \lambda[\overline{U} - U(q_1, q_2)]$. According to the envelope theorem (see the Calculus Appendix), at the optimum, $\partial E/\partial p_1 = \partial \mathcal{L}/\partial p_1 = q_1$, which is Equation 4.6. It shows that the derivative of the expenditure function with respect to p_1 is q_1, the quantity that the consumer demands.

One informal explanation for Equation 4.6 is that if p_1 increases by \$1 on each of the q_1 units that the consumer buys, then the minimum amount consumers must spend to keep their utility constant must increase by \$$q_1$. This expression can also be interpreted as the pure substitution effect on the quantity demanded because we are holding the consumer's utility constant as we change the price.

SOLVED PROBLEM 4.7

MyLab Economics
Solved Problem

A consumer has a Cobb-Douglas utility function $U = q_1^a q_2^{1-a}$. Derive the compensated demand function for Good q_1. Given that $a = 0.4$ in Jackie's utility function, what is her compensated demand function for music tracks, q_1?

Answer

1. *Write the formula for the expenditure function for this Cobb-Douglas utility function.* We derived the Cobb-Douglas expenditure function in Solved Problem 3.8:

$$E = \overline{U}\left(\frac{p_1}{a}\right)^a \left(\frac{p_2}{1-a}\right)^{1-a}. \tag{4.7}$$

2. *Differentiate the expenditure function in Equation 4.7 with respect to p_1 to obtain the compensated demand function for q_1, making use of Equation 4.6.* The compensated demand function is

$$q_1 = \frac{\partial E}{\partial p_1} = \overline{U}\left(\frac{a}{1-a}\frac{p_2}{p_1}\right)^{1-a}. \tag{4.8}$$

3. *Substitute Jackie's value of a in Equation 4.7 to obtain her expenditure function, and in Equation 4.8 to obtain her compensated demand function for tracks.* Given that her $a = 0.4$, Jackie's expenditure function is

$$E = \overline{U}\left(\frac{p_1}{0.4}\right)^{0.4}\left(\frac{p_2}{0.6}\right)^{0.6} \approx 1.96\overline{U}p_1^{0.4}p_2^{0.6}, \tag{4.9}$$

and her compensated demand function for tracks is

$$q_1 = \overline{U}\left(\frac{0.4}{0.6}\frac{p_2}{p_1}\right)^{0.6} \approx 0.784\overline{U}\left(\frac{p_2}{p_1}\right)^{0.6}. \tag{4.10}$$

Comment: We showed earlier that if Jackie's quarterly budget is $Y = £30$ and she faces prices of $p_1 = £0.5$ and $p_2 = £1$, she chooses $q_1 = 24$ and $q_2 = 18$. The corresponding indifference curve is $\overline{U} = 24^{0.4}18^{0.6} \approx 20.2$. Thus, at the initial prices, her compensated demand for tracks, Equation 4.10, is $q_1 \approx 0.784 \times 20.2(1/0.5)^{0.6} \approx 24$, which is reassuring because the compensated and uncompensated demand curves must cross at the initial prices.

Slutsky Equation

We have shown graphically that the total effect from a price change can be decomposed into a substitution effect and an income effect. That same relationship can be derived mathematically. We can use this relationship in a variety of ways. For example, we can apply it to determine how likely a good is to be a Giffen good based on whether the consumer spends a relatively large or small share of the budget on this good. We can also use the relationship to determine the effect of government policies that compensate some consumers.

The usual price elasticity of demand, ε, captures the total effect of a price change—that is, the change along an uncompensated demand curve. We can break this price elasticity of demand into two terms involving elasticities that capture the substitution and income effects. We measure the substitution effect using the pure *substitution elasticity of demand, ε**, which is the percentage that the quantity demanded falls for a given percentage increase in price if we compensate the consumer to keep the consumer's utility constant. That is, ε* is the elasticity of the compensated demand curve. The income effect is the income elasticity, ξ, times the share of the budget spent on that good, θ. This relationship among the price elasticity of demand, ε, the substitution elasticity of demand, ε*, and the income elasticity of demand, ξ, is the *Slutsky equation* (named after its discoverer, the Russian economist Eugene Slutsky):[12]

$$\text{total effect} = \text{substitution effect} + \text{income effect}$$
$$\varepsilon = \varepsilon^* + (-\theta\xi). \tag{4.11}$$

If a consumer spends little on a good, a change in its price does not affect the person's total budget significantly. For example, if the price of garlic triples, your purchasing power will hardly be affected (unless you are a vampire slayer). Thus, the total effect, ε, for garlic hardly differs from the substitution effect, ε*, because the price change has little effect on the consumer's income.

In Mimi's original optimal bundle, e_1 in Figure 4.2, where the price of beer was $12 and Mimi bought 26.7 gallons of beer per year, Mimi spent about three-quarters of her $419 beverage budget on beer: θ = 0.76 = (12 × 26.7)/419. Her income elasticity is ξ = 0.88, her price elasticity is ε = −0.76, and her substitution price elasticity is ε* = −0.09. Thus, Mimi's Slutsky equation is

$$\varepsilon = \varepsilon^* - \theta\xi$$
$$-0.76 \approx -0.09 - (0.76 \times 0.88).$$

Because beer is a normal good for Mimi, the income effect reinforces the substitution effect. Indeed, the size of the total change, ε = −0.76, is due more to the income effect, −θξ = −0.67, than to the substitution effect, ε* = −0.09. If the price of beer rises by 1% but Mimi is given just enough extra income so that her utility remains constant, Mimi would reduce her consumption of beer by less than a tenth of a percent

---

[12]When we derived the compensated demand function, H, we noted that it equals the uncompensated demand function, D, at the initial optimum where utility is $\overline{U}$.

$$q_1 = H(p_1, p_2, \overline{U}) = D(p_1, p_2, Y) = D(p_1, p_2, E(p_1, p_2, \overline{U})),$$

and $E(p_1, p_2, \overline{U})$, the expenditure function, is the minimum expenditure needed to achieve that level of utility. If we differentiate with respect to p_1, we find that

$$\frac{\partial H}{\partial p_1} = \frac{\partial D}{\partial p_1} + \frac{\partial D}{\partial E}\frac{\partial E}{\partial p_1} = \frac{\partial D}{\partial p_1} + \frac{\partial D}{\partial E}q_1,$$

where we know that $\partial E/\partial p_1 = q_1$ from Equation 4.6. Rearranging terms and multiplying all terms by p_1/q_1, and the last term by E/E, we obtain

$$\frac{\partial D}{\partial p_1}\frac{p_1}{q_1} = \frac{\partial H}{\partial p_1}\frac{p_1}{q_1} - q_1\frac{\partial D}{\partial E}\frac{p_1}{q_1}\frac{E}{E}.$$

This last expression is the Slutsky equation (Equation 4.11), where $\varepsilon = (\partial D/\partial p_1)(p_1/q_1)$, $\varepsilon^* = (\partial H/\partial p_1)(p_1/q_1)$, $\theta = p_1q_1/E$, and $\xi = (\partial D/\partial E)(E/q_1)$, because $E = Y$.

(substitution effect). Without compensation, Mimi reduces her consumption of beer by about three-quarters of a percent (total effect).

Similarly, in Jackie's original optimum, e_1 in Figure 4.5, the price of a track was £0.5, and Jackie bought 24 tracks per year. She spent $\theta = 0.4$ share of her budget on tracks (see Solved Problem 3.7). Her uncompensated demand function, Equation 4.3, is $q_1 = 0.4Y/p_1$, so her price elasticity of demand is $\varepsilon = -1$,[13] and her income elasticity is $\xi = 1$ (Solved Problem 4.2). Her compensated demand function, Equation 4.10, is $q_1 \approx 0.784\overline{U}(p_2/p_1)^{0.6} = 0.784\overline{U}p_2^{0.6}p_1^{-0.6}$. Because it is a constant elasticity demand function where the exponent on p_1 is -0.6, we know that $\varepsilon^* = -0.6$ (Chapter 2). Thus, her Slutsky equation is

$$
\begin{aligned}
\varepsilon &= \varepsilon^* &-& \theta\xi \\
-1 &= -0.6 &-& (0.4 \times 1).
\end{aligned}
$$

For a good to have an upward-sloping demand curve so that it is a Giffen good, ε must be positive. The substitution elasticity, ε^*, is always negative: Consumers buy less of a good when its price increases, holding utility constant. Thus, a Giffen good has an income effect, $-\theta\xi$, that is positive and large relative to the substitution effect. The income effect is more likely to be a large positive number if the good is very inferior (that is, ξ is a large negative number, which is not common) and the budget share, θ, is large (closer to one than to zero). One reason we don't see upward-sloping demand curves is that the goods on which consumers spend a large share of their budget, such as housing, are usually normal goods rather than inferior goods.

4.4 Cost-of-Living Adjustment

In spite of the cost of living, it's still popular. —Kathleen Norris

By knowing both the substitution and income effects, we can answer questions that we could not answer if we knew only the total effect of a price change. One particularly important use of consumer theory is to analyze how accurately the government measures inflation.

Many long-term contracts and government programs include *cost-of-living adjustments* (COLAs), which raise prices or incomes in proportion to an index of inflation. Not only business contracts, but also rental contracts, alimony payments, salaries, pensions, and Social Security payments use cost-of-living adjustments. We next use consumer theory to show that the cost-of-living measure that most of these contracts use overestimates how the true cost of living changes over time. Because of this overestimation, you overpay your landlord if the rent on your apartment rises with this measure.

Inflation Indexes

The prices of most goods rise over time. We call the increase in the overall price level *inflation*.

The actual price of a good is the *nominal price*. The price adjusted for inflation is the *real price*. Because the overall level of prices rises over time, nominal prices

---

[13]Differentiating $q_1 = 0.4Y/p_1$ with respect to p_1, we learn that $dq_1/dp_1 = -0.4Y/(p_1)^2 = -q_1/p_1$. Thus, the price elasticity of demand is $\varepsilon = (dq_1/dp_1)(p_1/q_1) = -1$.

usually increase more rapidly than real prices. For example, the nominal price of a McDonald's hamburger rose from 15¢ in 1940 (when the McDonald brothers opened their first restaurant) to $2.50 in 2018, a 1,667% increase. However, the real price of the burger fell because the prices of other goods rose more rapidly than that of the burger.

How do we adjust for inflation to calculate the real price? Governments measure the cost of a standard bundle of consumer goods (the market basket) to compare prices over time. This measure is the Consumer Price Index (CPI). Each month, the government reports how much it costs to buy the bundle of goods that an average consumer purchased in a *base* year (with the base year changing every few years).

By comparing the cost of buying this bundle over time, we can determine how much the overall price level has increased. In the United States, the CPI was 14.0 in 1940 and 252.1 in August 2018.[14] The cost of buying the bundle of goods increased 1,801% ($\approx$ 252.1/14.0) over this period.

We can use the CPI to calculate the real price of a McDonald's hamburger over time. In terms of 2018 dollars, the real price of the hamburger in 1940 was

$$\frac{\text{CPI for 2018}}{\text{CPI for 1940}} \times \text{price of a burger} = \frac{252.1}{14.0} \times 15¢ \approx \$2.70.$$

If you could have purchased the hamburger in 1940 with 2018 dollars—which are worth less than 1940 dollars—the hamburger would have cost $2.70. The real price in 2018 dollars (the nominal price) of the hamburger in 2018 was only $2.50. Thus, the real price fell by over 7%. If we compared the real prices in both years, using 1940 dollars, we would reach the same conclusion that the real price of hamburgers fell by about 7%.

The government collects data on the quantities and prices of 364 individual goods and services, such as housing, dental services, watch and jewelry repairs, college tuition fees, taxi fares, women's hairpieces and wigs, hearing aids, slipcovers and decorative pillows, bananas, pork sausage, and funeral expenses. These prices rise at different rates. If the government merely reported all these price increases separately, most of us would find this information overwhelming. It is much more convenient to use a single summary statistic, the CPI, which tells us how prices rose *on average*.

We can use an example with only two goods, clothing and food, to show how the CPI is calculated. In the first year, consumers buy C_1 units of clothing and F_1 units of food at prices p_C^1 and p_F^1. We use this bundle of goods, C_1 and F_1, as our base bundle for comparison. In the second year, consumers buy C_2 and F_2 units at prices p_C^2 and p_F^2.

The government knows from its survey of prices that the price of clothing in the second year is p_C^2/p_C^1 times as large as the price the previous year. Similarly, the price of food is p_F^2/p_F^1 times as large as the price the previous year. For example, if the price of clothing were $1 in the first year and $2 in the second year, the price of clothing in the second year would be $\frac{2}{1} = 2$ times, or 100%, larger than in the first year.

One way we can average the price increases of each good is to weight them equally. But do we really want to do that? Do we want to give as much weight to the price increase for skateboards as to the price increase for cars? An alternative approach is to assign a larger weight to the price change for goods with relatively large budget shares. In constructing its averages, the CPI weights using budget shares.[15]

---

[14]The number 252.1 is not an actual dollar amount. Rather, it is the actual dollar cost of buying the bundle divided by a constant. That constant was chosen so that the average expenditure in the period 1982–1984 was 100.

[15]This discussion of the CPI is simplified in many ways. Sophisticated adjustments are made to the CPI that are ignored here, including repeated updating of the base year (chaining). See Pollak (1989) and Diewert and Nakamura (1993).

The CPI for the first year is the amount of income it took to buy the market basket that was actually purchased that year:

$$Y_1 = p_C^1 C_1 + p_F^1 F_1. \tag{4.12}$$

The cost of buying the first year's bundle in the second year is

$$Y_2 = p_C^2 C_1 + p_F^2 F_1. \tag{4.13}$$

That is, in the second year, we use the prices for the second year but the quantities from the first year.

To calculate the rate of inflation, we determine how much more income it took to buy the first year's bundle in the second year, which is the ratio of Equation 4.13 to Equation 4.12:

$$\frac{Y_2}{Y_1} = \frac{p_C^2 C_1 + p_F^2 F_1}{p_C^1 C_1 + p_F^1 F_1}.$$

For example, from August 2017 to August 2018, the U.S. CPI rose by $1.027 \approx Y_2/Y_1$ from $Y_1 = 245.5$ to $Y_2 = 252.1$. Thus, it cost on average 2.7% more in August 2018 than in August 2017 to buy the same bundle of goods.

The ratio Y_2/Y_1 reflects how much prices rise on average. By multiplying and dividing the first term in the numerator by p_C^1 and multiplying and dividing the second term by p_F^1, we find that this index is equivalent to

$$\frac{Y_2}{Y_1} = \frac{\left(\frac{p_C^2}{p_C^1}\right)p_C^1 C_1 + \left(\frac{p_F^2}{p_F^1}\right)p_F^1 F_1}{Y_1} = \left(\frac{p_C^2}{p_C^1}\right)\theta_C + \left(\frac{p_F^2}{p_F^1}\right)\theta_F,$$

where $\theta_C = p_C^1 C_1/Y_1$ and $\theta_F = p_F^1 F_1/Y_1$ are the budget shares of clothing and food in the first, or base, year. The CPI is a *weighted average* of the price increase for each good, p_C^2/p_C^1 and p_F^2/p_F^1, where the weights are each good's budget share in the base year, θ_C and θ_F.

Effects of Inflation Adjustments

A CPI adjustment of prices in a long-term contract overcompensates for inflation. We use an example involving an employment contract to illustrate the difference between using the CPI to adjust a long-term contract and using a true cost-of-living adjustment, which holds utility constant.

CPI Adjustment. Klaas signed a long-term contract when he was hired. According to the COLA clause in his contract, his employer increases his salary each year by the same percentage that the CPI increases. If the CPI this year is 5% higher than last year, Klaas's salary rises automatically by 5%.

Klaas spends all his money on clothing and food. His budget constraint in the first year is $Y_1 = p_C^1 C + p_F^1 F$, which we rewrite as

$$C = \frac{Y_1}{p_C^1} - \frac{p_F^1}{p_C^1} F.$$

The intercept of the budget constraint, L^1, on the vertical (clothing) axis in Figure 4.7 is Y_1/p_C^1, and the slope of the constraint is $-p_F^1/p_C^1$. The tangency of his indifference curve I^1 and the budget constraint L^1 determine his optimal consumption bundle in the first year, e_1, where he purchases C_1 and F_1.

Figure 4.7 CPI Adjustment

In the first year, when Klaas has an income of Y_1, his optimal bundle is e_1, where indifference curve I^1 is tangent to his budget constraint, L^1. In the second year, the price of clothing rises more than the price of food. Because his salary increases in proportion to the CPI, his second-year budget constraint, L^2, goes through e_1, so he can buy the same bundle as in the first year. His new optimal bundle, however, is e_2, where I^2 is tangent to L^2. The CPI adjustment overcompensates Klaas for the increase in prices: He is better off in the second year because his utility is greater on I^2 than on I^1. With a smaller true cost-of-living adjustment, Klaas's budget constraint, L^*, is tangent to I^1 at e^*.

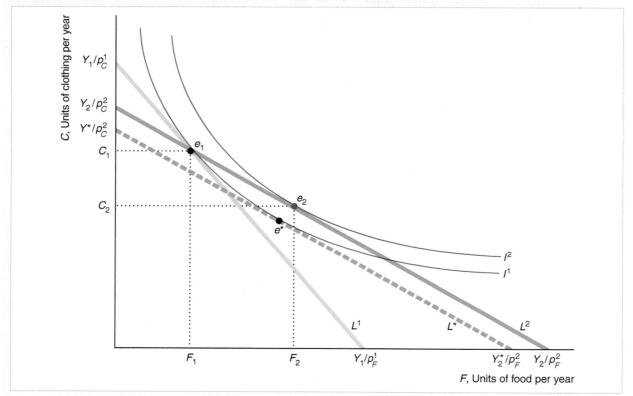

In the second year, his salary rises with the CPI to Y_2, so his budget constraint in that year, L^2, is

$$C = \frac{Y_2}{p_C^2} - \frac{p_F^2}{p_C^2} F.$$

The new constraint, L^2, has a flatter slope, $-p_F^2/p_C^2$, than L^1 because the price of clothing rose more than the price of food. The new constraint goes through the original optimal bundle, e_1, because by increasing his salary according to the CPI, the firm ensures that Klaas can buy the same bundle of goods in the second year that he bought in the first year.

He *can* buy the same bundle, but *does* he? The answer is no. His optimal bundle in the second year is e_2, where indifference curve I^2 is tangent to his new budget constraint, L^2. The movement from e_1 to e_2 is the *total effect* from the changes in the real prices of clothing and food. *This adjustment to his income does not keep him on his original indifference curve, I^1.*

Indeed, Klaas is better off in the second year than in the first. The CPI adjustment *overcompensates* him for the change in inflation in the sense that his utility increases.

Klaas is better off because the prices of clothing and food did not increase by the same amount. Suppose that the price of clothing and food had both increased by *exactly* the same amount. After a CPI adjustment, Klaas's budget constraint in the second year, L^2, would be exactly the same as in the first year, L^1, so he would choose exactly the same bundle, e_1, in the second year as he chose in the first year.

Because the price of food rose by less than the price of clothing, L^2 is not the same as L^1. Food became cheaper relative to clothing. Therefore, by consuming more food and less clothing, Klaas has a higher utility in the second year.

Had clothing become relatively less expensive, Klaas would have raised his utility in the second year by consuming relatively more clothing. Thus, it doesn't matter which good becomes relatively less expensive over time for Klaas to benefit from the CPI compensation; it's necessary only for one of the goods to become a relative bargain.

True Cost-of-Living Adjustment. We now know that a CPI adjustment overcompensates for inflation. What we want is a *true cost-of-living index*: an inflation index that holds utility constant over time.

How big an increase in Klaas's salary would leave him exactly as well off in the second year as he was in the first? We can answer this question by applying the same technique we used to identify the substitution and income effects. Suppose that his utility function is $U = 20\sqrt{CF}$, where C is his units of clothing and F is his units of food. We draw an imaginary budget line, L^*, in Figure 4.7, that is tangent to I^1 so that Klaas's utility remains constant but has the same slope as L^2. The income, Y^*, corresponding to that imaginary budget constraint is the amount that leaves Klaas's utility constant. Had Klaas received Y^* instead of Y_2 in the second year, he would have chosen Bundle e^* instead of e_2. Because e^* is on the same indifference curve, I^1, as e_1, Klaas's utility would be the same in both years.

The numerical example in Table 4.2 illustrates how the CPI overcompensates Klaas. Suppose that p_C^1 is \$1, p_C^2 is \$2, p_F^1 is \$4, and p_F^2 is \$5. In the first year, Klaas spends his income, $Y_1 = \$400$, on $C_1 = 200$ units of clothing and $F_1 = 50$ units of food, and he has a utility of 2,000, which is the level of utility on I^1. If his income did not increase in the second year, he would substitute toward the relatively inexpensive food, cutting his consumption of clothing in half but reducing his consumption of food by only a fifth. His utility would fall to 1,265.

If his second-year income increases in proportion to the CPI, he can buy the same bundle, e_1, in the second year as in the first. His second-year income is $Y_2 = \$650 (= p_C^2 C_1 + p_F^2 F_1 = \$2 \times 200 + \$5 \times 50)$. However, instead of buying the same bundle, he can substitute toward the relatively inexpensive food, buying less clothing than in the first year. This bundle is depicted by e_2. His utility then rises from 2,000 to approximately 2,055 (the level of utility on I^2). Clearly, Klaas is better off if his income increases to Y_2. In other words, the CPI adjustment overcompensates him.

Table 4.2 Cost-of-Living Adjustments

	p_C	p_F	Income, Y	Clothing	Food	Utility, U
First year	\$1	\$4	\$400	200	50	2,000
Second year	\$2	\$5				
No adjustment			\$400	100	40	1,265
CPI adjustment			\$650	162.5	65	2,055
True COLA			\$632.50	158.1	63.2	2,000

How much would his income have to rise to leave him *only* as well off as he was in the first year? If his second-year income is $Y^* \approx \$632.50$, by substituting toward food and the Bundle e^*, he can achieve the same level of utility, 2,000, as in the first year.

We can use the income that just compensates Klaas for the price changes, Y^*, to construct a true cost-of-living index. In our numerical example, the true cost-of-living index rose 58.1% [$\approx (632.50 - 400)/400$], while the CPI rose 62.5% [$= (650 - 400)/400$].

Size of the CPI Substitution Bias. We have just demonstrated that the CPI has an *upward bias* in the sense that an individual's utility rises if we increase the person's income by the same percentage by which the CPI rises. If we make the CPI adjustment, we are implicitly assuming—incorrectly—that consumers do not substitute toward relatively inexpensive goods when prices change, but they keep buying the same bundle of goods over time. We call this overcompensation a *substitution bias*.[16]

The CPI calculates the increase in prices as Y_2/Y_1. We can rewrite this expression as

$$\frac{Y_2}{Y_1} = \frac{Y^*}{Y_1} \frac{Y_2}{Y^*}.$$

The first term to the right of the equal sign, Y^*/Y_1, is the increase in the true cost of living. The second term, Y_2/Y^*, reflects the substitution bias in the CPI. It is greater than one because $Y_2 > Y^*$. In the example in Table 4.2, $Y_2/Y^* = 650/632.50 \approx 1.028$, so the CPI overestimates the increase in the cost of living by about 2.8%.

If all prices increase at the same rate so that relative prices remain constant, no substitution bias occurs. The faster some prices rise relative to others, the more pronounced the upward bias caused by the substitution that occurs toward less expensive goods.

APPLICATION

Reducing the CPI Substitution Bias

Several years ago, academic studies estimated that the inflation rate using the traditional CPI (which is called a *Laspeyres* index) was too high by about half a percentage point per year due to the substitution bias. In response to this finding, the U.S. Bureau of Labor Statistics (BLS) revised its methodology.

Since 2002, the BLS has updated the CPI weights (the market basket shares of consumption) every two years instead of only every decade. More frequent updating reduces the substitution bias in a Laspeyres index because market basket shares are frozen for a shorter period. According to the BLS, had it used updated weights between 1989 and 1997, the CPI would have increased by only 31.9% rather than the reported 33.9%. The BLS believes that this change reduces the rate of increase in the CPI by approximately 0.2 percentage points per year.

The BLS considered using an alternative index, a *Paasche* index. The Paasche index weights prices using the current quantities of goods purchased, whereas the Laspeyres index uses quantities from the earlier period. As a result, the Paasche index is likely to overstate the degree of substitution and thus to understate the change in the cost-of-living index. Hence, replacing the traditional Laspeyres index with the Paasche would merely replace an overestimate with an underestimate of the rate of inflation.

---

[16]The CPI has other biases as well. For example, Bils (2009) argues that CPI measures for consumer durables largely capture shifts to newer product models that display higher prices, rather than a price increase for a given set of goods. He estimates that as much as two-thirds of the price increase for new models is due to quality growth. Consequently, the CPI inflation for durables may have been overstated by almost two percentage points per year.

Another alternative is to take an average of the Laspeyres and Paasche indexes because the true cost-of-living index lies between these two biased indexes. Starting in 1999, the BLS used the *Fisher* index, which is the geometric mean of the Laspeyres and Paasche indexes (the square root of their product). Starting in 2015, the BLS announced it was using a constant elasticity of substitution index, which it calls the *Chained Consumer Price Index* (C-CPI).[17] The BLS reports both the traditional CPI and the C-CPI.

A biased estimate of the rate of inflation has important implications for U.S. society because union agreements, Social Security, various retirement plans, welfare, and many other programs include CPI-based cost-of-living adjustments. According to one estimate, the previous bias in the CPI alone was the fourth-largest "federal program" after Social Security, health care, and defense. For example, the U.S. Postal Service (USPS) has a CPI-based COLA in its union contracts. In 2017, the median USPS worker earned about $57,260 a year, so the estimated substitution bias of the old CPI of half a percent a year would have cost the USPS slightly more than $286 per employee. Because the USPS had over 500,000 career employees, the total cost of this bias would have been about $143 million.

4.5 Revealed Preference

We have seen that we can predict a consumer's purchasing behavior if we know that person's preferences. We can also do the opposite: We can infer a consumer's preferences by observing the consumer's buying behavior. If we observe a consumer's choice at many different prices and income levels, we can derive the consumer's indifference curves using the *theory of revealed preference* (Samuelson, 1947). We can also use this theory to demonstrate the substitution effect. Economists can use this approach to estimate demand curves merely by observing the choices consumers make over time.

Recovering Preferences

The basic assumption of the theory of revealed preference is that a consumer chooses bundles to maximize utility subject to a budget constraint: The consumer chooses the best bundle that the consumer can afford. We also assume that the consumer's indifference curve is convex to the origin so that the consumer picks a unique bundle on any budget constraint.

If such a consumer chooses a more expensive bundle of goods, *a*, over a less expensive bundle, *b*, then we say that the consumer *prefers* Bundle *a* to *b*. In panel a of Figure 4.8, when Linda's budget constraint is L^1, she chooses Bundle *a*, showing that she prefers *a* to *b*, which costs less than *a* because it lies strictly within her opportunity set.

If the consumer prefers Bundle *a* to *b* and Bundle *b* to *c*, then the consumer must prefer Bundle *a* to *c* because the consumer's preferences are transitive. In panel a, Linda chooses Bundle *a* over *b* when the budget line is L^1, and she picks Bundle *b* over *c* when the constraint is L^2; so, by transitivity, Linda prefers *a* to *c*. We say that

---

[17]The assumption behind the Fisher index is that the elasticity of substitution among goods is unitary, so the share of consumer expenditures on each item remains constant as relative prices change (in contrast to the Laspeyres' assumption that the quantities remain fixed).

Figure 4.8   Revealed Preference

(a) Linda chooses Bundle a on budget constraint L^1, so she prefers it to b, which costs less. On L^2, she chooses b, so she prefers it to c, which costs less. Thus, due to transitivity, Linda prefers a to c or any other of the *worse bundles*. She prefers the bundles in the shaded area above and to

the right of a according to the more-is-better property. (b) With more budget lines and choices, we learn more about the *better bundles*. Linda's indifference curve through a must lie in the white area between the worse and better bundles.

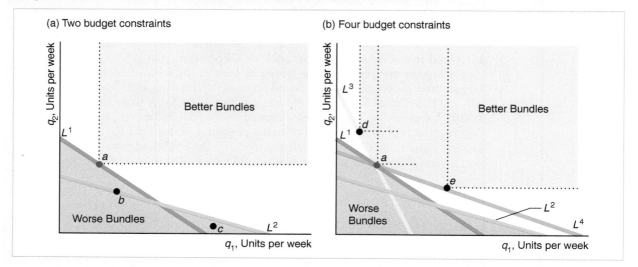

Bundle a is *revealed to be preferred* to Bundle c if Linda chooses a over c directly, or if we learn indirectly that Linda prefers a to b and b to c.

We know that Linda prefers a to any other bundle in the shaded area, labeled "Worse Bundles," by a sequence of direct or indirect comparisons. Due to the more-is-better property (Chapter 3), Linda prefers bundles in the area above and to the right of a. Thus, the indifference curve through a must lie within the white area between the worse and better bundles.

If we learn that Linda chooses d when faced with budget line L^3 and e given line L^4 as panel b shows, we can expand her *better bundle* area. We know that her indifference curve through a must lie within the white area between the better and worse bundle areas. Thus, if we observe a large number of choices, we can determine the shape of her indifference curves, which summarizes her preferences.

Substitution Effect

One of the clearest and most important results from consumer theory is that the substitution effect is negative: The Law of Demand holds for compensated demand curves. This result stems from utility maximization, given that indifference curves are convex to the origin. The theory of revealed preference provides an alternative justification without appealing to unobservable indifference curves or utility functions.

Suppose that Steven is indifferent between Bundle a, which consists of M_a music tracks and C_a candy bars, and Bundle b, with M_b tracks and C_b candy bars. That is, the bundles are on the same indifference curve.

The price of candy bars, C, remains fixed at p_C, but the price of songs changes. We observe that when the price for M is p_M^a, Steven chooses Bundle a—that is, a is revealed to be preferred to b. Similarly, when the price is p_M^b, he chooses b over a.

Because Steven is indifferent between the two bundles, the cost of the chosen bundle must be less than or equal to that of the other bundle. Thus, if he chooses a when the price is p_M^a, then $p_M^a M_a + p_C C_a \leq p_M^a M_b + p_C C_b$, or

$$p_M^a(M_a - M_b) + p_C(C_a - C_b) \leq 0. \qquad (4.14)$$

And, if he chooses b when the price is p_M^b, then $p_M^b M_b + p_C C_b \leq p_M^b M_a + p_C C_a$, or

$$p_M^b(M_b - M_a) + p_C(C_b - C_a) \leq 0. \qquad (4.15)$$

Adding Equations 4.14 and 4.15, we learn that

$$(p_M^a - p_M^b)(M_a - M_b) \leq 0. \qquad (4.16)$$

Equation 4.16 shows that the product of the difference in prices times the difference in quantities of music purchased is nonpositive. That result can be true only if the price and the quantity move in opposite directions: When the price rises, the quantity falls. Thus, we are able to derive the substitution effect result without using utility functions or making any assumptions about the curvature of indifference curves.

CHALLENGE SOLUTION

Paying Employees to Relocate

We conclude our analysis of consumer theory by returning to the Challenge posed in the introduction of this chapter: Do firms' standard compensation packages overcompensate workers, paying them more than is necessary to induce them to relocate? As we noted in the Challenge, most firms claim that they pay their employees enough in their new city to buy the same bundle of goods as in their original city. We want to investigate whether such firms are paying employees more than necessary to relocate. We illustrate our reasoning using an employee who cares about only two goods.

Alexx's firm wants to transfer him from its Seattle office to its London office, where he will face different prices and a higher cost of living. Alexx, who doesn't care whether he lives in Seattle or London, spends his money on housing and food. Like most firms, his employer will pay him an after-tax salary in British pounds such that he can buy the same bundle of goods in London that he is currently buying in Seattle. Will Alexx benefit by moving to London? Could his employer have induced him to relocate for less money?

Alexx's optimal bundle, s, in Seattle is determined by the tangency of his indifference curve, I^1, and his Seattle budget line, L^S, in the figure. In 2018, on average, it cost 17% more to live in London than in Seattle. If the prices of all goods are exactly 17% higher in London than in Seattle, the relative costs of housing and food are the same in both cities. In that case, if Alexx's firm raises his income by 17%, his budget line does not change and he buys the same bundle, s, and his level of utility is unchanged.

However, relative prices are not the same in both cities. Controlling for quality, housing is relatively more expensive and food is relatively less expensive in London than in Seattle. Thus, if Alexx's firm adjusts his income so that he can buy the same bundle, s, in London as he did in Seattle, his new budget line in London, L^L, must go through s but have a different slope. Because food is relatively less expensive than housing in London compared to Seattle, if Alexx

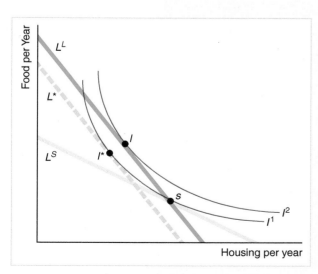

Food per Year

L^L

L^*

L^S

I

I^*

s

I^2

I^1

Housing per year

spends all his money on food, he can buy more in London than in Seattle. Similarly, if he spends all his money on housing, he can buy less in London than in Seattle. As a result, L^L hits the vertical axis at a higher point than the L^S line and cuts the L^S line at Bundle *s*.

Alexx's new optimal bundle, *l*, is determined by the tangency of I^2 and L^L. Thus, because relative prices are different in London and Seattle, Alexx is better off with the transfer after receiving the firm's 17% higher salary. He was on I^1 and is now on I^2. Alexx could buy his original bundle, *s*, but chooses to substitute toward food, which is relatively inexpensive in London, thereby raising his utility.

Consequently, his firm could have induced him to move for less compensation. If the firm lowers his income, the London budget line he faces will be closer to the origin but will have the same slope as L^L. The firm can lower his income until his lower-income London budget line, L^*, is tangent to his Seattle indifference curve, I^1, at Bundle l^*. Alexx still substitutes toward the relatively less expensive food in London, but he is only as well off as he was in Seattle (he remains on the same indifference curve as when he lived in Seattle). Thus, his firm can induce Alexx to transfer to London for less than what the firm would have to pay so that Alexx could buy his original Seattle consumption bundle in London.

SUMMARY

1. **Deriving Demand Curves.** We can derive an individual demand curve using information about the consumer's tastes, which are summarized in an indifference or preference map. Varying the price of one good, holding other prices and income constant, we find how the quantity demanded of a good varies with its price, which is the information we need to draw the demand curve. Consumers' tastes, which are captured by the indifference curves, determine the shape of the demand curve.

2. **Effects of an Increase in Income.** A consumer's demand curve shifts as the consumer's income rises. By varying income while holding prices constant, we determine how quantity demanded shifts with income, which is the information we need to show how the consumer's demand curve shifts. An Engel curve summarizes the relationship between income and quantity demanded, holding prices constant.

3. **Effects of a Price Increase.** An increase in the price of a good causes both a substitution effect and an income effect. The substitution effect is the amount by which a consumer's demand for a good falls because of a price increase if we compensate the consumer with enough extra income so that the consumer's utility does not change. The direction of the substitution effect is unambiguous: A compensated rise in a good's price always causes consumers to buy less of the good. Without compensation, a price increase reduces the consumer's opportunity set: The consumer can now buy less than before with the same income, which harms the consumer. Suppose instead that the prices are held constant, but the consumer's income is reduced by an amount that harms the consumer by as much as the price increase. The income effect is the change in the quantity demanded due to such an income adjustment. The income effect is negative if a good is normal (the income elasticity is positive) and positive if the good is inferior (the income elasticity is negative).

4. **Cost-of-Living Adjustment.** Traditionally, the government's major index of inflation, the Consumer Price Index (CPI), overestimated inflation by ignoring the substitution effect.

5. **Revealed Preference.** If we observe a consumer's choice at various prices and income levels, we can infer the consumer's preferences: the shape of the consumer's indifference curves. We can also use the theory of revealed preference to show that a consumer substitutes away from a good as its price rises.

EXERCISES

All exercises are available on MyLab Economics; * = *answer appears at the back of this book;* M = *mathematical problem.*

1. Deriving Demand Curves

1.1 Manufactured diamonds have become as big and virtually indistinguishable from the best natural diamonds (Hemali Chhapia Shah, "Pick Your Diamond, Get It Lab-Baked," *Times of India*, April 28, 2014). Suppose consumers change from believing that manufactured diamonds, q_1, were imperfect substitutes for natural diamonds, q_2, to perfect substitutes, so that their utility function becomes $U(q_1, q_2) = q_1 + q_2$. What effect would that have on the demand for manufactured diamonds? Derive the new demand curve for manufactured diamonds and draw it. **M**

1.2 How would your answer to Exercise 1.1 change if $U = \ln(q_1 + q_2)$, so that consumers have diminishing marginal utility of diamonds? **M**

1.3 Derive Ryan's demand curve for q_1, given his utility function is $U = q_1^\rho + q_2^\rho$. **M**

1.4 David consumes two things: gasoline (G) and bread (B). David's utility function is $U(q_1, q_2) = 10\, q_1^{0.25} q_2^{0.75}$.
   a. Derive David's demand curve for gasoline.
   b. If the price of gasoline rises, how much does David reduce his consumption of gasoline, $\partial q_1/\partial p_1$?
   c. For David, how does $\partial q_1/\partial p_1$ depend on his income? That is, how does David's change in gasoline consumption due to an increase in the price of gasoline depend on his income level? To answer these questions, find the cross-partial derivative, $\partial^2 q_1/(\partial p_1 \partial Y)$. **M**

1.5 If Philip's utility function is $U = 2q_1^{0.5} + q_2$, what are his demand functions for the two goods? **M**

1.6 Draw a figure to illustrate the Application "Cigarettes Versus E-Cigarettes." That is, show why, as the price of e-cigarettes rises, people consume fewer e-cigarettes but more combustible cigarettes. (*Hint*: Draw a figure like panel a of Figure 4.2 with e-cigarettes on the horizontal axis and combustible cigarettes on the vertical axis. Determine the slope of the price-consumption curve.)

*1.7 In 2005, a typical U.S. owner of a home theater (a television and a DVD player) bought 12 music CDs (q_1) per year and 6 Top-20 movie DVDs (q_2) per year. The average price of a CD was about $p_1 = \$15$, the average price of a DVD was roughly $p_2 = \$20$, and the typical consumer spent $300 on these entertainment goods.[18] Based on these data, we estimate a typical consumer's Cobb-Douglas utility function is $U = q_1^{0.6}q_2^{0.4}$. Draw a figure similar to Figure 4.2 using this utility function. Explain the shape of the price-consumption curve. **M**

2. Effects of an Increase in Income

2.1 Have your folks given you cash or promised to leave you money after they're gone? If so, they may think of such gifts as a good. They decide whether to spend their money on fun, food, drink, or cars, or give money to you. Hmmm. Altonji and Villanueva (2007) estimated that, for every extra dollar of expected lifetime resources, parents give their adult offspring between 2¢ and 3¢ in bequests and about 3¢ in transfers. Those gifts are about one-fifth of what they give their children under 18 and spend on their college education. Illustrate how an increase in your parents' income affects their allocations between bequests to you and all other goods ("fun") in two related graphs, where one shows an income-consumption curve and the other shows an Engel curve for bequests. (*Hint*: See the Application "Fast-Food Engel Curve.")

*2.2 Guerdon always puts half a sliced banana, q_1, on his bowl of cereal, q_2—the two goods are perfect complements. What is his utility function? Derive his demand curve for bananas graphically and mathematically. (*Hint*: See Solved Problem 4.1.) **M**

2.3 According to the U.S. Consumer Expenditure Survey for 2016, Americans with the lowest 10% of incomes spend 41% of their income on housing. What are the limits on their income elasticities of housing if housing and all other goods are normal? They spend 2% on cellular phone service. What are the limits on their income elasticities for cellular phone service if cell phones are normal? (*Hint*: See Solved Problem 4.3.) **M**

*2.4 Given the estimated Cobb-Douglas utility function in Exercise 1.7, $U = q_1^{0.6}q_2^{0.4}$, for CDs, q_1, and DVDs, q_2, derive a typical consumer's Engel curve for movie DVDs. Illustrate in a figure. **M**

2.5 Derive the income elasticity of demand for individuals with (a) Cobb-Douglas, (b) perfect substitutes, and (c) perfect complements utility functions. **M**

2.6 Ryan has a constant elasticity of substitution utility function $U = q_1^\rho + q_2^\rho$.
   a. What is his income elasticity for q_1? (*Hint*: See Solved Problem 4.2.)
   b. Derive his Engel curve for q_1. **M**

---

[18]Budget share, price, and quantity data were obtained from **www.leesmovieinfo.net**, the *New York Times*, and **http://ce.org**.

2.7 Sally's utility function is $U(q_1, q_2) = 4q_1^{0.5} + q_2$. Derive her Engel curves. **M**

3. Effects of a Price Increase

3.1 Under what conditions does the income effect reinforce the substitution effect? Under what conditions does it have an offsetting effect? If the income effect more than offsets the substitution effect for a good, what do we call that good? In a figure, illustrate that the income effect can more than offset the substitution effect (a Giffen good).

*3.2 Don spends his money on food and operas. Food is an inferior good for Don. Does he view an opera performance as an inferior or a normal good? Why? In a diagram, show a possible income-consumption curve for Don.

3.3 Pat eats eggs and toast for breakfast and insists on having three pieces of toast for every two eggs he eats. Derive his utility function. If the price of eggs increases but we compensate Pat to make him just as "happy" as he was before the price change, what happens to his consumption of eggs? Draw a graph and explain your diagram. Does the change in his consumption reflect a substitution or an income effect? (*Hint:* See Solved Problem 4.4.)

3.4 Use a figure to illustrate the effect of a change in the price of alcohol in the Application "Substituting Marijuana for Alcohol." Label the figure using the numbers for a typical female from the application. Is the percentage change in marijuana consumption due to a pure substitution effect or does it reflect both substitution and income effects?

3.5 The New York state cigarette tax applies equally to low-quality (generic) and high-quality cigarettes. However, the state cannot collect the tax on sales on Indian reservations. DeCicca, Kenkel, and Liu (2014) found that people purchase a larger share of low-quality cigarettes on Indian reservations compared to purchases elsewhere in New York. Why? (*Hint:* See Solved Problem 4.5.)

*3.6 Draw a figure to illustrate the answer given in Solved Problem 4.5. Use math and a figure to show whether applying an ad valorem tax rather than a specific tax changes the analysis. **M**

3.7 Lucy views Bayer aspirin and Tylenol as perfect substitutes. Initially the aspirin is cheaper. However, a price increase makes aspirin more expensive than Tylenol. In a diagram, show the substitution, income, and total effect of this price change.

*3.8 Siggi's quasilinear utility function is $U = 4q_1^{0.5} + q_2$. His budget for these goods is $Y = 10$. Originally, the prices are $p_1 = p_2 = 1$. However, the price of the first good rises to $p_1 = 2$. Discuss the substitution, income, and total effect on the demand for q_1. **M**

3.9 Remy views ice cream and fudge sauce as perfect complements. Is it possible that either of these goods or both of them are Giffen goods? (*Hint:* See Solved Problem 4.6.)

*3.10 Sylvia's utility function is $U(q_1, q_2) = \min(q_1, jq_2)$. Derive her compensated (Hicksian) demand and expenditure functions. **M**

3.11 Bill's utility function is $U = 0.5 \ln q_1 + 0.5 \ln q_2$. What is his compensated demand function for q_1? (*Hint:* See Solved Problem 4.7.) **M**

3.12 Sylvan's utility function is $U(q_1, q_2) = q_1 + 2q_2$. Derive his compensated (Hicksian) demand and expenditure functions. **M**

4. Cost-of-Living Adjustment

*4.1 Alix consumes only coffee and coffee cake and only consumes them together (they are perfect complements). If we calculate a CPI using only these two goods, by how much will this CPI differ from the true cost-of-living index?

4.2 Jean views coffee and cream as perfect complements. In the first year, Jean picks an optimal bundle of coffee and cream, e_1. In the second year, inflation occurs, the prices of coffee and cream change by different amounts, and Jean receives a cost-of-living adjustment (COLA) based on the consumer price index (CPI) for these two goods. After the price changes and she receives the COLA, her new optimal bundle is e_2. Show the two equilibria in a figure. Is she better off, worse off, or equally well off at e_2 compared to e_1? Explain.

4.3 Ann's only income is her annual college scholarship, which she spends exclusively on gallons of ice cream and books. Last year, when ice cream cost $10 and used books cost $20, Ann spent her $250 scholarship on 5 gallons of ice cream and 10 books. This year, the price of ice cream rose to $15 and the price of books increased to $25. So that Ann can afford the same bundle of ice cream and books that she bought last year, her college raised her scholarship to $325. Ann has the usual-shaped indifference curves. Will Ann change the amount of ice cream and books that she buys this year? If so, explain how and why. Will Ann be better off, as well off, or worse off this year than last year? Why?

4.4 *The Economist* magazine publishes the Big Mac Index, which is based on the price of a Big Mac at McDonald's in various countries over time. Under what circumstances would people find this index to be as useful as or more useful than the consumer price index in measuring how their true cost of living changes over time?

4.5 During his first year at school, Guojun buys eight new college textbooks at a cost of $50 each. Used books cost $30 each. When the bookstore announces a 20% price increase in new texts and a 10% increase in used texts for the next year, Guojun's father offers him $80 extra. Is Guojun better off, the same, or worse off after the price change? Why?

4.6 Use a graph to illustrate that the Paasche cost-of-living index (see the Application "Reducing the CPI Substitution Bias") underestimates the rate of inflation when compared to the true cost-of-living index.

*4.7 The Application "Reducing the CPI Substitution Bias" discusses the new inflation index, the C-CPI, which averages the Laspeyres and Paasche indexes. Give an example of circumstances such that the traditional CPI (Laspeyres) index would be superior to the new one.

4.8 Cynthia buys gasoline and other goods. The government considers imposing a lump-sum tax, $\mathcal{L}$ dollars, dollars per person, or a specific tax on gasoline of t dollars per gallon. Given that either tax will raise the same amount of tax revenue from Cynthia, which tax does she prefer and why? Show your answer using a graph or calculus. **M**

4.9 The price of a serving of McDonald's French fries in 1950 was 10¢. Using the internet, or visiting a McDonald's, determine the price of fries today. The federal government's urban CPI index is available at **www.bls.gov/cpi/data.htm**. Based on these data, has the real price of fries increased?

5. Revealed Preference

5.1 Remy spends her weekly income of $30 on chocolate, q_1, and shampoo, q_2. Initially, when the prices are $p_1 = \$2 = p_2$, she buys $q_1 = 10$ and $q_2 = 5$. After the prices change to $p_1 = \$1$ and $p_2 = \$3$, she purchases $q_1 = 6$ and $q_2 = 8$. Draw her budget lines and choices in a diagram. Use a revealed preference argument to discuss whether or not she is maximizing her utility before and after the price changes.

5.2 Analyze the problem in Exercise 5.1, making use of Equation 4.16. **M**

5.3 Felix chooses between clothing, q_1, and food, q_2. His initial income is $1,000 a month, $p_1 = 100$, and $p_2 = 10$. At his initial bundle, he consumes $q_1 = 2$ and $q_2 = 80$. Later, his income rises to $1,200 and the price of clothing rises to $p_1 = 150$, but the price of food does not change. As a result, he reduces his consumption of clothing to one unit. Using a revealed preference reasoning (that is, knowing nothing about his indifference curves), can you determine how he ranks the two bundles?

6. Challenge

6.1 In the Challenge Solution, suppose that housing was relatively less expensive and food was relatively more expensive in London than in Seattle, so that the L^L budget line cuts the L^S budget line from below rather than from above, as in the Challenge Solution's figure. Show that the conclusion that Alexx is better off after his move still holds. Explain the logic behind the following statement: "The analysis holds as long as the relative prices differ in the two cities. Whether one price or the other is relatively higher in London than in Seattle is irrelevant to the analysis."

5 Consumer Welfare and Policy Analysis

The welfare of the people is the ultimate law. —Cicero

CHALLENGE

Per-Hour Versus Lump-Sum Childcare Subsidies

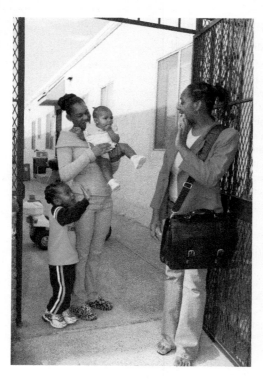

Childcare subsidies are common throughout the world. According to the Organization for Economic Cooperation and Development, in 2016, childcare spending as a percentage of gross domestic product averaged 0.7% across developed countries and was as high as 1.6% in Sweden and 1.8% in Iceland. In contrast, the United States spends less than 0.5%.

The increased employment of mothers outside the home has led to a steep rise in childcare over the past half century. In the United States today, nearly 7 out of 10 mothers work outside the home—more than twice the rate in 1970. Eight out of 10 employed mothers with children under age six are likely to have some form of nonparental childcare arrangement. Six out of 10 children under the age of six are in childcare, as are 45% of children under age one.

Childcare is a major burden for the poor, and the expense may prevent poor mothers from working. Paying for childcare for children under the age of five absorbed 25% of the earnings for families with annual incomes under $14,400, but only 6% for families with incomes of $54,000 or more. Guner, Kaygusuz, and Ventura (2017) estimated that a universal childcare subsidy that covered 75% of the cost would increase the labor force participation of married females by 8.8% (and 21.5% for those with less than a high school education). As one would expect, the subsidies have larger impacts on welfare recipients than on wealthier mothers.

In large part to help poor families obtain childcare so that the parents can work, the U.S. Child Care and Development Fund provided $5.2 billion to states in 2018. Childcare programs vary substantially across states in their generosity and in the form of the subsidy.[1] Most states provide an ad valorem or a specific subsidy (see Chapter 2) to lower the hourly rate that a poor family pays for childcare.

Rather than subsidizing the price of childcare, the Canadian government provides an unrestricted lump-sum payment that parents can spend on childcare or on all other goods, such as food and housing.

For a given government expenditure, does a per-hour subsidy or a lump-sum subsidy provide greater benefit to recipients? Which option increases the demand for childcare services by more? Which one inflicts less cost on other consumers of childcare?

---

[1]For example, in 2016, the monthly base reimbursement rate for toddlers was a little over $400 in Alabama, Kansas, and Louisiana, but about $1,000 in Connecticut and Washington, D.C., and about $1,200 in New York and Oregon.

To answer these kinds of questions, first we will use consumer theory to develop various measures of consumer welfare. Then we will examine how several types of government policies affect consumer well-being. Finally, we will use consumer theory to study individuals' labor supply and analyze the impact of income taxes.

In this chapter, we examine four main topics	1. **Uncompensated Consumer Welfare.** Information from a consumer's demand curve or utility function shows the degree to which an increase in the equilibrium price helps or harms the consumer.
	2. **Compensated Consumer Welfare.** We can use indifference curves, compensated demand curves, or expenditure functions to calculate how much more money we would have to give a consumer to offset the harm from a price increase.
	3. **Effects of Government Policies on Consumer Welfare.** We use our consumer welfare measures to determine the degree to which quotas, food stamps, or childcare subsidies help or hurt consumers.
	4. **Deriving Labor Supply Curves.** We derive a worker's labor supply curve using the individual's demand curve for leisure. We use the labor supply curve to determine how a reduction in the income tax rate affects consumer welfare, the supply of labor, and tax revenues.

5.1 Uncompensated Consumer Welfare

Economists and policymakers want to know by how much a shock that affects the equilibrium price and quantity of goods and services helps or hurts consumers. Examples of such shocks include price changes when new inventions reduce costs or when a government imposes a tax or subsidy, and quantity changes when a government sets a quota. To determine how these changes affect consumers, we need a measure of consumers' welfare.

If we knew a consumer's utility function, we could directly answer the question of how government actions, natural disasters, and other events affect consumers' welfare. If the price of beef increases, the budget line of someone who eats beef rotates inward, so the consumer is on a lower indifference curve at a new equilibrium. If we knew the levels of utility associated with the original indifference curve and the new indifference curve, we could measure the impact of the price change on the consumer's utility level.

However, this approach is not practical for a couple of reasons. First, we rarely know individuals' utility functions. Second, even if we had utility measures for various consumers, we would have no obvious way to compare the measures. One person might say that he gets 1,000 utils (units of utility) of pleasure from the same bundle that another consumer says gives her 872 utils. The first person is not necessarily happier—he may just be using a different scale.

Because it is more practical to compare dollars rather than utils across people, we *measure consumer well-being using dollars.* Instead of asking the question "How many utils would you lose if your daily commute increased by 15 minutes?" we could ask, "How much would you pay to avoid having your daily commute grow a quarter of an hour longer?" or "How much would it cost you if your daily commute were 15 minutes longer?"

Consumer well-being from a good is the benefit a consumer gets from consuming that good in excess of its cost. How much pleasure do you get from a good above and beyond its price? If you buy a good for exactly what it's worth to you, you are indifferent between making that transaction and not making it. Frequently, however, you buy things that are worth more to you than what they cost. Imagine that you've played tennis in the hot sun and are very thirsty. A nearby vending machine will sell you a soft drink for $1. You'd be willing to pay $2. You're better off making this purchase than not because you are willing to pay $1 more than the drink costs.

In this section, we examine *consumer surplus*, which is the most widely used measure of consumer well-being. Consumer surplus is relatively easy to calculate using the usual, uncompensated (Marshallian) demand function and approximates the true value of a consumer's welfare. Later in the chapter, we discuss approaches that provide exact values using compensated demand functions and examine how close consumer surplus comes to the exact values.

Willingness to Pay

If we can measure how much more you'd be willing to pay than you actually paid for a product, we'd know how much you gained from the transaction. Luckily, the demand curve contains the information we need to make this measurement. For convenience in most of the following discussion, we use the equivalent *inverse demand function*, which rearranges the demand function, $Q = D(p)$, to express a product's price as a function of the quantity of it demanded, $p = p(Q)$. For example, if the demand function is $Q = a - bp$, then the inverse demand function is $p = a/b - Q/b$.

To develop a welfare measure based on the inverse demand curve, we need to know what information is contained in an inverse demand curve. The inverse demand curve reflects a consumer's *marginal willingness to pay*: the maximum amount a consumer will spend for an extra unit. The consumer's marginal willingness to pay for a product is the *marginal value* the consumer places on buying one more unit.

David's inverse demand curve for magazines per week in panel a of Figure 5.1 indicates his marginal willingness to pay for various numbers of magazines. David places a marginal value of $5 on the first magazine. As a result, if the price of a magazine is $5, David buys one magazine, point *a* on the demand curve. His marginal willingness to buy a second magazine is $4, so if the price falls to $4, he buys two magazines, *b*. His marginal willingness to buy three magazines is $3, so if the price of magazines is $3, he buys three magazines, *c*.

An Individual's Consumer Surplus

Consumer surplus (*CS*) is the monetary difference between the maximum amount that a consumer is willing to pay for the quantity of the good purchased and what the good actually costs. Consumer surplus is a dollar-value measure of the extra pleasure the consumer receives from the transaction beyond its price.

For example, David's consumer surplus from each additional magazine is his marginal willingness to pay minus what he pays to obtain the magazine. His marginal willingness to pay for the first magazine, $5, is area $CS_1 + E_1$ in panel a of Figure 5.1. If the price is $3, his expenditure to obtain the magazine is area $E_1 = \$3$. Thus, his consumer surplus on the first magazine is area $CS_1 = (CS_1 + E_1) - E_1 = \$5 - \$3 = \$2$. Because his marginal willingness to pay for the second magazine is $4, his consumer surplus for the second magazine is the smaller area, $CS_2 = \$1$. His marginal willingness to pay for the third magazine is $3, which equals what he must pay to obtain it, so his consumer surplus is zero. He is indifferent between buying and not buying the third magazine.

At a price of $3, David buys three magazines. His total consumer surplus from the three magazines he buys is the sum of the consumer surplus he gets from each of these magazines: $CS_1 + CS_2 + CS_3 = \$2 + \$1 + \$0 = \$3$. This total consumer

Figure 5.1 Consumer Surplus

(a) David's inverse demand curve for magazines has a step-like shape. When the price is $3, he buys three magazines, point *c*. David's marginal value for the first magazine is $5, areas $CS_1 + E_1$, and his expenditure is $3, area E_1, so his consumer surplus is $CS_1 = $2. His consumer surplus is $1 for the second magazine, area CS_2, and is $0 for the third (he is indifferent between buying and not buying it).

Thus, his total consumer surplus is the blue shaded area $CS_1 + CS_2 = $3, and his total expenditure is the tan shaded area $E_1 + E_2 + E_3 = $9. (b) The market's willingness to pay for UberX rides is the height of the smooth inverse demand curve. At price p_1, the expenditure is $E (= p_1 Q_1)$, consumer surplus is CS, and the total value the market places on consuming Q_1 UberX rides per year is $CS + E$.

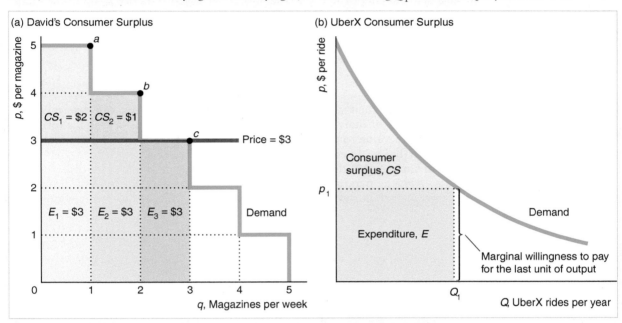

(a) David's Consumer Surplus

(b) UberX Consumer Surplus

surplus of $3 is the extra amount that David is willing to spend for the right to buy three magazines at $3 each. David is unwilling to buy a fourth magazine unless the price drops to $2 or less. If David's mother gives him a fourth magazine as a gift, the marginal value that David puts on that fourth magazine, $2, is less than what it cost his mother, $3.

Thus, an individual's consumer surplus is

- the extra value that a consumer gets from buying the desired number of units of a good in excess of the amount paid,
- the amount that a consumer would be willing to pay for the right to buy as many units as desired at the specified price, and
- the area under the consumer's inverse demand curve and above the market price up to the quantity of the product the consumer buys.

A Market's Consumer Surplus

Similarly, we can determine a market's consumer surplus associated with a smooth inverse demand curve in the same way as we did with David's unusual stair-like inverse demand curve. Panel b of Figure 5.1 shows the inverse demand curve for UberX rides

(Uber's most used service) rides. The height of this inverse demand curve measures the market's willingness to pay for one more ride. This willingness varies with the number of rides. The total value the market places on obtaining Q_1 rides per year is the area under the inverse demand curve up to Q_1, the areas CS and E. Area E is the expenditure on Q_1 rides. Because the price is p_1, the expenditure is $p_1 Q_1$ (the height of the rectangle is p_1 and its length is Q_1, so its area is $p_1 Q_1$). The market's consumer surplus from Q_1 is the value of consuming those rides, area $CS + E$, minus the expenditure E to obtain them, or CS. Thus, the market consumer surplus, CS, is the area under the inverse demand curve and above the horizontal line at the price p_1 up to the quantity purchased, Q_1.

Cohen et al. (2016) estimated that the UberX consumer surplus was $6.8 billion in 2015.[2] They also estimated that consumers received about $1.60 of consumer surplus for every dollar they spent, so the ratio of CS to E was about 1.6.[3]

APPLICATION

Willingness to Pay and Consumer Surplus on eBay

People differ in their willingness to pay for a given item. We can determine willingness to pay of individuals for an A.D. 238 Roman coin—a sesterce (originally equivalent in value to four asses) with the image of Emperor Balbinus—by how much they bid in an eBay auction. On its website, eBay correctly argues (as we show in Chapter 13) that an individual's best strategy is to bid his or her *willingness to pay*: the maximum value that the bidder places on the item. From what eBay reports, we know the maximum bid of each person except the winner, who paid the second-highest amount bid plus an increment.[4]

In the figure, the bids for the coin are arranged from highest to lowest. Because each bar on the graph indicates the bid for one coin, the figure shows how many units this group of bidders would have been willing to buy at various prices. That is, it is the market inverse demand curve.

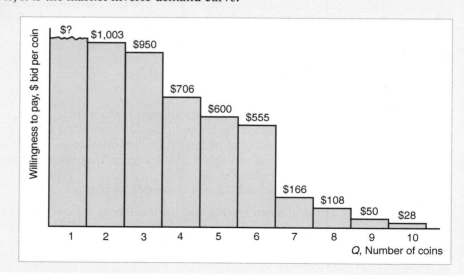

---

[3]In contrast, Hasker, Jiang, and Sickles (2014) estimated that the median CS from buying a computer monitor on eBay was $28 and that CS/E was about 19%.

[4]The increment depends on the size of the bid. It is $1 for the bids between $25 and $199.99 and $25 for bids between $1,000 and $2,499.99.

Figure 5.2 A Change in Consumer Surplus

As the price increases from £0.5 to £1, Jackie loses consumer surplus equal to areas $A + B$.

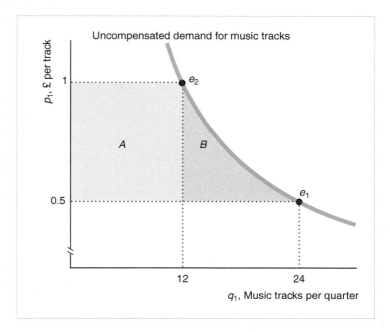

Effect of a Price Change on Consumer Surplus

If the price of a good rises, purchasers of that good lose consumer surplus. To illustrate this loss, we return to the estimated Cobb-Douglas utility, $U = q_1^{0.4}q_1^{0.6}$, for a typical young person, whom we call Jackie, who buys music tracks, q_1, and attends live music events, q_2 (see the Application "*MRS* Between Recorded Tracks and Live Music" in Chapter 3). In that chapter, we showed that her uncompensated demand curve for tracks is $q_1 = 0.4Y/p_1 = 12/p_1$ given that her music budget per quarter is $Y = $ £30. At the initial price of tracks $p_1 = $ £0.5, she bought $q_1 = 12/0.5 = 24$ song tracks.

Suppose that a government tax or a price increase causes the price of tracks to double to £1. Jackie now buys $q_1 = 12/1 = 12$ tracks. As Figure 5.2 illustrates, she loses the amount of consumer surplus (ΔCS) equal to area $A + B$: the area between £0.5 and £1 on the price axis to the left of her uncompensated demand curve. Due to the price increase, she now buys 12 tracks for which she pays £0.5 (= £1 − £0.5) more than originally, so area $A = $ £6 = £0.5 × 12. In addition, she loses surplus from no longer consuming 12 (= 24 − 12) of the original 24 tracks, area B.[5]

SOLVED PROBLEM 5.1

MyLab Economics Solved Problem

What is the exact change in Jackie's consumer surplus, $A + B$, in Figure 5.2? How large is area B?

Answer

1. *State Jackie's uncompensated demand function of music tracks given her initial budget.* From Chapters 3 and 4, we know that her demand function for tracks is $q_1 = 12/p_1$.

---

[5]If we replace the curved demand curve with a straight line, we slightly overestimate area B as the area of a triangle: $\frac{1}{2} \times $ £0.5 × 12 = £3. We calculate the exact amount in Solved Problem 5.1.

2. *Integrate between £0.5 and £1 to the left of Jackie's uncompensated demand curve for tracks.* Her lost consumer surplus is

$$\Delta CS = -\int_{0.5}^{1} \frac{12}{p_1} dp_1 = -12 \ln p_1 \Big|_{0.5}^{1}$$

$$= -12(\ln 1 - \ln 0.5) \approx -12 \times 0.69 \approx -8.28,$$

where we put a minus sign in front of the integrated area because the price increased, causing a loss of consumer surplus.

3. *Determine the size of area B residually.* Because areas $A + B = £8.28$ and $A = £6 (= [£1 - £0.5] \times 12)$, area B is £2.28 $(= £8.28 - £6)$.

Comment: A 100% increase in price causes Jackie's consumer surplus to fall by £8.28, which is 69% of the £12 she spends on tracks.

5.2 Compensated Consumer Welfare

Ideally, we want to measure how a consumer's utility changes in response to the change in a price. However, because utility is an ordinal measure, we use a monetary equivalent.

Initially, a consumer with an income of Y who faces prices (p_1, p_2) picks a bundle of goods that provides a level of utility of $\overline{U}$. The price of the first good rises so that the consumer now faces prices (p_1^*, p_2). To obtain the initial level of utility $\overline{U}$, the consumer now needs more income, Y^*. Thus, $Y - Y^*$ is a monetary measure of the change in utility due to the change in a price.

Unfortunately, the change in consumer surplus provides us with only an approximation of this measure. The problem with consumer surplus is that we calculate it using an uncompensated demand curve, which does not hold utility constant as the price changes (Chapter 4).

We start this section by using indifference curves to derive exact monetary measures of the change in utility due to a higher price. Then, we show that compensated demand curves capture this information.

Indifference Curve Analysis

To calculate the money measure of the harm to a consumer from a price increase, we need to decide which level of utility, $\overline{U}$, to use in deriving an exact monetary measure. The two choices are (1) the utility at the consumer's original optimal bundle before the price increase, $\overline{U}$; or (2) the utility after the price change, $\overline{U}^*$. We call the first of these measures the *compensating variation* and the second one the *equivalent variation*.

The **compensating variation** (*CV*) is the amount of money one would have to give a consumer to offset completely the harm from a price increase. That is, *CV* is the amount of extra income that would keep the consumer on the original indifference curve. We call this measure the compensating variation because we compensate the consumer for the harm from a higher price.

The **equivalent variation** (*EV*) is the amount of money one would have to take from a consumer to harm the consumer by as much as the price increase. That is, taking this amount of money causes the same, or equivalent, harm as does the price increase: It moves the consumer to the new, lower indifference curve.

Figure 5.3 Compensating Variation and Equivalent Variation

At the initial price, Jackie's budget constraint, L^a, is tangent to indifference curve I at a, where she buys 24 tracks. After the price of tracks doubles, her new budget constraint, L^b, is tangent to indifference curve I^* at b, where she buys 12 tracks. Because the price of a unit of live music is £1, L^b hits the vertical axis at Y. If Jackie were given CV extra income to offset the price increase, her budget line would be L^{CV} (which is parallel to L^b), and she would be tangent to her original indifference curve, I, at point c. The budget line L^{CV} hits the vertical axis at $Y + CV$, so the difference between where this budget line and the L^b line strike the vertical axis equals CV. Similarly, at the original price, if we removed income equal to EV, her budget line would shift down to L^{EV}, and Jackie would choose bundle d on I^*. Thus, taking EV away harms her as much as the price increase. The gap between where L^b and L^{EV} touch the vertical axis equals EV.

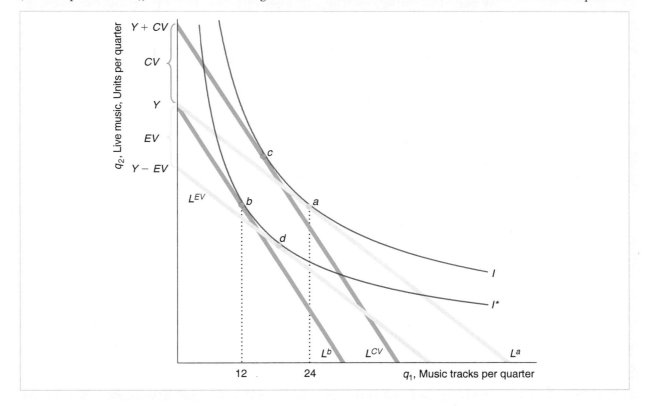

We illustrate how to determine CV and EV using Jackie's estimated utility function to draw her indifference curves in Figure 5.3. Initially, Jackie pays $p_1 = £0.5$ for each music track and $p_2 = £1$ for each unit of live music. Jackie has $Y = £30$ to spend on music tracks and live music. Her original budget constraint, $Y = p_1 q_1 + p_2 q_2 = 0.5q_1 + q_2$, labeled L^a, as a slope of $-p_1/p_2 = -0.5/1 = -0.5$. The budget constraint is tangent to indifference curve I at her optimal bundle, a, where she buys 24 tracks and 18 units of live music. Her utility is $\overline{U}$.

If the price of tracks doubles to $p_1^* = £1$ but her income remains unchanged at Y, Jackie's budget line rotates to L^b and has a slope of -1. The new budget line is tangent to indifference curve I^* at her new optimal bundle, b, where she buys 12 tracks and 18 units of live music. Jackie is harmed by the price increase: She is on a lower indifference curve I^* with utility $\overline{U}^*$, which is less than $\overline{U}$.

Compensating Variation. If Jackie receives enough extra income—the compensating variation CV—her utility remains at the original utility level $\overline{U}$ after the price of tracks doubles to $p_1^* = £1$. In Figure 5.3, the extra income CV causes a parallel shift upward of her budget line from L^b to L^{CV}, which is tangent to the original indifference curve I at bundle c. At c, her utility is the same as at a, $\overline{U}$.

Her expenditure at b is Y. Her expenditure at c is $Y + CV$. Thus, her compensating variation is her expenditure at c minus her expenditure at b: $CV = (Y + CV) - Y$.

Because the price of a unit of live music is £1 per unit, L^b hits the live music axis at Y, where she spends all her money on live music. Similarly, L^{CV} hits the live music axis at $Y + CV$. Thus, CV is the gap between the two intercepts, as Figure 5.3 shows.

Equivalent Variation. The equivalent variation, EV, is the amount of income that we would have to take from Jackie to lower her utility by the same amount as would a price increase for tracks from $p_1 = £0.5$ to $p_1^* = £1$. We know that if Jackie's income remains constant at Y when the price increases, her optimal bundle is b on indifference curve I^* with utility $\overline{U}^*$.

Leaving the price unchanged at p_1, a decrease in Jackie's income by EV causes a parallel shift downward of her original budget line, L^a, to L^{EV}, which is tangent to I^* at d. That is, losing EV amount of income reduces her utility as much as would the price increase.

Her expenditure at a is Y and her expenditure at d is $Y - EV$. Thus, her equivalent variation is $EV = Y - (Y - EV)$. Because the price of a unit of live music is £1 per unit, L^a intersects the live music axis at Y, and L^{EV} hits that axis at $Y - EV$. As Figure 5.3 shows, the gap between the two intercepts is EV.

Thus, CV and EV both provide an exact monetary measure of the utility harm from a higher price. The key distinction between these measures is that we calculate CV holding utility constant at $\overline{U}$ and EV holding utility at $\overline{U}^*$. That is, these measures provide exact, correct answers to different questions. Because the levels of utility they hold constant differ, CV generally does not equal EV.

APPLICATION

Compensating
Variation and
Equivalent Variation
for Smartphones
and Facebook

How much do you value using modern digital conveniences such as surfing the internet with your smartphone or using Facebook?

The Boston Consulting Group (BCG) surveyed consumers in 13 wealthy countries about their compensated variation, CV, and equivalent variation, EV (although the survey did not use those terms).

The surveyors asked consumers how much money they would want in exchange for giving up mobile internet access: their compensating variation. Across the 13 countries, the average CV was $4,000, seven times what consumers pay for the device and access. For all the consumers in these countries, the total CV is about $3.5 trillion.

The survey also asked an equivalent variation question: What would you give up for a year to maintain your mobile internet connection? That is, giving up what good or activity would hurt you as much as losing the internet? To keep mobile internet access, 74% of consumers would give up newspapers, 70% chocolate, 67% alcohol, 62% books, 49% television, 44% exercise, 27% sex, and 19% showering.

Many economists question whether answers to survey questions are reliable. For this reason, economists typically calculate consumer surplus, compensating variation, and equivalent variation by using estimated demand curves based on observed purchasing behavior.

Brynjolfsson, Eggers, and Gannamaneni (2018) estimated demand curves to determine the value consumers place on using Facebook. They examined whether people were willing to give up access to Facebook for a month in exchange for a certain amount of money. They estimated that the median CV was $48.49 per month in 2016, but it fell to $37.76 in 2017.

Compensated Demand Curves and Consumer Welfare

Because we typically do not know a consumer's indifference curves, we can't use them to measure CV or EV. However, we can use compensated (Hicksian) demand curves, which contain the same information.

As the price of a good rises, the compensated demand curve shows how many fewer units a consumer would purchase given that the consumer receives extra income that holds the consumer's utility constant. This change in the quantity demanded by the consumer reflects a pure substitution effect, as Figure 4.6 illustrates.

Figures 5.3 and 5.4 show the relationship between points a, b, c, and d on indifference curves and on the corresponding points on three demand curves. Initially, when Jackie's income is Y and the price is $p_1 = £0.5$, she buys 24 music tracks at point a in both figures. If the price increases to $p_1^* = £1$ but her income remains constant, she buys 12 tracks at point b in both figures. Points a and b lie on her uncompensated demand curve D in Figure 5.4.

If Jackie receives a payment of CV to compensate her for the price increase, her optimal point moves from a to c in both figures. Because a and c are on indifference curve I in Figure 5.3, both have the same level of utility $\overline{U}$. In Figure 5.4, a and c lie on H^{CV}, which is her compensated demand curve that holds utility at $\overline{U}$.

Alternatively, losing EV amount of income would lower her utility to $\overline{U}^*$ on indifference curve I^* in Figure 5.3, which equals the harm from the price increase. Holding her utility constant at $\overline{U}^*$, the price increase causes her optimal bundle to move from d to b, which lie on her compensated demand curve H^{EV} in Figure 5.4.

Figure 5.4 Comparing *CV*, *EV*, and *ΔCS*

At the initial price of tracks, $p_1 = £0.5$, Jackie buys 24 tracks at point a. If the price doubles to £1 and her income does not change, she buys 12 tracks at b on the uncompensated demand curve D. She loses consumer surplus, ΔCS, equal to $A + B$: the area to the left of D between £0.5 and £1. If she receives a compensating variation $CV = $ area $A + B + C$ that holds her utility at the initial level corresponding to point a, she buys the quantity at c on the compensated demand curve H^{CV}. Alternatively, at the utility that corresponds to point b, her compensated demand curve is H^{EV}. Here, Jackie's loss from the price increase is equal to a loss of income of $EV = $ area A associated with the move from d to b.

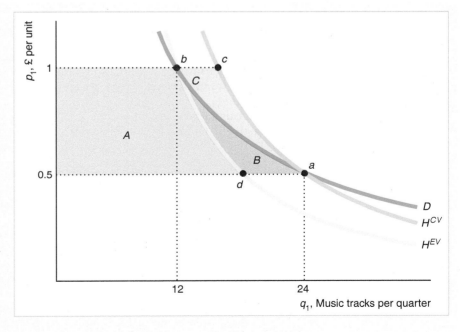

Associated with each compensated demand curve is an expenditure function (Equation 3.32), which is the minimal expenditure necessary to achieve a specific utility level $\overline{U}$ for a given set of prices,

$$E = E(p_1, p_2, \overline{U}). \tag{5.1}$$

The compensated demand function for q_1 is the partial derivative of the expenditure function with respect to p_1: The compensated demand function is $\partial E(p_1, p_2, \overline{U})/\partial p_1$ (Chapter 4). Thus, if we integrate with respect to price to the left of the compensated demand function, we get the expenditure function.

We can use the expenditure function to determine how much compensation Jackie would need to leave her as well off at a new set of prices as at the original prices. If we hold p_2 constant, and increase p_1 to p_1^*, the difference between the expenditures at these two prices is the change in the compensated (Hicksian) consumer surplus:

$$\Delta \text{ compensated } CS = E(p_1, p_2, \overline{U}) - E(p_1^*, p_2, \overline{U}). \tag{5.2}$$

Holding Jackie's utility constant at $\overline{U}$, the price increase causes her optimal bundles to change from a to c along indifference curve I in Figure 5.3 and along H^{CV} in Figure 5.4. Jackie's expenditure is $E(p_1, p_2, \overline{U}) = Y$ at point a and $E(p_1^*, p_2, \overline{U}) = Y + CV$ at point c. Thus, the change in her compensated CS is $-CV$ if we evaluate Equation 5.2 at $\overline{U}$.

Similarly, if we hold her utility at the lower level $\overline{U}^*$, as the price increases, Jackie's optimal bundles moves from point d to b along indifference curve I^* in Figure 5.3 and along H^{EV} in Figure 5.4. Her expenditure is $E(p_1^*, p_2, \overline{U}^*) = Y$ at b and $E(p_1, p_2, \overline{U}^*) = Y - EV$ at point d. Thus, the change in her compensated CS is $-EV$ if we evaluate Equation 5.2 at $\overline{U}^*$.

Comparing the Three Welfare Measures

Economists usually think of the change in consumer surplus as an approximation to the compensating variation and equivalent variation measures. Consumer surplus lies between these exact monetary measures of the change in utility due to a price change.

Which consumer welfare measure is larger depends on the sign of the product's income elasticity. If the good is a normal good (as a music track is for Jackie), $|CV| > |\Delta CS| > |EV|$. If the good is an inferior good, $|CV| < |\Delta CS| < |EV|$.

An Example. We illustrate the relative size of the three measures using Jackie's estimated Cobb-Douglas utility, in which a government tax causes the price of music tracks, p_1, to double from £0.5 to £1, so that she reduces her purchases from 24 to 12 tracks per quarter.

In Figure 5.4, her lost consumer surplus, ΔCS, is areas $A + B$: the area between £0.5 and £1 on the price axis to the left of her uncompensated demand curve, D. Her compensating variation is $A + B + C$, which is the area between £0.5 and £1 to the left of the compensated demand curve at the original utility level, H^{CV}. This amount of money is just large enough to offset the harm of the higher price, so that Jackie will remain on her initial indifference curve. Finally, her equivalent variation is A, which is the area between £0.5 and £1 to the left of the compensated demand curve at the new, lower utility level, H^{EV}. Losing this amount of money would harm Jackie as much as would the price increase.

We can calculate CV and EV as the change in Jackie's expenditure function as the price rises, holding the price of a unit of live music constant at $p_2 = £1$. Substituting this price into Jackie's Cobb-Douglas expenditure function (Equation 4.9), we find that

$$E(p_1, p_2, \overline{U}) = \overline{U}\left(\frac{p_1}{0.4}\right)^{0.4}\left(\frac{p_2}{0.6}\right)^{0.6} \approx 1.96\overline{U}p_1^{0.4}p_2^{0.6} = 1.96\overline{U}p_1^{0.4}. \qquad (5.3)$$

At Jackie's initial optimum, where $q_1 = 24$ and $q_2 = 18$, her utility is $\overline{U} = 24^{0.4}18^{0.6} \approx 20.195$. Thus, the expenditure function at the original optimum is $\overline{E}(p_1) \approx 39.582p_1^{0.4}$. At her new optimum after the price change, where $q_1 = 12$ and $q_2 = 18$, the utility level $\overline{U}^* = 12^{0.4}18^{0.6} \approx 15.305$, so the new expenditure function is $\overline{E}^*(p_1) \approx 29.998p_1^{0.4}$. Thus,

$$CV = \overline{E}(1) - \overline{E}(0.5) = 39.582(1^{0.4} - 0.5^{0.4}) \approx 39.582(0.242) \approx 9.579 \quad (5.4)$$

and

$$EV = \overline{E}^*(1) - \overline{E}^*(0.5) = 29.998(1^{0.4} - 0.5^{0.4}) \approx 29.998(0.242) \approx 7.260. \quad (5.5)$$

As Figure 5.4 shows, Jackie's equivalent variation, $EV = A = £7.26$ (Equation 5.5), is smaller than her consumer surplus loss, $\Delta CS = A + B = £8.28$ (Solved Problem 5.1), which is smaller than her compensating variation, $CV = A + B + C = £9.58$ (Equation 5.4).

By How Much Do These Measures Differ? Although in principle the three measures of welfare could differ substantially, for many goods they do not differ much for small changes in price. According to the Slutsky equation (Equation 4.11),

$$\varepsilon = \varepsilon^* - \theta\xi,$$

the uncompensated elasticity of demand, ε, equals the compensated elasticity of demand (pure substitution elasticity), ε^*, minus the budget share of the good, θ, times the income elasticity, ξ. Thus, if either the income elasticity or the budget share are near zero, the substitution elasticity nearly equals the uncompensated elasticity, so a price change has nearly the same effect on both the uncompensated demand curve and the compensated demand curve. Thus, the smaller the income elasticity or budget share, the closer the three welfare measures are to each other.

Because the budget shares of most goods are small, the three measures are often very close. Even for an aggregate good on which consumers spend a relatively large share of their budget, the differences between the three measures may be small because the income elasticity is relatively close to zero. Table 5.1 shows how EV and CV compare to ΔCS for various aggregate goods based on an estimated system of U.S. demand curves for a typical consumer. For each category of goods, the table shows the income elasticity; the budget share; the ratio of compensating variation to the change in consumer surplus, $|CV|/|\Delta CS|$; and the ratio of the equivalent variation to the change in consumer surplus, $|EV|/|\Delta CS|$, for a 50% increase in price.

If the ratios $|EV|/|\Delta CS|$ and $|CV|/|\Delta CS|$ nearly equal one (100%), the three welfare measures are virtually identical. That occurs for the alcohol and tobacco category, which has the smallest income elasticity and budget share of any of these aggregate goods. Because housing has the largest income elasticity and budget share, it has a relatively large gap between the measures. However, even for housing, the difference between the change in uncompensated consumer surplus and either of the compensating consumer surplus measures is only 7% ($|EV|/|\Delta CS| = 93\%$ and $|CV|/|\Delta CS| = 107\%$).

Willig (1976) showed theoretically that the three measures vary little for small price changes regardless of the size of the income effect. Indeed, for the seven goods in the table, if the price change were only a more realistic 10%—instead of the 50% in

Table 5.1 Welfare Measures

	Income Elasticity, ξ	Budget Share (%)	$\dfrac{\|EV\|}{\|\Delta CS\|}$	$\dfrac{\|CV\|}{\|\Delta CS\|}$
Alcohol and tobacco	0.39	4	99%	100.4%
Food	0.46	17	97	103
Clothing	0.88	8	97	102
Utilities	1.00	4	98	101
Transportation	1.04	8	97	103
Medical	1.37	9	95	104
Housing	1.38	15	93	107

Source: Calculations based on Blanciforti (1982).

the table—the differences between $|CV|$ or $|EV|$ and $|\Delta CS|$ are a small fraction of a percentage point for all goods except housing, where the difference is only about 1%.

Thus, the three measures of the welfare effect of a small price change give similar answers even for aggregate goods. As a result, economists frequently use the change in consumer surplus, which is relatively easy to calculate because it uses the uncompensated demand curve.

SOLVED PROBLEM 5.2

MyLab Economics Solved Problem

Lucy has a quasilinear utility function, Equation 3.9, $U(q_1, q_2) = u(q_1) + q_2$. When she maximizes her utility subject to her budget constraint, she chooses to consume both goods (an interior solution). The price of the second good, p_2, equals one. The price of q_1 increases from p_1 to p_1^*. Show that her compensating variation, CV, her equivalent variation, EV, and the change in her consumer surplus, ΔCS are all equal.

Answer

1. *Discuss Lucy's demand function for q_1 and write her utility function in terms of her expenditures.* From Chapter 4, we know that Lucy's demand for q_1 is independent of income for an interior solution. We can rearrange Lucy's expenditure function, $E = p_1 q_1 + q_2$, as $q_2 = E - p_1 q_1$. Substituting this expression into her utility function, we can write her utility as $u(q_1) + E - p_1 q_1$.

2. *Calculate the compensating variation at the two prices.* At p_1, Lucy demands $q_1 = q_1(p_1)$ and her utility is $u(q_1) + E - p_1 q_1$. At p_1^*, $q_1^* = q_1(p_1^*)$ and her utility is $u(q_1^*) + E - p_1^* q_1^*$. The compensating variation, CV, is the amount of extra money she needs to receive if her utility is to remain constant despite the increase in price: $u(q_1) + E - p_1 q_1 = u(q_1^*) + E + CV - p_1^* q_1^*$. Solving the equation for CV, we find that

$$CV = u(q_1) - u(q_1^*) + p_1^* q_1^* - p_1 q_1.$$

3. *Calculate the equivalent variation at the two prices and compare it to the compensating variation.* By similar reasoning, her equivalent variation, EV, is the amount that would have to be taken from her at the original price to lower her

utility to that at the higher price. We use the same approach as before by setting $u(q_1) + E - EV - p_1 q_1 = u(q_1^*) + E - p_1^* q_1^*$. Solving for EV, we learn that

$$EV = u(q_1) - u(q_1^*) + p_1^* q_1^* - p_1 q_1.$$

Thus, for a quasilinear utility function, $CV = EV$.

4. *Show that her change in consumer surplus equals the other two measures.* Because $|\Delta CS|$ lies between $|EV|$ and $|CV|$, if $EV = CV$, then $|EV| = |CV| = |\Delta CS|$.

Comment: We noted earlier that $|CV| > |\Delta CS| > |EV|$ for a normal good (the quantity demanded rises with income) and that $|CV| < |\Delta CS| < |EV|$ for an inferior good (the quantity demanded falls with income). With a quasilinear utility function, a change in income does not affect the quantity demanded of the first good if both goods are consumed (see Table 4.1), so $|CV| = |\Delta CS| = |EV|$.

5.3 Effects of Government Policies on Consumer Welfare

Economists use the various consumer welfare measures to answer questions about the effect on consumers of government programs and other events that shift consumers' budget constraints. If the government imposes a quota, which reduces the number of units that a consumer buys, or provides a consumer with a certain amount of a good (such as food), the government creates a kink in the consumer's budget constraint. In contrast, if the government subsidizes the price of a good (such as a childcare subsidy) or provides cash to the consumer, it causes a rotation or a parallel shift of the budget line.

Quotas

Consumers' welfare falls if they cannot buy as many units of a good as they want. As a promotion, firms often sell a good at an unusually low price but limit the number of units that one can purchase. Governments, too, frequently limit how much of a good one can buy by setting a quota.

During emergencies, for example, governments sometimes ration "essential" goods such as water, food, energy, and flu vaccines rather than let the prices of these goods rise. In the past few years, governments imposed water quotas in the United Kingdom, Fiji, China, Cyprus, Australia, and the United States (California, Georgia, Massachusetts, North Carolina, Oklahoma, and Texas). In recent years, the United States, the United Kingdom, China, and other countries limited or considered limiting energy use. Also, in recent years, the United States and many nations rationed bird, swine, and other flu vaccines.

To illustrate the effect of a quota, we return to Jackie's choice between music tracks and live music. In Figure 5.5, we divide Jackie's downward-sloping budget constraint into two line segments, L^1 and L^2. Without a quota, her optimal bundle occurs where L^2 is tangent to I^1 at e_1, which consists of 24 tracks and 18 units of live music per quarter.

Figure 5.5 The Equivalent Variation of a Quota

Originally, Jackie faces a budget constraint consisting of the line segments L^1 and L^2 and buys 24 song tracks and 18 units of live music at e_1 on indifference curve I^1. When a quota limits purchases of tracks to 12 per quarter (vertical line at 12), the L^2 segment is no longer available and the shaded triangle, A, is lost from the opportunity set. The best that Jackie can do now is to purchase e_2 on indifference curve I^2. Suppose that Jackie did not face a quota but lost an amount of income equal to EV that caused her budget constraint to shift down to L^3, which is tangent to indifference curve I^2 at e_3. Thus, the effect on her utility of losing EV amount of income—shifting her from I^1 to I^2—is equivalent to the effect of the quota.

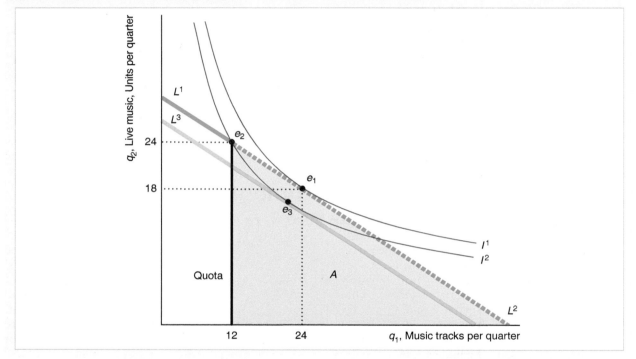

Now suppose that a government (or her mother) limits Jackie's purchases to no more than 12 tracks per quarter. Her new budget constraint is the same as the original for fewer than 12 tracks, L^1, and is vertical at 12 tracks. She loses part of the original opportunity set: the shaded triangle, area A, determined by the vertical line at 12 tracks, L^2, and the horizontal axis. Now, her best option is to purchase Bundle e_2—12 tracks and 24 units of live music—which is the highest point where the indifference curve I^2 touches the new constraint. However, I^2 is not tangent to the budget constraint. Thus, with a quota, a consumer could have an interior solution in which she buys some of all the goods, but the tangency condition does not hold because the limit causes a kink in the budget constraint (as in the corner solution in Chapter 3).

The quota harms Jackie because she is now on indifference curve I^2, which is below her original indifference curve, I^1. To determine by how much the quota harms her, we calculate her equivalent variation: the amount of money we would have to take from Jackie to harm her as much as the quota does. We draw a budget line, L^3, that is parallel to L^2 but that just barely touches I^2. The difference between the expenditure on the original budget line and the new expenditure is Jackie's equivalent variation.

We can use her expenditure function, Equation 5.3, $E \approx 1.96\overline{U}p_1^{0.4}$, to determine the expenditure on L^3. Substituting $p_1 = £0.5$ and her utility on I^2 at e_2, $\overline{U} = 12^{0.4}24^{0.6} \approx 18.19$, into her expenditure function, we find that her expenditure on L^3 is about £27. Because her original expenditure was £30, Jackie's equivalent variation is £30 − £27 = £3, which is 10% of her expenditure.

Food Stamps

I've known what it is to be hungry, but I always went right to a restaurant.
—Ring Lardner

We can use the theory of consumer choice to analyze whether poor people are better off receiving food or a comparable amount of cash. Poor U.S. households that meet income, asset, and employment eligibility requirements may receive coupons—food stamps—that they can use to purchase food from retail stores.

The U.S. Food Stamp Plan started in 1939. It was renamed the Food Stamp Program in 1964 and the Supplemental Nutrition Assistance Program (SNAP) in 2008. SNAP is one of the nation's largest social welfare programs, with nearly 42 million people (one in seven U.S. residents) receiving food stamps at a cost of $68 billion in 2017. The average benefits were $126 per person per month or $4.20 per day. The share of food-at-home spending funded by SNAP is between 10% and 16% overall and 50% for low-income households (Beatty and Tuttle, 2015).

In 2018, the U.S. Department of Agriculture reported that over half of SNAP participants were children, adults age 60 or older, or disabled nonelderly adults. By the time they reach 20 years of age, half of all Americans and 90% of African American children have received food stamps, at least briefly.[6]

Since the food stamp programs started, economists, nutritionists, and policymakers have debated "cashing out" food stamps by providing cash instead of coupons (or the modern equivalent, which is a debit card) that can be spent only on food. Legally, recipients may not sell food stamps (though a black market for them exists). Because of technological advances in electronic fund transfers, switching from food stamps to a cash program would lower administrative costs and reduce losses due to fraud and theft.

Would a switch to a comparable cash subsidy instead of food stamps increase the well-being of people who receive food assistance? Would recipients spend less on food and more on other goods?

Poor people who receive cash have more choices than those who receive a comparable amount of food stamps. With cash, recipients could buy either food or other goods—not just food, as with food stamps. As a result, a cash grant increases a recipient's opportunity set by more than do food stamps of the same value. Following this reasoning, many people overgeneralize about how many people would benefit from cash.

Common Confusion Most poor people would be better off with cash than with food stamps.

---

[6]According to Professor Mark Rank (Jason DeParle and Robert Gebeloff, "The Safety Net: Food Stamp Use Soars, and Stigma Fades," *New York Times*, November 29, 2009).

Figure 5.6 Food Stamps Versus Cash

The lighter line shows Felicity's original budget line given an income of Y per month. The heavier line shows her budget constraint with $100 worth of food stamps. The budget constraint with a grant of $100 in cash is a line between Y + 100 on both axes. The opportunity set increases by area B with food stamps but by B + C with cash. Given these indifference curves, Felicity consumes Bundle d (with less than 100 units of food) with no subsidy, e (Y units of all other goods and 100 units of food) with food stamps, and f (more than Y units of all other goods and less than 100 units of food) with a cash subsidy. Her utility is greater with a cash subsidy than with food stamps.

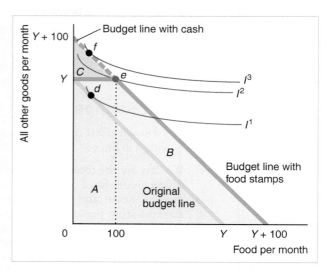

People are better off with cash only if the amount of food stamps they receive exceeds what they would spend on food if they had received cash instead, which is not true for most food stamp recipients. In Figure 5.6, one unit of food and one unit of all other goods each has a price of $1. Felicity has a monthly income of Y, so her budget line hits both axes at Y. Her opportunity set is area A.

If Felicity receives a subsidy of $100 in cash per month, her new monthly income is Y + $100. Her new budget constraint with cash hits both axes at Y + 100 and is parallel to the original budget constraint. Her opportunity set increases by B + C to A + B + C.

If, instead, Felicity receives $100 worth of food stamps, her food stamp budget constraint has a kink. Because she can use the food stamps only to buy food, her budget constraint shifts 100 units to the right for any quantity of other goods up to Y units. For example, if Felicity buys only food, she can purchase Y + 100 units of food. If she buys only other goods with the original Y income, she can get Y units of other goods plus 100 units of food. Because the food stamps cannot be turned into other goods, Felicity can't buy Y + 100 units of other goods, as she can under a cash-transfer program. The food stamps opportunity set is area A + B, which is larger than the pre-subsidy opportunity set by B. The opportunity set with food stamps is smaller than with the cash-transfer program by C.

Felicity benefits as much from cash or an equivalent amount of food stamps if she would have spent at least $100 on food if given cash. In other words, she is indifferent between cash and food stamps if her indifference curve is tangent to the downward-sloping section of the food stamp budget constraint. Here, the equivalent variation is $100.

Conversely, if she would spend less than $100 on food if given cash, she prefers receiving cash to food stamps. Given that she has the indifference curves in Figure 5.6, she prefers cash to food stamps. She chooses Bundle e (Y units of all other goods and 100 units of food) if she receives food stamps, but Bundle f (more than Y units of all other goods and less than 100 units of food) if she is given cash. She is on a higher indifference curve, I^2 rather than I^1, if given cash rather than food stamps. If we draw a budget line with the same slope as the original one (−1) that is tangent to I^2, we can calculate the equivalent variation as the difference between the expenditure on that budget line and the original one. The equivalent variation is less than $100.

Your food stamps will be stopped effective March 1992 because we received notice that you passed away. May God bless you. You may reapply if there is a change in your circumstances. —Department of Social Services, Greeneville, South Carolina

Consumer theory predicts that if the government were to give poor people an equivalent amount of cash instead of food stamps, their utility would remain the same or rise and some recipients would consume less food and more of other goods.

Whitmore (2002) estimated that between 20% and 30% of food stamp recipients would be better off if they were given cash instead of an equivalent value in food stamps. They would spend less on food than their food stamp benefit amount if they received cash instead of stamps, and therefore would be better off with cash. Of those who would trade their food stamps for cash, the average food stamp recipient values the stamps at 80% of their face value (although the average price on the underground economy is only 65%). Across all such recipients, giving food stamps rather than cash wasted $500 million.

Hoynes and Schanzenbach (2009) found that food stamps result in a decrease in out-of-pocket expenditures on food and an increase in overall food expenditures. For those households that would prefer cash to food stamps—those that spend relatively little of their income on food—food stamps cause them to increase their food consumption by about 22%, compared to 15% for other recipients, and 18% overall. Bruich (2014) estimated that each extra $1 of SNAP leads to 37¢ more in grocery store spending.

Lusk and Weaver (2017) examined the effects of giving food versus cash with a controlled experiment. They found that the 82% of subjects who would spend the cash on food behaved the same with either in-kind or cash transfers. However, for the other subjects, in-kind transfers increase food expenditures eight times more than an equivalent cash transfer.

5.4 Deriving Labor Supply Curves

So far, we've used consumer theory to examine consumers' demand behavior. Perhaps surprisingly, we can also apply the consumer theory model to derive a person's supply curve of labor. We start by using consumer theory to obtain the person's demand curve for leisure time. Then, we use that demand curve to derive the supply curve, which shows the hours the individual wants to work as a function of the wage. We then use our labor supply model to analyze how a change in the income tax rate affects the supply of labor and the revenue that the government collects.

Labor-Leisure Choice

The human race faces a cruel choice: work or daytime television.

People choose between working to earn money to buy goods and services and consuming *leisure*: all their time spent not working for pay. In addition to sleeping, eating, and playing, leisure—or more accurately nonwork, *N*—includes time spent cooking meals and fixing things around the house.

Hugo spends his total income, Y, on various goods. For simplicity, we assume that the price of these goods is \$1 per unit, so he buys Y goods. His utility, U, depends on how much leisure, N, and how many goods, Y, he consumes:

$$U = U(N, Y). \tag{5.6}$$

He faces an hours-worked constraint and an income constraint. The number of hours he works per day, H, equals 24 minus the hours he spends on leisure:

$$H = 24 - N. \tag{5.7}$$

The total income, Y, that Hugo has to spend on goods equals his earned income—his wage times the number of hours he works, wH—and his unearned income, Y^*, such as income from an inheritance or a gift from his parents:

$$Y = wH + Y^*. \tag{5.8}$$

Using consumer theory, we can determine Hugo's demand curve for leisure once we know the price of leisure. What does your time cost you if you watch TV, go to school, or do anything other than work for an hour? It costs you the wage, w, you could have earned from an hour's work: The price of leisure is forgone earnings, which is the opportunity cost of not working. The higher your wage, the more an hour of leisure costs you. Taking an afternoon off costs a lawyer who earns \$250 an hour much more than it costs a fast-food server who earns the minimum wage.

Panel a of Figure 5.7 shows Hugo's choice between leisure and goods. The vertical axis shows how many goods, Y, Hugo buys. The horizontal axis shows both hours of leisure, N, which we measure from left to right, and hours of work, H, which we measure from right to left. Hugo maximizes his utility given the *two* constraints he faces. First, he faces a time constraint, which is a vertical line at 24 hours of leisure. Because a day has only 24 hours, not all the money in the world will buy him more time. Second, Hugo faces a budget constraint. Because Hugo has no unearned income, his initial budget constraint, L^1, is $Y = w_1 H = w_1(24 - N)$. The slope of his budget constraint is $-w_1$, because each extra hour of leisure he consumes costs him w_1 goods.

If I get less than 8 hours sleep, I stay awake for more than 16 hours.

Hugo picks his optimal hours of leisure, $N_1 = 16$, so he is on the highest indifference curve, I^1, that touches his budget constraint. He works $H_1 = 24 - N_1 = 8$ hours per day and earns an income of $Y_1 = w_1 H_1 = 8w_1$.

We derive Hugo's demand curve for leisure using the same method by which we derived Mimi's demand curve for beer in Chapter 4. We raise the price of leisure—the wage—in panel a of Figure 5.7 to trace Hugo's demand curve for leisure in panel b. As the wage increases from w_1 to w_2, leisure becomes more expensive, and Hugo demands less of it.

We can also solve this problem using calculus. Hugo maximizes his utility, Equation 5.6, subject to the time constraint, Equation 5.7, and the income constraint, Equation 5.8. Although we can analyze this problem using the Lagrangian method, it is easier to do so by substitution. Substituting Equations 5.7 and 5.8 into 5.6 to replace N, we convert his constrained problem into an unconstrained maximization problem, where Hugo maximizes his utility through his choice of how many hours to work per day:

$$\max_{H} U = U(N, Y) = U(24 - H, wH). \tag{5.9}$$

Figure 5.7 The Demand Curve for Leisure

(a) Hugo chooses between leisure, N, and other goods, Y, subject to a time constraint (the vertical line at 24 hours) and a budget constraint, L^1, which is $Y = w_1H = w_1 \times (24 - N)$, and has a slope of $-w_1$. The tangency of his indifference curve I^1 with his budget constraint L^1 determines his optimal bundle, e_1, where he has $N_1 = 16$ hours of leisure and works $H_1 = 24 - N_1 = 8$ hours. If his wage rises from w_1 to w_2, Hugo shifts from optimal bundle e_1 to e_2. (b) Bundles e_1 and e_2 correspond to E_1 and E_2 on his leisure demand curve.

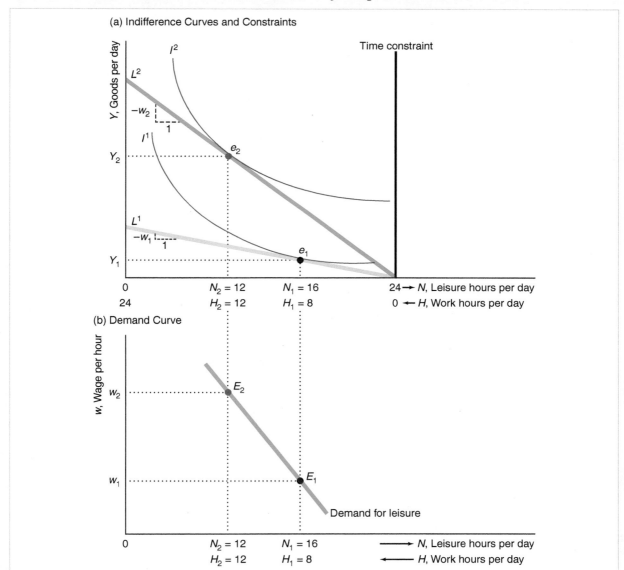

By using the chain rule of differentiation, we obtain the first-order condition for an interior maximum to the problem in Equation 5.9,

$$\frac{\partial U}{\partial N}\frac{dN}{dH} + \frac{\partial U}{\partial Y}\frac{dY}{dH} = -U_N + wU_Y = 0, \tag{5.10}$$

Figure 5.8 The Labor Supply Curve

(a) Hugo's demand for leisure is downward sloping. (b) At any given wage, the number of hours that Hugo works, H, and the number of hours of leisure, N, that he consumes

add to 24. Thus, his supply curve for hours worked, which equals 24 hours minus the number of hours of leisure he demands, is upward sloping.

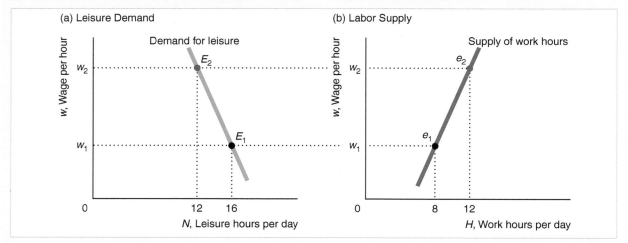

where $U_Y \equiv \partial U / \partial Y$ is the marginal utility of goods or income and $U_N \equiv \partial U / \partial N$ is the marginal utility of leisure. Rearranging Equation 5.10, we find that Hugo sets his marginal rate of substitution of income for leisure, $MRS = -U_N / U_Y$, equal to his marginal rate of transformation of income for leisure, $MRT = -w$, in the market:

$$MRS = -\frac{U_N}{N_Y} = -w = MRT. \tag{5.11}$$

We can rewrite Equation 5.11 as $U_N / w = U_Y$. That is, Hugo should choose his hours of leisure such that the last dollar's worth of leisure, U_N / w, equals his marginal utility from the last dollar's worth of goods, U_Y.

By subtracting Hugo's demand for hours of leisure at each wage—his demand curve for leisure in panel a of Figure 5.8—from 24, we obtain his labor supply curve—the hours he is willing to work as a function of the wage, $H(w)$—in panel b. His supply curve for hours worked is the mirror image of the demand curve for leisure: For every extra hour of leisure that Hugo consumes, he works one hour less.

SOLVED PROBLEM 5.3

MyLab Economics
Solved Problem

If Sofia has a Cobb-Douglas utility function, $U(N, Y) = (24 - H)^{1-a}(wH)^a$, what is her labor supply function? What is her supply function if $a = \frac{1}{3}$?

Answer

1. *To find the values that maximize her utility, set the derivative of Sofia's utility function with respect to H equal to zero.* Sofia's first-order condition is a special case of Equation 5.10:

   $$-U_N + wU_Y = -(1 - a)(wH)^a(24 - H)^{-a} + wa(wH)^{a-1}(24 - H)^{1-a} = 0.$$

   Simplifying, we find that $H = 24a$. Thus, Sofia works a fixed number of hours regardless of the wage.

2. *Substitute in the value $a = \frac{1}{3}$ to obtain the specific hours-worked function.* If $a = \frac{1}{3}$, she works $H = 8$ hours a day regardless of whether the wage is 50¢ or $50 per hour.

Figure 5.9 The Income and Substitution Effects of a Wage Change

A wage change causes both a substitution and an income effect. As the wage rises, Hugo's optimal bundle changes from e_1 to e_2. The movement from e_1 to e^* is the substitution effect, the movement from e^* to e_2 is the income effect, and the movement from e_1 to e_2 is the total effect. The compensating variation is $Y^* - Y_2$.

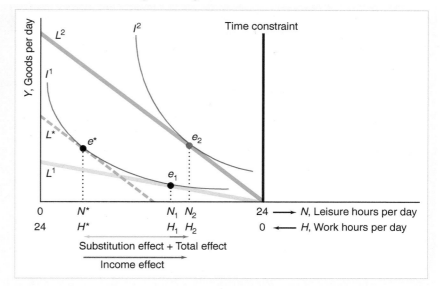

Income and Substitution Effects

An increase in the wage causes both income and substitution effects, which alter an individual's demand for leisure and supply of hours worked. The *total effect* of an increase in Hugo's wage from w_1 to w_2 is the movement from e_1 to e_2 in Figure 5.9. Hugo works $H_2 - H_1$ fewer hours and consumes $N_2 - N_1$ more hours of leisure.

By drawing an imaginary budget constraint, L^*, that is tangent to Hugo's original indifference curve and has the slope of the new wage, we can divide the total effect into substitution and income effects. The *substitution effect*, the movement from e_1 to e^*, must be negative: A compensating wage increase causes Hugo to consume fewer hours of leisure, N^*, and to work more hours, H^*. As his wage rises, if Hugo works the same number of hours as before, he has a higher income. The *income effect* is the movement from e^* to e_2. The figure shows that his income effect is positive—he consumes more leisure as his income rises—because he views leisure as a normal good.

When leisure is a normal good, the substitution and income effects work in opposite directions because an increase in the price of leisure (the wage) increases his income. Which effect dominates depends on the relative size of the two effects. In Figure 5.9, Hugo's income effect dominates the substitution effect, so the total effect for leisure is positive: $N_2 > N_1$. Given that the total number of hours in a day is fixed, if Hugo consumes more leisure when his wage rises, then he must work fewer hours. That is, his supply curve is downward sloping, so that it has the opposite slope of the one in panel b of Figure 5.8. (Such a supply curve is often referred to as *backward bending*.) Alternatively, if Hugo were to view leisure as an inferior good, both his substitution effect and income effect would work in the same direction, so that an increase in the wage would cause his hours of leisure to fall and his work hours to rise (as in Figure 5.8).

In Figure 5.9, by removing $Y^* - Y_2$ income from Hugo, we could offset the benefit of the wage increase by keeping him on indifference curve I^1. Thus, $Y^* - Y_2$ is the compensating variation.

**SOLVED PROBLEM
5.4**

Enrico receives a no-strings-attached scholarship that pays him an extra Y^* per day. How does this scholarship affect the number of hours he wants to work? Does his utility increase?

MyLab Economics
Solved Problem

Answer

1. *Show his consumer equilibrium before he receives the scholarship.* When Enrico had no unearned income from the scholarship, his budget constraint, L^1 in the graphs, hit the hours-leisure axis at 0 hours and had a slope of $-w$.

2. *Show how the unearned income affects his budget constraint.* The extra income causes a parallel upward shift of his budget constraint by Y^*. His new budget constraint, L^2, has the same slope as before, $-w$, because his wage does not change. The extra income cannot buy Enrico more time, of course, so L^2 cannot extend to the right of the time constraint. It hits the vertical time constraint at Y^*: If he works no hours, he has Y^* income.

3. *Show that the relative position of the new to the original equilibrium depends on his tastes.* The change in the number of hours he works depends on Enrico's tastes. Panels a and b show two possible sets of indifference curves. In both diagrams, when facing budget constraint L^1, Enrico chooses to work H_1 hours. In panel a, leisure is a normal good, so as his income rises, Enrico consumes more leisure: He moves from Bundle e_1 to Bundle e_2. In panel b, he views leisure as an inferior good and consumes fewer hours of leisure than at first: He moves from e_1 to e_3. (Another possibility is that the number of hours he works is unaffected by the extra unearned income.)

4. *Discuss how his utility changes.* Regardless of his tastes, Enrico has more income in the new equilibrium and is on a higher indifference curve after receiving the scholarship. In short, he believes that more money is better than less.

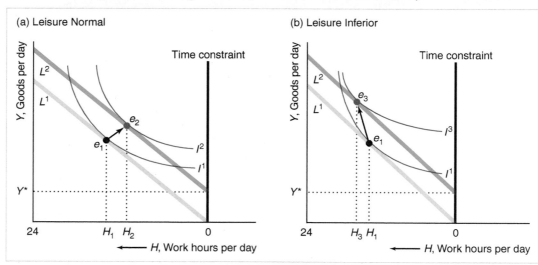

APPLICATION

Fracking Causes
Students to Drop Out

For many young people, attending high schools, colleges, universities, graduate schools, or technical schools is a major nonwork activity. However, as opportunities change, people change their allocation of time between work and schooling.

Over the past decade and a half, U.S. oil firms greatly increased the use of hydraulic fracturing (*fracking*) to extract oil and natural gas.[7] To operate these new fracking oil wells, firms significantly increased their demand for low-education, primarily male workers. The resulting higher wages for many male teens raised the opportunity cost of an education, making working more attractive than finishing high school.

Cascio and Narayan (2017) compared teens' education choices in areas with fracking firms to those in areas without fracking firms. They estimated that in areas with fracking firms, the gap in the high school dropout rate between 17- and 18-year-old men and women was 11% larger. That is, the opportunity of working for fracking companies caused relatively more young men than young women to drop out of high school.

SOLVED PROBLEM 5.5

MyLab Economics Solved Problem

Lance lives in Williston, North Dakota. The firms in town, such as the Walmart, pay teenagers without a high school degree the federal minimum wage of $7.25 an hour. Because his parents provide him Y^* (mostly in the form of room and board), Lance chooses to stay in school and not work. However, a new fracking firm starts production nearby so the wage rises to three times the minimum wage. Use a labor-leisure choice figure to show why he does not work initially but then works a substantial number of hours at the higher wage.

Answer

1. *Draw Lance's original budget constraint and show that he does not choose to work.* His initial budget constraint, L^1, meets the time constraint at Y^* and has a slope of $-\$7.25$. He maximizes his utility in a corner solution (see Chapter 3), where his indifference curve I^1 touches his budget constraint L^1 at e_1, where he does not work: $H_1 = 0$.

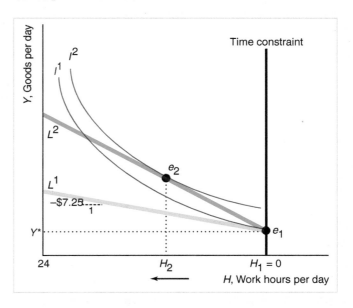

---

[7]Most new U.S. oil wells use fracking: pumping pressurized liquid consisting of water, sand, and chemicals to fracture oil shale (rock containing oil), which releases natural gas and oil.

2. *Draw Lance's new budget constraint after the fracking firm starts hiring and show that he chooses to work.* His new budget constraint, L^2, has three times the slope of his original constraint, L^1, and hits the time constraint at Y^*. His highest indifference curve that is tangent to L^2 is I^2 at e_2, where he works a positive number of hours, H_2.

Shape of the Labor Supply Curve

Whether the labor supply curve slopes upward, downward, or has both upward and downward sloping sections depends on the income elasticity of leisure. Suppose that a worker views leisure as an inferior good at low wages and a normal good at high wages. As the wage increases, the worker's demand for leisure first falls and then rises, and the hours supplied to the market first rise and then fall so that the labor supply curve is backward bending. (Alternatively, the labor supply curve may slope upward and then backward even if leisure is normal at all wages: At low wages, the substitution effect—working more hours—dominates the income effect—working fewer hours—while the opposite occurs at higher wages.)

The budget line rotates upward from L^1 to L^2 as the wage rises in panel a of Figure 5.10. Because leisure is an inferior good at low incomes, in the new optimal bundle, e_2, this worker consumes less leisure and buys more goods than at the original bundle, e_1. At higher incomes, however, leisure is a normal good. At an even higher wage, the new equilibrium is e_3 on budget line L^3, where the quantity of leisure demanded is higher and the number of hours worked is lower. Thus, the corresponding supply curve for labor slopes upward at low wages and bends backward at higher wages in panel b.

Do labor supply curves slope upward or backward? Economic theory alone cannot answer this question, as both forward-sloping and backward-bending supply curves are *theoretically* possible. Empirical research is necessary to resolve this question.

Figure 5.10 A Labor Supply Curve That Slopes Upward and Then Bends Backward

At low incomes, an increase in the wage causes the worker to work more hours: the movement from e_1 to e_2 in panel a or from E_1 to E_2 in panel b. At higher incomes, an increase in the wage causes the worker to work fewer hours: the movement from e_2 to e_3 or from E_2 to E_3.

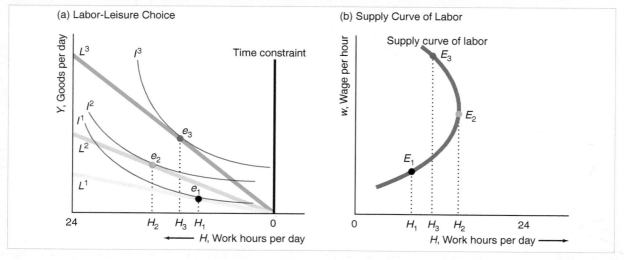

Most studies (see Keane, 2011; Kuroda and Yamamoto, 2008; and Evers, De Mooij, and Van Vuuren, 2008) find that the labor supply curves for U.S., U.K., Japanese, and Dutch men are relatively vertical because the income and the substitution effects are offsetting or both are small. Keane's average across all studies of U.S. and U.K. males' pure substitution wage elasticity for hours worked is about 0.31 (although most of the estimates are below 0.15). Most studies (see Keane's survey) find that the long-run wage elasticity estimates for females range from 1.25 to 5.6. That is, when the wage increases, men hardly change how many hours they work, whereas women work substantially more hours.

Income Tax Rates and the Labor Supply Curve

Why do we care about the shape of labor supply curves? One reason is that we can tell from the shape of the labor supply curve whether an increase in the income tax rate—a percentage of earnings—will cause a substantial reduction in the hours of work and possibly reduce tax revenues.

Various U.S. presidents have advocated tax cuts. Presidents John Kennedy, Lyndon Johnson, Ronald Reagan, and George W. Bush argued that cutting the *marginal tax rate*—the percentage of the last dollar earned that the government takes in taxes—would induce people to work longer and produce more, both desirable effects. They were pointing out an unintended effect of raising tax revenue through an income tax:

Unintended Consequence An income tax may reduce the hours that people work and hence reduce national output.

In addition, President Reagan predicted that the government's tax receipts would increase due to the additional work. Years of such claims by politicians has led to the belief among many that tax cuts must increase tax revenue:

Common Confusion Cutting the income tax rate increases tax revenue.

Although such cuts theoretically could increase tax revenue, little evidence exists to suggest that they have increased U.S. tax revenue.

We will examine the theory behind both the hours and revenue effects of changes in the income tax rate. An increase in the income tax rate lowers workers' after-tax wages. If people's supply curves are upward sloping, a small increase in the wage tax rate reduces hours worked, decreases production, and may lower the tax revenue collected. In contrast, if workers' supply curves are backward bending, a small rise in the tax rate increases hours worked (reducing leisure hours), boosts production, and increases the tax revenue collected.

As we've already discussed, most studies of labor supply curves conclude that males' labor supply curves are virtually vertical, so that a tax rate cut should have no effect on their hours worked and thus must reduce tax revenue. Because women's labor supply curves are upward sloping, a tax cut should increase their hours and might raise tax revenue.

Because tax rates have changed substantially over time, we have a natural experiment to test the tax-revenue hypothesis. The figure shows how the top U.S. federal marginal tax rate fell over time. It was 91% from World War II until the early 1960s.

Top U.S. Federal Marginal Income Tax Rate (%)

The Kennedy-Johnson tax cuts lowered this rate to 70% and other rates fell, too. A sequence of Reagan tax cuts lowered it to 28% by 1988. Today, it is 37%.[8]

If the tax does not affect the pre-tax wage, the effect of imposing a constant tax rate of $v = 25\% = 0.25$ is to reduce the effective wage from w to $(1 - v)w = 0.75w$. The tax reduces the after-tax wage by 25%, so a worker's budget constraint rotates downward, similar to rotating the budget constraint downward from L^2 to L^1 in Figure 5.10.

As we discussed, if the budget constraint rotates downward, the hours of work may increase or decrease, depending on whether a person considers leisure to be a normal or an inferior good. The worker in panel b of Figure 5.10 has a labor supply curve that at first slopes upward and then bends backward. If the worker's wage is very high, the worker is in the backward-bending section of the labor supply curve.

If so, the relationship between the marginal tax rate, v, and tax revenue, vwH, is bell-shaped, as in Figure 5.11. This figure is the estimated U.S. tax revenue curve (Trabandt and Uhlig, 2011, 2013). At the marginal rate for the typical person, $v = 28\%$, the government collects 100% of the amount of tax revenue it's currently collecting.[9] At a zero tax rate, a small increase in the tax rate *must* increase the tax revenue because no revenue was collected when the tax rate was zero. However, if the tax rate rises a little more, the tax revenue collected must rise even higher, for two reasons: First, the government collects a larger percentage of every dollar earned because the tax rate is higher. Second, employees work more hours as the tax rate rises because workers are in the backward-bending sections of their labor supply curves.

---

[8]Of more concern to individuals than the federal marginal tax rate is the *all-inclusive tax rate* that combines the income taxes collected by all levels of government. According to the Organization for Economic Cooperation and Development, the all-inclusive marginal tax rate in 2017 on the highest earners was 32% in Switzerland, 35% in Japan, 40% in Canada, 42% in Australia, 44% in the United States, 49% in the United Kingdom, 60% in France, 63% in Italy, 68% in Belgium, and 70% in Sweden. Thus, among high-income countries, the U.S. rate is in the middle of the pack. Those European countries with substantially higher marginal tax rates typically provide more services to their citizens and welfare transfers than does the United States.

[9]A 2012 and a 2017 University of Chicago Booth School of Business poll of 80 distinguished economists (including Republicans, Independents, and Democrats) did not find a single economist who believed that a U.S. tax cut would cause tax revenue to rise.

Figure 5.11 The Relationship of U.S. Tax Revenue to the Marginal Tax Rate

This curve shows how U.S. income tax revenue varies with the marginal income tax rate, v, according to Trabandt and Uhlig (2011). The typical person paid $v = 28\%$, which corresponds to 100% of the current tax revenue that the government collects. The tax revenue would be maximized at 130% of its current level if the marginal rate were set at $v^* = 63\%$. For rates below v^*, an increase in the marginal rate raises larger tax revenue. However, at rates above v^*, an increase in the marginal rate decreases tax revenue.

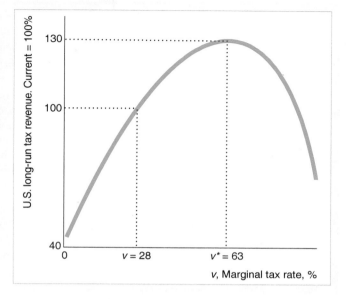

As the marginal rate increases, tax revenue rises until the marginal rate reaches $v^* = 63\%$, where the U.S. tax revenue would be 130% of its current level.[10] If the marginal tax rate increases more, workers are in the upward-sloping sections of their labor supply curves, so an increase in the tax rate reduces the number of hours worked. When the tax rate rises high enough, the reduction in hours worked more than offsets the gain from the higher rate, so the tax revenue falls.

It makes little sense for a government to operate at very high marginal tax rates in the downward-sloping portion of this bell-shaped curve. The government could get more output *and* more tax revenue by cutting the marginal tax rate.

SOLVED PROBLEM 5.6

MyLab Economics
Solved Problem

Suppose a worker's wage is w and the marginal income tax rate, v, is constant, so $\underline{w} = (1 - v)w$ is the worker's after-tax wage, and the worker supplies $H([1 - v]w) = H(\underline{w})$ hours of work. What is the effect of an increase in v on the tax revenue collected? Show that the change in tax revenue in response to an increase in v depends on a direct effect of a higher tax rate and the labor supply response to a higher tax rate. For what elasticity of supply of labor does tax revenue rise if v falls?

Answer

1. *Determine the government's tax revenue.* The government's tax revenue, T, is v times a worker's earnings (the wage, w, times the hours worked):

    $$T = vwH([1 - v]w) = vwH(\underline{w}). \qquad (5.12)$$

---

[10]On average for 14 European Union countries, v is also less than v^*, but raising the rate to v^* would raise European tax revenue by only 8% (Trabandt and Uhlig, 2011).

2. *By differentiating Equation 5.12 with respect to v, show how the tax revenue changes as the tax rate increases.* Using the product rule and the chain rule, the change in T as v increases is

$$\frac{dT}{dv} = wH(\underline{w}) + vw\,\frac{dH}{d\underline{w}}\,\frac{d\underline{w}}{dv} = wH(\underline{w}) - vw^2\,\frac{dH}{d\underline{w}}. \tag{5.13}$$

3. *Show that dT/dv reflects both a direct tax effect and labor supply response.* Equation 5.13 shows that a change in the tax rate has two effects. First, the government collects more revenue because of the higher tax rate: A one-unit increase in v causes the tax revenue to increase by $wH(\underline{w})$, the amount that the worker earns. Second, the change in the tax alters the hours worked. As the rate goes up, before-tax labor earnings, $wH(\underline{w})$, decrease if the labor supply is upward sloping, $dH/d\underline{w} > 0$, which reduces the tax revenue by $vw^2 dH/d\underline{w}$.

4. *Determine a condition under which tax revenue rises when the tax rate falls.* According to Equation 5.13, for the tax revenue to rise when the tax rate decreases (or to decrease when the tax rate increases), we need $dT/dv = wH(\underline{w}) - vw^2 dH/d\underline{w} < 0$. Using algebra, we can rewrite this condition as

$$\frac{1}{v} < \frac{dH}{d\underline{w}}\,\frac{w}{H(\underline{w})}. \tag{5.14}$$

5. *Express the condition in Equation 5.14 in terms of the elasticity of supply of labor.* If we multiply both sides of Equation 5.14 by $(1 - v)$, we obtain the condition that

$$\frac{1 - v}{v} < \frac{dH}{d\underline{w}}\,\frac{(1 - v)w}{H(\underline{w})} = \frac{dH}{d\underline{w}}\,\frac{w}{H(\underline{w})} = \eta. \tag{5.15}$$

where $\eta = [dH/d\underline{w}][\underline{w}/H(\underline{w})]$ is the elasticity of supply of work hours with respect to after-tax wages, $\underline{w}$.

Comment: Thus, for the tax revenue the government collects to rise from a small decrease in the tax rate, the elasticity of supply of labor must be greater than $(1 - v)/v$. In the United States in 2018, a single person with taxable income between \$38,701 and \$82,500 had a marginal tax rate of $v = 22\%$. For a small decrease in this rate to raise the tax revenue collected, such a person's η had to be greater than $0.78/0.22 \approx 3.5$, which is not likely. In the past, before the Kennedy-era tax cuts, the top U.S. marginal tax rate was $v = 91\%$. For this rate, the condition is met if the elasticity of supply is greater than about 0.11.

CHALLENGE SOLUTION

Per-Hour Versus Lump-Sum Childcare Subsidies

We now return to the questions raised in the Challenge at the beginning of the chapter: For a given government expenditure, does a childcare price subsidy or a lump-sum subsidy provide greater benefit to recipients? Which increases the demand for childcare services by more? Which inflicts less cost on other consumers of childcare?

To determine which program benefits recipients more, we employ a model of consumer choice. The figure shows a poor family that chooses between hours of childcare per day (Q) and all other goods per day. Given that the price of all other goods is \$1 per unit, the expenditure on all other goods is the income, Y, not spent on

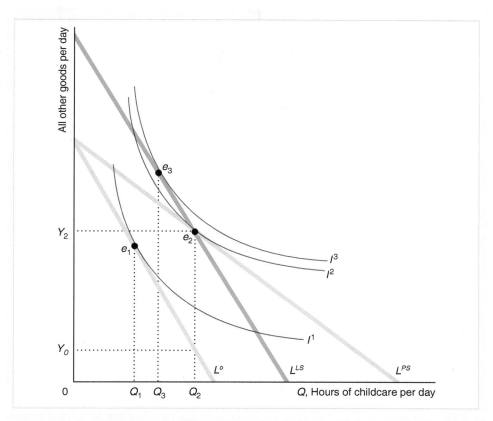

childcare. The family's original budget constraint is L^o. The family chooses Bundle e_1 on indifference curve I^1, where the family consumes Q_1 hours of childcare services.

If the government gives a childcare price subsidy, the new budget line, L^{PS}, rotates out along the childcare axis. Now the family consumes Bundle e_2 on (higher) indifference curve I^2. The family consumes more hours of childcare, Q_2, because childcare is now less expensive and it is a normal good.

One way to measure the value of the subsidy the family receives is to calculate how many *other goods* the family could buy before and after the subsidy. If the family consumes Q_2 hours of childcare, the family could have consumed Y_o other goods with the original budget constraint and Y_2 with the price-subsidy budget constraint. Given that Y_2 is the family's remaining income after paying for childcare, the family buys Y_2 units of all other goods. Thus, the value to the family of the childcare price subsidy is $Y_2 - Y_o$.

If, instead of receiving a childcare price subsidy, the family were to receive a lump-sum payment of $Y_2 - Y_o$, taxpayers' costs for the two programs would be the same. The family's budget constraint after receiving a lump-sum payment, L^{LS}, has the same slope as the original one, L^o, because the relative prices of childcare and all other goods are unchanged from their original levels. This budget constraint must go through e_2 because the family has just enough money to buy that bundle. However, given this budget constraint, the family would be better off if it buys Bundle e_3 on indifference curve I^3 (the reasoning is the same as that in the Chapter 4 Challenge Solution and the Consumer Price Index analysis in Figure 4.7). The family consumes less childcare with the lump-sum subsidy than with the price subsidy, Q_3 rather than Q_2, but more than it originally did, Q_1.

Poor families prefer the lump-sum payment to the price subsidy because indifference curve I^3 is above I^2. Taxpayers are indifferent between the two programs because they both cost the same. The childcare industry prefers the price subsidy because the demand curve for its service is farther to the right: At any given price, more childcare is demanded by poor families who receive a price subsidy rather than a lump-sum subsidy.

Given that most of the directly affected groups benefit more from lump-sum payments than price subsidies, why are price subsidies more heavily used? One possible explanation is that the childcare industry has very effectively lobbied for price subsidies; however, little such lobbying has occurred. Second, politicians might believe that poor families will not make intelligent choices about childcare, so they might see price subsidies as a way of getting such families to consume relatively more (or better-quality) childcare than they would otherwise choose. Third, politicians may prefer that poor people consume more childcare so that they can work more hours, thereby increasing society's wealth. Fourth, politicians may not understand this analysis.

SUMMARY

1. **Uncompensated Consumer Welfare.** The pleasure a consumer receives from a good in excess of its cost is called *consumer surplus*. Consumer surplus is the extra value that a consumer gets from a transaction over and above the amount paid. Consumer surplus is also the area under the consumer's inverse demand curve and above the market price up to the quantity the consumer buys. The degree of the harm to consumers from an increase in a product's price is the reduction in consumer surplus. The market consumer surplus—the sum of the welfare effect across all consumers—is the area under the market inverse demand curve above the market price.

2. **Compensated Consumer Welfare.** If we measure the harm to a consumer from a price increase using consumer surplus, we are not holding a consumer's utility constant. We can use compensated demand curves or the associated expenditure functions to obtain two measures that hold utility constant. The expenditure function enables us to determine how much a consumer's income (expenditure) would have to change to offset a change in price, holding the consumer's utility constant. The *compensating variation* is the amount of money one would have to give a consumer to offset completely the harm from a price increase—to keep the consumer on the original indifference curve. The *equivalent variation* is the amount of money one would have to take from a consumer to harm the consumer by as much as the price increase would. For small (and even large) price changes, the three measures of the effect of a price increase on a consumer's well-being—the change in consumer surplus,

the compensating variation, and the equivalent variation—are typically close. The smaller the income elasticity or the smaller the budget share of the good, the smaller the differences between these three measures.

3. **Effects of Government Policies on Consumer Welfare.** A government quota on the consumption of a good, food stamps, or a childcare price subsidy creates a kink in a consumer's budget constraint, which affects how much consumers purchase and their well-being. Many, but not most, consumers would be better off if the government gave them an amount of money equal to the value of the food stamps or the childcare subsidy instead of these subsidies.

4. **Deriving Labor Supply Curves.** Using consumer theory, we can derive a person's daily demand curve for leisure (time spent on activities other than work), which shows how hours of leisure vary with the wage rate, which is the price of leisure. The number of hours that a person works equals 24 minus that person's leisure hours, so we can determine a person's daily labor supply curve from that person's demand curve for leisure. The labor supply curve is upward sloping if leisure is an inferior good, and downward sloping if it is a normal good and the income effect dominates the substitution effect. The labor supply curve may be backward bending if a worker views leisure as an inferior good at low wages and a normal good at high wage. Whether a cut in the income tax rate will cause government tax revenue to rise or fall depends on the shape of the labor supply curve.

EXERCISES

*All exercises are available on MyLab Economics; * = answer appears at the back of this book; M = mathematical problem.*

1. Uncompensated Consumer Welfare

1.1 Observe an auction on an online website such as eBay. Use the bidding information to draw a demand curve for the item and indicate the total willingness to pay for the good by the auction participants. (*Hint*: See the Application "Willingness to Pay and Consumer Surplus on eBay.")

*1.2 If the inverse demand function for toasters is $p = 60 - q$, what is the consumer surplus if the price is 30? **M**

1.3 If the inverse demand function for radios is $p = a - bq$, what is the consumer surplus if the price is $a/2$? **M**

1.4 Hong and Wolak (2008) estimated that a 5% postal (stamp) price increase, such as the one in 2006, reduces postal revenue by $215 million and lowers consumer surplus by $333 million. Illustrate these results in a figure similar to that of Figure 5.2, and indicate the dollar amounts of areas A and B in the figure.

*1.5 Use the facts in Exercise 1.4:

    a. Hong and Wolak estimated that the elasticity of demand for postal services is -1.6. Assume that the market has a constant elasticity of demand function, $Q = Xp^{-1.6}$, where X is a constant. In 2006, the price of a first-class stamp went from 37¢ to 39¢. Given the information in the problem about the effect of the price increase on revenue, calculate X.

    b. Calculate the size of the triangle corresponding to the lost consumer surplus (area B in Exercise 1.4). *Note*: You will get a slightly larger total surplus loss than the amount estimated by Hong and Wolak because they estimated a slightly different demand function. (*Hint*: See Solved Problem 5.1.) **M**

1.6 Compare the consumer surplus effects between a lump-sum tax and an ad valorem (percentage) tax on all goods that raise the same amount of tax revenue. **M**

*1.7 Two linear demand curves go through the initial equilibrium, e_1. One demand curve is less elastic than the other at e_1. For which demand curve will a price increase cause the larger consumer surplus loss?

2. Compensated Consumer Welfare

2.1 In the Application "Compensating Variation and Equivalent Variation for Smartphones and Facebook," people were asked how much they would have to be paid not to use the internet or what else they'd have to give up to keep using it. Use a graph to illustrate the compensating variation and equivalent variation in this Application. What is a better way to determine the equivalent variation?

2.2 According to a 2018 survey, 41% of single, employed millennials without children would be willing to dump their partner for a $37,000 raise.[11] Was the survey asking a *CV* or an *EV* question? (*Hint*: See the Application "Compensating Variation and Equivalent Variation for Smartphones and Facebook.")

*2.3 Redraw Figure 5.4 for an inferior good. Use your diagram to compare the relative sizes of *CV*, ΔCS, and *EV*.

2.4 Suppose that Lucy's quasilinear utility function in Solved Problem 5.2 is $U(q_1, q_2) = 2q_1^{0.5} + q_2$, $\underline{p}_1 = 2, p_2 = 4, \overline{p}_1 = 4, \underline{q}_1 = q_1(\underline{p}_1) = 4, \overline{q}_1 = q_1(\overline{p}_1) = 1$. Compare her *CV*, *EV*, and ΔCS. **M**

2.5 Marvin has a Cobb-Douglas utility function, $U = q_1^{0.5} q_2^{0.5}$, his income is $Y = 100$, and, initially he faces prices of $p_1 = 1$ and $p_2 = 2$. If p_1 increases to 2, what are his *CV*, ΔCS, and *EV*? (*Hint*: See Solved Problems 5.1 and 5.2.) **M**

2.6 The local swimming pool charges nonmembers $10 per visit. If you join the pool, you can swim for $5 per visit, but you have to pay an annual fee of F. Use an indifference curve diagram to find the value of F such that you are indifferent between joining and not joining. Suppose that the pool charged you exactly F. Would you go to the pool more or fewer times than if you did not join? For simplicity, assume that the price of all other goods is $1.

2.7 Marcia spends her money on coffee and sugar, which she views as perfect complements. She adds one tablespoon of sugar to each cup of coffee. A cup of coffee costs $1, a tablespoon of sugar cost $0.20, and she spends $16.80 on coffee every week. Use graphs to show her compensating variation and equivalent variation if the price of sugar doubles. Discuss the relative sizes of the change in her consumer surplus, compensating variation, and equivalent variation.

---

[11]www.cometfi.com/young-single-career-oriented; www.washingtonpost.com/news/get-there/wp/2018/03/22/would-you-dump-your-honey-for-this-much-more-money/.

2.8 Kwabena's utility function is $U(q_1, q_2) = \min(q_1, q_2)$. The price of each good is $1, and his monthly income is $4,000. His firm wants him to relocate to another city where the price of q_2 is $3, but the price of q_1 and his income remain constant. Obviously, he would be worse off due to the move. What would be his equivalent variation and compensating variation? **M**

2.9 Fangwen's utility function is $U(q_1, q_2) = q_1 + q_2$. The price of each good is $1, and her monthly income is $4,000. Her firm wants her to relocate to another city where the price of q_2 is $2, but the price of q_1 and her income remain constant. What would be her equivalent variation or compensating variation? **M**

3. Effects of Government Policies on Consumer Welfare

3.1 Max chooses between water and all other goods. If he spends all his money on water, he can buy 12,000 gallons per week. Given that he has usual-shaped indifference curves, show his optimal bundle e_1 in a diagram. During a drought, the government limits the number of gallons per week that he may purchase to 10,000. Using diagrams, discuss under which conditions his new optimal bundle, e_2, will be the same as e_1. If the two bundles differ, can you state where e_2 must be located?

3.2 Ralph usually buys one pizza and two colas from the local pizzeria. The pizzeria announces a special: All pizzas after the first one are half price. Show the original and new budget constraints. What can you say about the bundle Ralph will choose when faced with the new constraint?

3.3 Since 1979, the U.S. government has given low-income recipients food stamps without charge. Before 1979, people bought food stamps at a subsidized rate. For example, to get $1 worth of food stamps, a household paid about 20¢ (the exact amount varied by household characteristics and other factors). Show the budget constraint facing an individual if that individual may buy up to $100 per month in food stamps at 20¢ per each $1 coupon. Compare this constraint to the original budget constraint (original income is Y) with no assistance and the budget constraint if the individual receives $100 of food stamps for free.

3.4 Is a poor person more likely to benefit from $100 a month worth of food stamps (that can be used only to buy food) or $100 a month worth of clothing stamps (that can be used only to buy clothing)? Why?

3.5 If a relatively wealthy person spends more on food than a poor person before receiving food stamps, is the wealthy person less likely than the poor person to have a tangency at a point such as f in Figure 5.6?

3.6 Recipients of federal housing choice vouchers can use the vouchers only for housing. Several empirical studies found that recipients increase their non-housing expenditures by 10% to 20% (Harkness and Newman, 2003). Show that recipients might—but do not necessarily—increase their spending on non-housing, depending on their tastes.

3.7 Federal housing choice vouchers ($19 billion in 2015) and food stamps ($74 billion in 2014) are two of the largest in-kind transfer programs for the poor. Many poor people are eligible for both programs: 30% of housing assistance recipients also used food stamps, and 38% of food stamp participants also received housing assistance (Harkness and Newman, 2003). Suppose Jill's income is $500 a month, which she spends on food and housing. The prices of food and housing are each $1 per unit. Draw her budget line. If she receives $100 in food stamps and $200 in a housing subsidy (which she can spend only on housing), how do her budget line and opportunity set change?

3.8 Governments increasingly use educational vouchers in various parts of the United States. Suppose that the government offers poor people $5,000 education vouchers that they may use only to pay for education. Doreen would be better off with $5,000 in cash than with the educational voucher. In a graph, determine the cash value, V, Doreen places on the education voucher (that is, the amount of cash that would leave her as well off as with the voucher). Show how much education and "all other goods" she would consume with the educational voucher versus the cash payment of V.

4. Deriving Labor Supply Curves

4.1 Under a welfare plan, poor people are given a lump-sum payment of L. If they accept this welfare payment, they must pay a high marginal tax rate, $v = \frac{1}{2}$, on anything they earn. If they do not accept the welfare payment, they do not have to pay a tax on their earnings. Show that whether an individual accepts welfare depends on the individual's tastes.

4.2 If an individual's labor supply curve slopes forward at low wages and bends backward at high wages, is leisure a Giffen good? If so, is leisure a Giffen good at high or low wage rates?

4.3 Bessie, who can currently work as many hours as she wants at a wage of w, chooses to work 10 hours a day. Her boss decides to limit the number of hours that she can work to 8 hours per day. Show how her budget constraint and choice of hours change. Is she unambiguously worse off as a result of this change? Why or why not?

4.4 Originally when he could work as many hours as he wanted at a wage w, Roy chose to work seven hours a day. The employer now offers him w for the first eight hours in a day and an overtime wage of $1.5w$ for every hour he works beyond a minimum of eight hours. Show how his budget constraint changes. Will he necessarily choose to work more than seven hours a day? Would your answer be different if he originally chose to work eight hours?

4.5 Jerome moonlights: He holds down two jobs. The higher-paying job pays w, but he can work at most eight hours. The other job pays w^*, but he can work as many hours as he wants. Show how Jerome determines how many total hours to work. Now suppose that the job with no restriction on hours was the higher-paying job. How do Jerome's budget constraint and behavior change?

4.6 Taxes during the fourteenth century were very progressive. The 1377 poll tax on the Duke of Lancaster was 520 times that on a peasant. A poll tax is a lump-sum (fixed amount) tax per person, which is independent of the hours a person works or earns. Use a graph to show the effect of a poll tax on the labor-leisure decision. Does knowing that the tax was progressive tell us whether a nobleman or a peasant—assuming they had identical tastes—worked more hours?

*4.7 Today, most developed countries have progressive income taxes. Under such a taxation program, is the marginal tax higher than, equal to, or lower than the average tax?

*4.8 As of 2015, at least 41 countries—including most of the formerly centrally planned economies of Central and Eastern Europe and Eurasia—use a flat personal income tax. Show that if each person is allowed a "personal deduction" whereby the first $10,000 earned by the person is untaxed, the flat tax can be a *progressive* tax in which rich people pay a higher average tax rate than poor people.

4.9 George views leisure as a normal good. He works at a job that pays w an hour. Use a labor-leisure analysis to compare the effects on the hours he works from a marginal tax rate on his wage, v, or a lump-sum tax (a tax collected regardless of the number of hours he works), T. If the per-hour tax is used, he works 10 hours and earns $(1 - v)10w$. The government sets $T = v10w$, so that it collects the same amount of money from either tax. Which tax is likely to reduce George's hours of work more, and why? (*Hint*: See Solved Problem 5.4.)

*4.10 Prescott (2004) argued that U.S. employees work 50% more than do German, French, and Italian employees because European employees face lower marginal tax rates. Assuming that workers in all four countries have the same tastes toward leisure and goods, must it necessarily be true that U.S. employees work longer hours? Use graphs to illustrate your answer, and explain why it is true or is not true. Does Prescott's evidence indicate anything about the relative sizes of the substitution and income effects? Why or why not?

*4.11 Originally, Julia could work as many hours as she wanted at a wage of w. She chose to work 12 hours per day. Then, her employer told her that, in the future, she may work as many hours as she wants up to a maximum of 8 hours (and she can find no additional part-time job). How does her optimal choice between leisure and goods change? Does this change hurt her?

4.12 Using calculus, show the effect of a change in the wage on the amount of leisure that an individual wants to consume. **M**

4.13 Suppose that Joe's wage varies with the hours he works: $w(H) = aH, a > 0$. Use both a graph and calculus to show how the number of hours he chooses to work depends on his tastes. **M**

4.14 Derive Sarah's labor supply function given that she has a quasilinear utility function, $U = Y^{0.5} + 2N$, and her income is $Y = wH$. What is the slope of her labor supply curve with respect to a change in the wage? (*Hint*: See Solved Problem 5.3.) **M**

4.15 Joe won $365,000 a year for life in the state lottery. Use a labor-leisure choice analysis to answer the following:

a. Show how Joe's lottery winnings affect the position of his budget line.

b. Joe's utility function for goods per day (Y) and hours of leisure per day (N) is $U = Y + 240N^{0.5}$. After winning the lottery, does Joe continue to work the same number of hours each day? What is the income effect of Joe's lottery gains on the amount of goods he buys per day? **M**

4.16 Redraw the figure in Solved Problem 5.5 to show that Lance might not choose to work at the higher wage.

4.17 In Solved Problem 5.5, suppose that Lance's parents will not give Lance Y^* if he drops out of high school to work. Use two figures to show that he might or might not choose to start working when the wage increases.

*4.18 The government collects a specific tax of t for each hour worked. Thus, a worker whose wage is w keeps $w - t$ after taxes and supplies $H(w - t)$ hours of work. The government wants to know if its tax revenue will increase or decrease if it lowers t. Show that how the tax revenue changes depends on the elasticity of supply of labor, η. (*Hint*: See Solved Problem 5.6.) **M**

5. Challenge

5.1 Governments generally limit the amount of the child-care subsidy. For example, in Washington State, the 2015 maximum subsidy for an infant is $31.47 per day. A binding limit on the subsidy creates a kink in the budget constraint. Show how a limit changes the analysis in the Challenge Solution.

*5.2 How are parents who do not receive subsidies affected by the two childcare programs analyzed in the Challenge Solution figure? (*Hint*: Use a supply-and-demand analysis.)

*5.3 How could the government set a smaller lump-sum subsidy that would make poor parents as well off as with the hourly childcare subsidy yet cost the government less? Given the tastes shown in the Challenge Solution figure, what would be the effect on the number of hours of childcare service that these parents buy? Are you calculating a compensating variation or an equivalent variation (given that the original family is initially at e_1 in the figure)?

Firms and Production

6

Hard work never killed anybody, but why take a chance?

Why has a measure of labor productivity—the output produced per worker—risen for many firms during recent recessions (Lazear, Shaw, and Stanton, 2016)? During the Great Recession (the fourth quarter of 2007 through the third quarter of 2009), labor productivity rose by 3.2% in nonfarm businesses. In contrast, in the two years before the Great Recession, labor productivity rose by only 2.2%.

Firms produce less output during recessions as demand for their products falls. In response, firms typically lay off workers during recessions. A 2017 U.S. Bureau of Labor Statistics study found that during the Great Recession, output declined by $753 billion and 8.1 million jobs were lost.

If we know about a firm's production process, can we predict whether output produced per worker will rise or fall with each additional layoff? We answer this question in the Challenge Solution, where we examine whether the productivity of a beer bottling plant rises or falls.

This chapter examines the nature of firms and how they choose their inputs to produce efficiently. Chapter 7 considers how firms choose the least costly among all possible efficient production processes. Then, Chapter 8 combines this information about costs with information about revenues to determine how firms select the output level that maximizes profit.

The main lesson of this chapter and the next is that firms are not black boxes that mysteriously transform inputs (such as labor, capital, and material) into outputs. Economic theory explains how firms make decisions about production processes, types of inputs to use, and the volume of output to produce.

In this chapter, we examine six main topics	
	1. **The Ownership and Management of Firms.** Decisions must be made about how a firm is owned and managed.
	2. **Production.** A firm converts inputs into outputs, using one of possibly many available technologies.

3. **Short-Run Production: One Variable and One Fixed Input.** In the short run, only some inputs can be varied, so the firm changes its output by adjusting its variable inputs.

4. **Long-Run Production: Two Variable Inputs.** The firm has more flexibility in how it produces and how it changes its output level in the long run, when all factors can be varied.

5. **Returns to Scale.** How the ratio of output to input varies with the size of the firm is an important factor in determining a firm's size.

6. **Productivity and Technical Change.** The amount of output that can be produced with a given quantity of inputs varies across firms and over time.

6.1 The Ownership and Management of Firms

A **firm** is an organization that converts *inputs* such as labor, materials, and capital into *outputs*, the goods and services that it sells. U.S. Steel combines iron ore, machinery, and labor to create steel. A local restaurant buys raw food, cooks it, and serves it. A landscape designer hires gardeners, rents machines, buys trees and shrubs, transports them to a customer's home, and supervises the project.

Private, Public, and Nonprofit Firms

Atheism is a non-prophet organization.

Firms operate in the private, public, or nonprofit sectors. The *private sector*, sometimes referred to as the *for-profit private sector*, consists of firms owned by individuals or other nongovernmental entities whose owners try to earn a profit. Throughout this book, we concentrate on these firms. In almost every country, this sector contributes the most to the gross domestic product (GDP, a measure of a country's total output).

The *public sector* consists of firms and organizations that are owned by governments or government agencies. For example, the National Railroad Passenger Corporation (Amtrak) is owned primarily by the U.S. government. The armed forces and the court system are also part of the public sector, as are most schools, colleges, and universities.

The *nonprofit* or *not-for-profit sector* consists of organizations that are neither government-owned nor intended to earn a profit. Organizations in this sector typically pursue social or public interest objectives. Well-known examples include Greenpeace, Alcoholics Anonymous, and the Salvation Army, along with many other charitable, educational, health, and religious organizations. According to the Federal Reserve Bank of St. Louis, in 2018, the private sector created 76% of the U.S. gross domestic product, the government sector was responsible for 11%, and nonprofits and households produced the remaining 13%.

Sometimes all three sectors play an important role in the same industry. For example, in the United States, the United Kingdom, Canada, and many other countries, for-profit, nonprofit, and government-owned hospitals coexist. A single enterprise may be partially owned by a government and partially owned by individuals. For example, during the 2007–2009 Great Recession, the U.S. government took a partial ownership position in many firms in the financial and automobile industries.

APPLICATION

Chinese State-Owned
Enterprises

Before 1978, virtually all Chinese industrial firms were state-owned enterprises (SOEs). Since then, China has been transitioning to a market-based economy, gradually increasing the role of private-sector firms. It has dramatically reduced the number of SOEs, keeping mainly the largest ones. By 1999, SOEs comprised only about 36% of Chinese industrial firms but still controlled nearly 68% of industrial assets (capital). Since 2000, the Chinese government has allowed many small SOEs to be privatized or go bankrupt, while it continues to subsidize many large SOEs. By 2017, SOEs accounted for only 29% of industrial assets, but still account for 30% to 40% of China's gross domestic product.

The Ownership of For-Profit Firms

The legal structure of a firm determines who is liable for its debts. The private sector has three primary legal forms of organization: a sole proprietorship, a general partnership, or a corporation.

Sole proprietorships are firms owned by an individual who is personally liable for the firm's debts.

General partnerships (often called *partnerships*) are businesses jointly owned and controlled by two or more people who are personally liable for the firm's debts. The owners operate under a partnership agreement. In most legal jurisdictions, if any partner leaves, the partnership agreement ends and a new partnership agreement is created if the firm is to continue operations.

Corporations are owned by *shareholders* in proportion to the number of shares or amount of stock they hold. The shareholders elect a board of directors to represent them. In turn, the board of directors usually hires managers to oversee the firm's operations. Some corporations are very small and have a single shareholder; others are very large and have thousands of shareholders. The legal name of a corporation often includes the term Incorporated (Inc.) or Limited (Ltd) to indicate its corporate status.

A fundamental characteristic of corporations is that the owners are not personally liable for the firm's debts; they have **limited liability**: The personal assets of corporate owners cannot be taken to pay a corporation's debts even if it goes into bankruptcy. Because corporations have limited liability, the most that shareholders can lose is the amount they paid for their stock, which typically becomes worthless if the corporation declares bankruptcy.[1]

The purpose of limiting liability was to allow firms to raise funds and grow beyond what was possible when owners risked personal assets on any firm in which they invested. According to the latest available figures (2012), U.S. corporations are responsible for 81% of business receipts and 58% of net business income even though they are only 18% of all nonfarm firms. Nonfarm sole proprietorships are 72% of firms but make only 4% of the sales revenue and earn 15% of net income. Partnerships are 10% of firms, account for 15% of revenue, and make 27% of net income.

---

[1]Only relatively recently, the United States (1996), the United Kingdom (2000), and other countries have allowed any sole proprietorship, partnership, or corporation to register as a *limited liability company* (LLC). Thus, all firms—not just corporations—can now obtain limited liability.

The Management of Firms

In a small firm, the owner usually manages the firm's operations. In larger firms, typically corporations and larger partnerships, a manager or a management team usually runs the company. In such firms, owners, managers, and lower-level supervisors are all decision makers.

As revelations about Enron, WorldCom, American International Group (AIG), MF Global, and JP Morgan Chase illustrate, various decision makers may have conflicting objectives. What is in the best interest of the owners may not be in the best interest of managers or other employees. For example, a manager may want a fancy office, a company car, a corporate jet, and other perks, but an owner would likely oppose those drains on profit.

The owner replaces the manager if the manager pursues personal objectives rather than the firm's objectives. In a corporation, the board of directors is responsible for ensuring that the manager stays on track. If the manager and the board of directors are ineffective, the shareholders can fire both or change certain policies through votes at the corporation's annual shareholders' meeting. Until Chapter 19, we'll ignore the potential conflict between managers and owners and assume that the owner *is* the manager of the firm and makes all the decisions.

What Owners Want

Economists usually assume that a firm's owners try to maximize profit. Presumably, most people invest in a firm to make money—lots of money, they hope. They want the firm to earn a positive profit rather than suffer a loss (a negative profit). A firm's **profit**, π, is the difference between its revenue, R, which is what it earns from selling a good, and its cost, C, which is what it pays for labor, materials, and other inputs:

$$\pi = R - C. \qquad (6.1)$$

Typically, revenue is p, the price, times q, the firm's quantity: $R = pq$. (For simplicity, we will assume that the firm produces only one product.)

In reality, some owners have other objectives, such as running as large a firm as possible, owning a fancy building, or keeping risks low. However, Chapter 8 shows that a firm in a highly competitive market is likely to be driven out of business if it doesn't maximize its profit.

To maximize its profit, a firm must produce as efficiently as possible. A firm achieves **production efficiency (technological efficiency)** if it cannot produce its current level of output with fewer inputs, given its existing knowledge about technology and how to organize production. Equivalently, a firm produces efficiently if, given the quantity of inputs used, no more output can be produced using existing knowledge.

If a firm does not produce efficiently, it cannot maximize its profit—so efficient production is *necessary* for maximizing profit. Even if a firm efficiently produces a given level of output, it will not maximize its profit if that output level is too high or too low or if it uses an excessively expensive production process. Thus, efficient production alone is not *sufficient* to ensure that a firm maximizes its profit.

A firm may use engineers and other experts to determine the most efficient ways to produce using a known method or technology. However, this knowledge does not indicate which of the many technologies, each of which uses different combinations of inputs, allows for production at the lowest cost or with the highest possible profit. How to produce at the lowest cost is an economic decision typically made by the firm's manager (see Chapter 7).

6.2 Production

A firm uses a *technology* or *production process* to transform *inputs* or *factors of production* into *outputs*. Firms use many types of inputs, most of which fall into three broad categories:

- **Capital services** (*K*): use of long-lived inputs such as land, buildings (such as factories and stores), and equipment (such as machines and trucks)
- **Labor services** (*L*): hours of work provided by managers, skilled workers (such as architects, economists, engineers, and plumbers), and less-skilled workers (such as custodians, construction laborers, and assembly-line workers)
- **Materials** (*M*): natural resources and raw goods (such as oil, water, and wheat) and processed products (such as aluminum, plastic, paper, and steel) that are typically consumed in producing, or incorporated in making, the final product

For brevity, we typically refer to *capital services* as *capital* and *labor services* as *labor*. The output can be a *service*, such as an automobile tune-up by a mechanic, or a *physical product*, such as a computer chip or a potato chip.

Production Functions

Firms can transform inputs into outputs in many different ways. Candy manufacturing companies differ in the skills of their workforce and the amount of equipment they use. While all employ a chef, a manager, and relatively unskilled workers, some candy firms also use skilled technicians and modern equipment. In small candy companies, the relatively unskilled workers shape the candy, decorate it, package it, and box it by hand. In slightly larger firms, these same-level workers use conveyor belts and other industrial equipment. In modern large-scale plants, the relatively unskilled laborers work with robots and other state-of-the-art machines maintained by skilled technicians. Before deciding which production process to use, a firm must consider its options.

The various ways that a firm can transform inputs into output are summarized in the **production function**: the relationship between the quantities of inputs used and the *maximum* quantity of output that can be produced, given current knowledge about technology and organization. The production function for a firm that uses labor and capital only is

$$q = f(L, K), \tag{6.2}$$

where *q* units of output (wrapped candy bars) are produced using *L* units of labor services (days of work by relatively unskilled assembly-line workers) and *K* units of capital (the number of conveyor belts).

The production function shows only the *maximum* amount of output that can be produced from given levels of labor and capital, because the production function includes efficient production processes only. A profit-maximizing firm is not interested in production processes that are inefficient and wasteful: Why would the firm want to use two workers to do a job that one worker can perform as efficiently?

Time and the Variability of Inputs

A firm can more easily adjust its inputs in the long run than in the short run. Typically, a firm can vary the amount of materials and relatively unskilled labor it uses comparatively quickly. However, it needs more time to find and hire skilled workers, order new equipment, or build a new manufacturing plant.

The more time a firm has to adjust its inputs, the more factors of production it can alter. The **short run** is a period so brief that at least one factor of production cannot be varied practically. A factor that a firm cannot vary practically in the short run is called a **fixed input**. In contrast, a **variable input** is a factor of production whose quantity the firm can change readily during the relevant period. The **long run** is a long enough period that all inputs can be varied—no inputs are fixed.

Suppose that one day a painting company has more work than its crew can handle. Even if it wanted to, the firm does not have time to buy or rent an extra truck and buy another compressor to run a power sprayer; these inputs are fixed in the short run. To complete the day's work, the firm uses its only truck to drop off a temporary worker, equipped with only a brush and a can of paint, at the last job. However, in the long run, the firm can adjust all its inputs. If the firm wants to paint more houses every day, it can hire more full-time workers, purchase a second truck, get another compressor to run a power sprayer, and buy a computer program to track its projects.

The time it takes for all inputs to be variable depends on the factors a firm uses. For a janitorial service whose only major input is workers, the long run is a brief period. In contrast, an automobile manufacturer may need many years to build a new manufacturing plant or design and construct a new type of machine. A pistachio farmer needs about a decade before newly planted trees yield a substantial crop of nuts.

For many firms over a short period, say, a month, materials and often labor are variable inputs. However, labor is not always a variable input. Finding additional highly skilled workers may take substantial time. Similarly, capital may be a variable or a fixed input. A firm can rent small capital assets (trucks and personal computers) quickly, but it may take years to obtain larger capital assets (buildings and large specialized pieces of equipment).

To illustrate the greater flexibility a firm has in the long run than in the short run, we examine the production function in Equation 6.2, in which output is a function of only labor and capital. We first look at the short-run and then at the long-run production process.

6.3 Short-Run Production: One Variable and One Fixed Input

In the short run, we assume that capital is a fixed input and that labor is a variable input, so the firm can increase output only by increasing the amount of labor it uses. In the short run, the firm's production function is

$$q = f(L, \overline{K}),$$ (6.3)

where q is output, L is workers, and $\overline{K}$ is the fixed number of units of capital. The short-run production function is also referred to as the **total product of labor**—the amount of output (or *total product*) that a given amount of labor can produce, holding the quantity of other inputs fixed.

The exact relationship between *output* or *total product* and *labor* is given in Equation 6.3. The **marginal product of labor** (MP_L) is the change in total output resulting from using an extra unit of labor, holding other factors (capital) constant. The marginal product of labor is the partial derivative of the production function with respect to labor,

$$MP_L = \frac{\partial q}{\partial L} = \frac{\partial f(L, K)}{\partial L}.$$

The **average product of labor** (AP_L) is the ratio of output to the number of workers used to produce that output,[2]

$$AP_L = \frac{q}{L}.$$

SOLVED PROBLEM
6.1

MyLab Economics
Solved Problem

A computer assembly firm's production function is $q = 0.1LK + 3L^2K - 0.1L^3K$. What is its short-run production function if capital is fixed at $\overline{K} = 10$? Give the formulas for its marginal product of labor and its average product of labor. Draw two figures, one above the other. In the top figure, show the relationship between output (total product) and labor. In the bottom figure, show the MP_L and AP_L curves. Is this production function valid for all values of labor?

Answer

1. *Write the formula for the short-run production function by replacing K in the production function with its fixed short-run value.* To obtain a production function in the form of Equation 6.3, set capital in the production function equal to 10:

$$q = 0.1L(10) + 3L^2(10) - 0.1L^3(10) = L + 30L^2 - L^3.$$

2. *Determine the MP_L by differentiating the short-run production function with respect to labor.* The marginal product of labor is[3]

$$MP_L = \frac{dq}{dL} = \frac{d(L + 30L^2 - L^3)}{dL} = 1 + 60L - 3L^2.$$

3. *Determine the AP_L by dividing the short-run production function by labor.* The average product of labor is

$$AP_L = \frac{q}{L} = \frac{L + 30L^2 - L^3}{L} = 1 + 30L - L^2.$$

4. *Draw the requested figures by plotting the short-run production function, MP_L, and AP_L equations.* Figure 6.1 shows how the total product of labor, marginal product of labor, and average product of labor vary with the number of workers.

5. *Show that the production function equation does not hold for all values of labor by noting that, beyond a certain level, extra workers lower output.* In the figure, the total product curve to the right of $L = 20$ is a dashed line, indicating that this section is not part of the true production function. Because output falls—the curve decreases—as the firm uses more than 20 workers, a rational firm would never use more than 20 workers. From the definition of a production function, we want the maximum quantity of output that the given inputs can produce, so if the firm had more than 20 workers, it could increase its output by sending the extra employees home. (The portions of the MP_L and AP_L curves beyond 20 workers also appear as dashed lines because they correspond to irrelevant sections of the short-run production function equation.)

---

[2]*Jargon alert*: Some economists call the MP_L the marginal physical product of labor and the AP_L the average physical product of labor.

[3]Because the short-run production function is solely a function of labor, $MP_L = dq/dL$. An alternative way to derive the MP_L is to differentiate the production function with respect to labor and then set capital equal to 10: $MP_L = \partial q/\partial L = \partial(0.1LK + 3L^2K - 0.1L^3K)/\partial L = 0.1K + 6LK - 0.3L^2K$. Evaluating at $\overline{K} = 10$, we obtain $MP_L = 1 + 60L - 30L^2$.

Interpretation of Graphs

Figure 6.1 shows how the total product of labor (computers assembled), the average product of labor, and the marginal product of labor vary with the number of workers. The figures are smooth curves because the firm can hire a "fraction of a worker" by employing a worker for a fraction of a day. The total product of labor curve in panel a shows that output rises with labor until the firm employs 20 workers.

Panel b illustrates how the average product of labor and the marginal product of labor vary with the number of workers. By lining up the two panels vertically, we can show the relationships between the total product of labor, marginal product of labor, and average product of labor curves.

Figure 6.1 Production Relationships with Variable Labor

(a) The short-run total product of labor curve, $q = L + 30L^2 - L^3$, shows how much output, q, can be assembled with 10 units of capital, which is fixed in the short run. Where extra workers reduce the amount of output produced, the total product of labor curve is a dashed line, which indicates that such production is inefficient production and not part of the production function. The slope of the line from the origin to point B is the average product of labor for 15 workers. (b) The marginal product of labor, MP_L, equals the average product of labor, AP_L, at the peak of the average product curve where the firm employs 15 workers.

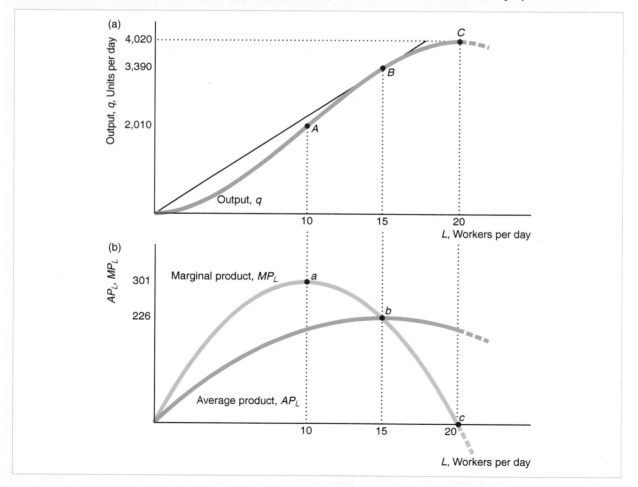

In most production processes—and as Figure 6.1 shows—the average product of labor first rises and then falls as labor increases. For example, the AP_L curve may initially rise because it helps to have more than two hands when assembling a computer. One worker holds a part in place while another worker bolts it down. As a result, output increases more than in proportion to labor, so the average product of labor rises. Similarly, output may initially rise more than in proportion to labor because of greater specialization of activities. With greater specialization, firms assign workers to tasks at which they are particularly adept, saving workers' time by not having workers move from one task to another.

However, as the number of workers rises further, output may not increase by as much per worker because workers have to wait to use a particular piece of equipment or because they get in each other's way. In Figure 6.1, as the number of workers exceeds 15, total output increases less than in proportion to labor, so the average product falls.

The three curves are geometrically related. First, we use panel b to illustrate the relationship between the average and marginal product of labor curves. Then, we use panels a and b to show the relationship between the total product of labor curve and the other two curves.

The average product of labor curve slopes upward where the marginal product of labor curve is above it and slopes downward where the marginal product curve is below it. If an extra worker adds more output—that worker's marginal product—than the average product of the initial workers, the extra worker raises the average product. As panel b shows, with fewer than 15 workers, the marginal product curve is above the average product curve, so the average product curve is upward sloping.

Similarly, if the marginal product of labor for a new worker is less than the former average product of labor, then the average product of labor falls. In the figure, the average product of labor falls beyond 15 workers. Because the average product of labor curve rises when the marginal product of labor curve is above it, and the average product of labor falls when the marginal product of labor is below it, the average product of labor curve reaches a peak, point *b* in panel b, where the marginal product of labor curve crosses it.[4]

We can determine the average product of labor curve, shown in panel b of Figure 6.1, using the total product of labor curve, shown in panel a. The AP_L for L workers equals the slope of a straight line from the origin to a point on the total product of labor curve for L workers in panel a. The slope ("rise over run") of this line equals output ("rise") divided by the number of workers ("run"), which is the definition of the average product of labor. For example, the slope of the straight line drawn from the origin to point B ($L = 15$, $q = 3,390$) is 226, which is the height of the AP_L curve in panel b when $L = 15$.

---

[4]We can use calculus to prove that the MP_L curve intersects the AP_L at its peak. Because capital is fixed, we can write the production function solely in terms of labor: $q = f(L)$. In the figure, $MP_L = dq/dL = df/dL > 0$ and $d^2f/dL^2 < 0$. A necessary condition to identify the amount of labor where the average product of labor curve, $AP_L = q/L = f(L)/L$, reaches a maximum is that the derivative of AP_L with respect to L equals zero:

$$\frac{dAP_L}{dL} = \left(\frac{dq}{dL} - \frac{q}{L} \right)\frac{1}{L} = 0.$$

At the L determined by this first-order condition, AP_L is maximized if the second-order condition is negative: $d^2AP_L/dL^2 = d^2f/dL^2 < 0$. From the necessary condition, $MP_L = dq/dL = q/L = AP_L$, at the peak of the AP_L curve.

The marginal product of labor also has a geometric interpretation in terms of the total product of labor curve. The slope of the total product of labor curve at a given point, dq/dL, equals the MP_L. That is, the MP_L equals the slope of a straight line that is tangent to the total output (product) curve for a given number of workers. For example, at point C in panel a with 20 workers, the line tangent to the total product curve is flat, so the MP_L is zero: A little extra labor has no effect on output. The total product curve is upward sloping with fewer than 20 workers, so the MP_L is positive. If the firm is foolish enough to hire more than 20 workers, the total product curve slopes downward (dashed line), so the MP_L would be negative: Extra workers lower output. Again, this portion of the MP_L curve is not part of the production function.

With 15 workers, the average product of labor equals the marginal product of labor. The reason is that the line from the origin to point B in panel a is tangent to the total product curve, so the slope of that line, 226, is the marginal product of labor and the average product of labor at point b in panel b.

SOLVED PROBLEM 6.2

MyLab Economics
Solved Problem

Tian and Wan (2000) estimated the production function for rice in China as a function of labor, fertilizer, and other inputs such as seed, draft animals, and equipment. Holding the other inputs besides labor fixed, the total product of labor is $\ln q = 4.63 + 1.29 \ln L - 0.2(\ln L)^2$. What is the marginal product of labor? What is the relationship of the marginal product of labor to the average product of labor? What is the elasticity of output with respect to labor?

Answer

1. *Totally differentiate the short-run production function to obtain the marginal product of labor.* Differentiating $\ln q = 4.63 + 1.29 \ln L - 0.2(\ln L)^2$ with respect to q and L, we obtain

$$\frac{dq/dL}{q} = \frac{1.29 - 0.4 \ln L}{L}.$$

   By rearranging terms, we find that the $MP_L = dq/dL = (q/L)(1.29 - 0.4 \ln L)$.

2. *Determine the relationship between MP_L and AP_L using the expression for MP_L.* Using the definition for $AP_L = q/L$, we can rewrite the expression we derived for the marginal product of labor as $MP_L = AP_L(1.29 - 0.4 \ln L)$, so the MP_L is $(1.29 - 0.4 \ln L)$ times as large as is the AP_L. Equivalently, $MP_L/AP_L = 1.29 - 0.4 \ln L$.

3. *Show that the elasticity of output with respect to labor is the ratio of the marginal product of labor to the average product of labor and make use of the equation relating the MP_L to the AP_L.* Given the general definition of an elasticity, the elasticity of output produced with respect to labor is $(dq/dL)(L/q)$. By substituting the definitions of $MP_L = dq/dL$ and $AP_L = q/L$ into this expression, we find that the elasticity of output with respect to labor is $(dq/dL)(L/q) = MP_L/AP_L = 1.29 - 0.4 \ln L$.

Law of Diminishing Marginal Returns

Next to *supply equals demand*, the most commonly used phrase of economic jargon is probably the *law of diminishing marginal returns*. This "law" determines the shapes of the total product and marginal product of labor curves as a firm uses more and more labor. As with the "law" of supply and demand, this "law" is not theoretically necessary, but it is an empirical regularity.

The *law of diminishing marginal returns* (or *diminishing marginal product*) holds that *if a firm keeps increasing an input, holding all other inputs and technology constant, the corresponding increases in output will eventually become smaller*. That is, if only one input is increased, *the marginal product of that input will eventually diminish*. The marginal product of labor diminishes if $\partial MP_L/\partial L = \partial(\partial q/\partial L)/\partial L = \partial^2 q/\partial L^2 = \partial^2 f(L, K)/\partial L^2 < 0$. That is, the marginal product falls with increased labor if the second partial derivative of the production function with respect to labor is negative.

Panel b of Figure 6.1 illustrates diminishing marginal product of labor. At low levels of labor, the marginal product of labor rises with the number of workers. However, when the number of workers exceeds 10, each additional worker reduces the marginal product of labor.

Unfortunately, when attempting to cite this empirical regularity, many people overstate it. Instead of talking about "diminishing *marginal* returns," they talk about "diminishing returns." These phrases have different meanings. With "diminishing marginal returns," the MP_L curve is falling—beyond 10 workers in panel b of Figure 6.1—but it may be positive, as the solid MP_L curve between 10 and 20 workers shows. With "diminishing returns," extra labor causes *output* to fall. Total returns diminish for more than 20 workers, and consequently the MP_L is negative, as the dashed MP_L line in panel b shows.

Thus, saying that a production process has diminishing returns is much stronger than saying that it has diminishing marginal returns. We often observe successful firms producing with diminishing marginal returns to labor, but we never see a well-run firm operating with diminishing total returns. Such a firm could produce more output by using fewer inputs.

Many people misstate the law of diminishing marginal returns:

Common Confusion Marginal product must fall as an input increases.

That claim is true only if as we add more of an input, we hold technology and other inputs constant. If we increase labor while simultaneously increasing other factors or adopting superior technologies, the marginal product of labor may rise indefinitely. Thomas Malthus provided the most famous example of this fallacy (as well as the reason some people refer to economics as the "dismal science").

APPLICATION

Malthus and the Green Revolution

[W]hoever makes two ears of corn, or two blades of grass, to grow upon a spot of ground where only one grew before, would deserve better of mankind, and do more essential service to his country, than the whole race of politicians put together. —Jonathan Swift, *Gulliver's Travels*

In 1798, Thomas Malthus—a clergyman and professor of modern history and political economy—predicted that population (if unchecked) would grow more rapidly than food production because the quantity of land was fixed. The problem, he believed, was that the fixed amount of land would lead to a diminishing marginal product of labor, so output would rise less than in proportion to the increase in farm workers. Malthus grimly concluded that mass starvation would result. Brander and Taylor (1998) argue that such a disaster may have occurred on Easter Island around 500 years ago.

Today, the earth supports a population about eight times as great as it was when Malthus made his predictions. Why haven't most of us starved to death? The simple explanation is that fewer workers using less land can produce much more food today than was possible when Malthus was alive. The output of a U.S. farm worker today is more than double that of an average worker just 50 years ago. We have not seen diminishing marginal returns to labor because the production function has changed due to substantial technological progress in agriculture and because farmers make greater use of other inputs such as fertilizers, capital, and superior seeds.

Two hundred years ago, most of the population had to work in agriculture to feed themselves. Today, less than 1% of the U.S. population works in agriculture. Over the past century, food production grew substantially faster than the population in most developed countries.

In 1850 in the United States, it took more than 80 hours of labor to produce 100 bushels of corn. Introducing mechanical power cut the required labor in half. Labor hours were again cut in half by the introduction of hybrid seed and chemical fertilizers, and then in half again by the advent of herbicides and pesticides. Biotechnology, with the introduction of herbicide-tolerant and insect-resistant crops, has reduced the labor required to produce 100 bushels of corn to about two hours—2.5% of the hours of work it took in 1850. Over the past 60 years, the output per worker has more than doubled, and the corn yield per acre has increased by 6.2 times.

Of course, the risk of starvation is more severe in developing countries. Nearly all (98%) of the world's hungry people live in developing countries. Luckily, one man decided to defeat the threat of Malthusian disaster personally. Do you know anyone who saved a life? A hundred lives? Do you know the name of the man who probably saved the most lives in history?

According to some estimates, during the second half of the twentieth century, Norman Borlaug and his fellow scientists prevented a *billion deaths* with their *Green Revolution*, which included development of drought- and insect-resistant crop varieties, improved irrigation, better use of fertilizer and pesticides, and improved equipment. Gollin, Hansen, and Wingender (2018) estimated that in developing countries, a 10% increase in high-yielding, green revolution crops raises gross domestic product per capital (loosely, average earnings) by 15%, while reducing infant and adult mortality.

However, as Dr. Borlaug noted in his 1970 Nobel Prize speech, superior science is not the complete answer to preventing starvation. We also need a sound economic system and a stable political environment.

Economic and political failures such as the breakdown of economic production and distribution systems due to wars have caused widespread starvation and malnutrition, particularly in parts of sub-Saharan Africa. Environmental problems such as shifting rainfall patterns due to global warming and soil degradation have also become a major concern. According to the 2017 annual report on food insecurity of the United Nations Food and Agriculture Organization, about 11% of the world's population suffers from significant undernourishment, with a particularly high concentration in sub-Saharan Africa. A 2018 report concluded that 60% of people facing food insecurity did so because of conflicts and 31% due to climate disasters, mainly droughts. If society cannot solve these economic, political, and climate problems, Malthus' prediction may prove to be right for the wrong reasons.

6.4 Long-Run Production: Two Variable Inputs

Eternity? When's it going to end?

We started our analysis of production functions by looking at a short-run production function in which one input—capital—is fixed, and the other—labor—is variable. However, in the long run, both of these inputs are variable. With both factors variable, a firm can produce a given level of output by using a great deal of labor and very little capital, a great deal of capital and very little labor, or moderate amounts of each. That is, the firm can substitute one input for another while continuing to produce the same level of output, in much the same way that a consumer can maintain a given level of utility by substituting one good for another.

Typically, a firm can produce in various ways, some of which require more labor than others. For example, a lumberyard can produce 200 planks an hour with 10 workers using handsaws, or 4 workers using handheld power saws, or 2 workers using bench power saws.

We can illustrate the basic idea using a Cobb-Douglas production function,

$$q = AL^aK^b, \tag{6.4}$$

where A, a, and b are constants.[5] If we redefine a unit of output as $1/A$, we can write the production function as $q = L^aK^b$, which is the form we generally use. Hsieh (1995) estimated a Cobb-Douglas production function for a U.S. firm producing electronics and other electrical equipment as

$$q = L^{0.5}K^{0.5}, \tag{6.5}$$

where L is labor (workers) per day and K is capital services per day. From inspection, many combinations of labor and capital can produce the same level of output.

Isoquants

We can summarize the possible combinations of inputs that will produce a given level of output using an **isoquant**, which is a curve that shows the efficient combinations of labor and capital that can produce a single (*iso*) level of output (*quant*ity). If the production function is $q = f(L, K)$, then the equation for an isoquant with output held constant at $\bar{q}$ is

$$\bar{q} = f(L, K). \tag{6.6}$$

For the particular production function, Equation 6.5, the isoquant is $\bar{q} = L^{0.5}K^{0.5}$.

Figure 6.2 shows an isoquant for $q = 6$, $q = 9$, and $q = 12$, which are three of the many possible isoquants. The isoquants show a firm's flexibility in producing a given level of output. These isoquants are smooth curves because the firm can use fractional units of each input.

Many combinations of labor and capital, (L, K), will produce 6 units of output, including (1, 36), (2, 18), (3, 12), (4, 9), (6, 6), (9, 4), (12, 3), (18, 2), and (36, 1). Figure 6.2 shows some of these combinations as points a through f on the $q = 6$ isoquant.

---

[5]The Cobb-Douglas production function (named after its inventors, Charles W. Cobb, a mathematician, and Paul H. Douglas, an economist and U.S. senator) is the most commonly used production function. The Cobb-Douglas production function has the same functional form as the Cobb-Douglas utility function, which we studied in Chapters 3 through 5. Unlike in those chapters, we do not require that $b = 1 - a$ in this chapter.

Figure 6.2 Family of Isoquants for a U.S. Electronics Manufacturing Firm

These isoquants for a U.S. firm producing electronics and other electrical equipment (Hsieh, 1995) show the combinations of labor and capital that produce various levels of output. Isoquants farther from the origin correspond to higher levels of output. Points a, b, c, d, e, and f are various combinations of labor and capital that the firm can use to produce $q = 6$ units of output. If the firm holds capital constant at 12 and increases labor from 3 (point b) to 12 (point g), the firm shifts from operating on the $q = 6$ isoquant to producing on the $q = 12$ isoquant.

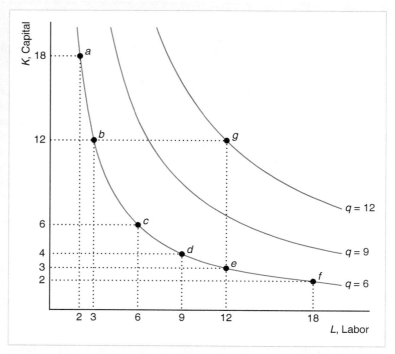

Properties of Isoquants. Isoquants have most of the same properties as indifference curves. The main difference is that an isoquant holds quantity constant, whereas an indifference curve holds utility constant. The quantities associated with isoquants have cardinal properties (for example, an output of 12 is twice as much as an output of 6), while the utilities associated with indifference curves have only ordinal properties (for example, 12 utils are associated with more pleasure than 6, but not necessarily twice as much pleasure).

We now consider four major properties of isoquants. Most of these properties result from efficient production by firms.

First, *the farther an isoquant is from the origin, the greater the level of output*. That is, the more inputs a firm uses, the more output it gets if it produces efficiently. At point e in Figure 6.2, the electronics firm is producing 6 units of output with 12 workers and 3 units of capital. If the firm holds the number of workers constant and adds 9 more units of capital, it produces at point g. Point g must be on an isoquant with a higher level of output—here, 12 units—if the firm is producing efficiently and not wasting the extra labor.

Second, *isoquants do not cross*. Such intersections are inconsistent with the requirement that the firm always produces efficiently. For example, if the $q = 15$ and $q = 20$ isoquants crossed, the firm could produce at either output level with the same combination of labor and capital where they intersect. The firm must be producing inefficiently if it produces $q = 15$ when it could produce $q = 20$. Thus, that labor-capital combination should not lie on the $q = 15$ isoquant, which should include only efficient combinations of inputs. So, productive efficiency requires that isoquants do not cross.

Third, *isoquants slope downward*. If an isoquant sloped upward, the firm could produce the same level of output with relatively few inputs or relatively many inputs. Producing with relatively many inputs would be inefficient. Consequently, because isoquants show only efficient production, an upward-sloping isoquant is impossible.

Fourth, *isoquants must be thin*. This result follows from virtually the same argument we just used to show that isoquants slope downward.

Shape of Isoquants. The curvature of an isoquant shows how readily a firm can substitute one input for another. The two extreme cases are production processes in which inputs are perfect substitutes and those in which inputs cannot be substituted for each other.

If the inputs are perfect substitutes, each isoquant is a straight line. Suppose either potatoes from Maine, x, or potatoes from Idaho, y, both of which are measured in pounds per day, can be used to produce potato salad, q, measured in pounds. This technology has a *linear production function*,

$$q = x + y.$$

A pound of potato salad can be produced by using one pound of Idaho potatoes and no Maine potatoes, one pound of Maine potatoes and no Idaho potatoes, or a half pound of each. The isoquant for $q =$ one pound of potato salad is $1 = x + y$, or $y = 1 - x$. The slope of this straight-line isoquant is -1. Panel a of Figure 6.3 shows the $q = 1$, 2, and 3 isoquants.

Sometimes it is impossible to substitute one input for the other: Inputs must be used in fixed proportions. Such a technology is called a *fixed-proportions production function*. For example, the inputs needed to produce a 12-ounce box of cereal, q, are cereal (12-ounce units per day), g, and cardboard boxes (boxes per day), b. This fixed-proportions production function is

$$q = \min(g, b),$$

where the min function means "the minimum number of g or b." For example, if the firm has $g = 4$ units of cereal and $b = 3$ boxes, it can produce only $q = 3$ boxes of cereal. Thus, in panel b of Figure 6.3, the only efficient points of production are the large dots along the 45° line, where the firm uses equal quantities of both inputs. Dashed lines show that the isoquants would be right angles if isoquants could include inefficient production processes.

Figure 6.3 Substitutability of Inputs

(a) If the inputs are perfect substitutes, each isoquant is a straight line. (b) If the inputs cannot be substituted at all, the isoquants are right angles (the dashed lines show that the isoquants would be right angles if we included inefficient production). (c) Typical isoquants lie between the extreme cases of straight lines and right angles. Along a curved isoquant, the ability to substitute one input for another varies.

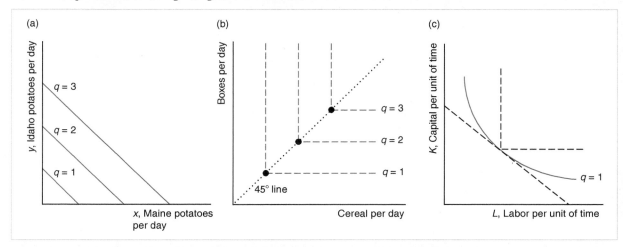

Other production processes allow imperfect substitution between inputs. These isoquants are convex (so the middle of the isoquant is closer to the origin than it would be if the isoquant were a straight line). They do not have the same slope at every point, unlike the straight-line isoquants. Most isoquants are smooth, slope downward, curve away from the origin, and lie between the extreme cases of straight lines (perfect substitutes) and right angles (nonsubstitutes), as panel c of Figure 6.3 illustrates.

APPLICATION

Self-Driving Trucks

We can show why isoquants curve away from the origin by deriving an isoquant for trucking.

Self-driving trucks are poised to revolutionize trucking. Otto (owned by Uber), Tesla, Embark, Peloton, and over 50 other companies are investing more than a $1 billion on developing self-driving truck and other high-tech trucking technologies.

Autonomous trucks are starting to hit the road. In 2016, an Otto self-driving truck carried 2,000 cases of Budweiser beer from Fort Collins, Colorado, to Colorado Springs along Interstate 25. In 2017, Empark autonomous trucks started hauling Frigidaire refrigerators 650 miles along the I-10 freeway from El Paso, Texas, to Palm Springs, California. Uber predicts that between 500,000 and 1.5 million self-driving trucks will be on the road by 2028.

Soon, a company that wants to transport a given amount of goods from one city to another will choose between two technologies:

- *Traditional*: A trucker drives the entire route.
- *Self-Driving*: A trucker drives the first and last few miles through complex urban roads, but an autonomous truck drives the highway portion unattended.

A driver is legally restricted to 11 hours of driving a day and 60 hours a week. Given that big rigs cost $150,000 or more, leaving them idle for part of the day is wasteful. A self-driving truck can operate around the clock, with various human drivers handling the short distances at either end of a route. The alternative is to have the traditional big-rig driven by several drivers.

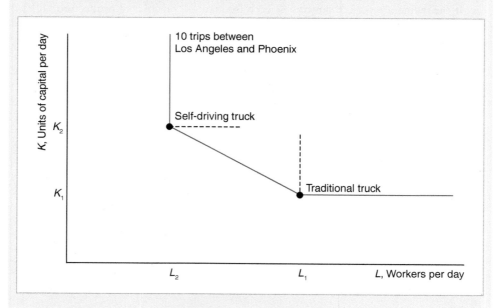

The diagram shows the isoquant for 10 trips between Los Angeles and Phoenix. The vertical axis measures the amount of capital, and the horizontal records the amount of labor. Both technologies use labor and capital in fixed proportions. The diagram shows the two right-angle isoquants corresponding to each of these technologies.

The traditional truck contains less capital, K_1, than does the self-driving truck, K_2, which also includes artificial intelligence (AI). However, the traditional technology uses more labor, L_1, than does the self-driving technology.

A truck company could use a combination of traditional and self-driving trucks. By doing so, the firm can produce using intermediate combinations of labor and capital, as the solid-line, kinked isoquant illustrates.

New processes are constantly being invented. As they are introduced, the isoquant will have more and more kinks (one for each new process) and will begin to resemble the smooth, convex isoquants we've been drawing.

Substituting Inputs

The slope of an isoquant shows the ability of a firm to replace one input with another while holding output constant. The slope of an isoquant is called the *marginal rate of technical substitution*:

$$MRTS = \frac{\text{Change in capital}}{\text{Change in labor}} = \frac{\Delta K}{\Delta L} = \frac{dK}{dL}.$$

The **marginal rate of technical substitution** (*MRTS*) tells us how many units of capital the firm can replace with an extra unit of labor while holding output constant. Because isoquants slope downward, the *MRTS* is negative.

To determine the slope at a point on an isoquant, we totally differentiate the isoquant, $\bar{q} = f(L, K)$, with respect to L and K. Along the isoquant, we can write capital as an implicit function of labor: $K(L)$. This function determines the level of capital that produces $\bar{q}$ units for the specified level of labor. Differentiating with respect to labor (and realizing that output does not change along the isoquant as we change labor, so $d\bar{q}/dL = 0$), we have

$$\frac{d\bar{q}}{dL} = 0 = \frac{\partial f}{\partial L} + \frac{\partial f}{\partial K}\frac{dK}{dL} = MP_L + MP_K\frac{dK}{dL}, \tag{6.7}$$

where $MP_K = \partial f/\partial K$ is the marginal product of capital.

Equation 6.7 has an appealing intuition. As we move down and to the right along an isoquant (such as the ones in Figure 6.2), we increase the amount of labor slightly, so we must decrease the amount of capital to stay on the same isoquant. A little extra labor produces MP_L amount of extra output, the marginal product of labor. For example, if the MP_L is 2 and the firm hires one extra worker, its output rises by 2 units. Similarly, a little extra capital increases output by MP_K, so the change in output due to the drop in capital in response to the increase in labor is $MP_K \times dK/dL$. If we are to stay on the same isoquant—that is, hold output constant—these two effects must offset each other: $MP_L = -MP_K \times dK/dL$.

By rearranging Equation 6.7, we find that the marginal rate of technical substitution, which is the change in capital relative to the change in labor, equals the negative of the ratio of the marginal products:

$$MRTS = \frac{dK}{dL} = -\frac{MP_L}{MP_K}. \tag{6.8}$$

SOLVED PROBLEM 6.3

What is the marginal rate of technical substitution for a general Cobb-Douglas production function, Equation 6.4, $q = AL^aK^b$?

**MyLab Economics
Solved Problem**

Answer

1. *Calculate the marginal products of labor and capital by differentiating the Cobb-Douglas production function first with respect to labor and then with respect to capital.* The marginal product of labor is $MP_L = \partial q/\partial L = aAL^{a-1}K^b = aq/L$, and the marginal product of capital is $MP_K = \partial q/\partial K = bAL^aK^{b-1} = bq/K$.

2. *Substitute the expression for MP_L and MP_K into Equation 6.8 to determine the MRTS.* Making the indicated substitutions,

$$MRTS = -\frac{MP_L}{MP_K} = -\frac{a\dfrac{q}{L}}{b\dfrac{q}{K}} = -\frac{a}{b}\frac{K}{L}. \qquad (6.9)$$

Thus, the *MRTS* for a Cobb-Douglas production function is a constant, $-a/b$, times the capital-labor ratio, K/L.

Diminishing Marginal Rates of Technical Substitution

We can illustrate how the *MRTS* changes along an isoquant using the estimated $q = 6 = L^{0.5}K^{0.5}$ isoquant for an electronics firm from Figure 6.2, which is reproduced in Figure 6.4. Setting $a = b = 0.5$ in Equation 6.9, we find that the slope along this isoquant is $MRTS = -K/L$.

At point c in Figure 6.4, where $K = 12$ and $L = 3$, the $MRTS = -4$. The dashed line that is tangent to the isoquant at that point has the same slope. In contrast, the $MRTS = -1$ at d ($K = 6$, $L = 6$), and the $MRTS = -0.25$ at e ($K = 3$, $L = 12$). Thus, as we move down and to the right along this curved isoquant, the slope becomes flatter—the slope gets closer to zero—because the ratio K/L grows closer to zero.

The curvature of the isoquant away from the origin reflects *diminishing marginal rates of technical substitution*. The more labor the firm has, the harder it is to replace the remaining capital with labor, so the *MRTS* falls as the isoquant becomes flatter.

In the special case in which isoquants are straight lines, isoquants do not exhibit diminishing marginal rates of technical substitution because neither input becomes more valuable in the production process: The inputs remain perfect substitutes. In our earlier example of producing potato salad, the *MRTS* is -1 at every point along the isoquant: One pound of Idaho potatoes always can be replaced by one pound of Maine potatoes. In the other special case of fixed proportions, where isoquants are right angles (or, perhaps more accurately, single points), no substitution is possible.

The Elasticity of Substitution

We've just seen that the marginal rate of technical substitution, the slope of the isoquant at a single point, varies as we move along a curved isoquant. It is useful to have a measure of this curvature, which reflects the ease with which a firm can substitute

Figure 6.4 How the Marginal Rate of Technical Substitution Varies Along an Isoquant

Moving from point c to d, a U.S. electronics firm (Hsieh, 1995) can produce the same amount of output, $q = 6$, using six fewer units of capital, $\Delta K = -6$, if it uses three more workers. The slope of the isoquant, the *MRTS*, at a point is the same as the slope of the dashed tangent line. The *MRTS* goes from -4 at point c to -1 at d to -0.25 at e. Thus, as we move down and to the right, the isoquant becomes flatter: The slope gets closer to zero. Because it curves away from the origin, this isoquant exhibits a diminishing marginal rate of technical substitution: With each extra worker, the firm reduces capital by a smaller amount as the ratio of capital to labor falls.

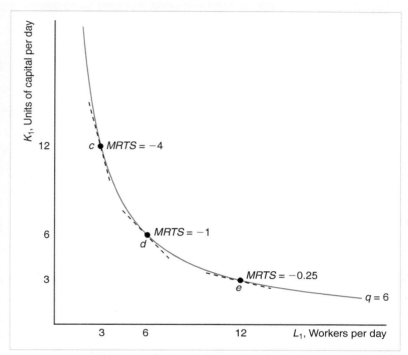

capital for labor. The best-known measure of the ease of substitution is the **elasticity of substitution**, σ (the Greek letter sigma), which is the percentage change in the capital-labor ratio divided by the percentage change in the *MRTS*:

$$\sigma = \frac{\dfrac{d(K/L)}{K/L}}{\dfrac{d\ MRTS}{MRTS}} = \frac{d(K/L)}{dMRTS}\ \frac{MRTS}{K/L}. \tag{6.10}$$

This measure tells us how the input factor ratio changes as the slope of the isoquant changes. If the elasticity is large—a small change in the slope results in a big increase in the factor ratio—the isoquant is relatively flat. The lower the elasticity, the more curved is the isoquant. As we move along the isoquant, both K/L and the absolute value of the *MRTS* change in the same direction (see Figure 6.4), so the elasticity is positive.

Both the factor ratio, K/L, and the absolute value of the *MRTS*, $|MRTS|$, are positive numbers, so the logarithm of each is meaningful. It is often helpful to write the elasticity of substitution as a logarithmic derivative:[6]

$$\sigma = \frac{d\ln(K/L)}{d\ln|MRTS|}. \tag{6.11}$$

---

[6]By totally differentiating, we find that $d\ln(K/L) = d(K/L)/(K/L)$ and $d\ln|MRTS| = dMRTS/MRTS$, so $[d\ln(K/L)]/[d\ln|MRTS|] = [d(K/L)/dMRTS][MRTS/(K/L)] = \sigma$.

Constant Elasticity of Substitution Production Function. In general, the elasticity of substitution varies along an isoquant. An exception is the *constant elasticity of substitution (CES)* production function,

$$q = (aL^\rho + bK^\rho)^{\frac{d}{\rho}}, \tag{6.12}$$

where $\rho < 1$ is a constant. For simplicity, we assume that $a = b = d = 1$, so

$$q = (L^\rho + K^\rho)^{\frac{1}{\rho}}. \tag{6.13}$$

The marginal rate of technical substitution for a CES isoquant is[7]

$$MRTS = -\left(\frac{L}{K}\right)^{\rho-1}. \tag{6.14}$$

That is, the *MRTS* varies with the labor-capital ratio. At every point on a CES isoquant, the constant elasticity of substitutions is[8]

$$\sigma = \frac{1}{1-\rho}. \tag{6.15}$$

The linear, fixed-proportion, and Cobb-Douglas production functions are special cases of the CES production function.

Chirinko and Mallick (2014) estimated a CES industry-level elasticity of substitution in various industries: 0.15 in paper, 0.29 in agriculture, 0.30 in rubber and miscellaneous plastics, 0.56 in primary metal, 0.744 in trade, and 1.16 in finance, insurance, and real estate.

Linear Production Function. Setting $\rho = 1$ in Equation 6.13, we get the linear production function $q = L + K$. At every point along a linear isoquant, the elasticity of substitution, $\sigma = 1/(1 - \rho) = 1/0$, is infinite: The two inputs are perfect substitutes.

Fixed-Proportion Production Function. As ρ approaches negative infinity, the CES production function approaches the fixed-proportion production function, which has right-angle isoquants (or, more accurately, single-point isoquants).[9] The elasticity of substitution is $\sigma = 1/(-\infty)$, which approaches zero: Substitution between the inputs is impossible.

Cobb-Douglas Production Function. As ρ approaches zero, a CES isoquant approaches a Cobb-Douglas isoquant, and hence the CES production function approaches a Cobb-Douglas production function.[10] According to Equation 6.14 for the CES production function, $MRTS = -(L/K)^{\rho-1}$. In the limit as ρ approaches zero, $MRTS = -K/L$. (We obtain the same result by setting $a = b$ in Equation 6.9.) The elasticity of substitution is $\sigma = 1/(1 - \rho) = 1/1 = 1$ at every point along a Cobb-Douglas isoquant.

---

[7]Using the chain rule, we know that the $MP_L = (1/\rho)(L^\rho + K^\rho)^{1/\rho-1}\rho L^{\rho-1} = (L^\rho + K^\rho)^{1/\rho-1}L^{\rho-1}$. Similarly, the $MP_K = (L^\rho + K^\rho)^{1/\rho-1}K^{\rho-1}$. Thus, the $MRTS = -MP_L/MP_K = -(L/K)^{\rho-1}$.

[8]From the *MRTS* Equation 6.14, we know that $K/L = |MRTS|^{1/(1-\rho)}$. Taking logarithms of both sides of this expression, we find that $\ln(K/L) = [1/(1 - \rho)]\ln|MRTS|$. We use the logarithmic derivative of the elasticity of substitution, Equation 6.11, to show that $\sigma = (d \ln K/L)/(d \ln|MRTS|) = 1/(1 - \rho)$.

[9]According to Equation 6.15, as ρ approaches $-\infty$, the *MRTS* approaches $-(L/K)^{-\infty}$. Thus, the *MRTS* is zero if $L > K$, and the *MRTS* goes to infinity if $K > L$.

[10]Balistreri, McDaniel, and Wong (2003) used a CES production function to estimate substitution elasticities for 28 industries that cover the entire U.S. economy and found that the estimated CES substitution elasticity did not differ significantly from the Cobb-Douglas elasticity in 20 of the 28 industries.

SOLVED PROBLEM 6.4

MyLab Economics
Solved Problem

What is the elasticity of substitution for the general Cobb-Douglas production function, Equation 6.4, $q = AL^a K^b$? (*Comment*: We just showed that the elasticity of substitution is one for a Cobb-Douglas production function where $a = b$. We want to know if that result holds for the more general Cobb-Douglas production function.)

Answer

1. *Using the formula for the marginal rate of technical substitution, determine d(K/L)/dMRTS and MRTS/(K/L), which appear in the elasticity of substitution formula.* The marginal rate of technical substitution of a general Cobb-Douglas production function, Equation 6.9, is $MRTS = -(a/b)(K/L)$. Rearranging these terms,

$$\frac{K}{L} = -\frac{b}{a} MRTS. \tag{6.16}$$

Differentiating Equation 6.16 with respect to $MRTS$, we find that $d(K/L)/dMRTS = -b/a$. By rearranging the terms in Equation 6.16, we also know that $MRTS/(K/L) = -a/b$.

2. *Substitute the two expressions from Step 1 into the elasticity of substitution formula and simplify.* The elasticity of substitution for a Cobb-Douglas production function is

$$\sigma = \frac{d(K/L)}{dMRTS} \frac{MRTS}{K/L} = \left(-\frac{b}{a}\right)\left(-\frac{a}{b}\right) = 1. \tag{6.17}$$

6.5 Returns to Scale

So far, we have examined the effects of increasing one input while holding the other input constant (the shift from one isoquant to another), or decreasing the other input by an offsetting amount (the movement along an isoquant). We now turn to the question of *how much output changes if a firm increases all its inputs proportionately.* The answer to this question helps a firm determine its *scale* or size in the long run.

In the long run, a firm can increase its output by building a second plant and staffing it with the same number of workers as in the first plant. The firm's decision about whether to build a second plant partly depends on whether its output increases less than in proportion, in proportion, or more than in proportion to its inputs.

Constant, Increasing, and Decreasing Returns to Scale

If, when all inputs are increased by a certain percentage, output increases by that same percentage, the production function is said to exhibit **constant returns to scale** (*CRS*). A firm's production process has constant returns to scale if, when the firm doubles its inputs—for example, builds an identical second plant and uses the same amount of labor and equipment as in the first plant—it doubles its output: $f(2L, 2K) = 2f(L, K)$. [More generally, a production function is homogeneous of degree g if $f(xL, xK) = x^g f(L, K)$, where x is a positive constant. Thus, constant returns to scale is homogeneity of degree one.]

We can check whether the linear potato salad production function has constant returns to scale. If a firm uses x_1 pounds of Idaho potatoes and y_1 pounds of Maine potatoes, it produces $q_1 = x_1 + y_1$ pounds of potato salad. If it doubles both inputs, using $x_2 = 2x_1$ Idaho potatoes and $y_2 = 2y_1$ Maine potatoes, it doubles its output:

$$q_2 = x_2 + y_2 = 2x_1 + 2y_1 = 2q_1.$$

This'll save a lot of time!

Thus, the potato salad production function exhibits constant returns to scale.

If output rises more than in proportion to an equal percentage increase in all inputs, the production function is said to exhibit **increasing returns to scale** (*IRS*). A technology exhibits increasing returns to scale if doubling inputs more than doubles the output: $f(2L, 2K) > 2f(L, K)$.

Why might a production function have increasing returns to scale? One reason is that although a firm could duplicate its small factory and double its output, it might be able to more than double its output by building a single large plant, which may allow for greater specialization of labor or capital. In the two smaller plants, workers must perform many unrelated tasks, such as operating, maintaining, and fixing machines. In the single large plant, some workers may specialize in maintaining and fixing machines, thereby increasing efficiency. Similarly, a firm may use specialized equipment in a large plant but not in a small one.

If output rises less than in proportion to an equal percentage increase in all inputs, the production function exhibits **decreasing returns to scale** (*DRS*). A technology exhibits decreasing returns to scale if doubling inputs causes output to rise less than in proportion: $f(2L, 2K) < 2f(L, K)$.

One reason for decreasing returns to scale is that the difficulty of organizing, coordinating, and integrating activities increases with firm size. An owner may be able to manage one plant well but may have trouble running two plants. In some sense, the owner's difficulties in running a larger firm may reflect our failure to consider some factor such as management in our production function. When the firm increases the various inputs, it does not increase the management input in proportion. Therefore, the decreasing returns to scale is really due to a fixed input. Another reason is that large teams of workers may not function as well as small teams in which each individual has greater personal responsibility.

SOLVED PROBLEM 6.5	Under what conditions does a general Cobb-Douglas production function, $q = AL^a K^b$, exhibit decreasing, constant, or increasing returns to scale?
MyLab Economics Solved Problem	**Answer**

Answer

1. *Show how output changes if both inputs are doubled.* If the firm initially uses L and K amounts of inputs, it produces $q_1 = AL^a K^b$. After the firm doubles the amount of both labor and capital, it produces

$$q_2 = A(2L)^a (2K)^b = 2^{a+b} AL^a K^b. \qquad (6.18)$$

That is, q_2 is 2^{a+b} times q_1. If we define $g = a + b$, then Equation 6.18 tells us that

$$q_2 = 2^g q_1. \tag{6.19}$$

Thus, if the inputs double, output increases by 2^g.

2. *Give a rule for determining the returns to scale.* If we set $g = 1$ in Equation 6.19, we find that $q_2 = 2^1 q_1 = 2q_1$. That is, output doubles when the inputs double, so the Cobb-Douglas production function has constant returns to scale. If $g < 1$, then $q_2 = 2^g q_1 < 2q_1$ because $2^g < 2$ if $g < 1$. That is, when input doubles, output increases less than in proportion, so this Cobb-Douglas production function exhibits decreasing returns to scale. Finally, the Cobb-Douglas production function has increasing returns to scale if $g > 1$ so that $q_2 > 2q_1$. Thus, the rule for determining returns to scale for a Cobb-Douglas production function is that the returns to scale are decreasing if $g < 1$, constant if $g = 1$, and increasing if $g > 1$.

Comment: Thus, g is a measure of the returns to scale. It is a *scale elasticity*: If all inputs increase by 1%, output increases by g%.

APPLICATION

Returns to Scale in Various Industries

Increasing, constant, and decreasing returns to scale are common. The table shows estimates of Cobb-Douglas production functions and returns to scale in various industries.

	Labor, *a*	Capital, *b*	Scale, *g* = *a* + *b*
Decreasing Returns to Scale			
U.S. tobacco products[a]	0.18	0.33	0.51
Bangladesh glass[b]	0.27	0.45	0.72
Danish food and beverages[c]	0.69	0.18	0.87
Chinese high technology[d]	0.28	0.66	0.94
Constant Returns to Scale			
Japanese synthetic rubber[e]	0.50	0.50	1.00
Japanese beer[e]	0.60	0.40	1.00
New Zealand wholesale trade[f]	0.60	0.42	1.02
Danish publishing and printing[c]	0.89	0.14	1.03
Increasing Returns to Scale			
New Zealand mining[f]	0.69	0.45	1.14
Bangladesh leather products[b]	0.86	0.27	1.13
Bangladesh fabricated metal[b]	0.98	0.28	1.26

[a]Hsieh (1995); [b]Hossain, Basak, and Majumber (2012); [c]Fox and Smeets (2011); [d]Zhang, Delgado, and Kumbhakar (2012); [e]Flath (2011); [f]Devine, Doan, and Stevens (2012).

The graphs use isoquants to illustrate the returns to scale for three firms: a Japanese beer firm, a U.S. tobacco firm, and a Bangladesh fabricated metal firm.

We measure the units of labor, capital, and output so that, for all three firms, 100 units of labor and 100 units of capital produce 100 units of output on the $q = 100$ isoquant in the three panels. These graphs illustrate that the spacing of the isoquant reflects the returns to scale. The closer together the $q = 100$ and $q = 200$ isoquants, the greater the returns to scale.

In panel a, the beer firm has constant returns to scale because $\gamma = 1$: A 1% increase in the inputs causes output to rise by 1%. If both its labor and capital are doubled from 100 to 200 units, output doubles to 200 ($= 100 \times 2^1$, multiplying the original output by the rate of increase using Equation 6.19).

In panel b, the tobacco firm has decreasing returns to scale because $\gamma = 0.51$. The same doubling of inputs causes output to rise to only 142 ($\approx 100 \times 2^{0.51}$) for the tobacco firm: Output rises less than in proportion to inputs.

In panel c, the fabricated metal firm exhibits increasing returns to scale because $\gamma = 1.26$. If it doubles its inputs, its output more than doubles, to 239 ($\approx 100 \times 2^{1.26}$), so the production function has increasing returns to scale.

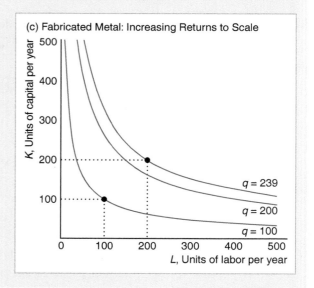

Varying Returns to Scale

Many production functions have increasing returns to scale for small amounts of output, constant returns for moderate amounts of output, and decreasing returns for large amounts of output. With a small firm, increasing labor and capital may produce gains from cooperation between workers and greater specialization of workers and equipment—*returns to specialization*—resulting in increasing returns to scale. Firm growth eventually exhausts returns to scale. With no more returns to specialization, the production process exhibits constant returns to scale. If the firm continues to grow, managing the staff becomes more difficult, so the firm suffers from decreasing returns to scale.

Figure 6.5 Varying Scale Economies

This production function exhibits varying returns to scale. Initially, the firm uses one worker and one unit of capital, point *a*. It repeatedly doubles these inputs to points *b*, *c*, and *d*, which lie along the dashed line. The first time the inputs are doubled, *a* to *b*, output more than doubles from $q = 1$ to $q = 3$, so the production function has increasing returns to scale. The next doubling, *b* to *c*, causes a proportionate increase in output, constant returns to scale. At the last doubling, from *c* to *d*, the production function exhibits decreasing returns to scale.

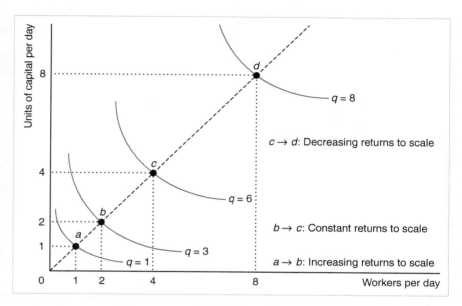

Figure 6.5 shows such a pattern. Again, the spacing of the isoquants reflects the returns to scale. Initially, the firm has one worker and one piece of equipment, point *a*, and produces one unit of output on the $q = 1$ isoquant. If the firm doubles its inputs, it produces at *b*, where $L = 2$ and $K = 2$, which lies on the dashed line through the origin and point *a*. Output more than doubles to $q = 3$, so the production function exhibits increasing returns to scale in this range. Another doubling of inputs to *c* causes output to double to $q = 6$, so the production function has constant returns to scale in this range. Another doubling of inputs to *d* causes output to increase by only one-third, to $q = 8$, so the production function has decreasing returns to scale in this range.

6.6 Productivity and Technical Change

Because firms may use different technologies and different methods of organizing production, the amount of output that one firm produces from a given amount of inputs may differ from that produced by another. Moreover, after a technical or managerial innovation, a firm can produce more today from a given amount of inputs than it could in the past.

Relative Productivity

This chapter has assumed that firms produce efficiently. A firm must produce efficiently to maximize its profit. However, even if each firm in a market produces as efficiently as possible, firms may not be equally *productive*. One firm may be able to produce more than another from a given amount of inputs.

A firm may be more productive than another if its management knows a better way to organize production or if it has access to a new invention. Union-mandated work rules, racial or gender discrimination, government regulations, or other institutional restrictions that affect only certain firms may lower the relative productivity of those firms.

Differences in productivity across markets may be due to differences in the degree of competition. In competitive markets, where many firms can enter and exit easily, less productive firms lose money and are driven out of business, so the firms that actually continue to produce are equally productive (see Chapter 8). In a less competitive market with few firms and no possibility of entry by new ones, a less productive firm may be able to survive, so firms with varying levels of productivity are observed.

Innovations

Maximum number of miles that Ford's most fuel-efficient 2003 car could drive on a gallon of gas: 36. Maximum number its 1912 Model T could: 35. —Harper's Index 2003

In its production process, a firm tries to use the best available technological and managerial knowledge. **Technical progress** is an advance in knowledge that allows more output to be produced with the same level of inputs. The invention of new products is a form of technical progress. The use of robotic arms increases the number of automobiles produced with a given amount of labor and raw materials. Better *management* or *organization of the production process* similarly allows the firm to produce more output from given levels of inputs.

Technical Progress. A technological innovation changes the production process. Last year, a firm produced

$$q_1 = f(L, K)$$

units of output using L units of labor services and K units of capital service. Due to a new invention used by the firm, this year's production function differs from last year's, so the firm produces 10% more output with the same inputs:

$$q_2 = 1.1f(L, K).$$

Surprisingly, those robo-arms increase productivity substantially.

This firm has experienced *neutral technical change*, in which it can produce more output using the same ratio of inputs. For example, a technical innovation in the form of a new printing press allows more output to be produced using the same ratio of inputs as before: one worker to one printing press.

Many empirical studies find that systematic neutral technical progress occurs over time. In these studies, the production function is

$$q = A(t)f(L, K), \tag{6.20}$$

where $A(t)$ is a function of time, t, that shows how much output grows over time for any given mix of inputs. For example, the annual rate at which computer and related goods output grew for given levels of inputs was 0.9% in the United Kingdom, 1.0% in Canada, 1.3% in the United States, 1.4% in France, and 1.5% in Australia.[11] Given that the U.S. annual growth rate is 1.3%, the U.S. computer production function, Equation 6.20, is $q = 1.013^t f(L,K)$, where t increases by 1 unit each year.

---

[11]OECD Productivity Database, December 17, 2004.

Non-neutral technical changes are innovations that alter the proportion in which inputs are used. Technological progress could be *capital saving*, where relatively less capital is used relative to other inputs. For example, the development of cell phones allowed firms to eliminate enough landline phones, fax machines, and computers to lower the capital-labor ratio for its sales or repair workers while increasing output.

Alternatively, technological progress may be *labor saving*. The development of self-driving trucks is an example of labor-saving technical progress. Basker (2012) found that the introduction of barcode scanners in grocery stores increased the average product of labor by 4.5% on average across stores. By 2017, Amazon was using at least 100,000 robots at its warehouses around the world to move items. Today, robots help doctors perform surgery more quickly and reduce patients' recovery times.

APPLICATION

Robots and the Food You Eat

Robots have been used in manufacturing for many years, and they are now gaining a foothold in agriculture. A strawberry-picking robot called the Agrobot costs about $100,000 and, despite the expense, is attracting buyers in California. The Hackney Nursery in Florida uses robots to assess whether flowers have adequate room to grow optimally and to move the flowers around accordingly. And fully autonomous cow-milking robots are widely used.

It is not just the farming end of the food business that is using robots. In 2016, KFC opened the world's first human-free fast food restaurant in Shanghai. In 2018, Spyce opened in Boston, claiming to be the first restaurant with a robotic kitchen that cooks complex meals.

The Dalu Robot Restaurant in Jinan, China, uses robots to wait on tables, greet customers, and provide entertainment. Each robot serving food has a motion sensor that tells it to stop when someone is in its path so customers can reach for dishes they want. But perhaps the most popular employee is a female robot, complete with batting eyelashes, who greets people with an electronic "welcome." First-time customer Li Xiaomei praised the robots, claiming that "they have a better service attitude than humans."

However, restaurant jobs may not be on their way out just yet. China's *Workers' Daily* newspaper reported that three restaurants in the Chinese city of Guangzhou fired their robotic staff for incompetence.

Organizational Change. Organizational change may also alter the production function and increase the amount of output produced by a given amount of inputs. In 1904, King C. Gillette used automated production techniques to produce a new type of razor blade that could be sold for 5¢—a fraction of the price charged by rivals—allowing working men to shave daily.

In the early 1900s, Henry Ford revolutionized mass production through two organizational innovations. First, he introduced interchangeable parts, which cut the time required to install parts because workers no longer had to file or machine individually made parts to get them to fit. Second, Ford introduced a conveyor belt and an assembly line to his production process. Before Ford, workers walked around the car, and each worker performed many assembly activities. In Ford's plant, each worker specialized in a single activity, such as attaching the right rear fender to the chassis. A conveyor belt moved the car at a constant speed from worker to worker along the assembly line. Because his workers gained proficiency from specializing in only a few activities, and because the conveyor belts reduced the number of movements workers had to make, Ford could produce more automobiles with the same number of workers. In 1908, the Ford Model T sold for $850, when rival vehicles sold for $2,000. By the early 1920s, Ford had increased production from fewer than 1,000 cars per year to 2 million cars per year.

APPLICATION A Good Boss Raises Productivity	Does a good supervisor make workers more productive? To answer this question, Lazear, Shaw, and Stanton (2015) looked at a large service-oriented company. Supervisor quality varied substantially, as measured by the boss's effect on worker productivity. Replacing one of the 10% worst bosses with one of the 10% best ones raised a team's output by about the same amount as adding one worker to a nine-member team. Thus, differences in managers can cause one firm to be more productive than another.

CHALLENGE SOLUTION **Labor Productivity During Downturns**	We can use what we've learned to answer the question posed at the beginning of the chapter about how labor productivity, as measured by the average product of labor, changes during a recession when a firm reduces its output by reducing the number of workers it employs. How much will the output produced per worker rise or fall with each additional layoff?

In the short run, when the firm holds its capital constant, layoffs have the positive effect of freeing up machines to be used by the remaining workers. However, if layoffs mean that the remaining workers might have to "multitask" to replace departed colleagues, the firm will lose the benefits from specialization. When a firm has many workers, the advantage of freeing up machines is important and increased multitasking is unlikely to be a problem. With only a few workers, freeing up more machines does not help much—some machines might stand idle part of the time—while multitasking becomes a more serious problem. As a result, laying off a worker might raise the average product of labor if the firm has many workers relative to the available capital, but might reduce average product if it has only a few workers.

For example, in panel b of Figure 6.1, the average product of labor rises with the number of workers up to 15 workers and then falls as the number of workers increases. As a result, the average product of labor falls if the firm initially has fewer than 15 workers and lays one off, but rises if the firm initially has more than 15 workers and lays off a worker.

However, for some production functions, layoffs always raise labor productivity because the AP_L curve is downward sloping everywhere. For such a production function, the positive effect of freeing up capital always dominates any negative effect of layoffs on the average product of labor.

Consider a Cobb-Douglas production function, $q = AL^aK^b$, where $AP_L = q/L = q = AL^{a-1}K^b$. If we increase labor slightly, the change in the average product of labor is $dAP_L/dL = (a - 1)AL^{a-2}K^b$. Thus, if $(a - 1)$ is negative (that is, $a < 1$), the AP_L falls with extra labor. This condition holds for all of the estimated Cobb-Douglas production functions listed in the Application "Returns to Scale in Various Industries" (though not necessarily in all industries).

For example, for the beer firm's estimated Cobb-Douglas production function (Flath, 2011), $q = AL^{0.6}K^{0.4}$, $a = 0.6$ is less than 1, so the AP_L curve slopes downward at every quantity. We can illustrate how much the AP_L rises with a layoff for this particular production function. If $A = 1$ and $L = K = 10$ initially, then the firm's output is $q = 10^{0.6} \times 10^{0.4} = 10$, and its average product of labor is $AP_L = q/L = 10/10 = 1$. If the number of workers is reduced by one, then output falls to $q = 9^{0.6} \times 10^{0.4} \approx 9.39$, and the average product of labor rises to $AP_L \approx 9.39/9 \approx 1.04$. That is, a 10% reduction in labor causes output to *fall* by 6.1%, but causes the average product of labor to *rise* by 4%. The firm's output falls less than 10% because each remaining worker is more productive.

This increase in labor productivity in many industries reduces the impact of a recession on output in the United States. However, this increase in labor productivity is not always observed in other countries that are less likely to lay off workers during a downturn. Until recently, most large Japanese firms did not lay off workers during recessions. Thus, in contrast to U.S. firms, their average product of labor decreased substantially during recessions because their output fell while labor remained constant.

Similarly, European firms show 30% less employment volatility over time than do U.S. firms, at least in part because European firms that fire workers are subject to a tax (Veracierto, 2008).[12] Consequently, with other factors held constant in the short run, recessions might be more damaging to the profit and output of a Japanese or European firm than to the profit and output of a comparable U.S. firm. However, retaining good workers over short-run downturns might be a good long-run policy for the firm as well as for workers.

SUMMARY

1. **The Ownership and Management of Firms.** Firms can be sole proprietorships, partnerships, or corporations. In small firms (particularly sole proprietorships and partnerships), the owners usually run the company. In large firms (such as most corporations), the owners hire managers to run the firms. Owners want to maximize profits. If managers have different objectives than owners, owners must keep a close watch to ensure that profits are maximized.

2. **Production.** Inputs, or factors of production—labor, capital, and materials—are combined to produce output using the current state of knowledge about technology and management. To maximize profits, a firm must produce as efficiently as possible: It must get the maximum amount of output from the inputs it uses, given existing knowledge. A firm may have access to many efficient production processes that use different combinations of inputs to produce a given level of output. New technologies or new forms of organization can increase the amount of output that can be produced from a given combination of inputs. A production function shows how much output can be produced efficiently from various levels of inputs. A firm can vary all its inputs in the long run but only some of its inputs in the short run.

3. **Short-Run Production: One Variable and One Fixed Input.** In the short run, a firm cannot adjust the quantity of some inputs, such as capital. The firm varies its output by adjusting its variable inputs, such as labor. If all factors are fixed except labor, and a firm that was using very little labor increases its labor, its output may rise more than in proportion to the increase in labor because of greater specialization of workers. Eventually, however, as more workers are hired, the workers get in each other's way or wait to share equipment, so output increases by smaller and smaller amounts. This phenomenon is described by the law of diminishing marginal returns: The marginal product of an input—the extra output from the last unit of input—eventually decreases as more of that input is used, holding other inputs fixed.

---

[12]Severance payments for blue-collar workers with ten years of experience may exceed one year of wages in some European countries, unlike in the United States.

4. **Long-Run Production: Two Variable Inputs.** In the long run, when all inputs are variable, firms can substitute between inputs. An isoquant shows the combinations of inputs that can produce a given level of output. The marginal rate of technical substitution is the slope of the isoquant. Usually, the more of one input the firm uses, the more difficult it is to substitute that input for another input. That is, the firm experiences diminishing marginal rates of technical substitution as the firm uses more of one input. The elasticity of substitution reflects the ease of replacing one input with another in the production process, or, equivalently, the curvature of an isoquant.

5. **Returns to Scale.** If, when a firm increases all inputs in proportion, its output increases by the same proportion, the production process exhibits constant returns to scale. If output increases less than in proportion to inputs, the production process has decreasing returns to scale; if it increases more than in proportion, it has increasing returns to scale. All these types of returns to scale are commonly observed in various industries. Many production processes first exhibit increasing, then constant, and finally decreasing returns to scale as the size of the firm increases.

6. **Productivity and Technical Change.** Although all firms in an industry produce efficiently, given what they know and what institutional and other constraints they face, some firms may be more productive than others: They can produce more output from a given bundle of inputs. Due to innovations such as technical progress and new methods of organizing production, firms can produce more today than they could in the past from the same bundle of inputs. Such innovations change the production function.

EXERCISES

All exercises are available on **MyLab Economics;** * = *answer appears at the back of this book;* **M** = *mathematical problem.*

1. The Ownership and Management of Firms

1.1 Are firms with limited liability likely to be larger than other firms? Why?

1.2 What types of firms would not normally maximize profit?

1.3 What types of organization allow owners of a firm to obtain the advantages of limited liability?

2. Production

2.1 With respect to production functions, how long is the *short run*?

2.2 Consider Boeing (a producer of jet aircraft), General Mills (a producer of breakfast cereals), and Wacky Jack's (which claims to be the largest U.S. provider of singing telegrams). For which of these firms is the *short run* the longest period of time? For which is the *long run* the shortest? Explain.

*2.3 Suppose that for the production function $q = f(L, K)$, if $L = 3$ and $K = 5$ then $q = 10$. Is it possible that $L = 3$ and $K = 6$ also produces $q = 10$ for this production function? Why or why not?

3. Short-Run Production: One Variable and One Fixed Input

*3.1 If each extra worker produces an extra unit of output, how do the total product of labor, the average product of labor, and the marginal product of labor vary with the number of workers?

3.2 Each extra worker produces an extra unit of output, up to six workers. After six, no additional output is produced. Draw the total product of labor, average product of labor, and marginal product of labor curves.

3.3 In the short run, a firm cannot vary its capital, $\overline{K} = 2$, but it can vary its labor, L. It produces output q. Explain why the firm will or will not experience diminishing marginal returns to labor in the short run if its production function is $q = 10L + K$. (See Solved Problem 6.1.) **M**

*3.4 Suppose that the Cobb-Douglas production function is $q = L^{0.75}K^{0.25}$.

   a. What is the average product of labor, holding capital fixed?

   b. What is the marginal product of labor?

   c. What are the AP_L and MP_L when $\overline{K} = 16$? (See Solved Problem 6.1.) **M**

3.5 If the Cobb-Douglas production function is $q = L^{0.75}K^{0.25}$, and $\overline{K} = 16$, what is the elasticity of output with respect to labor? (See Solved Problem 6.2.) **M**

3.6 In the short run, a firm cannot vary its capital, $K = 2$, but can vary its labor, L. It produces output q. Explain why the firm will or will not experience diminishing marginal returns to labor in the short run if its production function is

   a. $q = 10L + K$,

   b. $q = L^{0.5}K^{0.5}$. **M**

3.7 Based on the information in the Application "Malthus and the Green Revolution," how did the average product of labor in corn production change over time?

4. Long-Run Production: Two Variable Inputs

4.1 What are the differences between an isoquant and an indifference curve?

4.2 Why must isoquants be thin? (*Hint*: See the discussion of why indifference curves must be thin in Chapter 3.)

4.3 Suppose that a firm has a fixed-proportions production function in which 1 unit of output is produced using one worker and 2 units of capital. If the firm has an extra worker and no more capital, it still can produce only 1 unit of output. Similarly, 1 more unit of capital produces no extra output.

   a. Draw the isoquants for this production function.

   b. Draw the total product of labor, average product of labor, and marginal product of labor curves (you will probably want to use two diagrams) for this production function.

*4.4 To produce a book, $q = 1$, a firm uses one unit of paper, $x = 1$, and the services of a printing press, $y = 1$, for eight minutes. Draw an isoquant for this production process. Explain the reason for its shape.

4.5 What is the production function if L and K are perfect substitutes and each unit of q requires 1 unit of L or 1 unit of K (or a combination of these inputs that equals 1)? **M**

4.6 The production function at Ginko's Copy Shop is $q = 1{,}000 \times \min(L, 3K)$, where q is the number of copies per hour, L is the number of workers, and K is the number of copy machines. As an example, if $L = 4$ and $K = 1$, then $\min(L, 3K) = 3$, and $q = 3{,}000$.

   a. Draw the isoquants for this production function.

   b. Draw the total product of labor, average product of labor, and marginal product of labor curves for this production function for some fixed level of capital.

*4.7 At $L = 4$ and $K = 4$, the marginal product of labor is 2 and the marginal product of capital is 3. What is the marginal rate of technical substitution? **M**

*4.8 Mark launders his white clothes using the production function $q = B + 0.5G$, where B is the number of cups of Clorox bleach and G is the number of cups of generic bleach that is half as potent. Draw an isoquant. What are the marginal products of B and G? What is the marginal rate of technical substitution at each point on an isoquant?

4.9 The isoquant in the Application "Self-Driving Trucks" is based on two technologies. Suppose that a company develops a third technology that assists but does not replace a human driver. It uses more labor and less capital than the fully self-driving technology but less labor and more capital than the traditional technology. In the isoquant diagram, the input combination needed to produce 10 trips lies below the straight line joining the input combinations for the traditional and self-driving technologies. Illustrate the resulting isoquant.

4.10 Draw a circle in a diagram with labor services on one axis and capital services on the other. This circle represents all the combinations of labor and capital that produce 100 units of output. Now, draw the isoquant for 100 units of output. (*Hint*: Remember that the isoquant includes only the efficient combinations of labor and capital.)

4.11 Michelle's business produces ceramic cups using labor, clay, and a kiln. She can manufacture 25 cups a day with one worker and 35 cups with two workers. Does her production process illustrate *diminishing returns to scale* or *diminishing marginal returns to scale*? Give a plausible explanation for why output does not increase proportionately with the number of workers.

4.12 By studying, Will can produce a higher grade, G_W, on an upcoming economics exam. His production function depends on the number of hours he studies marginal analysis problems, A, and the number of hours he studies supply and demand problems, R. Specifically, $G_W = 2.5A^{0.36}R^{0.64}$. The grade production function of his roommate David is $G_D = 2.5A^{0.25}R^{0.75}$.

   a. What is Will's marginal productivity from studying supply and demand problems? What is David's?

   b. What is Will's marginal rate of technical substitution between studying the two types of problems? What is David's?

   c. Is it possible that Will and David have different marginal productivity functions but the same marginal rate of technical substitution functions? Explain. **M**

4.13 Show that the CES production function $q = (aL^{\rho} + bK^{\rho})^{1/\rho}$ can be written as $q = B(\rho)[cL^{\rho} + (1 - c) \times K^{\rho}]^{1/\rho}$. **M**

4.14 What is the *MRTS* of the CES production function $q = (aL^{\rho} + bK^{\rho})^{d/\rho}$? (See Solved Problem 6.3.) **M**

4.15 What is the elasticity of substitution, σ, of the CES production function $q = (aL^{\rho} + bK^{\rho})^{d/\rho}$? (See Solved Problem 6.4.) **M**

4.16 Electric power is often generated by burning oil or gas to create steam. That steam is used to drive the turbines and produce electricity. One barrel of crude oil produces about 5.6 million BTUs of energy, while 1,000 cubic feet of natural gas produces 1,027,000 BTUs (**www.physics.uci.edu/~silverma/units.html**). Thus, an electric generating company can substitute 1 barrel of crude oil with 5,648 cubic feet of natural gas. Draw a few isoquants for this production process. What is the marginal rate of technical substitution? **M**

5. Returns to Scale

5.1 To speed relief to isolated South Asian communities that were devastated by the December 2004 tsunami, the U.S. Navy doubled the number of helicopters from 45 to 90 soon after the first ship arrived. Navy Admiral Thomas Fargo, head of the U.S. Pacific Command, was asked if doubling the number of helicopters would "produce twice as much [relief]." He replied, "Maybe pretty close to twice as much." (Vicky O'Hara, *All Things Considered*, National Public Radio, NPR, January 4, 2005). Identify the inputs and outputs and describe the production process. Is the admiral discussing a production process with nearly constant returns to scale, or is he referring to another property of the production process?

5.2 Show in a diagram that a production function can have diminishing marginal returns to a factor and constant returns to scale.

5.3 Under what conditions do the following production functions exhibit decreasing, constant, or increasing returns to scale?

a. $q = L + K$, a linear production function,

b. $q = AL^aK^b$, a general Cobb-Douglas production function,

c. $q = L + L^aK^b + K$,

d. $q = (aL^\rho + [1 - a]K^\rho)^{d/\rho}$, a CES production function. (See Solved Problem 6.5.) **M**

*5.4 Haskel and Sadun (2012) estimated the production function for U.K. supermarkets is $Q = L^{0.23}K^{0.10}M^{0.66}$, where L is labor, K is capital, and M is materials. What kind of returns to scale, g, do these production functions exhibit? (*Hint:* See Solved Problem 6.5.) **M**

5.5 As asserted in the comment in Solved Problem 6.5, prove that g is a scale elasticity. **M**

5.6 Is it possible that a firm's production function exhibits increasing returns to scale while exhibiting diminishing marginal productivity of each of its inputs? To answer this question, calculate the marginal productivities of capital and labor for the production of U.S. tobacco products, Japanese synthetic rubber, and New Zealand mining, using the information listed in the Application "Returns to Scale in Various Industries." **M**

5.7 A production function is said to be homogeneous of degree g if $f(xL, xK) = x^gf(L, K)$, where x is a positive constant. That is, the production function has the same returns to scale for every combination of inputs. For such a production function, show that the marginal product of labor and marginal product of capital functions are homogeneous of degree $g - 1$. **M**

5.8 Show that with a constant-returns-to-scale production function, the *MRTS* between labor and capital depends only on the K/L ratio and not on the scale of production. (*Hint:* Use your result from Exercise 5.7.) **M**

5.9 Prove Euler's theorem that, if $f(L, K)$ is homogeneous of degree g (see Exercise 5.7), then $L(\partial f/\partial L) + K(\partial f/\partial K) = gf(L, K)$. Given this result, what can you conclude if a production function has constant returns to scale? Express your results in terms of the marginal products of labor and capital. **M**

6. Productivity and Technical Change

6.1 Are the robots in the Application "Robots and the Food You Eat" an example of neutral, labor-saving, or capital-saving innovation? Explain.

6.2 In a manufacturing plant, workers use a specialized machine to produce belts. A new labor-saving machine is invented. With the new machine, the firm can use fewer workers and still produce the same number of belts as it did using the old machine. In the long run, both labor and capital (the machine) are variable. From what you know, what is the effect of this invention on the AP_L, MP_L, and returns to scale? If you require more information to answer this question, specify what else you need to know.

6.3 Does it follow that, because we observe that the average product of labor is higher for Firm 1 than for Firm 2, Firm 1 is more productive in the sense that it can produce more output from a given amount of inputs? Why or why not?

*6.4 Firm 1 and Firm 2 use the same type of production function, but Firm 1 is only 90% as productive as Firm 2. That is, the production function of Firm 2 is $q_2 = f(L, K)$, and the production function of Firm 1 is $q_1 = 0.9f(L, K)$. At a particular level of inputs, how does the marginal product of labor differ between the firms? **M**

6.5 Is a boss a fixed or variable input in the Application "A Good Boss Raises Productivity"? How does having a good boss affect the marginal product of labor curve for this firm? Assuming that the production process also includes a capital input, what effect does a good boss have on a typical isoquant?

7. Challenge

7.1 If a firm lays off workers during a recession, how will the firm's marginal product of labor change?

*7.2 During recessions, American firms historically laid off a larger proportion of their workers than Japanese firms did. (Apparently, Japanese firms continued to produce at high levels and stored the output or sold it at relatively low prices during recessions.) Assuming that the production function was unchanged over many recessions and expansions, would you expect the average product of labor to have been higher in Japan or in the United States? Why?

7.3 For the CES production function $q = (aL^\rho + [1 - a]K^\rho)^{d/\rho}$, does $\partial AP_L/\partial L$ have an unambiguous sign? **M**

Costs

7

People want economy and they will pay any price to get it. —Lee Iacocca (former CEO of Chrysler)

A manager of a semiconductor manufacturing firm, who can choose from many different production technologies, must determine whether to use the same technology in its foreign plant that it uses in its domestic plant. U.S. semiconductor manufacturing firms have been moving much of their production abroad since 1961, when Fairchild Semiconductor built a plant in Hong Kong. According to the Semiconductor Industry Association, worldwide semiconductor billings from the Americas dropped from 66% in 1976, to 34% in 1998, to 17% in 2011, and then rose to 22% in early 2018.

Semiconductor firms moved their production abroad because of lower taxes, lower labor costs, and capital grants. Capital grants are funds provided by a foreign government to a firm to induce them to produce in that country. Such grants can reduce the cost of owning and operating an overseas semiconductor fabrication facility by as much as 25% compared to the costs of a U.S.-based plant. However, over the past decade, most Asian countries substantially raised their minimum wages, which reduces the incentive of U.S. firms to move production there. For example, the minimum wage in China increased almost three-fold from 2012 to 2018.

The semiconductor manufacturer can produce a chip using sophisticated equipment and relatively few workers or many workers and less complex equipment. In the United States, firms use a relatively capital-intensive technology, because doing so minimizes their cost of producing a given level of output. Will that same technology be cost minimizing if they move their production abroad?

A firm uses a two-step procedure to determine how to produce a certain amount of output efficiently. It first determines which production processes are *technologically efficient* so that it can produce the desired level of output with the least amount of inputs. As we saw in Chapter 6, the firm uses engineering and other information to determine its production function, which summarizes the many technologically efficient production processes available.

The firm's second step is to select the technologically efficient production process that is also **cost efficient**, minimizing the cost of producing a specified amount of output. To determine which process minimizes its cost of production, the firm uses information about the production function and the cost of inputs.

By reducing its cost of producing a given level of output, a firm can increase its profit. Any profit-maximizing competitive, monopolistic, or oligopolistic firm minimizes its cost of production.

In this chapter, we examine five main topics	1. **Measuring Costs.** Economists count both explicit costs and implicit (opportunity) costs.
	2. **Short-Run Costs.** To minimize its costs in the short run, a firm can adjust its variable factors (such as labor), but it cannot adjust its fixed factors (such as capital).
	3. **Long-Run Costs.** To minimize its costs in the long run, a firm can adjust all its inputs because all inputs are variable.
	4. **Lower Costs in the Long Run.** Long-run cost is as low as or lower than short-run cost because the firm has more flexibility in the long run, technological progress occurs, and workers and managers learn from experience.
	5. **Cost of Producing Multiple Goods.** If a firm produces several goods simultaneously, the cost of each may depend on the quantity of all the goods it produces.

Businesspeople and economists need to understand the relationship between the costs of inputs and production to determine the most cost-efficient way to produce. Economists have an additional reason for wanting to understand costs. As we will see in later chapters, the relationship between output and costs plays an important role in determining the nature of a market—how many firms are in the market and how high price is relative to cost.

7.1   Measuring Costs

How much would it cost you to stand at the wrong end of a shooting gallery?
—S. J. Perelman

To show how a firm's cost varies with its output, we first have to measure costs. Businesspeople and economists often measure costs differently. Economists include all relevant costs. To run a firm profitably, a manager must think like an economist and consider all relevant costs. However, this same manager may direct the firm's accountant or bookkeeper to measure costs in ways that are more consistent with tax laws and other laws so as to make the firm's financial statements look good to stockholders or to minimize the firm's taxes.[1]

To produce a particular amount of output, a firm incurs costs for the required inputs, such as labor, capital, energy, and materials. A firm's manager (or accountant) determines the cost of labor, capital, energy, and materials by multiplying the price of the factor by the number of units used. If workers earn $20 per hour and work 100 hours per day, then the firm's cost of labor is $20 \times 100 = \$2,000$ per day. The manager can easily calculate these *explicit costs*, which are its direct, out-of-pocket payments for inputs to its production process within a given period. While calculating explicit costs is straightforward, some costs are *implicit* in that they reflect only a forgone opportunity rather than an explicit, current expenditure. Properly taking account of forgone opportunities requires particularly careful attention when dealing with durable capital goods, as past expenditures for an input may be irrelevant to current cost calculations if that input has no current, alternative use.

---

[1]See "Tax Rules" in **MyLab Economics**, Chapter Resources, for Chapter 7.

Opportunity Costs

An economist is a person who, when invited to give a talk at a banquet, tells the audience there's no such thing as a free lunch.

The **economic cost** or **opportunity cost** of a resource is the value of the best alternative use of that resource. The opportunity cost may equal or exceed a firm's explicit cost. If a firm purchases an input in a market and uses that input immediately, the input's opportunity cost is the amount the firm pays for it, the market price. After all, if the firm does not use the input in its production process, its best alternative would be to sell it to someone else at the market price.

The concept of an opportunity cost becomes particularly useful when the firm uses an input that is not available for purchase in a market or was purchased in a market in the past. Here, the opportunity cost exceeds the explicit costs. A key example of such an opportunity cost is the value of an owner's time. For example, Maoyong owns and manages a firm. He pays himself only a small monthly salary of $1,000 because he also receives the firm's profit. However, Maoyong could work for another firm and earn $11,000 a month. Thus, the opportunity cost of his time is $11,000—from his best alternative use of his time—not the $1,000 he actually pays himself. As a result, his firm's total opportunity cost is the opportunity cost of his time plus the explicit amount he pays for inputs that he buys from markets.

The classic example of an implicit opportunity cost is captured in the phrase "There's no such thing as a free lunch." Suppose that your parents offer to take you to lunch tomorrow. You know that they will pay for the meal, but you also know that this lunch will not truly be free. Your opportunity cost for the lunch is the best alternative use of your time. Presumably, the best alternative use of your time is reading this chapter, but other possible alternatives include working at a job or watching TV. Often, such an opportunity cost is substantial. (What are you giving up to study opportunity costs?)

At one point or another, most of us have held the following false belief:

Common Confusion I can save money by doing things myself rather than buying goods and services from firms.

The fallacy in this belief is that we have ignored the opportunity cost of our time. Have you ever tried to fix a plumbing problem that ended up taking hours and that a professional plumber could have repaired in a few minutes? Doing that only makes sense if the opportunity cost of your time is very low (or the plumber's fee is very high). Similarly, growing our own food would cost most of us much more than buying it from a store once we take into account the value of our time.

APPLICATION

The Opportunity Cost of an MBA

During major economic downturns, do applications to MBA programs fall, hold steady, or rise? Knowledge of opportunity costs helps us answer this question.

The biggest cost of attending an MBA program is often the opportunity cost of giving up a well-paying job. Someone who leaves a job paying $6,000 per month to attend an MBA program is, in effect, incurring a $6,000 per month opportunity cost, in addition to the tuition and cost of textbooks (though this one is well worth the money).

Thus, it is not surprising that MBA applications rise in bad economic times when outside opportunities decline. People thinking of going back to school face a reduced opportunity cost of entering an MBA program if they think they might be laid off or might not be promoted during an economic downturn. As Stacey Kole, deputy dean for the MBA program at the University of Chicago's Graduate School of Business, observed, "When there's a go-go economy, fewer people decide to go back to school. When things go south, the opportunity cost of leaving work is lower."

During the Great Recession in 2008, when U.S. unemployment rose sharply and the economy was in poor shape, the number of people seeking admission to MBA programs also rose sharply. Applications continued to rise as unemployment remained high for several years. The U.S. unemployment rate peaked at 10% in late 2009 and did not fall below 8% until 2012. However, the U.S. unemployment rate dropped below 5% by late 2015, and has continued to fall. Correspondingly, U.S. MBA applications fell in the 2015, 2016, and 2017 admission years.

SOLVED PROBLEM 7.1

MyLab Economics
Solved Problem

Meredith's firm sends her to a conference for managers and has paid her registration fee. Included in the registration fee is admission to a class on how to price derivative securities such as options. She is considering attending, but her most attractive alternative opportunity is to attend a talk by Warren Buffett about his investment strategies, which is scheduled at the same time. Although she would be willing to pay $100 to hear his talk, the cost of a ticket is only $40. Given that she incurs no other costs to attend either event, what is Meredith's opportunity cost of attending the derivatives talk?

Answer

To calculate her opportunity cost, determine the benefit that Meredith would forgo by attending the derivatives class. Because she incurs no additional fee to attend the derivatives talk, Meredith's opportunity cost is the forgone benefit of hearing the Buffett speech. Because she values hearing the Buffett speech at $100, but only has to pay $40, her net benefit from hearing that talk is $60 (= $100 − $40). Thus, her opportunity cost of attending the derivatives talk is $60.

Opportunity Cost of Capital

Capital: Something—like a car, refrigerator, factory, or airplane—that is blown up in an action movie.

Determining the opportunity cost of capital, such as land or equipment, requires special considerations. Capital is a **durable good**: a product that provides services for a long period, typically for many years. Two problems may arise in measuring the cost of capital. The first is how to allocate the initial purchase cost over time. The second is what to do if the value of the capital changes over time.

We can avoid these two measurement problems if the firm rents capital instead of purchasing it. Suppose that a firm can rent a small pick-up truck for $400 a month or buy it outright for $20,000. If the firm rents the truck, the rental payment is the relevant opportunity cost per month. The truck is rented month-to-month, so the firm does not have to worry about how to allocate the purchase cost of a truck over time. Moreover, the rental rate will adjust if the cost of trucks changes over time. Thus, if the firm can rent capital for short periods, it calculates the cost of this capital in the same way that it calculates the cost of nondurable inputs, such as labor services or materials.

The firm faces a more complex problem in determining the opportunity cost of the truck if it purchases the truck. The firm's accountant may *expense* the truck's purchase price by treating the full $20,000 as a cost at the time that the truck is purchased, or the accountant may *amortize* the cost by spreading the $20,000 over the life of the truck, following rules set by an accounting organization or by a relevant government authority such as the Internal Revenue Service (IRS).

A manager who wants to make sound decisions does not expense or amortize the truck using such rules. The true opportunity cost of using a truck that the firm owns is the amount the firm could earn if it rented the truck to others. That is, regardless of whether the firm rents or buys the truck, the manager views the opportunity cost of this capital good as the rental rate for a given period. If the value of an older truck is less than that of a newer one, the rental rate for the truck falls over time.

But what if no rental market for trucks exists? It is still important to determine an appropriate opportunity cost. Suppose that the firm has two choices: It can choose not to buy the truck and keep the truck's purchase price of $20,000, or it can use the truck for a year and sell it for $17,000 at the end of the year. If the firm does not purchase the truck, it will deposit the $20,000 in a bank account that pays 5% per year, so the firm will have $21,000 at the end of the year. Thus, the opportunity cost of using the truck for a year is $21,000 − $17,000 = $4,000.[2] This $4,000 opportunity cost equals the $3,000 depreciation of the truck (= $20,000 − $17,000) plus the $1,000 in forgone interest that the firm could have earned over the year if the firm had invested the $20,000.

Because the values of trucks, machines, and other equipment decline over time, their rental rates fall, so the firm's opportunity costs decline. In contrast, the value of some land, buildings, and other forms of capital may rise over time. To maximize profit, a firm must properly measure the opportunity cost of a piece of capital even if its value rises over time. If a beauty parlor buys a building when similar buildings in the area rent for $1,000 per month, the opportunity cost of using the building is $1,000 a month. If land values increase so that rents in the area rise to $2,000 per month, the beauty parlor's opportunity cost of its building rises to $2,000 per month.

Sunk Costs

An opportunity cost is not always easy to observe but should always be considered when deciding how much to produce. In contrast, a **sunk cost**—a past expenditure that cannot be recovered—though easily observed, is not relevant to a manager when deciding how much to produce now. A sunk expenditure is not an opportunity cost.[3]

If a firm buys a forklift for $25,000 and can resell it for the same price a year later, it is not a sunk expenditure, and the opportunity cost of the forklift is $25,000. If instead the firm buys a specialized piece of equipment for $25,000 and cannot resell it, then the original expenditure is a sunk cost. Because this equipment has no alternative use, the firm cannot resell it, so its opportunity cost is zero and should not be included in the firm's current cost calculations. If the firm could resell the specialized equipment that originally cost $25,000 for $10,000, then only $15,000 of the original expenditure is a sunk cost, and the opportunity cost is $10,000.

---

[2]The firm would also pay for gasoline, insurance, licensing fees, and other operating costs, but these items would all be expensed as operating costs and would not appear in the firm's accounts as capital costs.

[3]Nonetheless, a sunk cost paid for a specialized input should still be deducted from income before paying taxes even if that cost is sunk, and must therefore appear in financial accounts.

To illustrate why a sunk cost should not influence a manager's current decisions, consider a firm that paid $300,000 for a piece of land for which the market value has fallen to $200,000. Now, the land's true opportunity cost is $200,000. The $100,000 difference between the $300,000 purchase price and the current market value of $200,000 is a sunk cost that the firm cannot recover. Suppose that the land is worth $240,000 to the firm if it builds a plant on this parcel. Is it worth carrying out production on this land or should the land be sold for its market value of $200,000? If the firm uses the original purchase price in its decision-making process, the firm will falsely conclude that using the land for production will result in a $60,000 loss: the $240,000 value of using the land minus the purchase price of $300,000. Instead, the firm should use the land because it is worth $40,000 more as a production facility than if the firm sells the land for $200,000, its next best alternative. Thus, the firm should use the land's opportunity cost to make its decisions and ignore the land's sunk cost. In short, "no use crying over spilt milk," "what's done is done," and "don't throw good money after bad."

7.2 Short-Run Costs

To make profit-maximizing decisions, a firm needs to know how its cost varies with output. As a firm increases its output, its cost rises. The short run is the period over which some inputs, such as labor, can be varied, while other inputs, such as capital, are fixed (Chapter 6). In contrast, the firm can vary all its inputs in the long run. For simplicity in our graphs, we concentrate on firms that use only two inputs: labor and capital. We focus on the case in which labor is the only variable input in the short run, and both labor and capital are variable in the long run. However, we can generalize our analysis to examine a firm that uses any number of inputs.

We start by examining various measures of cost, which we use to show the distinction between short-run and long-run costs. Then we show the relationship between the shapes of the short-run cost curves and the firm's production function.

Short-Run Cost Measures

We start by using a numerical example to illustrate the basic cost concepts. We then examine the graphic relationship between these concepts.

Fixed Cost, Variable Cost, and Total Cost. To produce a given level of output in the short run, a firm incurs costs for both its fixed and variable inputs. A **fixed cost** (F) is a cost that does not vary with the level of output. Fixed costs include expenditures on land, office space, production facilities, and other *overhead* expenses. The firm cannot avoid fixed costs by reducing output as long as it stays in business.

Fixed costs are often sunk costs, but not always. For example, a restaurant rents space for $2,000 per month on a month-to-month lease. This rent does not vary with the number of meals served (its output level), so it is a fixed cost. Because the restaurant has already paid this month's rent, this fixed cost is also a sunk cost: The restaurant cannot recover the $2,000 even if it goes out of business. Next month, if the restaurant stays open, it will have to pay the $2,000 rent. If the lease is a month-to-month rental agreement, this fixed cost of $2,000 is an *avoidable cost*, not a sunk cost. The restaurant can shut down, cancel its rental agreement, and avoid paying this fixed cost. In planning for next month, the restaurant should treat the $2,000 rent as a fixed cost but not as a sunk cost. Thus, the $2,000 per month rental fee is a fixed cost in both the short run (this month) and the long run, but it is a sunk cost only in the short run.

Fixed	Variable

A firm's **variable cost** (*VC*) is the production expense that changes with the quantity of output produced. The variable cost is the cost of the variable inputs—the inputs the firm can adjust to alter its output level, such as labor and materials.

A firm's **cost** (or **total cost**, *C*) is the sum of a firm's variable cost and fixed cost:

$$C = VC + F.$$

Because variable cost changes with the level of output, total cost also varies with the level of output.

To decide how much to produce, a firm uses measures of marginal and average costs. We derive four such measures using the fixed cost, the variable cost, and the total cost.

APPLICATION

The Sharing Economy and the Short Run

A construction company views workers' earnings as a variable cost and the capital that the firm owns—particularly heavy equipment such as bulldozers—as a fixed cost. The sharing economy is changing that.

When Platinum Pipeline Inc., a firm that installs water and sewer lines, won a new job, it needed a third bulldozer. Rather than buy one, the firm's president, Manuel de Freitas, merely called up an app on his phone and found a Caterpillar D6T dozer that he could rent for two months at $7,500 a month. The rental firm, Yard Club Inc., finds idle heavy equipment and rents it—much like Airbnb

Inc. does with spare bedrooms. Often, rental companies own this equipment.

Renting construction equipment is catching on. In 2014, rental companies owned 54% of U.S. construction equipment, up from 40% a decade earlier. According to one forecast, the share could top 60% within the next 5 to 10 years. In 2018, Global Market Insights predicted that the construction equipment rental market will grow at over 4% a year from 2018 to 2024.

If construction companies can rely on renting heavy equipment rather than owning it, all their inputs are variable. As a result, they face no distinction between the short run and the long run.

Marginal Cost. A firm's **marginal cost** (*MC*) is the amount by which a firm's cost changes if it produces one more unit of output. The marginal cost is

$$MC = \frac{dC(q)}{dq}. \tag{7.1}$$

Because only variable cost changes with output, we can also define marginal cost as the change in variable cost from a small increase in output, $MC = dVC(q)/dq$, where $VC(q)$ is the firm's variable cost function. Chapter 8 will show that a firm uses its marginal cost to decide whether changing its output level pays off.

Average Cost. Firms use three average cost measures. The **average fixed cost** (*AFC*) is the fixed cost divided by the units of output produced: $AFC = F/q$. The average fixed cost falls as output rises because the fixed cost is spread over more units: $dAFC/dq = -F/q^2 < 0$. The *AFC* curve approaches zero as the output level grows large.

The **average variable cost** (*AVC*) is the variable cost divided by the units of output produced: $AVC = VC/q$. Because the variable cost increases with output, the average variable cost may either increase or decrease as output rises. As Chapter 8 shows, a firm uses the average variable cost to determine whether to shut down operations when demand is low.

The **average cost** (AC)—or average total cost—is the total cost divided by the units of output produced: $AC = C/q$. Because total cost equals variable cost plus fixed cost, $C = VC + F$, when we divide both sides of the equation by q, we learn that

$$AC = \frac{C}{q} = \frac{VC}{q} + \frac{F}{q} = AVC + AFC. \tag{7.2}$$

That is, the average cost is the sum of the average variable cost and the average fixed cost. A firm uses its average cost to determine if it is making a profit.

SOLVED PROBLEM 7.2

MyLab Economics
Solved Problem

A manufacturing plant has a short-run cost function of $C(q) = 100q - 4q^2 + 0.2q^3 + 450$. What are the firm's short-run fixed cost and variable cost functions? Derive the formulas for its marginal cost, average variable cost, average fixed cost, and average cost. Draw two figures, one above the other. In the top figure, show the fixed cost, variable cost, and total cost curves. In the bottom figure, show the corresponding marginal cost curve and three average cost curves.

Answer

1. *Identify the fixed cost as the part of the short-run cost function that does not vary with output, q, and the remaining part of the cost function as the variable cost function.* The fixed cost is $F = 450$, the only part that does not vary with q. The variable cost function, $VC(q) = 100q - 4q^2 + 0.2q^3$, is the part of the cost function that varies with q.

2. *Determine the marginal cost by differentiating the short-run cost function (or variable cost function) with respect to output.* Differentiating, we find that

$$MC = \frac{dC(q)}{dq}$$
$$= \frac{d(100q - 4q^2 + 0.2q^3 + 450)}{dq}$$
$$= 100 - 8q + 0.6q^2.$$

3. *Calculate the three average cost functions using their definitions.*

$$AVC = \frac{VC(q)}{q} = \frac{100q - 4q^2 + 0.2q^3}{q} = 100 - 4q + 0.2q^2,$$
$$AFC = \frac{F}{q} = \frac{450}{q},$$
$$AC = \frac{C(q)}{q}$$
$$= \frac{100q - 4q^2 + 0.2q^3 + 450}{q}$$
$$= (100 - 4q + 0.2q^2) + \frac{450}{q}$$
$$= AVC + AFC.$$

4. *Use these cost, marginal cost, and average cost functions to plot the specified figures.* Figure 7.1 shows these curves.

Figure 7.1 Short-Run Cost Curves

(a) Because the total cost differs from the variable cost by the fixed cost, $F = \$450$, the cost curve, C, is parallel to the variable cost curve, VC. (b) The marginal cost curve, MC, cuts the average variable cost, AVC, and average cost, AC, curves at their minimums. The height of the AC curve at point a equals the slope of the line from the origin to the cost curve at A. The height of the AVC at b equals the slope of the line from the origin to the variable cost curve at B. The height of the marginal cost is the slope of either the C or VC curve at that quantity.

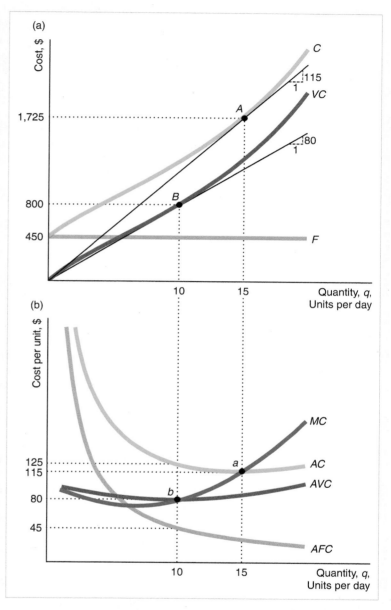

Short-Run Cost Curves

We illustrate the relationship between output and the various cost measures using the example in Solved Problem 7.2. Panel a of Figure 7.1 shows the variable cost, fixed cost, and total cost curves. The fixed cost, which does not vary with output, is a horizontal line at $450. The variable cost curve is zero when output is zero and rises as output increases. The total cost curve, which is the vertical sum of the variable cost curve and the fixed cost line, is $450 higher than the variable cost curve at every output level, so the variable cost and total cost curves are parallel.

Panel b shows the average fixed cost, average variable cost, average cost, and marginal cost curves. The average fixed cost curve falls as output increases. It approaches zero as output gets larger because the fixed cost is spread over many units of output. The average cost curve is the vertical sum of the average fixed cost and average variable cost curves. For example, at 10 units of output, the average variable cost is $80 and the average fixed cost is $45, so the average cost is $125.

The marginal cost curve cuts the U-shaped average cost and the average variable cost curves at their minimums.[4] The average cost (or average variable cost) curve rises where it lies below the marginal cost curve and falls where it lies above the marginal cost curve, so the marginal cost curve must cut the average cost curve at its minimum (by similar reasoning to that used in Chapter 6, where we discussed average and marginal products).

Production Functions and the Shape of Cost Curves

The production function determines the shape of a firm's cost curves. It shows the amount of inputs needed to produce a given level of output. The firm calculates its cost by multiplying the quantity of each input by its price and then summing these products.

If a firm produces output using capital and labor and its capital is fixed in the short run, the firm's variable cost is its cost of labor. Its labor cost is the wage per hour, w, times the number of hours of labor, L, so that its variable cost (labor cost) is $VC = wL$.

If input prices are constant, the production function determines the shape of the variable cost curve. We can write the short-run production function as $q = f(L, \overline{K}) = g(L)$ because capital does not vary. By inverting, we know that the amount of labor we need to produce any given amount of output is $L = g^{-1}(q)$. If the wage of labor is w, the variable cost function is $VC(q) = wL = wg^{-1}(q)$. Similarly, the cost function is $C(q) = VC(q) + F = wg^{-1}(q) + F$.

In the short run, when the firm's capital is fixed, the only way the firm can increase its output is to use more labor. If the firm increases its labor enough, it reaches the point of *diminishing marginal returns to labor*, where each extra worker increases output by a smaller amount. Because the variable cost function is the inverse of the short-run production function, its properties are determined by the short-run production function. If the production function exhibits diminishing marginal returns, then the variable cost rises more than in proportion as output increases.

Because the production function determines the shape of the variable cost curve, it also determines the shape of the marginal, average variable, and average cost curves. We now examine the shape of each of these cost curves in detail, because firms rely more on these per-unit cost measures than on total variable cost to make decisions about labor and capital.

---

[4]To determine the output level q where the average cost curve, $AC(q)$, reaches its minimum, we set the derivative of average cost with respect to q equal to zero:

$$\frac{dAC(q)}{dq} = \frac{d[C(q)/q]}{dq} = \left[\frac{dC(q)}{dq} - \frac{C(q)}{q}\right]\frac{1}{q} = 0.$$

This condition holds at the output q where $dC(q)/dq = C(q)/q$, or $MC = AC$. If the second-order condition holds at the same level for q, the average cost curve reaches its minimum at that quantity. The second-order condition requires that the average cost curve be falling to the left of this quantity and rising to the right. Similarly, $dAVC/dq = d[VC(q)/q]/dq = [dVC/dq - VC(q)/q](1/q) = 0$, so $MC = AVC$ at the minimum of the average variable cost curve.

Shape of the Marginal Cost Curve. The marginal cost is the change in variable cost as output increases by one unit: $MC = dVC/dq$. In the short run, capital is fixed, so the only way a firm can produce more output is to use extra labor. The extra labor required to produce one more unit of output is $dL/dq = 1/MP_L$. The extra labor costs the firm w per unit, so the firm's cost rises by $w(dL/dq)$. As a result, the firm's marginal cost is

$$MC = \frac{dV(q)}{dq} = w\frac{dL}{dq}.$$

The marginal cost equals the wage times the extra labor necessary to produce one more unit of output.

How do we know how much extra labor is needed to produce one more unit of output? This information comes from the production function. The marginal product of labor—the amount of extra output produced by another unit of labor, holding other inputs fixed—is $MP_L = dq/dL$. Thus, the extra labor needed to produce one more unit of output, dL/dq, is $1/MP_L$, so the firm's marginal cost is

$$MC = \frac{w}{MP_L}. \tag{7.3}$$

According to Equation 7.3, the marginal cost equals the wage divided by the marginal product of labor. If it takes four extra hours of labor services to produce one more unit of output, the marginal product of an hour of labor is $\frac{1}{4}$. If the wage is \$10 an hour, the marginal cost of one more unit of output is $w/MP_L = \$10/\frac{1}{4} = \$40$.

Equation 7.3 shows that the marginal cost moves in the opposite direction to that of the marginal product of labor. At low levels of labor, the marginal product of labor commonly rises with additional workers who may help the original workers to collectively make better use of the firm's equipment (Chapter 6). As the marginal product of labor rises, the marginal cost falls.

Eventually, however, as the number of workers increases, workers must share the fixed amount of equipment and may get in each other's way. Consequently, the marginal cost curve slopes upward due to diminishing marginal returns to labor. As a result, the marginal cost first falls and then rises, as panel b of Figure 7.1 illustrates.

Shape of the Average Cost Curve. Because diminishing marginal returns to labor affect the shape of the variable cost curve, they also determine the shape of the average variable cost curve. The average variable cost is the variable cost divided by output: $AVC = VC/q$. For a firm that has labor as its only variable input, variable cost is wL, so average variable cost is

$$AVC = \frac{VC}{q} = \frac{wL}{q}.$$

Because the average product of labor is q/L, average variable cost is the wage divided by the average product of labor:

$$AVC = \frac{w}{AP_L}. \tag{7.4}$$

With a constant wage, the average variable cost moves in the opposite direction to that of the average product of labor in Equation 7.4. As we saw in Chapter 6, the average product of labor tends to rise and then fall, so the average cost tends to fall and then rise, as panel b of Figure 7.1 shows.

The average cost curve is the vertical sum of the average variable cost curve and the average fixed cost curve, as in panel b. If the average variable cost curve is U-shaped, adding the strictly falling average fixed cost makes the average cost fall more steeply than the average variable cost curve at low output levels. At high output levels, the average cost and average variable cost curves differ by ever-smaller amounts, as the average fixed cost, F/q, approaches zero. Thus, the average cost curve is also U-shaped.

APPLICATION	We can derive the various short-run cost curves for a typical Japanese beer manufacturer using its estimated Cobb-Douglas production function (based on Flath, 2011)

Short-Run Cost Curves for a Japanese Beer Manufacturer

$$q = 1.52L^{0.6}K^{0.4}. \tag{7.5}$$

We assume that the firm's capital is fixed at $\overline{K} = 100$ units in the short run.

Given that the rental rate of a unit of capital is \$8, the fixed cost, F, is \$800, the average fixed cost is

$$AFC = F/q = 800/q.$$

An increase in output reduces the AFC, $dAFC/dq = -800/q^2 < 0$, so the AFC slopes down and asymptotically approaches the horizontal axis in the figure.

We can use the production function to derive the variable cost. Because capital is fixed in the short run, the short-run production function is solely a function of labor:

$$q = 1.52L^{0.6}100^{0.4} \approx 9.59L^{0.6}.$$

Rearranging this expression, we can write the number of workers, L, needed to produce q units of output, as a function solely of output:

$$L(q) = \left(\frac{q}{9.59}\right)^{\frac{1}{0.6}} = \left(\frac{1}{9.59}\right)^{1.67}q^{1.67} \approx 0.023q^{1.67}.$$

Now that we know how labor and output are related, we can calculate variable cost directly. The only variable input is labor, so if the wage is \$24, the firm's variable cost is

$$VC(q) = wL(q) = 24L(q).$$

Substituting for $L(q)$ from the previous equation into this variable cost equation, we learn how variable cost varies with output:

$$VC(q) = 24L(q) = 24(0.023q^{1.67}) \approx 0.55q^{1.67}.$$

Using this expression for variable cost, we can construct the other cost measures. Thus, to construct all the cost measures of the beer firm, we need only the production function and the prices of the inputs.

The average variable cost is $AVC = VC/q = 0.55q^{0.67}$. To obtain the equation for marginal cost as a function of output, we differentiate the variable cost, $VC(q)$, with respect to output:

$$MC(q) = \frac{dVC(q)}{dq} \approx \frac{d(0.55q^{1.67})}{dq} = 1.67 \times 0.55q^{0.67} \approx 0.92q^{0.67}.$$

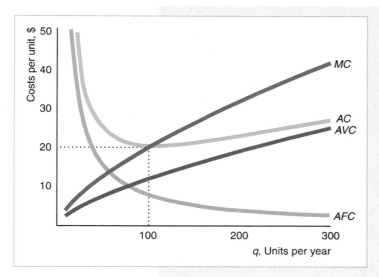

Total cost is $C = FC + VC = 800 + 0.55q^{1.67}$. Average cost is $AC = C/q = AFC + AVC = 800/q + 0.55q^{0.67}$. As the figure shows, the short-run average cost curve for a Japanese beer manufacturer is U-shaped, because the AC is the vertical sum of the strictly falling AFC and the strictly increasing AVC. The firm's marginal cost curve lies above the rising average variable cost curve for all positive quantities of output and cuts the average cost curve at its minimum at $q = 100$.

Effects of Taxes on Costs

Taxes applied to a firm shift some or all of the marginal and average cost curves. For example, suppose that the government collects a specific tax of $10 per unit of output. This specific tax, which varies with output, affects the firm's variable cost but not its fixed cost. As a result, it affects the firm's average cost, average variable cost, and marginal cost curves but not its average fixed cost curve.

At every quantity, the average variable cost and the average cost rise by the full amount of the tax. Thus, the firm's after-tax average variable cost, AVC^a, is its average variable cost of production—the before-tax average variable cost, AVC^b—plus the tax per unit, $10: AVC^a = AVC^b + \$10$.

The average cost equals the average variable cost plus the average fixed cost. For example, in the last Application, the Japanese beer firm's before-tax average cost is $AC^b = AVC + AFC = 0.55q^{0.67} + 800/q$. Because the tax increases average variable cost by $10 and does not affect the average fixed cost, average cost increases by $10: AC^a = AC^b + 10 = 0.55q^{0.67} + 800/q + 10$. The tax also increases the firm's marginal cost by $10 per unit. The beer manufacturer's pre-tax marginal cost is $MC^b = 0.92q^{0.67}$, so its after-tax marginal cost is $MC^a = 0.92q^{0.67} + 10$.

Figure 7.2 shows these shifts in the marginal and average cost curves. The new marginal cost curve and average cost curve are parallel to the old ones: $10 higher at each quantity. At first, it may not look like the shift of the average cost curve is parallel, but you can convince yourself that it is a parallel shift by using a ruler.

Similarly, we can analyze the effect of a franchise tax on costs. A franchise tax—also called a business license fee—is a lump sum that a firm pays for the right to operate a business. For example, a tax of $800 per year is levied "for the privilege of doing business in California." These taxes do not vary with output, so they affect firms' fixed costs only—not their variable costs.

Short-Run Cost Summary

We have examined three cost-level curves—total cost, fixed cost, and variable cost—and four cost-per-unit curves—average cost, average fixed cost, average variable cost, and marginal cost. Understanding the shapes of these curves and the relationships

Figure 7.2 Effect of a Specific Tax on a Japanese Beer Manufacturer's Cost Curves

A specific tax of $10 per unit shifts both the marginal cost and average cost curves upward by $10. Because of the parallel upward shift of the average cost curve, the minimum of both the before-tax average cost curve, AC^b, and the after-tax average cost curve, AC^a, occurs at the same output, 100 units.

among them is crucial to understanding the analysis of a firm's behavior in the rest of this book. The following basic concepts capture most of what you need to know about the relationships among the curves and their shapes:

- In the short run, the cost associated with inputs that cannot be adjusted is fixed, while the cost from inputs that can be adjusted is variable.
- Given constant input prices, the shapes of the cost, variable cost, marginal cost, and average cost curves are determined by the production function.
- Where a variable input has diminishing marginal returns, the variable cost and cost curves become relatively steep as output increases, so the average cost, average variable cost, and marginal cost curves rise with output.
- Both the average cost curve and the average variable cost curve fall at quantities where the marginal cost curve is below them and rise where the marginal cost is above them, so the marginal cost curve cuts both of these average cost curves at their minimum points.

7.3 Long-Run Costs

In the long run, a firm adjusts all its inputs to keep its cost of production as low as possible. The firm can change its plant size, design and build new equipment, and otherwise adjust inputs that were fixed in the short run.

Although firms may incur fixed costs in the long run, these fixed costs are *avoidable* rather than *sunk* costs, as in the short run. The rent of F per month paid by a restaurant is a fixed cost because it does not vary with the number of meals (output) served. In the short run, this fixed cost is also a sunk cost: The firm must pay F even if the restaurant does not operate. In the long run, this fixed cost is avoidable: The firm does not have to pay the rent if it shuts down. The long run is determined by the length of the rental contract, during which time the firm is obligated to pay rent.

The examples throughout this chapter assume that all inputs can be varied in the long run, so long-run fixed costs are zero ($F = 0$). As a result, the long-run total cost equals the long-run variable cost: $C = VC$. Thus, our firm concentrates on only three cost concepts in the long run—total cost, average cost, and marginal cost—rather than the seven cost concepts that it uses in the short run.

To produce a given quantity of output at minimum cost, our firm uses information about the production function and the price of labor and capital. In the long run, the firm chooses how much labor and capital to use, whereas in the short run, when capital is fixed, it chooses only how much labor to use. Consequently, the firm's long-run cost is lower than its short-run cost of production if it has to use the "wrong" level of capital in the short run. This section shows how a firm determines which combinations of inputs are cost minimizing in the long run.

Input Choice

A firm can produce a given level of output using many different *technologically efficient* combinations of inputs, as summarized by an isoquant (Chapter 6). From among the technologically efficient combinations of inputs, a firm wants to choose the particular bundle with the lowest cost of production, which is the *cost-efficient* combination of inputs. To do so, the firm combines information about technology from the isoquant with information about the cost of labor and capital.

We now show how information about cost can be summarized in an *isocost line*. Then we show how a firm can combine the information in isoquant and isocost lines to determine the cost-efficient combination of inputs.

Isocost Line. The cost of producing a given level of output depends on the price of labor and capital. The firm hires L hours of labor services at a wage of w per hour, so its labor cost is wL. The firm rents K hours of machine services at a rental rate of r per hour, so its capital cost is rK. (If the firm owns the capital, r is the implicit rental rate.) The firm's total cost is the sum of its labor and capital costs:

$$C = wL + rK. \tag{7.6}$$

The firm can hire as much labor and capital as it wants at these constant input prices.

The firm can use many combinations of labor and capital that cost the same amount. These combinations of labor and capital are plotted on an **isocost line**, which indicates all the combinations of inputs that require the same (*iso*) total expenditure (*cost*). Along an isocost line, cost is fixed at a particular level, $\overline{C}$, so by setting cost at $\overline{C}$ in Equation 7.6, we can write the equation for the $\overline{C}$ isocost line as

$$\overline{C} = wL + rK. \tag{7.7}$$

Figure 7.3 shows three isocost lines for the Japanese beer manufacturer where the fixed cost is $\overline{C} = \$1{,}000, \$2{,}000,$ or $\$3{,}000$; $w = \$24$ per hour; and $r = \$8$ per hour.

Using algebra, we can rewrite Equation 7.7 to show how much capital the firm can buy if it spends a total of $\overline{C}$ and purchases L units of labor:

$$K = \frac{\overline{C}}{r} - \frac{w}{r}L. \tag{7.8}$$

The equation for the isocost lines in the figure is $K = \overline{C}/8 - (24/8)L = \overline{C}/8 - 3L$. We can use Equation 7.8 to derive three properties of isocost lines.

Figure 7.3 Cost Minimization

The beer manufacturer minimizes its cost of producing 100 units of output by producing at x ($L = 50$ and $K = 100$). This cost-minimizing combination of inputs is determined by the tangency between the $q = 100$ isoquant and the lowest isocost line, \$2,000, that touches that isoquant. At x, the isocost line is tangent to the isoquant, so the slope of the isocost line, $-w/r = -3$, equals the slope of the isoquant, which is the negative of the marginal rate of technical substitution. That is, the rate at which the firm can trade capital for labor in the input markets equals the rate at which it can substitute capital for labor in the production process.

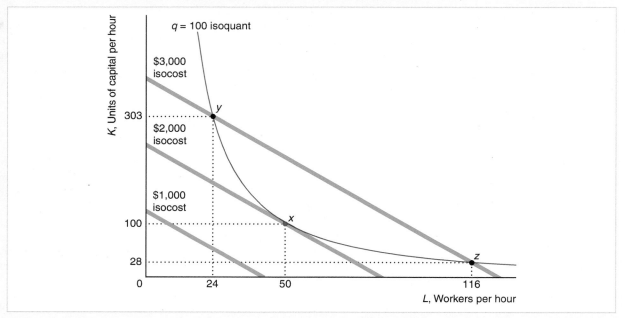

First, the point where the isocost lines hit the capital and labor axes depends on the firm's cost, $\overline{C}$, and the input prices. The $\overline{C}$ isocost line intersects the capital axis where the firm uses only capital. Setting $L = 0$ in Equation 7.8, we find that the firm buys $K = \overline{C}/r$ units of capital. Similarly, the intersection of the isocost line with the labor axis is at $\overline{C}/w$, which is the amount of labor the firm hires if it uses only labor.

Second, isocost lines that are farther from the origin have higher costs than those closer to the origin. Because the isocost lines intersect the capital axis at $\overline{C}/r$ and the labor axis at $\overline{C}/w$, an increase in the cost shifts these intersections with the axes proportionately outward.

Third, the slope of each isocost line is the same. By differentiating Equation 7.8, we find that the slope of any isocost line is

$$\frac{dK}{dL} = -\frac{w}{r}.$$

Thus, the slope of the isocost line depends on the relative prices of the inputs. Because all isocost lines are based on the same relative prices, they all have the same slope, so they are parallel.

The role of the isocost line in the firm's decision making is similar to the role of the budget line in a consumer's decision making. Both an isocost line and a budget line are straight lines with slopes that depend on relative prices. However, they differ in an important way. The single budget line is determined by the consumer's income.

The firm faces many isocost lines, each of which corresponds to a different level of expenditures the firm might make. A firm may incur a relatively low cost by producing relatively little output with few inputs, or it may incur a relatively high cost by producing a relatively large quantity.

Minimizing Cost. By combining the information about costs contained in the isocost lines with information about efficient production that is summarized by an isoquant, a firm determines how to produce a given level of output at the lowest cost. We examine how our beer manufacturer picks the combination of labor and capital that minimizes its cost of producing 100 units of output. Figure 7.3 shows the isoquant for 100 units of output and the isocost lines where the rental rate of a unit of capital is $8 per hour and the wage rate is $24 per hour.

The firm can choose any of three equivalent approaches to minimize its cost:

1. **Lowest-isocost rule.** Pick the bundle of inputs where the lowest isocost line touches the isoquant.
2. **Tangency rule.** Pick the bundle of inputs where the isoquant is tangent to the isocost line.
3. **Last-dollar rule.** Pick the bundle of inputs where the last dollar spent on one input gives as much extra output as the last dollar spent on any other input.

Using the *lowest-isocost rule*, the firm minimizes its cost by using the combination of inputs on the isoquant that lies on the lowest isocost line to touch the isoquant. The lowest possible isoquant that will allow the beer manufacturer to produce 100 units of output is tangent to the $2,000 isocost line. This isocost line touches the isoquant at the bundle of inputs x, where the firm uses $L = 50$ workers and $K = 100$ units of capital.

How do we know that x is the least costly way to produce 100 units of output? We need to demonstrate that other practical combinations of inputs produce fewer than 100 units or produce 100 units at greater cost.

If the firm spent less than $2,000, it could not produce 100 units of output. Each combination of inputs on the $1,000 isocost line lies below the isoquant, so the firm cannot produce 100 units of output for $1,000.

The firm can produce 100 units of output using other combinations of inputs besides x, but using these other bundles of inputs is more expensive. For example, the firm can produce 100 units of output using the combinations y ($L = 24, K = 303$) or z ($L = 116, K = 28$). Both these combinations, however, cost the firm $3,000.

If an isocost line crosses the isoquant twice, as the $3,000 isocost line does, another lower isocost line also touches the isoquant. The lowest possible isocost line to touch the isoquant, the $2,000 isocost line, is tangent to the isoquant at a single bundle, x. Thus, the firm may use the *tangency rule*: The firm chooses the input bundle where the relevant isoquant is tangent to an isocost line to produce a given level of output at the lowest cost.

We can interpret this tangency or cost minimization condition in two ways. At the point of tangency, the slope of the isoquant equals the slope of the isocost line. As we saw in Chapter 6, the slope of the isoquant is the marginal rate of technical substitution ($MRTS$). The slope of the isocost line is the negative of the ratio of the wage to the cost of capital, $-w/r$. Thus, to minimize its cost of producing a given level of output, a firm chooses its inputs so that the marginal rate of technical substitution equals the negative of the relative input prices:

$$MRTS = -\frac{w}{r}. \qquad (7.9)$$

The firm chooses inputs so that the rate at which it can substitute capital for labor in the production process, the MRTS, exactly equals the rate at which it can trade capital for labor in input markets, $-w/r$.

Equation 6.9 shows that, for a Cobb-Douglas production function, $MRTS = -(a/b)(K/L)$. Because the beer manufacturer's Cobb-Douglas production function, Equation 7.5, is $q = 1.52L^{0.6}K^{0.4}$, its marginal rate of technical substitution is $-(0.6/0.4)K/L = -1.5K/L$. At $K = 100$ and $L = 50$, its MRTS is -3, which equals the negative of the ratio of its input prices, $-w/r = -24/8 = -3$. In contrast, at y, the isocost line cuts the isoquant so that the slopes are not equal. At y, the MRTS is -18.9375, so the isoquant is steeper than the isocost line, -3. Because the slopes are not equal at y, the firm can produce the same output at lower cost. As Figure 7.3 shows, the cost of producing at y is $3,000, whereas the cost of producing at x is only $2,000.

We can interpret the condition in Equation 7.9 in another way. The marginal rate of technical substitution equals the negative of the ratio of the marginal product of labor to that of capital: $MRTS = -MP_L/MP_K$ (Equation 6.8). Thus, the cost-minimizing condition in Equation 7.9 is (taking the absolute value of both sides)

$$\frac{MP_L}{MP_K} = \frac{w}{r}. \tag{7.10}$$

Equation 7.10 may be rewritten as

$$\frac{MP_L}{w} = \frac{MP_K}{r}. \tag{7.11}$$

Equation 7.11 is the *last-dollar rule*: Cost is minimized if inputs are chosen so that the last dollar spent on labor adds as much extra output as the last dollar spent on capital.

To summarize, the firm can use three equivalent rules to determine the lowest-cost combination of inputs that will produce a given level of output when isoquants are smooth: the lowest-isocost rule; the tangency rule, Equations 7.9 and 7.10; and the last-dollar rule, Equation 7.11. If the isoquant is not smooth, the lowest-cost method of production cannot be determined by using the tangency rule or the last-dollar rule. The lowest-isocost rule always works, even when isoquants are not smooth.

SOLVED PROBLEM 7.3

MyLab Economics
Solved Problem

Using the estimated Japanese beer manufacturer's production function, Equation 7.5, $q = 1.52L^{0.6}K^{0.4}$, calculate the extra output produced by spending the last dollar on either labor or capital at points x and y in Figure 7.3. Show whether the last-dollar rule, Equation 7.11, holds at either of these points.

Answer

1. *Determine the general formula for the extra output from the last dollar spent on labor or capital.* The marginal product of labor is $MP_L = 0.6 \times 1.52L^{0.6-1}K^{0.4} = 0.6 \times 1.52L^{0.6}K^{0.4}/L = 0.6q/L$, and the marginal product of capital is $MP_K = 0.4q/K$.

2. *Calculate the extra output from the last-dollar expenditures at point x and check whether the last-dollar rule holds.* At point x ($L = 50, K = 100$), the beer firm's marginal product of labor is 1.2 ($= 0.6 \times 100/50$) and its marginal product of capital is 0.4 ($= 0.4 \times 100/100$). The last dollar spent on labor results in $MP/w = 1.2/24 = 0.05$ more units of output. Spending its last dollar

on capital, the firm produces $MP_K/r = 0.4/8 = 0.05$ extra output. Therefore, the last-dollar rule, Equation 7.11, holds at x: spending one more dollar on labor results in as much extra output as spending the same amount on capital. Thus, the firm is minimizing its cost of producing 100 units of output by producing at x.

3. *Repeat the analysis at point y.* If the firm produces at y ($L = 24, K = 303$), where it uses more capital and less labor, its MP_L is 2.5 ($= 0.6 \times 100/24$) and its MP_K is approximately 0.13 ($\approx 0.4 \times 100/303$). As a result, the last dollar spent on labor produces $MP_L/w = 2.5/24 \approx 0.1$ more units of output, whereas the last dollar spent on capital produces substantially less extra output, $MP_K/r \approx 0.13/303 \approx 0.017$, so the last-dollar rule does not hold.

Comment: At y, if the firm shifts \$1 from capital to labor, output falls by 0.017 due to the reduction in capital, but output increases by 0.1 due to the additional labor, for a net gain of 0.083 more output at the same cost. The firm should shift even more resources from capital to labor—thereby increasing the marginal product of capital and decreasing the marginal product of labor—until Equation 7.11 holds with equality at point x.

Using Calculus to Minimize Cost. Formally, the firm minimizes its cost, Equation 7.6, subject to the information about the production function that is contained in the isoquant formula, $\bar{q} = f(L, K)$, Equation 6.6. The corresponding Lagrangian problem is

$$\min_{L, K, \lambda} \mathcal{L} = wL + rK + \lambda[\bar{q} - f(L, K)]. \tag{7.12}$$

Assuming that we have an interior solution where both L and K are positive, the first-order conditions are

$$\frac{\partial \mathcal{L}}{\partial L} = w - \lambda \frac{\partial f}{\partial L} = 0, \tag{7.13}$$

$$\frac{\partial \mathcal{L}}{\partial K} = r - \lambda \frac{\partial f}{\partial K} = 0, \tag{7.14}$$

$$\frac{\partial \mathcal{L}}{\partial \lambda} = \bar{q} - f(L, K) = 0. \tag{7.15}$$

Equating the middle terms of Equation 7.13 and Equation 7.14 and dividing the resulting expression, we obtain the same expression as in Equation 7.10:

$$\frac{w}{r} = \frac{\dfrac{\partial f}{\partial L}}{\dfrac{\partial f}{\partial K}} = \frac{MP_L}{MP_K}. \tag{7.16}$$

That is, the firm minimizes cost where the factor-price ratio equals the ratio of the marginal products.[5]

_____

[5]Using Equations 7.13, 7.14, and 7.16, we find that $\lambda = w/MP_L = r/MP_K$. That is, the Lagrangian multiplier, λ, equals the ratio of the input price to the marginal product for each factor. As we already know, the input price divided by the factor's marginal product equals the marginal cost. Thus, the Lagrangian multiplier equals the marginal cost of production: It measures how much the cost increases if we produce one more unit of output.

SOLVED PROBLEM 7.4

Use calculus to derive the cost-minimizing capital-labor ratio for a constant elasticity of substitution (CES) isoquant, $\bar{q} = (L^\rho + K^\rho)^{1/\rho}$. Then, if $\rho = 0.5, w = r = 1$, and $\bar{q} = 4$, solve for the cost-minimizing L and K.

MyLab Economics
Solved Problem

Answer

1. *Write the Lagrangian expression for this cost-minimization problem.*

$$\mathcal{L} = wL + rK + \lambda(\bar{q} - [L^\rho + K^\rho]^{\frac{1}{\rho}}).$$

2. *Set the derivatives of the Lagrangian with respect to L, K, and λ equal to zero to obtain the first-order conditions.* The first-order conditions, which correspond to Equations 7.13–7.15, are

$$\frac{\partial \mathcal{L}}{\partial L} = w - \lambda\frac{1}{\rho}(L^\rho + K^\rho)^{\frac{1-\rho}{\rho}}\rho L^{\rho-1} = w - \lambda(L^\rho + K^\rho)^{\frac{1-\rho}{\rho}}L^{\rho-1} = 0, \quad (7.17)$$

$$\frac{\partial \mathcal{L}}{\partial K} = r - \lambda(L^\rho + K^\rho)^{\frac{1-\rho}{\rho}}K^{\rho-1} = 0, \quad (7.18)$$

$$\frac{\partial \mathcal{L}}{\partial \lambda} = \bar{q} - (L^\rho + K^\rho)^{\frac{1}{\rho}} = 0. \quad (7.19)$$

3. *Divide Equation 7.17 by Equation 7.18.* This ratio of first-order conditions, which corresponds to Equation 7.16, is

$$\frac{w}{r} = \frac{MP_L}{MP_K} = \frac{L^{\rho-1}}{K^{\rho-1}} = \left(\frac{L}{K}\right)^{\rho-1}. \quad (7.20)$$

The elasticity of substitution, Equation 6.15, is $\sigma = 1/(1 - \rho)$. Thus, if $\rho \to 0$, $\sigma \to 1$, so that the production function is Cobb-Douglas (Chapter 6), this condition is $w/r = K/L$. That is, a change in the factor-price ratio, w/r, has a proportional effect on the capital-labor ratio, K/L. The capital-labor ratio change is less than proportional if $\sigma < 1$, and more than proportional if $\sigma > 1$.

4. *Given that $\rho = 0.5, w = r = 1$, and $\bar{q} = 4$, solve Equations 7.19 and 7.20 for the cost-minimizing L and K.* Substituting $w = r = 1$, into Equation 7.20, we find that $1 = (K/L)^{0.5}$, or $K/L = 1$, or $K = L$. Substituting $K = L$ and $\bar{q} = 4$ into Equation 7.19, we discover that $4 = (2L^{0.5})^2 = 4L$, so $L = 1 = K$.

Maximizing Output. An equivalent or *dual* problem to minimizing the cost of producing a given quantity of output is maximizing output for a given level of cost. (In a similar pair of problems in Chapter 3, we examined how firms maximize utility for a given budget constraint and minimize expenditure for a given level of utility.) Here, the Lagrangian problem is

$$\max_{L, K, \lambda} \mathcal{L} = f(L, K) + \lambda(\bar{C} - wL - rK). \quad (7.21)$$

Assuming that we have an interior solution where both L and K are positive, the first-order conditions are

$$\frac{\partial \mathcal{L}}{\partial L} = \frac{\partial f}{\partial L} - \lambda w = 0, \quad (7.22)$$

$$\frac{\partial \mathscr{L}}{\partial K} = \frac{\partial f}{\partial K} - \lambda r = 0, \tag{7.23}$$

$$\frac{\partial \mathscr{L}}{\partial \lambda} = \overline{C} - wL - rK = 0. \tag{7.24}$$

By dividing Equation 7.22 by Equation 7.23, we obtain the same condition as when we minimized cost by holding output constant: $MP_L/MP_K = (\partial f/\partial L)/(\partial f/\partial K) = w/r$. That is, at the output maximum, the slope of the isoquant equals the slope of the isocost line. Figure 7.4 shows that the firm maximizes its output for a given level of cost by operating where the highest feasible isoquant, $q = 100$, is tangent to the $2,000 isocost line.

Shortcuts for Minimizing Cost and Maximizing Output. Rather than going through all the effort of using the Lagrangian method to solve for the optimal choice of inputs, we can use shortcuts to determine the two optimality conditions. We obtain these conditions using either the graphical or the Lagrangian approach for the general case.

We know that two conditions must hold to either minimize cost or maximize output (given smooth curves). The first condition is that the marginal rate of technical substitution (the slope of the isoquant) equals the rate at which a firm trades one input for the other (the slope of the isocost line), $MP_L/MP_K = w/r$, Equation 7.10. That is, the isoquant is tangent to the isocost line.

The second condition is the relevant constraint. To minimize cost, the constraint is the isoquant formula, $\overline{q} = f(L, K)$, Equation 6.6. The constraint when we maximize output is the isocost formula, $\overline{C} = wL + rK$ (Equation 7.7).

For example, in Solved Problem 7.4, in which we want to find the cost-minimizing choice of inputs for a CES production function, we use the two optimality conditions Equation 7.20 (the special case of the general tangency condition, Equation 7.10, for the CES) and Equation 7.19 (the special case of the general isoquant formula for the CES). We then solve these two equations for the two unknowns, L and K.

Figure 7.4 Output Maximization

The beer manufacturer maximizes its production at a cost of $2,000 by producing 100 units of output at x using $L = 50$ and $K = 100$. The $q = 100$ isoquant is the highest one that touches the $2,000 isocost line. The firm operates where the $q = 100$ isoquant is tangent to the $2,000 isocost line.

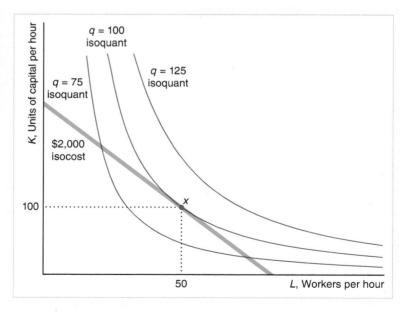

Factor Price Changes. Once the beer manufacturer determines the lowest-cost combination of inputs to produce a given level of output, it uses that method as long as the input prices remain constant. How should the firm change its behavior if the cost of one of the factors changes?

Suppose that the wage falls from $24 to $8 but the rental rate of capital stays constant at $8. Because of the wage decrease, the new isocost line in Figure 7.5 has a flatter slope, $-w/r = -8/8 = -1$, than the original isocost line, $-w/r = -24/8 = -3$. The change in the wage does not affect technological efficiency, so it does not affect the isoquant. The relatively steep original isocost line is tangent to the 100-unit isoquant at point x ($L = 50, K = 100$), while the new, flatter isocost line is tangent to the isoquant at v ($L = 77, K = 52$). Because labor is now relatively less expensive, the firm uses more labor and less capital. Moreover, the firm's cost of producing 100 units falls from $2,000 to $1,032 as a result of the decrease in the wage. This example illustrates that a change in the relative prices of inputs affects the combination of inputs that a firm selects and its cost of production.

Formally, we know from Equation 7.10 that the ratio of the factor prices equals the ratio of the marginal products: $w/r = MP_L/MP_K$. As we have already determined, this expression is $w/r = 1.5K/L$ for the beer manufacturer. Holding r fixed for a small change in w, the change in the factor ratio is $d(K/L)/dw = 1/(1.5r)$. For the beer manufacturer, where $r = 8$, $d(K/L)/dw = 1/12 \approx 0.083$. Because this derivative is positive, a small change in the wage leads to a higher capital-labor ratio because the firm substitutes some relatively less expensive capital for labor.

How Long-Run Cost Varies with Output

We now know how a firm determines the cost-minimizing combination of inputs for any given level of output. By repeating this analysis for different output levels, the firm determines how its cost varies with output.

Figure 7.5 Change in Factor Price

Originally the wage was $24 and the rental rate of capital was $8, so the lowest isocost line ($2,000) was tangent to the $q = 100$ isoquant at x ($L = 50, K = 100$). When the wage fell to $8, the isocost lines became flatter: Labor became relatively less expensive than capital. The slope of the isocost lines falls from $-w/r = -24/8 = -3$ to $-8/8 = -1$. The new lowest isocost line ($1,032) is tangent at v ($L = 77, K = 52$). Thus, when the wage falls, the firm uses more labor and less capital to produce a given level of output, and the cost of production falls from $2,000 to $1,032.

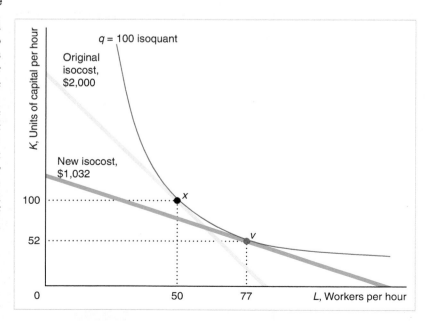

Figure 7.6 Expansion Path and Long-Run Cost Curve

(a) The curve through the tangency points between isocost lines and isoquants, such as x, y, and z, is called the expansion path. The points on the expansion path are the cost-minimizing combinations of labor and capital for each output level. (b) The beer manufacturer's expansion path shows the same relationship between long-run cost and output as the long-run cost curve.

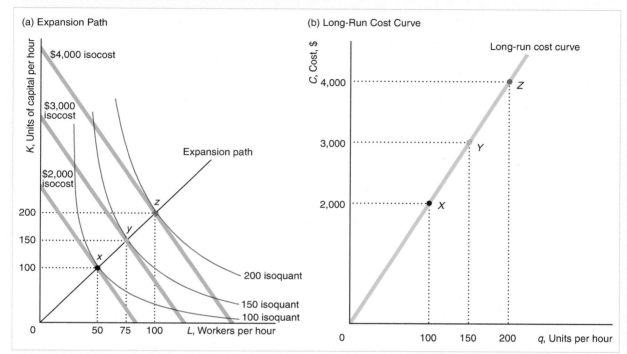

Expansion Path. Panel a of Figure 7.6 shows the relationship between the lowest-cost factor combinations and various levels of output for the beer manufacturer when input prices are held constant at $w = \$24$ and $r = \$8$. The curve through the tangency points is the long-run **expansion path**: the cost-minimizing combination of labor and capital for each output level. The lowest-cost method of producing 100 units of output is to use the labor and capital combination x ($L = 50$ and $K = 100$), which lies on the $2,000 isocost line. Similarly, the lowest-cost way to produce 200 units is to use z, which lies on the $4,000 isocost line. The expansion path for the beer manufacturer is a straight line through the origin and x, y, and z, which has a slope of 2: At any given output level, the firm uses twice as much capital as labor. (In general, the expansion path need not be a straight line but can curve up or down as input use increases.)

SOLVED PROBLEM 7.5

What is the expansion path function for a constant-returns-to-scale Cobb-Douglas production function $q = AL^a K^{1-a}$? What is the path for the estimated beer manufacturer, which has a production function of $q = 1.52L^{0.6}K^{0.4}$?

MyLab Economics Solved Problem

Answer

Use the tangency condition between the isocost line and the isoquant that determines the cost-minimizing factor ratio to derive the expansion path. Because the marginal product of labor is $MP_L = aq/L$ and the marginal product of capital is $MP_K = (1 - a)q/K$, the tangency condition is

$$\frac{w}{r} = \frac{aq/L}{(1 - a)q/K} = \frac{a}{1 - a}\frac{K}{L}.$$

Using algebra to rearrange this expression, we obtain the expansion path formula:

$$K = \frac{(1 - a)}{a}\frac{w}{r}L. \tag{7.25}$$

For the beer manufacturer in panel a of Figure 7.6, the expansion path, Equation 7.25, is $K = (0.4/0.6)(24/8)L = 2L$.

Long-Run Cost Function. The beer manufacturer's expansion path contains the same information as its long-run cost function, $C(q)$, which shows the relationship between the cost of production and output. As the expansion path plot in Figure 7.6 shows, to produce q units of output requires $K = q$ units of capital and $L = q/2$ units of labor. Thus, the long-run cost of producing q units of output is

$$C(q) = wL + rK = wq/2 + rq = (w/2 + r)q = (24/2 + 8)q = 20q.$$

That is, the long-run cost function corresponding to this expansion path is $C(q) = 20q$. This cost function is consistent with the expansion path in panel a: $C(100) = \$2,000$ at x on the expansion path, $C(150) = \$3,000$ at y, and $C(200) = \$4,000$ at z.

Panel b of Figure 7.6 plots this long-run cost curve. Points X, Y, and Z on the cost curve correspond to points x, y, and z on the expansion path. For example, the $\$2,000$ isocost line hits the $q = 100$ isoquant at x, which is the lowest-cost combination of labor and capital that can produce 100 units of output. Similarly, X on the long-run cost curve is at $\$2,000$ and 100 units of output. Consistent with the expansion path, the cost curve shows that as output doubles, cost doubles.

Solving for the cost function from the production function is not always easy. However, a cost function is relatively simple to derive from the production function if the production function is homogeneous of degree g so that $q = f(xL^*, xK^*) = x^g f(L^*, K^*)$, where x is a positive constant and L^* and K^* are particular values of labor and capital. That is, the production function has the same returns to scale for any given combination of inputs. Important examples of such production functions include the Cobb-Douglas ($q = AL^aK^b, g = a + b$), constant elasticity of substitution (CES), linear, and fixed-proportions production functions (see Chapter 6).

Because a firm's cost equation is $C = wL + rK$ (Equation 7.6), were we to double the inputs, we would double the cost. More generally, if we multiplied each output by x, the new cost would be $C = (wL^* + rK^*)x = \theta x$, where $\theta = wL^* + rK^*$. Solving the production function for x, we know that $x = q^{1/g}$. Substituting that expression in the cost equation, we find that the cost function for any homogeneous production function of degree g is $C = \theta q^{1/g}$. The constant in this cost function depends on factor prices and two constants, L^* and K^*. We would prefer to express the constant in terms of only the factor prices and parameters. We can do so by noting that the firm chooses the cost-minimizing combination of labor and capital, as summarized in the expansion path equation, as we illustrate in Solved Problem 7.6.

SOLVED PROBLEM 7.6 MyLab Economics Solved Problem	A firm has a Cobb-Douglas production function that is homogeneous of degree one: $q = AL^aK^{1-a}$. Derive the firm's long-run cost function as a function of only output and factor prices. What is the cost function that corresponds to the estimated beer manufacturer's production function $q = 1.52L^{0.6}K^{0.4}$?

Answer

1. *Combine the cost identity, Equation 7.6, with the expansion path, Equation 7.25, which shows how the cost-minimizing factor ratio varies with factor prices, to derive expressions for the inputs as a function of cost and factor prices.* From the expansion path, we know that $rK = wL(1 - a)/a$. Substituting for rK in the cost identity gives $C = wL + wL(1 - a)/a$. Simplifying shows that $L = aC/w$. Repeating this process to solve for K, we find that $K = (1 - a)C/r$.

2. *To derive the cost function, substitute these expressions of labor and capital into the production function.* By combining this information with the production function, we can obtain a relationship between cost and output. By substituting, we find that

$$q = A\left(\frac{aC}{w}\right)^a\left[\frac{(1-a)C}{r}\right]^{1-a}.$$

We can rewrite this equation as

$$C = \theta q, \tag{7.26}$$

where $\theta = w^a r^{1-a}/[Aa^a(1 - a)^{1-a}]$.

3. *To derive the long-run cost function for the beer firm, substitute the parameter values into $C = \theta q$.* For the beer firm, $C = [24^{0.6}8^{0.4}/(1.52 \times 0.6^{0.6}0.4^{0.4})]q \approx 20q$.

The Shape of Long-Run Cost Curves

The shapes of the average cost and marginal cost curves depend on the shape of the long-run cost curve. The relationships among total, marginal, and average costs are the same for both the long-run and short-run cost functions. For example, if the long-run average cost curve is U-shaped, the long-run marginal cost curve cuts it at its minimum.

The long-run average cost curve may be U-shaped, but the reason for this shape differs from those given for the short-run average cost curve. A key explanation for why the short-run average cost initially slopes downward is that the average fixed cost curve is downward sloping: Spreading the fixed cost over more units of output lowers the average fixed cost per unit. Because fixed costs are zero in the long run, fixed costs cannot explain the initial downward slope of the long-run average cost curve.

A major reason why the short-run average cost curve slopes upward at higher levels of output is diminishing marginal returns. In the long run, however, all factors can be varied, so diminishing marginal returns do not explain the upward slope of a long-run average cost curve.

As with the short-run curves, the shape of the long-run curves is determined by the production function relationship between output and inputs. In the long run, returns to scale play a major role in determining the shape of the average cost curve and the other cost curves. As we discussed in Chapter 6, increasing all inputs in proportion may cause output to increase more than in proportion (increasing returns to scale) at low levels of output, in proportion (constant returns to scale) at intermediate levels of output, and less than in proportion (decreasing returns to scale) at high levels of output. If a production function has this returns-to-scale pattern and the prices of inputs are constant, the long-run average cost curve must be U-shaped.

A cost function exhibits **economies of scale** if the average cost of production falls as output expands. Returns to scale is a sufficient condition for economies of scale. If a production function has increasing returns to scale, then the corresponding cost function has economies of scale: Doubling inputs more than doubles output, so average cost falls with higher output. However, if, for example, it is cost effective to switch to more capital-intensive production (such as using more robots and fewer workers) as the firm increases output, the cost function might exhibit economies of scale even if the production function does not have increasing returns to scale.

If an increase in output has no effect on average cost, then the production process has *no economies of scale*. Finally, a firm suffers from **diseconomies of scale** if average cost rises when output increases.

Average cost curves can have many different shapes. Perfectly competitive firms typically show U-shaped average cost curves. Average cost curves in noncompetitive markets may be U-shaped, L-shaped (average cost at first falls rapidly and then levels off as output increases), everywhere downward sloping, everywhere upward sloping, or take other shapes altogether. The shape of the average cost curve indicates whether the production process results in economies or diseconomies of scale. Some L-shaped average cost curves may be part of a U-shaped curve with long, flat bottoms, where we don't observe any firm producing enough to exhibit diseconomies of scale.

APPLICATION

3D Printing

Over the years, the typical factory has grown in size to take advantage of economies of scale to keep costs down. However, three-dimensional (3D) printing may reverse this trend by making it as inexpensive to manufacture one item as it is a thousand.

With 3D printing, an employee gives instructions—essentially a blueprint—to the machine, presses *Print*, and the machine builds the object from the ground up, either by depositing material from a nozzle or by selectively solidifying a thin layer of plastic or metal dust using drops of glue or a tightly focused beam.

Until recently, firms primarily used 3D printers to create prototypes in the aerospace, medical, and automotive industries. Then, they manufactured the final products using conventional techniques. However, costs have fallen to the point where manufacturing using 3D printers is often cost effective. According to Tucci Hot Rods (a car-customizing company) a hood vent for a Ford Fiesta ST modification costs $500 to build using machines and takes about three to four weeks to be delivered, compared to $15 to $17 in cost and 12 to 24 hours to 3D print.

Biomedical and aerospace companies are using 3D printing for just-in-time manufacturing. Printing can be used to fabricate small, highly customized batches of products as end-users need them. By 2018, Boeing and Airbus were each using thousands of different printed parts in their aircraft. The printers produce lighter parts, which lower the weight of planes (saving fuel) and can be quickly redesigned. Perhaps more striking, Airbus introduced the world's first entirely 3D-printed aircraft, a drone, in 2016. Some scientists and firms believe that 3D printing eventually will eliminate the need for many factories and may eliminate the manufacturing advantage of low-wage countries. Eventually, as the cost of printing drops, these machines may be used to produce small, highly customized batches as end-users need them.

Estimating Cost Curves Versus Introspection

Economists use statistical methods to estimate a cost function. However, we can sometimes infer the shape through casual observation and deductive reasoning.

For example, in the good old days, the Good Humor Company sent out herds of ice cream trucks to purvey its products. It seems likely that the company's production process had fixed proportions and constant returns to scale: If it wanted to sell more, Good Humor dispatched another truck and another driver. Drivers and trucks are almost certainly nonsubstitutable inputs (the isoquants are right angles). If the cost of a driver is w per day, the rental cost is r per day, and q is the quantity of ice cream sold per day, then the cost function is $C = (w + r)q$.

Such deductive reasoning can lead one astray, as I once discovered. A water-heater manufacturing firm provided me with many years of data on the inputs it used and the amount of output it produced. I also talked to the company's engineers about the production process and toured the plant (which resembled a scene from Dante's *Inferno*, with deafening noise levels and flames).

A water heater consists of an outside cylinder of metal, a liner, an electronic control unit, hundreds of tiny parts, and a couple of rods that slow corrosion. Workers cut out the metal for the cylinder, weld it together, and add the other parts. "Okay," I said to myself, "this production process must be one of fixed proportions because the firm needs one of each input to produce a water heater. How could you substitute a cylinder for an electronic control unit? Or substitute labor for metal?"

I then used statistical techniques to estimate the production and cost functions. Following the usual procedure, I did not assume that I knew the exact form of the functions. Rather, I allowed the data to "tell" me the type of production and cost functions. To my surprise, the estimates indicated that the production process was not one of fixed proportions. Rather, the firm could readily substitute between labor and metal.

"Surely I've made a mistake," I said to the plant manager after describing these results.

"No," he said, "that's correct. There's a great deal of substitutability between labor and metal."

"How can they be substitutes?"

"Easy," he said. "We can use a lot of labor and waste very little metal by cutting out exactly what we want and being very careful. Or we can use relatively little labor, cut quickly, and waste more metal. When the cost of labor is relatively high, we waste more metal. When the cost of metal is relatively high, we cut more carefully." This practice, as the manager explained, minimizes the firm's cost.

7.4 Lower Costs in the Long Run

In its long-term planning, a firm selects a plant size and makes other investments to minimize its long-run cost based on how many units it produces. Once it chooses its plant size and equipment, these inputs are fixed in the short run. Thus, the firm's long-run decisions determine its short-run cost. Because the firm cannot vary its capital in the short run but can in the long run, its short-run cost is at least as high as long-run cost and is higher if the "wrong" level of capital is used in the short run.

Long-Run Average Cost as the Envelope of Short-Run Average Cost Curves

As a result, the long-run average cost is always equal to or less than the short-run average cost. Figure 7.7 shows a firm with a U-shaped long-run average cost curve. Suppose initially that the firm has only three possible plant sizes. The firm's short-run

Figure 7.7 Long-Run Average Cost as the Envelope of Short-Run Average Cost Curves

(a) The firm can choose between only three possible plant sizes, with short-run average costs $SRAC^1$, $SRAC^2$, and $SRAC^3$, and the long-run average cost curve is the solid, scalloped portion of the three short-run curves. If the firm can pick any possible plant size, $LRAC$ is a smooth,

U-shaped long-run average cost curve. (b) Because the beer firm's production function has constant returns to scale, its long-run average cost and marginal cost curves are horizontal.

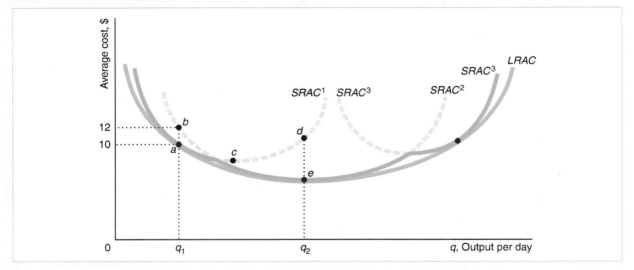

average cost curve is $SRAC^1$ for the smallest possible plant. The average cost of producing q_1 units of output using this plant, point *a* on $SRAC^1$, is $10. If instead the firm used the next larger plant size, its cost of producing q_1 units of output, point *b* on $SRAC^2$, would be $12. Thus, if the firm knows that it will produce only q_1 units of output, it minimizes its average cost by using the smaller plant. Its average cost of producing q_2 is lower on the $SRAC^2$ curve, point *e*, than on the $SRAC^1$ curve, point *d*.

In the long run, the firm chooses the plant size that minimizes its cost of production, so it selects the plant size with the lowest average cost for each possible output level. At q_1, it opts for the small plant, whereas at q_2, it uses the medium plant. Therefore, the long-run average cost curve is the solid, scalloped section of the three short-run cost curves.

But if a firm can pick whatever plant size it wants, the long-run average curve, $LRAC$, is smooth and U-shaped. The $LRAC$ includes one point from each possible short-run average cost curve. This point, however, is not necessarily the minimum point from a short-run curve. For example, the $LRAC$ includes point *a* on $SRAC^1$ and not the curve's minimum point, *c*. A small plant operating at minimum average cost cannot produce at as low an average cost as a slightly larger plant that takes advantage of economies of scale.

APPLICATION

A Beer Manufacturer's Long-Run Cost Curves

The figure shows the relationship between short-run and long-run average cost curves for the beer manufacturer (based on the estimates of Flath, 2011). Because this production function has constant returns to scale, doubling both inputs doubles output, so the long-run average cost, $LRAC$, is constant at $20 (as Solved Problem 7.6 shows, the long-run cost function is $C = 20q$, so $LRAC = C/q = 20$). If capital is fixed at 200 units, the firm's short-run average cost curve is $SRAC^1$. If the firm produces 200 units of output, its short-run and long-run average costs are equal. At any other output, its short-run cost is higher than its long-run cost.

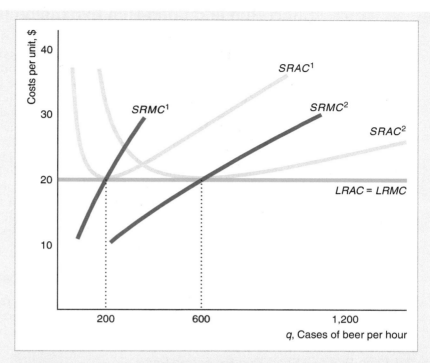

The short-run marginal cost curves, $SRMC^1$ and $SRMC^2$, are upward sloping and equal the corresponding U-shaped short-run average cost curves, $SRAC^1$ and $SRAC^2$, only at their minimum points of $20. In contrast, because the long-run average cost is horizontal at $20, the long-run marginal cost curve, $LRMC$, is horizontal at $20. Thus, the long-run marginal cost curve is not the envelope of the short-run marginal cost curves.

APPLICATION

Choosing an Inkjet or Laser Printer

You can buy a personal laser printer for $90 or an inkjet printer for $30. If you buy the inkjet printer, you immediately save $60. However, the laser printer costs less per page to operate. The cost of paper and ink or toner is about 4¢ per page for a laser printer compared to about 7¢ per page for an inkjet.

Thus, the average cost per page of operating a laser printer is $90/q + 0.04$, where q is the number of pages, while the average cost for an inkjet is $30/q + 0.07$. The graph shows the short-run average cost curves for the laser and inkjet printers. The average cost per page is lower with the inkjet printer until q reaches 2,000 pages, where the average cost of both is about 8.5¢ per page. For larger quantities, the laser is less expensive per page.

Short-Run and Long-Run Expansion Paths

Long-run cost is lower than short-run cost because a firm has more flexibility in the long run. To show the advantage of flexibility, we can compare the short-run and long-run expansion paths, which correspond to the short-run and long-run cost curves.

The beer manufacturer has greater flexibility in the long run. The tangency of the firm's isoquants and isocost lines determines the long-run expansion path in Figure 7.8. The firm expands output by increasing both its labor and capital, so its long-run expansion path is upward sloping. To increase its output from 100 to 200 units (that is, move from x to z), the firm doubles its capital from 100 to 200 units and its labor from 50 to 100 workers. As a result, its cost increases from $2,000 to $4,000.

In the short run, the firm cannot increase its capital, which is fixed at 100 units. The firm can increase its output only by using more labor, so its short-run expansion path is horizontal at $K = 100$. To expand its output from 100 to 200 units (move from x to y), the firm must increase its labor from 50 to 159 workers, and its cost rises from $2,000 to $4,616. Doubling output increases long-run cost by a factor of 2 and short-run cost by approximately 2.3.

How Learning by Doing Lowers Costs

Long-run cost is lower than short-run cost for three reasons. First, firms have more flexibility in the long run. Second, technological progress (Chapter 6) may lower cost over time. Third, the firm may benefit from **learning by doing**: the productive skills

Figure 7.8 Long-Run and Short-Run Expansion Paths

In the long run, the beer manufacturer increases its output by using more of both inputs, so its long-run expansion path is upward sloping. In the short run, the firm cannot vary its capital, so its short-run expansion path is horizontal at the fixed level of output. That is, it increases its output by increasing the amount of labor it uses. Expanding output from 100 to 200 raises the beer firm's long-run cost from $2,000 to $4,000 but raises its short-run cost from $2,000 to $4,616.

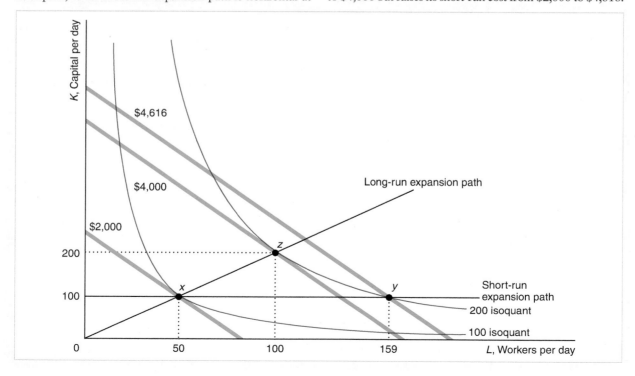

and knowledge of better ways to produce that workers and managers gain from experience. Workers who are given a new task may perform it slowly the first few times, but their speed increases with practice. Over time, managers may learn how to organize production more efficiently, determine which workers to assign to which tasks, and discover where inventories need to be increased and where they can be reduced. Engineers may optimize product designs by experimenting with various production methods. For these and other reasons, the average cost of production tends to fall over time, and the effect is particularly strong with new products.

Learning by doing might be a function of the time elapsed since a particular product or production process is introduced. More commonly, learning is a function of *cumulative output*: Workers become increasingly adept the more often they perform a task. We summarize the relationship between average costs and cumulative output with a **learning curve**. The learning curve for Intel central processing units (CPUs) in panel a of Figure 7.9 shows that Intel's average cost fell very rapidly with the first few million units of cumulative output, but then dropped relatively slowly with additional units (Salgado, 2008).

If a firm operates in the economies-of-scale section of its average cost curve, expanding output lowers its cost for two reasons: Its average cost falls today due to economies of scale, and for any given level of output, its average cost will be lower in the next period because of learning by doing.

In panel b of Figure 7.9, the firm currently produces q_1 units of output at point A on average cost curve AC^1. If it expands its output to q_2, its average cost falls in this period to point B due to economies of scale. Learning by doing in this period results in a lower average cost, AC^2, in the next period. If the firm continues to produce q_2 units of output in the next period, its average cost will fall to point b on AC^2.

Figure 7.9 Learning by Doing

(a) As Intel produces more cumulative central processing units (CPUs), the average cost of production per unit falls (Salgado, 2008). The horizontal axis measures the cumulative production. (b) In the short run, extra production reduces a firm's average cost owing to economies of scale: Because $q_1 < q_2 < q_3$, A is higher than B, which is higher than C. In the long run, extra production reduces average cost as a result of learning by doing. To produce q_2 this period costs B on AC^1, but to produce that same output in the next period would cost only b on AC^2. If the firm produces q_3 instead of q_2 in this period, its average cost in the next period is AC^3 instead of AC^2 due to additional learning by doing. Thus, extra output in this period lowers the firm's cost in two ways: It lowers average cost in this period due to economies of scale and lowers average cost for any given output level in the next period due to learning by doing.

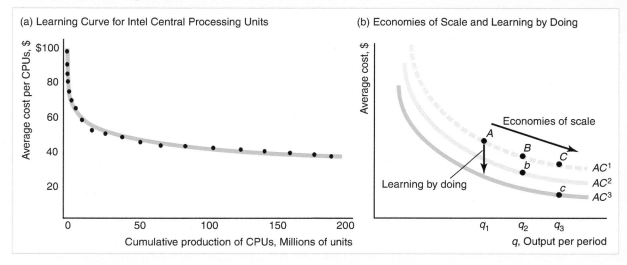

(a) Learning Curve for Intel Central Processing Units

(b) Economies of Scale and Learning by Doing

If instead of expanding output to q_2 in Period 1, the firm expands to q_3, its average cost is even lower in Period 1 (C on AC^1) due to even greater economies of scale. Moreover, its average cost curve, AC^3, in Period 2 is even lower due to the extra experience gained from producing more output in Period 1. If the firm continues to produce q_3 in Period 2, its average cost is c on AC^3. Thus, all else being the same, if learning by doing depends on cumulative output, firms have an incentive to produce more in the short run than they otherwise would to lower their costs in the future.

APPLICATION

Solar Power Learning Curves

Learning by doing substantially reduces the cost of installing solar photovoltaic systems, which makes installation much less expensive in some countries than in others. If you want solar power for your home, you need to buy the module, which converts sunlight to electricity, and install the system by paying for labor and components, such as cables, inverters, and mounts. Modules are sold globally. However, the installation costs vary by country due to labor and other differences as well as how many systems have been installed in the country.

Elshurafa et al. (2018) estimated learning curves for residential solar system installations, showing how the marginal cost varies with cumulative residential and commercial installations. On average, the global learning curve is 89%, which means that every time cumulative quantity doubles, the cost of installation falls to 89% of the previous level. The table shows these learning curve numbers for various countries or region.

Country or Region	Learning Curve (%)
Sweden	74
United Kingdom	84
Japan	87
Europe	91
Australia	93
Canada	93
Mexico	93
United States	93
China	96

7.5 Cost of Producing Multiple Goods

If a firm produces two or more goods, the cost of one good may depend on the output level of the other. Outputs are linked if a single input is used to produce both of them. For example, mutton and wool come from sheep, cattle provide beef and hides, and oil supplies heating fuel and gasoline. It is less expensive to produce beef and hides together than separately. If the goods are produced together, a single steer yields one unit of beef and one hide. If beef and hides are produced separately (throwing away the unused good), the same amount of output requires two steers and more labor.

A production process has **economies of scope** if it is less expensive to produce goods jointly than separately (Panzar and Willig, 1977, 1981). A measure of the degree of scope economies (SC) is

$$SC = \frac{C(q_1, 0) + C(0, q_2) - C(q_1, q_2)}{C(q_1, q_2)},$$

where $C(q_1, 0)$ is the cost of producing q_1 units of the first good by itself, $C(0, q_2)$ is the cost of producing q_2 units of the second good by itself, and $C(q_1, q_2)$ is the cost of producing both goods together. If the cost of producing the two goods separately, $C(q_1, 0) + C(0, q_2)$, is the same as the cost of producing them together, $C(q_1, q_2)$, then SC is zero. If it is cheaper to produce the goods jointly, SC is positive. If it is less expensive to produce the two goods separately, SC is negative and the production process has *diseconomies* of scope.

For example, a university may provide face-to-face classes, online classes, or both. Based on 37 public universities in Australia, Zhang and Worthington (2017) estimated that producing both jointly provides positive economies of scope, reducing cost by 16%.

To illustrate this idea, suppose that Laura spends one day collecting mushrooms and wild strawberries in the woods. Her **production possibility frontier**—a graph that shows the maximum amount of one good (say, mushrooms) that can be produced for any quantity of the other good (strawberries) using the available inputs (Laura's effort during one day) and technology—is PPF^1 in Figure 7.10. The production possibility frontier summarizes the trade-off Laura faces: She picks fewer mushrooms if she collects more strawberries in a day.

If Laura spends all day collecting only mushrooms, she picks eight pints; if she spends all day picking strawberries, she collects six pints. If she picks some of each, however, she can harvest more total pints: six pints of mushrooms and four pints of strawberries. The product possibility frontier is concave (the middle of the curve is farther from the origin than it would be if it were a straight line) because of the diminishing marginal returns to collecting only one of the two goods. If she collects only mushrooms, she must walk past wild strawberries without picking them. As a

Figure 7.10 Joint Production

With economies of scope, the production possibility frontier bows away from the origin, PPF^1. If instead the production possibility frontier is a straight line, PPF^2, the cost of producing both goods does not fall if they are produced together.

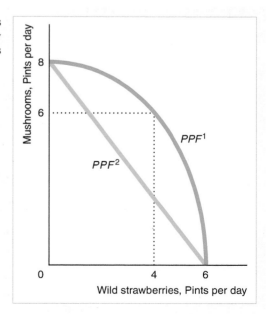

result, she has to walk farther if she collects only mushrooms than if she picks both. Thus, she can take advantage of the economies of scope by collecting both mushrooms and strawberries.

If instead the production possibility frontier were a straight line, the cost of producing the two goods jointly would not be lower. Suppose, for example, that mushrooms grow in one section of the woods and strawberries in another section. In that case, Laura can collect only mushrooms without passing any strawberries. That production possibility frontier is a straight line, PPF^2 in Figure 7.10. By allocating her time between the two sections of the woods, Laura can collect any combination of mushrooms and strawberries by spending part of her day in one section of the woods and part in the other.

<table>
<tr><td>

CHALLENGE SOLUTION

Technology Choice at Home Versus Abroad

</td><td>

If a U.S. semiconductor manufacturing firm shifts production from the firm's home plant to one abroad, should it use the same mix of inputs as at home? The firm may choose to use a different technology because the firm's cost of labor relative to capital is lower abroad than in the United States.

If the firm's isoquant is smooth, the firm uses a different bundle of inputs abroad than at home given that the relative factor prices differ (as Figure 7.5 shows).

However, semiconductor manufacturers have kinked isoquants.[6] Firms can use three different technologies to produce semiconductors. One technology is based on machines called *aligners*. This technology requires a relatively large amount of labor to reach any particular output level. The *stepper* technology uses more sophisticated machines and less labor, and advanced steppers called *wafer-handling steppers* represent an even larger capital input and correspondingly require less labor to reach any target output.

</td></tr>
</table>

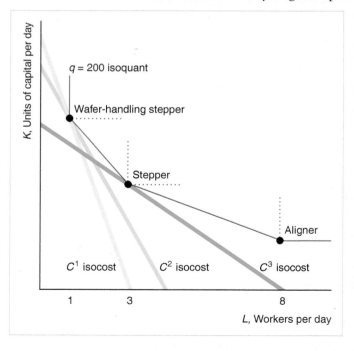

The figure shows a firm's $q = 200$ semiconductor chips isoquant. In its U.S. plant, the semiconductor manufacturing firm uses a wafer-handling stepper technology because the C^1 isocost line, which is the lowest isocost line that touches the isoquant, hits the isoquant at that technology.

The firm's cost of both inputs is less abroad than in the United States, and its cost of labor is relatively less than the cost of capital at its foreign plant than at its U.S. plant. The slope of its isocost line is $-w/r$, where w is the wage and r is the rental cost of the manufacturing equipment. The smaller w is relative to r, the less steeply sloped is its isocost line. Thus, the firm's foreign isocost line is flatter than its domestic C^1 isocost line.

If the firm's isoquant were smooth, the firm would certainly use a different technology at its foreign plant than in its home plant. However, its isoquant has kinks, so a small change in the relative input prices does not necessarily lead to a change in production technology. The firm could face either the C^2 or C^3 isocost

---

lines, both of which are flatter than the C^1 isocost line. If the firm faces the C^2 isocost line, which is only slightly flatter than the C^1 isocost, the firm still uses the capital-intensive wafer-handling stepper technology in its foreign plant. However, if the firm faces the much flatter C^3 isocost line, which hits the isoquant at the stepper technology, it switches technologies. (If the isocost line were even flatter, it could hit the isoquant at the aligner technology.)

Even if the wage change is small so that the firm's isocost line is C^2 and the firm does not switch technologies abroad, the firm's cost will be lower abroad with the same technology because C^2 is less than C^1. However, if the wage is low enough that it can shift to a more labor-intensive technology, its costs will be even lower: C^3 is less than C^2.

Thus, whether the firm uses a different technology in its foreign plant than in its domestic plant turns on the relative factor prices in the two locations and whether the firm's isoquant is smooth. If the isoquant is smooth, even a slight difference in relative factor prices will induce the firm to shift along the isoquant and use a different technology with a different capital-labor ratio. However, if the isoquant has kinks, the firm will use a different technology only if the relative factor prices differ substantially.

SUMMARY

From all available technologically efficient production processes, a firm chooses the one that is cost efficient. The cost-efficient production process is the technologically efficient process for which the cost of producing a given quantity of output is lowest, or the one that produces the most output for a given cost.

1. **Measuring Costs.** The economic or opportunity cost of a good is the value of its next best alternative use. Economic cost includes both explicit and implicit costs.

2. **Short-Run Costs.** In the short run, a firm can vary the costs of the factors that are adjustable, but the costs of other factors are fixed. The firm's average fixed cost falls as its output rises. If a firm has a short-run average cost curve that is U-shaped, its marginal cost curve lies below the average cost curve when average cost is falling and above the average cost curve when it is rising, so the marginal cost curve cuts the average cost curve at its minimum.

3. **Long-Run Costs.** In the long run, all factors can be varied, so all costs are variable. As a result, average cost and average variable cost are identical. A firm chooses the best combination of inputs to minimize its cost. To produce a given output level, it chooses the lowest isocost line to touch the relevant isoquant, which is tangent to the isoquant.

Equivalently, to minimize cost, the firm adjusts inputs until the last dollar spent on any input increases output by as much as the last dollar spent on any other input. If the firm calculates the cost of producing every possible output level given current input prices, it knows its cost function: Cost is a function of the input prices and the output level. If the firm's average cost falls as output expands, its cost function exhibits economies of scale. If the firm's average cost rises as output expands, it exhibits diseconomies of scale.

4. **Lower Costs in the Long Run.** The firm can always do in the long run what it does in the short run, so its long-run cost can never be greater than its short-run cost. Because some factors are fixed in the short run, the firm, to expand output, must greatly increase its use of other factors, a relatively costly choice. In the long run, the firm can adjust all factors, a process that keeps its cost down. Long-run cost may also be lower than short-run cost if technological progress or learning by doing occurs.

5. **Cost of Producing Multiple Goods.** If it is less expensive for a firm to produce two goods jointly rather than separately, the production process has economies of scope. With diseconomies of scope, it is less expensive to produce the goods separately.

EXERCISES

*All exercises are available on MyLab Economics; * = answer appears at the back of this book;* **M** = *mathematical problem.*

1. Measuring Costs

1.1 You have a ticket to go to a concert by one of your favorite groups, the Hives, which you cannot resell. However, you can buy a ticket for $30 to attend a talk by Steven Colbert, at the same time as the concert. You are willing to pay up to $90 to hear Colbert. Given that you incur no other costs involved in attending either event, what is your opportunity cost of attending the Hives concert? (*Hint*: See Solved Problem 7.1 and the Application "The Opportunity Cost of an MBA.")

1.2 Many corporations allow CEOs to use their firm's corporate jet for personal travel. The Internal Revenue Service (IRS) requires that the firm report personal use of its corporate jet as taxable executive income, and the Securities and Exchange Commission (SEC) requires that publicly traded corporations report the value of this benefit to shareholders. A firm may use any one of three valuation techniques. The IRS values a CEO's personal flight at or below the price of a first-class ticket. The SEC values the flight at the "incremental" cost of the flight: the additional costs to the corporation of the flight. The third alternative is the market value of chartering an aircraft. Of the three methods, the first-class ticket is least expensive and the chartered flight is most expensive.

   a. What factors (such as fuel) determine the marginal explicit cost to a corporation of an executive's personal flight? Does any one of the three valuation methods correctly determine the marginal explicit cost?

   b. What is the marginal opportunity cost to the corporation of an executive's personal flight?

*1.3 A firm purchased copper pipes a few years ago at $10 per pipe and stored them, using them only as the need arises. The firm could sell its remaining pipes in the market at the current price of $9. For each pipe, what is the opportunity cost and what is the sunk cost?

1.4 In 2015, the U.S. Supreme Court was hearing a case about a federal rule to promote reduced electricity use. In discussing this rule, Chief Justice John Roberts related the regulation to the pricing of hamburgers:[7]

   "If FERC is basically standing outside McDonald's and saying, 'We'll give you $5 not to go in,' and the price of the hamburger is $3 . . . the price of a hamburger is actually—I think most economists would say—$8, because if they give up the $5, they've still got to pay the $3."

Is he correct that the true opportunity cost of a hamburger is now $8? What is the explicit cost of the hamburger? What is the additional opportunity cost of eating the hamburger?

2. Short-Run Costs

*2.1 Nicolas has purchased a streaming audio service for $8.00 per month. As he now listens to more songs in a month, he spreads this fixed cost over a larger quantity, q. Derive an algebraic formula for his average fixed cost per song and draw it in a diagram. One of his friends says to Nicolas: "The more music you listen to the less you pay per song, so you should spend all your time listening to music." What is wrong with this reasoning?

2.2 A firm's short-run cost function is $C(q) = 200q - 6q^2 + 0.3q^3 + 400$. Determine the fixed cost, F; the average variable cost, AVC; the average cost, AC; the marginal cost, MC; and the average fixed cost, AFC. (*Hint*: See Solved Problem 7.2.) **M**

2.3 Give the formulas for and plot AFC, MC, AVC, and AC if the cost function is

   a. $C = 10 + 10q$,

   b. $C = 10 + q^2$,

   c. $C = 10 + 10q - 4q^2 + q^3$. (*Hint*: See Solved Problem 7.2.) **M**

2.4 A firm's cost curve is $C = F + 10q - bq^2 + q^3$, where $b > 0$.

   a. For what values of b are cost, average cost, and average variable cost positive? (From now on, assume that all these measures of cost are positive at every output level.)

   b. What is the shape of the AC curve? At what output level is the AC minimized?

   c. At what output levels does the MC curve cross the AC and the AVC curves?

   d. Use calculus to show that the MC curve must cross the AVC at its minimum point. **M**

*2.5 A firm builds wooden shipping crates. How does the cost of producing a 1-cubic-foot crate (each side is 1 foot square) compare to the cost of building an 8-cubic-foot crate if wood costs $1 per square foot and the firm has no labor or other costs? More generally, how does cost vary with volume?

---

[7]Bravender, Robin, "McDonald's helps Chief Justice Roberts Demystify FERC Rule," eenews.net.

2.6 The only variable input a janitorial service firm uses to clean offices is workers who are paid a wage, w, of $8 an hour. Each worker can clean four offices in an hour. Use math to determine the variable cost, the average variable cost, and the marginal cost of cleaning one more office. Draw a diagram similar to Figure 7.1 to show the variable cost, average variable cost, and marginal cost curves.

2.7 Gail works in a flower shop, where she produces 10 floral arrangements per hour. She is paid $10 an hour for the first eight hours she works and $15 an hour for each additional hour. What is the firm's cost function? What are its AC, AVC, and MC functions? Draw the AC, AVC, and MC curves. **M**

2.8 In 1796, Gottfried Christoph Härtel, a German music publisher, calculated the cost of printing music using an engraved plate technology and used these estimated cost functions to make production decisions. Härtel figured that the fixed cost of printing a musical page—the cost of engraving the plates—was 900 pfennigs. The marginal cost of each additional copy of the page was 5 pfennigs (Scherer, 2001).

a. Graph the total cost, average cost, average variable cost, and marginal cost functions.

b. Would the cost be lower if only one music publisher prints a given composition? Why?

c. Härtel used his data to do the following type of analysis: Suppose he expected to sell exactly 300 copies of a composition at 15 pfennigs per page. What is the highest price the publisher would be willing to pay the composer per page of the composition if he wants to at least break even? **M**

2.9 A Chinese high technology firm has a production function of $q = 10L^{0.28}K^{0.66}$ (Zhang, Delgado, and Kumbhakar, 2012). It faces factor prices of $w = 10$ and $r = 20$. What are its short-run marginal and average variable cost curves? **M**

2.10 A Japanese synthetic rubber manufacturer's production function is $q = 10L^{0.5}K^{0.5}$ (Flath, 2011). Suppose that its wage, w, is $1 per hour and the rental cost of capital, r, is $4.

a. Draw an accurate figure showing how the synthetic rubber manufacturer minimizes its cost of production.

b. What is the equation of the (long-run) expansion path for the manufacturer? Illustrate it in a graph.

c. Derive the long-run total cost curve equation as a function of q.

2.11 A firm has two plants that produce identical output. The cost functions are $C_1 = 10q - 4q^2 + q^3$ and $C_2 = 10q - 2q^2 + q^3$.

a. At what output level does the average cost curve of each plant reach its minimum?

b. If the firm wants to produce four units of output, how much should it produce in each plant? **M**

2.12 The estimated short-run cost function of a Japanese beer manufacturer is $C(q) = 0.55q^{1.67} + 800/q$ (see the Application "Short-Run Cost Curves for a Japanese Beer Manufacturer"). At what positive quantity does the average cost function reach its minimum? If a $400 lump-sum tax is applied to the firm, at what positive quantity is the after-tax average cost minimized? **M**

*2.13 What is the effect of a lump-sum franchise tax $\mathscr{L}$ on the quantity at which a firm's after-tax average cost curve reaches its minimum, given that the firm's before-tax average cost curve is U-shaped?

2.14 Platinum Pipeline Inc. needs a Caterpillar D6T dozer to install water and sewer lines. How does its fixed cost change if it can rent a dozer rather than buy one? (*Hint*: See the Application "The Sharing Economy and the Short Run.")

3. Long-Run Costs

*3.1 What is the long-run cost function if the production function is $q = L + K$? **M**

*3.2 A bottling company uses two inputs to produce bottles of the soft drink Sludge: bottling machines, K, and workers, L. The isoquants have the usual smooth shape. The machine costs $1,000 per day to run, and the workers earn $200 per day. At the current level of production, the marginal product of the machine is an additional 200 bottles per day, and the marginal product of labor is 50 more bottles per day. Is this firm producing at minimum cost? If it is minimizing cost, explain why. If it is not minimizing cost, explain how the firm should change the ratio of inputs it uses to lower its cost. (*Hint*: See Solved Problem 7.3.) **M**

*3.3 You have 60 minutes to complete an exam with two questions. You want to maximize your score. Toward the end of the exam, the more time you spend on either question, the fewer extra points per minute you get for that question. How should you allocate your time between the two questions? (*Hint*: Think about producing an output of a score on the exam using inputs of time spent on each of the problems. Then use an equation similar to Equation 7.11.)

3.4 Suppose that the government subsidizes the cost of workers by paying for 25% of the wage (the rate offered by the U.S. government in the late 1970s under the New Jobs Tax Credit program). What effect does this subsidy have on the firm's choice of labor and capital to produce a given level of output?

*3.5 The all-American baseball is made using cork from Portugal, rubber from Malaysia, yarn from Australia, and leather from France, and it is stitched (108 stitches exactly) by workers in Costa Rica. To assemble a baseball takes one unit of each of these inputs. Ultimately, the finished product must be shipped to its final destination—say, Cooperstown, New York. The materials used cost the same in any location. Labor costs are lower in Costa Rica than in a possible alternative manufacturing site in Georgia, but shipping costs from Costa Rica are higher. Would you expect the production function to exhibit decreasing, increasing, or constant returns to scale? What is the cost function? What can you conclude about shipping costs if it is less expensive to produce baseballs in Costa Rica than in Georgia?

3.6 A firm has a Cobb-Douglas production function, $Q = AL^aK^b$, where $a + b < 1$. What properties does its cost function have? (*Hint*: Compare this cost function to that of the Japanese beer manufacturer.) **M**

3.7 Replace the production function in Solved Problem 7.4 with a Cobb-Douglas $q = AL^aK^b$, and use calculus to find the cost-minimizing capital-labor ratio. **M**

3.8 Derive the long-run cost function for the constant elasticity of substitution production function $q = (L^\rho + K^\rho)^{d/\rho}$. (*Hint*: See Solved Problem 7.4.) **M**

3.9 For a Cobb-Douglas production function, how does the expansion path change if the wage increases while the rental rate of capital stays the same? (*Hint*: See Solved Problem 7.5.) **M**

3.10 The Bouncing Ball Ping Pong Company sells table tennis sets, which include two paddles and one net. What is the firm's long-run expansion path if it incurs no costs other than what it pays for paddles and nets, which it buys at market prices? How does its expansion path depend on the relative prices of paddles and nets? (*Hint*: See Solved Problem 7.5.)

3.11 Suppose that your firm's production function has constant returns to scale. What is the long-run expansion path?

3.12 A production function is homogeneous of degree g and involves three inputs, L, K, and M (materials). The corresponding factor prices are w, r, and e. Derive the long-run cost function. **M**

3.13 In Solved Problem 7.6, Equation 7.26 gives the long-run cost function of a firm with a constant-returns-to-scale Cobb-Douglas production function. Show how, for a given output level, cost changes as the wage, w, increases. Explain why. **M**

3.14 A water heater manufacturer produces q water heaters per day, q, using L workers and S square feet of sheet metal per day, using a constant elasticity of substitution production function, $q = (L^{-2} + S^{-2}/40)^{-0.5}$. The hourly wage rate is $20, and the price per square foot of sheet metal is 50¢.

   a. What is the marginal product of labor? What is the marginal product of capital?

   b. What is the expansion path equation? Draw the expansion path.

   c. Derive the long-run cost function.

   d. Suppose the price of sheet metal decreases to 25¢. Draw the new expansion path. Discuss the magnitude of the shift in the expansion path due to this price decrease. **M**

3.15 California's State Board of Equalization imposed a higher tax on "alcopops," flavored beers containing more than 0.5% alcohol-based flavorings, such as vanilla extract (Guy L. Smith, "On Regulation of 'Alcopops,'" *San Francisco Chronicle*, April 10, 2009). Until California banned alcopops in 2011, such beers were taxed as distilled spirits at $3.30 a gallon rather than as beer at 20¢ a gallon. In response, manufacturers reformulated their beverages to avoid the tax. By early 2009, instead of collecting a predicted $38 million a year in new taxes, the state collected only about $9,000. Use an isocost-isoquant diagram to explain the firms' response. (*Hint*: Alcohol-based flavors and other flavors may be close to perfect substitutes.)

3.16 See the Application "3D Printing." When fully incorporated by firms, how will 3D printing affect the shape of short-run and long-run cost curves?

3.17 Trader Joe's sells very cheap and popular wine produced by Bronco Wine.[8] When asked why the wine is so cheap, Bronco winemaker Ed Moody emphasizes the volume of output, stating that it is easier to make wine "in a 700,000-gallon tank than . . . in a 700-gallon one because there is less exposure to air and oxygen is the enemy in winemaking." Wine educator Keith Wallace emphasizes the role of machines: "The company uses machines to harvest the grapes, which helps keep labor costs low, but also increases the chances that bad grapes end up in the wine." One of these reasons is based on choosing input proportions to minimize cost and one is based on economies of scale. State which is which and explain.

4. Lower Costs in the Long Run

4.1 A U-shaped long-run average cost curve is the envelope of U-shaped short-run average cost curves. On

---

[8]Hayley Peterson, "The Real Reasons Trader Joe's Wine Is So Cheap," *Business Insider*, May 6, 2017.

what part of the curve (downward sloping, flat, or upward sloping) does a short-run curve touch the long-run curve? (*Hint*: Your answer should depend on where the two curves touch on the long-run curve.)

*4.2 A firm's average cost is $AC = aq^b$, where $a > 0$. How can you interpret a? (*Hint*: Suppose that $q = 1$.) What sign must b have if this cost function reflects learning by doing? What happens to average cost as q increases? Draw the average cost curve as a function of output for particular values of a and b. **M**

*4.3 A firm's learning curve, which shows the relationship between average cost and cumulative output (the sum of its output since the firm started producing), is $AC = a + bN^{-r}$, where AC is its average cost; N is its cumulative output; a, b, and r are positive constants; and $0 < r < 1$.

    a. What is the firm's AC if r is nearly zero? What can you say about the firm's ability to learn by doing?

    b. If r exceeds zero, what can you say about the firm's ability to learn by doing?

    c. What happens to its AC as its cumulative output, N, gets extremely large? Given this result, what is your interpretation of a? **M**

4.4 In the Application "Solar Power Learning Curves," the cost of solar power installations fell as the installed base (cumulative experience) in a given country rose. If N represents cumulative national experience, would the average cost curve $AC = a + bN^{-r}$, where a, b, and r are positive constants, exhibit such learning by doing? Explain.

5. Cost of Producing Multiple Goods

5.1 What can you say about Laura's economies of scope if her time is valued at $10 an hour and her production possibility frontier is PPF^1 in Figure 7.10?

*5.2 A refiner produces heating fuel and gasoline from crude oil in virtually fixed proportions. What can you say about economies of scope for such a firm? What is the sign of its measure of economies of scope, SC?

5.3 According to Haskel and Sadun (2012), the United Kingdom started regulating the size of grocery stores in the early 1990s, and today the average size of a typical U.K. grocery store is roughly half the size of a typical U.S. store and two-thirds the size of a typical French store. What implications would such a restriction on size have on a store's average costs? Discuss in terms of economies of scale and scope.

6. Challenge

*6.1 In the Challenge Solution, show that for some wage and rental cost of capital the firm is indifferent between using the wafer-handling stepper technology and the stepper technology. How does this wage/cost-of-capital ratio compare to those in the C^2 and C^3 isocost lines?

6.2 If it manufactures at home, a firm faces input prices for labor and capital of w and r and produces q units of output using L units of labor and K units of capital. Abroad, the wage and cost of capital are half as much as at home. If the firm manufactures abroad, will it change the amount of labor and capital it uses to produce q? What happens to its cost of producing q? **M**

*6.3 A U.S. synthetic rubber manufacturer is considering moving its production to a Japanese plant. Its estimated production function is $q = 10L^{0.5}K^{0.5}$ (Flath, 2011). In the United States, $w = 10 = r$. At its Japanese plant, the firm will pay a 10% lower wage and a 10% higher cost of capital: $w^* = 10/1.1$ and $r^* = 1.1 \times 10 = 11$. What are L and K, and what is the cost of producing $q = 100$ units in both countries? What would be the cost of production in Japan if the firm had to use the same factor quantities as in the United States? **M**

6.4 A U.S. apparel manufacturer is considering moving its production abroad. Its production function is $q = L^{0.7}K^{0.3}$ (based on Hsieh, 1995). In the United States, $w = 7$ and $r = 3$. At its Asian plant, the firm will pay a 50% lower wage and a 50% higher cost of capital: $w = 7/1.5$ and $r = 3 \times 1.5$. What are L and K, and what is the cost of producing $q = 100$ units in both countries? What would be the cost of production in Asia if the firm had to use the same factor quantities as in the United States? **M**

8 Competitive Firms and Markets

The love of money is the root of all virtue. —George Bernard Shaw

Businesses complain constantly about the costs and red tape that government regulations impose on them. U.S. truckers and trucking firms have a particular beef. In recent years, federal and state fees have increased substantially and truckers have had to adhere to many new regulations.

The Federal Motor Carrier Safety Administration (FMCSA), along with state transportation agencies in 41 states, administers interstate trucking licenses through the Unified Carrier Registration Agreement. As of 2018, the FMCSA's website lists 40 different areas of regulation, each of which contains multiple specific areas, ranging from regulations on noise, drivers, hazardous materials, preserving records, and transporting migrant workers. A trucker must also maintain minimum insurance coverage, pay registration fees, and follow policies that differ across states before the FMCSA will issue the actual authorities (grant permission to operate). The registration process is so complex and time consuming that firms pay substantial amounts to brokers who expedite the application process and take care of state licensing requirements.

For a large truck, the annual federal interstate registration fee can exceed $8,000. To operate, truckers and firms must pay for many additional fees and costly regulations. These largely lump-sum costs—which are not related to the number of miles driven—have increased substantially in recent years. In 2017, regulations took effect requiring each truck to have an electronic onboard recorder, which documents travel time and distance, at an annualized cost of several hundred dollars per truck.

What effect do these new fixed costs have on the trucking industry's market price and quantity? Are individual firms providing more or fewer trucking services? Does the number of firms in the market rise or fall? (As we'll discuss at the end of the chapter, the answer to one of these questions is surprising.)

To answer questions about industry price and quantity, we need to combine our understanding of demand curves with knowledge about firm and market supply curves to predict industry price. We start our analysis of firm behavior by addressing the fundamental question "How much should a firm produce?" To pick a level of output that maximizes its profit, a firm must consider its cost function and how much it can sell at a given price. The amount the firm thinks it can sell depends in turn on the market demand of consumers and the firm's beliefs about how other firms in the market will behave. The behavior of firms depends on the

market structure: the number of firms in the market, the ease with which firms can enter and leave the market, and the ability of firms to differentiate their products from those of their rivals.

In this chapter, we look at **perfect competition:** a market structure in which buyers and sellers are price takers. That is, neither firms nor consumers can sell or buy except at the market price. If a firm were to try to charge more than the market price, it would be unable to sell any of its output because consumers would buy the good at a lower price from other firms in the market. The market price summarizes everything that a firm needs to know about the demand of consumers *and* the behavior of its rivals. Thus, a competitive firm can ignore the specific behavior of individual rivals when deciding how much to produce.[1]

In this chapter, we examine four main topics

1. **Perfect Competition.** A perfectly competitive firm is a price taker, and as such, it faces a horizontal demand curve.

2. **Profit Maximization.** To maximize profit, any firm must make two decisions: what output level maximizes its profit (or minimizes its loss) and whether to produce at all.

3. **Competition in the Short Run.** In the short run, variable costs determine a profit-maximizing, competitive firm's supply curve, the market supply curve, and, with the market demand curve, the competitive equilibrium.

4. **Competition in the Long Run.** Firm supply, market supply, and competitive equilibrium are different in the long run than in the short run because firms can vary inputs that were fixed in the short run and new firms can enter the market.

8.1 Perfect Competition

Perfect competition is a market structure with very desirable properties, so it is useful to compare other market structures to competition. Many markets approximate perfect competition. In this section, we examine the properties of competitive firms and markets.

Price Taking

When most people talk about "competitive firms," they mean firms that are rivals for the same customers. By this interpretation, any market with more than one firm is competitive. However, to an economist, only some of these multifirm markets are competitive.

Economists say that a market is perfectly competitive if each firm in the market is a *price taker:* It cannot significantly affect the market price for its output or the prices at which it buys inputs. Why would a competitive firm be a price taker? Because it has no choice. The firm *has* to be a price taker if it faces a demand curve that is horizontal at the market price. If the demand curve is horizontal at the market price, the firm can sell as much as it wants at that price, so it has no incentive to lower its

---

[1]In contrast, in a market with a small number of firms, each firm must consider the behavior of each of its rivals, as we discuss in Chapters 13 and 14.

price. Similarly, the firm cannot increase the price at which it sells by restricting its output because it faces an infinitely elastic demand (see Chapter 2): A small increase in price results in its demand falling to zero.

Why a Firm's Demand Curve Is Horizontal

Perfectly competitive markets have five characteristics that force firms to be price takers:

1. The market consists of many small buyers and sellers.
2. All firms produce identical products.
3. All market participants have full information about price and product characteristics.
4. Transaction costs are negligible.
5. Firms can easily enter and exit the market.

Large Number of Small Firms and Consumers. In a market with many small firms, no single firm can raise or lower the market price. The more firms in a market, the less any one firm's output affects the market output and hence the market price.

For example, the 107,000 U.S. soybean farmers are price takers. If a typical grower drops out of the market, market supply falls by only 1/107,000 = 0.00093%, which would not noticeably affect the market price. A soybean farm can sell any feasible output it produces at the prevailing market equilibrium price. In other words, *the firm's demand curve is effectively a horizontal line at the market price.*

Similarly, perfect competition requires that buyers be price takers as well. For example, if firms sell to only a single buyer—such as producers of weapons that are allowed to sell to only the government—then the buyer can set the price and the market is not perfectly competitive.

Identical Products. Firms in a perfectly competitive market sell *identical* or *homogeneous* products. Consumers do not ask which farm grew a Granny Smith apple because they view all Granny Smith apples as essentially identical. If the products of all firms are identical, it is difficult for a single firm to raise its price above the going price charged by other firms.

In contrast, in the automobile market—which is not perfectly competitive—the characteristics of a BMW 5 Series and a Honda Civic differ substantially. These products are *differentiated* or *heterogeneous*. Competition from Civics would not be very effective in preventing BMW from raising its price.

Full Information. If buyers know that different firms are producing identical products and they know the prices charged by all firms, no single firm can unilaterally raise its price above the market equilibrium price. If it tried to do so, consumers would buy the identical product from another firm. However, if consumers are unaware that products are identical or they don't know the prices charged by other firms, a single firm may be able to raise its price and still make sales.

Negligible Transaction Costs. Perfectly competitive markets have very low transaction costs. Buyers and sellers do not have to spend much time and money finding each other or hiring lawyers to write contracts to execute a trade.[2] If transaction costs are low, it is easy for a customer to buy from a rival firm if the customer's usual supplier raises its price.

---

[2]Average number of hours per week that an American and a Chinese person, respectively, spend shopping: 4, 10. —*Harper's Index*, 2008.

In contrast, if transaction costs are high, customers might absorb a price increase from a traditional supplier. For example, because some consumers prefer to buy milk at a local convenience store rather than travel several miles to a supermarket, the convenience store can charge slightly more than the supermarket without losing all its customers.

In some perfectly competitive markets, many buyers and sellers are brought together in a single room, so transaction costs are virtually zero. For example, transaction costs are very low at FloraHolland's daily flower auctions in the Netherlands, which attract 7,000 suppliers and 4,500 buyers from around the world. It has 125,000 auction transactions every day, with 12 billion cut flowers and 1.3 billion plants trading in a year.

Free Entry and Exit. The ability of firms to enter and exit a market freely leads to a large number of firms in a market and promotes price taking. Suppose a firm can raise its price and increase its profit. If other firms are not able to enter the market, the firm will not be a price taker. However, if other firms can enter the market, the higher profit encourages entry until the price is driven back to the original level. Free exit is also important: If firms can freely enter a market but cannot exit easily if prices decline, they might be reluctant to enter the market in response to a short-run profit opportunity in the first place.[3] More generally, we assume perfect mobility of resources, which allows firms to alter their scale of production as well as to enter and exit an industry.

Perfect Competition in the Chicago Commodity Exchange

The Chicago Commodity Exchange, where buyers and sellers can trade wheat and other commodities, has the various characteristics of perfect competition, including thousands of buyers and sellers who are price takers. Anyone can be a buyer or seller. Indeed, a trader might buy wheat in the morning and sell it in the afternoon. They trade virtually *identical products*. Buyers and sellers have *full information* about products and prices, which is posted for everyone to see. Market participants waste no time finding someone who wants to trade and they can easily place buy or sell orders in person, over the telephone, or electronically without paperwork, so *transaction costs are negligible*. Finally, *buyers and sellers can easily enter this market and trade wheat*. These characteristics lead to an abundance of buyers and sellers and to price-taking behavior by these market participants.

Deviations from Perfect Competition

Many markets possess some, but not all, the characteristics of perfect competition but are still highly competitive so that buyers and sellers are, for all practical purposes, price takers. For example, a government may limit entry into a market, but if the market has many buyers and sellers, they may be price takers. Many cities use zoning laws to limit the number of certain types of stores or motels, yet these cities still have many such firms. Other cities impose moderately large transaction costs on entrants by requiring them to buy licenses, post bonds, and deal with a slow-moving city bureaucracy, yet a significant number of firms enter the market anyway. Similarly, even if only some customers have full information, that may be sufficient to

---

[3]Many national governments require that firms give workers a warning (for example, six months) before they exit a market.

prevent firms from deviating significantly from price taking. For instance, tourists do not know the prices at various stores, but locals do and they use their knowledge to prevent one store from charging unusually high prices.

Economists use the terms *competition* and *competitive* more restrictively than do real people. To an economist, a competitive firm is a price taker. In contrast, when most people talk about competitive firms, they mean that firms are rivals for the same customers. Even in an oligopolistic market—one with only a few firms—the firms compete for the same customers so they are competitive in this broader sense. From now on, we will use the terms *competition* and *competitive* to refer to all markets in which no buyer or seller can significantly affect the market price—they are price takers—even if the market is not perfectly competitive.

Derivation of a Competitive Firm's Demand Curve

Are the demand curves faced by individual competitive firms actually flat? To answer this question, we use a modified supply-and-demand diagram to derive the demand curve for an individual firm.

An individual firm faces a **residual demand curve**: the market demand that is not met by other sellers at any given price. The firm's residual demand function, $D^r(p)$, shows the quantity demanded from the firm at price p. A firm sells only to people who have not already purchased the good from another seller. We can determine the quantity that a particular firm can sell at each possible price using the market demand curve and the supply curve for all *other* firms in the market. The quantity the market demands is a function of the price: $Q = D(p)$. The supply curve of the other firms is $S^o(p)$. The residual demand function equals the market demand function, $D(p)$, minus the supply function of all other firms:

$$D^r(p) = D(p) - S^o(p). \tag{8.1}$$

At prices so high that the amount supplied by other firms, $S^o(p)$, is greater than the quantity demanded by the market, $D(p)$, the residual quantity demanded, $D^r(p)$, is zero.

In Figure 8.1, we derive the residual demand for a Canadian manufacturing firm that produces metal chairs. Panel b shows the market demand curve, D, and the supply curve of all but one manufacturing firm, S^o.[4] At $p = \$66$ per chair, the supply of the other firms, 500 units (where a unit is 1,000 metal chairs) per year, equals the market demand (panel b), so the residual quantity demanded of the remaining firm (panel a) is zero.

At prices below $66, the other chair firms are not willing to supply as much as the market demands. At $p = \$63$, for example, the market demand is 527 units, but other firms want to supply only 434 units. As a result, the residual quantity demanded from the individual firm at $p = \$63$ is 93 ($= 527 - 434$) units. Thus, the residual demand curve at any given price is the horizontal difference between the market demand curve and the supply curve of the other firms.

The residual demand curve that the firm faces in panel a is much flatter than the market demand curve in panel b. As a result, the elasticity of the residual demand curve is much higher than the market elasticity.

---

[4]The figure uses constant elasticity demand and supply curves (Chapter 2). The elasticity of supply is based on the estimated cost function from Robidoux and Lester (1988) for Canadian office furniture manufacturers. I estimated that the market elasticity of demand is $\varepsilon = -1.1$, using data from *Statistics Canada, Office Furniture Manufacturers*.

Figure 8.1 Residual Demand Curve

The residual demand curve, $D^r(p)$, faced by a single office furniture manufacturing firm is the market demand, $D(p)$, minus the supply of the other firms in the market, $S^o(p)$.

The residual demand curve is much flatter than the market demand curve.

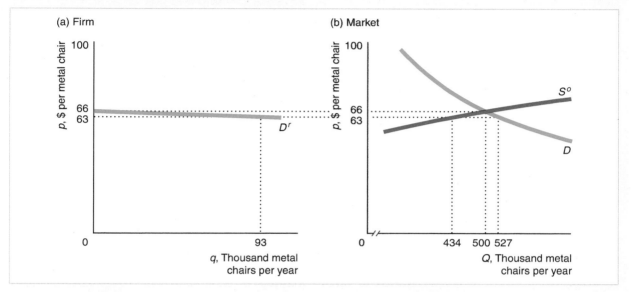

(a) Firm

(b) Market

In a market with n identical firms, the elasticity of demand, ε_i, facing Firm i is

$$\varepsilon_i = n\varepsilon - (n-1)\eta_o, \tag{8.2}$$

where ε is the market elasticity of demand (a negative number), η_o is the elasticity of supply of the other firms (typically a positive number), and $n - 1$ is the number of other firms.[5]

---

[5]To derive Equation 8.2, we start by differentiating the residual demand function, Equation 8.1, with respect to p:

$$\frac{dD^r}{dp} = \frac{dD}{dp} - \frac{dS^o}{dp}.$$

Because the n firms in the market are identical, each firm produces $q = Q/n$, where Q is total output. The output produced by the other firms is $Q_o = (n-1)q$. Multiplying both sides of the previous expression by p/q and multiplying and dividing the first term on the right side by Q/Q and the second term by Q_o/Q_o, this expression may be rewritten as

$$\frac{dD^r}{dp}\frac{p}{q} = \frac{dD}{dp}\frac{p}{Q}\frac{Q}{q} - \frac{dS^o}{dp}\frac{p}{Q_o}\frac{Q_o}{q},$$

where $q = D^r(p)$, $Q = D(p)$, and $Q_o = S^o(p)$. This expression can be rewritten as Equation 8.2 by noting that $Q/q = n$, $Q_o/q = (n-1)$, $(dD^r/dp)(p/q) = \varepsilon_i$, $(dD/dp)(p/Q) = \varepsilon$, and $(dS^o/dp)(p/Q_o) = \eta_o$.

SOLVED PROBLEM 8.1 MyLab Economics Solved Problem	The Canadian metal chair manufacturing market has $n = 78$ firms. The estimated elasticity of supply is $\eta = 3.1$, and the estimated elasticity of demand is $\varepsilon = -1.1$. Assuming that the firms are identical, calculate the elasticity of demand facing a single firm. Is its residual demand curve highly elastic?

Answer

1. *Use Equation 8.2 and the estimated elasticities to calculate the residual demand elasticity facing a firm.* If we assume that $\eta_o \approx \eta$, and we substitute the elasticities into Equation 8.2, we find that

$$\varepsilon_i = n\varepsilon - (n - 1)\eta_o$$
$$= [78 \times (-1.1)] - (77 \times 3.1)$$
$$= -85.8 - 238.7 = -324.5.$$

That is, a typical firm faces a residual demand elasticity of –324.5.

2. *Discuss whether this elasticity is high.* The estimated ε_i is nearly 300 times the market elasticity of -1.1. If a firm raises its price by one-tenth of a percent, the quantity it can sell falls by nearly one-third. Therefore, the competitive model assumption that this firm faces a horizontal demand curve with an infinite price elasticity is not much of an exaggeration.

Comment: As Equation 8.2 shows, if the supply curve slopes upward, the residual demand elasticity, ε_i, must be at least as elastic as $n\varepsilon$ because the second term makes the residual demand elasticity more elastic. Thus, if we do not know the supply elasticity, we can use $n\varepsilon$ as a conservative approximation of ε_i. For example, the soybean market has roughly 107,000 farms, so even though the market elasticity of demand for soybeans is very inelastic, -0.2, the residual demand facing a single farm must be at least $n\varepsilon = 107,000 \times (-0.2) = -21,400$, which is extremely elastic.

Why Perfect Competition Is Important

Perfectly competitive markets are important for two reasons. First, many markets can be reasonably described as competitive. Many agricultural and other commodity markets, stock exchanges, retail and wholesale, building construction, and other types of markets have many or all of the properties of a perfectly competitive market. The competitive supply-and-demand model works well enough in these markets that it accurately predicts the effects of changes in taxes, costs, incomes, and other factors on market equilibrium.

Second, a perfectly competitive market has many desirable properties. Economists compare the real-world market to this ideal market. Throughout the rest of this book, we show that society as a whole suffers if the properties of the perfectly competitive market fail to hold. From this point on, for brevity, we use the phrase *competitive market* to mean a *perfectly competitive market* unless we explicitly note an imperfection.

8.2 Profit Maximization

"Too caustic?" To hell with the cost. If it's a good picture, we'll make it.
—Samuel Goldwyn

Economists usually assume that *all* firms—not just competitive firms—want to maximize their profits. One reason is that many businesspeople say that their objective is to maximize profits. A second reason is that a firm—especially a competitive firm—that does not maximize profit is likely to lose money and be driven out of business.

In this section, we examine how any type of firm—not just a competitive firm—maximizes its profit. We then examine how a competitive firm in particular maximizes profit.

Profit

A firm's *profit*, π, is the difference between its revenues, R, and its cost, C:

$$\pi = R - C.$$

If profit is negative, $\pi < 0$, the firm suffers a *loss*.

Measuring a firm's revenue is straightforward: Revenue is price times quantity. Measuring cost is more challenging. From the economic point of view, the correct measure of cost is the *opportunity cost* or *economic cost*: the value of the best alternative use of any input the firm employs. As discussed in Chapter 7, the full opportunity cost of inputs used might exceed the explicit or out-of-pocket costs recorded in financial accounting statements. This distinction is important because a firm may make a serious mistake if it incorrectly measures profit by ignoring some relevant opportunity costs.

We always refer to *profit* or **economic profit** as revenue minus opportunity (economic) cost. For tax or other reasons, *business profit* may differ. For example, if a firm uses only explicit cost, then its reported profit may be larger than its economic profit. A couple of examples illustrate the difference in the two profit measures and the importance of this distinction in dispelling a misconception:

> **Common Confusion** It pays to run your own firm if you are making a business profit.

That conclusion may not follow because business profit ignores opportunity cost (unlike economic profit).

Suppose you start your own firm.[6] You have to pay explicit costs such as workers' wages and the price of materials. Like many owners, you do not pay yourself a salary. Instead, you take home a business profit, which is based on only explicit costs, of $40,000 per year.

Economists (well-known spoilsports) argue that your profit is less than $40,000. Economic profit equals your business profit minus any additional opportunity cost. Suppose that instead of running your own business, you could have earned $50,000 a year working for someone else. The opportunity cost of your time working for your business is $50,000—your forgone salary. So even though your firm made a business profit of $40,000, your economic loss (negative economic profit) is $10,000. Put another way, the price of being your own boss is $10,000.

By looking at only the explicit cost and ignoring opportunity cost, you conclude that running your business is profitable. However, if you consider economic profit, you realize that working for others maximizes your income.

Similarly, when a firm decides whether to invest in a new venture, it must consider the next best alternative use of its funds. A firm considering setting up a new branch in Tucson must evaluate all the alternatives: placing the branch in Santa Fe, depositing

---

[6]For example, Michael Dell started a mail-order computer company while he was in college. Today, his company is one of the world's largest personal computer companies. In 2018, *Forbes* estimated Mr. Dell's wealth at $24.3 billion.

the money it would otherwise spend on the new branch in the bank where it earns interest, and so on. If the best alternative use of the money is to put it in the bank and earn $10,000 per year in interest, the firm should build the new branch in Tucson only if it expects to make $10,000 or more per year in business profit. That is, the firm should create a Tucson branch only if the economic profit from the new branch is zero or greater. If the economic profit is zero, then the firm is earning the same return on its investment as it would from putting the money into its next best alternative, the bank.

Two Steps to Maximizing Profit

Any firm (not just a competitive firm) uses a two-step process to maximize profit. Because both revenue and cost vary with output, a firm's profit varies with its output level. Its profit function is

$$\pi(q) = R(q) - C(q), \tag{8.3}$$

where q is the number of units it produces, $R(q)$ is its revenue function, and $C(q)$ is its cost function. To maximize its profit, a firm must answer two questions:

1. **Output decision:** If the firm produces, what output level, q^*, maximizes its profit or minimizes its loss?
2. **Shutdown decision:** Is it more profitable to produce q^* or to shut down and produce no output?

We use the profit curve in Figure 8.2 to illustrate these two basic decisions. This firm makes losses at very low and very high output levels and makes positive profits at moderate output levels. The profit curve first rises and then falls, reaching a maximum profit of π^* when its output is q^*. Because the firm makes a positive profit at that output, it chooses to produce q^* units of output.

Output Rules. A firm can use one of three equivalent rules to choose how much output to produce. All types of firms maximize profit using the same rules. The most straightforward rule is:

Output Rule 1: *The firm sets its output where its profit is maximized.*
The profit curve in Figure 8.2 reaches its maximum, π^*, at output q^*. If the firm knows its entire profit curve, it can immediately set its output to maximize its profit.

Figure 8.2 Maximizing Profit

By setting its output at q^*, the firm maximizes its profit at π^*, where the profit curve is flat (has zero slope): $d\pi/dq = 0$.

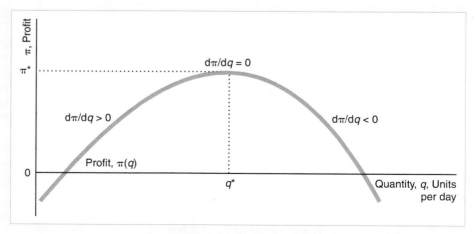

Even if the firm does not know the exact shape of its profit curve, it may be able to find the maximum by experimenting. The firm starts by slightly increasing its output. If profit increases, the firm increases the output more. The firm keeps raising output until its profit does not change. At that output, the firm is at the peak of the profit curve. If profit falls when the firm first increases its output, the firm tries decreasing its output. It keeps decreasing its output until it reaches the peak of the profit curve.

What the firm is doing is experimentally determining the slope of the profit curve. The slope of the profit curve is the firm's **marginal profit**: the change in the profit the firm gets from selling one more unit of output, $d\pi(q)/dq$. In the figure, the marginal profit or slope is positive when output is less than q^*, zero when output is q^*, and negative when output is greater than q^*. Thus,

Output Rule 2: *A firm sets its output where its marginal profit is zero.*

We obtain this result formally using the first-order condition for a profit maximum. We set the derivative of the profit function, Equation 8.3, with respect to quantity equal to zero:

$$\frac{d\pi(q^*)}{dq} = 0. \tag{8.4}$$

Equation 8.4 states that a necessary condition for profit to be maximized is that the quantity be set at q^* where the firm's marginal profit with respect to quantity equals zero.

Equation 8.4 is a necessary condition for profit maximization. Sufficiency requires, in addition, that the second-order condition hold:

$$\frac{d^2\pi(q^*)}{dq^2} < 0. \tag{8.5}$$

That is, for profit to be maximized at q^*, when we increase the output beyond q^*, the marginal profit must decline.

Because profit is a function of revenue and cost, we can obtain another necessary condition for profit maximization by setting the derivative of $\pi(q) = R(q) - C(q)$ with respect to output equal to zero:

$$\frac{d\pi(q^*)}{dq} = \frac{dR(q^*)}{dq} - \frac{dC(q^*)}{dq} = MR(q^*) - MC(q^*) = 0. \tag{8.6}$$

The derivative of cost with respect to output, $dC(q)/dq = MC(q)$, is its marginal cost (Chapter 7). The firm's **marginal revenue**, MR, is the change in revenue it gains from selling one more unit of output: dR/dq. Equation 8.6 shows that a necessary condition for profit to be maximized is that the firm set its quantity at q^* where the difference between the firm's marginal revenue and marginal cost is zero. Thus, a third, equivalent rule is

Output Rule 3: *A firm sets its output where its marginal revenue equals its marginal cost,*

$$MR(q^*) = MC(q^*). \tag{8.7}$$

The intuition for this result is that if the marginal revenue from this last unit of output exceeds its marginal cost, $MR(q) > MC(q)$, the firm's marginal profit is positive, $MR(q) - MC(q) > 0$, so it pays to increase output. The firm keeps increasing its output until its marginal profit $= MR(q) - MC(q) = 0$. At that output, its marginal revenue equals its marginal cost: $MR(q) = MC(q)$. If the firm produces more output where its marginal cost exceeds its marginal revenue, $MR(q) < MC(q)$, the extra output reduces the firm's profit, so the firm should reduce its output.

For profit to be maximized at q^*, the second-order condition must hold:

$$\frac{d^2\pi(q^*)}{dq^2} = \frac{d^2R(q^*)}{dq^2} - \frac{d^2C(q^*)}{dq^2} = \frac{dMR(q^*)}{dq} - \frac{dMC(q^*)}{dq} < 0. \qquad (8.8)$$

That is, for profit to be maximized at q^*, the slope of the marginal revenue curve, dMR/dq, must be less than the slope of the marginal cost curve, dMC/dq.

Shutdown Rules. The firm chooses to produce q^* if it can make a profit. But even if the firm maximizes its profit at q^*, should it produce output if doing so makes a loss? "Common sense" suggests that it should not.

Common Confusion A firm should shut down if it is making a loss.

This intuition holds if the firm is making a loss in the long run, but it may be wrong in the short run. The general rule, which holds for all types of firms in both the short and long run, is

Shutdown Rule 1: *The firm shuts down only if it can reduce its loss by doing so.*
In the short run, the firm has variable costs, such as labor and materials, as well as fixed costs, such as plant and equipment (Chapter 7). If the fixed cost is a *sunk* cost, this expense cannot be avoided by stopping operations—the firm pays this cost whether it shuts down or not. By shutting down, the firm stops receiving revenue and stops paying avoidable costs, but it is still stuck with its fixed cost. Thus, it pays for the firm to shut down only if its revenue is less than its avoidable cost.

Suppose that the firm's revenue is $R = \$2,000$, its variable cost is $VC = \$1,000$, and its fixed cost is $F = \$3,000$, which is the price it paid for a machine that it cannot resell or use for any other purpose. This firm is making a short-run loss:

$$\pi = R - VC - F = \$2,000 - \$1,000 - \$3,000 = -\$2,000.$$

If the firm operates, its revenue more than covers its avoidable, variable cost and offsets some of the fixed cost, so its profit is $-\$2,000$ (a loss of $\$2,000$). In contrast, if it shuts down, it loses $\$3,000$. Thus, the firm is better off operating.

However, if its revenue is only $\$500$, its loss is $\$3,500$, which is greater than the loss from the fixed cost alone of $\$3,000$. Because its revenue is less than its avoidable, variable cost, the firm reduces its loss by shutting down.

In conclusion, the firm compares its revenue to its variable cost only when deciding whether to stop operating. Because the fixed cost is sunk, the firm pays this cost whether it shuts down or not. The sunk fixed cost is irrelevant to the shutdown decision.

We usually assume that fixed cost is *sunk* (Chapter 7). However, if a firm can sell its capital for as much as it paid, its fixed cost is *avoidable*, so that the firm should consider it when deciding whether to shut down. A firm with a fully avoidable fixed cost always shuts down if it makes a short-run loss. If a firm buys a specialized piece of machinery for $\$1,000$ that can be used only for its business but can be sold for scrap metal for $\$100$, then $\$100$ of the fixed cost is avoidable and $\$900$ is sunk. Only the avoidable portion of a fixed cost is relevant for the shutdown decision.

In the long run, all costs are avoidable because the firm can eliminate them all by shutting down. Thus, in the long run, where the firm can avoid all losses by not operating, it pays to shut down if the firm faces any loss at all. As a result, we can restate the shutdown rule, which holds for all types of firms in both the short run and the long run, as

Shutdown Rule 2: *The firm shuts down only if its revenue is less than its avoidable cost.*
Both versions of the shutdown rule hold for all types of firms in both the short run and the long run.

8.3 Competition in the Short Run

Having considered how firms maximize profit in general, we now examine the profit-maximizing behavior of competitive firms, paying careful attention to firms' shutdown decisions. In this section, we focus on the short run, which is a period short enough that at least one input cannot be varied (Chapter 6).

Short-Run Competitive Profit Maximization

A competitive firm, like other firms, first determines the output at which it maximizes its profit (or minimizes its loss). Second, it decides whether to produce or to shut down.

Short-Run Output Decision. We've already seen that *any* firm maximizes its profit at the output where its marginal profit is zero or, equivalently, where its marginal cost equals its marginal revenue. *Because it faces a horizontal demand curve, a competitive firm can sell as many units of output as it wants at the market price, p.* Thus, a competitive firm's revenue, $R(q) = pq$, increases by p if it sells one more unit of output, so its marginal revenue equals the market price: $MR(q) = \mathrm{d}(pq)/\mathrm{d}q = p$. A competitive firm maximizes its profit by choosing its output such that

$$\frac{\mathrm{d}\pi(q^*)}{\mathrm{d}q} = \frac{\mathrm{d}(pq^*)}{\mathrm{d}q} - \frac{\mathrm{d}C(q^*)}{\mathrm{d}q} = p - MC(q^*) = 0. \qquad (8.9)$$

That is, because a competitive firm's marginal revenue equals the market price, a profit-maximizing competitive firm produces the amount of output q^* at which its *marginal cost equals the market price*: $MC(q^*) = p$.

For the quantity determined by Equation 8.9 to maximize profit, the second-order condition must hold: $\mathrm{d}^2\pi(q^*)/\mathrm{d}q^2 = \mathrm{d}p/\mathrm{d}q - \mathrm{d}MC(q^*)/\mathrm{d}q < 0$. Because the firm's marginal revenue, p, does not vary with q, $\mathrm{d}p/\mathrm{d}q = 0$. Thus, the second-order condition, which requires that the second derivative of the cost function with respect to quantity evaluated at the profit-maximizing quantity be negative, holds if the first derivative of the marginal cost function is positive:

$$\frac{\mathrm{d}MC(q^*)}{\mathrm{d}q} > 0. \qquad (8.10)$$

Equation 8.10 requires that the marginal cost curve be upward sloping at q^*.

To illustrate how a competitive firm maximizes its profit, we examine a representative firm in the highly competitive Canadian lime manufacturing industry. Lime is a nonmetallic mineral used in mortars, plasters, cements, bleaching powders, steel, paper, glass, and other products. The lime plant's estimated average cost curve, AC, first falls and then rises in panel a of Figure 8.3.[7] As always, the marginal cost curve, MC, intersects the average cost curve at its minimum point.

If the market price of lime is $p = \$8$ per metric ton, the competitive firm faces a horizontal demand curve (marginal revenue curve) at \$8. The MC curve crosses the firm's demand curve (or price or marginal revenue curve) at point e, where the firm's output is 284 units (where a unit is a thousand metric tons).

At a market price of \$8, the competitive firm maximizes its profit by producing 284 units. If the firm produced fewer than 284 units, the market price would be above

---

[7]The figure is based on Robidoux and Lester's (1988) estimated variable cost function. In the figure, we assume that the minimum of the average variable cost curve is \$5 at 50,000 metric tons of output. Based on information from *Statistics Canada*, we set the fixed cost so that the average cost is \$6 at 140,000 tons.

Figure 8.3 How a Competitive Firm Maximizes Profit

(a) A competitive lime manufacturing firm produces 284 units of lime where its marginal revenue, MR, which is the market price $p = \$8$, equals its marginal cost, MC. It maximizes its profit at $\pi = \$426,000$. (b) The corresponding profit curve reaches its peak at 284 units of lime. The estimated cost curves are based on Robidoux and Lester (1988).

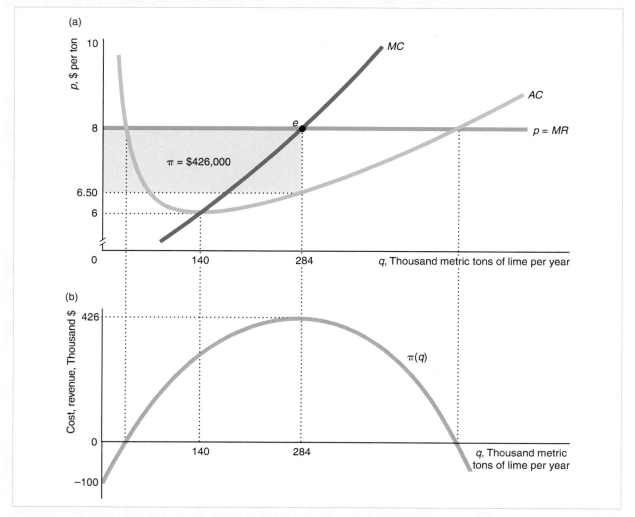

its marginal cost. The firm could increase its profit by expanding output because the firm earns more on the next ton, $p = \$8$, than it costs to produce it, $MC < \$8$. If the firm were to produce more than 284 units, the market price would be below its marginal cost, $MC > \$8$, and the firm could increase its profit by reducing its output. Thus, the competitive firm maximizes its profit by producing that output at which its marginal cost equals its marginal revenue, which is the market price.

At 284 units, the firm's profit is $\pi = \$426,000$, which is the shaded rectangle in panel a. The length of the rectangle is the number of units sold, $q = 284,000$ (or 284 units). The height of the rectangle is the firm's average profit per unit. Because the firm's profit is its revenue, $R(q) = pq$, minus its cost, $\pi(q) = R(q) - C(q)$, its average profit per unit is the difference between the market price (or average revenue), $p = R(q)/q = pq/q$, and its average cost, $AC = C(q)/q$:

$$\frac{\pi(q)}{q} = \frac{R(q)}{q} - \frac{C(q)}{q} = \frac{pq}{q} - \frac{C(q)}{q} = p - AC(q). \tag{8.11}$$

At 284 units, the lime firm's average profit per unit is $\$1.50 = p - AC(284) = \$8 - \$6.50$, and the firm's profit is $\pi = \$1.50 \times 284{,}000 = \$426{,}000$. Panel b shows that this profit is the maximum possible profit because it is the peak of the profit curve.

SOLVED PROBLEM 8.2 **MyLab Economics** Solved Problem	If a competitive firm's cost increases due to an increase in the price of a factor of production or a tax, the firm's manager can quickly determine by how much to adjust output by calculating how the firm's marginal cost has changed and applying the profit-maximization rule. Suppose that the Canadian province of Manitoba imposes a specific (per-unit) tax of t per ton of lime produced in the province. No other provincial government imposes such a tax. Manitoba has only one lime-producing firm, so the tax affects only that firm and hence has virtually no effect on the market price. Solve for the output that maximizes the firm's before-tax profit, and the output that maximizes its after-tax profit. Use comparative statics to show how the output changes. Show that the firm's profit must fall.

Answer

1. *Use calculus to find the firm's profit-maximizing output before the tax is imposed.* The firm's before-tax profit function is $\pi = pq - C(q)$. Its first-order condition for a profit maximum requires the firm to set its output, q_1, where $d\pi(q_1)/dq = p - dC(q_1)/dq = 0$, or $p = MC(q_1)$. As the figure shows, the firm maximizes its profit at e_1, where its MC^1 marginal cost curve crosses the market price line.

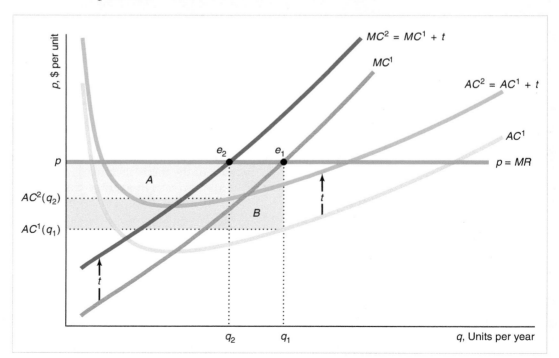

2. *Use calculus to find the firm's profit-maximizing output after the tax is imposed.*
The after-tax profit is $\bar{\pi} = pq - C(q) - tq$. The firm maximizes its profit at q_2 where

$$\frac{d\bar{\pi}(q_2)}{dq} = p - \frac{dC(q_2)}{dq} - t = 0, \tag{8.12}$$

or $p = MC(q_2) + t$. (If $t = 0$, we obtain the same result as in our before-tax analysis.) The figure shows that the firm's after-tax marginal cost curve shifts from MC^1 to $MC^2 = MC^1 + t$. Because the firm is a price taker and the government applies this tax to only this one firm, its marginal revenue before and after the tax is the market price, p. In the figure, the firm's new maximum is at e_2.

3. *Use comparative statics to determine how a change in the tax rate affects output.* Given the first-order condition, Equation 8.12, we can write the optimal quantity as a function of the tax rate: $q(t)$. Differentiating this first-order condition with respect to t, we obtain

$$-\frac{d^2C}{dq^2}\frac{dq}{dt} - 1 = -\frac{dMC}{dq}\frac{dq}{dt} - 1 = 0.$$

The second-order condition for a profit maximum, Equation 8.10, requires that dMC/dq be positive, so

$$\frac{dq}{dt} = -\frac{1}{dMC/dq} < 0. \tag{8.13}$$

At $t = 0$, the firm chooses q_1. As t increases, the firm reduces its output as Equation 8.13 shows. The figure shows that the tax shifts the firm's after-tax marginal cost curve up by t, so it produces less, reducing its output from q_1 to q_2. (*Note:* The figure shows a relatively large change in tax, whereas the calculus analysis examines a marginal change.)

4. *Show that the profit must fall using the definition of a maximum or by showing that profit falls at every output.* Because the firm's after-tax profit is maximized at q_1, when the firm reduces its output in response to the tax, its before-tax profit falls: $\pi(q_2) < \pi(q_1)$. Because its after-tax profit is lower than its before-tax profit, $\pi(q_2) - tq_2 < \pi(q_2)$, its profit must fall after the tax: $\bar{\pi}(q_2) < \pi(q_1)$.

We can also show this result by noting that the firm's average cost curve shifts up by t from AC^1 to $AC^2 = AC^1 + t$ in the figure, so the firm's profit at every output level falls because the market price remains constant. The firm sells fewer units (because of the increase in marginal cost) and makes less profit per unit (because of the increase in average cost). The after-tax profit is area $A = \bar{\pi}(q_2) = [p - AC(q_2) - t]q_2$, and the before-tax profit is area $A + B = \pi(q_1) = [p - AC(q_1)]q_1$, so profit falls by area B due to the tax.

Short-Run Shutdown Decision. Once a firm determines the output level that maximizes its profit or minimizes its loss, it must decide whether to produce that output level or to shut down and produce nothing. This decision is easy for the lime firm in Figure 8.3 because, at the output that maximizes its profit, it makes a positive economic profit. However, the question remains whether a firm should shut down if it is making a loss in the short run.

All firms—not just competitive firms—use the same shutdown rule: The firm shuts down only if it can reduce its loss by doing so. The firm shuts down only if its revenue is less than its avoidable variable cost: $R(q) < VC(q)$. For a competitive firm, this rule is

$$pq < VC(q). \tag{8.14}$$

By dividing both sides of Equation 8.14 by output, we can write this condition as

$$p < \frac{VC(q)}{q} = AVC. \tag{8.15}$$

Thus, a competitive firm shuts down if the market price is less than the minimum of its short-run average variable cost curve.

We illustrate the logic behind this rule using our lime firm example. We look at three cases where the market price is (1) above the minimum average cost (AC), (2) less than the minimum average cost but at least equal to or above the minimum average variable cost, or (3) below the minimum average variable cost.

The Market Price Is Above the Minimum AC. If the market price is above the firm's average cost at the quantity that it is producing, the firm makes a profit and so it operates. In panel a of Figure 8.3, the competitive lime firm's average cost curve reaches its minimum of $6 per ton at 140 units. Thus, if the market price is above $6, the firm makes a profit of $p - AC$ on each unit it sells and operates. In the figure, the market price is $8, and the firm makes a profit of $426,000.

The Market Price Is Between the Minimum AC and the Minimum AVC. The tricky case is when the market price is less than the minimum average cost but is at least as great as the minimum average variable cost. If the price is in this range, the firm makes a loss, but it reduces its loss by operating rather than shutting down.

Figure 8.4 reproduces the marginal and average cost curves for the lime firm from panel a of Figure 8.3 and adds the average variable cost curve. The lime firm's average cost curve reaches a minimum of $6 at 140 units, while its average variable cost curve hits its minimum of $5 at 50 units. If the market price is between $5 and $6, the lime firm loses money (its profit is negative) because the price is less than its AC, but the firm does not shut down.

For example, if the market price is $5.50, the firm minimizes its loss by producing 100 units where the marginal cost curve crosses the price line. At 100 units, the average cost is $6.12, so the firm's loss is $-62¢ = p - AC(100) = \$5.50 - \$6.12$ on each unit that it sells.

Why does the firm produce given that it is making a loss? The reason is that the firm reduces its loss by operating rather than shutting down because its revenue exceeds its variable cost—or equivalently, the market price exceeds its average variable cost.

If the firm shuts down in the short run, it incurs a loss equal to its fixed cost of $98,000, which is the sum of rectangles A and B.[8] If the firm operates and produces $q = 100$ units, its average variable cost is $AVC = \$5.14$, which is less than the market price of $p = \$5.50$ per ton. It makes $36¢ = p - AVC = \$5.50 - \$5.14$ more on each ton than its average variable cost. The difference between the firm's revenue and its variable cost, $R - VC$, is the rectangle $B = \$36,000$, which has a length

---

[8]The average cost is the sum of the average variable cost and the average fixed cost, $AC = AVC + F/q$ (Chapter 7). Thus, the gap between the average cost and the average variable cost curves at any given output is $AC - AVC = F/q$. Consequently, the height of the rectangle $A + B$ is $AC(100) - AVC(100) = F/100$, and the length of the rectangle is 100 units, so the area of the rectangle is F, or $98,000 = \$62,000 + \$36,000$.

Figure 8.4 The Short-Run Shutdown Decision

The competitive lime manufacturing plant operates if price is above the minimum of the average variable cost curve, point *a*, at $5. With a market price of $5.50, the firm produces 100 units because that price is above $AVC(100) = \$5.14$, so the firm more than covers its out-of-pocket, variable costs. At that price, the firm suffers a loss of area $A = \$62,000$ because the price is less than the average cost of $6.12. If it shuts down, its loss is its fixed cost, area $A + B = \$98,000$. Therefore, the firm does not shut down.

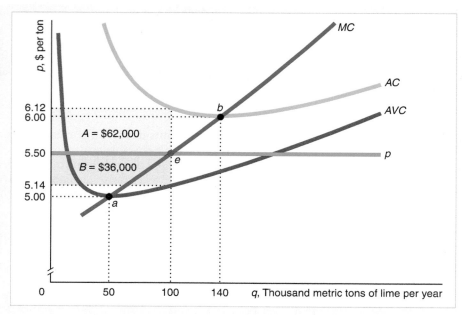

of 100 thousand tons and a height of 36¢. Thus, if the firm operates, it loses only $62,000 (rectangle A), which is less than its loss if it shuts down, $98,000. The firm makes a smaller loss by operating than by shutting down because its revenue more than covers its variable cost and hence helps to reduce the loss from the fixed cost.

The Market Price Is Less Than the Minimum AVC. If the market price dips below the minimum of the average variable cost, $5 in Figure 8.4, then the firm should shut down in the short run. At any price less than the minimum average variable cost, the firm's revenue is less than its variable cost, so it makes a greater loss by operating than by shutting down because it loses money on each unit sold in addition to the fixed cost that it loses if it shuts down.[9]

In summary, a competitive firm uses a two-step decision-making process to maximize its profit. First, the competitive firm determines the output that maximizes its profit or minimizes its loss when its marginal cost equals the market price (which is its marginal revenue): $p = MC$. Second, the firm chooses to produce that quantity unless it would lose more by operating than by shutting down. The competitive firm shuts down in the short run only if the market price is less than the minimum of its average variable cost, $p < AVC$.

APPLICATION

Fracking and Shutdowns

Oil production starts and stops in the short run as the market price fluctuates. In 1998–1999, when oil prices were historically low, U.S. oil-producing firms shut down or abandoned 74,000 of the 136,000 oil wells. History repeats itself. From 2011 through the first half of 2014, oil prices were above $100 per barrel—nearly hitting $130 at one point—so virtually all wells could produce profitably. However, when oil prices fell below $50 a barrel in 2015 and below $30 a barrel in 2016, many U.S. wells shut down. From 2014 through 2016, 1,764 wells under development were left incomplete.

---

[9]A firm cannot "lose a little on every sale but make it up on volume."

Conventional oil wells—which essentially stick a pipe in the ground and pump oil—have low enough minimum average variable costs that most could profitably operate in 2014 and 2015. Some Middle Eastern oil wells break even at a price as low as $10 a barrel. Older Texas wells often have a break-even point at $20 to $30 per barrel.

Most new U.S. oil wells use hydraulic fracturing (fracking). Fracking uses pressurized liquid consisting of water, sand, and chemicals to fracture oil shale (rock containing oil), which releases natural gas and oil.[10] Current fracking operations break even at between $50 and $77 per barrel, with an average of about $65. Thus, fracking operations were more likely to shut down than were conventional wells during the recent period of low prices.

By mid-2018, the price of oil exceeded $65, and many fracking wells were operating again. In addition, oil companies that had almost 7,000 wells that had been drilled but not fracked started bringing some of these wells online.

Short-Run Firm Supply Curve

We just analyzed how a competitive firm chooses its output for a given market price to maximize its profit. By repeating this analysis at different possible market prices, we can derive the firm's *short-run supply curve,* which shows how the quantity supplied by the competitive firm varies with the market price.

As the market price increases from $p_1 = \$5$ to $p_2 = \$6$ to $p_3 = \$7$ to $p_4 = \$8$, the lime firm increases its output from 50 to 140 to 215 to 285 units per year, as Figure 8.5 shows. The relevant demand curve—market price line—and the firm's marginal cost curve determine the equilibrium at each market price, e_1 through e_4. That is, as the market price increases, the equilibria trace out the marginal cost curve.

If the price falls below the firm's minimum average variable cost of $5, the firm shuts down. Thus, the competitive firm's short-run supply curve is its marginal cost curve above its minimum average variable cost.

---

[10]The first fracking experiment was in 1947. Initially, fracking wells had a minimum average variable cost that was too high to operate profitably. However, in recent years, technological innovation substantially lowered this cost, and the global price of oil was often high enough for fracking to be widely used. Due to fracking, U.S. oil production rose from 5.6 million barrels a day in 2010 to 9.3 million in 2015. Fracking is controversial because opponents fear it will create environmental problems and trigger earthquakes.

Figure 8.5 How the Profit-Maximizing Quantity Varies with Price

As the market price increases, the lime manufacturing firm produces more output. The change in the price traces out the marginal cost (*MC*) curve of the firm. The firm's short-run supply (*S*) curve is the *MC* curve above the minimum of its *AVC* curve (at e_1).

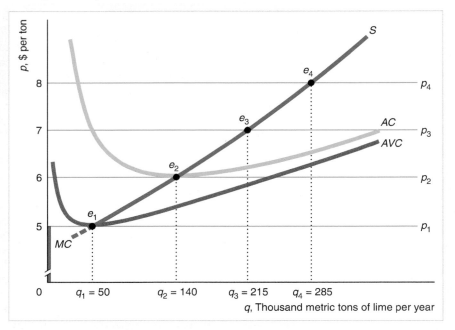

At prices above $5, the firm's short-run supply curve, *S*, is the same as the marginal cost curve. The supply is zero when price is less than the minimum of the *AVC* curve of $5. (From now on, for simplicity, the graphs will not show the supply curve at prices below the minimum *AVC*.)

SOLVED PROBLEM 8.3

Given that a competitive firm's short-run cost function is $C(q) = 100q - 4q^2 + 0.2q^3 + 450$, what is the firm's short-run supply curve? If the price is $p = 115$, how much output does the firm supply?

MyLab Economics
Solved Problem

Answer

1. *Determine the firm's supply curve by calculating for which output levels the firm's marginal cost is greater than its minimum average variable cost.* The firm's supply curve is its marginal cost curve above its minimum average variable cost. As we noted in Solved Problem 7.2, $MC(q) = dC(q)/dq = 100 - 8q + 0.6q^2$ and $AVC(q) = VC(q)/q = 100 - 4q + 0.2q^2$. We also know that the marginal cost curve cuts the average variable cost curve at its minimum (Chapter 7), so we can determine the q where the *AVC* reaches its minimum by equating the *AVC* and *MC* functions: $\bar{A}VC = 100 - 4q + 0.2q^2 = 100 - 8q + 0.6q^2 = MC$. Solving, the minimum is $q = 10$, as Figure 7.1 illustrates. Thus, the supply curve is the *MC* curve for output greater than or equal to 10.[11]

2. *Determine the quantity where $p = MC = 115$.* The firm operates where price equals marginal cost. At $p = 115$, the firm produces the quantity q such that $115 = MC = 100 - 8q + 0.6q^2$, or $q = 15$.

---

[11]An alternative approach is to set the derivative of the *AC* function equal to zero, to find the output at which the *AC* curve is at its minimum: $dAC/dq = 0 = -4 + 0.4q$, so $q = 10$.

Short-Run Market Supply Curve

The market supply curve is the horizontal sum of the supply curves of all the individual firms in the market (see Chapter 2). In the short run, the maximum number of firms in a market, n, is fixed because new firms need time to enter the market. If all the firms in a competitive market are identical, each firm's supply curve is identical, so the market supply at any price is n times the supply of an individual firm. Where firms have different shutdown prices, the market supply reflects a different number of firms at various prices even in the short run. We examine competitive markets first with firms that have identical costs and then with firms that have different costs.

Short-Run Market Supply with Identical Firms. To illustrate how to construct a short-run market supply curve, we suppose that the lime manufacturing market has $n = 5$ competitive firms with identical cost curves. Panel a of Figure 8.6 plots the short-run supply curve, S^1, of a typical firm—the MC curve above the minimum AVC—where the horizontal axis shows the firm's output, q, per year. Panel b illustrates the competitive market supply curve, the dark line S^5, where the horizontal axis is market output, Q, per year. The price axis is the same in the two panels.

If the market price is less than $5 per ton, no firm supplies any output, so the market supply is zero. At $5, each firm is willing to supply $q = 50$ units, as in panel a. Consequently, the market supply is $Q = 5q = 250$ units in panel b. At $6 per ton, each firm supplies 140 units, so the market supply is 700 ($= 5 \times 140$) units.

Suppose the market has fewer than five firms in the short run. The light-colored lines in panel b show the market supply curves for various other numbers of firms. The market supply curve is S^1 with one price-taking firm, S^2 with two firms, S^3 with three firms, and S^4 with four firms. The market supply curve flattens as the number of firms in the market increases because the market supply curve is the

Figure 8.6 Short-Run Market Supply with Five Identical Lime Firms

(a) The short-run supply curve, S^1, for a typical lime manufacturing firm is its MC above the minimum of its AVC. (b) The market supply curve, S^5, is the horizontal sum of the supply curves of each of the five identical firms. The curve S^4 shows the market supply curve with four firms in the market.

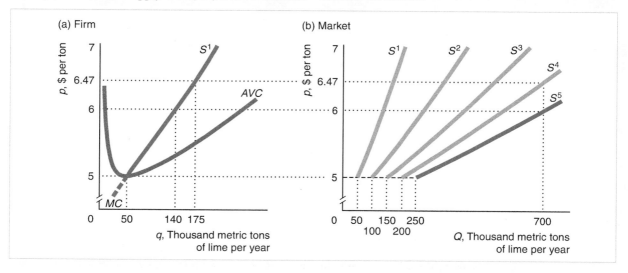

horizontal sum of more and more upward-sloping firm supply curves.[12] Thus, *the more identical firms producing at a given price, the flatter the short-run market supply curve at that price.*

The flatter the supply curve is at a given quantity, the more elastic is the supply curve. As a result, the more firms in the market, the less the price has to increase for the short-run market supply to increase substantially. Consumers pay $6 per ton to obtain 700 units of lime if the market has five firms, but they must pay $6.47 per ton to obtain that much with only four firms. As the number of firms grows very large, the market supply curve approaches a horizontal line at $5.

Short-Run Market Supply with Firms That Differ. If the firms in a competitive market have different minimum average variable costs, then not all firms produce at every price, a situation that affects the shape of the short-run market supply curve. Suppose that the only two firms in the lime market are our typical lime firm with a supply curve of S^1 and a second firm with a higher marginal and minimum average cost with the supply curve of S^2 in Figure 8.7. The first firm produces if the market price is at least $5, whereas the second firm does not produce unless the price is $6 or more. At $5, the first firm produces 50 units, so the quantity on the market supply curve, S, is 50 units. Between $5 and $6, only the first firm produces, so the market supply, S, is the same as the first firm's supply, S^1. If the price is $6 or more, both firms produce, so the market supply curve is the horizontal summation of their two individual supply curves. For example, at $7, the first firm produces 215 units, and the second firm supplies 100 units, so the market supply is 315 units.

Figure 8.7 Short-Run Market Supply with Two Different Lime Firms

The supply curve S^1 is the same as for the typical lime firm in Figure 8.6. A second firm has an MC that lies to the left of the original firm's cost curve and a higher minimum AVC. Thus, its supply curve, S^2, lies above and to the left of the original firm's supply curve, S^1. The market supply curve, S, is the horizontal sum of the two supply curves. When the price is $6 or higher, both firms produce, and the market supply curve is flatter than the supply curve of either individual firm.

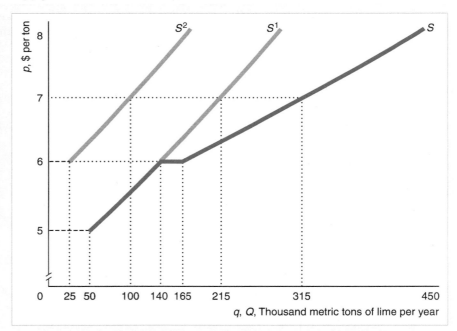

[12]In the figure, if the price rises by $\Delta p = 47$¢ from $6 to $6.47 per ton, each firm increases its output by $\Delta q = 35$ tons, so the slope (measured in cents per ton) of its supply curve over that range is $\Delta p/\Delta q = 47/35 \approx 1.34$. With two firms, $\Delta q = 70$, so the slope is $47/70 \approx 0.67$. Similarly, the slope is $47/105 \approx 0.45$ with three firms, 0.34 with four firms, and 0.27 with five firms. Although not shown in the figure, the slope is 0.13 with 10 firms and 0.013 with 100 firms.

As in a market with identical firms, where both firms produce, the market supply curve is flatter than that of either firm. Because the second firm does not produce at as low a price as the first firm, the short-run market supply curve has a steeper slope (less elastic supply) at relatively low prices than it would if the firms were identical.

Where firms differ, only the low-cost firm supplies goods at relatively low prices. As the price rises, the other, higher-cost firm starts supplying, creating a stair-like market supply curve. The more suppliers with differing costs, the more steps in the market supply curve. As price rises and more firms supply goods, the market supply curve flattens, so it takes a smaller increase in price to increase supply by a given amount. Stated another way, the more firms differ in costs, the steeper the market supply curve is at low prices. Differences in costs are one explanation for why some market supply curves are upward sloping.

Short-Run Competitive Equilibrium

By combining the short-run market supply curve and the market demand curve, we can determine the short-run competitive equilibrium. We examine first how to determine the equilibrium in the lime market and then how taxes change the equilibrium.

Suppose that the lime manufacturing market has five identical firms in the short run. Panel a of Figure 8.8 shows the short-run cost curves and the supply curve, S^1, for a typical firm, and panel b shows the corresponding short-run competitive market supply curve, S.

In panel b, the initial demand curve D^1 intersects the market supply curve at E_1, the market equilibrium. The equilibrium quantity is $Q_1 = 1,075$ units of lime per year, and the equilibrium market price is $7.

Figure 8.8 Short-Run Competitive Equilibrium in the Lime Market

(a) The short-run supply curve is the marginal cost above the minimum average variable cost of $5. At a price of $5, each firm makes a short-run loss of $98,500, $(p - AC)q = (\$5 - \$6.97) \times 50,000$, area $A + C$. At a price of $7, the short-run profit of a typical lime firm is $(p - AC)q = (\$7 - \$6.20) \times 215,000 = \$172,000$, area $A + B$. (b) If the lime market has only five firms in the short run, the market supply is S, and the market demand curve is D^1, then the short-run equilibrium is E_1, the market price is $7, and market output is $Q_1 = 1,075$ units. If the demand curve shifts to D^2, the market equilibrium is $p = \$5$ and $Q_2 = 250$ units.

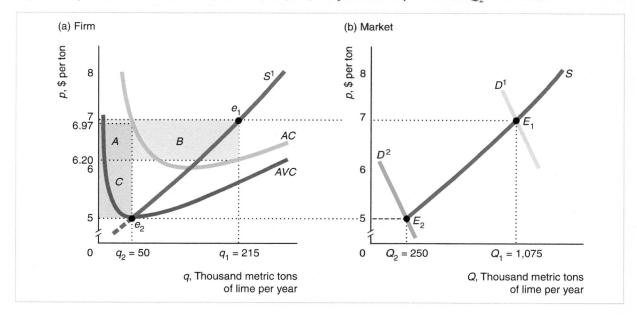

(a) Firm

(b) Market

In panel a, each competitive firm faces a horizontal demand curve at the equilibrium price of $7. Each price-taking firm chooses its output where its marginal cost curve intersects the horizontal demand curve at e_1. Because each firm maximizes its profit at e_1, no firm wants to change its behavior, so e_1 is each firm's equilibrium. In panel a, each firm makes a short-run profit of area $A + B = \$172,000$, which is the average profit per ton, $p - AC = \$7 - \$6.20 = 80¢$, times the firm's output, $q_1 = 215$ units. The equilibrium market output, Q_1, is the number of firms, n, times the equilibrium output of each firm: $Q_1 = nq_1 = 5 \times 215$ units $= 1{,}075$ units (panel b).

Now suppose that the demand curve shifts to D^2. The new market equilibrium is E_2, where the price is only $5. At that price, each firm produces $q = 50$ units, and market output is $Q = 250$ units. In panel a, each firm loses $98,500, area $A + C$, because it makes an average profit per ton of $(p - AC) = (\$5 - \$6.97) = -\$1.97$ and it sells $q_2 = 50$ units. However, such a firm does not necessarily shut down because the price equals the firm's average variable cost, so the firm is able to cover its out-of-pocket expenses.

SOLVED PROBLEM 8.4

What is the effect on the short-run equilibrium of a specific tax of t per unit that is collected from all n identical firms in a market? Does the consumer bear the full incidence of the tax (the share of the tax that falls on consumers)?

MyLab Economics
Solved Problem

Answer

1. *Show how the tax shifts a typical firm's marginal cost and average cost curves and hence its supply curve.* In Solved Problem 8.2, we showed that such a tax causes the marginal cost curve, the average cost curve, and (hence) the minimum average cost of the firm to shift up by t, as illustrated in panel a of the figure. As a result, the short-run supply curve of the firm, labeled $S^1 + t$, shifts up by t from the pre-tax supply curve, S^1.

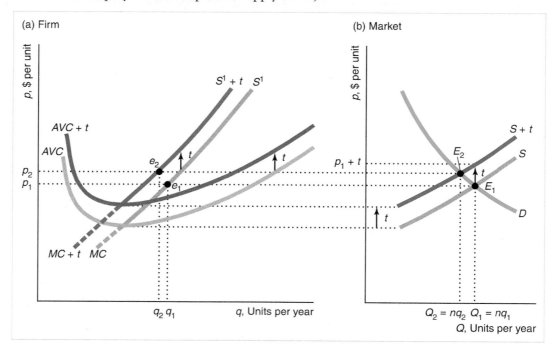

2. *Show how the market supply curve shifts.* The market supply curve is the sum of all the individual firm's supply curves, so it also shifts up by t, from S to $S + t$ in panel b of the figure.

3. *Determine how the short-run market equilibrium changes.* The pre-tax short-run market equilibrium is E_1, where the downward-sloping market demand curve D intersects S in panel b. In that equilibrium, price is p_1 and quantity is Q_1, which equals n (the number of firms) times the quantity q_1 that a typical firm produces at p_1. The after-tax short-run market equilibrium, E_2, determined by the intersection of D and the after-tax supply curve, $S + t$, occurs at p_2 and Q_2. Because the after-tax price p_2 is above the after-tax minimum average variable cost, all the firms continue to produce, but they produce less than before: $q_2 < q_1$. Consequently, the equilibrium quantity falls from $Q_1 = nq_1$ to $Q_2 = nq_2$.

4. *Discuss the incidence of the tax.* The equilibrium price increases, but by less than the full amount of the tax: $p_2 < p_1 + t$. Because the supply curve slopes up and the demand curve slopes down, consumers and producers share the incidence of the tax (Chapter 2).

8.4 Competition in the Long Run

Originally one thought that if there were a half dozen large computers in this country, hidden away in research laboratories, this would take care of all requirements we had throughout the country. —Howard H. Aiken, Harvard, 1952

In the long run, competitive firms can vary inputs that were fixed in the short run, so the long-run firm and market supply curves differ from the short-run curves. After briefly looking at how a firm determines its long-run supply curve that maximizes its profit, we examine the relationship between short-run and long-run market supply curves and competitive equilibria.

Long-Run Competitive Profit Maximization

A firm's two profit-maximizing decisions—how much to produce and whether to produce at all—are simpler in the long run than in the short run. In the long run, typically all costs are variable, so the firm does not have to consider whether fixed costs are sunk or avoidable costs.

The firm chooses the quantity that maximizes its profit using the same rules as in the short run. The company will pick the quantity that maximizes long-run profit, which is the difference between revenue and long-run cost. Equivalently, it operates where long-run marginal profit is zero and where marginal revenue equals long-run marginal cost.

After determining the output level, q^*, that maximizes its profit or minimizes its loss, the firm decides whether to produce or shut down. The firm shuts down if its revenue is less than its avoidable or variable cost. In the long run, however, all costs are variable. As a result, in the long run, the firm shuts down if it would suffer an economic loss by continuing to operate.

Long-Run Firm Supply Curve

A firm's long-run supply curve is its long-run marginal cost curve above the minimum of its long-run average cost curve (because all costs are variable in the long run). The firm is free to choose its capital in the long run, so the firm's long-run supply curve may differ substantially from its short-run supply curve.

Figure 8.9 The Short-Run and Long-Run Supply Curves

The firm's long-run supply curve, S^{LR}, is zero below its minimum average cost of $24 and equals the long-run marginal cost, $LRMC$, at higher prices. At a price of $35, the firm produces more in the long run than in the short run, 110 units instead of 50 units, and earns a higher profit, area $A + B$, instead of just area A.

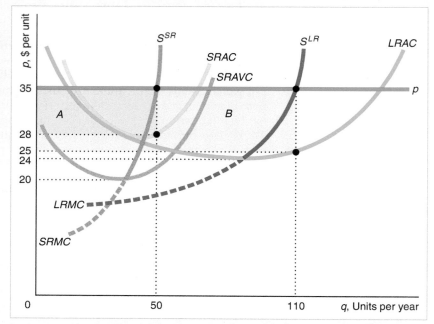

The firm chooses a plant size to maximize its long-run economic profit in light of its beliefs about the future. If its forecast is wrong, it may be stuck with a plant that is too small or too large for its chosen level of production in the short run. The firm corrects this mistake in plant size in the long run.

The firm in Figure 8.9 has different short- and long-run cost curves. In the short run, the firm uses a plant that is smaller than the optimal long-run size if the price is $35. The firm produces 50 units of output per year in the short run, where its short-run marginal cost, $SRMC$, equals the price, and makes a short-run profit equal to area A. The firm's short-run supply curve, S^{SR}, is its short-run marginal cost above the minimum, $20, of its short-run average variable cost, $SRAVC$.

If the firm expects the price to remain at $35, it builds a larger plant in the long run. Using the larger plant, the firm produces 110 units per year, where its long-run marginal cost, $LRMC$, equals the market price. It expects to make a long-run profit, area $A + B$, which is greater than its short-run profit by area B because it sells 60 more units, and its equilibrium long-run average cost, $LRAC = \$25$, is lower than its short-run average cost in equilibrium, $28.

The firm does not operate at a loss in the long run when all inputs are variable. It shuts down if the market price falls below the firm's minimum long-run average cost of $24. Thus, the competitive firm's long-run supply curve is its long-run marginal cost curve above $24.

APPLICATION

The Size of Ethanol Processing Plants

When a large number of firms initially built ethanol processing plants, they built relatively small ones. When the ethanol market took off in the first half decade of the twenty-first century, with the price reaching a peak of $4.23 a gallon in June 2006, many firms built larger plants or greatly increased their plant size. From 1999 to 2006, the number of plants nearly doubled and the average plant capacity nearly tripled (36 to 106 million gallons per year).

However, since then, the ethanol market price has collapsed. The price was generally below $3 and often below $1.50 from 2007 through 2018, hitting a low of $1.26 in January 2016. As a result, many firms closed plants or reduced their size. The average plant capacity fell by a third from 2006 to 2017 (106 to 78 million gallons per year).

Long-Run Market Supply Curve

The competitive market supply curve is the horizontal sum of the supply curves of the individual firms in both the short run and the long run. Because new firms cannot enter the market in the short run (it takes time to build a new plant, buy equipment, and hire workers), we add the supply curves of a known number of firms to obtain the short-run market supply curve. The only way for the market to supply more output in the short run is for existing firms to produce more.

However, in the long run, firms can enter the market. Thus, before we can add all the relevant firm supply curves to obtain the long-run market supply curve, we need to determine how many firms are in the market at each possible market price. We now look in detail at how market entry and exit affect the long-run market supply curve.

To construct the long-run market supply curve properly, we also have to determine how input prices vary with output. As the market expands or contracts substantially, changes in factor prices may shift firms' cost and supply curves. If so, we need to determine how such shifts in factor prices affect firm supply curves so that we can properly construct the market supply curve. The effect of changes in input prices is greater in the long run than in the short run because market output can change more dramatically in the long run.

Entry and Exit. *Entry* and *exit* by firms determines the long-run number of firms in a market. In the long run, each firm decides whether to enter or exit depending on whether it can make a long-run profit:

- A firm enters the market if it can make a long-run profit, $\pi > 0$.
- A firm exits the market to avoid a long-run loss, $\pi < 0$.

If firms in a market are making zero long-run profit, they are indifferent between staying in the market and exiting. We presume that if they are already in the market, they stay in the market when they are making zero long-run profit.

In December 2016, 239,000 private firms entered the U.S. market and 217,000 exited.[13] The annual rates of entry and exit are both about 10% of the total number of firms in most years.

Even in the long run, entry is limited in many markets, such as manufacturing, because firms face significant costs to enter, such as large start-up costs. In other markets, government restrictions create a barrier to entry. For instance, many city governments limit the number of liquor stores, creating an insurmountable barrier that prevents new ones from entering. Similarly, patent protection prevents new firms from producing the patented product until the patent expires.

However, in many unregulated, perfectly competitive markets, firms can enter and exit freely in the long run. Entry or exit is typically easy in many agriculture, construction, wholesale and retail trade, transportation, and service industries, unless governments regulate them. For example, many construction firms, which have no capital and provide only labor services, engage in *hit-and-run* entry and exit: They enter the market whenever they can make a profit and exit whenever they can't. These firms may enter and exit markets several times a year.

---

[13]**www.bls.gov/web/cewbd/table9_1.txt** (viewed July 11, 2018).

In markets with free entry, when the demand curve shifts to the right so that the market price and profit rise, entry occurs until the last firm to enter—the *marginal firm*—makes zero long-run profit. Similarly, in markets with free exit, if the demand curve shifts to the left so that the market price drops, firms with minimum average costs above the new, lower market price exit the market. Firms continue to leave the market until the next firm that considers leaving, the marginal firm, is again earning a zero long-run profit.

APPLICATION

Industries with High Entry and Exit Rates

In many competitive industries, firms frequently enter and exit. Firms can easily enter or exit most transportation markets unless governments regulate them. Trucking and shipping firms may serve a particular route, but entry is easy. Other firms quickly enter and serve a route as soon as a profit opportunity appears. Entrants shift their highly mobile equipment—trucks or ships—from less profitable routes to more profitable ones.

The annual entry and exit rates in construction were 10% in 2015. However, many construction firms enter and exit the market repeatedly over the year. When home construction booms during the spring and summer, the number of home construction firms in a market is large. During the slow winter months, many of these firms shut down, only to reenter the market as soon as the market picks up again.

In agriculture, even though farms may take substantial time to enter the market, about 7.5% of U.S. agricultural firms enter every year and about 8.5% exit. As a result, the number of farms fell in recent years.

Solar energy installation firms rapidly enter and exit the market. In California, which has half of all U.S. solar energy systems, the number of firms increased from 603 firms in 2008 to 1,057 in 2010 and 1,499 in 2018.

Long-Run Market Supply with Identical Firms and Free Entry. The *long-run market supply curve is flat* at the minimum long-run average cost *if firms can freely enter and exit* the market, an unlimited number of *firms have identical costs*, and *input prices are constant*. This result follows from our reasoning about the short-run supply curve, in which we showed that the more firms in the market, the flatter the market supply curve. With many firms in the market in the long run, the market supply curve is effectively flat. ("Many" is 10 firms in the vegetable oil market.)

The long-run supply curve of a typical vegetable oil mill, S^1 in panel a of Figure 8.10, is the long-run marginal cost curve above a minimum long-run average cost of $10. Because each firm shuts down if the market price is below $10, the long-run market supply curve is zero at a price below $10. If the price rises above $10, firms are making positive profits, so new firms enter, expanding market output until profits are driven to zero, where price is again $10. The long-run market supply curve in panel b is a horizontal line at the minimum long-run average cost of the typical firm, $10. At a price of $10, each firm produces $q = 150$ units (where one unit equals 100 metric tons). Thus, the total output produced by n firms in the market is $Q = nq = n \times 150$ units. Extra market output is obtained by new firms entering the market.

In summary, the long-run market supply curve is horizontal if the market has free entry and exit, an unlimited number of firms have identical costs, and input prices are constant. When these strong assumptions do not hold, the long-run market supply

Figure 8.10 Long-Run Firm and Market Supply with Identical Vegetable Oil Firms

(a) The long-run supply curve of a typical vegetable oil mill, S^1, is the long-run marginal cost curve above the minimum average cost of $10. (b) The long-run market supply curve is horizontal at the minimum of the long-run minimum average cost of a typical firm. Each firm produces 150 units, so market output is $150n$, where n is the number of firms.

curve has a slope, as we now show. In particular, the market supply curve has an upward slope if the number of firms in a market is limited in the long run, firms' cost functions differ, input prices increase as output rises, or a country demands a large share of a good sold on a world market. It may slope downward if input prices fall as output increases.

Long-Run Market Supply When Entry Is Limited. If the number of firms in a market is limited in the long run, the market supply curve slopes upward. The number of firms is limited if the government restricts that number, if firms need a scarce resource, or if entry is costly. An example of a scarce resource is the limited number of lots on which a luxury beachfront hotel can be built in Miami Beach. High entry costs restrict the number of firms in a market because firms enter only if the long-run economic profit is greater than the cost of entering.

The only way to increase output if the number of firms is limited is for existing firms to produce more. Because individual firms' supply curves slope upward, the long-run market supply curve is also upward sloping. The reasoning is the same as in the short run, as panel b of Figure 8.6 illustrates, given that no more than five firms can enter. The market supply curve is the upward-sloping S^5 curve, which is the horizontal sum of the five firms' upward-sloping marginal cost curves above minimum average cost.

Long-Run Market Supply When Firms Differ. A second reason why some long-run market supply curves slope upward is that firms' cost functions differ. Because firms with relatively low minimum long-run average costs enter the market at lower prices than do others, the long-run market supply curve slopes upward (similar to the short-run example in Figure 8.7).

Many markets have a number of low-cost firms and other higher-cost firms.[14] If lower-cost firms can supply as much output as the market wants, only low-cost firms produce, and the long-run market supply curve is horizontal at the minimum of the low-cost firm's average cost curve. The long-run supply curve is upward sloping *only* if lower-cost firms cannot produce as much output as the market demands because each of these firms has a limited capacity and the number of these firms is limited.

APPLICATION

Upward-Sloping Long-Run Supply Curve for Cotton

Many countries produce cotton. Production costs differ among countries because of differences in the quality of land, the amount of rainfall, irrigation and labor costs, and other factors.

The length of each step-like segment of the long-run supply curve of cotton in the graph is the quantity produced by the named country. The amount that the low-cost countries can produce must be limited, or we would not observe production by the higher-cost countries.

The height of each segment of the supply curve is the typical minimum average cost of production in that country. The average cost of production in Pakistan is less than half that in Iran. The supply curve has a step-like appearance because we are using an average of the estimated average cost in each country, which is a single number. If we knew the individual firms' supply curves in each of these countries, the market supply curve would have a smoother shape.

As the market price rises, the number of countries producing increases. At market prices below $1.08 per kilogram, only Pakistan produces. If the market price is below $1.50, the United States and Iran do not produce. If the price increases to $1.56, the United States supplies a large amount of cotton. In this range of the supply curve, supply is very elastic. For Iran to produce, the price has to rise to $1.71. Price increases in that range result in only a relatively small increase in supply. Thus, the supply curve is relatively inelastic at prices above $1.56.

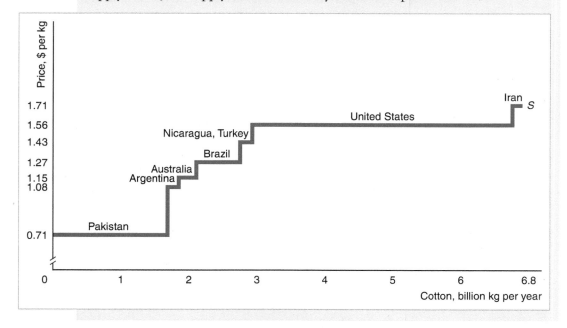

---

[14]Syverson (2004) estimated that, in the typical 4-digit (narrowly defined) U.S. manufacturing industry, the 90th percentile plant produces 90% more output from the same input as the 10th percentile plant.

Long-Run Market Supply When Input Prices Vary with Output. A third reason why market supply curves may slope upward is non-constant input prices. In markets where factor prices rise when output increases, the long-run supply curve slopes upward even if firms have identical costs and can freely enter and exit. (Similarly, the long-run supply slopes downward if factor prices fall when output increases.)

If a market's product uses a relatively small share of the total quantity of a factor of production, as that market's output expands, the price of the factor is not likely to change. For example, dentists do not hire enough receptionists to affect the market wage for receptionists.

In contrast, if the market's product uses a very large share of a factor, the price of that input is more likely to vary with that market's output. As jet plane manufacturers expand and buy more jet engines, the price of these engines rises because the jet plane manufacturers are the sole purchasers of these engines.

To produce a larger quantity in a market, firms must use more inputs. If as the firms use more of some or all inputs, the prices of those inputs may rise, so that the cost of producing the final good also rises. We call a market in which input prices rise with output an *increasing-cost market*. Few steelworkers lack a fear of heights and are willing to construct tall buildings, so their supply curve is steeply upward sloping. As the number of skyscrapers under construction skyrockets, the demand curve for these workers shifts to the right, the equilibrium moves up the supply curve, and their wage rises.

We now assume that all firms in a market have the same cost curves and that input prices rise as market output expands. We use the cost curves of a representative firm in panel a of Figure 8.11 to derive the upward-sloping market supply curve in panel b.

Figure 8.11 Long-Run Market Supply in an Increasing-Cost Market

With the initial demand curve D_1 and the relatively low market output, Q_1, in panel b, each firm's long-run marginal and average cost curves are MC^1 and AC^1 in panel a. When the demand shifts rightward to D^2, market quantity increases to Q_2, and higher input prices shift the cost curves upward to MC^2 and AC^2. Each firm produces at minimum average cost, such as points e_1 and e_2. The long-run market supply, S, in panel b is upward sloping.

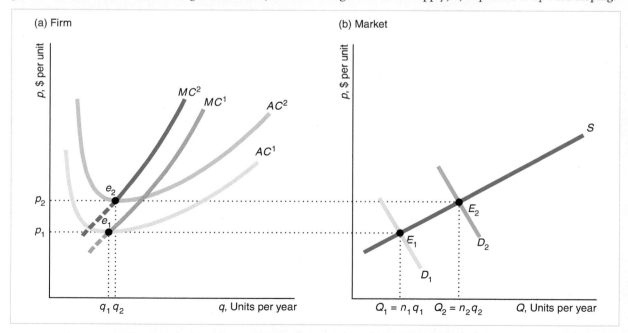

The initial demand curve is D^1 in panel b. The market price is p_1 and the market produces relatively little output, Q_1, so input prices are relatively low. In panel a, each firm has the same long-run marginal cost curve, MC^1, and average cost curve, AC^1. Each firm produces at minimum average cost, e_1, and sells q_1 units of output. The n_1 firms collectively sell $Q_1 = n_1 q_1$ units of output, which is point E_1 on the market supply curve in panel b.

If the market demand curve shifts outward to D^2 (panel b), the market price rises to p_2, new firms eventually enter, and market output rises to Q_2. The higher output causes input prices to rise, which is reflected in the upward shift of the marginal cost curve from MC^1 to MC^2 and of the average cost curve from AC^1 to AC^2. The typical firm produces at a higher minimum average cost, e_2. At this higher price, the market has n_2 firms, so market output is $Q_2 = n_2 q_2$ at point E_2 on the market supply curve.

Thus, in both an increasing-cost market and a *constant-cost market*—where input prices remain constant as output increases—firms produce at minimum average cost in the long run. The difference is that the minimum average cost rises as market output increases in an increasing-cost market, whereas minimum average cost remains constant in a constant-cost market. In conclusion, *the long-run supply curve is upward sloping in an increasing-cost market and flat in a constant-cost market.*

In a decreasing-cost market, as market output rises, at least some factor prices fall. As a result, in a decreasing-cost market, the long-run market supply curve is downward sloping.

Increasing returns to scale may cause factor prices to fall. For example, when firms introduced Blu-ray drives, they manufactured and sold relatively few drives, and the cost of manufacturing was relatively high. Due to the high price of Blu-ray drives and the lack of Blu-ray disks, consumers demanded fewer Blu-ray drives than today. As demand for Blu-ray drives increased, it became practical to automate more of the production process so firms could produce drives at a lower average cost. The resulting decrease in the price of these drives lowered the cost of personal computers with these drives.

Long-Run Market Supply Curve with Trade. A fourth reason why a market supply curve may slope is that a country demands a large share of a good sold on a world market. Many goods, such as cotton and oil, are traded on world markets. The world equilibrium price and quantity for a good are determined by the intersection of the world supply curve—the horizontal sum of the supply curves of each producing country—and the world demand curve—the horizontal sum of the demand curves of each consuming country.

A country that imports a good has a supply curve that is the horizontal sum of its domestic industry's long-run supply curve and the import supply curve. The domestic industry's long-run supply curve is the competitive long-run supply curve that we have just derived. However, we need to determine the import supply curve.

A country's import supply curve is the world's **residual supply curve**: the quantity that the market supplies that is not consumed by other demanders at any given price.[15] The country's import supply function is its residual supply function, $S^r(p)$, which is the quantity supplied to this country at price p. Because the country buys only that part of the world supply, $S(p)$, that is not consumed by any *other* demander elsewhere in the world, $D^o(p)$, its residual supply function is

$$S^r(p) = S(p) - D^o(p). \tag{8.16}$$

At prices so low that $D^o(p)$ is greater than $S(p)$, the residual supply, $S^r(p)$, is zero.

---

[15]*Jargon alert*: It is traditional to use the expression *excess supply* when discussing international trade and *residual supply* otherwise, though the terms are equivalent.

Figure 8.12 Residual Supply Curve

Japan's residual supply curve, S^r, for cotton is the horizontal difference between the world's supply curve, S, and the demand curve of the other countries in the world, D^o.

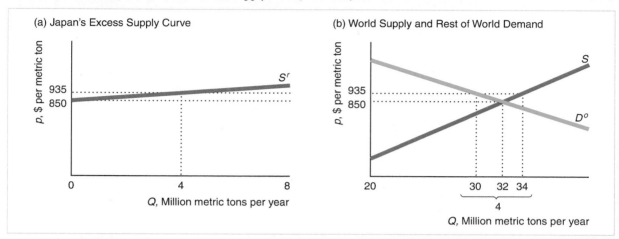

In Figure 8.12, we derive Japan's residual supply curve for cotton in panel a using the world supply curve, S, and the demand curve of the rest of the world, D^o, in panel b. The scales differ for the quantity axes in the two panels. At a price of $850 per metric ton, the demand in other countries exhausts world supply (D^o intersects S at 32 million metric tons per year), leaving no residual supply for Japan. At a much higher price, $935, Japan's residual supply, 4 million metric tons, is the difference between the world supply, 34 million tons, and the quantity demanded elsewhere, 30 million tons. As the figure illustrates, the residual supply curve facing Japan is much closer to horizontal than the world supply curve.

The elasticity of residual supply, η_r, facing a given country is[16]

$$\eta_r = \frac{\eta}{\theta} - \frac{1-\theta}{\theta}\varepsilon_o, \tag{8.17}$$

where η is the market supply elasticity, ε_o is the demand elasticity of the other countries, and $\theta = Q_r/Q$ is the importing country's share of the world's output.

If a country imports a small fraction of the world's supply, we expect it to face an almost perfectly elastic, horizontal residual supply curve. On the other hand, a relatively large consumer of the good might face an upward-sloping residual supply curve.

We can illustrate this difference for cotton, where $\eta = 0.5$ and $\varepsilon_o = -0.7$ (Green, Howitt, and Russo, 2005). The United States imports only $\theta = 0.1\%$ of the world's cotton, so its residual supply elasticity is

$$\eta_r = \frac{\eta}{0.001} - \frac{0.999}{0.001}\varepsilon_o$$
$$= 1{,}000\eta - 999\varepsilon_o$$
$$= (1{,}000 \times 0.5) - [999 \times (-0.7)] = 1{,}199.3,$$

[16]The derivation of this equation is similar to that of Equation 8.2.

which is 2,398.6 times more elastic than the world's supply elasticity. Canada's import share is 10 times larger, $\theta = 1\%$, so its residual supply elasticity is "only" 119.3. Nonetheless, its residual supply curve is nearly horizontal: A 1% increase in the price would induce imports to more than double, rising by 119.3%. Even Japan's $\theta = 2.5\%$ leads to a relatively elastic $\eta_r = 46.4$. In contrast, China imports 18.5% of the world's cotton, so its residual supply elasticity is 5.8. Even though its residual supply elasticity is more than 11 times larger than the world's elasticity, it is still small enough for its residual supply curve to be upward sloping.

Thus, if a country is *small*—it imports a small share of the world's output—then it faces a horizontal import supply curve at the world equilibrium price. If its domestic supply curve lies strictly above the world price, then the country only imports and faces a horizontal supply curve. If some portion of its upward-sloping domestic supply curve lies below the world price, then its total supply curve is the same as the upward-sloping domestic supply curve up to the world price and is horizontal at the world price (Chapter 9 shows this type of supply curve for oil).

This analysis of trade applies to trade within a country, too. The following Application shows that it can be used to look at trade across geographical areas or jurisdictions such as states.

APPLICATION

Reformulated Gasoline Supply Curves

You can't buy the gasoline sold in Milwaukee in other parts of Wisconsin. Houston gas isn't the same as western Texas gas. California, Minnesota, Nevada, and most of America's biggest cities use one or more of at least 46 specialized blends (sometimes called *boutique fuels*), while much of the rest of the country uses regular gas. The U.S. Clean Air Act Amendments, state laws, and local ordinances in areas with serious pollution problems require special, more highly refined blends that cut air pollution. For example, the objective of the federal Reformulated Fuels Program (RFG) is to reduce ground-level ozone-forming pollutants. It specifies both content criteria (such as benzene content limits) and emissions-based performance standards for refiners.

In states in which regular gasoline is used, wholesalers in one state ship gasoline to neighboring states with even slightly higher prices. Consequently, the residual supply curve for regular gasoline for a given state is close to horizontal.

In contrast, jurisdictions that require special blends rarely import gasoline. Few refiners produce any given special blend. Only one Wisconsin refinery produces Milwaukee's special low-polluting blend of gasoline. Because refineries require expensive upgrades to produce a new kind of gas, they generally do not switch from producing one type of gas to another type. Thus, even if the price of gasoline rises in Milwaukee, wholesalers in other states do not send gasoline to Milwaukee, because they cannot legally sell regular gasoline there and it would cost too much to start producing the reformulated gasoline.

Consequently, unlike the nearly horizontal residual supply curve for regular gasoline, the reformulated gasoline residual supply curve is eventually upward sloping. At relatively small quantities, refineries can produce more gasoline without incurring higher costs, so the supply curve in this region is relatively flat. However, to produce much larger quantities of gasoline, refiners have to run their plants around the clock and convert a larger fraction of each gallon of oil into gasoline, incurring higher costs of production. Because of this higher cost, they are willing to sell larger quantities in this range only at a higher price, so the supply curve slopes upward. When the refineries reach capacity, no matter how high the price gets, firms cannot produce more gasoline (at least until new refineries go online), so the supply curve becomes vertical.

Milwaukee and five other counties in southeastern Wisconsin use reformulated gasoline during warm months, while the rest of Wisconsin uses regular gasoline. At the beginning of spring, when the refinery starts switching to cleaner-burning reformulated gasoline and consumers drive more, Milwaukee operates in the steeply upward-sloping section of its supply curve. During March 2015, while reformulated gasoline was in particularly short supply, motorists in Milwaukee were paying 45¢ or one-fifth more for a gallon of regular than were motorists in Madison, Wisconsin, which uses regular gasoline. Nationally, in July 2018, reformulated gasoline cost 9% more than did regular gasoline.

**SOLVED PROBLEM
8.5**

**MyLab Economics
Solved Problem**

In the short run, what happens to the competitive market price of gasoline if the demand curve in a state shifts to the right as more people move to the state or start driving gas-guzzling SUVs? In your answer, distinguish between areas that use regular gasoline and jurisdictions that require special blends.

Answer

1. *Show the effect of a shift of the demand curve in areas that use regular gasoline.* In an area using regular gasoline, the supply curve is horizontal, as panel a of the figure shows. Thus, as the demand curve shifts to the right from D^1 to D^2, the equilibrium shifts along the supply curve from e_1 to e_2, and the price remains at p_1.

2. *Show the effects of both a small and large shift of the demand curve in a jurisdiction that uses a special blend.* The supply curve in panel b is drawn as described in the Application "Reformulated Gasoline Supply Curves." If the demand curve shifts to the right from D^1 to D^2, the price remains unchanged at p_1 because the demand curve continues to intersect the supply curve in the flat region. However, if the demand curve shifts farther to the right to D^3, then the new intersection is in the upward-sloping section of the supply curve and the price increases to p_3. Consequently, unforeseen "jumps" in demand are more likely to cause a *price spike*—a large increase in price—in jurisdictions that use special blends.

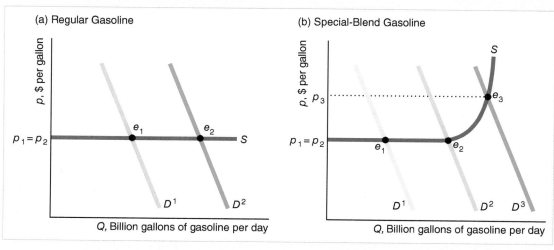

Long-Run Competitive Equilibrium

The intersection of the long-run market supply and demand curves determines the long-run competitive equilibrium. With identical firms, constant input prices, and free entry and exit, the long-run competitive market supply is horizontal at minimum long-run average cost, so the equilibrium price equals long-run average cost. A shift in the demand curve affects only the equilibrium quantity and not the equilibrium price, which remains constant at the minimum long-run average cost.

The market supply curve is different in the short run than in the long run, so the long-run competitive equilibrium differs from the short-run equilibrium. The relationship between the short- and long-run equilibria depends on where the market demand curve crosses the short- and long-run market supply curves. Figure 8.13 illustrates this point using the short- and long-run supply curves for the vegetable oil mill market.

The short-run supply curve for a typical firm in panel a is its marginal cost curve above the minimum, $7, of its short-run average variable cost curve, AVC^{SR}. At a price of $7, each firm produces 100 units, so the 20 firms in the market in the short run collectively supply 2,000 (= 20 × 100) units of oil in panel b. At higher prices, the short-run market supply curve slopes upward because it is the horizontal summation of the firm's upward-sloping marginal cost curves.

We assume that the firms use the same size plant in the short run and the long run so that the average cost curve is the same in both the short run and the long run, $AC^{SR,LR}$. The minimum average cost is $10 in both the short run and the long run. Because all firms have the same costs and can enter freely, the long-run market supply

Figure 8.13 The Short-Run and Long-Run Equilibria for Vegetable Oil

(a) A typical vegetable oil mill is willing to produce 100 units of oil at a price of $7,150 units at $10, or 165 units at $11. A firm's short-run supply curve is its marginal cost curve above the minimum, $7, of its short-run average variable cost curve, AVC^{SR}. (b) The short-run market supply curve, S^{SR}, is the horizontal sum of each firm's short-run supply curve. The long-run market supply curve,

S^{LR}, is horizontal at the minimum average cost, $10. If the demand curve is D^1 in the short-run equilibrium, F_1, 20 firms sell 2,000 units of oil at $7. In the long-run equilibrium, E_1, 10 firms sell 1,500 units at $10. If demand is D^2, the short-run equilibrium is F_2 ($11; 3,300 units; 20 firms) and the long-run equilibrium is E_2 ($10; 3,600 units; 24 firms).

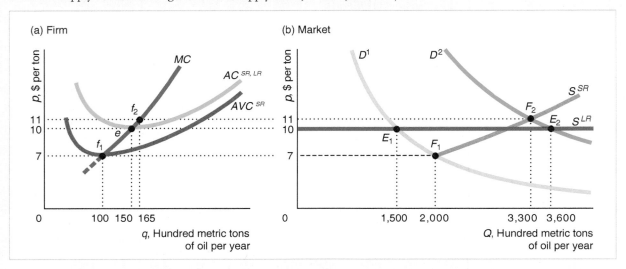

curve is flat at the minimum average cost, $10, in panel b. At prices between $7 and $10, firms supply goods at a loss in the short run but not in the long run.

If the market demand curve is D^1, the short-run market equilibrium, F_1, lies below and to the right of the long-run market equilibrium, E_1. This relationship is reversed if the market demand curve is D^2.[17]

In the short run, if the demand is as low as D^1, the market price in the short-run equilibrium, F_1, is $7. At that price, each of the 20 firms produces 100 units, at f_1 in panel a. The firms lose money because the price of $7 is below the average cost at 100 units. These losses drive some of the firms out of the market in the long run, so market output falls and the market price rises. In the long-run equilibrium, E_1, the price is $10, and each firm produces 150 units, e, and breaks even. As the market demands only 1,500 units, only 10 ($= 1,500/150$) firms produce, so half the firms that produced in the short run exit the market.[18] Thus, with the D^1 demand curve, price rises and output falls in the long run.

If demand expands to D^2 in the short run, each of the 20 firms expands its output to 165 units, f_2, and the price rises to $11, where the firms make profits: The price of $11 is above the average cost at 165 units. These profits attract entry in the long run, and the price falls. In the long-run equilibrium, each firm produces 150 units, e, and 3,600 units are sold in the market, E_2, by 24 ($= 3,600/150$) firms. Thus, with the D^2 demand curve, price falls and output rises in the long run.

Because firms may enter and exit in the long run, taxes can have a counterintuitive effect on the competitive equilibrium. For example, as the following Challenge Solution shows, a lump-sum franchise tax causes the competitive equilibrium output of a firm to increase even though market output falls.

CHALLENGE SOLUTION

The Rising Cost of Keeping On Truckin'

We return to the Challenge questions about the effects of higher annual fees and other lump-sum costs on the trucking market price and quantity, the output of individual firms, and the number of trucking firms (assuming that the demand curve remains constant). Because firms may enter and exit this industry in the long run, such higher lump-sum costs can have a counterintuitive effect on the competitive equilibrium.

All trucks of a certain size are essentially identical, and trucks can easily enter and exit the industry (government regulations aside). Panel a of the figure shows a typical firm's cost curves and panel b shows the market equilibrium.

The new, higher fees and other lump-sum costs raise the fixed cost of operating by $\mathcal{L}$. In panel a, a lump-sum, franchise tax shifts the typical firm's average cost curve upward from AC^1 to $AC^2 = AC^1 + \mathcal{L}/q$ but does not affect the marginal cost. As a result, the minimum average cost rises from e_1 to e_2.

Given that an unlimited number of identical truckers are willing to operate in this market, the long-run market supply is horizontal at minimum average cost. Thus, the market supply curve shifts upward in panel b by the same amount as the minimum average cost increases. Given a downward-sloping market demand curve D, the new equilibrium, E_2, has a lower quantity, $Q_2 < Q_1$, and higher price, $p_2 > p_1$, than the original equilibrium, E_1.

---

[17]Using data from *Statistics Canada*, I estimated that the elasticity of demand for vegetable oil is -0.8. Both D^1 and D^2 are constant -0.8 elasticity demand curves, but the demand at any price on D^2 is 2.4 times that on D^1.

[18]Which firms leave? If the firms are identical, the theory says nothing about which ones leave and which ones stay. The firms that leave make zero economic profit, and those that stay make zero economic profit, so firms are indifferent as to whether to stay or exit.

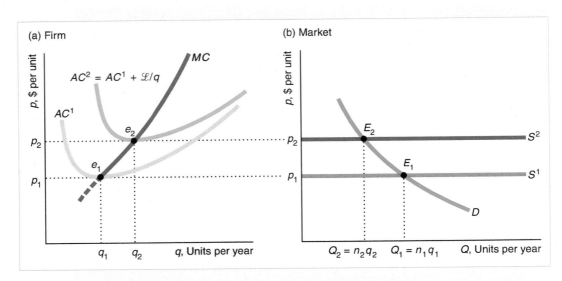

(a) Firm (b) Market

As the market price rises, the quantity that a firm produces rises from q_1 to q_2 in panel a. Because the marginal cost curve is upward sloping at the original equilibrium, when the average cost curve shifts up due to the higher fixed cost, the new minimum point on the average cost curve corresponds to a larger output than in the original equilibrium. Thus, any trucking firm still operating in the market produces at a larger volume.

Because the market quantity falls but each firm remaining in the market produces more, the number of firms in the market must fall. At the initial equilibrium, the number of firms was $n_1 = Q_1/q_1$. The new equilibrium number of firms, $n_2 = Q_2/q_2$, must be smaller than n_1 because $Q_2 < Q_1$ and $q_2 > q_1$.

Thus, these government policies have a number of negative effects:

Unintended Consequences Government lump-sum taxes and regulations that raise a firm's fixed cost cause the market price to rise, the market quantity to fall, and the number of trucking firms to fall.

Many people would expect these effects. However, these policies also have what most people would view as a surprising effect—that the policies cause the remaining firms to increase the amount of services they provide.

SUMMARY

1. **Perfect Competition.** Perfect competition is a market structure in which buyers and sellers are price takers. Each firm faces a horizontal demand curve. A firm's demand curve is horizontal because perfectly competitive markets have five characteristics: the market has a large number of small buyers and sellers, firms produce identical (homogeneous) products, buyers have full information about product prices and characteristics, transaction costs are negligible, and firms can freely enter and exit in the long run. Many markets are highly competitive—firms are very close to being price takers—even if they do not strictly possess all five of the characteristics associated with perfect competition.

2. **Profit Maximization.** Most firms maximize economic profit, which is revenue minus economic cost (explicit and implicit cost). Because business profit, which is revenue minus only explicit cost, does not include implicit cost, economic profit tends to be less than business profit. A firm earning zero economic profit is making as much as it could if its resources were devoted to their best alternative uses. To maximize profit, all firms (not just competitive firms) must make two decisions. First, the firm determines the quantity at which its profit is highest. Profit is maximized when marginal profit is zero or, equivalently, when marginal revenue equals marginal cost. Second, the firm decides whether to produce at all.   *MR=MC*

3. **Competition in the Short Run.** To maximize its profit, a competitive firm (like a firm in any other market structure) chooses its output level where marginal revenue equals marginal cost. Because a competitive firm is a price taker, its marginal revenue equals the market price, so it sets its output so that price equals marginal cost. New firms cannot enter in the short run. In addition, firms have some sunk fixed inputs. In this sense, firms cannot exit the industry in the short run. However, a profit-maximizing firm shuts down and produces no output if the market price is less than its minimum average variable cost. Thus, a competitive firm's short-run supply curve is its marginal cost curve above its minimum average variable cost. The

short-run market supply curve is the sum of the supply curves of the fixed number of firms producing in the short run. The intersection of the market demand curve and the short-run market supply curve determines the short-run competitive equilibrium.

4. **Competition in the Long Run.** In the long run, a competitive firm sets its output where the market price equals its long-run marginal cost. It shuts down if the market price is less than the minimum of its long-run average cost, because all costs are variable in the long run. Consequently, the competitive firm's supply curve is its long-run marginal cost above its minimum long-run average cost. The long-run supply curve of a firm may have a different slope than the short-run curve because the firm can vary its fixed factors in the long run. The long-run market supply curve is the horizontal sum of the supply curves of all the firms in the market. If all firms are identical, entry and exit are easy, and input prices are constant, the long-run market supply curve is flat at minimum average cost. If firms differ, entry is difficult or costly, input prices vary with output, or a country demands a large share of a good sold on a world market, the long-run market supply curve has an upward slope. The long-run market supply curve slopes upward if input prices increase with output and slopes downward if input prices decrease with output. The long-run market equilibrium price and quantity are different from the short-run price and quantity.

EXERCISES

All exercises are available on MyLab Economics; * = *answer appears at the back of this book;* **M** = *mathematical problem.*

1. Perfect Competition

1.1 A large city has nearly 500 restaurants, with new ones entering regularly as the population grows. The city decides to limit the number of restaurant licenses to 500. Which characteristics of this market are consistent with perfect competition and which are not? Is this restaurant market likely to be nearly perfectly competitive? Explain your answer.

1.2 Why would high transaction costs or imperfect information tend to prevent price-taking behavior?

1.3 Based on Roberts and Schlenker (2013), the corn demand elasticity is $\varepsilon = -0.3$, and the supply elasticity is $\eta = 0.15$. According to the 2007 Census of Agriculture, the United States has 347,760 corn farms. Assuming that the farms are of roughly equal size, what is the elasticity of demand facing a single farm? (*Hint*: See Solved Problem 8.1.) **M**

1.4 Based on Equation 8.2, by how much does the residual elasticity of demand facing a firm increase as the

number of firms increases by one firm? (*Hint*: See Solved Problem 8.1.) **M**

2. Profit Maximization

2.1 Should a competitive firm ever produce when it is losing money (making a negative economic profit)? Why or why not?

2.2 Should a firm shut down (and why) if its revenue is $R = \$1,000$ per week and

  a. its variable cost is $VC = \$500$, and its sunk fixed cost is $F = \$600$?

  b. its variable cost is $VC = \$1,001$, and its sunk fixed cost is $F = \$500$?

  c. its variable cost is $VC = \$500$, its fixed cost is $\$800$, of which $\$600$ is avoidable if it shuts down?

*2.3 A competitive firm's bookkeeper, upon reviewing the firm's books, finds that the company spent twice as much on its plant, a fixed cost, as the firm's manager had previously thought. Should the manager change the output level because of this new information? How does this new information affect profit?

2.4 The producers of *Spider-Man: Turn Off the Dark* spent $75 million bringing their musical to Broadway (Kevin Flynn and Patrick Healy, "How the Numbers Add Up [Way Up] for 'Spider-Man,'" *New York Times*, June 23, 2011). They spent $9 million alone on sets, costumes, and shoes. Their operating expenses were $1.2 million a week as of January 2011. Since then, they revamped the show and lowered their operating costs to about $1 million a week. The show is selling out but bringing in between $1.2 million and $1.3 million a week. The producers acknowledge that at the show's current earning level, *Spider-Man* would need to run more than seven years to pay back the investors. Only 18 Broadway shows have run for seven or more years. Should *Spider-Man* shut down or keep operating? Why?

2.5 Mercedes-Benz of San Francisco advertised on the radio that the same family had owned and operated the firm in the same location for half a century. It then made two claims: first, that it had lower overhead than other nearby auto dealers because it has owned this land for so long, and second, it charged a lower price for its cars because of its lower overhead. Discuss the logic of these claims.

*2.6 A firm's profit function is $\pi(q) = R(q) - C(q) = 120q - (200 + 40q + 10q^2)$. What is the positive output level that maximizes the firm's profit (or minimizes its loss)? What is the firm's revenue, variable cost, and profit? Should it operate or shut down in the short run?

2.7 A firm's profit function is $\pi(q) = R(q) - C(q) = 300q - (300 + 60q + 20q^2)$. What is the positive output level that maximizes the firm's profit (or minimizes its loss)? What is the firm's revenue, variable cost, and profit? Should it operate or shut down in the short run?

2.8 A firm decided to make decisions based on an alternative measure of profit = revenue − variable cost. Would it pick the output that maximizes the usual measure of profit? Would it make the correct shutdown decision?

3. Competition in the Short Run

*3.1 A marginal cost curve may be U-shaped. As a result, the *MC* curve may hit the firm's demand curve or price line at two output levels. Which is the profit-maximizing output? Why? **M**

3.2 The cost function for Acme Laundry is $C(q) = 10 + 10q + q^2$, where q is tons of laundry cleaned. What q should the firm choose to maximize

its profit if the market price is p? How much does it produce if $p = 50$? **M**

3.3 If the cost function for John's Shoe Repair is $C(q) = 100 + 10q - q^2 + \frac{1}{3}q^3$, what is the firm's marginal cost function? What is its profit-maximizing condition if the market price is p? What is its supply curve? **M**

3.4 The government imposes a specific tax of $t = 2$ on laundry. Acme Laundry's pre-tax cost function is $C(q) = 10 + 10q + q^2$. How much should the firm produce to maximize its after-tax profit if the market price is p? How much does it produce if $p = 50$? (*Hint:* See Exercise 3.2 and Solved Problem 8.2.) **M**

3.5 If the pre-tax cost function for John's Shoe Repair is $C(q) = 100 + 10q - q^2 + \frac{1}{3}q^3$, and it faces a specific tax of $t = 10$, what is its profit-maximizing condition if the market price is p? Can you solve for a single, profit-maximizing q in terms of p? (*Hint:* See Exercise 3.3 and Solved Problem 8.2.) **M**

3.6 If only one competitive firm receives a specific subsidy (negative tax) of s, how should that firm change its output level to maximize its profit, and how does its maximum profit change? Use a graph to illustrate your answer. (*Hint:* See Solved Problem 8.2.)

3.7 What is the effect of an ad valorem tax of v (the share of the price that goes to the government) on a competitive firm's profit-maximizing output given that the market price is unaffected? (*Hint:* See Solved Problem 8.2.)

3.8 According to the Application "Fracking and Shutdowns," conventional oil wells have lower shutdown points than those that use fracking. Use figures to compare the supply curves of firms with conventional wells and those that use fracking. On your figures, show the shutdown points and label the relevant costs on the vertical axes.

*3.9 In the summer of 2012, due to plentiful lobsters, the price of lobster in Maine fell to $1.25 a pound, which was 70% below normal and nearly a 30-year low. According to Bill Adler, head of the Massachusetts Lobstermen's Association, "Anything under $4 [a pound], lobstermen can't make any money" (Jerry A. Dicolo and Nicole Friedman, "Lobster Glut Slams Prices," *Wall Street Journal*, July 16, 2012). At least 30 boats announced that they would stay in port until the price rose. However, Canadian and other U.S. fishers continued to harvest lobsters. Why did some lobster boats stop fishing while others continued?

3.10 The last of California's operating gold mines closed after World War II because mining had become unprofitable when the price of gold was $34.71 an ounce (about \$446 in current dollars). However, in 2012, the price of gold approached historic highs, hovering around \$1,700 an ounce. Consequently, in 2012 and 2013, several large-scale hard rock gold mining operations reopened for the first time in more than half a century.

a. Show in a figure what this information implies about the shape of the gold extraction cost function.

b. Use the cost function you drew in part a to show how an increase in the market price of gold affects the amount of gold that a competitive firm extracts. Show the change in the firm's equilibrium profit.

*3.11 If a competitive firm's cost function is $C(q) = a + bq + cq^2 + dq^3$, where a, b, c, and d are constants, what is the firm's marginal cost function? What is the firm's profit-maximizing condition? (*Hint*: See Solved Problem 8.3.) **M**

3.12 A Christmas tree seller has a cost function $C = 6,860 + (p_T + t + 7/12)q + 37/27,000,000q^3$, where $p_T = \$11.50$ is the wholesale price of each tree and $t = \$2.00$ is the shipping price per tree. What is the seller's marginal cost function? What is the shutdown price? What is the seller's short-run supply function? If the seller's supply curve is $S(q, t)$, what is $\partial(q, t)/\partial t$? Evaluate it at $p_T = \$11.50$ and $t = \$2.00$. (*Hint*: See Solved Problem 8.3.) **M**

*3.13 Many marginal cost curves are U-shaped. Consequently, the MC curve can equal price at two output levels. Which is the profit-maximizing output? Why?

3.14 Each of the 10 firms in a competitive market has a cost function of $C = 25 + q^2$. The market demand function is $Q = 120 - p$. Determine the equilibrium price, quantity per firm, and market quantity. **M**

3.15 Given the information in the previous exercise, what effect does a specific tax of \$2.40 per unit have on the equilibrium price and quantities? (*Hint*: See Solved Problem 8.4.) **M**

3.16 Since 2013, most customers at California grocery and drug stores must pay an extra 10¢ for each paper bag that the store provides (the store keeps this fee). Does such a charge affect the marginal cost of any particular good? If so, by how much? Is this fee likely to affect the overall amount that consumers pay for groceries?

3.17 A firm has a cost function $C = q^3 - 36q^2 + 490q + 1,000$. The firm is a price taker and faces a market price of 250. What is its profit function? What quantity maximizes its profit? What is its profit? Should the firm operate or shut down?

4. Competition in the Long Run

4.1 In June 2005, Eastman Kodak announced that it no longer would produce black-and-white photographic paper—the type used to develop photographs by a traditional darkroom process. Kodak based its decision on the substitution of digital photography for traditional photography. In making its exit decision, did Kodak compare the price of its paper and average variable cost (at its optimal output)? Alternatively, did Kodak compare the price of its paper and average total cost (again at its optimal output)?

*4.2 What is the effect on firm and market equilibrium of the U.S. law requiring a firm to give its workers six months' notice before it can shut down its plant?

4.3 Redraw Figure 8.9 to show the situation where the short-run plant size is too large, relative to the optimal long-run plant size.

4.4 Each firm in a competitive market has a cost function of $C = q + q^2 + q^3$. The market has an unlimited number of potential firms. The market demand function is $Q = 24 - p$. Determine the long-run equilibrium price, quantity per firm, market quantity, and number of firms. How do these values change if a tax of \$1 per unit is collected from each firm? (*Hint*: See Solved Problem 8.4.) **M**

4.5 The major oil spill in the Gulf of Mexico in 2010 caused the oil firm BP and the U.S. government to greatly increase purchases of boat services, various oil-absorbing materials, and other goods and services to minimize damage from the spill. Use side-by-side firm and market diagrams to show the effects (number of firms, price, output, profits) of such a shift in demand in one such industry in both the short run and the long run. Explain how your answer depends on whether the shift in demand is expected to be temporary or permanent.

*4.6 Derive the residual supply elasticity in Equation 8.17 using the definition of the residual demand function in Equation 8.16. What is the formula with n identical countries? **M**

*4.7 The federal specific tax on gasoline is 18.4¢ per gallon, and the average state specific tax is 20.2¢, ranging from 7.5¢ in Georgia to 25¢ in Connecticut. A statistical study (Chouinard and Perloff, 2004) found that the incidence (Chapter 2) of the federal specific tax on consumers is substantially lower than that from state specific taxes. When the federal specific tax increases by 1¢, the retail price rises by about 0.5¢, so that retail consumers bear half the tax incidence. In contrast, when a state that uses regular gasoline increases its specific tax by 1¢, the retail price rises by nearly 1¢, so that the incidence of the tax falls almost entirely on consumers. (*Hint*: See Chapter 2 on tax incidence.)

a. What are the incidences of the federal and state specific gasoline taxes on firms?

b. Explain why the incidence on consumers differs between a federal and a state specific gasoline tax, assuming that the market is competitive. (*Hint*: Consider the residual supply curve facing a state compared to the supply curve facing the nation.)

c. Using the residual supply elasticity in Equation 8.17, estimate how much more elastic is the residual supply elasticity to one state than is the national supply elasticity. (For simplicity, assume that all 50 states are identical.) **M**

4.8 To reduce pollution, the California Air Resources Board requires the reformulation of gasoline sold in California. Since then, every few years, occasional disasters at California refineries have substantially cut the supply of gasoline and contributed to temporary large price increases. Environmentalists and California refiners (who had sunk large investments to produce the reformulated gasoline) opposed imports from other states, which would have kept prices down. To minimize fluctuations in prices in California, Severin Borenstein and Steven Stoft suggested setting a 15¢ surcharge on sellers of standard gasoline. In normal times, none of this gasoline would be sold, because it costs only 8¢ to 12¢ more to produce the California version. However, when disasters trigger a large shift in the supply curve of gasoline, firms could profitably import standard gasoline and keep the price in California from rising more than about 15¢ above prices in the rest of the United States. Use figures to evaluate Borenstein and Stoft's proposal. (*Hint*: See Solved Problem 8.5.)

4.9 Is the long-run supply curve for a good horizontal only if the long-run supply curves of all factors are horizontal? Explain.

4.10 Navel oranges are grown in California and Arizona. If Arizona starts collecting a specific tax per orange from its firms, what happens to the long-run market supply curve? (*Hint*: You may assume that all firms initially have the same costs. Your answer may depend on whether unlimited entry occurs.)

4.11 Draw a figure to illustrate why the size of ethanol processing plants has fallen in recent years (see the Application "The Size of Ethanol Processing Plants").

4.12 The Application "Upward-Sloping Long-Run Supply Curve for Cotton" shows a supply curve for cotton. Discuss the equilibrium if the world demand curve crosses this supply curve in either (a) a flat section labeled "Brazil" or (b) the vertical section to its right. What do farms in the United States do?

4.13 In late 2004 and early 2005, the price of raw coffee beans jumped as much as 50% from the previous year. In response, the price of roasted coffee rose about 14%. Similarly, in 2012, the price of raw beans fell by a third, yet the price of roasted coffee fell by only a few percentage points. Why would the roasted coffee price change less than in proportion to the rise in the cost of raw beans?

4.14 Before the late 1990s, people bought air tickets from a travel agent. When airline deregulation in the late 1970s led U.S. air travel to more than triple between 1975 and 2000, the number of travel agents grew from 45,000 to 124,000. In the late 1990s, internet travel sites such as Travelocity, Expedia, Priceline, and Orbitz entered the market. As a result, travel agents began to disappear. Of those travel agents working in 2000, 10% left in 2001, another 6% in 2002, and 43% by 2010 (Waldfogel, 2012). Use figures to explain what happened in the market for travel agents.

4.15 The long-run cost function of one of the identical carrot-producing firms is $C = 40q - q^2 + 0.01q^3$. The market demand curve is $Q = 5,000 - 200p$. What are the long-run equilibrium price, market quantity, and number of firms?

4.16 Now, the government starts collecting a specific tax t on the carrot market described in the previous problem.

a. What are the long-run equilibrium price, market quantity, and number of firms as functions of t?

b. How does the equilibrium market quantity change as t changes?

5. Challenge

5.1 In the Challenge Solution, would it make a difference to the analysis whether the government collects the lump-sum costs such as registration fees annually or only once when the firm starts operation? How would each of these franchise taxes affect the firm's long-run supply curve? Explain your answer.

5.2 Answer the Challenge for the short run rather than for the long run. (*Hint*: The answer depends on where the demand curve intersects the original short-run supply curve.)

5.3 The North American Free Trade Agreement provided for two-way, long-haul trucking across the U.S.–Mexican border. U.S. truckers objected, arguing that the Mexican trucks didn't have to meet the same environmental and safety standards as U.S.

trucks. They were concerned that the combination of these lower fixed costs and lower Mexican wages would cause them to lose business to Mexican drivers. Their complaints delayed implementation of this agreement (except for a small pilot program during the Bush administration, which was ended during the Obama administration). What would have been the short-run and long-run effects of allowing entry of Mexican drivers on market price and quantity and the number of U.S. truckers?

5.4 A perfectly competitive market has identical firms, free entry and exit, and an unlimited number of potential entrants. The government starts collecting a specific tax t; how do the long-run market and firm equilibria change?

*5.5 The finding that the average real price of abortions has remained relatively constant over the past 25 years suggests that the supply curve is horizontal. Medoff (1997) estimated that the price elasticity of demand for abortions ranges from -0.70 to -0.99. By how much would the market price of abortions and the number of abortions change if a lump-sum tax is assessed on abortion clinics that raises their minimum average cost by 10%? Use a figure to illustrate your answer. **M**

*5.6 Answer the Challenge problem using calculus. (*Note*: This comparative statics problem is difficult because you will need to solve two or three equations simultaneously, and hence you may need to use matrix techniques.) **M**

9 Properties and Applications of the Competitive Model

No more good must be attempted than the public can bear. —Thomas Jefferson

After you graduate, do you want to open a restaurant that serves drinks? If so, you'll need a liquor license, which, in some states, costs a lot of money.

Seventeen states and Washington, D.C., limit the number of liquor licenses.[1] Massachusetts issues one license per 2,000 residents; New Jersey, one per 3,000; and Utah, one per 4,925. In these limit or quota states, buying a liquor license from the state only costs a few hundred dollars. However, you probably can't get one from the state. You'll have to buy one from someone who already has one. Buying a license will cost you as much as $200,000 in the Philadelphia suburbs; $450,000 in Massachusetts; $1 million in Montana, New Mexico, or Utah; and $1.6 million in parts of New Jersey.

What effect does setting a limit on the number of liquor licenses have on the price of meals (including liquor)? What determines the value of a license? How much profit beyond the cost of the license can a restaurant earn? Who benefits and who loses from limiting the number of liquor licenses?

In this chapter, we illustrate how to use the competitive market model to answer these types of questions. One of the major strengths of the competitive market model is that it can predict how government policies, such as licensing, trade tariffs and quotas, global warming, and major cost-saving discoveries, will affect consumers and producers. We start by examining the properties of a competitive market and then consider how government actions and other shocks affect the market and its properties.

We concentrate on two main properties of a competitive market. First, firms in a competitive equilibrium make zero (economic) profit in the long run. Second, competition maximizes a measure of societal welfare.

To many people, the term *welfare* refers to the government's payments to the poor. In contrast, economists use *welfare* to refer to the well-being of various groups such

---

[1]Alaska, Arizona, California, Florida, Idaho, Kentucky, Massachusetts, Michigan, Minnesota, Montana, New Jersey, New Mexico, Ohio, Pennsylvania, South Dakota, Utah, and Washington.

as consumers and producers. They call an analysis of the impact of a change on various groups' well-being a study of *welfare economics*.

We introduced a measure of consumer well-being, *consumer surplus*, in Chapter 5. Here, we examine a similar concept for firms, *producer surplus*, which is closely related to profit and is used by economists to determine whether firms gain or lose when the equilibrium of a competitive market changes. The sum of producer surplus and consumer surplus equals the measure of welfare that we use in this chapter.

By predicting the effects of a proposed policy on consumer surplus, producer surplus, and welfare, economists can advise policymakers as to who will benefit, who will lose, and what the net effect of this policy will likely be. To decide whether to adopt a particular policy, policymakers may combine these predictions with their normative views (values), such as whether they are more interested in helping the group that gains or the group that loses.

In this chapter, we examine six main topics	1. **Zero Profit for Competitive Firms in the Long Run.** In the long-run competitive market equilibrium, profit-maximizing firms break even, so firms that do not try to maximize profits lose money and leave the market.
	2. **Producer Surplus.** How much producers gain or lose from a change in the equilibrium price is measured by producer surplus, which uses information from the marginal cost curve or the change in profit.
	3. **Competition Maximizes Welfare.** Competition maximizes a measure of social welfare based on consumer surplus and producer surplus.
	4. **Policies That Shift Supply or Demand Curves.** Government policies that shift supply or demand curves in perfectly competitive markets harm consumers and lower welfare.
	5. **Policies That Create a Wedge Between Supply and Demand Curves.** Government policies such as taxes, price floors, and tariffs that create a wedge between the supply and demand curves reduce the equilibrium quantity, raise the equilibrium price to consumers, and therefore lower welfare.
	6. **Comparing Both Types of Policies: Trade.** Policies that limit supply (such as quotas or bans on imports) or create a wedge between supply and demand (such as tariffs, which are taxes on imports) have different welfare effects when both policies reduce imports by equal amounts.

9.1 Zero Profit for Competitive Firms in the Long Run

Competitive firms earn zero profit in the long run whether or not entry is completely free. Consequently, competitive firms must maximize profit.

Zero Long-Run Profit with Free Entry

The long-run supply curve is horizontal if firms are free to enter the market, have identical costs, and face constant input prices. All firms in the market operate at minimum long-run average cost. That is, they are indifferent about whether or not to shut down because they are earning zero profit.

One implication of the shutdown rule is that firms are willing to operate in the long run even if they are making zero profit. This conclusion may seem strange unless you remember that we are talking about *economic profit*, which is revenue minus opportunity cost. Because opportunity cost includes the value of the next best investment, at a zero long-run economic profit, firms earn the normal business profit that they could gain by investing elsewhere in the economy.

For example, if a firm's owner had not built the plant the firm uses to produce, the owner could have spent that money on another business or put the money in a bank. The opportunity cost of the current plant, then, is the forgone profit from what the owner could have earned by investing the money elsewhere.

Because business cost does not include all opportunity costs, business profit is larger than economic profit. Thus, a profit-maximizing firm may stay in business if it earns zero long-run economic profit, but it shuts down if it earns zero long-run business profit.

Zero Long-Run Profit When Entry Is Limited

In some markets, firms cannot enter in response to long-run profit opportunities. The number of firms in these markets may be limited because the supply of an input is limited. For example, only so much land is suitable for mining uranium.

One might think that firms make positive long-run economic profits in such markets; however, that's not true. The reason firms earn zero economic profits is that firms bidding for the scarce input drive up its price until their profits are zero.

Suppose that the number of acres suitable for growing tomatoes is limited. Figure 9.1 shows a typical farm's average cost curve if the rental cost of land is zero (the average cost curve includes only the farm's costs of labor, capital, materials, and energy—not land). At the market price p^*, the firm produces q^* bushels of tomatoes and makes a profit of π^*, the shaded rectangle in the figure.

Figure 9.1 Rent

If farmers did not have to pay rent for their farms, a farmer with relatively high-quality land would earn a positive long-run profit of π^*. Due to competitive bidding for this land, however, the rent equals π^*, so the landlord reaps all the benefits of the superior land, and the farmer earns a zero long-run economic profit.

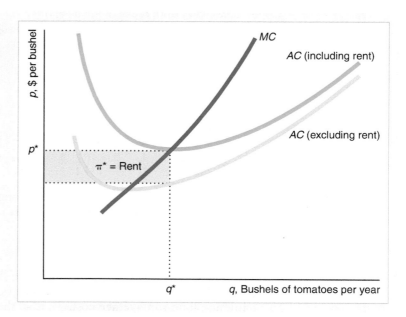

Thus, if the owner of the land does not charge rent, the farmer makes a profit. Unfortunately for the farmer, the landowner rents the land for π^*, so the farmer actually earns zero profit. Why does the landowner charge that much? The reason is that π^* is the opportunity cost of the land: The land is worth π^* to other potential farmers. These farmers will bid against each other to rent this land until the rent reaches π^*.

This rent is a fixed cost to the farmer because it does not vary with the amount of output. Thus, the rent affects the farm's average cost curve but not its marginal cost curve.

As a result, if the farm produces at all, it produces q^* where its marginal cost equals the market price, no matter what rent is charged. The higher average cost curve in the figure includes a rent equal to π^*. The minimum point of this average cost curve is p^* at q^* bushels of tomatoes, so the farmer earns zero economic profit.

If the demand curve shifts to the left so that the market price falls, the farmer suffers short-run losses. In the long run, the rental price of the land will fall enough that once again each farm earns zero economic profit.

Does it make a difference whether farmers own or rent the land? Not really. The opportunity cost to a farmer who owns superior land is the amount at which the farmer could rent the land in a competitive market. Thus, the economic profit of both owned and rented land is zero at the long-run equilibrium.

Good-quality land is not the only scarce resource. The price of any fixed factor will be bid up in a similar fashion until economic profit for the firm is zero in the long run. Similarly, the government may require that a firm have a license to operate and then limit the number of licenses available. The price of the license gets bid up by potential entrants, driving profit to zero. For example, the license fee is more than half a million dollars a year for a hot dog stand next to the steps of the Metropolitan Museum of Art in New York City.[2]

A scarce input—whether its fixed factor is a person with high ability or land—earns an extra opportunity value. This extra opportunity value is called a **rent**: a payment to the owner of an input beyond the minimum necessary for the factor to be supplied.

Bonnie manages a store for the salary of $40,000, the amount paid to a typical manager. Because she's a superior manager, however, the firm earns an economic profit of $50,000 a year. Other firms, seeing what a good job Bonnie is doing, offer her a higher salary. The bidding for her services drives her salary up to $90,000: her $40,000 base salary plus the $50,000 rent. After paying this rent to Bonnie, the store makes zero economic profit.

To summarize, if some firms in a market make short-run economic profits due to a scarce input, the other firms in the market bid for that input. This bidding drives up the price of the factor until all firms earn zero long-run profits. In such a market, the supply curve is flat because all firms have the same minimum long-run average cost.

---

[2]The auction value for this license hit $643,000 in 2009, but has fallen since then. (In the hot dog stand photo, I'm the fellow in the blue shirt with the dopey expression.) In 2013, the highest fee in New York City was $1.39 million a year to operate a hot dog cart outside the former Tavern on the Green restaurant in Central Park.

People with unusual abilities can earn staggering incomes, which are rents for their abilities. Though no law stops anyone from trying to become a professional entertainer or athlete, most of us do not have so much talent that others will pay to watch us perform.

According to **Forbes.com**, Floyd Mayweather earned $285 million in 2017, George Clooney $239 million, and Dwayne "the Rock" Johnson $124 million. Indeed, the estates of major celebrities continue to collect rents even after they die. People will still pay to listen to their music, view their cartoons, or use their image. In 2017, the estates of Michael Jackson earned $75 million, Charles Schulz $38 million, Elvis Presley $35 million, Dr. Seuss $16 million, and Albert Einstein $10 million.

To put these receipts in perspective, these amounts can exceed some small nations' gross domestic product (the value of the country's total output), such as the $42 million in 2017 for Tuvalu, with a population of 11,052 people.

The Need to Maximize Profit

The worst crime against working people is a company which fails to operate at a profit. —Samuel Gompers, first president of the American Federation of Labor

In a competitive market with identical firms and free entry, if most firms are profit-maximizing, profits are driven to zero at the long-run equilibrium. Any firm that does not maximize profit—that is, any firm that sets its output so that its marginal cost exceeds the market price or that fails to use the most cost-efficient methods of production—will lose money. Thus, *to survive in a competitive market, a firm must maximize its profit.*

9.2 Producer Surplus

Economists measure a firm's gain from participating in the market by its **producer surplus** (*PS*), which is the excess of the revenue from selling a good over the minimum amount necessary for the seller to be willing to produce the good. The minimum amount that a seller must receive to be willing to produce is the firm's avoidable production cost, which is usually its variable cost (Chapter 8). Producer surplus is analogous to the consumer surplus measure that we analyzed in Chapter 5.

Measuring Producer Surplus Using a Supply Curve

To determine a competitive firm's producer surplus, we use its supply curve: its marginal cost curve above its minimum average variable cost (Chapter 8). The firm's supply curve in panel a of Figure 9.2 looks like a staircase. The marginal cost of producing the first unit is $MC_1 = \$1$, which is the area below the marginal cost curve between 0 and 1. The marginal cost of producing the second unit is $MC_2 = \$2$, and so on. The variable cost, VC, of producing 4 units is the sum of the marginal costs for the first 4 units: $VC = MC_1 + MC_2 + MC_3 + MC_4 = \$1 + \$2 + \$3 + \$4 = \$10$.

If the market price, p, is $4, the firm's revenue from the sale of the first unit exceeds its cost by $PS_1 = p - MC_1 = \$4 - \$1 = \$3$, which is its producer surplus on the first unit. The firm's producer surplus is $2 on the second unit and $1 on the third unit. On the fourth unit, the price equals marginal cost, so the firm just breaks even. As a result, the firm's total producer surplus, *PS*, from selling 4 units at $4 each is the sum of its producer surplus on these 4 units: $PS = PS_1 + PS_2 + PS_3 + PS_4 = \$3 + \$2 + \$1 + \$0 = \$6$.[3]

---

[3]The firm is indifferent between producing the fourth unit or not. Its producer surplus would be the same if it produced only three units, because its marginal producer surplus from the fourth unit is zero.

Figure 9.2 Producer Surplus

(a) The firm's producer surplus, $6, is the area below the market price, $4, and above the marginal cost (supply curve) up to the quantity sold, 4. The area under the marginal cost curve up to the number of units actually produced is the variable cost of production. (b) The market producer surplus is the area above the supply curve and below the line at the market price, p^*, up to the quantity produced, Q^*. The area below the supply curve and to the left of the quantity produced by the market, Q^*, is the variable cost of producing that level of output.

Graphically, the total producer surplus is the area above the supply curve and below the market price up to the quantity actually produced. This same reasoning holds when the firm's supply curve is smooth.

The producer surplus is found by integrating the difference between the firm's demand function—the straight line at p—and its marginal cost function, $MC(q)$, up to the quantity produced, q^* (here $q^* = 4$ units):[4]

$$PS = \int_0^{q^*} [p - MC(q)]dq = pq^* - VC(q^*) = R(q^*) - VC(q^*), \quad (9.1)$$

where $R = pq^*$ is revenue. In panel a of Figure 9.2, revenue is $R = \$4 \times 4 = \$16$ and variable cost is $VC = \$10$, so producer surplus is $PS = \$6$.

Producer surplus is closely related to profit. Profit is revenue minus total cost, C, which equals variable cost plus fixed cost, F:

$$\pi = R - C = R - (VC + F). \quad (9.2)$$

[4]The marginal cost can be obtained by differentiating with respect to output either the variable cost function, $VC(q)$, or the total cost function, $C(q) = VC(q) + F$, because F is a constant (Chapter 7). When we integrate under the marginal cost function, we obtain the variable cost function—that is, we cannot recover the constant fixed cost.

Thus, the difference between producer surplus, Equation 9.1, and profit, Equation 9.2, is fixed cost, $PS - \pi = F$. If the fixed cost is zero (as often occurs in the long run), producer surplus equals profit.[5]

Another interpretation is that the producer surplus is the gain from trading. In the short run, if the firm produces and sells a good—that is, if the firm trades—it earns a profit of $\pi = R - VC - F$. If the firm shuts down—does not trade—it loses its fixed cost of $-F$. Thus, producer surplus equals the profit from trading minus the loss (fixed costs) it incurs from not trading:

$$PS = (R - VC - F) - (-F) = R - VC.$$

Using Producer Surplus

Even in the short run, we can use producer surplus to study the effects of any shock that does not affect the fixed cost of firms, such as a change in the price of a substitute or an input. Such shocks change profit by exactly the same amount as they change producer surplus, $\Delta\pi = \Delta PS$, because fixed costs do not change.

A major advantage of producer surplus is that we can use it to measure the effect of a shock on *all* the firms in a market without having to measure the profit of each firm separately. We can calculate market producer surplus using the market supply curve in the same way that we calculate a firm's producer surplus using its supply curve. The market producer surplus in panel b of Figure 9.2 is the area above the supply curve and below the market price line at p^* up to the quantity sold, Q^*. The market supply curve is the horizontal sum of the firms' supply curves (marginal cost curves) (Chapter 8).

SOLVED PROBLEM 9.1

MyLab Economics Solved Problem

Green, Howitt, and Russo (2005) estimated the inverse supply curve for California processed tomatoes as $p = 0.693Q^{1.82}$, where Q is the quantity of processing tomatoes in millions of tons per year and p is the price in dollars per ton. If the price falls from $60 (where the quantity supplied is about 11.6) to $50 (where the quantity supplied is approximately 10.5), how does producer surplus change? Illustrate in a figure. Show that you can obtain a good approximation using rectangles and triangles. (Round results to the nearest tenth.)

Answer

1. *Calculate the producer surplus at each price (or corresponding quantity) and take the difference to determine how producer surplus changes.* When the price is $60, the producer surplus is

$$PS_1 = \int_0^{11.6} (60 - 0.693Q^{1.82})dQ = 60Q - \frac{0.693}{2.82}Q^{2.82}\Big|_0^{11.6} \approx 449.3.$$

The producer surplus at the new price is

$$PS_2 = \int_0^{10.5} (50 - 0.693Q^{1.82})dQ \approx 338.7.$$

Thus, the change in producer surplus is $\Delta PS = PS_2 - PS_1 \approx 338.7 - 449.3 = -110.6$.

---

[5]Even though each competitive firm makes zero profit in the long run, owners of scarce resources used in that market may earn rents, as we discussed in Section 9.1. Thus, owners of scarce resources may receive positive producer surplus in the long run.

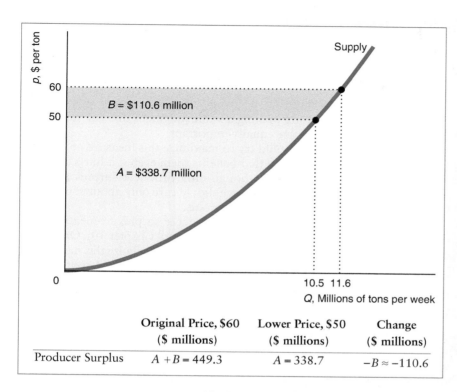

	Original Price, $60 ($ millions)	Lower Price, $50 ($ millions)	Change ($ millions)
Producer Surplus	$A + B = 449.3$	$A = 338.7$	$-B \approx -110.6$

2. *At each price, the producer surplus is the area above the supply curve and below the price up to the quantity sold.* In the figure, area A corresponds to PS_2 because it is the area above the supply curve, below the price of $50, up to the quantity 10.5. Similarly, PS_1 is the sum of areas A and B, so the loss in producer surplus, ΔPS, is area B.

3. *Approximate area B as the sum of a rectangle and a triangle.* Area B consists of a rectangle with a height of 10 (= 60 − 50) and a length of 10.5 and a shape that's nearly a triangle with a height of 10 and a base of 1.1 (= 11.6 − 10.5). The sum of the areas of the rectangle and the triangle is $(10 \times 10.5) + (\frac{1}{2} \times 10 \times 1.1)$ = 110.5, which is close to the value, 110.6, that we obtained by integrating.

9.3 Competition Maximizes Welfare

All is for the best in the best of all possible worlds. —Voltaire (*Candide*)

Perfect competition serves as an ideal or benchmark for other industries. This benchmark is widely used by economists and widely misused by politicians.

Most U.S. politicians have at one point or another in their careers stated (with a hand over their heart), "I believe in the free market." While I'm not about to bash free markets, I find this statement to be, at best, mysterious. What do the politicians mean by "believe in" and "free market?" It is hoped they realize that whether a free market is desirable is a scientific question rather than one of belief. Possibly, when they say they "believe in," they are making some claim that free markets are desirable for some unspecified reason. By "free market," they might mean a market without government regulation or intervention. This statement is a bad summary of what is probably the most important theoretical result in economics: *A perfectly competitive market maximizes an important measure of economic well-being.*[6]

---

[6] In 1776, Adam Smith, the father of modern economics, in his book *An Inquiry into the Nature and Causes of the Wealth of Nations*, was the first to observe that firms and consumers acting independently in their self-interest generate a socially desirable outcome. Economists call this insight the *invisible hand theorem* based on a phrase Smith used.

Measuring Welfare

How should we measure society's welfare? One commonly used measure of the welfare of society, W, is the sum of consumer surplus (Chapter 5) plus producer surplus:

$$W = CS + PS.$$

This measure implicitly weights the well-being of consumers and producers equally. By using this measure, we are making a value judgment that the well-being of consumers and that of producers are equally important.

Not everyone agrees that society should try to maximize this measure of welfare. Groups of producers argue for legislation that benefits them even if it hurts consumers by more than the producers gain—as though only producer surplus matters. Similarly, some consumer advocates argue that we should care only about consumers, so social welfare should include only consumer surplus.

In this chapter, we use consumer surplus plus producer surplus to measure welfare (and postpone a discussion of other welfare concepts until Chapter 10). One of the most striking results in economics is that competitive markets maximize this measure of welfare. If either less or more output than the competitive level is produced, welfare falls.

Why Producing Less Than the Competitive Output Lowers Welfare

Producing less than the competitive output lowers welfare. At the competitive equilibrium in Figure 9.3, e_1, where output is Q_1 and price is p_1, consumer surplus equals area $CS_1 = A + B + C$, producer surplus is $PS_1 = D + E$, and total welfare is $W_1 = A + B + C + D + E$. If output is reduced to Q_2 so that price rises to p_2 at e_2, consumer surplus is $CS_2 = A$, producer surplus is $PS_2 = B + D$, and welfare is $W_2 = A + B + D$.

The change in consumer surplus is

$$\Delta CS = CS_2 - CS_1 = A - (A + B + C) = -B - C.$$

Consumers lose B because they have to pay $p_2 - p_1$ more than they would at the competitive price for the Q_2 units they buy. Consumers lose C because they buy only Q_2 rather than Q_1 at the higher price.

The change in producer surplus is

$$\Delta PS = PS_2 - PS_1 = (B + D) - (D + E) = B - E.$$

Producers gain B because they now sell Q_2 units at p_2 rather than at p_1. They lose E because they sell $Q_2 - Q_1$ fewer units.

The change in welfare is

$$
\begin{aligned}
\Delta W &= W_2 - W_1 \\
&= (CS_2 + PS_2) - (CS_1 + PS_1) \\
&= (CS_2 - CS_1) + (PS_2 - PS_1) = \Delta CS + \Delta PS \\
&= (-B - C) + (B - E) \\
&= -C - E.
\end{aligned}
$$

Area B is a transfer from consumers to producers—the extra amount consumers pay for the Q_2 units goes to the sellers—so it does not affect welfare. Welfare drops because consumers' loss of C and producers' loss of E benefit no one. This reduction in welfare by $C + E$ is a **deadweight loss** (DWL): the net reduction in welfare from a loss of surplus by one group that is not offset by a gain to another group.

The deadweight loss results because consumers value extra output by more than the marginal cost of producing it. In the competitive equilibrium, **allocative efficiency**

Figure 9.3 Why Reducing Output from the Competitive Level Lowers Welfare

Reducing output from the competitive level Q_1 to Q_2 causes price to increase from p_1 to p_2. Consumers suffer: Consumer surplus is now A, a fall of $\Delta CS = -B - C$. Producers may gain or lose: Producer surplus is now $B + D$, a change of $\Delta PS = B - E$. Overall, welfare falls by $\Delta W = -C - E$, so the deadweight loss (DWL) to society is $C + E$.

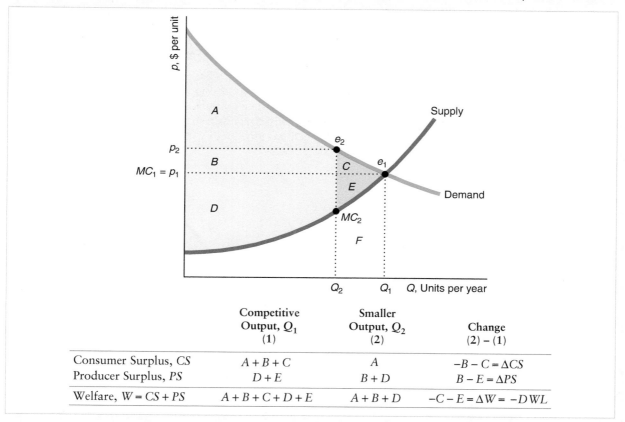

	Competitive Output, Q_1 (1)	Smaller Output, Q_2 (2)	Change (2) – (1)
Consumer Surplus, CS	$A + B + C$	A	$-B - C = \Delta CS$
Producer Surplus, PS	$D + E$	$B + D$	$B - E = \Delta PS$
Welfare, $W = CS + PS$	$A + B + C + D + E$	$A + B + D$	$-C - E = \Delta W = -DWL$

occurs: Every good or service is produced up to the point where no consumer is willing to pay more for it than the price at which someone else is willing to supply it. In Figure 9.3, where the output is less than the competitive equilibrium quantity, society suffers from *allocative inefficiency* because at each output between Q_2 and Q_1, consumers' marginal willingness to pay for another unit—the height of the demand curve—is greater than the marginal cost of producing the next unit—the height of the supply curve. For example, at e_2, consumers value the next unit of output at p_2, which is much greater than the marginal cost, MC_2, of producing it. Increasing output from Q_2 to Q_1 raises firms' variable cost by area F, the area under the marginal cost (supply) curve between Q_2 and Q_1. Consumers value this extra output by the area under the demand curve between Q_2 and Q_1, area $C + E + F$. Thus, consumers value the extra output by $C + E$ more than it costs to produce it.

Society would be better off producing and consuming extra units of this good than spending the deadweight loss on other goods. In short, *the deadweight loss is the opportunity cost of giving up some of this good to buy more of another good.*

A deadweight loss reflects a **market failure**: cost inefficiency or allocative inefficiency. It is often the result of the price not equaling the marginal cost. At the competitive equilibrium, demand equals supply, which ensures that price equals marginal cost. In other situations where consumers value the last unit by more than the marginal cost of production, increasing output would increase welfare.

SOLVED PROBLEM 9.2

MyLab Economics Solved Problem

Show that increasing output beyond the competitive level decreases welfare because the cost of producing this extra output exceeds the value consumers place on it.

Answer

1. *Illustrate that setting output above the competitive level requires the price to fall for consumers to buy the extra output.* The figure shows the effect of increasing output from the competitive level, Q_1, to Q_2. At the competitive equilibrium, e_1, the price is p_1. For consumers to buy the extra output at Q_2, the price must fall to p_2 at e_2 on the demand curve.

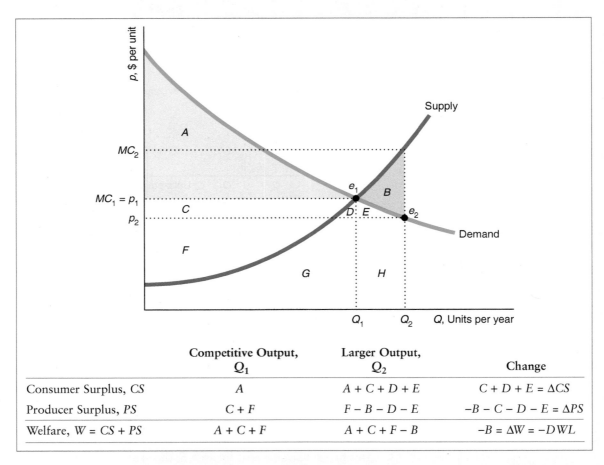

	Competitive Output, Q_1	Larger Output, Q_2	Change
Consumer Surplus, CS	A	$A + C + D + E$	$C + D + E = \Delta CS$
Producer Surplus, PS	$C + F$	$F - B - D - E$	$-B - C - D - E = \Delta PS$
Welfare, $W = CS + PS$	$A + C + F$	$A + C + F - B$	$-B = \Delta W = -DWL$

2. *Show how the consumer surplus and producer surplus change when the output level increases.* Because the price falls from p_1 to p_2, consumer surplus rises by $\Delta CS = C + D + E$, which is the area between p_2 and p_1 to the left of the demand curve. At the original price, p_1, producer surplus was $C + F$. The cost of producing the larger output is the area under the supply curve up to Q_2, $B + D + E + G + H$. The firms sell this quantity for only $p_2 Q_2$, area $F + G + H$. Thus, the new producer surplus is $F - B - D - E$. As a result, the increase in output causes producer surplus to fall by $\Delta PS = -B - C - D - E$.

3. *Determine how welfare changes by adding the change in consumer surplus and producer surplus.* Because producers lose more than consumers gain, the change in welfare is

$$\Delta W = \Delta CS + \Delta PS = (C + D + E) + (-B - C - D - E) = -B.$$

Thus, the deadweight loss to society is B.

4. *Explain why welfare changes due to setting the price different than the marginal cost.* The new price, p_2, is less than the marginal cost, MC_2, of producing Q_2. Too much is being produced. A net loss occurs because consumers value the $Q_2 - Q_1$ extra output by only $E + H$, which is less than the extra cost, $B + E + H$, of producing it. The reason that competition maximizes welfare is that price equals marginal cost at the competitive equilibrium. At the competitive equilibrium, price equals marginal cost, so consumers value the last unit of output by exactly the amount that it costs to produce it. If consumers value the last unit by less than its marginal cost, welfare is higher at a lower level of production.

APPLICATION

The Deadweight Loss of Christmas Presents

Just how much did you enjoy the expensive woolen socks with the dancing purple teddy bears that your Aunt Fern gave you last Christmas? Often the cost of a gift exceeds the value that the recipient places on it.

Until the advent of gift cards, only 10% to 15% of holiday gifts were monetary. A gift of cash typically gives at least as much pleasure to the recipient as a gift that costs the same but can't be exchanged for cash. (So what if giving cash is tacky?) Of course, it's possible that a gift can give more pleasure to the recipient than it cost the giver—but how often does that happen to you?

An *efficient gift* is one that the recipient values as much or more than as the gift costs the giver. If the price of the gift exceeds its value to the recipient, the difference is a deadweight loss to society. Based on surveys of Yale undergraduates, Waldfogel (1993, 2009) estimated that the deadweight loss is between 10% and 33% of the value of gifts. Waldfogel (2005) found that consumers value their own purchases at 10% to 18% more, per dollar spent, than items received as gifts.[7]

Waldfogel found that gifts from friends and "significant others" are most efficient, while noncash gifts from members of the extended family are least

---

[7]Gift recipients may exhibit an endowment effect (Chapter 3) in which their willingness to pay (WTP) for the gift is less than what they would have to be offered to give up the gift, their willingness to accept (WTA). Bauer and Schmidt (2008) asked students at the Ruhr University in Germany their WTP and WTA for three recently received Christmas gifts. On average over all students and gifts, the average WTP was 11% below the market price and the WTA was 18% above the market price.

efficient (one-third of the value is lost).[8] Luckily, grandparents, aunts, and uncles are most likely to give cash.

Waldfogel concluded that a conservative estimate of the deadweight loss of Christmas, Hanukkah, and other holidays with gift-giving rituals is about $12 billion. (And that's not counting about 2.8 billion hours spent shopping.) However, if the reason others don't give cash or gift cards is that they get pleasure from picking the "perfect" gift, the deadweight loss that adjusts for the pleasure of the giver is lower than these calculations suggest.

The question remains why people don't give cash instead of presents. Indeed, 77% of all Americans and 85% of those 25 to 34 years old give gift cards. (A gift card is similar to cash, though recipients can use some cards only in a particular store.) By one estimate, gift card sales will hit $180 billion in 2018. Indeed, 93% of consumers say that they would prefer receiving a $25 gift card to a gift that cost $25. Bah, humbug!

9.4   Policies That Shift Supply or Demand Curves

One of the main reasons that economists developed welfare tools was to predict the impact of government programs that alter a competitive equilibrium. Virtually all government actions affect a competitive equilibrium in one of two ways. Some government policies shift the demand curve or the supply curve, such as a limit on the number of firms in a market. Others, such as sales taxes, create a wedge or gap between price and marginal cost so that they are not equal, even though they were in the original competitive equilibrium.

These government interventions move us from an unconstrained competitive equilibrium to a new, constrained competitive equilibrium. Because welfare was maximized at the initial competitive equilibrium, the examples of government-induced changes that we consider here lower welfare. In later chapters, we show that government intervention may raise welfare in markets in which welfare was not maximized initially.

Although government policies may cause either the supply curve or the demand curve to shift, we concentrate on policies that limit supply because they are used frequently and have clear-cut effects. If a government policy causes the supply curve to shift to the left, consumers make fewer purchases at a higher price and welfare falls. For example, if the supply curve in Figure 9.3 shifts to the left so that it hits the demand curve at e_2, then output falls from Q_1 to Q_2, the price rises from p_1 to p_2,

---

[8]Some people return an unwanted gift to a store. For the 2014 holiday season, gift recipients returned 11% of holiday presents, valued at $65 billion. Other people may deal with a disappointing present by "regifting" it. Some families have been passing the same fruitcake among family members for decades. According to one survey, 33% of women and 19% of men admitted that they pass on an unwanted gift (and 28% of respondents said that they would not admit it if asked whether they had done so).

and the drop in welfare is $-C - E$. The only "trick" in this analysis is that we use the original supply curve to evaluate the effects on producer surplus and welfare.[9]

During World War II, most of the nations involved limited the sales of consumer goods so that the nations' resources could be used for the war effort. Similarly, a government may cause a supply curve to shift to the left by restricting the number of firms in a market, such as by licensing taxicabs, psychiatric hospitals, or restaurants to serve drinks. We examine the effect of such policies in the Challenge Solution at the end of this chapter.

Entry Barrier. A government may also cause the supply curve to shift to the left by raising the cost of entry. If its cost will be greater than that of firms already in the market, a potential firm might not enter a market even if existing firms are making a profit. Any cost that falls only on potential entrants and not on current firms discourages entry. A long-run **barrier to entry** is an explicit restriction or a cost that applies only to potential new firms—existing firms are not subject to the restriction or do not bear the cost.

At the time they entered, incumbent firms had to pay many of the costs of entering a market that new entrants incur, such as the fixed costs of building plants, buying equipment, and advertising a new product. For example, the fixed cost to McDonald's and other fast-food chains of opening a new fast-food restaurant is about $2 million. These fixed costs are *costs of entry* but are *not* barriers to entry because they apply equally to incumbents and entrants. Costs incurred by both incumbents and entrants do not discourage potential firms from entering a market if existing firms are making money. Potential entrants know that they will do as well as existing firms once they begin operations, so they are willing to enter as long as profit opportunities exist.

Large sunk costs can be barriers to entry under two conditions. First, if capital markets do not work efficiently so that new firms have difficulty raising money, new firms may be unable to enter profitable markets. Second, if a firm must incur a large *sunk* cost, which would increase the loss if it exits, the firm may be reluctant to enter a market in which it is uncertain of success.

APPLICATION Welfare Effects of Allowing Fracking	Technological advances have made hydraulic fracturing—fracking—a practical means to extract natural gas as well as oil from shale formations that previously could not be exploited (see the Application "Fracking and Shutdowns" in Chapter 8). Opponents of fracking fear that it pollutes air and water and triggers earthquakes. Due to their opposition, governments limit or prohibit fracking in parts of the United States and Europe. Hausman and Kellogg (2015) used estimated natural gas supply and demand curves to calculate the welfare effects of permitting fracking firms to enter the gas market. They found that the rightward shift of the supply curve reduced the U.S. natural gas price by 47% in 2013. As a result, consumer surplus increased substantially, particularly in the south central and midwestern United States, where the industrial and electric power industries use large quantities of gas. This drop in price was sufficient to reduce producer surplus. Hausman and Kellogg concluded that the total surplus increased by $48 billion, but noted that this calculation ignores any possible harmful environmental effects.

[9] Welfare falls when governments restrict the consumption of competitive products that we all agree are *goods*, such as food and medical services. In contrast, if most of society wants to discourage the use of certain products, such as hallucinogenic drugs and poisons, policies that restrict consumption may increase some measures of society's welfare.

Exit Restriction. U.S., European, and other governments have laws that delay how quickly some (typically large) firms may go out of business so that workers can receive advance warning that they will be laid off. Although these restrictions keep the number of firms in a market relatively large in the short run, they may reduce the number of firms in a market in the long run.

Why do exit restrictions reduce the number of firms in a market in the long run? Suppose that you are considering starting a construction firm with no capital or other fixed factors. Your firm's only input is labor. You know that the demand for construction services is low during business downturns and in the winter. To avoid paying workers when business is slack, you plan to shut down during those periods. Because you can avoid losses by shutting down during low-demand periods, you enter this market if your expected economic profits during good periods are zero or positive.

A law that requires you to give your workers six months' warning before laying them off prevents your firm from shutting down quickly. You know that you'll regularly suffer losses during business downturns because you'll have to pay your workers for up to six months during periods when you have nothing for them to do. Knowing that you'll incur these regular losses, you are less inclined to enter the market. Unless the economic profits during good periods are much higher than zero—high enough to offset your losses—you will not choose to enter the market. If exit barriers limit the number of firms, the same analysis that we used to examine entry barriers applies. Thus, a government's attempt to help workers may hurt consumers:

Unintended Consequences Exit barriers may raise prices, lower consumer surplus, and reduce welfare.

9.5 Policies That Create a Wedge Between Supply and Demand Curves

Never try to kill a government program—you'll only make it mad.

The most common government policies that create a wedge between supply and demand curves are sales taxes (or subsidies) and price controls. Because these policies create a gap between marginal cost and price, either too little or too much is produced. For example, a tax causes price to exceed marginal cost—that is, consumers value the good more than it costs to produce it—with the result that consumer surplus, producer surplus, and welfare fall (although tax revenue rises).

Welfare Effects of a Sales Tax

A new sales tax causes a rise in the price that consumers pay (Chapter 2), resulting in a loss of consumer surplus, $\Delta CS < 0$, and a fall in the price that firms receive, resulting in a drop in producer surplus, $\Delta PS < 0$. However, this tax provides the government with new tax revenue, $\Delta T = T > 0$, if tax revenue was zero before the new tax.

Assuming that the government does something useful with the tax revenue, we should include tax revenue in our definition of welfare:

$$W = CS + PS + T.$$

As a result, the change in welfare is

$$\Delta W = \Delta CS + \Delta PS + \Delta T.$$

Even when we include tax revenue in our welfare measure, a specific tax must lower welfare in, for example, the competitive market for tea roses. We show the welfare loss from a specific tax of $t = 11¢$ per rose stem in Figure 9.4, which is based on estimated demand and supply curves.

Without the tax, the intersection of the demand curve, D, and the supply curve, S, determines the competitive equilibrium, e_1, at a price of 30¢ per stem and a quantity of 1.25 billion rose stems per year. Consumer surplus is $A + B + C$, producer surplus is $D + E + F$, tax revenue is zero, and society faces no deadweight loss.

The specific tax shifts the effective supply curve up by 11¢, creating an 11¢ wedge or differential between the price consumers pay, 32¢, and the price producers receive, $32¢ - t = 21¢$. Equilibrium output falls from 1.25 to 1.16 billion stems per year.

The extra 2¢ per stem that buyers pay causes consumer surplus to fall by $B + C = \$24.1$ million per year (as the table under the figure shows). Due to the 9¢ drop in the price firms receive, they lose producer surplus of $D + E = \$108.45$ million

Figure 9.4 Welfare Effects of a Specific Tax on Roses

The $t = 11¢$ specific tax on roses creates an 11¢ per stem wedge between the price customers pay, 32¢, and the price producers receive, 21¢. Tax revenue is $T = tQ = \$127.6$ million per year. The deadweight loss to society is $C + E = \$4.95$ million per year.

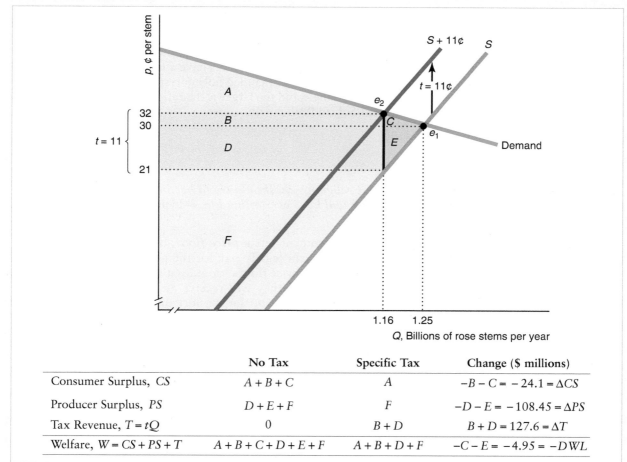

	No Tax	Specific Tax	Change (\$ millions)
Consumer Surplus, CS	$A + B + C$	A	$-B - C = -24.1 = \Delta CS$
Producer Surplus, PS	$D + E + F$	F	$-D - E = -108.45 = \Delta PS$
Tax Revenue, $T = tQ$	0	$B + D$	$B + D = 127.6 = \Delta T$
Welfare, $W = CS + PS + T$	$A + B + C + D + E + F$	$A + B + D + F$	$-C - E = -4.95 = -DWL$

per year. The government gains tax revenue of $tQ = 11¢$ per stem $\times$ 1.16 billion stems per year $=$ \$127.6 million per year, area $B + D$.

The combined loss of consumer surplus and producer surplus is only partially offset by the government's gain in tax revenue, so welfare drops by

$$\Delta W = \Delta CS + \Delta PS + \Delta T = -\$24.1 - \$108.45 + \$127.6$$
$$= -\$4.95 \text{ million per year.}$$

This deadweight loss is $C + E$.

Why does society suffer a deadweight loss? The reason is that the tax lowers output from the competitive level where welfare is maximized. An equivalent explanation for this loss to society is that the tax puts a wedge between price and marginal cost, which is an allocative inefficiency. At the new equilibrium, buyers are willing to pay $p = 32¢$ for one more rose stem, while the marginal cost to firms is only $21¢ (= p - t)$. Shouldn't more roses be produced and sold if consumers are willing to pay nearly a third more than the cost of producing it? That's what our welfare study indicates.

APPLICATION

The Deadweight Loss from Gas Taxes

The social cost of collecting tax revenue is the deadweight loss that the tax causes. Blundell, Horowitz, and Parey (2012) found that the deadweight loss per dollar of gasoline tax revenue raised is 4.3% for high-income, 9.2% for middle-income, and 3.9% for low-income U.S. consumers.[10]

Why is a gasoline tax more distorting for middle-income consumers? Part of the explanation is that middle-income U.S. and Canadian consumers are much more responsive to changes in gasoline prices than low-income and high-income consumers. That is, middle-income consumers have a more elastic demand curve. Typically, the more the quantity demanded falls in response to the tax, the wider is the deadweight loss triangle and the larger is the ratio of deadweight loss to tax revenue, as the next Solved Problem illustrates.

Welfare Effects of a Price Floor

No matter what your religion, you should try to become a government program, for then you will have everlasting life. —Lynn Martin (former U.S. Representative)

In some markets, the government sets a *price floor*, or minimum price, which is the lowest price a consumer can legally pay for the good. For example, in most countries, the government sets price floors for at least some agricultural products, which guarantee producers that they will receive at least a price of $\underline{p}$ for their good. If the market price is above $\underline{p}$, the support program is irrelevant. If the market price is below $\underline{p}$, however, the government buys as much output as necessary to drive the price up to $\underline{p}$. Since 1929 (the start of the Great Depression), the U.S. government has used price floors or similar programs to keep the prices of many agricultural products above the price that competition would determine in unregulated markets.

---

[10]The U.S. low-income group consists of the 25% lowest earners and has a median income of \$42,500 per year. The middle-income group has a median income of \$57,500. The median income of the high-income group is \$72,500. *These calculations ignore the environmental effects from reduced consumption of gasoline.*

Agricultural Price Support. Traditionally, the U.S. government supported agricultural prices by buying some of the crop and storing it.[11] We show the effect of such a price support using estimated supply and demand curves for the soybean market (Holt, 1992). The intersection of the market demand curve and the market supply curve in Figure 9.5 determines the competitive equilibrium, e, in the absence of a price support program, where the equilibrium price is $p_1 = \$4.59$ per bushel and the equilibrium quantity is $Q_1 = 2.1$ billion bushels per year.[12]

With a price support on soybeans of $\overline{p} = \$5.00$ per bushel and the government's pledge to buy as much output as farmers want to sell, quantity sold is $Q_s = 2.2$ billion bushels. At $\overline{p}$, consumers buy less output, $Q_d = 1.9$ billion bushels, than the Q_1 they would have bought at the market-determined price p_1. As a result, consumer surplus falls by $B + C = \$864$ million. The government buys $Q_g = Q_s - Q_d \approx 0.3$ billion bushels per year, which is the excess supply, at a cost of $T = \overline{p} \times Q_g = C + D + F + G = \$1.283$ billion.

The government cannot resell the output domestically, because if it tried to do so, it would succeed only in driving down the price consumers pay. Instead, the government stores the output or sends it abroad.

Although farmers gain producer surplus of $B + C + D = \$921$ million, this program is an inefficient way to transfer money to them. Assuming that the government's purchases have no alternative use, the change in welfare is $\Delta W = \Delta CS + \Delta PS - T = -C - F - G = -\$1.226$ billion per year.[13] The deadweight loss, $C + F + G$, reflects two distortions in this market:

1. **Excess production:** More output is produced than is consumed, so Q_g is stored, destroyed, or shipped abroad.
2. **Allocative inefficiency:** At the quantity they actually buy, Q_d, consumers are willing to pay $\$5$ for the last bushel of soybeans, which is more than the marginal cost, $MC = \$3.60$, of producing that bushel.

Thus, traditional government agricultural price support programs designed to help farmers hurt others.

---

[11]The wool and mohair price support program is my favorite. The U.S. government instituted wool price supports after the Korean War to ensure "strategic supplies" for uniforms. Later, Congress added mohair to the program, even though mohair has no military use. In some years, the extra amount that the government paid for mohair exceeded the amount consumers paid for mohair, and the government payments on wool and mohair reached a fifth of a billion dollars over the first half-century of the program. No doubt the Clinton-era end of these subsidies in 1995 endangered national security. Thanks to Senator Phil Gramm, a well-known fiscal conservative, and other patriots (primarily from Texas, where much mohair is produced), Congress resurrected the program in 2000. Representative Lamar Smith took vehement exception to people who questioned the need for the mohair program: "Mohair is popular! I have a mohair sweater! It's my favorite one!" The 2006 budget called for $11 million for wool and mohair with a loan rate of $4.20 per pound. Again in 2011, the program was ended as a cost-cutting measure. However, Congress restored the wool and mohair program in 2012, and the 2014 agricultural bill extended it at least through 2018. The House version of the 2018 farm bill extends it beyond 2018.

[12]The support or target price has increased slowly over time. It was $5.02 in 1985 and $6.00 in 2010–2012. The 2014 Farm Bill set the rate at $8.40 for 2014–2018.

[13]This measure of deadweight loss underestimates the true loss. The government also pays storage and administration costs. In 2018, the USDA had roughly 100,000 employees, or about 1 employee for every 8.2 farms that received assistance, although many of these employees had other job responsibilities (**www.downsizinggovernment.org/agriculture/subsidies; www.usda.gov/our-agency**).

Figure 9.5 Effect of Price Supports in Soybeans

Without government price supports, the equilibrium is *e*, where $p_1 = \$4.59$ per bushel and $Q_1 = 2.1$ billion bushels of soybeans per year (based on estimates in Holt, 1992). With the price support at $\underline{p} = \$5.00$ per bushel, output sold increases to Q_s and consumer purchases fall to Q_d, so the government must buy $Q_g = Q_s - Q_d$ at a cost of \$1.283 billion per year. The deadweight loss is $C + F + G = \$1.226$ billion per year, not counting storage and administrative costs.

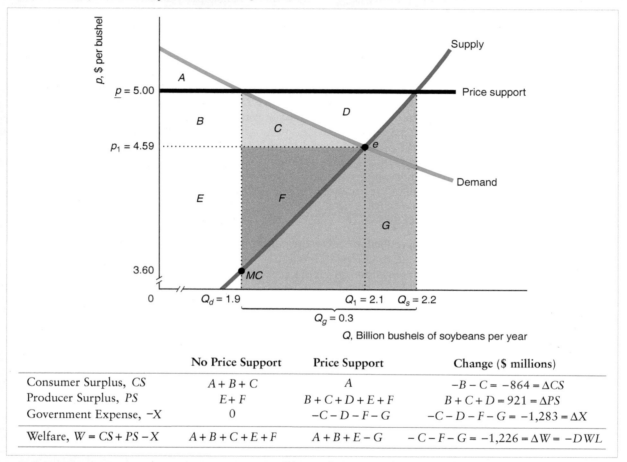

	No Price Support	Price Support	Change (\$ millions)
Consumer Surplus, *CS*	$A + B + C$	A	$-B - C = -864 = \Delta CS$
Producer Surplus, *PS*	$E + F$	$B + C + D + E + F$	$B + C + D = 921 = \Delta PS$
Government Expense, $-X$	0	$-C - D - F - G$	$-C - D - F - G = -1{,}283 = \Delta X$
Welfare, $W = CS + PS - X$	$A + B + C + E + F$	$A + B + E - G$	$-C - F - G = -1{,}226 = \Delta W = -DWL$

Unintended Consequences The traditional agricultural price support program caused excess production, raised the price, and reduced consumer surplus and welfare.

Alternative Price Support. Because of price supports, the government was buying and storing large quantities of food, much of which was allowed to spoil. Consequently, the government started limiting the amount farmers could produce. Because the government is uncertain about how much farmers will produce, it sets quotas or limits on the amount of land farmers may use, so as to restrict their output. Today, the government uses an alternative price support program. The government sets a support price, $\underline{p}$. Farmers decide how much to grow and sell all of their produce to consumers at the price, *p*, that clears the market. The government then gives the farmers a *deficiency payment* equal to the difference between the support and actual prices, $\underline{p} - p$, for every unit sold, so that farmers receive the support price on their entire crop.[14]

SOLVED PROBLEM 9.3	What are the effects in the soybean market of a $5-per-bushel deficiency-payment price support on the equilibrium price and quantity, consumer surplus, producer surplus, and deadweight loss?
MyLab Economics Solved Problem	**Answer**

1. *Describe how the program affects the equilibrium price and quantity.* Without a price support, the equilibrium is e_1 in the figure, where the price is $p_1 = \$4.59$ and the quantity is 2.1 billion bushels per year. With a support price of $5 per bushel, the new equilibrium is e_2. Farmers produce at the quantity where the price support line hits their supply curve at 2.2 billion bushels. The equilibrium price is the height of the demand curve at 2.2 billion bushels, or approximately $4.39 per bushel. Thus, the equilibrium price falls and the quantity increases.

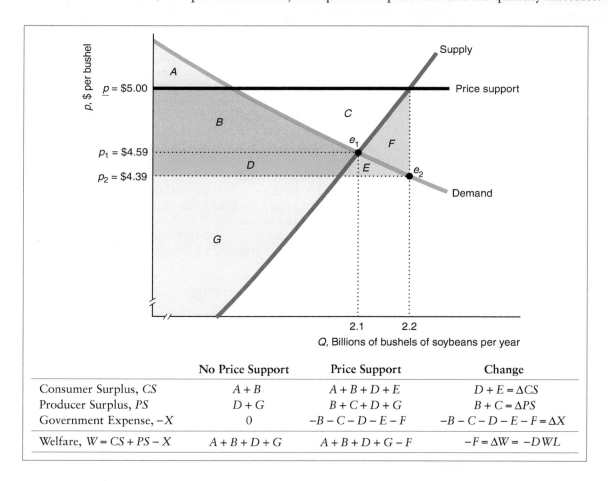

	No Price Support	Price Support	Change
Consumer Surplus, *CS*	$A + B$	$A + B + D + E$	$D + E = \Delta CS$
Producer Surplus, *PS*	$D + G$	$B + C + D + G$	$B + C = \Delta PS$
Government Expense, $-X$	0	$-B - C - D - E - F$	$-B - C - D - E - F = \Delta X$
Welfare, $W = CS + PS - X$	$A + B + D + G$	$A + B + D + G - F$	$-F = \Delta W = -DWL$

---

[14]The 2014 and 2018 Farm Bills expand the government's crop insurance programs, providing farmers with protection against low prices and low revenue. Farmers have a choice between three support programs.

2. *Show the welfare effects.* Because the price consumers pay drops from p_1 to p_2, consumer surplus rises by area $D + E$. Producers now receive $\underline{p}$ instead of p_1, so their producer surplus rises by $B + C$. Government payments are the difference between the support price, $\underline{p} = \$5$, and the price consumers pay, $p_2 = \$4.39$, times the number of units sold, 2.2 billion bushels per year, or the rectangle $B + C + D + E + F$. Because government expenditures exceed the gains to consumers and producers, welfare falls by the deadweight loss triangle F. Compared to the equivalent "buy-and-store" soybean price support program in Figure 9.5, the deficiency payment approach results in a smaller deadweight loss (less than a tenth of the original one) and lower government expenditures (though the expenditures need not be smaller in general).

APPLICATION

How Big Are Farm Subsidies and Who Gets Them?

Amount the EU paid to businessmen in Serbia–Montenegro for sugar subsidies before realizing that there was no sugar industry there: $1.2 million.
—Harper's Index, 2004

Virtually every country in the world showers its farmers with subsidies. Although government support to farmers has fallen in developed countries over the past decade, support remains high. Farmers in developed countries received $317 billion in agricultural producer support payments (subsidies) in 2015–2017.

These payments were 18% of actual farm sales in developed countries in 2017. The percentage of subsidies ranged from 53% in Norway, 51% in Switzerland, 49% in Japan, 18% in the European Union, 10% in Canada and the United States, 1.7% in Australia, 0.7% in New Zealand, to 2.3% in Vietnam.

In 2017, total U.S. agricultural support payments were $97 billion, or 0.5% of the U.S. gross domestic product. Each adult in the United States pays $387 a year to support agriculture. Did you get full value for your money? The 2018 Farm Bill is forecast to lower these outlays slightly.

The lion's share of U.S. farm subsidies goes to large agricultural corporations, not to poor farmers. According to the Environmental Working Group, 77% of the payments go to the largest and wealthiest 10% of farm operations and landlords, while nearly two-thirds of farmers receive no direct payments. Indeed, 33 members of Congress received payments of at least $15.3 million between 1995 and 2016.[15]

Welfare Effects of a Price Ceiling

In some markets, the government sets a *price ceiling*: the highest price that a firm can legally charge. If the government sets the ceiling below the unregulated competitive price, consumers demand more than the unregulated equilibrium quantity and firms supply less than that quantity (Chapter 2). Producer surplus must fall because firms receive a lower price and sell fewer units.

As a result of the price ceiling, consumers buy the good at a lower price but are limited in how much they can buy by sellers. Because less is sold than at the pre-control equilibrium, society suffers a deadweight loss: Consumers value the good more than the marginal cost of producing extra units.

This measure of the deadweight loss may *underestimate* the true loss for two reasons. First, because consumers want to buy more units than are sold, they may spend additional time searching for a store with units for sale. This (often unsuccessful) search activity is wasteful and thus an additional deadweight loss to society. Deacon and

---

[15]A farm owned in part by Representative Doug LaMalfa, a member of the House Agriculture Committee, received at least $5.3 million in farm subsidies between 1995 and 2016.

Sonstelie (1989) calculated that for every $1 consumers saved from lower prices due to U.S. gasoline price controls in 1973, they lost $1.16 in waiting time and other factors.[16]

Second, when a price ceiling creates excess demand, the customers who are lucky enough to buy the good may not be the consumers who value it most. In a market without a price ceiling, all consumers who value the good more than the market price buy it, and those who value it less do not, so that those consumers who value it most buy the good. In contrast with a price control whereby the good is sold on a first-come, first-served basis, the consumers who reach the store first may not be the consumers with the highest willingness to pay. With a price control, if a lucky customer who buys a unit of the good has a willingness to pay of p_0, while someone who cannot buy it has a willingness to pay of $p_1 > p_0$, then the *allocative inefficiency* of this unit being sold to the "wrong" consumer is $p_1 - p_0$.[17]

SOLVED PROBLEM 9.4

MyLab Economics Solved Problem

What is the effect on the equilibrium, consumer surplus, producer surplus, and welfare if the government sets a price ceiling, $\bar{p}$, below the unregulated competitive equilibrium price?

Answer

1. *Show the initial unregulated equilibrium.* The intersection of the demand curve and the supply curve determines the unregulated, competitive equilibrium e_1, where the equilibrium quantity is Q_1.

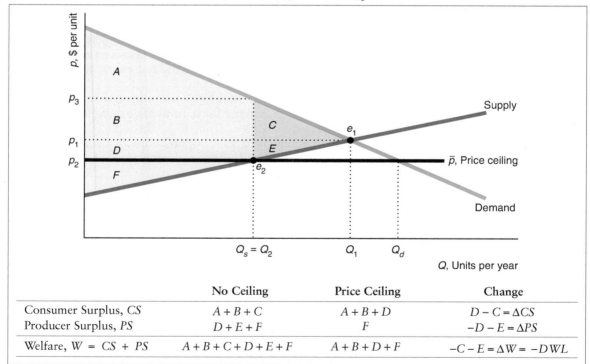

	No Ceiling	Price Ceiling	Change
Consumer Surplus, CS	$A + B + C$	$A + B + D$	$D - C = \Delta CS$
Producer Surplus, PS	$D + E + F$	F	$-D - E = \Delta PS$
Welfare, $W = CS + PS$	$A + B + C + D + E + F$	$A + B + D + F$	$-C - E = \Delta W = -DWL$

---

[16]This type of wasteful search does not occur if the good is efficiently but inequitably distributed to people according to a discriminatory criterion such as race, gender, or attractiveness because people who are suffering discrimination know it is pointless to search.

[17] This allocative cost will be reduced or eliminated with a resale market where consumers who place a high value on the good can buy it from consumers who place a lower value on the good but were lucky enough to be able to buy it initially.

2. *Show how the equilibrium changes with the price ceiling.* Because the price ceiling, $\bar{p}$, is set below the equilibrium price of p_1, the ceiling binds. At this lower price, consumer demand increases to Q_d while the quantity that firms are willing to supply falls to Q_s, so only $Q_s = Q_2$ units are sold at the new equilibrium, e_2. Thus, the price control causes the equilibrium quantity and price to fall, but consumers have excess demand of $Q_d - Q_s$.

3. *Describe the welfare effects.* Because consumers are able to buy Q_s units at a lower price than before the controls, they gain area D. Consumers lose consumer surplus of C, however, because they can purchase only Q_s instead of Q_1 units of output. Thus, consumers gain net consumer surplus of $D - C$. Because they sell fewer units at a lower price, firms lose producer surplus $-D - E$. Part of this loss, D, is transferred to consumers in the form of lower prices, but the rest, E, is a loss to society. The change in our usual welfare measure is $\Delta W = \Delta CS + \Delta PS = -C - E$. The total deadweight loss to society is $C + E$ plus any additional allocation cost to consumers.

APPLICATION

The Social Cost of a Natural Gas Price Ceiling

From 1954 through 1989, U.S. federal law imposed a price ceiling on interstate sales of natural gas. The law did not apply to sales within states in the Southwest that produced the gas—primarily Louisiana, Oklahoma, New Mexico, and Texas. Consequently, consumers in the Midwest and Northeast, where most of the gas was used, were less likely to be able to buy as much natural gas as they wanted, unlike consumers in the Southwest. Because they could not buy natural gas, some consumers who would have otherwise done so did not install natural gas heating. As heating systems last for years, even today, many homes use dirtier fuels such as heating oil due to this decades-old price control.

By comparing consumer behavior before and after the regulated period, Davis and Kilian (2011) estimated that demand for natural gas exceeded observed sales of natural gas by an average of 19.4% from 1950 through 2000. They calculated that the allocative cost averaged $3.6 billion annually during this half century. This additional loss was a third of the estimated annual deadweight loss from the price control of $10.5 billion (MacAvoy, 2000). The total loss was $14.1 (= $10.5 + $3.6) billion.[18]

9.6 Comparing Both Types of Policies: Trade

Traditionally, most of the United States' imports come from overseas.

We have examined examples of government policies that shift supply curves and policies that create a wedge between supply and demand. Governments use both types of policies to control international trade.

Allowing imports of foreign goods benefits the importing country. If a government reduces imports of a good, the domestic price rises; the profits increase for domestic

---

[18]Consumers' share of the deadweight loss, area C in the figure in Solved Problem 9.4, is $9.3 billion annually; the sellers' share, area E, is $1.2 billion; so the entire deadweight loss is $10.5 billion. Consumers who are lucky enough to buy the gas gain area $D = $6.9 billion from paying a lower price, which represents a transfer from sellers. Thus, altogether consumers lose $7.0 (= $9.3 + $4.6 − $6.9) billion and firms lose $8.1 (= $1.2 + $6.9) billion.

firms that produce the good but domestic consumers are hurt. Our analysis will show that the loss to consumers exceeds the gain to producers.

The government of the (potentially) importing country can use one of four trade policies:

1. **Allow free trade:** Any firm can sell in the importing country without restrictions.
2. **Ban all imports:** The government sets a quota of zero on imports.
3. **Set a tariff:** The government imposes a tax called a **tariff** (or a *duty*) only on imported goods.
4. **Set a positive quota:** The government limits imports to $\overline{Q}$.

We compare welfare under free trade to welfare under bans and quotas, which change the supply curve, and to welfare under tariffs, which create a wedge between supply and demand.

To illustrate the differences in welfare under these various policies, we examine the U.S. market for crude oil. We also assume, for the sake of simplicity, that transportation costs are zero and that the supply curve of the potentially imported good is horizontal at the world price. Given these two assumptions, the importing country, the United States, can buy as much of this good as it wants at the world price: It is a price taker in the world market because its demand is too small to influence the world price.

Free Trade Versus a Ban on Imports

No nation was ever ruined by trade. —Benjamin Franklin

Preventing imports raises the domestic market price. We now compare the equilibrium with and without free trade in the U.S. crude oil market.

The estimated U.S. daily demand function for oil is[19]

$$Q = D(p) = 48.71p^{-0.25}, \tag{9.3}$$

and the U.S. daily domestic supply function is

$$Q = S(p) = 3.45p^{0.25}. \tag{9.4}$$

Although the estimated U.S. domestic supply curve, S^a, in Figure 9.6 is upward sloping, the foreign supply curve is horizontal at the world price of $60. The total U.S. supply curve, S^1, is the horizontal sum of the domestic supply curve and the foreign supply curve. Thus, S^1 is the same as the upward-sloping domestic supply curve for prices below $60 and is horizontal at $60. Under free trade, the United States imports crude oil if its domestic price in the absence of imports would exceed the world price, $60 per barrel.

The intersection of S^1 and the demand curve determines the free-trade equilibrium, e_1, where the U.S. price equals the world price, $60. U.S. consumers demand 17.5 million barrels per day at that price. Because domestic firms produce only 9.6 million barrels, imports are $17.5 - 9.6 = 7.9$ million barrels per day.[20] U.S. consumer surplus is $A + B + C$, U.S. producer surplus is D, and U.S. welfare is $A + B + C + D$. Throughout our discussion of trade, we ignore welfare effects in other countries.

---

[19]These constant-elasticity supply and demand equations for crude oil are based on Baumeister and Peersman (2013), with rounding and updating using 2015 production and import data.

[20] Substituting $p = \$60$ into demand function in Equation 9.3, we find that the equilibrium quantity is $48.71(60^{-0.25}) \approx 17.5$ million barrels per day. At the equilibrium price of $60, domestic supply is $3.45(60^{0.25}) \approx 9.6$ million barrels per day.

Figure 9.6 Loss from Eliminating Free Trade

Because the supply curve that foreigners face is horizontal at the world price of $60, the total U.S. supply curve of crude oil is S^1 with free trade. The free-trade equilibrium is e_1. With a ban on imports, the equilibrium e_2 occurs where the domestic supply curve, $S^a = S^2$, intersects the demand curve. The ban increases producer surplus by $B = \$1{,}606$ million per day and decreases consumer surplus by $B + C = \$2{,}045$ million per day, so the deadweight loss is $C = \$439$ million per day or about $160 billion per year.

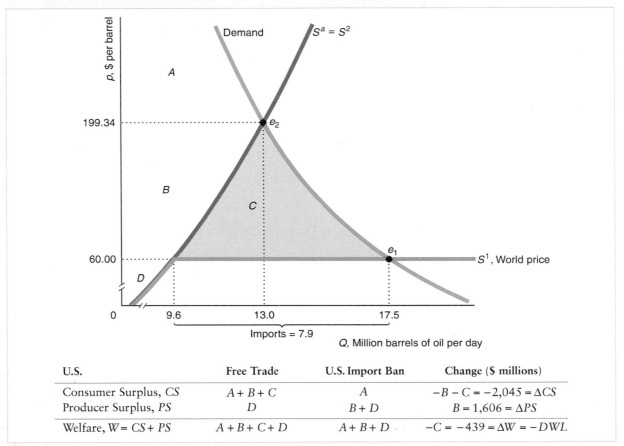

U.S.	Free Trade	U.S. Import Ban	Change ($ millions)
Consumer Surplus, CS	$A + B + C$	A	$-B - C = -2{,}045 = \Delta CS$
Producer Surplus, PS	D	$B + D$	$B = 1{,}606 = \Delta PS$
Welfare, $W = CS + PS$	$A + B + C + D$	$A + B + D$	$-C = -439 = \Delta W = -DWL$

If the U.S. government were to ban imports, the total U.S. supply curve, S^2, is the American domestic supply curve, S^a. The intersection of S^2 and the demand curve determines the no-trade equilibrium at e_2, where the equilibrium price is $199.34 and the quantity is 13.0.[21] Consumer surplus is only A, producer surplus is $B + D$, and welfare is $A + B + D$.

Thus, the ban helps producers but harms consumers. Because of the higher price, domestic firms gain producer surplus of $\Delta PS = B$. The change in consumer surplus is $\Delta CS = -B - C$. The change in total welfare, ΔW, is the difference between the gain to producers and the loss to consumers, $\Delta W = \Delta PS + \Delta CS = -C$, so the ban hurts society.

---

[21]Setting the right sides of Equations 9.3 and 9.4 equal, $48.71p^{-0.25} = 3.45p^{0.25}$, and solving for p, we find that the no-trade equilibrium price is about $199.34. Substituting $199.34 into Equation 9.3, we find that $Q = 48.71(199.34^{-0.25}) \approx 13.0$.

SOLVED PROBLEM 9.5

MyLab Economics
Solved Problem

Based on the estimates of the U.S. daily oil demand function in Equation 9.3 and the supply function in Equation 9.4, use calculus to determine the changes in producer surplus, consumer surplus, and welfare from eliminating free trade. (Round to the nearest million dollar.)

Answer

1. *Integrate the supply function with respect to price between the free-trade and no-trade prices to obtain the change in producer surplus.* If imports are banned, the gain in domestic producer surplus is the area to the left of the domestic supply curve between the free-trade price, $60, and the price with the ban in effect, $199.34, which is area *B* in Figure 9.6.[22] Integrating, we find that

$$\Delta PS = \int_{60}^{199.34} S(p)\,dp = \int_{60}^{199.34} 3.45 p^{0.25}\,dp = \left.\frac{3.45}{1.25} p^{1.25}\right|_{60}^{199.34}$$
$$= 2.76(199.34^{1.25} - 60^{1.25}) \approx 1{,}606.$$

2. *Integrate with respect to price between the free-trade and no-trade prices to obtain the change in consumer surplus.* To determine the lost consumer surplus, we integrate to the left of the demand curve between the relevant prices:

$$\Delta CS = -\int_{60}^{199.34} D(p)\,dp = -\int_{60}^{199.34} 48.71 p^{-0.25} = \left.-\frac{48.71}{0.75} p^{0.75}\right|_{60}^{199.34}$$
$$\approx 64.95(199.34^{0.75} - 60^{0.75}) \approx -2{,}045.$$

3. *To determine the change in welfare, sum the changes in consumer surplus and producer surplus.* The change in welfare is $\Delta W = \Delta CS + \Delta PS = -2{,}045 + 1{,}606 = -\$439$ million per day or about –$160 billion per year. This deadweight loss is 27% of the gain to producers: Consumers lose $1.27 for every $1 that producers gain from a ban.

APPLICATION

Russian Food Ban

Starting in 2014, many Western nations imposed a variety of sanctions on Russia because of its military activities in Ukraine. In retaliation, Russia banned imports of many agricultural products from the United States, the European Union, Canada, and other countries.

Russians, particularly in prosperous cities such as Moscow, depend heavily on imported foods from the West. The previous year, 2013, Russian agricultural imports were about $1 billion from the United States and 11.8 billion euros ($15.7 billion) from the European Union.

The ban imposes substantial costs on Russian consumers. In 2014, food prices soared 11.5%, which was 5.8% higher than the overall inflation rate. Prices for some types of food shot up by even more. Meat and poultry prices rose 18%

---

[22]In Section 9.2, we noted that we can also calculate the producer surplus by integrating below the price, above the supply (or marginal cost) function, up to the relevant quantity.

over the previous year, while the price of butter shot up by 17%. In early 2015, the Russian finance minister said that Russia's losses from the Western sanction were $50 billion. The ban had less of an effect on firms in exporting nations, which could sell their products elsewhere.

Of course, Russian food-producing firms benefited. For example, in the first quarter after the ban went into effect, the profit of Cherkizovo, a Russian producer of meat, rose eight-fold from the previous year. In 2017, the Agriculture Ministry said that during the past three years, food imports fell from $42 billion to $25 billion, while Russian agricultural production rose by 11%. The ban is scheduled to stay in effect at least until the end of 2019.

Free Trade Versus a Tariff

TARIFF, n. A scale of taxes on imports, designed to protect the domestic producer against the greed of his customers. —Ambrose Bierce

Governments use *specific tariffs* (t dollars per unit) and *ad valorem tariffs* (α percent of the sales price). Governments around the world use tariffs, particularly on agricultural products.[23] American policymakers have frequently debated the optimal tariff on crude oil as a way to raise revenue or to reduce dependence on foreign oil.

You may be asking yourself, "Why should we study tariffs if we've already looked at taxes? Isn't a tariff just another tax?" Good point! Tariffs are just taxes. If the only goods sold in the market were imported, the effect of a tariff in the importing country would be the same as for a sales tax. We study tariffs separately because a government applies a tariff to only imported goods, so it affects domestic and foreign producers differently. Because tariffs apply to only imported goods, all else the same, they do not raise as much tax revenue or affect equilibrium quantities as much as taxes applied to all goods in a market.

To illustrate the effect of a tariff clearly in our figures, we suppose that the U.S. government imposes a large specific tariff of $t = \$40$ per barrel of crude oil. Consequently, firms import oil into the United States only if the U.S. price is at least $40 above the world price. The tariff creates a wedge between the world price, $60, and the U.S. price, $100. The tariff shifts the U.S. total supply curve upward from S^1 to S^3 in Figure 9.7 so that S^3 equals the domestic supply curve for prices below $100 and is horizontal at $100.

In the new equilibrium, e_3, where S^3 intersects the demand curve, the equilibrium price is $100 and the quantity is 15.4 million barrels of oil per day. Domestic firms supply 10.9 million barrels, so imports are 4.5.

The tariff *protects* American producers from foreign competition. The larger the tariff, the fewer the imports, and hence the higher the price that domestic firms can charge. (With a large enough tariff, firms import nothing and the price rises to the no-trade level, $199.34.) With a tariff of $40, domestic firms' producer surplus increases by area $B = \$412$ million per day.

---

[23]After World War II, most trading nations signed the General Agreement on Tariffs and Trade (GATT), which limited their ability to subsidize exports or limit imports using quotas and tariffs. The rules prohibited most export subsidies and import quotas, except when imports threatened "market disruption" (a term that unfortunately was not defined). The GATT also required that any new tariff be offset by a reduction in other tariffs to compensate the exporting country. Modifications of the GATT and agreements negotiated by its successor, the World Trade Organization, have reduced or eliminated many tariffs.

Figure 9.7 Effect of a Tariff (or Quota)

A tariff of $t = \$40$ per barrel of oil imported or a quota of $Q = 3.4$ million barrels per day drives the U.S. price of crude oil to \$100, which is \$40 more than the world price of \$60. Under the tariff, the intersection of the S^3 total U.S. supply curve and the demand curve determines the equilibrium, e_3. Under the quota, e_3 is determined by a quantity wedge of 4.5 million barrels per day between the quantity demanded, 15.4 million barrels per day, and the quantity supplied, 10.9 million barrels per day. Compared to free trade, producers gain $B = \$412$ million per day and consumers lose $B + C + D + E = \$654$ million per day from the tariff or quota. The deadweight loss under the quota is $C + D + E = \$242$ million per day. With a tariff, the government's tariff revenue increases by $D = \$180$ million a day, so the deadweight loss is "only" $C + E = \$62$ million per day.

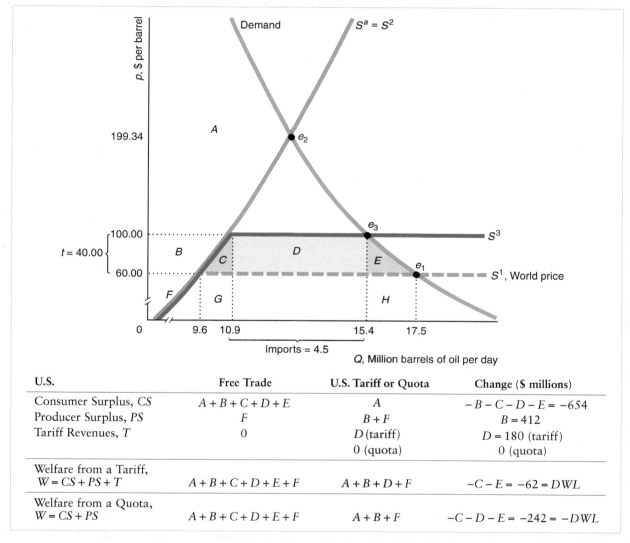

U.S.	Free Trade	U.S. Tariff or Quota	Change (\$ millions)
Consumer Surplus, CS	$A + B + C + D + E$	A	$-B - C - D - E = -654$
Producer Surplus, PS	F	$B + F$	$B = 412$
Tariff Revenues, T	0	D (tariff) 0 (quota)	$D = 180$ (tariff) 0 (quota)
Welfare from a Tariff, $W = CS + PS + T$	$A + B + C + D + E + F$	$A + B + D + F$	$-C - E = -62 = DWL$
Welfare from a Quota, $W = CS + PS$	$A + B + C + D + E + F$	$A + B + F$	$-C - D - E = -242 = -DWL$

Because the U.S. price rises from \$60 to \$100, consumer surplus falls by $B + C + D + E = \$654$ million per day. The government receives tariff revenues, T, equal to area $D = \$180$ million per day, which is $t = \$40$ times the quantity imported, 4.5 million.

The deadweight loss is the loss of consumer surplus, $B + C + D + E$, minus the tax revenue, D, minus the producer surplus gain, B. That is, the deadweight loss is $C + E = \$62$ million per day, or $22.6 billion per year. This deadweight loss is 15% of the gain to producers. Consumers lose $1.59 for each $1 that domestic producers gain. Because the tariff does not eliminate all imports, the welfare loss is smaller than from an import ban.

This deadweight loss has two components. First, C is a loss due to *cost inefficiency*: U.S. firms produce 10.9 million barrels per day instead of 9.6 million barrels per day at greater cost than this extra output could be purchased at the world price. Domestic firms produce this extra output because the tariff drives up the price from $60 to $100. The cost of producing these extra 1.3 million barrels of oil per day domestically is $C + G$, the area under the domestic supply curve, S^a, between 9.6 and 10.9. Had Americans bought this oil at the world price, the cost would have been only G. Thus, C is the additional cost of producing the extra 1.3 million barrels of oil per day domestically instead of importing it.

Second, E is a loss due to *allocative inefficiency* from U.S. consumers' buying too little oil, 15.4 instead of 17.5 million barrels, because the tariff increases the price from $60 to $100.[24] U.S. consumers place a value on this extra output of $E + H$, the area under their demand curve between 15.4 and 17.5. The cost of buying this extra oil from the world market is only H, the area below the line at $60 between 15.4 and 17.5. Thus, E is the difference between the value at the world price and the value U.S. consumers place on this extra 2.1 million barrels per day.

Thus, a government's use of a tariff to protect domestic producers harms consumers and the economy:

Unintended Consequences Tariffs cause cost and allocative inefficiencies, raising the price and reducing consumer surplus and welfare.

SOLVED PROBLEM 9.6

MyLab Economics
Solved Problem

Based on the estimates of the U.S. daily oil demand function in Equation 9.3, the supply function in Equation 9.4, and the preceding discussion, use calculus to determine the change in equilibrium quantity, the amount supplied by domestic firms, and their producer surplus from a marginal increase in a tariff, evaluated where the tariff is initially zero.

Answer

1. *Discuss the effect of the tariff on the U.S. equilibrium quantity and on the domestic supply of oil at the free-trade equilibrium.* Without the tariff, the U.S. supply curve of oil is horizontal at a price of $60 ($S^1$ in Figure 9.7), and the equilibrium is determined by the intersection of this horizontal supply curve with the demand curve. With a new, small tariff of t, the U.S. supply curve is horizontal at $60 + t$, and the new equilibrium quantity is determined by substituting $p = 60 + t$ into the demand function in Equation 9.3, $Q = 48.71(60 + t)^{-0.25}$. The domestic supply is determined by substituting $60 + t$ into the U.S. supply function in Equation 9.4, $Q = 3.45(\$60 + t)^{0.25}$. Evaluated at $t = 0$, the equilibrium quantity remains at the free-trade level, 17.5, and the domestic supply is 9.6 million barrels of oil per day.

---

[24]This analysis ignores the effect of oil consumption on the environment. We address that issue in Chapter 17.

2. *Differentiate the expression for producer surplus with respect to t and evaluate at* $t = 0$. The producer surplus is the area below \$60 and to the left of the supply curve (area $B + F$ in Figure 9.7):

$$PS = \int_0^{60+t} S(p)dp = \int_0^{60+t} 3.45p^{0.25}dp.$$

To see how a change in t affects producer surplus, we differentiate PS with respect to t:[25]

$$\frac{dPS}{dt} = \frac{d}{dt}\int_0^{60+t} S(p)dp = S(60 + t)$$

$$= \frac{d}{dt}\int_0^{60+t} 3.45p^{0.25}dp = 3.45(60 + t)^{0.25}.$$

If we evaluate this expression at $t = 0$, we find that $dPS/dt = S(60) = 3.45(60)^{0.25} \approx \$9.6$ million per day. Equivalently, $dPS = S(60 + t)dt$. If $dt = 1¢$, then the change in producer surplus is about \$96,000 per day.

A Tariff Versus a Quota

Many countries use quotas instead of tariffs, which may lead to a false belief:

Common Confusion Quotas are preferable to tariffs.

Although politicians have a variety of reasons to prefer quotas, countries usually benefit from employing a tariff rather than an equivalent quota—that reduces imports by the same amount—because only the tariff produces revenue for the government. Of course, countries would generally be better off using neither.

The market effects of a quota are similar to those of a tariff. In Figure 9.7, if the government limits imports to $\overline{Q} = 4.5$ million barrels per day, the quota is binding because firms import 7.9 million barrels per day under free trade. This quota on imports of 4.5 million barrels leads to the same equilibrium, e_3 in Figure 9.7, as a tariff of \$40. Given this binding quota, the equilibrium price is \$100, and the quantity demanded, 15.4 million barrels per day, minus the quantity supplied by domestic producers, 10.9 million barrels per day, equals the quantity imported, 4.5 million barrels per day.

The gain to domestic producers, B, and the loss to consumers, $B + C + D + E$, are the same as those with a tariff. However, unlike with a tariff, the government does not receive any revenue when it uses a quota (unless the government sells import licenses). Thus, the deadweight loss with this quota, $C + D + E = \$242$ million per day, is greater than the deadweight loss with the equivalent \$40 tariff, $C + E = \$62$ million

---

[25]We are using Leibniz's rule for differentiating a definite integral. According to Leibniz's rule,

$$\frac{d}{dt}\int_{a(t)}^{b(t)} f(t, p)dp = \int_{a(t)}^{b(t)} \frac{\partial f(t, p)}{\partial t}dp + f[t, b(t)]\frac{db(t)}{dt} - f[t, a(t)]\frac{da(t)}{dt}.$$

In our problem, neither a nor f is a function of t and $db(t)/dt = d(60 + t)dt = 1$.

per day. The extra deadweight loss from using the quota instead of a tariff is the forgone government tariff revenues, $D = \$180$ million per day. Under the quota, D may go to foreign exporters.

Thus, the importing country fares better using a tariff than setting a quota that reduces imports by the same amount. Consumers and domestic firms do as well under the two policies, but the government gains tariff revenues, D, only when the tariff is used.

However, if the government gives the quota licenses to domestic importing firms, then the United States does not lose D. Similarly, if the government sells the quota licenses to firms at a price equal to the tariff, then the government gets D.

Rent Seeking

Given that tariffs and quotas hurt the importing country, why do the Japanese, U.S., and other governments impose tariffs, quotas, or other trade barriers? The reason is that domestic producers stand to make large gains from such government actions, so the producers lobby the government to enact these trade policies. Although consumers as a whole suffer large losses, the loss to any one consumer is usually small. Moreover, consumers rarely organize to lobby the government about trade issues. Thus, in most countries, producers are often able to convince (cajole, influence, or bribe) legislators or government officials to aid them, even though the loss to consumers exceeds the gain to domestic producers.

If domestic producers can talk the government into a tariff, quota, or other policy that reduces imports, they gain extra producer surplus (rents), such as area B in Figure 9.7. Economists call efforts and expenditures to gain a rent or a profit from government actions **rent seeking**. If producers or other interest groups bribe legislators to influence policy, the bribe is a transfer of income and hence does not increase deadweight loss (except to the degree that a harmful policy is chosen). However, if this rent-seeking behavior—such as hiring lobbyists and engaging in advertising to influence legislators—uses up resources, the deadweight loss from tariffs and quotas understates the true loss to society. The domestic producers may spend an amount up to the gain in producer surplus to influence the government.[26]

Indeed, some economists contend that the government revenues from tariffs are completely offset by administrative costs and rent-seeking behavior. If so—and if the tariffs and quotas do not affect world prices—the loss to society from tariffs and quotas equals the entire change in consumer surplus, such as area $B + C + D + E$ in Figure 9.7.

Lopez and Pagoulatos (1994) estimated the deadweight loss and the additional losses due to rent-seeking activities in the United States in food and tobacco products. They estimated that the deadweight loss was $18.3 billion (in 2015 dollars), which was 2.6% of the domestic consumption of these products. The largest deadweight losses were in milk products and sugar manufacturing, which primarily use import quotas to raise domestic prices. The gain in producer surplus is $66.2 billion, or 9.5% of domestic consumption. The government obtained $2.7 billion in tariff revenues, or 0.4% of consumption. If all of producer surplus and government revenues were expended in rent-seeking behavior and other wasteful activities, the total loss would be $68.9 billion, or 12.5% of consumption, which is 4.75 times larger than the deadweight loss alone. In other words, the loss to society is somewhere between the deadweight loss of $18.3 billion and $87.2 billion.

---

[26]This argument was made in Tullock (1967) and Posner (1975). Fisher (1985) and Varian (1989) argued that the expenditure is typically less than the producer surplus.

CHALLENGE SOLUTION

Liquor Licenses

We can now answer the Challenge questions from the beginning of the chapter: What effect does setting a quota on the number of liquor licenses have on the price of meals (including liquor)? What determines the value of a license? How much profit beyond the cost of the license can a restaurant earn? Who benefits and who loses from limiting the number of liquor licenses?

By limiting the number of liquor licenses, the government causes the supply curve of restaurant meals to shift to the left, or become steeper. As a result, the equilibrium price of a meal rises and the equilibrium quantity falls. The quota harms consumers: They do not buy as much as they would at lower prices. Restaurants that are in the market when the government first imposes the limits benefit from higher profits.

For simplicity, we'll assume that all restaurants have identical costs and produce identical meals. Without a quota on the number of liquor licenses, a virtually unlimited number of potential restaurants could enter the market freely. Panel a of the figure shows a typical restaurant owner's marginal cost curve, MC, and average cost curve, AC^1. An increase in demand—a rightward shift of the demand curve—is met by new restaurants entering the market, so the long-run supply curve of restaurant meals, S^1 in panel b, is horizontal at the minimum of AC^1 (Chapter 8).

Given the market demand curve in the figure, the equilibrium is E_1, where the equilibrium price, p_1, equals the minimum of AC^1 of a typical restaurant. The total number of meals is $Q_1 = n_1 q_1$, where n_1 is the equilibrium number of restaurants and q_1 is the number of meals per month provided by a restaurant.

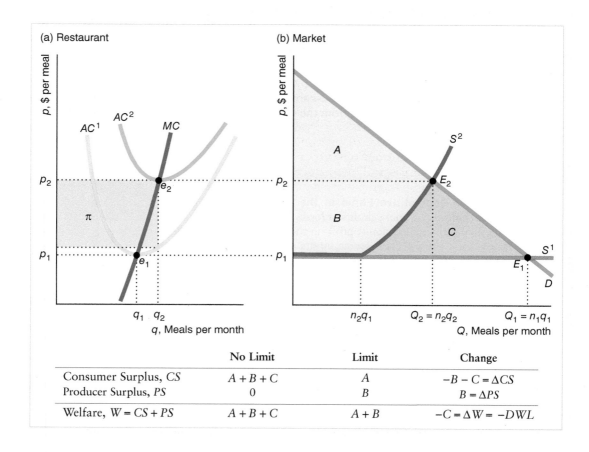

	No Limit	Limit	Change
Consumer Surplus, CS	$A + B + C$	A	$-B - C = \Delta CS$
Producer Surplus, PS	0	B	$B = \Delta PS$
Welfare, $W = CS + PS$	$A + B + C$	$A + B$	$-C = \Delta W = -DWL$

Consumer surplus, $A + B + C$, is the area under the market demand curve above p_1 up to Q_1. Restaurants receive no producer surplus because the supply curve is horizontal at the market price, which equals marginal and average cost. Thus, welfare is the same as consumer surplus.

The licensing quota limits the number of restaurants to $n_2 < n_1$. The market supply curve, S^2, is the horizontal sum of the marginal cost curves above the corresponding minimum average cost curves of the n_2 restaurants in the market. For the market to produce more than $n_2 q_1$ meals, the price must rise to induce the n_2 restaurants to supply more.

With the same demand curve as before, the equilibrium market price rises to p_2. At this higher price, each restaurant produces more meals, $q_2 > q_1$, but the total number of meals, $Q_2 = n_2 q_2$, falls because the number of restaurants, n_2, drops. Consumer surplus is A, producer surplus is B, and welfare is $A + B$.

Thus, because of the higher prices under a quota system, consumer surplus falls: $\Delta CS = -B - C$. The producer surplus of the lucky license holders rises by $\Delta PS = B$. As a result, total welfare falls,

$$\Delta W = \Delta CS + \Delta PS = (-B - C) + B = -C,$$

so the deadweight loss is C.

If a state prevents other restaurants from entering the market by limiting liquor licenses, it creates economic profit, the area labeled π in panel a, for each license holder. A license holder may sell the license, so the owner of the scarce resource—the license—can capture this unusual profit. The license sells at a price that captures the current value of all future profits. The government causes the license to have this value by creating an artificial scarcity of licenses.

The new owner's average cost rises to AC^2. Because the fee is a fixed cost that is unrelated to output, it does not affect the marginal cost. The new owner earns zero economic profits because the market price, p_2, equals the minimum of AC^2. The producer surplus, B, created by the limits on entry goes to the original owners of the licenses rather than to the current owners. Thus, the original license holders are the *only* ones who benefit from the restrictions, and their gains are less than the losses to others.

SUMMARY

1. **Zero Profit for Competitive Firms in the Long Run.** Although firms may make profits or losses in the short run, they earn zero economic profit in the long run. If necessary, the prices of scarce inputs adjust to ensure that competitive firms make zero long-run profit. Because profit-maximizing firms just break even in the long run, firms that do not try to maximize profits will lose money. Competitive firms must maximize profit to survive.

2. **Producer Surplus.** A firm's gain from trading is measured by its producer surplus. Producer surplus is the largest amount of money that could be taken from a firm's revenue and still leave the firm willing to produce. That is, the producer surplus is the amount that the firm is paid minus its variable cost of production, which is profit in the long run. It is the area below the price and above the supply curve up to the quantity that the firm sells. The effect of a change in price on a supplier is measured by the change in producer surplus, which equals the change in profit.

3. **Competition Maximizes Welfare.** A standard measure of welfare is the sum of consumer surplus and producer surplus. The more price exceeds marginal cost, the lower is this measure of welfare. In the competitive equilibrium, in which price equals marginal cost, welfare is maximized.

4. **Policies That Shift Supply or Demand Curves.** Government policies that shift supply or demand curves in perfectly competitive markets harm consumers and lower welfare. For example, governments frequently limit the number of firms in a market directly, by licensing them, or indirectly, by raising the costs of

entry to new firms or raising the cost of exiting. A reduction in the number of firms in a competitive market raises price, hurts consumers, helps producing firms, and lowers the standard measure of welfare. This reduction in welfare is a deadweight loss: The gain to producers is less than the loss to consumers.

5. **Policies That Create a Wedge Between Supply and Demand Curves.** Taxes and price floors create a gap between the price consumers pay and the price firms receive. These policies force price above marginal cost, which raises the price to consumers and lowers the amount sold. Price ceilings lower both the price and the amount sold. Each of these policies causes a deadweight loss: The reduction in total surplus that is not offset by increased taxes or by benefits to other groups.

6. **Comparing Both Types of Policies: Trade.** A government may use either a quantity restriction such as a quota, which shifts the supply curve, or a tariff, which creates a wedge, to reduce imports or achieve other goals. These policies may have different welfare implications. A tariff that reduces imports by the same amount as a quota has the same harms—a larger loss of consumer surplus than increased domestic producer surplus—but has a partially offsetting benefit—increased tariff revenues for the government. Rent-seeking activities are attempts by firms or individuals to influence a government to adopt a policy that favors them. By using up resources, rent seeking exacerbates the welfare loss beyond the deadweight loss caused by the policy itself. In a perfectly competitive market, government policies frequently lower welfare. As later chapters show, however, in markets that are not perfectly competitive, government policies may increase welfare.

EXERCISES

All exercises are available on MyLab Economics; * = *answer appears at the back of this book;* **M** = *mathematical problem.*

1. Zero Profit for Competitive Firms in the Long Run

1.1 Only a limited amount of high-quality, grape-growing land is available. The firms that farm the land are identical. Because the demand curve hits the market supply curve in its upward-sloping section, the firms initially earn positive profit.

   a. The owners of the land raise their rents to capture the profit. Show how the market supply curve changes (if at all).

   b. Suppose some firms own the land and some rent. Do these firms behave differently in terms of their shutdown decision or in any other way?

1.2 The reputations of some of the world's most prestigious museums have been damaged by accusations that they obtained antiquities that were looted or stolen in violation of international laws and treaties aimed at halting illicit trade in art and antiquities. A new wariness among private and public collectors to buy works whose provenance has not been rigorously established jeopardizes the business of even the most established dealers. Conversely, this fear has increased the value of antiquities that have a solid ownership history. The Aboutaam brothers, who are among the world's most powerful dealers of antiquities, back an international ban on trade in excavated antiquities. As Hicham Aboutaam said, "The more questionable works entering the antiquities market, the less their value and the larger the dark cloud that hangs over the field. That affects prices negatively. I think we could put an end to the new supply, and work comfortably with what we have."[27]

   a. What would be the effect of the ban on the current stock of antiquities for sale in the United States and Europe?

   b. Would such a ban differentially affect established dealers and new dealers?

   c. Why would established dealers back such a ban?

   d. Discuss the implications of a ban using the concept of an economic rent.

2. Producer Surplus

2.1 For a firm, how does the concept of *producer surplus* differ from that of *profit*?

2.2 If the supply curve is $q = 2 + 2p$, what is the producer surplus if the price is 10? **M**

2.3 If the supply function is $q = ap^\eta$, what is the producer surplus if price is p^*? (*Hint*: See Solved Problem 9.1.) **M**

3. Competition Maximizes Welfare

3.1 If society cared only about the well-being of consumers so that it wanted to maximize consumer surplus, would a competitive market achieve that goal given that the government cannot force or bribe firms to produce more than the competitive level of output? How would your answer change if society cared only about maximizing producer surplus?

[27]Ron Stodghill, "Do You Know Where That Art Has Been?" *New York Times*, March 18, 2007.

3.2 Suppose that the market demand function for 32-oz. wide-mouth Nalgene bottles is $Q = 50{,}000p^{-1.076}$, where Q is the quantity of bottles per week and p is the price per bottle. The market supply function is $Q = 0.01p^{7.208}$. What are the equilibrium price and quantity? What is the consumer surplus? What is the producer surplus? **M**

3.3 Suppose that the inverse market demand function for silicone replacement tips for Sony earbud headphones is $p = p_N - 0.1Q$, where p is the price per pair of replacement tips, p_N is the price of a new pair of headphones, and Q is the number of tips per week. Suppose that the inverse supply function of the replacement tips is $p = 2 + 0.012Q$.

   a. Find the effect of a change in the price of a new pair of headphones on the equilibrium price of replacement tips at the equilibrium, dp/dp_N.

   b. If $p_N = \$30$, what are the equilibrium p and Q? What is the consumer surplus? What is the producer surplus? **M**

3.4 Until recently, the U.S. Department of Agriculture's (USDA) minimum general recommendation has been to eat five servings of fruits and vegetables a day. Jetter, Chalfant, and Sumner (2004) estimated that if consumers followed that guideline, the equilibrium price and quantity of most fruits and vegetables would increase substantially. For example, the price of salad would rise 7.2%, output would increase 3.5%, and growers' revenues would jump 7.3% (presumably, health benefits would occur as well). Use a diagram to illustrate as many of these effects as possible and to show how consumer surplus and producer surplus change. Discuss how to calculate the consumer surplus (given that the USDA's recommendation shifts consumers' tastes or behavior).

3.5 Use an indifference curve diagram (gift goods on one axis and all other goods on the other) to illustrate that one is better off receiving cash than a gift. (*Hint*: See the discussion of gifts in this chapter and the discussion of food stamps in Chapter 5.) Relate your analysis to the Application "The Deadweight Loss of Christmas Presents."

3.6 The Application "Welfare Effects of Allowing Fracking" says that allowing fracking resulted in a loss in producer surplus and an increase in consumer surplus and welfare in the natural gas market. Illustrate these results in a figure.

4. Policies That Shift Supply or Demand Curves

4.1 The government imposes a restriction on firms that shifts the supply curve in Figure 9.3 so that it intersects the demand curve at e_2. Discuss the effects on CS, PS, welfare, and DWL.

4.2 The government forces firms to provide more output at each price so that the new supply curve in the figure in Solved Problem 9.2 intersects the demand curve at e_2. Discuss the effects on CS, PS, welfare, and DWL. (*Hint*: See Solved Problem 9.4.)

4.3 The park service wants to restrict the number of visitors to Yellowstone National Park to Q^*, which is fewer than the current volume. It considers two policies: (a) raising the price of admissions and (b) setting a quota. Compare the effects of these two policies on consumer surplus and welfare. Use a graph to show which policy is superior according to the welfare criterion.

5. Policies That Create a Wedge Between Supply and Demand Curves

5.1 If the inverse demand function for books is $p = 60 - q$ and the supply function is $q = p$, what is the initial equilibrium? What is the welfare effect of a specific tax of $t = \$2$ per unit on the equilibrium, CS, PS, welfare, and DWL? **M**

5.2 Suppose that the demand curve for wheat is $Q = 100 - 10p$ and that the supply curve is $Q = 10p$. What are the effects of a specific tax of $t = 1$ per unit on the equilibrium, government tax revenue, CS, PS, welfare, and DWL? **M**

5.3 The initial equilibrium is e, where the linear supply curve intersects the linear demand curve. Show the welfare effects of imposing a specific tax t. Now suppose the demand curve becomes flatter, but still goes through point e, so that it is more elastic at e than originally. Discuss how the tax affects the equilibrium, CS, PS, welfare, and DWL differently than with the original demand curve.

5.4 Suppose that the demand curve for wheat is $Q = 100 - 10p$ and that the supply curve is $Q = 10p$. What are the effects of a subsidy (negative tax) of $s = 1$ per unit on the equilibrium, government subsidy cost, CS, PS, welfare, and DWL? **M**

*5.5 Suppose that the government gives rose producers a specific subsidy of $s = 11¢$ per stem. (Figure 9.4 shows the original demand and supply curves.) What is the effect of the subsidy on the equilibrium prices and quantity, consumer surplus, producer surplus, government expenditures, welfare, and deadweight loss?

5.6 Suppose that the market demand function for cows is $Q = 1{,}000{,}000p^{-2}$, where Q is the number of cows per month and p is the price per cow. The market supply function is $Q = p$.

   a. What are the equilibrium price and quantity of cows? What is the consumer surplus, the producer surplus, and welfare?

   b. Now suppose that the government provides a subsidy of $\$100$ per cow. What are the new equilibrium price and quantity, the consumer surplus, the producer surplus, and welfare? Round your answers to whole numbers.

5.7 What is the welfare effect of an ad valorem sales tax, v, assessed on each competitive firm in a market?

*5.8 What is the long-run welfare effect of a profit tax (the government collects a specified percentage of a firm's profit) assessed on each competitive firm in a market?

*5.9 What is the welfare effect of a lump-sum tax, $\mathcal{L}$, assessed on each competitive firm in a market? (*Hint*: See the Challenge Solution in Chapter 8.)

5.10 The United States not only subsidizes producers of cotton (in several ways, including a water subsidy and a price support) but also pays $1.7 billion to U.S. agribusiness and manufacturers to buy American cotton. It has paid $100 million each to Allenberg Cotton and Dunavant Enterprises and large amounts to more than 300 other firms.[28] Assume for simplicity that specific subsidies (dollars per unit) are used. Use a diagram to show how applying both subsidies changes the equilibrium from the no-subsidy case. Show who gains and who loses.

*5.11 Suppose that the demand curve for wheat is $q = 100 - 10p$ and the supply curve is $q = 10p$. The government imposes a price support at $p = 6$ using a deficiency payment program.

    a. What is the quantity supplied, the price that clears the market, and the deficiency payment?

    b. What effect does this program have on consumer surplus, producer surplus, welfare, and deadweight loss? (*Hint*: See Solved Problem 9.3.) **M**

5.12 Suppose that the demand curve for wheat is $Q = 100 - 10p$ and the supply curve is $Q = 10p$. The government imposes a price ceiling of $p = 3$.

    a. Describe how the equilibrium changes.

    b. What effect does this ceiling have on consumer surplus, producer surplus, and deadweight loss? **M**

5.13 The government wants to drive the price of soybeans above the equilibrium price, p_1, to p_2. It offers growers a payment of x to reduce their output from Q_1 (the equilibrium level) to Q_2, which is the quantity demanded by consumers at p_2. Show in a figure how large x must be for growers to reduce output to this level. What are the effects of this program on consumers, farmers, and total welfare? Compare this approach to (a) offering a price support of p_2, (b) offering a price support and a quota set at Q_1, and (c) offering a price support and a quota set at Q_2.

5.14 What were the welfare effects (who gained, who lost, what was the deadweight loss) of the gasoline price ceiling described in Chapter 2? Add the relevant areas to a drawing like Figure 2.14. (*Hint*: See Solved Problem 9.4.)

5.15 What are the welfare effects of a binding minimum wage? Use a graphical approach to show what happens if all workers are identical. Then describe in writing what is likely to happen to workers who differ by experience, education, age, gender, and race.

5.16 A mayor wants to help renters in her city. She considers two policies that will benefit renters equally. One policy is *rent control*, which places a price ceiling, p, on rents. The other is a government housing subsidy of s dollars per month that lowers the amount renters pay (to p). Who benefits and who loses from these policies? Compare the effects of the two policies on the quantity of housing consumed, consumer surplus, producer surplus, government expenditure, and deadweight loss. Does the comparison of deadweight loss depend on the elasticities of supply and demand? (*Hint*: Consider extreme cases and see Solved Problem 9.4.) If so, how?

5.17 Draw and label a figure (including the dollar amount of the deadweight loss area) to illustrate the effects of a price control in the natural gas market as described in the Application "The Social Cost of a Natural Gas Price Ceiling."

6. Comparing Both Types of Policies: Trade

6.1 Although 23 states barred the sale of self-service gasoline in 1968, most removed the bans by the mid-1970s. By 1992, self-service outlets sold nearly 80% of all U.S. gas, and only New Jersey and Oregon continued to ban self-service sales (which Oregon stopped doing in 2018). Johnson and Romeo (2000) estimated that the ban in those two states raised the price of gasoline by approximately 3¢ to 5¢ per gallon. Why did the ban affect the price? Illustrate using a figure and explain. Show the welfare effects in your figure. Use a table to show who gains and who loses.

6.2 The U.S. Supreme Court ruled in May 2005 that people can buy wine directly from out-of-state vineyards. The Court held that state laws requiring people to buy directly from wine retailers within the state violate the Constitution's commerce clause.

    a. Suppose the market for wine in New York is perfectly competitive both before and after the Supreme Court decision. Use the analysis of Section 9.6 to evaluate the effect of the Court's decision on the price of wine in New York.

    b. Evaluate the increase in New York consumer surplus, producer surplus, and welfare.

6.3 Canada has 20% of the world's known freshwater resources, yet many Canadians believe that the country has little or none to spare. Over the years,

---

[28]Elizabeth Becker, "U.S. Subsidizes Companies to Buy Subsidized Cotton," *New York Times*, November 4, 2003, C1, C2.

U.S. and Canadian firms have struck deals to export bulk shipments of water to drought-afflicted U.S. cities and towns. Provincial leaders have blocked these deals in British Columbia and Ontario. Use graphs to show the likely outcome of such barriers to exports on the price and quantity of water used in Canada and in the United States if markets for water are competitive. Show the effects on consumer and producer surplus in both countries.

6.4 In Solved Problem 9.5, if the domestic demand curve is $Q = 20p^{-0.5}$, the domestic supply curve is $Q = 5p^{0.5}$, and the world price is 5, use calculus to determine the changes in producer surplus, consumer surplus, and welfare from eliminating free trade. **M**

*6.5 Based on the estimates of the U.S. daily oil demand function in Equation 9.3 and supply function in Equation 9.4, use calculus to determine the change in deadweight loss from a marginal increase in a tariff, evaluated where the tariff is initially zero. (*Hint*: You are being asked to determine how an area similar to that of $C + E$ in Figure 9.7 changes when a small tariff is initially applied. See Solved Problem 9.6.) **M**

6.6 In 2013, the U.S. government claimed that China and Vietnam were dumping shrimp in the United States at a price below cost, and proposed duties as high as 112%. Suppose that China and Vietnam were subsidizing their shrimp fisheries. In a diagram, show who gains and who loses in the United States (compared to the equilibrium in which those nations do not subsidize their shrimp fisheries). The United States imposed a 10.17% antidumping duty (essentially a tariff) on shrimp from these and several other countries. Use your diagram to show how the large tariff would affect government revenues and the welfare of consumers and producers.

6.7 Show that if the importing country faces an upward-sloping foreign supply curve (excess supply curve), a tariff may raise welfare in the importing country.

6.8 Given that the world supply curve is horizontal at the world price for a given good, can a subsidy on imports raise welfare in the importing country? Explain your answer.

6.9 After Mexico signed the North American Free Trade Agreement (NAFTA) with the United States in 1994, corn imports from the United States doubled within a year, and today U.S. imports make up nearly one-third of the corn consumed in Mexico. According to Oxfam (2003), the price of Mexican corn fell more than 70% since NAFTA took effect. Part of the reason for this flow south of our border is that the U.S. government subsidizes corn production to the tune of $10 billion a year. According to Oxfam, the 2002 U.S. cost of production was $3.08 per bushel, but the export price was $2.69 per bushel, with the difference reflecting an export subsidy of 39¢ per bushel. The United States exported 5.3 metric tons. Use graphs to show the effect of such a subsidy on the welfare of various groups and on government expenditures in the United States and Mexico.

6.10 In the first quarter of 2013, the world price for raw sugar, 24¢ per pound, was about 79% of the domestic price, 29¢ per pound, because of quotas and tariffs on sugar imports. Consequently, American-made corn sweeteners can be profitably sold domestically. A decade ago, the U.S. Commerce Department estimated that the quotas and price support reduce American welfare by about $3 billion a year, so each dollar of Archer Daniels Midland's profit from selling U.S. sugar costs Americans about $10. Model the effects of a quota on sugar in both the sugar and corn sweetener markets.

6.11 During the Napoleonic Wars, Britain blockaded North America, seizing U.S. vessels and cargo and impressing sailors. At President Thomas Jefferson's request, Congress imposed a nearly complete—perhaps 80%—embargo on international commerce from December 1807 to March 1809. Just before the embargo, exports were about 13% of the U.S. gross national product (GNP). Due to the embargo, U.S. consumers could not find acceptable substitutes for manufactured goods from Europe, and producers could not sell farm produce and other goods for as much as in Europe. According to Irwin (2005), the welfare cost of the embargo was at least 8% of the GNP in 1807. Use graphs to show the effects of the embargo on a market for an exported good and one for an imported good. Show the change in equilibria and the welfare effects on consumers and firms.

6.12 A government is considering a quota and a tariff, both of which will reduce imports by the same amount. Why might the government prefer one of these policies to the other?

7. Challenge

7.1 In 2002, Los Angeles imposed a ban on new billboards. Owners of existing billboards did not oppose the ban. Why? What are the implications of the ban for producer surplus, consumer surplus, and welfare? Who are the producers and consumers in your analysis? How else does the ban affect welfare in Los Angeles? (*Hint*: The demand curve for billboards shifts to the right over time.)

7.2 As the Challenge mentions, several state governments issue a fixed number of liquor licenses that are good forever, but allow the holder of a license to resell them. Alternatively, the government could charge a high enough license fee that firms buy the same number of licenses currently issued. Use figures to compare and contrast the equilibrium under each of these approaches. Discuss who wins and who loses under each plan, considering consumers, restaurant owners, the original holders of a license (if relevant), and society.

General Equilibrium and Economic Welfare

10

Capitalism is the astounding belief that the most wickedest of men will do the most wickedest of things for the greatest good of everyone. —John Maynard Keynes

CHALLENGE

Anti–Price Gouging Laws

After a disaster strikes, prices tend to rise. The average U.S. gasoline price increased by 46¢ per gallon after Hurricane Katrina in 2005 damaged most Gulf Coast oil refineries. Many state governments enforce anti–price gouging laws to prevent prices from rising, while prices may be free to adjust in neighboring states. For example, Louisiana's anti–price gouging law went into effect when Governor Bobby Jindal declared a state of emergency in response to the 2010 BP oil spill that endangered Louisiana's coast.

In 2018, California Governor Jerry Brown imposed price gouging protection for lodging, food, medical products, and building supplies, limiting price increases to 10%, in the wake of devastating wildfires in three counties.

On average, gasoline prices rose by a few cents immediately after Superstorm Sandy in 2012; however, some stations increased the retail markup over the wholesale prices by up to 135%. The New York Attorney General's office received over 500 consumer complaints about price gouging within a week of the storm. The attorney general pursued price gouging cases against 25 gas stations. Virginia in 2014 and Kentucky, New York, Pennsylvania, and West Virginia in 2015 declared storm emergencies that triggered anti–price gouging laws.

The District of Columbia and 34 states have anti–price gouging laws. Arkansas, California, Maine, New Jersey, Oklahoma, Oregon, and West Virginia set a "percentage increase cap limit" on how much price may be increased after a disaster, ranging from 10% to 25% of the price before the emergency. Sixteen states prohibit "unconscionable" price increases. Connecticut, Georgia, Hawaii, Kentucky, Louisiana, Mississippi, and Utah have outright bans on price increases during an emergency.

Generally, legislatures pass these laws after a major natural disaster.[1] California passed its law in 1994 after the Northridge earthquake. Georgia enacted its anti–price gouging

---

[1]Governments pass anti–price gouging laws because they are popular. After the post-Katrina gas price increases, an ABC News/*Washington Post* poll found that only 16% of respondents thought that the price increase was "justified," 72.7% thought that "oil companies and gas dealers are taking unfair advantage," 7.4% said both views were true, and the rest held another or no opinion.

statute after a 500-year flood in 1994. Consequently, often a state hit by a recent disaster has such a law, while a neighboring state does not.

In Chapter 2, we showed that a national price control causes shortages. However, does a binding price control that affects one state, but not a neighboring state, cause shortages? How does it affect prices and quantities sold in the two states? Which consumers benefit from these laws?

In addition to natural disasters, a change in government policies or other shocks often affect equilibrium price and quantity in more than one market. To determine the effects of such a change, we must examine the interrelationships among markets. In this chapter, we extend our analysis of equilibrium in a single market to equilibrium in all markets.

We also examine how a society decides whether a particular equilibrium (or change in equilibrium) in all markets is desirable. To do so, society must answer two questions: "Is the equilibrium efficient?" and "Is the equilibrium equitable?"

For an equilibrium to be efficient, both consumption and production must be efficient. Production is efficient only if it is impossible to produce more output at current cost given current knowledge (Chapter 6). Consumption is efficient only if goods cannot be reallocated among people so that at least someone is better off and no one is harmed. This chapter shows how we determine whether consumption is efficient.

Whether an equilibrium is efficient is a scientific question. It is possible that all members of society could agree on how to answer scientific questions concerning efficiency.

Deciding whether an equilibrium is equitable, however, involves making a value judgment as to whether each member of society receives one's fair or just share of all the goods and services. A common view in individualistic cultures is that each person is the best—and possibly, the only legitimate—judge of one's own welfare. Nonetheless, to make social choices about events that affect more than one person, we must make interpersonal comparisons, through which we decide whether one person's gain is more or less important than another person's loss. For example, we showed that a price ceiling lowers a measure of total welfare when the value judgment that the well-being of consumers, consumer surplus, and the well-being of the owners of firms, producer surplus, are weighted equally (Chapter 9). People of goodwill—and others—may disagree greatly about questions of equity.

As a first step in studying welfare issues, many economists use a narrow value criterion due to the Italian economist Vilfredo Pareto to rank different allocations of goods and services for which no interpersonal comparisons need to be made. According to the **Pareto principle**, society should favor a change that benefits some people without harming others. Thus, according to this principle, if everyone shares in the extra surplus when a government policy eliminates a market failure, then the government should make this change.

A **Pareto improvement** is a change, such as a reallocation of goods between people, that helps at least one person without harming anyone else. An example of a Pareto improvement is an exchange when a baseball card collector trades cards with another collector. Both are better off and no one else is harmed by the exchange. Once all possible Pareto improvements have occurred, the outcome is **Pareto efficient** because any possible reallocation of goods and services would harm at least one person.[2]

---

[2]Pareto efficiency is a more general concept than economic efficiency, which is based on maximization of welfare. If a market exhibits Pareto efficiency, the market is efficient: It maximizes welfare. Unlike the surplus concept, the Pareto concept can also be used in non-market situations. For example, if two people are happier after they marry, then that marriage is a Pareto improvement, even though we cannot reasonably define a related price or measure of consumer and producer surplus.

Presumably, you agree that a government policy that makes all members of society better off is desirable. Do you also agree that a policy that makes some members better off without harming others is desirable? What about a policy that helps one group more than it hurts another? Or how about a policy that hurts another group more than it helps your group? It is unlikely that all members of society will agree on how to answer these questions—much less agree on the answers.

Efficiency and equity questions arise even in small social units such as a family. Suppose that your family has gathered for the Thanksgiving holiday and everyone wants pumpkin pie. How much pie you bake will depend on the answer to efficiency and equity questions such as "How can we make the pie as large as possible with available resources?" and "How should we divide the pie?" It will probably be easier to agree about how to make the largest pie possible than about how to divide it equitably.

So far in this book (aside from Chapter 9's welfare analysis), we have used economic theory to answer the scientific efficiency question. We have concentrated on that question because the equity question requires a value judgment. (Strangely, most members of society seem to believe that economists are no better at making value judgments than anyone else.)

In this chapter, we examine various views on equity, focusing on five main topics

1. **General Equilibrium.** A shift in government policy or other shock in one market often affects other markets.

2. **Trading Between Two People.** When two people have goods but cannot produce more goods, both parties benefit from mutually agreeable trades.

3. **Competitive Exchange.** The competitive equilibrium has two desirable properties: Any competitive equilibrium is Pareto efficient, and competition can result in any Pareto-efficient allocation given an appropriate income distribution.

4. **Production and Trading.** The benefits from trade continue to hold when production is possible.

5. **Efficiency and Equity.** Because many Pareto-efficient allocations are possible, a society may use its views about equity to choose among them.

10.1 General Equilibrium

So far, we have used equalize **partial-equilibrium analysis**: an examination of equilibrium and changes in equilibrium in one market in isolation. In a partial-equilibrium analysis in which we hold the prices and quantities of other goods fixed, we implicitly ignore the possibility that events in this market affect other markets' equilibrium prices and quantities.

When stated this baldly, partial-equilibrium analysis sounds foolish, but it need not be. Suppose that the government puts a specific tax on the price of hula hoops. If the tax is sizable, it will dramatically affect hula hoop sales. However, even a very large tax on hula hoops is unlikely to affect the markets for automobiles, doctors' services, or orange juice. It is even unlikely to affect the demand for other toys much. Thus, a partial-equilibrium analysis of the effect of such a tax should serve us well. Studying all markets simultaneously to analyze this tax would be unnecessary at best and confusing at worst.

Sometimes, however, we need to use a **general-equilibrium analysis**: the study of how equilibrium is determined in all markets simultaneously. For example, the discovery of a major oil deposit in a small country raises the income of its citizens, and the increased income affects all of that country's markets.

Frequently, economists look at equilibrium in several—but not all—markets simultaneously. We would expect a tax on comic books to affect the price of comic books, which in turn would affect the price of video games because video games are substitutes for comics. But we would not expect a tax on comics to have a measurable effect on the demand for washing machines. Therefore, it is reasonable to conduct a *multimarket analysis* of the effects of a tax on comics by looking only at the markets for comics, video games, and a few other closely related markets, such as those for movies and trading cards. That is, a multimarket-equilibrium analysis covers the relevant markets, but not all markets, as a general-equilibrium analysis would.

Markets are closely related if an increase in the price in one market causes the demand or supply curve in another market to shift measurably. Suppose that a tax on coffee causes the price of coffee to increase. The rise in the price of coffee causes the demand curve for tea to shift outward (more tea is demanded at any given price of tea) because tea and coffee are substitutes. The price increase for coffee also causes the demand curve for cream to shift inward because coffee and cream are complements.

Similarly, supply curves in different markets may be related. If a farmer produces corn and soybeans, an increase in the price of corn will affect the relative amounts of both crops that the farmer chooses to produce.

Markets may also be linked if the output of one market is an input in another market. A shock that raises the price of computer chips will also raise the price of computers.

Thus, an event in one market may have a *spillover effect* on other, related markets for various reasons. Indeed, a single event may initiate a chain reaction of spillover effects that reverberates between markets.

Competitive Equilibrium in Two Interrelated Markets

Suppose that the demand functions for Good 1, Q_1, and Good 2, Q_2, depend on both prices, p_1 and p_2,

$$Q_1 = D_1(p_1, p_2),$$
$$Q_2 = D_2(p_1, p_2),$$

but that the supply function for each good depends only on the good's own price,

$$Q_1 = S_1(p_1),$$
$$Q_2 = S_2(p_2).$$

To determine the equilibrium p_1, p_2, Q_1, and Q_2, we solve these four equations in four unknowns simultaneously.

Doing so is straightforward with linear equations. Suppose that the demand functions are linear,

$$Q_1 = a_1 - b_1 p_1 + c_1 p_2, \tag{10.1}$$
$$Q_2 = a_2 - b_2 p_2 + c_2 p_1, \tag{10.2}$$

as are the supply functions,

$$Q_1 = d_1 + e_1 p_1, \tag{10.3}$$
$$Q_2 = d_2 + e_2 p_2, \tag{10.4}$$

where all the coefficients are positive numbers.

Equating the quantity demanded and supplied in both markets—setting the right-hand side of Equation 10.1 equal to the right-hand side of Equation 10.3, and similarly for Equations 10.2 and 10.4—we obtain

$$a_1 - b_1 p_1 + c_1 p_2 = d_1 + e_1 p_1, \tag{10.5}$$

$$a_2 - b_2 p_2 + c_2 p_1 = d_2 + e_2 p_2. \tag{10.6}$$

We now have two equations, 10.5 and 10.6, in two unknowns, p_1 and p_2, to solve. The solutions of these two equations are

$$p_1 = \frac{(b_2 + e_2)(a_1 - d_1) + c_1(a_2 - d_2)}{(b_1 + e_1)(b_2 + e_2) - c_1 c_2}, \tag{10.7}$$

$$p_2 = \frac{(b_1 + e_1)(a_2 - d_2) + c_2(a_1 - d_1)}{(b_1 + e_1)(b_2 + e_2) - c_1 c_2}. \tag{10.8}$$

Substituting these values for p_1 and p_2 in the demand functions 10.1 and 10.2 or in the supply functions 10.3 and 10.4, we obtain expressions for Q_1 and Q_2. Thus, by simultaneously solving the demand and supply curves for related markets, we can determine the equilibrium prices and quantities in both markets.

APPLICATION

Partial-Equilibrium Versus Multimarket-Equilibrium Analysis in Corn and Soybean Markets

Consumers and producers substitute between corn and soybeans, so the demand and supply curves in these markets are related according to the estimates of Holt (1992). The quantity of corn demanded and the quantity of soybeans demanded depend on the price of corn, the price of soybeans, and other variables. Similarly, the quantities of corn and soybeans supplied depend on their relative prices.

A shock in one market affects both markets. Given actual supply and demand curves for corn and soybeans, the original equilibrium price of corn is $2.15 per bushel, and the quantity is 8.44 billion bushels per year; and the equilibrium price of soybeans is $4.12 per bushel, and the quantity is 2.07 billion bushels per year (see the first row of the table).[3] Now suppose that a scare about the safety of corn causes a parallel shift to the left of the foreign demand curve for American corn so that at the original price, the export of corn falls by 10%.

If we were conducting a partial-equilibrium analysis, we would examine the new corn equilibrium, where the new U.S. corn demand curve intersects the corn supply curve. The second row of the table shows the partial equilibrium effects on the corn equilibrium, holding other prices (such as the price of soybeans) constant.

In a multimarket-equilibrium analysis, we consider how this shock to the corn market affects the soybean market, and how the changed soybean price in turn affects the corn market. The third row of the table shows the new multimarket equilibrium in both markets.

[3]Until recently, the corn and soybean markets were subject to price controls (Chapter 9). However, we use the estimated demand and supply curves to determine what would happen in these markets without price controls.

Equilibria	Corn		Soybeans	
	Price	*Quantity*	*Price*	*Quantity*
Original equilibria	2.15	8.44	4.12	2.07
New partial equilibrium	1.917	8.227		
New multimarket equilibria	1.905	8.263	3.82	2.05

Suppose that we were interested only in the effect of the shift in the foreign corn demand curve on the corn market. Could we rely on a partial-equilibrium analysis? According to a partial-equilibrium analysis, the price of corn falls 10.8% to $1.917. In contrast, in the multimarket-equilibrium analysis, the price falls 11.4% to $1.905, which is 1.2¢ less per bushel. That is, the partial-equilibrium analysis underestimates the price effect by 0.6 percentage points. Similarly, the fall in quantity is 2.5% according to the partial-equilibrium analysis and only 2.1% according to the multimarket-equilibrium analysis. Thus, in this market, the biases from using a partial-equilibrium analysis are small.[4]

Minimum Wages with Incomplete Coverage

We used a partial-equilibrium analysis in Chapter 2 to examine the effects of a minimum wage law that holds throughout the entire labor market. The minimum wage causes the quantity of labor demanded to be less than the quantity of labor supplied. Workers who lose their jobs cannot find work elsewhere and are unemployed.

Many people are familiar with that reasoning and over generalize:

Common Confusion A minimum wage must cause unemployment.

This result follows logically if the minimum wage applies to and is binding on the entire work force. However, the minimum wage may not cause unemployment if the minimum wage law covers workers in only some sectors of the economy, as we show using a general-equilibrium analysis.[5]

When a minimum wage is applied to a covered sector of the economy, the increase in the wage causes the quantity of labor demanded in that sector to fall. Workers who are displaced from jobs in the covered sector move to the uncovered sector, driving down the wage in that sector. When the U.S. minimum wage law was first passed in 1938, only 56% of workers were employed in covered sectors, so some economists joked that its purpose was to maintain family farms: The law drove workers out of manufacturing and other covered industries into the uncovered agricultural sector. Even today, a few small sectors are not covered by federal and state minimum wage laws.

Figure 10.1 shows the effect of a minimum wage when coverage is incomplete. The total demand curve, *D* in panel c, is the horizontal sum of the demand curve for labor services in the covered sector, D^c in panel a, and the demand curve in the uncovered sector, D^u in panel b. In the absence of a minimum wage law, the wage in both sectors

---

[4]For an example of where the bias from using a partial-equilibrium analysis instead of a multimarket- or general-equilibrium analysis is large, see "Sin Taxes" in **MyLab Economics**, Chapter Resources, Chapter 10.

[5]Also, in a market with a single employer, a *monopsony*, a minimum wage increases employment and does not cause unemployment (see Solved Problem 11.8).

Figure 10.1 Minimum Wage with Incomplete Coverage

In the absence of a minimum wage, the equilibrium wage is w_1. Applying a minimum wage, $\underline{w}$, to only one sector causes the quantity of labor services demanded in the covered sector to fall. The extra labor moves to the uncovered sector, driving the wage in that sector down to w_2.

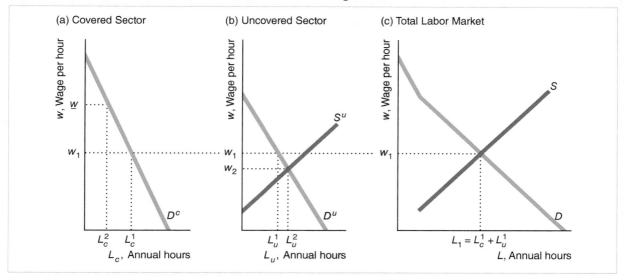

is w_1, which is determined by the intersection of the total demand curve, D, and the total supply curve, S. At that wage, L_c^1 annual hours of work are hired in the covered sector, L_u^1 annual hours are hired in the uncovered sector, and $L_1 = L_c^1 + L_u^1$ total annual hours of work are performed.

If a minimum wage of $\underline{w}$ is set in the covered sector only, employment in that sector falls to L_c^2. To determine the wage and level of employment in the uncovered sector, we first need to determine how much labor service is available to that sector.

Anyone unable to find work in the covered sector goes to the uncovered sector. The supply curve of labor to the uncovered sector in panel b is a *residual supply curve*: the quantity the market supplies that is not met by demanders in other sectors at any given wage (Chapter 8). With a binding minimum wage $\underline{w}$ in the covered sector, the residual supply function for the uncovered sector is

$$S^u(w) = S(w) - D^c(\underline{w}).$$

That is, the residual supply to the uncovered sector, $S^u(w)$, is the total supply, $S(w)$, at any given wage w minus the amount of labor used in the covered sector, $L_c^2 = D^c(\underline{w})$.

The intersection of D^u and S^u determines w_2, the new wage in the uncovered sector, and L_u^2, the new level of employment.[6] This general-equilibrium analysis shows that a minimum wage causes employment to drop in the covered sector, employment to rise (by a smaller amount) in the uncovered sector, and the wage in the uncovered sector to fall below the original competitive level. Thus, a minimum wage law with

---

[6]This analysis is incomplete if the minimum wage causes the price of goods in the covered sector to rise relative to those in the uncovered sector, which in turn causes the demands for labor in those two sectors, D^c and D^u, to shift. Ignoring that possibility is reasonable if labor costs are a small fraction of total costs (hence the effect of the minimum wage is minimal on total costs) or if the demands for the final goods are relatively price insensitive.

only partial coverage affects wage levels and employment levels in various sectors but need not create unemployment.

More than 140 U.S. cities and counties have enacted living-wage laws, a new type of minimum wage legislation where the minimum is high enough to allow a fully employed person to live above the poverty level in a given locale. Living-wage laws provide incomplete coverage, typically extending only to the employees of a government or to firms that contract with that government.

SOLVED PROBLEM 10.1

MyLab Economics Solved Problem

Initially, all workers are paid a wage of w_1 per hour. The government taxes the cost of labor by t per hour only in the *covered* sector of the economy. That is, if workers receive a wage of w_2 per hour, firms in the covered sector pay $w_2 + t$ per hour. Show how the wages in the covered and uncovered sectors are determined in the post-tax equilibrium. What effect does the tax have on total employment, L, employment in the covered sector, L_c, and employment in the uncovered sector, L_u?

Answer

1. *Determine the original equilibrium.* In the diagram, the intersection of the total demand curve, D^1, and the total supply curve of labor, S, determines the original equilibrium, e_1, where the wage is w_1, employment in the covered sector is L_c^1, employment in the uncovered sector is L_u^1, and total employment is $L_1 = L_c^1 + L_u^1$. The total demand curve is the horizontal sum of the demand curves in the covered, D_1^c, and uncovered, D^u, sectors.

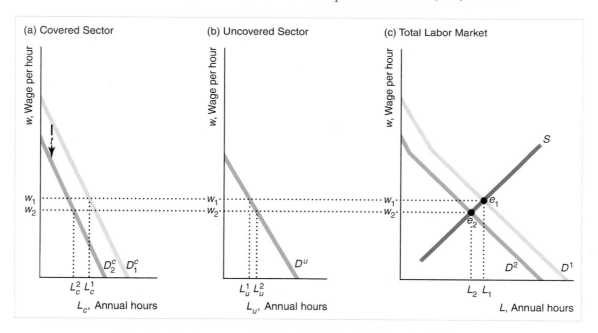

2. *Show the shift in the demand for labor in the covered sector and the resulting shift in the total demand curve.* The tax causes the demand curve for labor in the covered sector to shift downward from D_1^c to D_2^c. As a result, the total demand curve shifts inward to D^2.

3. *Determine the equilibrium wage using the total supply and demand curves, and then determine employment in the two sectors.* Workers shift between sectors

until the new wage is equal in both sectors at w_2, which is determined by the intersection of the new total demand curve, D^2, and the total supply curve, S. Employment in the covered sector is L_c^2, and employment in the uncovered sector is L_u^2.

4. *Compare the equilibria.* The tax causes the wage, total employment, and employment in the covered sector to fall and employment in the uncovered sector to rise.

Philadelphia and some other cities tax wages, while suburban areas do not (or they set much lower rates). Philadelphia collects a wage tax from residents whether or not they work in the city and from nonresidents who work in the city. Unfortunately, this situation drives people and jobs from Philadelphia to the suburbs. To offset such job losses, the city has gradually reduced the wage tax from a high of 4.96% from 1983–1995 to 3.88% for Philadelphia residents and 3.46% for nonresidents in 2018.

A study conducted for Philadelphia estimated that if the city were to lower the wage tax by 0.4175 percentage points, 30,500 more people would work in the city. Local wage tax cuts have greater effects than a federal income tax cut. Workers rarely leave the country to avoid taxes, but many will move to the suburbs to avoid a city tax. Indeed, growth over many years has been greater on the suburban side of City Line Avenue, which runs along Philadelphia's border, than on the side within city limits.

10.2 Trading Between Two People

In Chapter 9, we showed that tariffs, quotas, and other trade restrictions usually harm both importing and exporting nations because people who voluntarily trade benefit from that trade—otherwise, they would not have traded. In this section, we use a general-equilibrium model to show that free trade is Pareto efficient: After all voluntary trades occur, no reallocation of goods is possible that makes one person better off without harming another. Our analysis demonstrates that trade between two people is Pareto efficient and that the same property holds when many people trade in a competitive market.

Endowments

Suppose that Jane and Denise are neighbors in the wilds of Massachusetts. A nasty snowstorm hits, isolating them. They must trade with each other or consume only what they have at hand.

Collectively, they have 50 piles of firewood and 80 candy bars and no way of producing more of either good. Jane's **endowment**—her initial allocation of goods—is 30 piles of firewood and 20 candy bars. Denise's endowment is 20 (= 50 − 30) piles of firewood and 60 (= 80 − 20) candy bars. So Jane has relatively more wood, and Denise has relatively more candy.

We show these endowments in Figure 10.2. Panels a and b are typical indifference curve diagrams (Chapter 3) in which we measure piles of firewood on the vertical axis and candy bars on the horizontal axis. Jane's endowment is e_j (30 piles of wood and 20 candy bars) in panel a, and Denise's endowment is e_d in panel b. Both panels show the indifference curve through the endowment.

If we take Denise's diagram, rotate it, and put it on Jane's diagram, we obtain the box in panel c. This type of figure, called an *Edgeworth box* (after the English economist Francis Ysidro Edgeworth), illustrates trade between two people with

Figure 10.2 Endowments in an Edgeworth Box

(a) Jane's endowment is e_j. She has 20 candy bars and 30 piles of firewood. She is indifferent between that bundle and the others that lie on her indifference curve I_j^1. (b) Denise is indifferent between her endowment, e_d (60 candy bars and 20 piles of firewood), and the other bundles on I_d^1. (c) Their endowments are at e in the Edgeworth box formed by combining panels a and b. Jane prefers bundles in A and B to e. Denise prefers bundles in B and C to e. Thus, both prefer any bundle in area B to e.

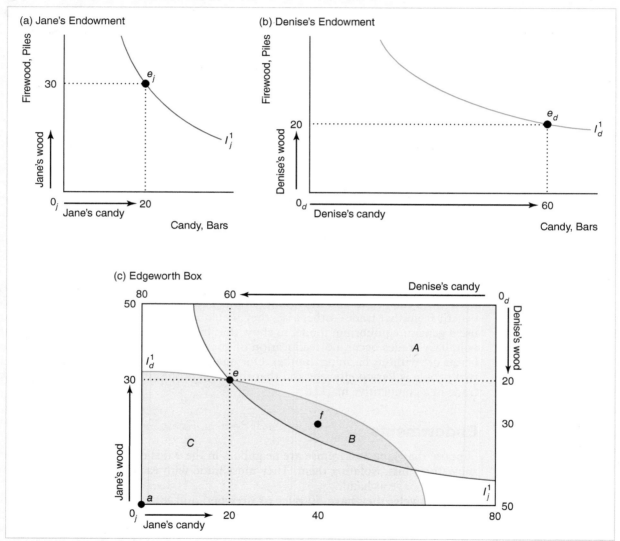

fixed endowments of two goods. We use this Edgeworth box to illustrate a general-equilibrium model in which we examine simultaneous trade in firewood and in candy.

The height of the Edgeworth box represents 50 piles of firewood, and the length represents 80 candy bars, which are the combined endowments of Jane and Denise. Bundle e shows both endowments. Measuring from Jane's origin, 0_j, at the lower-left corner of the diagram, we see that Jane has 30 piles of wood and 20 candy bars at endowment e. Similarly, measuring from Denise's origin, 0_d, at the upper-right corner, we see that Denise has 60 candy bars and 20 piles of wood at e.

Mutually Beneficial Trades

Should Jane and Denise trade? The answer depends on their tastes, which are summarized by their indifference curves. We make four assumptions about their tastes and behavior:

1. **Utility maximization:** Each person *maximizes* her *utility*.
2. **Non-satiation:** Each person has strictly positive *marginal utility* for each good, so each person wants as much of the good as possible (that is, neither person is ever satiated).
3. **Usual-shaped indifference curves:** Each person's indifference curves have the usual convex shape, which reflects a diminishing marginal rate of substitution.
4. **No interdependence:** Neither person's utility depends on the other's consumption (that is, neither person derives pleasure or displeasure from the other's consumption), and neither person's consumption harms the other person (that is, one person's consumption of firewood does not cause smoke pollution that bothers the other person).

Figure 10.2 reflects these assumptions. In panel a, Jane's indifference curve, I_j^1, through her endowment point, e_j, is convex to her origin, 0_j. Jane is indifferent between e_j and any other bundle on I_j^1. She prefers bundles that lie above I_j^1 to e_j and prefers e_j to points that lie below I_j^1. Panel c also shows her indifference curve I_j^1. The bundles that Jane prefers to her endowment are in the shaded areas A and B, which lie above her indifference curve I_j^1.

Similarly, Denise's indifference curve, I_d^1, through her endowment is convex to her origin, 0_d, in the lower-left corner of panel b. This indifference curve, I_d^1, is still convex to 0_d in panel c, but 0_d is in the upper-right corner of the Edgeworth box. (It may help to rotate this book 180° when viewing Denise's indifference curves in an Edgeworth box. Then again, possibly many points will be clearer if you hold this book upside down.) The bundles Denise prefers to her endowment are in shaded areas B and C, which lie on the other side of her indifference curve I_d^1 from her origin 0_d (above I_d^1 if you turn this book upside down).

At endowment e in panel c, Jane and Denise can both benefit from a trade. Jane prefers bundles in A and B to e, and Denise prefers bundles in B and C to e, so *both* prefer bundles in area B to their endowment at e.

Suppose that they trade, reallocating goods from Bundle e to Bundle f. Jane gives up 10 piles of wood for 20 more candy bars, and Denise gives up 20 candy bars for 10 more piles of wood. As Figure 10.3 illustrates, both gain from such a trade. Jane's indifference curve I_j^2 through allocation f lies above her indifference curve I_j^1 through allocation e, so she is better off at f than at e. Similarly, Denise's indifference curve I_d^2 through f lies above (if you hold the book upside down) her indifference curve I_d^1 through e, so she also benefits from the trade.

Now that they've traded to Bundle f, do Jane and Denise want to make additional trades? To answer this question, we can repeat our analysis. Jane prefers all bundles above I_j^2, her indifference curve through f. Denise prefers all bundles above (when the book is held upside down) I_d^2 to f. However, no bundle exists that both prefer because I_j^2 and I_d^2 are tangent at f. Neither Jane nor Denise wants to trade from f to a bundle such as e, which is below both of their indifference curves. Jane would love to trade from f to c, which is on her higher indifference curve I_j^3, but such a trade would make Denise worse off because this bundle is on a lower indifference curve, I_d^1. Similarly, Denise prefers b to f, but Jane does not. Thus, *any* move from f harms at least one of them.

The reason no further trade is possible at a bundle like f is that Jane's marginal rate of substitution (the slope of her indifference curve), MRS_j, between wood and

Figure 10.3 Contract Curve

The contract curve contains all the Pareto-efficient allocations. Any bundle for which Jane's indifference curve is tangent to Denise's indifference curve lies on the contract curve, because no further trade is possible, so we can't reallocate goods to make one of them better off without harming the other. Starting at an endowment of *e*, Jane and Denise will trade to a bundle on the contract curve in area *B*: bundles between *b* and *c*. The table shows how they would trade to Bundle *f*.

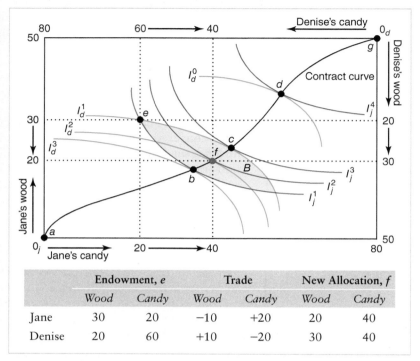

	Endowment, *e*		Trade		New Allocation, *f*	
	Wood	Candy	Wood	Candy	Wood	Candy
Jane	30	20	−10	+20	20	40
Denise	20	60	+10	−20	30	40

candy equals Denise's marginal rate of substitution, MRS_d. Jane's MRS_j is $-\frac{1}{2}$: She is willing to trade one pile of wood for two candy bars. Because Denise's indifference curve is tangent to Jane's, Denise's MRS_d must also be $-\frac{1}{2}$. When they both want to trade wood for candy at the same rate, they can't agree on additional trades.

In contrast, at a bundle such as *e* where their indifference curves are not tangent, MRS_j does not equal MRS_d. Denise's MRS_d is $-\frac{1}{3}$, and Jane's MRS_j is -2. Denise is willing to give up one pile of wood for three more candy bars or to sacrifice three candy bars for one more pile of wood. If Denise offers Jane three candy bars for one pile of wood, Jane will accept because she is willing to give up two piles of wood for one candy bar. This example illustrates that trades are possible where indifference curves intersect, because marginal rates of substitution are unequal.

To summarize, we can make four equivalent statements about allocation *f*:

1. The indifference curves of the two parties are tangent at *f*.
2. The parties' marginal rates of substitution are equal at *f*.
3. No further mutually beneficial trades are possible at *f*.
4. The allocation at *f* is Pareto efficient: One party cannot be made better off without harming the other.

Indifference curves are also tangent at Bundles *b*, *c*, and *d*, so these allocations, like *f*, are Pareto efficient. By connecting all such bundles, we draw the **contract curve**: the set of all Pareto-efficient bundles. The reason for this name is that only at these points are the parties unwilling to engage in further trades, or contracts—these allocations are the final contracts. A move from any bundle on the contract curve must harm at least one person.

SOLVED PROBLEM 10.2

MyLab Economics
Solved Problem

Are allocations *a* and *g* in Figure 10.3, where one person owns everything, part of the contract curve?

Answer

By showing that no mutually beneficial trades are possible at those points, demonstrate that those bundles are Pareto efficient. The allocation at which Jane has everything, *g*, is on the contract curve because no mutually beneficial trade is possible: Denise has no goods to trade with Jane. As a consequence, we cannot make Denise better off without taking goods from Jane. Similarly, when Denise has everything, *a*, we can make Jane better off only by taking wood or candy from Denise and giving it to Jane.

Deriving the Contract Curve

We can use calculus to derive the contract curve. We want to specify conditions where we make one individual as well off as possible without harming the other person.

Let Denise's utility function be $U_d(q_{d1}, q_{d2})$, where q_{d1} is the amount of candy and q_{d2} is the amount of wood belonging to Denise. Similarly, Jane's utility function is $U_j(q_{j1}, q_{j2})$. We want to determine the bundle that maximizes Jane's well-being, $U_j(q_{j1}, q_{j2})$, given that we hold Denise's utility constant at $\overline{U}_d = U_d(q_{d1}, q_{d2})$.

For example, in Figure 10.3, we take Denise's indifference curve I_d^2, along which her utility is $\overline{U}_d$, and ask what bundle places Jane on her highest indifference curve subject to Denise's being on I_d^2. That is, I_d^2 is the constraint (analogous to the budget line in earlier chapters) that Jane faces, and we pick a bundle on the highest one of Jane's indifference curves that touches I_d^2. As we already know, at Bundle *f*, Denise is on I_d^2 and Jane is on her highest feasible indifference curve, I_j^2.

Using a Lagrangian multiplier, λ, we can write the Lagrangian corresponding to the maximum problem as

$$\mathcal{L} = U_j(q_{j1}, q_{j2}) + \lambda[U_d(q_1 - q_{j1}, q_2 - q_{j2}) - \overline{U}_d], \quad (10.9)$$

where $q_1 = q_{d1} + q_{j1}$ is the total amount of candy available and q_2 is the total amount of wood. The first-order conditions are

$$\frac{\partial \mathcal{L}}{\partial q_{j1}} = \frac{\partial U_j}{\partial q_{j1}} - \lambda \frac{\partial U_d}{\partial q_{j1}} = 0, \quad (10.10)$$

$$\frac{\partial \mathcal{L}}{\partial q_{j2}} = \frac{\partial U_j}{\partial q_{j2}} - \lambda \frac{\partial U_d}{\partial q_{j2}} = 0, \quad (10.11)$$

$$\frac{\partial \mathcal{L}}{\partial \lambda} = U_d(q_1 - q_{j1}, q_2 - q_{j2}) - \overline{U}_d = 0. \quad (10.12)$$

If we equate the right-hand sides of Equations 10.10 and 10.11, we find that

$$MRS_j = \frac{\partial U_j/\partial q_{j1}}{\partial U_j/\partial q_{j2}} = \frac{\partial U_d/\partial q_{d1}}{\partial U_d/\partial q_{d2}} = MRS_d. \quad (10.13)$$

That is, Jane's marginal rate of substitution equals Denise's marginal rate of substitution at an optimal bundle. In geometric terms, this condition says that Jane's indifference curve is tangent to Denise's indifference curve along the contract curve.

SOLVED PROBLEM 10.3

MyLab Economics
Solved Problem

In a pure exchange economy with two goods, G and H, the two traders, Amos and Elise, have Cobb-Douglas utility functions. Amos's utility is $U_a = (G_a)^\alpha (H_a)^{1-\alpha}$, and Elise's is $U_e = (G_e)^\beta (H_e)^{1-\beta}$. Between them, Amos and Elise own 100 units of G and 50 units of H. Thus, if Amos has G_a and H_a, Elise owns $G_e = 100 - G_a$ and $H_e = 50 - H_a$. Solve for their contract curve. Solve for the contract curve if $\alpha = \beta$.

Answer

1. *Use Equation 10.13 and the information about their endowments to determine the necessary condition for Amos's and Elise's contract curve.* From Solved Problem 3.2, we know that Amos's marginal rate of substitution is $MRS_a = [\alpha/(1-\alpha)]H_a/G_a$ and that Elise's is $MRS_e = [\beta/(1-\beta)]H_e/G_e$. From Equation 10.13, we know that these marginal rates of substitution are equal along the contract curve: $MRS_a = MRS_e$. Equating the right-hand sides of the expressions for MRS_a and MRS_e and using the information about the endowments and some algebra, we can write the (quadratic) formula for the contract curve in terms of Amos's goods as

$$(\beta - \alpha)G_a H_a + \beta(\alpha - 1)50G_a + \alpha(1 - \beta)100\, H_a = 0.$$

2. *Substitute in $\alpha = \beta$ and solve.* If we set $\alpha = \beta$, then the contract curve is $(\beta^2 - \beta)50G_a + (\beta - \beta^2)100H_a = 0$. Dividing by $(\beta^2 - \beta)$ to obtain $50G_a - 100H_a = 0$, and using algebra, we conclude that the contract curve is a straight line: $G_a = 2H_a$.

Bargaining Ability

Corresponding to any allocation off the contract curve are allocations on the contract curve that benefit at least one person. If they start at endowment e, Jane and Denise should trade until they reach a point on the contract curve between Bundles b and c in Figure 10.3. All the allocations in area B are better for one or both of them. However, if they trade to any allocation in B that is not on the contract curve, further beneficial trades are possible because their indifference curves intersect at that allocation.

Where will they end up on the contract curve between b and c? That depends on who is the better negotiator. Suppose Jane is. She knows that the more she gets, the worse off Denise will be and that Denise will not agree to any trade that makes her worse off than she is at e. Thus, the best trade Jane can make is one that leaves Denise only as well off as at e, which are the bundles on I_d^1. If Jane could pick any point she wanted along I_d^1, she would choose the bundle on her highest possible indifference curve, Bundle c, where I_j^3 is just tangent to I_d^1. After this trade, Denise is no better off than before, but Jane is much happier. By similar reasoning, if Denise is better at bargaining, the final allocation will be at b.

10.3 Competitive Exchange

Most trading throughout the world occurs without one-on-one bargaining between people. When you go to the store for a bottle of shampoo, you check its price and decide whether to buy it. You've probably never tried to bargain with the store clerk over the price of shampoo: You're a price taker in the shampoo market.

If we don't know much about how Jane and Denise bargain, all we can say is that they will trade to some allocation on the contract curve. However, if we know the exact trading process they use, we can apply that process to determine the final allocation. In particular, we can examine the competitive trading process to determine the competitive equilibrium in a pure exchange economy.

In Chapter 9, we used a partial-equilibrium approach to show that one measure of welfare, W, is maximized in a competitive market in which many voluntary trades occur. We now use a general-equilibrium model to show that a competitive market has two desirable properties:

1. **The competitive equilibrium is efficient:** Competition results in a Pareto-efficient allocation—no one can be made better off without making someone worse off—in all markets.

2. **Any efficient allocations can be achieved by competition:** Any possible efficient allocations can be obtained by competitive exchange given an appropriate initial allocation of goods.

Economists call these results the *First Theorem of Welfare Economics* and the *Second Theorem of Welfare Economics,* respectively. These results hold under fairly weak conditions.

Competitive Equilibrium

When two people trade, they are unlikely to view themselves as price takers. However, if many people with tastes and endowments like Jane's and many with tastes and endowments like Denise's trade, each person would be a price taker in the markets for the two goods. We can use an Edgeworth box to examine how such price takers would trade.

Because they can trade only two goods, each person needs to consider only the relative price of the two goods when deciding whether to trade. If the price of a pile of wood, p_w, is \$2, and the price of a candy bar, p_c, is \$1, then a candy bar costs half as much as a pile of wood: $p_c/p_w = \frac{1}{2}$. An individual can sell one pile of wood and use that money to buy two candy bars.

At the initial allocation, e, Jane has goods worth \$80 = (\$2 per pile × 30 piles of firewood) + (\$1 per candy bar × 20 candy bars). At these prices, Jane could keep her endowment or trade to an allocation with 40 piles of wood and no candy, 80 candy bars and no firewood, or any combination in between, as the price line (budget line) in panel a of Figure 10.4 shows. The price line is all the combinations of goods that Jane could get by trading, given her endowment. The price line goes through point e and has a slope of $-p_c/p_w = -\frac{1}{2}$.

Given the price line, what bundle of goods will Jane choose? She wants to maximize her utility by picking the bundle where one of her indifference curves, I_j^2, is tangent to her budget or price line. Denise wants to maximize her utility by choosing a bundle in the same way.

In a competitive market, prices adjust until the quantity supplied equals the quantity demanded. An auctioneer could help determine the equilibrium price by calling out a price and asking how much is demanded and how much is offered for sale. If the quantity demanded does not equal the quantity supplied, the auctioneer calls out another price. When the quantity demanded equals the quantity supplied, the transactions occur at that price, and the auction stops. At some ports, fishers sell their catch to fish wholesalers at daily auctions run in this manner.

Panel a of Figure 10.4 shows that, when candy costs half as much as wood, the quantity demanded of each good equals the quantity supplied. Jane (and every similar person) wants to sell 10 piles of wood and use that money to buy 20 additional candy bars. Similarly, Denise (and everyone like her) wants to sell 20 candy bars and

Figure 10.4 Competitive Equilibrium

The initial endowment is e. (a) If, along the price line facing Jane and Denise, $p_w = \$2$ and $p_c = \$1$, they trade to point f, where Jane's indifference curve, I_j^2, is tangent to the price line and to Denise's indifference curve, I_d^2. (b) No other price line results in an equilibrium. If $p_w = \$1.33$ and $p_c = \$1$, Denise wants to buy 12 (= 32 − 20) piles of firewood at these prices, but Jane wants to sell only 8 (= 30 − 22) piles. Similarly, Jane wants to buy 10 (= 30 − 20) candy bars, but Denise wants to sell 17 (= 60 − 43). Thus, these prices are not consistent with a competitive equilibrium.

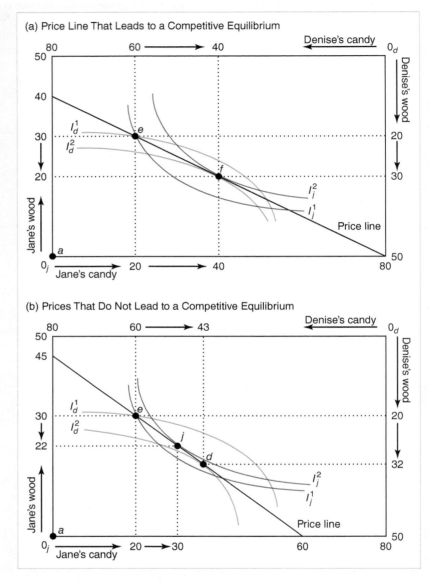

buy 10 piles of wood. Thus, the quantity of wood sold equals the quantity of wood bought, and the quantity of candy demanded equals the quantity of candy supplied. We can see in the figure that the quantities demanded equal the quantities supplied because the optimal bundle for both types of consumers is the same, Bundle f.

At any other price ratio, the quantity demanded of each good would not equal the quantity supplied. For example, if the price of candy remained constant at $p_c = \$1$ per bar but the price of wood fell to $p_w = \$1.33$ per pile, the price line would be steeper, with a slope of $-p_c/p_w = -1/1.33 = -3/4$ in panel b. At these prices, Jane wants to trade to Bundle j and Denise wants to trade to Bundle d. Because Jane wants to buy 10 extra candy bars but Denise wants to sell 17 extra candy bars, the quantity supplied does not equal the quantity demanded, so this price ratio does not result in a competitive equilibrium when the endowment is e.

SOLVED PROBLEM 10.4

MyLab Economics
Solved Problem

Continuing with the example in Solved Problem 10.3—a pure exchange economy with two goods, $G = 100$ and $H = 50$, and two traders, Amos and Elise, with Cobb-Douglas utility functions $U_a = (G_a)^\alpha (H_a)^{1-\alpha}$ and $U_e = (G_e)^\beta (H_e)^{1-\beta}$, respectively—what are the competitive equilibrium prices? (*Note:* We can solve only for the relative prices. We normalize the price of H to equal 1 and solve for p, the price of G.)

Answer

1. *Determine their demand curves.* If Amos's endowment is G_a and H_a, then his income is $Y_a = pG_a + H_a$. Similarly, Elise's endowment is $G_e = 100 - G_a$ and $H_e = 50 - H_a$, so her income is $Y_e = p(100 - G_a) + (50 - H_a)$. Using Equations 3.29 and 3.30 for a Cobb-Douglas utility function, we know that Amos's demand functions are $G_a = \alpha Y_a/p$ and $H_a = (1 - \alpha)Y_a/1$. Similarly, Elise's demand functions are $G_e = \beta Y_e/p$ and $H_e = (1 - \beta)Y_e/1$.

2. *To determine the competitive equilibrium price, equate the demand and supply curves.* The sum of their demands for G equals the fixed supply: $G_a + G_e = 100$. Rearranging the terms in this expression and then substituting for G_e and H_e, we find that the equilibrium price of G is

$$p = \frac{\alpha H_a + \beta H_e}{100 - \alpha G_a + \beta G_e} = \frac{50\beta + (\alpha - \beta)H_a}{100(1 - \beta) + (\beta - \alpha)G_a}.$$

The Efficiency of Competition

In a competitive equilibrium, the indifference curves of both types of consumers are tangent at the same bundle on the price line. As a result, the slope (MRS) of each person's indifference curve equals the slope of the price line, so the slopes of the indifference curves are equal:

$$MRS_j = -\frac{p_c}{p_w} = MRS_d. \tag{10.14}$$

The marginal rates of substitution are equal among consumers in the competitive equilibrium, so the competitive equilibrium must lie on the contract curve. Thus, we have demonstrated the First Theorem of Welfare Economics:

Any competitive equilibrium is Pareto efficient.

The intuition for this result is that people (who face the same prices) make all the voluntary trades they want in a competitive market. Because no additional voluntary trades can occur in a competitive equilibrium, no reallocation of goods would make someone better off without harming someone else. (If an involuntary trade occurs, it harms someone. For example, a person who steals goods from another person—an involuntary exchange—gains at the expense of the victim.)

Obtaining Any Efficient Allocation Using Competition

Of the many possible Pareto-efficient allocations, the government may want to choose one. Can it achieve that allocation using the competitive market mechanism?

Our previous example illustrates that the competitive equilibrium depends on the endowment: the initial distribution of wealth. For example, if the endowment were *a* in panel a of Figure 10.4—where Denise has everything and Jane has nothing—the competitive equilibrium would be *a* because no trades would be possible.

Thus, for competition to lead to a particular allocation—say, *f*—the trading must start at an appropriate endowment. If the consumers' endowment is *f*, a Pareto-efficient point, their indifference curves are tangent at *f*, so no further trades occur. That is, *f* is a competitive equilibrium.

Many other endowments will also result in a competitive equilibrium at *f*. Panel a of Figure 10.4 shows that the resulting competitive equilibrium is *f* if the endowment is *e*. In that figure, a price line goes through both *e* and *f*. If the endowment is any bundle along this price line—not just *e* or *f*—then the competitive equilibrium is *f*, because only at *f* are the indifference curves tangent.

To summarize, any Pareto-efficient bundle *x* can be obtained as a competitive equilibrium if the initial endowment is *x*. Moreover, competition results in that allocation if the endowment lies on a price line through *x*, where the slope of the price line equals the marginal rate of substitution of the indifference curves that are tangent at *x*. Thus, we have demonstrated the Second Theorem of Welfare Economics:

Competition can produce any Pareto-efficient equilibrium given an appropriate endowment.

The first welfare theorem tells us that society can achieve efficiency by allowing competition. The second welfare theorem adds that society can obtain the particular efficient allocation it prefers, based on its value judgments about equity, by appropriately redistributing endowments (income).

10.4 Production and Trading

So far our discussion has been based on a pure exchange economy with no production. We now examine an economy in which a fixed amount of a single input can produce two different goods.

Comparative Advantage

Jane and Denise can produce candy or chop wood using their own labor. However, they differ as to how much of each good they can produce in a day.

Production Possibility Frontier. Jane can produce either three candy bars or six piles of firewood in a day. By splitting her time between the two activities, she can produce various combinations of the two goods. If *t* is the fraction of a day she spends making candy and $1 - t$ is the fraction she spends cutting wood, she produces $3t$ candy bars and $6(1 - t)$ piles of wood.

By varying *t* between 0 and 1, we trace out the line in panel a of Figure 10.5. This line is Jane's *production possibility frontier* (PPF_j; Chapter 7), which shows the maximum combinations of candy and wood that she can produce from a given amount of input. If Jane works all day using the best technology (such as a sharp ax), she achieves *efficiency in production* and produces combinations of goods on PPF_j. If she relaxes part of the day or does not use the best technology, she produces an inefficient combination of candy and wood that lies inside PPF_j.

Marginal Rate of Transformation. The slope of the production possibility frontier is the *marginal rate of transformation* (MRT).[7] The marginal rate of transformation

---

[7]In Chapter 3, we called the slope of a consumer's budget line the marginal rate of transformation. For a price-taking consumer who obtains goods by buying them, the budget line plays the same role as the production possibility frontier for someone who produces the two goods.

Figure 10.5 Comparative Advantage and Production Possibility Frontiers

(a) Jane's production possibility frontier, PPF_j, shows that in a day, she can produce 6 piles of firewood or 3 candy bars or any combination of the two. Her marginal rate of transformation (MRT) is -2. (b) Denise's production possibility frontier, PPF_d, has an MRT of $\frac{1}{2}$. (c) Their joint production possibility frontier, PPF, has a kink at 6 piles of wood (produced by Jane) and 6 candy bars (produced by Denise) and is concave to the origin.

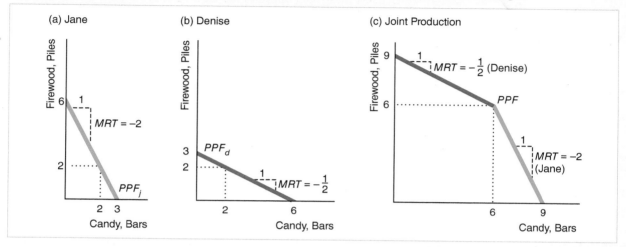

tells us how much more wood can be produced if the production of candy is reduced by one bar. Because Jane's PPF_j is a straight line with a slope of -2, her MRT is -2 at every allocation.

Denise can produce up to three piles of wood or six candy bars each day. Panel b shows her production possibility function, PPF_d, with an $MRT = -\frac{1}{2}$. Thus, with a day's work, Denise can produce relatively more candy, and Jane can produce relatively more wood, as reflected by their differing marginal rates of transformation.

The marginal rate of transformation shows how much it costs to produce one good in terms of the forgone production of the other good. Someone with the ability to produce a good at a lower opportunity cost than someone else has a **comparative advantage** in producing that good. Denise has a comparative advantage in producing candy (she forgoes less in wood production to produce a given amount of candy), and Jane has a comparative advantage in producing wood.

By combining their outputs, they have the joint production possibility frontier PPF in panel c. If Denise and Jane spend all their time producing wood, Denise produces three piles and Jane produces six piles for a total of nine piles, which is where the joint PPF hits the wood axis. Similarly, if they both produce candy, together they can produce nine bars. If Denise specializes in making candy and Jane specializes in cutting wood, they produce six candy bars and six piles of wood, a combination that appears at the kink in the PPF.

If they choose to produce a relatively large quantity of candy and a relatively small amount of wood, Denise produces only candy and Jane produces some candy and some wood. Jane chops the wood because that is her comparative advantage. The marginal rate of transformation in the lower portion of the PPF is Jane's, -2, because only she produces both candy and wood.

Similarly, if they produce little candy, Jane produces only wood and Denise produces some wood and some candy, so the marginal rate of transformation in the higher portion of the PPF is Denise's, $-\frac{1}{2}$. In short, the PPF has a kink at six piles of wood and six candy bars and is concave (bowed away from the origin).

Benefits of Trade. Because of the difference in their marginal rates of transformation, Jane and Denise can benefit from a trade. Suppose that Jane and Denise like to consume wood and candy in equal proportions. If they do not trade, each produces two candy bars and two piles of wood each day. If they agree to trade, Denise, who excels at making candy, spends all day producing six candy bars. Similarly, Jane, who has a comparative advantage at chopping wood, produces six piles of wood. If they split this production equally, they can each have three piles of wood and three candy bars—50% more than without trade.

They do better if they trade because each person uses her comparative advantage. Without trade, if Denise wants an extra pile of wood, she must give up two candy bars. Producing an extra pile of wood costs Jane only half a candy bar in forgone production. Denise is willing to trade up to two candy bars for a pile of wood, and Jane is willing to trade the wood as long as she gets at least half a candy bar. Thus, a mutually beneficial trade is possible.

SOLVED PROBLEM 10.5

MyLab Economics
Solved Problem

How does the joint production possibility frontier in panel c of Figure 10.5 change if Jane and Denise can also trade with Harvey, who can produce five piles of wood, five candy bars, or any linear combination of wood and candy in a day?

Answer

1. *Describe each person's individual production possibility frontier.* Panels a and b of Figure 10.5 show the production possibility frontiers of Jane and Denise. Harvey's production possibility frontier is a straight line that hits the firewood axis at five piles and the candy axis at five candy bars.

2. *Draw the joint PPF by starting at the quantity on the horizontal axis that is produced if everyone specializes in candy and then connecting the individual production possibility frontiers in order of comparative advantage in chopping wood.* If all three produce candy, they make 14 candy bars (on the horizontal axis of the accompanying graph). Jane has a comparative advantage at chopping wood over Harvey and Denise, and Harvey has a comparative advantage over Denise. Thus, Jane's production possibility frontier is the first frontier (starting at the lower right), then comes Harvey's, and then Denise's. The resulting *PPF* is concave to the origin. (If we change the order of the individual frontiers, the resulting *kinked line lies inside the PPF*. Thus, the new line cannot be the joint production possibility frontier, which shows the maximum possible production from the available labor inputs.)

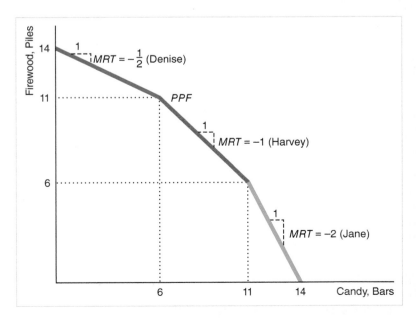

The Number of Producers. With only two ways of producing wood and candy—Denise's and Jane's methods with different marginal rates of transformation—the joint production possibility frontier has a single kink (panel c of Figure 10.5). If another method of production with a different marginal rate of transformation—Harvey's—is added, the joint production possibility frontier has two kinks (as in Solved Problem 10.5).

If many people can produce candy and firewood with different marginal rates of transformation, the joint production possibility frontier has even more kinks. As the number of people becomes very large, the *PPF* becomes a smooth curve that is concave to the origin, as in Figure 10.6.

Because the *PPF* is concave, the marginal rate of transformation decreases (in absolute value) as we move up the *PPF*. The *PPF* has a flatter slope at *a*, where the $MRT = -\frac{1}{2}$, than at *b*, where the $MRT = -1$. At *a*, giving up a candy bar leads to half a pile more wood production. In contrast, at *b*, which has relatively more candy, giving up producing a candy bar frees enough resources that they can produce an additional pile of wood.

The marginal rate of transformation along this smooth *PPF* tells us about the marginal cost of producing one good relative to the marginal cost of producing the other good. The marginal rate of transformation equals the negative of the ratio of the marginal cost of producing candy, MC_c, and wood, MC_w:

$$MRT = -\frac{MC_c}{MC_w}. \qquad (10.15)$$

Suppose that at point *a* in Figure 10.6, a person's marginal cost of producing an extra candy bar is $1, and the marginal cost of producing an additional pile of firewood is $2. As a result, the person can produce one extra candy bar or half a pile of wood at a cost of $1. The marginal rate of transformation is the negative of the

Figure 10.6 Optimal Product Mix

The optimal product mix, *a*, could be determined by maximizing an individual's utility by picking the allocation for which an indifference curve is tangent to the production possibility frontier. It could also be determined by picking the allocation where the relative competitive price, p_c/p_f, equals the slope of the *PPF*.

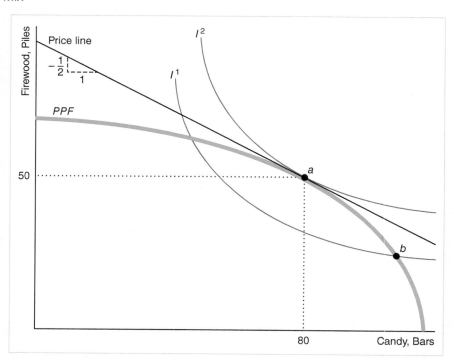

ratio of the marginal costs, $-(\$1/\$2) = -\frac{1}{2}$. To produce one more candy bar, the person must give up producing half a pile of wood.

Efficient Product Mix

Which combination of products along the *PPF* does society choose? If a single person were to decide on the product mix, that person would pick the allocation of wood and candy along the *PPF* that maximized his or her utility. A person with the indifference curves in Figure 10.6 would pick Allocation *a*, which is the point where the *PPF* touches indifference curve I^2.

Because I^2 is tangent to the *PPF* at *a*, that person's marginal rate of substitution (the slope of indifference curve I^2) equals the marginal rate of transformation (the slope of the *PPF*). The marginal rate of substitution, *MRS*, tells us how much a consumer is willing to give up of one good to get another. The marginal rate of transformation, *MRT*, tells us how much of one good we need to give up to produce more of another good.

If the *MRS* does not equal the *MRT*, the consumer will be happier with a different product mix. At Allocation *b*, the indifference curve I^1 intersects the *PPF*, so the *MRS* does not equal the *MRT*. At *b*, the consumer is willing to give up one candy bar to get a third of a pile of wood $\left(MRS = -\frac{1}{3}\right)$. But firms can produce one pile of wood for every candy bar not produced ($MRT = -1$). Thus at *b*, too little wood is being produced. If the firms increase wood production, the *MRS* will fall and the *MRT* will rise until they are equal at *a*, where $MRS = MRT = -\frac{1}{2}$.

We can extend this reasoning to look at the product mix choice of all consumers simultaneously. Each consumer's marginal rate of substitution must equal the economy's marginal rate of transformation, $MRS = MRT$, if the economy is to produce the optimal mix of goods for each consumer. How can we ensure that this condition holds for all consumers? One way is to use the competitive market.

Competition

Each price-taking consumer picks a bundle of goods so that the consumer's marginal rate of substitution equals the slope of the consumer's price line (the negative of the relative prices):

$$MRS = -\frac{p_c}{p_w}. \tag{10.16}$$

Thus, if all consumers face the same relative prices in the competitive equilibrium, all consumers will buy a bundle where their marginal rates of substitution are equal (Equation 10.14). Because all consumers have the same marginal rates of substitution, no further trades can occur. Thus, the competitive equilibrium achieves *consumption efficiency*: It is impossible to redistribute goods among consumers to make one consumer better off without harming another consumer. That is, the competitive equilibrium lies on the contract curve.

If competitive firms sell candy and wood, each firm sells a quantity of candy for which its price equals its marginal cost,

$$p_c = MC_c, \tag{10.17}$$

and a quantity of wood for which its price and marginal cost are equal,

$$p_w = MC_w. \tag{10.18}$$

Taking the ratio of Equations 10.17 and 10.18, we find that in competition, $p_c/p_w = MC_c/MC_w$. From Equation 10.15, we know that the marginal rate of transformation equals $-MC_c/MC_w$, so

$$MRT = -\frac{MC_c}{MC_w} = -\frac{p_c}{p_w}. \tag{10.19}$$

We can illustrate why firms want to produce where Equation 10.19 holds. Suppose that a firm were producing at b in Figure 10.6, where its MRT is -1, and that $p_c = \$1$ and $p_w = \$2$, so $-p_c/p_w = \frac{1}{2}$. If the firm reduces its output by one candy bar, it loses $1 in candy sales but makes $2 more from selling the extra pile of wood, for a net gain of $1. Thus at b, where the $MRT < -p_c/p_w$, the firm should reduce its output of candy and increase its output of wood. In contrast, if the firm is producing at a, where the $MRT = -p_c/p_w = \frac{1}{2}$, it has no incentive to change its behavior: The gain from producing a little more wood exactly offsets the loss from producing a little less candy.

Combining Equations 10.16 and 10.19, we find that in the competitive equilibrium, the MRS equals the ratio of relative prices, which equal the MRT:

$$MRS = -\frac{p_c}{p_w} = MRT.$$

Because competition ensures that the MRS equals the MRT, a competitive equilibrium achieves an *efficient product mix*: The rate at which firms can transform one good into another equals the rate at which consumers are willing to substitute between the goods, as reflected by their willingness to pay for the two goods.

By combining the production possibility frontier and an Edgeworth box, we can show the competitive equilibrium in both production and consumption. Suppose that firms produce 50 piles of firewood and 80 candy bars at a in Figure 10.7. The size of the Edgeworth box—the maximum amount of wood and candy available to consumers—is determined by point a on the PPF.

The prices consumers pay must equal the prices producers receive, so the price lines that consumers and producers face must have the same slope of $-p_c/p_w$. In equilibrium, the price lines are tangent to each consumer's indifference curve at f and to the PPF at a.

In this competitive equilibrium, supply equals demand in all markets. Consumers buy the mix of goods at f. Consumers like Jane, whose origin, 0_j, is at the lower-left corner, consume 20 piles of firewood and 40 candy bars. Consumers like Denise, whose origin is a at the upper right of the Edgeworth box, consume 30 (= 50 − 20) piles of firewood and 40 (= 80 − 40) candy bars.

The two key results concerning competition still hold in an economy with production. First, a competitive equilibrium is Pareto efficient, achieving efficiency in consumption and in output mix.[8] Second, any particular Pareto-efficient allocation between consumers can be obtained through competition, given that the government chooses an appropriate endowment.

---

[8]Competitive firms choose factor combinations so that their marginal rates of technical substitution between inputs equal the negative of the ratios of the relative factor prices (see Chapter 7). That is, competition also results in *efficiency in production*: Firms could not produce more of one good without producing less of another good.

Figure 10.7 Competitive Equilibrium

At the competitive equilibrium, the relative prices that firms and consumers face are the same (the price lines are parallel), so the $MRS = -p_c/p_w = MRT$.

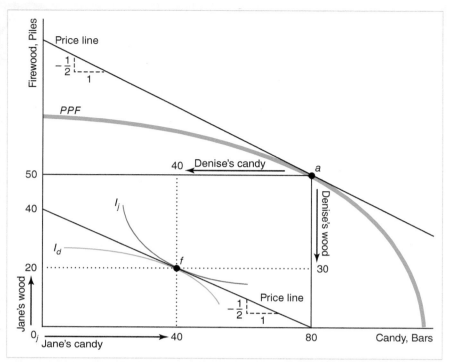

10.5 Efficiency and Equity

The welfare of a society's citizens depends on how society deals with efficiency (the size of the pie) and equity (the division of the pie between people). The outcome depends on individual choices and on government actions.

Role of the Government

By altering how efficiently society produces and distributes goods and the endowment of resources, governments help determine how much is produced and how goods are allocated. By redistributing endowments or by refusing to do so, governments, at least implicitly, are making value judgments about which members of society should get relatively more of society's goodies.

Virtually every government program, tax, or action redistributes wealth. Proceeds from a British lottery, played mostly by lower-income people, subsidize the Royal Opera House at Covent Garden, thereby transferring funds to the "rich toffs" who attend operas. Agricultural price support programs (Chapter 9) redistribute wealth to farmers from other taxpayers. Income taxes and food stamp programs (Chapter 5) redistribute income from better-off taxpayers to those less well off.

Efficiency

Many economists and political leaders make the value judgment that governments *should* use the Pareto principle, preferring reallocations of resources that make someone better off while harming no one else. Consequently, they believe that governments should allow voluntary trades, encourage competition, and otherwise try to prevent problems that reduce efficiency.

We can use the Pareto principle to rank allocations or government policies that alter allocations. The Pareto criterion ranks allocation x over allocation y if some people are better off at x and no one else is worse off. If so, we say that x is *Pareto superior* to y.

However, we cannot always use the Pareto principle to compare allocations. If both allocation x and allocation y are Pareto efficient, we cannot use this criterion to rank them. For example, if Denise has all the goods in x and Jane has all the goods in y, then we cannot rank these allocations using the Pareto rule.

To choose between two Pareto-efficient allocations, we have to make a value judgment based on interpersonal comparisons. Society must make interpersonal comparisons to evaluate most government policies.

Suppose that, when a country ends a ban on imports and allows free trade, domestic consumers benefit by many times more than domestic producers suffer. This policy change does not meet the Pareto efficiency criterion that someone may benefit without anyone else suffering. Of course, the government could adopt a more complex policy that meets the Pareto criterion. Because consumers benefit by more than producers suffer, the government could take enough of the free-trade gains from consumers to compensate the producers so that no one is harmed and some people benefit.

The government rarely uses policies that require winners to subsidize losers. If a policy does not require such subsidization, society must make additional value judgments involving interpersonal comparisons to decide whether to adopt that policy.

We have been using a welfare measure, $W =$ consumer surplus + producer surplus, that equally weights benefits and losses to consumers and producers. This measure is making an implicit interpersonal comparison by weighting consumers and producers equally. By this criterion, if a policy results in gains to consumers that outweigh the losses to producers, society should adopt that policy.

Thus, calling for policy changes that lead to Pareto-superior allocations is a weaker rule than calling for policy changes that increase the welfare measure W. We can rank more allocations using the welfare measure than using the Pareto rule. Any policy change that leads to a Pareto-superior allocation must increase W; however, some policy changes that increase W are not Pareto superior, because they produce both winners and losers.

Equity

If we are unwilling to use the Pareto principle or if that criterion does not allow us to rank the relevant allocations, we must make additional value judgments to rank these allocations. We can summarize these value judgments using a *social welfare function* that combines various consumers' utilities to provide a collective ranking of allocations. Loosely speaking, a social welfare function is a utility function for society.

We illustrate the use of a social welfare function using the pure exchange economy in which Jane and Denise trade wood and candy. The contract curve in Figure 10.3 consists of many possible Pareto-efficient allocations. Jane and Denise's utility levels

APPLICATION

Extremely Unequal Wealth

Money is better than poverty, if only for financial reasons. —Woody Allen

Wealth is unequally distributed, and the wealthiest are becoming wealthier over time. The six heirs to the Walmart fortune have as much wealth as the least wealthy 42% of U.S. families—49 million households. The Institute for Policy Studies calculates that the three wealthiest Americans—Jeff Bezos, Bill Gates, and Warren Buffet—have as much wealth as the entire bottom half of the U.S. population combined.

According to the charity Oxfam, the 42 richest people in the world—most of whom live in Europe or the United States—had as much wealth as did the poorest half of the world's population in 2017. That is, on average, each of these extremely wealthy people has as much wealth as about 88 million of the world's poorest people—about twice the number of people who live in Argentina. The world's richest man, Jeff Bezos, had $112 billion in wealth in 2018, which is the same as the 156 million poorest people. The wealthiest 1% had roughly the same amount of global wealth (50.1%) as did the poorest 99% (49.9%). The bottom four-fifths of people had only 5.5% of the wealth.

Share of Wealth of the Richest 1 Percent

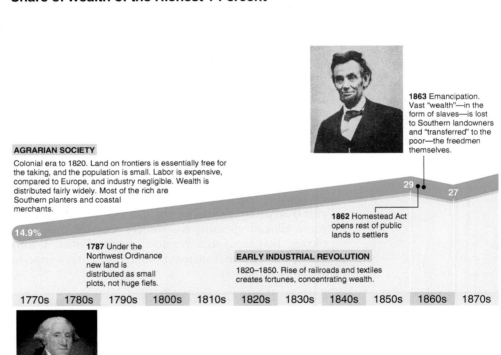

AGRARIAN SOCIETY

Colonial era to 1820. Land on frontiers is essentially free for the taking, and the population is small. Labor is expensive, compared to Europe, and industry negligible. Wealth is distributed fairly widely. Most of the rich are Southern planters and coastal merchants.

1863 Emancipation. Vast "wealth"—in the form of slaves—is lost to Southern landowners and "transferred" to the poor—the freedmen themselves.

1862 Homestead Act opens rest of public lands to settlers

14.9%

29

27

1787 Under the Northwest Ordinance new land is distributed as small plots, not huge fiefs.

EARLY INDUSTRIAL REVOLUTION

1820–1850. Rise of railroads and textiles creates fortunes, concentrating wealth.

1770s 1780s 1790s 1800s 1810s 1820s 1830s 1840s 1850s 1860s 1870s

North America and Europe have 64% of the world's wealth, China and other Asian-Pacific nations have 30%, while Latin America, India, and Africa combined have only 6%.

The United States has less equally distributed wealth than do other developed countries. According to Credit Suisse, as of 2017, the top 10% of U.S. households have 75% of U.S. wealth. The corresponding shares are 50% in France, 48% in Canada and in the United Kingdom, and 34% in Japan.

Since the founding of the United States, changes in its economy have altered the share of the nation's wealth held by the richest 1% of Americans (see the figure). An array of social changes—sometimes occurring during or after wars and often codified into new laws—have greatly redistributed wealth. For example, the emancipation of slaves in 1863 transferred vast wealth—the labor of the former slaves—from rich Southern landowners to the poor freed slaves.

The share of wealth—the total assets owned—held by the richest 1% generally increased until the Great Depression, declined through the mid-1970s, and has increased substantially since then. The greatest wealth concentration occurred in 1929 during the Great Depression and today, following the Great Recession.

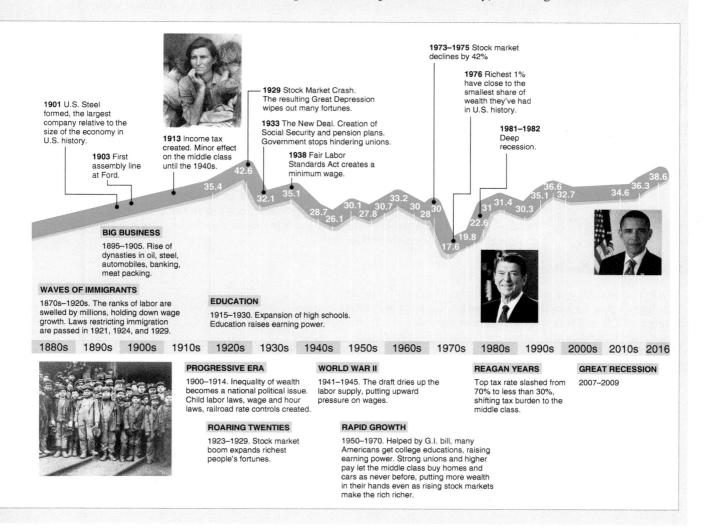

1973–1975 Stock market declines by 42%

1976 Richest 1% have close to the smallest share of wealth they've had in U.S. history.

1981–1982 Deep recession.

1929 Stock Market Crash. The resulting Great Depression wipes out many fortunes.

1933 The New Deal. Creation of Social Security and pension plans. Government stops hindering unions.

1938 Fair Labor Standards Act creates a minimum wage.

1901 U.S. Steel formed, the largest company relative to the size of the economy in U.S. history.

1903 First assembly line at Ford.

1913 Income tax created. Minor effect on the middle class until the 1940s.

BIG BUSINESS

1895–1905. Rise of dynasties in oil, steel, automobiles, banking, meat packing.

WAVES OF IMMIGRANTS

1870s–1920s. The ranks of labor are swelled by millions, holding down wage growth. Laws restricting immigration are passed in 1921, 1924, and 1929.

EDUCATION

1915–1930. Expansion of high schools. Education raises earning power.

Values along curve: 35.4, 42.6, 32.1, 35.1, 28.7, 26.1, 30.1, 27.8, 30.7, 33.2, 30, 30, 28, 17.6, 19.8, 22.6, 31, 31.4, 30.3, 35.1, 32.7, 36.6, 34.6, 36.3, 38.6

| 1880s | 1890s | 1900s | 1910s | 1920s | 1930s | 1940s | 1950s | 1960s | 1970s | 1980s | 1990s | 2000s | 2010s | 2016 |

PROGRESSIVE ERA

1900–1914. Inequality of wealth becomes a national political issue. Child labor laws, wage and hour laws, railroad rate controls created.

ROARING TWENTIES

1923–1929. Stock market boom expands richest people's fortunes.

WORLD WAR II

1941–1945. The draft dries up the labor supply, putting upward pressure on wages.

RAPID GROWTH

1950–1970. Helped by G.I. bill, many Americans get college educations, raising earning power. Strong unions and higher pay let the middle class buy homes and cars as never before, putting more wealth in their hands even as rising stock markets make the rich richer.

REAGAN YEARS

Top tax rate slashed from 70% to less than 30%, shifting tax burden to the middle class.

GREAT RECESSION

2007–2009

A major cause of the recent increased concentration of wealth is the change in the tax law. The top U.S. marginal income tax rate fell from 91% at the end of World War II to 70% under the Kennedy and Johnson Administrations, to less than 30% at the beginning of the Reagan administration, and to 37% today, shifting more of the tax burden to the middle class. Between 1989 and 2016, the wealth share of the top 1% of U.S. households rose from three-tenths to four-tenths. The top 5% of households own one-half of all U.S. wealth, and the top 20% have nine-tenths. The share of the lowest half of households dropped from a tiny 3% to an almost nonexistent 1%. Indeed, the poorest 20% of households have negative wealth because they owe more than the value of their assets. The major revision of the tax law that took effect in 2018 favors the wealthy, so it is likely to make the wealth distribution even more unequal.

vary along the contract curve. Figure 10.8 shows the *utility possibility frontier* (UPF): the set of utility levels corresponding to the Pareto-efficient allocations along the contract curve. Point *a* in Figure 10.8 corresponds to the end of the contract curve at which Denise has all the goods, and *c* corresponds to the allocation at which Jane has all the goods.

The curves labeled W^1, W^2, and W^3 in panel a are *isowelfare curves* based on the social welfare function. These curves are similar to indifference curves for individuals. They summarize all the allocations with identical levels of welfare. Society maximizes its welfare at point *b*.

Who decides on the welfare function? In most countries, government leaders make decisions about which allocations are most desirable. These officials may believe that transferring money from wealthy people to poorer people raises welfare, or vice versa. When government officials choose a particular allocation, they are implicitly or explicitly judging which consumers are relatively deserving and hence should receive more goods than others.

Voting. In a democracy, society votes on important government policies that determine the allocation of goods. Such democratic decision making is often difficult because people fundamentally disagree on how issues should be resolved and which groups the government should favor.

Figure 10.8 Welfare Maximization

Society maximizes welfare by choosing the allocation for which the highest possible isowelfare curve touches the utility possibility frontier, *UPF*. The isowelfare curves have the shape of a typical indifference curve. Society maximizes its welfare at point *b*.

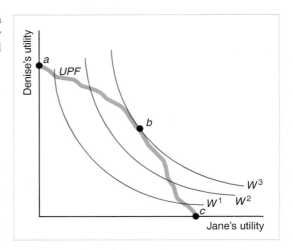

We assume (Chapter 3) that consumers can rank-order all bundles of goods in terms of their preferences (completeness) and that their rank over goods is transitive.[9] Suppose now that people have preferences over the allocations of goods among consumers. One possibility, as we assumed earlier, is that individuals care only about how many goods they receive—they do not care about how much others have. Another possibility is that because of envy, charity, pity, love, and other interpersonal feelings, individuals do care about how much everyone has.[10]

Let *a* be a particular allocation of goods that describes how much of each good an individual has. Each person can rank this allocation relative to Allocation *b*. For instance, individuals know whether they prefer an allocation in which everyone has equal amounts of all goods to another allocation in which people who work hard—or those of a particular skin color or religion—have relatively more goods than others.

Through voting, individuals express their rankings. One possible voting system requires that before the vote is taken, everyone agrees to be bound by the outcome in the sense that if a majority of people prefer Allocation *a* to Allocation *b*, then *a* is *socially preferred* to *b*.

Using majority voting to determine which allocations society prefers sounds reasonable, doesn't it? Such a system might work well. For example, if all individuals have the same transitive preferences, the social ordering has the same transitive ranking as that of each individual.

Unfortunately, sometimes voting does not work well, and the resulting social ordering of allocations is not transitive. To illustrate this possibility, suppose that three people have the transitive preferences. Individual 1 prefers Allocation *a* to Allocation *b* to Allocation *c*. Table 10.1 shows that the other two individuals have different transitive preferred orderings.

Two out of three of these individuals prefer *a* to *b*; two out of three prefer *b* to *c*; and two out of three prefer *c* to *a*. Thus, voting leads to nontransitive societal preferences, even though the preferences of each individual are transitive. As a result, no output is clearly socially preferred. A majority of people prefers some other allocation to any particular allocation. Compared to Allocation *a*, a majority prefers *c*. Similarly, a majority prefers *b* over *c*, and a majority prefers *a* over *b*.

If people have this type of ranking of allocations, the chosen allocation will depend crucially on the order of pairwise-comparison votes. Suppose that these three people first vote on whether they prefer *a* or *b* and then compare the winner to *c*. The majority prefers *a* to *b* in the first vote and *c* to *a* in the second vote, so they choose *c*. If instead they first compare *c* to *a* and the winner to *b*, then *b* is chosen. Thus, the

Table 10.1 Preferences over Allocations of Three People

	Individual 1	Individual 2	Individual 3
First choice	*a*	*b*	*c*
Second choice	*b*	*c*	*a*
Third choice	*c*	*a*	*b*

---

[9]The transitivity (or *rationality*) assumption is that a consumer's preference over bundles is consistent in the sense that if the consumer weakly prefers Bundle *a* to Bundle *b* and weakly prefers Bundle *b* to Bundle *c*, then the consumer weakly prefers Bundle *a* to Bundle *c*.

[10]To an economist, love is nothing more than interdependent utility functions. Thus, it's a mystery how each successive generation of economists is produced.

outcome depends on the political skill of various factions in determining the order of voting.

Similar problems arise with other types of voting schemes. Kenneth Arrow (1951), who received a Nobel Prize in economics in part for his work on social decision making, proved a startling and depressing result about democratic voting, which is now called Arrow's Impossibility Theorem. Arrow suggested that a socially desirable decision-making system, or social welfare function, should satisfy the following criteria:

■ Social preferences should be complete and transitive, like individual preferences (Chapter 3).
■ If everyone prefers Allocation *a* to Allocation *b*, *a* should be socially preferred to *b*.
■ Society's ranking of *a* and *b* should depend only on individuals' ordering of these two allocations, not on how they rank other alternatives.
■ Dictatorship is forbidden: Social preferences must not reflect the preferences of only a single individual.

Although each of these criteria seems reasonable—indeed, innocuous—Arrow proved that it is impossible to find a social decision-making rule that *always* satisfies all of these criteria. His result indicates that *democratic decision making* may fail—not that *democracy* must fail. After all, if everyone agrees on a ranking, these four criteria are satisfied.

If society is willing to give up one of these criteria, a democratic decision-making rule can guarantee that the other three criteria are met. For example, if we give up the third criterion, often referred to as the *independence of irrelevant alternatives*, certain complicated voting schemes in which individuals rank their preferences can meet the other criteria.

Social Welfare Functions. Philosophers, economists, newspaper columnists, politicians, radio talk-show hosts, and other deep thinkers have suggested various rules by which society might decide among various possible allocations. All these systems answer the question of which individuals' preferences should be given more weight in society's decision making. Determining how much weight to give to the preferences of various members of society is usually the key step in determining a social welfare function.

Probably the simplest and most egalitarian rule is that every member of society should receive exactly the same bundle of goods. If society forbids trading, this rule results in complete equality in the allocation of goods.

Jeremy Bentham (1748–1832) and his followers (including John Stuart Mill), the utilitarian philosophers, suggested that society should maximize the sum of the utilities of all members of society. Their social welfare function is the sum of the utilities of every member of society. The utilities of all people in society receive equal weight.[11] If U_i is the utility of Individual *i* and the society has *n* people, the utilitarian welfare function is

$$W = U_1 + U_2 + \cdots + U_n.$$

However, this social welfare function may not lead to an egalitarian distribution of goods. Indeed, under this system, society judges an allocation to be superior, all

---

[11]It is difficult to compare utilities across individuals because the scaling of utilities across individuals is arbitrary (Chapter 3). The welfare rule that we have been using avoids this utility comparison problem because it equally weights consumer surplus and producer surplus, which are denominated in dollars.

else the same, if people who get the most pleasure from consuming certain goods are given more of those goods.

A generalization of the utilitarian approach assigns different weights to various individuals' utilities. If the weight assigned to Individual i is α_i, this generalized utilitarian welfare function is

$$W = \alpha_1 U_1 + \alpha_2 U_2 + \cdots + \alpha_n U_n.$$

Society could give greater weight to adults, hardworking people, or those who meet other criteria. Under South Africa's former apartheid system, the utilities of people with white skin were given more weight than those with other skin colors.

John Rawls (1971), a Harvard University philosopher, believed that society should maximize the well-being of the worst-off member of society, the person with the lowest level of utility. In the social welfare function, the utility of the person with the lowest utility level should receive all the weight. The Rawlsian welfare function is

$$W = \min (U_1, U_2, \ldots , U_n).$$

Rawls's rule leads to a relatively egalitarian distribution of goods.

One final rule, frequently espoused by various members of Congress and by wealthy landowners in less-developed countries, is to maintain the status quo. Proponents of this rule believe that the current allocation is the best possible allocation, and they argue against any reallocation of resources from one individual to another. Under this rule, the final allocation is likely to be very unequal. Why else would the wealthy want it?

All of these rules or social welfare functions reflect value judgments involving interpersonal comparisons. Because each reflects value judgments, we cannot compare them on scientific grounds.

Efficiency Versus Equity

Given a particular social welfare function, *society might prefer an inefficient allocation to an efficient one.* We can show this result by comparing two allocations. In Allocation a, you have everything and everyone else has nothing. This allocation is Pareto efficient: It is impossible to make others better off without harming you. In Allocation b, everyone has an equal amount of all goods. Allocation b is not Pareto efficient: I would be willing to trade all my zucchini for just about anything else. Despite Allocation b's inefficiency, most people probably prefer b to a.

Although society might prefer an inefficient Allocation b to an efficient Allocation a, according to most social welfare functions, society would prefer some efficient allocation to b. Suppose that Allocation c is the competitive equilibrium that would be obtained if people were allowed to trade starting from Endowment b, in which everyone has an equal share of all goods. By the utilitarian social welfare functions, Allocation b might be socially preferred to Allocation a, but Allocation c is certainly socially preferred to b (ruling out envy and similar interpersonal feelings). After all, if everyone is as well off or better off in Allocation c than in b, c must be better than b regardless of weights on individuals' utilities. According to the egalitarian rule, however, b is preferred to c because only strict equality matters. Thus by most, but not all, of the well-known social welfare functions, *an efficient allocation is socially preferred to an inefficient allocation.*

A competitive equilibrium may not be very equitable even though it is Pareto efficient. Consequently, societies that believe in equity may tax the rich to give to the poor. If society transfers money from the rich to the poor, society moves from one Pareto-efficient allocation to another.

Sometimes, however, in an attempt to achieve greater equity, consumption efficiency is reduced. For example, advocates for the poor argue that providing public housing to the destitute leads to an allocation that is superior to the original competitive equilibrium. This reallocation is not efficient: The poor view themselves as better off receiving an amount of money equal to what the government spends on public housing. They could spend the money on the type of housing they like—rather than the type the government provides—or they could spend some of the money on food or other goods.[12]

Unfortunately, frequently society's goal of production efficiency and its goal of an equitable allocation conflict. When the government redistributes money from one group to another, it incurs significant costs from this redistribution. If tax collectors and other government bureaucrats produced goods rather than redistributing them, total output would increase. Similarly, income taxes discourage some people from working as hard as they otherwise would (Chapter 5). Nonetheless, probably few people believe that the status quo is optimal and that the government should engage in no redistribution at all (although some legislators vote for tax laws as though they believe that we should redistribute from the poor to the rich).

Theory of the Second Best

Many politicians and media pundits—influenced by the basic logic of the argument that competition maximizes efficiency and our usual welfare measure—argue that we should eliminate any distortion (such as tariffs and quotas). However, care must be taken in making this argument. The argument holds if we eliminate *all* distortions, but it does not necessarily hold if we eliminate only some of them.

Consider a competitive economy with no distortions. It is a *first-best equilibrium* in which any distortion will reduce efficiency. If a single distortion arises—such as one caused by a ban on trade—and that distortion is eliminated, efficiency must rise as the economy reverts to the first-best equilibrium (see Chapter 9). Everyone can gain—welfare rises—if losers (such as producers who lose the benefits of a ban on trade) are compensated.

However, according to the Theory of the Second Best (Lipsey and Lancaster, 1956), if an economy has at least two market distortions, correcting one of them may either increase or decrease welfare. For example, if a small country has a ban on trade and a subsidy on one good, permitting free trade may not raise efficiency.

Suppose that a wheat-producing country is a price taker on the world wheat market, where the world price is p_w. As we saw in Chapter 9, the country's total welfare is greater if it permits rather than bans free trade. Panel a of Figure 10.9 shows the gain to trade in the usual case. The domestic supply curve, S, is upward sloping, but the home country can import as much as it wants at the world price, p_w. In the free-trade equilibrium, e_1, the equilibrium quantity is Q_1 and the equilibrium price is the world price, p_w. With a ban on imports, the equilibrium is e_2, quantity falls to Q_2, and price rises to p_2. Consequently, the deadweight loss from the ban is area D.

Now suppose that the home government subsidizes its agricultural sector with a payment of s per unit of output. The subsidy creates a distortion: excess

---

[12]Letting the poor decide how to spend their income is efficient by our definition, even if they spend it on "sin goods" such as cigarettes, liquor, or illicit drugs. A similar argument was made regarding food stamps in Chapter 5.

Figure 10.9 Welfare Effect of Trade with and Without a Subsidy

Whether permitting trade raises welfare (consumer surplus plus producer surplus) depends on whether the economy has distortions. (a) If the only distortion is a trade ban, eliminating it must raise welfare. With free trade, the supply curve is the sum of the domestic supply curve and the world supply curve, which is horizontal at the world price, p_w. The equilibrium is e_1 where the supply curve intersects the domestic demand curve. In contrast, without trade, the equilibrium is e_2, where the domestic supply curve intersects the domestic demand curve. The deadweight loss from the ban is area D. (b) With a subsidy, the domestic supply curve shifts to S^*. The equilibrium with a trade ban is e_3 and the free-trade equilibrium is e_4. The gain to trade (ignoring government's subsidy cost) is area $A + B$. The expansion of domestic output increases the government's subsidy cost by area $B + C$. Welfare falls because area C is greater than area A.

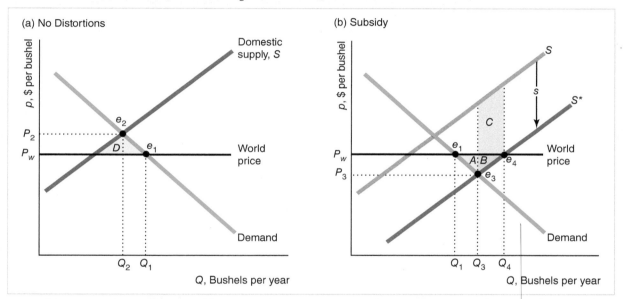

(a) No Distortions

(b) Subsidy

production (Chapter 9). The per-unit subsidy s causes the supply curve to shift down from S to S^* in panel b of Figure 10.9. With a trade ban, the equilibrium is at e_3, with a larger quantity, Q_3, than in the original free-trade equilibrium and a lower consumer price, p_3. Because the true marginal cost (the height of the S curve at Q_3) is above the consumer price, society suffers a deadweight loss.

With free trade, the Theory of the Second Best tells us that welfare does not necessarily rise, because the country still has the subsidy distortion. The free-trade equilibrium is e_4. Firms sell all their quantity, Q_4, at the world price, with Q_1 going to domestic consumers and $Q_4 - Q_1$ to consumers elsewhere. The private gain to trade—ignoring the government's cost of providing the subsidy—is area $A + B$. However, the expansion of domestic output increases the government's cost of the subsidy by area $B + C$ (the height of this area is the distance between the two supply curves, which is the subsidy, s, and the length is the extra output sold). Thus, if area C is greater than area A, a net welfare loss results from permitting trade. As the diagram is drawn, C is greater than A, so allowing trade lowers welfare, given that the subsidy is provided.

Does it follow from this argument that the country should prohibit free trade? No: To maximize efficiency, the country should allow free trade and eliminate the subsidy. However, unless winners compensate losers, not everyone will benefit.

We can use a multimarket model to analyze the Challenge questions about the effects of a binding price ceiling that applies to some states but not to others. The figure shows what happens if a binding price ceiling is imposed in the covered sector—those states that have anti–price gouging laws—and not in the uncovered sector—the other states.

We first consider what happens in the absence of the anti–price gouging laws. The demand curve for the entire market, D^1 in panel c, is the horizontal sum of the demand curve in the covered sector, D^c in panel a, and the demand curve in the uncovered sector, D^u in panel b. In panel c, the national supply curve S intersects the national demand curve D^1 at e_1, where the equilibrium price is p and the quantity is Q_1.

When the covered sector imposes a price ceiling at $\bar{p}$, which is less than p, it chops off the top part of the D^c above $\bar{p}$. Consequently, the new national demand curve, D^2, equals the uncovered sector's demand curve D^u above $\bar{p}$, is horizontal at $\bar{p}$, and is the same as D^1 below $\bar{p}$. The supply curve S intersects the new demand curve in the horizontal section at e_2, where the quantity is Q_2.[13] However, at a price of $\bar{p}$, national demand is Q, so the shortage is $Q - Q_2$.

How the available supply Q_2 is allocated between customers in the covered and uncovered sectors determines in which sector the shortage occurs. If some of the customers in the uncovered sector cannot buy as much as they want at $\bar{p}$, they can offer to pay a slightly higher price to obtain extra supplies. Because of the price control, customers in the covered sector cannot match a higher price.

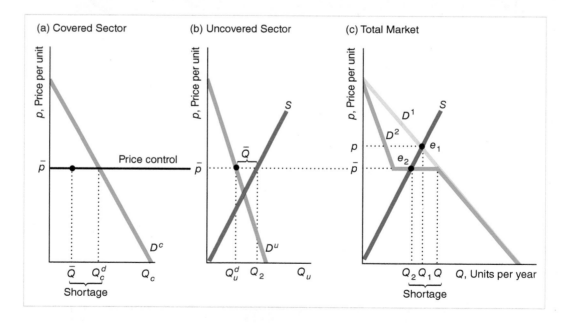

(a) Covered Sector   (b) Uncovered Sector   (c) Total Market

[13]If $\bar{p}$ were low enough that the supply curve hit D_2 in the downward-sloping section, suppliers would sell in only the uncovered sector. For example, in 2009, when West Virginia imposed anti–price gouging laws after flooding occurred in some parts of the state, Marathon Oil halted sales to independent gasoline retailers there and sold its gasoline in other states. Similarly, some Venezuelan firms avoid price controls by selling in neighboring Colombia (see the Chapter 2 Application "Venezuelan Price Ceilings and Shortages").

Consequently, customers in the uncovered sector can buy as much as they want, Q_u^d, at $\bar{p}$, as panel b shows.

For convenience, panel b also shows the national supply curve. At $\bar{p}$, the gap between the quantity demanded in the uncovered sector, Q_u^d, and the quantity that firms are willing to sell, Q_2, is $\overline{Q}$. Firms sell this extra amount, $\overline{Q}$, in the covered sector. That quantity is less than the amount demanded, Q_c^d, so the shortage in the covered sector is $Q_c^d - \overline{Q} \, (= Q - Q_2)$.

In conclusion, the anti–price gouging law lowers the price in both sectors to $\bar{p}$, which is less than the price p that would otherwise be charged. The consumers in the uncovered states do not suffer from a shortage in contrast to consumers in the covered sector. Thus, anti-gouging laws benefit residents of neighboring jurisdictions who can buy as much as they want at a lower price. Residents of jurisdictions with anti-gouging laws who can buy the good at a lower price benefit, but those who cannot buy the good are harmed.

SUMMARY

1. General Equilibrium. A shock to one market may have a spillover effect in another market. In a general-equilibrium analysis, we consider the direct effects of a shock in one market and the spillover effects in other markets. In contrast, in a partial-equilibrium analysis, we look at one market only and ignore spillover effects. The partial-equilibrium and general-equilibrium effects can differ substantially.

2. Trading Between Two People. If people make all the trades they want, the resulting equilibrium will be Pareto efficient: That is, by moving from this equilibrium, we cannot make one person better off without harming another. At a Pareto-efficient equilibrium, the marginal rates of substitution between people are equal because their indifference curves are tangent.

3. Competitive Exchange. Competition, in which all traders are price takers, leads to an allocation in which the ratio of relative prices equals the marginal rates of substitution of each person. Thus, every competitive equilibrium is Pareto efficient. Moreover, competition can result in any Pareto-efficient equilibrium given an appropriate initial endowment.

4. Production and Trading. When one person can produce more of one good and another person can produce more of another good at lower opportunity cost, specialization and trading can result in greater combined production.

5. Efficiency and Equity. The Pareto efficiency criterion reflects a value judgment that a change from one allocation to another is desirable if it makes someone better off without harming anyone else. This criterion does not allow all allocations to be ranked, because some people may be better off with one efficient allocation and others may be better off with another. Nor does majority voting necessarily allow society to produce a consensus, transitive ordering of allocations. Economists, philosophers, and others have proposed many criteria for ranking allocations, as summarized in welfare functions. Society may use a welfare function to choose among Pareto-efficient (or other) allocations. If an economy suffers from multiple distortions, correcting only one of them may not raise welfare.

EXERCISES

All exercises are available on **MyLab Economics;** * *= answer appears at the back of this book;* **M** *= mathematical problem.*

1. General Equilibrium

1.1 The demand functions for the only two goods in the economy are $Q_1 = 10 - 2p_1 + p_2$ and $Q_2 = 10 - 2p_2 + p_1$. Society has five units of each good. Solve for the equilibrium: $p_1, p_2, Q_1,$ and Q_2. **M**

1.2 The demand functions for each of two goods depend on the prices of the goods, p_1 and p_2: $Q_1 = 15 - 3p_1 + p_2$ and $Q_2 = 6 - 2p_2 + p_1$. However, each supply curve depends only on its own price: $Q_1 = 2 + p_1$ and $Q_2 = 1 + p_2$. Solve for the equilibrium: $p_1, p_2, Q_1,$ and Q_2. **M**

1.3 The market demand for medical checkups per day is $Q_F = 25(198 + n_C/20,000 - p_F)$, where n_C is the number of patients per day who are at least 40 years old, and p_F is the price of a checkup. The market demand for the number of dental checkups per day, Q_T, is $Q_T = 100(150 - p_T)/3$, where p_T represents the price of a dental checkup. The long-run market supply of medical checkups is $Q_F = 50p_F - 10p_T$. The long-run market supply of dentists is $Q_T = 50p_T - 10p_F$. The supplies are linked because people decide on a medical and dental career based in part on relative earnings.

a. If $n_C = 40,000$, what is the equilibrium number of medical and dental checkups? What are the equilibrium prices? How would an increase in n_C affect the equilibrium prices? Determine dp_F/dn_C and dp_T/dn_C.

b. Suppose that, instead of determining the price of medical checkups by a market process, large health insurance companies set their reimbursement rates, effectively determining all medical prices. A medical doctor receives $35 per checkup from an insurance company, and a patient pays only $10. How many checkups do doctors offer collectively? What is the equilibrium quantity and price of dental checkups?

c. What is the effect of a shift from a competitive medical checkup market to insurance-company-dictated medical-doctor payments on the equilibrium salaries of dentists? **M**

1.4 The demand curve in Sector 1 of the labor market is $L_1 = a - bw$. The demand curve in Sector 2 is $L_2 = c - dw$. The supply curve of labor for the entire market is $L = e + fw$. In equilibrium, $L_1 + L_2 = L$.

a. Solve for the equilibrium with no minimum wage.

b. Solve for the equilibrium at which the minimum wage is $\underline{w}$ in Sector 1 ("the covered sector") only.

c. Solve for the equilibrium at which the minimum wage $\underline{w}$ applies to the entire labor market. **M**

1.5 Philadelphia collects an ad valorem tax of 3.928% on its residents' earnings (see the Application "Urban Flight"), unlike the surrounding areas. Show the effect of this tax on the equilibrium wage, total employment, employment in Philadelphia, and employment in the surrounding areas. (*Hint*: See Solved Problem 10.1.)

*1.6 What is the effect of a subsidy of s per hour on labor in only one sector of the economy on the equilibrium wage, total employment, and employment in the covered and uncovered sectors? (*Hint*: See Solved Problem 10.1.)

1.7 Suppose that the government gives a fixed subsidy of T per firm in one sector of the economy to encourage firms to hire more workers. What is the effect on the equilibrium wage, total employment, and employment in the covered and uncovered sectors?

1.8 Competitive firms in Africa sell their output only in Europe and the United States (which do not produce the good themselves). The industry's supply curve is upward sloping. Europe puts a tariff of t per unit on the good, but the United States does not. What is the effect of the tariff on the total quantity of the good sold, the quantity sold in Europe, the quantity sold in the United States, and equilibrium price(s)?

2. Trading Between Two People

2.1 Initially, Michael has 10 candy bars and 5 cookies, and Tony has 5 candy bars and 10 cookies. After trading, Michael has 12 candy bars and 3 cookies. In an Edgeworth box, label the initial allocation A and the new allocation B. Draw some indifference curves that are consistent with this trade being optimal for both Michael and Tony.

2.2 Explain why point e in Figure 10.3 is not on the contract curve. (*Hint*: See Solved Problem 10.2.)

2.3 The two people in a pure exchange economy have identical utility functions. Will they ever want to trade? Why or why not?

2.4 Two people trade two goods that they cannot produce. Suppose that one consumer's indifference curves are bowed away from the origin—the usual type of curves—but the other's are concave to the origin. In an Edgeworth box, show that a point of tangency between the two consumers' indifference curves is not a Pareto-efficient bundle. (Identify another allocation that Pareto dominates.)

2.5 Adrienne and Stephen consume pizza, Z, and cola, C. Adrienne's utility function is $U_A = Z_A C_A$, and Stephen's is $U_A = Z_s^{0.5} C_s^{0.5}$. Their endowments are $Z_A = 10$, $C_A = 20$, $Z_S = 20$, and $C_S = 10$.

a. What are the marginal rates of substitution for each person?

b. What is the formula for the contract curve? Draw an Edgeworth box and indicate the contract curve. (*Hint*: See Solved Problem 10.3.) **M**

2.6 Continuing with Exercise 2.5, what are the competitive equilibrium prices, where one price is normalized to equal one? (*Hint*: See Solved Problem 10.4.) **M**

2.7 In a pure exchange economy with two goods, G and H, the two traders have Cobb-Douglas utility functions. Suppose that Tony's utility function is $U_t = G_t H_t$ and Margaret's utility function is

$U_m = G_m(H_m)^2$. Between them, they own 100 units of G and 50 units of H. Solve for their contract curve. (*Hint*: See Solved Problem 10.4.) **M**

2.8 Continuing with Exercise 2.7, determine p, the competitive price of G, where the price of H is normalized to equal one. (*Hint*: See Solved Problem 10.4.) **M**

3. Competitive Exchange

3.1 In an Edgeworth box, illustrate that a Pareto-efficient equilibrium, point a, can be obtained by competition, given an appropriate endowment. Do so by identifying an initial endowment point, b, located somewhere other than at point a, such that the competitive equilibrium (resulting from competitive exchange) is a. Explain.

4. Production and Trading

*4.1 In panel c of Figure 10.5, the joint production possibility frontier is concave to the origin. When the two individual production possibility frontiers are combined, however, the resulting *PPF* could have been drawn so that it was convex to the origin. How do we know which of these two ways of drawing the *PPF* to use?

*4.2 Pat and Chris can spend their non-leisure time working either in the marketplace or at home (preparing dinner, taking care of children, doing repairs). In the marketplace, Pat earns a higher wage, $w_p = \$20$, than Chris, $w_c = \$10$. Discuss how living together is likely to affect how much each of them works in the marketplace. In particular, discuss what effect marriage would have on their individual and combined budget constraints and their labor-leisure choices (see Chapter 5). In your discussion, take into account the theory of comparative advantage.

4.3 Suppose that Britain can produce 10 units of cloth or 5 units of food per day (or any linear combination) with available resources and that Greece can produce 2 units of food per day or 1 unit of cloth (or any combination). Britain has an *absolute advantage* over Greece in producing both goods. Does it still make sense for these countries to trade? Explain.

4.4 If Jane and Denise have identical, linear production possibility frontiers (see the Jane and Denise example in the text), can they gain from trade? Explain. (*Hint*: See Solved Problem 10.5.)

4.5 Modify Solved Problem 10.5 to show that the *PPF* more closely approximates a quarter of a circle with six people. One of these new people, Bill, can produce five piles of wood, or four candy bars, or any linear combination. The other, Helen, can produce four piles of wood, or five candy bars, or any linear combination.

4.6 Mexico and the United States can both produce food and toys. Mexico has 100 workers and the United States has 300 workers. If they do not trade, the United States consumes 10 units of food and 10 toys, and Mexico consumes 5 units of food and 1 toy. The following table shows how many workers are necessary to produce each good:

	Mexico	United States
Workers per pound of food	10	10
Workers per toy	50	20

a. In the absence of trade, how many units of food and toys can the United States produce? How many can Mexico produce?

b. Which country has a comparative advantage in producing food? In producing toys?

c. Draw the production possibility for each country and show where the two produce without trade. Label the axes accurately.

d. Draw the production possibility frontier with trade.

e. Show that both countries can benefit from trade. (*Hint*: See Solved Problem 10.5.) **M**

5. Efficiency and Equity

5.1 Give an example of a social welfare function that leads to the egalitarian allocation in which everyone receives exactly the same bundle of goods.

5.2 Suppose that society uses the "opposite" of a Rawlsian welfare function: It maximizes the well-being of the best-off member of society. Write this welfare function. What allocation maximizes welfare in this society?

5.3 Suppose that society cared only about the welfare of consumers so that it wanted to maximize consumer surplus. The government cannot force firms to produce more than the competitive level. Does competition maximize consumer surplus? Why? If not, what kind of policy would maximize consumer surplus?

6. Challenge

6.1 Modify the figure in the Challenge Solution to show how much is sold in both sectors in the absence of anti–price gouging laws. Discuss how these quantities differ from those that result from implementing such laws.

6.2 The market for peaches is competitive. The market has two types of demanders: consumers who eat fresh peaches and canners. If the government places a binding price ceiling only on peaches sold directly to consumers, what happens to prices and quantities of peaches sold for each use?

6.3   A central city imposes a rent control law that places a binding ceiling on the rent that a landlord may charge for an apartment. The suburbs of this city do not have rent control. What happens to the rental prices in the suburbs and to the equilibrium number of apartments in the total metropolitan area, in the city, and in the suburbs? (For simplicity, you may assume that people are indifferent as to whether they live in the city or in the suburbs.)

6.4   Initially, electricity sells in New York and in other states at a competitive single price. Now suppose that New York restricts the quantity of electricity that its citizens can buy. Show what happens to the price of electricity and the quantities sold in New York and elsewhere.

6.5   A competitive industry with an upward-sloping supply curve sells Q_h of its product in its home country and Q_f in a foreign country, so the total quantity it sells is $Q = Q_h + Q_f$. No one else produces this product. The shipping cost is zero. Determine the equilibrium price and quantity in each country. Now the foreign government imposes a binding quota, Q ($< Q_f$ at the original price). What happens to prices and quantities in both the home and the foreign market?

Monopoly and Monopsony

11

Monopoly: one parrot.

CHALLENGE

Brand-Name and Generic Drugs

A firm that creates a new drug may receive a *patent* that gives it the right to be the *monopoly* (sole producer) of the drug for up to 20 years. As a result, the firm can charge a price much greater than its marginal cost of production. For example, one of the world's best-selling drugs, the heart medication Plavix, sold for about $7 per pill, though it costs about 3¢ per pill to produce. A new drug to treat hepatitis C, Harvoni, sells for $1,350 a pill or $113,400 for a 12-week course of treatment. In 2015, Martin Shkreli, then the head of Turing Pharmaceuticals, raised the price of Daraprim, used to treat infections that are common in HIV/AIDS patients, from $13.50 to $750 per pill. The price rose to as high as $800 in 2018. Shkreli acknowledged that the drug costs "very little money" to make.

Every year, many pharmaceuticals lose their patent protection, as Plavix has. In 2018, patents for Apidra (diabetes), Ampyra (multiple sclerosis), Lyrica (nerve and muscle pain), and many other high-revenue drugs expired. In 2019, patent protection for Avastin (cancer), Azasite (bacterial eye infections), Ranexa (heart disease), and others end.

Generally, when a patent for a highly profitable drug expires, firms enter the market and sell generic (equivalent) versions of the brand-name drug. Generics' share of all U.S. prescriptions rose from about 18% in 1984 to nearly 80% currently.

The U.S. Congress, when it originally passed a law permitting generic drugs to quickly enter a market after a patent expires, expected that patent expiration would subsequently lead to sharp declines in drug prices.[1] If consumers view the generic product and the brand-name product as perfect substitutes, both goods will sell for the same price, and entry by many firms will drive the price down to the competitive level. Even if consumers view the goods as imperfect substitutes, one might expect the price of the brand-name drug to fall.

However, the prices of many brand-name drugs have increased after their patents expired and generics entered the market. The generic drugs are relatively inexpensive, but the brand-name drugs often continue to enjoy a significant market share and sell for high prices. Regan (2008), who studied the effects of generic entry on post-patent price competition for 18 prescription drugs, found an average 2% increase in brand-name prices. Studies based on older data have found up to a 7% average increase. Why do some brand-name prices rise after the entry of generic drugs?

---

[1]Under the 1984 Hatch-Waxman Act, the U.S. government allows a firm to sell a generic product after a brand-name drug's patent expires if the generic-drug firm can prove that its product delivers the same amount of active ingredient or drug to the body in the same way as the brand-name product. Sometimes the same firm manufactures both a brand-name drug and an identical generic drug, so the two have identical ingredients. Generics produced by other firms usually have a different appearance and name than the original product and may have different nonactive ingredients, but they have the same active ingredients.

Why can a firm with a patent-based monopoly charge a high price? Why might a brand-name pharmaceutical's price rise after its patent expires? To answer these questions, we need to understand the decision-making process for a **monopoly**: the sole supplier of a good that has no close substitute.

Monopolies have been common since ancient times. In the fifth century B.C., the Greek philosopher Thales gained control of most of the olive presses during a year of exceptionally productive harvests. The ancient Egyptian pharaohs controlled the sale of food. China's salt monopoly is 2,600 years old, and helped pay for stretches of the Great Wall. In England, until Parliament limited the practice in 1624, kings granted monopoly rights called royal charters or patents to court favorites. Particularly valuable royal charters went to companies that controlled trade with North America, the Hudson Bay Company, and with India, the British East India Company.

Today, government actions continue to play an important role in creating monopolies. Governments grant patents that allow the inventor of a new product, such as a new drug, to be the sole supplier of that product for up to 20 years, and sometimes grant monopoly rights for other reasons as well. Many utilities—water, gas, and electricity—are government-owned or government-protected monopolies.[2]

Some firms are able to gain monopoly power without government help. When first introduced, Apple's iPad had a near monopoly in the tablet market.

Unlike a competitive firm, which is a price taker (Chapter 8), a monopoly can *set* its price. A monopoly's output is the market output, and the demand curve a monopoly faces is the market demand curve. Because the market demand curve is downward sloping, the monopoly (unlike a competitive firm) doesn't lose all its sales if it raises its price. As a consequence, a profit-maximizing monopoly sets its price above marginal cost, the price that would prevail in a competitive market.

Consumers hate monopolies because monopolies charge high prices. They buy less at the relatively high monopoly price than they would at the competitive price.

We also examine a **monopsony**: the only buyer of a good in a market. We show that a profit-maximizing monopsony sets its price below the competitive level, which lowers welfare compared to a competitive market.

In this chapter, we examine seven main topics	1. **Monopoly Profit Maximization.** Like all firms, a monopoly maximizes its profit by setting its price or output so that its marginal revenue equals its marginal cost.
	2. **Market Power and Welfare.** How much the monopoly's price is above its marginal cost depends on the shape of the demand curve that the monopoly faces, and this gap between price and marginal cost lowers welfare relative to the competitive level.
	3. **Taxes and Monopoly.** Specific and ad valorem taxes increase the deadweight loss due to monopoly, may have consumer incidences in excess of 100%, and affect welfare differently from each other.
	4. **Causes of Monopolies.** Two major causes for a monopoly are a firm's cost advantage over other potential firms and government actions.
	5. **Government Actions That Reduce Market Power.** A government can regulate the price a monopoly charges or allow other firms to enter the market to reduce or eliminate the welfare loss from a monopoly.

---

[2]Whether the law views a firm as a monopoly depends on how broadly the market is defined. Is the market limited to a particular drug or the pharmaceutical industry as a whole? The manufacturer of the drug is a monopoly in the former case, but just one of many firms in the latter case. Thus, defining a market is critical in legal cases. A market definition depends on whether other products are good substitutes for those in that market.

6. **Internet Monopolies: Network Effects, Behavioral Economics, and Economies of Scale.** Network externalities and economies of scale facilitate internet monopolies.

7. **Monopsony.** A monopsony—a single buyer—maximizes its profit by paying a price below the competitive level, so welfare is lower than the competitive level.

11.1 Monopoly Profit Maximization

Competitive firms and monopolies alike maximize their profits using a two-step procedure (Chapter 8). First, the firm determines the output at which it makes the highest possible profit. Second, the firm decides whether to produce at that output level or to shut down, using the rules described in Chapter 8.

For a competitive firm, we distinguished between a lowercase q, which represented a firm's output, and an uppercase Q, which reflected the market quantity. Because a monopoly sells the entire market quantity, we use Q to indicate both the monopoly's quantity and the market quantity.

The Necessary Condition for Profit Maximization

A monopoly's first step is to pick its optimal output level. A monopoly, like any firm (Chapter 8), maximizes its profit by operating where its marginal revenue equals its marginal cost, as we now show formally.

A monopoly's profit function is $\pi(Q) = R(Q) - C(Q)$, where $R(Q)$ is its revenue function and $C(Q)$ is its cost function. The monopoly chooses output Q^* to maximize its profit by using the necessary condition that the derivative of its profit function with respect to output equals zero:

$$\frac{d\pi(Q^*)}{dQ} = \frac{dR(Q^*)}{dQ} - \frac{dC(Q^*)}{dQ} = 0, \tag{11.1}$$

where $dR/dQ = MR$ is its marginal revenue function (Chapter 8) and $dC/dQ = MC$ is its marginal cost function (Chapter 7). Thus, Equation 11.1 requires the monopoly to choose that output level Q^* such that *its marginal revenue equals its marginal cost*: $MR(Q^*) = MC(Q^*)$.

For profit to be maximized at Q^*, the second derivative of the profit function with respect to output must be negative:

$$\frac{d^2\pi(Q^*)}{dQ^2} = \frac{d^2R(Q^*)}{dQ^2} - \frac{d^2C(Q^*)}{dQ^2} < 0, \tag{11.2}$$

where d^2R/dQ^2 is the second derivative of the revenue function with respect to Q and d^2C/dQ^2 is the second derivative of the cost function. By definition, $d^2R/dQ^2 = dMR/dQ$ is the slope of its marginal revenue curve. Similarly, $d^2C/dQ^2 = dMC/dQ$ is the slope of the marginal cost curve. Thus, Equation 11.2 requires that, at the critical point Q^*, the slope of the marginal revenue curve be less than that of the marginal cost curve: $d^2R(Q^*)/dQ^2 < d^2C(Q^*)/dQ^2$ or $dMR(Q^*)/dQ < dMC(Q^*)/dQ$. Typically, this condition is met because the marginal cost curve is constant or increasing with output ($dMC/dQ \geq 0$) and the monopoly's marginal revenue curve is downward sloping ($dMR/dQ < 0$), as we show next.

Marginal Revenue and the Demand Curves

A firm's marginal revenue curve depends on its demand curve. We now demonstrate that a monopoly's marginal revenue curve is downward sloping and lies below its demand curve at any positive quantity because its demand curve is downward sloping. The following reasoning applies to any firm that faces a downward-sloping demand curve—not just to a monopoly.

The monopoly's inverse demand function shows the price it receives for selling a given quantity: $p(Q)$. That price, $p(Q)$, is the monopoly's *average revenue* for a given quantity, Q, because each unit sells for the same price. Its revenue function is its average revenue or price times the number of units it sells: $R(Q) = p(Q)Q$.

Using the product rule of differentiation, we can write the monopoly's marginal revenue function as

$$MR(Q) = \frac{dR(Q)}{dQ} = \frac{d[p(Q)Q]}{dQ} = p(Q)\frac{dQ}{dQ} + \frac{dp(Q)}{dQ}Q = p(Q) + \frac{dp(Q)}{dQ}Q. \quad (11.3)$$

The first term on the right-hand side of Equation 11.3, $p(Q)$, is the price or average revenue. The second term is the slope of the demand curve, $dp(Q)/dQ$, times the number of units sold, Q. Because the monopoly's inverse demand curve slopes downward, $dp(Q)/dQ < 0$, this second term is negative, so the marginal revenue curve also slopes downward. (In contrast, a competitive firm's inverse demand curve has a slope of zero because it is horizontal, so the second term is zero, and the competitive firm's marginal revenue equals the market price, as we saw in Chapter 8.) At a given positive quantity, a monopoly's marginal revenue is less than its price or average revenue by $[dp(Q)/dQ]Q$. Thus, *a monopoly's marginal revenue curve is downward sloping and lies below its inverse demand curve at any positive quantity.*

Figure 11.1 illustrates why a monopoly's marginal revenue is less than its price. The monopoly, which is initially selling Q units at p_1, can increase the number of units it sells by one unit to $Q = 1$ by lowering its price to p_2.

Figure 11.1 Average and Marginal Revenue

The demand curve shows the average revenue or price per unit of output sold. The monopoly's marginal revenue is less than the price p_2 by area C (the revenue lost due to a lower price on the Q units originally sold). The monopoly's initial revenue is $R_1 = p_1 Q = A + C$. If it sells one more unit, its revenue is $R_2 = p_2(Q + 1) = A + B = A + p_2$. Thus, its marginal revenue (if one extra unit is a very small increase in its output) is $MR = R_2 - R_1 = B - C = p_2 - C$, which is less than p_2.

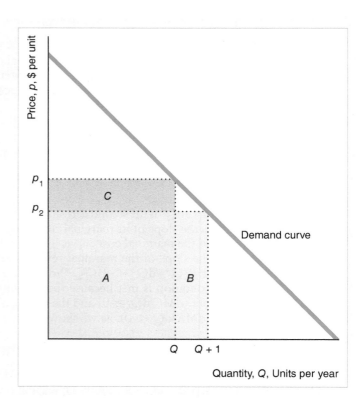

The monopoly's initial revenue is $R_1 = p_1 Q = A + C$. When it sells the extra unit, its revenue is $R_2 = p_2(Q + 1) = A + B$. Thus, its marginal revenue from selling one additional unit is

$$MR = R_2 - R_1 = (A + B) - (A + C) = B - C.$$

The monopoly sells the extra unit of output at the new price, p_2, so it gains extra revenue from that last unit of $B = p_2 \times 1 = p_2$, which corresponds to the $p(Q)$ term in Equation 11.3. Because it had to lower its price, the monopoly loses the difference between the new price and the original price, $\Delta p = (p_2 - p_1)$, on the Q units it originally sold, $C = \Delta p \times Q$, which corresponds to the $(dp/dQ)Q$ term in Equation 11.3. Thus, the monopoly's marginal revenue, $B - C = p_2 - C$, is less than the price it charges by an amount equal to area C.

In general, the relationship between the marginal revenue and demand curves depends on the shape of the demand curve. The relationship between the marginal revenue and demand curves is the same for all linear demand curves, as we show in Solved Problem 11.1.

SOLVED PROBLEM
11.1

MyLab Economics
Solved Problem

Show that if a monopoly's inverse demand curve is linear, its marginal revenue curve is also linear, has twice the slope of the inverse demand curve, intersects the vertical axis at the same point as the inverse demand curve, and intersects the horizontal axis at half the distance as does the inverse demand curve.

Answer

1. *Write a general formula for any downward-sloping linear inverse demand curve.* Any linear demand curve can be written as $p(Q) = a - bQ$, where a and b are positive constants.

2. *Derive the monopoly's revenue function and then derive its marginal revenue function by differentiating the revenue function with respect to its output.* The monopoly's revenue function is $R = p(Q)Q = aQ - bQ^2$. The marginal revenue function is the derivative of the revenue function with respect to quantity: $MR(Q) = dR/dQ = a - 2bQ$.

3. *Describe the properties of the marginal revenue function relative to those of the inverse demand function.* Both the marginal revenue function and the inverse demand functions are linear. Both hit the vertical (price) axis at a: $MR(0) = a - (2b \times 0) = a$ and $p(0) = a - (b \times 0) = a$. The slope of the marginal revenue curve, $dMR/dQ = -2b$, is twice the slope of the inverse demand curve $dp(Q)/dQ = -b$. Consequently, the MR curve hits the quantity axis at half the distance of the demand curve: $MR = 0 = a - 2bQ$, where $Q = a/(2b)$, and $p = 0 = a - bQ$, where $Q = a/b$.

Marginal Revenue Curve and the Price Elasticity of Demand

The marginal revenue at any given quantity depends on the inverse demand curve's height (the price) and the elasticity of demand. From Chapter 2, we know that the price elasticity of demand is $\varepsilon = (dQ/dp)/(p/Q) < 0$, which tells us the percentage by which quantity demanded falls as the price increases by 1%.

According to Equation 11.3, $MR = p + (dp/dQ)/Q$. By multiplying and dividing the second term by p, rearranging terms, and substituting using the definition of the elasticity of demand, we can write marginal revenue in terms of the elasticity of demand:

$$MR = p + \frac{dp}{dQ}Q = p + p\frac{dp}{dQ}\frac{Q}{P} = p\left[1 + \frac{1}{(dQ/dp)(p/Q)}\right] = p\left(1 + \frac{1}{\varepsilon}\right). \quad (11.4)$$

According to Equation 11.4, marginal revenue is closer to price as demand becomes more elastic. In the limit where $\varepsilon \rightarrow -\infty$, a monopoly faces a perfectly elastic demand curve (similar to that of a competitive firm), and its marginal revenue equals its price.

In Figure 11.2, we illustrate the relationship between the marginal revenue and the price elasticity of demand for a particular linear inverse demand function,

$$p(Q) = 24 - Q. \quad (11.5)$$

Its corresponding demand function is $Q(p) = 24 - p$. The slope of this demand function is $dQ/dp = -1$, so the elasticity of demand at a given output level is $\varepsilon = (dQ/dp)(p/Q) = -p/Q = -(24 - Q)/Q = 1 - 24/Q$.

From the results of Solved Problem 11.1, the monopoly's marginal revenue function is

$$MR(Q) = 24 - 2Q. \quad (11.6)$$

Where the demand curve hits the price axis ($Q = 0$), the demand curve is perfectly elastic, so the marginal revenue equals price: $MR = p$. At the midpoint of any linear demand curve, the demand elasticity is unitary (see Chapter 2), $\varepsilon = -1$, so, using Equation 11.4, we know that the marginal revenue is zero:

$$MR = p[1 + 1/\varepsilon] = p[1 + 1/(-1)] = 0.$$

Figure 11.2 Elasticity of Demand and Total, Average, and Marginal Revenue

The demand curve (or the average revenue curve), $p = 24 - Q$, lies above the marginal revenue curve, $MR = 24 - 2Q$.   Where the marginal revenue equals zero, $Q = 12$, and the elasticity of demand is $\varepsilon = -1$.

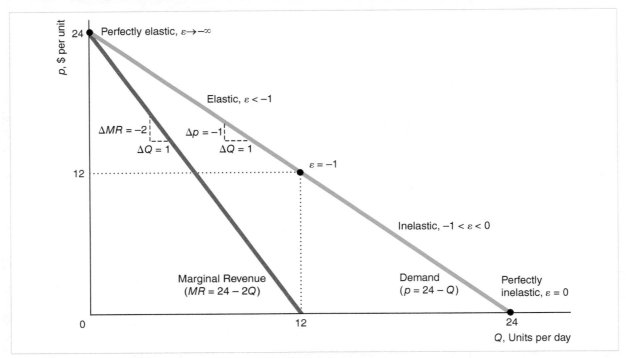

In our example at the midpoint of the demand curve where $Q = 12$, the elasticity is $\varepsilon = 1 - 24/12 = -1$, and the marginal revenue is $MR = 24 - (2 \times 12) = 0$. To the right of the midpoint of the demand curve, the demand curve is inelastic, $-1 \le \varepsilon \le 0$, so the marginal revenue is negative.

APPLICATION

Amazon Prime Revenue

In 2018, **Amazon.com** considered raising the annual price of its Amazon Prime shipping and streaming-video service from \$99 to \$119 per year, a 20% increase. Amazon was concerned that a price increase would result in many customers dropping the service. The number of customers that it would lose would depend on the price elasticity of demand for Amazon Prime. According to one analyst, Amazon expected to lose roughly 10% of its customers, going from 90 million members of its service to 81 million. That is, they estimated that the price elasticity of demand was $-10\%/20\% = -0.5$.

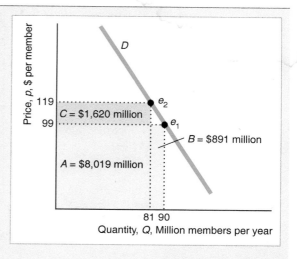

As a result, they predicted that area $C = 81 \times (119 - 99) = \$1,620$ million and area $B = (90 - 81) \times 99 = \$891$ million so the change in revenue would be positive: $\$1,620 - \$891$ million $= \$729$ million. Amazon decided to raise the price of Prime.

An Example of Monopoly Profit Maximization

In Chapter 8, we found that any type of firm maximizes its profit by selling its output such that its marginal cost equals its marginal revenue. We now examine how a monopoly maximizes its profit using an example with the linear inverse demand function in Equation 11.5, $p(Q) = 24 - Q$, and a quadratic short-run cost function,

$$C(Q) = VC(Q) + F = Q^2 + 12, \tag{11.7}$$

where the monopoly's variable cost is $VC(Q) = Q^2$ and its fixed cost is $F = 12$ (see Chapter 7). The firm's marginal cost function is

$$MC(Q) = \frac{dC(Q)}{dQ} = 2Q. \tag{11.8}$$

The average variable cost is $AVC = Q^2/Q = Q$, so it is a straight line through the origin with a slope of 1. The average cost is $AC = C/Q = (Q^2 + 12)/Q = Q + 12/Q$, which is U-shaped. Panel a of Figure 11.3 shows the MC, AVC, and AC curves.

The Profit-Maximizing Output. The firm's highest possible profit is obtained by producing at the quantity Q^* where its marginal revenue equals its marginal cost function:

$$MR(Q^*) = 24 - 2Q^* = 2Q^* = MC(Q^*).$$

Figure 11.3 Maximizing Profit

(a) At $Q = 6$, where marginal revenue, MR, equals marginal cost, MC, profit is maximized. The rectangle showing the maximum profit $60 is average profit per unit, $p - AC = \$18 - \$8 = \$10$, times six units. (b) Profit is maximized at a smaller quantity, $Q = 6$ (where marginal revenue equals marginal cost), than revenue is maximized, $Q = 12$ (where marginal revenue is zero).

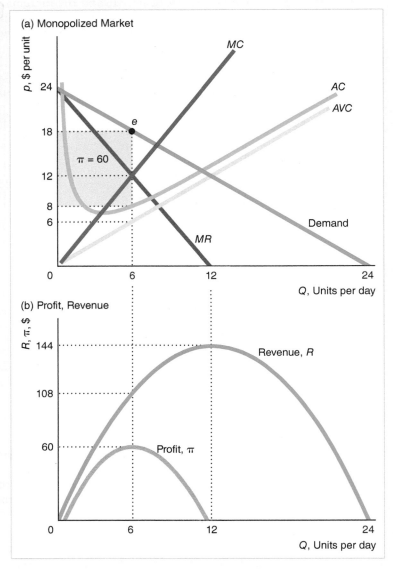

Solving this expression, we find that $Q^* = 6$. Panel a of Figure 11.3 shows that the monopoly's marginal revenue and marginal cost curves intersect at $Q^* = 6$.

Panel b shows the corresponding profit and revenue curves. The profit curve reaches its maximum at 6 units of output, where marginal profit—the slope of the profit curve—is zero. Because *marginal profit equals marginal revenue minus marginal cost* (Chapter 8), marginal profit is zero where the marginal revenue curve intersects the marginal cost curve at 6 units in panel a. The height of the demand curve at the profit-maximizing quantity is $p = 18$. Thus, the monopoly maximizes its profit at point e, where it sells 6 units per day at a price of $18 per unit.

Why does the monopoly maximize its profit by producing 6 units where its marginal revenue equals its marginal cost? At smaller quantities, the monopoly's marginal revenue is greater than its marginal cost, so its marginal profit is positive. By increasing its output slightly, it raises its profit. Similarly, at quantities greater than 6 units, the monopoly's marginal cost is greater than its marginal revenue, so it can increase its profit by reducing its output slightly.

The profit-maximizing quantity is smaller than the revenue-maximizing quantity. The revenue curve reaches its maximum at $Q = 12$, where the slope of the revenue curve, the marginal revenue, is zero (panel a). In contrast, the profit curve reaches its maximum at $Q = 6$, where marginal profit equals zero so that marginal revenue equals marginal cost. Because marginal cost is positive, marginal revenue must be positive when profit is maximized. Given that the marginal revenue curve has a negative slope, marginal revenue is positive at a smaller quantity than where it equals zero. Thus, the profit curve must reach a maximum at a smaller quantity, 6, than the revenue curve, 12.

As we already know, marginal revenue equals zero at the quantity where the demand curve has a unitary elasticity. Because a linear demand curve is more elastic at smaller quantities, *monopoly profit is maximized in the elastic portion of the demand curve.* (Here, profit is maximized at $Q = 6$ where the elasticity of demand is -3.) Equivalently, *a monopoly never operates in the inelastic portion of its demand curve.*

APPLICATION

Apple's iPad

Apple's iPad was the first commercially successful tablet. Users interact with the iPad using Apple's multi-touch, finger-sensitive touchscreen (rather than the pressure-triggered stylus that most previous tablets used) and a virtual onscreen keyboard (rather than a physical one). Most importantly, the iPad offers an intuitive interface and is well integrated with Apple's iTunes, eBooks, and various application programs.

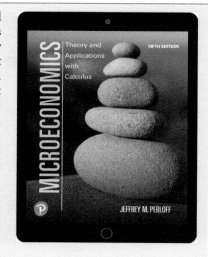

People loved the original iPad. Even at $499 for the basic model, Apple had a virtual monopoly in its first year in 2010, with 87% of the tablet market. Moreover, the other tablets available in 2010 were not viewed by most consumers as close substitutes. Apple reported that it sold 25 million iPads worldwide in its first full year.

Unfortunately for Apple, its monopoly was short lived. Within a year of the iPad's introduction, over a hundred iPad want-to-be tablets were available. Apple's share of the tablet market fell to 29% by early 2018.

SOLVED PROBLEM 11.2

MyLab Economics
Solved Problem

When the iPad was introduced, Apple's constant marginal cost of producing its top-of-the-line iPad was about $220, its fixed cost was $2,000 million (= $2 billion), and we estimate that its inverse demand function was $p = 770 - 11Q$, where Q is the millions of iPads purchased.[3] What was Apple's average cost function?

---

[3]See the Application "Apple's iPad" in the Sources at the end of this book for details on these estimates.

What was its marginal revenue function? What were its profit-maximizing price and quantity? What was its profit? Show Apple's profit-maximizing solution in a figure.

Answer

1. *Derive the average cost function using the information about Apple's marginal and fixed costs.* Given that Apple's marginal cost was constant, its average variable cost, AVC, equaled its marginal cost, $220. Its average fixed cost, AFC, was its fixed cost divided by the quantity produced, $2,000/Q$. Thus, its average cost was $AC = AVC + AFC = 220 + 2,000/Q$.

2. *Derive Apple's marginal revenue function using the information about its demand function.* Because the inverse demand function was $p = 770 - 11Q$, Apple's revenue function was $R = 770Q - 11Q^2$, so $MR = dR/dQ = 770 - 22Q$.

3. *Derive Apple's profit-maximizing price and quantity by equating the marginal revenue and marginal cost functions and solving.* Apple maximized its profit where

$$MR = 770 - 22Q = 220 = MC.$$

Solving this equation for the profit-maximizing output, we find that $Q = 25$ million iPads. By substituting this quantity into the inverse demand equation, we determine that the profit-maximizing price was $p = $495 per unit, as the figure shows.

4. *Calculate Apple's profit using the profit-maximizing price and quantity and the average cost.* At $Q = 25$, the firm's average cost was $AC = 220 + 2,000/25 = $300. The firm's profit was $\pi = (p - AC)Q = [495 - 300]25 = $4,875 million (= $4.875 billion). The figure shows that the profit is a rectangle with a height of $(p - AC) = $195 and a length of $Q = 25$.

The Shutdown Decision. Should a profit-maximizing monopoly produce at the output level determined by its first-order condition, Q^*, or shut down? In the short run, the monopoly shuts down if the monopoly-optimal price is less than its average variable cost. In our short-run example in Figure 11.3, at the profit-maximizing output, the average variable cost is $AVC(6) = 6$, which is less than the price, $p(6) = 18$, so the firm chooses to produce. Equivalently, using the inverse demand function in Equation 11.5, the firm's revenue, $R(6) = p(6)6 = 18 \times 6 = 108$, exceeds its variable (or avoidable) cost, $VC(6) = 6^2 = 36$, so the firm chooses to produce.

Indeed, the monopoly makes a positive profit. Because its profit is $\pi = p(Q)Q - C(Q)$, its average profit is $\pi/Q = p(Q) - C(Q)/Q = p(Q) - AC$. Thus, its average profit (and hence its profit) is positive only if price is above the average cost. At $Q^* = 6$, its average cost, $AC(6) = 8$, is less than its price, $p(6) = 18$. Its profit is $\pi = 60$, which is the shaded rectangle with a height equal to the average profit per unit, $p(6) - AC(6) = 18 - 8 = 10$, and a width of 6 units.

Choosing Price or Quantity

Unlike a competitive firm, a monopoly can adjust its price, so it has the choice of setting its price *or* its quantity to maximize its profit. (A competitive firm must set its quantity to maximize profit because it cannot affect market price.)

The monopoly is constrained by the market demand curve. Because the demand curve slopes downward, the monopoly faces a trade-off between a higher price and a lower quantity or a lower price and a higher quantity. The monopoly chooses the point on the demand curve that maximizes its profit. Unfortunately for the monopoly, it cannot set both its quantity and its price and thereby pick a point that is above the demand curve. If it could, the monopoly would choose an extremely high price and an extremely high output level and would become exceedingly wealthy.

If the monopoly sets its price, the demand curve determines how much output it sells. If the monopoly picks an output level, the demand curve determines the price. Because the monopoly wants to operate at the price and output at which its profit is maximized, it chooses the same profit-maximizing solution whether it sets the price or the output. We usually (but not always) assume that the monopoly sets the quantity rather than price.

APPLICATION

Taylor Swift Concert Pricing

Taylor Swift's 2015 concert tour was a huge success, breaking the Rolling Stones' North American tour revenue record. Her 2018 "Reputation" tour is poised to be even more successful, opening to rave reviews and enthusiastic crowds. But not all her 2018 concerts are selling out. Why would the exceptionally popular pop music icon have empty seats at her concerts?

The main reason for the empty seats is high prices. Ms. Swift can earn more profit by charging high prices and selling fewer tickets. We examine why in the following Solved Problem.

SOLVED PROBLEM 11.3

MyLab Economics
Solved Problem

Illustrate why charging a higher price, p_1, than the price that causes the concert to sell out, p_2, increases profit. For simplicity, assume that the marginal cost of selling tickets is constant at m until the stadium's capacity is reached, and that fixed cost is zero. Explain why setting a price high enough that the show does not sell out increases profit.

Answer

1. *Draw the marginal cost curve and explain its shape.* The marginal cost curve is horizontal at m until capacity is reached at Q_2. Because no more than Q_2 seats are available, the marginal cost of providing an additional seat becomes infinite at Q_2. That is, the marginal cost curve is vertical at Q_2.

2. *Add the demand curve and marginal revenue curve to the diagram, and show the profit-maximizing price and quantity.* The intersection of the marginal revenue and marginal cost curve determines the profit-maximizing quantity, Q_1. The corresponding price on the demand curve at point *a* is p_1.

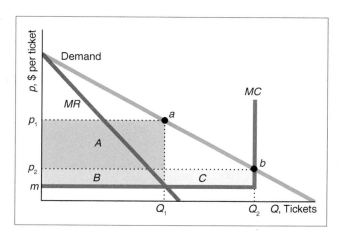

3. *Show the profit at Q_1.* Without a fixed cost, the average cost equals the marginal cost, m. Thus the profit is $\pi_1 = (p_1 - m)Q_1$, which is area $A + B$.

4. *Show the price such that ticket sales reach full capacity and the corresponding profit.* To reach capacity by selling Q_2 tickets, the price must fall to p_2 at point b on the demand curve. The corresponding profit is $\pi_2 = (p_2 - m)Q_2$, which is area $B + C$.

5. *Explain why not selling out the show is profit maximizing.* By charging a higher price and selling fewer tickets, Ms. Swift earns a higher profit: $\pi_1 > \pi_2$. We know that profit is maximized where marginal revenue equals marginal cost. To sell each additional seat, she has to lower the price by enough that the marginal revenue is less than the marginal cost, which reduces profit.

Effects of a Shift of the Demand Curve

Shifts in the demand curve or marginal cost curve affect the monopoly optimum and can have a wider variety of effects in a monopolized market than in a competitive market. In a competitive market, the effect of a shift in demand on a competitive firm's output depends only on the marginal cost curve (Chapter 8). In contrast, the effect of a shift in demand on a monopoly's output depends on the marginal cost curve and the demand curve.

A competitive firm's marginal cost curve tells us everything we need to know about the amount that the firm will supply at any given market price. The competitive firm's supply curve is its upward-sloping marginal cost curve above its minimum average variable cost. A competitive firm's supply behavior does not depend on the shape of the market demand curve because the firm always faces a horizontal residual demand curve at the market price. Thus, if you know a competitive firm's marginal cost curve, you can predict how much the firm will produce at any given market price.

In contrast, a monopoly's output decision depends on its marginal cost curve and its demand curve. Unlike a competitive firm, *a monopoly does not have a supply curve.* Knowing the monopoly's marginal cost curve is not sufficient for us to predict how much a monopoly will sell at any given price.

Figure 11.4 illustrates that the relationship between price and quantity is unique in a competitive market but not in a monopoly market. If the market is competitive, the initial equilibrium is e_1 in panel a, where the original demand curve D^1 intersects the supply curve, MC, which is the sum of the marginal cost curves of a large number of competitive firms. When the demand curve shifts to D^2, the new competitive equilibrium, e_2, has a higher price and quantity. A shift of the demand curve maps out competitive equilibria along the marginal cost curve, so every equilibrium quantity has a single corresponding equilibrium price.

Now consider the monopoly example in panel b with the same demand curves. As the demand curve shifts from D^1 to D^2, the monopoly optimum changes from E_1 to E_2, so the price rises but the quantity stays constant, $Q_1 = Q_2$. Thus, *a given quantity can correspond to more than one monopoly-optimal price.* Alternatively, a shift in the demand curve may cause the monopoly-optimal price to stay constant and the quantity to change, or both price and quantity to change.

Figure 11.4 Effects of a Shift of the Demand Curve

(a) A shift of the demand curve from D^1 to D^2 causes the competitive equilibrium to move from e_1 to e_2 along the supply curve (the horizontal sum of the marginal cost curves of all the competitive firms). Because the competitive equilibrium lies on the supply curve, each quantity corresponds to only one possible equilibrium price. (b) With a monopoly, this same shift of demand causes the monopoly optimum to change from E_1 to E_2. The monopoly quantity stays the same, but the monopoly price rises. Thus, a shift in demand does not map out a unique relationship between price and quantity in a monopolized market: The same quantity, $Q_1 = Q_2$, is associated with two different prices, p_1 and p_2.

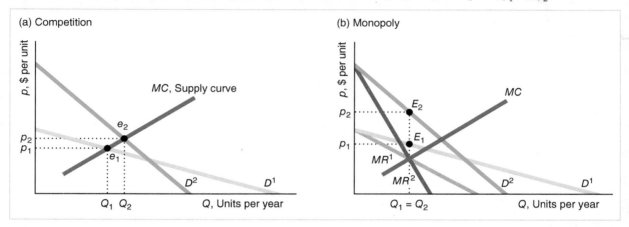

(a) Competition

(b) Monopoly

11.2 Market Power and Welfare

A monopoly has **market power**: the ability of a firm to charge a price above marginal cost and earn a positive profit. What determines how high a price a monopoly can charge? In this section, we examine the factors that determine how much above its marginal cost a monopoly sets its price and its effect on welfare.

Market Power and the Shape of the Demand Curve

Many people falsely believe that the biggest monopolies have the most power over prices:

Common Confusion The larger the monopoly, the more it can mark up its price over its cost.

Size doesn't matter. Rather, the degree to which the monopoly raises its price above its marginal cost depends on the shape of the demand curve at the profit-maximizing quantity. A profit-maximizing monopoly marks up price over marginal cost more if consumers are less sensitive to price (the demand curve is less elastic). For example, some of the drugs mentioned in the Challenge at the beginning of the chapter do not have a large volume of sales but have extremely high prices because they are crucial for a small segment of the population.

If the monopoly faces a highly elastic—nearly flat—demand curve at the profit-maximizing quantity, it would lose substantial sales if it raised its price by even a small amount. Conversely, if the demand curve is not very elastic (is relatively steep) at that quantity, the monopoly would lose fewer sales from raising its price by the same amount.

We can derive the relationship between market power and the elasticity of demand at the profit-maximizing quantity using the expression for marginal revenue in Equation 11.4 and the firm's profit-maximizing condition that marginal revenue equals marginal cost:

$$MR = p\left(1 + \frac{1}{\varepsilon}\right) = MC. \qquad (11.9)$$

By rearranging terms, we can rewrite Equation 11.9 as

$$\frac{p}{MC} = \frac{1}{1 + (1/\varepsilon)}. \qquad (11.10)$$

According to Equation 11.10, the ratio of the price to marginal cost depends *only* on the elasticity of demand at the profit-maximizing quantity.

In our linear demand example in panel a of Figure 11.3, the elasticity of demand is $\varepsilon = -3$ at the monopoly optimum where $Q^* = 6$. As a result, the ratio of price to marginal cost is $p/MC = 1/[1 + 1/(-3)] = 1.5$, or $p = 1.5MC$. The profit-maximizing price, $18, in panel a is 1.5 times the marginal cost of $12.

Table 11.1 illustrates how the ratio of price to marginal cost varies with the elasticity of demand. When the elasticity is -1.01, which is only slightly elastic, the monopoly's profit-maximizing price is 101 times larger than its marginal cost: $p/MC = 1/[1 + 1/(-1.01)] \approx 101$. As the elasticity of demand approaches negative infinity (becomes perfectly elastic), $1/\varepsilon$ approaches zero, so the ratio of price to marginal cost shrinks to $p/MC = 1$.

The table illustrates that not all monopolies can set high prices. A monopoly that faces a horizontal, perfectly elastic demand curve sets its price equal to its marginal cost—as a price-taking competitive firm does. If this monopoly were to raise its price, it would lose all its sales, so it maximizes its profit by setting its price equal to its marginal cost.

All else the same, the more close substitutes for the monopoly's good, the more elastic the demand the monopoly faces. For example, Pearson has the monopoly right to produce and sell this textbook. However, many other publishers have the rights to produce and sell similar microeconomics textbooks (although you wouldn't like them as much). The demand Pearson faces is much more elastic than it would be if no substitutes were available. If you think this textbook is expensive, imagine the cost if no substitutes were available!

Table 11.1 Elasticity of Demand, Price, and Marginal Cost

	Elasticity of Demand, ε	Price/Marginal Cost Ratio, $p/MC = 1/[1 + (1/\varepsilon)]$	Lerner Index, $(p - MC)/p = -1/\varepsilon$
↑	−1.01	101	0.99
less elastic	−1.1	11	0.91
	−2	2	0.50
	−3	1.5	0.33
	−5	1.25	0.20
more elastic	−10	1.11	0.10
	−100	1.01	0.01
↓	−∞	1	0

The Lerner Index

Another way to show how the elasticity of demand affects a monopoly's price relative to its marginal cost is to look at the firm's *Lerner Index*. A **Lerner Index** is the ratio of the difference between price and marginal cost to the price: $(p - MC)/p$.[4] This measure is zero for a competitive firm because a competitive firm cannot raise its price above its marginal cost. The greater the difference between price and marginal cost, the larger the Lerner Index and the greater the monopoly's ability to set price above marginal cost.

If the firm is maximizing its profit, we can express the Lerner Index in terms of the elasticity of demand by rearranging Equation 11.10:

$$\frac{p - MC}{p} = -\frac{1}{\varepsilon}. \tag{11.11}$$

Because $MC \geq 0$ and $p \geq MC$, $0 \leq p - MC \leq p$ and the Lerner Index ranges from 0 to 1 for a profit-maximizing firm.[5] Equation 11.11 confirms that a competitive firm has a Lerner Index of zero because its demand curve is perfectly elastic. As Table 11.1 illustrates, the Lerner Index for a monopoly increases as the demand becomes less elastic. If $\varepsilon = -5$, the monopoly's Lerner Index is $\frac{1}{5} = 0.2$; if $\varepsilon = -2$, the Lerner Index is $\frac{1}{2} = 0.5$; and if $\varepsilon = -1.01$, the Lerner Index is 0.99. Monopolies that face demand curves that are only slightly elastic set prices that are multiples of their marginal cost and have Lerner Indexes close to 1.

SOLVED PROBLEM 11.4	The EpiPen is a small portable device that can quickly deliver the drug epinephrine to stop a potentially life-threatening allergic reaction. The manufacturer of the EpiPen faces virtually no competition from other firms. The price for a pair of EpiPens is $630 for people without insurance, while two industry experts estimate that its marginal cost is $30.[6] What is its Lerner Index? If the firm is maximizing its short-run profit, what is its elasticity of demand?
MyLab Economics Solved Problem	

Answer

1. *Determine the Lerner Index by substituting into the Lerner definition.* The EpiPen's Lerner Index is

$$\frac{p - MC}{p} = \frac{630 - 30}{630} \approx 0.952.$$

2. *Use Equation 11.11 to infer the elasticity.* According to that equation, a profit-maximizing monopoly operates where $(p - MC)/p = -1/\varepsilon$. Combining that equation with the Lerner Index from the previous step, we learn that $0.952 = -1/\varepsilon$, or $\varepsilon \approx -1.05$.

---

[4]This index is named after its inventor, Abba Lerner.

[5]For the Lerner Index to be above 1, ε would have to be a negative fraction, indicating that the demand curve was inelastic at the monopoly optimum. However, a profit-maximizing monopoly never operates in the inelastic portion of its demand curve.

[6]www.nbcnews.com/business/consumer/industry-insiders-estimate-epipen-costs-no-more-30-n642091.

Sources of Market Power

What factors cause a monopoly to face a relatively elastic demand curve and hence have little market power? Ultimately, the elasticity of demand of the market demand curve depends on consumers' tastes and options. The more consumers want a good—the more willing they are to pay "virtually anything" for it—the less elastic is the demand curve.

Other things equal, the demand curve a firm (not necessarily a monopoly) faces becomes more elastic as (1) *better substitutes* for the firm's product are introduced, (2) *more firms* enter the market selling the same or similar products (as happened with Apple's iPad), or (3) firms that provide the same service *locate closer* to this firm.

Effect of Market Power on Welfare

By exercising market power, a monopoly lowers welfare relative to that of competition. As before, we define welfare, *W*, as the sum of consumer surplus, *CS*, and producer surplus, *PS*. In Chapter 9, we showed that competition maximizes welfare because price equals marginal cost. By setting its price above its marginal cost, a monopoly causes consumers to buy less than the competitive level of the good, and society suffers a deadweight loss (Chapter 9).

We illustrate this deadweight loss using our linear example. If the monopoly were to act like a competitive market and operate where its inverse demand curve, Equation 11.5, intersects its marginal cost (supply) curve, Equation 11.8,

$$p = 24 - Q = 2Q = MC,$$

it would sell $Q_c = 8$ units of output at a price of \$16, as Figure 11.5 shows. At this competitive price, consumer surplus is area $A + B + C$ and producer surplus is area $D + E$.

If the firm acts like a monopoly and operates where its marginal revenue equals its marginal cost, only 6 units are sold at the monopoly price of \$18, and consumer surplus is only A. Part of the lost consumer surplus, B, goes to the monopoly; but the rest, C, is lost.

By charging the monopoly price of \$18 instead of the competitive price of \$16, the monopoly receives \$2 more per unit and earns an extra profit of area $B = 12 on the $Q_m = 6$ units it sells. The monopoly loses area E, however, because it sells less than the competitive output. Consequently, the monopoly's producer surplus increases by $B - E$ over the competitive level. We know that its producer surplus increases, $B - E > 0$, because the monopoly had the option of producing at the competitive level and chose not to do so.

Social welfare with a monopoly is lower than with a competitive industry by $-C - E$. Thus, the deadweight loss of monopoly is $C + E$, which represents the consumer surplus and producer surplus lost because the monopoly output is smaller than the competitive output. As in the analysis of a tax in Chapter 9, the deadweight loss is due to the gap between price and marginal cost at the monopoly output. At $Q_m = 6$, the price, \$18, is above the marginal cost, \$12, so consumers are willing to pay more for the last unit of output than it costs to produce it. The inefficiency of monopoly pricing is another example of a *market failure* (see Chapter 9), a non-optimal allocation of goods and services such that a market does not achieve economic efficiency.

Of course you could get it done for less if I weren't the only plumber in town.

Figure 11.5 Deadweight Loss of Monopoly

A competitive market would produce $Q_c = 8$ at $p_c = \$16$, where the demand curve intersects the marginal cost (supply) curve. A monopoly produces only $Q_m = 6$ at $p_m = \$18$, where the marginal revenue curve intersects the marginal cost curve. Under monopoly, consumer surplus is A, producer surplus is $B + D$, and the lost welfare or deadweight loss of monopoly is $C + E$.

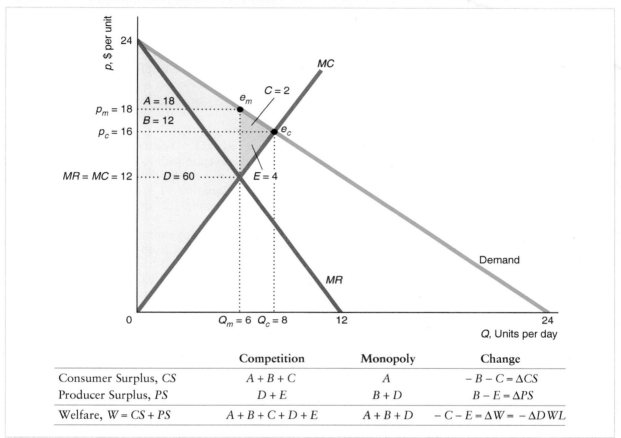

	Competition	Monopoly	Change
Consumer Surplus, CS	$A + B + C$	A	$-B - C = \Delta CS$
Producer Surplus, PS	$D + E$	$B + D$	$B - E = \Delta PS$
Welfare, $W = CS + PS$	$A + B + C + D + E$	$A + B + D$	$-C - E = \Delta W = -\Delta DWL$

11.3 Taxes and Monopoly

Monopolies may face specific taxes (the government charges t dollars per unit) or ad valorem taxes (the government collects vp per unit of output, where v is the ad valorem tax rate (see Chapter 2), a fraction, and p is the price it charges consumers). Both types of tax raise the price that consumers pay and lower welfare—the same effect as when a government taxes a competitive market (Chapter 2). However, taxes affect a monopoly differently than they affect a competitive industry in two ways.

First, the tax incidence on consumers—the change in the consumers' price divided by the change in the tax—can exceed 100% in a monopoly market but not in a competitive market. Second, if the ad valorem tax rate v and the specific tax, t, are set so that both produce the same after-tax output, the government is indifferent between the taxes for a competitive market but prefers the ad valorem tax for a monopoly. Compared to a specific tax, the ad valorem tax raises the same amount of tax revenue in a competitive market (Chapter 2), but more tax revenue with a monopoly.

Effects of a Specific Tax

If the government imposes a specific tax of t dollars per unit on a monopoly, the monopoly will reduce its output and raise its price. The incidence of the tax on consumers may exceed 100%.

The monopoly's before-tax cost function is $C(Q)$, so its after-tax cost function is $C(Q) + tQ$. The monopoly's after-tax profit is $R(Q) - C(Q) - tQ$. To obtain a necessary condition for the monopoly to maximize its after-tax profit, we set the derivative of the monopoly's after-tax profit to zero:

$$\frac{dR(Q)}{d(Q)} - \frac{dC(Q)}{dQ} - t = 0, \tag{11.12}$$

where dR/dQ is its marginal revenue and $dC/dQ + t$ is its after-tax marginal cost. That is, the monopoly equates its marginal revenue with its relevant (after-tax) marginal cost: $dR/dQ = dC/dQ + t$. At $t = 0$, this condition gives the before-tax necessary condition for profit maximization, Equation 11.1. For any t, the sufficient condition is the same as the before-tax Equation 11.2, $d^2R/dQ^2 - d^2C/dQ^2 < 0$, because $dt/dQ = 0$.

We can use comparative statics techniques to determine the effect of imposing a specific tax by asking how output changes as t goes from zero to a small positive value. Based on the necessary condition, Equation 11.12, we can write the monopoly's optimal quantity as a function of the tax: $Q(t)$: $dR(Q(t)/dQ - dC(Q(t))/dQ$. Differentiating the necessary condition with respect to t, we find that

$$\frac{d^2R}{dQ^2}\frac{dQ}{dt} - \frac{d^2C}{dQ^2}\frac{dQ}{dt} - 1 = 0,$$

or

$$\frac{dQ}{dt} = \frac{1}{\dfrac{d^2R}{dQ^2} - \dfrac{d^2C}{dQ^2}}. \tag{11.13}$$

The denominator of the right-hand-side of Equation 11.13 is negative by the second-order condition, Equation 11.2, so $dQ/dt < 0$. That is, as the specific tax rises, the monopoly reduces its output. Because its demand curve is downward sloping, when the monopoly lowers its output, it raises its price by $dp(Q(t))/dt = (dp/dQ)(dQ/dt) > 0$.

In a competitive market, the incidence of a specific or ad valorem tax on consumers is less than or equal to 100% of the tax (Chapter 2). In contrast, in a monopoly market, the incidence of a specific tax falling on consumers can exceed 100%: The price consumers pay may rise by an amount greater than the tax.

We use an example to demonstrate this possibility. Suppose that a monopoly's marginal cost is constant at m and that its demand curve has a constant elasticity of ε, so its inverse demand function is $p = Q^{1/\varepsilon}$. Consequently, the monopoly's revenue function is $R = pQ = Q^{1+1/\varepsilon}$, and the marginal revenue function is $MR = dQ^{1+1/\varepsilon}/dQ = (1 + 1/\varepsilon)Q^{1/\varepsilon}$.

To maximize its profit, the monopoly equates its after-tax marginal cost, $m + t$, with its marginal revenue function:

$$m + t = \left(1 + \frac{1}{\varepsilon}\right)Q^{1/\varepsilon}.$$

Solving this equation for the profit-maximizing output, the monopoly chooses to produce $Q = [(m + t)/(1 + 1/\varepsilon)]^\varepsilon$. Substituting this Q into its inverse demand function, $p = Q^{1/\varepsilon}$, we find that the monopoly's price is

$$p = \frac{m + t}{1 + 1/\varepsilon}. \tag{11.14}$$

To determine the effect of a change in the tax on the price that consumers pay, we differentiate Equation 11.14 with respect to the tax: $dp/dt = 1/(1 + 1/\varepsilon)$. We know that dp/dt is greater than one because a monopoly never operates in the inelastic portion of its demand curve, so $\varepsilon < -1$. Thus, the incidence of the tax that falls on consumers exceeds 100%. However, for other types of demand curves, the tax incidence on consumers may be less than 100%, as the following Solved Problem shows.

SOLVED PROBLEM **11.5** MyLab Economics Solved Problem	If the government imposes a specific tax of $t = \$8$ per unit on the monopoly in Figure 11.3, how does the monopoly change its profit-maximizing quantity and price? Use a figure to show how the tax affects tax revenue, consumer surplus, producer surplus, welfare, and deadweight loss. What is the incidence of the tax on consumers?

Answer

1. *Determine how imposing the tax affects the monopoly's optimum quantity by equating marginal revenue and after-tax marginal cost, and substitute the optimum quantity into the inverse demand function to find the profit-maximizing price.* Because the monopoly must pay the tax, its before-tax marginal cost, Equation 11.8, $2Q$, shifts to an after-tax marginal cost of $MC = 2Q + 8$.[7] The monopoly's marginal revenue, Equation 11.6, remains unchanged at $MR = 24 - 2Q$. The monopoly picks the output, Q^*, that equates its after-tax marginal cost and its marginal revenue: $2Q^* + 8 = 24 - 2Q^*$. Solving, we find that $Q^* = 4$. Because the monopoly's inverse demand function, Equation 11.5, is $p = 24 - Q$, it charges $p^* = 24 - 4 = 20$.

   The graph shows that the intersection of the marginal revenue curve, MR, and the before-tax marginal cost curve, MC^1, determines the before-tax monopoly's optimum quantity, $Q_1 = 6$. At the before-tax optimum, e_1, the price is $p_1 = \$18$. The specific tax causes the monopoly's before-tax marginal cost curve, $MC^1 = 2Q$, to shift upward by $\$8$ to $MC^2 = MC^1 + 8 = 2Q + 8$. After the tax is applied, the monopoly operates where $MR = 24 - 2Q = 2Q + 8 = MC^2$. In the after-tax monopoly optimum, e_2, the quantity is $Q_2 = 4$ and the price is $p_2 = \$20$. Thus, output falls by $\Delta Q = 2$ units and the price increases by $\Delta p = \$2$.

2. *Show the change in tax revenue and the various welfare measures.* In the figure, area G is the tax revenue collected by the government, $\$32$, because its height is the distance between the two marginal cost curves, $t = \$8$, and its length is

---

[7]The government can impose a tax on the seller (here, the monopoly) or the buyers (Chapter 2). Here, because the seller must pay the tax, the tax shifts its marginal cost curve, but not the demand or marginal revenue curves. In the next section, we assume that the government imposes the tax on the buyers so that it shifts the demand marginal revenue curves and not the marginal cost curve.

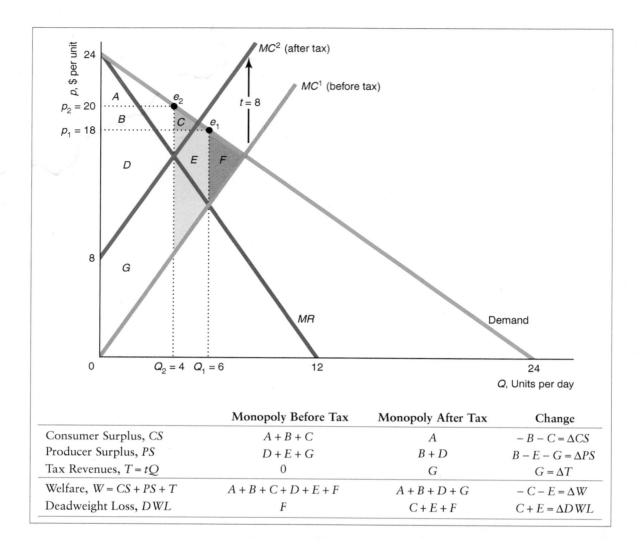

	Monopoly Before Tax	Monopoly After Tax	Change
Consumer Surplus, CS	$A + B + C$	A	$-B - C = \Delta CS$
Producer Surplus, PS	$D + E + G$	$B + D$	$B - E - G = \Delta PS$
Tax Revenues, $T = tQ$	0	G	$G = \Delta T$
Welfare, $W = CS + PS + T$	$A + B + C + D + E + F$	$A + B + D + G$	$-C - E = \Delta W$
Deadweight Loss, DWL	F	$C + E + F$	$C + E = \Delta DWL$

the after-tax output, $Q = 4$. The tax reduces consumer and producer surplus and increases the deadweight loss. Consumer surplus falls by area $B + C$ from $A + B + C$ to A. The monopoly's producer surplus falls from $D + E + G$ to $B + D$, so the change in producer surplus is $B - E - G$. We know that producer surplus falls because (a) the monopoly could have produced this reduced output level in the absence of the tax but did not because it was not the profit-maximizing output, so its before-tax profit falls, and (b) the monopoly must now pay taxes. The before-tax deadweight loss due to monopoly pricing was F. The after-tax deadweight loss is $C + E + F$, so the increase in deadweight loss (or loss in welfare) due to the tax is $C + E$.

3. *Calculate the incidence of the tax.* Because the tax goes from $0 to $8, the change in the tax is $\Delta t = \$8$. The incidence of the tax on consumers is $\Delta p / \Delta t = \$2/\$8 = \frac{1}{4}$. That is, the monopoly absorbs $6 of the tax and passes on only $2.

Welfare Effects of Ad Valorem Versus Specific Taxes

Why do governments generally use ad valorem sales taxes rather than specific taxes? In a market with a monopoly, a government raises more tax revenue with an ad valorem tax v than with a specific tax t when v and t are set so that the after-tax output (and hence the deadweight loss) is the same with either tax, as we now show.[8]

In Figure 11.6, the before-tax market demand curve is D, and the corresponding marginal revenue is MR. The before-tax monopoly optimum is e_1. The MR curve intersects the MC curve at Q_1 units, which sell at a price of p_1.

We assume that the government imposes the tax on consumers rather than on the firm, so that the tax shifts the demand and marginal revenue curves rather than the marginal cost curve. If the government imposes a specific tax t, the monopoly's after-tax demand curve is D^s, which is the market demand curve D shifted downward by t dollars. The corresponding marginal revenue curve, MR^s, intersects the marginal cost curve at Q_2. In this after-tax monopoly optimum, e_2, consumers pay p_2 and the monopoly receives $p_s = p_2 - t$ per unit. The government's revenue from the specific tax is area $A = tQ_2$.

If the government imposes an ad valorem tax, the demand curve facing the monopoly is D^a. The gap between D^a and D—which equals the tax per unit, vp—is greater at higher prices. By setting v appropriately, the corresponding marginal revenue curve, MR_a, intersects the marginal cost curve at Q_2, where consumers again pay p_2. Although the ad valorem tax reduces output by the same amount as the specific tax, the ad valorem tax raises more revenue, area $A + B = vp_2Q_2$.

Figure 11.6 Ad Valorem Versus Specific Tax

A specific tax (t) and an ad valorem tax (α) that reduce the monopoly output by the same amount (from Q_1 to Q_2) raise different amounts of tax revenues for the government. The tax revenue from the specific tax is area $A = tQ_2$. The tax revenue from the ad valorem tax is area $A + B = vp_2Q_2$.

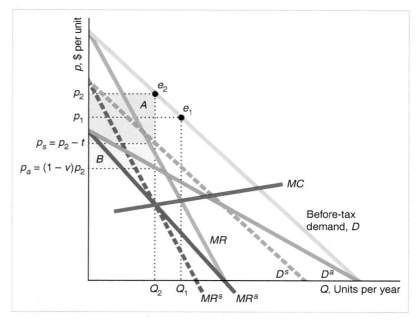

---

[8]Chapter 2 shows that both taxes raise the same tax revenue in a competitive market. However, the taxes raise different amounts when applied to monopolies or other noncompetitive firms. See Delipalla and Keen (1992), Skeath and Trandel (1994), and Hamilton (1999).

Both sales taxes harm consumers by the same amount because they raise the price consumers pay from p_1 to p_2 and reduce the quantity purchased from Q_1 to Q_2. The ad valorem tax transfers more revenue from the monopoly to the government, so the government prefers the ad valorem tax and the monopoly prefers the specific tax. (Equivalently, if the government set t and v so that they raised the same amount of tax revenue, the ad valorem tax would reduce output and consumer surplus less than the specific tax.) Amazingly, it makes sense for the government to employ an ad valorem tax, and state and local governments use ad valorem taxes for most goods (the likely exceptions are alcohol, tobacco, fuels, communications, and transportation).

11.4   Causes of Monopolies

Is it right that only one firm sells the game Monopoly?

Why are some markets monopolized? Two key reasons are that a firm has a cost advantage over other firms or a government created the monopoly.[9]

Cost Advantages

If a low-cost firm profitably sells at a price so low that potential competitors with higher costs would incur losses, no other firm enters the market. A firm can have a cost advantage over potential rivals because it has an essential facility, it has a superior technology or organization, or it is a natural monopoly.

Essential Facility. A firm may have a lower cost than potential rivals if it controls an **essential facility**: a scarce resource that a rival must use to survive. For example, a firm that owns the only quarry in a region is the only firm that can profitably sell gravel to local construction firms. Similarly, in 2012, Canadian pipeline giant Enbridge Inc. refused to allow the pipeline of a small Colorado firm to connect Enbridge's highway of pipelines that bring Canadian oil sands crude oil into the United States.[10]

Superior Technology or Organization. A firm may have lower costs if it uses a superior technology or has a better way of organizing production. Henry Ford's methods of organizing production using assembly lines and standardization allowed him to produce cars at lower cost than rival firms until they copied his organizational techniques.

Natural Monopoly. One firm can produce the total market output at lower cost than several firms could if it is a **natural monopoly**. If the cost for any firm to produce q is $C(q)$, the condition for a natural monopoly is

$$C(Q) < C(q_1) + C(q_2) + \cdots + C(q_n), \tag{11.15}$$

---

[9]In Section 11.6, we discuss how network externalities may lead to a monopoly. In later chapters, we discuss three other causes of monopolies. First, the original firm in a market may use strategies that discourage other firms from entering the market (Chapter 13). Second, a merger into a single firm (Chapter 14) of all the firms in an industry creates a monopoly if new firms fail to enter the market. Third, firms may coordinate their activities and set their prices as a monopoly would (Chapter 14). Such a group of firms is called a *cartel*.

[10]Hannah Northey, "U.S. Producers Accuse Canadian Pipeline Company of Refusing to Carry Their Crude," *Greenwire*, July 12, 2012.

Figure 11.7 Natural Monopoly

This natural monopoly has a strictly declining average cost.

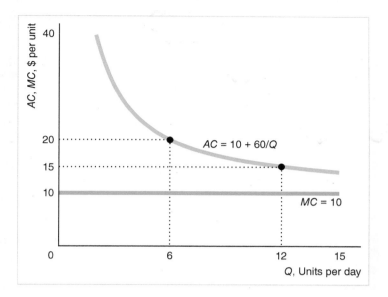

where $Q = q_1 + q_2 + \cdots + q_n$ is the sum of the output of any $n \geq 2$ firms and where the condition holds for all output levels that could be demanded by the market. With a natural monopoly, it is more efficient to have only one firm produce than to have more than one firm produce.[11] Believing that they are natural monopolies, governments frequently grant monopoly rights to *public utilities* to provide essential goods or services, such as water, gas, electric power, and mail delivery.

Suppose that a public utility has economies of scale (Chapter 7) at all levels of output, so its average cost curve falls as output increases for any observed level of output. If all potential firms have the same strictly declining average cost curve, this market has a natural monopoly, as we now consider.[12]

A company that supplies water to homes incurs a high fixed cost, F, to build a plant and connect houses to the plant. The firm's marginal cost, m, of supplying water is constant, so its marginal cost curve is horizontal and its average cost, $AC = m + F/Q$, declines as output rises. (The iPad cost function in Solved Problem 11.2 has this functional form.)

Figure 11.7 shows such marginal and average cost curves where $m = \$10$ and $F = \$60$. If the market output is 12 units per day, one firm produces that output

---

[11]A natural monopoly is the most efficient market structure only in the sense that the single firm produces at lowest cost. However, society's welfare may be greater with more firms producing at higher cost, because competition drives down the price from the monopoly level. One solution that allows society to maximize welfare is for the government to allow only one firm to produce but the government forces it to charge a price equal to marginal cost (as we discuss later in this chapter).

[12]A firm may be a natural monopoly even if its cost curve does not fall at all levels of output. If a U-shaped average cost curve reaches its minimum at 100 units of output, it may be less costly for only one firm to produce an output of 101 units even though its average cost curve is rising at that output. Thus, a cost function with economies of scale everywhere is a sufficient but not a necessary condition for a natural monopoly.

at an average cost of $15, or a total cost of $180 (= $15 × 12). If two firms each produce 6 units, the average cost is $20, and the cost of producing the market output is $240 (= $20 × 12), which is greater than the cost with a single firm.

If the two firms were to divide the total production in any other way, their costs of production would still exceed the cost of a single firm (as Solved Problem 11.6 asks you to prove).[13] The reason is that the marginal cost per unit is the same no matter how many firms produce, but each additional firm adds a fixed cost, which raises the total cost of producing a given quantity. If only one firm provides water, society avoids the cost of building a second plant and a second set of pipes.

SOLVED PROBLEM
11.6

A firm that delivers Q units of water to households has a total cost of $C(Q) = mQ + F$. If any entrant would have the same cost, does this market have a natural monopoly?

MyLab Economics
Solved Problem

Answer

Determine whether costs rise if two firms produce a given quantity. Let q_1 be the output of Firm 1 and q_2 be the output of Firm 2. The combined cost of these firms producing $Q = q_1 + q_2$ is

$$C(q_1) + C(q_2) = (mq_1 + F) + (mq_2 + F) = m(q_1 + q_2) + 2F = mQ + 2F.$$

If a single firm produces Q, its cost is $C(Q) = mQ + F$. Thus the cost of producing any given Q is greater with two firms than with one firm, so this market has a natural monopoly.

Government Actions That Create Monopolies

Governments create many monopolies by establishing barriers to entry to potential competitors. A government may own and manage a monopoly. In the United States, as in most other countries, the postal service is a government monopoly. Indeed, the U.S. Constitution explicitly grants the government the right to establish a postal service. Many local governments own and operate public utility monopolies that provide garbage collection, electricity, water, gas, phone services, and other utilities. Most national governments grant patents to the inventor of a new product that gives the patent holder monopoly rights for 20 years.

Licenses and Auctions. By preventing other firms from entering a market, governments create monopolies. Governments typically create monopolies by making it difficult for new firms to obtain a license to operate or by auctioning the rights to be a monopoly.

Frequently, firms need government licenses to operate. If a government makes it difficult for new firms to obtain licenses, the first firm to become licensed can maintain its monopoly. Until recently, many U.S. cities required new hospitals or other

---

[13]See "Electric Power Utilities" in MyLab Economics, Chapter Resources, Chapter 11.

inpatient establishments to demonstrate the need for a new facility by securing a certificate of need, which allowed them to enter the market.

Governments around the world have privatized many state-owned monopolies in the past several decades. By auctioning its monopolies to private firms, a government can capture the future value of monopoly earnings. Alternatively, a government could "auction" the rights to the firm that offers to charge customers the lowest price for a service such as cable television, so as to maximize social welfare.[14]

Public Utilities. Government grants of monopoly rights have been common for public utilities. Instead of running a public utility itself, a government gives a private company the monopoly rights to operate the utility. A government may capture some of the monopoly's profits by charging a high rent to the monopoly. Alternatively, government officials may capture the rents for monopoly rights through bribery.

Patents. If a firm cannot prevent imitation by keeping its discovery secret, it may obtain government protection to prevent other firms from duplicating its discovery and entering the market. Virtually all countries provide such protection through a **patent**: an exclusive right granted to the inventor to sell a new and useful product, process, substance, or design for a fixed time. A patent grants an inventor the right to be the monopoly provider of the good for a number of years. (Similarly, a copyright gives its owner the exclusive production, publication, or sales rights to artistic, dramatic, literary, or musical works.)

The length of a patent varies across countries. The U.S. Constitution explicitly gives the government the right to grant authors and inventors exclusive rights to their writings (copyrights) and to their discoveries (patents) for limited periods of time. Traditionally, U.S. patents lasted 17 years from the date they were *granted*, but in 1995, the United States agreed to change its patent law as part of an international agreement. Now, U.S. patents last for 20 years after the date the inventor *files* for patent protection. The length of protection is likely to be shorter under the new rules because frequently it takes more than three years after filing to obtain final approval of a patent.

A firm with a patent monopoly sets a high price, which results in deadweight loss. Why, then, do governments grant patent monopolies? The main reason is that inventive activity would fall if inventors could not obtain patent monopolies. The costs of developing a new drug or new computer chip are often hundreds of millions or even billions of dollars. If anyone could copy a new drug or computer chip and compete with the inventor, few individuals or firms would undertake the costly research. Thus, the government is explicitly trading off the long-run benefits of additional inventions against the shorter-term harms of monopoly pricing during the period of patent protection.[15]

---

[14]*Jargon alert*: Many economists refer to such a low-price auction as a Demsetz auction.

[15]Although patents may increase innovation, abuses of patent law may inhibit innovation. For example, *patent trolls* obtain minor patents that they sue to block other more serious inventors unless they pay a *ransom*. In addition, the large number of patents and patent holders in many areas, such as information technology and biotechnology, impose large transaction costs on potential inventors. Thus, while a well-designed patent system provides strong incentives for innovation, a poorly designed system can be counterproductive.

APPLICATION

The Botox Patent Monopoly

Ophthalmologist Dr. Alan Scott turned the deadly poison botulinum toxin into a miracle drug to treat two eye conditions: strabismus, a condition in which the eyes are not properly aligned, and blepharospasm, an uncontrollable closure of the eyes. Strabismus affects about 4% of children and blepharospasm left about 25,000 Americans functionally blind before Scott's discovery. Allergan, Inc. sells his patented drug, Botox.

Dr. Scott has been amused to see several of the unintended beneficiaries of his research at the annual Academy Awards. Even before the government explicitly approved using Botox for cosmetic use, many doctors were injecting Botox into the facial muscles of actors, models, and others to smooth out their wrinkles. (The drug paralyzes the muscles, so those injected with it also lose their ability to frown or smile—and, some would say, act.) The treatment is only temporary, lasting up to 120 days, so repeated injections are necessary.

Allergan has a near-monopoly in the treatment of wrinkles, although plastic surgery and collagen, Restylane, hyaluronic acids, and other filler injections provide limited competition. However, now 54% of its sales are for other uses, including as a treatment for chronic migraine and overactive bladder.

Allergan had Botox sales of $800 million in 2004 and about $2.8 billion in 2016. Indeed, Botox's value may increase. As Allergan finds new uses for Botox, its sales continue to increase. According to one forecast, Botox's global sales will reach $3.2 billion by the end of 2018 and $4.6 billion by 2024.

Dr. Scott can produce a vial of Botox in his lab for about $25. Allergan sells the potion to doctors for about $400. Assuming that the firm is setting its price to maximize its short-run profit, we can rearrange Equation 11.11 to determine the elasticity of demand for Botox:

$$\varepsilon = -\frac{p}{p - MC} = -\frac{400}{400 - 25} \approx -1.067.$$

Thus, the demand that Allergan faces is only slightly elastic: A 1% increase in price causes quantity to fall by slightly more than 1%.

If the demand curve is linear and the elasticity of demand is −1.067 at the 2002 monopoly optimum, e_m (1 million vials sold at $400 each, producing revenue of $400 million), then Allergan's inverse demand function is[16]

$$p = 775 - 375Q.$$

This demand curve (see the graph) has a slope of −375 and hits the price axis at $775 and the quantity axis at about 2.07 million vials per year. Thus, its revenue is $R = 775Q - 375Q^2$, so its marginal revenue curve is

$$MR = dR/dQ = 775 - 750Q.$$

The *MR* curve strikes the price axis at $775 and has twice the slope, −750, of the demand curve.

The intersection of the marginal revenue and marginal cost curves,

$$MR = 775 - 750Q = 25 = MC,$$

---

[16]The graph shows an inverse linear demand curve of the form $p = a - bQ$. Such a linear demand curve has an elasticity of $\varepsilon = -(1/b)(p/Q)$. Given that the elasticity of demand is $-400/375 = -(1/b)(400/1)$, where Q is measured in millions of vials, then $b = 375$. Solving $p = 400 = a - 375$, we find that $a = 775$.

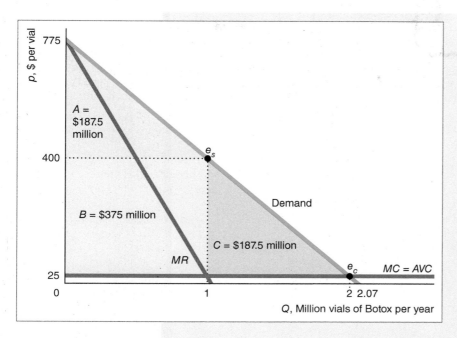

determines the monopoly optimum at the profit-maximizing quantity of 1 million vials per year and at a price of $400 per vial.

Were the company to sell Botox at a price equal to its marginal cost of $25 (as a competitive industry would), consumer surplus would equal area $A + B + C$. The height of triangle $A + B + C$ is $750 = $775 − 25, and its length is 2 million vials, so its area is $750 (= \frac{1}{2} \times 750 \times 2)$ million. At the higher monopoly price of $400, the consumer surplus is $A = 187.5 million. Compared to the competitive solution, e_c, buyers lose consumer surplus of $B + C = 562.5 million per year. Part of this loss, $B = 375 million per year, is transferred from consumers to Allergan. The rest, $C = 187.5 million per year, is the deadweight loss from monopoly pricing. Allergan's profit is its producer surplus, B, minus its fixed costs.

11.5 Government Actions That Reduce Market Power

Some governments act to reduce or eliminate monopolies' market power. Many governments directly regulate monopolies, especially those created by the government, such as public utilities. Most high-income countries have laws to prevent a firm from driving other firms out of the market so as to monopolize it. A government may destroy a monopoly by breaking it up into smaller, independent firms (as the government did with Alcoa, the former aluminum monopoly).

Regulating Monopolies

Governments limit monopolies' market power in various ways. For example, most utilities are subject to direct regulation. Today, the most commonly used approach to regulating monopoly pricing is to impose a price ceiling, called a *price cap*. Price cap regulation is used for telecommunications monopolies in 33 U.S. states and in many countries, including Australia, Canada, Denmark, France, Germany, Mexico, Sweden, and the United Kingdom (Sappington and Weisman, 2010).

Optimal Price Regulation. In some markets, the government can eliminate the deadweight loss of a monopoly by requiring that it charge no more than the competitive price. We use our earlier linear example to illustrate this type of regulation in Figure 11.8.

Figure 11.8 Optimal Price Regulation

If the government sets a price ceiling at $16, where the monopoly's marginal cost curve hits the demand curve, the new demand curve that the monopoly faces has a kink at 8 units, and the corresponding marginal revenue curve, MR^r, "jumps" at that quantity. The regulated monopoly sets its output where $MR^r = MC$, selling the same quantity, 8 units, at the same price, $16, as a competitive industry would. The regulation eliminates the monopoly deadweight loss, $C + E$. Consumer surplus, $A + B + C$, and producer surplus, $D + E$, are the same as under competition.

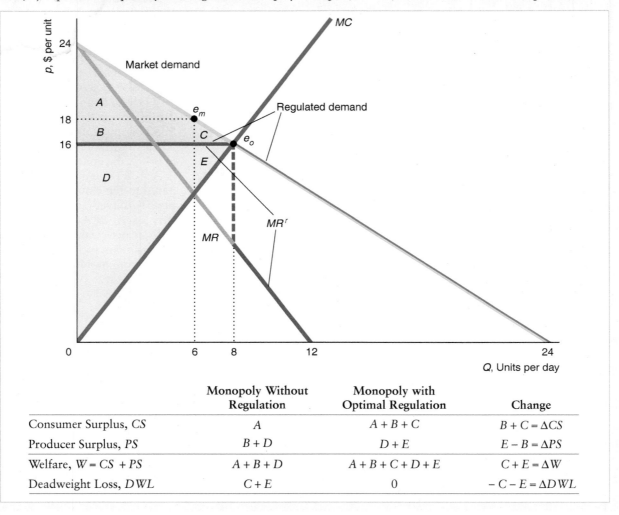

	Monopoly Without Regulation	Monopoly with Optimal Regulation	Change
Consumer Surplus, CS	A	$A + B + C$	$B + C = \Delta CS$
Producer Surplus, PS	$B + D$	$D + E$	$E - B = \Delta PS$
Welfare, $W = CS + PS$	$A + B + D$	$A + B + C + D + E$	$C + E = \Delta W$
Deadweight Loss, DWL	$C + E$	0	$-C - E = \Delta DWL$

If the government doesn't regulate the profit-maximizing monopoly, the monopoly optimum is e_m, at which 6 units are sold at the monopoly price of $18. Suppose that the government sets a ceiling price of $16, the price at which the marginal cost curve intersects the market demand curve. Because the monopoly cannot charge more than $16 per unit, the monopoly's regulated demand curve is horizontal at $16 (up to 8 units) and is the same as the market demand curve at lower prices. The marginal revenue curve corresponding to the regulated demand curve, MR^r, is horizontal where the regulated demand curve is horizontal (up to 8 units) and equals the marginal revenue curve, MR, corresponding to the market demand curve at larger quantities.

The regulated monopoly sets its output at 8 units, where MR^r equals its marginal cost, MC, and charges the maximum permitted price of $16. The regulated firm still makes a profit because its average cost is less than $16 at 8 units. The optimally regulated monopoly optimum, e_o, is the same as the competitive equilibrium, where marginal cost (supply) equals the market demand curve.[17] Thus, setting a price ceiling where the MC curve and market demand curve intersect eliminates the deadweight loss of monopoly.

How do we know that this regulation is optimal? The answer is that this regulated outcome is the same as would occur if this market were competitive, where welfare is maximized (Chapter 9). As the table accompanying Figure 11.8 shows, the deadweight loss of monopoly, $C + E$, is eliminated by this optimal regulation.

Nonoptimal Price Regulation. If the government sets the price ceiling at any point other than the optimal level, society incurs a deadweight loss. Suppose that the government sets the regulated price below the optimal level, which is $16 in Figure 11.8. If it sets the price below the firm's minimum average cost, the firm shuts down, so the deadweight loss equals the sum of the consumer plus producer surplus under optimal regulation, $A + B + C + D + E$.

Many consumers want the government to set regulated monopoly price as low as possible:

> **Common Confusion** Consumers benefit the lower the government sets the regulated price that a monopoly may charge (without causing the firm to shut down).

A very low regulated price may help some consumers, but hurt others. If the government sets the price ceiling below the optimally regulated price but high enough that the firm does not shut down, consumers who are lucky enough to buy the good benefit because they can buy it at a lower price than they could with optimal regulation. As we show in Solved Problem 11.7, society suffers a deadweight loss because less output is sold than with optimal regulation.

SOLVED PROBLEM 11.7

MyLab Economics Solved Problem

Suppose that the government sets a price ceiling at p_2, which is below the socially optimal level, p_1, but above the monopoly's minimum average cost. How do the price, quantity sold, quantity demanded, and welfare under this regulation compare to those under optimal regulation?

Answer

1. *Describe the optimally regulated outcome.* With optimal regulation, e_1, the price is set at p_1, where the market demand curve intersects the monopoly's marginal cost curve on the accompanying graph. The optimally regulated monopoly sells Q_1 units.

2. *Describe the outcome when the government regulates the price at p_2.* Where the market demand is above p_2, the regulated demand curve for the monopoly is horizontal at p_2 (up to Q_d). The corresponding marginal revenue curve, MR^r, is horizontal where the regulated demand curve is horizontal and equals the

---

[17]The monopoly produces at e_o only if the regulated price, $16, is greater than its average variable cost. Given the cost function in Equation 11.7, the average variable cost at 8 units is $VC(8) = Q = 8. Indeed, the firm makes a profit because $AC(8) = Q + 12/Q = $9.50 < 16.

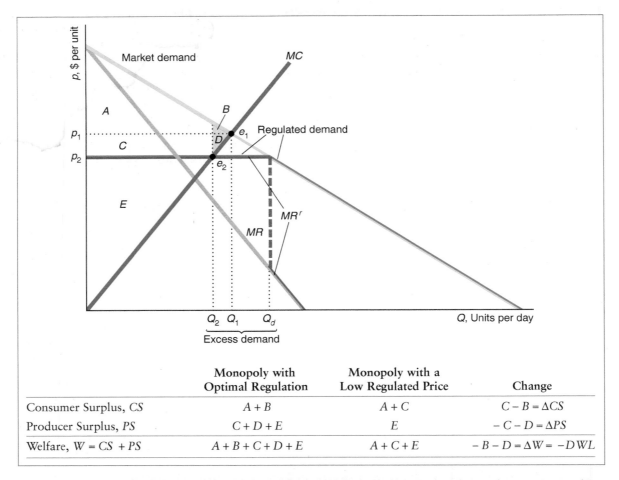

	Monopoly with Optimal Regulation	Monopoly with a Low Regulated Price	Change
Consumer Surplus, CS	$A + B$	$A + C$	$C - B = \Delta CS$
Producer Surplus, PS	$C + D + E$	E	$-C - D = \Delta PS$
Welfare, $W = CS + PS$	$A + B + C + D + E$	$A + C + E$	$-B - D = \Delta W = -DWL$

marginal revenue curve corresponding to the market demand curve, MR, where the regulated demand curve is downward sloping. The monopoly maximizes its profit by selling Q_2 units at p_2. The new regulated monopoly optimum is e_2, where MR^r intersects MC. The firm does not shut down when regulated as long as its average variable cost at Q_2 is less than p_2.

3. *Compare the outcomes.* The quantity that the monopoly sells falls from Q_1 to Q_2 when the government lowers its price ceiling from p_1 to p_2. At that lower price, consumers want to buy Q_d, so the excess demand is $Q_d - Q_2$. Compared to optimal regulation, welfare is lower by at least $B + D$.

Comment: The welfare loss is greater if unlucky consumers waste time trying to buy the good unsuccessfully or if goods are not allocated optimally among consumers. A consumer who values the good at only p_2 may be lucky enough to buy it, while a consumer who values the good at p_1 or more may not be able to obtain it, which is an allocative inefficiency (Chapter 9).

Problems in Regulating. Governments often fail to regulate monopolies optimally for at least three reasons. First, due to limited information about the demand and marginal cost curves, governments may set a price ceiling above or below the competitive level.

Second, regulation may be ineffective when regulators are *captured*: influenced by the firms they regulate. Typically, this influence is more subtle than an outright bribe. Because many regulators worked in the industry before becoming regulators, they are sympathetic to the industry. For many other regulators, the reverse is true: They aspire to obtain good jobs in the industry eventually, so they do not want to offend potential employers. And some regulators, relying on industry experts for their information, may be misled or at least heavily influenced by the industry. U.S. Food and Drug Administration advisers voted 15 to 11 to recommend approval of four Bayer AG birth-control pills, but three of the advisers, who voted favorably, had ties to Bayer, serving as consultants, speakers, or researchers.[18] Arguing that these influences are inherent, some economists contend that price and other types of regulation are unlikely to result in efficiency.

Third, because regulators generally cannot subsidize the monopoly, they may be unable to set the price as low as they want because the firm may shut down:

Unintended Consequence Very aggressive price regulation can cause a firm to shut down.

In a natural monopoly where the average cost curve is strictly above the marginal cost curve, if the regulator sets the price equal to the marginal cost so as to eliminate deadweight loss, the firm cannot afford to operate. If the regulators cannot subsidize the firm, they must raise the price to a level where the firm at least breaks even.

APPLICATION

Natural Gas Regulation

Because U.S. natural gas monopolies are natural monopolies and regulators generally cannot subsidize them, the regulated price is set above marginal cost, causing a deadweight loss. The figure uses the estimates of Davis and Muehlegger (2010).[19] If unregulated, this monopoly would sell 12.1 trillion cubic feet of natural gas per year, where its marginal revenue and marginal cost curves intersect. It would charge the corresponding price on the demand curve at point *a*. Its profit would equal the rectangle *A*, with a length equal to the quantity, 12.1 trillion cubic feet, and a height equal to the difference between the price at *a* and the corresponding average cost.

To eliminate deadweight loss, the government could set the price ceiling equal to the marginal cost of $5.78 per thousand cubic feet of natural gas so that the monopoly behaves like a price taker. The price ceiling or marginal cost curve hits the demand curve at *c* where the quantity is 24.2 billion cubic feet per year— double the unregulated quantity. At that quantity, the regulated utility would lose money. The regulated price, $5.78, is less than the average cost at that quantity of $7.78, so it would lose $2 on each thousand cubic feet it sells, or $48.2 billion in total. The monopoly is willing to sell this quantity at this price only if it receives a government subsidy to cover its losses.

---

[18]Thomas M. Burton, "FDA Panelists Had Ties to Bayer," *Wall Street Journal*, January 11, 2012.

[19]We use their most conservative estimate, the one that produces the smallest deadweight loss. We approximate their demand curve with a linear one that has the same price elasticity of demand of 0.2 at point *b*. This figure represents the aggregation of state-level monopolies to the national level.

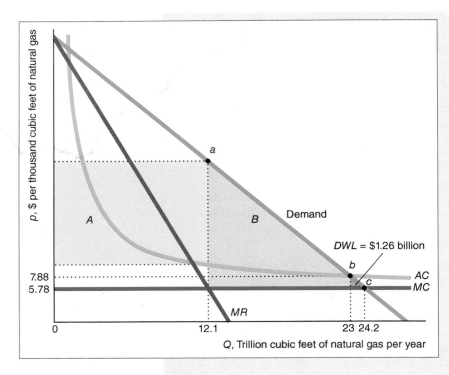

Typically, it is politically infeasible for a government regulatory agency to subsidize a monopoly. On average, the natural gas regulatory agencies try to set the price at $7.88 per thousand cubic feet, where the demand curve intersects the average cost curve and the monopoly breaks even, point *b*. The monopoly sells 23 trillion cubic feet per year. The corresponding price, $7.88, is 36% above marginal cost, $5.78. The deadweight loss is $1.26 billion annually, which is the small, dark gray triangle labeled *DWL*. Without regulation, the deadweight loss would be much greater: this deadweight loss area plus area *B*.

Of course, an alternative to regulating a monopoly's price to eliminate inefficiency is to make the market more competitive. The government has moved in that direction (Oliver and Mason, 2018).

Increasing Competition

Encouraging competition is an alternative to regulation as a means of reducing the harms of monopoly. When a government has created a monopoly by preventing entry, it can quickly reduce the monopoly's market power by allowing other firms to enter, as Canada did with its medical marijuana market in 2015. As new firms enter the market, the former monopoly must lower its price to compete, so welfare rises.

Similarly, a government may end a ban on imports so that a domestic monopoly faces competition from foreign firms. If costs for the domestic firm are the same as costs for the foreign firms and many foreign firms enter the market, the former monopoly becomes just one of many competitive firms. As the market becomes competitive, consumers pay the competitive price, which eliminates the deadweight loss of monopoly.

Globally, governments are increasing competition in previously monopolized markets. For example, many governments around the world forced former telephone and energy monopolies to compete.

Similarly, under pressure from the World Trade Organization, many countries are reducing or eliminating barriers that protected domestic monopolies. The entry of foreign competitive firms into a market can create a new, more competitive market structure.

APPLICATION

Movie Studios Attacked by 3D Printers!

Disney, Marvel, Lucas, and a variety of other companies make a fortune from selling figurines and other plastic toys based on their movies, such as Disney's *Incredibles 2*. These firms hold monopoly rights to produce their toys under copyright laws, which give the creators of original works such as comics and movies the exclusive right to its use and distribution for a limited time.

However, 3D printers are undermining their monopolies. Fans upload high-quality designs to the Web, which anyone with a 3D printer can use to produce pirated versions of these toys. The online marketplace for 3D designs and objects include comic-book heroes, cartoon characters, Angelina Jolie's headdress in the movie *Maleficent*, Homer Simpson, and even Walt Disney's head.

A movie firm is no longer a monopoly. It is a *dominant firm* that faces a *competitive fringe* made up of small, price-taking firms. If the movie firms can't block such pirating using the legal system, they may have to drop the prices for their toys to compete. The competitive fringe limits the movie firm's price much as government regulation would. The movie firm's main advantage is that its mass-production marginal costs are lower than the 3D-printer marginal costs of hobbyists and pirates, but 3D-printing costs are falling.

SOLVED PROBLEM 11.8

MyLab Economics
Solved Problem

How does the presence of pirated, 3D toys affect the price that Disney charges for an *Incredibles 2* or *Moana* figurine? Assume that Disney has a constant marginal cost MC. It faces a large number of identical, higher-cost rivals—the competitive fringe—which act like (competitive) price takers so that their collective supply curve is horizontal at $p_2 = MC + x$, which is the marginal cost of a fringe firm.

Answer

1. *Show how Disney prices a toy figurine if it is a monopoly by equating its marginal revenue and marginal cost.* The figure shows Disney's original (market) demand curve for its toy as a light-blue line. The light-purple line is the corresponding marginal revenue curve. Its profit-maximizing outcome was e_1 when Disney set its quantity, Q_1, where its MR curve hit its MC curve, and the corresponding price was p_1.

2. *Show how the competitive supply curve alters the demand curve facing Disney.* The competitive supply curve acts like a government price ceiling. Now, Disney cannot charge more than $p_2 = MC + x$. Thus, its dark-blue residual demand curve is flat at $MC + x$ and the same as the original downward-sloping demand curve at lower prices. (That is, the residual demand curve for the toy is similar to that of the regulated monopoly in Figure 11.8.)

3. *Determine Disney's new optimal outcome by equating its new marginal revenue with its marginal cost.* Disney acts like a monopoly with respect to its residual demand curve (rather than to its original demand curve). Corresponding to Disney's residual demand curve in the figure is a dark-purple, kinked marginal revenue curve, MR^r, that crosses Disney's marginal cost line at Q_2.[20] Disney maximizes its profit by selling Q_2 units for p_2 at e_2. That is, Disney sells more toys at a lower price than before the other firms entered the market. Once Disney lowers its price, the fringe sells virtually nothing.

11.6 Internet Monopolies: Networks Effects, Behavioral Economics, and Economies of Scale

A number of technology giants, such as Facebook (95% of young adults on the internet use one of their services), Google (89% of internet searches), and Amazon (75% of electronic book sales), have such large shares of their markets that they are nearly monopolies.[21] Why are they dominant? Two important reasons concern *networks* and natural monopoly.

The demand for many goods and services depends on who else consumes them. These consumers form a **network**: an interconnected group of people or things. Facebook, LinkedIn, and Twitter users form networks, as no one would be interested in such internet social media services unless others also used them.

Another characteristic that is more common on the internet than elsewhere in the economy is a cost structure with low or zero marginal cost and high fixed cost. These firms have economies of scale, which leads to natural monopoly.

Network Externalities

A good has a **network externality** if one person's demand depends on the consumption of a good by others.[22] If a good has a *positive* network externality, its value to a consumer grows as the number of units sold increases. Network externalities are an important source of monopoly power. They arise in many parts of the economy but are particularly important on the internet.

When a firm introduces a new good with a network externality, it faces a chicken-and-egg problem: Ali won't buy the good unless Shan buys it, and Shan won't buy it unless Ali does. The firm wants its customers to coordinate or to make their purchase decisions simultaneously.

The telephone provides a classic example of a positive network externality. When the phone was introduced, potential adopters had no reason to get phone service unless their family and friends did. Why buy a phone if there's no one to call? For

---

[20]If MC crossed MR^r in the downward-sloping section, Disney would be a monopoly because its monopoly price would be less than $MC + x$.

[21]www.wsj.com/articles/the-antitrust-case-against-facebook-google-amazon-and-apple-1516121561.

[22]In Chapter 16, we discuss the more general case of an *externality*, which occurs when a person's well-being or a firm's production capability is directly affected by the actions of other consumers or firms rather than indirectly through changes in prices.

Bell's phone network to succeed, it had to achieve a *critical mass* of users—enough adopters that others wanted to join. Had it failed to achieve this critical mass, demand would have withered and the network would have died.

Behavioral Network Externalities. Network externalities depend on the size of the network, because customers want to interact with each other. However, sometimes consumers' behavior depends on beliefs or tastes that can be explained by psychological and sociological theories, which economists study in *behavioral economics* (Chapter 3).

One such explanation for a direct network externality effect is based on consumer attitudes toward other consumers. Harvey Leibenstein (1950) suggested that consumers sometimes want a good because "everyone else has it." A fad or other popularity-based explanation for a positive network externality is called a **bandwagon effect**: A person places greater value on a good as more and more people possess it.[23] The continued success of the iPad today may be partially due to its early popularity.

The opposite, negative network externality is a **snob effect**: A person places greater value on a good as fewer and fewer people possess it. Some people prefer an original painting by an unknown artist to a lithograph by a star because no one else can possess that painting. (As Yogi Berra said, "Nobody goes there anymore; it's too crowded.")

Network Externalities as an Explanation for Monopolies. Because of the need for a critical mass of customers in a market with a positive network externality, we frequently see only one or a few large firms surviving.

The Windows operating system largely dominates the market—not because it is technically superior to Apple's operating system or Linux—but because it has a critical mass of users. Consequently, a developer can earn more producing software that works with Windows than with other operating systems, and the larger number of software programs makes Windows increasingly attractive to users. Similarly, Engström and Forsell (2013) found that a 10 percentile increase in the displayed number of downloads of Android apps on Google Play increases downloads by about 20%.

But having obtained a monopoly, a firm does not necessarily keep it. History is filled with examples where one product knocks off another: "The king is dead; long live the king." Google replaced Yahoo! as the predominant search engine. Explorer displaced Netscape as the big-dog browser, and then Chrome displaced Explorer.

APPLICATION Critical Mass and eBay	In the early years, eBay's online auction site, which started in 1995, faced competition from a variety of other internet sites including Yahoo! Auctions that the then mighty Yahoo! created in 1998. At the time, many commentators correctly predicted that whichever auction site first achieved a critical mass of users would drive the other sites out of business. Indeed, most of these alternative sites died or faded into obscurity. For example, Yahoo! Auctions closed its U.S. and Canada sections of the site in 2007, but its Hong Kong, Taiwanese, and Japanese sites continue to operate. Apparently the convenience of having one site where virtually all buyers and sellers congregate—which lowers buyers' search cost—and creating valuable reputations by having a feedback system (Brown and Morgan, 2006) more than compensates sellers for the lack of competition in sellers' fees. Brown and Morgan

---

[23]*Jargon alert*: Some economists use *bandwagon effect* to refer to any positive network externality—not just those that are based on popularity.

(2010) found that, prior to the demise of the Yahoo! Auction site, the same type of items attracted an average of two additional bidders on eBay and, consequently, the prices on eBay were consistently 20% to 70% percent higher than Yahoo! Auction prices.

Today, we see a battle to gain a critical mass between ridesharing companies, such as Uber and Lyft. This competition drove Sidecar from the market in 2016. Short-term rental sites such as Airbnb, VRBO, and Tripping are waging a similar battle.

Introductory Prices: A Two-Period Monopoly Model

A monopoly may be able to solve the chicken-and-egg problem of getting a critical mass for its product by initially selling the product at a low introductory price. By doing so, the firm maximizes its long-run profit but not its short-run profit.

Suppose that a monopoly sells its good—say, root-beer-scented sandals—for only two periods (after that, the demand goes to zero as a new craze hits the market). If the monopoly sells less than a critical quantity of output, Q, in the first period, its second-period demand curve lies close to the price axis. However, if the good is a success in the first period—selling at least Q units—the second-period demand curve shifts substantially to the right.

If the monopoly maximizes its short-run profit in the first period, it charges p^* and sells Q^* units, which is fewer than Q. To sell Q units, it would have to lower its first-period price to $\underline{p} < p^*$, which would reduce its first-period profit from π^* to $\underline{\pi}$.

In the second period, the monopoly maximizes its profit given its second-period demand curve. If the monopoly sold only Q^* units in the first period, it earns a relatively low second-period profit of π_l. However, if it sold Q units in the first period, it makes a relatively high second-period profit, π_h.

Should the monopoly charge a low introductory price in the first period? Its objective is to maximize its long-run profit: the sum of its profit in the two periods.[24] It maximizes its long-run profit by charging a low introductory price in the first period if the extra profit in the second period, $\pi_h - \pi_l$, from achieving a critical mass in the first period is greater than its forgone profit in the first period, $\pi^* - \underline{\pi}$.

This policy must be profitable for some firms: A 2018 internet search found 1.6 million web pages touting introductory prices.

A closely related strategy used for many internet services is to start by offering a free version, then, after creating a large enough user base, offer a premium version at a positive (and profitable) price, as Yahoo! Mail does.

Two-Sided Markets

A **two-sided market** or **two-sided network** is an economic platform that has two or more user groups that provide each other with network externalities. Two common types of *economic platforms* are online matchmakers and innovation platforms.

Economic platforms such as Airbnb (short-term rentals), Lyft (driver service), and Monster.com (an employment site) match sellers with buyers. The more drivers available on Lyft, the greater the demand for this service by customers, which is a network externality. Similarly, the more customers who use the service, the more drivers who want to use Lyft.

---

[24]In Chapter 15, we discuss why firms place lower value on profit in the future than profit today. However, for simplicity in this analysis, we assume that the monopoly places equal value on profit in either period.

An innovation platform provides a technology upon which other firms can build and customers use. Google's Android operating system for cell phones is an innovation platform. Developers produce apps that function on this operating system. The more apps, the more users. The more users, the more developers producing apps.

The internet itself is an innovation platform. In the early days of the internet, connecting to it over phone lines was slow and costly. Because the internet had relatively little content, many people found that the cost of connecting to the internet and using it exceeded the benefit. But, once a large enough number of customers had internet service, more suppliers found it profitable to provide internet content such as news media and downloadable music, movies, and computer software. As content increased, more people used the internet. And, with more customers, more firms started selling on the internet.

Many non-internet industries also have two-sided networks. Both cardholders and merchants use credit cards. Gamers and game developers link using video-game consoles. Doctors and patients connect through health maintenance organizations and hospitals.

Economies of Scale on the Internet

Many internet services require a large up-front fixed cost—primarily for development and promotion—but have a low marginal cost, sometimes nearly zero. As a result, such firms have downward-sloping average cost curves, reflecting economies of scale. Under such a cost structure, a natural monopoly (or near-monopoly) may emerge after a brief period of internet competition.[25]

Google is an example of such a natural monopoly. It has high fixed costs, but it incurs virtually zero marginal cost when someone uses its search engine. It can therefore easily accommodate more users. And because Google offers this service free to users, a potential competitor providing an identical service cannot undercut Google, short of offering a subsidy, and would struggle to cover its fixed costs. Because Google's large user base is attractive to advertisers, it earns large advertising revenues and has substantial profits even after covering its fixed costs.

Some firms, such as Facebook, benefit from both a natural monopoly cost structure and network externalities. Like Google, Facebook has high fixed costs and can add users at negligible marginal cost. It continuously expands its user base by offering free use of its service. In addition, because of network externalities, users increasingly want to join Facebook as its network becomes larger, further enhancing the value of Facebook to advertisers.

Disruptive Technologies

The internet facilitates the introduction of disruptive technologies with strong network externalities and economies of scale. Because these new internet technologies have network externalities, low marginal costs, and decreasing average cost curves, they often can drive out existing technologies, sometimes creating near-monopolies.

---

[25]If internet sites provide differentiated products, then several sites may coexist even though average costs are strictly decreasing. In 2007, commentators were predicting the emergence of monopolies in social networks such as MySpace, an early social networking site. MySpace lost dominance to Facebook. In turn, Facebook may eventually lose ground to a similar site; to newer variants, such as Instagram (which Facebook acquired), Snapchat (which Facebook tried to acquire), and Twitter; or to sites that cater to specialized audiences such as LinkedIn.

Online news is driving print newspapers out of business. Streaming movies killed off most of the movie videotape/CD/Blu-ray rental stores. Streaming music has largely eliminated record-CD sales.

Disruptions often lead to market power. The taxi industry traditionally has been competitive, but the disruptive innovation created by Uber in providing rides to passengers has given Uber an unprecedented level of market power in the industry.

The ease of finding and purchasing books on the internet using Amazon has attracted many consumers. Moreover, Amazon has much lower marginal and average costs than traditional brick-and-mortar bookstores. Its Kindle reader provides a two-sided market for online books. For all these reasons, Amazon is driving many traditional bookstores out of business and dominating this market.

11.7   Monopsony

We've seen that a *monopoly*, a single *seller*, picks a point—a price and a quantity combination—on the market *demand curve* that maximizes its profit. A *monopsony*, a single *buyer* in a market, chooses a price-quantity combination from the industry *supply curve* that maximizes its profit. A monopsony is the mirror image of monopoly, and it exercises its market power by buying at a price *below* the price that competitive buyers would pay.

Many fisheries have a single, monopsonistic buyer of fish. U.S. professional baseball teams, which act collectively, are the only U.S. firms that hire professional baseball players.[26] Because an American manufacturer of state-of-the-art weapon systems can legally sell only to the federal government, the government is a monopsony (though it is not trying to maximize a profit).

Monopsony Profit Maximization

Suppose that a firm is the sole employer in town—a monopsony in the local labor market. The firm uses only one factor, labor, L, to produce a final good. The value that the firm places on the last worker it hires is the value of the extra output the worker produces, which is the height of the firm's labor demand curve for the number of workers the firm employs.

The firm has a downward-sloping demand curve in Figure 11.9. The firm faces an upward-sloping supply curve of labor: The higher its daily wage, w, the more people want to work for the firm. The firm's *marginal expenditure* (*ME*)—the additional cost of hiring one more worker—depends on the shape of the supply curve.

The supply curve shows the average expenditure, or wage, that the monopsony pays to hire a certain number of workers. For example, the monopsony's average expenditure or wage is w_m if it hires L_m workers per day. If the monopsony wants to hire one more worker, it must raise its wage because the supply curve is upward sloping. Because it pays all workers the same wage, the monopsony must also pay more to each worker that it was already employing. Thus, the monopsony's marginal expenditure on the last worker is greater than that worker's wage.

The monopsony's total expenditure is $E = w(L)L$, where $w(L)$ is the wage given by the market labor supply curve. Its marginal expenditure is

$$ME = w(L) + \frac{\mathrm{d}w}{\mathrm{d}L}L, \qquad (11.16)$$

---

[26]Baseball players belong to a union that acts collectively, like a monopoly, in an attempt to offset the monopsony market power of the baseball teams.

Figure 11.9 The Market and Welfare Effects of Monopsony

The marginal expenditure (ME) curve—the monopsony's marginal cost of hiring one more worker—lies above the upward-sloping market supply curve. The monopsony optimum quantity, L_m, occurs where the marginal expenditure curve intersects the monopsony's demand curve. The monopsony optimum, e_m, shows the monopsony-optimal wage, w_m, and quantity, L_m. If the market were competitive, in the equilibrium, e_c, the wage would be w_c and L_c workers would be employed. The monopsony hires fewer workers and pays a lower wage. By setting the wage, w_m, below the competitive wage, w_c, a monopsony hires too few workers, thereby reducing welfare, causing a deadweight loss of $C + E$.

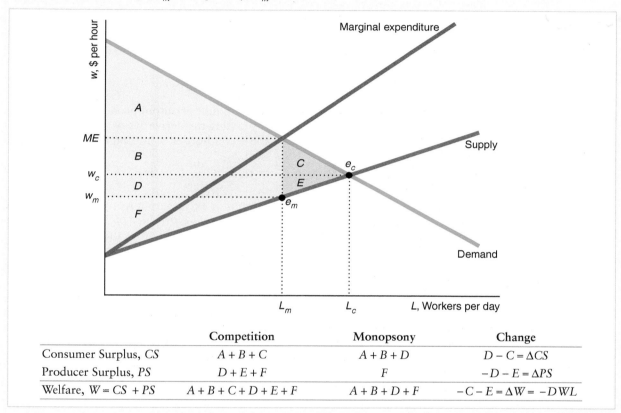

	Competition	Monopsony	Change
Consumer Surplus, CS	$A + B + C$	$A + B + D$	$D - C = \Delta CS$
Producer Surplus, PS	$D + E + F$	F	$-D - E = \Delta PS$
Welfare, $W = CS + PS$	$A + B + C + D + E + F$	$A + B + D + F$	$-C - E = \Delta W = -DWL$

where $w(L)$ is the wage paid the additional worker and $L[dw(L)/dL]$ is the extra amount the monopsony pays the current workers. Because the supply curve is upward sloping, $dw(L)/dL > 0$, the marginal expenditure, ME, is greater than the average expenditure, $w(L)$.

In contrast, if the firm were a competitive price taker in the labor market, it would face a supply curve that was horizontal at the market wage. Consequently, such a competitive firm's marginal expenditure to hire an additional worker would be the market wage.

Any profit-maximizing firm—a monopsony and a competitive firm alike—*buys labor services up to the point at which the marginal value of the last unit of a factor equals the firm's marginal expenditure.* If the last unit is worth more to the buyer than its marginal expenditure, the buyer purchases another unit. Similarly, if the last unit is less valuable than its marginal expenditure, the buyer purchases one less unit.

In the figure, the monopsony optimum occurs at e_m, where the monopsony employs L_m workers and pays a wage of w_m. The intersection of its marginal expenditure curve and its demand curve determines the monopsony quantity. The monopsony's marginal expenditure at L_m workers is the value it places on the labor services of the last worker, ME, which is the height of its demand curve. It pays only w_m, which is the height of its supply curve at L_m. In other words, the monopsony values the last unit at $ME - w_m$ more than it actually has to pay.

If the market in Figure 11.9 were competitive, the intersection of the market demand curve and the market supply curve would determine the competitive equilibrium at e_c, where buyers hire L_c workers at w_c per hour. Thus, the monopsony hires fewer workers, L_m versus L_c, than a competitive market would hire and pays a lower wage, w_m versus w_c.

We can also use calculus to analyze the labor monopsony's behavior. For simplicity, we assume that the firm is a price taker in the output market. It chooses how much labor to hire to maximize its profit,

$$\pi = pQ(L) - w(L)L,$$

where $Q(L)$ is the production function, the amount of output produced using L hours of labor. The firm maximizes its profit by setting the derivative of profit with respect to labor equal to zero (assuming that the second-order condition holds):

$$MRP_L = p\frac{dQ}{dL} = w(L) + \frac{dw}{dL}L = ME, \tag{11.17}$$

where dQ/dL is the marginal product of labor or extra output from one more worker, so $MRP_L = p(dQ/dL)$, called the *marginal revenue product of labor*, is the extra revenue from one more worker. Thus, Equation 11.17 shows that the monopsony hires labor up to the point where the marginal revenue product from employing the last worker, $MRP_L = p(dQ/dL)$, equals the marginal expenditure on the last worker, $ME = w + (dw/dL)L$.

Monopsony power is the ability of a single buyer to pay less than the competitive price profitably. The size of the gap between the value the monopsony places on the last worker (the height of its demand curve) and the wage it pays (the height of the supply curve) depends on the elasticity of supply of labor, η, at the monopsony optimum. Using algebra, we can express the marginal expenditure, Equation 11.16, in terms of the elasticity of supply of labor:

$$ME = w(L) + \frac{dw}{dL}L = w(L)\left(1 + \frac{dw}{dL}\frac{L}{w}\right) = w(L)\left(1 + \frac{1}{\eta}\right), \tag{11.18}$$

By rearranging the terms in Equation 11.18, we derive a type of Lerner Index:

$$\frac{ME - w}{w} = \frac{1}{\eta}. \tag{11.19}$$

Equation 11.19 shows that gap between the marginal expenditure (which equals the value to the monopsony) and the wage divided by the wage, $(ME - w)/w$, is inversely proportional to the elasticity of the supply of labor. Only if the firm is a price taker, so that η is infinite, does the wage equal the marginal expenditure. The less elastic the supply curve at the optimum, the greater the gap between marginal expenditure and the wage.

Welfare Effects of Monopsony

By creating a wedge between the value to the monopsony and the value to the suppliers, the monopsony causes a welfare loss in comparison to a competitive market. In

Figure 11.9, workers or sellers lose producer surplus, $D + E$, because the monopsony price, w_m, is below the competitive wage, w_c. Area D is a transfer from the sellers to the monopsony and represents the savings of $w_c - w_m$ on the L_m workers that the monopsony employs. The monopsony loses C because, at the monopsony's low price, suppliers sell it only L_m, which is less than L_c.

Thus, the deadweight loss of monopsony is $C + E$. This loss is due to the wedge between the value the monopsony places on the L_m units, the monopoly expenditure ME in the figure, and the wage it pays, w_m. The greater the difference between L_c and L_m and the larger the gap between ME and w_m, the greater the deadweight loss.

SOLVED PROBLEM 11.9

MyLab Economics Solved Problem

How does the outcome in a labor market with a monopsony employer change if a minimum wage is set at the competitive level?

Answer

1. *Determine the original monopsony optimum.* Given the supply curve in the graph, the marginal expenditure curve is ME^1. The intersection of ME^1 and the demand curve determines the monopsony optimum, e_1. The monopsony hires L_1 workers at a wage of w_1.

2. *Determine the effect of the minimum wage on the marginal expenditure curve.* The minimum wage makes the supply curve, as viewed by the monopsony, flat in the range where the minimum wage is above the original supply curve (fewer than L_2 workers). The new marginal expenditure curve, ME^2, is flat where the supply curve is flat. Where the supply curve is upward sloping, ME^2 is the same as ME^1.

3. *Determine the post-minimum-wage outcome.* The monopsony operates where its new marginal expenditure curve, ME^2, intersects the demand curve. With the minimum wage, the demand curve crosses the ME^2 curve at the end of the flat section. Thus, at the new outcome, e_2, the monopsony pays the minimum wage, w_2, and employs L_2 workers.

4. *Compare the outcomes.* The post-minimum-wage monopoly optimum is the same as the competitive equilibrium determined by the intersection of the demand and supply curves. Workers receive a higher wage, and more people are employed than in the unregulated monopsony outcome. Thus, imposing the minimum wage helps workers and hurts the monopsony.

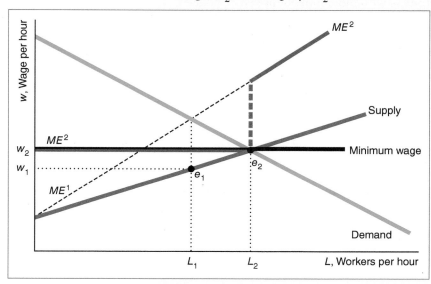

When generic drugs enter the market after the patent on a brand-name drug expires, the demand curve facing the brand-name firm shifts to the left. Why do many brand-name drug companies raise their prices after generic rivals enter the market? The reason is that the demand curve not only shifts to the left but it rotates so that it is less elastic at the original price.

The price the brand-name firm sets depends on the elasticity of demand. When the firm has a patent monopoly, it faces the linear demand curve D^1 in the figure. The intersection of the corresponding marginal revenue curve MR^1 and the marginal cost curve determines the monopoly optimum, e_1. (Because MR^1 is twice as steeply sloped as D^1, it intersects the MC curve at Q_1, while the demand curve D^1 intersects the MC curve at $2Q_1$.) The monopoly sells the Q_1 units at a price of p_1.

After the generic drugs enter the market, the linear demand curve facing the original patent holder shifts leftward to D^2 and becomes steeper and less elastic at the original price. The firm now maximizes its profit at e_2, where the quantity, Q_2, is smaller than Q_1 because D^2 lies to the left of D^1. However, the new price, p_2, is higher than the initial price, p_1, because the D^2 demand curve is less elastic at the new optimum quantity Q_2 than is the D^1 curve at Q_1.

Why might the demand curve rotate and become less elastic at the initial price? One explanation is that the brand-name firm has two types of consumers with different elasticities of demand who differ in their willingness to switch to a generic. One group of consumers is relatively price-sensitive and switches to the lower-priced generics. However, the brand-name drug remains the monopoly supplier to the remaining brand-loyal customers whose demand is less elastic than that of the price-sensitive consumers. These loyal customers prefer the brand-name drug because they are more comfortable with a familiar product, worry that new products may be substandard, or fear that differences in the inactive ingredients might affect them.

Older customers are less likely to switch brands than younger people. A survey by the American Association of Retired Persons found that people aged 65 and older were 15% less likely than people aged 45 to 64 to request generic versions of a drug from their doctor or pharmacist. Similarly, patients with generous insurance plans may be more likely to pay for expensive drugs (if their insurer permits) than customers with more limited insurance policies.

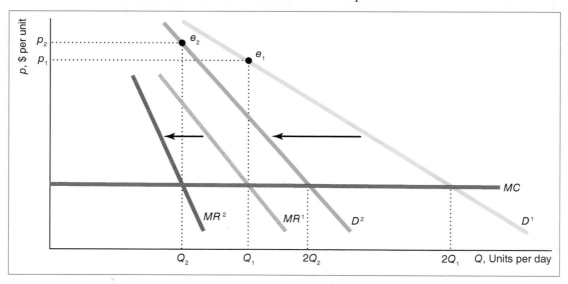

SUMMARY

1. **Monopoly Profit Maximization.** Like any firm, a monopoly—a single seller—maximizes its profit by setting its output so that its marginal revenue equals its marginal cost. The monopoly makes a positive profit if its average cost is less than the price at the profit-maximizing output. Because a monopoly does not have a supply curve, the effect of a shift in demand on a monopoly's output depends on the shapes of both its marginal cost curve and its demand curve. As a monopoly's demand curve shifts, price and output may change in the same direction or in different directions.

2. **Market Power and Welfare.** Market power is the ability of a firm to charge a price above marginal cost and earn a positive profit. The more elastic the demand the monopoly faces at the quantity at which it maximizes its profit, the closer its price to its marginal cost and the closer the Lerner Index, $(p - MC)/p$, is to zero, which is the competitive level. Because a monopoly's price is above its marginal cost, too little output is produced, and society suffers a deadweight loss. The monopoly makes higher profit than it would if it acted as a price taker. Consumers are worse off, buying less output at a higher price.

3. **Taxes and Monopoly.** A specific or an ad valorem tax exacerbates the deadweight loss of a monopoly by further reducing sales and driving up the price to consumers. Unlike in a competitive market, the tax incidence on consumers can exceed 100% in a monopoly market. In a monopoly, the welfare losses from an ad valorem tax are less than from a specific tax that reduces output by the same amount (unlike in a competitive market where both taxes reduce welfare by the same amount).

4. **Causes of Monopolies.** A firm may be a monopoly if it controls a key input, has superior knowledge about producing or distributing a good, or has substantial economies of scale. In markets with substantial economies of scale, the single seller is called a natural monopoly because total production costs would rise if more than one firm produced. Governments may establish government-owned-and-operated monopolies. They may also create private monopolies by establishing barriers to entry that prevent other firms from competing. For example, patents give inventors monopoly rights for a limited time.

5. **Government Actions That Reduce Market Power.** A government can eliminate the welfare harm of a monopoly by forcing the firm to set its price at the competitive level. If the government sets the price at a different level or otherwise regulates non-optimally, welfare at the regulated monopoly optimum is lower than in the competitive equilibrium. A government can eliminate or reduce the harms of monopoly by allowing or facilitating entry.

6. **Internet Monopolies: Network Effects, Behavioral Economics, and Economies of Scale.** One important reason for the emergence of near-monopoly firms on the internet is network externalities. For products with positive network externalities, the value to one user increases with the number of other users. Behavioral economics provides an explanation for some network externalities, such as bandwagon effects and snob effects. Many of these firms operate in a two-sided market, serving as a platform for sellers and buyers. The more buyers or sellers, the greater the network externalities. Many internet products also have high fixed costs and very low marginal costs, leading to economies of scale and natural monopoly. The combination of network externalities and economies of scale may allow a firm that first establishes critical mass to become a monopoly.

7. **Monopsony.** A profit-maximizing monopsony—a single buyer—sets its price so that the marginal value to the monopsony equals the firm's marginal expenditure. Because the monopsony pays a price below the competitive level, fewer units are bought than in a competitive market, producers of factors are worse off, the monopsony earns higher profits than it would if it were a price taker, and society suffers a deadweight loss.

EXERCISES

All exercises are available on MyLab Economics; * = *answer appears at the back of this book;* **M** = *mathematical problem.*

1. Monopoly Profit Maximization

1.1 Redraw Figure 11.1 for a competitive firm, which faces a horizontal demand curve. Use the same type of reasoning that we used in Figure 11.1 to explain why the competitive firm's *MR* curve is the same as its demand curve.

1.2 If the inverse demand function is $p = 300 - 3Q$, what is the marginal revenue function? Draw the demand and marginal revenue curves. At what quantities do the demand and marginal revenue lines hit the quantity axis? (*Hint*: See Solved Problem 11.1.) **M**

1.3 If the inverse demand curve a monopoly faces is $p = 10Q^{-0.5}$, what is the firm's marginal revenue curve? (*Hint*: See Solved Problem 11.1.) **M**

1.4 Given that the inverse demand function is $p(Q) = a - bQ + (c/2)Q^2$, derive the marginal revenue function. Compare the corresponding marginal revenue curve to the linear one (where $c = 0$) and show how its curvature depends on whether c is positive or negative. (*Hint*: See Solved Problem 11.1.) **M**

*1.5 Show that the elasticity of demand is unitary at the midpoint of a linear inverse demand function and hence that a monopoly will not operate to the right of this midpoint. **M**

1.6 The inverse demand curve that a monopoly faces is $p = 100 - Q$. The firm's cost curve is $C(Q) = 10 + 5Q$. What is the firm's profit-maximizing quantity and price? How does your answer change if $C(Q) = 100 + 5Q$? (*Hint*: See Solved Problem 11.2.) **M**

1.7 The inverse demand curve that a monopoly faces is $p = 10Q^{-0.5}$. The firm's cost curve is $C(Q) = 5Q$. What is the profit-maximizing quantity and price? (*Hint*: See Solved Problem 11.2.) **M**

1.8 Suppose that the inverse demand function for a monopolist's product is $p = 9 - Q/20$. Its cost function is $C = 10 + 10Q - 4Q^2 + \frac{2}{3}Q^3$. Draw marginal revenue and marginal cost curves. At what outputs does marginal revenue equal marginal cost? What is the profit-maximizing output? Check the second-order condition, $d^2\pi/dQ^2$, at the monopoly optimum. (*Hint*: See Solved Problem 11.2.) **M**

1.9 If a monopoly's inverse demand curve is $p = 13 - Q$ and its cost function is $C = 25 + Q + 0.5Q^2$, what Q^* maximizes the monopoly's profit (or minimizes its loss)? At Q^*, what is the price and the profit? Should the monopoly operate or shut down? (*Hint*: See Solved Problem 11.2.) **M**

1.10 Given that a monopoly's marginal revenue curve is strictly downward sloping, use math and a graph (such as Figure 11.3) to show why a monopoly's revenue curve reaches its maximum at a larger quantity than does its profit curve. **M**

1.11 AT&T Inc., the large U.S. phone company and the one-time monopoly, left the payphone business at the beginning of 2009 because people were switching to wireless phones. U.S. consumers owning cellphones reached 80% by 2007 and 91% by 2013 (and with 64% owning smartphones by 2015) according to the Pew Research Center. The number of payphones fell from 2.6 million at the peak in 1998 to 1 million in 2006 and half a million in 2016. (Where will Clark Kent go to change into Superman now?) Use graphs to explain why a monopoly exits a market when its demand curve shifts to the left.

1.12 Show why a monopoly may operate in the upward- or downward-sloping section of its long-run average cost curve but a competitive firm operates only in the upward-sloping section.

1.13 Are major league baseball clubs profit-maximizing monopolies? Some observers of this market contend that baseball club owners want to maximize attendance or revenue. Alexander (2004) said that one test of whether a firm is a profit-maximizing monopoly is to check whether it is operating in the elastic portion of its demand curve, which, according to his analysis, is true. Why is that a relevant test? What would the elasticity be if a baseball club were maximizing revenue?

1.14 Show that after a shift in the demand curve, a monopoly's price may remain constant but its output may rise.

1.15 In 2013, the Oakland A's were one of the hottest teams in baseball. They were regularly drawing "sellout" crowds, with many more fans wanting tickets. However, the A's did not sell all of the 56,000 seats. The A's removed or put tarps over roughly 20,000 seats in most of the third deck and the outfield stands. The A's management said that the reason was to create a more intimate feeling for the fans. What's another explanation? (*Hint*: See Solved Problem 11.3.)

2. Market Power and Welfare

2.1 Under what circumstances does a monopoly set its price equal to its marginal cost? (*Hint*: Consider the elasticity of demand.)

*2.2 Gilead Sciences' drug Sovaldi is an effective treatment for hepatitis C. The price for a 12-week regimen of Sovaldi is $84,000, which is more than 617 times the estimated marginal cost of $136.[27] What is the firm's Lerner Index? What elasticity of demand did the firm face if it was engaging in short-run profit maximization? (*Hint*: See Solved Problem 11.4.) **M**

2.3 The U.S. Postal Service (USPS) has a constitutionally guaranteed monopoly on first-class mail. In 2018, it charged 50¢ for a stamp, which was not the profit-maximizing price—the USPS goal, allegedly, is to break even rather than to turn a profit. Following the

---

[27]www.huffingtonpost.com/entry/why-hepatitis-c-drugs-are-expensive_us_5642840be4b08cda34868c8a.

postal services in Australia, Britain, Canada, Switzerland, and Ireland, the USPS allowed Stamps.com to sell a sheet of twenty 50¢ stamps with a photo of your dog, your mommy, or whatever image you want for $23.99 (that's $1.20 per stamp, or a 140% markup). Stamps.com keeps the extra beyond the 50¢ it pays the USPS. What is the firm's Lerner Index? If Stamps.com is a profit-maximizing monopoly, what elasticity of demand does it face for a customized stamp? (*Hint*: See Solved Problem 11.4.) **M**

*2.4 When the iPod was introduced, Apple's constant marginal cost of producing its top-of-the-line iPod was $200 (iSuppli), its fixed cost was approximately $736 million, and I estimate that its inverse demand function was $p = 600 - 25Q$, where Q is units measured in millions. What was Apple's average cost function? Assuming that Apple was maximizing short-run monopoly profit, what was its marginal revenue function? What were its profit-maximizing price and quantity, profit, and Lerner Index? What was the elasticity of demand at the profit-maximizing level? Show Apple's profit-maximizing solution in a figure. (*Hint*: See Solved Problem 11.4.) **M**

2.5 In 2015, Apple introduced the Apple Watch. According to HIS, the cost of producing the 38mm Apple Watch Sport was $84. The price was $349. What was Apple's price/marginal cost ratio? What was its Lerner Index? If Apple is a short-run profit-maximizing monopoly, what elasticity of demand did Apple believe it faced? (*Hint*: See Solved Problem 11.4.) **M**

2.6 Draw an example of a monopoly with a linear demand curve and a constant marginal cost curve.

   a. Show the profit-maximizing price and output, p^* and Q^*, and identify the areas of consumer surplus, producer surplus, and deadweight loss. Also show the quantity, Q_c, that would be produced if the monopoly were to act like a price taker.

   b. Now suppose that the demand curve is a smooth concave-to-the-origin curve (which hits both axes) that is tangent to the original demand curve at the point (Q^*, p^*). Explain why this monopoly optimum is the same as with the linear demand curve. Show how much output the firm would produce if it acted like a price taker. Show how the welfare areas change.

   c. How would your answer in part a change if the demand curve is a smooth convex-to-the-origin curve (which hits both axes) that is tangent to the original demand curve at the point (Q^*, p^*)?

2.7 Suppose that many similar price-taking consumers (such as Denise in Chapter 10) have a single good (candy bars). Jane has a monopoly in wood, so she

can set prices. Assume that no production is possible. Using an Edgeworth box, illustrate the monopoly optimum and show that it does not lie on the contract curve (that is, it isn't Pareto efficient).

3. Taxes and Monopoly

3.1 If the inverse demand function facing a monopoly is $p(Q)$ and its cost function is $C(Q)$, show the effect of a specific tax, t, on the monopoly's profit-maximizing output. How does imposing t affect its profit? **M**

3.2 A monopoly with a constant marginal cost m has a profit-maximizing price of p_1. It faces a constant elasticity demand curve with elasticity ε. After the government applies a specific tax of $1, its price is p_2. What is the price change $p_2 - p_1$ in terms of ε? How much does the price rise if the demand elasticity is -2? (*Hint*: Use Equation 11.10.) **M**

3.3 In 1996, Florida voted on (and rejected) a 1¢-per-pound excise tax on refined cane sugar in the Florida Everglades Agricultural Area. Swinton and Thomas (2001) used linear supply and demand curves (based on elasticities estimated by Marks, 1993) to calculate the incidence from this tax given that the market is competitive. Their inverse demand curve was $p = 1.787 - 0.0004641Q$, and their inverse supply curve was $p = -0.4896 + 0.00020165Q$, where price is measured in dollars. Calculate the incidence of the tax that falls on consumers (Chapter 2) for a competitive market. If producers merged to form a monopoly, and the supply curve becomes the monopoly's marginal cost curve, what is the incidence of the tax? (*Hint*: The incidence that falls on consumers is the difference between the price with and without the tax divided by the tax. Show that the incidence is 70% in a competitive market and 41% with a monopoly. See Solved Problem 11.5.) **M**

*3.4 Only Indian tribes can run casinos in California. These casinos are spread around the state so that each is a monopoly in its local community. In 2004, California Governor Arnold Schwarzenegger negotiated with the state's tribes, getting them to agree to transfer a fraction of their profits to the state in exchange for concessions. In 2004, he first proposed that the state get 25% of casino profits and then he dropped the level to 15%. He announced a deal with two tribes at 10% in 2005. How does a profit tax affect a monopoly's output and price? How would a monopoly change its behavior if the profit tax were 10% rather than 25%? (*Hint*: You may assume that the profit tax refers to the tribe's economic profit.) **M**

3.5 If the inverse demand curve is $p = 120 - Q$ and the marginal cost is constant at 10, how does charging the monopoly a specific tax of $t = 10$ per unit affect the monopoly optimum and the welfare of consumers, the monopoly, and society (where society's welfare includes the tax revenue)? What is the incidence of the tax on consumers? (*Hint*: See Solved Problem 11.5.) **M**

3.6   What is the effect of a franchise (lump-sum) tax on a monopoly? (*Hint*: Consider the possibility that the firm may shut down.)

3.7   In a figure, show the effect of an ad valorem tax (see Chapter 2) on a monopoly optimum, consumer surplus, producer surplus, welfare, and deadweight loss.

4. Causes of Monopolies

*4.1   Can a firm be a natural monopoly if it has a U-shaped average cost curve? Why or why not? (*Hint*: See Solved Problem 11.6.)

4.2   Can a firm operating in the upward-sloping portion of its average cost curve be a natural monopoly? Explain. (*Hint*: See Solved Problem 11.6.)

4.3   In the Application "The Botox Patent Monopoly," what would happen to the monopoly-optimal price and quantity if the government had collected a specific tax of $75 per vial of Botox? What welfare effects would such a tax have? **M**

4.4   In the Application "The Botox Patent Monopoly," consumer surplus, area *A*, equals the deadweight loss, area *C*. Show that this equality is a result of the linear demand and constant marginal cost assumptions. **M**

4.5   Once the copyright runs out on a book or musical composition, the work can legally be posted on the internet for anyone to download. U.S. copyright law protects the monopoly for 95 years after the original publication. But in Australia and Europe, the copyright holds for only 50 years. Thus, an Australian website can post *Gone With the Wind*, a 1936 novel, or Elvis Presley's 1954 single "That's All Right," while a U.S. site cannot. Obviously, this legal nicety won't stop American fans from downloading from Australian or European sites. Discuss how limiting the length of a copyright would affect the pricing used by the publisher of a novel.

5. Government Actions That Reduce Market Power

5.1   Water bottles are the best-selling item in airport stores. In many airports, the price charged is whatever the market will bear. However, some airports limit the price. San Francisco International and Dallas–Fort Worth International set a cap at "street prices" plus 10% (Scott McCartney, "The Price You Pay for Water at the Airport," *Wall Street Journal*, April 22, 2015.) Assume that one firm runs all the stores in the airport and that a competitive market determines the street price of water bottles outside the airport. Use a figure to show how the regulated price differs from the unregulated price. (*Hint*: See Solved Problem 11.7.)

5.2   Describe the effects on output and welfare if the government regulates a monopoly so that it may not charge a price above $\bar{p}$, which lies between the unregulated monopoly price and the optimally regulated price (determined by the intersection of the firm's marginal cost and the market demand curve). (*Hint*: See Solved Problem 11.7.)

5.3   In the Application "The Botox Patent Monopoly," what would happen to the price and quantity if the government had set a price ceiling of $200 per vial of Botox? What welfare effects would such a price ceiling have? (*Hint*: See Solved Problem 11.7.) **M**

5.4   A monopoly drug company produces a lifesaving medicine at a constant cost of $10 per dose. The demand for this medicine is perfectly inelastic at prices less than or equal to the $100 (per day) income of the 100 patients who need to take this drug daily. At a higher price, consumers buy nothing. Show the monopoly-optimal price and quantity and the consumer and producer surplus in a graph. Now the government imposes a price ceiling of $30. Show how the outcome, consumer surplus, and producer surplus change. What is the deadweight loss, if any, from this price control?

5.5   Bleyer Industries Inc., the only U.S. manufacturer of plastic Easter eggs, manufactured 250 million eggs each year. However, imports from China cut into its business. In 2005, Bleyer filed for bankruptcy because the Chinese firms could produce the eggs at much lower costs. Use graphs to show how a competitive import industry could drive a monopoly out of business. (*Hint*: Look at Solved Problems 11.7 and 11.8.)

5.6   Malaysia's monopoly auto manufacturer produces the Proton, which the government protects from imports by a specific tariff, *t*, on imported goods. The monopoly's profit-maximizing price is p^*. The world price of the good (comparable autos) is p_w, which is less than p^*. Because the price of imported goods with the tariff is $p_w + t$, no foreign goods are imported. Under pressure from the World Trade Organization, the government removes the tariff so that the supply of foreign goods to the country's consumers is horizontal at p_w. Show how much the former monopoly produces and what price it charges. Show who gains and who loses from removing the tariff. (*Hint*: Look at Solved Problems 11.7 and 11.8.)

6. Internet Monopolies: Network Effects, Behavioral Economics, and Economies of Scale

*6.1 A monopoly produces a good with a network externality at a constant marginal and average cost of $2. In the first period, its inverse demand curve is $p = 10 - Q$. In the second period, its demand is $p = 10 - Q$ unless it sells at least $Q = 8$ units in the first period. If it meets or exceeds this target, then the demand curve rotates out by b (that is, it sells b times as many units for any given price), so that its inverse demand curve is $p = 10 - Q/b$. The monopoly knows that it can sell no output after the second period. The monopoly's objective is to maximize the sum of its profits over the two periods. In the first period, should the monopoly set the output that maximizes its profit in that period? How does your answer depend on b? (*Hint*: See the discussion about introductory prices in Section 11.6.) **M**

6.2 A monopoly chocolate manufacturer faces two types of consumers. The larger group, the hoi polloi, loves desserts and has a relatively flat, linear demand curve for chocolate. The smaller group, the snobs, is interested in buying chocolate only if the hoi polloi do not buy it. Given that the hoi polloi do not buy the chocolate, the snobs have a relatively steep, linear demand curve. Show the monopoly's possible outcomes—high price and low quantity, or low price and high quantity—and explain the condition under which the monopoly chooses to cater to the snobs rather than to the hoi polloi.

7. Monopsony

7.1 Suppose that the original labor supply curve, S^1, for a monopsony shifts to the right to S^2 if the firm spends $1,000 in advertising. Under what condition should the monopsony engage in this advertising? (*Hint*: See the analysis of monopoly advertising.)

7.2 What happens to the monopsony outcome if the minimum wage is set slightly above or below the competitive wage? (*Hint*: See Solved Problem 11.9.)

7.3 Can a monopsony exercise monopsony power—that is, profitably set its price below the competitive level—if the supply curve it faces is horizontal? Why or why not?

7.4 What effect does a price support have on a monopsony? In particular, describe the monopsony optimum if the price support is set at the price where the supply curve intersects the demand curve.

7.5 A monopsony faces a supply curve of $p = 10 + Q$. What is its marginal expenditure curve? If the monopsony has a demand curve of $p = 50 - Q$, what are the monopsony-optimal quantity and price? How does this monopsony optimum differ from the competitive equilibrium? **M**

*7.6 For general functions, solve for the monopsony's first-order condition if it is also a monopoly in the product market. **M**

8. Challenge

8.1 Under what circumstances will a drug company charge more for its drug after its patent expires?

8.2 Does the Challenge Solution change if the entry of the generic causes a parallel shift to the left of the patent monopoly's linear demand curve?

8.3 Some people propose reducing the patent length for drugs, but their critics argue that such a change would result in even higher prices during the patent period, as companies would need to recover drug development costs more quickly. Is this argument valid if drug companies maximize profit?

12

Pricing and Advertising

Everything is worth what its purchaser will pay for it. —Publilius Syrus
(first century B.C.)

CHALLENGE

Sale Price

Because many firms use *sales*—temporarily setting the price below the usual price—some customers pay lower prices than others over time. Grocery stores are particularly likely to put products on sale frequently. In large U.S. supermarkets, a soft drink brand is on sale 94% of the time. Either Coke or Pepsi is on sale half the weeks in a year.

Heinz ketchup controlled 62% of the U.S. ketchup market in 2015. Its market share was 70% in Canada, and nearly 80% in the United Kingdom. In 2015, Heinz reported that it sold over 650 million bottles of ketchup in more than 140 countries. Kraft Heinz had annual sales of more than $6.9 billion in 2017.

When Heinz goes on sale, *switchers*—ketchup customers who normally buy whichever brand is least expensive—purchase Heinz rather than the low-price generic ketchup. How can Heinz's managers design a pattern of sales that maximizes Heinz's profit by obtaining extra sales from switchers without losing substantial sums by selling to its loyal customers at a discount price? Under what conditions does it pay for Heinz to have a policy of periodic sales?

Until now, we have examined how a monopoly (or other price-setting firm) chooses a single price given that it does not advertise. We need to extend this analysis because many price-setting firms set multiple prices and advertise. The analysis in this chapter helps to answer many real-world questions such as: Why do firms put products on sale periodically? Why are airlines' fares substantially less if you book in advance? Why do the spiritualists who live at the Wonewoc Spiritualist Camp give readings for $40 for half an hour, but charge seniors only $35 on Wednesdays?[1] Why are some goods, including computers and software, bundled and sold at a single price? To answer these questions, we need to examine how monopolies and other noncompetitive firms set prices.

In Chapter 11, we examined how a monopoly maximizes its profit when it uses **uniform pricing:** charging the same price for every unit sold of a particular good. However, it is possible for monopolies (and other firms with market power) to employ more sophisticated pricing methods.

---

[1]**www.campwonewoc.org/index.html,** August 20, 2018.

We now show that a monopoly can increase its profits if it can use **nonuniform pricing**, where a firm charges consumers different prices for the same product or charges a single customer a price that depends on the number of units the customer buys. In this chapter, we analyze nonuniform pricing for monopolies, but similar principles apply to any firm with market power.

As we saw in Chapter 11, a monopoly that sets a high single price sells only to the customers who value the good enough to buy it at the monopoly price, and those customers receive some consumer surplus. The monopoly does not sell the good to other customers who value the good at less than the single price, even if those consumers would be willing to pay more than the marginal cost of production. These lost sales cause *deadweight loss*, which is the forgone value of these potential sales in excess of the cost of producing the good.

A firm with market power can earn a higher profit using nonuniform pricing than by setting a uniform price for two reasons. First, the firm captures some or all of the single-price consumer surplus. Second, the firm converts at least some of the single-price deadweight loss into profit by charging a price below the uniform price to some customers who would not purchase at the single-price level. A monopoly that uses nonuniform pricing can lower the price to these otherwise excluded consumers without lowering the price to consumers who are willing to pay high prices.

In this chapter, we examine several types of nonuniform pricing including price discrimination, two-part pricing, and bundling. The most common form of nonuniform pricing is **price discrimination**: charging consumers different prices for the same good based on individual characteristics of consumers, on membership in an identifiable subgroup of consumers, or on the quantity purchased by the consumers. For example, for a full-year combination print and online subscription, the *Wall Street Journal* charges $99.95 to students, who are price sensitive, and $348 to other subscribers, who are less price sensitive.

Some firms with market power use other forms of nonuniform pricing to increase profits. A firm may use *two-part pricing*, charging a customer one fee for the right to buy the good and an additional fee for each unit purchased. For example, cable television companies often charge a monthly fee for basic service and an additional fee (pay-per-view) for certain shows. Similarly, mobile phone users pay a monthly fee for phone and text service and then may incur an additional charge for each text message.

Another type of nonuniform pricing is *bundling*, where several products are sold together as a package. For example, many restaurants provide full-course dinners for a fixed price that is less than the sum of the prices charged if the items (appetizer, main dish, and dessert) are ordered separately (à la carte).

A monopoly may also increase its profit by advertising. A monopoly (or another firm with market power) may advertise to shift its demand curve so as to raise its profit, taking into account the cost of advertising.

In this chapter, we examine seven main topics

1. **Conditions for Price Discrimination.** A firm can increase its profit by price discriminating if it has market power, can identify which customers are more price sensitive than others, and can prevent customers who pay low prices from reselling to those who pay high prices.

2. **Perfect Price Discrimination.** If a monopoly can charge the maximum that each customer is willing to pay for each unit of output, the monopoly captures all potential consumer surplus and sells the efficient (competitive) level of output.

3. **Group Price Discrimination.** Firms that cannot perfectly price discriminate may charge a group of consumers with relatively elastic demands a lower price than they charge other groups.

4. **Nonlinear Price Discrimination.** Some firms profit by charging different prices for large purchases than they charge for small ones, which is another form of price discrimination.

5. **Two-Part Pricing.** By charging consumers a fee for the right to buy any number of units and a price per unit, firms earn higher profits than they do by charging a single price per unit.

6. **Tie-In Sales.** By requiring customers to buy a second good or service along with the first, firms make higher profits than they do by selling the goods or services separately.

7. **Advertising.** A monopoly advertises to shift its demand curve and to increase its profit.

12.1 Conditions for Price Discrimination

We start by studying the most common form of nonuniform pricing, *price discrimination*, whereby a firm charges various consumers different prices for a good.[2] Many people complain that price discrimination is irrational:

Common Confusion It can't pay for a firm to charge some consumers a different price than others.

However, many (but not all) firms can profit by price discriminating.

Why Price Discrimination Pays

For almost any good or service, some consumers are willing to pay more than others. A firm that sets a single price faces a trade-off between charging consumers who really want the good as much as they are willing to pay and charging a sufficiently low price that the firm does not lose sales to less enthusiastic customers. As a result, the firm usually sets an intermediate price. A price-discriminating firm that varies its prices across customers avoids this trade-off.

A firm earns a higher profit from price discrimination than from uniform pricing for two reasons. First, a price-discriminating firm charges a higher price to customers who are willing to pay more than the uniform price, capturing some or all of their consumer surplus—the difference between what a good is worth to a consumer and what the consumer pays—under uniform pricing. Second, a price-discriminating firm sells to some people who are not willing to pay as much as the uniform price.

Which Firms Can Price Discriminate

For a firm to profitably price discriminate, three conditions must be met.

First, a firm must have *market power*; otherwise it cannot charge any consumer more than the competitive price. A monopoly, an oligopoly firm, a monopolistically competitive firm, or a cartel may be able to price discriminate. A competitive firm cannot price discriminate.

Second, for a firm to profitably charge various consumers different prices, the **reservation price**—the maximum amount a person is willing to pay for a unit of output—must *vary* across consumers, and a firm must be able to *identify* which consumers are willing to pay relatively more. A movie theater manager may know that

---

[2]Price discrimination is generally legal in the United States unless it harms competition between firms, as specified in the Robinson-Patman Act of 1936.

senior citizens have a lower reservation price for admission than do other adults. Theater employees can identify senior citizens by observation or by checking their driver's licenses. Even if all customers are identical, a firm may be able to price discriminate over the number of units each purchases. If a firm knows how each individual's reservation price varies with the number of units, it can charge each customer a higher price for the first unit of a good than it charges for subsequent units.

Third, a firm must be able to *prevent or limit resale* from those customers it charges a relatively low price to those it charges a relatively high price. Price discrimination is ineffective if resale is easy, because ease of reselling would inhibit the firm's ability to make higher-price sales. A movie theater owner can charge senior citizens a lower price than other adults because as soon as the seniors buy their tickets they enter the theater and don't have time to resell them.

Except for competitive firms, most firms have some market power, and many of those firms can identify which groups of customers have a relatively high reservation price. Usually, the biggest obstacle to price discrimination is a firm's inability to prevent resale. However in some markets, resale is inherently difficult or impossible, firms can take actions that prevent resale, or government actions or laws prevent resale.

APPLICATION

Disneyland Pricing

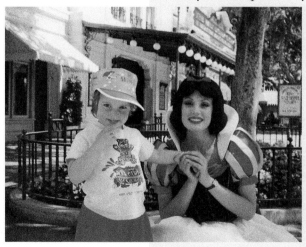

Disneyland, in southern California, is a well-run operation that rarely misses a trick when it comes to increasing its profit. (Indeed, Disneyland mints money: When you enter the park, you can exchange U.S. currency for Disney dollars, which you can spend only in the park.)[3]

For part of 2018, Disneyland offered local, Southern Californians two-day and three-day theme park tickets at a 25% discount. This policy of charging locals a discounted price makes sense if out-of-town visitors are willing to pay more than locals and if Disneyland can prevent locals from selling discounted tickets to nonlocals. Imagine a Midwesterner who's never been to Disneyland and wants to visit. Travel accounts for most of the trip's cost, so spending a few extra dollars to enter the park makes little percentage difference in the total cost of the visit and hence does not greatly affect that person's decision about visiting Disneyland. In contrast, for a local who has been to Disneyland many times and for whom the entrance price is a larger share of the total cost, a slightly higher entrance fee might prevent a visit.

Charging both groups the same price is not in Disney's best interest. If Disney were to charge the higher price to everyone, many locals wouldn't visit the park. If Disney were to use the lower price for everyone, it would be charging nonresidents much less than they are willing to pay.

Preventing Resale

Resale is difficult or impossible for most *services* and when *transaction costs are high*. If Joe the plumber charges you less than he charges your neighbor for clearing a pipe, you cannot make a deal with your neighbor to resell this service. The higher

---

[3]According to **www.babycenter.com/cost-of-raising-child-calculator**, it costs $334,860 for an average U.S. family to raise a child from cradle through college. Parents can cut that total in half, however: They don't *have* to take their kids to Disneyland.

the transaction costs a consumer must incur to resell a good, the less likely is a resale. Suppose that you are able to buy a jar of pickles for $1 less than the usual price. Could you practically buy and sell this jar to someone, or would the transaction costs be prohibitive? The more valuable a product or the more widely consumed it is, the more likely it is that transaction costs are low enough that resale occurs.

Some firms act to raise transaction costs or otherwise make resale difficult. Disneyland prevents resale by checking a purchaser's driver's license and requiring that the ticket be used for same-day entrance. If your college requires someone with a student ticket to show a student ID card before being admitted to a sporting event, it would be difficult to resell your low-price tickets to nonstudents, whom your college charges a higher price. When students at some universities buy computers at lower-than-usual prices, they must sign a contract that forbids them to resell it.

Similarly, a firm can prevent resale by *vertically integrating*: participating in more than one successive stage of the production and distribution chain for a good or service. Alcoa, the former aluminum monopoly, wanted to sell aluminum ingots to producers of aluminum wire at a lower price than it set for producers of aluminum aircraft parts. If Alcoa did so, however, the wire producers could easily resell their ingots. By starting its own wire production firm, Alcoa prevented resale and was able to charge high prices to firms that manufactured aircraft parts (Perry, 1980).

Governments frequently establish policies to promote price discrimination and to bar resale. For example, U.S. federal and some state governments require that milk producers, under penalty of law, price discriminate by selling milk at a higher price for fresh use than for processing (cheese, ice cream), and forbid resale. Government *tariffs* (taxes on imports) limit resale by making it expensive to buy goods in a low-price country and resell them in a high-price country. In some cases, laws prevent such reselling explicitly. Under U.S. trade laws, certain brand-name perfumes may not be sold in the United States except by their manufacturers.

APPLICATION

Preventing Resale of Designer Bags

During the holiday season, stores often limit how many of the hottest items—such as this year's best-selling toy—a customer can buy. But it may surprise you that websites of luxury-goods retailers such as Saks Fifth Avenue, Neiman Marcus, and Bergdorf Goodman limit how many designer handbags one can buy. For example, the Bergdorf Goodman site won't let you order more than one Prada Lizard Trimmed Nylon Shoulder Bag at $4,190 (darn!).

Some websites explain that they impose limits due to "popular demand." The more plausible explanation is that the restriction facilitates international price discrimination. The handbag manufacturers force U.S. retailers to limit the number of bags that one person can buy to prevent people from buying large numbers of bags and reselling them in Europe or Asia, where the same Prada and Gucci item often costs 20% to 40% more. When purchasing from Prada's U.S. online site, one must agree that the purchase is solely for private household use, that commercial resale or sale outside the United States is not authorized, and that the company reserves the right to reject orders and to limit order quantities.

Not All Price Differences Are Price Discrimination

Not every seller who charges consumers different prices is price discriminating. Hotels charge newlyweds more for bridal suites. Is that price discrimination? Some hotel managers say no. They contend that honeymooners, more than other guests, steal mementos, so the price differential reflects an actual cost differential.

Similarly, e-book, hardcopy print book, and audiobook CD of the same book sell for different prices in part because their costs differ. As of August 2018, the price of the 2018 Pulitzer Prize–winning novel *Less* by Andrew Sean Greer was $9.99 as a Kindle e-book, $17.68 as a hardcover, and $18.41 as an audio CD. These price differences reflect the much lower marginal cost of the e-book than of the hardcover or CD versions. Thus, these price differences do not reflect pure price discrimination.

Types of Price Discrimination

Firms use three main types of price discrimination. With **perfect price discrimination**—also called *first-degree price discrimination*—the firm sells each unit at the maximum amount each customer is willing to pay, so prices differ across customers, and a given customer may pay more for some units than for others.

With **group price discrimination** (*third-degree price discrimination*), the firm charges different groups of customers different prices but charges a given customer the same price for every unit sold. Typically, not all customers pay different prices—the firm sets different prices only for a few groups of customers. Because this type of discrimination is the most common, the term *price discrimination* is often used to mean *group price discrimination*.

With **nonlinear price discrimination** (*second-degree price discrimination*), the price varies with the quantity purchased, but all customers who buy a given quantity pay the same price. That is, the consumer's expenditure on an item does not rise linearly (proportionately) with the amount purchased, which it would if the price were a constant.

In addition to price discriminating, many firms use other, more complicated types of nonuniform pricing. Later in this chapter, we examine two other frequently used forms of nonlinear pricing: two-part pricing and tie-in sales.

12.2 Perfect Price Discrimination

A firm with market power that knows exactly how much each customer is willing to pay for each unit of its good, and that can prevent resale, can charge each person his or her reservation price. Such an all-knowing firm can *perfectly price discriminate*. By selling each unit of its output to the customer who values it the most at the maximum price that person is willing to pay, the perfectly price-discriminating monopoly captures all possible consumer surplus. This type of discrimination might be called *individual price discrimination*.

Perfect price discrimination is rare because firms do not have perfect information about their customers. Nevertheless, it is useful to examine perfect price discrimination because it is the most efficient form of price discrimination and provides a benchmark against which we compare other types of nonuniform pricing.

We now show how a firm with full information about consumer reservation prices can use that information to perfectly price discriminate. Next, we compare the market outcomes (price, quantity, surplus) of a perfectly price-discriminating monopoly to those of perfectly competitive and uniform-price monopoly firms.

How a Firm Perfectly Price Discriminates

A firm with market power that can prevent resale and has full information about its customers' willingness to pay price discriminates by selling each unit at its reservation price—the maximum amount any consumer would pay for it.

Graphical Analysis. The height of the demand curve at an output level is the maximum price consumers are willing to pay for that amount of output. In the demand curve facing a monopoly in Figure 12.1, the first customer is willing to pay $6 for a unit, the next is willing to pay $5, and so forth. A perfectly price-discriminating firm sells its first unit of output for $6. Having sold the first unit, the firm can get at most $5 for its second unit. The firm must drop its price by $1 for each successive unit it sells.

A perfectly price-discriminating monopoly's marginal revenue is the same as its price. As the figure shows, the firm's marginal revenue is $MR_1 = \$6$ on the first unit, $MR_2 = \$5$ on the second unit, and $MR_3 = \$4$ on the third unit, and so on. As a result, *the firm's marginal revenue curve is its demand curve.*

This firm has a constant marginal cost of $3 per unit. It pays for the firm to produce the first unit because the firm sells that unit for $6, so its marginal revenue exceeds its marginal cost by $3. Similarly, the firm certainly wants to sell the second unit for $5 and the third unit for $4, which also exceed its marginal cost. The firm breaks even when it sells the fourth unit for $3. The firm is unwilling to sell more than four units because its marginal cost would exceed its marginal revenue on successive units. Thus, like any profit-maximizing firm, a perfectly price-discriminating firm produces at point *e*, where its marginal revenue curve intersects its marginal cost curve. (If you find it upsetting that the firm is indifferent between producing three and four units, assume that the firm's marginal cost is $2.99, so it definitely wants to produce four units.)

This perfectly price-discriminating firm's revenue is $MR_1 + MR_2 + MR_3 + MR_4 = \$6 + \$5 + \$4 + \$3 = \$18$, which is the area under its marginal revenue curve up to the number of units it sells, four. If the firm has no fixed cost, its cost of producing four units is $\$12 = \$3 \times 4$, so its profit is $6.

Calculus Analysis. A perfectly price-discriminating monopoly charges each customer the reservation price $p = D(Q)$, where $D(Q)$ is the inverse market demand

Figure 12.1 Perfect Price Discrimination

The monopoly can charge $6 for the first unit, $5 for the second, and $4 for the third, as the demand curve shows. Its marginal revenue is $MR_1 = \$6$ for the first unit, $MR_2 = \$5$ for the second, and $MR_3 = \$4$ for the third. Thus, the demand curve is also the marginal revenue curve. Because the firm's marginal and average cost is $3 per unit, it is unwilling to sell at a price below $3, so it sells four units, point *e*, and breaks even on the last unit.

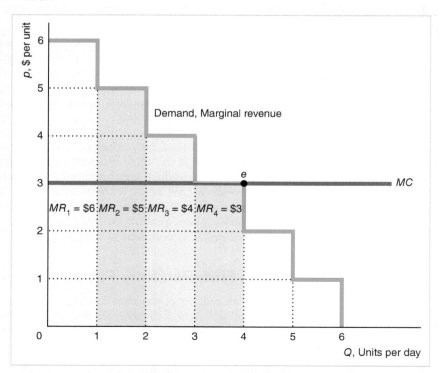

function and Q is total output. The discriminating monopoly's revenue, R, is the area under the demand curve up to the quantity, Q, it sells,

$$R = \int_0^Q D(z)dz,$$

where z is a placeholder for quantity. Its objective is to maximize its profit through its choice of Q:

$$\max_Q \pi = \int_0^Q D(z)dz - C(Q). \tag{12.1}$$

Its first-order condition for a maximum is found by differentiating Equation 12.1 (using Leibniz's rule,[4] to obtain

$$\frac{d\pi}{dQ} = D(Q) - \frac{dC(Q)}{dQ} = 0. \tag{12.2}$$

According to Equation 12.2, the discriminating monopoly sells units up to the quantity, Q, where the reservation price for the last unit, $D(Q)$, equals its marginal cost, $dC(Q)/dQ$.

For this solution to maximize profits, the second-order condition must hold:

$$\frac{d^2\pi}{dQ^2} = \frac{dD(Q)}{dQ} - \frac{d^2C(Q)}{dQ^2} < 0.$$

Given that the demand curve has a negative slope, the second-order condition holds if the marginal cost curve is upward sloping, $d^2C(Q)/dQ^2 > 0$, or if the demand curve has a greater (absolute) slope than the marginal cost curve. The perfectly price-discriminating monopoly's profit is

$$\pi = \int_0^Q D(z)dz - C(Q).$$

SOLVED PROBLEM 12.1

MyLab Economics
Solved Problem

Given that $D(Q) = a - bQ$, solve for the perfect price discrimination equilibrium. What quantity does a perfectly price-discriminating monopoly sell if $a = 100$, $b = 1$, and marginal cost is constant at $MC = 10$?

Answer

1. *Write the profit function for this demand curve given that the monopoly price discriminates.* The profit function is

$$\pi = \int_0^Q (a - bz)dz - C(Q) = aQ - \frac{b}{2}Q^2 - C(Q). \tag{12.3}$$

---

[4]According to Leibniz's rule for differentiating a definite integral,

$$\frac{d}{dt}\int_{a(t)}^{b(t)} f(t, z)dz = \int_{a(t)}^{b(t)} \frac{\partial f(t, z)}{\partial t}dz + f[t, b(t)]\frac{db(t)}{dt} - f[t, a(t)]\frac{da(t)}{dt}.$$

In our problem, a is not a function of t (= Q).

2. *Solve for the optimal quantity by setting the derivative of profit in Equation 12.3 with respect to quantity equal to zero*: The first-order condition to maximize profit is:

$$a - bQ - \frac{dC(Q)}{dQ} = 0.$$

By rearranging terms, we find that $D(Q) = a - bQ = dC(Q)/dQ = MC$, as in Equation 12.2. Thus, the monopoly produces the quantity at which the demand curve hits the marginal cost curve. If $a = 100$, $b = 1$, and $MC = 10$, this condition is $100 - Q = 10$, or $Q = 90$.

Perfect Price Discrimination Is Efficient but Harms Some Consumers

Perfect price discrimination is efficient: It maximizes the sum of consumer surplus and producer surplus. Therefore, both perfect competition and perfect price discrimination maximize welfare. However *with perfect price discrimination, the entire surplus goes to the firm, whereas the surplus is shared under competition.*

If the market in Figure 12.2 is competitive, the intersection of the demand curve and the marginal cost curve, MC, determines the competitive equilibrium at e_c, where price is p_c and quantity is Q_c. Consumer surplus is $A + B + C$, producer surplus is $D + E$, and society suffers no deadweight loss. The market is efficient because the price, p_c, equals the marginal cost, MC_c.

With a single-price monopoly (which charges all customers the same price because it cannot distinguish among them), the intersection of the MC curve and the single-price monopoly's marginal revenue curve, MC_s, determines the monopoly's optimum at e_s, where output is Q_s and price is p_s.[5] The deadweight loss from single-price monopoly is $C + E$. This efficiency loss is due to the monopoly's charging a price, p_s, that is above its marginal cost, $MC_s(Q_s)$, so less is sold than if the market were competitive.

The quantity, Q_d, that a perfectly price-discriminating monopoly produces is determined by the intersection of the marginal cost curve, MC, and the demand curve or marginal revenue curve, MR^d. A perfectly price-discriminating monopoly's producer surplus from selling Q_d units is the area below its demand curve and above its marginal cost curve, $A + B + C + D + E$. Its profit is the producer surplus minus its fixed cost, if any. Consumers receive no consumer surplus because each consumer pays his or her reservation price. With a perfectly price-discriminating monopoly, society suffers *no deadweight loss* because the last unit is sold at a price, p_c, equal to the marginal cost, $MC_c(Q_c)$, as in a competitive market. Thus, both a perfect price discrimination outcome and a competitive equilibrium are efficient.

The perfect price discrimination solution differs from the competitive equilibrium in two important ways. First, whereas everyone pays a price equal to the equilibrium marginal cost, $p_c = MC_c$ in the competitive equilibrium, the perfectly price-discriminating monopoly sells only the last unit at that price. The monopoly sells the other units at customers' reservation prices, which exceed p_c. Second, consumer surplus is $A + B + C$ in a competitive market; whereas a perfectly price-discriminating monopoly captures all the surplus or potential gains from trade. Thus, perfect price

---

[5]We assume that if we convert a monopoly into a competitive industry, the industry's marginal cost curve—the lowest cost at which any firm can produce an additional unit—is the same as the monopoly MC curve. The industry MC curve is the industry supply curve (Chapter 8).

Figure 12.2 Competitive, Single-Price, and Perfect Discrimination Equilibria

In the competitive market equilibrium, e_c, price is p_c, quantity is Q_c, consumer surplus is $A + B + C$, producer surplus is $D + E$, and society suffers no deadweight loss. In the single-price monopoly equilibrium, e_s, price is p_s, quantity is Q_s, consumer surplus falls to A, producer surplus is $B + D$, and deadweight loss is $C + E$. In the perfect discrimination equilibrium, the monopoly sells each unit at the customer's reservation price on the demand curve, which is also its marginal revenue curve, MR^d. It sells Q_d ($= Q_c$) units, where the last unit is sold at its marginal cost. Customers have no consumer surplus, but society suffers no deadweight loss.

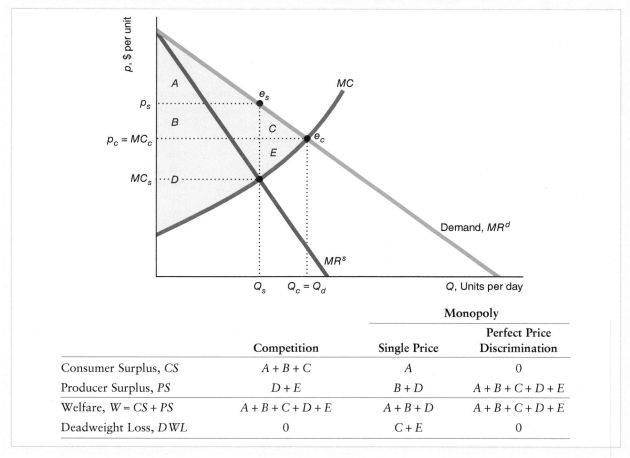

	Competition	Monopoly	
		Single Price	Perfect Price Discrimination
Consumer Surplus, CS	$A + B + C$	A	0
Producer Surplus, PS	$D + E$	$B + D$	$A + B + C + D + E$
Welfare, $W = CS + PS$	$A + B + C + D + E$	$A + B + D$	$A + B + C + D + E$
Deadweight Loss, DWL	0	$C + E$	0

discrimination does not reduce efficiency—both output and total surplus are the same as under competition—but it does redistribute income away from consumers. Consumers are better off under competition.

Is a single-price or perfectly price-discriminating monopoly better for consumers? A single-price monopoly takes less consumer surplus from consumers than does a perfectly price-discriminating monopoly. Consumers who put a very high value on the good have some consumer surplus under single-price monopoly, whereas they have none with perfect price discrimination. Consumers with lower reservation prices who purchase from the perfectly price-discriminating monopoly but not from the single-price monopoly have no consumer surplus in either case. But consumers who have low reservation prices and would not purchase from a single-price monopoly buy from a perfectly price-discriminating monopoly. All the social gain from the extra output goes to the perfectly price-discriminating monopoly. Consumer surplus is greatest with competition, lower with a single-price monopoly, and eliminated by a perfectly price-discriminating monopoly.

Thus, although a monopoly engages in perfect price discrimination to increase its profit, it benefits society.

Unintended Consequences Perfect price discrimination increases welfare and allows some consumers to buy the good who would not purchase it from a single-price monopoly.

APPLICATION			
Botox and Price Discrimination			

To show how perfect price discrimination differs from competition and single-price monopoly, we revisit the Application "Botox Patent Monopoly" in Chapter 11. The graph shows our estimated linear demand curve for Botox and a constant marginal cost (and average variable cost) of $25 per vial. If the market had been competitive (so that price equals marginal cost at e_c), consumer surplus would have been triangle $A + B + C = \$750$ million per year, and producer surplus and deadweight loss would be zero. In the single-price monopoly optimum, e_s, the firm sells one million Botox vials at $400 each. The corresponding consumer surplus is triangle $A = \$187.5$ million per year, producer surplus is rectangle $B = \$375$ million, and the deadweight loss is triangle $C = \$187.5$ million.

If Allergan, the manufacturer of Botox, could perfectly price discriminate, its producer surplus would double to $A + B + C = \$750$ million per year, and consumers would obtain no consumer surplus. The marginal consumer would pay the marginal cost of $25, the same as in a competitive market.

Allergan's inability to perfectly price discriminate costs the company and society dearly. The profit of the single-price monopoly, $B = \$375$ million per year, is lower than what it could earn if it could use perfect price discrimination, $A + B + C = \$750$ million per year. Society's welfare under single-price monopoly is lower than from perfect price discrimination by the deadweight loss, C, of $187.5 million per year, whereas consumers have no surplus with perfect price discrimination.

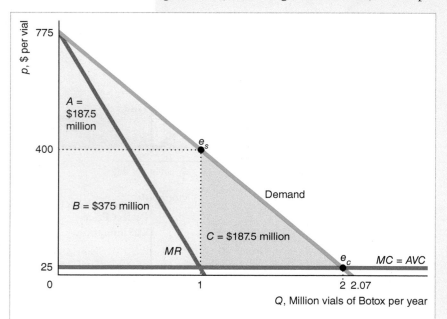

		Monopoly	
	Competition	Single Price	Perfect Price Discrimination
Consumer Surplus, CS	$A + B + C$	A	0
Producer Surplus, PS	0	B	$A + B + C$
Welfare, $W = CS + PS$	$A + B + C$	$A + B$	$A + B + C$
Deadweight Loss, DWL	0	C	0

Transaction Costs and Perfect Price Discrimination

Some firms come close to perfect price discrimination. For example, the managers of the Suez Canal set tolls individually, considering many factors such as weather and each ship's alternative routes. However, many more firms set a single price or use another nonuniform pricing method.

Transaction costs are a major reason these firms do not perfectly price discriminate: It is too difficult or costly to gather information about each customer's price sensitivity. Recent advances in computer technologies, however, have lowered these costs, allowing hotels, car- and truck-rental companies, cruise lines, and airlines to price discriminate more often.

Private colleges request and receive financial information from students, which allows the schools to nearly perfectly price discriminate. The schools give partial scholarships as a means of reducing tuition to relatively poor students. Epple et al. (2017) estimated that private schools raise tuition by an average of $210 to $510 for every $10,000 increase in family income.

Many auto dealerships try to increase their profit by perfectly price discriminating, charging each customer the maximum the customer is willing to pay. These firms hire salespeople to ascertain potential customers' willingness to pay and to bargain with them. Even if firms cannot achieve perfect price discrimination, imperfect individual price discrimination can increase their profits significantly.

APPLICATION

Google Uses Bidding for Ads to Price Discriminate

Which ads appear next to your Google search results depend on the terms in your search. That is, Google allows advertisers to *contextually target* people who search for particular phrases (Goldfarb, 2014). By making searches for unusual topics easy and fast, Google helps advertisers reach difficult-to-find potential customers with targeted ads. For example, a lawyer specializing in toxic mold lawsuits can place an ad that appears only when someone searches for "toxic mold lawyer."

Google uses auctions to price ads. Advertisers place higher bids for the first listing on Google's search page. Goldfarb and Tucker (2011) found that the amount lawyers are willing to pay for context-based ads varies inversely with the difficulty of making a match. The fewer the number of self-identified potential customers (the fewer people searching for a particular topic), the more lawyers are willing to pay per search request to advertise.

They also found that lawyers bid more when other methods of reaching potential clients are limited. Some states have anti-ambulance-chaser regulations, which prohibit personal injury lawyers from directly contacting potential clients by snail mail, phone, or e-mail for a few months after an accident. Search engine advertising prices per click are 5–7% higher in those states than in others.

By taking advantage of advertisers' desire to reach small, targeted segments of the population and varying the price according to advertisers' willingness to pay, Google is essentially perfectly price discriminating.

12.3 Group Price Discrimination

Most firms have no practical way to estimate the reservation price for each of their customers. But many of these firms know which groups of customers are likely to have higher reservation prices on average than others. A firm engages in *group price discrimination* by dividing potential customers into two or more groups and setting different prices for each group. Consumer groups may differ by age (such as adults and children), by location (such as by country), or in other ways. The monopoly sells all units of the good to customers within a group at a single price. As with perfect (individual) price discrimination, to engage in group price discrimination, a firm must have market power, be able to identify groups with different reservation prices, and prevent resale.

For example, first-run movie theaters with market power charge seniors a lower ticket price than they charge younger adults because the elderly typically are not willing to pay as much to see a movie. By admitting seniors as soon as they prove their age and buy tickets, the theater prevents resale.

How does a firm set its prices if it sells to two (or more) groups of consumers with different demand curves and if resale between the two groups is impossible? Suppose that a monopoly can divide its customers into two (or more) groups—for example, consumers in two countries. It sells Q_1 to the first group and earns revenues of $R_1(Q_1)$, and it sells Q_2 units to the second group and earns $R_2(Q_2)$. Its cost of producing total output $Q = Q_1 + Q_2$ units is $C(Q)$. The monopoly can maximize its profit through its choice of prices or quantities to each group. We examine its problem when it chooses quantities:

$$\max_{Q_1, Q_2} \pi = R_1(Q_1) + R_2(Q_2) - C(Q_1 + Q_2). \tag{12.4}$$

We obtain the first-order conditions by partially differentiating profit, π, from Equation 12.4 with respect to Q_1 and Q_2 and setting these partial derivatives equal to zero:

$$\frac{\partial \pi}{\partial Q_1} = \frac{dR_1(Q_1)}{dQ_1} - \frac{dC(Q)}{dQ} \frac{\partial Q}{\partial Q_1} = 0, \tag{12.5}$$

$$\frac{\partial \pi}{\partial Q_2} = \frac{dR_2(Q_2)}{dQ_2} - \frac{dC(Q)}{dQ} \frac{\partial Q}{\partial Q_2} = 0. \tag{12.6}$$

Equation 12.5 says that the marginal revenue from sales to the first group, $MR^1 = dR_1(Q_1)/dQ_1$, should equal the marginal cost of producing the last unit of total output, $MC = dC(Q)/dQ$, because $\partial Q/\partial Q_1 = 1$. Similarly, Equation 12.6 shows that the marginal revenue from the second group, MR^2, should also equal the marginal cost. By combining Equations 12.5 and 12.6, we find that the two marginal revenues are equal where the monopoly is profit maximizing:

$$MR^1 = MC = MR^2. \tag{12.7}$$

APPLICATION

Tesla Price Discrimination

A patent gives Tesla the legal monopoly to produce and sell the Tesla S electric car. When Tesla started selling the Model S in 2012, it was the only luxury electric car. Even by 2018, it faced little competition from all-electric luxury cars. Tesla engages in group price discrimination by charging different prices in various countries. Resale is not a problem because Tesla honors its warranty only in the region or country where the car is sold.

How should Tesla set its prices or equivalently its quantities in the United States and in Europe to maximize its total profit? Because Tesla currently manufactures in a single plant, its marginal cost is the same for all customers. A group price-discriminating monopoly with a constant marginal cost maximizes its total profit by maximizing its profit from each group separately, as a single-price monopoly would. Tesla sets its quantities so that the marginal revenue for each group equals the common marginal cost, m, which is about $30 thousand per car according to Elon Musk, the head of Tesla. In 2017, American consumers bought about $Q_A = 30$ thousand cars at $p_A = \$80$ thousand. Europeans bought $Q_E = 16$ thousand cars at $p_E = \$130$ thousand (€110,000).

Figure 12.3 shows our estimates of the linear demand curves in the two areas. In panel a, Tesla maximizes its U.S. profit by selling $Q_A = 30$ thousand cars, where its marginal revenue equals its marginal cost $MR^A = m = \$30$ thousand, as in Equation 12.5 (where U.S. consumers are group 1), and charging $p_A = \$80$ thousand. Similarly, in panel b, Tesla maximizes its European profit by selling $Q_E = 16$ thousand cars, where $MR^E = m = \$30,000$, Equation 12.6, at $p_B = \$130$ thousand.

Figure 12.3 Group Pricing of the Tesla S Car.

Tesla, the monopoly producer of the Model S all-electric car, charges more in Europe, $p_E = \$130$ thousand, than in the United States, $p_A = \$80$ thousand, because demand is more elastic in the United States. Tesla sets the quantity independently in each country. It maximizes profit by operating where its marginal revenue for each area equals its common, constant marginal cost, $m = \$30$ thousand. Consequently, the marginal revenues in the two countries are equal: $MR^A = m = MR^E$.

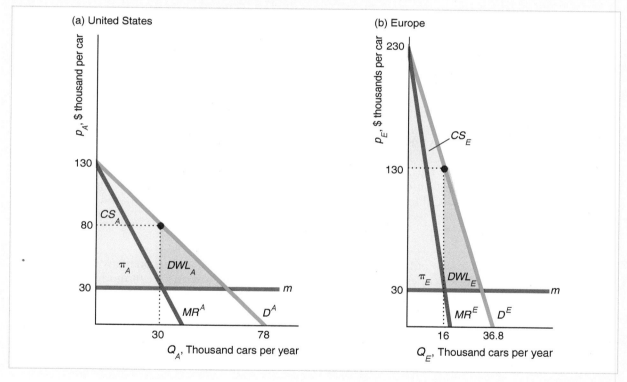

Prices and Elasticities

The ratio of the prices that a group-discriminating monopoly charges two groups depends solely on the price elasticities of demand at the profit-maximizing outputs. As Chapter 11 showed, marginal revenue is a function of the price and the price elasticity of demand: $MR^i = p_i(1 + 1/\varepsilon_i)$, where ε_i is the price elasticity of demand for group $i = 1$ or 2. Rewriting Equation 12.7, $MR^1 = MC = MR^2$, using these expressions for marginal revenue, we find that

$$MR^1 = p_1\left(1 + \frac{1}{\varepsilon_1}\right) = MC = p_2\left(1 + \frac{1}{\varepsilon_2}\right) = MR^2. \qquad (12.8)$$

By rearranging Equation 12.8, we learn that the ratio of prices in the two countries depends solely on demand elasticities in those countries:

$$\frac{p_2}{p_1} = \frac{1 + 1/\varepsilon_1}{1 + 1/\varepsilon_2}. \tag{12.9}$$

We can illustrate this result using the Tesla example. Given that $MC = m = \$30$ thousand, $p_A = \$80$ thousand, and $p_E = \$130$ thousand in Equation 12.8, Tesla must believe that $\varepsilon_A = p_A/[m - p_A] = 80/[30 - 80] = -1.6$.[6] Similarly, it believes that $\varepsilon_E = p_E/[m - p_E] = 130/[30 - 130] = -1.3$. Substituting the prices and the demand elasticities into Equation 12.9, we see that

$$\frac{p_E}{p_A} = \frac{\$130}{\$80} = 1.625 = \frac{1 + 1/(-1.6)}{1 + 1/(-1.3)} = \frac{1 + 1/\varepsilon_A}{1 + 1/\varepsilon_E}.$$

Thus, Tesla apparently believes that the European demand curve is less elastic at its profit-maximizing price than is the U.S. demand curve. Specifically, $\varepsilon_E = -1.3$ is closer to zero than is $\varepsilon_A = -1.6$. Consequently, Tesla charges European consumers 62.5% more than it charges U.S. customers.

APPLICATION
 	
Age Discrimination
	Firms can generally price discriminate between people except if based on race, religion, nationality, or gender. Firms often discriminate based on age.
	    You've probably noticed that movie theaters offer discount admission to children and senior citizens. Thus, it was probably a large shock to Tinder, an online dating app, when it was sued for price discriminating based on age.
	    Allan Candelore filed a class-action lawsuit on behalf of himself and others over the age of 30 who had to pay \$19.99 a month to use the app's premium service, Tinder Plus, while those under 30 paid only \$9.99 to \$14.99. In a 2018 ruling that, under California state law, Tinder was unlawfully discriminating against users over 30, a California state appeals court said that "we swipe left, and reverse," using Tinder's terminology to express disapproval.[7]

SOLVED PROBLEM 12.2 MyLab Economics Solved Problem	Greyhound Lines is the monopoly long-distance bus line on many routes in North America, especially those connecting small towns. Greyhound offers a senior discount to passengers aged 62 or older. Suppose that for a particular route, Greyhound faces an hourly linear inverse demand function of $p_1 = 60 - 5Q_1$ for seniors and $p_2 = 90 - 10Q_2$ for other passengers ("adults"). The marginal cost of an extra passenger is 10. What price would a profit-maximizing monopoly charge for each age group if it is allowed to price discriminate? What price would it charge if price discrimination by age is prohibited?

Answer

If price discrimination by age is legal:

1. *Determine the profit-maximizing price that the bus line sets for each age group by setting the relevant marginal revenue equal to the marginal cost. If the*

---

[6]We obtain the expression that $\varepsilon_i = p_i/(m - p_i)$ by rearranging the expression in Equation 12.8: $p_i(1 + 1/\varepsilon_i) = m$.

[7]Under U.S. law, typically firms can legally price discriminate against consumers unless the discrimination is based on gender, nationality, race, or religion. Individual states may choose stricter laws regarding price discrimination.

monopoly can price discriminate, it sets a monopoly price independently for each group. The revenue function for group 1 is $R_1 = p_1 Q_1 = 60Q_1 - 5Q_1^2$. Thus, the marginal revenue is $dR_1/dQ_1 = MR^1 = 60 - 10Q_1$. The marginal revenue curve is twice as steeply sloped as is the linear inverse demand curve (see Solved Problem 11.1), as panel a of the figure illustrates. The monopoly maximizes its profit where its marginal revenue function equals its marginal cost, $MR^1 = 60 - 10Q_1 = 10 = MC$. Solving, we find that its profit-maximizing output is $Q_1 = 5$. Substituting this quantity into the inverse demand curve for group 1, we learn that the monopoly's profit-maximizing price is $p_1 = 60 - (5 \times 5) = 35$, as panel a shows.

Similarly, for group 2, the inverse demand curve is $p_2 = 90 - 10Q_2$, so the monopoly chooses Q_2 such that $MR^2 = 90 - 20Q_2 = 10 = MC$. Thus, it maximizes its profit for group 2 where $Q_2 = 4$ and $p_2 = 50$ in panel b.

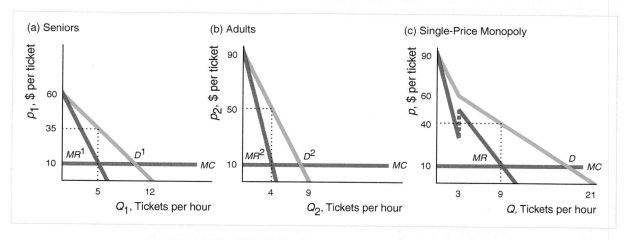

If price discrimination by age is not legal:

2. *Derive the total demand curve.* If Greyhound cannot price discriminate, it charges the same price, p, to all users. The company faces the total demand curve in panel c, which is the horizontal sum of the demand curves for each of the two age groups in panels a and b (Chapter 2). If the price is between 60 and 90, the quantity demanded is positive only for the adults, so the total demand curve (panel c) is just the adults' demand curve (panel b). If the price is less than 60, then both groups demand a positive quantity, and the total demand curve in panel c is the horizontal sum of the two age groups' demand curves (panels a and b).[8] As panel c shows, the total demand curve has a kink at $p = 60$, because the quantity demanded by seniors is positive at only lower prices.

3. *Determine the marginal revenue curve corresponding to the total demand curve.* Because the total demand curve has a kink at $p = 60$, the corresponding marginal revenue curve has two sections. At prices greater than 60, the marginal revenue curve is that of the adults, group 2. At prices less than 60,

---

[8]Rearranging the inverse demand functions, we find that the seniors' demand function is $Q_1 = 12 - 0.2p_1$ and the adults' demand function is $Q_2 = 90 - 0.1p_2$. As a result for a price less than 60, the total demand function is $Q = (12 - 0.2p) + (9 - 0.1p) = 21 - 0.3p$, where $Q = Q_1 + Q_2$ is the total quantity that the monopoly sells and p is the common price.

the inverse total demand function is $p = 70 - (1/0.3)Q$, so the revenue function is $R = 70 - (1/0.3)Q^2$ and the marginal revenue function is $dR/dQ = MR = 70 - (2/0.3)Q$. Panel c shows that the marginal revenue curve *jumps*—is discontinuous—at the quantity where the total demand curve has a kink.

4. *Solve for the single-price monopoly solution.* Greyhound maximizes its profit where its marginal revenue equals its marginal cost. From inspecting panel c, we learn that the intersection occurs in the section where both age groups have positive demand, so that $MR = 70 - (2/0.3)Q = 10 = MC$. Solving this equation, we find that the profit-maximizing output is $Q = 9$. Substituting that quantity into the inverse total demand function, we learn that Greyhound charges $p = 40$. Thus, if it can set only a single price, Greyhound's price, 40, lies between the two prices it would charge if it could price discriminate: $35 < 40 < 50$.

Identifying Groups

Firms use two approaches to divide customers into groups. One method is to divide buyers into groups based on *observable characteristics* of consumers that the firm believes are associated with relatively high or relatively low price elasticities. For example, movie theaters price discriminate using the age of customers. Similarly, some firms charge customers in one country higher prices than those in another country. Such differences reflect group price discrimination.

Another approach is to identify and divide consumers based on their *actions*. The firm allows consumers to self-select the group to which they belong.

For example, firms use differences in the value customers place on their time to discriminate by making people wait in line and other time-intensive methods of selling goods. Store managers who believe that high-wage people are unwilling to "waste their time shopping" may have sales that require consumers to visit the store and pick up the good themselves, while consumers who order over the phone or online pay a higher price. This type of price discrimination increases profit if people who put a high value on their time also have less elastic demand for the good.

APPLICATION	Firms use various approaches to induce consumers to indicate whether they have relatively high or low elasticities of demand. For each of these methods, consumers must incur some cost, such as their time, to receive a discount. Otherwise, all consumers would get the discount. By spending extra time to obtain a discount, price-sensitive consumers differentiate themselves.

Buying Discounts

Coupons. Many firms use discount coupons to group price discriminate. Through this device, firms divide customers into two groups, charging coupon clippers less than nonclippers. Offering coupons makes sense if the people who do not clip coupons are less price sensitive on average than those who do. People who are willing to spend their time clipping coupons buy cereals and other goods

You've got to you really want a discount!

at lower prices than those who value their time more. As of mid-2018, firms distributed 143 billion print and digital coupons for packaged goods, of which 92.5 million (about 0.6%) were redeemed. The introduction of digital coupons (for example, **EverSave.com**) has made it easier for firms to target appropriate groups, but has lowered consumers' costs of using them.

Airline Tickets. By choosing between two different types of tickets, airline customers indicate whether they are likely to be business or recreational travelers. Airlines give customers a choice between high-price tickets with no strings attached and low-price fares that must be purchased long in advance with many restrictions.

Airlines know that many business travelers have little advance warning before they book a flight and have relatively inelastic demand curves. In contrast, vacation travelers usually plan their trip in advance and have relatively high elasticities of demand for air travel. The airlines' rules ensure that vacationers with relatively elastic demand obtain low fares, while most business travelers with relatively inelastic demand buy high-price tickets (often more than four times higher than the plan-ahead rate). The average difference between the high and low price for passengers on the same U.S. route is 36% of an airline's average ticket price.

Reverse Auctions. Priceline.com and other online merchants use a name-your-own-price or "reverse" auction to identify price-sensitive customers. A customer enters a relatively low-price bid for a good or service, such as an airline ticket. Merchants decide whether to accept that bid. To prevent their less price-sensitive customers from using these methods, airlines force successful Priceline bidders to be flexible: to fly at off hours, to make one or more connections, and to accept any type of aircraft. Similarly, when bidding on groceries, a customer must list "one or two brands you like." As Jay Walker, Priceline's founder, explained, "The manufacturers would rather not give you a discount, of course, but if you prove that you're willing to switch brands, they're willing to pay to keep you."

Rebates. Why do many firms offer a rebate of, say, $5 instead of reducing the price on their product by $5? The reason is that a consumer must incur the postal cost plus an extra, time-consuming step to receive the rebate. Thus, only those consumers who are price sensitive or place a low value on their time will actually apply for the rebate. According to a *Consumer Reports* survey, 47% of customers always or often apply for a rebate, 23% sometimes apply, 25% never apply, and 5% responded that the question was not applicable to them.

SOLVED PROBLEM 12.3

MyLab Economics
Solved Problem

A monopoly producer with a constant marginal cost of $m = 20$ sells in two countries and can prevent reselling between the two countries. The inverse linear demand curve is $p_1 = 100 - Q_1$ in Country 1 and $p_2 = 100 - 2Q_2$ in Country 2. What price does the monopoly charge in each country? What quantity does it sell in each country? Does it price discriminate? Why or why not?

Answer

1. *Determine the profit-maximizing price and quantity that the monopoly sets in each country by setting the relevant marginal revenue equal to the marginal cost.* In Country 1, the inverse demand curve is $p_1 = 100 - Q_1$, so the revenue function is $R^1 = 100Q_1 - (Q_1)^2$, and hence the marginal revenue function is $MR^1 = dR^1/dQ_1 = 100 - 2Q_1$. It equates its marginal revenue to its marginal cost to determine its profit-maximizing quantity: $100 - 2Q_1 = 20$. Solving, the monopoly sets $Q_1 = 40$. Substituting this quantity into its inverse demand function, we learn that the monopoly's price is $p_1 = 100 - 40 = 60$. Similarly, in Country 2, the inverse demand curve is $p_2 = 100 - 2Q_2$, so the revenue function is $R^2 = 100Q_2 - 2(Q_2)^2$, and hence the marginal revenue function is $MR^2 = dR^2/dQ_2 = 100 - 4Q_2$. Equating marginal revenue and marginal cost, $100 - 4Q_2 = 20$, and solving, the monopoly sets $Q_2 = 20$ in Country 2. Its price is $p_2 = 100 - (2 \times 20) = 60$. Thus, the monopoly sells twice as much in Country 1 as in Country 2 but charges the same price in both countries.

2. *Explain, by solving for a general linear inverse demand function, why the monopoly does not price discriminate.* Although the firm has market power, can prevent reselling, and faces consumers in the two countries with different demand functions, it does not pay for the monopoly to price discriminate. Consider the monopoly's problem with a general linear inverse demand function: $p = a - bQ$. Here, revenue is $R = aQ - bQ^2$, so $MR = dR/dQ = a - 2bQ$. Equating marginal revenue and marginal cost, $a - 2bQ = m$, and solving for Q, we find that $Q = (a - m)/(2b)$. Consequently, the price is $p = a - b(a - m)/(2b) = (a + m)/2$. Thus, the price depends only on the inverse demand function's intercept on the vertical axis, a, and not on its slope, b. Because both inverse demand functions in this example have the same vertical intercept—they differ only in their slopes—the monopoly sets the same equilibrium price in both countries. In equilibrium, the elasticity of demand is the same in both countries. Thus, while the monopoly could price discriminate, it chooses not to do so.

Welfare Effects of Group Price Discrimination

Group price discrimination results in inefficient production and consumption. As a result, welfare under group price discrimination is lower than it is under competition or perfect price discrimination. Welfare may be lower or higher with group price discrimination than with a single-price monopoly, however.

Group Price Discrimination Versus Competition. Consumer surplus is greater and more output is produced with competition (or perfect price discrimination) than with group price discrimination. In Figure 12.3, consumer surplus with group price discrimination is CS_A (for American consumers in panel a) and CS_E (for European consumers in panel b). Under competition, consumer surplus is the area below the demand curve and above the marginal cost curve: $CS_A + \pi_A + DWL_A$ in panel a and $CS_E + \pi_E + DWL_E$ in panel b.

Thus, group price discrimination transfers some of the competitive consumer surplus to the monopoly as additional profit, π_A and π_E, and causes the deadweight losses DWL_A and DWL_E. The deadweight loss is due to the group price-discriminating monopoly's charging prices above marginal cost, which results in reduced production from the optimal competitive level.

Group Price Discrimination Versus Single-Price Monopoly. From theory alone, it is impossible to tell whether welfare is higher if the monopoly uses group price discrimination or if it sets a single price. Both types of monopolies set price above marginal cost, so they produce less than would a competitive market. Output may rise as the firm starts discriminating if groups that did not buy when the firm charged a single price start buying.

The closer the group price-discriminating monopoly comes to perfect price discrimination (say, by dividing its customers into many groups rather than just two), the greater is its output and the less deadweight loss it causes. However, unless a group price-discriminating monopoly sells significantly more output than it would if it had to set a single price, welfare is likely to be lower with discrimination because of consumption inefficiency and time wasted shopping. These two inefficiencies do not occur with a monopoly that charges all consumers the same price. As a result, consumers place the same marginal value (the single sales price) on the good, so they have no incentive to trade with each other. Similarly, if everyone pays the same price, consumers have no incentive to search for lower prices.

12.4 Nonlinear Price Discrimination

Many firms are unable to determine which customers or groups of customers have the highest reservation prices. However, firms may know that most customers are willing to pay more for the first unit than for successive units: The typical customer's demand curve is downward sloping. Such firms can price discriminate by letting the price that each customer pays vary with the number of units purchased. The firm uses second-degree price discrimination. Here, the price varies with quantity but each customer faces the same nonlinear pricing schedule.[9] To use nonlinear price discrimination, a firm must have market power and be able to prevent customers who buy at a low price from reselling to those who would otherwise pay a high price.

In 2018, a package of 48 Duracell Energizer AA batteries cost $18.98 (40¢ per battery). A 24-pack of the same battery cost $12.34 (51¢ per battery). The difference in the price per battery is nonlinear price discrimination unless the price difference is due to cost differences. This quantity discount results in customers who make large purchases paying less per unit than those who make small purchases.

Many utilities use *block-pricing* schedules, by which they charge one price for the first few units (a *block*) of usage and a different price for subsequent blocks. Gas, electric, water, and other utilities commonly use declining-block or increasing-block pricing schemes.

The block-pricing utility monopoly in Figure 12.4 faces a linear demand curve for each (identical) customer. The demand curve hits the vertical axis at $90 and the horizontal axis at 90 units. The monopoly has a constant marginal and average cost of $m = \$30$. Panel a shows how this monopoly maximizes its profit if it can quantity discriminate by setting two prices (and both prices lie on the demand curve).

---

[9]A consumer's expenditure is a linear function of quantity only if the price is constant. If the price varies with quantity, then the expenditure is nonlinear.

Figure 12.4 Block Pricing

If this monopoly engages in block pricing with quantity discounting, it makes a larger profit (producer surplus) than it does if it sets a single price, and welfare is greater. (a) With block pricing, its profit is $B = \$1,200$ and welfare is $A + B + C = \$1,600$. (b) If it sets a single price (so that its marginal revenue equals its marginal cost), the monopoly's profit is $F = \$900$, and welfare is $E + F = \$1,350$.

	Block Pricing	Single Price
Consumer Surplus, CS	$A + C = \$400$	$E = \$450$
Producer Surplus or Profit, $PS = \pi$	$B = \$1,200$	$F = \$900$
Welfare, $W = CS + PS$	$A + B + C = \$1,600$	$E + F = \$1,350$
Deadweight Loss, DWL	$D = \$200$	$G = \$450$

The monopoly faces an inverse demand curve $p = 90 - Q$, and its marginal and average cost is $m = 30$. Consequently, the quantity-discounting utility's profit is

$$\pi = p(Q_1)Q_1 + p(Q_2)(Q_2 - Q_1) - mQ_2$$
$$= (90 - Q_1)Q_1 + (90 - Q_2)(Q_2 - Q_1) - 30Q_2,$$

where Q_1 is the largest quantity for which the first-block rate, $p_1 = 90 - Q_1$, is charged and Q_2 is the total quantity that a consumer purchases. The utility chooses Q_1 and Q_2 to maximize its profit. It sets the derivative of profit with respect to Q_1 equal to zero (holding Q_2 constant), $\partial\pi/\partial Q_1 = Q_2 - 2Q_1 = 0$, and the derivative of profit with respect to Q_2 (holding Q_1 constant) equal to zero, $\partial\pi/\partial Q_2 = Q_1 - 2Q_2 + 60 = 0$.

By solving these two first-order conditions simultaneously, the utility determines its profit-maximizing quantities, $Q_1 = 20$ and $Q_2 = 40$. The corresponding block prices are $p_1 = 90 - 20 = 70$ and $p_2 = 50$. That is, the monopoly charges a price of $70 on any quantity up to 20—the first block—and $50 on any units beyond the first 20—the second block. (The point that determines the first block, $70 and 20 units, lies on the demand curve.)

The consumer gains consumer surplus equal to A on the first block and C on the second block, for a total of $A + C$. The quantity-discriminating monopoly's profit or producer surplus is area B. Society suffers a deadweight loss of D because price, $50, is above marginal cost, $30, on the last unit, 40, purchased.

If the monopoly can set only a single price (panel b), it produces where its marginal revenue equals its marginal cost, selling 30 units at $60 per unit. Thus, by using nonlinear pricing instead of using a single price, the utility sells more units, 40 instead of 30, and makes a higher profit, $B = \$1,200$ instead of $F = \$900$.

Many consumers draw a false inference about quantity discounts.

Common Confusion Quantity discounts help consumers.

Charging lower prices for high-volume purchases allows firms to charge higher prices for low-volume purchases than they otherwise would.

In our example, consumer surplus with quantity discounting is lower, $A + C = \$400$ instead of $E = \$450$; welfare (consumer surplus plus producer surplus) is higher, $A + B + C = \$1,600$ instead of $E + F = \$1,350$; and deadweight loss is lower, $D = \$200$ instead of $G = \$450$. Thus, in this example, the firm and society are better off with quantity discounting, but consumers as a group suffer.

The more block prices the monopoly can set, the closer the monopoly can get to perfect price discrimination, where it captures all potential consumer surplus. A deadweight loss results if the monopoly sets a price above marginal cost so it sells too few units. The more prices the monopoly sets, the lower the last price and hence the closer it is to marginal cost.

12.5 Two-Part Pricing

We now turn to another form of nonlinear pricing: *two-part pricing*. With two-part pricing, the average price per unit paid by a consumer varies with the number of units purchased by that consumer.

With **two-part pricing**, the firm charges each consumer a lump-sum *access fee* for the right to buy as many units of the good as the consumer wants at a per-unit *price*.[10] Thus, the overall payment consists of two prices: an access fee and a per-unit price. Because of the access fee, the average amount per unit that consumers pay is greater if they buy a small number of units than if they buy a larger number.

Two-part pricing is commonly used. Many fitness clubs charge a yearly access fee and a price per session. Many warehouse stores require that customers buy an annual membership to be able to buy goods at relatively low prices. Some car rental firms charge a rental or access fee for the day and an additional price per mile driven. To buy season tickets to the Dallas Cowboys football games, a fan first must buy a *personal seat license* (PSL), giving the fan the right to buy season tickets for the next 30 years. Most PSLs sell for between $10,000 and $125,000.

To profit from two-part pricing, a firm must have market power and must successfully prevent resale. In addition, a firm must know how individual demand curves vary across its customers. We start by examining a firm's two-part pricing problem in the extreme case in which all customers have the same demand curve. We then consider what happens when the demand curves of individual customers differ.

---

[10]*Jargon alert*: The prices used in two-part pricing are often referred to as *two-part tariffs*.

Two-Part Pricing with Identical Consumers

If all its customers are identical, a firm that knows its customers' demand curve can set a two-part price that has the same two important properties that perfect price discrimination has. First, the efficient quantity is sold because the price of the last unit equals marginal cost. Second, all potential consumer surplus is transferred from consumers to the firm.

To illustrate these points we consider a monopoly that has a constant marginal cost of $MC = 10$ and no fixed cost, so its average cost is also constant at 10. All of the monopoly's customers have the same demand curve, $q = 80 - p$. Panel a of Figure 12.5 shows the demand curve, D^1, of one such customer, Valerie.

Total surplus is maximized if the monopoly sets its price, p, equal to its constant marginal cost of 10. The firm breaks even on each unit sold and has no producer surplus and no profit. Valerie buys $q = 70$ units. Her consumer surplus is area $A = \frac{1}{2}(80 - p)q = \frac{1}{2}([80 - 10] \times 70) = 2{,}450$.

However, if the firm also charges a lump-sum access fee of $\mathscr{L} = 2{,}450$, it captures this 2,450 as its producer surplus or its profit per customer, and leaves Valerie with no consumer surplus. The firm's total profit is 2,450 times the number of identical customers.

The firm maximizes its profit by setting its price equal to its marginal cost and charging an access fee that captures the entire potential consumer surplus. If the firm were to charge a price above its marginal cost of 10, it would sell fewer units and make a smaller profit. In panel b of Figure 12.5, the firm charges $p = 20$. At that higher price, Valerie buys only 60 units, which is less than the 70 units that she buys at a price of 10 in panel a. The firm's profit from selling these 60 units is $B_1 = (20 - 10) \times 60 = 600$. For Valerie to agree to buy any units, the monopoly has to lower its access fee to 1,800 ($= \frac{1}{2} \times 60 \times 60$), the new potential consumer surplus,

Figure 12.5 Two-Part Pricing with Identical Consumers

(a) Because all customers have the same individual demand curve as Valerie, D^1, the monopoly captures the entire potential consumer surplus using two-part pricing. The monopoly charges a per-unit fee price, p, equal to the marginal cost of 10, and a lump-sum access fee, $\mathscr{L} = A = 2{,}450$, which is the blue triangle under the demand curve and above the per-unit price of $p = 10$. (b) Were the monopoly to set a price at 20, which is above

its marginal cost, it would earn less. It makes a profit of $B_1 = 600$ from the 10 it earns on the 60 units that Valerie buys at this higher price. However, the largest access fee the firm can charge now is $\mathscr{L} = A_1 = 1{,}800$, so its total profit is 2,400, which is less than the 2,450 it makes if it sets its price equal to marginal cost. The difference is a deadweight loss of $C_1 = 50$, which is due to fewer units being sold at the higher price.

area A_1. The firm's total profit from Valerie is $A_1 + B_1 = 1{,}800 + 600 = 2{,}400$. This amount is less than the 2,450 (= A in panel a) profit the firm earns if it sets price equal to marginal cost, 10, and charges the higher access fee. Area A in panel a equals $A_1 + B_1 + C_1$ in panel b. By charging a price above marginal cost, the firm loses $C_1 = \$50$, which is the deadweight loss due to selling fewer units.

Similarly, if the firm were to charge a price below its marginal cost, it would also earn less profit. It would sell too many units and make a loss on each unit that it could not fully recapture by a higher access fee.

Two-Part Pricing with Differing Consumers

Two-part pricing is more complex if consumers have different demand curves. Suppose that the monopoly has two customers (or two groups of identical customers), Valerie, Consumer 1, and Neal, Consumer 2. Valerie's demand curve, $q_1 = 80 - p$, is D^1 in panel a of Figure 12.6 (which is the same as panel b of Figure 12.5), and Neal's demand curve, $q_2 = 100 - p$, is D^2 in panel b. The monopoly's marginal cost, $MC = m$, and average cost are constant at 10 per unit.

If the firm knows each customer's demand curve, can prevent resale, and can charge its customers different prices and access fees, it can capture the entire potential consumer surplus. The monopoly sets its price for both customers at $p = m = 10$ and sets its access fee equal to each customer's potential consumer surplus. At

Figure 12.6 Two-Part Pricing with Differing Consumers

The monopoly faces two consumers. Valerie's demand curve is D^1 in panel a, and Neal's demand curve is D^2 in panel b. If the monopoly can set different prices and access fees for its two customers, it charges both a per-unit price of $p = 10$, which equals its marginal cost, and it charges an access fee of $\mathscr{L}_1 = 2{,}450 (= A_1 + B_1 + C_1)$ to Valerie and $\mathscr{L}_2 = 4{,}050 (= A_2 + B_2 + C_2)$ to Neal. The market has no deadweight loss. If the monopoly cannot charge its customers different prices, it sets its per-unit price at $p = 20$, where Valerie purchases 60 and Neal buys 80 units. The firm charges both the same access fee of $\mathscr{L} = 1{,}800 = A_1$, which is Valerie's potential consumer surplus. (The highest access fee that the firm could charge and have Neal buy is 3,200, but at that level, Valerie would not buy, which would lower the firm's profit.) By charging a price above its marginal cost, the firm captures $B_1 = 600$ from Valerie and $B_2 = 800$ from Neal. Thus, its total profit is 5,000 (= [2 × 1,800] + 600 + 800), which is less than the 6,500 (= 2,450 + 4,050) it makes if it can charge separate access fees to each customer. The deadweight loss is 100 (= 50 + 50).

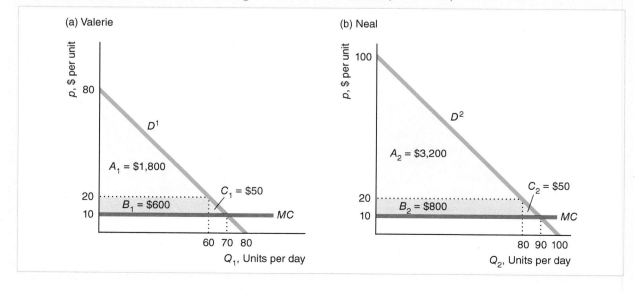

$p = 10$, Valerie buys 70 units (panel a), and Neal buys 90 units (panel b). If no access fee were charged, Valerie's consumer surplus, $CS_1 = \frac{1}{2}(80 - p)q_1 = \frac{1}{2}(80 - p)^2$, would equal the triangle below her demand curve and above the price line at 10, $A_1 + B_1 + C_1$, which is 2,450 ($= \frac{1}{2} \times 70 \times 70$). Similarly, Neal's consumer surplus, $CS_2 = \frac{1}{2}(100 - p)^2$, would be 4,050 ($= \frac{1}{2} \times 90 \times 90$), which is the triangle $A_2 + B_2 + C_2$. Thus, the monopoly charges a lump-sum access fee of $\mathcal{L}_1 = 2,450$ to Valerie and $\mathcal{L}_2 = 4,050$ to Neal, so that the customers receive no consumer surplus. The firm's total profit, $\mathcal{L}_1 + \mathcal{L}_2 = 2,450 + 4,050 = 6,500$, is the maximum possible profit, because the monopoly has captured the maximum potential consumer surplus from both customers. Thus, the market has no deadweight loss.

Now suppose that the monopoly has to charge each consumer the same lump-sum fee, $\mathcal{L}$, and the same per-unit price, p. For example, because of legal restrictions, a telephone company charges all residential customers the same monthly fee and the same fee per call, even though the company knows that consumers' demands vary. As with group price discrimination, the monopoly does not capture the entire consumer surplus.

If the monopoly charges the lower fee, $\mathcal{L} = CS_1 = \frac{1}{2}(80 - p)^2$, it sells to both consumers and its profit is

$$\pi = 2\mathcal{L} + (p - m)(q_1 + q_2) = (80 - p)^2 + (p - 10)(180 - 2p),$$

because total output is $q_1 + q_2 = 180 - 2p$. Setting the derivative of π with respect to p equal to zero, $-2(80 - p) + (180 - 2p) - 2(p - 10) = 0$. Solving this expression for p, we find that the profit-maximizing price is $p = 20$. The monopoly charges a fee of $\mathcal{L} = CS_1 = \frac{1}{2}(80 - 20)^2 = 1,800$. Valerie buys 60 units, and Neal buys 80 units. The monopoly makes $(p - m) = (20 - 10) = 10$ on each unit, so it earns $B_1 + B_2 = 600 + 800 = 1,400$ from the units it sells. Its total profit is $2\mathcal{L} + B_1 + B_2 = (2 \times 1,800) + 1,400 = 5,000$. The deadweight loss is $C_1 + C_2 = \$100$.

If the monopoly charges the higher fee, $\mathcal{L} = CS_2$, it sells only to Consumer 2, and its profit is

$$\pi = \mathcal{L} + (p - m)q_2 = \frac{1}{2}(100 - p)^2 + (p - 10)(100 - p).$$

The monopoly's profit-maximizing price is $p = 10$, and its profit is $\mathcal{L} = CS_2 = 4,050$. Hence, the monopoly makes more by setting $\mathcal{L} = CS_1$ and selling to both customers at $p = 20$. The deadweight loss from not selling to Valerie is large: $A_1 + B_1 + C_1 = \$2,450$.

Thus, the monopoly maximizes its profit by setting the lower lump-sum fee and charging a price $p = 20$, which is above marginal cost. The monopoly earns less than if it could charge each customer a separate access fee: $5,000 < 6,500$. Valerie has no consumer surplus, but Neal enjoys a consumer surplus of 1,400 ($= 3,200 - 1,800$).

Why does the monopoly charge a price above marginal cost when using two-part pricing? By raising its price, the monopoly earns more per unit from both types of customers but lowers its customers' potential consumer surplus. Thus, if the monopoly can capture each customer's potential surplus by charging different lump-sum fees, it sets its price equal to marginal cost. However, if the monopoly cannot capture all the potential consumer surplus because it must charge everyone the same lump-sum fee, the increase in profit from Neal due to the higher price more than offsets the reduction in the lump-sum fee from Valerie.[11]

---

[11]If the monopoly lowers its price from 20 to the marginal cost of 10, it loses B_1 from Valerie, but it can raise its access from A_1 to $A_1 + B_1 + C_1$, so its total profit from Valerie increases by $C_1 = 50$. The access fee it collects from Neal also rises by $B_1 + C_1 = 650$, but its profit from unit sales falls by $B_2 = 800$, so its total profit decreases by 150. The loss from Neal, -150, more than offsets the gain from Valerie, 50. Thus, the monopoly makes 100 more by charging a price of 20 rather than 10.

APPLICATION

Pricing iTunes

Prior to 2009, Apple's iTunes music store, the giant of music downloading, used *uniform pricing*, whereby it sold songs at 99¢ each. However, some of its competitors, such as Amazon MP3, did not use uniform pricing. Some record labels told Apple that they would not renew their contracts if Apple continued to use uniform pricing. Apparently responding to this pressure and the success of some of its competitors, Apple switched in 2009 to selling each song at one of three prices.

Did Apple's one-price-for-all-songs policy cost it substantial potential profit? How do consumer surplus and deadweight loss vary with pricing methods such as a single price, song-specific prices, price discrimination, and two-part pricing? To answer such questions, Shiller and Waldfogel (2011) surveyed nearly 1,000 students and determined each person's willingness to pay for each of 50 popular songs. Then they used this information to calculate optimal pricing under various pricing schemes.

First, under uniform pricing, Apple charges the same price for every song. Second, under variable pricing, each song sells at its individual profit-maximizing price. Third, the firm uses two-part pricing, charging a monthly or annual fee for access and then a fixed price for each download.

If we know the demand curve and the marginal cost, we can determine the producer surplus (*PS*), the consumer surplus (*CS*), or profit, and the deadweight loss (*DWL*) from each pricing regime. By dividing each of these surplus measures by the total available surplus—the area under the demand curve and above the marginal cost curve—Shiller and Waldfogel estimated the percentage shares of *PS*, *CS*, and *DWL* under each of the three pricing methods:

Pricing	PS	CS	DWL
Uniform	28	42	29
Variable	29	45	26
Two-part price	37	43	20

If these students have tastes similar to those of the general market, then deadweight loss decreases under either of the alternatives to uniform pricing. Consumers do best with variable pricing, but two-part pricing is also better for consumers than uniform pricing.

Apple raised its profit by switching from uniform pricing to variable pricing (see the *PS* column in the table). However, these results suggest that Apple could do even better using two-part pricing. Perhaps in response to this opportunity, Apple added iTunes Match (2011) and Apple Music (2015), which effectively use two-part pricing.

12.6 Tie-In Sales

Another type of nonuniform pricing is a **tie-in sale**, in which customers can buy one product or service only if they agree to purchase another as well. Firms use two forms of tie-in sales.

The first type is a **requirement tie-in sale**, in which customers who buy one product from a firm are required to make all their purchases of another product from that firm. Some firms sell durable machines such as copiers under the condition that customers buy copier services and supplies from them in the future. Because the amount of services and supplies that each customer buys differs, the per-unit price of copiers varies across customers.

The second type of tie-in sale is **bundling** (or a *package tie-in sale*), in which two goods are combined so that customers must buy both goods. For example, a Whirlpool refrigerator comes with shelves.

Most tie-in sales increase efficiency by lowering transaction costs. Indeed, tie-ins for efficiency purposes are so common that we hardly think about them. Presumably, no one would want to buy a shirt without buttons attached, so selling shirts with buttons lowers transaction costs. Because virtually everyone wants certain basic software, most companies sell computers with that software installed. Firms also often use tie-in sales to increase profits, as we now consider.

Requirement Tie-In Sales

Frequently, a firm cannot tell which customers are going to use its product the most and hence are willing to pay the most for it. These firms may be able to use a requirement tie-in sale to identify heavy users of the product and charge them more.

APPLICATION

Ties That Bind

Unfortunately for printer manufacturers, the Magnuson-Moss Warranty Improvement Act of 1975 forbids a manufacturer from using such tie-in provisions as a condition of warranty. To get around this Act, printer firms such as Brother, Canon, Epson, and Hewlett-Packard (HP) write their warranties to strongly encourage consumers to use only their cartridges and not to refill them. The warranty for an HP inkjet printer says that it does not apply if printer failure or damage is attributable to a non-HP or refilled cartridge.

Is this warning sufficient to induce most consumers to buy cartridges only from HP? Apparently so. In 2018 HP sold its Deskjet 1112 printer for only $29.99. That is, HP is virtually giving away an impressive machine that will print up to 7.5 pages per minute in black and white and 5.5 pages per minute in color in up to 4800 × 1200 optimized dots per inch (dpi) in color. HP charges $37.99 for its tri-color ink cartridge. If most customers bought inexpensive cartridges or refills from other firms, HP would not sell its printer at a rock-bottom price. Thus, HP demonstrates that the benefits of requirement tie-in sales can be achieved through careful wording of warranties and advertising.

Bundling

Firms sometimes bundle even when bundling has no production advantages and transaction costs are small. Bundling allows firms to increase their profit by charging different prices to different consumers based on the consumers' willingness to pay. For example, a computer firm may sell a package including a computer and a printer for a single price even if selling these products together does not lower costs.

Firms use two types of bundling. Some firms engage in *pure bundling*, in which they offer only a package deal, as when a cable company sells a bundle of internet, phone, and television services for a single price but does not allow customers to purchase the individual services separately. Other firms use *mixed bundling*, in which the goods are available on a stand-alone basis in addition to being available as part of a bundle, such as a cable company that allows consumers to buy the bundle or the individual services they want.

Pure Bundling. The two major component programs in Microsoft Office, Word and Excel, were originally sold as stand-alone products. A consumer who wanted both had to buy both separately. Later, Microsoft bundled both Word and Excel into Microsoft Office and also sold the products on a stand-alone basis. At present, if you try to purchase Word or Excel from Microsoft, you are directed only to the bundled product, MS Office.

Whether it pays Microsoft to sell a bundle or sell the programs separately depends on how reservation prices for the components vary across customers. We use an example to show that a firm that sells word processing and spreadsheet programs bundles them if doing so results in a higher profit than if it sells the programs separately.

The marginal cost of producing an extra copy of either type of software is essentially zero, so the firm's revenue equals its profit. The firm must charge all customers the same price—it cannot price discriminate.

The firm has two customers, Alisha and Bob. The first two columns of Table 12.1 show the reservation prices for each consumer for the two products. Alisha's reservation price for the word processing program, 120, is greater than Bob's, 90; however, Alisha's reservation price for the spreadsheet program, 50, is less than Bob's, 70. The reservation prices are *negatively correlated*: The customer who has the higher reservation price for one product has the lower reservation price for the other product. The third column of the table shows each consumer's reservation price for the bundle, which is the sum of the reservations prices for the two underlying products.

Table 12.1 Negatively Correlated Reservation Prices

	Word Processor	Spreadsheet	Bundle
Alisha	120	50	170
Bob	90	70	160
Profit maximizing price	90	50	160
Units sold	2	2	2

If the firm sells the two products separately, it maximizes its profit by charging 90 for the word processor and selling to both consumers, so that its profit is 180, rather than charging 120 and selling only to Alisha. If it charges between 90 and 120, it still only sells to Alisha and earns less than if it charges 120. Similarly, the firm maximizes its profit by selling the spreadsheet program for 50 to both consumers, earning 100, rather than charging 70 and selling to only Bob. The firm's total profit from selling the programs separately is 280 (= 180 + 100).

If the firm sells the two products in a bundle, it maximizes its profit by charging 160, selling to both customers, and earning 320. This is a better outcome than charging 170 and selling only to Alisha. Pure bundling is more profitable for the firm because it earns 320 from selling the bundle and only 280 from selling the programs separately.

Pure bundling is more profitable because the firm captures more of the consumers' potential consumer surplus—their reservation prices. With separate prices, Alisha has consumer surplus of 30 (= 120 − 90) from the word processing program and none from the spreadsheet program. Bob receives no consumer surplus from the word processing program and 20 from the spreadsheet program. Thus, the total consumer surplus is 50. With pure bundling, Alisha gets 10 of consumer surplus and Bob gets none, so the total is only 10. Thus, the pure bundling approach captures 40 more potential consumer surplus than does pricing separately.

Whether pure bundling increases the firm's profit depends on the reservation prices. Table 12.2 shows the reservation prices for two different consumers, Carol and Dmitri. Carol has higher reservation prices for both products than does Dmitri. These reservation prices are *positively correlated*: A higher reservation price for one product is associated with a higher reservation price for the other product.

Table 12.2 Positively Correlated Reservation Prices

	Word Processor	Spreadsheet	Bundle
Carol	100	90	190
Dmitri	90	40	130
Profit maximizing price	90	90	130
Units sold	2	1	2

If the programs are sold separately, the firm charges 90 for the word processor, sells to both consumers, and earns 180. However, it makes more charging 90 for the spreadsheet program and selling only to Carol, than it does charging 40 for the spreadsheet, selling to both consumers, and earning 80. The firm's total profit if it prices separately is 270 (= 180 + 90).

If the firm uses pure bundling, it maximizes its profit by charging 130 for the bundle, selling to both customers, and making 260. Because the firm earns more selling the programs separately, 270, than when it bundles them, 260, pure bundling is not profitable in this example.

Mixed Bundling. Restaurants, computer software firms, and many other companies commonly use mixed bundling, and allow consumers to buy the pure bundle or to buy any of the bundle's components separately. The following example illustrates that mixed bundling may be more profitable than pure bundling or only selling components separately because it may capture more of the potential consumer surplus.

A firm that sells word processing and spreadsheet programs has four potential customers with the reservation prices in Table 12.3. Again, the firm's cost of production is zero, so maximizing its profit is equivalent to maximizing its revenue.

Table 12.3 Reservation Prices and Mixed Bundling

	Word Processor	Spreadsheet	Suite (Bundle)
Aaron	120	30	150
Brigitte	110	90	200
Charles	90	110	200
Dorothy	30	120	150

Aaron, a writer, places high value on the word processing program but has relatively little use for a spreadsheet program. Dorothy, an accountant, has the opposite pattern of preferences—placing a high value on having the spreadsheet program but little value on a word processing program. Brigitte and Charles have intermediate reservation prices. These reservation prices are negatively correlated: Customers with a relatively high reservation price for one product have a relatively low reservation price for the other program. To determine its best pricing strategy, the firm calculates its profit by pricing the components separately, using pure bundling, and engaging in mixed bundling.

If the firm prices each program separately, it maximizes its profit by charging 90 for each product and selling each to three out of the four potential customers. It sells the word processing program to Aaron, Brigitte, and Charles. It sells the spreadsheet program to Brigitte, Charles, and Dorothy. Thus, it makes $270 (= 3 \times 90)$ from each program or 540 total, which exceeds what it could earn by setting any other price per program.[12]

However, the firm can make a higher profit by engaging in pure bundling. It can charge 150 for the bundle, sell to all four consumers, and earn 600, 60 more than the 540 it makes from selling the programs separately.

With mixed bundling, the firm obtains an even larger profit. It charges 200 for the bundle and 120 for each product separately. The firm earns 400 from Brigitte and Charles, who buy the bundle. Aaron buys only the word processing program for 120, and Dorothy buys only the spreadsheet for another 120, so that the firm makes 240 from its individual program sales. Thus, its profit is $640 (= 400 + 240)$ from mixed bundling, which exceeds the 600 from pure bundling, and the 540 from individual sales. We could construct other examples with different numbers where selling the programs separately would dominate (such as where reservation prices are positively correlated as in Table 12.2) or where the pure bundle does best (as in Table 12.1).

12.7 Advertising

You can fool all the people all the time with a big enough advertising budget.

In addition to setting its price or quantity, a monopoly has to make other decisions, one of the most important of which is how much to advertise to maximize its net profit.[13] As we will show, the rule for setting the profit-maximizing amount of advertising is the same as that for setting the profit-maximizing amount of output: Set advertising or quantity where the marginal benefit (the extra gross profit from one more unit of advertising or the marginal revenue from one more unit of output) equals its marginal cost.

Advertising is only one way to promote a product. Other promotional activities include providing free samples and using sales agents. Some promotional tactics are

---

[12]If it sets a price of a program as low as 30, it sells both programs to all four customers, but makes only 240. If it charges 110 it sells each program to two customers and earns 440. If it charges 120, it makes a single sale of each program, so it earns 240.

[13]For example, Ford spends more on advertising, $4.1 billion in 2017, than anything except R&D (John D. Stoll, "Behind Ford's New Approach to Advertising," *Wall Street Journal*, May 21, 2018). The Japanese space startup, iSpace Technologies, raised $90 million to launch a spacecraft into lunar orbit so that it can offer a "projection mapping service" to advertise on the moon's surface (**www .slate.com/articles/health_and_science/science/2017/12/ispace_wants_to_advertise_on_the_moon_ is_that_legal.html**).

subtle. For example, grocery stores place sugary breakfast cereals on lower shelves so they are at a child's eye level.[14]

A successful advertising or promotional campaign shifts the monopoly's demand curve by changing consumers' tastes or informing consumers about new products. The monopoly may be able to change the tastes of some consumers by telling them that a famous athlete or performer uses the product. Children and teenagers are frequently the targets of such advertising. If the advertising convinces some consumers that they can't live without the product, the monopoly's demand curve may shift outward and become less elastic at the new equilibrium, at which the firm charges a higher price for its product.

If the firm informs potential consumers about a new use for the product, demand at each price increases. For example in 1927, a Heinz advertisement suggested that putting its baked beans on toast was a good way to eat beans for breakfast as well as dinner. By so doing, it created a British national dish and shifted the demand curve for its product to the right.

Deciding Whether to Advertise

I have always believed that writing advertisements is the second most profitable form of writing. The first, of course, is ransom notes . . . —Philip Dusenberry

Even if advertising succeeds in shifting demand, it may not pay for the firm to advertise. If advertising shifts demand outward or makes it less elastic, the firm's *gross profit*, ignoring the cost of advertising, must rise. The firm undertakes this advertising campaign, however, only if it expects its *net profit* (gross profit minus the cost of advertising) to increase.

If the monopoly does not advertise, it faces the demand curve D^1 in Figure 12.7. If it advertises, its demand curve shifts from D^1 to D^2.

The monopoly's marginal cost, MC, is constant and equals its average cost, AC. Before advertising, the monopoly chooses its output, Q_1, where its marginal cost hits its marginal revenue curve, MR^1, which corresponds to the demand curve, D^1. The profit-maximizing equilibrium is e_1, and the monopoly charges a price of p_1. The monopoly's profit, π_1, is a box whose height is the difference between the price and the average cost and whose length is the quantity, Q_1.

After its advertising campaign shifts its demand curve to D^2, the monopoly chooses a higher quantity, $Q_2 (> Q_1)$, where the MR^2 and MC curves intersect. In this new equilibrium, e_2, the monopoly charges p_2. Despite this higher price, the monopoly sells more units after advertising because of the outward shift of its demand curve.

Consequently, the monopoly's gross profit rises. Its new gross profit is the rectangle $\pi_1 + B$, where the height of the rectangle is the new price minus the average cost, and the length is the quantity, Q_2. Thus, the benefit, B, to the monopoly from advertising at this level is the increase in its gross profit. If its cost of advertising is less than B, its net profit rises, and it pays for the monopoly to advertise at this level rather than not to advertise at all.

---

[14]According to a survey of 27 supermarkets nationwide by the Center for Science in the Public Interest, the average position of 10 child-appealing brands (44% sugar) was on the next-to-bottom shelf, while the average position of 10 adult brands (10% sugar) was on the next-to-top shelf.

Figure 12.7 Advertising

If the monopoly does not advertise, its demand curve is D^1. At its actual level of advertising, its demand curve is D^2. Advertising increases the monopoly's gross profit (ignoring the cost of advertising) from π_1 to $\pi_2 = \pi_1 + B$. Thus, if the cost of advertising is less than the benefits from advertising, B, the monopoly's net profit (gross profit minus the cost of advertising) rises.

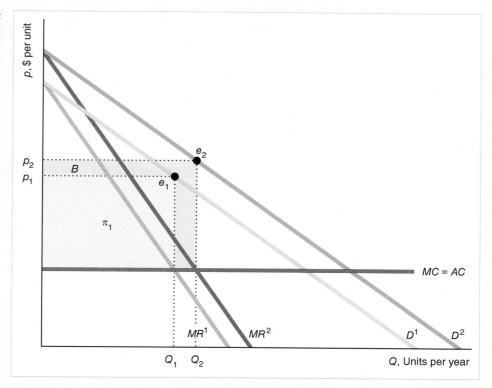

How Much to Advertise

The man who stops advertising to save money is like the man who stops the clock to save time.

In general, how much should a monopoly advertise to maximize its net profit? To answer this question, we consider what happens if the monopoly raises or lowers its advertising expenditures by $1, which is its marginal cost of an additional unit of advertising. If a monopoly spends an additional $1 on advertising and its gross profit rises by more than $1, its net profit rises, so the extra advertising pays. In contrast, the monopoly should reduce its advertising if the last dollar spent on advertising raises its gross profit by less than $1, causing its net profit to fall. Thus, the monopoly's level of advertising maximizes its net profit if the last dollar spent on advertising increases its gross profit by $1. In short, the rule for setting the profit-maximizing amount of advertising is the same as that for setting the profit-maximizing amount of output: Set advertising or quantity where the marginal benefit (the extra gross profit from one more unit of advertising or the marginal revenue from one more unit of output) equals its marginal cost.

Formally, to maximize its profit, a monopoly sets its quantity, Q, and level of advertising, A, to maximize its profit. Again, for simplicity, we assume that advertising affects only current sales, so that the inverse demand function the monopoly faces is $p = p(Q, A)$. That is, the price the monopoly charges to clear the market depends on how many units it sells and the amount of advertising. Consequently, the firm's revenue is $R = p(Q, A)Q = R(Q, A)$.

The firm's cost of production is $C(Q) + A$, where $C(Q)$ is the cost of manufacturing Q units and A is the cost of advertising because each unit of advertising costs $1 (by choosing the units of measurement appropriately).

The monopoly maximizes its profit through its choice of quantity and advertising:

$$\max_{Q,\,A} \pi = R(Q, A) - C(Q) - A. \qquad (12.10)$$

Its first-order conditions are found by differentiating the profit function in Equation 12.10 with respect to Q and A in turn:

$$\frac{\partial \pi(Q, A)}{\partial Q} = \frac{\partial R(Q, A)}{\partial Q} - \frac{dC(Q)}{dQ} = 0, \qquad (12.11)$$

$$\frac{\partial \pi(Q, A)}{\partial A} = \frac{\partial R(Q, A)}{\partial A} - 1 = 0. \qquad (12.12)$$

The profit-maximizing output and advertising levels are the Q^* and A^* that simultaneously satisfy Equations 12.11 and 12.12. Equation 12.11 says that output should be chosen so that the marginal revenue from one more unit of output, $\partial R/\partial Q$, equals the marginal cost, dC/dQ. According to Equation 12.12, the monopoly should advertise to the point where its marginal revenue or marginal benefit from the last unit of advertising, $\partial R/\partial A$, equals the marginal cost of the last unit of advertising, $1.

SOLVED PROBLEM 12.4

MyLab Economics Solved Problem

A monopoly's inverse demand function is $p = 800 - 4Q + 0.2A^{0.5}$. Its marginal cost of production is 2, and its marginal cost of a unit of advertising is 1. What are the firm's profit-maximizing price, quantity, and level of advertising?

Answer

1. *Write the firm's profit function using its inverse demand function.* The monopoly's profit is

$$\pi = (800 - 4Q + 0.2A^{0.5})Q - 2Q - A = 798Q - 4Q^2 + 0.2A^{0.5}Q - A.$$

2. *Set the partial derivatives of the profit function with respect to Q and A to zero to obtain the equations that determine the profit-maximizing levels, as in Equations 12.11 and 12.12.* The first-order conditions are

$$\frac{\partial \pi}{\partial Q} = 798 - 8Q + 0.2A^{0.5} = 0, \qquad (12.13)$$

$$\frac{\partial \pi}{\partial A} = 0.1A^{-0.5}Q - 1 = 0. \qquad (12.14)$$

3. *Solve this pair of equations in two unknowns, Q and A, for the profit-maximizing levels of Q and A.* Rearranging Equation 12.14, we find that $A^{0.5} = 0.1Q$. Substituting this expression into Equation 12.13, we learn that $798 - 8Q + 0.02Q = 0$, or $Q = 100$. Thus, $A^{0.5} = 0.1 \times 100 = 10$, so $A = 100$.

APPLICATION

Super Bowl
Commercials

Super Bowl commercials are the most expensive commercials on U.S. television. A 30-second spot during the Super Bowl averaged more than $5 million in 2018. A high price for these commercials is not surprising because the cost of commercials generally increases with the number of viewers (*eyeballs* in industry jargon), and the Super Bowl is the most widely watched show, with 103 million viewers in 2018. Super Bowl advertising costs 2.5 times as much per viewer as other TV commercials.

However, a Super Bowl commercial is much more likely to influence viewers than commercials on other shows. Not only is the Super Bowl a premier sports event, but it also showcases the most memorable commercials of the year, such as Apple's classic 1984 Macintosh ad, which is still discussed and rebroadcast annually. Indeed, many Super Bowl viewers are not even football fans—they watch to see these superior ads. Super Bowl commercials receive extra exposure because these ads often *go viral* on the internet.

Given that Super Bowl ads are more likely to be remembered by viewers, are these commercials worth the extra price? Obviously, many advertisers believe so, as their demand for these ads has bid up the price. Kim, Freling, and Grisaffe (2013) found that immediately after a Super Bowl commercial airs, the advertising firm's stock value rises. Thus, investors apparently believe that Super Bowl commercials raise a firm's profits despite the high cost of the commercial. Ho, Dhar, and Weinberg (2009) found that for the typical movie with a substantial advertising budget, a Super Bowl commercial advertising the movie raises theater revenues by more than the same expenditure on other television advertising. They also concluded that movie firms' advertising during the Super Bowl was at (or close to) the profit-maximizing amount.

**CHALLENGE
SOLUTION**

Sale Price

By putting Heinz ketchup on sale periodically, Kraft Heinz can price discriminate. To maximize its profit, how often should Heinz put its ketchup on sale? Under what conditions does it pay for Kraft Heinz to have sales? To answer these questions, we study a simplified market in which Heinz competes with one other ketchup brand, which we refer to as generic ketchup.[15] Every n days, the typical consumer buys either Heinz or generic ketchup. (The number of days between purchases is determined by the storage space in consumers' homes and how frequently they eat ketchup.)

Switchers are price sensitive and buy the least expensive ketchup. They pay attention to price information and always know when Heinz is on sale.

Heinz considers holding periodic sales to capture switchers' purchases. The generic is sold at a competitive price equal to its marginal cost of production of $2.01 per unit. Suppose that Heinz's marginal cost is $MC = \$1$ per unit (due to its large scale) and that, if it only sold to its loyal customers, it would charge a monopoly price of $p = \$3$. Heinz's managers face a trade-off. If Heinz is

---

[15]The rest of the U.S. market consists primarily of Hunt ketchup (15%) and generic or house brands (22%). In the following discussion, we assume that customers who are loyal to Hunt or generic ketchup are unaffected by a Heinz sale, and hence ignore them.

infrequently on sale for less than the generic price, Heinz sells little to switchers. On the other hand, if Heinz is frequently on sale, it loses money on its sales to loyal customers.

We start by supposing that Heinz pricing policy is to charge a low, sales price, $2, once every n days. For the other $n - 1$ days, Heinz sells at the regular, non-sale (monopoly) price of $3, which is the monopoly price given the demand curve of the loyal customers. During a sale, the switchers buy enough Heinz to last them for n days until it is on sale again. Consequently, the switchers never buy the generic product. (Some other customers are loyal to the generic, so they buy it even when Heinz is on sale.)

If the loyal customers find that Heinz is on sale, which happens $1/n$ of all days, they buy n days' worth at the sale price. Otherwise, they are willing to pay the regular price. If the other loyal customers were aware of this pattern and got on a schedule such that they always bought on sale too, this strategy would not be profit maximizing. However, their shopping schedules are determined independently: They buy many goods and are not willing to distort their shopping patterns solely to buy this one good on sale.[16]

Could Heinz make more money by altering its promotion pattern? It does not want to place its good on sale more frequently because it would earn less from its loyal customers without making more sales to switchers. If it pays to hold sales at all, it does not want to have a sale less frequently because it would sell fewer units to switchers. During a promotion, Heinz wants to charge the highest price it can and yet still attract switchers, which is $2. If it sets a lower price, the quantity sold is unchanged, so its profit falls. If Heinz sets a sale price higher than $2, it loses all switchers.

Does it pay for the firm to have sales? Whether it pays depends on the number of switchers, S, relative to the number of brand-loyal customers, B. If each customer buys one unit per day, then Heinz's profit per day if it sells only to loyals is $\pi = (p - MC)B = (3 - 1)B = 2B$, where $p = 3$ is Heinz's regular price and $MC = 1$ is its marginal and average cost. If Heinz uses the sale pricing scheme, its average profit per day is

$$\pi^* = 2B(n - 1)/n + (B + S)/n.$$

The first term is the profit it makes, $2 per unit, selling B units to loyal customers for the fraction of days that Heinz ketchup is not on sale, $(n - 1)/n$. The second term is the profit it makes, $1 per unit, selling $B + S$ units on the $1/n$ days that Heinz ketchup is on sale.

Thus, it pays to put Heinz on sale if $\pi < \pi^*$, or $2B < 2B(n - 1)/n +(B + S)/n$. Using algebra, we can simplify this expression to $B < S$. Thus, if the market has more switchers than loyal customers, the sales policy is more profitable than selling at a uniform price to only loyal customers.[17]

---

[16]We make this assumption for simplicity. In the real world, firms achieve a similar result by having random sales or by placing ads announcing sales where primarily switchers will see the ads.

[17]Hendel and Nevo (2013) examined the soft-drink market. They found that some price-sensitive consumers buy during sales and stockpile, while less price-sensitive consumers do not stockpile. As a result, sales capture 25–30% of the gap between the non-price-discriminating profit and the profit from (unattainable) price discrimination in which the seller can identify consumer types and prevent arbitrage.

SUMMARY

1. **Conditions for Price Discrimination.** A firm can price discriminate if it has market power, knows which customers will pay more for each unit of output, and can prevent customers who pay low prices from reselling to those who pay high prices. A firm earns a higher profit from price discrimination than from uniform pricing because (a) the firm captures some or all of the consumer surplus of customers who are willing to pay more than the uniform price and (b) the firm sells to some people who would not buy at the uniform price.

2. **Perfect Price Discrimination.** To perfectly price discriminate, a firm must know the maximum amount each customer is willing to pay for each unit of output. If a firm charges customers the maximum that each is willing to pay for each unit of output, the monopoly captures all potential consumer surplus and sells the efficient (competitive) level of output. Compared to competition, total welfare is the same, consumers are worse off, and firms are better off under perfect price discrimination.

3. **Group Price Discrimination.** A firm that does not have enough information to perfectly price discriminate may know the relative elasticities of demand of groups of its customers. Such a profit-maximizing firm charges groups of consumers prices in proportion to their elasticities of demand, the group of consumers with the least elastic demand paying the highest price. Welfare is less under group price discrimination than under competition or perfect price discrimination, but may be greater or less than that under single-price monopoly.

4. **Nonlinear Pricing.** Some firms charge customers different prices depending on how many units they purchase. If consumers who want more water have less elastic demands, a water utility can increase its profit by using declining-block pricing, in which the price for the first few gallons of water is higher than that for additional gallons.

5. **Two-Part Pricing.** By charging consumers one fee for the right to buy and a separate price per unit, firms may earn higher profits than if they charge only for each unit sold. If a firm knows its customers' demand curves, it can use two-part pricing (instead of perfect price discrimination) to capture the entire consumer surplus. Even if the firm does not know each customer's demand curve or cannot vary two-part pricing across customers, it can use two-part pricing to make a larger profit than it could get if it set a single price.

6. **Tie-In Sales.** A firm may increase its profit by using a tie-in sale that allows customers to buy one product only if they also purchase another product. In a requirement tie-in sale, customers who buy one good must make all of their purchases of another good or service from that firm. With bundling (a package tie-in sale), a firm sells only a bundle of two goods together. Prices differ across customers under both types of tie-in sales.

7. **Advertising.** A monopoly advertises or engages in other promotional activities to shift its demand curve to the right or to make it less elastic so as to raise its profit (taking account of its advertising expenses).

EXERCISES

All exercises are available on **MyLab Economics**; * = *answer appears at the back of this book;* **M** = *mathematical problem.*

1. Conditions for Price Discrimination

1.1 Many pharmaceutical companies provide low-income older people with a card guaranteeing them discounts on prescription medicines. As of 2018, such companies included GlaxoSmithKline, Merck, Pfizer, and Roche, along with many others. Why would these firms provide discount drug cards?

1.2 Alexx's monopoly currently sells its product at a single price. What are the necessary conditions so that he can profitably price discriminate?

*1.3 Spenser's Superior Stoves advertises a one-day sale on electric stoves. The ad specifies that the store will not accept phone orders and that the purchaser must transport the stove. Why does the firm include these restrictions?

*1.4 Many colleges provide students from low-income families with scholarships, subsidized loans, and other programs so that they pay lower tuitions than students from high-income families. Explain why universities behave this way.

1.5 Disneyland price discriminates by charging lower entry fees for children than for adults and for local residents than for other visitors. Why does it not have a resale problem? (*Hint*: See the Application "Disneyland Pricing.")

1.6 The 2002 production run of 25,000 new Thunderbirds included only 2,000 cars for Canada. Yet potential buyers besieged Canadian Ford dealers. Many hoped to make a quick profit by reselling the cars in the United States. Reselling was relatively easy, and shipping costs were comparatively low. When the Thunderbird with the optional hardtop first became available at the end of 2001, Canadians paid C$56,550 for the vehicle, while U.S. customers spent up to C$73,000 in the United States. Why? Why did Ford require Canadian dealers to sign an agreement that prohibited moving vehicles to the United States? (*Hint*: See the Application "Preventing Resale of Designer Bags.")

1.7 Hertz and other car rental companies charge much more for rentals of luxury cars such as Ferraris and Bentleys than for compact cars such as the Toyota Yaris or Chevrolet Sonic. Is this practice an example of price discrimination? Explain.

1.8 The European Commission charged six U.S. studios and a U.K. pay television company, Sky UK, with unfairly blocking access to films and other content. The charges challenge the studios' requirement under contracts that Sky UK block access for consumers outside Britain and Ireland. The studios have separate contracts with broadcasters in other countries. Why do the studios want such restrictions?

2. Perfect Price Discrimination

2.1 If a monopoly faces an inverse demand curve of $p = 90 - Q$, has a constant marginal and average cost of 30, and can perfectly price discriminate, what is its profit? What are the consumer surplus, welfare, and deadweight loss? How would these results change if the firm were a single-price monopoly? (*Hint*: See Solved Problem 12.1.) **M**

2.2 Using the information in the Application "Botox and Price Discrimination" and the Application "Botox Patent Monopoly" in Chapter 11, determine how much Allergan loses by being a single-price monopoly rather than a perfectly price-discriminating monopoly. Explain.

2.3 See the Application "Google Uses Bidding for Ads to Price Discriminate," which discusses how advertisers on Google's website bid for the right for their ads to be posted when people search for certain phrases. Should a firm that provides local services (such as plumbing or pest control) expect to pay more or less for an ad in a small town or a large city? Why?

2.4 To promote her platinum-selling CD *Feels Like Home* in 2005, singer Norah Jones toured the country giving live performances. However, she sold an average of only two-thirds of the tickets available for each show, T^* (Robert Levine, "The Trick of Making a Hot Ticket Pay," *New York Times*, June 6, 2005, C1, C4). Suppose that the local promoter is the monopoly provider of each concert. Each concert hall has a fixed number of seats.

a. Assume that the promoter's cost is independent of the number of people who attend the concert

(Ms. Jones received a guaranteed payment). Graph the promoter's marginal cost curve for the concert hall, where the number of tickets sold is on the horizontal axis. Be sure to show T^*.

b. If the monopoly can charge a single market price, does the concert's failure to sell out prove that the monopoly set too high a price? Explain.

c. Would your answer in part b be the same if the monopoly can perfectly price discriminate? Use a graph to explain.

2.5 A firm is a natural monopoly (see Chapter 11). Its marginal cost curve is flat, and its average cost curve is downward sloping (because it has a fixed cost). The firm can perfectly price discriminate. Use a graph to show how much the monopoly produces, Q^*. Show graphically and mathematically that a monopoly might shut down if it can only set a single price but operate if it can perfectly price discriminate. **M**

3. Group Price Discrimination

3.1 A monopoly has a marginal cost of zero and faces two groups of consumers. At first, the monopoly could not prevent resale, so it maximized its profit by charging everyone the same price, $p = \$5$. No one from the first group chose to purchase. Now the monopoly can prevent resale, so it decides to price discriminate. Will total output expand? Why or why not? What happens to profit and consumer surplus?

3.2 A firm charges different prices to two groups. Would the firm ever operate where it was suffering a loss from its sales to the low-price group? Explain.

3.3 A monopoly sells in two countries, and resale between the countries is impossible. The demand curves in the two countries are $p_1 = 100 - Q_1$ and $p_2 = 120 - 2Q_2$. The monopoly's marginal cost is $m = 30$. Solve for the equilibrium price in each country. (*Hint*: See Solved Problems 12.2 and 12.3.) **M**

3.4 Hershey Park sells tickets at the gate and at local municipal offices to two groups of people. Suppose that the demand function for people who purchase tickets at the gate is $Q_G = 10,000 - 100p_G$ and that the demand function for people who purchase tickets at municipal offices is $Q_G = 9,000 - 100p_G$. The marginal cost of each patron is 5.

a. If Hershey Park cannot successfully segment the two markets, what are the profit-maximizing price and quantity? What is its maximum possible profit?

b. If the people who purchase tickets at one location would never consider purchasing them at the other and Hershey Park can successfully price discriminate, what are the profit-maximizing price and quantity? What is its maximum possible profit? (*Hint*: See Solved Problem 12.2.) **M**

3.5 The estimated Tesla demand function for the S 100D car is $Q_A = 78 - 0.6p_A$ in the United States and $Q_E = 36.8 - 0.16p_E$ in Europe, as Figure 12.3 illustrates. Using that and other information from the Application "Tesla Price Discrimination," confirm that Tesla's profit-maximizing prices and quantities are those in Figure 12.3. **M**

*3.6 A patent gave Sony a legal monopoly to produce a robot dog called Aibo ("eye-BO"). The Chihuahua-sized robot could sit, beg, chase balls, dance, and play an electronic tune. When Sony started selling the toy in July 1999, it announced that it would sell 3,000 Aibo robots in Japan for about $2,000 each and a limited litter of 2,000 in the United States for about $2,500 each. Suppose that Sony's marginal cost of producing Aibos is $500. I estimate that its inverse demand curve was $p_J = 3,500 - \frac{1}{2}Q_J$ in Japan and $p_A = 4,500 - Q_A$ in the United States. Solve for the equilibrium prices and quantities (assuming that U.S. customers cannot buy robots from Japan). Show how the profit-maximizing price ratio depended on the elasticities of demand in the two countries. What are the deadweight losses in each country, and in which is the loss from monopoly pricing greater? (*Hint*: See Solved Problems 12.2 and 12.3.) **M**

*3.7 A monopoly sells its good in the U.S. and Japanese markets. The American inverse demand function is $p_A = 100 - Q_A$, and the Japanese inverse demand function is $p_J = 80 - 2Q_J$, where both prices, p_A and p_J, are measured in dollars. The firm's marginal cost of production is $m = 20$ in both countries. If the firm can prevent resale, what price will it charge in both markets? (*Hint*: The monopoly determines its optimal price in each country separately because customers cannot resell the good.) (*Hint*: See Solved Problems 12.2 and 12.3.) **M**

3.8 Universal Studios sold the *Mamma Mia!* DVD around the world. Universal charged $21.40 in Canada and $32 in Japan—more than the $20 it charged in the United States. Given that Universal had a constant marginal cost of $1, determine what the elasticities of demand must be in Canada and in Japan if Universal was profit maximizing. **M**

3.9 A copyright gives Warner Brothers the legal monopoly to produce and sell the *Harry Potter and the Deathly Hallows Part 2* DVD. Warner Brothers engaged in group price discrimination by charging different prices in the United States and the United Kingdom. Warner Brothers can ignore the problem of resale between the countries because the DVDs have incompatible formats. The DVD was released during the holiday season of 2011–2012 and sold $Q_A = 5.8$ million copies to American consumers at $p_A = 29 and $Q_B = 2.0$ million copies to British consumers at

$p_B = 39 (£25). Thus, Warner engaged in group price discrimination by charging different prices in various countries. We estimate that the inverse demand functions are $p_A = 57 - 4.8Q_A$ for the United States and $p_B = 77 - 19Q_B$ for the United Kingdom. Warner's constant marginal cost was $1 in both countries.

a. Solve for Warner's optimal prices and quantities in the two countries.

b. Illustrate in a figure similar to Figure 12.3.

c. Show that the ratio of the U.S. and U.K. prices is consistent with Equation 12.9. **M**

*3.10 Warner Home Entertainment sold the *Harry Potter and the Prisoner of Azkaban* two-DVD movie set in China for about $3, which was only one-fifth the U.S. price, and sold about 100,000 units. The price was extremely low in China because Chinese consumers are less wealthy and because (lower-quality) pirated versions were available in China for 72¢–$1.20, compared to the roughly $3 required to purchase the legal version. Assuming a marginal cost of $1, what is the Chinese elasticity of demand? Derive the demand function for China and illustrate Warner's policy in China using a figure similar to those in Figure 12.3. **M**

3.11 A monopoly sells its good in the United States, where the elasticity of demand is -2, and in Japan, where the elasticity of demand is -5. Its marginal cost is 10. At what price does the monopoly sell its good in each country if resale is impossible? **M**

3.12 How would the analysis in Solved Problem 12.2 change if $m = 70$ or if $m = 40$? (*Hint*: Where $m = 40$, the marginal cost curve crosses the *MR* curve three times—if we include the vertical section. The single-price monopoly will choose one of these three points where its profit is maximized.)

*3.13 A monopoly sells to n_1 consumers in Country 1 and n_2 in Country 2, where each person in Country 1 has a constant elasticity demand function of $q_1 = p^{\varepsilon_1}$ and every person in Country 2 has a demand function of $q_2 = p^{\varepsilon_2}$. Thus, the country demand functions are $Q_1 = n_1 p^{\varepsilon_1}$ and $Q_2 = n_2 p^{\varepsilon_2}$. The monopoly manufactures the output at constant marginal cost m. What prices does the monopoly charge in the two countries if it can group price discriminate? If the monopoly cannot price discriminate, what price does it charge?

3.14 Show that the equilibrium elasticities in the two countries must be equal in Solved Problem 12.3. **M**

3.15 According to a report from the Foundation for Taxpayer and Consumer Rights, gasoline costs twice as much in Europe as in the United States because taxes are higher in Europe. However, the amount per gallon net of taxes that U.S. consumers pay is higher than that paid by Europeans. The report concludes that "U.S. motorists are essentially subsidizing European drivers, who pay more for taxes but substantially less into oil company profits" (Tom Doggett, "US Drivers Subsidize European Pump Prices," Reuters, August 31, 2006). Given that oil companies have market power and can price discriminate across countries, is it reasonable to conclude that U.S. consumers are subsidizing Europeans? Explain your answer.

3.16 Does a monopoly's ability to price discriminate between two groups of consumers depend on its marginal cost curve? Why or why not? [Consider two cases: (a) The marginal cost is so high that the monopoly is uninterested in selling to one group; (b) the marginal cost is low enough that the monopoly wants to sell to both groups.]

4. Nonlinear Price Discrimination

4.1 Are all the customers of the monopoly that uses block pricing in panel a of Figure 12.4 worse off than they would be if the firm set a single price (panel b)? Why or why not?

4.2 In panel b of Figure 12.4, the single-price monopoly faces a demand curve of $p = 90 - Q$ and a constant marginal (and average) cost of $m = \$30$. Find the profit-maximizing quantity (or price) using math. Determine the profit, consumer surplus, welfare, and deadweight loss. **M**

4.3 Suppose that the nonlinear price-discriminating monopoly in panel a of Figure 12.4 can set three prices, depending on the quantity a consumer purchases. The firm's profit is

$$\pi = p_1 Q_1 + p_2(Q_2 - Q_1) + p_3(Q_3 - Q_2) - mQ_3,$$

where p_1 is the high price charged on the first Q_1 units (first block), p_2 is a lower price charged on the next $Q_2 - Q_1$ units, p_3 is the lowest price charged on the $Q_3 - Q_2$ remaining units, Q_3 is the total number of units actually purchased, and $m = \$30$ is the firm's constant marginal and average cost. Use calculus to determine the profit-maximizing $p_1, p_2,$ and p_3. **M**

4.4 Consider the nonlinear price discrimination analysis in panel a of Figure 12.4.

a. Suppose that the monopoly can make consumers a take-it-or-leave-it offer. The monopoly sets a price, p^*, and a minimum quantity, Q^*, that a consumer must pay to be able to purchase any units at all. What price and minimum quantity should it set to achieve the same outcome as it would if it perfectly price discriminated?

b. Now suppose that the monopoly charges a price of $90 for the first 30 units and a price of $30 for subsequent units, but requires that a consumer buy at least 30 units to be allowed to buy any units. Compare this outcome to the one in part a and to the perfectly price-discriminating outcome. **M**

5. Two-Part Pricing

5.1 Using math, show why two-part pricing causes customers who purchase few units to pay more per unit than customers who buy more units. **M**

5.2 Knoebels Amusement Park in Elysburg, Pennsylvania, charges an access fee, $\mathscr{L}$, to enter its Crystal Pool. It also charges p per trip down the pool's water slides. Suppose that 400 teenagers visit the park, each of whom has a demand function of $q_1 = 5 - p$. In addition, 400 seniors visit, each of whom has a demand function of $q_2 = 4 - p$. Knoebels' objective is to set $\mathscr{L}$ and p so as to maximize its profit given that it has no (non-sunk) cost and must charge both groups the same prices. What are the optimal $\mathscr{L}$ and p? **M**

5.3 Joe has just moved to a small town with only one golf course, the Northlands Golf Club. His inverse demand function is $p = 120 - 2q$, where q is the number of rounds of golf that he plays per year. The manager of the Northlands Club negotiates separately with each person who joins the club and can therefore charge individual prices. This manager has a good idea of what Joe's demand curve is and offers Joe a special deal, where Joe pays an annual membership fee and can play as many rounds as he wants at $20, which is the marginal cost his round imposes on the club. What membership fee would maximize profit for the club? The manager could have charged Joe a single price per round. How much extra profit does the club earn by using two-part pricing? **M**

5.4 Joe in Question 5.3 marries Susan, who is also an enthusiastic golfer. Susan wants to join the Northlands Club. The manager believes that Susan's inverse demand curve is $p = 100 - 2q$. The manager has a policy of offering each member of a married couple the same two-part prices, so he offers them both a new deal. What two-part pricing deal maximizes the club's profit? Will this new pricing have a higher or lower access fee and per-unit fee than in Joe's original deal? How much more would the club make if it charges Susan and Joe separate prices? **M**

5.5 As described in the Application "Pricing iTunes," Shiller and Waldfogel (2011) estimated that if iTunes used two-part pricing charging an annual access fee and a low price per song, it would raise its profit by about 30% relative to what it would earn using uniform pricing or variable pricing. Assume that iTunes uses two-part pricing and assume that the marginal cost of an additional download is zero. How should iTunes set its profit-maximizing price per song if all consumers are identical? Illustrate profit-maximizing two-part pricing in a diagram for the identical consumer case. Explain why the actual profit-maximizing price per song is positive.

5.6 Explain why charging a higher or lower price than $p = 10$ reduces the monopoly's profit in Figure 12.5. Show the monopoly's profit if $p = 20$ and compare it to its profit if $p = 10$.

6. Tie-In Sales

6.1 A monopoly sells two products, of which consumers want only one. Assuming that it can prevent resale, can the monopoly increase its profit by bundling them, forcing consumers to buy both goods? Explain.

6.2 A computer hardware firm sells both laptop computers and printers. Through the magic of focus groups, their pricing team determines that they have an equal number of three types of customers, and that these customers' reservation prices are

	Laptop	Printer	Bundle
Customer A	$800	$100	$900
Customer B	$1,000	$50	$1,050
Customer C	$600	$150	$750

a. If the firm were to charge only individual prices (not use the bundle price), what prices should it set for its laptops and printers to maximize profit? Assuming for simplicity that the firm has only one customer of each type, how much does it earn in total?

b. An outside consultant claims that the company could make more money from its customers if it sold laptops and printers together as a bundle instead of separately. Is the consultant right? Assuming again that the firm has one customer of each type, how much does the firm earn in total from pure bundling?

c. Why does bundling pay or not pay?

6.3 The publisher Elsevier uses mixed-bundling pricing strategy. The publisher sells a university access to a bundle of 930 of its journals for $1.7 million for one year. It also offers the journals separately at individual prices. Because Elsevier offers the journals online (with password access), universities can track how often their students and faculty access journals and then cancel those journals that they seldom read. Suppose that a publisher offers a university only three journals—A, B, and C—at the unbundled, individual annual subscription prices of $p_A = \$1,600$, $p_B = \$800$, and $p_C = \$1,500$. Suppose a university's willingness to pay for each of the journals is $v_A = \$2,000$, $v_B = \$1,100$, and $v_C = \$1,400$.

a. If the publisher offers the journals only at the individual subscription prices, to which journals does the university subscribe?

b. Given these individual prices, what is the highest price that the university is willing to pay for the three journals bundled together?

c. Now suppose that the publisher offers the same deal to a second university with willingness to pay $v_A = \$1,800$, $v_B = \$100$, and $v_C = \$2,100$. With the two universities, calculate the revenue-maximizing individual and bundle prices. **M**

6.4 Why do Honda service departments emphasize to customers the importance of using "genuine Honda parts" when servicing and tuning Honda cars and motorcycles? Is Honda likely to be as successful as Hewlett-Packard in the Application "Ties That Bind"?

7. Advertising

7.1 Show how a monopoly would solve for its optimal price and advertising level if it sets price instead of quantity. **M**

7.2 The demand a monopoly faces is

$$p = 100 - Q + A^{0.5},$$

where Q is its quantity, p is its price, and A is its level of advertising. Its marginal cost of production is 10, and its cost of a unit of advertising is 1. What is the firm's profit equation? Solve for the firm's profit-maximizing price, quantity, and level of advertising. (*Hint*: See Solved Problem 12.4.) **M**

7.3 What is the monopoly's profit-maximizing output, Q, and level of advertising, A, if it faces a demand curve of $p = a - bQ + cA^\alpha$, its constant marginal cost of producing output is m, and the cost of a unit of advertising is 1? (*Hint*: See Solved Problem 12.4.) **M**

7.4 For every dollar spent on advertising pharmaceuticals, revenue increases by about $4.20 (CNN, December 17, 2004). If this number is accurate and the firms are operating rationally, what (if anything) can we infer about marginal production and distribution costs? **M**

7.5 Use a diagram similar to Figure 12.7 to illustrate the effect of social media on the demand for Super Bowl commercials. (*Hint*: See the Application "Super Bowl Commercials.")

8. Challenge

8.1 Each week, a department store places a different item of clothing on sale. Give an explanation based on price discrimination for why the store conducts such regular sales.

8.2 In the Challenge Solution, did the sales method achieve the same group-price-discrimination outcome that Heinz would achieve if it could set separate prices for loyal customers and for switchers? Why or why not?

13

Game Theory

A camper awakens to the growl of a hungry bear and sees his friend putting on a pair of running shoes. "You can't outrun a bear," scoffs the camper. His friend coolly replies, "I don't have to. I only have to outrun you!"

Intel and Advanced Micro Devices (AMD) dominate the central processing unit (CPU) market for personal computers, with over 99% of total sales and the graphic chips market with 82% of total sales in 2018. Intel uses aggressive advertising—its very successful *Intel Inside* campaign—and charges relatively high prices, while AMD traditionally used little advertising and relied on the appeal of its lower prices. Intel controls more than 78% of the processor market and 67% of the graphic chip market.

According to Salgado's (2008) estimated demand functions, consumers were willing to pay a large premium for the Intel brand for processors. He found that, if Intel increased its advertising by 10% (holding prices constant), the total market demand would increase by 1%, while Intel's relative share would rise by more than 3%. Demand for AMD products would therefore fall. Salgado's work indicates that the two firms' shares would be roughly equal if they advertised equally (regardless of the level).

From the start of the personal computer era, Intel has been the 800-pound gorilla in the CPU market. Intel created the first commercial microprocessor chip in 1971. In 1991, Intel launched the Intel Inside® marketing and branding campaign. Intel offered to share costs for any manufacturer's PC print ads if they included the Intel logo. Not only did these funds reduce the computer manufacturers' costs, but also the logo assured consumers that their computers were powered by the latest technology. Within six months, 300 computer manufacturers had agreed to support the campaign. After the manufacturers' ads started to appear, Intel advertised globally to explain the significance of the logo to consumers. The Intel Inside campaign was one of the first successful attempts at *ingredient branding*.

Advanced Micro Devices (AMD) entered the microchip market in 1975, when it started selling a reverse-engineered clone of the Intel 8080 microprocessor. In 1982, AMD and Intel signed a contract allowing AMD to be a licensed second-source manufacturer of Intel's 8086 and 8088 processors because IBM would use these chips in its PCs only if it had two microchip sources.

Why does Intel advertise aggressively while AMD engages in relatively little advertising? At the end of the chapter, we discuss a possible explanation: Intel was able to act first and thereby gain an advantage. (In contrast, in Solved Problem 13.1, we examine the possible outcomes if both firms had acted simultaneously.)

In deciding how to price its products or how much to advertise, Procter and Gamble considers the pricing and advertising of its main rivals, Johnson and Johnson and Unilever. In such markets with a small number of firms, called an *oligopoly*, the firms know that their actions significantly affect each other's profit, so their actions depend on how they think their rivals will act. To understand how such oligopolistic firms interact, we employ **game theory**: a set of tools used by economists and others to analyze strategic decision making.

Game theory has many practical applications. Economists use it to study how oligopolistic firms set prices, quantities, and advertising levels; bargaining between unions and management or between the buyer and seller of a car or a home; interactions between polluters and those harmed by pollution; negotiations between parties with different amounts of information (such as between car owners and auto mechanics); bidding in auctions; and for many other economic interactions. Game theory is used by political scientists and military planners for avoiding or fighting wars, by biologists for analyzing evolutionary biology and ecology, and by philosophers, computer scientists, and many others.

In this chapter, we concentrate on how oligopolistic firms behave within a *game*. A **game** is an interaction between players (such as individuals or firms) in which players use strategies. A **strategy** is a battle plan that specifies the *actions* or *moves* that a player will make conditional on the information available at each move and for any possible contingency. For example, a firm may use a simple business strategy where it produces 100 units of output regardless of what a rival does. In such a case, the strategy consists of a single action—producing 100 units of output. However, a strategy can consist of a combination of actions or moves, possibly contingent on what a rival does. For example, a firm might decide to produce a small quantity as long as its rival produced a small amount in the previous period, and a large quantity otherwise.

Payoffs are the benefits received by players from a game's outcome, such as profits for firms or incomes or utilities for individuals. A *payoff function* specifies each player's payoff as a function of the strategies chosen by all players. We normally assume that players seek to maximize their payoffs. In essence, this assumption simply defines what we mean by payoffs. Payoffs include all relevant benefits experienced by the players. Therefore, rational players should try to obtain the highest payoffs they can.

The **rules of the game** include the *timing* of players' moves (such as whether one player moves first), the various actions that are possible at a particular point in the game, and possibly other specific aspects of how the game is played. A full description of a game normally includes a statement of the players, the rules of the game (including the possible actions or strategies), and the payoff function, along with a statement regarding the information available to the players.

We start by examining how firms interact strategically in a single period, and then turn to strategic interactions in games that last for more than one period. The single-period game is called a **static game**, in which each player acts only once and the players act simultaneously (or, at least, each player acts without knowing its rivals' actions). For example, each of two rival firms might make simultaneous one-time-only decisions about where to locate its new factory.

In a **dynamic game**, players move either repeatedly or sequentially. Therefore, dynamic games may be repeated games or sequential games. In a *repeated game*, a basic component game or *constituent game* is repeated, perhaps many times. Firms choose from the same set of possible actions again and again. In a *sequential game*, one player moves before another moves, possibly making alternating moves, as in chess or tic-tac-toe. A game is also sequential if players have a sequence of different decisions to make, even if moves are made simultaneously with a rival. For example, two firms might play a game in which they initially simultaneously choose how much capital to invest and then later simultaneously decide how much output to produce.

To analyze a game, we must know how much information participants have. We start by assuming that the relevant information is *common knowledge* to the players and then we relax that assumption. **Common knowledge** is a piece of information known by all players, and it is known by all players to be known by all players, and it is known to be known to be known, and so forth. In particular, we initially assume that players have **complete information**, a situation in which the strategies and payoffs of the game are *common knowledge*.

The information possessed by firms affects the outcome of a game. The outcome of a game in which a particular piece of information is known by all firms may differ from the outcome when some firms are uninformed. A firm may suffer a worse outcome if it does not know the potential payoffs of other firms.

In this chapter, we examine five main topics

1. **Static Games.** A static game is played once by players who act simultaneously and, hence, at the time they make a decision, do not know how other players will act.

2. **Repeated Dynamic Games.** If a static game is repeated over many periods, firms may use more complex strategies than in the static one-period game because a firm's action in one period may affect its rivals' actions in subsequent periods.

3. **Sequential Dynamic Games.** If one firm acts before its rival, it may gain an advantage by converting what would be an empty threat to its rival into a credible, observable action.

4. **Auctions.** An auction is a game where bidders have incomplete information about the value that other bidders place on the auctioned good or service.

5. **Behavioral Game Theory.** Some people make biased decisions based on psychological factors rather than using a rational strategy.

13.1 Static Games

We begin by examining static games, in which the players choose their actions simultaneously, have complete information about the possible strategies and payoff functions, and play the game once. Our example is a simplified version of the real-world competition between United Airlines and American Airlines on the Los Angeles–Chicago route (based on the estimates of Brander and Zhang, 1990), where we allow the firms to choose only one of two possible quantities.

The game has the following characteristics. The two *players* or firms are United and American. They play a *static game*—they compete only once. The *rules* of the game specify the possible actions or strategies that the firms can take and when they can take them. Each firm has only two possible *actions*: Each can fly either 48 thousand or 64 thousand passengers per quarter between Chicago and Los Angeles.[1] Other than announcing their output levels, the firms cannot communicate, so they cannot make side deals or otherwise coordinate their actions. Each firm's *strategy* is to take one of the two actions, choosing either a low output (48 thousand passengers per quarter) or a high output (64 thousand). The firms announce their actions or strategies *simultaneously*.

The firms have *complete information*: They are aware of the possible strategies and the corresponding payoff (profit) to each firm. However, their information is imperfect in one important respect. Because they choose their output levels simultaneously, neither airline knows what action its rival will take when it makes its output decision.

---

[1]We relax this assumption in Chapter 14 where we allow the firms to choose any output level, and call that game the Cournot game.

Normal-Form Games

[W]hen you have eliminated the impossible, whatever remains, however improbable, must be the truth. —Sherlock Holmes (Sir Arthur Conan Doyle)

We examine a **normal-form** representation of a static game of complete information, which specifies the players in the game, their possible strategies, and the payoff function that specifies the players' payoffs for each combination of strategies. The normal-form representation of this static game is the *payoff matrix (profit matrix)* in Table 13.1.

This payoff matrix shows the profits for each of the four possible combinations of the strategies that the firms may choose. For example, if American chooses a large quantity, $q_A = 64$ units per quarter, and United chooses a small quantity, $q_U = 48$ units per quarter, the firms' profits are in the cell in the lower-left corner of the profit matrix. That cell shows that American's profit is 5.1 ($5.1 million) per quarter in the upper-right corner, and United's profit is 3.8 ($3.8 million) per quarter in the lower-left corner. We now have a full description of the game, including a statement of the players, the rules, a list of the allowable actions or strategies, the payoffs, and the available information.

Because the firms choose their strategies simultaneously, each firm selects a strategy that maximizes its profit *given what it believes the other firm will do*. The firms are playing a *noncooperative game of imperfect information* in which each firm must choose an action before observing the simultaneous action of its rival. Thus, while the players have complete information about all players' strategies and payoffs, they have imperfect information about how the other will act.

We can predict the outcome of some games by using the insight that rational players will avoid strategies that are *dominated* by other strategies. First, we show that in some games we can predict a game's outcome if each firm has a single best strategy that dominates all others. Then, we show that in other games, by sequentially eliminating dominated strategies, we are left with a single outcome. Finally, we note that the outcome of a broader class of games can be precisely predicted based on each player's choosing a *best response* to the other players' actions—the response that produces the largest possible payoff.

Dominant Strategies. We can precisely predict the outcome of any game in which every player has a **dominant strategy**: a strategy that produces a higher payoff than any other strategy the player can use for every possible combination of its rivals' strategies. When a firm has a dominant strategy, a firm could have no belief about

Table 13.1 Dominant Strategies in a Quantity Setting, Prisoners' Dilemma Game

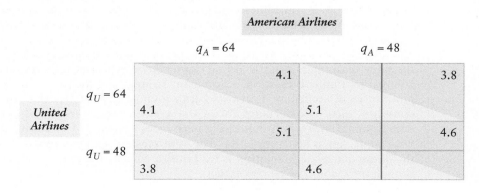

Note: Quantities are in thousands of passengers per quarter; (rounded) profits are in millions of dollars per quarter.

its rivals' choice of strategies that would cause it to choose one of its other, strictly *dominated strategies*.

Although firms do not always have dominant strategies, they have them in our airline game. American can determine its dominant strategy using the following reasoning:

- *If United chooses the high-output strategy ($q_U = 64$), American's high-output strategy maximizes its profit*: Given United's strategy, American's profit is 4.1 ($4.1 million) with its high-output strategy ($q_A = 64$) and only 3.8 with its low-output strategy ($q_A = 48$). Thus, American is better off using a high-output strategy if United chooses its high-output strategy.
- *If United chooses the low-output strategy ($q_U = 48$), American's high-output strategy maximizes its profit*: Given United's strategy, American's profit is 5.1 with its high-output strategy and only 4.6 with its low-output strategy.
- *Thus, the high-output strategy is American's dominant strategy*: Whichever strategy United uses, American's profit is higher if it uses its high-output strategy. We show that American won't use its low-output strategy (because that strategy is dominated by the high-output strategy) by drawing a vertical, dark red line through American's low-output cell in Table 13.1.

By the same type of reasoning, United's high-output strategy is also a dominant strategy. We draw a horizontal, light red line through United's low-output strategy. Because the high-output strategy is a dominant strategy for both firms, we can predict that the outcome of this game is the pair of high-output strategies, $q_A = q_U = 64$.

This game has a surprising feature that is inconsistent with most people's intuition:

Common Confusion   Rival firms always choose a set of strategies that benefits all of them.

A striking feature of this game is that the players choose strategies that do not maximize their joint profit. Each firm would earn 4.6 if $q_A = q_U = 48$ rather than the 4.1 they actually earn by setting $q_A = q_U = 64$. In this type of game—called a **prisoners' dilemma** game—all players have dominant strategies that lead to a profit (or another payoff) that is inferior to what they could achieve if they cooperated and pursued alternative strategies.

The prisoners' dilemma takes its name from a classic cops-and-robbers example. The police arrest Larry and Duncan and put them in separate rooms so that they cannot talk to each other. An assistant district attorney (DA) tells Larry, "We have enough evidence to convict you both of a minor crime for which you will each serve a year in prison. If you confess and give evidence against your partner while he stays silent, we can convict him of a major crime for which he will serve five years and you will go free. If you both confess, you will each get two years."

Meanwhile, another assistant DA is proposing an identical offer to Duncan. By the same reasoning as in the airline example, we expect both Larry and Duncan to confess because confessing is a dominant strategy for each of them. From Larry's point of view, confessing is always better no matter what Duncan does. If Duncan confesses, then by confessing also, Larry gets two years instead of five. If Duncan does not confess, then by confessing Larry goes free instead of serving a year. Either way, confessing is better for Larry. The same reasoning applies to Duncan. Therefore, the dominant strategy solution is for both to confess and get two years in jail, even though they would be better off, getting just one year in jail, if they both kept quiet.

Best Response and Nash Equilibrium.   Many games do not have a dominant strategy solution. For these games, we use a more general approach. For any given set of strategies chosen by rivals, a player wants to use its **best response**: the strategy that maximizes a player's payoff given its beliefs about its rivals' strategies.

A dominant strategy is a strategy that is a best response to *all possible* strategies that a rival might use. Thus, a dominant strategy is a best response. However, even if a dominant strategy does not exist, each firm can determine its best response to *any possible* strategies chosen by its rivals.

The idea that players use best responses is the basis for the Nash equilibrium, a solution concept for games formally introduced by John Nash (1951). A set of strategies is a **Nash equilibrium** if, when all other players use these strategies, no player can obtain a higher payoff by choosing a different strategy. An appealing property of the Nash equilibrium is that it is self-enforcing: If each player uses a Nash equilibrium strategy, then no player would want to deviate by choosing another strategy. In other words, no player regrets its strategy choice when it learns the strategies chosen by the other players. Each player says "given the strategies chosen by my rivals, my strategy was my best response."

The Nash equilibrium is the primary solution concept used by economists in analyzing games. It allows us to find solutions to more games than just those with a dominant strategy solution. If a game has a dominant strategy solution then that solution must also be a Nash equilibrium. However, many games that do not have dominant strategy solutions have a Nash equilibrium.

To illustrate these points, we examine a more complex simultaneous-move game in which American and United can produce an output of 96, 64, or 48 (thousand passengers per quarter). This game has nine possible output combinations, as the 3×3 profit matrix in Table 13.2 shows. Neither American nor United has a single, dominant strategy, but we can find a Nash equilibrium by using a two-step procedure. First, we determine each firm's best response to any given strategy of the other firm. Second, we determine if any pairs of strategies (a cell in the profit table) are best responses for both firms, so that the strategies in this cell are a Nash equilibrium.

We start by determining American's best response for each of United's possible actions. If United chooses $q_U = 96$ (thousand passengers per quarter), the first row of the table, then American's profit is 0 if it sets $q_A = 96$ (the first column), 2.0 if it chooses $q_A = 64$ (the second column), and 2.3 if it selects $q_A = 48$ (the third column). Thus, American's best response if United sets $q_U = 96$ is to select $q_A = 48$. We indicate American's best response by coloring the upper triangle in the last (third column) cell in this row dark green. Similarly, if United sets $q_U = 64$ (second row),

Table 13.2 Best Responses in a Quantity Setting, Prisoners' Dilemma Game

		American Airlines		
		$q_A = 96$	$q_A = 64$	$q_A = 48$
United Airlines	$q_U = 96$	0 / 0	2.0 / 3.1	2.3 / 4.6
	$q_U = 64$	3.1 / 2.0	4.1 / 4.1	3.8 / 5.1
	$q_U = 48$	4.6 / 2.3	5.1 / 3.8	4.6 / 4.6

Note: Quantities are in thousands of passengers per quarter; (rounded) profits are in millions of dollars per quarter.

American's best response is to set $q_A = 64$, where it earns 4.1, so we color the upper triangle in the middle cell (second column) of the second row dark green. Finally, if United sets $q_U = 48$ (third row), American's best response is $q_A = 64$, where it earns 5.1, so we color the upper triangle in the middle cell of the third row dark green.

We can use the same type of reasoning to determine United's best responses to each of American's strategies. If American chooses $q_A = 96$ (first column), then United's best response is $q_U = 48$ where its profit is 2.3, which we indicate by coloring the lower triangle light green in the lower left cell of the table. Similarly, we show that United's best response is $q_U = 64$, if American sets $q_A = 64$ or 48, which we show by coloring the relevant lower left triangles light green.

We now look for a Nash equilibrium, which is a pair of strategies where both firms are using a best-response strategy so that neither firm would want to change its strategy. This game has only one cell in which both the upper and lower triangles are green: $q_A = q_U = 64$. Given that its rival uses this strategy, neither firm wants to deviate from using this strategy. For example, if United continued to set $q_U = 64$, but American raised its quantity to 96, American's profit would fall from 4.1 to 3.1. Or, if American lowered its quantity to 48, its profit would fall to 3.8. Thus, American does not want to change its strategy.

Because no other cell has a pair of strategies that are best responses (green lower and upper triangles), at least one of the firms would want to change its strategy in each of these other cells. For example, at $q_A = q_U = 48$, either firm could raise its profit from 4.6 to 5.1 million by increasing its output to 64. At $q_A = 48$ and $q_U = 64$, American can raise its profit from 3.8 to 4.1 million by increasing its quantity to $q_A = 64$. Similarly, United would want to increase its output when $q_A = 64$ and $q_U = 48$. None of the other strategy combinations is a Nash equilibrium because at least one firm would want to deviate. Thus, we can find the single Nash equilibrium to this game by determining each firm's best responses.[2]

Failure to Maximize Joint Profits

The dominant-strategy analysis in Table 13.1 and the best-response analysis in Table 13.2 show that noncooperative firms may not reach the joint-profit-maximizing outcome. Whether players achieve the outcome that maximizes joint profit depends on the profit matrix.

We illustrate this idea using an advertising example.

Common Confusion If firms in a market decide to advertise, doing so raises their profits.

We'll show that, for some profit matrices, all the firms would benefit if they could agree not to advertise.

Table 13.3 shows an advertising game in which each firm can choose to advertise or not, with two possible profit matrices. In the Nash equilibrium, collective profit is not maximized in the first game but is maximized in the second game.

In the game in panel a, a firm's advertising does not bring new customers into the market but only has the effect of stealing business from the rival firm. Because each firm must decide whether or not to advertise at the same time, neither firm knows the strategy of its rival when it chooses its strategy.

---

[2]In these airline examples, we have assumed that the firms can only pick between a small number of output levels. However, in Chapter 14, we use game theory to find the Nash equilibrium in games in which the firms can choose any output level.

Table 13.3 Advertising Games: Prisoners' Dilemma or Joint-Profit-Maximizing Outcome?

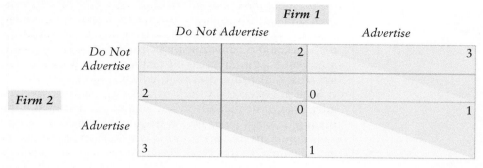

(a) Advertising Only Takes Customers from Rivals

		Firm 1	
		Do Not Advertise	Advertise
Firm 2	Do Not Advertise	2 / 2	3 / 0
	Advertise	0 / 3	1 / 1

(b) Advertising Attracts New Customers to the Market

		Firm 1	
		Do Not Advertise	Advertise
Firm 2	Do Not Advertise	2 / 2	4 / 3
	Advertise	3 / 4	5 / 5

If neither firm advertises, then each firm makes a profit of 2 (say, $2 million), as the upper-left cell of the profit matrix in panel a shows. If Firm 1 advertises but Firm 2 does not, then Firm 1 takes business from Firm 2 and raises its profit to 3, while the profit of Firm 2 is reduced to 0. The gain to Firm 1 is less than the loss to Firm 2 because the revenue that is transferred from Firm 2 to Firm 1 as customers shift is partially offset by the cost of Firm 2's advertising. If both firms advertise, then each firm gets a profit of 1, as the cell on the lower right shows.

Advertising is a dominant strategy for both firms.[3] We use red lines to show that the firms do not use the dominated do-not-advertise strategies. The outcome in which both firms advertise is therefore a dominant strategy solution. Advertising for both firms is also a Nash equilibrium because each firm is choosing its best response to the other firm's strategy.

In this Nash equilibrium, each firm earns 1, which is less than the 2 it would make if neither firm advertised. Thus, *the sum of the firms' profits is not maximized in this simultaneous-choice one-period game.*

---

[3]Firm 1 goes through the following reasoning. "If my rival does not advertise, I get 2 if I do not advertise and I get 3 if I do advertise, so advertising is better. If my rival does advertise, I get 0 if I do not advertise and I get 1 if I do advertise, so advertising is still better." Regardless of what Firm 2 does, advertising is better for Firm 1, so advertising is a dominant strategy for Firm 1 (and not advertising is a dominated strategy). Firm 2 faces a symmetric problem and would also conclude that advertising is a dominant strategy.

Many people are surprised when they see this result. Why don't the firms cooperate, refrain from advertising, and earn 2 instead of 1? This game is an example of a prisoners' dilemma: The game has a dominant strategy solution in which the players receive lower profits than they would get if the firms could cooperate. Each firm makes more money by advertising regardless of the strategy used by the other firm, even though their joint profit is maximized if neither advertises.

In the advertising game in panel b, advertising by a firm brings new customers to the market and consequently helps both firms. That is, each firm's advertising has a market expansion effect. If neither firm advertises, both earn 2. If only one firm advertises, its profit rises to 4, which is more than the 3 that the other firm makes. If both advertise, they each earn 5 and are collectively better off than if only one advertises or neither advertises. Again, advertising is a dominant strategy for a firm because it earns more by advertising regardless of the strategy the other firm uses. This dominant strategy solution is a Nash equilibrium, but this game is not a prisoners' dilemma. In this Nash equilibrium, the firms' combined profits are maximized, which is the same outcome that would arise if the firms could cooperate. Thus, whether the Nash equilibrium maximizes the combined profit for the players depends on the properties of the game that are summarized in the profit matrix.

APPLICATION

Strategic Advertising

Firms with market power, such as oligopolies, often advertise.[4] Comcast Corporation, which provides cable television, internet, and telephone services, spent $5.7 billion on U.S. advertising in 2017, the most of any corporation. The next largest U.S. advertisers were Procter & Gamble ($4.4 billion), AT&T ($3.5 billion), Amazon ($3.4 billion), and General Motors ($3.2 billion). Procter & Gamble is the largest global advertiser, spending $10.5 billion. The largest advertisers outside the United States include Samsung Electronics (South Korea, electronics), Nestlé (Switzerland, foods), and Unilever (U.K./Netherlands, consumer goods such as food, personal care, and cleaning products).

In oligopoly markets, firms consider the likely actions of their rivals when deciding how much to advertise. How much a firm should spend on advertising depends critically on whether the advertising helps or harms its rival.

For example, when a firm advertises to inform consumers about a new use for its product, its advertising may cause the quantity demanded for its own *and* rival brands to rise, as happened with toothpaste ads. Before World War I, only 26% of Americans brushed their teeth. By 1926, in part because of ads like those in Ipana's "pink toothbrush" campaign, which detailed the perils of bleeding gums, the share of Americans who brushed rose to 40%. Ipana's advertising helped all manufacturers of toothbrushes and toothpaste.[5]

Alternatively, a firm's advertising might increase demand for its product by taking customers away from other firms. A firm may use advertising to differentiate its products from those of rivals. The advertising may describe actual physical differences in the products or try to convince customers that essentially identical products differ. If a firm succeeds with this latter type of advertising, the products are described as *spuriously* differentiated.

A firm can raise its profit if it can convince consumers that its product is superior to other brands. From the 1930s through the early 1970s, *secret ingredients*

---

[4]Under perfect competition, there is no reason for an individual firm to advertise, as a firm can sell as much as it wants at the market price.

[5]Although it's difficult to believe, starting in the 1970s, Wisk liquid detergent claimed that it solved a major social problem: ring around the collar (**www.youtube.com/watch?v=e3N_skYSGoY**). Presumably, some consumers—even among those who were gullible enough to find this ad compelling—could generalize that applying other liquid detergents would work equally well.

were a mainstay of consumer advertising. These ingredients were given names combining letters and numbers to suggest that they were developed in laboratories rather than by Madison Avenue. Dial soap boasted that it contained AT-7. Rinso detergent had Solium, Comet included Chlorinol, and Bufferin had Di-Alminate. Among the toothpastes, Colgate had Gardol, Gleem had GL-70, Crest had Fluoristan, and Ipana had Hexachlorophene and Durenamel.

Empirical evidence indicates that the impact of a firm's advertising on other firms varies across industries. The cola market is an example of the extreme case in which a firm's advertising brings few new customers into the market and primarily serves to steal business from rivals. Gasmi, Laffont, and Vuong (1992) reported that Coke or Pepsi's gain from advertising comes at the expense of its rivals; however, cola advertising has almost no effect on total market demand, as in panel a. Similarly, advertising by one brand of an erectile dysfunction drug increases its share and decreases that of its rivals (David and Markowitz, 2011).

At the other extreme is cigarette and beer advertising. Roberts and Samuelson (1988) found that cigarette advertising increases the size of the market but does not change market shares substantially, as in panel b.[6] Similarly, Shapiro (2018) finds a positive spillover of a prescription antidepressant manufacturer's advertising onto its rivals. Intermediate results include Canadian fast foods, where advertising primarily increases general demand but has a small effect on market share (Richards and Padilla, 2009), and CPUs, where Intel's advertising has a smaller effect on total market demand than on Intel's share (Salgado, 2008).

Pricing Games in Two-Sided Markets

We can use game theory to analyze strategic rivalry in two-sided markets. A two-sided market is an economic platform that has two or more user groups that provide each other with network externalities (Chapter 11).

A credit card, such as MasterCard or Visa, connects merchants and consumers. The more consumers who use a card, the more attractive accepting that card is to merchants. The more merchants who accept the card, the more likely consumers want to use it.

The strategic rivalry between MasterCard and Visa determines the equilibrium prices they charge the two user groups. We assume that these firms choose one of two possible pricing strategies: balanced pricing, in which both merchants and consumers pay fees, and unbalanced pricing, in which only merchants pay. In Table 13.4,

Table 13.4 Unbalanced Pricing in a Two-Sided Market

		Visa	
		Balanced	*Unbalanced*
MasterCard	*Balanced*	7 / 7	9 / 2
	Unbalanced	2 / 9	4 / 4

---

[6]However, the Centers for Disease Control and Prevention's evidence suggests that advertising may shift the brand loyalty of youths.

Table 13.5   Balanced Pricing in a Two-Sided Market

		eHarmony	
		Balanced	*Unbalanced*
Match.com	*Balanced*	7 / 7	5 / 6
	Unbalanced	6 / 5	4 / 4

unbalanced pricing is the dominant strategy for each firm, so both use this strategy in the Nash equilibrium. This example is a prisoners' dilemma game. The firms would earn more if they used balanced pricing, 7 each, instead of unbalanced pricing, 4 each.

In contrast, consider a different game between the eHarmony and Match.com dating platforms. Each firm can use a balanced pricing strategy, charging both men and women, or it can use an unbalanced pricing strategy, charging only one group. The example in Table 13.5 is not a prisoners' dilemma game. Balanced pricing is the dominant strategy for each firm. The solution maximizes the joint payoffs to the firms.

Multiple Equilibria

In accordance with our principles of free enterprise and healthy competition, I'm going to ask you two to fight to the death for it. —Monty Python

Many oligopoly games have more than one Nash equilibrium. We illustrate this possibility with an entry game. Two firms are each considering opening a gas station at a highway rest stop that has no gas stations. The rest stop has enough physical space for at most two gas stations. The profit matrix in Table 13.6 shows that the demand for gasoline is adequate for only one station to operate profitably. If both firms enter,

Table 13.6 Simultaneous-Entry Game

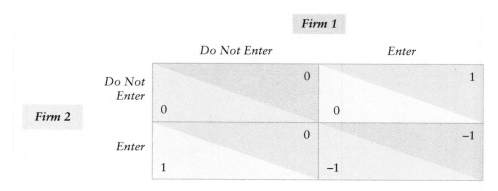

		Firm 1	
		Do Not Enter	*Enter*
Firm 2	*Do Not Enter*	0 / 0	0 / 1
	Enter	1 / 0	−1 / −1

each loses $1 (hundred thousand). Neither firm has a dominant strategy. Each firm's best action depends on what the other firm does.

By examining the firm's best responses, we can identify two Nash equilibria: Firm 1 *enters* and Firm 2 *does not enter*, or Firm 2 *enters* and Firm 1 *does not enter*. Each is a Nash equilibrium because neither firm wants to change its behavior. Given that Firm 2 does not enter, Firm 1 does not want to change its strategy from entering to staying out of the market. If it changed its behavior, it would go from earning $1 to earning $0. Similarly, given that Firm 1 enters, Firm 2 does not want to switch its behavior and enter because it would lose $1 instead of making $0. The outcome in which only Firm 2 enters is also a Nash equilibrium by the same type of reasoning.

How do the players know which (if any) Nash equilibrium will result? They *don't* know. It is difficult to see how the firms choose strategies unless they collude and can enforce their agreement. For example, the firm that enters could pay the other firm to stay out of the market. Without an enforceable collusive agreement, even discussions between the firms before they make decisions are unlikely to help. These pure Nash equilibria are unappealing because they call for identical firms to use different strategies.

SOLVED PROBLEM 13.1

MyLab Economics Solved Problem

Intel and AMD are the dominant central processing unit manufacturers. Assume they play the following game once and act simultaneously. Their profits are symmetric. If both choose low levels of advertising, Intel's profit, π_I, and AMD's profit, π_A, are each 2. If both choose high, each earns 3. If Intel's advertising is high and AMD's is low, $\pi_I = 8$ and $\pi_A = 4$. If Intel's advertising is low and AMD's is high, $\pi_I = 4$ and $\pi_A = 8$. Describe how each firm chooses its strategy? Describe the Nash equilibrium or equilibria.

Answer

1. *Use a profit matrix to show the firms' best responses.* The payoff matrix shows the four possible pairs of strategies and the associated profits. If Intel chooses a low level of advertising (top row), AMD's profit is 2 if its advertising is low and 8 if it is high, so its best response is high, as indicated by the dark green triangle in the upper right of the top right cell. If Intel's advertising is high (bottom row), AMD's profit is 4 if its advertising is low and 3 if it is high, so its best response is low, as indicated by the dark green triangle in the upper right of the lower-left cell. Similarly, we use light green triangles in the lower left of cells to show Intel's best responses.

2. *Identify the Nash equilibria using the best responses.* For a pair of strategies to be a Nash equilibrium, both firms must be using a best response. Thus, this game has two Nash equilibria: Intel's advertising is high and AMD's is low (lower-left cell) and Intel's advertising is low and AMD's is high (upper-right cell).

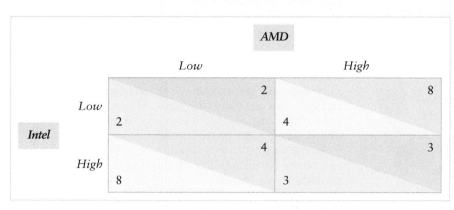

Mixed Strategies

In each of the games we have considered so far, including the entry game, we have assumed that the firms use a **pure strategy**: Each player chooses a single action. In addition to using a pure strategy, a firm in this entry game may employ a **mixed strategy** in which the player chooses among possible actions according to probabilities the player assigns. A pure strategy assigns a probability of 1 to a single action, whereas a mixed strategy is a probability distribution over actions. That is, a pure strategy is a rule telling the player what action to take, whereas a mixed strategy is a rule telling the player which dice to throw, coin to flip, or other random method of choosing an action.

A firm chooses a best-response strategy: one that produces the highest expected payoff given the strategy chosen by its rival. We start by describing a mixed strategy for the entry game and explaining why it is a best response. Then, we'll discuss how to derive such a mixed strategy.

In the entry game, both firms may use the same mixed strategy: Both firms enter with a probability of one-half—say, if a flipped coin comes up heads. This pair of mixed strategies is a Nash equilibrium because neither firm wants to change its strategy, given that the other firm uses its Nash equilibrium mixed strategy.

If both firms use this mixed strategy, each of the four outcomes in the payoff matrix in Table 13.6 is equally likely. The probability that the outcome in a particular cell of the matrix occurs is the product of the probabilities that each firm chooses the relevant action. The probability that a firm chooses a given action is $\frac{1}{2}$. Given that each firm flips its coin independently, the probability that both firms will choose a given pair of actions is $\frac{1}{2} \times \frac{1}{2} = \frac{1}{4}$. Consequently, Firm 1 has a one-fourth chance of earning \$1 (upper-right cell), a one-fourth chance of losing \$1 (lower-right cell), and a one-half chance of earning \$0 (upper-left and lower-left cells). Thus, Firm 1's expected profit—the firm's profit in each possible outcome times the probability of that outcome—is

$$\left(\$1 \times \frac{1}{2} \right) + \left(-\$1 \times \frac{1}{4} \right) + \left(\$0 \times \frac{1}{2} \right) = \$0.$$

Given that Firm 1 uses this mixed strategy, Firm 2 cannot achieve a higher expected profit by using a pure strategy. If Firm 2 uses the pure strategy of entering with probability 1, it earns \$1 half the time and loses \$1 the other half, so its expected profit is \$0. If Firm 2 stays out with certainty, it earns \$0 with certainty.

In general, if Firm 2 believes that Firm 1 will use its equilibrium mixed strategy, Firm 2 is indifferent as to which pure strategy it uses (of the strategies that have a positive probability in that firm's mixed strategy). In contrast, if one of the actions in the equilibrium mixed strategy has a higher expected payoff than some other action, it would pay to increase the probability that Firm 2 takes the action with the higher expected payoff. However, if all of the pure strategies that have positive probabilities in a mixed strategy have the same expected payoff, then the expected payoff of the mixed strategy must also have that expected payoff. Thus, Firm 2 is indifferent as to whether it uses any of these pure strategies or any mixed strategy over these pure strategies.

In our example, why would a firm pick a mixed strategy where its probability of entering is one-half? Let the probability of entering be θ_t for Firm i. Firm 2's payoff from entering is $[\theta_1 \times (-1)] + [(1 - \theta_1) \times 1] = 1 - 2\theta_1$, given that it believes that Firm will enter with probability

How business decisions are made.

θ_1. Its payoff from not entering is $[\theta_1 \times 0] + [(1 - \theta_1) \times 0] = 0$. For Firm 2 to use a mixed strategy, it must be indifferent between entering or not. That is, these two expected profits must be equal. Equating these two expected profits, $1 - 2\theta_1 = 0$, and solving, we find that $\theta_1 = \frac{1}{2}$. Using the same analysis for Firm 1, we find that $\theta_2 = \frac{1}{2}$.

The entry game has two pure-strategy Nash equilibria—one firm employing the pure strategy of entering and the other firm pursuing the pure strategy of not entering—and a mixed-strategy Nash equilibrium. If Firm 1 decides to *enter* with a probability of $\frac{1}{2}$, Firm 2 is indifferent between choosing to enter with a probability of 1 (the pure strategy of *enter*), 0 (the pure strategy of *do not enter*), or any fraction in between these extremes. However, for the firms' strategies to constitute a mixed-strategy Nash equilibrium, both firms must choose to enter with a probability of one-half. Thus, both firms using a mixed strategy where they enter with a probability of one-half is a Nash equilibrium.[7]

An important reason for introducing the concept of a mixed strategy is that some games have no pure-strategy Nash equilibria. However, Nash (1950) proved that every static game with a finite number of players and a finite number of actions has at least one Nash equilibrium, which may involve mixed strategies.

Some game theorists argue that mixed strategies are implausible because firms do not flip coins to choose strategies. One response is that firms may only appear to be unpredictable. In this game with no dominant strategies, neither firm has a strong reason to believe that the other will choose a pure strategy. It may think about its rival's behavior as random. However, in actual games, a firm may use some information or reasoning that its rival does not observe so that it chooses a pure strategy. Or, a firm may confront a different rival in each of many markets, where one-half of those firms use a pure entry strategy and one-half use the pure-no-entry strategy, which resembles a mixed strategy across firms. Another response is that a mixed strategy may be appealing in some games, such as the entry game, where a random strategy and symmetry between players are plausible.

APPLICATION

Boomerang Millennials

We can use game theory to explain many interactions between parents and their kids. In the United States, the term *boomerang generation* refers to young adults who return home after college, a first job, or the military to live with their parents. (The Japanese call them *parasite singles*.)

The Great Recession hit young people particularly hard, and the recovery was slow and uneven. The U.S. unemployment rate for 20- to 24-year-olds went from 8.5% in 2007 to 11% in 2008, then rose to 16% in 2009, and stayed above 13% through 2012, but fell to 7% by mid-2018.

As a result, many adults moved back to live with their parents after college. The share of 25- to 34-year-olds who lived with their parents was 15% in 2016 (Millennials) compared to 10% in 2000 (Gen Xers). In the European Union, 39% of 25- to 29-year-olds and 73% of 20- to 24-year-olds lived with their parents in 2016.

In many parents' minds the question arises of whether by supporting their kids, they discourage them from working. Rather than unconditionally supporting their children, would they help their kids more by engaging in tough love: kicking their kids out and making them support themselves? Solved Problem 13.2 addresses this question.

[7]"Solving for Mixed Strategies Using Calculus" in MyLab Economics, Chapter Resources, Chapter 13 shows how to solve for this mixed-strategy equilibrium using calculus.

| SOLVED PROBLEM 13.2 | Mimi wants to support her son Jeff if he looks for work but not otherwise. Jeff wants to try to find a job only if Mimi will not support his life of indolence. Their payoff matrix is: |

MyLab Economics
Solved Problem

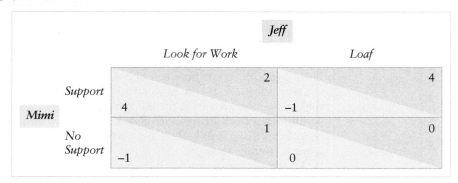

If Jeff and Mimi choose actions simultaneously, what are the pure- or mixed-strategy equilibria?

Answer

1. *Check whether any of the four possible pairs of pure strategies is a Nash equilibrium.* The four possible pure-strategy equilibria are support-look, support-loaf, no support-look, and no support-loaf. None of these pairs of pure strategies is a Nash equilibrium because one or the other player would want to change his or her strategy. The pair of strategies support-look is not a Nash equilibrium because, given that Mimi provides support, Jeff would have a higher payoff loafing, 4, than looking for work, 2. Support-loaf is not a Nash equilibrium because Mimi prefers not to support the idler, 0, to providing support, -1. We can reject no support-loaf because Jeff would prefer to look for work, 1, out of desperation rather than loaf, 0. Finally, no support-look is not a Nash equilibrium because Mimi would prefer to support her wonderful son, 4, rather than to feel guilty about not rewarding his search efforts, -1.

2. *By equating expected payoffs, determine the mixed-strategy equilibrium.* If Mimi provides support with probability θ_M, Jeff's expected payoff from looking for work is $2\theta_M + [1 \times (1 - \theta_M)] = 1 + \theta_M$, and his expected payoff from loafing is $4\theta_M + [0 \times (1 - \theta_M)] = 4\theta_M$. Jeff is indifferent between loafing and looking for work if his expected payoffs are equal: $1 + \theta_M = 4\theta_M$, or $\theta_M = \frac{1}{3}$. If Jeff looks for work with probability θ_J, then Mimi's expected payoff from supporting him is $4\theta_J + [(-1) \times (1 - \theta_J)] = 5\theta_J - 1$, and her expected payoff from not supporting him is $-\theta_J + [0 \times (1 - \theta_J)] = -\theta_J$. By equating her expected payoffs, $5\theta_J - 1 = -\theta_J$, we determine that his mixed-strategy probability is $\theta_J = \frac{1}{6}$.

Comment: Although this game has no pure-strategy Nash equilibria, it does have a mixed-strategy Nash equilibrium.

13.2 Repeated Dynamic Games

In static, normal-form games, players have imperfect information about how other players will act because everyone moves simultaneously and only once. In contrast, in *dynamic games*, players move sequentially or move simultaneously repeatedly over time, so a player has perfect information about other players' previous moves.

We consider two types of dynamic games. We start with a *repeated* or *multiperiod* game in which a single-period, simultaneous-move game, such as the airline prisoners' dilemma game, is played at least twice and possibly many times. Although the players move simultaneously in each period, they know about their rivals' moves in previous periods, so a rival's previous move may affect a player's current action. As a result, it is a dynamic game.

In the next section, we turn to *sequential games*. We examine a *two-stage game*, which is played once and hence can be said to occur in a "single period." In the first stage, Player 1 moves. In the second stage, Player 2 moves and the game ends with the players receiving payoffs based on their actions.

Strategies and Actions in Dynamic Games

A major difference between static and dynamic games is that dynamic games require us to distinguish between strategies and actions. An *action* is a single move that a player makes at a specified time, such as choosing an output level or a price. A *strategy* is a battle plan that specifies the full set of actions that a player will make throughout the game and may involve actions that are conditional on prior actions of other players or on additional information available at a given time.

For example, American's strategy might state that it will fly 64 thousand passengers between Chicago and Los Angeles this quarter if United flew 64 thousand last quarter, but that it will fly only 48 thousand this quarter if United flew 48 thousand last quarter. This distinction between an action and a strategy is moot in a simultaneous-move static game, where an action and a strategy are effectively the same because the game is played only once.

Cooperation in a Repeated Prisoners' Dilemma Game

To illustrate the difference between a static game and a repeated game, we consider a repeated prisoners' dilemma game. Each period has a single stage in which both players move simultaneously. However, these are dynamic games because Player 1's move in period t precedes Player 2's move in period $t + 1$; hence, the earlier action may affect the later one. Such a repeated game is a *game of almost perfect information*: The players know all the moves from previous periods, but they do not know each other's moves within a single period because they act simultaneously.

We showed that if American and United engage in a single-period prisoners' dilemma game, Table 13.1, the two firms produce more than they would if they had colluded. Yet cartels do form. What's wrong with this theory, which says that cartels won't occur? One explanation is that markets last for many periods, and collusion is more likely to occur in a multiperiod game than in a single-period game.

In a single-period game, one firm cannot punish the other firm for cheating on a cartel agreement. But if the firms play period after period, a wayward firm can be punished by the other.

Suppose now that the airlines' single-period prisoners' dilemma game is repeated quarter after quarter. If they play a single-period game, each firm takes its rival's strategy as a given and assumes that it cannot affect that strategy. When the same game is played repeatedly, a firm may devise a strategy for this period that depends on its rival's previous actions. For example, a firm may set a low output level for this period only if its rival set a low output level in the previous period.

Signaling. When antitrust laws make a firm hesitant to contact its rival directly, it may try to influence its rival's behavior by *signaling*. For example, American could use a low-quantity strategy for a couple of periods to signal United that it desires the two firms to cooperate and produce that low quantity in the future. If United does not respond by lowering its output in future periods, then American suffers lower profits for only a couple of periods. However, if United responds to this signal and lowers its quantity, both firms can profitably produce at the low quantity thereafter.

If the low-output strategy is so lucrative for everyone, why don't firms always cooperate when engaging in such indefinitely repeated games? One reason is that the cooperative outcome is not the only possible Nash equilibrium. This game has another Nash equilibrium in which each firm chooses the high output every period. If United believes that American will produce the high output in every period, then its best response is to produce the high output every period. This same reasoning also applies to American. Each firm's belief about its rival will be confirmed by experience, and neither firm will have an incentive to change its strategy.

Threatening to Punish. In addition to or instead of signaling, a firm can threaten to punish a rival for not restricting output. We use the profit matrix in Table 13.1 to illustrate how the airlines could threaten to punish rivals to ensure collusion. Suppose that American announces or somehow indicates to United that it will use the following two-part strategy:

- American will produce the smaller quantity each period as long as United does the same.
- If United produces the larger quantity in period t, American will produce the larger quantity in period $t + 1$ and all subsequent periods.

If United believes that American will follow this strategy, United knows that it will make $4.6 million each period if it produces the smaller quantity. Although United can make a higher profit, $5.1 million, in period t by producing the larger quantity, by doing so it lowers its potential profit to $4.1 million in each subsequent period. Thus, United gains half a million dollars relative to the cooperative payoff ($\$0.5 = \$5.1 - \$4.6$) in the period when it first defects from the cooperative output, but it loses half a million dollars relative to cooperation ($-\$0.5 = \$4.1 - \$4.6$) in each subsequent period. After only two punishment periods, the loss would be much larger in magnitude than the initial gain. Thus, United's best policy is to produce the lower quantity in each period unless it cares greatly about current profit and little about future profits.[8]

American is using a *trigger strategy*: a strategy in which a rival's defection from a collusive outcome triggers a punishment. In this case, the trigger strategy is extreme because a single defection calls for a firm to punish its rival forever by producing the high output in all subsequent periods.[9] However, if both firms adopt this trigger strategy, the outcome is a Nash equilibrium in which both firms choose the low output and obtain the collusive profit in every period: Defection and punishment need not occur. The firms may use less extreme trigger strategies. For example, a strategy that involved just two periods of punishment for a defection may make defection unattractive in this example.

---

[8]Presumably, a firm discounts future gains or losses (Chapter 16) because a dollar today is worth more than a dollar in the future. However, the effect of such discounting over a period as short as a few quarters is small.

[9]American does not have to punish United forever to induce it to cooperate. All it has to do is punish it for enough periods that it does not pay for United to deviate from the low-quantity strategy in any period.

<table>
<tr><td>

SOLVED PROBLEM 13.3

MyLab Economics
Solved Problem

</td><td>

Show that if American and United Airlines know they will play the game just described repeatedly for exactly T periods, the firms are unlikely to cooperate.

Answer

Start with the last period and work backward. In the last period, T, the firms know that they're not going to play again, so they know they can cheat—produce a large quantity—without fear of punishment. As a result, the last period is like a single-period game, and both firms produce the large quantity. That makes the $T - 1$ period the last interesting period. By the same reasoning, the firms will cheat in $T - 1$ because they know that they will both cheat in the last period and hence no additional punishment can be imposed. Continuing this type of argument, we conclude that maintaining an agreement to produce the small quantity will be difficult if the game has a known stopping point.

Comment: Playing the same game many times does not necessarily help the firms cooperate. With a known end period, cooperating is difficult. However, if the players know that the game will end but aren't sure when, cheating is less likely to occur. Cooperation is therefore more likely in a game that will continue forever or will end at an unknown period than in a game with a known final period.

</td></tr>
</table>

13.3 Sequential Game

We now turn to sequential dynamic games, in which one firm moves before another. We show how to represent these games diagrammatically and predict their outcomes.

Game Tree

Rather than use the normal form, economists analyze sequential dynamic games in their **extensive form**, which specifies the n players, the sequence in which they make their moves, the actions they can take at each move, the information that each player has about players' previous moves, and the payoff function over all possible strategies. In this section, we assume that players not only have complete information about the strategies and payoff functions but also have perfect information about the previous plays of the game.

We illustrate a sequential-move or two-stage game using the airline example where American can choose its output level before United does. This game is called a *Stackelberg game*.[10] The striking result of this analysis is that when one player can move before the other, the outcome is different from that in a game where they have to move simultaneously. For simplicity, we assume that United and American can choose only output levels of 96, 64, and 48 thousand passengers per quarter.

Using Table 13.2, the normal-form representation of this game, we derived the Nash equilibrium when both firms moved simultaneously. To demonstrate the role of sequential moves, we use an *extensive-form diagram* or *game tree*, Figure 13.1, which shows the order of the firms' moves, each firm's possible actions at the time of its move, and the resulting profits at the end of the game.

In the figure, each box is a point of decision by one of the firms, called a *decision node*. The name in the decision node box indicates that it is that player's turn to move. The lines or *branches* extending out of the box represent a complete list of the possible actions the player can make at that point in the game. On the left side of the figure, American, the leader, starts by picking one of the three output levels.

---

[10]We discuss a generalized version of this game in Chapter 14.

Figure 13.1 Airlines Game Tree

American, the leader firm, chooses its output level first. Given American's choice, United, the follower, picks an output level. The firms' profits that result from these decisions are shown on the right-hand side of the figure. Two red lines through an action line show that the firm rejects that action. The action that each firm chooses is indicated by a dark blue line.

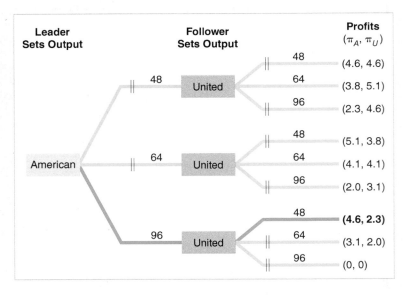

In the middle of the figure, United, the follower, chooses one of the three quantities after learning the output level American chose. The right side of the figure shows the profits that American and United earn, given that they sequentially took the actions to reach this final branch. For instance, if American selects 64 and then United chooses 96, American earns 2.0 ($2 million) profit per quarter and United earns 3.1.

Within this game are *subgames*. At a given stage, a **subgame** consists of all the subsequent decisions that players may make given the actions already taken. The game in Figure 13.1 has four subgames. The subgame at the time of American's first-stage decision is the entire game. The second stage has three subgames in which United makes a decision given each of American's three possible first-stage actions.

Subgame Perfect Nash Equilibrium

In solving a problem of this sort, the grand thing is to be able to reason backward.
—Sherlock Holmes (Sir Arthur Conan Doyle)

To predict the outcome of this sequential game, we introduce a stronger version of the Nash equilibrium concept. A set of strategies forms a **subgame perfect Nash equilibrium** if the players' strategies are a Nash equilibrium in every subgame. As the entire dynamic game is a subgame, a subgame perfect Nash equilibrium is also a Nash equilibrium. In contrast, in a simultaneous-move game such as the static prisoners' dilemma, the only subgame is the game itself, so the Nash equilibrium and the subgame perfect Nash equilibrium are the same.

Table 13.2 shows the normal-form representation of this game in which the Nash equilibrium in the simultaneous-move game is for each firm to choose 64. However, if the firms move sequentially, the subgame perfect Nash equilibrium results in a different outcome.

We can solve for the subgame perfect Nash equilibrium using **backward induction**, where we first determine the best response by the last player to move, next determine the best response for the player who made the next-to-last move, and then repeat the process until we reach the first move of the game. In our example, we work backward from the decision by the follower, United, to the decision by the leader, American, moving from the right to the left side of the game tree.

How should American, the leader, select its output in the first stage? For each possible quantity it can produce, American predicts what United will do and picks the output level that maximizes its own profit. Thus, to predict American's action in the first stage, American determines what United, the follower, will do in the second stage, given each possible output choice by American in the first stage. Using its conclusions about United's second-stage reaction, American makes its first-stage decision.

Which quantity that United, the follower, chooses depends on the quantity that American previously chose. If American chose 96, United's profit is 2.3 if its output is 48, 2.0 if it produces 64, and 0 if it picks a quantity of 96. Thus, if American chose 96, United's best response in this subgame is 48. The double lines through the other two action lines show that United will not choose those actions.

Using the same reasoning, American determines how United will respond to each of American's possible actions, as the right-hand side of the figure illustrates. American predicts the following:

- If American chooses 48, United selects 64, so American's profit will be 3.8.
- If American chooses 64, United selects 64, so American's profit will be 4.1.
- If American chooses 96, United selects 48, so American's profit will be 4.6.

Thus, to maximize its profit, American chooses 96 in the first stage. United's strategy is to make its best response to American's first-stage action: United selects 64 if American chooses 48 or 64, and United picks 48 if American chooses 96. Thus, United responds in the second stage by selecting 48. In this subgame perfect Nash equilibrium, neither firm wants to change its strategy. Given that American Airlines sets its output at 96, United is using a strategy that maximizes its profit, $q_U = 48$, so it doesn't want to change. Similarly, given how United will respond to each possible American output level, American cannot make more profit than if it chooses 96.

The subgame perfect Nash equilibrium requires players to believe that their opponents will act optimally—in their own best interests. No player has an incentive to deviate from the equilibrium strategies. The reason for adding the requirement of subgame perfection is that we want to explain what will happen if a player does not follow the equilibrium path. For example, if American does not choose its equilibrium output in the first stage, subgame perfection requires that United will still follow the strategy that maximizes its profit in the second stage conditional on American's actual output choice.

Not all Nash equilibria are subgame perfect Nash equilibria. For example, suppose that American's strategy is to pick 96 in the first stage, and United's strategy is to choose 96 if American selects 48 or 64, and 48 if American chooses 96. The outcome is the same as the subgame perfect Nash equilibrium we just derived because American selects 96, United chooses 48, and neither firm wants to deviate.[11] Due to each firm's unwillingness to deviate, this set of strategies is a Nash equilibrium. However, this set of strategies is not a subgame perfect Nash equilibrium. Although this Nash equilibrium has the same equilibrium path as the subgame perfect Nash equilibrium, United's strategy differs out of the equilibrium path. If American had selected 48 (or 64), United's strategy would not result in a Nash equilibrium. United would receive a higher profit if it produced 64 rather than the 96 that this strategy requires. Therefore, this Nash equilibrium is not subgame perfect.

The subgame perfect Nash equilibrium differs from the simultaneous-move equilibrium in Table 13.2. If American can move first, its output is 96, which is 50% more

---

[11]Given United's strategy, American does not have any incentive to deviate. If American chooses 48 it will get 2.3, and if it chooses 64 it will get 2.0, both of which are less than 4.6 if it chooses 96. And given American's strategy, no change in United's strategy would raise its profit.

than the 64 that it would fly if both firms move simultaneously. Similarly, American earns 4.6 if it moves first, which is 15% more than the 4.1 it would earn if both firms move simultaneously. If United moves second, it selects a smaller quantity, 48, and earns a lower profit, 2.3, than it would if both firms moved simultaneously, where it would fly 64 and earn 4.1. Thus, although United has more information in the sequential-move game than it does in the simultaneous-move game—it knows American's output level—it is worse off than if both firms chose their actions simultaneously.

Credibility

Why do the simultaneous-move and sequential-move games have different outcomes? Given the option to act first, American chooses a large output level to make it in United's best interest to pick a relatively small output level, 48. American benefits from moving first and choosing a relatively large quantity.

In the simultaneous-move game, why doesn't American announce that it will fly 96 thousand customers so as to induce United to pick a small quantity, 48? The answer is that when the firms move simultaneously, United doesn't believe American's warning that it will produce a large quantity, because it is not in American's best interest to produce that large a quantity of output. For a firm's announced

Come here! Don't make me run after you!

strategy to be a **credible threat**, rivals must believe that the firm's strategy is rational in the sense that it is in the firm's best interest to use it.[12] If American chose the first mover's equilibrium level of output, 96, and United produced the simultaneous-move equilibrium level, 64, American's profit would be lower than if it too chose the simultaneous-move level. Because American cannot be sure that United will believe its threat and reduce its output in the simultaneous-move game, American produces the simultaneous-move equilibrium output level, 64. In contrast, in the sequential-move game, because American moves first, its commitment to produce a large quantity is credible because it has already set that quantity.

The intuition for why commitment makes a threat credible is that of "burning bridges." If the general burns the bridge behind the army so that the troops can only advance and not retreat, the army becomes a more fearsome foe—like a cornered animal.[13] Similarly, by limiting its future options, a firm makes itself stronger.[14]

---

[12]You may have been in a restaurant and listened to an exasperated father trying to control his brat with such extreme threats as "If you don't behave, you'll have to sit in the car while we eat dinner" or "If you don't behave, you'll never watch television again." The kid, of course, does not view such threats as credible and continues to terrorize the restaurant—proving that the kid is a better game theorist than the father.

[13]"On hemmed-in ground, I would block any way of retreat. On desperate ground, I would proclaim to my soldiers the hopelessness of saving their lives." Sun Tzu, *On the Art of War*.

[14]Some psychologists use the idea of commitment to treat behavioral problems. An author tells a psychologist that she has writer's block. The psychologist advises her to set up an irreversible procedure: If the author's book is not finished by a certain date, the author's check for $10,000 will be sent to the group the author hates most in the world—be it the Nazi Party, the Ku Klux Klan, or the National Save the Skeets Foundation. Such an irreversible commitment encourages the author to complete the project by raising the cost of failure: We can imagine the author playing a game against the author's better self.

Not all firms can make credible threats, however, because not all firms can make commitments. Typically, for a threat to succeed, a firm must have an advantage that allows it to harm the other firm before that firm can retaliate. Identical firms that act simultaneously cannot credibly threaten each other. However, a firm may be able to make its threatened behavior believable if firms differ. An important difference is the ability of one firm to act before the other. For example, an incumbent firm could lobby for the passage of a law that forbids further entry.

Dynamic Entry Game

We can illustrate the use of laws as a form of commitment by using the entry game. In some markets, by moving first, a firm can act strategically to prevent potential rivals from entering the market. How can an *incumbent*, monopoly firm deter a (potential) *rival* from entering that market? Does the incumbent gain from taking an action that deters entry?

The incumbent can prevent entry if it can make a credible threat. However, a firm cannot deter entry merely by telling a potential rival, "Don't enter! This market ain't big enough for the two of us." The potential rival would merely laugh and suggest that the first firm exit if it doesn't want to share the market. The following examples demonstrate how, by acting first, a firm can make a credible threat that deters entry.

Exclusion Contract. We consider an example where the incumbent can pay a third party to prevent entry. An airport has a single book store, the incumbent firm. We consider an example where the incumbent can pay a third party, the city government that owns the airport, to prevent entry.[15] If this payment is made, the landlord agrees to rent the remaining space only to a restaurant, a toy store, or some other business that does not sell books. Should the book store pay?

Yes, I pay you to keep rivals out of our territory. But, I don't want to hear all the gory details.

The game tree, Figure 13.2, shows the two stages of the game involving the incumbent and its potential rival, another book store. In the first stage, the incumbent decides whether to pay b to prevent entry. In the second stage, the potential rival decides whether to enter. If it enters, it incurs a fixed fee of F to build its store in the airport.

The right side of the figure shows the incumbent's and the potential rival's profits (π_i, π_r) for each of the three possible outcomes. The outcome at the top of the figure shows that if the incumbent does not buy exclusivity and the potential rival does not enter, the incumbent earns the "monopoly" profit of $\pi_i = 10$ ($10 thousand) per month and its potential rival earns nothing, $\pi_r = 0$. The middle outcome shows that if the incumbent does not pay the exclusivity fee and the potential rival enters, the incumbent earns a duopoly profit of $\pi_i = 4$ and the rival earns the duopoly profit less its fixed cost, F, of entering, $\pi_r = 4 - F$. In the bottom outcome, the

---

[15]Dallas–Fort Worth, Fort Lauderdale–Hollywood, San Francisco, and other airports sell the exclusive rights to provide a particular product or service at their airports. For example, San Francisco International Airport put out a call for bids for the exclusive right to provide a book store with the minimum acceptable bid of $400,000 for one year.

Figure 13.2 Game Tree: Whether an Incumbent Pays to Prevent Entry

If the potential rival stays out of the mall, it makes no profit, $\pi_r = 0$, and the incumbent firm makes the monopoly profit, $\pi_i = 10$. If the potential rival enters, the incumbent earns the duopoly profit of 4 and the rival makes $4 - F$, where F is its fixed cost of entry. If the duopoly profit, 4, is less than F, entry does not occur. Otherwise, entry occurs unless the incumbent acts to deter entry by paying for exclusive rights to be the only firm in the mall. The incumbent pays the landlord only if $10 - b > 4$.

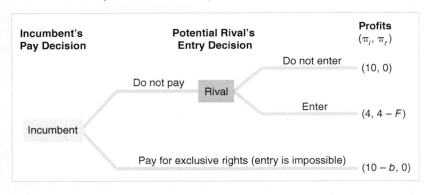

incumbent pays b for the exclusivity right so that it earns the monopoly profit less the exclusivity fee, $\pi_i = 10 - b$, and its potential rival earns nothing, $\pi_r = 0$.

To solve for the subgame perfect Nash equilibrium, we work backward, starting with the last decision, the potential rival's entry decision. The top portion of the game tree shows what happens if the incumbent does not pay the landlord to prevent entry. The potential rival enters if it earns more from entering, $\pi_r = 4 - F$, than if it stays out of the market, $\pi_r = 0$. That is, the potential rival enters if $F \le 4$. In the bottom portion of the game tree where the incumbent pays b for an exclusive contract that prevents entry, the potential rival has no possible action.

Which of the three possible outcomes occurs depends on the parameters b (the incumbent's exclusivity fee) and F (the potential rival's fixed cost of entering the market):

- **Blockaded entry** ($F > 4$): The potential rival chooses not to enter even if the incumbent does not pay to have an exclusive contract, so $\pi_r = 0$. The incumbent avoids spending b and still earns the monopoly profit, $\pi_i = 10$.
- **Deterred entry** ($F \le 4, b \le 6$): Because $F \le 4$, entry will occur unless the incumbent pays the exclusivity fee. The incumbent chooses to pay the exclusivity fee, b, because its profit from doing so, $\pi_i = 10 - b \ge 4$, which is at least as large as what it earns if it permits entry and earns the duopoly profit, $\pi_i = 4$. Because the rival does not enter, it earns nothing: $\pi_r = 0$.
- **Accommodated entry** ($F \le 4, b > 6$): Entry will occur unless the incumbent pays the fee because the rival's fixed costs are less than or equal to 4. However, the incumbent does not pay for an exclusive contract. The exclusivity fee is so high that the incumbent earns more by allowing entry, $\pi_i = 4$, than it earns if it pays for exclusivity $\pi_i = 10 - b < 4$. Thus, the incumbent earns the duopoly profit, $\pi_i = 4$ and the rival makes $\pi_r = 4 - F$.

In short, the incumbent does not pay for an exclusive contract if the potential rival's cost of entry is prohibitively high ($F > 4$) or if the cost of the exclusive contract is too high ($b > 6$).

The next Solved Problem uses dynamic game theory to reject the following false belief:

Common Confusion A firm invests in new equipment only if the variable cost savings outweigh the fixed cost of the investment.

SOLVED PROBLEM 13.4

MyLab Economics Solved Problem

Use the following game tree to demonstrate that an incumbent faced with potential entry may invest in new equipment even when the investment does not lower its variable cost by as much as the fixed cost of the investment. In the first stage of the game tree in the figure, the incumbent firm decides whether to invest in new robotic equipment, which will lower its marginal cost of production. In the second stage, a potential rival decides whether to enter the market.

Answer

1. *Determine the potential rival's response in the second stage to each possible action taken by the incumbent in the first stage.* To solve for the subgame perfect Nash equilibrium, we work backward from the potential rival's entry decision in the second stage of the game. If the incumbent does not invest, its rival enters because its profit from entering, $\pi_r = 4$, exceeds its zero profit if it does not enter. If the incumbent does invest, its potential rival stays out of the market because entry would be unprofitable: $\pi_r = -1 < 0$.

2. *Determine the incumbent's decision given its potential rival's responses.* If the incumbent does not invest and the rival enters, the incumbent earns $\pi_i = 4$. If it invests and potential rival does not enter, the incumbent earns $\pi_i = 8$. Thus, the incumbent invests.

Incumbent's Investment Decision	Potential Rival's Entry Decision		Profits (π_i, π_r)
No investment → Entrant	Do not enter		(10, 0)
	Enter		(4, 4)
Investment → Entrant	Do not enter		(8, 0)
	Enter		(2, −1)

Comment: This investment would not pay without a threat of entry. Investing would cause the incumbent's profit to fall from $\pi_i = 10$ to 8.

APPLICATION

Keeping Out Casinos

Suppose you own the only casino in town. You know that the larger your casino, the more games and entertainment you can provide, so the more customers your casino will attract. You face a trade-off because as the casino becomes larger, your costs increase. Thus, you must pick the optimal size to maximize your monopoly profit.

A complication arises if, at the monopoly-profit-maximizing size, it is profitable for a new firm to enter. If so, it may pay to expand your casino. You can credibly commit to maintaining a larger casino because such investments are costly to reverse. Given a large enough casino, a potential entrant will lose money by building a competing casino and hence won't enter.

A casino owner learns about entry plans when a potential entrant begins contacting a network of vendors and suppliers. Cookson (2018) estimated that incumbent casinos expand their floor space by 13 to 16% in response to an entry threat. He also found that entry is half as likely (33% versus 66%) if the incumbent invests in a large expansion rather than one that is 20,000 square feet smaller.

Limit Pricing. An incumbent firm sets a **limit price** (or, equivalently, an output) so that another firm cannot enter the market profitably. For example, the incumbent could set a price below the potential rival's marginal cost so entry would be unprofitable. Or, the incumbent could produce so much output that the price is very low and too few customers remain for the potential rival to make a profit. However, to limit price successfully, a firm must have an advantage over its rivals, as the following example illustrates.

An incumbent firm is making a large, monopoly profit, which attracts the interest of a potential rival. The incumbent could threaten that it will limit price if entry occurs. It could announce that, after entry, it will charge a price so low that the other firm will make a loss. This threat will only work if the threat is credible. It is not credible if the two firms have identical costs and market demand is adequate to support both firms. Once entry occurs, it is in the incumbent's best interest to charge the price that maximizes its profit in this subgame, so it makes a profit rather than charge such a low price that everyone loses money. Realizing that the incumbent won't actually limit price, the potential rival ignores the threat and enters.

For the threat of limit pricing to be credible, the incumbent must have an advantage over its rival. For example, if the incumbent's costs are lower than those of the potential rival, the incumbent can charge a price so low that the rival would lose money while the incumbent earns a higher profit than if it allows entry.

Another example is an extreme form of the Stackelberg oligopoly example. The Stackelberg leader acts first and produces a large quantity so that the follower produces a smaller quantity. Depending on the demand curve and the firms' costs, it may be even more profitable for the leader to produce such a large quantity that the follower cannot earn a profit. That is, the leader makes limit pricing credible by committing to provide a very large output level.

**SOLVED PROBLEM
13.5**

**MyLab Economics
Solved Problem**

In the first stage of a game between an incumbent and a potential rival, the incumbent builds its plant using either an inflexible technology that allows it to produce only a (large) fixed quantity, or a flexible technology that allows it to produce small or large quantities. In the second stage, the potential rival decides whether to enter. With the inflexible technology, the incumbent makes so much output that its threat to limit price is credible, as the following game tree illustrates. What strategy (technology) maximizes the incumbent's profit?

Answer

1. *Work backward by determining the potential rival's best strategy conditional on each possible action by the incumbent.* This game has two proper subgames. The upper-right subgame shows the profits if the potential rival enters or if it does not enter given that the incumbent uses the inflexible technology. The potential rival loses money ($\pi_r = -1$) if it enters, but breaks even ($\pi_r = 0$) if it doesn't, so it does not enter. In the lower-right subgame, the potential rival decides whether to enter given that the incumbent is using the

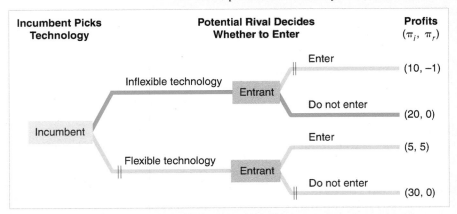

flexible technology. Here, the potential rival prefers to enter and earn a profit of $\pi_r = 5$ rather than stay out and earn nothing.

2. *Given the responses by the potential rival to each of the incumbent's strategies, determine the incumbent's best strategy.* If the incumbent uses the flexible technology, entry occurs, and the incumbent earns $\pi_i = 5$. However, if the incumbent uses the inflexible technology, the other firm does not enter, and the incumbent's profit is $\pi_i = 20$. Thus, the incumbent chooses the inflexible technology.

Comment: The incumbent would earn an even higher profit with the flexible technology if no entry occurs. However, if the incumbent chooses the flexible technology, its rival will enter, so the incumbent is better off committing to the inflexible technology. The inflexible technology serves as a credible threat that the incumbent will limit price.

13.4 Auctions

To this point, we have examined games in which players have complete information about payoff functions. We now turn to an important game, the auction, in which players devise bidding strategies without knowing other players' strategies or payoff functions.

An **auction** is a sale in which a good or service is sold to the highest bidder. A substantial amount of exchange takes place through auctions. Government contracts are typically awarded using procurement auctions. In recent years, governments have auctioned portions of the airwaves for radio stations, mobile phones, and wireless internet access and have used auctions to set up electricity and transport markets. Other goods commonly sold at auction are natural resources such as timber, as well as houses, cars, agricultural produce, horses, antiques, and art. In this section, we first consider the various types of auctions and then investigate how the rules of the auction influence buyers' strategies.

Elements of Auctions

Before deciding what strategy to use when bidding in an auction, one needs to know the rules of the game. Auctions have three key components: the number of units being sold, the format of the bidding, and the value that potential bidders place on the good.

Number of Units. Auctions can be used to sell one or many units of a good. The U.S. Department of the Treasury holds regular auctions of U.S. government bonds, selling bonds to many different buyers in the same auction. In many other auctions, a single good—such as an original painting—is sold. For simplicity in this discussion, we concentrate on auctions where a single, indivisible item is sold.

Format. Virtually all auctions are variants of the *English auction*, the *Dutch auction*, the *sealed-bid auction*, or the *double auction*.

- **English auction:** In the United States and Britain, almost everyone has seen an *English* or *ascending-bid auction*, at least in the movies. The auctioneer starts the bidding at the lowest price that is acceptable to the seller and then repeatedly encourages potential buyers to bid more than the previous highest bidder. The auction ends when no one is willing to bid more than the current highest bid by the time the auctioneer has called out "Going, going, gone!" The good is sold to the last bidder for the highest bid. Sotheby's and Christie's use English auctions to sell art and antiques.

- **Dutch auction:** A *Dutch auction* or *descending-bid auction* ends dramatically with the first "bid." The seller starts by asking if anyone wants to buy at a high price. The seller reduces the price by given increments until someone accepts the offered price and then buys at that price. Variants of Dutch auctions are often used to sell multiple goods simultaneously, such as in Google's initial public offering auction and the U.S. Treasury's sales of Treasury bills.
- **Sealed-bid auction:** In a *sealed-bid auction*, everyone submits a bid simultaneously without seeing the other bids (for example, by submitting each bid in a sealed envelope), and the highest bidder wins. The price the winner pays depends on whether it is a first-price auction or a second-price auction. In a *first-price auction*, the winner pays its own, highest bid. Governments often use this type of auction. In a *second-price auction*, the winner pays the amount bid by the second-highest bidder.
- **Double auction.** All potential buyers and sellers in a *double auction* may make public offers stating prices at which they are willing buy or sell. They may accept another participant's offer to buy or sell. Traditionally, most financial exchanges in which people trade stocks, options, or other securities were *oral* double auctions. Traders stood in *open pits* and would shout, wave cards in the air, or use hand signals to convey their offers or to signal agreements to trade. In recent years, almost all of these exchanges have switched to *electronic* double-auction systems.

Many online auction houses use a variant of the second-price auction. For example, you bid on eBay by specifying the maximum amount you are willing to bid. If your maximum is greater than the maximum bid of the other participants, eBay's computer places a bid on your behalf that is a small increment above the maximum bid of the second-highest bidder. This system differs from the traditional sealed-bid auction in that people can continue to bid until the official end of the auction, and potential bidders know the current bid price (but not the maximum that the highest bidder is willing to pay). Thus, eBay has some characteristics of an English auction.

Value. Auctioned goods are normally described as having a *private value* or a *common value*. Typically, this distinction turns on whether the good is unique.

- **Private value:** If each potential bidder places a different personal value on a good, we say that the good has a *private value*. Individual bidders know how much the good is worth to them but not how much other bidders value it. An archetypical example is an original work of art, which can be valued very differently by many people.
- **Common value:** Many auctions involve a good that has the same fundamental value to everyone, but no buyer knows exactly what that *common value* is. For example, in a timber auction, firms bid on all the trees in a given area. All firms know the current price of lumber; however, they do not know exactly how many board feet of lumber are contained in the trees.

In many actual auctions, goods have both private value and common value. For example, in the tree auction, bidding firms may differ not only in their estimates of the amount of lumber in the trees (common value), but also in their costs of harvesting (private value).

Bidding Strategies in Private-Value Auctions

A potential buyer's optimal strategy depends on the number of units, the format, and the type of values in an auction. For specificity, we examine auctions in which each bidder places a different private value on a single, indivisible good.

Second-Price Auction Strategies. According to eBay, if you choose to bid on an item in its second-price auction, you should "enter the maximum amount you are willing to spend."[16] Is eBay's advice correct?

In a traditional sealed-bid, second-price auction, bidding your highest value *weakly dominates* all other bidding strategies: The strategy of bidding your maximum value leaves you *as well off* as, or *better off* than, bidding any other value. The amount that you bid affects whether you win, but it does not affect how much you pay if you win, which equals the second-highest bid.

Suppose that you value a folk art carving at $100. If the highest amount that any other participant is willing to bid is $85 and you place a bid greater than $85, you will buy the carving for $85 and receive $15 (= $100 − $85) of consumer surplus. Other bidders pay nothing and gain no consumer surplus.

Should you ever bid more than your value? Suppose that you bid $120. You have three possibilities. First, if the highest bid of your rivals is greater than $120, then you do not buy the good and receive no consumer surplus. This outcome is the same as what you would have received if you had bid $100, so bidding higher than $100 does not benefit you.

Second, if the highest alternative bid is less than $100, then you win and receive the same consumer surplus that you would have received had you bid $100. Again, bidding higher does not affect the outcome.

Third, if the highest bid by a rival were an amount between $100 and $120—say, $110—then bidding more than your maximum value causes you to win, but you purchase the good for more than you value it, so you receive negative consumer surplus: −$10 (= $100 − $110). In contrast, if you had bid your maximum value, you would not have won, and your consumer surplus would have been zero—which is better than losing $10. Thus, bidding more than your maximum value can never make you better off than bidding your maximum value, and you may suffer.

Should you ever bid less than your maximum value, say, $90? No, because you only lower the odds of winning without affecting the price that you pay if you do win. If the highest alternative bid is less than $90 or greater than your value, you receive the same consumer surplus by bidding $90 as you would by bidding $100. However, if the highest alternative bid lies between $90 and $100, you will lose the auction and give up positive consumer surplus by underbidding.

Thus, you do as well or better by bidding your value than by overbidding or underbidding. This argument does not turn on whether or not you know other bidders' valuation. If you know your own value but not other bidders' values, bidding your value is your best strategy. If everyone follows this strategy, the person who places the highest value on the good will win and will pay the second-highest value.

English Auction Strategy. Suppose instead that the seller uses an English auction to sell the carving to bidders with various private values. Your best strategy is to raise the current highest bid as long as your bid is less than the value you place on the good, $100. If the current bid is $85, you should increase your bid by the smallest permitted amount, say, $86, which is less than your value. If no one raises the bid further, you

---

[16] See **pages.ebay.com/education/gettingstarted/bidding.html**.

win and receive a positive surplus of $14. By the same reasoning, it always pays to increase your bid up to $100, where you receive zero surplus if you win.

However, it never pays to bid more than $100. The best outcome that you can hope for is to lose and receive zero surplus. Were you to win, you would have negative surplus.

If all participants bid up to their value, the winner will pay slightly more than the value of the second-highest bidder. Thus, the outcome is essentially the same as in the sealed-bid, second-price auction.

Equivalence of Auction Outcomes. For Dutch or first-price sealed-bid auctions, one can show that participants will *shade* their bids to less than their value. The basic intuition is that you do not know the values of the other bidders. Reducing your bid lowers the probability that you will win but increases your consumer surplus if you do win. Your optimal bid, which balances these two effects, is lower than your actual value. Your bid depends on your beliefs about the strategies of your rivals. It can be shown that the best strategy is to bid an amount that is equal to or slightly greater than what you expect will be the second-highest bid, given that your value is the highest.

The expected outcome is the same under each format for private-value auctions: The winner is the person with the highest value, and the winner pays roughly the second-highest value. According to the Revenue Equivalence Theorem (Klemperer, 2004), under certain plausible conditions we would expect the same revenue from any auction in which the winner is the person who places the highest value on the good.

Winner's Curse

The **winner's curse** is that the auction winner's bid exceeds the common-value item's value. Such overbidding occurs when bidders are uncertain about the true value of the good. This phenomenon occurs in common-value auctions, but not in private-value auctions.

When the government auctions off timber on a plot of land, potential bidders may differ in their estimates of how many board feet of lumber are available on that land. The higher one's estimate, the more likely that one will make the winning bid. If the average bid is accurate, then the high bid is probably excessive. Thus, the winner's curse is paying too much.

Each bidder thinks, "I can minimize the likelihood of falling prey to the winner's curse by *shading* my bid below my estimate. I know that if I win, I am probably overestimating the value of the good. The amount by which I should shade my bid depends on the number of other bidders, because the more bidders, the more likely that the winning bid is an overestimate."

Because intelligent bidders shade their bids, sellers generally receive more money with an English auction than with a sealed-bid auction. In an English auction, bidders revise their views about the object's value as they watch others bid.

APPLICATION

Bidder's Curse

What's the maximum you would bid for an item that you know you can buy for a fixed price of p? No matter how much you value the good, it doesn't make sense to bid more than p. Yet, people commonly do that on eBay. Lee and Malmendier (2011) call bidding more than what should be one's valuation—here, the fixed price—*bidder's curse*.

They examined eBay auctions of a board game, Cashflow 101, a game that is supposed to help people better understand their finances. A search on eBay for

Cashflow 101 not only listed the auctions but also the availability of the game for a fixed price. During the period studied, the game was continuously available for a fixed price on the eBay site (with identical or better quality and seller reputation and lower shipping cost).

Even if only a few buyers overbid, they affect the auction price and who wins. The auction price exceeded the fixed price in 42% of the auctions. The average overpayment was 10% of the fixed price. This overbidding was caused by a small number of bidders—only 17% bid above the fixed price. However, people who bid too much are disproportionately likely to win the auction and, hence, determine the winning price.

One possible behavioral economics explanation is that bidders paid limited attention to the fixed-price option. Lee and Malmendier found that overbidding was less likely the closer the fixed price appeared on the same screen to the auction and hence the more likely that bidders would notice the fixed-price listing.

Another explanation is lack of bidding experience. Garratt, Walker, and Wooders (2012) and Feng, Fay, and Sivakumar (2016) found that inexperienced bidders were more likely to overbid than were experienced bidders.

13.5 Behavioral Game Theory

We normally assume that people are rational in the sense that they optimize using all available information. However, they may be subject to psychological biases and may have limited powers of calculation that cause them to act irrationally, as described in the Application "Bidder's Curse." Such possibilities are the domain of behavioral economics (Chapters 3 and 11), which seeks to augment the rational economic model so as to better understand and predict economic decision making.

Another example of nonoptimal strategies occurs in *ultimatum games*. People often face an *ultimatum*, where one person (the *proposer*) makes a "take it or leave it" offer to another (the *responder*). No matter how long the parties have negotiated, once an ultimatum is issued, the responder has to accept or reject the offer with no opportunity to make a counteroffer. An ultimatum can be viewed as a sequential game in which the proposer moves first and the responder moves second.

APPLICATION

GM's Ultimatum

In 2009, General Motors (GM), facing bankruptcy, planned to shut down about one-fourth of its dealerships in the United States and one-third in Canada. Because GM was concerned that dealer opposition could cause delays and impose other costs, it offered dealers slated for termination an ultimatum. They would receive a (small) payment from GM if they did not oppose the restructuring plan.

Dealers could accept the ultimatum and get something, or they could reject the offer, oppose the reorganization, and receive nothing. Although it was irrational, some dealers rejected the ultimatum and loudly complained that GM was "high-handed, oppressive, and patently unfair." In 2011, some terminated Canadian dealerships filed a class-action suit against GM of Canada, which they lost in 2017.

An Experiment. The possibility that someone might turn down an offer even at some personal cost is important in business and personal negotiations. To gain insight into real decisions, Camerer (2003) conducted an ultimatum experiment.

A group of student participants meets in a computer lab. Each person is designated as either a proposer or a responder. Using the computers, each proposer is matched (anonymously) with one responder. The game is based on dividing $10. Each proposer makes an ultimatum offer to the responder of a particular amount. A responder who accepts receives the amount offered and the proposer gets the rest of the $10. If the responder rejects the offer, both players get nothing.

To find the rational, subgame perfect solution, we use backward induction. In the second stage, the responder should accept if the offer x is positive. Thus in the first stage, the proposer should offer the lowest possible positive amount.

However, such rational behavior is not a good predictor of actual outcomes. The lowest possible offer is rarely made and, when it is, it is usually rejected. Thus, a proposer who makes the mistake of expecting the responder to be fully rational is likely to receive nothing. The most common range for offers is between $3 and $4—far more than the "rational" minimum offer. Offers less than $2 are relatively rare and, when they do occur, are turned down about half the time.

One concern about such experiments is that the payoffs are small enough that not all participants take the game seriously. However, when the total amount to be divided was increased to $100, the results were essentially unchanged: The typical offer remained between 30% and 40% of the total. If anything, responders are even more likely to turn down lowball offers when the stakes are higher.

Reciprocity. Some responders who reject lowball offers feel the proposer is being greedy and would prefer to make a small sacrifice rather than reward such behavior. Some responders are angered by low offers, some feel insulted, and some feel that they should oppose "unfair" behavior. Most proposers anticipate such feelings and offer a significant amount to the responder, but almost always less than 50%.

Apparently, most people accept that the advantage of moving first should provide some extra benefit to proposers, but not too much. Moreover, they believe in *reciprocity*. If others treat us well, we want to return the favor. If they treat us badly, we want to "get even" and will retaliate if the cost does not seem excessive. Thus, if a proposer makes a low offer, many responders are willing to give up something to punish the proposer, using "an eye for an eye" philosophy.

Eckel and Grossman (1996) found that men are more likely than women to punish if the personal cost is high in an ultimatum game. They speculate that this difference may explain gender patterns in wages and unemployment during downturns, where men are more likely to rigidly insist on a given wage than are women, who are more flexible.

CHALLENGE SOLUTION

Intel and AMD's Advertising Strategies

As we've seen, when one firm in a market acts before another, the first mover may gain an advantage large enough to discourage the second firm from entering the market. In a less extreme case, the original firm may gain a smaller advantage so that the second firm enters, but it produces less than the original firm (as in the airlines' Stackelberg model). We can use this insight to provide a possible explanation for the Challenge: In the market for CPUs for personal computers, why does Intel advertise substantially while AMD does not?

In Solved Problem 13.1, we examined a game where Intel and AMD act simultaneously and have symmetric profits (which is consistent with the estimates of Salgado, 2008). That game has two pure-strategy equilibria. In each, one firm advertises

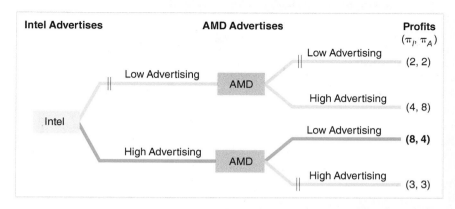

Intel Advertises	AMD Advertises	Profits (π_I, π_A)

at a low level while the other firm sets a high level. Exercise 5.2 asks you to show this game also has a mixed-strategy equilibrium in which each firm sets its advertising low with probability $\frac{1}{7}$ (and has an expected profit of about 3.71).

In contrast, the game has a clear outcome given that Intel acted first, as actually happened. The game tree shows that Intel decides on how much to advertise before AMD can act. AMD then decides how much to advertise. We solve for the subgame perfect, Nash equilibrium by working backward. For the profits in this game, if Intel were to have a minimal advertising campaign, AMD makes more if it advertises a lot ($\pi_A = 8$) than if it too has a low level of advertising ($\pi_A = 2$). If Intel advertises heavily, AMD makes more with a low-level advertising campaign ($\pi_A = 4$) than with a high-level campaign ($\pi_A = 3$). Given how it expects AMD to behave, Intel intensively advertises because doing so produces a higher profit ($\pi_I = 8$) than does the lower level of advertising ($\pi_I = 4$).

Thus, because Intel acts first and can commit to advertising aggressively, it can place AMD in a position where it makes more with a low-key advertising campaign. Of course, the results might vary if the profits in the game tree differ, but this example provides a plausible explanation for why the firms' strategies differ.

SUMMARY

Economists use game theory to analyze conflict and cooperation among players (such as firms). Each player adopts a strategy or battle plan to compete with other firms. Economists typically assume that players have *common knowledge* about the rules of the game, the strategies and payoff functions, and other players' knowledge about these issues.

1. **Static Games.** In a static game, such as the prisoners' dilemma game, players each make one move simultaneously. Economists use a normal-form representation or payoff matrix to analyze a static game. Typically, economists study static games in which players have complete information about the payoff function—the payoff to any player conditional on the actions all players take—but imperfect information about how their rivals behave because they act simultaneously. The set of players' strategies is a Nash equilibrium if, given that all other players use these strategies, no player can obtain a higher payoff by choosing a different strategy. Both pure-strategy and mixed-strategy Nash equilibria are possible in static games, and there may be multiple Nash equilibria for a given game.

There is no guarantee that Nash equilibria in static games maximize the joint payoffs of all the players.

2. **Repeated Dynamic Games.** In some dynamic games, a static game is repeated, such as when firms make price or quantity decisions every quarter. Therefore, a firm may use a strategy in which it makes a particular move contingent on its rival's actions in previous periods. By using contingent strategies, such as a tit-for-tat strategy or another trigger strategy, it is often easier for firms to maximize their joint payoff—achieve a collusive solution—in a repeated game than in a single-period game.

3. **Sequential Dynamic Games.** In other dynamic games, firms move sequentially, with one player acting before another. By moving first, a firm is able to make a *commitment* or *credible threat*. Consequently, the first mover may receive a higher profit than if the firms act simultaneously. For example, in the Stackelberg oligopoly model, one firm is a *leader* in a sequential game and therefore chooses its output level before rival firms (followers) choose theirs. Applying

backward induction, the leader anticipates a follower's reaction and chooses its best output accordingly in the first stage. This first-stage output is a commitment that allows the leader to gain a first-mover advantage. The leader produces more output and earns higher profits than does a follower firm with the same costs.

4. **Auctions.** Auctions are games of incomplete information because bidders do not know the valuation others place on a good. Buyers' optimal strategies depend on the characteristics of an auction. Under fairly general conditions, if the auction rules result in a win by the person placing the highest value on a good that various bidders value differently, the expected price is the same in all auctions. For example, the expected price in various types of private-value auctions is the value of the good to the person who values it second highest. In auctions where everyone values the good the same, though they may differ in their estimates of that value, the successful bidder may suffer from the winner's curse—paying too much—unless bidders shade their bids to compensate for their overoptimistic estimation of the good's value.

5. **Behavioral Game Theory.** People may not use rational strategies because of psychological bias, lack of reasoning ability, or their belief that others will not use rational strategies. The ultimatum game illustrates that people commonly use irrational strategies in certain circumstances.

EXERCISES

All exercises are available on **MyLab Economics**; * = *answer appears at the back of this book;* **M** = *mathematical problem.*

1. Static Games

*1.1 Show the payoff matrix and explain the reasoning in the prisoners' dilemma example where Larry and Duncan, possible criminals, will get one year in prison if neither talks; if one talks, one goes free and the other gets five years; and if both talk, both get two years. (*Note*: The payoffs are negative because they represent years in jail, which is a bad.)

1.2 Show that advertising is a dominant strategy for both firms in both panels of Table 13.3. Explain why that pair of strategies is a Nash equilibrium.

*1.3 Two firms must simultaneously decide which quality to manufacture. The profit matrix (in tens of thousands of euros) is

			Firm 1			
		Low		Medium		High
Firm 2	Low		1		21		12
		11		19		6
	Medium		25		2		4
		16		3		23
	High		24		26		11
		5		14		17

Identify all the Nash equilibria in this game. (See Solved Problem 13.1.)

1.4 Suppose Procter & Gamble (PG) and Johnson & Johnson (JNJ) are simultaneously considering new advertising campaigns. Each firm may choose a high, medium, or low level of advertising. What are each firm's best responses to its rival's strategies? Does either firm have a dominant strategy? What is the Nash equilibrium in this game? (See Solved Problem 13.1.)

			PG		
		High	Medium	Low
JNJ	High	1 / 1	2 / 3	3 / 5
	Medium	3 / 2	4 / 4	5 / 6
	Low	5 / 3	6 / 5	5 / 7

1.5 Lori employs Max. She wants him to work hard rather than to loaf. She considers offering him a bonus or not giving him one. All else the same, Max prefers to loaf. The payoff matrix is

			Max	
		Work	Loaf
Lori	Bonus	2 / 1	3 / −1
	No Bonus	−1 / 3	0 / 0

If they choose actions simultaneously, what are their strategies? (See Solved Problem 13.2.) **M**

1.6 Suppose that two firms face the following payoff matrix:

Firm 1

	Low Price	High Price
Low Price	2 \ 0	1 \ 2
High Price	0 \ 7	6 \ 6

(Firm 2 on the left axis, rows: Low Price, High Price)

Given these payoffs, Firm 2 wants to match Firm 1's price, but Firm 1 does not want to match Firm 2's price. What, if any, are the pure-strategy Nash equilibria of this game?

*1.7 What is the mixed-strategy Nash equilibrium for the game in Exercise 1.6? **M**

*1.8 Suppose that Toyota and GM are considering entering a new market for self-driving trucks and that their profits (in millions of dollars) from entering or staying out of the market are

GM

	Enter	Do Not Enter
Enter	10 \ −40	250 \ 0
Do Not Enter	0 \ 200	0 \ 0

(Toyota on the left axis, rows: Enter, Do Not Enter)

If the firms make their decisions simultaneously, which firms enter? How would your answer change if the U.S. government committed to paying GM a lump-sum subsidy of $50 million on the condition that it would produce this new type of truck?

1.9 In the *battle of the sexes* game, the husband likes to go to the mountains on vacation, and the wife prefers the ocean, but they both prefer to take their vacations together.

Husband

	Mountains	Beach
Mountains	2 \ 1	−1 \ −1
Beach	−1 \ −1	1 \ 2

(Wife on the left axis, rows: Mountains, Beach)

What are the Nash equilibria? Discuss whether this game and equilibrium concept make sense for analyzing a couple's decisions. How might you change the game's rules so that it makes more sense? **M**

1.10 Takashi Hashiyama, president of the Japanese electronics firm Maspro Denkoh Corporation, was torn between commissioning Christie's or Sotheby's to auction the company's $20 million art collection, which included a van Gogh, a Cézanne, and an early Picasso (Carol Vogel, "Rock, Paper, Payoff," *New York Times*, April 29, 2005, A1, A24). He resolved the issue by having the two auction houses' representatives compete in the playground game of rock-paper-scissors. A rock (fist) breaks scissors (two extended fingers), scissors cut paper (flat hand), and paper smothers rock. At stake were several million dollars in commissions. Christie's won: Scissors cut paper. Show the profit or payoff matrix for this rock-paper-scissors game. (*Hint*: You may assume that the payoff is −1 if you lose, 0 if you tie, and 1 if you win.) What pure or mixed strategy would you have recommended, and why? **M**

1.11 Suppose that Panasonic and LG are the only two firms that can produce a new type of holographic TV. The payoff matrix shows the firms' profits (in millions of dollars):

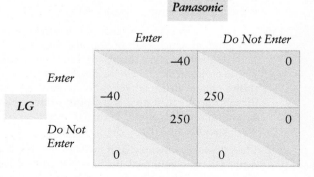

Panasonic

	Enter	Do Not Enter
Enter	−40 \ −40	250 \ 0
Do Not Enter	0 \ 250	0 \ 0

(LG on the left axis, rows: Enter, Do Not Enter)

a. If both firms move simultaneously, does either firm have a dominant strategy? Explain.

b. What are the Nash equilibria given that both firms move simultaneously?

c. The South Korean government commits to pay LG a lump-sum subsidy of $50 million if it enters this market. What is the Nash equilibrium?

1.12 Two guys (suffering from testosterone poisoning) engage in the game of chicken. They drive toward each other in the middle of a road. As they approach the impact point, each has the option of continuing to drive down the middle of the road or to swerve. Both believe that if only one driver swerves, that driver loses face (payoff = 0) and the other gains in self-esteem (payoff = 2). If neither swerves, they are maimed or killed (payoff = −10). If both swerve, neither is harmed (payoff = 1). Show the payoff matrix for the two drivers engaged in this game of chicken. Determine the Nash equilibria for this game. **M**

1.13 Modify the payoff matrix in the game of chicken in Exercise 1.12 so that the payoff is −2 if neither driver swerves. How does the equilibrium change? **M**

1.14 In the novel and film *The Princess Bride*, the villain Vizzini kidnaps the princess. In an attempt to rescue her, the hero, Westley, challenges Vizzini to a battle of wits. Consider this variation on the actual plot. (I do not want to reveal the story.) In the battle, Westley puts two identical glasses of wine behind his back, out of Vizzini's view, and adds iocane powder to one glass. Iocane is "odorless, tasteless, dissolves instantly in liquid, and is among the more deadly poisons known to man." Westley decides which glass to put on the table closest to Vizzini and which to put closest to himself. Then, with Westley's back turned so that he cannot observe Vizzini's move, Vizzini decides whether to switch the two glasses. Assume the two simultaneously drink all the wine in their respective glasses. Assume also that each player's payoff from drinking the poisoned wine is −3 and the payoff from drinking the safe wine is +1. Write the payoff matrix for this simultaneous-moves game. Specify the possible Nash equilibria. Is there a pure-strategy Nash equilibrium? Is there a mixed-strategy Nash equilibrium? **M**

1.15 Suppose that you and a friend play a *matching pennies* game in which each of you uncovers a penny. If both pennies show heads or both show tails, you keep both. If one shows heads and the other shows tails, your friend keeps them. Show the payoff matrix. What, if any, is the pure-strategy Nash equilibrium to this game? Is there a mixed-strategy Nash equilibrium? If so, what is it? **M**

1.16 The 100-meter Olympic gold medalist and the 200-meter Olympic gold medalist have agreed to a 150-meter duel. Before the race, each athlete decides whether to improve his performance by taking anabolic steroids. Each athlete's payoff is 20 from winning the race, 10 from tying, and 0 from losing. Furthermore, each athlete's utility of taking steroids is −6. Model this scenario as a game in which the players simultaneously decide whether to take steroids.

a. What is the Nash equilibrium? Is the game a prisoners' dilemma? Explain.

b. Suppose that one athlete's utility of taking steroids is −12, while the other's remains at −6. What is the Nash equilibrium? Is the game a prisoners' dilemma? **M**

1.17 In the Application "Strategic Advertising," would the cola advertising or cigarette advertising game be an example of a prisoners' dilemma game?

1.18 For the examples of two-sided markets in Tables 13.4 and 13.5, would the firms change their strategies were they to merge (form one firm) or collude (coordinate activities)?

2. Repeated Dynamic Games

2.1 In a repeated game, how does the outcome differ if firms know that the game will be (a) repeated indefinitely, (b) repeated a known, finite number of times, or (c) repeated a finite number of times but the firms are unsure as to which period will be the last period? (*Hint*: See Solved Problem 13.3.)

*2.2 The airlines play the game in Table 13.1 repeatedly. What happens if the players know the game will last five periods? What happens if they repeat the game indefinitely but one or both firms care only about current profit?

2.3 You and your best friend swear that if either of you reveals the other person's secrets, that person will never speak to you again. How is this scenario like the repeated games described in this chapter? Discuss the circumstances under which this oath will result in neither of you revealing the other's secrets.

3. Sequential Dynamic Games

3.1 Two firms are planning to sell 10 or 20 units of their goods and face the following profit matrix:

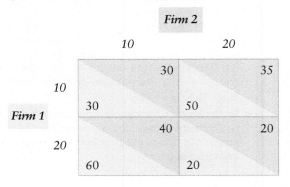

a. What is the Nash equilibrium if both firms make their decisions simultaneously?

b. Draw the game tree if Firm 1 can decide first. What is the outcome? Why?

c. Draw the game tree if Firm 2 can decide first. What is the outcome? Why?

3.2 How does your analysis change if the government imposes a lump-sum franchise tax of 40 on each firm (that is, the payoffs in the matrix are all reduced by 40). Explain how your analysis would change if the firms have an additional option of shutting down and avoiding the lump-sum tax rather than producing 10 or 20 units and paying the tax.

3.3 Suppose that Exercise 1.8 were modified so that GM has no subsidy but does have a head start over Toyota and can move first. What is the Nash equilibrium? Explain.

3.4 A small tourist town has two Italian restaurants, Romano's and Giardino's. Normally both restaurants prosper with no advertising. Romano's could take some of Giardino's customers by running radio ads and Giardino's could do the same thing. The one-month profit matrix (showing payoffs in thousands of dollars) is

		Romano's	
		Do Not Advertise	*Advertise*
Giardino's	*Do Not Advertise*	3 / 3	4 / 0
	Advertise	0 / 4	1 / 1

a. What is the Nash equilibrium in the static (one-month) game?

b. Describe one or more possible Nash equilibria if the game is repeated indefinitely.

c. Are there multiple equilibria if the game repeats indefinitely?

3.5 In Solved Problem 13.2, suppose that Mimi can move first. What are the equilibria, and why? Now repeat your analysis if Jeff can move first.

3.6 Solve for the Stackelberg subgame perfect Nash equilibrium for the following game tree. What is the joint-profit-maximizing outcome? Why is that not the outcome of this game?

Leader Sets Output	Follower Sets Output		Profits (π_1, π_2)
	Firm 2 (180)	48	(64.9, 64.8)
		64	(54.0, 72.0)
		96	(32.1, 64.8)
Firm 1	Firm 2 (240)	48	(72.0, 54.0)
		64	(57.6, 57.6)
		96	(28.8, 43.2)
	Firm 2 (360)	48	(64.8, 32.4)
		64	(43.2, 28.8)
		96	(0, 0)

3.7 A criminal wants the contents of a safe and is threatening the owner, the only person who knows the code, to open the safe. "I will kill you if you don't open the safe, and let you live if you do." Should the information holder believe the threat and open the safe? The table shows the value that each person places on the various possible outcomes.

	Thug	Safe's Owner
Open the safe, thug does not kill	4	3
Open the safe, thug kills	2	1
Do not open, thug kills	1	2
Do not open, thug does not kill	3	4

Such a game appears in many films, including *Die Hard*, *Crimson Tide*, and *The Maltese Falcon*.

a. Draw the game tree. Who moves first?

b. What is the equilibrium?

c. Does the safe's owner believe the thug's threat?

d. Does the safe's owner open the safe?

3.8 Levi Strauss and Wrangler are planning new-generation jeans and must decide on the colors for their products. The possible colors are white, black, and violet. The payoff to each firm depends on the color it chooses and the color chosen by its rival, as the profit matrix shows:

		Levi Strauss		
		White	*Black*	*Violet*
Wrangler	*White*	10 / 10	30 / 20	40 / 30
	Black	20 / 30	0 / 0	35 / 15
	Violet	15 / 40	20 / 35	0 / 0

a. Given that the firms move simultaneously, identify any dominant strategies in this game, and find any pure-strategy Nash equilibria.

b. Now suppose the firms move sequentially, with Wrangler moving first. Draw a game tree and identify any subgame perfect Nash equilibria in this sequential-move game.

*3.9 A monopoly manufacturing plant currently uses many workers to pack its product into boxes. It can replace these workers with an expensive set of robotic arms. Although the robotic arms raise the monopoly's fixed cost substantially, they lower its marginal cost because it no longer has to hire as many workers. Buying the robotic arms raises its total cost: The monopoly can't sell enough boxes to make the machine pay for itself, given the market demand curve. Suppose the incumbent does not invest. If its rival does not enter, it earns $0 and the incumbent earns $900. If the rival enters, it earns $300 and the incumbent earns $400. Alternatively, the incumbent invests. If the rival does not enter, it earns $0 and the incumbent earns $500. If the rival enters, the rival loses $36 and the incumbent makes $132. Show the game tree. Should the monopoly buy the machine anyway? (See Solved Problem 13.4.)

*3.10 Suppose that an incumbent can commit to producing a large quantity of output before the potential entrant decides whether to enter. The incumbent chooses whether to commit to produce a small quantity or a large quantity. The rival then decides whether to enter. If the incumbent commits to the small output level and if the rival does not enter, the rival makes $0 and the incumbent makes $900. If it does enter, the rival makes $125 and the incumbent earns $450. If the incumbent commits to producing the large quantity, and the potential entrant stays out of the market, the potential entrant makes $0 and the incumbent makes $800. If the rival enters, the best the entrant can make is $0, the same amount it would earn if it didn't enter, but the incumbent earns only $400. Show the game tree. What is the subgame perfect Nash equilibrium? (See Solved Problem 13.4 and 13.5.)

*3.11 Before entry, the incumbent earns a monopoly profit of $\pi_m = \$10$ (million). If entry occurs, the incumbent and entrant each earn the duopoly profit, $\pi_d = \$3$. Suppose that the incumbent can induce the government to require all firms to install pollution-control devices that cost each firm $4. Show the game tree. Should the incumbent urge the government to require pollution-control devices? Why or why not? (See Solved Problem 13.4.)

3.12 Due to learning by doing (Chapter 7), the more that an incumbent firm produces in the first period, the lower its marginal cost in the second period. If a potential entrant expects the incumbent to produce a large quantity in the second period, it does not enter. Draw a game tree to illustrate why an incumbent would produce more in the first period than the single-period profit-maximizing level. Now change the payoffs in the tree to show a situation in which the firm does not increase production in the first period. (See Solved Problem 13.4.)

3.13 In 2007, Italy announced that an Italian journalist who had been held hostage for 15 days by the Taliban in Afghanistan had been ransomed for five Taliban prisoners. Governments in many nations denounced the act as a bad idea because it rewarded terrorism and encouraged more abductions. Use an extensive-form game tree to analyze the basic arguments. Can you draw any hard and fast conclusions about whether the Italians' actions were a good or bad idea? (*Hint*: Does your answer depend on the relative weight one puts on future costs and benefits relative to those today?)

3.14 Salgado (2008) found that AMD's cost of manufacturing computer chips was about 12% higher than Intel's cost because AMD had less learning by doing (Chapter 7), as it had produced fewer units. The more an incumbent firm produces in the first period, the lower its marginal cost in the second period. If a potential entrant expects the incumbent to produce a large quantity in the second period, it does not enter. Draw a game tree to illustrate why an incumbent would produce more in the first period than the single-period profit-maximizing level. Now change the payoffs in the tree to show a situation in which the firm does not increase production in the first period. (*Hint*: See Solved Problems 13.4 and 13.5.)

4. Auctions

4.1 Suppose that Anna, Bill, and Cameron are the only people interested in the paintings of the Bucks County artist Walter Emerson Baum. His painting *Sellers Mill* is being auctioned by a second-price sealed-bid auction. Suppose Anna's value of the painting is $20,000, Bill's is $18,500, and Cameron's is $16,800. Each bidder's consumer surplus is $v_i - p$ if he or she wins the auction and 0 if he or she loses. The values are private. What is each bidder's optimal bid? Who wins the auction, and what price does he or she pay? **M**

4.2 At the end of performances of his Broadway play *Cyrano de Bergerac*, Kevin Kline, who starred as Cyrano, the cavalier poet with a huge nose, auctioned his prosthetic proboscis, which he and his co-star, Jennifer Garner, autographed to benefit Broadway Cares in its fight against AIDS. They used an English auction. One night, a television producer grabbed the nose for $1,400, while the next night it fetched $1,600. On other nights, it sold for $3,000 and $900. Why did the value fluctuate substantially from night to night? Which bidder's bid determined the sales price? How did the audience's knowledge that the proceeds would go to charity affect the auction price?

4.3 Charity events often use silent auctions. A donated item or event, such as a meal with a movie star (Colin Firth and Scarlett Johansson in 2008) or a former president (Bill Clinton in 2013) or Warren Buffett (in 2018), is put up for bid. In a silent auction, bidders write down bids and submit them. Some silent auctions use secret bids, which bidders submit in sealed envelopes, and which are confidential. Other silent auctions are open: Bidders write a bid on a bulletin board that everyone present can see. Which kind of auction would you expect to raise more revenue for the charity?

5. Behavioral Game Theory

5.1 Draw a game tree that represents the ultimatum game in which the proposer is a first mover who decides how much to offer a responder and the responder then decides to accept or reject the offer. The total amount available is $50 if agreement is reached, but both players get nothing if the responder rejects the offer.

5.2 A prisoners' dilemma game is played for a fixed number of periods. The fully rational solution is for each player to defect in each period. However, in experiments with students, players often cooperate for a significant number of periods if the total number of periods is fairly large (such as 10 or 20). What explanation can you give for this behavior?

6. Challenge

6.1 In the game between Intel and AMD in the Challenge Solution, suppose that each firm earns a profit of 9 if both firms advertise. What is the new subgame perfect Nash equilibrium outcome? Show in a game tree.

6.2 Derive the mixed-strategy equilibrium if both Intel and AMD act simultaneously in the game in the Challenge Solution. What is the expected profit of each firm? (*Hint:* See Solved Problems 13.1 and 13.2 and the Challenge Solution.) **M**

14 Oligopoly and Monopolistic Competition

Anyone can win unless there happens to be a second entry. —George Ade

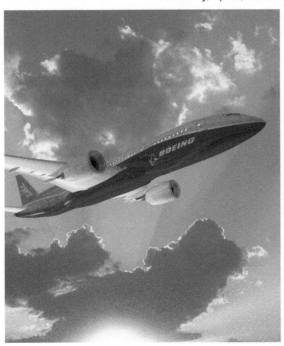

Aircraft manufacturers lobby their governments for subsidies, which they use to better compete with rival firms. Airbus SAS, based in Europe, and the Boeing Co., based in the United States, are the only two major manufacturers of large commercial jet aircraft. France, Germany, Spain, and the United Kingdom subsidize Airbus, which competes in the wide-body aircraft market with Boeing. The U.S. government decries the European subsidies to Airbus despite giving lucrative military contracts to Boeing, which the Europeans view as implicit subsidies.

This government largesse does not magically appear. Managers at both Boeing and Airbus lobby strenuously for this support. For example, in 2017–2018, Boeing spent over $24 million on lobbying and was represented by 105 lobbyists, 76 of whom previously held government jobs.

Washington and the European Union have repeatedly charged each other before the World Trade Organization (WTO) with illegally subsidizing their respective aircraft manufacturers. In 2012, the WTO ruled that Boeing and Airbus both received improper subsidies. In 2015, the WTO agreed to investigate a complaint about Washington State subsidies to Boeing, and Boeing questioned government loans to Airbus. In 2018, the WTO concluded that the European Union and members France, Germany, Spain, and the United Kingdom "failed to comply with an earlier WTO panel ruling by maintaining illegal subsidies" for Airbus. Thus, the cycle of subsidies, charges, agreements, and new subsidies continues. . . .

If only one government subsidizes its firm, what are the price and quantity effects in the aircraft manufacturing market (see Solved Problem 14.3)? What happens if both governments subsidize their firms (see the Challenge Solution)?

The major airlines within a country compete with relatively few other firms. Consequently, each firm's profit depends on its own actions and those of its rivals. Similarly, three firms—Nintendo, Microsoft, and Sony—dominate the $13 billion U.S. video game market, and each firm's profit depends on how its price stacks up to those of its rivals and whether its product has better features.

The group of airlines and the group of video game firms are each an **oligopoly**: a small group of firms in a market with substantial barriers to entry. Because relatively few firms compete in such a market, each can influence the price, and hence its actions affect rival firms. The need to consider the behavior of rival firms makes an oligopolistic firm's profit maximization decision more difficult than that of a monopoly or competitive firm. A monopoly has no rivals, and a competitive firm ignores the behavior of individual rivals—it considers only the market price and its own costs in choosing its profit-maximizing output.

An oligopolistic firm that ignores or inaccurately predicts its rivals' behavior is likely to suffer a loss of profit. For example, as its rivals produce more cars, the price that Ford can get for its cars falls. If Ford underestimates how many cars Toyota and Honda will produce, Ford may produce too many automobiles and lose money.

Oligopolistic firms may act independently or coordinate their actions. If firms coordinate setting their prices or quantities, the firms **collude**. A group of firms that collude is a **cartel**. If all the firms in a market collude and behave like a monopoly, the members of a cartel collectively earn the monopoly profit—the maximum possible profit. Generally, collusion is illegal in most developed countries.

How do oligopolistic firms behave if they do not collude? Although economists have only one model of competition and only one model of monopoly, we have many models of oligopolistic behavior that have many possible equilibrium prices and quantities.

The appropriate model depends on the characteristics of the market, including the type of *actions* firms take—such as setting quantity or price—and whether firms act simultaneously or sequentially. We examine the three best-known oligopoly models in turn. In the *Cournot model*, firms simultaneously choose quantities without colluding. In the *Stackelberg model*, a leader firm chooses its quantity and then the follower firms independently choose their quantities. In the *Bertrand model*, firms simultaneously and independently choose prices.

To compare market outcomes within the various models, we must be able to characterize the oligopoly equilibrium. Because oligopolistic firms may take many possible actions (such as setting price or quantity, or choosing an advertising level), the oligopoly equilibrium rule needs to refer to firms' behavior more generally than just setting output. Thus, we use the Nash equilibrium concept that we introduced in Chapter 13: A set of strategies is a *Nash equilibrium* if, when all other players use these strategies, no player can obtain a higher payoff by choosing a different strategy. In most models in this chapter, we use a special case of that definition that is appropriate for single-period oligopoly models in which the only action that a firm can take is to set either its quantity or its price. That is, a set of actions that the firms take is a *Nash equilibrium* if, holding the actions of all other firms constant, no firm can obtain a higher profit by choosing a different action.

If oligopolistic firms do not collude, they collectively earn less than the monopoly profit. Yet because the market has few firms, oligopolistic firms that act independently may earn positive economic profits in the long run, unlike competitive firms.

In an oligopolistic market, one or more barriers to entry keep the number of firms small. In a market with no barriers to entry, firms enter the market until the last entrant earns zero profit. In perfectly competitive markets, enough entry occurs that firms face a horizontal demand curve and are price takers. However, in other markets, even after entry has driven profits to zero, each firm faces a downward-sloping demand curve. Because of this slope, the firm can charge a price above its marginal cost, creating a *market failure*: inefficient (too little) consumption (Chapter 9). **Monopolistic competition** is a market structure in which firms have market power (the ability to raise price profitably above marginal cost) but no additional firm can enter and earn a positive profit.

In this chapter, we examine cartelized, oligopolistic, and monopolistically competitive markets in which firms set quantities or prices. As we saw in Chapter 11, the monopoly equilibrium is the same whether a monopoly sets price or quantity. In contrast, the oligopolistic and monopolistically competitive equilibria differ if firms set prices instead of quantities.

In this chapter, we examine six main topics	
	1. **Market Structures.** The number of firms, price, profits, and other properties of markets vary depending on whether the market is monopolistic, oligopolistic, monopolistically competitive, or competitive.
	2. **Cartels.** If firms successfully coordinate their actions, they can collectively behave like a monopoly, so each firm makes a higher profit than if they were to act independently.
	3. **Cournot Oligopoly Model.** In a Cournot model, in which firms simultaneously set their output levels without colluding, market output and firms' profits lie between the competitive and monopoly levels.
	4. **Stackelberg Oligopoly Model.** In a Stackelberg model, in which a *leader* firm chooses its output level before follower rival firms choose their output levels, market output is greater than if all firms choose their output simultaneously, and the leader makes a higher profit than the other firms.
	5. **Bertrand Oligopoly Model.** In a Bertrand model, in which firms simultaneously set their prices without colluding, the equilibrium depends critically on the degree of product differentiation.
	6. **Monopolistic Competition.** When firms can freely enter the market but face downward-sloping demand curves in equilibrium, firms charge prices above marginal cost but make no profit.

14.1 Market Structures

Markets differ according to the number of firms in the market, the ease with which firms may enter and leave the market, and the ability of firms in a market to differentiate their products from those of their rivals. Table 14.1 lists characteristics and

Table 14.1 Properties of Monopoly, Oligopoly, Monopolistic Competition, and Competition

	Monopoly	Oligopoly	Monopolistic Competition	Perfect Competition
1. Number of firms	1	Few	Few or many	Many
2. Entry conditions	No entry	Limited entry	Free entry	Free entry
3. Long-run profit	≥ 0	≥ 0	0	0
4. Ability to set price	Price setter	Price setter	Price setter	Price taker
5. Price level	Very high	High	High	Low
6. Strategy dependent on individual rival firms' behavior	No (has no rivals)	Yes	Yes	No (cares about market price only)
7. Products	Single product	May be differentiated	May be differentiated	Undifferentiated
8. Example	Local natural gas utility	Automobile manufacturers	Books, restaurants	Apple farmers

properties of the four major market structures: monopoly, oligopoly, monopolistic competition, and perfect competition. In the table, we assume that the firms face many price-taking buyers.

The first row describes the number of firms in each market structure. A monopoly is a single (*mono*) firm in a market. An *oligopoly* usually has a small number (*oligo*) of firms. A *monopolistically competitive* market may have a few or many firms. A *perfectly competitive* market has many firms.

The reason why a monopoly and an oligopoly have few firms is because the markets have insurmountable barriers, such as government licenses or patents, that restrict entry (row 2). In contrast, in monopolistically and perfectly competitive markets, entry occurs until no new firm can profitably enter, so that long-run economic profit is zero (row 3). A monopoly and oligopolistic firms can earn positive long-run profits.

Perfectly competitive firms face horizontal demand curves, so they are price takers. Monopolistically competitive markets have fewer firms than perfectly competitive markets do. Each of monopolistically competitive firms is large relative to the market, so each firm faces a downward-sloping demand curve, as do monopolistic and oligopolistic firms. Thus, noncompetitive firms are price setters (row 4). That is, all but perfectly competitive firms have some degree of market power—the ability to set price above marginal cost—so a market failure occurs in each of these noncompetitive market structures because the price is above marginal cost. Typically, the fewer the firms in a market, the higher is the price (row 5).

Oligopolistic and monopolistically competitive firms pay attention to rival firms' behavior, in contrast to monopolistic or perfectly competitive firms (row 6). A monopoly has no rivals. A perfectly competitive firm ignores the behavior of individual rivals in choosing its output because the market price tells the firm everything it needs to know about its competitors.

Oligopolistic and monopolistically competitive firms may produce differentiated products (row 7). For example, oligopolistic car manufacturers produce automobiles that differ in size, weight, and various other dimensions. In contrast, perfectly competitive apple farmers sell undifferentiated (homogeneous) products.

14.2 Cartels

People of the same trade seldom meet together, even for merriment and diversion, but the conversation ends in a conspiracy against the public, or some contrivance to raise prices. —Adam Smith, 1776

Oligopolistic firms have an incentive to form cartels in which they collude in setting prices or quantities to increase their profits. The Organization of Petroleum Exporting Countries (OPEC) is a well-known example of an international cartel; however, many cartels operate within a single country.

Typically, each member of a cartel agrees to produce less output than it would if it acted independently. As a result, the market price rises and the firms earn higher profits. If the firms reduce market output to the monopoly level, they achieve the highest possible collective profit.

Luckily for consumers, cartels often fail because of government policies that forbid cartels or because members of the cartel "cheat" on the agreement. Each member has an incentive to cheat, because it can raise its profit if it increases its output while other cartel members stick to the agreement.

Why Cartels Form

A cartel forms if members of the cartel believe that they can raise their profits by coordinating their actions. But if a firm maximizes its profit when acting independently, why should joining a cartel increase its profit? The answer involves a subtle argument. When a firm acts independently, it considers how increasing its output affects its own profit only. The firm does not care that when it increases its output, it lowers the profits of other firms. A cartel, in contrast, takes into account how changes in any one firm's output affect the profits of all members of the cartel. Therefore, the aggregate profit of a cartel can exceed the combined profits of the same firms acting independently.

Although cartels are most common in oligopolistic markets, occasionally we see cartels formed in what would otherwise be highly competitive markets, as in markets of professionals. If a competitive firm lowers its output, it raises the market price very slightly—so slightly that the firm ignores the effect not only on other firms' profits but also on its own. If all the identical competitive firms in an industry lower their output by this same amount, however, the market price will change noticeably. Recognizing this effect of collective action, a cartel chooses to produce a smaller market output than is produced by a competitive market.

Figure 14.1 illustrates this difference between a competitive market and a cartel. This oligopolistic market has *n* firms, and no further entry is possible. Panel a shows the marginal and average cost curves of a typical perfectly competitive firm. If all firms are price takers, the market supply curve, *S* in panel b, is the

Figure 14.1 Competition Versus Cartel

(a) The marginal cost and average cost of one of the *n* firms in the market are shown. A competitive firm produces q_c units of output, whereas a cartel member produces $q_m < q_c$. At the cartel price, p_m, each cartel member has an incentive to increase its output from q_m to q^* (where the dotted line at p_m intersects the MC curve). (b) The competitive equilibrium, e_c, has more output and a lower price than the cartel equilibrium, e_m.

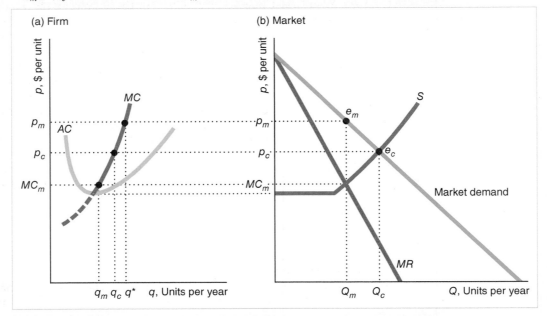

horizontal sum of the individual marginal cost curves above minimum average cost. At the competitive price, p_c, each price-taking firm produces q_c units of output (which is determined by the intersection in panel a of MC and the dotted line at p_c).[1] The market output is $Q_c = nq_c$ (where S intersects the market demand curve in panel b).

Now suppose that the firms form a cartel. Should they reduce their output? At the competitive output, the cartel's marginal cost (which is the competitive industry supply curve, S in panel b) is greater than its marginal revenue, so the cartel's profit rises if it reduces output. The cartel's collective profit rises until output is reduced to where its marginal revenue equals its marginal cost at Q_m, the monopoly output. If the profit of the cartel increases, the profit of each of the n members of the cartel also increases. To achieve the monopoly output level, each firm in the cartel must reduce its output to $q_m = Q_m/n$, as panel a shows.

Why must the firms form a cartel to achieve these higher profits? A competitive firm produces q_c, where its marginal cost equals the market price. If only one firm reduces its output, it loses profit because it sells fewer units at essentially the same price. By getting all the firms to lower their output together, the cartel raises the market price and hence individual firms' profits. The less elastic the market demand the potential cartel faces, all else the same, the higher the price the cartel sets and the greater the benefit from cartelizing. If the penalty for forming an illegal cartel is relatively low, some unscrupulous businesspeople may succumb to the lure of extra profits and join.

Why Cartels Fail

In most developed countries, cartels are generally illegal, firms in the cartel may incur fines, and the owners or managers of these firms may be subject to individual fines and jail terms.[2] Further, many cartels fail even without legal intervention.

Some cartels fail because they do not control enough of the market to raise the price significantly. For example, copper producers tried four times to form an international cartel between 1918 and 1988. In the most recent attempt, the Intergovernmental Council of Copper Exporting Countries controlled less than a third of the noncommunist world's copper production and faced additional competition from firms that recycle copper from scrap materials. Because of this competition from noncartel members, the cartel could not successfully increase copper prices and dissolved in 1988.

Members of a cartel have incentives to cheat on the cartel agreement. The owner of a participating firm may reason, "I joined the cartel to encourage others to reduce their output, which raises the market price and increases profits for everyone. However, I can make even more if I cheat on the cartel agreement by producing extra output. I can get away with cheating if the other firms can't tell who is producing the extra output because my firm is just one of many firms and my increase in output will hardly affect the market price." By this reasoning, it is in each firm's best interest for all *other* firms to honor the cartel agreement—thus driving up the market price—while it ignores the agreement and makes extra profitable sales at the high price.

---

[1]In the figure, the competitive price exceeds the minimum average cost. These competitive firms earn a profit because the number of firms is fixed.

[2]With rare exceptions, it is illegal for firms to collude over prices, quantities, market areas, or the equivalent. However, in most jurisdictions, firms are allowed to coordinate R&D efforts or technical standards if they wish.

Figure 14.1 illustrates why firms want to cheat. At the cartel output, q_m in panel a, each cartel member's marginal cost is MC_m. A firm that does not restrict its output to the cartel level can increase its profit. It can earn the market price, p_m, on each extra unit it sells because each individual firm's output has little effect on the market price. That is, the firm can act like a price taker, so its marginal revenue equals the market price. The firm maximizes its profit by selling q^* units, which is determined by the intersection of its marginal cost curve and the dotted line at p_m. Because its marginal revenue is above its marginal cost for all the extra units it sells (those between q_m and q^*), it makes extra money by violating the cartel agreement. As more and more firms leave the cartel, the cartel price falls. Eventually, if enough firms quit, the cartel collapses.

Laws Against Cartels

In the late nineteenth century, cartels (or, as they were called then, *trusts*) were legal and common in the United States. Oil, railroad, sugar, and tobacco trusts raised prices substantially above competitive levels.[3]

In response to the trusts' high prices, the U.S. Congress passed the Sherman Antitrust Act in 1890, and the Clayton Antitrust Act and the Federal Trade Commission Act in 1914, to prohibit firms from *explicitly* agreeing to take actions that substantially lessen competition.[4] In particular, cartels that are formed to jointly set price are strictly prohibited. In legal jargon, price fixing is a *per se* violation: It is against the law, and firms have no possible mitigating justifications. By imposing penalties on firms caught colluding, government agencies seek to discourage cartels from forming.

The Antitrust Division of the Department of Justice (DOJ) and the Federal Trade Commission (FTC) divide the responsibility for U.S. antitrust policy. The U.S. Department of Justice, quoting the Supreme Court that collusion was the "supreme evil of antitrust," stated that prosecuting cartels was its "top enforcement priority." The FTC's objective is "to prevent unfair methods of competition in commerce" and "to administer . . . other consumer protection laws." Both U.S. agencies can use criminal and civil law to attack cartels, price fixing, and other anticompetitive actions.

However, cartels persist despite these laws, for three reasons. First, international cartels and cartels within certain countries operate legally. International cartels, such as OPEC, that are organized by countries rather than by firms operate legally.

Second, some illegal cartels operate believing that they can avoid detection or, if caught, that the punishment will be insignificant. At least until recently, they were generally correct. For example, in 1996, Archer Daniels Midland (ADM) paid to settle three civil price-fixing-related cases: $35 million in a case involving citric acid (used in many consumer products), $30 million to shareholders as compensation for lost stock value after the citric acid price-fixing scandal became public, and $25 million in a lysine (an animal feed additive) case. ADM paid a $100 million fine in a federal criminal case for fixing the price of lysine and citric acid in 1996, but only eight years later, ADM settled a fructose corn syrup price-fixing case for $400 million.

---

[3]Nineteenth-century and early-twentieth century robber barons who made fortunes due to these cartels include John Jacob Astor (real estate, fur), Andrew Carnegie (railroads, steel), Henry Clay Frick (steel), Jay Gould (finance, railroads), Mark Hopkins (railroads), J. P. Morgan (banking), John D. Rockefeller (oil), Leland Stanford (railroads), and Cornelius Vanderbilt (railroads, shipping).

[4]U.S. law does not prohibit all cartels. A bizarre Supreme Court decision largely exempted Major League Baseball from antitrust laws (**www.slate.com/id/2068290**). Unions are explicitly exempt from antitrust laws. Workers may act collectively to raise wages. A historical justification for exempting labor unions was that the workers faced employers that could exercise monopsony power (see Chapter 11). As long as they do not discuss such issues as prices and quantities, firms may coordinate R&D efforts or technical standards.

We can't legally discuss price. However, look at how many sugar cubes I can stack!

Third, some firms are able to coordinate their activities without explicitly colluding and thereby running afoul of competition laws. To determine guilt, U.S. antitrust laws use evidence of conspiracy—explicit agreements—rather than the economic effect of the suspected cartel. The law does not prohibit firms from charging monopoly-level prices—it prohibits explicitly agreeing to raise prices. As a result, some groups of firms charge monopoly-level prices without violating competition laws. These firms may *tacitly collude* without meeting by signaling to each other through their actions. One firm may raises its price and keep it high only if other firms follow its lead. As long as the firms do not explicitly communicate, that behavior is not necessarily illegal.

For example, shortly before Thanksgiving in 2012, United Airlines announced a fare increase. However, when rivals failed to match this increase, United rolled back its fares the next day. Shortly thereafter, the president of US Airways observed that if Southwest Airlines, the firm that carried the most passengers, failed to match an increase by other airlines, rivals canceled the increase.[5]

Canada enacted the world's first antitrust statute in 1889, one year before the U.S. Sherman Act. As under U.S. law, price-fixing cartels are *per se* illegal and are subject to civil and criminal punishment. Australia and New Zealand have laws on cartels that are similar to those in Canada and the United States. In recent years, the European Union and most developed countries have followed Canada and the United States in strictly prohibiting cartels.

The DOJ, the FTC, the Canadian Competition Bureau, and the European Union authorities have become increasingly aggressive in recent years, prosecuting many more cases and increasing fines dramatically. Increasingly, antitrust authorities from around the world are cooperating. Cooperation agreements exist between authorities in Canada, Mexico, Europe, Australia, New Zealand, and the United States, among others. Such cooperation is critical given the increasingly global scope of the firms engaged in collusion and other anticompetitive activities.

APPLICATION

Employer "No-Poaching" Cartels

How would you get a higher wage than your current employer is paying? Probably you'd seek a job offer from another firm in the same field. But, if that other firm agrees not to hire anyone employed by your current firm, you're out of luck. That's what happened to many skilled engineers. Such an employer conspiracy is an example of a buyers' cartel, which is similar to the sellers' cartels we've been discussing.

In 2005, when demand for Silicon Valley engineers was skyrocketing, Apple's Steve Jobs agreed on a secret, illegal "no-poaching" deal with Google's Eric Schmidt (who was also on Apple's board of directors) to keep their employees' wages low by agreeing not to recruit each other's workers, by sharing wage information, and by punishing a firm that violated the agreement. Intuit, Pixar, and Lucasfilm joined the cartel. It is alleged that many other major tech firms also joined, affecting over a million employees.

---

[5]Charisse Jones, "United Airlines Hikes Fares; Will Rivals Follow?" *USA Today*, October 11, 2012; "US Airways President Talks about Southwest Fares," *Businessweek*, October 24, 2012.

In 2014, Intuit, Pixar, and Lucasfilm agreed to a $20 million settlement of a class-action lawsuit alleging that they conspired to suppress wages. In 2015, Apple, Google, Intel, and Adobe agreed to pay $415 million to settle a similar lawsuit.

A similar cartel affected animation workers. In 2017, these workers obtained a $100 million settlement with the Walt Disney Company, Pixar, and Lucasfilm from a class-action lawsuit concerning wage fixing using non-poaching agreements.

Krueger and Ashenfelter (2017) found no-poaching agreements in 58% of major franchisors' contracts across a wide range of industries, including firms such as Jiffy Lube and H&R Block, as well as fast-food restaurants. Starr, Prescott, and Bishara (2018) concluded that nearly one in five U.S. workers was bound by noncompete clauses that limit the other firms for which they can work, and that nearly 40% had signed at least one noncompete clause in the past.

In 2018, seven fast-food chains—including Arby's, Cinnabon, and McDonald's—agreed to end no-poaching rules. These rules prevented employees from moving between franchises within a restaurant chain, affecting an estimated 25,000 U.S. restaurants. By settling the lawsuits rather than risk losing in a trial, these companies avoided the costs of a trial and the risk of larger fines.

Maintaining Cartels

To keep firms from violating the cartel agreement, the cartel must be able to detect cheating and punish violators. Further, members of a cartel must keep their illegal behavior hidden from customers and government agencies.

Detection and Enforcement Cartels use various techniques to detect cheating. Some cartels, for example, give members the right to inspect each other's accounts. Cartels may also divide the market by region or by customers, making it more likely that the cartel knows if a firm steals another firm's customers, as in the two-country mercury cartel (1928–1972) that allocated the Americas to Spain and Europe to Italy. Another option is for a cartel to turn to industry organizations that collect data on market share by firm. A cheating cartel's market share would rise, tipping off the other firms that it cheated.

You perhaps have seen "low price" ads in which local retail stores guarantee to meet or beat the prices of any competitors. These ads may, in fact, be a way for the firm to induce its customers to report cheating by other firms on an explicit or implicit cartel agreement (Salop, 1986).

Cartels use various methods to enforce their agreements. For example, GE and Westinghouse, the two major sellers of large steam-turbine generators, included "most-favored-customer" clauses in their contracts. These contracts stated that the seller would not offer a lower price to any other current or future buyer without offering the same price decrease to the firms that signed these contracts. This type of rebate clause creates a penalty for cheating on the cartel: If either company cheats by cutting prices, it has to lower prices to all previous buyers as well. Threats of violence are another means of enforcing a cartel agreement.[6]

Governments often enable cartels indirectly:

Unintended Consequence Requiring government agencies to report which company submitted the lowest bid for a government contract and the amount of the bid can facilitate cartels.

---

[6]See **MyLab Economics** Chapter Resources, Chapter 11, "Bad Bakers."

Although society benefits in many ways from government transparency, disclosing bidding information can help a cartel enforce its agreement. If the government reports that the "wrong" cartel member submitted the low bid and won the contract, then the other cartel members know immediately that a firm cheated on the cartel agreement. Electric equipment and heavy construction cartels have made use of such government information.

Government Support. Sometimes governments help create and enforce cartels, exempting them from antitrust and competition laws. By successfully lobbying the U.S. Congress for a special exemption, professional baseball teams have not been subject to most U.S. antitrust laws since 1922. As a result, they can use the courts to help enforce certain aspects of their cartel agreement.

The international airline market provides an example where governments first created a cartel and then later acted to end it. In 1944, 52 countries signed the Convention on International Civil Aviation, which established rules ("freedoms") that enabled airlines to fly between countries. Rather than having the market determine international airfares, bilateral governmental agreements determined them. These countries exempted airlines from their cartel laws, which allowed the firms to discuss prices through the International Air Transport Association (IATA). In the late 1970s, the United States deregulated its airline industry. Soon thereafter, European countries started to deregulate, allowing nongovernment-owned airlines to enter the market. Countries negotiated bilateral *open skies* agreements that weakened IATA's price-fixing role.[7]

APPLICATION Cheating on the Maple Syrup Cartel	Most maple syrup comes from Quebec—not Vermont (as many Americans assume). Quebec has many, many trees and about 13,500 maple syrup producers. How could they band together and effectively run a cartel? The provincial government passed a law creating the cartel: the Federation of Quebec Maple Syrup Producers. Simon Trépanier, the federation's executive director, has referred to the federation as the OPEC of maple syrup.

The federation is half a century old. However, technological change, such as the use of plastic pipes, caused a large increase in supply and a drop in price. Since 1990, the federation has been the province's only wholesale seller of syrup. A majority of the federation's members voted to establish mandatory production quotas starting in 2004, which limit how much farmers can sell in a year. Moreover, farmers have to sell all their syrup through the federation. Thus, the federation restricts supply to raise the price of maple syrup. The price rose 36% from 2004 to 2015 (13% in real terms).

So, are all the farmers happy? According to Mr. Trépanier, "Three-quarters of our members are happy or very happy with what we are doing." And the rest? Some of them are "cheating" on the cartel.

If the federation suspects that farmers are producing and selling outside the federation, it posts guards on their properties. Then it seeks fines, or, in extreme circumstances, it seizes production. In other words, it has powers that illegal cartels can only envy.

But does the federation stop all cheating? It is in a battle with farmers like Robert Hodge, who break the law by not participating in the federation's system. The federation did not catch Mr. Hodge from 2004 through 2008. In 2009, the federation demanded C$278,000 from Mr. Hodge for not joining and selling

---

[7]The European Court of Justice struck down the central provisions of aviation treaties among the United States and eight other countries in 2002.

outside the system, which exceeded his annual sales of about C$50,000 by more than fivefold.

In 2015, the federation hired guards to keep watch over Mr. Hodge's sugar farm. After watching the farm for several weeks, they seized his entire annual production of 20,400 pounds of maple syrup, worth about C$60,000 ($46,000). He remains intransigent, contending that he should be free to choose how much to produce and to whom to sell regardless of the law. He says, "They call us rebels, say we're in a sugar war or something." His 20-year-old daughter observed, "A war over maple syrup, like how pathetic can you get?"

Similarly, in 2018, the Sûreté du Québec seized the maple syrup of producers Nathalie Bombardier and Daniel Gaudreau because they refused to sell through the federation.

Barriers to Entry. Barriers to entry that limit the number of firms help the cartel detect and punish cheating. The fewer the firms in a market, the more likely it is that other firms will know if a given firm cheats and the easier it is to impose penalties. Cartels with a large number of firms are relatively rare, except those involving professional associations.

When new firms enter their market, cartels frequently fail. For example, when only Italy and Spain sold mercury, they were able to establish and maintain a stable cartel. When a larger group of countries joined them, their attempts to cartelize the world mercury market repeatedly failed (MacKie-Mason and Pindyck, 1986).

Mergers

If antitrust or competition laws prevent firms from colluding, firms may try to merge instead. Consequently, many governments limit mergers to prevent all the firms in a market from combining and forming a monopoly.

U.S. laws restrict the ability of firms to merge if the effect would be anticompetitive. In recent years, the European Commission has been actively reviewing and blocking mergers. For example, in 2011, the DOJ and the European Commission blocked a proposed merger between the world's two largest stock exchanges, the New York Stock Exchange and NASDAQ.

Would it be a good idea to ban all mergers? No, because some mergers result in more efficient production. Formerly separate firms may become more efficient because of greater scale, the sharing of trade secrets, or the closure of duplicative retail outlets. For example, when Chase and Chemical banks merged, they closed or combined seven Manhattan branches that were located within two blocks of other branches. Thus, whether a merger raises or lowers welfare depends on which of its two offsetting effects—reducing competition and increasing efficiency—is larger.

APPLICATION

Airline Mergers

In recent years, mergers involving six U.S. legacy airlines reduced the number of firms to three. Delta merged with Northwest in 2008, United with Continental in 2010, and American with US Airways in 2013.

Carlton et al. (forthcoming) examined whether these mergers raised or lowered airfares. They concluded that the mergers reduced fares on routes where the merger partners previously competed. That is, in these mergers, the efficiency effects outweighed the effect of a reduction in the number of firms.

14.3 Cournot Oligopoly Model

How do oligopolistic firms behave if they do not collude? The French economist and mathematician Antoine-Augustin Cournot introduced the first formal model of oligopoly in 1838. Cournot explained how oligopolistic firms behave if they simultaneously choose how much they produce.

The firms act independently and have imperfect information about their rivals, so each firm must choose its output level before knowing what the other firms will choose. The quantity that one firm produces directly affects the profits of the other firms because the market price depends on total output. Thus, in choosing its strategy to maximize its profit, each firm considers its beliefs about the output its rivals will sell. Cournot introduced an equilibrium concept that is the same as the Nash definition in which each firm's action is to choose quantities.

To illustrate this model as simply as possible, we start by making four restrictive assumptions. First, we assume that the market lasts for only one period. Consequently, each firm chooses its quantity or price only once.

Second, we assume in this section that the firms act simultaneously. In our discussion of the Stackelberg model, we change this assumption so that one firm acts before the other.

Third, we initially assume that all firms are identical in the sense that they have the same cost functions and produce identical, *undifferentiated* products. Then, we show how the market outcomes change if costs differ or if consumers believe that the products differ across firms.

Fourth, we initially illustrate each of these oligopoly models for a **duopoly**: an oligopoly with two (*duo*) firms. Then, we examine the equilibrium changes as the number of firms increases.

The Duopoly Nash-Cournot Equilibrium

To illustrate the basic idea of the Cournot model, we start with a duopoly model. We examine the actual market where American Airlines and United Airlines compete for customers on flights between Chicago and Los Angeles.[8] The total number of passengers flown by these two firms, Q, is the sum of the number of passengers flown on American, q_A, and those flown on United, q_U. No other companies can enter this market because they cannot obtain landing rights at both airports.[9]

How many passengers does each airline firm choose to carry? To answer this question, we determine the Nash equilibrium for this model. This Nash equilibrium, in which firms choose quantities, is also called a **Nash-Cournot equilibrium** or a **Cournot equilibrium** (or a *Nash-in-quantities equilibrium*): a set of quantities chosen by firms such that, holding the quantities of all other firms constant, no firm can obtain a higher profit by choosing a different quantity.

We studied this airline market in our normal-form game example in Chapter 13, where we assumed that the firms chose between two or three output levels only. That analysis illustrates a Nash-Cournot equilibrium. Here, we first generalize the analysis so that the firms can consider using any possible output level, and then we generalize the

---

[8]This example is based on Brander and Zhang (1990). They reported data for economy and discount passengers taking direct flights between the two cities in the third quarter of 1985. In calculating the profits, we assume that Brander and Zhang's estimate of the firms' constant marginal cost is the same as the firms' relevant long-run average cost.

[9]Existing airline firms have the right to buy, sell, or rent landing slots. However, by controlling landing slots, existing firms can make entry difficult.

model to allow for a larger number of players, n. We determine each firm's *best response* (Chapter 13)—the strategy that maximizes a player's payoff given its beliefs about its rivals' strategies—and use that information to solve for the Nash-Cournot equilibrium.

To determine the Nash-Cournot equilibrium, we must establish how each firm chooses its quantity. We start by using the total demand curve for the Chicago–Los Angeles route and a firm's belief about how much its rival will sell to determine its *residual demand curve*: the market demand that is not met by other sellers at any given price (Chapter 8). Next, we examine how a firm uses its residual demand curve to determine its best response: the output level that maximizes its profit given its belief about how much its rival will produce. Finally, we use the information contained in the firms' best-response functions to determine the Nash-Cournot equilibrium quantities.

The quantity that each firm chooses depends on the residual demand curve it faces and its marginal cost. American Airlines' profit-maximizing output depends on how many passengers it believes United will fly.

The estimated airline market demand function is linear,

$$Q = 339 - p, \qquad (14.1)$$

where price, p, is the dollar cost of a one-way flight, and the total quantity of the two airlines combined, Q, is measured in thousands of passengers flying one way per quarter. Panels a and b of Figure 14.2 show that this market demand curve, D, is a straight line that hits the price axis at $339 and the quantity axis at 339 units (thousands of passengers) per quarter. Each airline has a constant marginal cost, MC, and an average cost, AC, of $147 per passenger per flight. Using only this information and our economic model, we can determine the Nash-Cournot equilibrium quantities for the two airlines.

Figure 14.2 illustrates two possibilities. If American Airlines were a monopoly, it wouldn't have to worry about United Airlines' actions. American's demand would

Figure 14.2 American Airlines' Profit-Maximizing Output

(a) If American is a monopoly, it picks its profit-maximizing output, $q_A = 96$ units (thousand passengers) per quarter, so that its marginal revenue, MR, equals its marginal cost, MC. (b) If American believes that United will fly $q_U = 64$ units per quarter, its residual demand curve, D^r, is the market demand curve, D, minus q_U. American maximizes its profit at $q_A = 64$, where its marginal revenue, MR^r, equals MC.

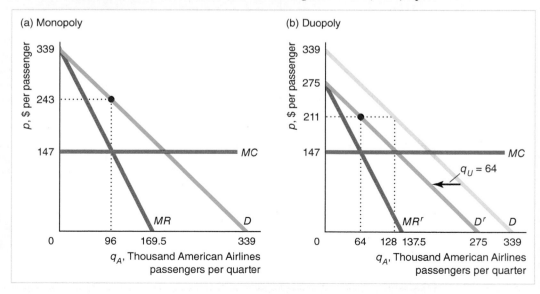

be the market demand curve, D in panel a. To maximize its profit, American would set its output so that its marginal revenue curve, MR, intersected its marginal cost curve, MC, which is constant at $147 per passenger. Panel a shows that the monopoly output is 96 units (thousands of passengers) per quarter and that the monopoly price is $243 per passenger (one way).

But because American competes with United, American must consider United's behavior when choosing its profit-maximizing output. American's demand is not the entire market demand. Rather, American is concerned with its residual demand curve. In general, if the market demand function is $D(p)$, and the supply of other firms is $S^o(p)$, then the residual demand function, $D^r(p)$, is

$$D^r(p) = D(p) - S^o(p).$$

Thus, if United flies q_U passengers regardless of the price, American transports only the residual demand, $Q = D(p) = 339 - p$ (Equation 14.1), minus the q_U passengers, so $q_A = Q - q_U$. The residual demand that American faces is

$$q_A = Q(p) - q_U = (339 - p) - q_U. \tag{14.2}$$

In panel b, American believes that United will fly $q_U = 64$, so American's residual demand curve, D^r, is the market demand curve, D, moved to the left by $q_U = 64$. For example, if the price is $211, the total number of passengers who want to fly is $Q = 128$. If United transports $q_U = 64$, American flies $Q - q_U = 128 - 64 = 64 = q_A$.

What is American's best-response, profit-maximizing output if its managers believe that United will fly q_U passengers? *American can think of itself as having a monopoly with respect to the people who don't fly on United.* That is, American can think of itself as having a monopoly with respect to its residual demand curve, D^r. We will use our analysis based on the residual demand curve to derive American's *best-response function*, $q_A = B_A(q_U)$, which shows American's best-response or profit-maximizing output, q_A, as a function of United's output, q_U.[10]

To maximize its profit, American sets its output so that its marginal revenue corresponding to this residual demand, MR^r, equals its marginal cost. Thus, our first step is to determine American's marginal revenue. Rearranging the terms in Equation 14.2 shows that American's residual inverse demand function is

$$p = 339 - q_A - q_U. \tag{14.3}$$

Consequently, its revenue function based on its residual demand function is

$$R^r(q_A) = pq_A = (339 - q_A - q_U)q_A = 339q_A - (q_A)^2 - q_U q_A.$$

American views its revenue as a function solely of its own output, $R^r(q_A)$, because American treats United's quantity as a constant. Thus, American's marginal revenue with respect to its residual demand function is

$$MR^r = \frac{dR^r(q_A)}{dq_A} = 339 - 2q_A - q_U. \tag{14.4}$$

Equating its marginal revenue with its marginal cost, $147, American derives its best-response function, $MR^r = 339 - 2q_A - q_U = 147 = MC$, or

$$q_A = 96 - \frac{1}{2}q_U = B_A(q_U). \tag{14.5}$$

---

[10]*Jargon alert:* Many economists refer to the best-response function as the reaction function.

Figure 14.3 plots American Airlines' best-response function, Equation 14.5, which shows how many tickets American sells for each possible q_U. As the best-response curve shows, American sells the monopoly number of tickets, 96, if American thinks United will fly no passengers, $q_U = 0$. The negative slope of the best-response curve shows that American sells fewer tickets the more people American thinks that United will fly. American sells $q_A = 64$ if it thinks q_U will be 64. American shuts down, $q_A = 0$, if it thinks q_U will be 192 or more, because operating wouldn't be profitable.

We can derive United's best-response function, $q_U = B_U(q_A)$, similarly. Given that the two firms have identical marginal costs and face the same market demand function, United's best-response function is the same as American's with the quantity subscripts reversed:

$$q_U = 96 - \frac{1}{2}q_A = B_U(q_A). \qquad (14.6)$$

We obtain the Nash-Cournot equilibrium quantities by solving Equations 14.5 and 14.6 simultaneously for q_A and q_U.[11] This solution is the point where the firms' best-response curves intersect at $q_A = q_U = 64$. In a Nash-Cournot equilibrium, neither firm wants to change its output level given that the other firm is producing the equilibrium quantity. If American expects United to sell $q_U = 64$, American wants to sell $q_A = 64$. Because this point is on its best-response curve, American doesn't want to change its output from 64. Similarly, if United expects American to sell $q_A = 64$, United doesn't want to change q_U from 64. Thus, this pair of outputs is a Nash equilibrium: Given its correct belief about its rival's output, each firm is maximizing its profit, and neither firm wants to change its output.

Figure 14.3 American's and United's Best-Response Curves

The best-response curves show the output that each firm picks to maximize its profit, given its belief about its rival's output. The Nash-Cournot equilibrium occurs at the intersection of the best-response curves.

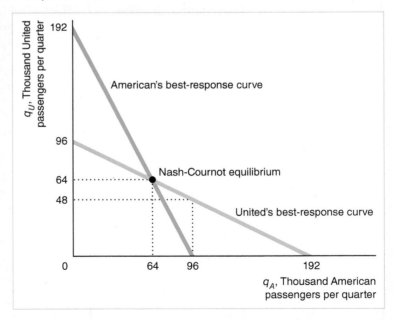

---

[11]For example, we can substitute for q_U in Equation 14.5 using Equation 14.6 to obtain an equation in only q_A. Then we can substitute that value of q_A in Equation 14.6 to obtain q_U. Alternatively, because the firms are identical, $q_A = q_U = q$, so we can replace both q_A and q_U with q in either best-response function and solve for q.

Any pair of quantities other than the pair at an intersection of the best-response functions is *not* a Nash-Cournot equilibrium. If either firm is not on its best-response curve, it wants to change its output to increase its profit. For example, the output pair $q_A = 96$ and $q_U = 0$ is not a Nash-Cournot equilibrium. American is perfectly happy producing the monopoly output if United doesn't operate at all: American is on its best-response curve. United, however, would not be happy with this outcome because it is not on United's best-response curve. As its best-response curve shows, if it knows that American will sell $q_A = 96$, United maximizes its profit by selling $q_U = 48$. Only if $q_A = q_U = 64$ does neither firm want to change its action. Based on statistical tests, Brander and Zhang (1990) reported that they could not reject the hypothesis that the Cournot model is consistent with American's and United's behavior.[12]

The Cournot Model with Many Firms

We've seen that the price is lower if two firms set output independently than in a market with one firm or firms that collude. As the number of firms acting independently increases, the Nash-Cournot equilibrium price falls. We illustrate this result for general demand and marginal cost functions for n firms. Then, we examine the case of a linear inverse demand function and a constant marginal cost and apply that analysis to our airline example.

General Case. If output is homogeneous, the market inverse demand function is $p(Q)$, where Q, the total market output, is the sum of the output of each of the n firms: $Q = q_1 + q_2 + \ldots + q_n$. Each of the n identical firms has the same cost function, $C(q_i)$. To analyze a Cournot market of identical firms, we first examine the behavior of a representative firm. Firm 1 wants to maximize its profit through its choice of q_1:

$$\max_{q_1} \pi_1(q_1, q_2, \ldots, q_n) = q_1 p(q_1 + q_2 + \cdots + q_n) - C(q_1)$$

$$= q_1 p(Q) - C(q_1). \tag{14.7}$$

Firm 1 views the outputs of the other firms as fixed, so $q_2, q_3, \ldots, q_n$ are constants. Firm 1's first-order condition is the partial derivative of its profit with respect to q_1 set equal to zero:[13]

$$\frac{\partial \pi}{\partial q_1} = p(Q) + q_1 \frac{dp(Q)}{dQ} \frac{\partial Q}{\partial q_1} - \frac{dC(q_1)}{dq_1} = 0. \tag{14.8}$$

Given that the other firms' outputs are constants,

$$\partial Q / \partial q_1 = \partial(q_1 + q_2 + \ldots + q_n)/\partial q_1 = dq_1/dq_1 = 1.$$

Making this substitution and rearranging terms, we see that the firm's first-order condition implies that Firm 1 equates is marginal revenue and its marginal cost:

$$MR = p(Q) + q_1 \frac{dp(Q)}{dQ} = \frac{dC(q_1)}{dq_1} = MC. \tag{14.9}$$

---

[12]Because the model described here is a simplified version of the Brander and Zhang (1990) model, the predicted output levels, $q_A = q_U = 64$, differ slightly from theirs. Nonetheless, our predictions are very close to the actual observed outcome, $q_A = 65.9$ and $q_U = 62.7$.

[13]We use a partial derivative to show that we are changing only q_1 and not the other outputs, $q_2, \ldots, q_n$. However, given that Firm 1 views those other outputs as constants so that the only variable in its profit function is q_1, we could use a derivative instead of a partial derivative.

Equation 14.9 gives the firm's best-response function, allowing the firm to calculate its optimal q_1 for any given set of outputs of other firms. We can write Firm 1's best-response function as an implicit function of the other firm's output levels: $p(q_1 + q_2 + \ldots + q_n) + q_1(dp/dQ) - dC(q_1)/dq_1 = 0$. Thus, for any given set of $q_2, \ldots, q_n$, the firm can solve for the profit-maximizing q_1 using this expression.

Solving the best-response functions for all the firms simultaneously, we obtain the Nash-Cournot equilibrium quantities $q_1, q_2, \ldots, q_n$. Because all the firms are identical, in equilibrium $q_1 = q_2 = \ldots = q_n = q$.

The marginal revenue expression can be rewritten as $p[1 + (q/p)(dp/dQ)]$. Multiplying and dividing the last term by n, noting that $Q = nq$ (given that all firms are identical), and observing that the market elasticity of demand, ε, is defined as $(dQ/dp)(p/Q)$, we can rewrite the first-order conditions, such as Equation 14.9, as

$$MR = p\left(1 + \frac{1}{n\varepsilon}\right) = \frac{dC(q)}{dq} = MC. \tag{14.10}$$

In Equation 14.10, the firm's marginal revenue is expressed in terms of the elasticity of demand of its residual demand curve, $n\varepsilon$, which is the number of firms, n, times the market demand elasticity, ε. For example, if $n = 2$, the elasticity of demand of either firm's residual demand curve is twice as elastic as the market demand curve at the equilibrium.

We can rearrange Equation 14.10 to determine the Nash-Cournot equilibrium price:

$$p = \frac{MC}{\left(1 + \dfrac{1}{n\varepsilon}\right)}. \tag{14.11}$$

That is, the Nash-Cournot equilibrium price is above the MC by $1/(1 + [n\varepsilon]) > 1$.[14] Holding ε constant, the more firms, the more elastic is the residual demand curve, which causes the price to fall. For example, if the market elasticity ε is constant at -1, then $p = MC/(1 - \frac{1}{2}) = 2MC$ if $n = 2$, $p = MC/(1 - \frac{1}{3}) = 1.5MC$ if $n = 3$, and $p = MC/(1 - \frac{1}{4}) \approx 1.33MC$ if $n = 4$. As n grows without bound, the price approaches MC.

By further rearranging Equation 14.11, we obtain an expression for the Lerner Index, $(p - MC)/p$, in terms of the market demand elasticity and the number of firms:

$$\frac{p - MC}{p} = \frac{1}{n\varepsilon}. \tag{14.12}$$

The larger the Lerner Index, the greater the firm's market power. As Equation 14.12 shows, if we hold the market elasticity constant and increase the number of firms, the Lerner Index falls. As n approaches ∞, the elasticity facing any one firm approaches $-\infty$, so the Lerner Index approaches 0 and the market is competitive.

Linear Case. We cannot explicitly solve for a firm's best-response function or the Nash-Cournot equilibrium given general functional forms, but we can for specific

---

[14]From the Law of Demand, we know that $\varepsilon < 0$, so $1/[n\varepsilon] < 0$. Given that each firm is operating in the elastic portion of its residual demand curve (using the same argument as we did in Chapter 11 to show that a monopoly would not operate in the inelastic portions of its demand curve), $n\varepsilon < -1$, so $1 > -1/[n\varepsilon]$. Thus, $1/(1 + [n\varepsilon]) > 1$.

functions, as we now show for the linear case. Suppose that the inverse market demand function is linear,

$$p = a - bQ,$$

and that each firm's marginal cost is m, a constant, and it has no fixed cost.

For this linear model, we can rewrite Firm 1's profit-maximizing objective, Equation 14.7, as

$$\max_{q_1} \pi_1(q_1) = q_1[a - b(q_1 + q_2 + \cdots + q_n)] - mq_1. \qquad (14.13)$$

Firm 1's first-order condition, Equation 14.9, is

$$MR = a - b(2q_1 + q_2 + \ldots + q_n) = m = MC. \qquad (14.14)$$

Because all firms have the same cost function, $q_2 = q_3 = \ldots = q_n \equiv q$ in equilibrium. Substituting these equalities into Equation 14.14, we find that the first firm's best-response function, B_1, is

$$q_1 = B_1(q_2, q_3, \cdots, q_n) = \frac{a - m}{2b} - \frac{n - 1}{2}q. \qquad (14.15)$$

The right-hand sides of the other firms' best-response functions are identical.

All these best-response functions must hold simultaneously. The intersection of the best-response functions determines the Nash-Cournot equilibrium. Given that all the firms are identical, all choose the same output level in equilibrium. Thus, we can solve for the equilibrium by setting $q_1 = q$ in Equation 14.15 and rearranging terms to obtain

$$q = \frac{a - m}{(n + 1)b}. \qquad (14.16)$$

Total market output, $Q = nq$, equals $n(a - m)/[(n + 1)b]$. The corresponding price is obtained by substituting this expression for market output into the demand function:

$$p = \frac{a + nm}{n + 1}. \qquad (14.17)$$

Setting $n = 1$ in Equations 14.16 and 14.17 yields the monopoly quantity and price. As n becomes large, each firm's quantity approaches zero, total output approaches $(a - m)/b$, and price approaches m, which are the competitive levels.[15] The Lerner Index is

$$\frac{p - MC}{p} = \frac{a - m}{a + nm}. \qquad (14.18)$$

As n grows large, the denominator in Equation 14.18 goes to infinity (∞), so the Lerner Index goes to 0, and market power is eliminated.

Airline Example. We can illustrate these results using our airline example, where $a = 339$, $b = 1$, $m = 147$, and $n = 2$. Suppose that additional airlines with an identical marginal cost of $m = \$147$ were to fly between Chicago and Los Angeles. Table 14.2 shows how the Nash-Cournot equilibrium price and the Lerner Index vary with the number of firms. Using the equations for the general linear model, we know that each firm's Nash-Cournot equilibrium quantity is

---

[15]As the number of firms goes to infinity, the Nash-Cournot equilibrium goes to perfect competition only if average cost is nondecreasing (Ruffin, 1971).

Table 14.2 Nash-Cournot Equilibrium Varies with the Number of Firms

Number of Firms, n	Firm Output, q	Market Output, Q	Price, p	Market Elasticity, ε	Residual Demand Elasticity, $n\varepsilon$	Lerner Index, $(p - m)/p = -1/(n\varepsilon)$
1	96	96	243	−2.53	−2.53	0.40
2	64	128	211	−1.65	−3.30	0.30
3	48	144	195	−1.35	−4.06	0.25
4	38.4	154	185.40	−1.21	−4.83	0.21
5	32	160	179	−1.12	−5.59	0.18
10	17.5	175	164.45	−0.94	−9.42	0.11
50	3.8	188	150.76	−0.80	−40.05	0.02
100	1.9	190	148.90	−0.78	−78.33	0.01
200	1.0	191	147.96	−0.77	−154.89	0.01

$q = (339 - 147)/(n + 1) = 192/(n + 1)$ and the Nash-Cournot equilibrium price is $p = (339 + 147n)/(n + 1)$.

As we already know, a single firm in the market would produce the monopoly quantity, 96, at the monopoly price, $243. We also know that each duopoly firm's output is 64, so market output is 128 and price is $211. The duopoly market elasticity is $\varepsilon = -1.65$, so the residual demand elasticity that each duopoly firm faces is twice as large as the market elasticity, $2\varepsilon = -3.3$.

As the number of firms increases, each firm's output falls toward zero, but total output approaches 192, the quantity on the market demand curve where price equals the marginal cost of $147. Although the market elasticity of demand falls as the number of firms grows, the residual demand curve for each firm becomes increasingly horizontal (perfectly elastic). As a result, the price approaches the marginal cost, $147. Similarly, as the number of firms increases, the Lerner Index approaches the price-taking level of zero.

The table shows that having extra firms in the market benefits consumers. When the number of firms rises from 1 to 4, the price falls by a quarter and the Lerner Index is cut nearly in half. At 10 firms, the price is one-third less than the monopoly level, and the Lerner Index is one-quarter of the monopoly level.

APPLICATION

Mobile Number Portability

An inability of consumers to switch from an old provider of a service to a new provider has a similar demand curve effect to that of differentiating the services. When mobile phones were introduced in most European countries, a monopoly provided the service. After governments opened their markets to new entrants, customers were slow to switch firms because of large switching costs, such as having to obtain a new phone number and new handsets. Preventing customers from transferring their phone number if they switch carriers makes the demand curve facing a given firm less elastic.

To reduce switching costs and increase competition by new firms, many governments require Mobile Number Portability (MNP), which allows consumers to move their phone number to another mobile phone carrier.[16] Cho, Ferreira, and Telang (2016) estimated that the introduction of MNP in European countries—and the increase in effective competitors—decreased phone service prices by 7.9% and increased consumer surplus by 2.86€ ($3.86) per person per quarter.

---

[16]The United States has required wireless local number portability nationwide since 2003, and Canada since 2007. In 2002, the European Commission mandated that MNP be enacted in each European Community country. At least 63 countries have MNP.

The Cournot Model with Nonidentical Firms

For simplicity, we initially assumed that the firms were identical: All firms had identical costs and produced identical products. However, costs often vary across firms, and firms often differentiate the products they produce from those of their rivals.

Unequal Costs. In the Cournot model, the firm sets its output to equate its marginal revenue to its marginal cost, as specified by its first-order condition. If firms' marginal costs vary, then so will the firms' first-order conditions and hence their best-response functions. In the resulting Nash-Cournot equilibrium, the relatively low-cost firm produces more, as Solved Problem 14.1 illustrates. However, as long as the products are undifferentiated, the firms charge the same price.

SOLVED PROBLEM 14.1

MyLab Economics Solved Problem

If the inverse market demand function facing a duopoly is $p = a - bQ$, what are the Nash-Cournot equilibrium quantities if the marginal cost of Firm 1 is m and that of Firm 2 is $m + x$, where $x > 0$? Which firm produces more and which has the higher profit?

Answer

1. *Determine each firm's best-response function.* Firm 1's profit is the same as in Equation 14.13 where $n = 2$: $\pi_1 = [a - b(q_1 + q_2)]q_1 - mq_1$. Consequently, its best-response function is the same as Equation 14.15,

$$q_1 = \frac{a - m - bq_2}{2b}. \qquad (14.19)$$

   Firm 2's profit is the same as in Equation 14.13 except that m is replaced by $m + x$. That is, $\pi_2 = q_2[a - b(q_1 + q_2)] - (m + x)q_2$. Setting the derivative of Firm 2's profit with respect to q_2 (holding q_1 fixed) equal to zero, and rearranging terms, we find that the first-order condition for Firm 2 to maximize its profit is $MR_2 = a - b(2q_2 + q_1) = m + x = MC_2$. Rearranging this expression shows that Firm 2's best-response function is

$$q_2 = \frac{a - (m + x) - bq_1}{2b}. \qquad (14.20)$$

2. *Use the best-response functions to solve for the Nash-Cournot equilibrium.* To determine the equilibrium, we solve Equations 14.19 and 14.20 simultaneously for q_1 and q_2:[17]

$$q_1 = \frac{a - m + x}{3b}, \qquad (14.21)$$

$$q_2 = \frac{a - m - 2x}{3b}. \qquad (14.22)$$

---

[17]By substituting the expression for q_1 from Equation 14.19 into Equation 14.20, we obtain

$$q_2 = \left[a - m - x - b\left(\frac{a - m - bq_2}{2b} \right) \right] / (2b).$$

Solving for q_2, we derive Equation 14.22. Substituting that expression into Equation 14.19 and simplifying, we get Equation 14.21.

3. *Use the Nash-Cournot equilibrium quantity equations to determine which firm produces more.* By inspection of Equations 14.21 and 14.22, $q_1 = [a - m + x]/[3b] > q_2 = [a - m - 2x]/[3b]$, because $x > 0$. As x increases, q_1 increases by $dq_1/dx = 1/[3b]$ and q_2 falls by $dq_2/dx = -2/[3b]$.

4. *Substitute the Nash-Cournot equilibrium quantity equations into the profit functions to determine which firm has a higher profit.* The low-cost firm has the higher profit. Using Equations 14.21 and 14.22, $q_1 + q_2 = (2a - 2m - x)/(3b)$. Substituting this expression and the expression for q_1 from Equation 14.21 into the profit function for Firm 1, we find that

$$\pi_1 = [a - m - b(q_1 + q_2)]q_1$$
$$= [a - m - (2a - 2m - x)/3](a - m + x)/(3b)$$
$$= (a - m + x)^2/[9b]$$

and, by similar reasoning, $\pi_2 = (a - m - 2x)^2/[9b]$. Thus,

$$\pi_1 = \frac{(a - m + x)^2}{9b} > \frac{(a - m - 2x)^2}{9b} = \pi_2.$$

APPLICATION

How Do Costs, Price Markups, and Profits Vary Across Airlines?

Average costs per passenger vary substantially across airlines. The average cost per passenger mile in 2017 was 19% higher for "network" carriers such as American, Delta, and United than for "value" carriers such as JetBlue and Southwest.

As a result, the price markup or Lerner Index, $(p - MC)/p$, varies across firms: Southwest 21.8%, JetBlue 19.2%, Delta 18.8%, United 14%, and American 13.8% in 2017. The average profit per passenger varies as well: $29 on JetBlue, $22 on Southwest, $19 on Delta, $14 on United, and $10 on American.

Differentiated Products. Firms differentiate their products to increase their profits. By differentiating its product from those of a rival, an oligopolistic firm can shift its demand curve to the right and make it less elastic. The less elastic the demand curve, the more the firm can charge. Consumers are willing to pay more for a product that they perceive as being superior.

One way to differentiate a product is to give it unique, "desirable" attributes.[18] In 2010, Kimberly-Clark introduced a new Huggies disposable diaper with a printed denim pattern, including seams and back pockets, which boosted their sales 15%. The Exo protein bar uses flour made from ground crickets, and Epic Bar has one that is beef liver flavored. Campbell Soup Co. developed slightly more than 100 varieties in its first 90 years, but four times that number in the most recent 30 years.

A firm can differentiate its product by advertising, using colorful labels, and engaging in other promotional activities to convince consumers that its product is superior in some (possibly unspecified) way even though it is

---

[18]The Cow Protection Department of the Rashtriya Swayamsevak Sangh (RSS), India's largest and oldest Hindu nationalist group, announced that it was introducing a new, highly differentiated soft drink called gau jal, or "cow water," made from cow urine—a truly differentiated product. (Jeremy Page, "India to Launch Cow Urine as Soft Drink," *Times Online*, February 11, 2009.)

virtually identical to its rivals physically or chemically. Economists call this practice *spurious differentiation*.

Bayer charges more for its chemically identical aspirin than other brands because Bayer has convinced consumers that its product is safer or superior in some other way. Similarly, Clorox's customers must believe that its product is superior in some way because they pay more for it than for the chemically identical bleach sold by its rivals.

Even if the products are physically identical, if consumers think products differ, the Nash-Cournot quantities and prices will differ across firms. Each firm faces a different inverse demand function and hence charges a different price. For example, suppose that Firm 1's inverse demand function is $p_1 = a - b_1 q_1 - b_2 q_2$, where $b_1 > b_2$ if consumers believe that Good 1 is different from Good 2, and $b_1 = b_2 = b$ if the goods are identical. Given that consumers view the products as differentiated and Firm 2 faces a similar inverse demand function, we replace the single-market demand with these individual demand functions in the Cournot model. Solved Problem 14.2 shows how to solve for the Nash-Cournot equilibrium in an actual market.

SOLVED PROBLEM 14.2

MyLab Economics
Solved Problem

Intel and Advanced Micro Devices (AMD) are the only firms that produce central processing units (CPUs), which are the brains of personal computers. Both because the products differ physically and because Intel's *Intel Inside* advertising campaign has convinced some consumers of its superiority, customers view the CPUs as imperfect substitutes. Consequently, the two firms' inverse demand functions differ:

$$p_A = 197 - 15.1q_A - 0.3q_I, \tag{14.23}$$

$$p_I = 490 - 10q_I - 6q_A, \tag{14.24}$$

where price is dollars per CPU, quantity is in millions of CPUs, the subscript I indicates Intel, and the subscript A represents AMD.[19] Each firm faces a constant marginal cost of $m = \$40$ per unit. (We can ignore the firms' fixed costs because we know that the firms operate and the fixed costs do not affect the marginal costs.) Solve for the Nash-Cournot equilibrium quantities and prices.

Answer

1. *Determine each firm's best-response function.* Substituting the inverse demand Equations 14.23 and 14.24 into the definition of profit and setting $m = 40$, we find that the firms' profit functions are

$$\pi_A = (p_A - m)q_A = (157 - 15.1q_A - 0.3q_I)q_A, \tag{14.25}$$

$$\pi_I = (p_I - m)q_I = (450 - 10q_I - 6q_A)q_I. \tag{14.26}$$

The first-order conditions corresponding to Equations 14.25 and 14.26 are $\partial \pi_A / \partial q_A = 157 - 30.2q_A - 0.3q_I$ and $\partial \pi_I / \partial q_I = 450 - 20q_I - 6q_A$. Rearranging these expressions, we obtain the best-response functions:

$$q_A = \frac{157 - 0.3q_I}{30.2}, \tag{14.27}$$

$$q_I = \frac{450 - 6q_A}{20}. \tag{14.28}$$

---

[19] I thank Hugo Salgado for estimating these inverse demand functions and providing evidence that this market is well described by a Nash-Cournot equilibrium.

2. *Use the best-response functions to solve for the Nash-Cournot equilibrium.* Solving the system of best-response functions 14.27 and 14.28, we find that the Nash-Cournot equilibrium quantities are $q_A \approx 5$ million CPUs, and $q_I \approx 21$ million CPUs. Substituting these values into the inverse demand functions, we obtain the corresponding prices: $p_A = \$115.20$ and $p_I = \$250$ per CPU.

APPLICATION

Differentiating Bottled Water Through Marketing

Bottled water is the most dramatic recent example of *spurious product differentiation*, where the products do not significantly differ physically. Firms convince consumers that their products differ through marketing.

One product that you might think is difficult to differentiate is water. Capehart and Berg (2018) found that in a blind taste test, consumers cannot distinguish bottled waters or tap water. Water can be carbonated or flavored, but doing so caters to only a subset of the $16 billion U.S. bottled water market, which grew rapidly from 2010 through 2018.

How did Coca-Cola and Pepsico differentiate their uncarbonated, unflavored water? Primarily through marketing. Pepsico's top-selling bottled water, Aquafina, has a colorful blue label and a logo showing the sun rising over the mountains. From that logo, consumers may infer that the water comes from some bubbling spring high in an unspoiled wilderness. If so, they're wrong. Pepsi's best-selling bottled water comes from the same place as tap water: public-water sources. Pepsi also claims that it adds value by filtering the water using a state-of-the-art "HydRO-7 purification system," implying that such filtering (which removes natural minerals) is desirable. Similarly, Coke's marketing distinguishes its Dasani bottled water, even though it, too, is basically bottled public water.

In a recent "blind" taste test reported in *Slate*, no one could distinguish between Aquafina and Dasani, and both are equally clean and safe. However, many consumers, responding to perceived differences created by marketing, strongly prefer one or the other of these brands and pay a premium for these products.[20]

14.4   Stackelberg Oligopoly Model

In the Cournot model, both firms announce their output decisions simultaneously. In contrast, suppose that one of the firms, called the *leader*, can set its output before its rival, the *follower*, does. This type of situation, where one firm acts before the other, arises naturally if one firm enters a market before the other. Would the firm that acts first have an advantage?

To answer this question, the German economist Heinrich von Stackelberg showed how to modify the Cournot model. We introduced the Stackelberg model

---

[20]Having succeeded in differentiating water, Coca-Cola turned to milk. In 2015, it started selling its Fairlife "super milk." Using a special filtration process, it has more "natural" protein and calcium, and less sugar. Sandy Douglas, President of Coca-Cola North America, said, "It's basically the premiumization of milk. . . . We'll charge twice as much for it as the milk we're used to buying in a jug."

in Chapter 13, where United and American Airlines could choose among only three possible output levels. Here, we consider the more general problem where the airlines are free to choose any output level they want.

How does the leader decide to set its output? The leader realizes that once it sets its output, the rival firm will use its Cournot best-response curve to select its best-response output. Thus, the leader predicts what the follower will do before the follower acts. Using this knowledge, the leader chooses its output level to "manipulate" the follower, thereby benefiting at the follower's expense.

Calculus Solution

We start by deriving the Stackelberg equilibrium for a general, linear model, and then we apply that analysis to the airlines example. We can use calculus to derive the Stackelberg equilibrium for a general linear inverse demand function, $p(Q) = a - bQ$, where two firms have identical constant marginal costs, m. Because Firm 1, the Stackelberg leader, chooses its output first, it knows that Firm 2, the follower, will choose its output using its best-response function. Setting the number of firms $n = 2$ in Equation 14.15, we know that Firm 2's best-response function, B_2, is

$$q_2 = B_2(q_1) = \frac{a - m}{2b} - \frac{1}{2}q_1. \tag{14.29}$$

The market price depends on the output of both firms, $p(q_1 + q_2)$. Consequently, the Stackelberg leader's profit is a function of its own and the follower's output: $\pi_1(q_1 + q_2) = p(q_1 + q_2)q_1 - mq_1$. By replacing the follower's output with the follower's best-response function Equation 14.29 so that the leader's profit depends only on its own output, we can write the leader's profit function, $\pi(q_1, q_2)$, as

$$\begin{aligned}
\pi_1(q_1, B_2(q_1)) &= [p(q_1 + B_2(q_1)) - m]q_1 \\
&= [a - b(q_1 + B_2(q_1)) - m]q_1 \\
&= \left[a - b\left(q_1 + \frac{a - m}{2b} - \frac{1}{2}q_1\right) - m\right]q_1 \\
&= \left(\frac{a - m - bq_1}{2}\right)q_1. \tag{14.30}
\end{aligned}$$

The Stackelberg leader's objective is to choose q_1 to maximize its profit in Equation 14.30. The leader's first-order condition is derived by setting the derivative of its profit with respect to q_1 equal to zero: $(a - m - 2bq_1)/2 = 0$. Solving this expression for q_1, we find that the profit-maximizing output of the leader is

$$q_1 = \frac{a - m}{2b}. \tag{14.31}$$

Substituting the expression for q_1 in Equation 14.31 into the follower's best-response function 14.29 gives the equilibrium output of the follower:

$$q_2 = \frac{a - m}{4b}.$$

Thus, given a linear demand curve and constant marginal cost, the leader produces twice as much as the follower.[21]

---

[21]Here, the leader produces the same quantity as a monopoly would, and the follower produces the same quantity as it would in the cartel equilibrium. These relationships are due to the linear demand curve and the constant marginal cost—they do not hold more generally.

We can use this analysis to ask what would happen in our airline example if American Airlines can act before United Airlines, so that American is a Stackelberg leader and United is a Stackelberg follower. Replacing the parameters in our linear analysis with the specific values for the airlines, $a = 339$, $b = 1$, $m = 147$, and $n = 2$, we find that American's output is $q_1 = (339 - 147)/2 = 96$, and United's output is $q_2 = (339 - 147)/4 = 48$.

Graphical Solution

We can illustrate this airline analysis with graphs. American, the Stackelberg leader, uses its residual demand curve to determine its profit-maximizing output. American knows that when it sets q_A, United will use its Cournot best-response function to pick its best-response q_U. Thus, American believes it faces a residual demand curve, D^r (panel a of Figure 14.4), that is the market demand curve, D

Figure 14.4 Stackelberg Equilibrium

(a) The residual demand that the Stackelberg leader faces is the market demand minus the quantity produced by the follower, q_U, given the leader's quantity, q_A. The leader chooses $q_A = 96$ so that its marginal revenue, MR^r, equals its marginal cost. The total output, $Q = 144$, is the sum of the output of the two firms. (b) The quantity that the follower produces is its best response to the leader's output, as given by its Cournot best-response curve.

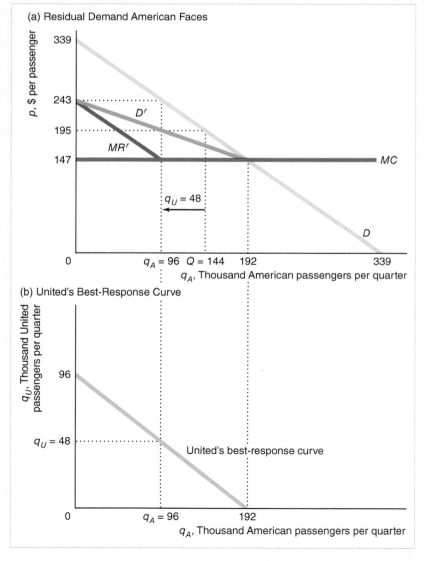

(panel a), minus the output United will produce as summarized by United's best-response curve (panel b). For example, if American sets $q_A = 192$, United's best response is $q_U = 0$ (as United's best-response curve in panel b shows). As a result, the residual demand curve and the market demand curve are identical at $q_A = 192$ (panel a).

Similarly, if American set $q_A = 0$, United would choose $q_U = 96$, so the residual demand at $q_A = 0$ is 96 less than demand. The residual demand curve hits the vertical axis, where $q_A = 0$, at $p = \$243$, which is 96 units to the left of demand at that price. When $q_A = 96$, $q_U = 48$, so the residual demand at $q_A = 96$ is 48 units to the left of the demand.

American chooses its profit-maximizing output, $q_A = 96$, where its marginal revenue curve that corresponds to the residual demand curve, MR^r, equals its marginal cost, \$147. At $q_A = 96$, the price, which is the height of the residual demand curve, is \$195. Total demand at \$195 is $Q = 144$. At that price, United produces $q_U = Q - q_A = 48$, its best response to American's output of $q_A = 96$. Thus, as Figure 14.4 shows, the Stackelberg leader produces twice as much as the follower.

Why Moving Sequentially Is Essential

Why don't we get the Stackelberg equilibrium when both firms move simultaneously? Why doesn't American announce that it will produce the Stackelberg leader's output to induce United to produce the Stackelberg follower's output level? As we discussed in Chapter 13, the answer is that when the firms move simultaneously, United doesn't view American's warning that it will produce a large quantity as a *credible threat*.

If United believed that threat, it would indeed produce the Stackelberg follower's output level. But United doesn't believe the threat because it is not in American's best interest to produce that large a quantity of output. If American produced the leader's level of output and United produced the Cournot level, American's profit would be lower than if it, too, produced the Cournot level. Because American cannot be sure that United will believe its threat and reduce its output, American will produce the Cournot output level.

Indeed, each firm may make the same threat and announce that it wants to be the leader. Because neither firm can be sure that the other will be intimidated and produce the smaller quantity, both produce the Cournot output level. In contrast, when one firm moves first, its threat to produce a large quantity is credible because it has already *committed* to producing the larger quantity, thereby carrying out its threat.

Strategic Trade Policy: An Application of the Stackelberg Model

Suppose that two identical firms in two different countries compete in a world market. Both firms act simultaneously, so neither firm can make itself the Stackelberg leader. However, a government may intervene to make its firm a Stackelberg leader. For example, the Japanese and French governments often help their domestic firms compete with international rivals; occasionally, so do U.S., British, Canadian, and many other governments. If only one government intervenes, it can make its domestic firm's threat to produce a large quantity of output credible, causing foreign rivals to produce the Stackelberg follower's level of output (Spencer and Brander, 1983).

We have already conducted a similar analysis in Solved Problem 14.1, where we showed that a firm with a lower marginal cost would produce more than its higher-cost rival in a Nash-Cournot equilibrium. Thus, a government can subsidize its domestic firm to make it a more fearsome rival to the unsubsidized firm.

Government Subsidy for an Airline. By modifying our airline example, we can illustrate how one country's government can aid its firm. Suppose that United Airlines were owned by one country and American Airlines by another. Initially, United and American are in a Nash-Cournot equilibrium. Each firm has a marginal cost of $147 and flies 64 thousand passengers per quarter at a price of $211.

Now suppose that United's government gives United a $48-per-passenger subsidy, but the other government doesn't help American. As a result, American's marginal cost remains at $147, while United's marginal cost after the subsidy drops to only $99.

The firms continue to act as in the Cournot model, but the playing field is no longer level.[22] How does the Nash-Cournot equilibrium change? Your intuition probably tells you that United's output increases relative to that of American, as we now show.

Nothing changes for American, so its best-response function is unchanged. United's best response to any given American output is the output at which its marginal revenue corresponding to its residual demand, MR^r, equals its new, lower marginal cost. Because United's marginal cost curve fell, United wants to produce more than before for any given level of American's output.

Panel a of Figure 14.5 illustrates this reasoning. United's MR^r curve is unaffected, but its marginal cost curve shifts down from MC^1 to MC^2. Suppose we fix American's output at 64 units. Consequently, United's residual demand, D^r, lies 64 units to the left of the market demand, D. United's corresponding MR^r curve intersects its original marginal cost curve, $MC^1 = \$147$, at 64 and its new marginal cost, $MC^2 = \$99$, at 88. Thus, if we hold American's output constant at 64, United produces more as its marginal cost falls.

Because this reasoning applies for any level of output American chooses, United's best-response curve in panel b of Figure 14.5 shifts outward as its after-subsidy marginal cost falls. As a result, the before-subsidy, Nash-Cournot equilibrium, e_1, at which both firms sold 64, moves to e_2, at which United sells 96 and American sells 48. Thus, the $48 subsidy to United causes it to sell the Stackelberg leader quantity and American to sell the Stackelberg follower quantity. The subsidy works by convincing American that United will produce large quantities of output.

Using the market demand Equation 14.1, we find that the market price drops from $211 to $195, benefiting consumers. United's profit increases from $4.1 million to $9.2 million, while American's profit falls to $2.3 million. Consequently, United Airlines and consumers gain and American Airlines and taxpayers lose from the drop in United's marginal cost.

This example illustrates that a government subsidy to one firm *can* lead to the same outcome as in a Stackelberg equilibrium. Would a government *want* to give the subsidy that leads to the Stackelberg outcome?

The answer depends on the government's objective. Suppose that the government is interested in maximizing its domestic firm's profit net of (not including) the government's subsidy. The subsidy is a transfer from some citizens (taxpayers) to others (the owners of United). We assume that the government does not care about consumers—as is certainly true if they live in another country. Given this objective, the government maximizes its objective by setting the subsidy so as to achieve the Stackelberg equilibrium.

---

[22]Don't you think that anyone who uses the phrase "level playing field" should have to pay a fine?

Figure 14.5 Effect of a Government Subsidy on a Duopoly Nash-Cournot Equilibrium

(a) Due to a government subsidy, United's marginal cost falls from $MC^1 = \$147$ to $MC^2 = \$99$. If American produces $q_a = 64$, United's best response is to increase its output from $q_U = 64$ to 88 given its lower marginal cost. (b) Given that both airlines' marginal cost is $147 before the subsidy, the Nash-Cournot equilibrium is e_1. After United's marginal cost falls to $99, its best-response function shifts outward. It now sells more tickets in response to any given American output than previously. At the new Nash-Cournot equilibrium, e_2, United sells $q_U = 96$, while American sells only $q_A = 48$.

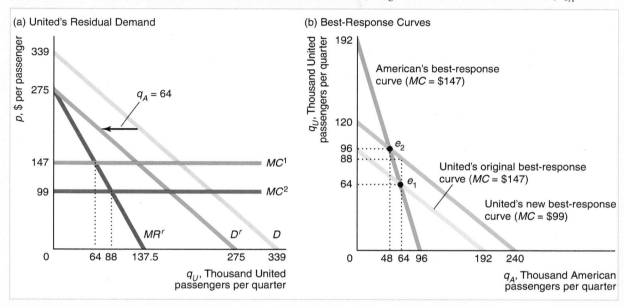

(a) United's Residual Demand

(b) Best-Response Curves

Table 14.3 shows the effects of various subsidies and a tax (a negative subsidy). If the subsidy is zero, we have the usual Nash-Cournot equilibrium. A $48-per-passenger subsidy leads to the same outcome as in the Stackelberg equilibrium and maximizes the government's welfare measure. At a larger subsidy, such as $60, United's profit rises, but by less than the cost of the subsidy to the government. Similarly, at smaller subsidies or taxes, welfare is also lower.

Table 14.3 Effects of a Subsidy Given to United Airlines

Subsidy, s	United			American	
	q_U	π_U	Welfare, $\pi_U - sq_U$	q_A	π_A
60	104	$10.8	$4.58	44	$1.9
48	96	$9.2	$4.61	48	$2.3
30	84	$7.1	$4.50	54	$2.9
0	64	$4.1	$4.10	64	$4.1
−30	44	$1.9	$3.30	74	$5.5

Notes: The subsidy is in dollars per passenger (and is a tax if negative). Output units are in thousands of passengers per quarter. Profits and welfare (defined as United's profits minus the subsidy) are in millions of dollars per quarter.

SOLVED PROBLEM 14.3

MyLab Economics
Solved Problem

In our duopoly airline example, the government gives United a $48-per-passenger subsidy. Use calculus to show that the subsidy causes a parallel shift out of United's best-response curve. Assuming that only United is subsidized, use math to solve for the new equilibrium quantities.

Answer

1. *Set United's marginal revenue function equal to its subsidized marginal cost, and solve for United's best-response function.* United's marginal revenue with respect to its residual demand function is the same as Equation 14.4 with the A and U subscripts reversed: $MR_U = 339 - 2q_U - q_A$. Because United's original marginal cost was 147, its new marginal cost is $147 - 48 = 99$. Equating United's marginal revenue and marginal cost and solving for q_U, we find that United's best-response function is

$$q_U = 120 - \frac{1}{2}q_A. \tag{14.32}$$

This best-response function calls for United to provide more output for any given q_A than in the original best-response function, Equation 14.6, where $q_U = 96 - \frac{1}{2}q_A$. Because only the constants differ, these two best-response functions are parallel.

2. *Substitute for q_A from American's original best-response function into United's new best-response function and solve for United's new Nash-Cournot equilibrium quantity, then substitute that value into American's best-response function to find American's equilibrium quantity.* The subsidy does not affect American, so its best-response function remains the same, Equation 14.5: $q_A = 96 - \frac{1}{2}q_U$. Substituting this expression for q_A into United's best-response function from Equation 14.32, we learn that

$$q_U = 120 - \frac{1}{2}q_A = 120 - \frac{1}{2}\left(96 - \frac{1}{2}q_U\right) = 72 + \frac{1}{4}q_U. \tag{14.33}$$

Solving Equation 14.33 for q_U, we find that $q_U = \frac{4}{3} \times 72 = 96$. Plugging this value into American's best-response function, we conclude that $q_A = 96 - (\frac{1}{2} \times 96) = 48$. Thus, compared to the original equilibrium where both firms produced 64, United produces more and American less in this new equilibrium.

Problems with Government Intervention. Thus, in theory, a government may want to subsidize its domestic firm to make it produce the same output as it would if it were a Stackelberg leader. However, if such subsidies are to work as desired, four conditions must hold:

1. The other government must not retaliate. (See the Challenge Solution.)
2. The government must be able to set its subsidy before the firms choose their output levels. The idea behind this intervention is that one firm cannot act before the other, but its government can act first.
3. The government's actions must be credible. If the foreign firm's country doesn't believe that the government will subsidize its domestic firm, the foreign firm produces the Cournot level. The foreign firm may not believe

Table 14.4 Comparison of the Duopoly Airline Competitive, Stackelberg, Cournot, and Collusive Equilibria

	Competition	Stackelberg	Cournot	Collusion
Total output, Q (thousands)	192	144	128	96
Price, p ($)	147	195	211	243
Consumer surplus ($ million)	18.4	10.4	8.2	4.6
Profit, π ($ million)	0	6.9	8.2	9.2

in the subsidies because governments have difficulty in committing to long-term policies.[23]

4. The government must know enough about how the firms behave to intervene appropriately. If it doesn't know the demand function and the costs of all firms or whether they are engaged in a Cournot game, the government may intervene inappropriately.

Comparison of Collusive, Nash-Cournot, Stackelberg, and Competitive Equilibria

The Nash-Cournot and Stackelberg equilibrium prices, quantities, consumer surplus, and profits lie between those of the collusive and competitive equilibria. Table 14.4 compares the four market structures for the airline example.

We've already determined the equilibrium price, quantities, and profits for the Cournot and Stackelberg cases. If the firms were to act as price takers, they would each produce where their residual demand curve intersects their marginal cost curve, so the equilibrium price would equal the marginal cost of $147. The price-taking equilibrium is $q_A = q_U = 96$. The quantities produced by both the firms are 192 (= 96 + 96) in the competitive equilibrium.

If American and United were to collude, they would maximize joint profits by producing the monopoly output, $q_A + q_U = 96$. American could act as a monopoly and serve all the passengers, $q_A = 96$ and $q_U = 0$, and give United some of the profits. Or they could reverse roles so that United served everyone, $q_A = 0$ and $q_U = 96$. Or the two airlines could share the passengers in any combination such that the sum of the airlines' passengers equals the monopoly quantity, or, equivalently,

$$q_U = 96 - q_A. \tag{14.34}$$

Figure 14.6 plots Equation 14.34, the set of possible collusive outcomes, which it labels the *Contract curve*. In the figure, we assume that the collusive firms split the market equally so that $q_A = q_U = 48$.

Table 14.4 and Figure 14.6 show that the equilibrium market quantity ranges from a low of 96 under collusion, to 128, Cournot; 144, Stackelberg; and a high of 192,

---

[23]For example, during the 1996 Republican presidential primaries, many candidates said that, if elected, they would reverse President Clinton's trade policies. The 2004 Democratic presidential candidates promised to change President George W. Bush's trade policies. The major Democratic presidential candidates in the 2008 election had conflicting views on optimal trade policies. Governor Romney, the 2012 Republican presidential candidate, said that he would reverse many of President Obama's trade policies.

Figure 14.6 Duopoly Equilibria

The intersection of the best-response curves determines the Nash-Cournot equilibrium, where each firm produces 64. The possible cartel equilibria lie on the contract curve: $q_U = 96 - q_A$. The figure shows the symmetric cartel case where each firm produces 48. If the firms act as price takers, each firm produces where its residual demand equals its marginal cost, 96. In the Nash-Stackelberg equilibrium, the leader produces more, 96, than the follower, 48.

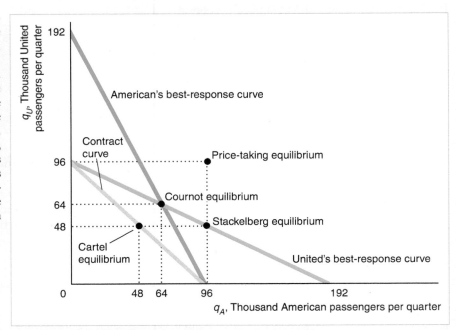

competitive. Consequently, the order of the equilibrium market price is the opposite: $147, competitive; $195, Stackelberg; $211, Cournot; and $243, collusive.

Consumers prefer the lower prices and have greater consumer surplus, the more competitive the market structure. The cartel profits are the highest-possible level of profits that the firms can earn. The monopoly profit is $9.2 million per quarter, so each firm earns $4.6 million if the firms split the profit equally. In contrast, if the firms act independently, each earns the Cournot profit of approximately $4.1 million. The Stackelberg leader earns more than the Cournot profit, $4.6 million, while the follower earns less, $2.3 million. The competitive firms earn zero.

We showed that the Nash-Cournot equilibrium approaches the competitive, price-taking equilibrium as the number of firms grows. Similarly, we can show that the Nash-Stackelberg equilibrium approaches the price-taking equilibrium as the number of Stackelberg followers grows. As a result, the differences between the Cournot, Stackelberg, and price-taking market structures shrink as the number of firms grows.

14.5 Bertrand Oligopoly Model

We have examined how oligopolistic firms set quantities to try to maximize their profits. However, many such firms set prices instead of quantities and allow consumers to decide how much to buy. The market equilibrium is different if firms set prices rather than quantities.

In monopolistic and competitive markets, the issue of whether firms set quantities or prices does not arise. Competitive firms have no choice: They cannot affect price and hence can choose only quantity (Chapter 8). The monopoly equilibrium is the same whether the monopoly sets price or quantity (Chapter 11).

In 1883, the French mathematician Joseph Bertrand rejected Cournot's assumption that oligopolistic firms set quantities. He argued that oligopolies set prices and then consumers decide how many units to buy. The resulting Nash equilibrium is called a **Nash-Bertrand equilibrium** or **Bertrand equilibrium** (or *Nash-in-prices equilibrium*): a set of prices such that no firm can obtain a higher profit by choosing a different price if the other firms continue to charge these prices.

We will show that the price and quantity in a Nash-Bertrand equilibrium are different from those in a Nash-Cournot equilibrium. In addition, the properties of the Nash-Bertrand equilibrium depend on whether firms are producing identical or differentiated products.

Nash-Bertrand Equilibrium with Identical Products

We start by examining a price-setting oligopoly in which firms have identical costs and produce identical goods. The resulting Nash-Bertrand equilibrium price equals the marginal cost, as in the price-taking equilibrium. To show this result, we use best-response curves to determine the Nash-Bertrand equilibrium, as we did in the Nash-Cournot model.

Best-Response Curves. Suppose that each of two price-setting oligopolistic firms in a market produces an identical product and faces a constant marginal and average cost of $5 per unit. What is Firm 1's best response—what price should it set—if Firm 2 sets a price of $p_2 = \$10$? If Firm 1 charges more than $10, it makes no sales because consumers will buy from Firm 2. Firm 1 makes a profit of $5 on each unit it sells if it also charges $10 per unit. If the market demand is 200 units and both firms charge the same price, we would expect Firm 1 to make half the sales, so its profit is $500.

Suppose, however, that Firm 1 slightly undercuts its rival's price by charging $9.99. Because the products are identical, Firm 1 captures the entire market. Firm 1 makes a profit of $4.99 per unit and a total profit of $998. Thus, Firm 1's profit is higher if it slightly undercuts its rival's price. By similar reasoning, if Firm 2 charges $8, Firm 1 also charges slightly less than Firm 2.

Figure 14.7 shows that, if Firm 2 sets its price above $5, Firm 1's best response is to undercut Firm 2's price slightly so its best-response curve is above the 45° line by the smallest amount possible. (The distance of the best-response curve from the 45° line is exaggerated in the figure for clarity.)

Now imagine that Firm 2 charges $p_2 = \$5$. If Firm 1 charges more than $5, it makes no sales. The firms split the market and make zero profit if Firm 1 charges $5. If Firm 1 undercuts its rival, it captures the entire market, but it suffers a loss on each unit. Thus, Firm 1 will undercut only if its rival's price is higher than Firm 1's marginal and average cost of $5. By similar reasoning, if Firm 2 charges less than $5, Firm 1 chooses not to produce. The two best-response functions intersect only at e, where each firm charges $5. If its rival were to charge less than $5, a firm would choose not to produce.

It does not pay for either firm to change its price as long as the other charges $5, so e is a Nash-Bertrand equilibrium. In this equilibrium, each firm makes zero profit. Thus, *the Nash-Bertrand equilibrium when firms produce identical products is the same as the price-taking, competitive equilibrium.*[24] This result remains the same for larger numbers of firms.

---

[24]This result depends heavily on the firms' facing a constant marginal cost. If firms face a binding capacity constraint so that the marginal cost eventually becomes large (infinite), the Nash-Bertrand equilibrium may be the same as the Nash-Cournot equilibrium (Kreps and Scheinkman, 1983).

Figure 14.7 Nash-Bertrand Equilibrium with Identical Products

With identical products and constant marginal and average costs of $5, Firm 1's best-response curve starts at $5 and then lies slightly above the 45° line. That is, Firm 1 undercuts its rival's price as long as its price remains above $5. The best-response curves intersect at *e*, the Bertrand or Nash equilibrium, where both firms charge $5.

Bertrand Versus Cournot. This Nash-Bertrand equilibrium differs substantially from the Nash-Cournot equilibrium. We can calculate the Nash-Cournot equilibrium price for firms with constant marginal costs of $5 per unit, using Equation 14.11:

$$p = \frac{MC}{1 + 1/(n\varepsilon)} = \frac{\$5}{1 + 1/(n\varepsilon)}, \tag{14.35}$$

where n is the number of firms and ε is the market demand elasticity. For example, if the market demand elasticity is $\varepsilon = -1$ and $n = 2$, the Nash-Cournot equilibrium price is $\$5/(1 - \frac{1}{2}) = \$10$, which is double the Nash-Bertrand equilibrium price.

When firms produce identical products and have a constant marginal cost, the Nash-Cournot model is more plausible than the Nash-Bertrand model. The Nash-Bertrand model—unlike the Nash-Cournot model—appears inconsistent with real oligopoly markets in at least two ways.

First, the Nash-Bertrand model's "competitive" equilibrium price is implausible. In a market with few firms, why would the firms compete so vigorously that they would make no profit, as in the Nash-Bertrand equilibrium? In contrast, the Nash-Cournot equilibrium price with a small number of firms lies between the competitive price and the monopoly price. Because oligopolies typically charge a higher price than competitive firms, the Nash-Cournot equilibrium is more plausible.

Second, the Nash-Bertrand equilibrium price, which depends only on cost, is insensitive to demand conditions and the number of firms. In contrast, the Nash-Cournot equilibrium price, Equation 14.11, depends on demand conditions and the number of firms as well as on costs. In our last example, if the number of firms rises from two to three, the Cournot price falls from $10 to $\$5/(1 - \frac{1}{3}) = \$7.50$, but the Nash-Bertrand equilibrium price remains constant at $5. Again, the Cournot model is more plausible because we usually observe market price changing with the number of firms and demand conditions, not just with changes in costs. Thus, for both of these reasons, economists are much more likely to use the Cournot model than the Bertrand model to study markets in which firms produce identical goods.

Nash-Bertrand Equilibrium with Differentiated Products

Why don't they make mouse-flavored cat food?

If most markets were characterized by firms producing homogeneous goods, the Bertrand model would probably have been forgotten. However, markets with differentiated goods—such as those for automobiles, stereos, computers, toothpaste, and spaghetti sauce—are extremely common, as is price setting by firms. In such markets, the Nash-Bertrand equilibrium is plausible, and the two problems of the homogeneous-goods Bertrand model disappear. That is, firms set prices above marginal cost, and prices are sensitive to demand conditions.

Indeed, many economists believe that price-setting models are more plausible than quantity-setting models when goods are differentiated. If products are differentiated and firms set prices, then consumers determine quantities. In contrast, if firms set quantities, it is not clear how the prices of the differentiated goods are determined in the market.

The main reason the differentiated-goods Bertrand model differs from the undifferentiated-goods version is that one firm can charge more than another for a differentiated product without losing all its sales. For example, Coke and Pepsi produce similar but not identical products; many consumers prefer one to the other.[25] If the price of Pepsi were to fall slightly relative to that of Coke, most consumers who prefer Coke to Pepsi would not switch. Thus, neither firm has to match its rival's price cut exactly to continue to sell cola.

Product differentiation allows a firm to charge a higher price because the differentiation causes its residual demand curve to become less elastic. That is, a given decrease in the price charged by a rival lowers the demand for this firm's product by *less*, the less substitutable the two goods. In contrast, if consumers view the goods as perfect substitutes, a small drop in the rival's price causes this firm to lose all its sales. For this reason, differentiation leads to higher equilibrium prices and profits in both the Bertrand and the Cournot models. As a result, a firm aggressively differentiates its products so as to raise its profit.[26]

General Demand Functions. We can use calculus to determine the Nash-Bertrand equilibrium for a duopoly. We derive equilibrium for general demand functions, and then we present the solution for the cola market. In both analyses, we first determine the best-response functions for each firm and then solve these best-response functions simultaneously for the equilibrium prices for the two firms.

Each firm's demand function depends on its own price and the other firm's price. The demand function for Firm 1 is $q_1 = q_1(p_1, p_2)$ and that of Firm 2 is $q_2 = q_2(p_1, p_2)$.

---

[25]The critical issue is whether consumers believe products differ rather than whether the products physically differ because the consumers' beliefs affect their buying behavior. Although few consumers can reliably distinguish Coke from Pepsi in blind taste tests, many consumers strongly prefer buying one product over the other. I have run blind taste tests in my classes over the years involving literally thousands of students. Given a choice between Coke, Pepsi, and a generic cola, a very small fraction can consistently identify the products. However, people who do not regularly drink these products generally admit that they can't tell the difference. Indeed, relatively few of the regular cola drinkers can clearly distinguish among the brands.

[26]Chance that a British baby's first word is a brand name: 1 in 4. —*Harper's Index 2004*.

For simplicity, we assume that marginal cost for both firms is constant, m, and neither has a fixed cost.

Firm 1's objective is to set its price so as to maximize its profit,

$$\max_{p_1} \pi_1(p_1, p_2) = (p_1 - m)q_1(p_1, p_2), \tag{14.36}$$

where $(p_1 - m)$ is the profit per unit. Firm 1 views p_2 as a constant. Firm 1's first-order condition corresponding to Equation 14.36 is the derivative of its profit with respect to p_1 set equal to zero:

$$\frac{\partial \pi_1}{\partial p_1} = q_1(p_1, p_2) + (p_1 - m)\frac{\partial q_1(p_1, p_2)}{\partial p_1} = 0. \tag{14.37}$$

Equation 14.37 contains the information in Firm 1's best-response function: $p_1 = B_1(p_2)$.

Similarly, we can derive Firm 2's best-response function. Solving the two best-response functions simultaneously, we obtain the Nash-Bertrand equilibrium prices: p_1 and p_2. We illustrate this procedure for Coke and Pepsi.

Cola Market. Because many consumers view Coke and Pepsi as imperfect substitutes, the demand for each good depends on both firms' prices. Gasmi, Laffont, and Vuong (1992) estimated the Coke demand function as [27]

$$q_C = 58 - 4p_C + 2p_P, \tag{14.38}$$

where q_C is the quantity of Coke demanded in tens of millions of cases (a case is 24 twelve-ounce cans) per quarter, p_C is the price of 10 cases of Coke, and p_P is the price of 10 cases of Pepsi. Partially differentiating Equation 14.38 with respect to p_C (that is, holding the price of Pepsi constant), we find that the change in quantity for every dollar change in price is $\partial q_C/\partial p_C = -4$, so a $1-per-unit increase in the price of Coke causes the quantity of Coke demanded to fall by 4 units. Similarly, the demand for Coke rises by 2 units if the price of Pepsi rises by $1 while the price of Coke remains constant: $\partial q_C/\partial p_P = 2$.

If Coke faces a constant marginal and average cost of m per unit, its profit is

$$\pi_C(p_C) = (p_C - m)q_C = (p_C - m)(58 - 4p_C + 2p_P). \tag{14.39}$$

To determine Coke's profit-maximizing price given that Pepsi's price is held constant, we set the partial derivative of the profit function, Equation 14.39, with respect to the price of Coke equal to zero,

$$\frac{\partial \pi_C}{\partial p_C} = q_C + (p_C - m)\frac{\partial q_C}{\partial p_C} = q_C - 4(p_C - m) = 0, \tag{14.40}$$

and solve for p_C as a function of p_P and m to find Coke's best-response function:

$$p_C = 7.25 + 0.25p_P + 0.5m. \tag{14.41}$$

Coke's best-response function tells us the price Coke charges that maximizes its profit as a function of the price Pepsi charges. Equation 14.41 shows that Coke's best-response price is 25¢ higher for every extra dollar that Pepsi charges and 50¢ higher for every extra dollar of Coke's marginal cost. Figure 14.8 plots Coke's best-response

---

[27]Their estimated model allows the firms to set both prices and advertising. We assume that the firms' advertising is held constant. The Coke equation is Gasmi, Laffont, and Vuong's estimates (with slight rounding). Prices (to retailers) and costs are in real 1982 dollars per 10 cases.

Figure 14.8 Nash-Bertrand Equilibrium with Differentiated Products

If both firms have a constant marginal cost of $5, the best-response curves of Coke and Pepsi intersect at e_1, where each sets a price of $13 per unit. If Coke's marginal cost rises to $14.50, its best-response curve shifts up. In the new equilibrium, e_2, Coke charges a higher price, $18, than does Pepsi, $14.

curve given that Coke's average and marginal cost of production is $5 per unit, so its best-response function is

$$p_C = 9.75 + 0.25 p_P. \tag{14.42}$$

If $p_P = \$13$, then Coke's best response is to set p_C at $13.
Pepsi's demand function is[28]

$$q_P = 63.2 - 4p_P + 1.6p_C. \tag{14.43}$$

Using the same approach as we used for Coke, we find that Pepsi's best-response function (for $m = \$5$) is

$$p_P = 10.4 + 0.2 p_C. \tag{14.44}$$

Thus, neither firm's best-response curve in Figure 14.8 lies along a 45° line through the origin. The Bertrand best-response curves have different slopes than the Cournot best-response curves in Figure 14.3. The Cournot best-response curves—which plot relationships between quantities—slope downward, showing that a firm produces less the more it expects its rival to produce (as Figure 14.3 illustrates for identical goods, and Solved Problem 14.2 shows for differentiated goods). In Figure 14.8, the Bertrand best-response curves—which plot relationships between prices—slope upward, indicating that a firm charges a higher price the higher the price the firm expects its rival to charge.

The intersection of Coke's and Pepsi's best-response functions, Equations 14.42 and 14.44, determines the Nash equilibrium. By substituting Pepsi's best-response function, Equation 14.44, for p_P in Coke's best-response function, Equation 14.42, we find that

$$p_C = 9.75 + 0.25(10.4 + 0.2p_C).$$

[28]I have rescaled Gasmi, Laffont, and Vuong's estimate so that the equilibrium prices of Coke and Pepsi are equal.

The solution to this equation is that p_C—the equilibrium price of Coke—is \$13. Substituting $p_C = \$13$ into Equation 14.44, we discover that the equilibrium price of Pepsi is also \$13, as Figure 14.8 illustrates.

In this Nash-Bertrand equilibrium, each firm sets its best-response price *given the price the other firm is charging*. Neither firm wants to change its price because neither firm can increase its profit by doing so.

Figure 14.8 also shows what happens if Pepsi's marginal cost remains at \$5, but Coke's marginal cost rises to \$14.50. Coke's best-response curve shifts up, so that in the new equilibrium e_2, Coke charges a higher price, \$18, than does Pepsi, \$14.

Product Differentiation and Welfare. We've seen that prices are likely to be higher when products are differentiated than when they are identical, all else the same. We also know that welfare falls as the gap between price and marginal cost rises. Does it follow that differentiating products lowers welfare? Not necessarily. Although differentiation leads to higher prices, which harm consumers, differentiation is desirable in its own right. Consumers value having a choice, and some may greatly prefer a new brand to existing ones.

One way to illustrate the importance of this second effect is to consider the value of introducing a new, differentiated product. This value reflects how much extra income consumers would require to be as well off without the good as with it.

APPLICATION

Rising Market Power

Cournot, Bertrand, and other oligopoly models predict that price exceeds marginal cost. How large are these markups?

Hall (2018) examined U.S. firms' markups, which he defined as the ratio of price to marginal cost, across all sectors of the economy. He found that the markup ratio grew from 1.12 in 1988 to 1.38 in 2015. The growth rates were particularly high in the finance and insurance and the utilities sectors.

De Loecker and Eeckhout (2018) examined the same markup for 70,000 firms in 134 countries. They estimated that the average global markup increased from about 1.1 in 1980 to around 1.6 in 2016. The markup increased the most in North America and Europe and the least in Latin America and Asia.

14.6 Monopolistic Competition

So far, we've concentrated on oligopolistic markets where the number of firms is fixed because of barriers to entry. We've seen that these firms in an oligopoly (such as the airlines in our example) may earn positive economic profits. We now consider firms in monopolistically competitive markets without barriers to entry, so firms enter the market until no more firms can enter profitably in the long run.

If both competitive and monopolistically competitive firms make zero economic profits, what distinguishes these two market structures? Competitive firms face horizontal residual demand curves and charge prices equal to marginal cost. In contrast, monopolistically competitive firms face downward-sloping residual demand curves and thus charge prices above marginal cost. Monopolistically competitive firms face downward-sloping residual demand curves because (unlike competitive firms) they have relatively few rivals or sell differentiated products.

The fewer monopolistically competitive firms, the less elastic is the residual demand curve each firm faces. As we saw, the elasticity of demand for an individual Cournot firm is $n\varepsilon$, where n is the number of firms and ε is the market elasticity. Thus, the fewer the firms in a market, the less elastic the residual demand curve.

When monopolistically competitive firms benefit from economies of scale at high levels of output (the average cost curve is downward sloping), so that each firm is relatively large in comparison to market demand, the market has room for only a few firms. In the short run, if fixed costs are large and marginal costs are constant or diminishing, firms have economies of scale (Chapter 7) at all output levels, so the market has room for relatively few firms. In an extreme case with substantial enough economies of scale, the market may have room for only one firm: a natural monopoly (Chapter 11). The number of firms in equilibrium is smaller the greater the economies of scale and the farther to the left the market demand curve.

Monopolistically competitive firms also face downward-sloping residual demand curves if each firm differentiates its product so that at least some consumers believe that product is superior to other brands. If some consumers believe that Tide laundry detergent is better than Cheer and other brands, Tide won't lose all its sales even if Tide charges a slightly higher price. Thus, Tide faces a downward-sloping demand curve—not a horizontal one.

APPLICATION

Monopolistically Competitive Food Truck Market

One of the hottest food phenomena in the United States is gourmet food trucks, which started in major West Coast cities such as Los Angeles, Portland, and Seattle. Now, flocks of food trucks ply their business in previously underserved areas of cities across the country. The mobile restaurant business has been exploding. As William Bender, a food service consultant in Santa Clara, California, said, "The limited menu approach, high quality, and low operating costs have opened up an entirely new sector."

Even top restaurant chefs have entered this business. Celebrity Los Angeles chef Ludovic Lefebvre created LudoTruck, a mobile fried chicken outlet. San Francisco's Chez Spencer has a "French takeaway," Spencer on the Go, that serves bistro food such as foie gras torchon and toast for $12.

Opening a new restaurant is very risky. If demand is less than anticipated, a brick-and-mortar firm loses its (large) fixed cost. A food truck has two advantages over a traditional restaurant. The cost of entry is very low, ranging from $50,000 to lease the equipment and pay ancillary expenses, to $250,000 or more for a deluxe truck and top-of-the-line cooking and refrigeration facilities. Moreover, if the manager of a food truck's first guess as to where to locate is wrong, it is easy to drive to another neighborhood.

How do firms identify profit opportunities? "Lunch is our consistent bread-and-butter market," said Matthew Cohen, proprietor of Off the Grid, a food truck promoter and location finder in the San Francisco Bay Area. When lines in front of his trucks grow longer at lunch time, he sets up additional trucks. Having started with about a dozen trucks in June 2010, Off the Grid now has over 200 in 2018.

Monopolistically Competitive Equilibrium

In a monopolistically competitive market, each firm tries to maximize its profit, but each makes zero economic profit due to entry. Two conditions hold in a monopolistically competitive equilibrium: *Marginal revenue equals marginal cost* because firms set output to maximize profit, and *price equals average cost* because firms enter until no further profitable entry is possible.

Figure 14.9 shows a monopolistically competitive long-run market equilibrium. A typical monopolistically competitive firm faces a residual demand curve D^r. To maximize its profit, the firm sets its output, q, where its marginal revenue curve corresponding to the residual demand curve intersects its marginal cost curve: $MR^r = MC$. At that quantity, the firm's average cost curve, AC, is tangent to its residual demand

Figure 14.9 Monopolistically Competitive Equilibrium

A monopolistically competitive firm, facing residual demand curve D^r, sets its output where its marginal revenue equals its marginal cost: $MR^r = MC$. Because firms can enter this market, the profit of the firm is driven to zero, so price equals the firm's average cost: $p = AC$.

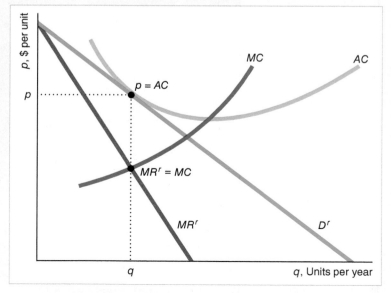

curve. Because the height of the residual demand curve is the price, at the tangency point price equals average cost, $p = AC$, and the firm makes zero profit.

If the average cost were less than price at that quantity, firms would make positive profits and entrants would be attracted. If average cost were above price, firms would lose money, so firms would exit until the marginal firm was breaking even.

The smallest quantity at which the average cost curve reaches its minimum is referred to as *full capacity* or **minimum efficient scale**. The firm's full capacity or minimum efficient scale is the quantity at which the firm no longer benefits from economies of scale. Because a monopolistically competitive equilibrium occurs in the downward-sloping section of the average cost curve (where the average cost curve is tangent to the downward-sloping demand curve), a monopolistically competitive firm operates at less than full capacity in the long run.

Fixed Costs and the Number of Firms

The number of firms in a monopolistically competitive equilibrium depends on firms' costs. The larger each firm's fixed cost, the smaller the number of monopolistically competitive firms in the market equilibrium.

Although entry is free, if the fixed costs are high, few firms may enter. In the automobile industry, just to develop a new fender costs $8 to $10 million.[29] Developing a new pharmaceutical drug could cost more than $350 million.

We can illustrate this relationship using the airlines example, where we now modify our assumptions about entry and fixed costs. Recall that American and United are the only airlines providing service on the Chicago–Los Angeles route. Until now, we have assumed that a barrier to entry—such as an inability to obtain landing rights at both airports—prevented entry and that the firms had no fixed costs. If fixed cost is zero and marginal cost is constant at $147 per passenger, average cost is also constant at $147 per passenger. As we showed earlier, each firm in this oligopolistic market flies $q = 64$ thousand passengers per quarter at a price of $p = \$211$ and makes a profit of $4.1 million per quarter.

Now suppose that the market has no barriers to entry and each airline incurs a fixed cost, F, due to airport fees, capital expenditure, or other factors.[30] Each firm's marginal cost remains $147 per passenger, but its average cost,

$$AC = 147 + \frac{F}{q},$$

falls as the number of passengers rises, as panels a and b of Figure 14.10 illustrate for $F = \$2.3$ million.

In a monopolistically competitive market, what must the fixed costs be so that the two firms earn zero profit? We know that these firms each receive a profit of $4.1 million in the absence of fixed costs. As a result, the fixed cost must be $4.1 million per firm for the firms to earn zero profit. With this fixed cost, the monopolistically competitive price and quantity are the same as in the oligopolistic equilibrium, $q = 64$ and $p = \$211$, and the number of firms is the same, but now each firm's profit is zero.

---

[29]James B. Treece ("Sometimes, You've Still Gotta Have Size," *Business Week*, Enterprise 1993: 2000–2001) illustrates the importance of fixed costs on entry in the following anecdote: "In 1946, steel magnate Henry J. Kaiser boasted to a Detroit dinner gathering that two recent stock offerings had raised a huge $50 million to invest in his budding car company. Suddenly, a voice from the back of the room shot out: 'Give that man one white chip.'"

[30]See "Virgin America's Fixed Costs" in **MyLab Economics**, Chapter Resources, Chapter 19.

Figure 14.10 Monopolistic Competition Among Airlines

(a) If each identical airline has a fixed cost of $2.3 million, and the market has two firms, each firm flies $q = 64$ units (thousands of passengers) per quarter at a price of $p = \$211$ per passenger and makes a profit of $1.8 million.

This profit attracts entry. (b) After a third firm enters, the residual demand curve shifts, so each firm flies $q = 48$ units at $p = \$195$ and makes zero profit, which is the monopolistically competitive equilibrium.

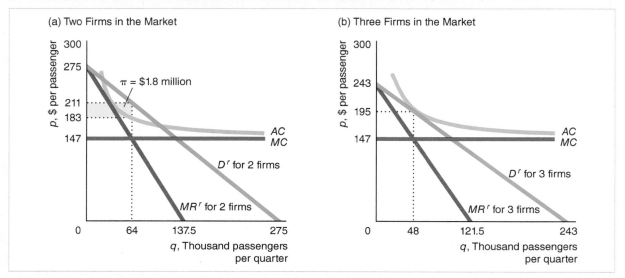

If the fixed cost is only $2.3 million and the market has only two firms, each firm makes a profit, as panel a shows. Each duopoly firm faces a residual demand curve (labeled "D^r for 2 firms"), which is the market demand minus its rival's Nash-Cournot equilibrium quantity, $q = 64$. Given this residual demand, each firm produces $q = 64$, which equates its marginal revenue, MR^r, and its marginal cost, MC. At $q = 64$, the firm's average cost is $AC = \$147 + (\$2.3 \text{ million})/(64 \text{ units}) \approx \$183$, so each firm makes a profit of $\pi = (p - AC)q \approx (\$211 - \$183) \times 64$ units per quarter $\approx \$1.8$ million per quarter.

This substantial economic profit attracts an entrant. The entry of a third firm causes the residual demand for any one firm to shift to the left in panel b. In the new equilibrium, each firm sets $q = 48$ and charges $p = \$195$. At this quantity, each firm's average cost is $195, so the firms break even. No other firms enter because if one did, the residual demand curve would shift even farther to the left and all the firms would lose money. Thus, if the fixed cost is $2.3 million, the market has three firms in the monopolistically competitive equilibrium. This example illustrates a general result: *The lower the fixed costs, the more firms in the monopolistically competitive equilibrium.*

SOLVED PROBLEM
14.4

MyLab Economics
Solved Problem

What is the monopolistically competitive airline equilibrium if each firm has a fixed cost of $3 million?

Answer

1. *Determine the number of firms.* We already know that the monopolistically competitive equilibrium has two firms if the fixed cost is $4.1 million and three firms if the fixed cost is $2.3 million. With a fixed cost of $3 million, if the

market has only two firms, each makes a profit of $1.1 (= $4.1 − 3) million. If another firm enters, though, each firm's loss is −$0.7 (= $2.3 − 3) million. Thus, the monopolistically competitive equilibrium has two firms, each of which earns a positive profit that is too small to attract another firm. This outcome is a monopolistically competitive equilibrium because no other firm wants to enter.

2. *Determine the equilibrium quantities and prices.* We already know that each duopoly firm produces $q = 64$, so $Q = 128$ and $p = 211.

APPLICATION

Subsidizing the Entry Cost of Dentists

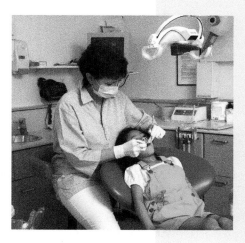

Markets for dentists are normally monopolistically competitive. Dentists provide similar services. As the number of dentists in a local market increases, dentists' profits fall.

In areas with relatively few dentists, the price for their services is high. Dunne et al. (2013) estimated that relative to an area with five dentists, the profit of each dentist is 10% higher in a market with four dentists, 36% higher with three dentists, 47% higher with two dentists (a duopoly), and 69% higher with one dentist (a monopoly). Thus, the fewer the dentists, the higher the profit.

The U.S. Health Resource and Services Administration identifies underserved areas, called Health Professional Shortage Areas (HPSAs). The government subsidizes the entry costs of primary care physicians, dentists, and mental health professionals in HPSAs. Subsidies range from $30,000 to $200,000 per dentist, depending on how long they commit to serve the HPSA. A typical subsidy is $60,000 for a full-time, two-year commitment.

To enter a market, a dentist incurs fixed costs for equipment and office construction. An entrant must construct a new office that has multiple treatment rooms with specialized electrical, plumbing, and X-ray equipment. The study estimates that on average, the mean entry cost is 11% lower in these subsidized markets, which leads to an average of one-half an additional dentist per market.

CHALLENGE SOLUTION

Government Aircraft Subsidies

At various times over the years, the United States has subsidized its aircraft manufacturer, Boeing, and various European countries have subsidized their aircraft manufacturer, Airbus. What happens if both firms are government subsidized?

To keep our answers to these questions as simple as possible, we assume that Airbus and Boeing compete in a Cournot model, they produce identical products with identical costs, and they face a linear demand curve. (Our analysis would be similar in a Cournot or Bertrand model with differentiated products.)

In Solved Problem 14.3 and Figure 14.5, we showed that a government per-unit subsidy to one firm causes its marginal cost to fall and its best-response curve to shift out. If only one firm is subsidized, the subsidized firm produces more and the other firm less than they would in the absence of a subsidy.

If both governments give identical subsidies that lower each firm's marginal cost, then both firms' best-response curves shift out as the figure shows. The original, unsubsidized equilibrium, e_1, is determined by the intersection of the original

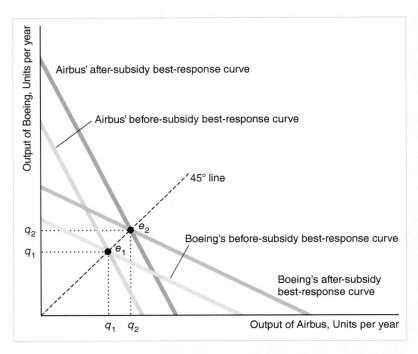

best-response curves. The new, subsidized equilibrium, e_2, occurs where the new best-response curves intersect. Both firms produce more in the new equilibrium than in the original: $q_2 > q_1$. Thus, total equilibrium output increases, which causes the equilibrium price to fall.

We can show these results mathematically, for the general linear model where the inverse demand function is $p = a - bQ$, and the marginal cost of each firm is m. A per-unit subsidy, s, reduces a firm's after-subsidy marginal cost to $m - s$. Thus, we can use the same equations we derived for the Cournot model for two firms ($n = 2$) where we replace the original marginal cost m by $m - s$. The subsidy changes the best-response function for Firm 1 from Equation 14.15 to

$$q_1 = \frac{a - m + s}{2b} - \frac{1}{2}q_2. \tag{14.45}$$

Similarly, Firm 2's best-response function is the same as Equation 14.45 with the 1 and 2 subscripts reversed.

The equilibrium output ($q = q_1 = q_2$) expression, formerly Equation 14.16, becomes

$$q = \frac{a - m + s}{3b}. \tag{14.46}$$

Differentiating Equation 14.46 with respect to s, we find that the equilibrium output of each firm increases by $dq/ds = 1/(3b) > 0$. (In the American and United Airlines example, a \$1 subsidy would cause the equilibrium output to rise by a third of a unit, or about 333 passengers per quarter.)

Unlike the situation in which only one government subsidizes its firm, each subsidized firm increases its equilibrium output by the same amount so that the price falls. Each government is essentially subsidizing final consumers in other countries without giving its own firm a strategic advantage over its rival.[31]

Each government's welfare function is the sum of its firm's profit including the subsidy minus the cost of the subsidy, which is the firm's profit ignoring the subsidy. Because the firms produce more than in the Nash-Cournot equilibrium, both firms earn less (ignoring the subsidies), so both countries are harmed. However, if a government did not provide a subsidy, its firm would be at a strategic disadvantage. Hence, both firms strongly lobby their governments for subsidies.

---

[31]In 1992, a U.S.–EU agreement on trade in civil aircraft limited government subsidies, including a maximum direct subsidy limit of 33% of development costs and various limits on variable costs. Irwin and Pavcnik (2004) found that aircraft prices increased by about 3.7% after this agreement. This price hike is consistent with a 5% increase in firms' marginal costs after the subsidy cuts.

A widely held view is that export subsidies are desirable:

Common Confusion If a country's government subsidizes a firm's exports, the firm and the country benefit.

Most economists who analyze strategic trade policies strongly oppose them because they are difficult to implement and mean-spirited, "beggar thy neighbor" policies. If only one government intervenes, another country's firm is harmed. If both governments intervene, both countries may suffer. For these reasons, the World Trade Organization (WTO) has forbidden the use of all explicit export subsidies.

SUMMARY

1. **Market Structures.** Prices, profits, and quantities in a market equilibrium depend on the market's structure. Because profit-maximizing firms set marginal revenue equal to marginal cost, price is above marginal revenue—and hence marginal cost—only if firms face downward-sloping demand curves. In monopoly, oligopoly, and monopolistically competitive markets, firms face downward-sloping demand curves, in contrast to firms in a competitive market. Firms can earn positive profits when entry is blocked with a monopoly or an oligopoly, in contrast to the zero profits that competitive or monopolistically competitive firms earn with free entry. Oligopoly and monopolistically competitive firms, in contrast to competitive and monopoly firms, must pay attention to their rivals.

2. **Cartels.** If firms successfully collude, they produce the monopoly output and collectively earn the monopoly level of profit. Although their individual and collective profits rise if all firms collude, each individual firm has an incentive to cheat on the cartel arrangement so as to raise its own profit even higher. For cartel prices to remain high, cartel members must be able to detect and prevent cheating, and noncartel firms must be unable to supply very much output. When antitrust laws or competition policies prevent firms from colluding, firms may try to merge if permitted by law.

3. **Cournot Oligopoly Model.** If oligopolistic firms act independently, market output and firms' profits lie between the competitive and monopoly levels. In a Cournot model, each oligopoly firm sets its output simultaneously. In the Nash-Cournot equilibrium, each firm produces its best-response output—the output that maximizes its profit—given the output its rival produces. As the number of Cournot firms increases, the Nash-Cournot equilibrium price, quantity, and profits approach the price-taking levels.

4. **Stackelberg Oligopoly Model.** If one firm, the Stackelberg leader, chooses its output before its rivals, the Stackelberg followers, the leader produces more and earns a higher profit than each identical-cost follower firm. A government may subsidize a domestic oligopolistic firm so that the firm produces the Stackelberg leader quantity, which it sells in an international market. For a given number of firms, the Stackelberg equilibrium output is less than the efficient (competitive market) level but exceeds that of the Nash-Cournot equilibrium, which exceeds that of the collusive equilibrium (which is the same as a monopoly produces). Correspondingly, the Stackelberg price is more than marginal cost but less than the Cournot price, which is less than the collusive or monopoly price. For a given number of firms, the Stackelberg equilibrium output exceeds that of the Nash-Cournot equilibrium, which is greater than that of the collusive or monopoly equilibrium. Correspondingly, the Stackelberg price is less than the Cournot price, which is less than the collusive or monopoly price, but greater than the competitive price.

5. **Bertrand Oligopoly Model.** In many oligopolistic or monopolistically competitive markets, firms set prices instead of quantities. If the product is homogeneous and firms set prices, the Nash-Bertrand equilibrium price equals marginal cost (which is lower than the Nash-Cournot equilibrium price). If the products are differentiated, the Nash-Bertrand equilibrium price is above marginal cost. Typically, the markup of price over marginal cost is greater the more the goods are differentiated.

6. Monopolistic Competition. In monopolistically competitive markets after all profitable entry occurs, the market has few enough firms such that each firm faces a downward-sloping demand curve. Consequently, the firms charge prices above marginal cost. These markets are not perfectly competitive because they have relatively few firms—possibly because of high fixed costs or economies of scale that are large relative to market demand—or because the firms sell differentiated products.

EXERCISES

All exercises are available on **MyLab Economics**; * = *answer appears at the back of this book;* **M** = *mathematical problem.*

1. Market Structures

1.1 Which market structure best describes (a) airplane manufacturing, (b) electricians in a small town, (c) farms that grow tomatoes, and (d) cable television in a city? Why?

2. Cartels

2.1 Many retail stores offer to match or beat the price offered by a rival store. Explain why firms that belong to a cartel might make this offer.

*2.2 A market has an inverse demand curve $p = 100 - 2Q$ and four firms, each of which has a constant marginal cost of $MC = 20$. If the firms form a profit-maximizing cartel and agree to operate subject to the constraint that each firm will produce the same output level, how much does each firm produce? (*Hint:* See Chapter 11's treatment of monopoly.) **M**

2.3 The European Union fined Sotheby's auction house more than €20 million for operating a price-fixing cartel with Christie's auction house (see "The Art of Price Fixing" in **MyLab Economics**, Chapter Resources, Chapter 14). The two auction houses were jointly setting the commission rates sellers must pay. Let r denote the jointly set auction commission rate, $D_i(r)$ represent the demand for auction house i's services by sellers of auctioned items, p denote the average price of auctioned items, F represent an auction house's fixed cost, and v denote its average variable cost of auctioning an object. At the agreed-upon commission rate r, the profit of an auction house i is $\pi_i = rpD_i(r) - [F + vD_i(r)]$.

   a. What is the sum of the profits of auction houses i and j?

   b. Characterize the commission rate that maximizes the sum of profits. That is, show that the commission rate that maximizes the sum of profits satisfies an equation that looks something like the monopoly's Lerner Index profit-maximizing condition $(p - MC)/p = -1/\varepsilon$ (Equation 11.11).

   c. Do the auction houses have an incentive to cheat on their agreement? If Christie's changes its rate while Sotheby's continues to charge r, what will happen to their individual and collective profits? **M**

2.4 The Federation of Quebec Maple Syrup Producers supplies over three-quarters of the world's maple syrup (see the Application "Cheating on the Maple Syrup Cartel"). Under government rules, the member firms jointly market their syrup through the federation, which sets quotas on how much each firm can produce. Show this cartel's price determination process using a graph similar to Figure 14.1. Show how much profit a firm would gain by cheating: by producing more than the cartel's quota.

2.5 In 2013, a federal judge ruled that Apple colluded with five major U.S. publishers to artificially drive up the prices of e-books (which could be read on Apple's iPad). Apple collects a 30% commission on the price of a book from the publisher. Why would Apple want to help publishers raise their price? Given Apple's commission, what price would a book cartel want to set? (*Hint:* The marginal cost of an e-book is virtually zero.)

2.6 In 2012, the U.S. government sued to block the world's biggest beer maker, Anheuser-Busch InBev, from buying Mexico's Grupo Modelo (which manufactures Corona and other beers) for $20 billion (Brent Kendall and Valerie Bauerlein, "U.S. Sues to Block Big Beer Merger," *Wall Street Journal*, January 31, 2013). Currently, Anheuser-Busch InBev has 39% of the U.S. beer market, MillerCoors has 26%, and Grupo Modelo has 7%. When the suit was announced, both firms' stock prices dropped sharply. Why?

2.7 In 2013, the U.S. Federal Trade Commission allowed the number two and number three office supply companies, OfficeMax Inc. and Office Depot, Inc., to merge. Office Depot's market value was $1.3 billion and OfficeMax's was $933 million. Reportedly, the efficiency gains from merging would save the new company between $400 and $500 million. However, in 2015, a federal judge agreed with the U.S. Federal Trade Commission (FTC) and blocked a merger valued at $6.3 billion between Office Depot and Staples, the largest office supply company. Why might the FTC permit the earlier merger attempt but not the Staples-Office Depot merger?

3. Cournot Oligopoly

*3.1 What is the duopoly Nash-Cournot equilibrium if the market demand function is $Q = 1000 - 1000p$ and each firm's marginal cost is 28¢ per unit? **M**

3.2 In the initial Cournot oligopoly equilibrium, both firms have constant marginal costs, m, and no fixed costs, and the market has a barrier to entry. Use calculus to show what happens to the best-response function of firms if both firms now face a fixed cost of F. **M**

3.3 According to Robert Guy Matthews, "Fixed Costs Chafe at Steel Mills," *Wall Street Journal*, June 10, 2009, stainless steel manufacturers were increasing prices even though the market demand curve had shifted to the left. In a letter to its customers, one of these companies announced that "Unlike mill increases announced in recent years, this is obviously not driven by increasing global demand, but rather by fixed costs being proportioned across significantly lower demand." If the firms are oligopolistic, produce a homogeneous good, face a linear market demand curve and have linear costs, and the market outcome is a Nash-Cournot equilibrium, does the firm's explanation as to why the market equilibrium price is rising make sense? (*Hint*: See Exercise 3.2.) What is a better explanation? **M**

3.4 From June 2017 to June 2018, the price of jet fuel jumped 33%.

  a. Based on a general Cournot model, use calculus to show how much a marginal change in the marginal cost, m, affects the equilibrium price.

  b. In 2018, fuel cost was about 23% of airlines' costs. Calculate how much a one-third increase in fuel costs would have affected the equilibrium price in the airline model in this chapter. Why did prices rise less than in proportion to per-passenger-per-day cost? **M**

*3.5 In a Nash-Cournot equilibrium, each of the n firms faces a constant marginal cost m, the inverse market demand function is $p = a - bQ$, and the government assesses a specific tax of τ per unit. What is the incidence of this tax on consumers? **M**

*3.6 Your college is considering renting space in the student union to one or two commercial textbook stores. The rent the college can charge per square foot of space depends on the profit (before rent) of the firms and hence on the number of firms. Which number of stores is better for the college in terms of rent? Which is better for students? Why?

3.7 Connecticut sets a maximum fee that bail-bond businesses can charge for posting a given-size bond (Ayres and Waldfogel, 1994). The bail-bond fee is set at virtually the maximum amount allowed by law in cities with only one active firm (Plainville, 99%; Stamford, 99%; and Wallingford, 99%). The price is as high in cities with a duopoly (Ansonia, 99.6%; Meriden, 98%; and New London, 98%). In cities with three or more firms, however, the price falls well below the maximum permitted price. The fees are only 54% of the maximum in Norwalk (3 firms), 64% in New Haven (8 firms), and 78% in Bridgeport (10 firms). Give possible explanations for this pattern.

3.8 In 2005, the prices for 36 prescription painkillers shot up as much as 15% after Merck yanked its once-popular arthritis drug Vioxx from the market due to fears that it caused heart problems. Can this product's exit be the cause of the price increases if the prices reflect a Nash-Cournot equilibrium? Explain.

3.9 Consider the Cournot model with n firms. The inverse linear market demand function is $p = a - bQ$. Each of the n identical firms has the same cost function $C(q) = Aq_i + \frac{1}{2}Bq_i^2$, where $a > A$. In terms of n, what is each firm's Nash equilibrium output and profit and the equilibrium price? As n gets very large (approaches infinity), does each firm's equilibrium profit approach zero? Why? **M**

3.10 Using Table 14.2 and other information from the chapter, show how the deadweight loss varies in the airline market as the number of firms increases from one to three. **M**

*3.11 The viatical settlement industry enables terminally ill consumers, typically HIV patients, to borrow against equity in their existing life insurance contracts to finance their consumption and medical expenses. The introduction and dissemination of effective anti-HIV medication in 1996 reduced AIDS mortality, extending patients' lives, and hence delayed when the viatical settlement industry would receive the insurance payments. However, viatical settlement payments (what patients can borrow) fell more than can be explained by greater life expectancy. The number of viatical settlement firms dropped from 44 in 1995 to 24 in 2001. Sood, Alpert, and Bhattacharya (2005) found that an increase in market power of viatical settlement firms reduced the value of life insurance holdings of HIV-positive persons by about $1 billion. When marginal cost rises and the number of firms falls, what happens to the Nash-Cournot equilibrium price? Use graphs or math to illustrate your answer. (*Hint*: If you use math, it may be helpful to assume that the market demand curve has a constant elasticity throughout.) **M**

*3.12 Why does differentiating its product allow an oligopoly to charge a higher price?

3.13 A duopoly faces an inverse market demand function of $p = 120 - Q$. Firm 1 has a constant marginal cost of 20. Firm 2's constant marginal cost is 40. Calculate the output of each firm, market output, and price in (a) a collusive equilibrium or (b) a Nash-Cournot equilibrium. (*Hint*: See Solved Problem 14.1.) **M**

3.14 Graph the best-response curve of the second firm in Solved Problem 14.1 if its marginal cost is m and if it is $m + x$. Add the first firm's best-response curve and show how the Nash-Cournot equilibrium changes as its marginal cost increases.

3.15 In 2015, Spirit reported that its "average cost per available seat mile excluding special items and fuel" was 5.7¢ compared to 8.5¢ for Southwest. Assuming that Spirit and Southwest compete on a single route, use a graph to show that their equilibrium quantities differ. (*Hint*: See Solved Problem 14.1.)

3.16 How would the Nash-Cournot equilibrium change in the airline example if United's marginal cost were $100 and American's were $200? (*Hint*: See Solved Problem 14.1.) **M**

* 3.17 To examine the trade-off between efficiency and market power from a merger, consider a market with two firms that sell identical products. Firm 1 has a constant marginal cost of 1, and Firm 2 has a constant marginal cost of 2. The market demand is $Q = 15 - p$.

    a. Solve for the Nash-Cournot equilibrium price, quantities, profits, consumer surplus, and deadweight loss. (*Hint*: See Solved Problem 14.1.)

    b. If the firms merge and produce at the lower marginal cost, how do the equilibrium values change?

    c. Discuss the change in efficiency (average cost of producing the output) and welfare—consumer surplus, producer surplus (or profit), and deadweight loss. **M**

3.18 The firms in a duopoly produce differentiated products. The inverse demand for Firm 1 is $p_1 = 52 - q_1 - 0.5q_2$. The inverse demand for Firm 2 is $p_2 = 40 - q_2 - 0.5q_1$. Each firm has a marginal cost of $m = 1$. Solve for the Nash-Cournot equilibrium quantities. (*Hint*: See Solved Problem 14.2.) **M**

* 3.19 An incumbent firm, Firm 1, faces a potential entrant, Firm 2, that has a lower marginal cost. The market demand curve is $p = 120 - q_1 - q_2$. Firm 1 has a constant marginal cost of $20, while Firm 2's is $10.

    a. What are the Nash-Cournot equilibrium price, quantities, and profits without government intervention?

    b. To block entry, the incumbent appeals to the government to require that the entrant incur extra

costs. What happens to the Nash-Cournot equilibrium if the legal requirement causes the marginal cost of the second firm to rise to that of the first firm, $20?

    c. Now suppose that the barrier leaves the marginal cost alone but imposes a fixed cost. What is the minimal fixed cost that will prevent entry? (*Hint*: See Solved Problem 14.3.) **M**

4. Stackelberg Oligopoly Model

*4.1 Duopoly quantity-setting firms face the market demand

$$p = 150 - q_1 - q_2.$$

Each firm has a marginal cost of $60 per unit.

    a. What is the Nash-Cournot equilibrium?

    b. What is the Stackelberg equilibrium when Firm 1 moves first? **M**

4.2 Determine the Stackelberg equilibrium with one leader firm and two follower firms if the market demand curve is linear and each firm faces a constant marginal cost, m, and no fixed cost. **M**

4.3 Show the effect of a subsidy on Firm 1's best-response function in Solved Problem 14.3 if the firm faces a general demand function $p(Q)$. **M**

4.4 Two firms, each in a different country, sell homogeneous output in a third country. Government 1 subsidizes its domestic firm by s per unit. The other government does not react. In the absence of government intervention, the market has a Nash-Cournot equilibrium. Suppose demand is linear, $p = 1 - q_1 - q_2$, and each firm's marginal and average costs of production are constant at m. Government 1 maximizes net national income (it does not care about transfers between the government and the firm, so it maximizes the firm's profit net of the transfers). Show that Government 1's optimal s results in its firm producing the Stackelberg leader quantity and the other firm producing the Stackelberg follower quantity in equilibrium. (*Hint*: See Solved Problem 14.3.) **M**

4.5 Zipcar (now owned by Avis) initiated the business of renting cars by the hour and is still the industry leader. However, car2go (owned by Daimler), Enterprise CarShare, and Hertz 24/7 have more recently entered the market. As of 2015, the four companies control about 95% of the U.S. car sharing market. Zipcar's large network of members and cars may allow it to be a Stackelberg leader. Use graphs to show how the entry of rivals affects Zipcar. Discuss the difference between a market with a Stackelberg leader and one follower versus a market with three followers.

5. Bertrand Oligopoly Model

5.1 What happens to the homogeneous-good Nash-Bertrand equilibrium price if the number of firms increases? Why?

*5.2 Will price be lower if duopoly firms set price or if they set quantity? Under what conditions can you give a definitive answer to this question?

*5.3 Suppose that identical duopoly firms have constant marginal costs of $10 per unit. Firm 1 faces a demand function of $q_1 = 100 - 2p_1 + p_2$, where q_1 is Firm 1's output, p_1 is Firm 1's price, and p_2 is Firm 2's price. Similarly, the demand Firm 2 faces is $q_2 = 100 - 2p_2 + p_1$. Solve for the Nash-Bertrand equilibrium. **M**

5.4 Solve for the Nash-Bertrand equilibrium for the firms described in Exercise 5.3 if both firms have a marginal cost of $0 per unit. **M**

5.5 Solve for the Nash-Bertrand equilibrium for the firms described in Exercise 5.3 if Firm 1's marginal cost is $30 per unit and Firm 2's marginal cost is $10 per unit. **M**

5.6 In the Coke and Pepsi example, what is the effect of a specific tax, τ, on the equilibrium prices? (*Hint*: What does the tax do to the firm's marginal cost? You do not have to use math to provide a qualitative answer to this problem.)

5.7 At a busy intersection on Route 309 in Quakertown, Pennsylvania, the convenience store and gasoline station, Wawa, competes with the service and gasoline station, Fred's Sunoco. In the Nash-Bertrand equilibrium with product differentiation competition for gasoline sales, the demand for Wawa's gas is $q_W = 680 - 500p_W + 400p_S$, and the demand for Fred's gas is $q_W = 680 - 500p_S + 400p_W$. Assume that the marginal cost of each gallon of gasoline is $m = \$2$. The gasoline retailers simultaneously set their prices.

    a. What is the Bertrand-Nash equilibrium?

    b. Suppose that for each gallon of gasoline sold, Wawa earns a profit of 25¢ from its sale of salty snacks to its gasoline customers. Fred sells no products that are related to the consumption of his gasoline. What is the Nash equilibrium? (*Hint*: See Solved Problem 14.3.) **M**

5.8 In February 2005, the U.S. Federal Trade Commission (FTC) went to court to undo the January 2000 takeover of Highland Park Hospital by Evanston Northwestern Healthcare Corp. The FTC accused Evanston Northwestern of antitrust violations by using its post-merger market power in the Evanston hospital market to impose 40% to 60% price increases (Bernard Wysocki, Jr., "FTC Targets Hospital Merger in Antitrust Case," *Wall Street Journal*, January 17, 2005, A1). Hospitals, even within the same community, are geographically differentiated as well as possibly quality differentiated. Suppose that the demand for an appendectomy at Highland Park Hospital is a function of the price of the procedure at Highland Park and Evanston Northwestern Hospital: $q_H = 50 - 0.01p_H + 0.005p_N$. The comparable demand function at Evanston Northwestern is $q_N = 500 - 0.01p_N + 0.005p_H$. At each hospital, the fixed cost of the procedure is $20,000 and the marginal cost is $2,000.

    a. Use the product-differentiated Bertrand model to analyze the prices the hospitals set before the merger. Find the Nash equilibrium prices of the procedure at the two hospitals.

    b. After the merger, find the profit-maximizing monopoly prices of the procedure at each hospital. Include the effect of each hospital's price on the profit of the other hospital.

    c. Does the merger result in increased prices? Explain. **M**

5.9 Two pizza parlors are located within a few feet of each other on the Avenue of the Americas in New York City. Both were selling a slice of pizza for $1.[32] Then, Bombay Fast Food/6th Ave. Pizza lowered its price to 79¢. The next morning, 2 Bros. Pizza dropped its price to 75¢, which Bombay quickly matched. These price cuts led to long lines of customers. However, both firms claimed that they were losing money. The two proprietors had a meeting on the sidewalk. According to one, they reached an agreement and raised their prices back to a dollar. Can the identical-goods, Bertrand, or cartel models be used to explain this series of events? Why or why not?

5.10 Firms use marketing to differentiate their bottled water products (see the Application "Differentiating Bottled Water Through Marketing"). If the firms in this market engage in a Bertrand game, what is the effect of this differentiation on prices? What is the effect on welfare?

5.11 A Bertrand duopoly produces differentiated products. The firms face demand curves: $q_i = q(p_1, p_2)$. Each firm has a marginal cost of m. What are the firms' best-response functions? Describe how to determine the Nash-Bertrand equilibrium. **M**

6. Monopolistic Competition

6.1 What is the effect of a government subsidy that reduces the fixed cost of each firm in an industry in a Cournot monopolistic competition equilibrium?

---

[32]Matt Flegenheimer, "$1 Pizza Slice Is Back After a Sidewalk Showdown Ends Two Parlors' Price War," *New York Times*, September 5, 2012.

6.2 In the monopolistically competitive airlines model, what is the equilibrium if firms face no fixed costs?

6.3 In a monopolistically competitive market, the government applies a specific tax of $1 per unit of output. What happens to the profit of a typical firm in this market? Does the number of firms in the market change? Why?

6.4 Does an oligopoly or a monopolistically competitive firm have a supply curve? Why or why not? (*Hint*: See the discussion in Chapter 11 of whether a monopoly has a supply curve.)

*6.5 Show that a monopolistically competitive firm maximizes its profit where it is operating at less than *full capacity* or *minimum efficient scale*, which is the smallest quantity at which the average cost curve reaches its minimum (the bottom of a U-shaped average cost curve). The firm's minimum efficient scale is the quantity at which the firm no longer benefits from economies of scale.

6.6 Exercise 6.5 shows that a monopolistically competitive firm maximizes its profit where it is operating at less than full capacity. Does this result depend upon whether firms produce identical or differentiated products? Why?

6.7 In Solved Problem 14.4, what fixed cost would result in four firms operating in the monopolistically competitive equilibrium? What are the equilibrium quantities and prices?

7. Challenge

7.1 In the Challenge Solution's mathematical model, how much does Firm 1's best-response curve shift as the subsidy, s, increases?

7.2 Using the Challenge Solution's mathematical model, how much does Firm 1's profit (ignoring the subsidy) change as the subsidy, s, increases?

Factor Markets

15

I have often thought that if there had been a good rap group around in those days, I would have chosen a career in music instead of politics. —Richard Nixon

For most of your childhood, your parents, teachers, or other adults urged you to go to college. Is college worth the cost?

According to a 2018 poll, when asked whether a four-year college degree is "a key to future success" or "not worth the cost," 61% of Americans say it is crucial to future success. Many people calculate that it is personally worth it. In the fall of 2017, two-thirds of high school graduates were enrolled in colleges or universities. Enrollment in U.S. colleges and universities rose by 5% between fall 2006–2007 and fall 2017–2018. The share of adults over 25 who have completed a bachelor's or higher degree increased from 21% in 1990 to 34% in 2017.

Going to college is expensive. In the 2017–2018 school year, the average total cost of tuition and fees was $9,970 at a public four-year school in-state, $25,620 out-of-state, and $34,740 at private nonprofit schools. According to the College Board, the average college grad earns 66% more than does a typical high school grad over a 40-year working life. How should we weigh the costs and benefits to determine if an investment in a college education pays financially?

CHALLENGE

Does Going to College Pay?

This chapter examines factor markets, such as the markets for labor and capital. We want to answer questions such as Nokia faces when manufacturing cell phones: How many workers should Nokia hire? How much equipment does it need? Should it invest in a new factory? Its decisions depend on wages, the rental price of capital, and the interest rate, which the labor and capital factor markets determine.

We first look at factor markets, such as the market for labor. We look at *nondurable* services, such as one hour of work by an engineer or a daily truck rental. Nondurable services are those consumed when they are purchased or soon thereafter.

Additional analytical complications arise when the input is *capital* or other *durable goods*: products that are usable for years. Firms use durable goods—such as manufacturing plants, machines, and trucks—to produce and distribute goods and services. Consumers spend one out of eight dollars on durable goods such as houses, cars, and refrigerators.

If a firm rents a durable good by the week, it faces a decision similar to its decision in buying a nondurable good or service. If the firm must buy or build a capital good rather than rent it, the firm cannot apply this rule based on current costs and benefits alone. A firm cannot rent many types of specialized capital, such as custom-built factories or custom equipment.

We examine how purchases of durable goods or investments in college depend critically on the interest rate, which is also determined by the capital market. The interest rate also has a critical effect on how fast prices rise in natural resources markets, such as those for coal and oil.

In this chapter, we examine three main topics

1. **Factor Markets.** The intersection of the factor supply curve and the factor demand curve (which depends on firms' production functions and on the market price for output) determines the equilibrium quantity in a competitive factor market, which is greater quantity than in a noncompetitive factor market.

2. **Capital Markets and Investing.** Investing money in a project pays if the return from that investment is greater than that from the best alternative.

3. **Exhaustible Resources.** Scarcity, rising costs of extraction, and positive interest rates may cause the price of exhaustible resources, such as coal and gold, to rise exponentially over time.

15.1 Factor Markets

Virtually all firms rely on factor markets for at least some inputs, such as labor. The firms that buy factors may be competitive price takers or noncompetitive price setters, such as a monopsony firm. Competitive, monopolistically competitive, oligopolistic, and monopolistic firms sell factors.

We start with competitive factor markets. Factor markets are competitive if they have many small sellers and buyers. FloraHolland's daily flower auction in Amsterdam typifies such a competitive market with many sellers and buyers. The sellers supply inputs—flowers in bulk—to buyers, who sell outputs—trimmed flowers in vases and wrapped bouquets—at retail to final customers.

Our earlier analysis of the competitive supply curve applies to factor markets. Chapter 5 derives the supply curve of labor by examining how individuals' choices between labor and leisure depend on tastes and the wage rate. Chapter 8 determines the competitive supply curves of firms in general, including those that produce factors for other firms. Given that we know the supply curve, once we determine the factor's demand curve, we can analyze the market for a competitive factor.

A firm chooses inputs so as to maximize its profit. We illustrate this decision for a firm that combines labor, L, and capital, K, to produce output, q, where its production function is $q = q(L, K)$.[1] Using the theory of the firm (Chapters 6 and 7), we show how the amount of each input that the firm demands depends on the prices of the factors and the price of the final output. We begin by considering the firm's short-run problem when the firm can adjust only labor because capital is fixed. We then examine its long-run problem when both inputs are variable.

A Firm's Short-Run Factor Demand Curve

In the short run, the firm's capital is fixed at $\overline{K}$ so the firm can increase its output only by using more labor. That is, the short-run production function might be written as $q = \tilde{q}(L, \overline{K}) = q(L)$ to show that it is solely a function of labor.

---

[1]In Chapters 6 and 7, we wrote the production function as $q = f(L, K)$. Here, for notational simplicity, we write the function as $q(L, K)$.

The firm chooses how many workers to hire to maximize its profit. The firm is a price taker in the labor markets, so it can hire as many workers as it wants at the market wage, w. Thus, the firm's short-run cost is $C = wL + F$, where F is the fixed cost. The firm's revenue function is $R(q(L))$.

The firm's profit function is its revenue function minus its cost function. The firm's objective is to maximize its profit through its labor choice:

$$\max_{L} \ \pi = R(q(L)) - wL - F. \tag{15.1}$$

We use the chain rule to derive the firm's first-order condition for a profit maximum:[2]

$$\frac{d\pi}{dL} = \frac{dR}{dq}\frac{dq}{dL} - w = 0,$$

hence,

$$\frac{dR}{dq}\frac{dq}{dL} = w. \tag{15.2}$$

According to Equation 15.2, a profit-maximizing firm chooses L so that the additional revenue it receives from employing the last worker equals the wage it must pay for the last worker. The additional revenue from the last unit of labor, $(dR/dq)(dq/dL)$, is called the **marginal revenue product of labor** (MRP_L). That is, the firm's marginal benefit equals its marginal cost from one extra hour of work.

The marginal revenue product of labor is the marginal revenue from the last unit of output, $MR = dR/dq$, times the marginal product of labor, $MP_L = dq/dL$, which is the extra output produced by the last unit of labor (Chapter 6):

$$MRP_L = MR \times MP_L.$$

A Competitive Firm's Short-Run Factor Demand Curve. A competitive firm faces an infinitely elastic demand for its output at the market price, p, so its marginal revenue is p (Chapter 8), and its marginal revenue product of labor is

$$MRP_L = p\frac{dq}{dL} = pMP_L.$$

The marginal revenue product for a competitive firm is also called the *value of the marginal product* because the marginal revenue product equals the market price or value times the marginal product of labor, which is the market value of the extra output from the last unit of labor.

Thus, for a competitive firm, Equation 15.2 is

$$MRP_L = pMP_L = w. \tag{15.3}$$

Equation 15.3 is the firm's short-run labor demand function. It shows that the marginal revenue product of labor curve is the firm's demand curve for labor when capital is fixed. One interpretation of Equation 15.3 is that the MRP_L determines the maximum wage a firm is willing to pay to hire a given number of workers (or vice versa). Dividing both sides of Equation 15.3 by p, we find that the marginal product of labor

---

[2]We assume that the second-order condition, $(dR/dq)(d^2q/dL^2) < 0$, holds and that the firm does not want to shut down.

equals the ratio of the wage to the output price, $MP_L = dq(L)/dL = w/p$, which is sometimes called the *real wage*. Because the marginal product of labor is a function of labor, this expression can be restated so that the quantity of labor demanded by a competitive firm is a function of the real wage: $L = L(w/p)$.

We can illustrate these calculations using an estimated Cobb-Douglas production function for a paper firm (Hossain et al., 2012): $q = L^{0.6}K^{0.2}$. If the firm's capital is fixed at $\overline{K} = 32$ units in the short run, its short-run production function is $q = L^{0.6}32^{0.2} = 2L^{0.6}$. The firm's marginal product of labor is $MP_L = d(2L^{0.6})/dL = 1.2L^{-0.4}$. As a result, Equation 15.3 becomes

$$MRP_L = 1.2pL^{-0.4} = w. \qquad (15.4)$$

If the firm faces a price of $p = \$50$ per unit and a wage of $w = \$15$ an hour, Equation 15.4 becomes $MRP_L = 60L^{-0.4} = 15$, so the firm should employ $L = 32$ workers. More generally, when we solve Equation 15.4 for L in terms of p and w, the paper firm's demand for labor function is

$$L = \left(\frac{1}{1.2}\frac{w}{p}\right)^{1/(-0.4)} \approx 1.577\left(\frac{w}{p}\right)^{-2.5}. \qquad (15.5)$$

Figure 15.1 plots Equation 15.4, the paper firm's MRP_L or labor demand curve, for $p = \$50$. The wage line at $w = 15$ is the supply curve of labor that the firm faces. The firm can hire as many workers as it wants at a constant wage of $15. The marginal revenue product of labor curve, MRP_L, is the firm's demand curve for labor when other inputs are fixed. The MRP_L shows the maximum wage that a firm is willing to pay to hire a given number of workers. Thus, the intersection of the supply curve of labor facing the firm and the firm's demand curve for labor determines the profit-maximizing number of workers.

Effect of a Change in the Wage. What happens to the short-run demand for labor if the wage increases or decreases? The firm's labor demand curve is usually downward sloping because of the law of diminishing marginal returns (Chapter 6). The marginal product from extra workers, MP_L, of a firm with fixed capital eventually falls as the firm increases the amount of labor it uses. Because the marginal product of labor declines as more workers are hired, the marginal revenue product of labor (which equals a constant price times the marginal product of labor) or the demand curve must slope downward as well.

Figure 15.1 Short-Run Labor Demand of a Paper Firm

In the short run, capital is fixed at 32 units. If the market price is $50 per unit and the wage is $w = \$15$ per hour, a paper firm hires 32 workers at point a, where the labor supply curve intersects the mill's short-run labor demand curve. If the wage falls to $10, the mill hires 88 workers at point b.

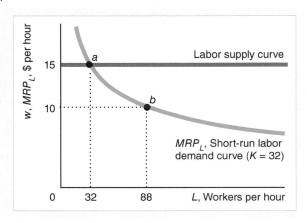

According to Equation 15.3, the firm hires labor until the value of its marginal product of labor equals the wage: $pMP_L = w$. If w increases and p remains constant, the only way for the firm to maintain this equality is to adjust its labor force so as to cause its marginal product of labor to rise. If the firm operates where the production function exhibits diminishing marginal returns to labor, its marginal product of labor rises when it reduces its labor force. Thus, the firm's demand curve for labor is downward sloping.

We can confirm this reasoning using a formal comparative static analysis. Because Equation 15.3 is an identity, it must hold for all values of w; hence we can write the amount of labor demanded as an implicit function of the wage: $L(w)$. To show how labor demand varies with the wage, we differentiate Equation 15.3 with respect to w:

$$p \frac{dMP_L}{dL} \frac{dL}{dw} = 1.$$

Rearranging terms,

$$\frac{dL}{dw} = \frac{1}{p \dfrac{dMP_L}{dL}}. \qquad (15.6)$$

Thus, if the firm is operating where the production function exhibits diminishing marginal product of labor, $dMP_L/dL = d^2q/dL^2 < 0$, $dL/dw < 0$, and the demand curve for labor slopes downward.

Figure 15.1 shows that the paper firm's short-run labor demand curve is downward sloping: The quantity of labor services demanded rises from 32 to 88 workers if the wage falls from \$15 to \$10. The reason the firm's demand curve is downward sloping is that its marginal product of labor, $MP_L = 1.2L^{-0.4}$, falls as the firm uses more labor: $dMP_L/dL = -0.48L^{-1.4} < 0$. Indeed, because this inequality holds for any L, the production function exhibits diminishing marginal product of labor at any quantity of labor, and hence the mill's labor demand curve slopes downward everywhere.

SOLVED PROBLEM 15.1

MyLab Economics
Solved Problem

How does a competitive firm adjust its short-run demand for labor if the local government collects a specific tax of t on each unit of output, where this tax does not affect other firms in the market because they are located in other communities?

Answer

1. *Give intuition.* Because the government applies the tax to only one competitive firm, it does not affect p or w measurably. The specific tax lowers the after-tax price per unit that the firm receives, so we can apply the same type of analysis that we would use to show the comparative statics effect of a change in the output price. For a given amount of labor, the marginal revenue product of labor falls from $pMP_L(L)$ to $(p - t)MP_L(L)$. The marginal revenue product of labor curve—the labor demand curve—shifts downward until it is only $(p - t)/p$ as high as the original labor demand curve at any quantity of labor, so the firm demands less labor at any given wage. We now use calculus to derive this result formally.

2. *Differentiate the profit-maximizing condition with respect to the tax.* The firm's profit-maximizing condition, Equation 15.3, is $(p - t)MP_L = w$ (which we evaluate at $t = 0$ before the tax is imposed). Given that this identity holds for all t, the labor demanded is an implicit function of the tax: $L(t)$. Differentiating this identity with respect to t, we find that

$$-MP_L + (p - t)\frac{dMP_L}{dL}\frac{dL}{dt} = 0,$$

where the right-hand side of the equation is zero because w does not vary with t. Rearranging terms,

$$\frac{dL}{dt} = \frac{MP_L}{(p - t)\dfrac{dMP_L}{dL}}.$$

Because MP_L and $(p - t)$ are positive, the sign of this expression is the same as that of dMP_L/dL. Thus, if the production process exhibits diminishing marginal product of labor, the quantity of labor demanded falls with the tax: $dL/dt < 0$.

A Noncompetitive Firm's Short-Run Factor Demand Curve. Factor demand curves vary with market power. As we have seen in earlier chapters, the marginal revenue of profit-maximizing Firm i, $MR = p(1 + 1/\varepsilon_i)$, is a function of the elasticity of demand, ε_i, facing the firm and of the market price, p. Thus, the firm's marginal revenue product of labor function is

$$MRP_L = p\left(1 + \frac{1}{\varepsilon_i}\right)MP_L.$$

The labor demand curve is $p \times MP_L$ for a competitive firm because it faces an infinitely elastic demand at the market price, so its marginal revenue equals the market price.

A monopoly operates in the elastic section of its downward-sloping market demand curve (Chapter 11), so its demand elasticity is less than -1 and finite: $-\infty < \varepsilon < -1$. As a result, at any given price, the monopoly's labor demand, $p(1 + 1/\varepsilon)MP_L$, lies below the labor demand curve, pMP_L, of a competitive firm with an identical marginal product of labor curve.

Figure 15.2 shows the short-run market labor demand curve for an actual competitive paper firm and the corresponding curve for a monopoly. In the short run, the paper firm's marginal product function is $MP_L = 1.2L^{-0.4}$. The labor demand is $p \times 1.2L^{-0.4}$ for a competitive firm and $p(1 + 1/\varepsilon) \times 1.2L^{-0.4}$ for a monopoly. In the figure, we assume that $\varepsilon = -2$.

A Cournot firm faces an elasticity of demand of $n\varepsilon$, where n is the number of identical firms and ε is the market elasticity of demand (Chapter 14). If the market has a constant elasticity demand curve with an elasticity of ε, the demand elasticity faced by a duopoly Cournot firm is twice that, 2ε, of a monopoly. Consequently, a Cournot duopoly firm's labor demand curve, $p[1 + 1/(2\varepsilon)]MP_L$, lies above that of a monopoly but below that of a competitive firm. Figure 15.2 shows the short-run market labor demand curve for one of two identical Cournot paper firms is $p[1 + 1/(2\varepsilon)] \times 1.2L^{-0.4}$.

Figure 15.2 How a Paper Firm's Labor Demand Varies with Market Structure

For all profit-maximizing firms, the labor demand curve is the marginal revenue product of labor: $MRP_L = MR \times MP_L$. Because marginal revenue differs with market structure, so does the MRP_L. At a given wage, a competitive paper firm demands more workers than a Cournot duopoly firm, which demands more workers than a monopoly.

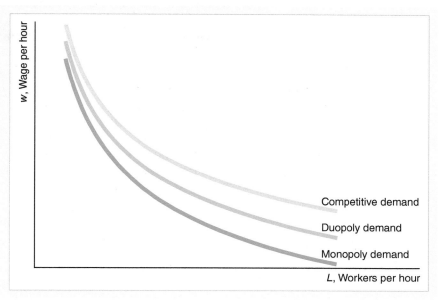

A Firm's Long-Run Factor Demand Curves

In the long run, the firm is free to vary all of its inputs. Thus, in the long run, if the wage rises, the firm adjusts both labor and capital. As a result, the short-run marginal revenue product of labor curve that holds capital fixed is not the firm's long-run labor demand curve. The long-run labor demand curve takes account of changes in the firm's use of capital as the wage rises.

In the long run, the firm chooses both labor and capital so as to maximize its profit. If the firm is a price taker in these factor markets, then the firm's cost is $C = wL + rK$, where w is the wage and r is the rental cost of capital. Because the firm's production process is $q = q(L, K)$, its revenue function is $R(q(L, K))$.

The firm's profit function is its revenue function minus its costs. The firm's objective is to maximize its profit through its choice of inputs:

$$\max_{L, K} \pi = R(q(L, K)) - wL - rK. \tag{15.7}$$

The firm's first-order conditions for a profit maximum are

$$\frac{\partial \pi}{\partial L} = \frac{\partial R}{\partial q} \frac{\partial q}{\partial L} - w = 0,$$

$$\frac{\partial \pi}{\partial K} = \frac{\partial R}{\partial q} \frac{\partial q}{\partial K} - r = 0.$$

These first-order conditions are closely analogous to the short-run profit-maximizing condition. They show that the firm sets its marginal revenue product of labor equal to the wage and its marginal revenue product of capital equal to the rental price of capital:

$$MRP_L = MR \times MP_L = \frac{\partial R}{\partial q} \frac{\partial q}{\partial L} = w, \tag{15.8}$$

$$MRP_K = MR \times MP_K = \frac{\partial R}{\partial q}\frac{\partial q}{\partial K} = r. \tag{15.9}$$

A Competitive Firm's Long-Run Factor Demand Curve. Again, if the firm is competitive, $MR = p$, so Equations 15.8 and 15.9 can be written as

$$MRP_L = pMP_L = p\frac{\partial q}{\partial L} = w, \tag{15.10}$$

$$MRP_K = pMP_K = \frac{\partial q}{\partial K} = r. \tag{15.11}$$

That is, each input's factor price equals the value of its marginal product. Equations 15.10 and 15.11 are the competitive firm's long-run factor demand equations.

For example, if the production function is Cobb-Douglas, $q = AL^aK^b$, then Equations 15.10 and 15.11 are

$$paAL^{a-1}K^b = w,$$

$$pbAL^aK^{b-1} = r.$$

Solving these equations for L and K, we find that the factor demand functions are

$$L = \left(\frac{a}{w}\right)^{(1-b)/d}\left(\frac{b}{r}\right)^{b/d}(Ap)^{1/d}, \tag{15.12}$$

$$K = \left(\frac{a}{w}\right)^{a/d}\left(\frac{b}{r}\right)^{(1-a)/d}(Ap)^{1/d}, \tag{15.13}$$

where $d = 1 - a - b$.[3] By differentiating the input demand Equations 15.12 and 15.13, we can show that the demand for each factor decreases with respect to its own factor price, w or r, and increases with p. Given the parameters for the estimated paper firm's production function, $a = 0.6$, $b = 0.2$, and $A = 1$, the long-run labor demand Equation 15.12 is $L = (0.6/w)^4(0.2/r)p^5$, and the long-run capital demand Equation 15.13 is $K = (0.6/w)^3(0.2/r)^2p^5$.

The shares of its total revenue that a competitive firm pays to labor and to capital do not vary with factor or output prices if the firm has a Cobb-Douglas production function, $q = AL^aK^b$. A competitive firm with a Cobb-Douglas production function pays its labor the value of its marginal product, $w = pMP_L = apAL^{a-1}K^b = apq/L$. As a result, the share of the firm's revenue that it pays to labor is $\omega_L = wL/(pq) = a$. Similarly, $\omega_K = rK/(pq) = b$. Thus, the payment shares to labor and to capital for the competitive firm are fixed and independent of prices with a Cobb-Douglas production function.

Comparing Short-Run and Long-Run Labor Demand Curves. In both the short run and the long run, the labor demand curve is the marginal revenue product of labor curve. In the short run, the firm cannot vary capital, so the short-run MP_L curve and hence the short-run MRP_L curve are relatively steep. In the long run, when the firm can vary all inputs, its long-run MP_L curve and MRP_L curve are flatter.

Figure 15.3 illustrates this difference for the paper firm, where $p = \$50$ per unit and $r = \$5$ per hour. On the short-run labor demand curve where capital is fixed at

---

[3]If the Cobb-Douglas production function has constant returns to scale, $d = 0$, then Equations 15.12 and 15.13 are not helpful. The problem with constant returns to scale is that a competitive firm does not care how much it produces (and hence how many inputs it uses) as long as the market price and input prices are consistent with zero profit.

Figure 15.3 Labor Demand Curves of a Paper Firm

If the long-run market price is $50 per unit, the rental rate of capital services is $r = \$5$, and the wage is $w = \$15$ per hour, a paper firm hires 32 workers (and uses 32 units of capital) at point a on its long-run labor demand curve. In the short run, if capital is fixed at $\overline{K} = 32$, the firm still hires 32 workers per hour at point a on its short-run labor demand curve. If the wage drops to $10 and capital remains fixed at $\overline{K} = 32$, the firm would hire 88 workers, point b on the short-run labor demand curve. In the long run, however, it would increase its capital to $K = 108$ and hire 162 workers, point c on the long-run labor demand curve and on the short-run labor demand curve with $\overline{K} = 108$.

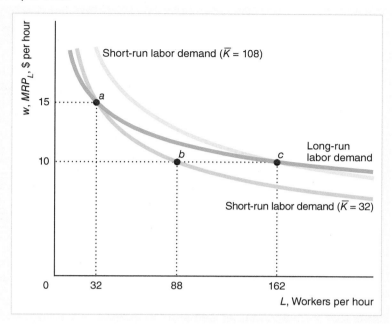

$\overline{K} = 32$ the firm hires 32 workers per hour at $w = \$15$. Using 32 workers and 32 units of capital is profit maximizing in the long run, so point a is also on the firm's long-run labor demand curve. The short-run labor demand curve is steeper than the long-run curve at point a.[4]

In the short run, if the wage fell to $10, the firm could not increase its capital, so it would hire 88 workers, point b on the short-run labor demand curve, where $\overline{K} = 32$. However, in the long run, the firm would employ more capital and even more labor (because it can sell as much output as it wants at the market price). It would hire 162 workers and use 108 units of capital, which is point c on both the long-run labor demand curve and the short-run labor demand curve for $\overline{K} = 108$.

Competitive Factor Markets

To determine the competitive equilibrium in a factor market, we aggregate the individual firms' demand curves to obtain the factor market demand curve, and then we determine where the factor market demand curve intersects the factor market supply curve.

A Factor Market Demand Curve. A factor market demand curve is the horizontal sum of the factor demand curves of the various firms that use the input. Determining a factor market demand curve is more difficult than deriving consumers' market demand for a final good. When horizontally summing the demand curves for

---

[4]If $p = \$50$, the paper firm's short-run labor demand equation is $L \approx 27{,}885.48 w^{-2.5}$. In contrast, if $r = \$5$, its long-run labor demand equation is $L = 1{,}620{,}000 w^{-4}$. At $w = \$15$, the two curves intersect at $L = 32$, as Figure 15.3 shows. At that point, the change in labor with respect to a change in the wage on the short-run labor demand curve is $dL/dw \approx -2.5(27{,}885.48) w^{-1.5} \approx -1{,}200$, and the corresponding derivative along the long-run curve is $dL/dw = -4(1{,}620{,}000) \times w^{-3} = -1{,}920$. Thus, the slope of the short-run labor demand curve, dw/dL, is steeper than that of the long-run curve.

individual consumers in Chapter 2, we were concerned with only a single market. However, inputs such as labor and capital are used in many output markets. Thus, to derive the labor market demand curve, we first determine the labor demand curve for each output market and then sum across output markets to obtain the factor market demand curve.

Earlier, we derived the factor demand of a competitive firm that took the output market price as given. However, the output market price depends on the factor's price. As the factor's price falls, each firm, taking the original market price as given, uses more of the factor to produce more output. This extra production by all the firms in the market causes the market price to fall. As the market price falls, each firm reduces its output and hence its demand for the input. Thus, a fall in an input price causes less of an increase in factor demand than would occur if the market price remained constant, as Figure 15.4 illustrates.

At the initial output market price of $9 per unit, the competitive firm's labor demand curve (panel a of Figure 15.4) is $MRP_L(p = \$9) = \$9 \times MP_L$. When the wage is $25 per hour, the firm hires 50 workers: point a. The 10 firms in the market (panel b) demand 500 hours of work: point A on the demand curve $D(p = \$9) = 10 \times \$9 \times MP_L$. If the wage falls to $10 while the market price remains fixed at $9, each firm hires 90 workers, point c, and all the firms in the market would hire 900 workers, point C. However, the extra output drives the price down to $7, so each firm hires 70 workers,

Figure 15.4 Firm and Market Demand for Labor

When the output price is $p = \$9$, the individual competitive firm's labor demand curve is $MRP_L(p = \$9)$. If $w = \$25$ per hour, the firm hires 50 workers, point a in panel a, and the 10 firms in the market demand 500 workers, point A on the labor demand curve $D(p = \$9)$ in panel b. When the wage falls to $10, each firm would hire 90 workers, point c, if the market price stayed fixed at $9. The extra output, however, drives the price down to $7, so each firm hires 70 workers, point b. The market's demand for labor that takes price adjustments into account, D(price varies), goes through points A and B.

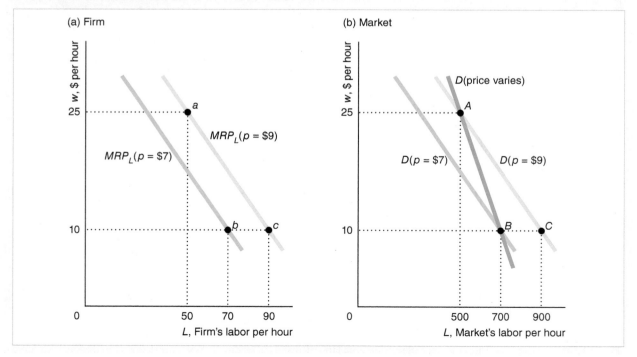

point b, and the firms collectively demand 700 workers, point B. The market labor demand curve for this output market that accounts for price adjustments, D(price varies), goes through points A and B. Thus, the market's demand for labor is steeper than it would be if output prices were fixed.

Competitive Factor Market Equilibrium. The intersection of the factor market demand curve and the factor market supply curve determines the competitive factor market equilibrium. We've just derived the factor market demand curve. A market supply curve for capital, material, and other factors is a typical supply curve. The long-run factor supply curve for each firm is its marginal cost curve above the minimum of its average cost curve, and the factor market supply curve is the horizontal sum of the firms' supply curves. We discussed the labor supply curve in Chapter 5. Because we've already analyzed competitive market equilibria for markets in general in Chapters 2, 8, and 9, there's no point in repeating the analysis. Been there. Done that.

Factor prices are equalized across markets (Chapter 10). For example, if wages were higher in one industry than in another, workers would shift from the low-wage industry to the high-wage industry until the wages were equalized.

APPLICATION

Black Death Raises Wages

The Black Death—bubonic plague—wiped out between one-third and one-half of the population of medieval Western Europe, resulting in a large increase in the real wage and sizable drops in the real rents on land and capital. Why?

The plague is characterized by large, dark lumps in the groin or armpits followed by livid black spots on the arms, thighs, and other parts of the body. In virtually all its victims, the Black Death led to a horrible demise within one to three days of onset.

In England, the plague struck in 1348–1349, 1360–1361, 1369, and 1375. According to one historian, the population fell by 40% over the entire period: from 3.76 million in 1348 to 3.13 million in 1348–1350, 2.75 million in 1360, 2.45 million in 1369, and 2.25 million in 1374.

In England, nominal wages rose in the second half of the fourteenth century compared to the first half: Thatchers earned 35% more, thatchers' helpers 105%, carpenters 40%, masons 48%, mowers 24%, oat threshers 73%, and oat reapers 61%. Adjusting for output price changes (at a medieval consumer price index), the average real wage rose by about 25%. In Pistoia, Italy, rents in-kind on land fell by about 40%, and the rate of return on capital fell by about the same proportion.

Because the plague wiped out one-half to two-thirds of the labor force, labor became scarce relative to capital and land, which, of course, were unaffected by the disease. The scarcity of labor caused the marginal product of labor, MP_L, to rise: The remaining workers had lots of capital and land to use and hence were very productive. In competitive markets, workers are paid a wage equal to the value of their marginal product (marginal revenue product), $w = pMP_L$. If we rearrange this expression, the real wage, w/p, equals the marginal product of labor, $w/p = MP_L$. Hence, a large increase in the marginal product of labor causes a comparable increase in the real wage. Similarly, the fall in labor reduced the marginal products of capital and land, resulting in a drop in the real prices that these factors of production received.

**SOLVED PROBLEM
15.2**

**MyLab Economics
Solved Problem**

For simplicity, suppose that medieval England was a single, large, price-taking firm that produced one type of output with a constant-returns-to-scale Cobb-Douglas production function, $q = L^{0.5}K^{0.5}$. Labor and capital have inelastic supply curves. Everyone, $L = 100$, works and all capital, $K = 100$, is used. Suppose that the Black Death killed three-fourths of the workers, causing the number of workers to fall from L to $L^* = \frac{1}{4}L$. Show how much the wage, w, rose. Given that p is normalized to 1, calculate the changes in the factor prices.

Answer

1. *Show how output falls due to a reduction in labor.* When labor falls from L to $L^* = \frac{1}{4}L$, output falls from $q = L^{0.5}K^{0.5}$ to $q^* = (\frac{1}{4}L)^{0.5}K^{0.5} = \frac{1}{4}^{0.5}L^{0.5}K^{0.5} = \frac{1}{4}^{0.5}q = \frac{1}{2}q$. That is, when labor falls to one-fourth its original level, output falls less than in proportion to one-half its initial level.

2. *Given the effect of the plague on output, show how the marginal product of labor changed and hence how the real wage changed.* We know that the marginal product of labor for a Cobb-Douglas production function is $MP_L = \frac{1}{2}q/L$. The output-to-labor ratio changes from q/L to $q^*/L^* = \frac{1}{2}q/(\frac{1}{4}L) = 2q/L > q/L$. Consequently, the marginal product of labor rose from $MP_L = \frac{1}{2}q/L$ to $MP_L^* = q/L = 2MP_L$. The competitive labor demand equation is determined by equating the marginal product of labor to the real wage, $MP_L = w/p$. For this equation to hold when the marginal product of labor rose, the real wage of labor, $w^*/p = MP_L^*$, had to rise in proportion to MP_L^*.

3. *Show the corresponding effect on capital.* Because output fell and capital remained the same, the marginal product of capital fell from $MP_K = \frac{1}{2}q/K$ to $MP_K^* = \frac{1}{4}^{0.5} \times 0.5 \times q/K = \frac{1}{2}MP_K$. Consequently, the real price of capital, $r^*/p = MP_K$, dropped.

4. *Calculate the changes in wages and the rental price of capital.* The initial output was $q = L^{0.5}K^{0.5} = 100^{0.5}100^{0.5} = 100$. The marginal product of labor was $MP_L = \frac{1}{2}q/L = \frac{1}{2}(100/100) = \frac{1}{2}$, so the real wage was $w/p = \frac{1}{2}$, given that $p = 1$. Similarly, the marginal product of capital was $MP_K = \frac{1}{2}q/K = \frac{1}{2}$, and the real price of capital was $r/p = \frac{1}{2}$. After the plague, the labor force fell to $L^* = \frac{1}{4}L = 25$, and output dropped to $q = 25^{0.5}100^{0.5} = 50$. Consequently, the marginal product of labor rose to $MP_L^* = \frac{1}{2}(50/25) = 1$, so the real wage rose to $w^*/p = 1$. Similarly, the marginal product of capital and the real price of capital fell to $MP_K^* = \frac{1}{2}(50/100) = \frac{1}{4} = r^*/p$. Thus, the real wage doubled and the real rental rate on capital dropped by half.

15.2 Capital Markets and Investing

If a firm rents a durable good by the week, it faces a decision similar to the one it encounters when buying a nondurable good or service. A firm demands workers' services (or other nondurable input) up to the point at which its *current* marginal cost (the wage) equals its *current* marginal benefit (the marginal revenue product of the workers' services). A firm that rents a durable good, such as a truck, by the week can use the same rule to decide how many trucks to rent per week. The firm rents trucks up to the point at which the *current* marginal rental cost equals its *current* marginal benefit—the marginal revenue product of the trucks.

If a firm must buy or build a capital good rather than rent it, the firm cannot apply this rule based on current costs and benefits alone. A firm cannot rent many types of specialized capital, such as a factory or a customized piece of equipment. In deciding whether to build a factory that will last for many years, a firm must compare the *current* cost of the capital to the *future* higher profits it will make over time by using the plant.

Such comparisons may involve both *stocks* and *flows*. A **stock** is a quantity or value that is measured independently of time. Because a durable good lasts for many periods, its stock is discussed without reference to its use within a particular time period. We say that a firm owns "an apartment building *this* year" (not "an apartment building *per* year"). If a firm buys the apartment building for $5 million, we say that it has a capital stock worth $5 million today.

A **flow** is a quantity or value that is measured per unit of time. The consumption of nondurable goods, such as the number of ice-cream cones you eat per week, is a flow. Similarly, the stock of a durable good provides a flow of services. A firm's apartment building—its capital stock—provides a flow of housing services (apartments rented per month or year) to tenants. In exchange for these housing services, the firm receives a flow of rental payments from the tenants. If the capital good or *asset* provides a monetary flow, it is called a *financial asset*.

Does it pay for a firm to buy an apartment building? To answer this question, we need to extend our analysis in two ways. First, we must compare a flow of dollars in the future to a dollar today, which we do in this chapter. Second, we need to consider the role of uncertainty about the future. For example, can a firm that builds an apartment house rent all its units each month? We address uncertainty in Chapter 16.

We start by showing how we can use interest rates to compare money in the future to money today. Then, we show how we can use interest rates to compare streams of payments or streams of returns from investment over time to money today. Finally, we use these means of comparison to analyze how a firm chooses between two investments.

Interest Rates

Because virtually everyone values having a dollar today more than having a dollar in the future, you would not loan a bank a dollar today (that is, place money in a savings account) unless the bank agreed to pay back more than a dollar in the future. How much more you must be paid in the future is specified by an **interest rate**: the percentage more that must be repaid to borrow money for a fixed period.[5] In the following discussion, we assume that the rate of inflation is zero and concentrate on real interest rates.

It is crucial that you understand how to use interest rates to make rational decisions about saving and investing. Unfortunately, most people do not understand how interest rates work:

> **Common Confusion** In making saving and investment decisions, you just need to look at the current interest rate.

You also need to pay attention to how frequently the interest compounds, which is "interest on interest."

---

[5]For simplicity, we refer to *the* interest rate, but most economies have many interest rates. For example, a bank charges a higher interest rate to lend you money than the interest rate it pays you to borrow your money. (See "Usury" in MyLab Economics, Chapter Resources, Chapter 15, for a discussion of ancient people's opposition to paying interest, and current restrictions on Islamic banks.)

If you save a *present value* of PV dollars this year and the bank pays *i* percent interest per year, the bank will return a *future value* of PV × (1 + *i*) next year. If you leave your money in the bank for many years, you will earn interest in later years on the interest paid in the earlier years, which is called *compounded interest*. Thus, if you deposit PV dollars in the bank today and allow the interest to compound for *t* years, the future value FV is

$$FV = PV \times (1 + i)^t. \tag{15.14}$$

Equivalently, we can ask what the *present value* is of an investment that pays FV next year. At an interest rate of *i*, the present value is $PV = FV/(1 + i)$. By rearranging Equation 15.14, we find that the amount of money you would have to put in the bank today to get FV in *t* years at an interest rate of *i* is

$$PV = \frac{FV}{(1 + i)^t}. \tag{15.15}$$

The frequency of compounding matters. If a bank's annual interest rate is $i = 10\%$, but it pays interest two times a year, the bank pays you half a year's interest, $i/2 = 5\%$, every six months. For every dollar in your account, the bank pays you $(1 + i/2) = 1.05$ dollars after six months. If you leave the interest in the bank, at the end of the year, the bank must pay you interest on your original dollar and on the interest you received at the end of the first six months. At the end of the year, the bank owes you $(1 + i/2) \times (1 + i/2) = (1 + i/2)^2 = (1.05)^2 = \$1.1025$, which is your original \$1 plus 10.25¢ in interest. With daily compounding, the bank pays about 1.1052. At 18%, the interest compounded once a year is 18¢, but it is over 19.7¢ compounded daily.

Discount Rate

You may value future consumption more or less than other members of society do. If you knew you had two years to live, you would place less value on payments three or more years in the future than most other people would. We call an individual's personal "interest" rate that person's **discount rate**: a rate reflecting the relative value an individual places on future consumption compared to current consumption.

People's willingness to borrow or lend depends on whether their discount rate is greater or less than the market interest rate. If your discount rate is nearly zero—you view current and future consumption as equally desirable—you would gladly lend money in exchange for a positive interest rate. Similarly, if your discount rate is high—current consumption is much more valuable to you than future consumption—you would be willing to borrow at a lower interest rate. In the following discussion, we assume for simplicity that an individual's discount rate is the same as the market interest rate unless we explicitly state otherwise.

Stream of Payments

Many people pay a certain amount each month over time for their purchases. These payments are flow measures—in contrast to a present value and a future value, which are stock measures. For example, a firm may pay for a new factory by making monthly mortgage payments. In deciding whether to purchase the factory, the firm compares the present value of the stock (the factory) to a flow of payments over time.

One way to evaluate this investment is to determine the present value of the stream of payments and compare this value directly to the present value of the factory. The present value of the stream of payments is the sum of the present value of each future payment. Thus, if the firm makes a *future payment* of f per year for t years at an interest rate of i, the present value (stock) of this flow of payments is[6]

$$PV = f\left[\frac{1}{(1+i)^1} + \frac{1}{(1+i)^2} + \cdots + \frac{1}{(1+i)^t}\right]$$

$$= \frac{f}{i}\left[1 - \frac{1}{(1+i)^t}\right]. \tag{15.16}$$

If these payments must be made at the end of each year forever, the present value formula is easier to calculate than Equation 15.16. If the firm invests PV dollars into a bank account earning an interest rate of i, it receives interest or future payments of $f = i \times PV$ at the end of each year. Dividing both sides of this expression by i, we find that to get a payment of f each year forever, the firm would have to put

$$PV = \frac{f}{i} \tag{15.17}$$

in the bank.[7]

This payment-in-perpetuity formula, Equation 15.17, provides a good approximation of a payment for a large but finite number of years. At a 5% interest rate, the present value of a payment of $10 a year for 100 years, $198, is close to the present value of a permanent stream of payments, $200. At higher interest rates, this approximation is nearly perfect. At 10%, the present value of payments for 100 years is $99.9927 compared to $100 for perpetual payments. This approximation works better at high rates because $1 paid more than 50 or 100 years from now is essentially worthless today at high rates.

We just calculated the present value of a stream of payments. This type of computation can help a firm decide whether to buy something today that it will pay for over time. Alternatively, the firm may want to know the future value of a bank account if it invests f each year. At the end of t years, the account has[8]

$$FV = f[1 + (1+i)^1 + (1+i)^2 + \cdots + (1+i)^{t-1}] = \frac{f}{i}[(1+i)^t - 1]. \tag{15.18}$$

---

[6]To obtain the last line of Equation 15.16, we first multiply both sides of the first line by $(1+i)$:

$$PV(1+i) = f\left[1 + \frac{1}{(1+i)} + \frac{1}{(1+i)^2} + \cdots + \frac{1}{(1+i)^{t-1}}\right] = f\left[1 + \frac{PV}{f} - \frac{1}{(1+i)^t}\right].$$

Rearranging terms, we obtain the second line of Equation 15.16.

[7]In Equation 15.16, if the number of periods is infinite, the present value is

$$PV = \frac{f}{1+i} + \frac{f}{(1+i)^2} + \frac{f}{(1+i)^3} + \cdots .$$

Factoring $1/(1+i)$ out of the right side, we rewrite the equation as

$$PV = \frac{1}{1+i}\left[f + \frac{f}{1+i} + \frac{f}{(1+i)^2} + \frac{f}{(1+i)^3} + \cdots \right] = \frac{1}{1+i}(f + PV).$$

Rearranging terms, we obtain Equation 15.17. This result also follows by taking the limit of the second line of Equation 15.16 as t goes to infinity.

[8]To obtain the expression after the second equality, multiply both sides of the first equality in Equation 15.18 by $(1+i)$ to obtain

$$FV(1+i) = f[(1+i) + (1+i)^2 + (1+i)^3 + \cdots + (1+i)^t] = FV + f[(1+i)^t - 1].$$

Rearranging terms, we obtain the second equality.

If all goes well, you'll live long enough to retire. Will you live like royalty off your savings, or will you have to depend on Social Security to provide enough income so that you can avoid having to eat dog food to stay alive? (When I retire, I'm going to be a Velcro farmer.)

You almost certainly don't want to hear this now, but it isn't too early to think about saving for retirement. Thanks to the power of compounding (earning interest on interest), if you start saving when you're young, you don't have to save as much per year as you would if you start saving when you're middle aged.

Suppose that you plan to work full time from age 22 until you retire at 70 and that you can earn 5% on your retirement savings account. Let's consider two approaches:

1. **Early bird:** You save $5,000 a year for the first 15 years of your working life and then let your savings accumulate interest until you retire.

2. **Late bloomer:** After not saving for the first 15 years, you save $5,000 a year for the next 33 years until you retire.

Which scenario leads to a bigger retirement nest egg? To answer this question, we calculate the future value at retirement of each of these streams of investments.

The early bird adds $5,000 each year for 15 years into a retirement account. Using Equation 15.18, we calculate that the account has

$$\frac{\$5,000}{0.05}[(1.05)^{15} - 1] = \$107,892.82$$

at the end of 15 years. Leaving this amount in the retirement account for the next 33 years increases the fund about 5 times, to

$$\$107,898.82 \times 1.05^{33} = \$539,808.12.$$

The late bloomer makes no investments for 15 years and then invests $5,000 a year until retirement. Again using Equation 15.18, we calculate that the funds at retirement are

$$\frac{\$5,000}{0.05}[(1.05)^{33} - 1] = \$400,318.85.$$

Thus, even though the late bloomer contributes to the account for more than twice as long as the early bird, the late bloomer has saved slightly less than three-quarters as much at retirement. Indeed, to have roughly the same amount at retirement as the early bird, the late bloomer would have to save nearly $6,742.22 a year for 33 years. (By the way, someone who saved $5,000 each year for 48 years would have $539,808 + $400,319 = $940,127 salted away by retirement.)

Investing

Frequently, firms must choose between two or more investments that have different streams of payments and streams of returns. For example, MGM, a conglomerate, may decide whether to produce a movie starring a muscle-bound hero who solves the pollution problem by beating up an evil capitalist, to build a new hotel in Reno, to buy a television studio, or to put money in a long-term savings account.

For simplicity, we start by analyzing a firm's choice between two financial assets with no uncertainty and no inflation. In such a scenario, all assets must have the same rate of return, because no one would invest in any asset that had less than the highest available rate of return.

Just as you would not lend money to a bank unless it paid interest, a firm will not invest—tie up its funds for a while—in either a financial asset or a piece of capital unless it expects a payoff greater than its initial outlay. The *rate of return on an investment* is the payoff from that investment expressed as a percentage per time period. For example, a bond might pay a 5% rate of return per year.

One possible investment is to put $1 (or $1 million) in a bank and earn interest of i per year. For example, i might be 4%. The value of this investment next year is $1 + i$. A second possible investment is to buy an asset this year at $1 and sell it with certainty next year for FV, the future value of the asset. The firm is indifferent between these two investments only if $FV = 1 + i$.

We now consider more complex investments. As a general rule, a firm makes an investment if the expected return from the investment is greater than the opportunity cost (Chapter 7). The opportunity cost is the best alternative use of its money, which is what it would earn in the next best use of the money.

Thus, to decide whether to make an investment, the firm needs to compare the potential outlay of money to the firm's best alternative. One possibility is that its best alternative is to put the money that it would otherwise spend on this investment in an interest-bearing bank account. We consider two methods for making this comparison: the *net present value* approach and the *internal rate of return* approach.

Net Present Value Approach. A firm has to decide whether to buy a truck for $20,000. Because the opportunity cost is $20,000, the firm should make the investment only if the present value of expected future returns from the truck is greater than $20,000.

More generally, *a firm should make an investment only if the present value of the expected return exceeds the present value of the costs*. If R is the present value of the expected returns to an investment and C is the present value of the costs of the investment, the firm should make the investment if $R > C$.[9]

This rule is often restated in terms of the net present value, $NPV = R - C$, which is the difference between the present value of the returns, R, and the present value of the costs, C. *A firm should make an investment only if the net present value is positive*:

$$NPV = R - C > 0.$$

Assume that the initial year is $t = 0$, the firm's revenue in year t is R_t, and its cost in year t is C_t. If the last year in which either revenue or cost is nonzero is T, the net present value rule holds that the firm should invest if

$$NPV = R - C$$

$$= \left[R_0 + \frac{R_1}{(1 + i)^1} + \frac{R^2}{(1 + i)^2} + \cdots + \frac{R_T}{(1 + i)^T} \right]$$

$$- \left[C_0 + \frac{C_1}{(1 + i)^1} + \frac{C_2}{(1 + i)^2} + \cdots + \frac{C_T}{(1 + i)^T} \right] > 0.$$

Instead of comparing the present values of the returns and costs, we can examine whether the present value of the *cash flow* in each year (loosely, the annual *profit*),

---

[9]This rule holds when future costs and returns are known with certainty and investments can be reversed but not delayed (Dixit and Pindyck, 1994).

$\pi_t = R_t - C_t$, is positive. By rearranging the terms in the previous expression, we can rewrite the net present value rule as

$$NPV = (R_0 - C_0) + \frac{R_1 - C_1}{(1 + i)^1} + \frac{R_2 - C_2}{(1 + i)^2} + \cdots + \frac{R_T - C_T}{(1 + i)^T}$$

$$= \pi_0 + \frac{\pi_1}{(1 + i)^1} + \frac{\pi_2}{(1 + i)^2} + \cdots + \frac{\pi_T}{(1 + i)^T} > 0. \qquad (15.19)$$

This rule does not restrict the firm to making investments only where its cash flow is positive each year. For example, a firm buys a piece of equipment for $100 and spends the first year learning how to use it, so it makes no revenue from the machine and has a negative cash flow that year: $\pi_0 = -100$. The next year, its revenue is $350 and the machine's maintenance cost is $50, so its second year's cash flow is $\pi_1 = \$300$. At the end of that year, the machine wears out, so the annual cash flow from this investment is zero thereafter. Using Equation 15.19, the firm calculates the investment's net present value at $i = 5\%$ as

$$NPV = -100 + 300/1.05 \approx \$185.71.$$

Because this net present value is positive, the firm buys the equipment.

SOLVED PROBLEM 15.3

MyLab Economics Solved Problem

In 2010, Joe Labob and Peter Guber bought the Golden State Warriors basketball team for $450 million. *Forbes* magazine estimated the team's net income at that time to be $12 million.[10] If these owners believed that they would continue to earn this annual profit (after adjusting for inflation), $f = \$12$ million, forever, was this investment more lucrative than putting the $450 million in a savings account that pays a real interest rate of $i = 2\%$?

Answer

Determine the net present value of the team. The net present value of buying the Warriors is positive if the present value of the expected returns, $12 million/0.02 = $600 million, minus the present value of the cost, which is the purchase price of $450 million, is positive:

$$NPV = \$600 \text{ million} - \$450 \text{ million} = \$150 \text{ million} > 0.$$

Thus, it paid to buy the Warriors if the owners' best alternative investment paid 2%.

Internal Rate of Return Approach. Whether the net present value of an investment is positive depends on the interest rate. In Solved Problem 15.3, the investors buy the basketball team, given an interest rate of 2%. However, if the interest rate were 10%, the net present value would be $12 million/0.1 − $450 million = −$330 million, and the investors would not buy the team.

At what discount rate (rate of return) is a firm indifferent between making an investment and not doing so? The **internal rate of return** (*irr*) is the discount rate such that the net present value of an investment is zero. Replacing the interest rate, i, in

---

[10]By 2015, when they won the league championship, their income was $45 million.

Equation 15.19 with *irr* and setting the *NPV* equal to zero, we implicitly determine the internal rate of return by solving

$$NPV = \pi_0 + \frac{\pi_1}{1 + irr} + \frac{\pi_2}{(1 + irr)^2} + \cdots + \frac{\pi_T}{(1 + irr)^T} = 0$$

for *irr*.

It is easier to calculate *irr* when the investment pays a steady stream of profit, *f*, forever and when the cost of the investment is *PV*. The investment's rate of return is found by rearranging Equation 15.17 and replacing *i* with *irr*:

$$irr = \frac{f}{PV}. \tag{15.20}$$

Instead of using the net present value rule, we can decide whether to invest by comparing the internal rate of return to the interest rate. If the firm is borrowing money to make the investment, *it pays for the firm to borrow to make the investment if the internal rate of return on that investment exceeds that of the next best alternative* (which we assume is the interest rate):[11]

$$irr > i.$$

SOLVED PROBLEM 15.4

Joe Labob and Peter Guber can buy the Golden State Warriors basketball team for a *PV* = $450 million. They expect an annual real flow of payments (profits) of *f* = $12 million forever. If the interest rate is 2%, do they buy the team?

MyLab Economics Solved Problem

Answer

Determine the internal rate of return to this investment and compare it to the interest rate. Using Equation 15.20, we calculate that the internal rate of return from buying the Warriors is

$$irr = \frac{f}{PV} = \frac{\$12 \text{ million}}{\$450 \text{ million}} \approx 2.667\%.$$

Because this rate of return, 2.667%, is greater than the interest rate, 2%, the investors buy the team.

Durability

Many firms must decide how durable to make the products they sell or those they produce for their own use. Should they make long-lasting products at a relatively high cost or less-durable goods at a lower cost?

Suppose the company can vary the quality of a factor (a machine) that it uses in its own production process. If it needs exactly one machine, it must replace the machine when it wears out. Thus, *the firm should pick the durability level for the machine that minimizes the present discounted cost of having a machine forever.*

---

[11]The net present value approach always works. The internal rate of return method is inapplicable if *irr* is not unique. In Solved Problem 15.4, *irr* is unique, and using this approach gives the same answer as the net present value approach.

APPLICATION

Durability of
Telephone Poles

Pacific Gas & Electric (PG&E), a western power utility, must decide how durable to make its 132 million wooden utility poles. The poles are a capital stock for PG&E, which uses them to provide a flow of services: supporting power and phone lines year after year. A wooden utility pole provides the same services each year for T years under normal use. After T years, the pole breaks and is replaced because it can't be repaired, but the flow of services must be maintained. Until recently, PG&E used poles with a life span of $T = 25$ years.

The constant marginal cost of manufacturing and installing the poles depends on how long they last, $m(T)$. For an additional cost, the firm can extend the life span of a pole by treating it with chemicals to prevent bug infestations and rot, reinforcing it with metal bands, varying its thickness, or using higher-quality materials. Because the marginal cost increases with the pole's expected life span, a pole that lasts 50 years costs more than one that lasts 25 years: $m(50) > m(25)$.

The replacement cost of a pole that lasts 25 years is $m(25) = \$1,500$. Thus, replacing all of PG&E's poles today would cost $198 billion—which is more than the cost of many giant power plants.

PG&E believes that it can save money by switching to a longer-lasting pole. The firm picks the duration, T, that minimizes its cost of maintaining its forest of poles. Because the utility keeps the same number of poles in place every year, after a pole wears out at T years, the firm incurs an expense of $m(T)$ to replace it. The present value of providing each pole is the cost of producing it today, $m(T)$, plus the discounted cost of producing another one in T years, $m(T)/(1 + i)^T$, plus the discounted cost of producing another one in $2T$ years, $m(T)/(1 + i)^{2T}$, and so on.

The table shows the present value of the cost of maintaining one pole for the next 100 years given that the utility faces an interest rate of 5%. Because the cost of producing a pole that lasts for 25 years is $m(25) = \$1,500$, the present value of the cost of providing a pole for the next 100 years is $2,112 (column 2). If the cost of a pole that lasts 50 years were $m(50) = \$1,943$ (column 4), the present value would be the same as that for the 25-year pole. If so, the utility would be indifferent between using poles that last 25 years and poles that last 50 years.

	25-Year Pole	50-Year Pole	
Marginal cost, $m(T)$:	$1,500	$1,650	$1,943
Year			
0	$1,500	$1,650	$1,943
25	443	0	0
50	131	144	169
75	39	0	0
Present value of the cost of providing a pole for 100 years:	$2,112	$1,794	$2,112

Note: Due to rounding, column 2 does not add to the present value.

Thus, PG&E will not use 50-year poles if the extra cost is greater than $443 = \$1,943 - \$1,500$ but will use them if the difference in cost is less. The actual extra cost is about $150, so $m(50) = \$1,650$. Thus, the present value of the cost of a 50-year pole is only about $1,794 (column 3 of the table). Because using the 50-year poles reduces the present value by $318, or about 15% per pole, the utility wants to use the longer-lasting poles. By so doing, PG&E cuts the present value of the cost of maintaining all its poles for 100 years by about $42 billion. Thus, the length of time one maintains a durable good depends on the alternatives and the rate of interest.

Time-Varying Discounting

Tomorrow: One of the greatest labor saving devices of today.

People want immediate gratification.[12] We want rewards now and costs delayed until later: "Rain, rain, go away; come again some other day; we want to go out and play; come again some other day."

Time Consistency. So far in this chapter, we have explained such impatience by assuming that people discount future costs or benefits by using *exponential discounting*, as in Equation 15.15: The present value is the future value divided by $(1 + i)^t$, where the number of years, t, is the exponent and the discount rate, i, is constant over time. If people use this approach, their preferences are *time consistent*: They will discount an event that occurs a decade from the time they're asked by the same amount today as they will one year from now.

However, many of us indulge in immediate gratification in a manner that is inconsistent with our long-term preferences: Our "long-run self" disapproves of the lack of discipline of our "short-run self." Even though we plan today not to overeat tomorrow, tomorrow we may overindulge. We have *present-biased preferences*: When considering the trade-off between two future moments, we put more weight on the earlier moment as it gets closer. For example, if you are offered $100 in 10 years or $200 in 10 years and a day, you will almost certainly choose the larger amount one day later. After all, what's the cost of waiting one extra day a decade from now? However, if you are offered $100 today or $200 tomorrow, you may choose the smaller amount today because an extra day is an appreciable delay when your planning horizon is short.

Behavioral Economics. One explanation that behavioral economists (see Chapter 11) give for procrastination and other time-inconsistent behavior is that people's personal discount rates are smaller in the far future than in the near future. For example, suppose you know that you can mow your lawn today in two hours, but if you wait until next week, it will take you two-and-a-quarter hours because the grass will be longer. Your displeasure (negative utility) from spending two hours mowing is -20 and from spending two-and-a-quarter hours mowing is -22.5. The present value of mowing next week is $-22.5/(1 + i)$, where i is your personal discount rate for a week. If today your discount rate is $i = 0.25$, then your present value of mowing in a week is $-22.5/1.25 = -18$, which is not as bad as -20, so you delay mowing. However, if you were asked six months in advance, your discount rate might be much smaller, say, $i = 0.1$. At that interest rate, the present value is $-22.5/1.1 \approx -20.45$, which is worse than -20, so you would plan to mow on the first of the two dates. Thus, falling discount rates may explain this type of time-inconsistent behavior.

Falling Discount Rates and the Environment. A social discount rate that declines over time may be useful in planning for global warming or other future environmental disasters (Karp, 2005). Suppose that the harmful effects of greenhouse gases will not be felt for a century and that society used traditional, exponential discounting. We would be willing to invest at most 37¢ today to avoid a dollar's worth of damages in a century if society's constant discount rate is 1%, and only 2¢ if the discount rate is 4%. Thus, even such modest discount rates makes us callous toward our distant descendants: We are unwilling to incur even moderate costs today to avoid large damages far in the future.

---

[12]This section draws heavily on Rabin (1998), O'Donoghue and Rabin (1999), and Karp (2005).

One alternative is for society to use a declining discount rate, although doing so will make our decisions time inconsistent. Parents today may care more about their existing children than about their unborn grandchildren, and therefore may be willing to discount the welfare of their grandchildren significantly relative to that of their children. They probably have a smaller difference in their relative emotional attachment to the tenth future generation relative to the eleventh generation. If society agrees with such reasoning, our future social discount rate should be lower than our current rate. By reducing the discount rate over time, we are saying that the weights we place on the welfare of any two successive generations in the distant future are more similar and lower than the weights on two successive generations in the near future.

APPLICATION

Behavioral Economics: Falling Discount Rates and Self-Control

If people's discount rates fall over time, they have a *present bias* or a *self-control problem*, which means that they prefer immediate gratification to delayed gratification.[13] Several recent studies argue that governments should help people with this bias by providing self-control policies.

Shapiro (2004) found that food stamp recipients' caloric intake declines by 10% to 15% over the food stamp month, implying that they prefer immediate consumption. With a constant discount rate, they would be more likely to spread their consumption evenly over the month. Governments can help people with a present bias by delivering food stamps at two-week intervals instead of once a month, as several states do with welfare payments.

Cigarette smokers often have inconsistent preferences with respect to smoking. Individuals with declining discount rates lack self-control and perpetually postpone quitting smoking. A 2018 Gallup poll found that three-quarters of U.S. smokers would like to give up smoking. Consequently, a smoker who wants to quit may support the government's impositions of control devices. Based on a survey in Taiwan, Kan (2007) finds that a smoker who intends to quit is more likely to support a smoking ban and a cigarette tax increase. In 2012, most (59%) New Zealand smokers supported more government action on tobacco, and nearly half (46%) supported banning sales of cigarettes in 10 years, provided effective nicotine substitutes were available. In 2014, 39% of smokers favored higher taxes (up from 29% in 2002). However, only 1 in 10 U.S. smokers favor outlawing smoking.

In 2009, President Obama—a smoker who wanted to quit—signed a law bringing tobacco products under federal law for the first time. He said that this law, aimed at stopping children from starting to smoke, would have prevented him from taking up smoking. Perhaps the most striking evidence of smokers' mixed feelings is that Gruber and Mullainathan (2005) found that cigarette taxes make people with a propensity to smoke happier in both the United States and Canada.

Capital Markets, Interest Rates, and Investments

We've seen that an individual's decision about whether to make an investment depends on the market interest rate. The interest rate is determined in the capital market, where the interest rate is the price, the quantity supplied is the amount of funds loaned, and the quantity demanded is the amount of funds borrowed.

---

[13]In the famous marshmallow test, small children are offered one marshmallow now or a second one if they wait. See an excellent reenactment at **www.youtube.com/watch?v=QX_oy9614HQ**. Children who could delay gratification did slightly better later in life (Watts, Duncan, and Quan, 2018).

If the government borrows to pay for its spending, it affects the market interest rate:

Unintended Consequences Government borrowing increases your cost of borrowing.

If the government borrows to pay for its spending, it affects the market interest rate, which affects your cost of investment, such as how much you pay to borrow money for college.

Because the capital market is competitive, the interest rate and the quantity of funds loaned and borrowed are determined by the intersection of the supply curve for funds and the demand curve for funds. Funds are demanded by individuals buying homes or paying for a college education, governments borrowing money to build roads or wage wars, and firms investing in new plants or equipment. The demand curve is downward sloping because more is borrowed as the interest rate falls.

The supply curve reflects loans made by individuals and firms. Many people, when their earnings are relatively high, save money in bank accounts and buy bonds (which they convert back to money for consumption when they retire or during lean times). Firms that have no alternative investments with higher returns may also lend money to banks or others. Higher interest rates induce greater savings by both groups, so the supply curve is upward sloping.

SOLVED PROBLEM 15.5

MyLab Economics
Solved Problem

Suppose the government wants to borrow money to pay for fighting a war in a foreign land. Show that increased borrowing by the government—an increase in the government's demand for money at any given interest rate—raises the equilibrium interest rate, which discourages or *crowds out* private investment.

Answer

Using three side-by-side graphs, show how an outward shift of the government's demand curve affects the equilibrium interest rate and thereby reduces private

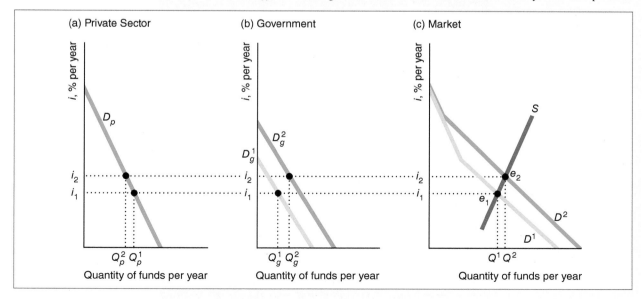

investment. In the figure, panel a shows the private-sector demand curve for funds, D_p, which are funds that private firms and individuals borrow to make investments. Panel b shows that the government-sector demand curve shifts to the right from D_g^1 to D_g^2. As a result, in panel c, the total demand curve—the horizontal sum of the private and government demand curves—shifts from D^1 to D^2. Panel c also shows the supply curve of money, S.

The initial equilibrium, e_1 in panel c, is determined by the intersection of the initial total demand for funds, D^1, and the supply curve, S, where the interest rate is i_1 and the quantity of funds borrowed is Q^1. After the government demand curve shifts out, the new equilibrium is e_2, where the interest rate is higher, $i_2 > i_1$, and more funds are borrowed, $Q^2 > Q^1$.

The higher market interest rate causes private investment to fall from Q_p^1 to Q_p^2 (panel a). That is, the government borrowing crowds out some private investment.

15.3 Exhaustible Resources

The meek shall inherit the earth, but not the mineral rights.—J. Paul Getty

Discounting plays an important role in decision making about how fast to consume oil, gold, copper, uranium, and other **exhaustible resources**: nonrenewable natural assets that cannot be increased, only depleted. An owner of an exhaustible resource decides when to extract and sell it so as to maximize the present value of the resource. Scarcity of the resource, mining costs, and market structure affect whether the price of such a resource rises or falls over time.

When to Sell an Exhaustible Resource

Suppose that you own a coal mine. In what year do you mine the coal, and in what year do you sell it to maximize its present value? To illustrate how to answer these questions, we assume that the rate of inflation is zero, you have no uncertainty, you can sell the coal only this year or next year in a competitive market, the interest rate is i, and that the cost of mining each pound of coal, m, stays constant over time.

Given the last two of these assumptions, the present value of the cost of mining a pound of coal is m if you mine this year and $m/(1 + i)$ if you mine next year. As a result, if you're going to sell the coal next year, you're better off mining it next year because you postpone incurring the cost of mining. You mine the coal this year only if you plan to sell it this year.

Now that you have a rule that specifies when to mine the coal—at the last possible moment—your remaining problem is when to sell it. That decision depends on how the price of a pound of coal changes from one year to the next. Suppose you know that the price of coal will increase from p_1 this year to p_2 next year.

To decide in which year to sell, you compare the present value of selling today to that of selling next year. The present value of your profit per pound of coal is $p_1 - m$ if you sell your coal this year and $(p_2 - m)/(1 + i)$ if you sell it next year. Thus, to maximize the present value from selling your coal:

- *You sell all the coal this year* if the present value of selling this year is greater than the present value of selling next year: $p_1 - m > (p_2 - m)/(1 + i)$.
- *You sell all the coal next year* if $p_1 - m < (p_2 - m)/(1 + i)$.
- *You sell all the coal in either year* if $p_1 - m = (p_2 - m)/(1 + i)$.

The intuition behind these rules is that storing coal in the ground is like keeping money in the bank. You can sell a pound of coal today, netting $p_1 - m$, invest the money in the bank, and have $(p_1 - m)(1 + i)$ next year. Alternatively, you can keep the coal in the ground for a year and then sell it. If the amount you'll get next year, $p_2 - m$, is less than what you can earn from selling now and keeping the money in a bank, you sell the coal now. In contrast, if the price of coal is rising so rapidly that the coal will be worth more in the future than the wealth left in a bank, you leave your wealth in the mine.

Price of a Scarce Exhaustible Resource

This two-period analysis generalizes to many time periods (Hotelling, 1931). We use a multiperiod analysis to show how the price of an exhaustible resource changes over time.

The resource is sold both this year, year t, and next year, $t + 1$, only if the present value of a pound sold now is the same as the present value of a pound sold next year: $p_t - m = (p_{t+1} - m)/(1 + i)$, where the price is p_t in year t and is p_{t+1} in the following year. Using algebra to rearrange this equation, we obtain an expression that tells us how price changes from one year to the next:

$$p_{t+1} = p_t + i(p_t - m). \tag{15.21}$$

If you're willing to sell the coal in both years, the price next year must exceed the price this year by $i(p_t - m)$, which is the interest payment you'd receive if you sold a pound of coal this year and put the profit in a bank that paid interest at rate i.

The gap between the price and the constant marginal cost of mining grows over time, as Figure 15.5 shows. To see why, we subtract p_t from both sides of Equation 15.21 to obtain an expression for the change in the price from one year to the next:

$$\Delta p \equiv p_{t+1} - p_t = i(p_t - m).$$

This equation shows that the gap between this year's price and next year's price widens as your cash flow this year, $p_t - m$, increases. Thus, the price rises over time,

Figure 15.5 Price of an Exhaustible Resource

The price of an exhaustible resource in year $t + 1$ is higher than the price in year t by the interest rate times the difference between the price in year t and the marginal cost of mining, $i(p_t - m)$. Thus, the gap between the price line and the marginal cost line, $p_t - m$, grows exponentially with the interest rate.

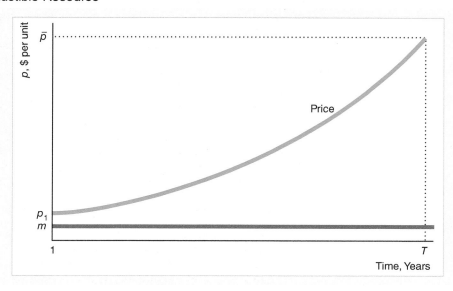

and the gap between the price line and the flat marginal cost of mining line grows, as the figure illustrates.

Although we now understand how price changes over time, we need more information to determine the price in the first year and hence in each subsequent year. Suppose mine owners know that the government will ban the use of coal in year T (or that a superior substitute will become available that year). They want to price the coal so that all of it is sold by year T, because any resource that is unsold by then is worthless. The restriction that all the coal is used up by T and Equation 15.21 determine the price in the first year and the increase in the price thereafter.

Price in a Two-Period Example. To illustrate how the price is determined in each year, we assume that the market has many identical competitive mines, no more coal will be sold after the second year because of a government ban, and the marginal cost of mining is zero in each period. Setting $m = 0$ in Equation 15.21, we learn that the price in the second year equals the price in the first year plus the interest rate times the first-year price:

$$p_2 = p_1 + (i \times p_1) = p_1(1 + i). \tag{15.22}$$

Thus, the price increases with the interest rate from the first year to the second year.

The mine owners face a resource constraint: They can't sell more coal than they have in their mines. The coal they sell in the first year, Q_1, plus the coal they sell in the second year, Q_2, equals the total amount of coal in the mines, Q. The mine owners want to sell all their coal within these two years because any coal they don't sell does them no good.

Suppose that the demand curve for coal is $Q_t = 200 - p_t$ in each year t. If the amount of coal in the ground is less than would be demanded at a zero price, the sum of the amount demanded in both years equals the total amount of coal in the ground:

$$Q_1 + Q_2 = (200 - p_1) + (200 - p_2) = Q.$$

Substituting the expression for p_2 from Equation 15.22 into this resource constraint to obtain $(200 - p_1) + [200 - p_1(1 + i)] = Q$ and rearranging terms, we find that

$$p_1 = \frac{400 - Q}{2 + i}. \tag{15.23}$$

Thus, the first-year price depends on the amount of coal in the ground and the interest rate.

If the mines initially contain $Q = 169$ pounds of coal, then p_1 is $110 at a 10% interest rate and $105 at a 20% interest rate, as Table 15.1 shows. At the lower interest rate, the difference between the first- and second-year prices is smaller ($11 versus $21), so relatively more of the original stock of coal is sold in the second year (47% versus 44%).

Rents. If coal is a scarce good, its competitive price is above the marginal cost of mining the coal ($m = 0$ in our example). How can we reconcile this result with our earlier finding that price equals marginal cost in a competitive market? The answer is that when coal is scarce, it earns a *rent*: a payment to the owner of an input beyond the minimum necessary for the input to be supplied (Chapter 9).

The owner of the coal need not be the same person who mines the coal. A miner could pay the owner for the right to take the coal out of the mine. After incurring the marginal cost of mining the coal, m, the miner earns $p_1 - m$. However, the owner of the mine charges that amount in rent for the right to mine this scarce resource, rather than giving any of this profit to the miner. Even if the owner of the coal and the miner are the same person, the amount beyond the marginal mining cost is a rent to scarcity.

Table 15.1 Price and Quantity of Coal Reflecting the Amount of Coal and the Interest Rate

	$Q = 169$		$Q = 400$
	$i = 10\%$	$i = 20\%$	Any i
$p_1 = (400 - Q)/(2 + i)$	$110	$105	$0
$p_2 = p_1(1 + i)$	$121	$126	$0
$\Delta p \equiv p_2 - p_1 = i \times p_1$	11	21	0
$Q_1 = 200 - p_1$	90	95	200
$Q_2 = 200 - p_2$	79	74	200
Share sold in Year 2	47%	44%	50%

If the coal were not scarce, no rent would be paid, and the price would equal the marginal cost of mining. Given the demand curve in the example, the most coal that anyone would buy in a year is 200 pounds, which is the amount demanded at a price of zero. If the initial quantity of coal in the ground is 400 pounds of coal—enough to provide 200 pounds in each year—the coal is not scarce, so the price of coal in both years is zero, as Table 15.1 illustrates.[14] As Figure 15.6 shows, the less coal in the ground initially, Q, the higher the initial price of coal.

Figure 15.6 First-Year Price in a Two-Period Model

In a two-period model, the price of coal in the first year, p_1, falls as the initial amount of coal in the ground, Q, increases. This figure is based on an interest rate of 10%.

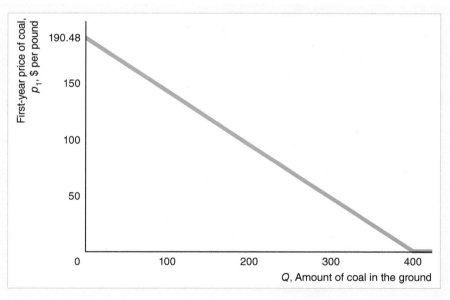

[14]Equation 15.23 holds only when coal is scarce: $Q \leq 400$. According to this equation, $p_1 = 0$ when $Q = 400$. If the quantity of coal in the ground is even greater, $Q > 400$, coal is not scarce—people don't want all the coal even if the price is zero—so the price in the first year equals the marginal mining cost of zero. That is, the price is not negative, as Equation 15.23 would imply if it held for quantities greater than 400.

Rising Prices. Thus, according to our theory, the price of an exhaustible resource rises if the resource (1) is scarce, (2) can be mined at a marginal cost that remains constant over time, and (3) is sold in a competitive market. The rate of increase in the price of old-growth redwood trees is predicted by this theory.

APPLICATION

Redwood Trees

Many of the majestic old-growth redwood trees in America's western forests are several hundred to several thousand years old. If a mature redwood is cut, young redwoods will not grow to a comparable size within our lifetimes. Thus, an old-growth redwood forest, like fossil fuels, is effectively a nonrenewable resource, even though new redwoods are being created (very slowly). In contrast, many other types of trees, such as those grown as Christmas trees, are quickly replenished and therefore are renewable resources like fish.

The exponential trend line on the graph shows that the real price of redwoods rose from 1953 to 1983 at an average rate of 8% a year. By the end of this period, virtually no redwood trees were available for sale. The trees either had been harvested or were growing in protected forests. The last remaining privately owned stand was purchased by the U.S. government and the state of California from the Maxxam Corporation in 1996.

The unusually high prices observed in the late 1960s through the 1970s were in large part due to actions of the federal government, which used its power of eminent domain to buy, at the market price, a considerable fraction of all remaining old-growth redwoods for the Redwood National Park. The government bought 1.7 million million-board feet (MBF) in 1968 and 1.4 million MBF in 1978. The latter purchase represented about two-and-a-quarter years of cutting at previous rates. These two government purchases combined equaled 43% of private holdings in 1978 of about 7.3 million MBF. Thus, the government purchases were so large that they moved up the time of exhaustion of privately held redwoods by several years, causing the price to jump to the level it would have reached several years later.

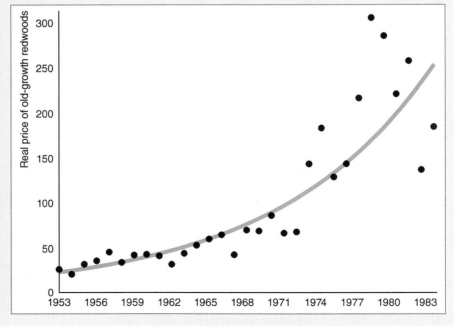

Why Price Might Not Rise

If any one of the three conditions we've been assuming—*scarcity, constant marginal mining costs*, and *competition*—is not met, the price of an exhaustible resource may remain steady or fall.[15] Most exhaustible resources, such as aluminum, coal, lead, natural gas, silver, and zinc, have had decades-long periods of falling or constant real prices. Indeed, the real price of each major mineral and metal is lower today than in 1948.

Abundance. As we've seen, the initial price is set at essentially the marginal cost of mining if the exhaustible resource is not scarce. The gap between the price and the marginal cost grows with the interest rate. If the good is so abundant that the initial gap is zero, the gap does not grow and the price stays constant at the marginal cost. Further, if the gap is initially very small, it has to grow for a long time before the increase becomes noticeable.

Because of abundance, the real prices for many exhaustible resources have remained relatively constant for decades. Moreover, the price falls when the discovery of a large deposit of the resource is announced.

The amount of a resource that can be profitably recovered using current technology is called a reserve. Known reserves of some resources are enormous; others are more limited.[16] The world has enough silicon (from sand) and magnesium to last virtually forever at current rates of extraction. Known reserves of zinc will last 19 years; lead, 17 years; gold, 19 years; and silver, 23 years. Known reserves of aluminum (bauxite) will last 106 years, and firms are constantly discovering additional reserves. Because of this abundance, the real price of aluminum has remained virtually constant for the past 50 years.

Technical Progress. Steady technical progress over many years has reduced the marginal cost of mining and thereby lowered the price of many natural resources. A large enough drop in the marginal mining cost may more than offset the increase in the price due to the interest rate, so the price falls from one year to the next.[17]

Many advances in mining occurred in the years spanning the end of the nineteenth century and the beginning of the twentieth century. As a result of technical progress and discoveries of new supplies, the real prices of many exhaustible resources fell. For example, the real price of aluminum in 1945 was only 12% of the price 50 years earlier. Eventually, as mines play out, prospectors have to dig ever deeper to find resources, causing marginal costs to increase and prices to rise faster than they would with constant marginal costs.

Changing Market Power. Changes in market structure can result in either a rise or a fall in the price of an exhaustible resource. The real price of oil remained virtually constant from 1880 through 1972. But when the Organization of Petroleum

---

[15]The following discussion of why prices of exhaustible resources might not rise and the accompanying examples are based on Berck and Roberts (1996) and additional data supplied by these authors. Their paper also shows that pollution controls and other environmental controls can keep resource prices from rising. Additional data are from Brown and Wolk (2000).

[16]minerals.usgs.gov/minerals/pubs/mcs/2018/mcs2018.pdf.

[17]When the marginal cost of mining is constant at m, Equation 15.21 shows that $p_{t+1} = p_t + i(p_t - m)$, so p_{t+1} must be above p_t. If we allow mining costs to vary from year to year, then

$$p_{t+1} = p_t + i(p_t - m_t) + (m_{t+1} - m_t).$$

Thus, if the drop in the mining costs, $m_{t+1} - m_t$, is greater than $i(p_t - m_t)$, p_{t+1} is less than p_t.

Exporting Countries (OPEC) started to act as a cartel in 1973, the price of oil climbed rapidly. At its peak in 1981, the real price of oil was nearly five times higher than its nearly constant level during the period 1880–1972. When Iran and Iraq went to war in 1980, the OPEC cartel began to fall apart, and the real price of oil sank to traditional levels, where it remained through the 1990s. Since then, wars have caused the price to fluctuate substantially.

CHALLENGE SOLUTION

Does Going to College Pay?

Probably the most important human capital decision you've had to make was whether to attend college. If you opted to go to college solely to increase your lifetime earnings, did you make a good investment?

Let's look at your last year of high school. During that year, you have to decide whether to invest in a college education or go directly into the job market. If you go straight into the job market, we assume that you work full time from age 18 until you retire at age 70.

If your motivation for attending college is to increase your lifetime earnings, you should start college upon finishing high school so that you can earn a higher salary for as long as possible. To keep the analysis relatively simple, we'll assume that you graduate from college in four years, during which time you do not work and you spend $30,000 a year on tuition and other schooling expenses such as books and fees. When you graduate from college, you will work full time from age 22 to 70. Thus, the opportunity cost of a college education includes the tuition payments plus the four years of forgone earnings for someone with a high school diploma. The expected benefit is the stream of higher earnings in the future.

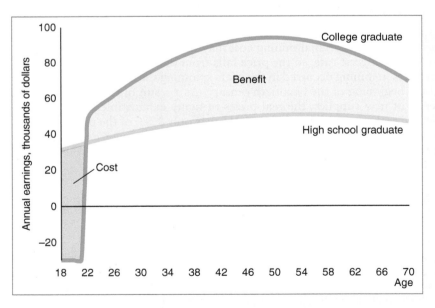

The figure shows how much the typical person earns with a high school diploma and with a college degree at each age.[18] At age 22, a typical college grad earns $49,782 and those with only a high school diploma earn $35,405. The college grad's earnings peak at 49 years of age, at $94,211. A high school grad's earnings reach a maximum at 54 years, at $50,551.

If one stream of earnings is higher than the other at every age, we would pick the higher stream. Because these streams of earnings cross at age 22, we cannot use that simple approach to answer the question. One way to decide whether investing in a college education pays is to compare

---

[18]The statistical analysis controls for age, education, and demographic characteristics but not innate ability. See Sources for Applications for information about the data. We assumed that wages increase at the same rate as inflation, so real earnings are constant over time. No adjustment was made for the greater incidence of unemployment among high school graduates, which was more than twice that of college graduates in 2018.

Discount Rate, %	Present Value, Thousands of 2017 Dollars	
	High School	College
0	2,417	3,884
2	1,463	1,218
4	970	1,355
6	695	877
8	531	595
9.72	438	438
10	426	418
12	355	301

the present values at age 18 of the two earnings streams. The present values depend on the interest rate used, as the table shows.

If potential college students can borrow money at an interest rate of 0%, money in the future is worth as much as money today, so the present value equals the sum of earnings over time. According to the table, the sum of a college graduate's earnings (including the initial negative earnings) is $3.884 million (first row of the table), which is 61% more than the lifetime earnings of a high school grad, $2.417 million. Thus, it pays to go to college if the interest rate is 0%. The figure also illustrates that attending college pays at a 0% discount rate because the benefit area is larger than the cost areas.

The table demonstrates that the present value of earnings for a college grad equals that of a high school grad at an interest rate of 9.72%. That is, the average internal rate of return to the college education is 9.72%. Because the present value of earnings for a college grad exceeds that of a high school grad if the real interest rate at which they can borrow or invest is less than 9.72%, income-maximizing people should go to college if the real interest rate is less than that rate.[19]

According to www.Payscale.com in 2018, the average internal rate of return of going to college is higher for students at some schools than others: 13.0% at SUNY Maritime College; 11.9%, Georgia Institute of Technology; 10.2%, Purdue and Texas A&M; 9.9%, Iowa State and Utah State; 9.8%, U.C. Berkeley; 9.6%, University of Washington; 8.9%, Rutgers; 8.6%, UCLA and University of Connecticut; 8.5%, MIT; 7.4%, Stanford; 7.2%, Harvard; 6.9%, Lehigh University; 6.3%, Columbia University; 4.5%, University of Chicago; 2.6%, Moody Bible Institute; 0%, Chatham University; and –0.9%, Wesleyan College.[20]

The decision whether to go to college is more complex for people for whom education has a consumption component. Somebody who loves school may go to college even if alternative investments pay more. Someone who hates going to school invests in a college education only if the financial rewards are much higher than those for alternative investments.

---

[19]The government-subsidized nominal interest rate on federal Stafford loans was 4.45% in 2017–2018. Some poor people who cannot borrow to pay for college at all—effectively, they face extremely high interest rates—do not go to college, unlike wealthier people with comparable abilities.

[20]For more schools, see www.payscale.com/college-roi. The Payscale's calculations, though similar to the one used in this Challenge Solution, differ in not controlling for individual characteristics and in several other ways.

SUMMARY

1. **Factor Markets.** Any firm maximizes its profit by choosing the quantity of a factor such that the marginal revenue product (MRP) of that factor—the marginal revenue times the marginal product of the factor—equals the factor price. The MRP is the firm's factor demand. A competitive firm's marginal revenue is the market price, so its MRP is the market price times the marginal product. The factor demand curves of a noncompetitive firm lie to the left of those of a competitive firm. The firm's long-run factor demand is usually flatter than its short-run demand because the firm can adjust more factors, and thus benefit from more flexibility. The market demand for a factor reflects how changes in factor prices affect output prices and hence output levels in product markets. The intersection of the market factor demand curve and the market factor supply curve determines the factor market equilibrium.

2. **Capital Markets and Investing.** Inflation aside, most people value money in the future less than money today. An interest rate reflects how much more people value a dollar today than a dollar in the future. To compare a payment made in the future to one made today, we can express the future value in terms of current dollars—its present value—by discounting the future payment using the interest rate. Similarly, a flow of payments over time is related to the present or future value of these payments by the interest rate. A firm may choose between two options with different cash flows over time by picking the one with the higher present value. Similarly, a firm invests in a project if its net present value is positive or its internal rate of return is greater than the interest rate.

3. **Exhaustible Resources.** Nonrenewable resources, such as coal, gold, and oil, are depleted over time and cannot be replenished. If these resources are scarce, the marginal cost of mining them is constant or increasing, and the market structure remains unchanged, their prices rise rapidly over time because of positive interest rates. However, if the resources are abundant, the marginal cost of mining falls over time, or the market becomes more competitive, nonrenewable resource prices may remain constant or fall over time.

EXERCISES

All exercises are available on **MyLab Economics**; * = *answer appears at the back of this book;* **M** = *mathematical problem.*

1. Factor Markets

1.1 What does a competitive firm's labor demand curve look like at quantities of labor such that the marginal product of labor is negative? Why?

*1.2 If a local government starts collecting an ad valorem tax of α on the revenue of a competitive firm (and all other firms are located outside this jurisdiction), what happens to the firm's demand curve for labor? (*Hint*: See Solved Problem 15.1.)

1.3 How does a fall in the rental price of capital affect a firm's demand for labor in the long run?

1.4 Oil companies, prompted by improvements in technology and increases in oil prices, are drilling in deeper and deeper water. Using a marginal revenue product and marginal cost diagram of drilling in deep water, show how improvements in drilling technology and increases in oil prices result in more deep-water drilling.

1.5 Georges, the owner of Maison d'Ail, earned his coveted Michelin star rating by smothering his dishes in freshly minced garlic. Georges knows that he can save labor costs by using less garlic, albeit with a reduction in quality. If Georges puts g garlic cloves in a dish, the dish's quality, z, is $z = 1/2g^{0.5}$. Georges always fills his restaurant to its capacity, 250 seats. He knows that he can raise the price of each dish by 40¢ for each unit increase in quality and continue to fill his restaurant. Jacqueline, who earns \$10 per hour, minces Georges' garlic at a rate of 120 garlic cloves per hour.

   a. What is Jacqueline's value of marginal revenue product?

   b. How many hours per afternoon (while the kitchen prep work is being done) does Jacqueline work?

   c. How many minced cloves of fresh garlic does Georges put in each dish? **M**

1.6 Show that the quantity of labor or capital that a firm demands decreases with a factor's own factor price and increases with the output price when the production function is Cobb-Douglas as in Equations 15.12 and 15.13. **M**

1.7 The estimated Cobb-Douglas production function for a U.S. tobacco products firm is $q = L^{0.2}K^{0.3}$ ("Returns to Scale in Various Industries" Application, Chapter 6).

Derive the marginal revenue product of labor for this firm. **M**

*1.8 A competitive firm has a constant elasticity production function, $q = (L^\rho + K^\rho)^{1/\rho}$. What is its marginal revenue product of labor? $q = (L^\rho + K^\rho)^{1/\rho}$

1.9 Suppose that a firm's production function is $q = L + K$. Can it be a competitive firm? Why?

1.10 A monopoly with a Cobb-Douglas production function, $Q = (L^\rho + K^\rho)^{1/\rho}$, faces a constant elasticity demand curve. What is its marginal revenue product of labor? **M**

1.11 How does a monopoly's demand for labor shift if a second firm enters its output market and the result is a Cournot duopoly equilibrium?

1.12 Does a shift in the supply curve of labor have a greater effect on wages if the output market is competitive or if it is monopolistic? Explain.

1.13 What is a monopoly's demand for labor if it uses a fixed-proportions production function in which each unit of output takes one unit of labor and one unit of capital?

1.14 In Solved Problem 15.2, show how the results change if the share of workers killed by the Black Death was one-half.

1.15 An economic consultant explaining the effect on labor demand of increasing health care costs, interviewed for the *Wall Street Journal*'s Capital column (David Wessel, "Health-Care Costs Blamed for Hiring Gap," March 11, 2004, A2), states, "Medical costs are rising more rapidly than anything else in the economy—more than prices, wages or profits. It isn't only current medical costs, but also the present value of the stream of endlessly high cost increases that retards hiring."

a. Why does the present value of the stream of health care costs, and not just the current health care costs, affect a firm's decision whether to create a new position?

b. Why should an employer discount future health care costs in deciding whether to create a new position? **M**

2. Capital Markets and Investing

*2.1 How does an individual with a zero discount rate compare current and future consumption? How does your answer change if the discount rate is infinite?

2.2 If you buy a car for $100 down and $100 a year for two more years, what is the present value of these payments at a 5% interest rate? If the interest rate is i? **M**

2.3 How much money do you have to put into a bank account that pays 10% interest compounded annually to receive annual payments of $200? **M**

2.4 Pacific Gas and Electric sent its customers a comparison showing that a person could save $80 per year in gas, water, and detergent expenses by replacing a traditional clothes washer with a new tumble-action washer. Suppose that the interest rate is 5%. You expect your current washer to die in five years. If the cost of a new tumble-action washer is $800, should you replace your washer now or in five years? Explain. **M**

2.5 You plan to buy a used refrigerator this year for $200 and to sell it when you graduate in two years. Assuming that you can get $100 for the refrigerator at that time, the rate of inflation is zero, and the interest rate is 5%, what is the true cost (your current outlay minus the resale value in current terms) of the refrigerator to you? **M**

2.6 You want to buy a room air conditioner. The price of one machine is $200. It costs $20 a year to operate. The price of another air conditioner is $300, but it costs only $10 a year to operate. Assuming that both machines last 10 years, which is a better deal? (Do you need to do extensive calculations to answer this question?) **M**

*2.7 Two different teams offer a professional basketball player contracts for playing this year. Both contracts are guaranteed, and payments will be made even if the athlete is injured and cannot play. Team A's contract would pay him $1 million today. Team B's contract would pay him $500,000 today and $2 million 10 years from now. Assuming that the rate of inflation is zero, our pro is concerned only about which contract has the highest present value, and his personal discount rate is 5%, which contract does he accept? Does your answer change if the discount rate is 20%? (*Hint*: See the Application "Saving for Retirement.") **M**

2.8 You are buying a new $20,000 car and have the option to pay for the car with a 0% loan or to receive $500 cash back at the time of the purchase. With the loan, you pay $5,000 down when you purchase the car and then make three $5,000 payments, one at the end of each year of the loan. You currently have $50,000 in your savings account.

a. The rate of interest on your savings account is 4% and will remain so for the next three years. Which payment method should you choose?

b. What interest rate, i, makes you indifferent between the two payment methods? **M**

2.9 Discussing the $350 price of a ticket for one of her concerts, Barbra Streisand said, "If you amortize the money over 28 years, it's $12.50 a year. So is it worth $12.50 a year to see me sing? To hear me sing live?"[21] Under what condition is it useful for an individual to apply Ms. Streisand's rule to decide whether to go to the concert? What do we know about the discount rate of a person who makes such a purchase?

2.10 If you spend $4 a day on a latte (in real dollars) for the rest of your life (essentially forever), what is your present discounted value at a 3% interest rate? **M**

2.11 At a 10% interest rate, do you prefer to buy a phone for $100 or to rent the same phone for $10 a year? Does your answer depend on how long you think the phone will last? **M**

*2.12 A firm is considering an investment in which its cash flow is $\pi_1 = \$1$ (million), $\pi_2 = -\$12$, $\pi_3 = \$20$, and $\pi_t = 0$ for all other t. The interest rate is 7%. Use the net present value rule to determine whether the firm should make the investment. Can the firm use the internal rate of return rule to make this decision? **M**

2.13 With the end of the Cold War, the U.S. government decided to *downsize* the military. Along with a pink slip, the government offered ex-military personnel their choice of $8,000 a year for 30 years or an immediate lump-sum payment of $50,000. The lump-sum option was chosen by 92% of enlisted personnel and 51% of officers (Warner and Pleeter, 2001). What is the break-even personal discount rate at which someone would be indifferent between the two options? What can you conclude about the personal discount rates of the enlisted personnel and officers? **M**

2.14 Dell Computer makes its suppliers wait 37 days on average to be paid for their goods; however, Dell is paid by its customers immediately. Thus, Dell earns interest on this *float*, the money that it is implicitly borrowing. If Dell can earn an annual interest rate of 4%, what is this float worth to Dell per dollar spent on inputs? **M**

2.15 According to the Associated Press, in 2015, Max Scherzer became the highest-paid right-handed pitcher in major league history by agreeing to a "$210 million, seven-year contract" with the Washington Nationals that includes a "record $50 million signing bonus." Reportedly, he will be paid $10 million in 2015, $15 million in 2016–2018, and $35 million in 2019–2021.[22] However, the $105 million (= 3 × $35 million) for the years 2019–2021 will be deferred without interest until 2028. In addition, the $50 million signing bonus will be spread equally over the seven years of the contract. At what interest rate is the present value $210 million? What is the present value of this contract if the interest rate is 3%? **M**

*2.16 Your gas-guzzling car gets only 10 miles to the gallon and has no resale value, but you are sure that it will last five years. You know that you can always buy a used car for $8,000 that gets 20 miles to the gallon. A gallon of gas costs $2 and you drive 6,000 miles a year. If the interest rate is 5% and you are interested only in saving money, should you buy a car now rather than wait until your current car dies? Would you make the same decision if you faced a 10% interest rate? **M**

2.17 What would the net present value be in Solved Problem 15.3 if the interest rate were 3% instead of 2%? **M**

2.18 In 2005, Lewis Wolff and his investment group bought the Oakland A's baseball team for $180 million. *Forbes* magazine estimated their net income in 2005 to be $5.9 million. Suppose the new owners believe that they will continue to earn this annual profit (after adjusting for inflation), $f = \$5.9$ million, forever. Calculate the internal rate of return. If the interest rate is 3%, did it pay to buy the team? (*Hint*: See Solved Problem 15.4.) **M**

2.19 If the government bars foreign lenders from loaning money to its citizens, how does the capital market equilibrium change?

2.20 In the figure in Solved Problem 15.5, suppose that the government's demand curve remains constant at D_g^1 but the government starts to tax private earnings, collecting 1% of all interest earnings. How does the capital market equilibrium change? What is the effect on private borrowers?

2.21 You may have read that the Dutch got a good deal buying Manhattan from the original inhabitants in 1626 for about $24 worth of beads and trinkets. However, if those Native Americans had had the opportunity to sell the beads and invest in tax-free bonds with an APR of 7%, what would the bond be worth today? **M**

2.22 You put $100 in the bank. The bank pays 8% interest, which is compounded quarterly. How much interest do you receive at the end of a year? **M**

---

[21]"In Other Words . . . ," *San Francisco Chronicle*, January 1, 1995: Sunday Section, p. 3. She divided the $350 ticket price by 28 years to get $12.50 as the payment per year.

[22]**http://mlb.nbcsports.com/2015/01/22/details-of-max-scherzers-seven-year-210-million-contract-with-the-nationals**.

2.23 Starting in 2019, the Golden State Warriors basketball team plans to start a "membership" program. A fan must pay a one-time fee for the right to buy a season ticket for the next 30 years. However, the Warriors promise to pay back that fee after 30 years. If the fee is $10,000 and the interest rate is 5% (and you expect no inflation), what is the present value of this membership fee: the upfront expenditure minus the present value of the repayment? **M**

2.24 You win a lottery. Your prize is either two annual payments of $50,000 at the end of each year or a lump-sum payment of $87,000 today. You expect the interest rate to be 4%. Which prize has a higher present value? **M**

3. Exhaustible Resources

3.1 You can sell a barrel of oil today for p dollars. Assuming no inflation and no storage cost, how high would the price have to be next year for you to sell the oil next year rather than now? **M**

3.2 If all the coal in the ground, Q, is to be consumed in two years and the demand for coal is $Q_t = A(p_t)^\varepsilon$ in each year t where ε is a constant demand elasticity, what is the price of coal each year? **M**

3.3 Trees, wine, and cattle become more valuable over time and then possibly decrease in value. Draw a figure with present value on the vertical axis and years (age) on the horizontal axis and show this relationship. Show in what year the owner should "harvest" such a good, assuming that the cost of harvesting is zero. (*Hint*: If the good's present value is P_0 and we take that money and invest it at interest rate i, which is a small number such as 0.02 or 0.04, then its value in year t is $P_0(1 + i)^t$; or, if we allow continuous compounding, $P_0 e^{it}$.) Such a curve increases exponentially over time and looks like the curve labeled "Price" in Figure 15.5. Draw curves with different possible present values. Use those curves to choose the optimal harvest time. How would your

answer change if the interest rate were zero? Show in a figure. **M**

4. Challenge

4.1 If the interest rate is near zero, should an individual go to college, given the information in the figure in the Challenge Solution? State a simple rule for determining whether this individual should go to college in terms of the areas labeled "Benefit" and "Cost" in the figure.

4.2 At current interest rates, it pays for Bob to go to college if he graduates in four years. If it takes an extra year to graduate from college, does going to college still pay? Show how the figure in the Challenge Solution changes. Illustrate how the present value calculation changes using a formula and variables.

4.3 Which is worth more to you: (a) a $10,000 payment today or (b) a $1,000-per-year higher salary for as long as you work? At what interest rate would (a) be worth more to you than (b)? Does your answer depend on how many years you expect to work?

4.4 In 2012, the Clarkson Community Schools in Clarkson, Michigan, paid its starting teachers $38,087 with a bachelor's degree and $41,802 with a master's degree. (For simplicity, assume that these salaries stay constant and do not increase with experience.) Suppose you know that you want to work for this school district and want to maximize your lifetime earnings. To get a master's degree takes one extra year of schooling and costs $20,000. Should you get the master's if you cannot work during that year? Should you get your master's degree if you can work while studying for your master's? In your calculations, assume that you'll work for 40 years and then retire and consider interest rates of 3% and 10%. (*Hint*: You can solve exactly using Equation 15.16 or get a reasonable approximation by assuming that you work forever and use Equation 15.17.)

16 Uncertainty

In America anyone can be president. That's one of the risks you take. —Adlai Stevenson

On April 20, 2010, a massive explosion occurred on the Transocean Deepwater Horizon oil rig, which was leased by the oil company BP. The explosion killed 11 workers and seriously injured 17 others. In addition, many of the 90,000 workers who participated in the cleanup suffered significant health problems from exposure to various toxins. Safeguards in the well

to automatically cap the oil in case of an accident did not work as expected. Consequently, a massive spill of roughly 200 million gallons of oil polluted the Gulf of Mexico before the well was finally capped. This catastrophic oil spill inflicted gigantic costs for cleaning up Louisiana and other Gulf states and inflicted very large losses on the Gulf fishing and tourism industries.

A bad outcome does necessarily imply that BP made bad decisions before the event. BP could have taken reasonable safety precautions and merely been unlucky. However, government agencies concluded that the explosion and the resulting massive oil leak were largely due to a failure to take appropriate safety and other precautions by BP and its subcontractors.

BP may have ignored or underestimated the chance of these expensive calamities, improperly reasoning that such major disasters had not happened to them before and would therefore never happen in the future (or at least that the chances were miniscule). However, a more likely explanation for BP's behavior is that it did not expect to bear the full cost if a catastrophe occurred. In 1990, Congress passed a law that limited liability beyond cleanup costs to $75 million for a rig spill, a tiny fraction of the harm in this case.

In the face of international condemnation for the massive Gulf spill, BP agreed to waive this cap. In 2015, BP struck a $20.8 billion agreement to settle damages with Gulf Coast states and the federal government. By the start of 2018, BP's total costs arising from the disaster were $65.1 billion, about 870 times larger than $75 million. These losses are substantial compared to BP shareholders' equity of $188 billion at the time of the disaster.

BP made a calculated choice about the risks that a catastrophic oil spill would happen, presumably taking the $75 million cap on liability into account in making their decisions. How does a cap on liability affect a firm's willingness to make a risky investment or to invest less than the optimal amount in safety? How does a cap affect the amount of risk that the firm and others in society bear? How does a cap affect the amount of insurance against the costs of an oil spill that a firm buys?

Life is a series of gambles. Will your plane crash? Will you receive Social Security benefits when you retire? Will you win the lottery tomorrow? Will your stocks' value increase this year? In this chapter, we look at how uncertainty affects consumer choice (Chapters 3 through 5), such as how much insurance to buy, and investment decisions (Chapter 15).

When making decisions about investments and other matters, consumers and firms consider the possible *outcomes* under various circumstances, or *states of nature*. Suppose that a regulator will approve or reject a new drug, so the two states of nature are *approve* or *reject*. The outcome varies with these states of nature. The pharmaceutical firm's stock will be worth $100 per share if the regulator approves the drug and only $75 if the regulator rejects it.

We do not know with certainty what will happen in the future, but we may know that some outcomes are more likely than are others. Often we can assign a probability to each possible outcome. For example, if we toss a coin, the probability of a head or of a tail is 50%. Quantifiable uncertainty is called **risk**: the situation in which the likelihood of each possible outcome is known or can be estimated, and no single possible outcome is certain to occur. All of the examples in this chapter concern quantifiable uncertainty.[1]

Consumers and firms behave differently as the degree of risk varies. Most people will buy more insurance or take additional preventive actions in riskier situations. Most of us will choose a riskier investment over a less risky one only if we expect a higher return from the riskier investment.

In this chapter, we examine five main topics	1. **Assessing Risk.** Probability, expected value, and variance are important concepts that are used to assess the degree of risk and the likely profit from a risky undertaking.
	2. **Attitudes Toward Risk.** Whether people choose a risky option over a nonrisky option depends on their attitudes toward risk and on the expected payoffs of each option.
	3. **Reducing Risk.** People try to reduce their overall risk by not making risky choices, taking actions to lower the likelihood of a disaster, combining offsetting risks, and insuring.
	4. **Investing Under Uncertainty.** Whether people make an investment depends on the riskiness of the payoff, the expected return, their attitudes toward risk, the interest rate, and whether it is profitable to alter the likelihood of a good outcome.
	5. **Behavioral Economics and Uncertainty.** Because some people do not choose among risky options the way that traditional economic theory predicts, some researchers have switched to new models that include psychological factors.

16.1 Assessing Risk

Gregg, a promoter, is considering whether to schedule an outdoor concert on July 4th. Booking the concert is a gamble: He stands to make a tidy profit if the weather is good, but he'll lose a substantial amount if it rains.

To analyze this decision, Gregg needs a way to describe and quantify risk. A particular *event*—such as holding an outdoor concert—has a number of possible *outcomes*—here, either it rains or it does not rain. When deciding whether to schedule

---

[1]Uncertainty is unquantifiable when we do not know enough to assign meaningful probabilities to different outcomes or if we do not even know what the possible outcomes are. If asked "Who will be the U.S. President in 20 years?" most of us do not even know the likely contenders, let alone the probabilities.

the concert, Gregg quantifies how risky each outcome is using a *probability* and then uses these probabilities to determine what he can expect to earn.

Probability

A *probability* is a number between 0 and 1 that indicates the likelihood that a particular outcome will occur. If an outcome cannot occur, it has a probability of 0. If the outcome is sure to happen, it has a probability of 1. If the chance of rain on July 4 is one in four, the probability of rain is $\frac{1}{4}$ or 25%.

These weather outcomes that it rains or does not rain are *mutually exclusive*: Only one of these outcomes can occur. This list of outcomes is also *exhaustive*, as no other outcomes are possible. If outcomes are mutually exclusive and exhaustive, exactly one of these outcomes will occur, and the probabilities sum to 100%.

How can Gregg estimate the probability of rain on July 4? Usually the best approach is to use the *frequency*, which tells us how often an uncertain event occurred in the past. Otherwise, one has to use a *subjective probability*: estimate the probability using other information, such as informal "best guesses" of experienced weather forecasters.

Frequency. The probability is the actual chance that an outcome will occur. People do not know the true probability, so they have to estimate it. Because Gregg (or the weather department) knows how often it rained on July 4 over many years, he can use that information to estimate the probability that it will rain this year. He calculates θ (theta), the frequency that it rained, by dividing n, the number of years that it rained on July 4, by N, the total number of years for which he has data:

$$\theta = \frac{n}{N}.$$

Then Gregg uses θ, the frequency, as his estimate of the true probability that it will rain this year.

Subjective Probability. Unfortunately, if an event occurs infrequently, we cannot use a frequency calculation to calculate a probability. For example, the disastrous magnitude 9.0 earthquake that struck Japan in 2011, with an accompanying tsunami and nuclear reactor crisis, was unprecedented in modern history.

We use whatever information we have to form a *subjective probability*, which is a best estimate of the likelihood that the outcome will occur—that is, our best, informed guess. The subjective probability can combine frequencies and all other available information—even information that is not based on scientific observation.

If Gregg is planning a concert months in advance, he bases his estimate of the probability of rain on the frequency of rain in the past. However, as the event approaches, a weather forecaster can give him a better estimate that takes into account atmospheric conditions and other information in addition to the historical frequency. Because the forecaster's probability estimate uses personal judgment in addition to an observed frequency, it is a subjective probability.[2]

---

[2]With repeated events, we can compare our subjective probabilities to observed frequencies. We can compare our subjective probability that it rains 50% of the days in January to the frequency of rain in January during the recorded history. However if an event is not going to be repeated, it may not be possible to check whether our subjective probability is reasonable or accurate by comparing it to a frequency. We might believe that the chance of dry weather tomorrow is 75%. If it does rain tomorrow, that doesn't mean we were wrong. Only if we believed that the probability of rain was 0% would observing rain tomorrow prove us wrong.

APPLICATION	Cyberattacks—attempts to gain illegal access to computer systems to steal information or harm the system—are one of the newest and largest sources of risk facing major corporations. A cyberattack on Target Corporation exposed personal information of nearly 70 million of their customers. News of the attack resulted in reduced customer traffic and many expenses. Target's earnings before interest and taxes fell by nearly 30%, or $1.58 billion, from the year before the attack. Its breach-related expenses were $292 million, including the settlement of class-action lawsuits. After the 2017 announcement of the cyberattack on Equifax, a consumer credit report firm, its stock price fell by almost one-quarter.
Risk of a Cyberattack	

Which firms should put a high, subjective probability on an attack? According to Kamiya et al. (2018), cyberattacks are more likely to afflict large, visible firms; highly valued firms; firms with more intangible assets; and firms whose board pays inadequate attention to risk management. They also found that firms suffer major losses when consumer financial information is stolen, but attacks have relatively little effect otherwise.

Probability Distributions. A *probability distribution* relates the probability of occurrence to each possible outcome. Panel a of Figure 16.1 shows a probability distribution over five possible outcomes: zero to four days of rain per month in a relatively dry city. The probability that it rains no days during the month is 10%, as is the probability of exactly four days of rain. The chance of two rainy days is 40%, and the chance of one or three rainy days is 20% each. The probability that it rains five or more days in a month is 0%. These weather outcomes are mutually exclusive

Figure 16.1 Probability Distribution

The probability distribution shows the probability of occurrence for each of the mutually exclusive outcomes. Panel a shows five possible mutually exclusive outcomes. The probability that it rains exactly two days per month is 40%. The probability that it rains more than four days per month is 0%. The probability distributions in panels a and b have the same expected value or mean. The variance is smaller in panel b, where the probability distribution is more concentrated around the mean than the distribution in panel a.

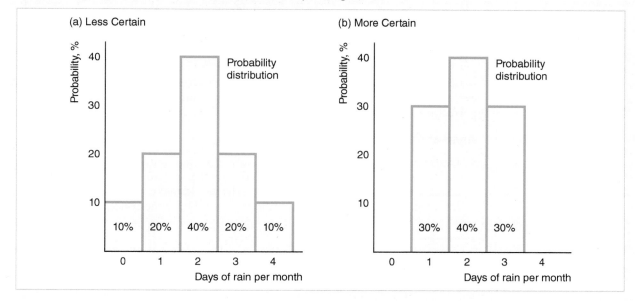

and exhaustive, so exactly one of these outcomes will occur, and the probabilities must sum to 100%. For simplicity in the following examples, we concentrate mainly on situations with only two possible outcomes.

Expected Value

One of the common denominators I have found is that expectations rise above that which is expected.—George W. Bush

Gregg's earnings from his outdoor concert will depend on the weather. If it doesn't rain, his profit or value from the concert is $V = 15$ ($15,000). If it rains, he'll have to cancel the concert and he will lose the money, $V = -5$, that he must pay the band. Although Gregg does not know what the weather will be with certainty, he knows that the weather department forecasts a 50% chance of rain.

Gregg may use the *mean* or the *average* of the values from both outcomes as a summary statistic of the likely payoff from booking this concert. The amount Gregg expects to earn is called his *expected value* (here, his *expected profit*). The **expected value** is the weighted average of the values of each possible outcome, where the weights are the probability of each outcome. That is, the expected value, EV, is the sum of the product of the probability and the value of each outcome:[3]

$$EV = [Pr(\text{no rain}) \times \text{Value(no rain)}] + [Pr(\text{rain}) \times \text{Value(rain)}]$$
$$= \left[\tfrac{1}{2} \times 15\right] + \left[\tfrac{1}{2} \times (-5)\right] = 5,$$

where *Pr* is the probability of an outcome, so *Pr*(rain) is the "probability that rain occurs."

The expected value is the amount Gregg would earn on average if he held the event many times. If he puts on such concerts on the same date over many years and the weather follows historical patterns, he will earn 15 at half of the concerts (those without rain), and he will get soaked for -5 at the other half of the concerts, when it rains. Thus, he'll earn an average of 5 per concert over a long period of time. More generally, with *n* possible outcomes—*states of nature*—and corresponding payoffs or values $V_i, i = 1, \ldots, n$, and associated probabilities θ_i, the expected value is

$$EV = \sum_{i=1}^{n} \theta_i V_i. \tag{16.1}$$

SOLVED PROBLEM 16.1

MyLab Economics Solved Problem

Suppose that Gregg could obtain perfect information so that he can accurately predict whether it will rain far enough before the concert that he could book the band only if needed. How much would he expect to earn, knowing that he will eventually have this perfect information? How much does he gain by having this perfect information?

Answer

1. *Determine how much Gregg would earn if he had perfect information in each state of nature.* If Gregg knew with certainty that it would rain at the time of the concert, he would not book the band, so he would make no loss or profit: $V = 0$. If Gregg knew that it would not rain, he would hold the concert and make 15.

[3]The expectation operator, E, tells us to take the weighted average of all possible values, where the weights are the probabilities that a particular value will be observed. Given *n* possible outcomes, the value of outcome *i* is V_i, and the probability of that outcome is Pr_i, then the expected value is $EV = Pr_1 V_1 + Pr_2 V_2 + \ldots + Pr_n V_n$.

2. *Determine how much Gregg would expect to earn before he learns with certainty what the weather will be.* Gregg knows that he'll make 15 with a 50% probability $(= \frac{1}{2})$ and 0 with a 50% probability because the weather department forecasts a 50% chance of rain, so his expected value, given that he'll receive perfect information in time to act on it, is

$$\left(\tfrac{1}{2} \times 15\right) + \left(\tfrac{1}{2} \times 0\right) = 7.5.$$

3. *Calculate his gain from perfect information as the difference between his expected earnings with perfect information and his expected earnings with imperfect information.* Gregg's gain from perfect information is the difference between the expected earnings with perfect information, 7.5, and the expected earnings without perfect information, 5. Thus, Gregg expects to earn 2.50 (= 7.50 − 5) more with perfect information than with imperfect information.[4]

Variance and Standard Deviation

From the expected value, Gregg knows how much he is likely to earn on average if he books many similar concerts. However, he cannot tell from the expected value how risky the concert is.

If Gregg's earnings are the same whether it rains or not, he faces no risk and the actual return that he receives is the expected value.[5] With risk, the possible outcomes differ from one another.

We can measure the risk Gregg faces in various ways. The most common approach is to use a measure based on how much the values of the possible outcomes differ from the expected value, EV. If it does not rain, the *difference* between Gregg's actual earnings, 15, and his expected earnings, 5, is 10. The difference if it does rain is −5 − 5 = −10. Because we have two differences—one difference for each state of nature (possible outcome)—it is convenient to combine them in a single measure of risk.

One such measure of risk is the *variance*, which measures the spread of the probability distribution. For example, the probability distributions in the two panels in Figure 16.1 have the same means (two days of rain) but different variances. The variance in panel a, where the probability distribution ranges from zero to four days of rain per month, is greater than the variance in panel b, where the probability distribution ranges from one to three days of rain per month.

Formally, the variance is the probability-weighted average of the squares of the differences between the observed outcome and the expected value. Given n possible outcomes with an expected value of EV, the value of outcome i is V_i, and the probability of that outcome is θ_i, the variance is

$$\text{Variance} = \sum_{i=1}^{n} \theta_i (V_i - EV)^2. \tag{16.2}$$

The variance puts more weight on large deviations from the expected value than on smaller ones. Instead of describing risk using the variance, economists and

---

[4]We can derive this answer directly. Perfect weather information is valuable to Gregg because he can avoid hiring the band when it rains. (Having information has no value if it has no use.) The value of this information is his expected savings from not hiring the band when it rains: $\frac{1}{2} \times 5 = 2.50$.

[5]The Tappet brothers (the hosts of National Public Radio's *Car Talk*) offered a risk-free investment. Their Capital Depreciation Fund guaranteed a 50% return: If you sent them $100, they would send you back $50.

businesspeople often report the *standard deviation*, which is the square root of the variance. The usual symbol for the standard deviation is σ (sigma), so the symbol for variance is σ^2.

Gregg faces the probability $\theta_1 = \frac{1}{2}$ if it does not rain and $\theta_2 = \frac{1}{2}$ if it rains. The value of the concert is $V_1 = 15$ without rain and $V_2 = -5$ with rain, and $EV = 5$. Thus, the variance of the value that Gregg obtains from the outdoor concert is

$$\sigma^2 = \left[\theta_1 \times (V_1 - EV)^2\right] + \left[\theta_2 \times (V_2 - EV)^2\right]$$
$$= \left[\tfrac{1}{2} \times (15 - 5)^2\right] + \left[\tfrac{1}{2} \times (-5 - 5)^2\right]$$
$$= \left[\tfrac{1}{2} \times (10)^2\right] + \left[\tfrac{1}{2} \times (-10)^2\right] = 100.$$

Because the variance of the payoff from the outdoor concert is $\sigma^2 = 100$, the standard deviation is $\sigma = 10$.

Holding the expected value constant, the smaller the standard deviation or variance, the smaller the risk. Suppose that Gregg's expected value of profit is the same if he stages the concert indoors, but that the standard deviation of his profit is less. The indoor theater does not hold as many people as the outdoor venue, so the most that Gregg can earn if it does not rain is $10. Rain discourages attendance even at the indoor theater, so he just breaks even, earning $0. The expected value of the indoor concert, $EV = (\frac{1}{2} \times 10) + (\frac{1}{2} \times 0) = 5$, is the same as that of the outdoor concert. Staging the concert indoors involves less risk, however. The variance of his earnings from the indoor concert is

$$\sigma^2 = \left[\tfrac{1}{2} \times (10 - 5)^2\right] + \left[\tfrac{1}{2} \times (0 - 5)^2\right] = \left[\tfrac{1}{2} \times (5)^2\right] + \left[\tfrac{1}{2} \times (-5)^2\right] = 25,$$

which is only one-fourth of the variance if he holds the event outside.

16.2   Attitudes Toward Risk

Given the risks Gregg faces if he schedules a concert, will Gregg stage the concert? To answer this question, we need to know Gregg's attitude toward risk.

Expected Utility Theory

If Gregg did not care about risk, then he would decide whether to promote the concert based on its expected value (profit) regardless of any difference in the risk. However, most people care about risk as well as expected value. Indeed, most people are *risk averse*—they dislike risk. They will choose a riskier option over a less risky option only if the expected value of the riskier option is sufficiently higher than that of the less risky one.

We need a formal means to judge the trade-off between expected value and risk—to determine if the expected value of a riskier option is sufficiently higher to justify the greater risk. The most commonly used method is to extend the model of utility maximization. In Chapter 3, we noted that one can describe an individual's preferences over various bundles of goods by using a utility function. John von Neumann and Oskar Morgenstern (1944) extended the standard utility-maximizing model to include risk.[6] They did so by treating utility as a cardinal measure rather

---

[6]This approach to handling choice under uncertainty is the most commonly used method. Schoemaker (1982) discusses the logic underlying this approach, the evidence for it, and several variants. Machina (1989) discusses a number of alternative methods.

than an ordinal measure (as we did in Chapters 3 through 5). In von Neumann's and Morgenstern's reformulation, a rational person maximizes *expected utility*. Expected utility, E*U*, is the probability-weighted average of the utility, $U(\cdot)$, from each possible outcome:

$$EU = \sum_{i=1}^{n} \theta_i U(V_i). \tag{16.3}$$

For example, Gregg's expected utility, E*U*, from the outdoor concert is

$$EU = [\theta_1 \times U(V_1)] + [\theta_2 \times U(V_2)] = [\tfrac{1}{2} \times U(15)] + [\tfrac{1}{2} \times U(-5)],$$

where his utility function, *U*, depends on his earnings. For example, $U(15)$ is the amount of utility Gregg gets from his earnings of 15. (People have preferences over the goods they consume. However, for simplicity we assume that a person receives utility from earnings or wealth, which can be spent on consumption goods.)

In short, the expected utility calculation is similar to the expected value calculation. Both are weighted averages in which the weights are the probabilities that a state of nature will occur. The difference is that the expected value is the probability-weighted average of the monetary value, whereas the expected utility is the probability-weighted average of the utility from the monetary value.

If we know how an individual's utility increases with wealth, we can determine how that person reacts to risky propositions. We can classify people in terms of their willingness to make a **fair bet**: a wager with an expected value of zero. An example of a fair bet is one in which you pay 1 if a flipped coin comes up heads and receive 1 if it comes up tails. Because you expect to win half the time and lose half the time, the expected value of this bet is zero:

$$[\tfrac{1}{2} \times (-1)] + [\tfrac{1}{2} \times 1] = 0.$$

In contrast, a bet in which you pay 2 if you lose the coin flip and receive 4 if you win is an unfair bet that favors you, with an expected value of

$$[\tfrac{1}{2} \times (-2)] + [\tfrac{1}{2} \times 4] = 1.$$

Someone who is unwilling to make a fair bet is **risk averse**. A person who is indifferent about making a fair bet is **risk neutral**. A person who is **risk preferring** will make a fair bet.

Risk Aversion

We can use our expected utility model to examine how Irma, who is risk averse, makes a choice under uncertainty. Figure 16.2 shows Irma's utility function. The utility function is concave to the wealth axis, indicating that Irma's utility rises with wealth but at a diminishing rate. Irma's utility from wealth *W* is $U(W)$. She has positive marginal utility from extra wealth, $dU(W)/dW > 0$; however, her utility increases with wealth at a diminishing rate, $d^2U(W)/dW^2 < 0$. That is, she has *diminishing marginal utility of wealth*: The extra pleasure she gets from each extra dollar of wealth is smaller than the pleasure she gets from the previous dollar. An individual whose utility function is concave to the wealth axis is risk averse, as we now illustrate.

Unwillingness to Take a Fair Bet. We can demonstrate that *a person whose utility function is concave picks the less-risky choice if both choices have the same expected value.* Suppose that Irma has an initial wealth of 40 and two options. One option is

Figure 16.2 Risk Aversion

Initially, Irma's wealth is 40, so her utility is $U(40) = 120$, point d. If she buys the stock and it's worth 70, her utility is $U(70) = 140$ at point c. If she buys the stock and it's worth only 10, she is at point a, where $U(10) = 70$. If her subjective probability that the stock will be worth 70 is 50%, her expected value of the stock is $40 = (0.5 \times 10) + (0.5 \times 70)$ and her expected utility from buying the stock is $0.5U(10) + 0.5U(70) = 105$ at point b, which is the midpoint of the line between the good outcome, point c, and the bad outcome, point a. Thus, her expected utility from buying the stock, 105, is less than her utility from having a certain wealth of 40, $U(40) = 120$, so she does not buy the stock. In contrast, if Irma's subjective probability that the stock will be worth 70 is 90%, her expected utility from buying the stock is $0.1U(10) + 0.9U(70) = 133$, point f, which is more than her utility with a certain wealth of 40, $U(40) = 120$, d, so she buys the stock.

Stockbrokers at Work

...for a small fee, I can place a bet for you.

to do nothing and keep the 40, so her utility is $U(40) = 120$ (point d in Figure 16.2) with certainty.

Her other option is to buy a share (a unit of stock) in a start-up company. Her wealth will be 70 if the start-up is a big success and 10 otherwise. Irma's subjective probability is 50% that the firm will be a big success. Her expected value of wealth remains

$$40 = \left(\tfrac{1}{2} \times 10\right) + \left(\tfrac{1}{2} \times 70\right).$$

Thus, buying the stock is a fair bet because she has the same expected wealth whether she purchases the stock or not.

If Irma only cared about her expected value and didn't care about risk, she would be indifferent between buying the stock or not. However, because Irma is risk averse, Irma prefers not buying the stock because both options have the same expected wealth and buying the stock carries more risk.

We can show that her expected utility is lower if she buys the stock than if she does not. If she buys the stock, her utility if the stock does well is $U(70) = 140$, point c. If it doesn't do well, her utility is $U(10) = 70$, point a. Thus, her expected utility from buying the stock is

$$[\tfrac{1}{2} \times U(10)] + [\tfrac{1}{2} \times U(70)] = [\tfrac{1}{2} \times 70] + [\tfrac{1}{2} \times 140] = 105.$$

Figure 16.2 shows that her expected utility is point b, the midpoint of a line (called a *chord*) between a and c.[7]

Because Irma's utility function is concave, her utility from certain wealth, 120 at point d, is greater than her expected utility from the risky activity, 105 at point b. As a result, she does not buy the stock. Buying this stock, which is a fair bet, increases the risk she faces without changing her expected wealth. *A person whose utility function is concave picks the less risky choice if both choices have the same expected value.*

Common Confusion A risk-averse person always chooses the least risky option.

A risk-averse person chooses a riskier option only if it has a sufficiently higher expected value. Given her wealth of $40, if Irma were much more confident that the stock would be valuable, her expected value would rise and she would buy the stock, as Solved Problem 16.2 shows.

SOLVED PROBLEM 16.2

MyLab Education
Solved Problem

Suppose that Irma's subjective probability is 90% that the stock will be valuable. What is her expected wealth if she buys the stock? What is her expected utility? Does she buy the stock?

Answer

1. *Calculate Irma's expected wealth.* Her expected value or wealth is 10% times her wealth if the stock bombs plus 90% times her wealth if the stock does well:

$$(0.1 \times 10) + (0.9 \times 70) = 64.$$

In Figure 16.2, 64 is the distance along the wealth axis corresponding to point f.

2. *Calculate Irma's expected utility.* Her expected utility is the probability-weighted average of her utility under the two outcomes:

$$[0.1 \times U(10)] + [0.9 \times U(70)] = [0.1 \times 70] + [0.9 \times 140] = 133.$$

Her expected utility is the height on the utility axis of point f. Point f is nine-tenths of the distance along the line connecting point a to point c.

3. *Compare Irma's expected utility to her certain utility if she does not buy.* Irma's expected utility from buying the stock, 133 (point f), is greater than her certain utility, 120 (point d), if she does not. Thus, if Irma is this confident that the stock will do well, she buys it. Although the risk is greater from buying than from not buying, her expected wealth is sufficiently higher (64 instead of 40) that it's worth taking the chance.

---

[7]The chord represents all the possible weighted averages of the utility at point a and the utility at point c. When the probabilities of the two outcomes are equal, the expected value is the midpoint.

The Risk Premium. The **risk premium** is the amount that a risk-averse person would pay to avoid taking a risk. For example, an individual may buy insurance to avoid risk. Equivalently, the risk premium is the minimum extra compensation (premium) that a decision maker would require to willingly incur a risk.

To calculate a risk premium, we can use the **certainty equivalent**: the amount of certain wealth that would yield the same utility as a risky prospect. We can use Figure 16.2, where Irma owns the stock that has a 50% chance of being worth 70 and a 50% chance of being worth 10, to determine her risk premium. The risk premium is the difference between her expected wealth from the risky stock and her certainty equivalent.

Irma's expected wealth from holding the stock is 40. Her corresponding expected utility is 105. The certainty equivalent income is 26, because the utility Irma gets from having 26 with certainty is $U(26) = 105$, the same as her expected utility from owning the stock. She would therefore be willing to sell the stock for a price of 26. Thus, her risk premium, which is the difference between the expected value and the certainty equivalent, is $40 - 26 = 14$, as the figure shows.

SOLVED PROBLEM
16.3

MyLab Economics
Solved Problem

Jen has a concave utility function of $U(W) = \sqrt{W}$. Her only major asset is shares in an internet start-up company. Tomorrow she will learn her stock's value. She believes that it is worth \$144 with probability $\frac{2}{3}$ and \$225 with probability $\frac{1}{3}$. What is her expected utility? What risk premium, P, would she pay to avoid bearing this risk?

Answer

1. *Calculate Jen's expected wealth and her expected utility.* Her expected wealth is

$$EW = \left(\tfrac{2}{3} \times 144\right) + \left(\tfrac{1}{3} \times 225\right) = 96 + 75 = 171.$$

Her expected utility is

$$\begin{aligned}
EU &= \left[\tfrac{2}{3} \times U(144)\right] + \left[\tfrac{1}{3} \times U(225)\right] \\
&= \left[\tfrac{2}{3} \times \sqrt{144}\right] + \left[\tfrac{1}{3} \times \sqrt{225}\right] \\
&= \left[\tfrac{2}{3} \times 12\right] + \left[\tfrac{1}{3} \times 15\right] = 8 + 5 = 13.
\end{aligned}$$

2. *Solve for P such that her expected utility equals her utility from her expected wealth minus P.* Jen would pay up to an amount P to avoid bearing the risk, where $U(EW - P)$ equals her expected utility from the risky stock, EU. That is,

$$U(EW - P) = U(171 - P) = \sqrt{171 - P} = 13 = EU.$$

Squaring both sides, we find that $171 - P = 169$, or $P = 2$. That is, Jen would accept an offer for her stock today of \$169 (or more), which reflects a risk premium of \$2.

APPLICATION

Stocks' Risk Premium

The value of most stocks is more variable over time than are bonds. Because stocks are riskier than bonds, for both to sell in the market to risk-averse investors, the anticipated rates of return on investing in stocks must exceed those on bonds over the period that the investor plans to hold these investments. This greater return is an investor's risk premium for stocks.

For example, a U.S. government bond is essentially free of any risk that the U.S. government will default. As Figure 16.2 illustrates, an investor will buy a stock only if it provides a risk premium over a risk-free U.S. government bond. That is, the investor buys the stock only if the expected return on the stock exceeds the rate of return on the bond.

In 2017, the stocks in the Standard and Poor's index of 500 leading stocks, the S&P 500, had a return of 21.6%, which exceeded the 2.8% return on 10-year U.S. treasury bonds by a large margin. However, stocks do not always outperform safe government bonds. In certain years, such as 2008 and 2011, stocks have performed worse than bonds.

Nonetheless, stocks have had a higher rate of return over the long run. For the 50-year period 1968–2017, the annualized return was 10.0% for S&P 500 stocks and 6.8% on long-term bonds. Jorda et al. (2017) estimated that the annual real rate of return from 1870 to 2015 across 16 high-income nations was 6.89% for stocks and 2.50% for bonds.

Risk Neutrality

Someone who is risk neutral has a constant marginal utility of wealth: Each extra dollar of wealth raises that person's utility by the same amount as the previous dollar. With constant marginal utility of wealth, the utility curve is a straight line in a utility and wealth graph. As a consequence, a risk-neutral person's utility depends only on wealth and not on risk.

Suppose that Irma is risk neutral and has the straight-line utility function in panel a of Figure 16.3. She would be indifferent between buying the stock and not buying

Figure 16.3 Risk Neutrality and Risk Preference

(a) If Irma's utility curve is a straight line, she is risk neutral and is indifferent as to whether or not to make a fair bet. Her expected utility from buying the stock, 105 at *b*, is the same as from a certain wealth of 40 at *b*. (b) If Irma's utility curve is convex to the horizontal axis, Irma has increasing marginal utility to wealth and is risk preferring. She buys the stock because her expected utility from buying the stock, 105 at *b*, is higher than her utility from a certain wealth of 40, 82 at *d*.

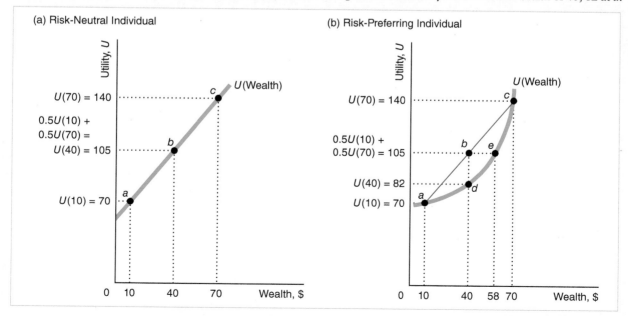

it if her subjective probability is 50% that it will do well. Her expected utility from buying the stock is the average of her utility at points *a* (10) and *c* (70):

$$\left[\tfrac{1}{2} \times U(10)\right] + \left[\tfrac{1}{2} \times U(70)\right] = \left[\tfrac{1}{2} \times 70\right] + \left[\tfrac{1}{2} \times 140\right] = 105.$$

Her expected utility exactly equals her utility with certain wealth of 40 (point *b*) because the line connecting points *a* and *c* lies on the utility function and point *b* is the midpoint of that line.

Here, Irma is indifferent between buying and not buying the stock, a fair bet, because she doesn't care how much risk she faces. Because the expected wealth from both options is 40, she is indifferent between them.

In general, *a risk-neutral person chooses the option with the highest expected value because maximizing expected value maximizes utility.* A risk-neutral person chooses the riskier option if it has even a slightly higher expected value than the less risky option. Equivalently, the risk premium for a risk-neutral person is zero.

Risk Preference

An individual with an increasing marginal utility of wealth is risk preferring: that is, willing to take a fair bet. If Irma has the utility curve in panel b of Figure 16.3, she is risk preferring. Her expected utility from buying the stock, 105 at point *b*, is higher than her certain utility if she does not buy the stock, 82 at point *d*. Therefore, she buys the stock.

A risk-preferring person is willing to pay for the right to make a fair bet (a negative risk premium). As the figure shows, Irma's expected utility from buying the stock is the same as the utility from a certain wealth of 58. Given her initial wealth of 40, if you offer her the opportunity to buy the stock or offer to give her 18, she is indifferent. With any payment smaller than 18, she prefers to buy the stock.

APPLICATION	Most people say that they don't like bearing risk. Consistent with such statements, most consumers purchase insurance such as car insurance, homeowner's insurance, medical insurance, and other forms of insurance that reduce the risks they face. But many of these same people gamble.
Gambling	

According to one estimate, global gaming revenues were $138 billion in 2018, over half of which were generated in the United States and China. Over half of the countries in the world have lotteries.

Not only do many people gamble, but they make unfair bets, in which the expected value of the gamble is negative. That is, if they play the game repeatedly, they are likely to lose money in the long run. For example, the British government keeps half of the total amount bet on its lottery. Americans lose 7% of all legal money bet.

According to a *Wall Street Journal* study, internet gamblers win money 30% of the days they wager, but only 11% were in the black over two years (and most of those were ahead by less than $150). Of the top 10% most frequent bettors, 95% lost money. One estimate put U.S. gamblers' losses at $119 billion in legal betting in 2018.

Why do people take unfair bets? Some people gamble because they are risk preferring or because they have a compulsion to gamble.[8] However, neither of these observations is likely to explain noncompulsive gambling by most people who exhibit risk-averse behavior in the other aspects of their lives, such as buying insurance. Risk-averse people may make unfair bets because they get pleasure from participating in the game or because they falsely believe that the gamble favors them.

The first explanation is that gambling provides entertainment as well as risk. Risk-averse people insure their property, such as their homes, because they do not want to bear the risk of theft, flooding, and fire. However, these same people may play poker or bet on horse races because they get enough pleasure from playing those games to put up with the financial risk and the expected loss.

Many people definitely like games of chance. One survey found that 65% of Americans say that they engage in games of chance even when the games involve no money or only trivial sums. That is, they play because they enjoy the games. The anticipation of possibly winning and the satisfaction and excitement arising from a win generate greater benefits than the negative feelings associated with a loss.

Instead, or in addition, people may gamble because they make mistakes.[9] People either do not know the true probabilities or cannot properly calculate expected values, so they do not realize that they are participating in an unfair bet. And some gamblers are simply overconfident: They overestimate their likelihood of winning.

Degree of Risk Aversion

Figures 16.2 and 16.3 illustrate that whether Irma is risk averse depends on the shape of her utility function over wealth, $U(W)$. Economists sometimes use quantitative measures of the curvature of the utility function to describe the degree of an individual's risk aversion.

Arrow-Pratt Measure of Risk Aversion. One of the most commonly used measures is the Arrow-Pratt measure of risk aversion (Pratt, 1964):

$$\rho(W) = -\frac{d^2 U(W)/dW^2}{dU(W)/dW}. \tag{16.4}$$

Because Irma's marginal utility of wealth is positive, $dU(W)/dW > 0$, $\rho(W)$ has the opposite sign of $d^2 U(W)/dW^2$. Irma is risk averse if her utility function is concave to the horizontal axis, so she has diminishing marginal utility of wealth, $d^2 U(W)/dW^2 < 0$. Thus, if she is risk averse, the Arrow-Pratt measure is positive.

---

[8]Friedman and Savage (1948) suggest that some gamblers are risk averse with respect to small gambles but risk preferring for large ones, such as a lottery.

[9]Economists, who know how to calculate expected values and derive most of their excitement from economic models, are apparently less likely to gamble than are other people. A number of years ago, an association of economists met in Reno, Nevada. Reno hotels charge low room rates on the assumption that they'll make plenty from guests' gambling losses. However, the economists gambled so little that they were asked pointedly not to return.

If Irma has the concave utility function $U(W) = \ln W$, then $dU(W)/dW = 1/W$ and $d^2U(W)/dW^2 = -1/W^2$, so her Arrow-Pratt measure is $\rho(W) = 1/W > 0$. Her degree of risk aversion falls with wealth. In contrast, if she has an exponential utility function, $U(W) = -e^{-aW}$, where $a > 0$, her Arrow-Pratt measure is $\rho(W) = -(-a^2 e^{-aW})/(ae^{-aW}) = a$, so her measure of risk aversion is constant over all possible values of wealth.

The Arrow-Pratt measure is zero if Irma is risk neutral. For example, if her utility function is $U(W) = aW$, then $dU(W)/dW = a$, $d^2U(W)/dW^2 = 0$, and her Arrow-Pratt risk aversion measure is $\rho(W) = -0/a = 0$. The Arrow-Pratt measure is negative if Irma is risk preferring.

Arrow-Pratt Measure and the Willingness to Gamble. We can show that the smaller the Arrow-Pratt measure of risk aversion, the more small gambles that an individual will take. Suppose Ryan's house is currently worth W. He considers painting it bright orange, which he believes will lower its value by A with probability θ and raise it by B with probability $1 - \theta$. He takes this gamble if his expected utility is higher than his certain utility when he does not gamble: $\theta U(W - A) + (1 - \theta)U(W + B) > U(W)$. Let $B(A)$ show how large B must be for a given value of A such that Ryan's expected utility equals his certain utility:

$$\theta U(W - A) + (1 - \theta)U[W + B(A)] = U(W). \tag{16.5}$$

From Equation 16.5, if $A = 0$, $B(0) = 0$. Given that A is initially 0, how much does B change as we slightly increase A? That is, how much does the house's value have to rise in the good state of nature to offset the drop in value in the bad state such that Ryan is willing to take the gamble on painting his house? To answer these questions, we differentiate Equation 16.5 with respect to A,

$$-\theta \frac{dU(W - A)}{dA} + (1 - \theta)\frac{dU(W + B(A))}{dA}\frac{dB(A)}{dA} = 0, \tag{16.6}$$

and evaluate at $A = 0$:

$$-\theta \frac{dU(W)}{dA} + (1 - \theta)\frac{dU(W)}{dA}\frac{dB(0)}{dA} = 0.$$

Rearranging this last expression, we learn that

$$\frac{dB(0)}{dA} = \frac{\theta}{1 - \theta}. \tag{16.7}$$

That is, Ryan will be willing to engage in this gamble if the increase in B in response to an increase in A equals the odds $\theta/(1 - \theta)$.

For a given θ, A, and B, Ryan is more likely to take this gamble, the less risk averse he is. How risk averse he is depends on the curvature of his utility function, which is reflected by the second derivative of his utility function. Differentiating the identity in Equation 16.6 again with respect to A and evaluating at $A = 0$, we discover that

$$\theta \frac{d^2U(W)}{dA^2} + (1 - \theta)\frac{d^2U(W)}{dA^2}\left[\frac{dB(0)}{dA}\right]^2 + (1 - \theta)\frac{dU(W)}{dA}\frac{d^2B(0)}{dA^2} = 0. \tag{16.8}$$

Substituting Equation 16.7 into Equation 16.8, rearranging terms, and finally substituting in the definition from Equation 16.4, we obtain

$$\frac{d^2B(0)}{dA^2} = \frac{\theta}{(1 - \theta)^2}\left[-\frac{d^2U(W)/dA^2}{dU(W)/dA}\right] = \frac{\theta}{(1 - \theta)^2}\rho(W).$$

That is, $d^2B(0)/dA^2$ is proportional to the Arrow-Pratt risk-aversion measure. The larger d^2B/dA^2, the greater the rate that B must increase as A increases for Ryan to be willing to gamble. Thus, for a given θ, A, and B, he is more likely to take the gamble, the smaller his Arrow-Pratt measure.

SOLVED PROBLEM 16.4 **MyLab Economics** Solved Problem	Jen's utility function is $U(W) = W^{0.5}$, while Ryan's is $U(W) = W^{0.25}$. Use the Arrow-Pratt measure to show that Ryan is more risk averse. Next, suppose that each owns a home worth 100 (for simplicity) and is considering painting it orange. If each does so, each house is worth 81 with a 50% probability and is worth 121 with a 50% probability. Will either person take this gamble?

Answer

1. *Calculate their Arrow-Pratt measures using Equation 16.4.* Differentiating Jen's utility function, $U(W) = W^{0.5}$, with respect to W, we find that $dU/dW = 0.5W^{-0.5}$. Differentiating again, we learn that $d^2U/dW^2 = -0.25W^{-1.5}$. Thus, her Arrow-Pratt risk measure is $\rho_J = -(d^2U/dW^2)/(dU/dW) = 0.25W^{-1.5}/0.5W^{-0.5} = 0.5/W$. Ryan's utility function is $U(W) = W^{0.25}$, so $dU/dW = 0.25W^{-0.75}$, $d^2U/dW^2 = -0.1875W^{-1.75}$, and his Arrow-Pratt risk measure is $\rho_R = 0.1875W^{-1.75}/0.25W^{-0.75} = 0.75/W$. Subtracting one Arrow-Pratt risk measure from the other shows that $\rho_R - \rho_J = (0.75 - 0.5)/W > 0$ or $\rho_R > \rho_J$. Thus, Ryan is more risk averse than Jen.

2. *By comparing their expected utility with the gamble to their utility without the gamble, determine if either is willing to take the gamble.* Without the gamble, Jen's utility is $U(100) = 100^{0.5} = 10$. With the gamble, her expected utility is $0.5U(81) + 0.5U(121) = (0.5 \times 9) + (0.5 \times 11) = 10$. Consequently, she is indifferent to the gamble. Ryan's certain utility is $U(100) = 100^{0.25} \approx 3.1623$. With the gamble, his expected utility is $0.5U(81) + 0.5U(121) \approx (0.5 \times 3) + (0.5 \times 3.3166) = 3.1583$, which is less than 3.1623, so he is unwilling to take the gamble. Thus, Jen may take this gamble, unlike Ryan, who is more risk averse.

16.3 Reducing Risk

Risk-averse people want to eliminate or reduce the risks they face. Risk-neutral people avoid unfair bets that are stacked against them, and even risk-preferring people avoid very unfair bets. Individuals can avoid optional risky activities, but often they can't escape risk altogether. Property owners, for instance, always face the possibility that their property will be damaged or stolen. However, they may be able to reduce the probability that bad events (such as earthquakes, tornadoes, fires, floods, and thefts) happen to them.

Individuals can avoid optional risky activities, but they can't escape risk altogether. Property owners, for instance, face the possibility that their property will be damaged or stolen or will burn down. They may be able to reduce the probability that bad states of nature occur, however.

Just Say No

The simplest way to avoid risk is to abstain from optional risky activities. No one forces you to bet on the lottery, work in a high-risk environment, or invest in a start-up biotech firm.

Even when you can't avoid risk altogether, you can take precautions to reduce the probability of bad states of nature happening or the magnitude of any loss that might occur. By maintaining your car as the manufacturer recommends, you reduce the probability that it will break down. By locking your apartment door, you lower the chance of having your television stolen. Getting rid of the four-year-old collection of newspapers in your basement lessens the likelihood that your house will burn down. In 2015, DuPont Pioneer introduced a corn seed that it claims is more drought resistant than traditional seeds, which farmers can use to reduce their risk from drought.

Obtaining Information

Collecting accurate information before acting is one of the most important ways in which people can reduce risk and increase expected value and expected utility, as Solved Problem 16.1 illustrated. Armed with information, people may avoid making a risky choice, or may be able to take actions that reduce the probability of a disaster or the size of a loss.

Before buying a car or refrigerator, many people read *Consumer Reports* to determine how frequently a particular brand is likely to need repairs. By collecting such information before buying, they can reduce the likelihood of making a costly mistake.[10]

Diversification

Although it may sound paradoxical, individuals and firms can reduce their overall risk by making many risky investments instead of only one. This practice is called *risk pooling* or *diversifying*. As your grandparents may have told you, "Don't put all your eggs in one basket."[11]

The extent to which diversification reduces risk depends on the degree to which various events are correlated over states of nature. The degree of correlation ranges from negatively correlated to uncorrelated to positively correlated.[12]

If two investments are positively correlated, one performs well when the other performs well. If two investments are negatively correlated, when one performs well, the other performs badly. If the performances of two investments move *independently*—do not move together predictably—their payoffs are uncorrelated.

Diversification can eliminate risk if two events are perfectly negatively correlated. Suppose that two firms are competing for a government contract and have an equal chance of winning. Because only one firm can win, the other must lose, so the two events are *perfectly negatively correlated*. You can buy a share of stock in either firm for $20. The stock of the firm that wins the contract will be worth $40, while the

---

[10]See "Bond Ratings" in MyLab Economics, Chapter Resources, Chapter 16 for a discussion of how the riskiness of bonds is reported.

[11]Unlike the supermarket manager who left all his baskets in one exit, where they were smashed by a car.

[12]A measure of the *correlation* between two random variables x and y is

$$\rho = E\left(\frac{x - \bar{x}}{\sigma_x} \frac{y - \bar{y}}{\sigma_y}\right),$$

where the $E(\cdot)$ means "take the expectation" of the term in parentheses, $\bar{x}$ and $\bar{y}$ are the means, and σ_x and σ_y are the standard deviations of x and y. This correlation can vary between -1 and 1. If $\rho = 1$ these random variables are perfectly positively correlated, if $\rho = -1$ they have a perfect negative correlation, and if $\rho = 0$ they are uncorrelated.

stock of the loser will be worth $10. If you buy two shares of one firm, the expected value of the two shares is

$$EV = \left(\tfrac{1}{2} \times 80\right) + \left(\tfrac{1}{2} \times 20\right) = 50$$

with a variance of

$$\sigma^2 = \left[\tfrac{1}{2} \times (80 - 50)^2\right] + \left[\tfrac{1}{2} \times (20 - 50)^2\right] = 900.$$

However, if you buy one share of each firm, your two shares will be worth $40 + 10 = 50$ no matter which firm wins, and the variance is zero.

Diversification can reduce (but not eliminate) risk even when investments are not perfectly negatively correlated. Indeed, diversification reduces risk even if the two investments are uncorrelated or imperfectly positively correlated.

Now suppose that the two stocks' values are uncorrelated: Whether one firm wins a contract is independent of whether the other firm gets one. Each of the two firms has a 50% chance of receiving a government contract. The chance that each firm's share is worth 40 is $\tfrac{1}{4}$, the chance that one is worth 40 and the other is worth 10 is $\tfrac{1}{2}$, and the chance that each is worth 10 is $\tfrac{1}{4}$. If you buy one share of each firm, the expected value of these two shares is

$$EV = \left(\tfrac{1}{4} \times 80\right) + \left(\tfrac{1}{2} \times 50\right) + \left(\tfrac{1}{4} \times 20\right) = 50,$$

and the variance is

$$\sigma^2 = \left[\tfrac{1}{4} \times (80 - 50)^2\right] + \left[\tfrac{1}{2} \times (50 - 50)^2\right] + \left[\tfrac{1}{4} \times (20 - 50)^2\right] = 450.$$

The expected value is the same as when buying two shares of one firm, but the variance is only half as large. Thus, diversification lowers risk when the values are uncorrelated.

You may find it surprising that diversification can reduce risk even if the investments are positively correlated, provided that the correlation is not perfect. However, *diversification does not reduce risk if two investments have a perfect positive correlation.* For example, if the government awards contracts only to both firms or to neither firm, the risks are perfectly positively correlated. The expected value of the stocks and the variance are the same whether you buy two shares of one firm or one share of each firm.

Because the stock price of any given firm is not perfectly positively correlated with the stock price of other firms, an investor or a manager can reduce risk by buying the stocks of many companies rather than the stock of just one firm. One way to effectively own shares in a number of companies at once is by buying shares in a *mutual fund* of stocks. A mutual fund share is issued by a company that buys stocks in many other companies.

One well-known type of mutual fund is the *Standard & Poor's Composite Index of 500 Stocks (S&P 500)*, which is a value-weighted average of 500 large firms' stocks.[13] The S&P 500 companies constitute only about 7% of all the publicly traded firms in the United States, but they represent approximately 80% of the total value of the U.S. stock market.

However, a stock mutual fund has a *market-wide risk*, a risk that is common to the overall market, which arises because the prices of almost all stocks tend to rise when the economy is expanding and to fall when the economy is contracting. You cannot avoid the systematic risks associated with shifts in the economy that have a similar effect on most stocks even if you buy a diversified mutual stock fund.

---

[13]The Calvert, Domini Social Investments, Pax World Funds, and hundreds of other mutual funds have portfolios consisting of only socially responsible firms (by their criteria). An alternative, the Barrier Fund (formerly the Vice Fund), invests in only sin stocks. Adding additional restrictions may lower the returns to mutual funds.

APPLICATION	Foolishly, many corporate employees fail to diversify their portfolios. Much of
Failure to Diversify	their wealth is tied up in their employer's stock. Managers and other corporate

APPLICATION

Failure to Diversify

Foolishly, many corporate employees fail to diversify their portfolios. Much of their wealth is tied up in their employer's stock. Managers and other corporate employees may receive stock bonuses, which they do not sell. For others, their employer matches their investment in the company's retirement plans with company stock. Others invest voluntarily as a sign of loyalty.

If the firm fails, these employees lose not only their jobs but also much of the value of their retirement portfolio, as happened to many of Radio Shack's employees when it declared bankruptcy in 2015. That's typical. Duan et al. (2015) analyzed 20 years of data for 729 troubled, large, publicly traded companies. They found that employees kept the amounts of money they held in company stock relatively stable during periods of trouble. Pension losses were particularly bad during the Great Recession of 2007–2009.

Many investment advisors recommend investing at most 5% in employer stock—much less than the 26% level found by a 2006 survey of large U.S. pension plans. The good news is that the share of company stock in pension plans has decreased in recent years as participants have become more educated, and both employees and firms have taken the lessons of the Great Recession to heart. Many firms now restrict employees' ability to invest their pension savings in company stock. The 2018 *Investment Company Fact Book* reports that younger workers were down to holding only about 5% of their pension savings in company stock.

Insurance

I detest life-insurance agents; they always argue that I shall some day die, which is not so. —Stephen Leacock

People and firms can also avoid or reduce risk by purchasing insurance. As we've seen, a risk-averse person is willing to pay money—a risk premium—to avoid risk. The demand for risk reduction is met by insurance companies, which bear the risk for anyone who buys an insurance policy. Many risk-averse individuals and firms buy insurance, leading to an industry of enormous size. According to the Swiss Re Institute, global insurance premiums in 2017 were about $4.9 trillion, which is more than 6% of world GDP.[14]

Determining the Amount of Insurance to Buy. Many individuals and firms buy insurance to shift some or all of the risk they face to an insurance company. A risk-averse person or firm pays a premium to the insurance company, and the insurance company transfers money to the policyholder if a bad outcome occurs, such as sickness, an accident, or property loss due to theft or fire.

Because Scott is risk averse, he wants to insure his home, which is worth 500. The probability that his home will burn next year is 20%. If a fire occurs, the home will be worth nothing.

With no insurance, the expected value of his home is

$$EV = (0.2 \times 0) + (0.8 \times 500) = 400.$$

Scott faces a good deal of risk. The variance of the value of his home is

$$\sigma^2 = [0.2 \times (0 - 400)^2] + [0.8 \times (500 - 400)^2] = 40,000.$$

---

[14]institute.swissre.com/research/overview/sigma/3_2018.html.

Suppose that an insurance company offers **fair insurance**: a contract between an insurer and a policyholder in which the expected value of the contract to the policyholder is zero. That is, the insurance is a fair bet. With fair insurance, for every $1 that Scott pays the insurance company, the *premium*, the insurance company will pay Scott $5 to cover the damage if the fire occurs, so that he has $1 less if the fire does not occur, but $4 (=5 − 1) more if it does occur.

Because Scott is risk averse and the insurance is fair, he wants to *fully insure* by buying enough insurance to eliminate his risk altogether. That is, he wants to buy the amount of fair insurance that will leave him equally well off in both states of nature. That is, he pays a premium of x so that he has $500 - x$ if the fire does not occur, and has $4x$ if the fire occurs, such that $500 - x = 4x$, or $x = 100$.[15] If no fire occurs, he pays a premium of 100 and has a home worth 500 for a net value of 400. If a fire occurs, Scott pays 100 but receives 500 from the insurance company for a net value of 400. Thus, Scott's wealth is 400 in either case.

Although Scott's expected value with full and fair insurance is the same as his expected value without insurance, the variance he faces drops from 10,000 without insurance to 0 with insurance. Scott is better off with full fair insurance because he has the same expected value and faces no risk. A risk-averse person always wants full insurance if the insurance is fair.

Sometimes insurance companies put limits on the amount of insurance offered. For example, the insurance company could offer Scott fair insurance but only up to a maximum gross payment of, for example, 400 rather than 500. Given this limit, Scott would buy the maximum amount of fair insurance that he could.

SOLVED PROBLEM 16.5

MyLab Economics Solved Problem

The local government collects a property tax of 20 on Scott's home. If the tax is collected whether or not the home burns, how much fair insurance does Scott buy? If the tax is collected only if the home does not burn, how much fair insurance does Scott buy?

Answer

1. *Determine the after-tax expected value of the house with and without insurance.* If the tax is always collected, the house is worth $480 = 500 - 20$ if it does not burn and −20 if it does burn. Thus, the expected value of the house is

$$380 = [0.2 \times (-20)] + [0.8 \times 480].$$

If the tax is collected only if the fire does not occur, the expected value of the house is

$$384 = [0.2 \times 0] + [0.8 \times 480].$$

2. *Calculate the amount of fair insurance Scott buys if the tax is always collected.* Because Scott is risk averse, he wants to fully insure so that the after-tax value of his house is the same in both states of nature. If the tax is always collected, he pays a premium of x such that $500 - x - 20 = 4x - 20$, so $x = 100$. If no fire occurs, his net wealth is $500 - 100 - 20 = 380$. If a fire occurs, the insurance company pays 500, or a net payment of 400 above the cost of the insurance, and Scott pays 20 in taxes, leaving him with 380 once again. That is, he buys the same amount of insurance as he would without any taxes. The tax has no effect on his insurance decision because he owes the tax regardless of the state of nature.

---

[15]The expected value of Scott's insurance contract is $[0.8 \times (-100)] + [0.2 \times 400] = 0$, which shows that the insurance is fair.

3. *Calculate the amount of fair insurance Scott buys if the government collects the tax only if a fire occurs.* With this tax rule, Scott pays a premium of x such that $500 - x - 20 = 4x$, so $x = 96$.

Scott pays the insurance company 96 and receives 480 if a fire occurs. Without a fire, Scott's wealth is $500 - 96 - 20 = 384$. If a fire occurs, the insurance company pays 480, so Scott's wealth is $480 - 96 = 384$. Thus, he has the same after-tax wealth in both states of nature.

Comment: Because the tax system is partially insuring Scott by dropping the tax in the bad state of nature, he purchases less private insurance, 480, than the 500 he buys if the tax is collected in both states of nature. That is,

Unintended Consequence Property taxes encourage risk-averse people to "underinsure."

Fairness and Insurance. We have been examining situations where the insurance is fair so that the customer's insurance contract has an expected value of zero. However, an insurance company could not stay in business if it offered fair insurance. With fair insurance, the insurance company's expected payments would equal the premiums that the insurance company collects. Because the insurance company has operating expenses, it loses money if it provides fair insurance. Thus, we expect that real-world insurance companies offer unfair insurance, charging a premium that exceeds the fair-insurance premium. Although a risk-averse consumer fully insures if offered fair insurance, they will buy less than full insurance if insurance is unfair.[16]

How much can insurance companies charge for insurance? A monopoly insurance company could charge an amount up to the risk premium a person is willing to pay to avoid risk. For example, in Figure 16.2, Irma would be willing to pay up to $14 for an insurance policy that would compensate her if her stock did not perform well. The more risk averse an individual is, the more a monopoly insurance company can charge. If many insurance companies compete, the price of an insurance policy is less than the maximum that risk-averse individuals are willing to pay—but still high enough that the firms can cover their operating expenses.

APPLICATION	*That airline that doesn't kill me makes me stronger.*
Flight Insurance	Many folks fear flying: "If flying is so safe, why do they call the airport the terminal?" Many companies such as Travel Guard (TG) offer accidental death insurance for individual flights. If, just before I take my next regularly scheduled commercial flight, I pay TG $25 and I die on that flight, TG will pay my family $500,000. (Although I can get much larger amounts of air travel insurance, it seems a bad idea to make myself worth more to my family dead than alive.)

Is Travel Guard (TG) flight insurance fair? If θ is my probability of dying on a flight, my family's expected value from this bet with TG is $[\theta \times 500,000] + [(1 - \theta) \times (-25)]$. For this insurance to be fair, this expected value must be zero, which is true if $\theta \approx 0.000115$. That is, one in every 20,040 passengers dies.

---

[16]As Solved Problem 16.5 shows, tax laws may offset the problem of unfair insurance, so that some insurance may be fair or more than fair after taxes.

But dear! Flying is safer than driving.

How great *is* the danger of being in a fatal commercial airline crash? According to the National Transportation Safety Board, no fatalities occurred on scheduled U.S. commercial airline flights in 2002, 2007, 2008, and from 2010 through at least August 2018.

In 2001, the probability was much higher than any other year because of the 525 on-board deaths caused by the terrorist hijacking and crashes on September 11 and the subsequent sharp reduction in the number of flights. However, even in 2001, the probability was 0.00000077, or 1 in 1.3 million fliers—much lower than the probability that makes TG's insurance a fair bet. For the decade 2008–2017, the probability was 0.00000000531, or one fatality per 188 million fliers.

Given that probability, if I fly each day for 100 years, the probability of avoiding a fatal crash is 99.98%. The probability drops to 99.81% after flying every day for 1,000 years and to 98.07% after 10,000 years of flying every day. (For most people, the greatest risk of an airplane trip is the drive to and from the airport. More than twice as many people are killed in vehicle-deer collisions than in plane crashes.)

Given that my chance of dying in a fatal crash is $\theta = 0.00000000531$ (the rate for the decade 2008–2017), the fair rate to pay for $500,000 of flight insurance is about 0.27¢. Thus, TG is offering to charge me 9,259 times more than the fair rate for this insurance.

I would have to be incredibly risk averse to be take TG up on their kind offer. Even if I were that risk averse, I would be much better off buying general life insurance, which is much less expensive than flight insurance and covers accidental death from all types of accidents and diseases.

Insurance Only for Diversifiable Risks. Why is an insurance company willing to sell policies and take on risk? By pooling the risks of many people, the insurance company can lower its risk much below that of any individual. If the probability that one car is stolen is independent of whether other cars are stolen, the risk to an insurance company of insuring one person against car theft is much greater than the average risk of insuring many people.

However, if the risks from disasters to its policyholders are highly positively correlated, an insurance company is not well diversified just by holding many policies. A war affects all policyholders, so the outcomes that they face are perfectly correlated. Because wars are *nondiversifiable risks*, insurance companies normally do not offer policies insuring against wars.

APPLICATION

Flooded by
Insurance Claims

Global economic losses from natural disasters in 2017 were $337 billion. About 43% of these losses, $144 billion, were insured, setting a new annual record for insured natural disaster losses. Hurricanes Harvey, Irma, and Maria and the associated flooding accounted for $92 billion of this loss.

In recent years, many insurance companies have started viewing some major natural disasters as nondiversifiable risks because such catastrophic events cause many insured people to suffer losses at the same time. As people build more homes in flood-prone areas, the size of the potential losses to insurers from nondiversifiable risks has grown. Thus, in disaster-prone areas, private flood insurance is generally not available. Homeowners rely on government programs, such as the U.S. National Flood Insurance Program (NFIP).

A few insured properties account for a disproportionate share of NFIP claims. Brian Harman's property in Texas is one of several million insured by NFIP. Shortly after completing major home renovations in 2017, Mr. Harman was flooded by Hurricane Harvey. The flood should not have been a surprise. Mr. Harmon's house, situated in a flood plain of the San Jacinto River, has flooded 22 times since 1979. Between 1979 and 2015, the NFIP paid out almost $2 million—much more than the property is worth—to fix the house multiple times.

For many frequently flooded properties, it would be cheaper for the NFIP to buy them and return them to an undeveloped state rather than repeatedly repair flood damage. The U.S. government is trying to do just that, but homeowners often do not want to move, and local governments often oppose losing developed properties from their tax base.

Largely because of such "frequent flooders," NFIP has taken in much less in premiums than it has paid out in recent years. Even before the 2017 floods, the NFIP owed the U.S. Treasury $24.6 billion. For a combination of political and other reasons, premiums for the high-risk properties are less than the actuarially fair value. In addition, President Trump rescinded an executive order signed by President Obama requiring that projects receiving federal building funds consider future effects of flooding in their construction plans.

16.4   Investing Under Uncertainty

Don't invest with anyone named Slick.

We now investigate how uncertainty affects the investment decision. In particular, we examine how attitudes toward risk affect individuals' willingness to invest, how people evaluate risky investments that last for many periods, and how investors pay to alter their probabilities of success.

In the following examples, the owner of a monopoly decides whether to open a new store. Because the firm is a monopoly, the owner's return from the investment does not depend on the actions of other firms. As a result, the owner faces no strategic considerations. The owner knows the cost of the investment but is unsure about how many people will patronize the new store; hence, the profits are uncertain.

How Investing Depends on Attitudes Toward Risk

We start by considering an investor who is only interested in the uncertain payoff for this year, so that we can ignore the problem of discounting the future profits. Whether the owner invests depends on how risk averse he or she is and on the risks involved.

We first consider the decision of Chris, a risk-neutral owner. Because she is risk neutral, she invests if the expected value of the firm rises due to the investment. Any action that increases her expected value must also increase her expected utility because she is indifferent to risk. In contrast, in the next example, Ken is risk averse, so he might not make an investment that increases his firm's expected value if the investment is very risky. That is, maximizing expected value does not necessarily maximize his expected utility.

Risk-Neutral Investing. Chris, the risk-neutral owner of the monopoly, uses a *decision tree* (panel a of Figure 16.4) to decide whether to invest. The rectangle, called a *decision node*, indicates that she must make a decision about whether to invest or not. The circle, a *chance node*, denotes that a random process determines the outcome (consistent with the given probabilities). If Chris does not open the new store, she makes 0. If she opens the new store, she expects to make 200 with 80% probability and to lose 100 with 20% probability. The expected value from a new store (see the circle in panel a) is

$$EV = (0.8 \times 200) + [0.2 \times (-100)] = 140.$$

Because she is risk neutral, she prefers an expected value of 140 to a certain one of 0, so she invests. Thus, her expected value in the rectangle is 140.

Risk-Averse Investing. We can compare Chris's decision to that of Ken, a risk-averse owner of a monopoly who faces the same investment decision. Ken invests in the new store if his expected utility from investing is greater than his certain utility from not investing. Panel b of Figure 16.4 shows the decision tree for a particular risk-averse utility function. The circle shows that Ken's expected utility from the investment is

$$EU = [0.2 \times U(-100)] + [0.8 \times U(200)]$$
$$= (0.2 \times 0) + (0.8 \times 40) = 32.$$

Ken's certain utility from not investing is $U(0) = 35$, which is greater than 32. Thus, Ken does not invest. As a result, his expected utility in the rectangle is 35 (his certain utility from not investing).

Figure 16.4 Investment Decision Tree with Uncertainty

Chris and Ken, each the owner of a monopoly, must decide whether to invest in a new store. (a) The expected value of the investment is 140, so it pays for Chris, who is risk neutral, to invest. (b) Ken is so risk averse that he does not invest even though the expected value of the investment is positive. His expected utility falls if he makes this risky investment.

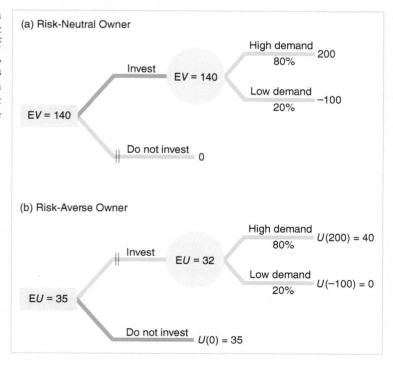

Figure 16.5 Investment Decision Tree with Uncertainty and Discounting

The risk-neutral owner invests if the expected net present value is positive. The expected value, EV, of the revenue from the investment next year is $110. With an interest rate of 10%, the expected present value, EPV, of the revenue is $100. The expected net present value, ENPV, is EPV = $100 minus the $25 cost of the investment this year, which is $75. The owner therefore invests.

Investing with Uncertainty and Discounting

Now suppose that the uncertain returns or costs from an investment are spread out over time. In Chapter 15, we derived an investment rule when we know future costs and returns with certainty. We concluded that an investment pays if its *net present value* (calculated by discounting the difference between the return and the cost in each future period) is positive.

How does this rule change if the returns are uncertain? A risk-neutral person chooses to invest if the *expected net present value* is positive. We calculate the expected net present value by discounting the difference between expected return and expected cost in each future period.

Sam is risk neutral. His decision tree, Figure 16.5, shows that his cost of investing is $C = \$25$ this year. Next year, he receives uncertain revenues from the investment of $125 with 80% probability or $50 with 20% probability. Thus, the expected value of the revenues next year is

$$EV = (0.8 \times \$125) + (0.2 \times \$50) = \$110.$$

With a real interest rate of 10%, the expected present value of the revenues is

$$EPV = \$110/1.1 = \$100.$$

Subtracting the $25 cost incurred this year, Sam determines that his expected net present value is $ENPV = \$75$. As a result, he invests.

SOLVED PROBLEM 16.6

MyLab Economics Solved Problem

We have been assuming that nature dictates the probabilities of various possible events. However, sometimes we can alter the probabilities at some expense. Gautam, who is risk neutral, is considering whether to invest in a new store, as the figure shows. After investing, he can increase the probability that demand will be high at the new store by advertising at a cost of $50 (thousand). If he makes the investment but does not advertise, he has a 40% probability of making 100 and a 60% probability of losing 100. Should he invest in the new store?

Answer

1. *Calculate the expected value of the investment and determine if it pays if Gautam does not advertise.* If Gautam makes the investment but does not advertise, the expected value of his investment is

$$[0.4 \times 100] + [0.6 \times (-100)] = -20.$$

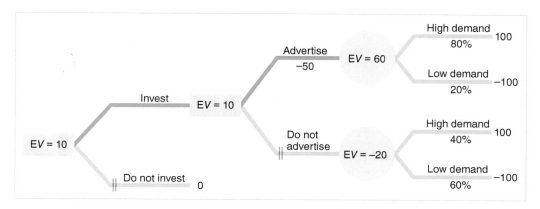

Thus, if he does not advertise, he expects to lose money if he makes this investment.

2. *Calculate the expected value of the investment and determine if it pays given that Gautam advertises.* With advertising, Gautam's expected value before paying for the advertisements is

$$[0.8 \times 100] + [0.2 \times (-100)] = 60.$$

Thus, his expected value after paying for the advertisements is 10 (= 60 − 50). As a result, he is better off investing and advertising than not investing at all or investing without advertising.

16.5 Behavioral Economics and Uncertainty

In the expected utility model, as in the standard utility model, we assume that people make rational choices (Chapter 3). However, many individuals make choices that are inconsistent with the predictions of the expected utility model. Economists and psychologists use behavioral economics to explain some of these departures from the predictions of the expected utility model. Researchers have established that some people have difficulty determining probabilities or making probability calculations. Through experiments, they've shown that how people behave under similar circumstances differs. New theories have been developed to explain behavior that is inconsistent with expected utility theory.

Biased Assessment of Probabilities

People often have mistaken beliefs about the probability that an event will occur. These biases in estimating probabilities come from several sources, including false beliefs about causality and overconfidence.

Gambler's Fallacy. Many—perhaps most—people subscribe to the *gambler's fallacy*:

Common Confusion Past events affect current, independent outcomes.[17]

---

[17]The false belief that one event affects another independent event is captured by the joke about a man who brings a bomb on board a plane whenever he flies because he believes that "The chance of having one bomb on a plane is very small, so the chance of having two bombs on a plane is near zero!"

For example, suppose that you flip a fair coin and it comes up heads six times in a row. What are the odds that you'll get a tail on the next flip? Because past flips do not affect this one, the chance of a tail remains 50%, yet many people believe that a head is much more likely because they're on a "run." Others hold the opposite but equally false view that the chance of a tail is high because a tail is "due."

Suppose that you have an urn with three black balls and two red ones. If you draw a ball without looking, your probability of getting a black ball is $\frac{3}{5} = 60\%$. If you replace the ball and draw again, the chance of a picking a black ball remains the same. However, if you draw a black ball and do not replace it, the probability of drawing a black ball again falls to $\frac{2}{4} = 50\%$. Thus, the belief that a tail is due after several heads are tossed in a row is analogous to falsely believing that you are drawing without replacement when you are actually drawing with replacement.

Overconfidence. Another common explanation for why some people engage in gambles that the rest of us avoid like the plague is that these gamblers are overconfident. For example, Golec and Tamarkin (1995) found that football bettors tend to make low-probability bets because they greatly overestimate their probabilities of winning certain types of exotic football bets (an *exotic bet* depends on the outcome of more than one game). In a survey, gamblers estimated their chance of winning a particular bet at 45% when the objective probability was 20%.

Few groups exhibit more overconfidence than male high school athletes. Many U.S. high school basketball and football players believe they will get an athletic scholarship to attend college, but less than 5% receive one. Only 1% of high school basketball players play in Division I (the top level) of college basketball. Of those, three-quarters believe that it is at least "somewhat" likely that they will play professionally. Only 1.2% are drafted into the National Basketball Association (and not all of them play). Thus, only about 0.01% of high school basketball athletes make it to the pros.[18]

APPLICATION

Biased Estimates

Factor by which Americans are more likely to be killed by a cow than by a shark: 27. — Harper's Index 2015

Do scare stories in newspapers, TV shows, and movies cause people to overestimate relatively rare events and underestimate relatively common ones? Newspapers are more likely to publish "man bites dog" stories than the more common "dog bites man" reports.[19]

If you have seen the movie *Jaws*, you can't help but think about sharks before wading into the ocean. In 2018, news media around the world reported shark attacks along the Florida, New York, Western Australia, Brazil, and Egypt coasts. Do you worry about shark attacks? You really shouldn't.

Only eight people were killed by sharks in U.S. waters in the decade from 2008 through 2017—fewer than one a year. Being killed by a shark is less likely than suffocating in a beanbag chair. The annual number of deaths from potable

---

[18]See Rossi and Armstrong (1989), **www.ncaa.org/about/resources/research/probability-competing-beyond-high-school** (viewed September 7, 2015) and **www.insidehighered.com/news/2015/01/27/college-athletes-greatly-overestimate-their-chances-playing-professionally**.

[19]For example, Indian papers reported on a man bites snake story, noting that Neeranjan Bhaskar has eaten more than 4,000 snakes (*Calcutta Telegraph*, August 1, 2005) and the even stranger "Cobra Dies after Biting Priest of Snake Temple!" (*Express India*, July 11, 2005).

pool drownings is 23, car–deer collisions 211; motorcycles 2,500; firearm homicides 11,000; all homicides 16,000; car crashes 34,000; prostate cancer 40,000; breast cancer 46,000; cancer 500,000; tobacco-related causes 500,000; and heart disease 734,000.

Benjamin, Dougan, and Buschena (2001) reported that, when asked to estimate the frequency of deaths from various causes for the entire population, people overestimate the number of deaths from infrequent causes and underestimate those from more common causes. In contrast, if asked to estimate the number of deaths among their own age group from a variety of causes, their estimates are essentially unbiased. That is not to say that people know the true probabilities—only that their mistakes are not systematic. (However, you should know that, despite the widespread warnings issued every Christmas season, no one has died from a poinsettia.)

Violations of Expected Utility Theory

Over the years, economists and psychologists have shown that some people's choices vary with circumstances, which contradicts expected utility theory. One important class of violations arises because people change their choices in response to inessential changes in how choices are described or *framed*, even when the underlying probabilities and events do not change. Another class of violations arises because of a bias toward certainty.

Framing. A widely held view is that people are generally rational:

Common Confusion People react the same way when given equivalent choices no matter how they are posed.

However, experiments show that many people reverse their preferences when a problem is presented, or *framed*, in different but equivalent ways. Tversky and Kahneman (1981) posed the problem that the United States expects an unusual disease, such as avian flu, to kill 600 people. The government is considering two alternative programs to combat the disease. The "exact scientific estimates" of the consequences of these programs are

- If Program A is adopted, 200 people will be saved.
- If Program B is adopted, 600 people will be saved with a one-third probability and no one will be saved with a two-thirds probability.

When college students were asked to choose, 72% opted for the certain gains of Program A over the riskier, but less likely, gains of Program B.

A second group of students was asked to choose between an alternative pair of programs, and were told

- If Program C is adopted, 400 people will die.
- If Program D is adopted, no one will die with a one-third probability, and 600 people will die with a two-thirds probability.

When faced with this choice, 78% chose the uncertain, but more likely, losses of Program D over the certain losses of Program C. These results are surprising if people maximize their expected utility: Program A is identical to Program C, and Program B is the same as Program D in the sense that these pairs have identical expected outcomes. Thus, expected utility theory predicts consistent choices for the two pairs of programs.

In many similar experiments, researchers have repeatedly observed this pattern, called the *reflection effect*: Attitudes toward risk are reversed (reflected) for gains versus losses. People are often risk averse when making choices involving gains, but they are often risk preferring when making choices involving losses.

Certainty Effect. Many people put excessive weight on outcomes that they consider to be certain relative to risky outcomes. This *certainty effect* (or *Allais effect*, named for the French economist who first noticed it) can be illustrated using an example from Kahneman and Tversky (1979). First, a group of subjects were asked to choose between two options:

- **Option A.** You receive $4,000 with probability 80% and $0 with probability 20%.
- **Option B.** You receive $3,000 with certainty.

The vast majority, 80%, chose the certain outcome, B.
   Then, the subjects were given another set of options:

- **Option C.** You receive $4,000 with probability 20% and $0 with probability 80%.
- **Option D.** You receive $3,000 with probability 25% and $0 with probability 75%.

Now, 65% prefer C.
   Kahneman and Tversky found that more than half the respondents violated expected utility theory by choosing B in the first experiment and C in the second one. If $U(0) = 0$, then choosing B over A implies that the expected utility from B is greater than the expected utility from A, so that $U(3,000) > 0.8U(4,000)$, or $U(3,000)/U(4,000) > 0.8$. Choosing C over D implies that $0.2U(4,000) > 0.25U(3,000)$, or $U(3,000)/U(4,000) < 0.8 (= 0.2/0.25)$. Thus, these choices are inconsistent with each other, and hence inconsistent with expected utility theory.

Expected utility theory is based on gambles with known probabilities, whereas most real-world situations involve unknown or subjective probabilities. Ellsberg (1961) pointed out that expected utility theory cannot account for an ambiguous situation where many people are reluctant to put substantial decision weight on any outcome. He illustrated the problem in a "paradox." You know that one urn has 50 red and 50 black balls. You know that another urn has 100 red and black balls, but you do not know the ratio of red to black balls. Most of us would agree that the known probability of drawing a red from the first urn equals the subjective probability of drawing a red from the second urn. Yet, most people would prefer to bet that a red ball will be drawn from the first urn rather than from the second urn.

Prospect Theory

Kahneman and Tversky's (1979) *prospect theory*, an alternative theory of decision making under uncertainty, can explain some of the choices people make that are inconsistent with expected utility theory. According to *prospect theory*, people are concerned about gains and losses—the changes in wealth—rather than the level of wealth, as in expected utility theory. People start with a reference point and consider lower outcomes as losses and higher ones as gains.

Comparing Expected Utility and Prospect Theories

We can illustrate the differences in the two theories by comparing how people would act under the two theories when facing the same situation. Both Muzhe and Rui have initial wealth W. They may choose a gamble whereby they get A dollars with probability θ or B dollars with probability $1 - \theta$. For example, A might be negative, reflecting a loss, and B might be positive, indicating a gain.

Muzhe wants to maximize his expected utility. If he does not gamble, his utility is $U(W)$. To calculate his expected utility if he gambles, Muzhe uses the probabilities θ and $1 - \theta$ to weight the utilities from the two possible outcomes:

$$EU = \theta U(W + A) + (1 - \theta)U(W + B),$$

where $U(W + A)$ is the utility he gets from his after-gambling wealth if A occurs and $U(W + B)$ is the utility if he receives B. He chooses to gamble if his expected utility from gambling exceeds his certain utility from his initial wealth: $EU > U(W)$.

In contrast, Rui's decisions are consistent with prospect theory. Rui compares the gamble to her current reference point, which is her initial situation where she has W with certainty. The value she places on her reference point is $V(0)$, where 0 indicates that she has neither a gain nor a loss with this certain outcome. The negative value that she places on losing is $V(A)$, and the positive value from winning is $V(B)$.

To determine the value from taking the gamble, Rui does not calculate the expectation using the probabilities θ and $1 - \theta$, as she would with expected utility theory. Rather, she uses *decision weights* $w(\theta)$ and $w(1 - \theta)$, where the w function assigns a weight that differs from the original probability. If people assign disproportionately high weights to rare events (see the Application "Biased Estimates"), the weight $w(\theta)$ exceeds θ for low values of θ and is less for high values of θ.

Properties of Prospect Theory. To resolve various choice mysteries, the prospect theory value function, V, corresponds to an S-shaped curve, as in Figure 16.6. This curve has three properties. First, the curve passes through the reference point at the origin, because gains and losses are determined relative to the initial situation that has neither gain nor loss.

Second, both sections of the curve are concave to the horizontal, outcome axis. Because of this curvature, Rui is less sensitive to a given change in the outcome for large gains or losses than for small ones. For example, she cares more about whether she has a loss of $1 instead of $2 than she does about a loss of $1,001 instead of $1,002.

Third, the curve is asymmetric with respect to gains and losses. People treat gains and losses differently, in contrast to the predictions of expected utility theory. The S-curve in the figure shows that people suffer more from a loss than they benefit from a comparable size gain. That is, the value function reflects *loss aversion*: People dislike making losses more than they like making gains.

Given the subjective weights, valuations based on gains and losses, and the shape of the value curve, prospect theory can resolve some of the behavioral mysteries of choice under uncertainty. Because the S-shaped curve shows that people treat gains and losses differently, it can explain the reflection effect in the disease experiment described earlier in this section, where people make different choices when identical outcomes are stated in terms of lives saved instead of lives lost. It also provides an explanation of why some people engage in unfair lotteries: They put heavier weight on rare events than the true probability used in expected utility theory.

Similarly, we could use a weighting function to resolve the Ellsberg paradox. For example, with the urn containing an unknown ratio of black and red balls, an individual might put 40% on getting a black ball, 40% on getting a red ball, and

Figure 16.6 Prospect Theory Value Function

The prospect theory value function has an S shape. It passes through the reference point at the origin because gains and losses are measured relative to the initial condition. Because both sections of the curve are concave to the outcome axis, decision makers are less sensitive to a given change in the outcome for large gains or losses than for small ones. Because the curve is asymmetric with respect to gains and losses, people treat gains and losses differently. This S-curve shows a bigger impact to a loss than to a comparable size gain, reflecting loss aversion.

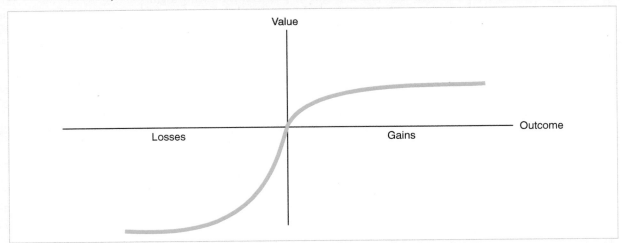

leave 20% to capture an unwillingness to take a gamble when faced with substantial ambiguity. Doing so reduces the expected value of the gamble relative to that of the initial, certain situation in which one does not gamble.

CHALLENGE SOLUTION

BP and Limited Liability

As the Challenge at the beginning of this chapter noted, firms such as BP and Transocean that have deepwater oil rigs may face limited liability for a major spill. Although it is possible that BP and Transocean underestimated the true probabilities of disaster prior to the 2010 spill, a cap on the firms' liability may have also influenced these firms' behavior and led to the disaster. In particular, we now address the three questions raised in the Challenge: How does a cap on liability affect a firm's willingness to make a risky investment or to invest less than the optimal amount in safety? How does a cap affect the amount of risk borne by the firm and by the rest of society? How does a cap affect the amount of insurance that a firm buys?

To illustrate the basic ideas, suppose that an oil rig firm expects to earn $1 billion in the absence of a spill on its new rig and to lose $39 billion if a spill occurs. The probability of a spill is θ. We start by considering whether the firm invests in a new rig (the analysis would be similar if it were deciding to invest in a given safety feature for a rig).

If the firm is risk neutral, then it invests in the new rig only if the expected return is positive, $[(1 - \theta) \times 1] + [\theta \times (-39)] > 0$, or if $\theta < 1/40 = 2.5\%$.[20] If the firm is risk averse, this *threshold probability*—the highest probability at which the firm is willing to invest—is less than 2.5%.

---

[20]The firm compares the expected return to that of the second-best investment opportunity, which we assume is zero for simplicity.

Now suppose that the firm's liability is capped at $19 billion. If the firm is risk neutral, it invests in the new rig if $[(1 - \theta) \times 1] + [\theta \times (-19)] > 0$, or if $\theta < 1/20 = 5\%$. Similarly, if the firm is risk averse, the threshold probability is higher than it would be without the limit on liability.

A limit on liability increases society's total risk if it encourages the drilling company to drill when it would not otherwise do so. If the drilling company is risk neutral, the probability of a spill is $\theta = 3\%$, and the firm bears the full liability for the damages from a spill, then the company's expected earnings are $[0.97 \times 1] + [0.03 \times (-39)] = -0.2 < 0$, so it would not drill. However, if its liability is capped at $19 billion, then its expected gain from drilling is $[0.97 \times 1] + [0.03 \times (-19)] = 0.4 > 0$, so it would drill. Because the firm is more likely to drill because of the liability cap, the cap causes the rest of society's total risk to increase. Moreover, the rest of society bears the risk from the $20 billion ($39 billion − $19 billion) for which it is now responsible if a spill occurs.

If the firm is risk averse, it wants to buy fair insurance to cover its risk. To illustrate the effect of the cap on its decision regarding how much insurance the firm buys, we now assume that the probability of a disaster is $\theta = 1\%$. Without either a liability cap or insurance, the firm's expected gain is $[0.99 \times 1] + [0.01 \times (-39)] = \$0.6$ billion. If an insurance company would provide fair insurance, the drilling firm could buy $100 of insurance for each $1 spent. Given that the drilling company is risk averse, it fully insures, so that if a spill occurs, the insurance company pays $39 billion. To buy this much insurance, the drilling company pays $0.39 billion, so that the expected value of the insurance contract is $-0.39 + [0.01 \times 39] = \$0$. With the insurance, the company earns $[0.99 \times 1] - 0.39 = \$0.6$ billion whether or not a spill occurs.

If the drilling company's liability is capped at $19 billion, it buys $19 billion worth of insurance for $0.19 billion, so that its expected gain in either state of nature is $[0.99 \times 1] + [0.01 \times (-19)] = \$0.8$ billion. Therefore, the drilling company's expected profit increases by $0.2 billion due to the limit on its liability. This amount is a transfer from the rest of society to the firm, because society will be responsible for the extra $20 billion in damages if the spill occurs.

SUMMARY

1. **Assessing Risk.** A probability measures the likelihood that a particular state of nature occurs. People use historical frequencies to calculate probabilities. If they lack frequencies, people may form subjective estimates of a probability using other information. The expected value is the probability-weighted average of the values in each state of nature. One widely used measure of risk is the variance (or the standard deviation, which is the square root of the variance). The variance is the probability-weighted average of the squared difference between the value in each state of nature and the expected value.

2. **Attitudes Toward Risk.** Whether people choose a risky option over a nonrisky one depends on their attitudes toward risk and the expected payoffs of the various options. Most people are *risk averse*. They choose a riskier option only if its expected value is sufficiently higher than that of a less risky option. *Risk-neutral* people choose the option with the highest rate of return because they do not care about risk. *Risk-preferring* people may choose the riskier option even if it has a lower rate of return because they like risk. They will give up some expected return to take on more risk. A utility function reflects a person's attitude toward risk. People pick the option with the highest expected utility. Expected utility is the probability-weighted average of the utility from the outcomes in the various states of nature. The larger an individual's Arrow-Pratt measure of risk aversion, the less likely that person will take a small gamble.

3. Reducing Risk. People reduce their risk in several ways. They can avoid some risks and take actions to lower the probabilities of bad events. They might act to reduce the harm from bad events. Investors make better choices if they have more information. Unless returns to the different investments are perfectly positively correlated, diversification reduces risk. Insurance companies diversify by pooling risks across many individuals.

Insurance is fair if the expected return to the policyholder is zero: The expected payout equals the premium paid. Risk-averse people fully insure if fair insurance is available. Because insurance companies must earn enough income to cover their costs, they offer unfair insurance. Risk-averse people often buy unfair insurance, but they buy less than full insurance. When buying unfair insurance, policyholders exchange the risk of a large loss for the certainty of a smaller loss (paying the premium).

4. Investing Under Uncertainty. Whether an individual invests depends on the uncertainty of the payoff, the expected return, the individual's attitudes toward risk, the interest rate, and the cost of altering the likelihood of a good outcome. An investment pays for risk-neutral people if the expected net present value is positive. Risk-averse people invest only if investing raises their expected utilities. Thus, risk-averse people make risky investments if those investments pay higher rates of return than do safer investments. If an investment takes place over time, a risk-neutral investor invests if the expected net present value is positive. People pay to alter the probabilities of various outcomes from an investment if doing so raises their expected utility.

5. Behavioral Economics and Uncertainty. Some people's actions in uncertain situations are inconsistent with expected utility theory. Their choices may be due to biased estimates of probabilities or different objectives than maximizing expected utility. Prospect theory explains some of these puzzling choices. Under this theory, people may care more about losses than gains and weight outcomes differently than with the probabilities used in expected utility theory.

EXERCISES

All exercises are available on **MyLab Economics;** * *= answer appears at the back of this book;* **M** *= mathematical problem.*

1. Assessing Risk

1.1 In a neighborhood with 1,000 houses, 5 catch fire (but are not damaged by high winds), 7 are damaged by high winds (but do not catch fire), and the rest are unharmed during a one-year period. What is the probability that a fire or high winds damage the house? **M**

*1.2 Asa buys a painting. With a 20% probability, the artist will become famous and the painting will be worth $1,000. With a 10% probability, a fire will destroy the painting so that it becomes worthless. If the painting is not destroyed and the artist does not become famous, it will be worth $500. What is the expected value of the painting? **M**

*1.3 By next year, your stock has a 25% chance of being worth $400 and a 75% probability of being worth $200. What are the expected value and the variance? **M**

1.4 The EZ Construction Company is offered a $20,000 contract to build a new deck for a house. The company's profit if it does not have to sink piers (vertical supports) down to bedrock will be $4,000. However, if it has to sink the piers, it will lose $1,000. The probability it has to put in the piers is 25%. What is the expected value of this contract? Now, EZ learns that it can obtain a seismic study of the property that would specify whether piers have to be sunk before EZ must accept or reject this contract.

By how much would the seismic study increase EZ's expected value? What is the most that it will pay for such a study? (*Hint*: See Solved Problem 16.1.) **M**

1.5 What is the difference—if any—between an individual gambling at a casino and gambling by buying a stock? What is the difference for society?

*1.6 To discourage people from breaking the traffic laws, society can increase the probability that someone exceeding the speed limit will be caught and punished, or it can increase the size of the fine for speeding. Explain why either method can be used to discourage speeding. Which approach is a government likely to prefer, and why?

1.7 Suppose that most people will not speed if the expected fine is at least $500. The actual fine for speeding is $800. How high must the probability of being caught and convicted be to discourage speeding? **M**

1.8 A drug development company develops a new antiviral medication. It applies for a patent and for Federal Drug Administration (FDA) approval to sell it. The firm estimates that the patent application has a 60% chance of success and that FDA approval has a probability of 50%. The firm believes these events are independent. If both applications are successful, the drug can be sold to a major drug producer for $10 million. If FDA approval is obtained but the patent application is unsuccessful, the drug can be sold for $4 million. If the drug is not approved by the FDA, it is worth nothing. What are the expected value and variance of this drug? (Work in units of $1 million.) **M**

2. Attitudes Toward Risk

2.1 Guojun offers to bet Kristin that if a six-sided die comes up with one or two dots showing, he will pay her $3, but if it comes up with any other number of dots, she'll owe him $2. Is that a fair bet for Kristin? **M**

2.2 Jen's utility function with respect to wealth is $U(W) = \sqrt{W}$. Plot her utility function. Use your figure and calculus to show that Jen is risk averse. (*Hint*: You can also use calculus to see if she is risk averse by determining the sign of the second derivative of the utility function.) **M**

*2.3 Jen, in Exercise 2.2, may buy Stock A or Stock B. Stock A has a 50% chance of being worth $100 and 50% of being worth $200. Stock B's value is $50 with a chance of a half or $250 with a probability of 50%. Show that the two stocks have an equal expected value but different variances. Show that Jen prefers Stock A to Stock B because her expected utility is higher with Stock A. **M**

2.4 Suppose that an individual is risk averse and has to choose between $100 with certainty and a risky option with two equally likely outcomes: $100 − x$ and $100 + x$. Use a graph (or math) to show that this person's risk premium is smaller, the smaller x is (the less variable the gamble is).

*2.5 Given the information in Solved Problem 16.2, Irma prefers to buy the stock. Show graphically how high her certain wealth would have to be for her to choose not to buy the stock.

2.6 In Solved Problem 16.3, what is Jen's risk premium if her utility function were $\ln(W)$? **M**

*2.7 Hugo has a concave utility function of $U(W) = W^{0.5}$. His only asset is shares in an internet start-up company. Tomorrow he will learn the stock's value. He believes that it is worth $144 with probability $\frac{2}{3}$ and $225 with probability $\frac{1}{3}$. What is his expected utility? What risk premium would he pay to avoid bearing this risk? (*Hint*: See Solved Problem 16.3.) **M**

2.8 Mary's utility function is $U(W) = W^{0.33}$, where W is wealth. Is she risk averse? Mary has an initial wealth of $27,000. How much of a risk premium would she require to participate in a gamble that has a 50% probability of raising her wealth to $29,791 and a 50% probability of lowering her wealth to $24,389? (*Hint*: See Solved Problem 16.3 and the discussion of the risk premium in Figure 16.2.) **M**

2.9 Would risk-neutral people ever buy insurance that was not fair (that was biased against them)? Explain.

2.10 Lisa just inherited a vineyard from a distant relative. In good years (with no rain or frost during harvest season), she earns $100,000 from the sale of grapes from the vineyard. If the weather is poor, she loses $20,000. Lisa's estimate of the probability of good weather is 60%.

a. Calculate the expected value and the variance of Lisa's income from the vineyard.

b. Lisa is risk averse. Ethan, a grape buyer, offers Lisa a guaranteed payment of $70,000 each year in exchange for her entire harvest. Will Lisa accept this offer? Explain.

c. Why might Ethan make such an offer?

2.11 Joanna is considering three possible jobs. The following table shows the possible incomes she might get in each job.

	Outcome A		Outcome B	
	Probability	Earnings	Probability	Earnings
Job 1	0.5	20	0.5	40
Job 2	0.3	15	0.7	45
Job 3	1	30		

For each job, calculate the expected value, the variance, and the standard deviation. If Joanna is averse to risk (as measured by variance), what can you predict about her job choice? What if she is risk neutral?

2.12 Suppose that Irma's utility function with respect to wealth is $U(W) = 100 + 100W - W^2$. Show that for $W < 10$, Irma's Arrow-Pratt risk-aversion measure increases with her wealth. (*Hint*: See Solved Problem 16.4.) **M**

2.13 Carolyn and Sanjay are neighbors. Each owns a car valued at $10,000. Neither has comprehensive insurance (which covers losses due to theft). Carolyn's wealth, including the value of her car, is $80,000. Sanjay's wealth, including the value of his car, is $20,000. Carolyn and Sanjay have identical utility of wealth functions, $U(W) = W^{0.4}$. Carolyn and Sanjay can park their cars on the street or rent space in a garage. In their neighborhood, a street-parked car has a 50% probability of being stolen during the year. A garage-parked car will not be stolen.

a. What is the largest amount that Carolyn is willing to pay to park her car in a garage? What is the maximum amount that Sanjay is willing to pay?

b. Compare Carolyn's willingness-to-pay to Sanjay's. Why do they differ? Include a comparison of their Arrow-Pratt measures of risk aversion. (*Hint*: See Solved Problem 16.4.) **M**

2.14 Based on the information in the Application "Gambling," provide at least three reasons why many risk-averse people gamble in casinos.

2.15 Do the following utility functions imply risk aversion, risk neutrality, or risk preference?

a. $U(W) = \ln(W)$

b. $U(W) = W^{0.4}$

c. $U(W) = W^2$

d. $U(W) = 2W$ **M**

3. Reducing Risk

3.1 Lori, who is risk averse, has two pieces of jewelry, each worth $1,000. She plans to send them to her sister's firm in Thailand, which will sell them there. She is concerned about the safety of shipping them. She believes that the probability that any box shipped will not reach its destination is θ. Is her expected utility higher if she sends the articles together or in two separate shipments? **M**

3.2 Helen, the owner of Dubrow Labs, worries about the firm being sued for botched results from blood tests. If it isn't sued, the firm expects to earn a profit of 100, but if it is successfully sued, its profit will be 10. Helen believes that the probability of a successful suit is 5%. If fair insurance is available and Helen is risk averse, how much insurance will she buy? **M**

3.3 Jill possesses $160,000 worth of valuables. She faces a 0.2 probability of a burglary, where she would lose jewelry worth $70,000. She can buy an insurance policy for $15,000 that would fully reimburse the $70,000. Her utility function is $U(X) = 4X^{0.5}$.

a. What is the actuarially fair price for the insurance policy?

b. Should she buy this insurance policy?

c. What is the most she is willing to pay for an insurance policy that fully covers her valuables against loss? **M**

3.4 An insurance agent (interviewed in Jonathan Clements, "Dare to Live Dangerously: Passing on Some Insurance Can Pay Off," *Wall Street Journal*, July 23, 2005, D1) states, "On paper, it never makes sense to have a policy with low deductibles or carry collision on an old car." But the agent notes that raising deductibles and dropping collision coverage can be a tough decision for people with a low income or little savings. Collision insurance is the coverage on a policyholder's own car for accidents where another driver is not at fault.

a. Suppose that the loss is $4,000 if an old car is in an accident. During the six-month coverage period, the probability that the insured person is found at fault in an accident is $\frac{1}{36}$. Suppose

that the price of the coverage is $150. Should a wealthy person purchase the coverage? Should a poor person purchase the coverage? Do your answers depend on the policyholder's degree of risk aversion? Does the policyholder's degree of risk aversion depend on his or her wealth?

b. The agent advises wealthy people not to purchase insurance to protect against possible small losses. Why? **M**

3.5 Using information in the Application "Flight Insurance," show how to calculate the price of fair insurance if the probability of being in a crash were as high as the frequency in 2001, 0.00000077? Use a graph to illustrate why a risk-averse person might buy unfair insurance. Show on the graph the risk premium that the person would be willing to pay.

3.6 After Hurricane Katrina in 2005, the government offered subsidies to people whose houses were destroyed. How does the expectation that the government will offer subsidies for future major disasters affect the probability that risk-averse people will buy insurance and the amount they buy? Use a utility function for a risk-averse person to illustrate your answer. (*Hint*: See the Application "Flooded by Insurance Claims" and Solved Problem 16.5.)

4. Investing Under Uncertainty

*4.1 Andy and Kim live together. Andy may invest $10,000 (possibly by taking on an extra job to earn the additional money) in Kim's MBA education this year. This investment will raise the current value of Kim's earnings by $24,000. If they stay together, they will share the benefit from the additional earnings. However, the probability is $\frac{1}{2}$ that they will split up in the future. If they were married and then split, Andy would get half of Kim's additional earnings. If they were living together without any legal ties and they split, then Andy would get nothing. Suppose that Andy is risk neutral. Will Andy invest in Kim's education? Does your answer depend on the couple's legal status? **M**

4.2 Use a decision tree to illustrate how a risk-neutral plaintiff in a lawsuit decides whether to settle a claim or go to trial. The defendants offer $50,000 to settle now. If the plaintiff does not settle, the plaintiff believes that the probability of winning at trial is 60%. If the plaintiff wins, the amount awarded is x. How large can x be before the plaintiff refuses to settle? How does the plaintiff's attitude toward risk affect this decision? **M**

4.3 Use a decision tree to illustrate how a patient with kidney disease would decide whether to have a transplant operation. The patient currently uses a dialysis machine, which lowers her utility. If the operation is successful, her utility will return to its level before the onset of her kidney disease. However, she has a 5% probability of dying if she has the operation. (If it will help, make up utility numbers to illustrate your answer.)

4.4 Robert Green repeatedly and painstakingly applied herbicides to kill weeds that would harm his beet crops in 2007. However, in 2008, he planted beets genetically engineered to withstand Monsanto's Roundup herbicide. Roundup destroys weeds but leaves the crop unharmed, thereby saving a farmer thousands of dollars in tractor fuel and labor (Andrew Pollack, "Round 2 for Biotech Beets," *New York Times*, November 27, 2007). However, this policy is risky. In the past when beet breeders announced they were going to use Roundup-resistant seeds, sugar-using food companies like Hershey and Mars objected, fearing consumer resistance. Now, though, sensing that consumer concerns have subsided, many processors have cleared their growers to plant the Roundup-resistant beets. A Kellogg spokeswoman said her company was willing to use such beets, but Hershey and Mars declined to comment. Thus, a farmer like Mr. Green faces risks by switching to Roundup Ready beets. Use a decision tree to illustrate the analysis that a farmer in this situation needs to do.

4.5 In Solved Problem 16.6, advertising increases the probability of high demand to 80%. What is the minimum probability of high demand resulting from advertising such that Gautam decides to invest and advertise? **M**

4.6 Because a state's governor can substantially influence new laws, uncertainty about the outcome of a gubernatorial election may affect whether firms make new investments. Shelton and Falk (2018) estimate that in a state with average partisan polarization, doubling the electoral uncertainty causes a 2.7% drop in manufacturing firms' investments. Explain a possible reason for this result. Does your explanation require that the firms' managers are risk averse?

4.7 A risk-neutral firm believes that the probability of a harmful cyberattack (see Application "Risk of a Cyberattack") is 25%. It expects to make a profit of $200 million if no attack occurs and $120 million if it is attacked. The firm can spend $5 million to increase its electronic defenses, which reduces the probability of a successful cyberattack to 10%. Use a decision tree similar to Figure 16.4 to assess whether the firm should make this investment.

4.8 R&D investments are a major source of business uncertainty. Do all risk-averse managers fail to invest in R&D? Why or why not?

5. Behavioral Economics and Uncertainty

5.1 Before reading the rest of this exercise, answer the following two questions about your preferences:

a. You are given $5,000 and offered a choice between receiving an extra $2,500 with certainty or flipping a coin and getting $5,000 more if heads or $0 if tails. Which option do you prefer?

b. You are given $10,000 if you will make the following choice: return $2,500 or flip a coin and return $5,000 if heads and $0 if tails. Which option do you prefer?

Most people choose the sure $2,500 in the first case but flip the coin in the second. Explain why this behavior is not consistent. What do you conclude about how people make decisions concerning uncertain events? **M**

5.2 What are the major differences between expected utility theory and prospect theory?

5.3 Draw an individual's utility curve to illustrate that the person is risk averse with respect to a loss but is risk preferring with respect to a gain.

5.4 Evan is risk seeking with respect to gains and risk averse with respect to losses. Louisa is risk seeking with respect to losses and risk averse with respect to gains. Illustrate both utility functions. Which person's attitudes toward risk are consistent with prospect theory?

5.5 Is someone who acts as described in prospect theory always more likely or less likely to take a gamble than someone who acts as described by expected utility theory? Why? What conditions (such as on the weights), if any, allow you to answer this question definitively?

6. Challenge

6.1 Global Gas International offers to subcontract the Halidurton Heavy Construction Corporation to build an oil pipeline from Canada to New Orleans for $500 million. The probability that the oil pipeline will leak, causing environmental damage, is θ. If so, the legal liabilities will be $600 million.

a. If Halidurton is risk neutral and liable for the damages from a leak, what is the θ such that it is indifferent between accepting or rejecting the contract?

b. If Halidurton is risk averse and fair insurance is offered, how much insurance would it buy?

c. If Global Gas International will partially indemnify Halidurton so that the largest damages that Halidurton would have to pay is $200 million, what is the θ that leaves it indifferent about accepting the contract?

d. If partially indemnified, how much fair insurance will Halidurton buy?

17 Property Rights, Externalities, Rivalry, and Exclusion

I shot an arrow in the air and it stuck.

CHALLENGE

Trade and Pollution

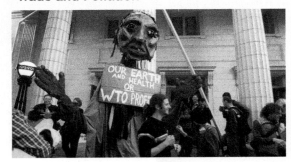

An estimated 3.3 million people a year die from air pollution (Lelieveld et al., 2015). Does free trade cause much of this pollution? That's what protestors in many countries allege. For years, these protesters have disrupted meetings of the World Trade Organization (WTO), which promotes free trade among its 161 member countries. The WTO forbids member countries from passing laws that unreasonably block trade, including environmental policies. The environmental protesters argue that when rich countries with relatively strong pollution laws import from poor countries without controls, world pollution rises. Even a country that cares only about its own welfare wants to know the answer to the question: Does exporting benefit a country if it does not regulate its domestic pollution?

In this chapter, we show that a market failure is likely if no one has a **property right**: ownership that confers exclusive control of a good. By owning this book, you have a property right to read it and to stop others from reading or taking it. But, many goods have incomplete or unclear property rights.

Unclearly defined property rights may cause *externalities*, which occur when someone's consumption or production activities help or harm someone else outside of a market. An externality occurs when a manufacturing plant spews pollution, harming neighboring firms and individuals. When people lack a property right to clean air, factories, drivers, and others pollute the air rather than incur the cost of reducing their pollution.

Indeed, if no one holds a property right for a good or a bad (like pollution), it is unlikely to have a price. If you had a property right to be free from noise pollution, you could use the courts to stop your neighbor from playing loud music. Or, you could sell your right, permitting your neighbor to play the music. If you did not have this property right, no one would be willing to pay you a positive price for it.

Some of the most important bad externalities arise as a by-product of production (such as water pollution from manufacturing) and consumption (such as congestion or air pollution from driving). A competitive market produces more pollution than a market that is optimally regulated by the government, but a monopoly may not create as much of a pollution problem as a competitive market. Clearly defined property rights may reduce externality problems.

Market failures due to externalities also occur if a good lacks exclusion. A good has *exclusion* if its owner has clearly defined property rights and can prevent others from consuming it. You have a legal right to stop anyone from eating your apple. However, a country's national defense cannot protect some citizens without protecting all citizens, so it does not have exclusion.

Market failures may also occur if a good lacks *rivalry*, where only one person can consume it, such as an apple. National defense lacks rivalry because my consumption does not prevent you from consuming it.

We look at three types of markets that lack exclusion or rivalry or both. An *open-access common property* is an unregulated resource, such as an ocean fishery, where *exclusion* of potential users is impossible. A *club good*, such as a swimming pool, is a good or service that allows for exclusion but is *nonrival*: One person's consumption does not use up the good, and others can also consume it (at least until capacity is reached). A *public good*, such as national defense, is both nonexclusive and nonrival. Goods that lack exclusion or rivalry may not have a market or the market undersupplies or oversupplies these goods.

When such market failures arise, government intervention may raise welfare. A government may regulate an externality such as pollution directly, or indirectly control an externality through taxation or laws that make polluters liable for the damage they cause. Similarly, a government may provide a public good.

In this chapter, we examine six main topics

1. **Externalities.** By-products of consumption and production may benefit or harm others.

2. **The Inefficiency of Competition with Externalities.** A competitive market produces too much of a harmful externality.

3. **Regulating Externalities.** Taxation or regulation can prevent overproduction of pollution and other externalities.

4. **Market Structure and Externalities.** With a harmful externality, a noncompetitive market equilibrium may be closer to the socially optimal level than that of a competitive equilibrium.

5. **Allocating Property Rights to Reduce Externalities.** Clearly assigning property rights allows exchanges that reduce or eliminate externality problems.

6. **Rivalry and Exclusion.** If goods lack rivalry or exclusion, competitive markets suffer from a market failure.

17.1 Externalities

Tragedy is when I cut my finger. Comedy is when you walk into an open sewer and die. —Mel Brooks

An **externality** occurs when the action of consumers or firms directly affects another person's well-being or a firm's production capability rather than indirectly through changes in prices. A firm whose production process generates fumes that harm its neighbors is creating an externality for which no market exists. In contrast, the firm is not causing an externality when it harms a rival by selling extra output that lowers the market price.

Externalities may either help or harm others. A *negative externality* harms others. For example, a chemical plant spoils a lake's beauty when it dumps its waste products into the water and in so doing harms a firm that rents boats for use on that waterway. In Sydney, government officials played loud Barry Manilow music to drive away late-night revelers from a suburban park—and in the process drove local residents out of their minds.

A *positive externality* benefits others.[1] By installing attractive shrubs and sculptures around its store, a firm provides a positive externality to its neighbors.

A single action may confer positive externalities on some people and negative externalities on others. For example, some people think that their wind chimes are pleasing to their neighbors, but anyone with an ounce of sense would realize that those chimes are annoying! Similarly, according to one report, the efforts to clean the air in Los Angeles, while enabling people to breathe more easily, caused radiation levels to increase much faster than if the air had remained dirty.

APPLICATION

Disney's Positive Externality

A firm may be able to capture a positive externality that it would otherwise create for another company. Walt Disney made relatively few mistakes. But one that he greatly regretted concerned the positive externalities from his widely successful theme park, Disneyland.

When he built Disneyland in Anaheim, California, in the early 1950s, this little town was surrounded by acres of orange groves. Disney purchased 160 acres of orange groves and built his Magic Kingdom. Eventually, it grew to 300 acres.

Soon after the park opened, it was surrounded by hotels, gift shops, restaurants, and other businesses that benefited from the crowds that Disneyland attracted. Not only was Disney losing that business, but he also worried that the tackiness of the surrounding businesses could harm his theme park.

He vowed that he'd never make that mistake again. Early in the 1960s, he set up dozens of dummy corporations (with names like "M. T. Lott") to buy land southwest of Orlando. The Walt Disney Company acquired 30,000 acres or 47 square miles of land, which is the size of San Francisco, California, and twice as big as Manhattan. Eventually, the company built four theme parks including Walt Disney World, but they occupied only 7,100 acres.

Because Disney owns all the surrounding land, a visitor to Walt Disney World who wants to stay at a hotel, eat at a restaurant, or buy a souvenir now deals directly with Disney, and no one else. That is, Disney captured the potential externality for itself.

17.2   The Inefficiency of Competition with Externalities

Competitive firms and consumers do not have to pay for the harms of their negative externalities, so they create excessive amounts. Similarly, because producers are not compensated for the benefits of a positive externality, too little of these externalities is produced.

To illustrate why externalities lead to nonoptimal production, we examine a competitive market in which paper mills produce paper and by-products of the production process—such as air and water pollution—that harm people who live nearby. We'll call the pollution *gunk*. Each ton of paper produced increases the amount of gunk by one unit. The only way to decrease the volume of gunk is to reduce the amount of paper manufactured. No less-polluting technologies are available, and it is not possible to locate plants where the gunk bothers no one.

---

[1]See the Application "Positive Externality: The Superstar Effect" in MyLab Economics, Chapter 17.

Paper firms do not have to pay for the harm from the pollution they cause. As a result, each firm's **private cost**—the cost of production only, not including externalities—includes its direct costs of labor, energy, and wood pulp but not the indirect costs of the harm from gunk. The true **social cost** is the private cost plus the cost of the harms from externalities.

Supply-and-Demand Analysis

The paper industry is the major industrial source of water pollution. We use a supply-and-demand diagram for the paper market in Figure 17.1 to illustrate that a competitive market produces excessive pollution because each firm's private cost is less than the social cost. In the competitive equilibrium, a firm considers only its private costs when making decisions and ignores the harms of the pollution externality it inflicts on

Figure 17.1 Welfare Effects of Pollution in a Competitive Market

The competitive equilibrium, e_c, is determined by the intersection of the demand curve and the competitive supply or private marginal cost curve, MC^p, which ignores the cost of pollution. The social optimum, e_s, is at the intersection of the demand curve and the social marginal cost curve, $MC^s = MC^p + MC^g$, where MC^g is the marginal cost of the pollution (gunk). Private producer surplus is based on the MC^p curve, and social producer surplus is based on the MC^s curve.

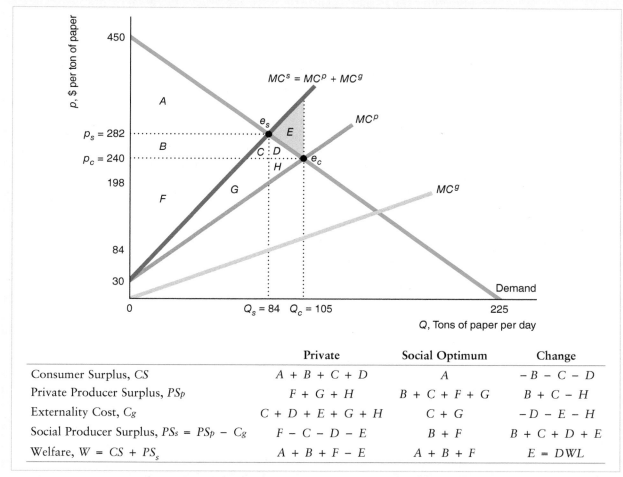

	Private	Social Optimum	Change
Consumer Surplus, CS	$A + B + C + D$	A	$-B - C - D$
Private Producer Surplus, PS_p	$F + G + H$	$B + C + F + G$	$B + C - H$
Externality Cost, C_g	$C + D + E + G + H$	$C + G$	$-D - E - H$
Social Producer Surplus, $PS_s = PS_p - C_g$	$F - C - D - E$	$B + F$	$B + C + D + E$
Welfare, $W = CS + PS_s$	$A + B + F - E$	$A + B + F$	$E = DWL$

others. The market supply curve is the aggregate private marginal cost curve, MC^p, which is the horizontal sum of the private marginal cost curves above their minimum average variable cost of each of the paper manufacturing plants.

The intersection of the market demand curve and the market supply curve for paper determines the competitive equilibrium, e_c. The inverse market demand function in the figure is $p = 450 - 2Q$. The inverse market supply function—the sum of the private marginal cost curves of the individual firms—is $MC^p = 30 + 2Q$. Equating these functions and solving (or looking at the figure), we find that the competitive equilibrium quantity is $Q_c = 105$ tons per day, and the competitive equilibrium price is $p_c = \$240$ per ton.

The firms' *private producer surplus* is the producer surplus of the paper mills based on their *private marginal cost* curve: the area $F + G + H$, which is below the market price and above MC^p up to the competitive equilibrium quantity, 105. The competitive equilibrium maximizes the sum of consumer surplus and private producer surplus (Chapter 9). Without an externality, the sum of consumer surplus and private producer surplus would equal welfare, so competition would maximize welfare.

Because of the pollution externality, however, the competitive equilibrium does *not* maximize welfare. Competitive firms produce too much gunk because they do not have to pay for the harm it causes. This *market failure* (Chapter 9) results from competitive forces that equalize the price and *private marginal cost* rather than *social marginal cost*, which includes both the private costs of production and the externality damage.

Good news. Production's up 13%!

For a given amount of paper production, the full cost of one more ton of paper to society, the *social marginal cost* (MC^s), is the cost to the paper firms of manufacturing one more ton of paper plus the additional externality damage to people in the community from producing this last ton of paper. Thus, the height of the social marginal cost curve, MC^s, at any given quantity equals the vertical sum of the height of the private marginal cost curve, MC^p, plus the height of the marginal externality damages curve, $MC^g = Q$ at that quantity: $MC^s(Q) = MC^p(Q) + MC^g(Q) = (30 + 2Q) + Q = 30 + 3Q$.

The social marginal cost curve intersects the demand curve at the socially optimal quantity, $Q_s = 84$, and price $p_s = 282$. At smaller quantities, the price—the value consumers place on the last unit of the good sold—is higher than the social marginal cost. That is, the gain to consumers of paper exceeds the full cost of producing an extra unit of output, which includes the cost of an extra unit of gunk. At larger quantities, the price is below the social marginal cost, so the gain to consumers is less than the cost of producing an extra unit.

Welfare is the sum of consumer surplus and social producer surplus. The *social producer surplus* is the area below the price and above the *social marginal cost* curve (rather than the *private marginal cost* curve) up to the quantity produced. *Equating the price and social marginal cost maximizes welfare.* At the social optimum, e_s, welfare equals $A + B + F$: the area between the demand curve and the MC^s curve up to the optimal quantity, 84 tons of paper.

Welfare at the competitive equilibrium, e_c, is lower: $A + B + F - E$, the area between the demand curve and the MC^s curve up to 105 tons of paper. The area between these curves from 84 to 105, E, is a deadweight loss because the social cost exceeds the value that consumers place on the last 21 tons of paper. *A deadweight loss results because the competitive market equates price with private marginal cost instead of with social marginal cost.*

Welfare is higher at the social optimum than at the competitive equilibrium because the gain from reducing pollution from the competitive to the socially optimal level more than offsets the loss to consumers and paper producers. The cost of the pollution to people who live near the factories is the area under the MC^g curve between zero and the quantity produced. By construction, this area is the same as the area between the MC^p and the MC^s curves. The total damage from the gunk is $C + D + E + G + H$ at the competitive equilibrium and only $C + G$ at the social optimum. Consequently, the extra pollution damage from producing the competitive output rather than the socially optimal quantity is $D + E + H$.

Paper buyers lose if the market produces at the social optimal level rather than at the competitive output level. Their price per ton of paper increases from \$240 to \$282. Their consumer surplus falls to A from $A + B + C + D$. The corresponding change in private producer surplus is $B + C - H$, which is positive in this figure.

The figure illustrates two main results with respect to negative externalities. First, *a competitive market produces excessive negative externalities.* Because the price of the pollution to the firms is zero, which is less than the marginal cost that the last unit of pollution imposes on society, an unregulated competitive market produces more pollution than is socially optimal. Second, *the optimal amount of pollution is greater than zero.* Even though pollution is harmful and we'd like to have none of it, we cannot wipe it out without eliminating virtually all production and consumption. Making paper, dishwashers, and televisions creates air and water pollution. Agricultural fertilizers pollute the water supply, and people pollute the air by driving by your home.

Cost-Benefit Analysis

We've used a supply-and-demand analysis to show that a competitive market produces excessive pollution because the price of output equals the marginal private cost rather than the marginal social cost. By using a cost-benefit analysis, we obtain another interpretation of the pollution problem in terms of the marginal cost and benefit of pollution.

Let $H = \overline{G} - G$ be the amount that gunk, G, is reduced from the competitive level, $\overline{G}$. Let $B(H)$ be the benefit to society of reducing the units of gunk produced by H, and $C(H)$ be the associated social cost due to the forgone consumption of the good so as to reduce gunk. Society wants to maximize welfare, which is defined as the benefit net of the cost: $W = B(H) - C(H)$. To find the optimal amount of gunk to remove to maximize this measure of welfare, we set the derivative of welfare with respect to H equal to zero:

$$\frac{dW(H)}{dH} = \frac{dB(H)}{dH} - \frac{dC(H)}{dH} = 0.$$

Thus, welfare is maximized when marginal benefit, $dB(H)/dH$, equals marginal cost, $dC(H)/dH$.

In the cost-benefit diagram, panel a of Figure 17.2 (which corresponds to Figure 17.1), the quantity on the horizontal axis starts at the competitive level, 105 tons, and *decreases to the right.* That is, H is zero at the origin of the axis and increases as G diminishes. Thus, a movement to the right indicates a reduction in paper and gunk.

The benefit of reducing output is the reduced damage from gunk. At any given quantity, the height of the benefit curve in panel a is the difference between the pollution harm at that quantity and the harm at the competitive quantity. The cost of reducing

Figure 17.2 Cost-Benefit Analysis of Pollution

(a) The benefit curve reflects the reduction in harm from pollution as the amount of gunk falls from the competitive level. The cost of reducing the amount of gunk is the fall in output, which reduces consumer surplus and private producer surplus. Welfare is maximized at 84 tons of paper and 84 units of gunk, the quantities at which the difference between the benefit and cost curves, the net benefit, is greatest. (b) The net benefit is maximized where the marginal benefit, *MB*, which is the slope of the benefit curve, equals the marginal cost, *MC*, the slope of the cost curve.

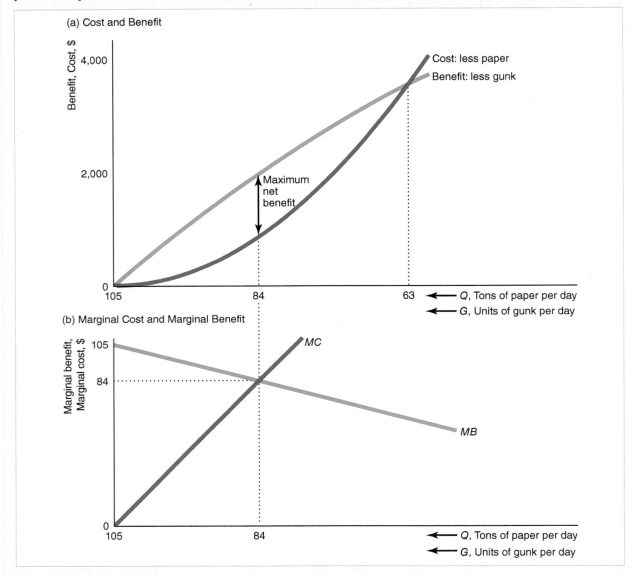

output is the fall in consumer surplus plus private producer surplus. The height of the cost curve at a given quantity is the sum of consumer surplus and private producer surplus at that quantity minus the corresponding value at the competitive quantity.

If society reduced output to 63 tons, the quantity at which the total benefit equals the total cost, society would be no better off than it is in the competitive equilibrium. To maximize welfare, we want to set output at 84 tons, the quantity at which the gap between the total benefit and total cost is greatest. At that quantity, the slope of the benefit curve, the marginal benefit, *MB*, equals the slope of the cost curve, the marginal cost, *MC*, as panel b of the figure shows.[2] Thus, *reducing output and pollution until the marginal benefit from less pollution equals the marginal cost of less output maximizes welfare.*

APPLICATION Spam: A Negative Externality	Spam—unsolicited bulk e-mail messages—inflicts a major negative externality on businesses and individuals around the world by forcing people to waste time removing it, by inducing people to reveal private information unintentionally, and by infecting computers with malicious software. Spammers take advantage of the open-access nature of e-mail. A spammer targets people who might be interested in the information provided in the spam message. This target group is relatively small compared to the vast majority of recipients who do not want the message and who incur the costs of reading and removing it. (Moreover, many spam messages are scams.) In 2018, 14.5 billion spam messages were sent daily, constituting 45% of global e-mail traffic. The worldwide cost of spam is enormous. Firms incur large costs to delete spam by installing spam filters and using employees' labor. A study at a German university found that the working time losses caused by spam were approximately 1,200 minutes or 2.5 days per employee per year (Caliendo et al., 2012). The Radicati research group estimated that the annual cost to business of spam grew almost 13-fold from $20.5 billion in 2012 to $257 billion in 2018. Various estimates of the cost range from $20 billion to $50 billion per year. Yahoo! researchers Rao and Reiley (2012) concluded that society loses $100 for every $1 of profit to a spammer, a rate that is "at least 100 times higher than that of automobile pollution."

17.3 Regulating Externalities

Because competitive markets produce excessive negative externalities, government intervention may increase welfare. In 1952, London suffered from a thick "pea souper" fog—pollution so dense that people had trouble finding their way home—that killed an estimated 4,000 to 12,000 people. Those dark days prompted the British government to pass the first Clean Air Act in 1956. The United States passed a Clean Air Act in 1970.

Now virtually the entire world is concerned about pollution. Burning fossil fuels is the primary source of additional carbon dioxide (CO_2), which is a major contributor to global warming and causes additional damage, such as to marine life. China and the United States are by far the largest producers of CO_2 from industrial production, as Table 17.1 shows. China produces 28% of the world's CO_2, the United States spews out 16%, India is responsible for 6%, and Russia emits nearly 5%. Thus, these four countries are responsible for 55% of the world's CO_2.

Emissions grew very rapidly from 2006 to 2016 in India and China, but decreased in relatively rich countries. The amount of CO_2 per person is extremely high in the United States, Canada, and Russia.

Developing countries spend little on controlling pollution, and many developed countries' public expenditures on pollution regulation have fallen in recent years. In response, various protests have erupted. China and India now face regular pollution protests.

---

[2] The marginal cost curve, *MC*, in Figure 17.2 reflects the social cost of removing the last unit of paper, whereas the social marginal cost curve, MC^s, in Figure 17.1 captures the extra cost to society from providing the last unit of paper, which includes the cost from one more unit of gunk.

Table 17.1 Industrial CO_2 Emissions Production, 2016

	CO_2, Million Metric Tons	Global share of CO_2 (%)	Change 2006 to 2016 (%)	CO_2 Tons per Capita
China	10,151	28.2	56	6.6
United States	5,312	16.0	−12	15.5
India	2,431	6.2	87	1.6
Russian Federation	1,635	4.5	−1	10.2
Japan	1,209	3.7	−6	9.0
Germany	802	2.2	−9	8.9
Canada	563	1.7	−1	15.3
United Kingdom	389	1.1	−31	6.0
France	343	1.0	−17	4.4

Source: www.statista.com/statistics/270499/co2-emissions-in-selected-countries/, www.statista.com/statistics/270508/co2-emissions-per-capita-by-country/, www.statista.com/statistics/271748/the-largest-emitters-of-co2-in-the-world/ (viewed on September 4, 2018).

Politicians around the world disagree about how and whether to control pollution. In 2012 at the United Nations (U.N.) Rio + 20 meeting, 120 heads of state and 50,000 environmentalists, social activists, and business leaders met to encourage sustainable, green growth in poor countries. They argued and accomplished little. The one bright spot is the 2015 Paris Agreement. Each U.N. member country that signed agreed to implement national goals to restrict greenhouse emissions. By the end of 2016, almost the entire U.N. membership had ratified the agreement, including the United States. Russia and Iran were the notable hold-outs. However, President Donald Trump gave formal notice in 2017 that the United States would withdraw from the agreement at the first legal opportunity in 2020.

However, suppose that a government wants to regulate pollution and it has full knowledge about the marginal damage from pollution, the demand curve, the costs, and the production technology. The government could optimally control pollution directly by restricting the amount of pollution that firms produce or by taxing the pollution they create. A limit on the amount of air or water pollution that may be released is a *pollution standard*. A tax on air pollution is an *emissions fee*, and a tax on discharges into the air or waterways is an *effluent charge*.

Frequently, however, a government controls pollution indirectly, through quantity restrictions or taxes on outputs or inputs. Whether the government restricts or taxes outputs or inputs may depend on the nature of the production process. It is generally better to regulate pollution directly than to regulate output, because direct regulation of pollution encourages firms to adopt efficient, new technologies to control pollution (a possibility we ignore in our paper example).

Regulation can effectively reduce pollution. Shapiro and Walker (2015) observe that emissions of the most common air pollutants from U.S. manufacturing fell by 60% between 1990 and 2008 even though U.S. manufacturing output increased substantially. They estimated that at least 75% of the reduction was due to environmental regulation.

Emissions Standard

We can use the paper mill example in Figure 17.1 to illustrate how a government may use an emissions standard to reduce pollution. Here, the government can achieve the social optimum by forcing the paper mills to produce no more than 84 units of paper

per day. (Because, in this example, output and pollution move in lockstep, regulating either reduces pollution in the same way.)

Unfortunately, the government usually does not know enough to regulate optimally. To set quantity restrictions on output optimally, the government must know how the marginal social cost curve, the demand for paper curve, and pollution vary with output. The ease with which the government can monitor output and pollution may determine whether it sets an output restriction or a pollution standard.

Even if the government knows enough to set the optimal regulation, it must enforce this regulation to achieve the desired outcome. The U.S. Environmental Protection Agency (EPA) periodically tightens its ozone standard, which is currently 0.075 parts per million. In 2018, 50 areas were marginally out of compliance with this rule, seven moderately, two seriously, two severely, and two extremely (the Los Angeles–South Coast Air Basin and the San Joaquin Valley, California).[3]

Emissions Fee and Effluent Charge

The government may impose costs on polluters by taxing their output or the amount of pollution produced. (Similarly, a law could make a polluter legally liable for damages.) In our paper mill example, taxing output works as well as taxing the pollution directly because the relationship between output and pollution is fixed. However, if firms can vary the output-pollution relationship by varying inputs or adding pollution-control devices, then the government should tax pollution rather than output.

In our paper mill example, if the government knows the marginal cost of the gunk, MC^g, it can set the output tax equal to this marginal cost curve, $t(Q) = MC^g$, so that the tax varies with output, Q. Figure 17.3 illustrates the manufacturers' after-tax marginal cost, $MC^s = MC^p + t(Q)$.

Figure 17.3 Taxes to Control Pollution

Placing a tax on firms equal to the harm from the gunk, $t(Q) = MC^g$, causes them to internalize the externality, so their private marginal cost is the same as the social marginal cost, MC^s. As a result, the competitive after-tax equilibrium is the same as the social optimum, e_s. Alternatively, applying a specific tax of $t = \$84$ per ton of paper, which is the marginal harm from the gunk at $Q_s = 84$, also results in the social optimum.

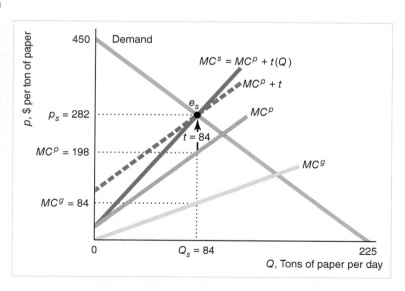

[3]See **www.epa.gov/sites/production/files/2018-04/documents/placeholder_0.pdf** (viewed on August 6, 2018) and **www.epa.gov/green-book** for details on noncompliance with EPA standards, and **scorecard.goodguide.com/** to learn about environmental risks in your area.

The output tax causes a manufacturer to **internalize the externality**: to bear the cost of the harm that it inflicts on others. The after-tax private marginal cost or supply curve is the same as the social marginal cost curve. As a result, the after-tax competitive equilibrium is the social optimum.

Usually, the government sets a specific tax rather than a tax that varies with the amount of pollution, as MC^g does. As Solved Problem 17.1 shows, applying an appropriate specific tax results in the socially optimal level of production.

Presumably because they expect carbon emissions will soon carry a price, in 2017, almost 1,400 companies, such as Microsoft and Shell, reported that they put an internal price on carbon for planning purposes.[4]

SOLVED PROBLEM 17.1	For the market with pollution in Figure 17.1, what constant, specific tax, t, on output could the government set to maximize welfare?
MyLab Economics **Solved Problem**	**Answer** *Set the specific tax equal to the marginal harm of pollution at the socially optimal quantity.* At the socially optimal quantity, $Q_s = 84$, the marginal harm from the gunk is \$84, as Figure 17.3 shows. If the specific tax is $t = \$84$, the after-tax private marginal cost (the after-tax competitive supply curve), $MC_p + t$, equals the social marginal cost at the socially optimal quantity. Consequently, the after-tax competitive supply curve intersects the demand curve at the socially optimal quantity. By paying this specific tax, the firms internalize the cost of the externality at the social optimum. All that is required for optimal production is that the tax equals the marginal cost of pollution at the optimum quantity; the tax need not equal the marginal cost of pollution at other quantities.

APPLICATION **Why Tax Drivers**	Driving causes many externalities including pollution, congestion, and accidents. Taking account of pollution from producing fuel and driving, Hill et al. (2009) estimated that burning one gallon of gasoline (including all downstream effects) causes a carbon dioxide–related climate change cost of 37¢ and a health-related cost of conventional pollutants associated with fine particulate matter of 34¢.

A driver imposes delays on other drivers during congested periods. Parry, Walls, and Harrington (2007) estimated that this cost is \$1.05 per gallon of gas on average across the United States.

Edlin and Karaca-Mandic (2006) measured the accident externality from additional cars by the increase in the cost of insurance. These externalities are big in states with a high concentration of traffic but not in states with low densities. In California, with lots of cars per mile, an extra driver raises the total statewide insurance costs of other drivers by between \$1,725 and \$3,239 per year, and a 1% increase in driving raises insurance costs 3.3% to 5.4%. While the state could build more roads to lower traffic density and hence accidents, it's cheaper to tax the externality.

Vehicles are inefficiently heavy because owners of heavier cars ignore the greater risk of death that they impose on other drivers and pedestrians in accidents

---

[4]www.cdp.net/en/campaigns/commit-to-action/price-on-carbon and www.c2es.org/2017/09/companies-set-their-own-price-on-carbon/ (viewed on September 2, 2018).

(Anderson and Auffhammer, 2014). Raising the weight of a vehicle that hits you by 1,000 pounds increases your chance of dying by 47%. The higher externality risk due to the greater weight of vehicles since 1989 is 26¢ per gallon of gasoline, and the total fatality externality roughly equals a gas tax of between 97¢ and $2.17 per gallon. Taking account of both carbon dioxide emissions and accidents, Sheehan-Connor (2015) estimates that the optimal flat tax is $1.14 per gallon.

Traditionally, governments have relied mainly on gasoline taxes to address driving externalities and to pay for roads. Vehicle taxes and carbon taxes have also been used. However, such taxes have been much lower than the marginal cost of the externalities and have not been adequately sensitive to vehicle weight or the time of day when the vehicle is driven. In California, a tax equal to the marginal externality cost of accidents would raise $66 billion annually—more than the $57 billion raised by all existing state taxes—and over $220 billion nationally.

Gasoline taxes target consumption of gasoline, but gasoline use is not the only problem. Even electric vehicles contribute to congestion and accidents but do not pay a gasoline tax. Some governments have adopted a *vehicle miles traveled tax* (VMT) to either supplement or replace gasoline taxes. Such a tax can be linked to vehicle weight or time of day. As of 2018, Germany, Austria, Slovakia, the Czech Republic, Poland, Hungary, and Switzerland had some form of a VMT. The state of Oregon has a voluntary VMT system in place, and several other U.S. states are considering a similar approach.

Benefits Versus Costs from Controlling Pollution

The Clean Air Act of 1970 and the Clean Air Act Amendments of 1990 cleansed U.S. air. Between 1980 and 2017, the national average of sulfur dioxide (SO_2) plummeted 90%, carbon monoxide (CO) fell 84%, lead dove 99%, nitrogen dioxide (NO_2) tumbled 60%, and ozone dropped 32%.[5]

The EPA believes that the Clean Air Act saves over 160,000 lives a year; avoids more than 100,000 hospital visits; prevents millions of cases of respiratory problems; and saves 13 million lost workdays. The EPA (2011) estimated the costs of complying with the Clean Air Act in 2010 were $53 billion, but the benefits were $1.3 trillion. Thus, benefits outweighed costs by nearly 25 to 1.

Taxes Versus Standards Under Uncertainty

To control pollution, the United States is more likely to use standards and the European Union is more likely to use taxes. Is it better to tax pollution or to set standards? With full information, a government can induce a firm to produce efficiently by setting either a tax or a standard optimally. However, if the government is uncertain about the cost of pollution abatement, which approach is better depends on the shape of the marginal benefit and marginal cost curves for abating pollution (Weitzman, 1974).

Figure 17.4 shows the government's knowledge about the shape and location of the marginal benefit (*MB*) curve of reducing gunk, a pollutant, and the marginal cost (*MC*) of abating it. We assume that the government knows the *MB* curve, which the figure shows, but is uncertain about the *MC* curve. The government believes that it is equally likely that the true marginal cost of abatement curve is MC^1 or MC^2.

To start our analysis, we ask how the government would regulate if it were certain that the *MC* curve equaled the expected marginal cost of abatement curve in

---

[5]According to **www3.epa.gov/airtrends/** (viewed on November 25, 2018).

Figure 17.4 Fees Versus Standards Under Uncertainty

The government knows the marginal benefit curve but is uncertain about the marginal cost curve from abating gunk. If the government uses the expected marginal cost curve to set a fee of $70 or a standard of 100, the deadweight loss from the fee will be smaller than the deadweight loss from the standard regardless of whether the actual marginal cost curve is MC^1 or MC^2.

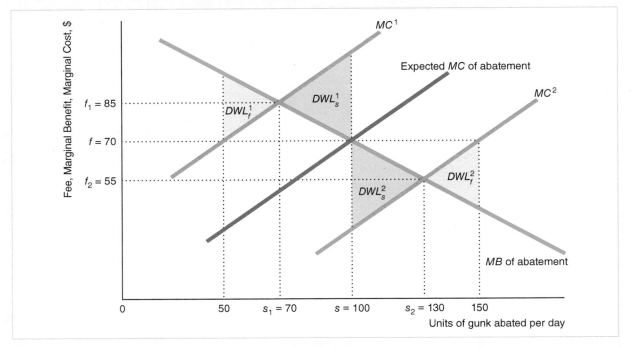

the figure, to set an emissions standard, s, on emissions (gunk) or an emissions fee, f, per unit. The government would set an emissions standard at $s = 100$ units or an emissions fee at $f = \$70$ per unit, both of which are determined by the intersection of the MB and the expected MC curves.

Although either regulation would be optimal in a world of certainty, these regulations are not optimal if the actual marginal cost curve is higher or lower than the expected curve. For example, if the true marginal cost of abatement curve is MC^1, which is higher than the expected marginal cost curve, the optimal standard is $s_1 = 70$ and the optimal fee is $f_1 = \$85$. Thus, if the government uses the expected MC curve, it sets the emissions standard too high and the fee too low. In this example, the deadweight loss from too high an emissions standard, DWL_s^1, is greater than the deadweight loss from too low a fee, DWL_f^1, as the figure illustrates.

If the true marginal cost is less than expected, MC^2, the government has set the standard too low and the fee too high. Again, the deadweight loss from the wrong standard, DWL_s^2 is greater than that from the wrong fee, DWL_f^2. Consequently, in this figure, if the government is uncertain about the marginal cost curve, it should use the fee.

However, if we redraw the figure with a much steeper marginal benefit curve, the deadweight loss from the fee will be greater than that from the standard. Thus, whether it is optimal to use fees or standards depends on the government's degree of uncertainty and the shape of the marginal benefit and marginal cost curves.

17.4 **Market Structure and Externalities**

Two of the main results concerning competitive markets and negative externalities—too much pollution is produced and a tax equal to the marginal social cost of the externality solves the problem—do not hold for other market structures. Although a competitive market always produces too many negative externalities, a noncompetitive market may produce more or less than the optimal level of output and pollution. If a tax is set so that firms internalize the externalities, a competitive market produces the social optimum, whereas a noncompetitive market does not.

Monopoly and Externalities

We use the paper mill example to illustrate these results. In Figure 17.5, the monopoly equilibrium, e_m, is determined by the intersection of the marginal revenue, MR, and private marginal cost, MC^p, curves. Like the competitive firms, the monopoly ignores the harm its pollution causes, so it considers just its direct, private costs in making decisions.

Figure 17.5 Monopoly, Competition, and Social Optimum with Pollution

At the competitive equilibrium, e_c, more is produced than at the social optimum, e_s. As a result, the deadweight loss in the competitive market is D. The monopoly equilibrium, e_m, quantity, 70, is determined by the intersection of the marginal revenue and the private marginal cost, MC^p, curves. The social welfare (based on the marginal social cost, MC^s, curve) under monopoly is $A + B$. Here, the deadweight loss of monopoly, C, is less than the deadweight loss under competition, D.

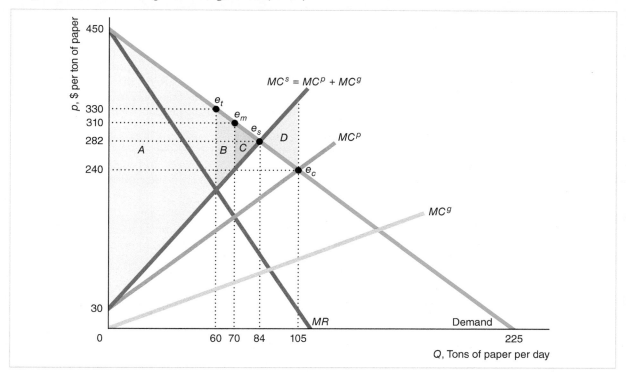

Output is only 70 tons in the monopoly equilibrium, e_m, which is less than the 84 tons at the social optimum, e_s.[6] Thus, this figure illustrates that *the monopoly outcome may be less than the social optimum even with an externality.*

Although the competitive market with an externality always produces more output than the social optimum, a monopoly may produce more than, the same as, or less than the social optimum. The reason that a monopoly may produce too little or too much is that it faces two offsetting effects. The monopoly tends to produce too little output because it sets its price above its marginal cost. However, the monopoly tends to produce too much output because its decisions depend on its private marginal cost instead of the social marginal cost.

Which effect dominates depends on the elasticity of demand for the output and on the extent of the marginal damage the pollution causes. If the demand curve is very elastic, the monopoly markup is small. As a result, the monopoly equilibrium is close to the competitive equilibrium, e_c, and is greater than the social optimum, e_s. If extra pollution causes little additional harm—when MC^g is close to zero at the equilibrium—the social marginal cost essentially equals the private marginal cost, and the monopoly produces less than the social optimum.

Monopoly Versus Competitive Welfare with Externalities

In the absence of externalities, welfare is greater under competition than under an unregulated monopoly (Chapter 11). However, with an externality, welfare may be greater with a monopoly than with competition.[7]

If both monopoly and competitive outputs are greater than the social optimum, welfare must be greater under monopoly because the competitive output is larger than the monopoly output. If the monopoly produces less than the social optimum, we must check which distortion is greater: the monopoly's producing too little or the competitive market's producing too much.

Welfare is lower at the monopoly equilibrium, area $A + B$, than at the social optimum, $A + B + C$, in Figure 17.5. The deadweight loss of monopoly, C, results from the monopoly's producing less output than is socially optimal.

In this figure, the deadweight loss from monopoly, C, is less than the deadweight loss from competition, D, so welfare is greater under monopoly. The monopoly produces only slightly too little output, whereas competition produces excessive output—and hence far too much gunk.

SOLVED PROBLEM 17.2	In Figure 17.5, what is the effect on output, price, and welfare of taxing the monopoly an amount equal to the marginal harm of the externality?
	Answer
MyLab Economics Solved Problem	1. *Show how the monopoly equilibrium shifts if the firm is taxed.* A tax equal to the marginal cost of the pollution causes the monopoly to internalize the externality

---

[6]Given that the inverse demand function is $p = 450 - 2Q$, the monopoly's revenue function is $R = 450Q - 2Q^2$, so its marginal revenue function is $MR = 450 - 4Q$. If the monopoly is unregulated, its equilibrium is found by equating its marginal revenue function and its private marginal cost function, $MC^p = 30 + 2Q$, and solving: $Q_m = 70$ and (using the inverse demand function) $p_m = 310$.

[7]Alabama, Idaho, New Hampshire, North Carolina, Pennsylvania, Utah, Virginia, and Washington use state-owned or county-owned monopolies to sell liquor. By charging high prices, they may reduce the externalities created by alcohol consumption, such as drunk driving (though New Hampshire does not do that).

and to view the social marginal cost as its private cost. The intersection of the marginal revenue, MR, curve and the social marginal cost, MC^s, curve determines the taxed-monopoly equilibrium, e_t. The tax causes the equilibrium quantity to fall from 70 to 60 and the equilibrium price to rise from $310 to $330.

2. *Determine how this shift affects the deadweight loss of monopoly.* The sum of consumer and producer surplus is only A after the tax, compared to $A + B$ before the tax. Thus, welfare falls. Welfare at the social optimum, $A + B + C$, minus A is $B + C$, which is the deadweight loss from the taxed monopoly. The tax exacerbates the monopoly's tendency to produce too little output. The deadweight loss increases from C to $B + C$. The monopoly produced too little before the tax; the taxed monopoly produces even less.

Taxing Externalities in Noncompetitive Markets

Many people argue that the government should tax firms an amount equal to the marginal harm of pollution because such a tax achieves the social optimum in a competitive market. That contention is true in a competitive market, but not necessarily in a noncompetitive market.

> **Unintended Consequence** Taxing firms an amount equal to the marginal harm of pollution may lower welfare in a noncompetitive market.

Solved Problem 17.2 shows an example where such a tax lowers welfare when applied to a monopoly. The tax definitely lowers welfare if the untaxed monopoly produces less than the social optimum. If the untaxed monopoly was originally producing more than the social optimum, a tax may cause welfare to increase.

If the government has enough information to determine the social optimum, it can force either a monopolized or a competitive market to produce the social optimum. If the social optimum is greater than the unregulated monopoly output, however, the government has to subsidize (rather than tax) the monopoly to get it to produce as much output as is desired.

In short, trying to solve a negative externality problem is more complex in a noncompetitive market than it is in a competitive market. To achieve a social optimum in a competitive market, the government only has to reduce the externality, possibly by decreasing output. In a noncompetitive market, the government must eliminate problems arising from both externalities *and* the exercise of market power. Thus, the government needs more information to regulate a noncompetitive market optimally and may require more tools, such as a subsidy. To the degree that the problems arising from market power and pollution are offsetting, however, the failure to regulate a noncompetitive market is less harmful than the failure to regulate a competitive market.

17.5 Allocating Property Rights to Reduce Externalities

Instead of controlling externalities directly through emissions fees and emissions standards, the government may take an indirect approach by assigning a *property right*: an exclusive privilege to use an asset. If no one holds a property right for a good or a bad, the good or bad is unlikely to have a price. If you had a property right that assured you of the right to be free from air pollution, you could go to court to stop a nearby factory from polluting the air. Or you could sell your right, permitting the factory to pollute. If you did not have this property right, no one would be willing to pay you a positive price for it. Because of this lack of a price, a polluter's private marginal cost of production is less than the full social marginal cost.

Coase Theorem

Before Ronald Coase published his classic paper in 1960, economists, like other people, suffered from a

> **Common Confusion** A polluter will necessarily pollute more if the government grants it the right to pollute than if the government grants the victim of pollution the right to be free from pollution.

According to the Coase Theorem (Coase, 1960), a polluter and its victim can achieve the optimal levels of pollution if property rights are clearly defined and they can bargain at low cost. Coase's Theorem is not a practical solution to most pollution problems. Rather, it demonstrates that a lack of clearly defined property rights is the root of the externality problem.

To illustrate the Coase Theorem, we consider two adjacent firms, Alice's Auto Body Shop and Theodore's Tea House. The noise from the auto body shop hurts the tea house's business, as Table 17.2 illustrates. As the auto body shop works on more cars per hour, its profit increases, but the resulting extra noise reduces the tea house's profit. The last column shows the total profit of the two firms. Having the auto body shop work on one car at a time maximizes their joint profit: the socially optimal solution.

No Property Rights. Initially, no one has clearly defined property rights concerning noise. Alice won't negotiate with Theodore. After all, why would she reduce her output and the associated noise, if Theodore has no legal right to be free of noise? Why would Theodore pay Alice to reduce the noise if he harbors the hope that the courts will eventually declare that he has a right to be free from noise pollution? Thus, Alice's shop works on two cars per hour, which maximizes her profit at 400. The resulting excessive pollution drives Theodore out of business, so their joint profit is 400.

Property Right to Be Free of Pollution. Now, suppose that the courts grant Theodore the right to silence. He can force Alice to shut down, so that he makes 400 and their joint profit is 400. However, if Alice works on one car, her gain is 300, while Theodore's loss is 200. They should be able to reach an agreement whereby she pays him between 200 and 300 for the right to work on one car. As a result, they maximize their joint profit at 500.

Why doesn't Alice buy the rights to work on two cars instead of one? Her gain of 100 from working on the second car is less than Theodore's loss of 200, so they cannot reach a deal to let her work on the second car.

Table 17.2 Daily Profits Vary with Production and Noise

Auto Body Shop's Output, Cars per Hour	Profits, $		
	Auto Body Shop	Tea House	Total
0	0	400	400
1	300	200	500
2	400	0	400

Property Right to Pollute. Alternatively, suppose the court says that Alice has the right to make as much noise as she wants. Unless Theodore pays her to reduce the noise, he has to shut down. The gain to Theodore of 200 from Alice working on one rather than two cars is greater than the 100 loss to Alice. They should be able to reach a deal in which Theodore pays Alice between 100 and 200, she works on only one car, and they maximize their joint profit at 500.

Summary. This example illustrates the three key results of the Coase Theorem:

1. Without clearly assigned property rights, one firm pollutes excessively and joint profit is not maximized.
2. Clearly assigning property rights results in the social optimum, maximizing joint profit, regardless of who gets the rights.
3. However, who gets the property rights affects how they split the joint profit. Because the property rights are valuable, the party without property rights pays the party with the property rights.

Problems with the Coase Approach. To achieve the socially optimal outcome, the two sides must bargain successfully with each other. However, the parties may not be able to bargain successfully for at least three important reasons.

First, if transaction costs are very high, it might not pay for the two sides to meet. For example, if a manufacturing plant pollutes the air, thousands or even millions of people may be affected. The cost of getting all of them together to bargain is prohibitive.

Second, if firms engage in strategic bargaining behavior, the firms may not be able to reach an agreement. For instance, if one party says, "Give me everything I want" and will not budge, reaching an agreement may be impossible.

Third, if either side lacks information about the costs or benefits of reducing pollution, the outcome is likely not to be optimal. It is difficult to know how much to offer the other party and to reach an agreement if you do not know how the polluting activity affects the other party.

For these reasons, Coasian bargaining is likely to occur in relatively few situations. Where bargaining cannot occur, the allocation of property rights affects the amount of pollution.

APPLICATION

Buying a Town

When the EPA stated that the James Gavin American Electric Power plant was violating the Clean Air Act by polluting Cheshire, Ohio, the EPA effectively gave the residents the right to be free from pollution. To avoid the higher cost of litigation and installing new equipment and other actions to reduce pollution at its plant, the company bought the town for $20 million, inducing the residents to pack up and leave. As of 2018, only 129 people still live in Cheshire.

Thus, once clear property rights are established, a firm may find it less expensive to purchase those rights from others rather than incur endless litigation and pollution-reduction costs.

Markets for Pollution

If high transaction costs preclude bargaining, society may be able to overcome this problem by using a market, which facilitates exchanges between individuals. Starting in the early 1980s, the U.S. federal government, some state governments, and many governments around the world introduced a cap-and-trade system. Under a *cap-and-trade* system, the government distributes a fixed number of permits that allow firms to produce a specified amount of pollution. These permits not only create a property right to pollute but also limit or cap the total amount of pollution. Firms can trade these permits in a market, often by means of an auction. Firms that do not use all their permits sell them to other firms that want to pollute more—much as sinners bought indulgences in the Middle Ages.

Firms whose products are worth a lot relative to the harm from pollution they create buy rights from firms that make less valuable products. Suppose that the cost in terms of forgone output from eliminating each ton of pollution is $200 at one firm and $300 at another. If the government reduces the permits it gives to each firm so that each must reduce its pollution by 1 ton, the total cost is $500. With tradable permits, the first firm can reduce its pollution by 2 tons and sell one permit to the second firm, so the total social cost is only $400. The trading maximizes the value of the output for a given amount of pollution damage, thus increasing efficiency.

If the government knew enough, it could assign the optimal amount of pollution to each firm, and trading would be unnecessary. By using a market, the government does not have to collect this type of detailed information to achieve efficiency. It only has to decide how much total pollution to allow.

APPLICATION

Acid Rain Program

The purpose of the Acid Rain Program, which was part of the 1990 U.S. Clean Air Act, was to reduce the primary components of acid rain, sulfur dioxide (SO_2) and nitrogen oxides (NO_x). Between 1990 and 2017 by 90%, it reduced the SO_2 by 90% and the NO_x by 60%.

Under the law, the EPA issues SO_2 permits to firms that collectively equal an aggregate emission cap, which the EPA lowers over time. Each permit allows a firm to emit 1 ton of SO_2 annually. The government fines a firm $2,000 per ton on emissions above its allowance. If a company's emissions are less than its allowance, it may sell the extra permits to another firm, thus providing the firm with an incentive to reduce its emissions.

The EPA holds an annual spot auction for permits that firms may use in the current year and an advanced auction for permits effective in seven years. Anyone can purchase allowances. In some years, environmental groups, such as the Acid Rain Retirement Fund, the University of Tampa Environmental Protection Coalition, University of Tampa Environmental Protection Coalition, and Bates College Environmental Economics classes, purchased permits and withheld them from firms to reduce pollution further. (You can see the outcome of the annual auctions at **www.epa.gov/airmarkets/so2-allowance-auctions**.)

According to some estimates, pollution reduction under this market program costs about a quarter to a third less than it would cost if permits were not tradable—a savings on the order of $225 to $375 million per year. Moreover, the EPA calculated the Acid Rain Program's annual benefits in 2010 at approximately $359 billion (in 2016 dollars), at an annual cost of about $8.4 billion, or a 43-to-1 benefit-to-cost ratio.

17.6 Rivalry and Exclusion

Until now, we've focused on *private goods*, which have the properties of rivalry and exclusion. A good is **rival** if only one person can consume the good. If Jane eats an orange, that orange is gone. **Exclusion** means that the owner of a good can prevent others from consuming it. If Jane owns an orange, she can easily prevent others from consuming that orange by, for example, locking it in her home. Thus, an orange is subject to rivalry and exclusion.

If a good lacks rivalry, everyone can consume the same good, such as clean air or national defense. If a market charges a positive price for that good, market failure occurs because the marginal cost of providing the good to one more person is zero.

If the good lacks exclusion, such as clean air, no one can be stopped from consuming it because no one has an exclusive property right to the good. Consequently, a market failure may occur as when people who don't have to pay for the good overexploit it, as when they pollute the air. If the market failure is severe, as it often is for open-access common resources and for public goods, governments may play an important role in provision or control of the good. For example, governments usually pay for streetlights.

We can classify goods by whether they exhibit rivalry and exclusion. Table 17.3 outlines the four possibilities: private good (which has rivalry and exclusion); open-access common property (rivalry, no exclusion); club good (no rivalry, exclusion); and public good (no rivalry, no exclusion).

Open-Access Common Property

An **open-access common property** is an unregulated resource that is nonexclusive but rival, such as an open-access fishery or an aquifer that provides water for municipal or agricultural use. Everyone has free access and an equal right to exploit this resource.

Many fisheries have common access such that anyone can fish and no one has an exclusive property right to a fish until someone catches it. Each fisher wants to land a fish before others do to gain the property right to that fish, which is rival. The lack of clearly defined property rights leads to overfishing. Fishers have an incentive to catch more fish than they would if the fishery were private property.

Suppose instead that each fisher owns a private lake. No externality occurs because each fisher has clearly defined property rights. Each owner is careful not to overfish in any one year to maintain the stock (or number) of fish in the future.

Most ocean fisheries are open-access and no property rights. Like polluting manufacturers, ocean fishers look only at their private costs. In calculating these costs, fishers include the cost of boats, other equipment, a crew, and supplies. They do not include the cost that they impose on future generations by decreasing the stock of fish today, which reduces the number of fish in the sea next year. The fewer fish in the sea, the harder it is to catch any, so reducing the population today raises the cost of catching fish in the future. As a result, fishers do not forgo fishing now to leave fish for the future.

Table 17.3 Rivalry and Exclusion

	Exclusion	No Exclusion
Rivalry	*Private good*: apple, pencil, computer, car	*Open-access common property*: fishery, freeway, park
No Rivalry	*Club good*: cable television, concert, tennis club	*Public good*: national defense, clean air, lighthouse

The social cost of catching a fish is the private cost plus the *externality cost* from reduced current and future populations of fish. Thus, the market failure arising from open-access common property can be viewed as a special type of negative externality.

Other important examples of open-access common property are petroleum, water, and other fluids and gases that are extracted from a *common pool*. Owners of wells drawing from a common pool compete to remove the substance most rapidly, thereby gaining ownership of the good. This competition creates an externality by lowering fluid pressure, which makes further pumping more difficult. Iraq justified its invasion of Kuwait, which led to the Persian Gulf War in 1991, on the grounds that Kuwait was overexploiting common pools of oil underlying both countries.[8]

If many people try to access a single website at one time, congestion may slow traffic to a crawl. In addition, everyone can send e-mail messages freely, even though the messages may impose handling costs on recipients, leading to excessive amounts of unwanted or junk e-mail, a negative externality (as the Application "Spam: A Negative Externality" discusses).

If you own a car, you have a property right to drive that car, but public roads and freeways are common property. But, because you lack an exclusive property right to the highway on which you drive, you cannot exclude others from driving on the highway and must share it with them. Each driver, however, claims a temporary property right in a portion of the highway by occupying it, thereby preventing others from occupying the same space. Competition for space on the highway leads to congestion, a negative externality that slows every driver.

To prevent overuse of a common resource, a government can clearly define property rights, restrict access, or tax users. Many developing countries over the past century have broken up open-access, common agricultural land into smaller private farms with clearly defined property rights. Governments frequently grant access to a resource on a first-come, first-served basis, such as at some popular national parks.

Alternatively, the government can impose a tax or fee to use the resource. Only those people who value the resource most gain access. Governments often charge an entrance fee to a park or a museum. Tolls are common on highways and bridges. By applying a tax or fee equal to the externality harm that each individual imposes on others (such as the value of increased congestion on a highway), the government forces each person to internalize the externality.

APPLICATION

Road Congestion

Roads and freeways belong to all of us. Anyone can drive on them for free. When many people try to use them at the same time, the resulting congestion—a negative externality—harms all drivers. That is, roads are a common resource that are overexploited or congested.

The cost in time, gasoline, and pollution from road congestion is extremely high in most developed nations. A study estimated that congestion cost U.S. drivers nearly $305 billion in 2017, which is an average of $1,445 per driver. Commuters wasted 8 billion hours in traffic, which exceeds the time it would take to drive to Pluto (given the existence of a road and no congestion).

The typical U.S. consumer lost 41 hours to traffic delay. The hours spent in congestion were 102 in Los Angeles (12% of total drive time in congestion), 91 in Moscow (26%) and New York (13%), 86 in Sao Paulo, Brazil (22%), and 79 in San Francisco (12%).

---

[8]Similarly, the State of Alaska proposed leasing land next to the federal Alaska National Wildlife Reserve, which would allow the leasing companies to drill and potentially drain oil from the Reserve, where drilling is prohibited. Phil Taylor, "Alaska Unveils Plan to 'Drain' Federal Crude from ANWR," *E&E News*, June 30, 2011.

Charging to use roads, such as tolls on some bridges and highways, decreases the number of drivers, reducing congestion. For example, people must pay a toll to drive on the Golden Gate Bridge into San Francisco or through the Callahan Tunnel into Boston. London has a congestion charge for cars driving in Central London.

Club Goods

A **club good** is a good that is nonrival but is subject to exclusion, such as swimming clubs or golf clubs. These clubs exclude people who do not pay membership fees, but the services they provide, swimming or golfing, are nonrival. An extra person can swim or golf without reducing the enjoyment of others until congestion occurs as capacity is reached.

However, the most significant club goods do not involve actual clubs. An important example is cable television. A cable television company, such as Comcast, can supply service to additional consumers at almost no additional cost (provided they have the cable in place). The service lacks rivalry, as adding one more viewer does not impair the viewing experience of other viewers (and the marginal cost is nearly zero).[9] However, a cable television company can easily exclude people. Only people who pay for the service receive the signal and can view the channel. As a result, some cable subscribers who are willing to pay to view a channel (but less than the current price) cannot watch it, which is a deadweight loss to society.

Although club goods create a market failure, government intervention is rare because it is difficult for the government to help. As with regulation, an attempt to eliminate deadweight loss by forcing a cable television company to charge a price equal to its zero marginal cost would be self-defeating, as the service would not be produced and even more total surplus would be lost. However, some local governments try (generally ineffectively) to cap the price of cable television. If they could set the price equal to average cost, they would reduce but would not eliminate the deadweight loss.

APPLICATION

Microsoft Word Piracy

One of the most important examples of a good that is not rival but does allow for exclusion is computer software, such as Microsoft Word. Software is nonrival. At almost no extra cost, Microsoft can provide a copy of the software program to another consumer. Because Microsoft charges a (high) positive price, a market failure results in which Microsoft sells too few units.

However, Microsoft has problems enforcing its property right to allow it to exclude nonpayers. Severe *pirating* of its software—the use of software without paying for it—could cause an even greater market failure: Microsoft could stop producing the product altogether. (This problem is severe in the music industry.)

In countries where the cost of excluding nonpaying users is high, computer software is pirated and widely shared, which reduces the profitability of producing and selling software. In its 2018 report, the Business Software Alliance (BSA) estimated that the share of software installed on personal computers globally that was pirated was 37%. They estimated that the share of unlicensed software exceeds 50% in the majority of countries, and ranges from relatively low levels of 15% in the United States, 20% in Germany, and 21% in the United Kingdom, to higher rates in poorer countries: 59% in Mexico, 56% in India, 66% in China, and 89% in Venezuela.

---

[9]Club goods with a zero marginal cost are generally natural monopolies (Chapter 11).

Public Goods

A **public good** is nonrival and nonexclusive. Clean air is a public good. One person's enjoyment of clean air does not stop other people from enjoying clean air as well, so clean air is nonrival. In addition, if we clean up the air, we cannot prevent others who live nearby from benefiting, so clean air is nonexclusive.

A public good is a special type of externality. If a firm reduces the amount of pollution it produces, it provides a nonpriced benefit to its neighbors, which is a positive externality.

Free Riding. Unfortunately, markets undersupply public goods due to a lack of clearly defined property rights. Because people who do not pay for the good cannot be excluded from consuming it, the provider of a public good cannot exercise property rights over the services provided by the public good. This problem is due to **free riding**: benefiting from the actions of others without paying. That is, free riders want to benefit from a positive externality. Consequently, it is very difficult for firms to provide a public good profitably because few people want to pay for the good no matter how valuable it is to them.

We illustrate the free rider problem using an example in which a market underprovides a public good. Two families, Family 1 and Family 2, live at the end of a road outside town. They would both benefit equally from streetlights along their road. They must pay for the lights themselves.

Figure 17.6 shows the demand curves for the two families, D^1 and D^2. Each family's demand curve reflects its willingness to pay for a given number of lights. Family 1's demand curve, D^1, lies below Family 2's demand curve, D^2. For example, to install six streetlights, Family 1 is willing to pay $80 each (point a) and Family 2 is willing to pay $160 each (point b).

The figure also shows the market or social demand curve, D. The market demand curve for a public good differs from that for a private good.

The social marginal benefit of a private good is the same as the marginal benefit to the individual who consumes that good. Thus, the market demand or social marginal

Figure 17.6 Inadequate Provision of a Public Good

Only two families live at the end of a road outside town. They must pay to install streetlights. The social demand curve D is the vertical sum of the families' individual demand curves D^1 and D^2. The supply curve is horizontal at the marginal cost of $240 per streetlight. The social optimum occurs where the social demand curve intersects the supply curve at e_s, where the families pay for six streetlights. If the families act independently, Family 2 buys four streetlights at e_p, where D^2 intersects the supply curve. The supply curve is everywhere above D^1, so Family 1 buys no streetlights and free rides on Family 2's four streetlights. Thus, the families buy too few streetlights if they act independently.

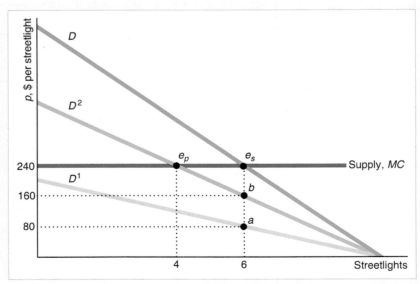

benefit curve for private goods is the *horizontal* sum of the demand curves of each individual (Chapter 2).

In contrast, the social marginal benefit of a public good is the sum of the marginal benefit to each person who consumes the good. Because a public good lacks rivalry, all people can get pleasure from the same unit of output. Consequently, the *social demand curve* or *social willingness-to-pay curve* for a public good is the *vertical* sum of the demand curves of each individual. For example, the social willingness to pay for six streetlights is $240 (point e_s), which is the sum of the amounts each of the two families are willing to pay, $80 + $160.

The competitive supply curve is horizontal at $240 per streetlight, which is the social marginal cost. In the social optimum, e_s, the social marginal cost equals the social willingness to pay. That is, the social optimum, e_s, occurs where the competitive supply curve intersects the social demand curve. In the social optimum, the families buy six streetlights.

However, if the families act independently, they buy only four streetlights at the market equilibrium, e_p. The supply curve intersects D^2 at e_p, where Family 2 buys four streetlights. It is above D^1 everywhere, so Family 1 does not want to buy any streetlights: Family 1 free rides on Family 2's streetlights. Family 1 benefits from the streetlights without paying because the streetlights are a public good. Thus, the competitive market provides fewer streetlights, four, than the socially optimal six.

In more extreme cases, no public good is provided because people who don't pay cannot be stopped from consuming the good. Usually, if the government does not provide a nonexclusive public good, no one provides it.

SOLVED PROBLEM 17.3

MyLab Economics
Solved Problem

The only two stores in a mall decide whether to hire one guard or none—extra guards provide no extra protection. The guard patrolling the mall provides a service without rivalry, simultaneously protecting both stores. A guard costs 20 per hour. The benefit to each store is 16 per hour. The stores play a game in which they act independently. The table shows their payoffs. What is the outcome of this game? What is the social optimum?

Answer

1. *Use a best-response analysis (Chapter 13) to determine the Nash equilibrium to this game.*

   If Store 1 hires a guard, Store 2's payoff is −4 if it hires a guard and 16 if it does not, so its best response is to not hire. The light-green triangle in the lower-left cell shows this choice. Similarly, if Store 1 does not hire a guard, Store 2's payoff is −4 if it hires and 0 if it does not, so its best response is not to hire. Thus, Store 2 has a dominant strategy of not hiring. Using a similar analysis, Store 1 also has a dominant strategy of not hiring (as the dark-green triangles show). The only Nash equilibrium to this game is for neither store to hire.

2. *Calculate the benefits and costs of hiring a guard to determine the social optimum.* The cost of a guard is 20, but the payoff to the two stores combined is 32, so it pays to hire a guard.

Comment: Acting independently, the stores do not achieve the social optimum because each firm tries to free ride. This game is an example of the prisoners' dilemma (Chapter 14).

APPLICATION

Free Riding on Measles Vaccinations

Measles vaccination is a public good. A person who gets a vaccination provides a positive externality to other free-riding people by helping to limit the spread of the disease. Immunizing most of the population against measles reduces the risk of exposure for everyone in the community, including people who refuse vaccinations: The populace has *herd immunity*. That is, a vaccinated person provides a positive externality to others, lowering their probability of getting the disease.

In contrast, when too many people free ride by forgoing vaccination, the entire herd becomes more vulnerable. A person with the disease inflicts a negative externality on others. Measles is so contagious that 90% of people who are exposed become infected. One sick person typically infects 12 to 18 others who lack immunity.

The disease spreads rapidly in areas that lack herd immunity. Before the introduction of the measles vaccine in 1963, measles infected 90% of Americans by the time they were 15. One in every 1,000 children who contracts the disease develops brain damage and two die from complications. The vaccine has prevented an estimated 35 million cases since 1963.

The United States declared measles eliminated in 2000. However, travelers from other countries continue to import the disease. The United States had 667 cases in 2014, 118 cases in 2017, and 124 cases through August, 2018.

The best estimate is that herd immunity requires at least a 92% to 94% vaccination rate. Vaccination of schoolchildren is mandatory in Mississippi, where 99.7% of kindergarten students receive vaccinations, so the state has herd immunity. However, in recent years, several states allowed families to avoid vaccinating their children for religious or other reasons. In large part because some people believe a discredited study that the vaccine causes autism, vaccination rates are low in some of these states. In 2014, seven states and Washington, D.C., had vaccination rates below 90%. After the major outbreak of measles in that year, several states tightened their rules. By the 2016–2017 school year, the national median rate was 94%. However, rates remain below 90% in Alaska, Colorado, Idaho, Indiana, Kansas, and the District of Columbia.

Optimal Provision of a Public Good. To illustrate how to determine the socially optimal level of a public good, we use an example of a society consisting of two people. Individual i's utility, $U_i(G, P_i)$, is a function of a public good, G, and that person's consumption of a private good, P_i. Each has an income, Y_i, which can be used to pay for a unit of either good at a price of $1 per unit. Thus, Individual i buys G_i amount of the public good and $P_i = Y_i - G_i$ of the private good. Thus, $U_i(G, P_i) = U_i(G_1 + G_2, Y_i - G_i)$.

We use the Pareto concept to evaluate society's optimal policy (Chapter 10). Any reallocation that increases one person's utility while holding the other person's utility constant is Pareto superior. Thus, to allocate resources efficiently, society chooses G_1

and G_2 to maximize Person 1's utility while holding Person 2's utility at a given level, $\overline{U}_2$ (or vice versa). The corresponding Lagrangian expression is

$$\mathscr{L} = U_1(G_1 + G_2, Y_1 - G_1) + \lambda[U_2(G_1 + G_2, Y_2 - G_2) - \overline{U}_2], \quad (17.1)$$

where λ is the Lagrangian multiplier. The first-order conditions are

$$\frac{\partial \mathscr{L}}{\partial G_1} = \frac{\partial U_1}{\partial G}\frac{dG}{dG_1} + \frac{\partial U_1}{\partial P_1}\frac{dP_1}{dG_1} + \lambda\frac{\partial U_2}{\partial G}\frac{dG}{dG_1} = \frac{\partial U_1}{\partial G} - \frac{\partial U_1}{\partial P_1} + \lambda\frac{\partial U_2}{\partial G} = 0, \quad (17.2)$$

and

$$\frac{\partial \mathscr{L}}{\partial G_2} = \frac{\partial U_1}{\partial G}\frac{dG}{dG_2} + \lambda\left(\frac{\partial U_2}{\partial G}\frac{dG}{dG_2} + \frac{\partial U_2}{\partial P_2}\frac{dP_2}{dG_2}\right)$$

$$= \frac{\partial U_1}{\partial G} + \lambda\left(\frac{\partial U_2}{\partial G} - \frac{\partial U_2}{\partial P_2}\right) = 0. \quad (17.3)$$

By subtracting Equation 17.3 from Equation 17.2, we learn that $\partial U_1/\partial P_1 = \lambda\partial U_2/\partial P_2$. Dividing Equation 17.2 by $\partial U_1/\partial P_1$ and substituting $\lambda\partial U_2/\partial P_2$ for $\partial U_1/\partial P_1$ in the second term, we find that

$$\frac{\partial U_1/\partial G}{\partial U_1/\partial P_1} + \frac{\partial U_2/\partial G}{\partial U_2/\partial P_2} = 1, \quad (17.4)$$

or

$$MRS_1 + MRS_2 = 1. \quad (17.5)$$

That is, the sum of the marginal rates of substitution of all the members of society equals one.

An individual chooses a bundle of two goods to equate the consumer's marginal rate of substitution between the goods with the marginal rate of transformation in the market (Chapter 3). Here, the marginal rate of transformation between the public good and a private good is one: You can trade one unit of the public good for one unit of the private good. With a public good, instead of equating one person's marginal rate of substitution with the marginal rate of transformation, we equate the sum of the marginal rates of substitution for the two people with the marginal rate of transformation. Because both people suffer if one person contributes less to the public good, society's marginal rate of substitution must reflect how much of the public good all members of society are willing to give up for one more unit of the private good.

For example, suppose that the individuals have Cobb-Douglas utility functions, $U_i(G, P_i) = a_i \ln G + \ln P_i$. The marginal utilities are $\partial U_i/\partial G = a_i/G$ and $\partial U_i/\partial P_i = 1/P_i$. Substituting these expressions into Equation 17.4, we obtain $a_1 P_1/G + a_2 P_2/G = 1$, or

$$G = a_1 P_1 + a_2 P_2. \quad (17.6)$$

We know that the two individuals can each allocate Y_i to the goods, so the total constraint on this society is

$$P_1 + P_2 + G = Y_1 + Y_2. \quad (17.7)$$

We have two equations, Equations 17.6 and 17.7, to determine three values, P_1, P_2, and G.[10] Thus, these equations restrict the optimal set of allocations, but an infinite number of combinations of G, P_1, and P_2 are consistent with these equations, so we do not obtain a unique solution.

_____

[10]Or, substituting Equation 17.6 into Equation 17.7, we have $(1 + a_1)P_1 + (1 + a_2)P_2 = Y_1 + Y_2$, so we have one equation to determine $P_1 + P_2$ (with G determined residually) for given Y_1 and Y_2.

SOLVED PROBLEM 17.4

MyLab Economics Solved Problem

What is the optimal level of the public good if the utility functions are quasilinear, $U_i(G, P_i) = a_i \ln G + P_i$?

Answer

Rewrite the optimality Equation 17.4 using these specific utility functions and solve for G. The marginal utilities are $\partial U_i / \partial G = a_i / G$ and $\partial U_i / \partial P_i = 1$. Thus, Equation 17.4 becomes $a_1 / G + a_2 G = 1$, or

$$G = a_1 + a_2. \tag{17.8}$$

Thus, we have determined a unique G that is optimal if society has adequate resources so that this G does not violate Equation 17.7. That is, $G \le Y_1 + Y_2$.

Reducing Free Riding

Unfortunately, individuals rarely contribute the optimal amounts toward a public good. One solution to the free riding problem is for the government to provide it. Governments provide public defense, roads, and many other public goods.

Alternatively, governmental or other collective actions can reduce free riding. Methods that may be used include social pressure, mergers, privatization, and compulsion.

Social pressure may reduce or eliminate free riding, especially for a small group. Such pressure may cause most firms in a mall to contribute "voluntarily" to hire security guards. The firms may cooperate in a repeated prisoners' dilemma game, especially if the mall has relatively few firms.

A direct way to eliminate free riding by firms is for them to *merge* into a single firm and thereby internalize the positive externality. The sum of the benefit to the individual stores equals the benefit to the merged firm, so it hires guards optimally.

If the independent stores sign a contract that commits them to share the cost of the guards, they achieve the practical advantage from a merger. However, the question remains as to why they would agree to sign the contract, given the prisoners' dilemma problem (Chapter 13).

Privatization—exclusion—eliminates free riding. A good that would be a public good if anyone could use it becomes a private good if access to it is restricted. An example is clean water, which water utilities can monitor and price using individual meters.

Another way to overcome free riding is through *mandates*. Some outside entity such as the government may mandate (dictate) a solution to a free-riding problem. For example, the management of a mall with many firms may require tenants to sign a rental contract committing them to pay fees to hire security guards that are determined through tenants' votes. If the majority votes to hire guards, all must share the cost. Although a firm might be unwilling to pay for the guard service if it has no guarantee that others will also pay, it may vote to assess everyone—including itself—to pay for the service.

APPLICATION

What's Their Beef?

Under U.S. federal law, agricultural producers can force all industry members to contribute to public goods if the majority of firms agrees. Under the Beef Promotion and Research Act, all beef producers must pay a $1-per-head fee on cattle sold in the United States. The $80 million raised by this fee annually finances research, educational programs on mad cow disease, and collective advertising, such as its 2012 "Stay Home. Grill Out" campaign and its 2015, 2016, and 2018 "Beef: It's What's for Dinner" campaign. Supporters of this collective advertising estimate that producers receive $5.67 in additional marginal revenue for every dollar they contribute.

Valuing Public Goods

To ensure the production of a public good, a government usually produces it or compels others to do so. Issues faced by a government when it provides such a public good include whether to provide it at all and, if so, how much of the good to provide. When grappling with these questions, the government needs to know the cost—usually the easy part—and the value of the public good to many individuals—the hard part.

Through surveys or voting results, the government may try to determine the value that consumers place on the public good. A major problem with these methods is that most people do not know how much a public good is worth to them. How much would you pay to maintain the National Archives? How much does reducing air pollution improve your health? How much better do you sleep at night knowing that the Army stands ready to protect you?

Even if people know how much they value a public good, they have an incentive to lie on a survey. Those who value the good highly and want the government to provide it may exaggerate its value. Similarly, people who place a low value on it may report *too low* a value—possibly even a negative one—to discourage government action.

Rather than relying on surveys, a government may ask its citizens to vote on public goods. Suppose the government holds a separate, majority-rule vote on whether to install a traffic signal—a public good—for each of several street corners. If the majority vote for a signal, the government taxes all voters equally to pay for it. An individual votes to install a signal if the value of the signal to that voter is at least as much as the tax that each voter must pay for the signal.

Whether the majority votes for the signal depends on the preferences of the *median voter*: the voter with respect to whom half the populace values the project less and half values the project more. If the median voter wants to install a signal, then at least half the voters agree, so the vote carries. Similarly, if the median voter is against the project, at least half the voters are against it, so the vote fails.

It is *efficient* to install the signal if the value of the signal to society is at least as great as its cost. Does majority voting result in efficiency? The following examples illustrate that efficiency may not occur.

Each signal costs $300 to install. Each of the three voters votes for the signal only if that person values the signal at least $100, which is the tax each person pays if the signal is installed. Table 17.4 shows the value that each voter places on installing a signal at each of three intersections.

For each of the proposed signals, Hayley is the median voter, so her views "determine" the outcome. If Hayley, the median voter, likes the signal, then she and Asa, a majority, vote for it. Otherwise, Nancy and Hayley vote against it. The majority favors installing a signal at corners *A* and *C* and is against doing so at corner *B*. It would be efficient to install the signal at corner *A*, where the social value is $300, and at corner *B*, where the social value is $375, because each value equals or exceeds the cost of $300.

Table 17.4 Voting on $300 Traffic Signals

Signal Location	Value to Each Voter, $			Value to Society, $	Outcome of Vote*
	Nancy	Hayley	Asa		
Corner *A*	50	100	150	300	Yes
Corner *B*	50	75	250	375	No
Corner *C*	50	100	110	260	Yes

*An individual votes to install a signal at a particular corner if and only if that person thinks the signal is worth at least $100, the tax that the individual must pay if the signal is installed.

At corner *A*, the citizens vote for the signal, and that outcome is efficient. The other two votes lead to inefficient outcomes. They vote against a signal at corner *B*, where society values the signal at more than $300. However, they vote for a signal at corner *C*, where society values the signal at less than $300.

The problem with yes-no votes is that they ignore the intensity of preferences. Voters indicate only whether they value the project by more or less than a certain amount. Thus, such majority voting fails to value the public good fully and hence does not guarantee the efficient provision of a public good.[11]

CHALLENGE SOLUTION **Trade and Pollution**	In the Challenge at the beginning of the chapter, we asked whether free trade benefits a country if it does not regulate its domestic pollution. This issue is increasingly important as nations move toward free trade and trade expands. The United States has signed free-trade agreements (FTA) that eliminate or reduce tariffs and quotas and liberalize rules on foreign investment to increase trade with Australia, Bahrain, Canada, Chile, Costa Rica, Dominican Republic, El Salvador, Guatemala, Honduras, Israel, Jordan, Mexico, Morocco, Nicaragua, Oman, Panama, Peru, Singapore, and South Korea (with several additional treaties under negotiation as of 2018). As of April 2018, FTA countries accounted for 47% of U.S. exports and 34% of imports. However, the Trump administration has acted to end several free-trade agreements and impose new tariffs.

Liberalized trade has expanded trade. Trade was 27% of the U.S. gross domestic product (GDP) in 2016, compared to slightly less than 10% in 1965. The GDP share of trade is greater in many other countries: 31% in Japan, 38% in China, 41% in India, 62% in the United Kingdom, 64% in Canada, 78% in Mexico, and 86% in the European Union.

Everyone can gain from free trade if winners compensate losers and if domestic markets are perfectly competitive (not distorted by taxes, tariffs, or pollution). Business and jobs lost in one sector from free trade are more than offset by gains in other sectors. However, if an economy has at least two market distortions, correcting one of them may either increase or decrease welfare.[12] For example, if a country bars trade and has uncontrolled pollution, then allowing free trade without controlling pollution may not increase welfare.

What are the welfare effects of permitting trade if a country's polluting export industry is unregulated? To analyze this question, we couple the trade model from Chapter 9 with the pollution model from this chapter.

Suppose that the country's paper industry is a price taker on the world paper market. The world price is p_w. Panel a of the figure shows the gain to trade in the usual case without pollution or where pollution is optimally regulated by the government. The domestic supply curve, *S*, is upward sloping, but the home country can import as much as it wants at the world price, p_w. In the free-trade

---

[11]Although voting does not reveal how much a public good is worth, Tideman and Tullock (1976) and other economists have devised taxing methods that can sometimes induce people to reveal their true valuations. However, these methods are rarely used.

[12]In the economics literature, this result is referred to as the *Theory of the Second Best*.

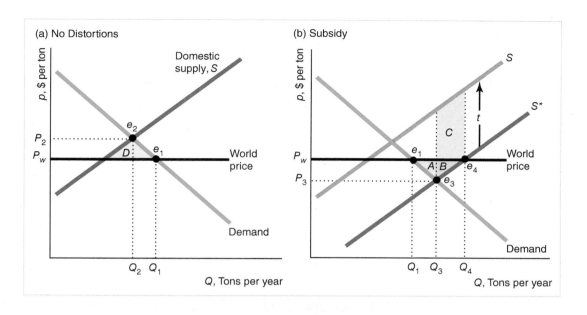

equilibrium, e_1, the equilibrium quantity is Q_1 and the equilibrium price is the world price, p_w. With a ban on imports, the equilibrium is e_2, quantity falls to Q_2, and price rises to p_2. Consequently, the deadweight loss from the ban is area D. (See the discussion of Figure 9.8 for a more thorough analysis.)

In panel b, we include pollution in the analysis. The supply curve S^* is the sum of the firms' private marginal cost curves where the firms do not bear the cost of the pollution (and similar to curve MC^p in Figure 17.1). If the government imposes a specific tax, t, that equals the marginal cost of the pollution per ton of paper, then the firms internalize the cost of pollution, and the resulting supply curve is S (similar to MC^s in Figure 17.1).

If the government does not tax or otherwise regulate pollution, the private supply curve S^* lies below the social supply curve, which results in excess domestic production. If trade is banned, the equilibrium is e_3, with a larger quantity, Q_3, than in the original free-trade equilibrium and a lower consumer price, p_3. Because the true marginal cost (the height of the S curve at Q_3) is above the consumer price, society suffers a deadweight loss.

With free trade, the Theory of the Second Best tells us that welfare does not necessarily rise, because the country still has the pollution distortion. The free-trade equilibrium is e_4. Firms sell all their quantity, Q_4, at the world price, with Q_1 going to domestic consumers and $Q_4 - Q_1$ to consumers elsewhere. The private gain to trade—ignoring the government's cost of providing the subsidy—is area $A + B$. However, the expansion of domestic output increases society's cost due to excess pollution from producing Q_4 rather than Q_3, which is area $B + C$. The height of this area is the distance between the two supply curves, which is the marginal and average costs of the pollution damage (t), and the length is the extra output sold ($Q_4 - Q_3$). Thus, if area C is greater than area A, trade results in a net welfare loss. In this diagram, C is greater than A, so allowing trade lowers welfare if pollution is not taxed.

Should the country prohibit free trade? No, the country should allow free trade and regulate pollution to maximize welfare.

SUMMARY

1. **Externalities.** An externality occurs when a consumer's well-being or a firm's production capabilities are directly affected by the actions of other consumers or firms rather than indirectly affected through changes in prices. An externality that harms others is a negative externality, and one that helps others is a positive externality. Some externalities benefit one group and harm another.

2. **The Inefficiency of Competition with Externalities.** Because producers do not pay for a negative externality such as pollution, the private costs are less than the social costs. Consequently, competitive markets produce more negative externalities than are optimal. If the only way to cut externalities is to decrease output, the optimal solution is to set output where the marginal benefit from reducing the externality equals the marginal cost to consumers and producers from less output. It is usually optimal to have some negative externalities, because eliminating all of them requires eliminating desirable outputs and consumption activities as well. If the government has sufficient information about demand, production cost, and the harm from the externality, it can use taxes or quotas to force the competitive market to produce the social optimum. It may tax or limit the negative externality, or it may tax or limit output.

3. **Regulating Externalities.** Governments may use taxes (emissions fees or effluent charges) or pollution standards to control externalities. If the government has full knowledge, it can set a tax equal to the marginal harm of the externality that causes firms to internalize the externality and produce the socially optimal output. Similarly, the government can set a standard that achieves the social optimum. However, if the government lacks full information, whether it should use a tax or standard depends on a number of factors.

4. **Market Structure and Externalities.** Although a competitive market produces excessive output and negative externalities, a noncompetitive market may produce more or less than the optimal level. With a negative externality, a noncompetitive equilibrium may be closer

than a competitive equilibrium to the social optimum. Although a tax equal to the marginal social harm of a negative externality results in the social optimum when applied to a competitive market, such a fee may lower welfare when applied to a noncompetitive market.

5. **Allocating Property Rights to Reduce Externalities.** Externalities arise because property rights are not clearly defined. According to the Coase Theorem, allocating property rights to either of two parties results in an efficient outcome if the parties can bargain. However, the assignment of the property rights affects income distribution because the rights are valuable. Unfortunately, bargaining is usually not practical, especially when many people are involved. In such cases, using markets for permits to produce externalities may overcome the externality problem.

6. **Rivalry and Exclusion.** Private goods are subject to rivalry—if one person consumes a unit of the good, it cannot be consumed by others—and to exclusion—others can be stopped from consuming the good. Some goods lack one or both of these properties. Open-access common property, such as an ocean fishery, is nonexclusive but is subject to rivalry. This lack of exclusion causes overfishing because users of the fishery do not take into account the costs they impose on others (forgone fish) when they go fishing. A club good is nonrival but exclusive. For example, a swimming club lacks rivalry up to capacity but can exclude nonmembers. A market failure occurs if a positive price is charged for such a good while the club has extra capacity, because the marginal cost of providing the good to one more person is zero, which is less than the price. A public good such as public defense is both nonrival and nonexclusive. The lack of exclusion causes a free rider problem in a market: People use the good without paying for it. Therefore, potential suppliers of such goods are not adequately compensated and underprovide the good. Because private markets tend to underprovide nonprivate goods, governments often produce or subsidize such goods.

EXERCISES

All exercises are available on **MyLab Economics;** * = *answer appears at the back of this book;* **M** = *mathematical problem.*

1. Externalities

1.1 According to a study in the *New England Journal of Medicine*, your friendships or "social networks" are more likely than your genes to make you obese (Jennifer Levitz, "Can Your Friends Make You Fat?" *Wall Street Journal*, July 26, 2007, D1). If it is true

that people who have overweight friends are more likely to be overweight, all else the same, is that an example of a negative externality? Why? (*Hints*: Is this relationship a causal one, or do heavier people choose heavier friends? Also, people with thinner friends may be thinner.)

1.2 According to the digital media company Captivate Network, employees viewing the 2012 Olympics instead of working caused a $1.38 billion loss in productivity for U.S. companies. Is this productivity loss an example of a negative externality? Explain.

1.3 Other sports teams benefit financially from playing a team with a superstar whom fans want to see. Do such positive externalities lower social welfare? If not, why not? If so, what could the teams do to solve that problem?

1.4 Many of the Florida manatees have made a startling discovery: The warm water pouring out of power plants makes an excellent winter refuge. The warm water prevents them from dying from cold stress. As a result, manatees were reclassified from *endangered* to *threatened* in 2016. Do power plants provide an externality? What type?

2. The Inefficiency of Competition with Externalities

2.1 Why isn't zero pollution the best solution for society? Can society have too little pollution? Why or why not?

2.2 In Figure 17.1, explain why area $D + E + H$ is the externality cost difference between the social optimum and the private equilibrium.

2.3 Let $H = \overline{G} - G$ be the amount that gunk, G, is reduced from the competitive level, $\overline{G}$. The benefit of reducing gunk is $B(H) = AH^\alpha$. The cost is $C(H) = H^\beta$. If the benefit is increasing but at a diminishing rate as H increases, and the cost is rising at an increasing rate, what are the possible ranges of values for A, α, and B? **M**

2.4 Applying the model in Exercise 2.3, use calculus to determine the optimal level of H. **M**

2.5 More than four times as many antibiotics are used for promoting growth and preventing disease in animals than for human use (Teillant and Laxminarayan, 2015). The extensive use of antibiotics in livestock contributes to the increase in drug-resistant pathogens in animals that might be transmitted to humans, harming their health. Use graphs to analyze the equilibrium and welfare effects of using growth hormones in livestock.

2.6 In 2009, when the world was worried about the danger of the H1N1 influenza virus (swine flu), Representative Rosa DeLauro and Senator Edward Kennedy proposed the Healthy Families Act in Congress to guarantee paid sick days to all workers. Although the Centers for Disease Control and Prevention urges ill people to stay home from work or school to keep from infecting others, many workers—especially those who do not receive paid sick days—ignore this advice. Evaluate the efficiency and welfare implications of the proposed law, taking account of externalities.

3. Regulating Externalities

3.1 Various countries, including Australia, Ireland, and the United States, require that firms sell more fuel-efficient light bulbs (such as compact fluorescent bulbs) instead of incandescent light bulbs. These restrictions were designed to reduce carbon and global warming. What alternative approaches could be used to achieve the same goals? What are the advantages and disadvantages of a ban relative to the alternatives?

3.2 Markowitz (2012) found that limiting the number of liquor stores reduces crime. To maximize welfare, taking into account the harms associated with alcohol sales, how should a regulatory agency set the number of liquor licenses? Should the profit-maximizing owner of a liquor store lobby for or against tighter restrictions on licenses? (*Hint:* See the Challenge Solution in Chapter 9.)

3.3 Many jurisdictions strictly limit sales of hard liquor (liquor with a significantly higher alcohol content than wine) in an effort to limit the associated negative externalities (de Mello et al., 2013). One approach is to impose a high tax on sales of such products. Another approach is to require sellers to obtain licenses and to limit the number of licenses to the socially desirable number. Often the government sells these licenses to the highest bidder. However, in other jurisdictions, the government sets the price of licenses at a low enough level that extensive excess demand for licenses occurs.

   a. Under what circumstances would auctioning licenses be equivalent to a tax?

   b. Why might regulators or politicians favor underpricing of liquor licenses? (*Hint:* Such licenses often end up in the hands of political donors or of friends and associates of donors.)

3.4 In 1998, the National Highway Traffic Safety Administration distributed the film *Without Helmet Laws, We All Pay the Price*. Two reasons for this title are that some injured motorcyclists are treated at public expense (Medicaid) and that the dependents of those killed in accidents receive public assistance.

   a. Does the purchase of a motorcycle by an individual who does not wear a helmet create a negative externality? Explain.

   b. If so, how should government set a no-helmet tax that would lead to a socially desirable level of motorcycle sales?

*3.5 In the paper mill example in this chapter, what are the optimal emissions fee and the optimal tax on output (assuming that only one fee or tax is applied)?

3.6 In Figure 17.1, could the government use a price ceiling or a price floor to achieve the optimal level of production?

3.7 In Figure 17.3, the government may optimally regulate the paper market by taxing output. Given that the output tax remains constant, what are the welfare implications of a technological change that drives down the private marginal cost of production?

*3.8 Suppose that the inverse demand curve for paper is $p = 200 - Q$, the private marginal cost (unregulated competitive market supply) is $MC^p = 80 + Q$, and the marginal harm from gunk is $MC^g = Q$.

   a. What is the unregulated competitive equilibrium?

   b. What is the social optimum?

   c. What specific tax t (per unit of output of gunk) results in the social optimum? (*Hint*: See Solved Problem 17.1.) **M**

3.9 Connecticut announced that commercial fleet operators would get a tax break if they converted vehicles from ozone-producing gasoline to what the state said were cleaner fuels, such as natural gas and electricity. For every dollar spent on the conversion of their fleets or building alternative fueling stations, operators could deduct 50¢ from their corporate tax. Is this approach likely to be a cost-effective way to control pollution?

3.10 If global warming occurs, output of three of the major U.S. cash crops could decline by as much as 80% according to Roberts and Schlenker (2013). Crop yields increase on days when the temperature rises above 50°, but fall precipitously on days when it is above 86°. Given this relationship between agricultural output and temperature, what would be the government's optimal policy if it can predictably control pollution and hence temperature (and this agricultural effect is the only externality from global warming)? Can you use either a tax or an emissions standard to achieve your optimal policy? How does your policy recommendation change if the government is uncertain about its ability to control pollution or predict the temperature?

*3.11 Suppose that the government knows the marginal cost, *MC*, curve of reducing pollution but is uncertain about the marginal benefit, *MB*, curve. With equal probability, the government faces a relatively high or a relatively low *MB* curve, so its expected *MB* curve is the same as the one in Figure 17.4. Should the government use an emissions fee or an emissions standard to maximize expected welfare? Explain. (*Hint*: Use an analysis similar to that employed in Figure 17.4.)

3.12 Spam imposes significant negative externalities on e-mail users (see the Application "Spam: A Negative Externality"). If the sender had to pay a small fee for each e-mail, would the extent and impact of this negative externality decline? What effect would such a charge have on the net benefits arising from non-spam e-mails? How would the charge affect the proportion of spam in overall e-mail traffic?

3.13 Countries around the world provide consumers with fossil fuel subsidies (Coady et al., 2017). In 2015, the subsidies reached $5.3 trillion (6.5% of global gross domestic product). Davis (2017) estimated that subsidies cause $4 billion in external costs annually. In a figure, show the effect of these subsidies and compare the post-subsidy equilibrium to the pre-subsidy equilibrium and to the social optimum, which accounts for pollution harms.

4. Market Structure and Externalities

4.1 Suppose that the only way to reduce pollution from paper production is to reduce output. The government imposes a tax on the monopoly producer that is equal to the marginal harm from the pollution. Show that the tax may raise welfare. (*Hint*: See Solved Problem 17.2.)

4.2 In the following, use the model in Exercise 3.8.

   a. What is the unregulated monopoly equilibrium?

   b. How could you optimally regulate the monopoly? What is the resulting (socially optimal) equilibrium? (*Hint*: See Solved Problem 17.2.) **M**

5. Allocating Property Rights to Reduce Externalities

5.1 List three specific examples where Coasian bargaining may result in the social optimum.

5.2 Analyze the following statement. Is garbage a positive or a negative externality? Why is a market solution practical here?

Since the turn of the twentieth century, hog farmers in New Jersey fed Philadelphia garbage to their pigs. Philadelphia saved $3 million a year and reduced its garbage mound by allowing New Jersey farmers to pick up leftover food scraps for their porcine recyclers. The city paid $1.9 million to the New Jersey pig farmers for picking up the waste each year, which was about $79 a ton. Otherwise, the city would have had to pay $125 a ton for curbside recycling of the same food waste.

5.3 Austin is going on holiday with his infant daughter and has a first-class air ticket. He values being in first class instead of coach at $300. A CEO has the seat adjacent to him and is considering offering to pay Austin to move to one of the empty seats in coach.

   a. The CEO values quiet at $600. Can Austin and the CEO reach a mutually agreeable price for Austin to move to coach?

b. If instead the CEO values quiet at $200, can Austin and the CEO reach a mutually agreeable price for Austin to move to coach?

c. Assuming efficient bargaining, for what range of the CEO's value of quiet will Austin move to coach?

6. Rivalry and Exclusion

6.1 List three examples of goods that do not fit neatly into the categories in Table 17.3 because they are not strictly rivalrous or exclusive.

6.2 Are heavily used bridges, such as the Bay Bridge, Brooklyn Bridge, and Golden Gate Bridge, commons? If so, what can be done to mitigate externality problems?

6.3 States and cities are increasingly using tolls on express lanes to reduce highway congestion. The tolls increase as traffic builds. However, Los Angeles and Miami have put caps on tolls, which limit the maximum amount of toll they can pay.[13] Show why a toll based on the amount of traffic can increase welfare. Show the effect of a cap on the toll. (*Hint*: The marginal cost is the cost per trip.)

6.4 To prevent overfishing, could one set a tax on fish or on boats? Explain and illustrate with a graph.

6.5 After Hurricane Katrina destroyed much of New Orleans, the Louisiana Road Home rebuilding grant program helped individuals pay for rebuilding their homes. Fu and Gregory (forthcoming) estimated that each additional rebuilt home generated positive externalities of $4,950 to other people who wanted to rebuild their homes but weren't eligible for the grant. Use a supply-and-demand figure to illustrate how the grant affected the market for rebuilding homes.

6.6 You and your roommate have a stack of dirty dishes in the sink. Either of you would wash the dishes if the decision were up to you; however, neither will do it, in the expectation (hope?) that the other will deal with the mess. Explain how this example illustrates the problem of public goods and free riding.

6.7 Do publishers sell the optimal number of intermediate microeconomics textbooks? Discuss in terms of public goods, rivalry, and exclusion.

6.8 A pandemic influenza (akin to the severe 1918 flu epidemic) that kills 2 million or more people could also cause annual income loss of 4% to 5% of global national income (see Fan, Jamison, and Summers, 2016). Using the concepts in this chapter (such as externalities, free riding, and public goods), explain the effects of a pandemic. Is government intervention necessary to help prevent pandemics, or can society rely solely on markets? (*Hint*: See the Application "Free Riding on Measles Vaccinations.")

*6.9 According to the Application "What's Their Beef?" collective generic advertising produces $5.67 in additional marginal revenue for every dollar contributed by producers. Is the industry advertising optimally (see Chapter 12)? Explain.

6.10 Guards patrolling a mall protect the mall's two stores. The electronics store's demand curve for guards is greater at all prices than that of the ice-cream parlor. The marginal cost of a guard is $10 per hour. Use a diagram to show the equilibrium, and compare that to the socially optimal equilibrium. Now suppose that the mall's owner will provide a subsidy of s per-hour-per-guard. Show in your graph the optimal s that leads to the socially optimal outcome for the two stores.

6.11 Two tenants of a mall are protected by the guard service, q. The number of guards per hour demanded by the electronics store is $q_1 = a_1 + b_1 p$, where p is the price of one hour of guard services. The ice-cream parlor's demand is $q_2 = a_2 + b_2 p$. What is the social demand for this service? **M**

6.12 In the analysis of the optimal level of a public good, suppose that each person's utility function is quasi-linear: $U_i(G) + P_i$. Show that the optimal G is unique and independent of P_1 and P_2 if society has adequate resources. (*Hint*: See Solved Problem 17.4.) **M**

6.13 Anna and Bess are assigned to write a joint paper within a 24-hour period about the Pareto optimal provision of public goods. Let A denote the number of hours that Anna contributes to the project and B the number of hours that Bess contributes. The numeric grade that Anna and Bess earn is a function, $23 \ln(A + B)$, of the total number of hours that they contribute to the project. If Anna contributes t_A, then she has $(24 - A)$ hours in the day for leisure. Anna's utility function is $U_A = 23 \ln(A + B) + \ln(24 - A)$; and Bess' utility function is $U_B = 23 \ln(A + B) + \ln(24 - B)$. If they choose the hours to contribute simultaneously and independently, what is the Nash equilibrium number of hours that each will provide? What is the number of hours each should contribute to the project that maximizes the sum of their utilities? **M**

6.14 Patent trolls are firms that buy patents in the hope of bringing patent infringement lawsuits against major firms rather than producing goods themselves. Recently, 53 firms such as Google, Microsoft, Ford Motor Company, JP Morgan Chase, Solar City, and Uber have joined the LOT (License of Transfer)

---

[13]Scott Calvert, "Why Not All Tolls Rise to Nearly $50," *Wall Street Journal*, May 4, 2018.

Network.[14] These companies control about 360,000 patents. If any fall into the hands of a troll, these companies automatically cross-license the patent to all members so that the troll cannot sue them. Ken Seddon, LOT executive director, says that this program is similar to the herd immunity conferred by vaccines. Moreover, the more companies that join, the more attractive it is for additional companies to join. Explain this reasoning. (*Hint*: See the Application "Free Riding on Measles Vaccinations.")

6.15   In Solved Problem 17.3, suppose that the firms will split the cost of a guard if they both vote to hire one. Show the new payoff matrix. Do they hire a guard?

6.16   People who use AirBnb, a home-sharing platform, to rent apartments often leave reviews, which provides a means of tracking the number of times properties are rented. Alyakoob and Rahman (2018) found that if Airbnb activity (reviews per household) increases by 2%, Yelp restaurant reviews in the area arise by 7% and restaurant employment in that neighborhood rises by 3%. This effect demonstrates which economic concepts?

6.17   In 2018, the U.S. Centers for Disease Control and Prevention (CDC) cut 80% of its epidemic prevention activities overseas. The former chief of the CDC says that this decision "would significantly increase the chance an epidemic will spread without our knowledge and endanger lives in our country and around the world."[15] What economic concepts does this story reflect?

7. Challenge

*7.1   Redraw panel b of the Challenge Solution figure to show that it is possible for trade to increase welfare even when pollution is not taxed or otherwise regulated.

*7.2   In the Challenge Solution, if society does not have a pollution problem (as in panel a of the figure), how do we know that winners from trade can compensate losers and still have enough left over to benefit themselves?

---

[14]Carolyn Said, "Tech, Auto Companies Join Forces to Thwart Patent Trolls," *San Francisco Chronicle*, January 28, 2016.
[15]www.cnn.com/2018/02/03/health/cdc-slashes-global-epidemic-programs-outrage/index.html.

Asymmetric Information

18

The buyer needs a hundred eyes, the seller not one. —George Herbert (1651)

In part because of the differing amounts that firms invest in safety, jobs in some firms are more dangerous than in others. Thousands of U.S. workers are killed on the job every year— 5,190 in 2016 or about 14 per day.

Major disasters have occurred in many countries. An apparel factory collapse in Bangladesh killed 1,129 workers in 2013. A warehouse explosion in the port of Tianjin, China, in 2015 killed over 100 workers. In 2017, a power plant explosion in Unchahar, India, killed 38 workers and seriously injured about 100 others. The International Labor Organization estimates that over two million workers die in industrial accidents or due to work-related illnesses every year.

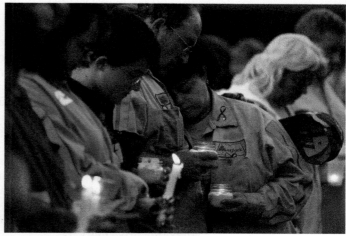

Injury rates vary dramatically by industry. For 2016, the financial services industry, the safest industry, had a rate of only 0.4 fatal injuries per 100,000 workers. Rates are relatively low in health care, 0.7, and education, 1.07 (although students risk dying of boredom). Construction and mining, 10.1, agriculture, 20.9, and truck driving, 25.6, are much more dangerous. The most dangerous industries are fishing, hunting, and trapping, 69.1, and logging, 100.1.[1]

If people are rational and fear danger, they agree to work in a dangerous job only if that job pays a sufficiently higher wage than less-risky alternative jobs. Economists find that workers receive *compensating wage differentials* in industries and occupations that government statistics show are relatively risky.

However, if workers are unaware of the greater risks at certain firms within an industry, they may not receive compensating wage differentials from more dangerous employers within that industry. Workers are likely to have a sense of the risks associated with an industry: Everyone knows that mining is relatively risky—but they do not know which mining companies are particularly risky until a major accident occurs. For example, in the decade before Massey Energy was acquired by Alpha Natural Resources in 2011, 54 coal miners were killed

---

[1]Government statistics also tell us that males have an accident rate, 6.0, that is an order of magnitude greater than that of females, 0.7. Some of this difference is due to different occupations and some to different attitudes toward risk. How many women are injured after saying, "Hey! Watch this!"?

in Massey mines, a much higher rate than at other mines, yet there's no evidence that these workers received higher pay than workers at other mining firms.[2]

One justification often given for government intervention is that firms have more information than workers do about job safety at their plants. Prospective employees often do not know the injury rates at individual firms but may know the *average* injury rate over an entire industry, in part because governments report such data. Does such a situation cause firms to underinvest in safety? Can government intervention overcome such safety problems?

So far, we've examined models in which everyone is equally knowledgeable or equally uninformed: They have *symmetric information*. In the competitive model, everyone knows the relevant facts. In uncertainty models in Chapter 16, the companies that sell insurance and the people who buy it may be equally uncertain about future events. In contrast, in this chapter's models, people have **asymmetric information**: One party to a transaction has relevant information that another party lacks. For example, the seller knows the quality of a product and the buyer does not.

Two important types of asymmetric information are *hidden characteristics* and *hidden actions*. A **hidden characteristic** is an attribute of a person or thing that is known to one party but unknown to others. For example, the owner of a property may possess extensive information about the mineral composition of the land that is unknown to a mining company that is considering buying the land.

A **hidden action** is an act by one party to a transaction that is unknown by the other parties. An example is a firm's manager using a company jet for personal use without the owners' knowledge.

When both parties to a transaction have equal information or equally limited information, neither has an advantage over the other. However, asymmetric information leads to **opportunistic behavior**, where one party takes economic advantage of another when circumstances permit. Such *opportunistic behavior* due to asymmetric information leads to market failures, and destroys many desirable properties of competitive markets.

Two problems of opportunistic behavior arise from asymmetric information. One—*adverse selection*—is due to hidden characteristics, while the other—*moral hazard*—is associated with hidden actions. The problem of **adverse selection** arises when one party to a transaction possesses information about a hidden characteristic that is unknown to other parties and takes economic advantage of this information. For example, if a roadside vendor sells a box of oranges to a passing motorist and only the vendor knows that the oranges are of low quality, the vendor may allege that the oranges are of high quality and charge a premium price for them. That is, the seller seeks to benefit from an informational asymmetry due to a hidden characteristic, the quality of the oranges. If potential buyers worry about such opportunistic behavior, they may be willing to pay only low prices or may forgo purchasing the oranges entirely.

The primary problem arising from hidden action is **moral hazard**, which occurs when an informed party takes an action that the other party cannot observe and

---

[2] The U.S. Mine Safety and Health Administration issued Massey 124 safety-related citations in 2010 prior to the April 2010 accident at Massey's Upper Big Branch mine in West Virginia that killed 29 workers. Massey had 515 violations in 2009. Mine Safety and Health Administration safety officials concluded in 2011 that the 2010 explosion that took 29 lives could have been prevented by Massey. The former head of security at the mine was prosecuted and convicted of two felonies and ultimately sentenced to 36 months in prison.

that harms the less-informed party. If you pay a mechanic by the hour to fix your car, and you do not actually watch the repairs, then the time spent by the mechanic on your car is a hidden action. Moral hazard occurs if the mechanic bills you for excessive hours.

This chapter focuses on adverse selection and unobserved characteristics. Adverse selection often leads to markets in which some desirable transactions do not take place or even the market as a whole cannot exist. We also discuss methods that sometimes solve adverse selection problems. Chapter 19 concentrates on moral hazard problems due to unobserved actions and on the use of contracts to deal with them.

In this chapter, we examine five main topics	1. **Adverse Selection.** Adverse selection may prevent desirable transactions from occurring, possibly eliminating a market.
	2. **Reducing Adverse Selection.** Government regulations, contracts between involved parties, and means of equalizing information may reduce or eliminate the harms from adverse selection.
	3. **Price Discrimination Due to False Beliefs About Quality.** If some consumers incorrectly think that quality varies across identical products, a firm may price discriminate.
	4. **Market Power from Price Ignorance.** Firms gain market power from consumers' ignorance about the price that each firm charges.
	5. **Problems Arising from Ignorance When Hiring.** Attempts to eliminate information asymmetries in hiring may raise or lower social welfare.

18.1 Adverse Selection

One of the most important problems associated with adverse selection is that consumers may not make purchases to avoid being exploited by better-informed sellers. As a result, not all desirable transactions occur, and potential consumer and producer surplus is lost. Indeed, in the extreme case, adverse selection may prevent a market from operating at all. We illustrate this idea using two important examples of adverse selection problems: insurance and products of unknown quality.

Insurance Markets

Hidden characteristics and adverse selection are very important in the insurance industry. Were a health insurance company to provide fair insurance by charging everyone a rate for insurance equal to the average cost of health care for the entire population, the company would lose money due to adverse selection. Many unhealthy people—people who expect to incur health care costs that are higher than average—would view this insurance as a good deal and would buy it. In contrast, unless they were very risk averse, healthy people would not buy it because the premiums exceed their expected health care costs. Given that a disproportionately large share of unhealthy people would buy the insurance, the market for health insurance would exhibit adverse selection, and the insurance company's average cost of medical care for covered people would exceed the population's average.

Adverse selection results in an inefficient market outcome because the sum of producer and consumer surplus is not maximized. The loss of potential surplus occurs because some potentially beneficial sales of insurance to relatively healthy individuals do not occur. These consumers are willing to buy insurance at a lower rate that is closer to the fair rate for them given their superior health. The insurance company is willing to offer such low rates only if it is sure that these individuals are healthy.

Products of Unknown Quality

Anagram for General Motors: or great lemons.

Adverse selection often arises because sellers of a product have better information about the product's quality—a hidden characteristic—than do buyers. Used cars that appear to be identical on the outside often differ substantially in the number of repairs they will need. Some cars—*lemons*—are cursed. They have a variety of insidious problems that become apparent to the owner only after driving the car for a while. Thus, the owner knows from experience if a used car is a lemon, but a potential buyer does not.

If buyers have the same information as sellers, no adverse selection problem arises. However, when sellers have more information than buyers, adverse selection is likely to occur. In this case, many people believe that

> **Common Confusion** If consumers know that some goods are low quality and others are high quality, but not which is which, all the goods will sell for the average price of the two types of goods.

As intuitively appealing as this belief is, it is generally untrue.

If consumers don't know the quality before they buy a good, the presence of low-quality goods in the market may drive high-quality products out of the market (Akerlof, 1970). Why? Used-car buyers worry that a used car might be a lemon. As a result, they will not pay as high a price as they would if they knew the car was of good quality. They will only buy if the price is low enough to reflect the possibility of getting a lemon. Given that sellers of excellent used cars do not want to sell their cars for that low a price, they do not enter the market. Adverse selection has driven the high-quality cars out of the market, leaving only the lemons.

In the following example, we assume that sellers cannot alter the quality of their used cars and that the number of potential used-car buyers is large. All potential buyers are willing to pay $4,000 for a lemon and $8,000 for a good used car: The demand curve for lemons, D^L, is horizontal at $4,000 in panel a of Figure 18.1, and the demand curve for good cars, D^G, is horizontal at $8,000 in panel b.

Although the number of potential buyers is virtually unlimited, only 1,000 owners of lemons and 1,000 owners of good cars are willing to sell. The *reservation price* of lemon owners—the lowest price at which they will sell their cars—is $3,000. Consequently, the supply curve for lemons, S^L in panel a, is horizontal at $3,000 up to 1,000 cars, where it becomes vertical (no more cars are for sale at any price). The reservation price of owners of high-quality used cars is v, which is less than $8,000. Panel b shows two possible values of v. If $v = $5,000$, the supply curve for good cars, S^1, is horizontal at $5,000 up to 1,000 cars and then becomes vertical. If $v = $7,000$, the supply curve is S^2.

Market Equilibrium with Symmetric Information. If sellers and buyers know the quality of all the used cars before any sales take place (they have full, symmetric

Figure 18.1 Markets for Lemons and Good Cars

If everyone has full information, the equilibrium in the lemons market is e (1,000 cars sold for $4,000 each), and the equilibrium in the good-car market is E (1,000 cars sold for $8,000 each). If buyers can't tell quality before buying but assume that equal numbers of the two types of cars are for sale, their demand in both markets is D^*, which is horizontal at $6,000. If the good-car owners' reservation price is $5,000, the supply curve for good cars is S^1, and 1,000 good cars (point F) and 1,000 lemons (point f) sell for $6,000 each. If their reservation price is $7,000, the supply curve is S^2. No good cars are sold; 1,000 lemons sell for $4,000 each (point e).

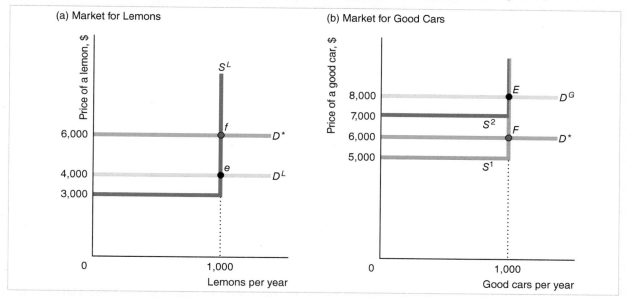

information), all 2,000 cars are sold, and the good cars sell for more than the lemons. In panel a of Figure 18.1, the intersection of the lemons demand curve D^L and the lemons supply curve S^L determines the equilibrium at e in the lemons market, where 1,000 lemons sell for $4,000 each. Regardless of whether the supply curve for good cars is S^1 or S^2 in panel b, the equilibrium in the good-car market is E, where 1,000 good cars sell for $8,000 each.

This market is efficient because the goods go to the people who value them the most. All current owners, who value the cars less than the potential buyers, sell their cars.

More generally, all buyers and sellers may have symmetric information by being equally informed or equally uninformed. *All the cars are sold if everyone has the same information.* It does not matter whether they all have full information or all lack information—it's the equality of information that matters. However, *the amount of information they have affects the price at which the cars sell*. With full information, good cars sell for $8,000 and lemons sell for $4,000.

If information is symmetric because buyers and sellers are equally uninformed (neither group knows if a car is good or a lemon), all cars sell for the same price. A buyer has an equal chance of buying a lemon or a good car. The expected value of a used car is

$$(\tfrac{1}{2} \times \$4,000) + (\tfrac{1}{2} \times \$8,000) = \$6,000.$$

Suppose buyers and sellers are risk neutral (Chapter 16). Buyers are willing to pay $6,000 for a car of unknown quality. Because sellers cannot distinguish between the cars either, sellers accept this amount and sell all the cars.[3] Thus, this market is efficient because the cars go to people who value them more than their original owners.

If only lemons were sold, they would sell for $4,000. The presence of good-quality cars raises the price received by sellers of lemons to $6,000. Similarly, if only good cars were sold, they would sell for $8,000. The presence of lemons lowers the price that sellers of good cars receive to $6,000. Thus, *sellers of good-quality cars are effectively subsidizing sellers of lemons.*

Market Equilibrium with Asymmetric Information. If sellers know the quality but buyers do not, the market may be inefficient: Possibly, owners sell none of the better-quality cars even though buyers value good cars more than the owners do. The equilibrium in this market depends on whether the value that the owners of good cars place on their cars, v, is greater or less than the expected value of buyers, $6,000. The two possible equilibria are: (1) All cars sell at the average price, or (2) only lemons sell at a price equal to the value that buyers place on lemons.

Initially, let's assume that the sellers of good cars value their cars at $v = \$5,000$, which is less than the buyers' expected value of the cars, $6,000, so transactions can occur. The equilibrium in the good-car market is determined by the intersection of S^1 and D^* at point F, where 1,000 good cars sell for $6,000. Similarly, owners of lemons, who value their cars at only $3,000, are very happy to sell them for $6,000. The new equilibrium in the lemons market is f.

Thus, all cars sell at the same price. Consequently, here *asymmetric information does not cause an efficiency problem, but it does have equity implications.* Sellers of lemons benefit and sellers of good cars suffer from consumers' inability to distinguish quality. Consumers who buy the good cars get a bargain, and buyers of lemons are left with a sour taste in their mouths.

Now suppose that the sellers of good cars place a value of $v = \$7,000$ on their cars, so they are unwilling to sell them for $6,000. As a result, the *lemons drive good cars out of the market.* Buyers realize that they can buy only lemons at any price less than $7,000. Consequently, in equilibrium, the 1,000 lemons sell for the expected (and actual) price of $4,000, and no good cars change hands. This equilibrium is inefficient because high-quality cars remain in the hands of people who value them less than potential buyers do.

In summary, if buyers have less information about product quality than sellers do, the result might be a lemons problem in which high-quality cars do not sell, even though potential buyers value the cars more than their current owners do. If so, the asymmetric information causes a competitive market to lose its desirable efficiency and welfare properties. However, if the information is symmetric, the lemons problem does not occur. That is, if buyers and sellers of used cars know the quality of the cars, each car sells for its true value in a perfectly competitive market. Moreover, if, as with new cars, neither buyers nor sellers can identify lemons, both good cars and lemons sell at a price equal to the expected value rather than at their (unknown) true values.

**SOLVED PROBLEM
18.1**

**MyLab Economics
Solved Problem**

Suppose that everyone in our used-car example is risk neutral; potential car buyers value lemons at $4,000 and good used cars at $8,000; the reservation price of lemon owners is $3,000; and the reservation price of owners of high-quality used cars is $7,000. The share of current owners who have lemons is θ. (In our previous example, the share was $\theta = \frac{1}{2} = 1{,}000/[1{,}000 + 1{,}000]$). For what values of θ do all the potential sellers sell their used cars? Describe the equilibrium.

---

[3]Risk-neutral sellers place an expected value of $(\frac{1}{2} \times \$3{,}000) + \frac{1}{2}v = \$1{,}500 + \frac{1}{2}v$ on a car of unknown quality. If $v = 7{,}000$, this expected value is $\$1{,}500 + \$3{,}500 = \$5{,}000$. If $v = \$5{,}000$ this expected value is only $4,000. In either case, sellers are happy to sell their cars for $6,000.

Answer

1. *Determine how much buyers are willing to pay if all cars are sold.* Because buyers are risk neutral, if they believe that the probability of getting a lemon is θ, the most they are willing to pay for a car of unknown quality is

$$p = [\$8,000 \times (1 - \theta)] + (\$4,000 \times \theta) = \$8,000 - (\$4,000 \times \theta). \quad (18.1)$$

For example, $p = \$6,000$ if $\theta = \frac{1}{2}$ and $p = \$7,000$ if $\theta = \frac{1}{4}$.

2. *Solve for the values of θ such that all the cars are sold, and describe the equilibrium.* All owners will sell if the market price equals or exceeds their reservation price, $7,000. Using Equation 18.1, we know that the market (equilibrium) price is $7,000 or more if a quarter or fewer of the used cars are lemons, $\theta \leq \frac{1}{4}$. Thus, for $\theta \leq \frac{1}{4}$, all the cars are sold at the price given in Equation 18.1.

Varying Quality with Asymmetric Information. Most firms can adjust their product's quality. If consumers cannot identify high-quality goods before purchase, they pay the same for all goods regardless of quality. Because the price that firms receive for top-quality goods is the same they receive for low-quality items, they do not produce top-quality goods. Such an outcome is inefficient if consumers are willing to pay sufficiently more for top-quality goods.

This unwillingness to produce high-quality products is due to an externality (Chapter 17): *A firm does not completely capture the benefits from raising the quality of its product.* By selling a better product than what other firms offer, a seller raises the average quality in the market, so buyers are willing to pay more for all products. As a result, the high-quality seller shares the benefits from its high-quality product with sellers of low-quality products by raising the average price to all. *The social value of raising the quality*, as reflected by the increased revenues shared by all firms, *is greater than the private value*, which is only the higher revenue received by the firm with the good product.

SOLVED PROBLEM 18.2

MyLab Economics Solved Problem

It costs $10 to produce a low-quality wallet and $20 to produce a high-quality wallet. Consumers cannot distinguish between the products before purchase, do not make repeat purchases, and value the wallets at the cost of production. The five firms in the market produce 100 wallets each. Each firm produces only high-quality or only low-quality wallets. Consumers pay the expected value of a wallet. Do any of the firms produce high-quality wallets?

Answer

1. *Calculate the expected value of wallet.* If all five firms make a low-quality wallet, consumers pay $10 per wallet. If one firm makes a high-quality wallet and all the others make low-quality wallets, the probability that a consumer buys a high-quality wallet is $\frac{1}{5}$. Thus, the expected value per wallet to consumers is

$$(\$10 \times \tfrac{4}{5}) + (\$20 \times \tfrac{1}{5}) = \$12.$$

2. *Show that it does not pay for a single firm to make high-quality wallets if the other firms make low-quality wallets due to asymmetric information.* If one

firm raises the quality of its product, all firms benefit because the wallets sell for $12 instead of $10. The high-quality firm receives only a fraction of the total benefit from raising quality but bears the entire cost. It gets $2 extra per high-quality wallet sold, which is less than the extra $10 it costs to make the better wallet. (In contrast, the other firms benefit from the higher price without incurring the extra cost.) Therefore, due to asymmetric information, no firm produces high-quality goods even though consumers are willing to pay for the extra quality.

18.2 Reducing Adverse Selection

Because adverse selection results from one party exploiting asymmetric information about a hidden characteristic, the two main methods for solving adverse selection problems are to *equalize information* among the parties and to *restrict the ability of the informed party to take advantage of hidden information*. Responses to adverse selection problems increase welfare in some markets, but may do more harm than good in others.

Equalizing Information

Providing information to all parties eliminates adverse selection problems. Either informed or uninformed parties can act to eliminate or reduce informational asymmetries. Three methods for reducing informational asymmetries are:

1. An uninformed party (such as an insurance company) can use **screening** to infer the information possessed by informed parties.
2. An informed party (such as a person seeking to buy health insurance) can use **signaling** to send information to a less-informed party.
3. A third party, such as a firm or a government agency, not directly involved in the transaction may collect information and sell or give it to the uninformed party.

Screening. Uninformed people may eliminate their disadvantage by screening to gather information on the hidden characteristics of informed people. Life insurance companies reduce adverse selection problems by requiring medical exams. Based on this information, a firm may decide not to insure high-risk individuals or to charge them a higher premium as compensation for the extra risk.

It is costly to collect information on a person's health or dangerous habits such as smoking, drinking, or skydiving. As a result, insurance companies collect information only up to the point at which the marginal benefit from the extra information they gather equals the marginal cost of obtaining it. Over time, insurance companies have increasingly concluded that it pays to collect information about whether individuals exercise, have a family history of dying young, or engage in potentially life-threatening activities.

Consumers can use screening techniques, too. For example, a potential customer can screen a used car by test-driving it; by having an objective, trustworthy

Congratulations! You qualify for our auto insurance.

mechanic examine the car; or by paying a company such as CARFAX to check the history of the repairs on the vehicle. As long as the consumers' costs of securing information are less than the private benefits, they obtain the information, transactions occur, and markets function smoothly.

In some markets, consumers can avoid the adverse selection problem by buying only from a firm that has a *reputation* for providing high-quality goods. For example, consumers know that a used-car dealer that expects repeat purchases has a stronger incentive not to sell defective cars than does an individual.

Signaling. An informed party may signal the uninformed party to eliminate adverse selection. However, signals solve the adverse selection problem only when the recipients view them as credible. Smart consumers may place little confidence in a firm's unsubstantiated claims. Do you believe that a used car runs well just because an ad tells you so?

If only high-quality firms find it worthwhile to send a signal, then a signal is credible. Producers of high-quality goods often try to signal to consumers that their products are of better quality than those of their rivals. If consumers believe their signals, these firms can charge higher prices for their goods.

But if the signals are to be effective, they must be credible. For example, a firm may distribute a favorable review of its product by an independent testing agency to try to convince buyers that its product is of high quality. Only if low-quality firms cannot obtain such a report from a reliable independent testing agency do consumers believe this signal.

A warranty may serve as both a signal and a guarantee. It is less expensive for the manufacturer of a reliable product to offer a warranty than it is for a firm that produces low-quality products. Consequently, if one firm offers a warranty and another does not, then a consumer may infer that the firm with the warranty produces a superior product. Of course, sleazy firms may try to imitate high-quality firms by offering a warranty that they do not intend to honor.

An applicant for life insurance can present an insurance company with a written statement from the doctor as a signal of good health. If only people who believe they can show that they are better than others want to send a signal, insurance companies may rely upon it. However, an insurance company may not trust such a signal if it is easy for people to find unscrupulous doctors who will report falsely that they are in good health. Here, screening by the insurance company using its own doctors may work better because the information is more credible.

APPLICATION

Discounts for Data

Are you healthy? Your insurance company wants to know. And it wants to keep you healthy. Life insurance companies in Australia, Europe, Singapore, and South Africa use the internet to allow customers to signal that they're healthy.

When Andrew Thomas swipes his membership card upon arriving at his gym, his South African life insurance company, Vitality, receives instant information. The company checks whether he's still there 30 minutes later by tracking his location using his smartphone. In return for sharing medical and exercise information with his insurance company, Mr. Thomas earns points, which reduce his insurance premium by 9%.

John Hancock was the first U.S. life insurance company to introduce a similar program. The company provides customers with Fitbit monitors that automatically upload their activity levels. The most active customers will earn a discount of up to 15% on their life insurance premium, Amazon gift cards, and half-price stays at Hyatt hotels.

U.S. health insurance companies also provide incentives. In 2017, Humana started providing members with incentives for a range of exercise and other activities. United Healthcare provides incentives of up to $1,460 a year, which it puts into a health savings account. One-quarter of its members were wearing a fitness device in 2017, up from 13% the previous year.

Thus, life and health insurance companies are helping their customers signal that they're healthy, reducing the adverse selection problem. In addition, the companies are using this information to provide incentives for their customers to lead healthier lives so that their families have to wait longer to collect on their life insurance.

Third-Party Information. In some markets, consumer groups, nonprofit organizations, and government agencies provide buyers with information about the quality of different goods and services. If this information is credible, it can reduce adverse selection by enabling consumers to avoid buying low-quality goods or paying less for poorer-quality products.

For an outside organization to provide believable information, it must convince consumers that it is trustworthy. Consumers Union, which publishes the product evaluation guide *Consumer Reports*, tries to establish its trustworthiness by refusing to accept advertising or other payments from firms.

Unfortunately, experts undersupply information because it is a *public good* (nonrivalrous and only sometimes exclusive—see Chapter 17). Consumers Union does not capture the full value of its information through sales of its *Consumer Reports* because buyers lend their copies to friends, libraries stock it, and newspapers report on its findings. As a result, Consumers Union conducts less research than is socially optimal.

Auditing is another important example of third-party assessment, in which an independent accounting firm assesses the financial statements of a firm or other organization. Sometimes a firm obtains an audit voluntarily to enhance its reputation (a signal). Sometimes audits are required as a condition of being listed on a particular exchange or of participating in a particular transaction, and sometimes laws require audits be performed (screening).

Governments, consumer groups, industry groups, and others may establish a **standard**, which is a metric or scale for evaluating the quality of a particular product. For example, the R-value of insulation tells how effectively insulation works. Consumers learn of a brand's quality through **certification**: a report that a particular product meets or exceeds a given standard level.

Many industry groups set their own standards and get an outside group or firm, such as Underwriters Laboratories (UL) or Factory Mutual Engineering Corporation (FMEC), to certify that their products meet specified standard levels. For example, by setting standards for the size of the thread on a screw, we ensure that screws work in products regardless of brand.

When standard and certification programs inexpensively and completely inform consumers about the relative quality of all goods in a market and do not restrict the goods available, the programs are socially desirable. Licenses or certifications that restrict entry raise the average quality in the industry by eliminating low-quality goods and services. However, they drive up prices to consumers by restricting supply. As a result, welfare may go up or down, depending on whether the increased-quality effect or the higher-price effect dominates.

APPLICATION

Adverse Selection and Remanufactured Goods

Because consumers can't see a good before buying it over the internet, it's easy for a shady seller to misrepresent its quality. In the worst-case lemons-market scenario, low-quality goods drive out high-quality goods.

Adverse selection concerns are particularly strong for electronic goods sold on eBay, as consumers cannot screen by inspecting the product ("squeeze the orange") before purchase. That this market exists on eBay indicates that sellers have found ways to signal quality or consumers have found ways to screen.

Consumers know that selling on eBay creates an enforceable contract, so sellers' signals reduce adverse selection on eBay. Sellers have a variety of ways to signal. Some sellers offer money back guarantees or warranties. Some pay extra to eBay to post flashy displays. One important signal is whether the good is new, remanufactured, or used. For years, manufacturers of cameras, computers, mobile phones, MP3 players, and other consumer durables have refurbished or upgraded returned products before trying to sell them again. Even though these remanufactured products may be comparable to new ones, consumers do not perceive them that way, so they are willing to pay a premium for new ones.

Neto, Bloemhof, and Corbett (2016) studied sales on eBay of three types of iPods: the Classic, the Touch, and the Nano. They found, for example, that the average price of a used iPod Nano was 65% of a new one, while a remanufactured Nano was 82% of a new one. Thus, the signal of the good's type affects the price.

What about other signals, such as positive descriptions? Consumers view used goods as varying more in quality than remanufactured or new products: The prices of used goods have greater variance than those of the others. As a result, quality claims may be more likely to affect the price of used goods than those of new and remanufactured goods. Positive descriptions affect the price of most types of used iPods, but not new and remanufactured iPods.

Consumers can also screen using eBay's feedback (reputation) score: the percentage of positive ratings by past customers. A sleazy seller will have a bad feedback score. Subramanian and Subramanyam (2012) studied the sales of electronic goods on eBay. They found that a higher seller feedback score reduced the price differential between new and remanufactured goods. They also discovered that consumers pay higher prices for products remanufactured by the original manufacturer or their authorized factories than for those remanufactured by third parties.

Thus, third-party information in the form of ratings from previous customers, which consumers use to screen, and a variety of signals from firms help reduce the adverse selection problem for used and remanufactured goods.

Laws to Prevent Opportunism

In addition to setting standards and certifying goods and services, governments and various organizations prevent opportunism in several ways. Three common examples are disclosure requirements, product liability laws, and universal coverage requirements.

Disclosure Requirements. Governments often require the informed party to disclose all relevant information to the uninformed party. For example, many local governments require that sellers disclose all relevant facts about a house to potential buyers, such as its age and any known defects in the electrical work or plumbing. By doing so, these governments protect buyers against adverse selection due to undisclosed defects.

Product Liability Laws. In many countries, product liability laws protect consumers from being stuck with nonfunctional or dangerous products. Moreover, many U.S. state supreme courts have concluded that new products carry an implicit understanding that they will safely perform their intended functions. If they do not, consumers can sue the seller even in the absence of product liability laws. If consumers can rely on explicit or implicit product liability laws to force a manufacturer to compensate consumers for defective products, they do not need to worry about adverse selection. However, the transaction costs of going to court are very high.

Universal Coverage. Health insurance markets have adverse selection because low-risk consumers do not buy insurance at prices that reflect the average risk. Such adverse selection can be eliminated by providing insurance to everyone or by mandating that everyone buy insurance. Firms often provide mandatory health insurance as a benefit to all employees, rather than paying them a higher wage and allowing them to decide whether to buy such insurance on their own. By doing so, firms reduce adverse selection problems for their insurance carriers: Both healthy and unhealthy people are covered. As a result, firms can buy medical insurance for their workers at a lower cost per person than workers can obtain on their own.

Similarly, Canada, the United Kingdom, and many other countries provide basic health insurance to all residents, financed by a combination of mandatory premiums and taxes. The U.S. Supreme Court confirmed the constitutionality of the "individual mandate" in the 2010 Patient Protection and Affordable Care Act, which required virtually all Americans to have health care coverage or pay a penalty. However, effective 2019, Congress removed the penalty for violating the mandate on the grounds that the government shouldn't force people to buy health insurance.

Unintended Consequence Eliminating universal coverage raises the price of insurance.

As only relatively unhealthy or risk-averse people will buy the insurance after the mandate ends, the price will rise.[4]

18.3 Price Discrimination Due to False Beliefs About Quality

We've seen that bad products can drive out good products if consumers cannot distinguish lemons from good-quality products at the time of purchase. The market outcome also changes if consumers falsely believe that identical products differ in quality. Consumers pay more for a product that they believe is of higher quality.

If some consumers know that two products are identical while others believe that they differ in quality, a firm can profitably price discriminate. The firm takes advantage of the less-informed customers by charging them a high price for the allegedly superior product. The firm does not want to charge informed customers this same high price. Doing so would reduce profit because the resulting drop in sales would exceed the gain from the higher price.

Asymmetric information on the part of some, but not all, consumers makes price discrimination possible. However, if all customers are informed or all are uninformed about the quality of different products, firms charge a single price.

By intentionally increasing consumer uncertainty, a firm may be better able to exploit uninformed consumers and earn a higher profit (Salop, 1977). One way in which firms confuse consumers is to create *noise* by selling virtually the same product under various brand names. A *noisy monopoly* may be able to sell a product under its own brand name at a relatively high price and supply grocery or discount stores with a virtually identical product that sells at a lower price under a *private-label* (house or store) brand. For example, Campbell Soup produces Prego spaghetti sauce and similar house brands for various grocery stores.

---

[4]By one forecast, the price of health plans will rise by 2.5% to 7.5% to compensate for the loss of the mandate (**www.vox.com/policy-and-politics/2018/4/13/17226566/obamacare-penalty-2018-individual-mandate-still-in-effect**).

If some consumers know that two products are identical while others believe that their qualities differ, a firm can engage in a special type of price discrimination (Chapter 12). For example, a food manufacturer may take advantage of less-informed customers by charging a higher price for the allegedly superior national brand, while informed customers buy a less expensive but equally good private-label brand.

Brand proliferation pays if the cost of producing multiple brands is relatively low and the share of consumers who are willing to buy the higher-price product is relatively large. Otherwise, the firm makes a higher profit by selling a single product at a moderate price than by selling one brand at a low price and another at a high price.

APPLICATION

Reducing Consumers' Information

By selling the same product under more than one brand name, firms can charge uninformed consumers higher prices. For decades, Amana, Caloric, GE, Gibson, Jenn-Air, Toshiba, and Whirlpool manufactured products that Sears, Roebuck & Company sold under its house brand names—Kenmore, DieHard, and Craftsman.

Frequently, the Kenmore product was identical to or even superior to the brand-name product and cost less. Knowledgeable consumers, realizing that the two brands were identical except for the label, bought the Sears brand at the lower price. But customers who falsely believed that the name brand was better than the Kenmore product paid more for the name brand. Amazon is currently following this approach, with its Amazon Basic and many other private-label brands.

Over time, as consumers have become familiar with private-label brands and recognized their quality, private-label products have rapidly gained market share. According to the Nielsen Company's 2018 report, the private-label value share was 16.7% globally, 31.4% in the European Union, and 17.7% in North America. As consumers gain more knowledge about the quality of private-label brands, the advantage from maintaining multiple brands diminishes, which partially explains why Sears sold its Craftsman brand in 2017 and put the Kenmore brand up for sale in 2018.

18.4 Market Power from Price Ignorance

We've seen that consumer ignorance about quality can keep high-quality goods out of markets. We now illustrate that consumer ignorance about price variation across firms gives firms market power. As a result, firms have an incentive to make it difficult for consumers to collect pricing information. Because of this incentive, some stores won't quote prices over the phone.

If consumers (unlike sellers) do not know how prices vary across firms, *firms may gain market power and set prices above marginal cost*. Suppose that you go to Store A to buy a television set. If you know that Store B is charging $499 for the same TV, you are willing to pay Store A at most $499 (or perhaps a little more to avoid having to go to Store B). *Knowledge is power*. However, if you don't know Store B's price for that TV, Store A might charge you much more than $499. *Ignorance costs*.

In this section, we examine why asymmetric pricing information leads to noncompetitive pricing in a market that would otherwise be competitive. Suppose that many stores in a town sell the same good. If consumers have *full information* about prices, all stores charge the full-information competitive price, p^*. If one store raises its price above p^*, the store loses all its business. Each store faces a residual demand curve that is horizontal at the going market price and has no market power.

In contrast, if consumers have *limited information* about the price that firms charge for a product, one store can charge more than others and not lose all its customers. Customers who do not know that the product is available for less else-where buy from the high-price store.[5] Thus, each store faces a downward-sloping residual demand curve and has some market power.

Tourist-Trap Model

We now show that if such a market has a single price, it is higher than p^*. Suppose you arrive in a small town in California near the site of the discovery of gold. Souvenir shops crowd the street. Wandering by one of them, you see that it sells the town's distinctive snowy: a plastic ball filled with water and imitation snow featuring a model of the Donner Party. You decide that you must buy at least one of these tasteful souvenirs—perhaps more if the price is low enough. Your bus is leaving soon, so you can't check the price at each shop to find the lowest price. Moreover, determining which shop has the lowest price won't be useful to you in the future because you do not intend to return anytime soon.

Let's assume that you and other tourists have a guidebook that reports how many souvenir shops charge each possible price for the snowy, but it does not provide the price at any particular shop.[6] You and the other tourists have identical demand functions.

It costs each tourist c in time and expenses to visit a shop to check the price or buy a snowy. Thus, if the price is p, the cost of buying a snowy at the first shop you visit is $p + c$. If you go to two souvenir shops before buying at the second shop, the cost of the snowy is $p + 2c$.

When Price Is Not Competitive. Will all souvenir shops charge the same price? If so, what is it? We start by considering whether each shop charges the full-information, competitive price, p^*.

The full-information, competitive price is the equilibrium price only if no firm has an incentive to charge a different price. No firm charges less than p^*, which equals marginal cost, because it would lose money on each sale.

However, a shop can gain by charging a higher price than p^*, so p^* is *not* an equilibrium price. If all other shops charge p^*, a shop can profitably charge $p_1 = p^* + M$, where M, a small positive number, is the shop's price markup. Suppose you walk into this shop and learn that it sells the snowy for p_1. You know from your guidebook that all the other souvenir shops charge only p^*. You say to yourself, "How unfortunate [or other words to that effect]! I've wandered into the only expensive shop in town." Annoyed, you consider going elsewhere. Nonetheless, you do not go to another shop if this first shop's markup, $M = p_1 - p^*$, is less than c, the cost of going to another shop.

As a result, it pays for this shop to raise its price by an amount that is just slightly less than the cost of an additional search, thereby deviating from the proposed equilibrium where all other shops charge p^*. Thus, *if consumers have limited information about price, an equilibrium in which all firms charge the full-information, competitive price is impossible.*

Monopoly Price. We've seen that the market price cannot be lower than or equal to the full-information, competitive price. Can an equilibrium exist in which all stores charge the same price and that price is higher than the competitive price? In

---

[5]A grave example concerns the ripping-off of the dying and their relatives. A cremation arranged through a memorial society—which typically charges a nominal enrollment fee of $10 to $25—often costs half or less than the same service when it is arranged through a mortuary. Consumers who know about memorial societies—which get competitive bids from mortuaries—can obtain a relatively low price.

[6]We make this assumption about the guidebook to keep the presentation as simple as possible. This assumption is not necessary to obtain the following result.

particular, can an equilibrium exist in which all shops charge $p_1 = p^* + M$? No, because shops would deviate from this proposed equilibrium for the same reason that they would deviate from charging the competitive price. A shop can profitably raise its price to $p_2 = p_1 + M = p^* + 2M$. Again, it does not pay for a tourist who is unlucky enough to enter that shop to go to another shop as long as $M < c$. Thus, p_1 is not the equilibrium price. By repeating this reasoning, we can reject other possible equilibrium prices that are above p^* and less than the monopoly price, p_m.

However, the monopoly price may be an equilibrium price. No firm wants to raise its price above the monopoly level because its profit would fall due to reduced sales. When tourists learn the price at a particular souvenir shop, they decide how many snowies to buy. If the price is set too high, the shop's lost sales more than offset the higher price, so its profit falls. Thus, although the shop can charge a higher price without losing all its sales, it chooses not to do so.

The only remaining question is whether a shop would like to charge a price lower than p_m if all other shops charge that price. If not, p_m is an equilibrium price.

Should a shop reduce its price below p_m by less than c? If it does so, it does not pay for consumers to search for this low-price firm. The shop makes less on each sale, so its profits must fall. Thus, a shop should not deviate by charging a price that is only slightly less than p_m.

Does it pay for a shop to drop its price below p_m by more than c? If the town has few shops, consumers may search for this low-price shop. Although the shop makes less per sale than the high-price shops, its profits may be higher because of greater sales volume. However, if the town has many shops, consumers do not search for the low-price shop because their chances of finding it are low. As a result, when the presence of a large number of shops makes searching for a low-price shop impractical, no firm lowers its price, so p_m is the equilibrium price. Thus, *when consumers have asymmetric information and when search costs and the number of firms are large, the only possible single-price equilibrium is at the monopoly price.*

If a firm charging a low price can break the single-price equilibrium at p_m, then no single-price equilibrium is possible. Either the market has no equilibrium or it has an equilibrium in which prices vary across shops (see Stiglitz, 1979, or Carlton and Perloff, 2005). Multiple-price equilibria are common.

SOLVED PROBLEM 18.3

MyLab Economics
Solved Problem

Initially, many souvenir shops compete. Each charges p_m (because consumers do not know the shops' prices). Buyers' search costs are c. If the government pays for half of consumers' search costs, is a single-price equilibrium at a price less than p_m possible?

Answer

Show that the argument we used to reject a single-price equilibrium at any price except the monopoly price does not depend on the size of the search cost. If all other stores charge any single price p, where $p^* \leq p < p_m$, a firm profits from raising its price. As long as it raises its price by no more than $c/2$ (the new cost of search to a consumer), unlucky consumers who stop at this deviant store will not search further. This profitable deviation shows that the proposed single-price equilibrium is not an equilibrium. Again, the only possible single-price equilibrium is at p_m.[7]

---

[7]If the search cost is low enough, a firm can break the single-price equilibrium at p_m by profitably charging a low price, so only a multiple-price equilibrium is possible. If the search cost falls to zero, consumers have full information, so the only possible equilibrium is at the full-information, competitive price.

Advertising and Prices

The U.S. Federal Trade Commission (FTC), a consumer protection agency, opposes groups that want to forbid price advertising; the FTC argues that advertising about price benefits consumers. If a firm informs consumers about its unusually low price, it may be able to gain enough additional customers to more than offset its loss from the lower price. If low-price stores advertise their prices and attract many customers, they can break the monopoly-price equilibrium that occurs when consumers must search store by store for low prices. The more successful the advertising, the larger these stores grow and the lower the average price in the market. If enough consumers become informed, all stores may charge the low price. Thus, without advertising, no store may find it profitable to charge low prices, but with advertising, all stores may charge low prices.

18.5 Problems Arising from Ignorance When Hiring

Asymmetric information is frequently a problem in labor markets. Prospective employees may have less information about working conditions than firms do. Firms may have less information about potential employees' abilities than potential workers do.

Information asymmetries in labor markets lower welfare below the full-information level. Workers may signal and firms may screen to reduce the asymmetry in information about workers' abilities. Signaling and screening may raise or lower welfare, as we now consider.

Cheap Talk

Honesty is the best policy—when there is money in it. —Mark Twain

We now consider situations in which workers have more information about their ability than firms do. We look first at inexpensive signals sent by workers, then at expensive signals sent by workers, and finally at screening by firms.

When an informed person voluntarily provides information to an uninformed person, the informed person engages in **cheap talk**: unsubstantiated claims or statements (see Farrell and Rabin, 1996). People use cheap talk to distinguish themselves or their attributes at low cost. Even though informed people may lie when it suits them, it is often in their and everyone else's best interest for them to tell the truth. Nothing stops me from advertising that I have a chimpanzee for sale, but doing so serves no purpose if I actually want to sell a refrigerator. One advantage of cheap talk, if it is effective, is that it is a less-expensive method of signaling ability to a potential employer than paying to have that ability tested.

Suppose that a firm plans to hire Cyndi to do one of two jobs. The demanding job requires someone with high ability. The undemanding job can be performed better by someone with low ability because the job bores more able people, who then work poorly.

Cyndi knows whether her ability level is high or low, but the firm is unsure, initially thinking that either level is equally likely. Panel a of Table 18.1 shows the payoffs to Cyndi and the firm under various possibilities.[8] If Cyndi has high ability, she enjoys the demanding job: Her payoff is 3 (which includes her wage and the dollar value of the pleasure or displeasure from working at this job). If she has low

---

[8]Previously, we used a 2 × 2 matrix to show a simultaneous-move game, in which both parties choose an action simultaneously. In contrast, in Table 18.1, only the firm can make a move. Cyndi does not take an action, because she cannot choose her ability level.

Table 18.1   Employee-Employer Payoffs

(a) *When Cheap Talk Works*

		Job That the Firm Gives to Cyndi	
		Demanding	*Undemanding*
Cyndi's Ability	*High*	3 2	1 1
	Low	1 1	2 4

(b) *When Cheap Talk Fails*

		Job That the Firm Gives to Cyndi	
		Demanding	*Undemanding*
Cyndi's Ability	*High*	3 2	1 1
	Low	3 1	2 4

ability, she finds the demanding job too stressful—her payoff is only 1—but she has a payoff of 2 at the undemanding job. The payoff to the firm is greater if Cyndi is properly matched to the job: She is given the demanding job if she has high ability and the undemanding job if she has low ability.

We can view this example as a two-stage game. In the first stage, Cyndi tells the firm something. In the second stage, the firm decides which job she gets.

Cyndi could make many possible statements about her ability. For simplicity, though, we assume that she says either, "My ability is high" or "My ability is low." This two-stage game has an equilibrium in which Cyndi tells the truth, and the firm, believing her, assigns her to the appropriate job. If she claims to have high ability, the firm gives her the demanding job.

If the firm reacts to her cheap talk in this manner, Cyndi has no incentive to lie. If she does, the firm would make a mistake, and a mistake would be bad for both parties. Cyndi and the firm want the same outcome, so cheap talk works.

In many other situations, however, cheap talk does not work. Given the payoffs in panel b, Cyndi and the firm do not want the same outcome. The firm still wants Cyndi in the demanding job if she has high ability and in the undemanding job otherwise. But Cyndi wants the demanding job regardless of her ability, so she claims to have high ability regardless of the truth. Knowing her incentives, the firm views her statement as meaningless—it does not change the firm's view that her ability is equally likely to be high or low.

Given that belief, the firm gives her the undemanding job, for which its expected payoff is higher. The firm's expected payoff is $(\frac{1}{2} \times 1) + (\frac{1}{2} \times 4) = 2.5$ if it gives her the undemanding job and $(\frac{1}{2} \times 2) + (\frac{1}{2} \times 1) = 1.5$ if it assigns her to the demanding job. Thus, given the firm's asymmetric information, the outcome is inefficient if Cyndi has high ability.

When the interests of the firm and the individual diverge, cheap talk does not provide a credible signal. Here, an individual has to send a more expensive signal to be believed. We now examine such a signal.

APPLICATION

Cheap Talk in eBay's
Best Offer Market

In addition to auctions, eBay allows a seller to offer to sell a good for a specified price. The buyer may allow a potential buyer to respond with a *best offer* of a lower price. The seller may accept the best-offer bid, decline it, or make a counteroffer. The transaction is completed when a buyer or the seller accept the other side's offer.[9]

Backus, Blake, and Tadelis (forthcoming) suggested that some sellers use cheap talk by posting an initial price that is a multiple of $100. Items listed in multiples of $100 receive offers 6 to 11 days sooner that are 5% to 8% lower, and are 3% to 5% more likely to sell than are items listed at similar "precise" prices such as $99 or $109. Thus, these round numbers may provide information that helps both parties: The seller makes a quick sale, and the customer buys at a low price.

Education as a Signal

No doubt you've been told that you should go to college to get a good job. Going to college may result in a better job because you obtain valuable training. Or, a college degree may land you a good job because it signals your ability to employers. If high-ability people are more likely to go to college than low-ability people, schooling signals ability to employers (Spence, 1974).

To illustrate how such signaling works, we'll make the extreme assumptions that graduating from an appropriate school serves as the signal and that schooling provides no useful training to firms (Stiglitz, 1975). High-ability workers are θ share of the workforce, and low-ability workers are $1 - \theta$ share. For a firm, the value of output produced by a high-ability worker is worth w_h, and that of a low-ability worker is w_l (over their careers). If competitive employers knew workers' ability levels, they would pay this value of the marginal product to each worker, so a high-ability worker receives w_h and a low-ability worker earns w_l.

However, suppose that employers cannot directly determine a worker's skill level. For example, when production is a group effort a firm cannot determine the productivity of a single employee.

Two types of equilibria are possible, depending on whether employers can distinguish high-ability workers from others. If employers have no way of distinguishing workers, the outcome is a **pooling equilibrium**: Dissimilar people are treated (paid) alike or behave alike. Employers pay all workers the average wage:

$$\overline{w} = \theta w_h + (1 - \theta)w_l. \tag{18.2}$$

Risk-neutral, competitive firms expect to break even because they underpay high-ability people by enough to offset the losses from overpaying low-ability workers.

We assume that high-ability individuals can get a degree by spending c to attend a school, but low-ability people cannot graduate from the school (or that the cost of doing so is prohibitively high). If high-ability people graduate and low-ability people do not, a degree is a signal of ability to employers. Given such a clear signal, the outcome is a **separating equilibrium**: One type of people takes actions (such as sending a signal) that allow them to be differentiated from other types of people. Here, a successful signal causes high-ability workers to receive w_h and others to receive w_l, so wages vary with ability.

We now examine whether a pooling or a separating equilibrium is possible. We consider whether anyone would want to change behavior in an equilibrium. If no one wants to change, the equilibrium is feasible.

---

[9]Because this game (Chapter 13) is very complicated, participants have difficulty devising optimal strategies.

Separating Equilibrium. In a separating equilibrium, high-ability people pay c to get a degree and are employed at a wage of w_h, while low-ability individuals do not get a degree and work at a wage of w_l. The low-ability people have no choice, because they can't get a degree. High-ability individuals have the option of not going to school. Without a degree, however, they are viewed as having low ability once they are hired, so they receive w_l. If they go to school, their net earnings are $w_h - c$. Thus, it pays for a high-ability person to go to school if $w_h - c > w_l$. Rearranging terms in this expression, we find that a high-ability person chooses to get a degree if

$$w_h - w_l > c. \tag{18.3}$$

Equation 18.3 says that the benefit from graduating, the extra pay $w_h - w_l$, exceeds the cost of schooling, c. If Equation 18.3 holds, no worker wants to change behavior, so a separating equilibrium is feasible.

   Suppose that $c = \$15,000$ and that high-ability workers are twice as productive as others: $w_h = \$40,000$ and $w_l = \$20,000$. Here, the benefit to a high-ability worker from graduating, $w_h - w_l = \$20,000$, exceeds the cost by $5,000. Thus, no one wants to change behavior in this separating equilibrium.

Pooling Equilibrium. In a pooling equilibrium, all workers are paid the average wage from Equation 18.2, $\overline{w}$. Again, because low-ability people cannot graduate, they have no choice. A high-ability person must choose whether or not to go to school. Without a degree, that individual is paid the average wage. With a degree, the worker is paid w_h. It does not pay for the high-ability person to graduate if the benefit from graduating, the extra pay $w_h - \overline{w}$, is less than the cost of schooling:

$$w_h - \overline{w} < c. \tag{18.4}$$

If Equation 18.4 holds, no worker wants to change behavior, so a pooling equilibrium persists.

   For example, if $w_h = \$40,000$, $w_l = \$20,000$, and $\theta = \frac{1}{2}$, then

$$\overline{w} = \left(\tfrac{1}{2} \times \$40,000\right) + \left(\tfrac{1}{2} \times \$20,000\right) = \$30,000.$$

If the cost of going to school is $c = \$15,000$, the benefit to a high-ability person from graduating, $w_h - \overline{w} = \$10,000$, is less than the cost, so a high-ability individual does not want to go to school. As a result, a pooling equilibrium exists.

SOLVED PROBLEM 18.4

MyLab Economics Solved Problem

If $c = \$15,000$, $w_h = \$40,000$, and $w_l = \$20,000$, for what values of θ is a pooling equilibrium possible?

Answer

1. *Determine the values of θ for which it pays for a high-ability person to go to school.* From Equation 18.4, we know that a high-ability individual does not go to school if $w_h - \overline{w} < c$. Using Equation 18.2, we substitute for $\overline{w}$ in Equation 18.4 and rearrange terms to find that high-ability people do not go to school if $w_h - [\theta w_h + (1 - \theta)w_l] < c$, or

$$\theta > 1 - \frac{c}{w_h - w_l}. \tag{18.5}$$

If almost everyone has high ability, so θ is large, a high-ability person does not go to school. The intuition is that, as the share of high-ability workers, θ, gets large (close to 1), the average wage approaches w_h (Equation 18.2), so the benefit, $w_h - \overline{w}$, of going to school shrinks.

2. *Solve for the possible values of θ for the specific parameters.* If we substitute $c = \$15,000$, $w_h = \$40,000$, and $w_l = \$20,000$ into Equation 18.5, we find that high-ability people do not go to school—that is, a pooling equilibrium is possible—when $\theta > \frac{1}{4}$.

Unique Equilibrium or Multiple Equilibria. Depending on differences in abilities, the cost of schooling, and the share of high-ability workers, only one type of equilibrium may be possible or both may be possible. In the following examples, using Figure 18.2, $w_h = \$40,000$ and $w_l = \$20,000$.

Only a pooling equilibrium is possible if schooling is very costly: $c > w_h - w_l = \$20,000$, so Equation 18.3 does not hold. The horizontal line in Figure 18.2 shows where $c = w_h - w_l = \$20,000$. Only a pooling equilibrium is feasible above that line, $c > \$20,000$, because it is not worthwhile for high-ability workers to go to school.

Equation 18.5 shows that if the market has few high-ability people (relative to the cost and earnings differential), only a separating equilibrium is possible. The figure shows a sloped line where $\theta = 1 - c/(w_h - w_l)$. Below that line, $\theta < 1 - c/(w_h - w_l)$, relatively few people have high ability, so the average wage, $\overline{w}$, is low. A pooling equilibrium is not possible because high-ability workers would want to signal. Thus, below this line, only a separating equilibrium is possible. Above this line, Equation 18.5 holds,

Figure 18.2 Pooling and Separating Equilibria

If firms know workers' abilities, high-ability workers are paid $w_h = \$40,000$ and low-ability workers get $w_l = \$20,000$. The type of equilibrium depends on the cost of schooling, c, and on the share of high-ability workers, θ. If $c > \$20,000$, only a pooling equilibrium, in which everyone gets the average wage, is possible. If the market has relatively few high-ability people, $\theta < 1 - c/\$20,000$, only a separating equilibrium is possible. Between the horizontal and sloped lines, either type of equilibrium may occur.

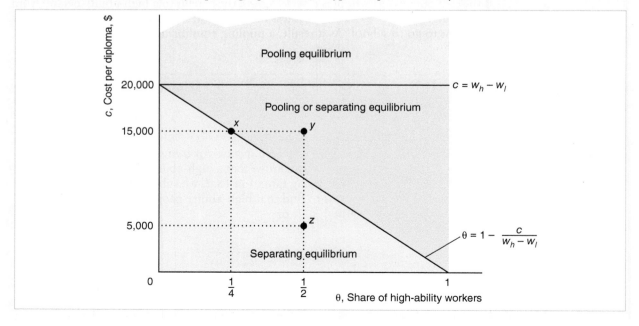

so a pooling equilibrium is possible. (The answer to Solved Problem 18.3 shows that no one wants to change behavior in a pooling equilibrium if $c = \$15,000$ and $\theta > \frac{1}{4}$, which are points to the right of x in the figure, such as y.)

Below the horizontal line where the cost of signaling is less than $20,000 and above the sloped line where the market has relatively many high-ability workers, either equilibrium may occur. For example at y, where $c = \$15,000$ and $\theta = \frac{1}{2}$, Equations 18.3 and 18.4 (or, equivalently, Equation 18.5) hold, so both a separating equilibrium and a pooling equilibrium are possible. In the pooling equilibrium, no one wants to change behavior, so that equilibrium is possible. Similarly, no one wants to change behavior in a separating equilibrium.

A government could ensure that one or the other of these equilibria occurs. It can achieve a pooling equilibrium by banning schooling (and other possible signals). Alternatively, the government can create a separating equilibrium by subsidizing schooling for some high-ability people. Once some individuals start to signal, so that firms pay either a low or a high wage (not a pooling wage), it is worthwhile for other high-ability people to signal.

Efficiency. In our example of a separating equilibrium, high-ability people get an otherwise useless education solely to show that they differ from low-ability people. An education is privately useful to the high-ability workers if it serves as a signal that gets them higher net pay. In our extreme example, education is socially inefficient because it is costly and provides no useful training.

Signaling changes the distribution of wages. Without signaling, everyone receives the average wage. With signaling, high-ability workers earn more than low-ability workers. Nonetheless, the total amount that firms pay is the same, so firms make zero expected profits in both equilibria.[10] Moreover, everyone is employed in both the pooling and screening equilibria, so total output is the same.

Nonetheless, everyone may be worse off in a separating equilibrium. At point y in Figure 18.2 ($w_h = \$40,000$, $w_l = \$20,000$, $c = \$15,000$, and $\theta = \frac{1}{2}$), either a pooling equilibrium or a separating equilibrium is possible. In the pooling equilibrium, each worker is paid $\overline{w} = \$30,000$ and no wasteful signaling occurs. In the separating equilibrium, high-ability workers make $w_h - c = \$25,000$ and low-ability workers make $w_l = \$20,000$.

High-ability people earn less in the separating equilibrium, $25,000, than they would in the pooling equilibrium, $30,000. Nonetheless, if anyone signals, all the other high-ability workers want to send a signal to prevent their wage from falling to that of a low-ability worker. High-ability workers net an extra $[w_h - c] - w_l = \$25,000 - \$20,000 = \$5,000$. The reason socially undesirable signaling happens is that the private return to signaling, $5,000, exceeds the net social return to signaling. The gross social return to the signal is zero because the signal changes only the distribution of wages. The net social return is negative because the signal is costly.

This inefficient expenditure on education is due to asymmetric information and the desire of high-ability workers to signal their ability. The government can increase total social wealth by banning wasteful signaling (eliminating schooling). Both low-ability and high-ability people benefit from such a ban.

In other cases, however, high-ability people do not want a ban. At point z (where $\theta = \frac{1}{2}$ and $c = \$5,000$), only a separating equilibrium is possible without government intervention. In this equilibrium, high-ability workers earn $w_h - c = \$35,000$

---

[10] Firms pay high-ability workers more than they pay low-ability workers in a separating equilibrium, but the average amount they pay per worker is $\overline{w}$, the same as in a pooling equilibrium.

and low-ability workers make $w_l =$ \$20,000. If the government bans signaling, both types of workers earn \$30,000 in the resulting pooling equilibrium, so high-ability workers are harmed, losing \$5,000 each. Thus, although the ban raises efficiency by eliminating wasteful signaling, high-ability workers oppose the ban.

In this example, efficiency can always be increased by banning signaling because signaling is unproductive. However, some signaling is socially efficient because it increases total output. Education may raise output because its signal results in a better matching of workers and jobs or because it provides useful training and serves as a signal. Also, education may make people better citizens. In conclusion, *total social output falls with signaling if signaling is socially unproductive but may rise with signaling if signaling also raises productivity or serves some other desirable purpose.*

Empirical evidence on the importance of signaling is mixed. For example, Tyler, Murnane, and Willett (2000) find that, for the least-skilled high school dropouts, passing the General Educational Development (GED) credential (the equivalent of a high school diploma) increases white dropouts' earnings by 10% to 19% but does not have a statistically significant effect on nonwhite dropouts.

Screening in Hiring

Firms screen prospective workers in many ways. An employer may hire someone based on a characteristic that the employer believes is correlated with ability, such as how a person dresses or speaks. Or a firm may use a test. Further, some employers engage in statistical discrimination, believing that an individual's gender, race, religion, or ethnicity is a proxy for ability.

Interviews and Tests. Most societies accept the use of interviews and tests by potential employers. Firms commonly assess abilities using interviews and tests. If such screening devices are accurate, firms benefit by selecting superior workers and assigning them to appropriate tasks. However, as with signaling, these costly activities are inefficient if they do not increase output. In the United States, the use of hiring tests may be challenged and rejected by the courts if the employer cannot demonstrate that the tests accurately measure skills or abilities required on the job.

Statistical Discrimination. If employers think that people of a certain age, gender, race, religion, or ethnicity have higher ability than others on average, they may engage in statistical discrimination (Aigner and Cain, 1977) and hire only people with that characteristic. Employers may engage in this practice even if they know that the correlation between these factors and ability is imperfect.[11]

Figure 18.3 illustrates one employer's belief that members of Race 1 have, on average, lower ability than members of Race 2: Much of the distribution curve for Race 2 lies to the right of the curve for Race 1. Nonetheless, the figure also shows that the employer believes that the highest-skilled members of Race 1 have higher ability than the lowest-skilled members of Race 2: Part of the Race 1 curve lies to the right of part of the Race 2 curve. Still, because the employer believes that a group characteristic, race, is an (imperfect) indicator of individual ability, the employer hires only people of Race 2 if enough of them are available.

The employer may claim not to be prejudiced but to be concerned only with maximizing profit. Nonetheless, this employer's actions harm members of Race 1 as much as they would if they were due to racial hatred.

---

[11] Other common sources of employment discrimination are prejudice (Becker, 1971) and the exercise of monopsony power (Madden, 1973).

Figure 18.3 Statistical Discrimination

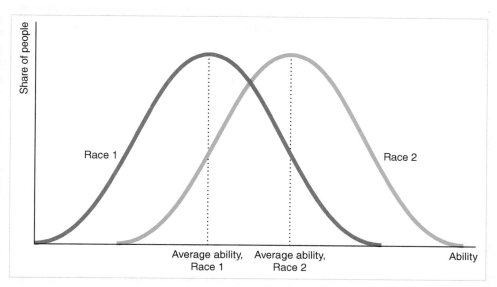

This figure shows the beliefs of an employer who thinks that people of Race 1 have less ability on average than people of Race 2. This employer hires only people of Race 2 even though the employer believes that some members of Race 1 have greater ability than some members of Race 2. Because this employer never employs members of Race 1, the employer may never learn that workers of both races have equal ability.

Even though ability distributions are identical across races, eliminating statistical discrimination is difficult. If all employers share the belief that members of Race 1 have such low ability that it is not worth hiring them, people of that race are never hired, so employers never learn that their beliefs are incorrect. Here, false beliefs can persist indefinitely. Such discrimination lowers social output by preventing skilled members of Race 1 from performing certain jobs.

However, statistical discrimination may be based on true differences between groups. For example, insurance companies offer lower auto insurance rates to young women than to young men because young men are more likely, *on average*, to have an accident. The companies report that this practice lowers their costs of providing insurance by reducing moral hazard. Nonetheless, this practice penalizes young men who are unusually safe drivers, and benefits young women who are unusually reckless drivers.

CHALLENGE SOLUTION

Dying to Work

In the Challenge at the beginning of the chapter, we asked whether a firm under-invests in safety if the firm knows how dangerous a job is but potential employees do not. Can the government intervene to improve this situation?

Consider an industry with two firms that are simultaneously deciding whether to make costly safety investments, such as sprinkler systems in a plant or escape tunnels in a mine. Unlike the firms, potential employees do not know how safe it is to work at each firm. They know only how risky it is to work in this industry. If only Firm 1 invests, workers do not know that safety has improved at Firm 1's plant only. Because the government's accident statistics for the industry fall, workers realize that it is safer to work in the industry, so both firms pay lower wages.

The profit table shows how the firms' profits depend on their safety investments. Firm 1 has a dominant strategy (Chapter 13). If Firm 2 invests (compare profits in the cells in the right column), Firm 1's *no investment* strategy has a higher profit, 250, than its *investment* strategy, 225. Similarly, if Firm 2 does not invest (compare the cells in the left column), Firm 1's profit is higher if it doesn't invest, 200, than if it does. Thus, not investing is its dominant strategy and investing is the dominated strategy, as is indicated by the horizontal red line through the investing strategy. Because the game is symmetric, Firm 2's dominant strategy is not to invest.

		Firm 2		
		No Investment	Investment	
Firm 1 No Investment	200	200	250	100
Investment	100	250	225	225

The pair of dominant strategies where neither firm invests (the upper-left cell) is the Nash equilibrium. Both firms receive an equilibrium profit of 200. If both firms invest in safety (the lower-right cell), each earns 225, which is more than they earn in the Nash equilibrium. However, the pair of strategies where both firms invest is not an equilibrium, because each firm can increase its profit from 225 to 250 by not investing if the other firm invests.

The firms are engaged in a prisoners' dilemma game. *Because each firm bears the full cost of its safety investments but derives only some of the benefits, the firms underinvest in safety.*

This prisoners' dilemma outcome results because workers do not know which firm is safer. If workers know how safe each firm is, a firm that invests in safety could hire at a lower wage than one that does not. Because that changes the profits, firms are more likely to invest in safety. Thus, if the government or a union collects and provides workers with firm-specific safety information, the firms might opt to invest. However, they will collect and provide this information only if their cost of doing so is sufficiently low.

SUMMARY

Asymmetric information causes market failures when informed parties engage in opportunistic behavior at the expense of uninformed parties. Two types of problems arise from opportunism. Adverse selection occurs when someone with a characteristic that is unknown by other parties to a deal exploits this information to the detriment of the less informed. Moral hazard occurs when an informed party takes advantage of a less-informed party through a hidden action.

1. **Adverse Selection.** Adverse selection creates problems in insurance markets because people with low risk do not buy insurance, which drives up the price for high-risk people. Due to adverse selection, not all desirable transactions take place. As a result, low-quality items tend to be overrepresented in transactions, as with the lemons problem associated with used cars and many other products. Bad products may drive good products out of the market.

2. **Reducing Adverse Selection.** Methods for dealing with adverse selection problems include consumer screening (such as by using experts or relying on firms' reputations), signaling by firms (including establishing brand names and providing guarantees or warranties), the provision of information by third parties such as government agencies or consumer groups, and laws limiting the ability of informed parties to exploit their private information.

3. **Price Discrimination Due to False Beliefs About Quality.** Firms may price discriminate if some consumers incorrectly think that quality varies across identical products. Because only some consumers collect information about quality, only those consumers know whether the quality differs between products in some markets. Firms can exploit uninformed consumers by creating noise: selling the same good under two different brand names at different prices.

4. **Market Power from Price Ignorance.** If consumers do not know how prices vary across firms, a firm can raise its price without losing all its customers. Consequently, consumers' ignorance about price creates market power. In a market that would be competitive with full information, consumer ignorance about price may lead to a monopoly price or a distribution of prices.

5. **Problems Arising from Ignorance When Hiring.** Companies use signaling and screening to try to eliminate information asymmetries in hiring. Where prospective employees and firms share common interests—such as assigning the right worker to the right task—everyone benefits from eliminating the information asymmetry by having informed job candidates honestly tell the firms—through cheap talk—about their abilities. When the two parties do not share common interests, cheap talk does not work. Potential employees may inform employers about their abilities by using an expensive signal such as a college degree. An unproductive signal (as when education serves only as a signal and provides no training) may be privately beneficial but socially harmful. A productive signal (as when education provides training or leads to greater output due to more appropriate job assignments) may be privately and socially beneficial. Firms may also screen. Job interviews, objective tests, and other screening devices that lead to a better matching of workers and jobs may be socially beneficial. However, screening by statistical discrimination harms the discriminated-against groups. Employers who discriminate based on a particular group characteristic may never learn that their discrimination is based on false beliefs because they never test these beliefs.

EXERCISES

All exercises are available on **MyLab Economics**; * = *answer appears at the back of this book;* **M** = *mathematical problem.*

1. Adverse Selection

1.1 According to the Federal Trade Commission, millions of U.S. consumers were victims of weight-loss fraud, ranging from a tea that promised to help people shed pounds to fraudulent clinical trials and fat-dissolving injections. Do these frauds illustrate adverse selection or moral hazard?

1.2 A grocery advertises a low price on its milk as a "loss leader" to induce customers to shop there. It finds that some people buy only milk there and do their other grocery shopping elsewhere. Is that an example of adverse selection or moral hazard?

1.3 You want to determine whether a lemons problem occurs in the market for single-engine airplanes. Can you use any of the following information to help answer this question? If so, how?

    a. Repair rates for original-owner planes versus resold planes.

    b. The fraction of planes resold in each year after purchase.

1.4 Suppose that half the population is healthy and the other half is unhealthy. The cost of getting sick is $1,000 for healthy people and $10,000 for unhealthy people. In a given year, any one person (regardless of health) either becomes sick or does not become sick. The probability that any one person gets sick is 0.4. Each person's utility of wealth function is $U(Y) = Y^{0.5}$, where Y is the person's wealth. Each worker's initial wealth is $30,000. Although each person knows whether he or she is healthy, the insurance company does not have this information. The insurance company offers complete, actuarially fair insurance. Because the insurance company cannot determine whether a person is healthy or not, it must offer each person the same coverage at the same price. The only costs to the company are the medical expenses of the coverage. Under these conditions, the insurance company covers all the medical expenses of its policyholders, and its expected profit is zero.

    a. If everyone purchases insurance, what is the price of the insurance?

    b. At the price you determined in part a, do healthy people purchase the optimal amount of insurance?

    c. If only unhealthy people purchase insurance, what is the price?

d. At the price you determined in part c, do unhealthy people purchase the optimal amount of insurance?

e. Given that each person has the option to purchase insurance, which type actually purchases insurance? What is the price of the insurance? Discuss the adverse selection problem. **M**

1.5 If you buy a new car and try to sell it in the first year—indeed, in the first few days after you buy it—the price that you get is substantially less than the original price. Use your knowledge about signaling and Akerlof's lemons model to explain this much-lower price.

1.6 What are the answers to Solved Problem 18.1 if customers are willing to pay $10,000 for a good used car?

*1.7 Many potential buyers value high-quality used cars at the full-information market price of p_1 and lemons at p_2. A limited number of potential sellers value high-quality cars at $v_1 \leq p_1$ and lemons at $v_2 \leq p_2$. Everyone is risk neutral. The share of lemons among all the used cars that might potentially be sold is θ. Under what conditions are all the cars sold? When are only lemons sold? Under what, if any, conditions are no cars sold? (*Hint*: See Solved Problem 18.1.) **M**

1.8 Suppose that the buyers in the previous question incur a transaction cost of $200 to purchase a car. This transaction cost is the value of their time to find a car. What is the equilibrium? Is it possible that no cars are sold? (*Hint*: See Solved Problem 18.1.) **M**

1.9 Suppose that everyone in the used-car example in the text is risk neutral, potential car buyers value lemons at $2,000 and good used cars at $10,000, the reservation price of lemon owners is $1,500, and the reservation price of owners of high-quality used cars is $8,000. The share of current owners who have lemons is θ. For what values of θ do all the potential sellers sell their used cars? Describe the equilibrium. (*Hint*: See Solved Problem 18.1.) **M**

1.10 It costs $12 to produce a low-quality electric stapler and $16 to produce a high-quality stapler. Consumers cannot distinguish good staplers from poor staplers when they make their purchases. Four firms produce staplers. Consumers value staplers at their cost of production and are risk neutral. Will any of the four firms be able to produce high-quality staplers without making losses? What happens if consumers are willing to pay $36 for high-quality staplers? (*Hint*: See Solved Problem 18.2.) **M**

1.11 In Solved Problem 18.2, show that, if all the other firms produce a high-quality wallet, it pays for one firm to start producing a low-quality wallet. **M**

1.12 In Solved Problem 18.2, will any of the firms produce high-quality wallets if the cost of producing a higher-quality wallet is only $11? Explain. **M**

1.13 Many wineries in the Napa Valley region of California enjoy strong reputations for producing high-quality wines and want to protect those reputations. Fred T. Franzia, the owner of Bronco Wine Co., sold Napa-brand wines that do not contain Napa grapes (Julia Flynn, "In Napa Valley, Winemaker's Brands Divide an Industry," *Wall Street Journal*, February 22, 2005, A1). Other Napa wineries sued Mr. Franzia, contending that his wines, made from lower-quality grapes, damaged the reputation of the Napa wines. Suppose that the wine market has 2,000 wineries, and each sells one bottle of wine. Half, 1,000, have Napa grapes that they can turn into wine, and half have Central Valley grapes. The marginal opportunity cost of selling a Napa wine is $20, and the marginal opportunity cost of selling a Central Valley wine is $5. A large number of risk-neutral consumers with identical tastes are willing to buy an unlimited number of bottles at their expected valuations. Each consumer values a wine made from Napa grapes at $25 and a wine made from Central Valley grapes at $10. By looking at the bottles, consumers cannot distinguish between the Napa and the Central Valley wines.

a. If all of the wineries choose to sell wine, what is a consumer's expected value of the wine? If only the wineries with Central Valley grapes sell wine, what is a consumer's expected value of the wine?

b. What is the market equilibrium price? In the market equilibrium, which wineries choose to sell wine?

c. Suppose that wine bottles clearly label where the grapes are grown. What are the equilibrium price and quantity of Napa wine? What are the equilibrium price and quantity of wine made from Central Valley grapes?

d. Does the market equilibrium exhibit a lemons problem? If so, does clearly labeling the origin of the grapes solve the lemons problem? **M**

2. Reducing Adverse Selection

2.1 Some states prohibit insurance companies from using car owners' home addresses to set auto insurance rates. Why do insurance companies use home addresses? What are the efficiency and equity implications of forbidding such practices?

*2.2 California set up its own earthquake insurance program for homeowners. The rates vary by zip code, depending on the proximity of the nearest fault line. However, critics claim that the people who set the rates ignored soil type. Some houses rest on bedrock; others sit on unstable soil. What are the implications of such rate setting?

*2.3 A firm spends a great deal of money in advertising to inform consumers of the brand name of its mushrooms. Should consumers conclude that its mushrooms are likely to be of higher quality than unbranded mushrooms? Why or why not?

2.4 According to Edelman (2011), the widely used online "trust" authorities issue certifications without adequate verification, giving rise to adverse selection. Edelman finds that TRUSTe certified sites are more than twice as likely to be untrustworthy as uncertified sites. Explain why.

2.5 What actions do John Hancock Life Insurance and other insurance companies take to reduce adverse selection? (*Hint:* See the Application "Discounts for Data.")

2.6 Grocery stores, hotels, and other firms give their customers free *loyalty cards*. A customer who uses the card receives a discount. Are these firms signaling, screening, price discriminating, or engaging in other activities?

2.7 The Application "Adverse Selection and Remanufactured Goods" reports that, for electronic goods sold on eBay, higher seller feedback scores reduce the price differential between new goods and remanufactured goods. Explain why this pattern is consistent with the theory of adverse selection. Would you also expect higher seller feedback to reduce the price differential between new goods and used (but not remanufactured) goods?

3. Price Discrimination Due to False Beliefs About Quality

3.1 Explain how a monopoly firm can price discriminate by advertising sales in newspapers or magazines that only some of its customers see. Is it a noisy monopoly?

3.2 Some food manufacturers sell a national brand product for more than an identical private-label product. Is such a firm a noisy monopoly (or oligopoly)?

3.3 Some firms sell the same product under two brand names at different prices. For example, although the Chevy Tahoe and the GMC Yukon are virtually twins, General Motors sold the 2018 Yukon for $1,600 more than the 2018 Tahoe. Give an asymmetric information explanation as to why the firm might use pairs of brand names and why one product might sell for more than another.

4. Market Power from Price Ignorance

*4.1 In Solved Problem 18.3, if the vast majority of all consumers knows the true prices at all stores and only a few shoppers have to incur a search cost to learn the prices, is the equilibrium a single price at the monopoly level, p_m?

4.2 The Federal Trade Commission objected to the California Dental Association's prohibitions against its members engaging in advertising about prices, calling them restraints on trade. What effect should such restraints have on equilibrium prices?

5. Problems Arising from Ignorance When Hiring

5.1 In the education signaling model, suppose that firms can pay c^* to have a worker's ability determined by a test. Does it pay for a firm to make this expenditure?

5.2 Some universities do not give letter grades. One rationale is that eliminating the letter-grade system reduces pressure on students, thus enabling them to learn more. Does this policy help or hurt students? (*Hint:* Consider the role grades play in educating and signaling.)

5.3 Some firms are willing to hire only high school graduates. Based on past experience or statistical evidence, these companies believe that, on average, high school graduates perform better than nongraduates. How does this hiring behavior compare to statistical discrimination by employers on the basis of race or gender? Discuss the equity and efficiency implications of this practice.

5.4 Suppose that you are given w_h, w_l, and θ in the education signaling model. For what value of c are both a pooling equilibrium and a separating equilibrium possible? For what value of c are both types of equilibria possible, and do high-ability workers have higher net earnings in a separating equilibrium than in a pooling equilibrium? (*Hint:* See Solved Problem 18.4.) **M**

5.5 Education is a continuous variable, where e_h is the years of schooling of a high-ability worker and e_l is the years of schooling of a low-ability worker. The cost per period of education for these types of workers is c_h and c_l, respectively, where $c_l > c_h$. The wages they receive if employers can tell them apart are w_h and w_l. Under what conditions is a separating equilibrium possible? How much education will each type of worker get? (*Hint:* See Solved Problem 18.4.) **M**

5.6 In Exercise 4.5, under what conditions is a pooling equilibrium possible? (*Hint:* See Solved Problem 18.4.) **M**

5.7 In Exercises 4.5 and 4.6, describe the equilibrium if $c_l \leq c_h$. (*Hint:* See Solved Problem 18.4.) **M**

5.8 When is statistical discrimination privately inefficient? When is it socially inefficient? Does it always harm members of the discriminated-against group? Explain.

6. Challenge

6.1 In the Challenge Solution, what is the minimum fine the government could levy on firms that do not invest in safety that would lead to a Nash equilibrium in which both firms invest?

6.2 Can you change the payoffs in the table in the Challenge Solution so that the firms choose to invest in safety? Explain. **M**

19 Contracts and Moral Hazards

The contracts of at least 33 major league baseball players have incentive clauses providing a bonus if that player is named the Most Valuable Player in a Division Series. Unfortunately, no such award is given for a Division Series.[1]

Clawing Back Bonuses

A major cause of the 2007–2009 worldwide financial crisis was that managers and other employees of banks, insurance companies, and other firms took excessive risks. Looking back on the events that led to the financial meltdown, Goldman Sachs Chief Executive Lloyd Blankfein admitted that Wall Street firms, caught up in the pursuit of profits, had ignored risks, and that these firms needed to dramatically change compensation practices. As he said, "Decisions on compensation and other actions taken and not taken, particularly at banks that rapidly lost a lot of shareholder value, look self-serving and greedy in hindsight."

Bank managers threw accepted lending practices out the window, rewarding their mortgage brokers for bringing in large numbers of new mortgages regardless of risk. For example, they often granted loans to risky borrowers without requiring any down payment. A borrower who does not make a down payment is more likely to default (stop paying the mortgage) than one who makes a sizeable down payment.

For example, Wells Fargo managers had employees engage in outrageous behavior, such as opening as many as 1.5 million bank accounts and 565,000 credit card accounts without the authorization of customers. Managers who encouraged and permitted this risky and unethical behavior were rewarded based on the increased (short-run) profits. The manager in charge of the relevant division received stock grants of about $19 million. The chief executive received at least $41 million in equity awards.

When this behavior became widely known, the bank paid dearly. Its reputation was damaged, and some customers took their money elsewhere. For fraudulently opening accounts, Wells Fargo was fined $185 million. For a variety of bad actions dating back to the Great Recession, Wells Fargo has paid fines of $12.6 billion between 2000 and 2018.

One response to bad managerial behavior was the 2010 Dodd-Frank Consumer Protection Act. That act instructed the Security and Exchange Commission (SEC) to develop rules requiring firms to institute *clawback* provisions that would allow firms to claw back, or reclaim, some earlier bonus payments to managers if their past actions resulted in

We're now tying annual executive bonuses to performance. You owe us $100,000.

---

[1]Tom FitzGerald, "Top of the Sixth," *San Francisco Chronicle*, January 31, 1997, C6.

later losses. Many firms instituted such provisions voluntarily. While only 18% of Fortune 100 companies reported having a clawback policy in 1986, almost 90% had such a provision by 2013. In 2015, the U.S. SEC proposed a rule that would require all U.S. publicly traded corporations to have clawback provisions, but it still has not finalized these rules as of 2018.

Three years after its accounts scandal, Wells Fargo's directors acted to claw back $60 million in stock grants from two top executives. However, such clawbacks remain relatively rare.

An alternative policy to a clawback is for a firm to withhold bonuses and other compensation for an extended period (often several years) so that managers are rewarded only for the long-run success arising from their decisions.

In Solved Problem 19.1, we address the question: Why did executives at these banks take extra risks that resulted in major lost shareholder value? In the Challenge Solution, we analyze the question: Does evaluating a manager's performance over a longer period using delayed compensation or clawback provisions lead to better management?

A firm's manager takes extreme risks. A dentist caps your tooth, not because you need it, but because he wants to purchase a new flat-screen TV. An employee cruises the internet for jokes instead of working when the boss is not watching. A driver of a rental car takes it off the highway and risks ruining its suspension.

Each of these examples illustrates an inefficient use of resources due to a *moral hazard*, where an informed person takes advantage of a less-informed person, often through an *unobserved action* (Chapter 18). In this chapter, we examine how to design contracts that *eliminate inefficiencies* due to moral hazard problems *without shifting risk to people who hate bearing risk*—or contracts that at least reach a good compromise between these two goals.

For example, insurance companies face a trade-off between reducing moral hazards and increasing the risk of insurance buyers. Because an insurance company pools risks, it acts as though it is risk neutral (Chapter 16). The firm offers insurance contracts to risk-averse homeowners so that they can reduce their exposure to risk. If homeowners can buy full insurance so that they will suffer no loss if a fire occurs, some of them fail to take reasonable precautions. For example, they might store flammable liquids and old newspapers, increasing the chance of a catastrophic fire.

A contract that avoids this moral hazard problem specifies that the insurance company will not pay in the event of a fire if the company can show that a policyholder was negligent by storing flammable materials in the home. If this approach is impractical, however, the insurance company might offer a contract that provides incomplete insurance, covering only a fraction of the damage from a fire. The less complete the coverage, the greater the incentive for policyholders to avoid dangerous activities but the greater the risk that risk-averse homeowners must bear.

To illustrate methods of controlling moral hazards and the trade-off between moral hazards and risk, we focus on contracts between a principal—such as an employer—and an agent—such as an employee. The *principal* contracts with the *agent* to take some *action* that benefits the principal. Until now, we have assumed that firms can produce efficiently. However, if a principal cannot practically monitor an agent constantly, the agent may steal, **shirk**—a moral hazard in which agents do not provide all the services they are paid to provide—or engage in other opportunistic behavior that lowers productivity.[2]

Opportunistic behavior by an informed agent harms a less-informed principal. Sometimes the losses are so great that both parties would be better off if each had full information and if opportunistic behavior were impossible.

In this chapter, we examine six main topics

1. **Principal-Agent Problem.** How an uninformed principal contracts with an informed agent determines whether moral hazards occur and how the parties share risks.

2. **Production Efficiency.** The agent's output depends on the type of contract used and the ability of the principal to monitor the agent's actions.

3. **Trade-Off Between Efficiency in Production and in Risk Bearing.** A principal and an agent may agree to a contract that does not eliminate moral hazards or optimally share risk but strikes a balance between these two objectives.

4. **Monitoring to Reduce Moral Hazard.** Employees work harder if an employer monitors their behavior and makes it worthwhile for them to avoid being fired.

5. **Contract Choice.** By observing which type of contract an agent picks when offered a choice, a principal may obtain enough information to reduce moral hazards.

6. **Checks on Principals.** To avoid moral hazard, an employer may agree to contractual commitments that make it in the employer's best interest to tell employees the truth.

19.1 Principal-Agent Problem

In a **principal-agent relationship**, a principal contracts with an agent to take an action on behalf of the principal. If you contract with people whose actions you cannot observe or evaluate, they may take advantage of you. If you pay someone by the hour to prepare your tax return, you do not know whether that person worked all the hours billed. If you retain a lawyer to represent you in a suit arising from an accident, you do not know whether the settlement that the lawyer recommends is in your best interest or the lawyer's. Moral hazard in a principal-agent relationship is referred to as a **principal-agent problem** or **agency problem**.

Moral hazard problems are frequent and extremely important in principal-agent employment relationships. According to the Association of Certified Fraud Examiners (2018), companies lose about 5% of their annual revenues to various forms of internal fraud alone. They suffer additional losses due to shirking.

Of course, many people behave honorably even if they have opportunities to exploit others. Also, many people honestly believe that they are putting in a full day's work even when they are not working as hard as they might. Paul, the *p*rincipal, hires Amy, the *a*gent, to manage his ice-cream store. Paul pays Amy an hourly wage. She

---

[2]The average U.S. employee fails to work six hours during the March Madness collegiate basketball tournament. One estimate puts the loss in productivity from U.S. employees watching the 2018 World Cup at $3.6 billion. **www.theladders.com/career-advice/watching-the-world-cup-drains-offices-of-3-6-billion-in-productivity** (viewed on September 8, 2018).

works every hour she is supposed to, even though Paul rarely checks on her. Nonetheless, Amy may not be spending her time as effectively as possible. She politely (but impersonally) asks everyone who enters the shop, "May I help you?" However, if she were to receive an appropriate financial incentive—say, a share of the shop's profit—she would memorize the names of her customers, greet them enthusiastically by name when they enter the store, and devise incentives for customers, such as frequent shopper discounts to increase sales.

A Model

We can describe many principal-agent interactions using a model in which the output or profit from this relationship and the risk borne by the two parties depend on the actions of the agent and the state of nature.

In a typical principal-agent relationship, the principal owns some property, such as a firm, or has a property right such as the right to sue for damages from an injury. The principal hires or contracts with an agent to take some action, *a*, that increases the value of his property or that produces profit, π, from using his property.

The principal and the agent need each other. If Paul hires Amy to run his ice-cream shop, Amy needs Paul's shop, and Paul needs Amy's efforts to sell ice cream. The profit from the ice cream sold, π, depends on the actions, *a*, that Amy takes at work. The profit may also depend on the outcome of θ, which represents the *state of nature*:

$$\pi = \pi(a, \theta).$$

For example, profit may depend on whether the ice-cream machine breaks, $\theta = 1$, or does not break, $\theta = 0$. Or it may depend on whether it is a hot day, $\theta =$ the temperature.

In extreme cases, the profit function depends only on the agent's actions or only on the state of nature. At one extreme, profit depends only on the agent's action, $\pi = \pi(a)$, if only one state of nature is possible so they face no uncertainty due to random events. In our example, the profit function has this form if demand does not vary with weather and if the ice-cream machine is reliable.

At the other extreme, profit depends only on the state of nature, $\pi = \pi(\theta)$, such as in an insurance market in which profit or value depends only on the state of nature and not on the actions of an agent. For instance, a couple buys insurance against rain on their wedding day. The value they place on their outdoor wedding ceremony is $\pi(\theta)$, which depends only on the weather, θ, because no actions are involved.

Types of Contracts

A verbal contract isn't worth the paper it's written on. —Samuel Goldwyn

When a formal market exists, the principal may deal impersonally with an anonymous agent by buying a good or service of known quality at the market price, so that opportunism cannot occur. We focus on transactions outside formal markets where a principal and an agent agree on a customized contract that is designed to reduce opportunism.

A contract between a principal and an agent determines how the outcome of their partnership (such as the profit or output) is split between them. Three common types of contracts are fixed-fee, hire, and contingent contracts.

In a *fixed-fee contract*, the payment to the agent, F, is independent of the agent's actions, a; the state of nature, θ; or the outcome, π. The principal keeps the *residual profit*, $\pi(a, \theta) - F$. Alternatively, the principal may get a fixed amount and the agent may receive the residual profit. For example, the agent may pay a fixed rent for the right to use the principal's property.[3]

In a *hire contract*, the payment to the agent depends on the agent's actions as the principal observes them. Two common types of hire contracts pay employees an *hourly rate*—a wage per hour—or a *piece rate*—a payment per unit of output produced. If w is the wage per hour (or the price per piece of output) and Amy works a hours (or produces a units of output), then Paul pays Amy wa and keeps the residual profit $\pi(a, \theta) - wa$.

In a *contingent contract*, the payoff to each person depends on the state of nature, which may not be known to the parties at the time they write the contract. For example, Penn agrees to pay Alexis a higher amount to fix his roof if it is raining than if it is not.

One type of contingent contract is a *splitting* or *sharing contract*, where the payoff to each person is a fraction of the total profit (which is observable). Alain sells Pamela's house for her for $\pi(a, \theta)$ and receives a commission of 7% on the sales price. He receives $0.07\pi(a, \theta)$, and she keeps $0.93\pi(a, \theta)$.

Efficiency

The type of contract selected depends on what the parties can observe. A principal is more likely to use a hire contract if the principal can easily monitor the agent's actions. A contingent contract may be chosen if the state of nature can be observed after the work is completed. A fixed-fee contract does not depend on observing anything, so it can be used anytime.

Ideally, the principal and agent agree to an **efficient contract**: an agreement with provisions that ensure that no party can be made better off without harming the other party. Using an efficient contract results in *efficiency in production* and *efficiency in risk sharing*.

Efficiency in production requires that the principal's and agent's combined value (profits, payoffs) is maximized. We say that production is efficient if Amy manages Paul's firm so that the sum of their profits cannot be increased. In our examples, the moral hazard hurts the principal more than it helps the agent, so total profit falls. Thus, achieving efficiency in production requires preventing the moral hazard.

Efficiency in risk bearing requires that risk sharing is optimal in that the person who least minds facing risk—the risk-neutral or less-risk-averse person—bears more of the risk. In Chapter 16, we saw that risk-averse people are willing to pay a risk premium to avoid risk, whereas risk-neutral people do not care if they face fair risk or not. Suppose that Arlene is risk averse and is willing to pay a risk premium of $100 to avoid a particular risk. Peter is risk neutral and would bear the risk without a premium. Arlene and Peter can strike a deal whereby Peter agrees to bear *all* of Arlene's risk in exchange for a payment of between $0 and $100.[4]

---

[3]Jefferson Hope says in the Sherlock Holmes mystery *A Study in Scarlet*, "I applied at a cab-owner's office, and soon got employment. I was to bring a certain sum a week to the owner, and whatever was over that I might keep for myself."

[4]For simplicity, we concentrate on situations in which one party is risk averse and the other is risk neutral. Generally, if both parties are risk averse, with one more risk averse than the other, both can be made better off if the less-risk-averse person bears more but not all of the risk.

If everyone has full information—no uncertainty and no asymmetric information—efficiency can be achieved. The principal contracts with the agent to perform a task for some specified reward and observes whether the agent completes the task properly before paying, so no moral hazard problem arises. Production inefficiency is more likely when either the agent has more information than the principal or both parties are uncertain about the state of nature.

With only one state of nature, if the agent has more information than the principal, contracts can achieve efficiency in production by ensuring that the principal gets adequate information. Alternatively, incentives in the contract may discourage the informed person from engaging in opportunistic behavior. The contracts do not have to address efficiency in risk bearing because they face no uncertainty.

Given that they face both asymmetric information and risk, the parties try to contract to achieve efficiency in production and efficiency in risk bearing. Often, however, both objectives cannot be achieved, so the parties must trade off between them. For example:

Unintended Consequence Paying a manager a share of revenue to encourage hard work may result in the manager engaging in excessive risky behavior.

The following Solved Problem illustrates this unintended consequence.

SOLVED PROBLEM 19.1

MyLab Economics
Solved Problem

An S&L can make one of two types of loans. It can lend money on home mortgages, where it has a 75% probability of earning $100 million and a 25% probability of earning $80 million. Alternatively, it can lend money to oil speculators, where it has a 25% probability of earning $400 million and a 75% probability of losing $160 million (due to loan defaults by the speculators). Bernie, the manager of the S&L who will make the lending decision, receives 1% of the firm's earnings. He believes that if the S&L loses money, he can walk away from his job without repercussions, although without compensation. Bernie and the shareholders of the company are risk neutral. Which decision would Bernie make if all he cares about is maximizing his personal expected earnings? Which investment would the stockholders prefer?

Answer

1. *Determine the S&L's expected return on the two investments.* If the S&L makes home mortgage loans, its expected return is

$$(0.75 \times 100) + (0.25 \times 80) = 95$$

million dollars. Alternatively, if it loans to the oil speculators, its expected return is

$$(0.25 \times 400) + [0.75 \times (-160)] = -20$$

million dollars, an expected loss.

2. *Compare the S&L manager's expected profits on the two investments.* Bernie expects to earn 1% of $95 million, or $950,000, from investing in mortgages. His take from investing in oil is 1% of $400 million, or $4 million, with a

probability of 25% and no compensation with a probability of 75%. Thus, he expects to earn

$$(0.25 \times 4) + (0.75 \times 0) = 1$$

million dollars from investing in oil. Because he is risk neutral and does not care a whit about anyone else, he invests in oil.

3. *Compare the shareholders' expected profits on the two investments.* The shareholders expect to receive 99% of the profit from the mortgages, or $0.99 \times \$95$ million = \$94.05 million. With the oil loans, they earn 99% of the \$400 million, or \$396 million, if the investment is good, and bear the full loss in the case of defaults, \$160 million, so their expected profit (loss) is

$$(0.25 \times 396) + [0.75 \times (-160)] = -21$$

million dollars. Thus, the shareholders would prefer that the S&L invest in mortgages.

Comment: Given the manager has the wrong incentives (and no integrity), he makes the investment that is not in the shareholders' interest. One solution to the problem of their divergent interests is to change the manager's compensation package, as we discuss in the Challenge Solution.

APPLICATION

Honest Cabbie?

You arrive in a strange city and get in a cab. Will the driver take you to your destination by the shortest route, or will you get ripped off?

To find out, Balafoutas, Kerschbamer, and Sutter (2017) ran an experiment in Athens. Four native-speaking Greeks took 400 taxi trips. For each trip, they said, "I would like to get to [name of a destination]. Do you know where it is? I am not from Athens." A few seconds after the ride began, the passenger said either, "Can I get a receipt at the end of the ride?" or "Can I get a receipt at the end of the ride? I need it in order to have my expenses reimbursed by my employer."

The experimenters expected that fraudulent behavior would be less likely in the former (control) case than in the latter ("moral hazard") case, where passengers would have weaker incentives to control or report a longer than necessary trip or overcharging. Overcharging (mostly bonus surcharges) occurred 36.5% of the time for the moral hazard rides compared to 19.5% for the control rides. Overall, the fare for the moral hazard trips averaged 17% more than for the control trips.

19.2 Production Efficiency

We start by examining situations with no risk due to random events, so that total profit, $\pi(a)$, is solely a function of the agent's action, a. Production efficiency is achieved by maximizing total or joint profit: the sum of the principal's and the agent's individual profits.

Efficient Contract

Some people believe that only the total compensation paid to a worker is important.

Common Confusion It doesn't matter whether someone is paid a lump-sum, by the hour, a percentage of the revenue, or in other ways.

On the contrary, in many situations the way someone is paid has a major effect on the outcome. In principal-agent settings, a skillfully designed payment contract may reduce or eliminate moral hazard problems. For example, Shearer (2004) found that when tree planters were randomly assigned piece-rate pay or fixed hourly wages, they were 19% more productive when paid by per tree planted.

To be efficient and to maximize joint profit, the contract that a principal offers to an agent must have two properties. First, the contract must provide a large enough payoff that the *agent is willing to participate* in the contract. We know that the principal's payoff is adequate to ensure the principal's participation because the principal offers the contract.

Second, the contract must be **incentive compatible**: It provides inducements such that the agent wants to perform the assigned task rather than engage in opportunistic behavior. That is, it is in the agent's best interest to act to maximize joint profit. If the contract is not incentive compatible so the agent tries to maximize personal profit rather than joint profit, efficiency is achieved only if the principal monitors the agent and forces the agent to maximize joint profit.

We use an example to illustrate why only some types of contracts lead to efficiency. Paula, the principal, owns a store called Buy-A-Duck (located near a canal) that sells wooden duck carvings. Arthur, the agent, manages the store. Paula and Arthur's joint profit is

$$\pi(a) = R(a) - ma, \qquad (19.1)$$

where $R(a)$ is the sales revenue from selling a carvings, and ma is the cost of the carvings. Arthur has a constant marginal cost m to obtain and sell each duck, including the amount he pays a local carver and the opportunity value (best alternative use) of his time.

Because Arthur bears the full marginal cost of selling one more carving, he wants to sell the joint-profit-maximizing output only if he also gets the full marginal benefit from selling one more duck. To determine the joint-profit-maximizing solution, we can ask what Arthur would do if he owned the shop and received all the profit, giving him an incentive to maximize total profit.

How many ducks, a, must Arthur sell to maximize the parties' joint profit, Equation 19.1? To obtain the first-order condition to maximize profit, we set the derivative of Equation 19.1 with respect to a equal to zero:

$$\frac{d\pi}{da} = \frac{dR(a)}{da} - m = 0. \qquad (19.2)$$

According to Equation 19.2, joint profit is maximized by choosing the number of ducks such that marginal revenue, $dR(a)/da$, equals marginal cost, m.

Suppose the marginal cost is $m = 12$. The inverse demand function is $p = 24 - \frac{1}{2}a$ so that the revenue function is $R(a) = 24a - \frac{1}{2}a^2$. The marginal revenue function is $MR(a) = dR(a)/da = 24 - a$. Substituting the marginal revenue function and the marginal cost into Equation 19.2, we find that $MR = 24 - a = 12 = m = MC$, or $a = 12$. Panel a of Figure 19.1 illustrates this result: The marginal revenue curve, MR, intersects the marginal cost curve, $MC = m = \$12$, at the equilibrium point e. The corresponding price is $18. Panel b shows that total profit, π, reaches a maximum of $72 at point E.

Figure 19.1 Maximizing Joint Profit When the Agent Gets the Residual Profit

(a) If the agent, Arthur, gets all the joint profit, π, he maximizes his profit by selling 12 carvings at e, where the marginal revenue curve intersects his marginal cost curve: $MR = MC = 12$.   If he pays the principal, Paula, a fixed rent of $48, he maximizes his profit by selling 12 carvings. (A fixed rent does not affect either his marginal revenue or his marginal cost.) (b) Joint profit at 12 carvings is $72, point E. If Arthur pays a rent of $48 to Paula, Arthur's profit is $\pi - \$48$. By selling 12 carvings and maximizing joint profit, Arthur also maximizes his profit.

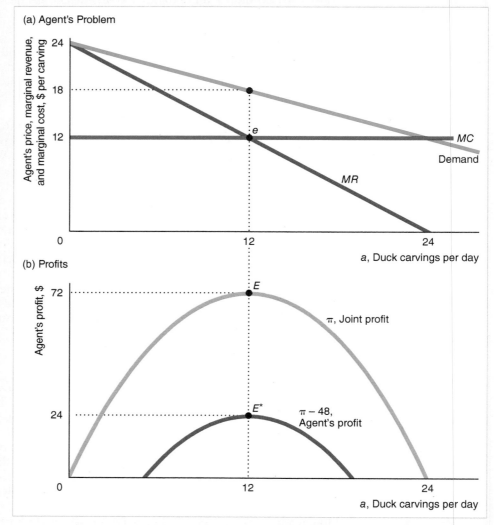

Which types of contracts lead to production efficiency? To answer this question, we first examine which contracts yield that outcome when both parties have full information and then consider which contracts bring the desired result when the principal is relatively uninformed. It is important to remember that we are considering a special case: Contracts that work here may not work in some other settings, and contracts that do not work here may be effective elsewhere.

Full Information

Suppose that both Paula and Arthur have full information. Each knows the actions Arthur takes—the number of carvings sold—and the effect of those actions on profit. Because she has full information, Paula can dictate exactly what Arthur is to do. Do incentive-compatible contracts exist that do not require such monitoring and supervision? To answer this question, we consider four kinds of contracts: a fixed-fee rental contract, a hire contract, and two types of contingent contracts.

Fixed-Fee Rental Contract. If Arthur contracts to rent the store from Paula for a fixed fee, F, joint profit is maximized. Arthur earns a residual profit equal to the joint profit minus the fixed rent he pays Paula, $\pi(a) - F$. Because the amount that Paula makes is fixed, Arthur gets the entire marginal profit from selling one more duck. As a consequence, the amount, a, that maximizes Arthur's profit,

$$\pi(a) - F = R(a) - ma - F, \tag{19.3}$$

also maximizes joint profit, $\pi(a)$. To show this result, we note that his first-order condition based on Equation 19.3,

$$\frac{d[\pi(a) - F]}{da} = \frac{dR(a)}{da} - m - \frac{dF}{da} = \frac{dR(a)}{da} - m = 0, \tag{19.4}$$

is identical to the first-order condition in Equation 19.2.

In Figure 19.1, Arthur pays Paula $F = \$48$ rent. This fixed payment does not affect his marginal cost. As a result, he maximizes his profit after paying the rent, $\pi - \$48$, by equating his marginal revenue to his marginal cost: $MR = MC = 12$ at point e in panel a.

Because Arthur pays the same fixed rent no matter how many units he sells, his profit curve in panel b lies $48 below the joint-profit curve at every quantity. As a result, Arthur's net-profit curve peaks (at point E^*) at the same quantity, 12, where the joint-profit curve peaks (at E). Thus, the fixed-fee rental contract is incentive compatible. Arthur participates in this contract because he earns $24 after paying the rent and for the carvings.

Hire Contract. Now suppose that Paula contracts to pay Arthur for each carving he sells. If she pays him $12 per carving, Arthur just breaks even on each sale. He is indifferent between participating and not. Even if he chooses to participate, he does not sell the joint-profit-maximizing number of carvings unless Paula supervises him. If she does supervise him, she instructs him to sell 12 carvings, and she gets all the joint profit of $72.

For Arthur to want to participate and to sell carvings without supervision, he must receive more than $12 per carving. If Paula pays Arthur $14 per carving, for example, he makes a profit of $2 per carving. He now has an incentive to sell as many carvings as he can (even if the price is less than the cost of the carving), which does not maximize joint profit, so this contract is not incentive compatible.

Even if Paula can control how many carvings Arthur sells, joint profit is not maximized. Paula keeps the revenue minus what she pays Arthur, $14 times the number of carvings,

$$R(a) - 14a.$$

Thus, her objective differs from the joint-profit-maximizing objective, which is to choose a to maximize $\pi(a) = R(a) - 12a$. Joint profit is maximized when marginal revenue equals the marginal cost of $12. Because Paula's marginal cost, $14, is larger, she directs Arthur to sell fewer than the optimal number of carvings. Paula maximizes $R - 14a = (24a - \frac{1}{2}a^2) - 14a = 10a - \frac{1}{2}a^2$. Given her first-order condition, where the derivative of Paula's profit with respect to a equals zero, $10 - a = 0$, she maximizes her profit by selling 10 carvings. Joint profit (based on a marginal cost of 12) is only $12a - \frac{1}{2}a^2 = 120 - 50 = \$70$ at 10 carvings, compared to $144 - 72 = \$72$ at the optimal 12 carvings.

Revenue-Sharing Contract. If Paula and Arthur use a *contingent contract* whereby they share the *revenue*, joint profit is not maximized. Suppose that Arthur receives three-quarters of the revenue, $\frac{3}{4}R$, and Paula gets the rest, $\frac{1}{4}R$. Panel a of Figure 19.2 shows the marginal revenue that Arthur obtains from selling an extra carving, $MR^* = \frac{3}{4}$. He maximizes his profit at $24 by selling eight carvings, for which $MR^* = MC$ at e^*. Paula gets the remaining profit of $40, which is the difference between their total profit from selling eight ducks per day, $\pi = \$64$, and Arthur's profit.

Thus, their joint profit in panel b at $a = 8$ is $64, which is $8 less than the maximum possible profit of $72 (point *E*). Arthur has an incentive to sell fewer than the optimal number of ducks because he bears the full marginal cost of each carving he sells, $12, but gets only three-quarters of the marginal revenue.

Even if Paula controls how many carvings are sold, joint profit is not maximized. Because the amount she makes, $\frac{1}{4}R$, depends only on revenue and not on the cost of obtaining the carvings, she wants the revenue-maximizing quantity sold. Revenue

Figure 19.2 Why Revenue Sharing Reduces Agent's Efforts

(a) Joint profit is maximized at 12 carvings, where $MR = MC = 12$ at equilibrium point *e*. If Arthur gets three-quarters of the revenue and Paula gets the rest, Arthur maximizes his profit by selling 8 carvings per day, where his new marginal revenue curve, $MR^* = \frac{3}{4}MR$, equals his marginal cost at point e^*. (b) Joint profit reaches a maximum of $72 at *E*, where they sell 12 carvings per day. If they split the revenue, Arthur sells 8 duck carvings per day and gets $24 at E^*, and Paula receives the residual, $40 (= $64 − $24).

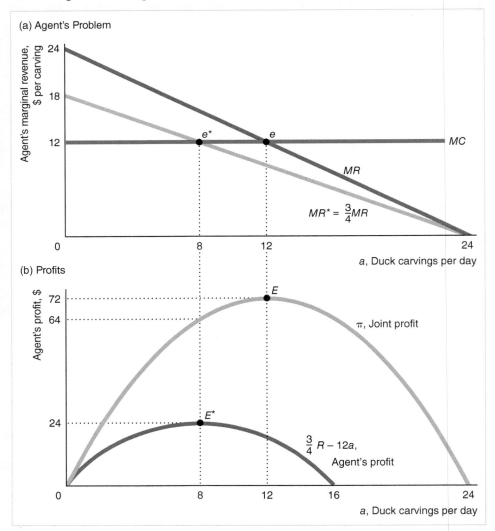

is maximized where marginal revenue is zero at $a = 24$ (panel a). Arthur will not participate if the contract grants him only three-quarters of the revenue but requires him to sell 24 carvings, because he will lose money.

SOLVED PROBLEM **19.2** **MyLab Economics** Solved Problem	Use calculus to show that, if Arthur receives three-quarters of the revenue, $\frac{3}{4}R$, and Paula gets the rest, he does not sell the joint-profit-maximizing quantity. **Answer**

1. *Write Arthur's profit function, calculate his first-order condition, and solve for his profit-maximizing output.* Arthur's profit is $\frac{3}{4}R(a) - 12a = \frac{3}{4}(24a - \frac{1}{2}a^2) - 12a$. To maximize his profit, he needs to choose a, such that his marginal profit with respect to a equals zero: $\frac{3}{4}dR(a)/da - 12 = \frac{3}{4}(24 - a) - 12 = 0$. Thus, the output that maximizes his profit is $a = 8$.

2. *Compare this solution to the joint-profit-maximizing output.* We know that the joint profit is maximized at 72, where $a = 12$. With revenue sharing, $a = 8$ and joint profits are only 64.

   Comment: Arthur produces too little output because he bears the full marginal cost, 12, but earns $\frac{3}{4}(24 - a)$, which is only three-quarters of the marginal benefit (marginal revenue) from the joint-profit-maximizing problem, $24 - a$.

Profit-Sharing Contract. Paula and Arthur may use a contingent contract by which they divide the economic profit π. If they can agree that the true marginal and average cost is \$12 per carving (which includes Arthur's opportunity cost of time), the contract is incentive compatible. Only by maximizing total profit can Arthur maximize his share of profit.

As Figure 19.3 shows, Arthur receives one-third of the joint profit and chooses to produce the level of output, $a = 12$, that maximizes joint profit. Arthur's share is $\frac{1}{3}\pi = \frac{1}{3}(R - C) = \frac{1}{3}R - \frac{1}{3}C$, where R is revenue and C is cost. He maximizes his

Figure 19.3 Why Profit Sharing Is Efficient

If the agent, Arthur, gets one-third of the joint profit, he maximizes his profit, $\frac{1}{3}\pi$, by maximizing joint profit, π.

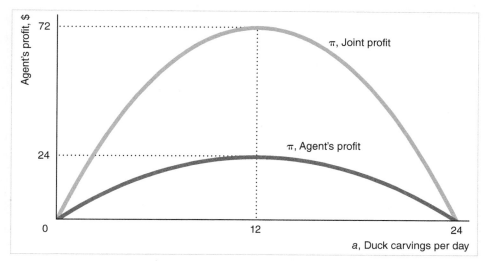

Table 19.1 Production Efficiency and Moral Hazard Problems for Buy-A-Duck

Contract	Full Information Production Efficiency	Asymmetric Information Production Efficiency	Moral Hazard Problem
Fixed-fee rental contract			
Rent (to principal)	Yes	Yes	No
Hire contract, per unit pay			
Pay equals marginal cost	No[a]	No[b]	Yes
Pay is greater than marginal cost	No[c]	No	Yes
Contingent contract			
Share revenue	No	No[b]	Yes
Share profit	Yes	No[b]	Yes

[a]The agent may not participate and has no incentive to sell the optimal number of carvings. Efficiency can be achieved only if the principal supervises.
[b]Unless the agent steals all the revenue (or profit) from an extra sale, inefficiency results.
[c]The agent sells too many or the principal directs the agent to sell too few carvings.

profit where $d[\frac{1}{3}\pi(a)]/da = \frac{1}{3}MR - \frac{1}{3}MC = 0$, or $\frac{1}{3}MR = \frac{1}{3}MC$. Although he receives only one-third of the marginal revenue, he bears only one-third of the marginal cost. Dividing both sides of the equation by $\frac{1}{3}$, we find that this condition is the same as the one for maximizing total profit: $MR = MC$. Arthur earns $24, so he is willing to participate.

Summary. The second column of Table 19.1 summarizes our analysis with full information. Whether production is efficient depends on the type of contract that the principal and the agent use. If the principal has full information (knows the agent's actions), the principal achieves production efficiency without having to supervise by using one of the incentive-compatible contracts: fixed-fee rental or profit-sharing.

Asymmetric Information

Now suppose that the principal, Paula, has less information than the agent, Arthur. She cannot observe the number of carvings he sells or the revenue. As Table 19.1 shows, with asymmetric information, only the fixed-rent contract results in production efficiency and no moral hazard problem. All the other contracts result in inefficiency, and Arthur has an opportunity to take advantage of Paula.

Fixed-Fee Rental Contract. Arthur pays Paula the fixed rent that she is due because Paula would know if she were paid less. Arthur receives the residual profit, joint profit minus the fixed rent, so he wants to sell the joint-profit-maximizing number of carvings.

Hire Contract. If Paula offers to pay Arthur the actual marginal cost of $12 per carving and he is honest, he may refuse to participate in the contract because he makes no profit. Even if he participates, he has no incentive to sell the optimal number of carvings.

If he is dishonest, he may **underreport** sales and pocket some of the extra revenue. Unless he can steal all the extra revenue from an additional sale, he sells less than the joint-profit-maximizing quantity.

If Paula pays him more than the actual marginal cost per carving, he has an incentive to sell too many carvings, whether or not he steals. If he also steals, he has an even greater incentive to sell too many carvings.

Revenue-Sharing Contract. Even with full information, the revenue-sharing contract is inefficient. Asymmetric information adds a moral hazard problem: The agent may steal from the principal. If Arthur can steal a larger share of the revenues than the contract specifies, he has less of an incentive to undersell than he does with full information. Indeed, if the agent can steal all the extra revenue from an additional sale, the agent acts efficiently to maximize joint profit, all of which the agent keeps.

Profit-Sharing Contract. If they use a contingent contract and split the economic profit, Arthur has to report both the revenue and the cost to Paula so that they can calculate their shares. If he can overreport cost or underreport revenue, he has an incentive to produce a nonoptimal quantity. Only if Arthur can appropriate all the profit does he produce efficiently.

APPLICATION Sing for Your Supper	The concert producer of one of the world's largest music festivals, Outside Lands Music & Arts Festival, negotiates with dozens of food and drink vendors to sell goods at his annual event. According to his contract with them, they owe him the larger of a minimum amount (the "guarantee") and his share of the revenues. He worries that the vendors might underreport their revenues, as he cannot easily monitor them. To minimize the moral hazard problem, he took two actions. First, he compares reported revenues across vendors. The vast majority of vendors report comparable revenues within their categories. He does not invite the 10% of vendors who report substantially smaller amounts back in following years. Thus, substantial cheating by vendors cost them the opportunity to participate in the event in the future. Second, he requires that to buy wine, concertgoers must use an electronic payment system, which keeps track of sales. The year he introduced this system, revenue increased by over 30% from the previous year due to more accurate reporting. Thus, by making information closer to symmetric, he has reduced his moral hazard problem.

19.3   Trade-Off Between Efficiency in Production and in Risk Bearing

Writing an efficient contract is difficult if the agent knows more than the principal, the principal never learns the truth, and both face risk. Usually, a contract does not achieve efficiency in production and in risk bearing. Contract clauses that increase production efficiency may reduce efficiency in risk bearing, and vice versa. If these goals are incompatible, the parties may write imperfect contracts that compromise between the two objectives. To illustrate the trade-offs involved, we consider a common situation in which it is difficult to achieve efficiency: contracting with an expert such as a lawyer.

Pam, the principal, is injured in a traffic accident and is a plaintiff in a lawsuit. Alfredo, the agent, is her lawyer. Pam faces uncertainty due to risk and to asymmetric information. The jury award at the conclusion of the trial, $\pi(a, \theta)$, depends on a, the number of hours Alfredo works preparing and trying the case, and θ, the state of nature: the unknown attitudes of jury members. All else the same, the more time Alfredo spends on the case, a, the larger the expected π. Pam never learns the jury's attitude, θ, so she cannot accurately judge Alfredo's efforts even after the trial. For example, if she loses the case, she won't know whether she lost because Alfredo didn't work hard (low a) or because the jury disliked her (bad θ).

Contracts and Efficiency

How hard Alfredo works depends on his attitude toward risk and his knowledge of the payoff for his trial preparations. For any hour that he does not devote to Pam's case, Alfredo can work on other cases. The most lucrative of these forgone opportunities is his marginal cost of working on Pam's case.

Who benefits from Alfredo's extra work depends on his contract with Pam. If Alfredo is risk neutral and gets the entire marginal benefit from any extra work, he sets his expected marginal benefit equal to his marginal cost, works the optimal number of hours, and maximizes the expected joint payoff.

The choice of various possible contracts between Pam and Alfredo affects whether efficiency in production or in risk bearing is achieved. They choose among fixed-fee, hire (hourly wage), and contingent contracts. Table 19.2 summarizes the outcomes under each of these contracts.

Lawyer Gets a Fixed Fee. If Pam pays Alfredo a fixed fee, F, he gets paid the same amount no matter how much he works. Thus, he has little incentive to work hard

Table 19.2   Efficiency of Client-Lawyer Contracts

Type of Contract	Fixed Fee to Lawyer	Fixed Payment to Client	Lawyer Paid by the Hour	Contingent Contract
Lawyer's payoff	F	$\pi(a, \theta) - F$	wa	$\alpha\pi(a, \theta)$
Client's payoff	$\pi(a, \theta) - F$	F	$\pi(a, \theta) - wa$	$(1 - \alpha)\pi(a, \theta)$
Production efficiency?	No*	Yes	No*	No*
Who bears risk?	Client	Lawyer	Client	Shared

*Production efficiency is possible if the client can monitor and enforce optimal effort by the lawyer.

on this case, and his production is inefficient.[5] Production efficiency can be achieved only if Pam can monitor Alfredo and force him to act optimally. However, most individual plaintiffs cannot monitor a lawyer and therefore cannot determine whether the lawyer is behaving appropriately.

Whether the fixed-fee contract leads to efficiency in risk bearing depends on the attitudes toward risk on the part of the principal and agent. Alfredo gets F regardless, so he bears no risk. Pam bears all the risk: Her net payoff $\pi(a, \theta) - F$ varies with the unknown state of nature, θ.

A lawyer who handles many similar cases may be less risk averse than an individual client whose financial future depends on a single case. If Alfredo has had many cases like Pam's and if Pam's future rests on the outcome of this suit, their choice of this type of contract leads to inefficiency in both production and risk bearing. Not only is Alfredo not working hard enough, but Pam bears the risk, even though she is more risk averse than Alfredo.

In contrast, if Alfredo is a self-employed lawyer working on a major case for Pam, who runs a large insurance company with many similar cases, Alfredo is risk averse and Pam is risk neutral. Here, having the principal bear all the risk is efficient. If the insurance company can monitor Alfredo's behavior, it is even possible to achieve production efficiency. Indeed, many insurance companies employ lawyers in this manner.

SOLVED PROBLEM 19.3

Alfredo, the lawyer, pays Pam, the client, a *fixed payment*, F, for the right to try the case and collect the entire verdict less the payment to Pam, $\pi(a, \theta) - F$. Does such a contract lead to efficiency? Are the parties willing to sign such a contract?

MyLab Economics Solved Problem

Answer

1. *Show that Alfredo has an incentive to put in the optimal number of hours.* Alfredo works until his marginal cost—the opportunity cost of his time—equals the marginal benefit—the extra amount he gets if he wins at trial. Because he has already paid Pam, all extra amounts earned at trial go to Alfredo. Therefore, Alfredo has an incentive to put in the optimal number of hours.

2. *Show that whether efficiency in risk bearing occurs depends on the parties' attitudes toward risk.* Alfredo bears all the risk related to the outcome of the trial. Thus, if he's risk neutral and Pam is risk averse, this contract results in efficient risk bearing, but not otherwise.

3. *Explain why the parties are hesitant to sign the contract because of asymmetric information and moral hazard.* No matter how risk averse Pam is, she may hesitate to agree to this contract. Because she is not an expert on the law, she cannot easily predict the jury's likely verdict. Thus, she does not know how large a fixed fee she should insist on receiving. They have no practical way in which Alfredo's superior information about the likely outcome of the trial can be credibly revealed to her. She suspects that it is in his best interest to tell her that the likely payout is lower than he truly believes. Similarly, Alfredo may be hesitant to offer Pam a fixed fee. How well they do in court depends on the merits of her case. At least initially, Alfredo does not know how good a case she has. Initially, she has an incentive to try to convince him that the case is very strong.

---

[5]His main incentive to work hard (other than honesty) is to establish a reputation as a good lawyer so as to attract future clients. For simplicity, we will ignore this effect, because it applies for all types of contracts.

Lawyer Is Hired by the Hour. If Pam pays Alfredo a wage of w per hour for the a hours that he works, Alfredo could bill her for more hours than he actually worked unless she can monitor him.[6] Even if Pam could observe how many hours he works, she would not know whether Alfredo worked effectively and whether the work was necessary. Thus it would be difficult, if not impossible, for Pam to monitor Alfredo's work.

Pam bears all the risk. Alfredo's earnings, wa, are determined before the outcome is known. Pam's return, $\pi(a, \theta) - wa$, varies with the state of nature and is unknown before the verdict.

Fee Is Contingent. Some lawyers offer plaintiffs a contract whereby the lawyer works for "free"—receiving no hourly payment—in exchange for splitting the compensation awarded in court or in a pre-trial settlement. The lawyer receives a **contingent fee**: a payment that is a share of the award in a court case (usually after legal expenses are deducted) if the client wins and nothing if the client loses. If the lawyer's share of the award is b and the jury awards $\pi(a, \theta)$, the lawyer receives $b\pi(a, \theta)$ and the principal gets $(1 - b)\pi(a, \theta)$. This approach is attractive to many plaintiffs because they cannot monitor how hard the lawyer works and are unable or unwilling to make payments before the trial is completed.

How they split the award affects the amount of risk each bears. If Alfredo gets one-quarter of the award, $b = \frac{1}{4}$, and Pam gets three-quarters, Pam bears more risk than Alfredo does. Suppose that the award is either 0 or 40 with equal probability. Alfredo receives either 0 or 10, so his average award is 5. His variance (Chapter 16) is $\sigma_a^2 = \frac{1}{2}(0 - 5)^2 + \frac{1}{2}(10 - 5)^2 = 25$. Pam makes either 0 or 30, so her average award is 15 and her variance is $\sigma_p^2 = \frac{1}{2}(0 - 15)^2 + \frac{1}{2}(30 - 15)^2 = 225$. Thus, the variance in Pam's payoff is greater than Alfredo's.

Whether splitting the risk in this way is desirable depends on how risk averse each party is. If one is risk neutral and the other is risk averse, it is efficient for the risk-neutral person to bear all the risk. If they are equally risk averse, a splitting rule in which $b = \frac{1}{2}$ and they face equal risk may be optimal.[7]

A sharing contract encourages shirking: Alfredo is likely to put in too little effort. He bears the full cost of his labors—the forgone use of his time—but gets only b share of the returns from this effort. Thus, this contract results in production inefficiency and may or may not lead to inefficient risk bearing.

Choosing the Best Contract

Which contract is best depends on the parties' attitudes toward risk, the degree of risk, the difficulty in monitoring, and other factors. If Alfredo is risk neutral, they can achieve both efficiency goals if Alfredo charges Pam a fixed fee. He has the incentive to put in the optimal amount of work and does not mind bearing the risk.

However, if Alfredo is risk averse and Pam is risk neutral, they may not be able to achieve both objectives. Contracts that provide Alfredo a fixed fee or a wage rate allocate all the risk to Pam and lead to inefficiency in production because Alfredo has too little incentive to work hard.

---

[6]A lawyer dies in an accident and goes to heaven. A host of angels greet him with a banner that reads, "Welcome Oldest Man!" The lawyer is puzzled: "Why do you think I'm the oldest man? I was only 47 when I died." One of the angels replies, "You can't fool us; you were at least 152 when you died. We saw the hours you billed!"

[7]If Pam and Alfredo split the award equally and each receives either 0 or 20 with equal probability, each has a variance of $\frac{1}{2}(0 - 10)^2 + \frac{1}{2}(20 - 10)^2 = 100$.

Often when the parties find that they cannot achieve both objectives, they choose a contract that attains neither goal. For example, they may use a contingent contract that fails to achieve efficiency in production and may not achieve efficiency in risk bearing. The contingent contract strikes a compromise between the two goals. Alfredo has more of an incentive to work if he splits the payoff than if he receives a fixed fee. He is less likely to work excessive hours with the contingent fee than if he were paid by the hour. Moreover, neither party has to bear all the risk—they share it under the contingent contract.

Lawyers usually work for a fixed fee only if the task or case is very simple, such as writing a will or handling an uncontested divorce. The client has some idea of whether the work is done satisfactorily, so monitoring is relatively easy and little risk is involved.

In riskier situations, the other types of contracts are more common. When the lawyer is relatively risk averse or when the principal is very concerned that the lawyer works hard, an hourly wage may be used.

Contingent fee arrangements are particularly common for plaintiffs' lawyers who specialize in auto accidents, medical malpractice, and product liability. Because these plaintiffs' lawyers can typically pool risks across clients, they are less concerned than their clients are about risk. As a consequence, these attorneys are willing to accept contingent fees (and might agree to pay a fixed fee to the plaintiff). Moreover, accident victims often lack the resources to pay for a lawyer's time before winning at trial, so they often prefer contingent contracts.

APPLICATION

Health Insurance and Moral Hazard

The 2010 U.S. Patient Protection and Affordable Care Act (ACA) resulted in more coverage of low-income people. The number of uninsured, nonelderly Americans fell from 44 million in 2013 (the year before the major coverage provisions kicked in) to fewer than 28 million by the end of 2016. However, as the program changed under the Trump administration, the number of Americans without insurance rose by 3.2 million people in 2017 and continued to increase in the first quarter of 2018.

Society benefits by shifting risk from these previously uncovered, risk-averse people to risk-neutral insurance companies (Chapter 16). However, many analysts argue that extending insurance coverage results in more moral hazard. For example, patients may use the medical system excessively, driving up costs to everyone. Do insured people use health care services excessively?

The adult dependent coverage provision of the ACA allows young adults up to age 26 to stay on their parents' health care policies. Prior to that, about one in three young adults ages 19–25 lacked insurance. Jhamb, Dave, Colman (2015) estimated that this provision raised insurance coverage among young adults by 7.4% and the number of doctor visits by 3%.

Kowalski (2018) found that the Oregon state health insurance program enrollees increased their emergency room (ER) utilization, but that subsequent enrollees will be healthier and will decrease their ER utilization. Simon, Soni, and Cawley (2017) found that the ACA increased the use of certain forms of preventive care, did not increase risky health behavior (a form of moral hazard), and modestly increased self-assessed health. Thus, studies to date find that the moral hazard effects are relatively small.

**SOLVED PROBLEM
19.4**

**MyLab Economics
Solved Problem**

Gary's demand for doctor visits depends on his health. Half the time his health is good and his demand is D^1 in the figure. When his health is poor, his demand is D^2. Gary is risk averse. Without medical insurance, he pays $50 a visit. With full insurance, he pays a fixed fee at the beginning of the year, and the insurance company pays the full cost of any visit. Alternatively, with a contingent contract, Gary pays a smaller premium at the beginning of the year, and the insurance company covers only $20 per visit, with Gary paying the remaining $30. How likely is a moral hazard problem to occur with each of these contracts? What is Gary's risk (the variance of his medical costs) with no insurance and with each of the two types of insurance? Compare the contracts in terms of the trade-offs between risk and moral hazard.

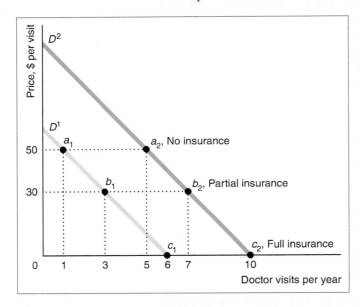

Answer

1. *Describe the moral hazard for each demand curve for each contract.* Given that Gary's health is good, if he does not have insurance, Gary pays the doctor $50 a visit and goes to the doctor once, at point a_1 on D^1 in the figure. In contrast, with full insurance, where he pays nothing per visit, he visits the doctor six times, at c_1. Similarly, if his health is poor, he goes to the doctor five times, a_2, without insurance, and 10 times, c_2, with full insurance. Thus, regardless of his health, he makes five extra visits a year with full insurance. These extra visits are the moral hazard.

With a contingent contract, Gary pays $30 a visit. He makes three visits if his health is good (at point b_1)—only two more than at a_1. If his health is poor, he makes seven visits, once again two more than if he were paying the full fee (five visits at point a_2). Thus, this contingent contract reduces the moral hazard problem: He makes only two extra visits.

2. *Calculate the variance of Gary's medical expenses for no insurance and for the two insurance contracts.* Without insurance, his average number of visits is $3 = (\frac{1}{2} \times 1) + (\frac{1}{2} \times 5)$, so his average annual medical cost is $150. Thus, the variance of his medical expenses without insurance is

$$\sigma_n^2 = \tfrac{1}{2}[(1 \times \$50) - \$150]^2 + \tfrac{1}{2}[(5 \times 50) - \$150]^2$$
$$= \tfrac{1}{2}(\$50 - \$150)^2 + \tfrac{1}{2}(\$250 - \$150)^2$$
$$= \$10,000.$$

If he has full insurance, he makes a single fixed payment each year, so his payments do not vary with his health: His variance is $\sigma_f^2 = 0$. Finally, with partial insurance, he averages 5 visits with an average cost of $150, so his variance is

$$\sigma_p^2 = \tfrac{1}{2}(\$90 - \$150)^2 + \tfrac{1}{2}(\$210 - \$150)^2 = \$3,600.$$

Thus, $\sigma_n^2 > \sigma_p^2 > \sigma_f^2$.

3. *Discuss the trade-offs.* Because Gary is risk averse, efficiency in risk bearing requires the insurance company to bear all the risk, as with full insurance. However, full insurance results in the largest moral hazard. Removing insurance eliminates the moral hazard, but forces Gary to bear all the risk. The contingent contract is a compromise in which both the moral hazard and the degree of risk lie between the extremes.

19.4 Monitoring to Reduce Moral Hazard

When a firm cannot pay workers in proportion to the work they do (a piece rate) or share the firm's profit with the workers, the firm usually pays fixed-fee salaries or hourly wages, which may lead to employees shirking. A firm can reduce such shirking by intensively supervising or monitoring workers. Monitoring eliminates the asymmetric information problem: Both the employee and the employer know how hard the employee works. If the cost of monitoring workers is low enough, it pays to prevent shirking by carefully monitoring and firing employees who do not work hard.

Firms experiment with various means of lowering the cost of monitoring. Requiring employees to punch a time clock and recording employees' work efforts by installing video cameras are examples of firms' attempts to use capital to monitor job performance. By using assembly lines that force employees to work at a set pace, employers can control employees' work rate. In 2018, Amazon patented a wristband to be worn by employees that would allow the firm to monitor whether employees stop working.

According to a survey by the American Management Association, nearly two-thirds of employers record employees' voice mail, e-mail, and phone calls; review employee computer files; or videotape workers. A quarter of the firms that use surveillance don't tell their employees. The most common types of surveillance are tallying outgoing phone calls and recording their duration (37%), videotaping the workplace (16%), storing and reviewing e-mails (15%), storing and reviewing computer files (14%), and taping and reviewing phone conversations (10%). Monitoring and surveillance are most common in the financial sector, in which 81% of firms use these techniques. Rather than watching all employees all the time, companies usually monitor selected workers randomly.

For some jobs, however, monitoring is counterproductive or not cost effective. Monitoring may lower employees' morale, reducing productivity. Several years ago, Northwest Airlines removed the doors from bathroom stalls to prevent workers from using them to slack off. When new management changed this policy (and made many other changes as well), productivity increased.

It is usually impractical for firms to monitor how hard salespeople work if they spend most of their time away from the main office. As telecommuting increases, monitoring workers may become increasingly difficult.

When direct monitoring is very costly, firms may use various financial incentives to reduce the amount of monitoring that is necessary. Each of these incentives—bonding, deferred payments, and efficiency (unusually high) wages—acts as a *hostage* for good behavior (Williamson, 1983). Workers who are caught shirking or engaging in other undesirable acts not only lose their jobs but also give up the hostage. The more valuable the hostage, the less monitoring is necessary to deter bad behavior.

Bonding

One way to ensure agents behave well is to require that they deposit funds guaranteeing their good behavior, just as a landlord requires tenants to post security deposits to ensure they will not damage an apartment. Typically, the agent posts (leaves) this bond with the principal or another party, such as an insurance company, before starting the job.

Many couriers who transport valuable shipments (such as jewels) or guards who protect them post bonds against theft and other moral hazards. Similarly, bonds prevent employees from quitting immediately after receiving costly training (Salop and Salop, 1976). Most of the other approaches that we will examine for controlling shirking can be viewed as forms of bonding.

Bonding to Prevent Shirking. Some employers require a worker to post a bond that is forfeited if the worker is discovered shirking. For example, a professional athlete faces a specified fine (the equivalent of a bond) for skipping a meeting or game. The higher the bond, the less frequently the employer needs to monitor to prevent shirking.

Let G be the value that a worker puts on taking it easy on the job. If a worker's only potential punishment for shirking is dismissal if caught, some workers will shirk.

Shirking is less likely if the worker must post a bond of B that is forfeited if the employee is caught not working. Given the firm's level of monitoring, the probability that a worker is caught is θ. Thus, a worker who shirks expects to lose θB.[8] A risk-neutral worker chooses not to shirk if the certain gain from shirking, G, is less than or equal to the expected penalty, θB, from forfeiting the bond if caught: $G \leq \theta B$. Thus, the minimum bond that discourages shirking is

$$B = \frac{G}{\theta}. \tag{19.5}$$

Equation 19.5 shows that the bond must be larger, the higher the value that the employee places on shirking and the lower the probability that the worker will be caught.

Thus, the larger the bond, the less monitoring is necessary to prevent shirking. Suppose that a worker places a value of $G = \$1,000$ a year on shirking. A bond that is large enough to discourage shirking is $\$1,000$ if the probability of the worker being caught is 100%, $\$2,000$ at 50%, $\$5,000$ at 20%, $\$10,000$ at 10%, and $\$20,000$ at 5%.

**SOLVED PROBLEM
19.5**

MyLab Economics
Solved Problem

Workers post bonds of B that are forfeited if they are caught stealing (but no other punishment is imposed). Each extra unit of monitoring, M, raises the probability that a firm catches a worker who steals, θ, by 5%. A unit of M costs $\$10$. A worker can steal a piece of equipment and resell it for its full value of G dollars. What is the optimal M that the firm uses if it believes workers are risk neutral? In particular, if $B = \$5,000$ and $G = \$500$, what is the optimal M?

Answer

1. *Determine how many units of monitoring are necessary to deter stealing.* The least amount of monitoring that deters stealing is the amount at which a worker's gain from stealing equals the worker's expected loss if caught. A worker is just deterred from stealing when the gain, G, equals the expected penalty, θB. Thus, the worker is deterred when the probability of being caught is $\theta = G/B$. The number of units of monitoring effort is $M = \theta/0.05$, because each extra unit of monitoring raises θ by 5%.

---

[8]The expected penalty is $\theta B + (1 - \theta)0 = \theta B$, where the first term on the left-hand side is the probability of being caught times the fine of B and the second term is the probability of not being caught and facing no fine.

2. *Determine whether monitoring is cost effective.* It pays for the firm to pay for M units of monitoring only if the expected benefit to the firm is greater than the cost of monitoring, $10 \times M$. The expected benefit if stealing is prevented is G, so monitoring pays if $G > \$10 \times M$, or $G/M > \$10$.

3. *Solve for the optimal monitoring in the special case.* The optimal level of monitoring is

$$M = \frac{\theta}{0.05} = \frac{G/B}{0.05} = \frac{500/5{,}000}{0.05} = \frac{0.1}{0.05} = 2.$$

It pays to engage in this level of monitoring because $G/M = \$500/2 = \$250 > \$10$.

Problems with Bonding. Employers like the bond-posting solution because it reduces the amount of employee monitoring that is necessary to discourage moral hazards such as shirking and theft. Nonetheless, firms use explicit bonding only occasionally to prevent stealing, and they rarely use it to prevent shirking.

Having an agent post a bond has two major problems. First, an unscrupulous employer might falsely accuse an employee of stealing. Employees who fear such employer opportunism are unwilling to post a bond. To avoid this problem, the firm may develop a reputation for not behaving in this manner or to make the grounds for forfeiture of the bond objective and verifiable by others.

Second, workers may not have enough wealth to post them. In our example, if the worker could steal $10,000, and if the probability of being caught were only 5%, shirking would be deterred only if a risk-neutral worker posted a bond of at least $200,000.

Consequently, bonds are more common in contracts between firms than between an employer and employees. Construction contractors sometimes post bonds to guarantee that they will satisfactorily finish their work by a given date. It is easy to verify whether the contract has been completed on time, and firms may post a bond more easily than employees.

APPLICATION

Capping Oil and Gas Bankruptcies

Why are most onshore gas and oil producers small? A major reason is to avoid liability. Being small allows them to produce as much as they can and if they cause environmental damages—water pollution, toxic gas releases, or explosions—greater than their assets, they avoid liability by declaring bankruptcy. They are "judgment proof." A large firm with substantial assets would pay the damages and stay in business.

Texas has roughly 5,000 oil- and gas-producing firms. Most of these have less than two million dollars in annual revenue—much less than their liability exposure. However, as of 2001, Texas required these firms to post a *surety bond*, which is an insurance contract that obligates the insurer to compensate the state for environmental damages by the insured oil or gas producer. Insurance companies set a high premium for a firm with a bad safety record or one that has little incentive to act prudently because it is financially weak. In contrast, a large, financially secure firm is less likely to act irresponsibly and hence pays a lower premium.

Boomhower (forthcoming) showed that the bond requirement improves firms' safety incentives. As soon as the bond mandate went into effect, 6% of firms exited the market (twice the usual rate). These firms were primarily small firms with poor environmental records. These exiting firms transferred 88% of their oil and gas leases to larger firms. The smallest 80% of the remaining firms reduced oil production, while the large firms' production was unaffected. That is, the ability to avoid responsibility prior to bonding inflated the number of small firms and their production.

> The amount of environmental damage fell after the bond mandate went into effect. Many fewer firms left their wells unplugged at the end of production, which causes a serious risk of groundwater pollution. Well blowouts and water protection violations also fell substantially.

Deferred Payments

Effectively, firms can post bonds for their employees by using deferred payments. For example, a firm pays new workers a low wage for some initial period of employment. Over time, workers caught shirking are fired, and those who remain are paid higher wages. Pensions are another form of deferred wages that reward only hard workers who stay with the firm until their retirement. Deferred payments function like bonds. They raise the cost of being fired, so less monitoring is necessary to deter shirking.

Workers care about the present value (Chapter 15) of their earnings stream over their lifetime. A firm may offer its workers one of two wage payment schemes. In the first, the firm pays w per year for each year that the worker is employed by the firm. In the second arrangement, the starting wage is less than w but rises over the years to a wage that exceeds w.

If hard workers can borrow against future earnings, those who work for one company their entire careers are indifferent between the two wage payment schemes if those plans have identical present values. However, the firm prefers the deferred-payment method because employees work harder to avoid being fired and losing the high future earnings.

Reducing shirking results in greater output. If the employer and the employee share the extra output through higher profit and lifetime earnings, both prefer the deferred-payment scheme that lowers incentives to shirk.

A drawback of the deferred-payment approach is that employers may engage in opportunistic behavior. For example, an employer might fire nonshirking senior workers to avoid paying their higher wages, and then replace them with less-expensive junior workers. However, if the firm can establish a reputation for not firing senior workers unjustifiably, the deferred-payment system can help prevent shirking.

Efficiency Wages

As we've seen, the use of bonds and deferred payments discourages shirking by raising an employee's cost of losing a job. An alternative is for the firm to pay an **efficiency wage:** an unusually high wage that a firm pays workers as an incentive to avoid shirking.[9] If a worker who is fired for shirking can immediately go to another firm and earn the same wage, the worker risks nothing by shirking. However, if the firm pays each worker an efficiency wage w, which is more than the wage $\underline{w}$ that an employee would earn elsewhere after being fired for shirking, it discourages shirking.[10] The less frequently the firm monitors workers, the greater the wage differential must be between w and $\underline{w}$ to prevent shirking.

---

[9]The discussion of efficiency wages is based on Yellen (1984), Stiglitz (1987), and especially Shapiro and Stiglitz (1984).

[10]Economists have other explanations for why efficiency wages lead to higher productivity. Some economists claim that in less-developed countries, employers pay an efficiency wage—more than they need to hire workers—to ensure that workers can afford to eat well enough to work hard. Other economists (Akerlof, 1982) and management experts contend that the higher wage acts like a gift, making workers feel beholden or loyal to the firm, so that little or no monitoring is needed.

An efficiency wage acts like a bond to prevent shirking. A risk-neutral worker decides whether to shirk by comparing the expected loss of earnings from getting fired to the value, G, that the worker places on shirking. An employee who never shirks is not fired and earns the efficiency wage, w. A fired worker goes elsewhere and earns the lower wage, $\underline{w}$. Consequently, a shirking worker expects to lose $\theta(w - \underline{w})$, where θ is the probability that a shirking worker is caught and fired and where the term in parentheses is the lost earnings from being fired. Thus, the expected value to a shirking employee is $\theta\underline{w} + (1 - \theta)w + G$, where $\theta\underline{w}$ is the probability of being caught shirking, θ, times earnings elsewhere if caught and fired; $(1 - \theta)w$ is the probability of not being caught times the efficiency wage; and G is the value that a worker derives from shirking.

The worker chooses not to shirk if the efficiency wage, w, exceeds the expected return from shirking: $w \geq \theta\underline{w} + (1 - \theta)w + G$. Subtracting the first two right-hand-side terms from both sides of the equation, we find that a worker does not shirk if the expected loss from being fired, $\theta(w - \underline{w})$, is greater than or equal to the gain from shirking, G:

$$\theta(w - \underline{w}) \geq G. \tag{19.6}$$

The smallest amount by which w can exceed $\underline{w}$ and prevent shirking is determined when Equation 19.6 holds with equality, $\theta(w - \underline{w}) = G$, or

$$w - \underline{w} = \frac{G}{\theta}. \tag{19.7}$$

The extra earnings, $w - \underline{w}$, in Equation 19.7 serve the same function as the bond, B, in Equation 19.5 in discouraging bad behavior.

Suppose that the value of the pleasure that a worker gets from not working hard is $G = \$1,000$, and the wage elsewhere is $\underline{w} = \$20,000$ a year. If the probability that a shirking worker is caught is $\theta = 20\%$, then the efficiency wage must be at least $w = \$25,000$ to prevent shirking. With greater monitoring, so that θ is 50%, the minimum w that prevents shirking is $\$22,000$. From the possible pairs of monitoring levels and efficiency wages that deter shirking, the firm picks the combination that minimizes its labor cost.

APPLICATION

Walmart's Efficiency Wages

Walmart was famous for cutting its costs and paying rock-bottom wages to raise its profit. However, it may have gone too far in 2015. Shoppers complained about dirty bathrooms, empty shelves, endless checkout lines, and impossible-to-find employees. Only 16% of stores met its customer service goals. Sales were down.

Walmart responded by trying an experiment: It raised its employees' wages by 16%. By 2016, the proportion of stores hitting their targeted customer-service rating increased to 75% and sales rose. Apparently, Walmart believed that it had set the wage about right, as its wage was little changed by 2018.

After-the-Fact Monitoring

So far, we've concentrated on monitoring by employers checking for bad behavior as it occurs. If shirking or other bad behavior is detected after the fact, the offending employee is fired or otherwise disciplined. If payment occurs after the principal checks for bad behavior, after-the-fact monitoring discourages bad behavior.[11]

---

[11]Learning about a moral hazard after it occurs is too late if the wrongdoer cannot be punished at that time. Although it's upsetting to find that you've been victimized, you may not be able to do anything beyond trying to prevent the situation from happening again.

Often detecting bad behavior as it occurs is difficult, but detecting it after the fact is relatively easy. For example, after an employer finds that the quality of an employee's work is substandard, the employer can force the employee to correct it or refuse to pay.

Insurance firms try to avoid extreme moral hazard by offering contracts that do not cover spectacularly reckless, stupid, or malicious behavior. An auto insurance company will not pay damages for a traffic accident if the insured driver was drunk at the time. A home insurance company disallows claims due to an explosion that resulted from an illegal activity such as making methamphetamine on the premises and claims by arsonists who torch their own property. Life insurance companies may refuse to pay benefits to the family of someone who commits suicide soon after buying the policy (as in the play *Death of a Salesman*).

19.5 Contract Choice

By offering an agent a choice of contracts, the principal may obtain enough information to prevent agent opportunism. Firms want to avoid hiring workers who shirk. Employers know that not all workers shirk, even when given an opportunity to do so. So, rather than focusing on stopping lazy workers from shirking, an employer may concentrate on hiring only industrious people. With this approach, the firm seeks to avoid *moral hazard* by preventing *adverse selection*, where lazy employees falsely assert that they are hardworking.

The firm makes potential job candidates select between two contracts in which payment depends on how hard they work. Suppose that a firm wants to hire a salesperson to run its Cleveland office and that the potential employees are risk neutral. A hardworking salesperson sells $200,000 worth of goods a year, but a lazy one sells only $120,000 worth (see Table 19.3). A hard worker can earn $50,000 from other firms, so the firm considers using a contingent contract that pays a salesperson a 30% commission on sales.

If the firm succeeds in hiring a hard worker, the salesperson makes $200,000 \times 0.30 = $60,000. The firm's share of sales is $140,000. For simplicity, we assume that the firm has no other costs, so the firm's profit is $140,000. If the firm hires a lazy salesperson under the same contract, the salesperson makes $36,000, and the firm's profit is $84,000.

To determine if potential employees are hardworking, the firm offers each a choice of contracts:

- Contingent contract: no salary and 30% of sales,
- Fixed-fee contract: annual salary of $50,000, regardless of sales.

Table 19.3   Firm's Spreadsheet

	Contingent Contract (30% of Sales), $	Fixed-Fee Contract ($50,000 Salary), $
Hard Worker		
Sales	200,000	200,000
− Salesperson's pay	−60,000	−50,000
= Firm's profit	140,000	150,000
Lazy Worker		
Sales	120,000	120,000
− Salesperson's pay	−36,000	−50,000
= Firm's profit	84,000	70,000

A prospective employee who doesn't mind hard work would earn $10,000 more by choosing the contingent contract. In contrast, a lazy candidate would make $14,000 more from a salary than from commissions. If an applicant chooses the fixed-fee contract, the firm knows that the person does not intend to work hard and decides not to hire that person.

The firm learns what it needs to know by offering this contract choice as long as the lazy applicant does not pretend to be a hard worker by choosing the contingent contract. Under the contingent contract, the lazy person makes only $36,000, but that offer may dominate others available in the market. If this pair of contracts fails to sort workers, the firm may try different pairs. If all these choices fail to sort the potential employees, the firm must use other means to prevent shirking.

19.6   Checks on Principals

Because employers (principals) often pay employees (agents) after work is completed, employers have many opportunities to exploit workers. For example, a dishonest employer can underpay after falsely claiming that a worker took time off or that some of the worker's output was substandard. Employers who provide bonuses can underreport the firm's output or profit.

Efficient contracts prevent or reduce such moral hazard problems. Requiring a firm to post a bond can be an effective method of deterring the firm's opportunistic behavior. For example, a firm may post bonds to ensure that it has the means of paying current wages and future pensions.

A firm cannot act opportunistically if information is symmetric because it reveals relevant information to employees. An employer can provide access to such information by allowing employee representatives to sit on the company board to monitor the firm's behavior. To induce workers to agree to profit sharing, a firm may provide workers with information about the company's profit by allowing them (or an independent auditor) to check its accounts. A firm may argue that its stock closely mirrors its profit and suggest that the known stock price be used for incentive payments.

Firms may rely on a good reputation. For instance, a firm may publicize that it does not make a practice of firing senior employees to avoid paying pensions. The better the firm's reputation, the more likely workers are to accept a deferred-payment scheme, which deters shirking.

When these approaches are infeasible, a firm may use less efficient contracts such as one that bases employee payments on easily observed revenues rather than less reliable profit reports. The next application discusses a particularly damaging but common type of inefficient contract.

APPLICATION

Layoffs Versus
Pay Cuts

During recessions and depressions, demand for most firms' products fall. Many firms respond by laying off workers and reducing production rather than by lowering wages and keeping everyone employed. The average real U.S. weekly earnings fluctuated in a narrow band—$333 to $354 (in 1982–1984 dollars)—from 2002 through 2012. It then fluctuated between $351 and $372 from 2013 through July 2018. In contrast, the U.S. unemployment rate over this period has fluctuated substantially. It started at 5.7% in 2002, rose to 6.1% in 2003, dropped to 4.4% in 2007, rose to 10.0% in 2009, and fell to 3.9% by July 2018.

If both sides agree to it, a wage reduction policy benefits firms and workers alike. Collectively, workers earn more than they would if they were laid off.

Because the firm's costs would fall, it sells more during the downturn than it otherwise could, so its profit is higher than with layoffs. Firms that provide relatively low wages and then share profits with employees achieve this type of wage flexibility.

Why, then, are wage reductions less common than layoffs? A major explanation involves asymmetric information: Unlike the firm, workers don't know whether the firm is actually facing a downturn, so they refuse to cut wages. They fear that the firm will falsely claim that economic conditions are bad to justify a wage cut. Workers believe that if the firm has to lay off workers—an action that hurts the firm as well as the workers—the firm is more likely to be telling the truth about economic conditions.[12]

We illustrate this reasoning in the following matrix, which shows the payoffs if wages are reduced during downturns. The value of output produced by each worker is $21 during good times and $15 during bad times. The lower left of each cell is the amount the firm pays workers. The firm pays employees $12 per hour if it reports that economic conditions are good and $8 if it says that conditions are bad. The amount the firm keeps is in the upper right of each cell. If economic conditions are bad, the firm earns more by reporting these bad conditions, $7, than it earns if it says that conditions are good, $3. Similarly, if conditions are good, the firm earns more if it claims that conditions are bad, $13, than if it says that they are good, $9. Thus, regardless of the true state, the firm benefits by always claiming that conditions are bad.

Wage Cut

Actual Conditions	Firm's Claim About Conditions	
	Bad	Good
Bad	8 / 7	12 / 3
Good	8 / 13	12 / 9

To shield themselves from such systematic lying, employees may insist that the firm lay off workers whenever it says that conditions are bad. This requirement provides the firm with an incentive to report the true conditions. In the next matrix, the firm must lay off workers for half of each period if it announces that times are bad, causing the value of output to fall by one-third. Because they now work only half the time, workers earn only half as much, $6, as they earn during good times, $12. If conditions are bad, the firm makes more by telling the truth, $4, than by claiming that conditions are good, $3. In good times, the firm makes more by announcing that conditions are good, $9, than by claiming that they are bad, $8. Thus, the firm reports conditions truthfully.

[12]In 2010, after several years of the Great Recession (when everyone knew that the downturn was real), layoffs were increasingly replaced with pay cuts, especially by state and local government employers. Similarly, Sub-Zero, which makes refrigerators and other appliances, told its workers it might close one or more factories and lay off 500 employees unless they accepted a 20% cut in wages and benefits.

Worker Layoff (for half of any period the firm claims is bad)

		Firm's Claim About Conditions	
		Bad	Good
Actual Conditions	Bad	6 4	12 3
	Good	6 8	12 9

With the wage-cut contract in which the firm always says that conditions are bad, workers earn $8 regardless of actual conditions. If economic conditions are good half the time, the firm earns an average of $10 = (\frac{1}{2} \times \$7) + (\frac{1}{2} \times \$13)$. Under the contract that requires layoffs, the workers earn an average of $9 = (\frac{1}{2} \times \$6) + (\frac{1}{2} \times \$12)$ and the firm earns an average of $6.50 = (\frac{1}{2} \times \$4) + (\frac{1}{2} \times \$9)$.

Therefore, the firm prefers the wage-cut contract and the workers favor the layoff contract. However, if the workers could observe actual conditions, both parties would prefer the wage-cut contract. Workers would earn an average of $10 = (\frac{1}{2} \times \$8) + (\frac{1}{2} \times \$12)$, and the firm would make $8 = (\frac{1}{2} \times \$7) + (\frac{1}{2} \times \$9)$. With the layoff contract, total payoffs are lower because of lost production. Thus, socially inefficient layoffs may be used because of the need to keep relatively well-informed firms honest.

CHALLENGE SOLUTION

Clawing Back Bonuses

The Challenge at the beginning of the chapter asks whether evaluating a manager's performance over a longer time period using delayed compensation or clawback provisions benefits shareholders. The answer depends on whether the reward a manager receives in the short run induces the manager to sacrifice long-run profit for short-run gains.

Managers prefer to be paid sooner rather than later because money today is worth more than the same amount later. Typically, a manager receives a bonus based on a firm's annual profit. If a manager can move a major sale from January of next year to December of this year, the firm's total profits over the two years are unchanged, but the manager receives the resulting performance-based bonus this year rather than next year. The owners of the firm are probably not very concerned with such shifts over time, as they are unlikely to lower long-run profits substantially.

Of more concern are managers who increase this year's profit in a way that lowers profits in later years. Many firms pay a bonus on a positive profit but do not impose fines or penalties (negative bonuses) for a loss (negative profit). Suppose that a particular policy results in a large profit this year, but a larger loss next year. If the manager gets a bonus based on each year's profit, the manager receives a large bonus this year and no bonus next year.

In an extreme case, a manager engages in reckless behavior that increases this year's profit but bankrupts the firm next year. The manager plans to grab this year's bonus and then disappear. Many mortgage and financial instrument managers engaged in such reckless and irresponsible behavior leading up to the

2007–2009 financial meltdown. Bad decisions at Merrill Lynch, a wealth management firm, cost shareholders billions of dollars, but senior managers kept bonuses despite the negative effects of their decisions on shareholders.

One solution to bad managerial incentives is to base bonuses on more than one year. Starting in 2012, Morgan Stanley paid bonuses to high-income employees over a three-year period.

To illustrate why paying over time provides a better incentive structure, we examine the case of Jim, who is an executive in a company that provides auto loans. We look at a two-year period. Initially, Jim receives 10% of the amount of the loans he makes in the first year. He may loan to two groups of customers. Customers in one group have excellent financial histories and repay their loans on time. Loans in this group produce revenue of $10 million this year, so that over the two-year period, the firm nets $9 million after paying Jim. Customers in the other group are much more likely to default. That group produces $30 million in revenue this year, but their defaults in the second year cost the firm $40 million. After paying Jim $3 million in the first year, the firm suffers a $13 million loss over the two years (ignoring discounting).

Because Jim prefers receiving $4 million by loaning to both groups to $1 million from loaning to only the good risks, he may expose the firm to devastating losses in the second year. He may be happy earning a gigantic amount in the first year even if he's fired in the second year. In contrast, if his bonus is based on profits over two years, he has an incentive to avoid making loans to the risky group.

SUMMARY

1. **Principal-Agent Problem.** A principal contracts with an agent to perform some task. The size of their joint profit depends on any assets that the principal contributes, the actions of the agent, and the state of nature. If the principal cannot observe the agent's actions, the agent may engage in opportunistic behavior. This moral hazard reduces the joint profit. An efficient contract leads to efficiency in production (joint profit is maximized by eliminating moral hazards) and efficiency in risk bearing (the less-risk-averse party bears more of the risk). Three common types of contracts are fixed-fee contracts, whereby one party pays the other a fixed fee and the other keeps the rest of the profits; hire contracts, in which the principal pays the agent a wage or pays for each piece of output produced; and contingent contracts, wherein the payoffs vary with the amount of output produced or in some other way. Because a contract that reduces the moral hazard may increase the risk for a relatively risk-averse person, a contract is chosen to achieve the best trade-off between the twin goals of efficiency in production and efficiency in risk bearing.

2. **Production Efficiency.** Whether efficiency in production is achieved depends on the type of contract that the principal and the agent use and on the degree to which their information is asymmetric. For the agent in our example to put forth the optimal level of effort, the agent must get the full marginal profit from that effort or the principal must monitor the agent. When the parties have full information, an agent with a fixed-fee rental or profit-sharing contract gets the entire marginal profit and produces optimally without being monitored. If the principal cannot monitor the agent or does not observe profit and cost, only a fixed-fee rental contract prevents moral hazard problems and achieves production efficiency.

3. **Trade-Off Between Efficiency in Production and in Risk Bearing.** A principal and an agent may agree to a contract that strikes a balance between reducing moral hazards and allocating risk optimally. Contracts that eliminate moral hazards require the agent to bear the risk. If the agent is more risk averse than the principal, the parties may trade off a reduction in production efficiency to lower risk for the agent.

4. **Monitoring to Reduce Moral Hazard.** Because of asymmetric information, an employer must normally monitor workers' efforts to prevent shirking. Less

monitoring is necessary as the employee's interest in keeping the job increases. The employer may require the employee to post a large bond that is forfeited if the employee is caught shirking, stealing, or otherwise misbehaving. If an employee cannot afford to post a bond, the employer may use deferred payments or efficiency wages—unusually high wages—to make it worthwhile for the employee to keep the job. Employers may also be able to prevent shirking by engaging in after-the-fact monitoring. However, such monitoring works only if bad behavior can be punished after the fact.

5. **Contract Choice.**   A principal may be able to prevent moral hazard problems from adverse selection by observing choices made by potential agents. For example, an employer may present potential employees with a choice of contracts, prompting hardworking job applicants to choose a contract that compensates the worker for working hard and lazy candidates to choose a different contract that provides a guaranteed salary.

6. **Checks on Principals.**   Often both agents and principals can engage in opportunistic behavior. If a firm must reveal its actions to its employees, it is less likely to be able to take advantage of the employees. To convey information, an employer may let employees participate in decision-making meetings or audit the company's books. Alternatively, an employer may make commitments so that it is in the employer's best interest to tell employees the truth. These commitments, such as laying off workers rather than reducing wages during downturns, may reduce moral hazards but lead to nonoptimal production.

EXERCISES

All exercises are available on **MyLab Economics**; * = *answer appears at the back of this book;* **M** = *mathematical problem.*

1. Principal-Agent Problem

1.1 A California state agency sells earthquake insurance. Because the agency has few staff members, it pays private insurance carriers to handle claims for earthquake damage. These insurance firms receive 9% of each approved claim. Is this compensation scheme likely to lead to opportunistic behavior by insurance companies? Explain. What would be a better way to handle the compensation?

*1.2 Some sellers offer to buy back a good later at some prespecified price. Why would a firm make such a commitment?

1.3 A flyer from one of the world's largest brokers says, "Most personal investment managers base their fees on a percentage of assets managed. We believe this is in your best interest because your manager is paid for investment management, not solely on the basis of trading commissions charged to your account. You can be assured your manager's investment decisions are guided by one primary goal—increasing your assets." Is this policy in a customer's best interest? Why or why not?

1.4 A study by Jean Mitchell found that urologists in group practices that profit from tests for prostate cancer order more of them than doctors who send samples to independent laboratories. Doctors' groups that perform their own lab work bill Medicare for analyzing 72% more prostate tissue samples per biopsy and detect fewer cases of cancer than doctors who use outside labs (Christopher Weaver, "Prostate-Test Fees Challenged," *Wall Street*

Journal, April 9, 2012). Explain these results. Do these results necessarily demonstrate moral hazard or can you provide another possible explanation?

1.5 In 2012, a California environmental group found that 14 plum and ginger candies imported from Asia contained 4 to 96 times the level of lead allowed under California law (Stephanie M. Lee, "Lead Found in Asian Candies," *San Francisco Chronicle*, August 14, 2012). Some observers predicted that U.S. consumers would face significant price increases if U.S. law were changed to require third-party testing by manufacturers and sellers. Suppose instead that candies could be reliably labeled "tested" or "untested," and untested candy sold at a discount. Would consumers buy cheaper, untested goods or would they fear a moral hazard problem? Discuss.

1.6 A publication of a major clinical trial showed that a common knee operation does not improve outcomes for patients with osteoarthritis. Howard, David, and Hockenberry (2017) examined all these operations in Florida from 1998 to 2010. They discovered that after the publication of this article, the number of these operations fell, but the number fell by less in physician-owned surgery centers than in hospitals. Explain why.

1.7 The U.S. government provides home insurance for floods (see Chapter 16's Application "Flooded by Insurance Claims"). The government will pay no matter how many times floods destroy a home. Does this policy create a moral hazard problem? Explain.

2. Production Efficiency

*2.1 When I was in graduate school, I shared an apartment with a fellow who was madly in love with a woman who lived in another city. They agreed to split the costs of their long-distance phone calls equally, regardless of who placed the calls. (In those days, long-distance calls were expensive and billed separately from general phone service.) What was the implication of this fee-sharing arrangement for their total phone bill? Why?

*2.2 Zhihua and Pu are partners in a store in which they do all the work. They split the store's business profit equally (ignoring the opportunity cost of their own time in calculating this profit). Does their business profit-sharing contract give them an incentive to maximize their joint economic profit if neither can force the other to work? (*Hint*: Imagine Zhihua's thought process late one Saturday night when he is alone in the store, debating whether to keep the store open a little later or go out on the town. See Solved Problem 19.2.)

2.3 In Solved Problem 19.2, does joint profit increase, decrease, or remain the same as the share of revenue going to Arthur increases?

*2.4 In the duck-carving example with full information (summarized in the second column of Table 19.1), is a contract efficient if it requires Paula to give Arthur a fixed-fee salary of $168 and leaves all the decisions to Arthur? If so, why? If not, what additional steps, if any, can Paula take to ensure that Arthur sells the optimal number of carvings?

*2.5 A promoter arranges for various restaurants to set up booths to sell Cajun-Creole food at a fair. Appropriate music and other entertainment are provided. Customers can buy food using only "Cajun Cash," which is scrip that has the same denominations as actual cash and is sold by the fair promoter. Why aren't the food booths allowed to sell food directly for cash? (*Hint*: See the Application "Sing for Your Supper.")

2.6 In the duck-carving example with limited information (summarized in the third and fourth columns of Table 19.1), is a fixed-fee contract efficient? If so, why? If not, what additional steps, if any, can Paula take to ensure efficiency?

2.7 The author of a science fiction novel is paid a royalty of b share of the revenue from sales, where the revenue is $R = pq$, p is the competitive market price for novels, and q is the number of copies of this book sold. The publisher's cost of printing and distributing the book is $C(q)$. Determine the equilibrium, and compare it to the outcome that maximizes the sum of the payment to the author plus the firm's profit. Answer using both math and a graph. **M**

2.8 John manages Rachel's used CD music store. To provide John with the incentive to sell CDs, Rachel offers him 50% of the store's profit. John has the opportunity to misrepresent sales by fraudulently recording sales that actually did not take place. Let t represent his fraudulent profit. John's expected earnings from reporting the fraudulent profit is $0.5t$. Rachel tries to detect such fraud and either detects all or none of it. The probability that Rachel detects the entire fraud is $t/(1 + t)$ and the probability that Rachel does not detect the fraud is $1 - t/(1 + t)$. Hence, Rachel's probability of detecting fraud is zero if John reports no fraudulent profit, increases with the amount of fraudulent profit he reports, and approaches 1 as the amount of fraud approaches infinity. If Rachel detects the fraud, then $x > 0.5$ is the fine that John pays Rachel per dollar of fraud. John's expected fine of reporting fraudulent profit t is $t^2 x/(1 + t)$. In choosing the level of fraud, John's objective is to maximize his expected earnings from the fraud, $0.5t$, less his expected fine, $t^2 x/(1 + t)$. As a function of x, what is John's optimal fraudulent profit? (*Hint*: Check the second-order condition.) Show that $\partial t/\partial x < 0$. Also show that as $x \to \infty$, John's optimal reported fraudulent profit goes to zero. (*Hint*: See Solved Problem 19.2.) **M**

2.9 In the National Basketball Association (NBA), the owners share revenue but not costs. Suppose that one team, the L.A. Clippers, sells only general-admission seats to a home game with the visiting Philadelphia 76ers (Sixers). The inverse demand for the Clippers-Sixers tickets is $p = 100 - 0.004Q$. The Clippers' cost function of selling Q tickets and running the franchise is $C(Q) = 10Q$.

a. Find the Clippers' profit-maximizing number of tickets sold and the price if the Clippers must give 50% of their revenue to the Sixers. At the maximum, what are the Clippers' profit and the Sixers' share of the revenues?

b. Instead, suppose that the Sixers set the Clippers' ticket price based on the same revenue-sharing rule. What price will the Sixers set, how many tickets are sold, and what revenue payment will the Sixers receive? Explain why your answers to parts a and b differ.

c. Now suppose that the Clippers must share their profit rather than their revenue. The Clippers keep 45% of their profit and share 55% with the Sixers. The Clippers set the price. Find the Clippers' profit-maximizing price and determine how many tickets the team sells and its share of the profit.

d. Compare your answers to parts a and c using marginal revenue and marginal cost in your explanation. (*Hint*: See Solved Problem 19.2.) **M**

2.10 Book retailers can return unsold copies to publishers. Effectively, retailers pay for the books they order only after they sell them. Dowell's Books believes that it will sell, with $\frac{1}{2}$ probability each, either zero or one copy of *The Fool's Handbook of Macroeconomics*. The bookstore also believes that it will sell, with $\frac{1}{2}$ probability each, either zero or one copy of *The Genius' Handbook of Microeconomics*. The retail price of each book is $100. Suppose that the marginal cost of manufacturing another copy of a book is $24. The publisher's value of a returned copy is $0. The *Microeconomics* publisher charges a $52 wholesale price and offers a full refund for returned, unsold books. While the *Macroeconomics* publisher charges a low $42 wholesale price, it pays a retailer only $32 if it returns an unsold book. Dowell's places an order for one copy of each title. When the two books arrive, Dowell's has space to shelve only one. Which title does Dowell's return? Comment on how Dowell's decision about which title to return depends on the books' wholesale prices and on the compensation from the publishers for returned unsold books. **M**

2.11 Topside Tiles, which produces roofing tiles, is a local monopoly. Its inverse demand function is $p = 50 - 2Q$, and its constant marginal cost is 10. The owner has delegated the decision of how much output to produce to the plant manager. The manager's income, Y, is 10% of revenue: $Y = 0.1R$. Show that a manager who wishes to maximize income, Y, will choose an output that exceeds the profit-maximizing level. Is there a conflict of interest between the owner and manager? Is this situation an agency problem? **M**

2.12 Now suppose that the owner of Topside Tiles in the previous question changes the manager's compensation to a fixed share (15%) of profit: $Y = 0.15\pi$. The situation is otherwise the same as in Exercise 3.11. Are the interests of the owner and manager aligned or in conflict? Is there an agency problem in this case? **M**

2.13 In 2012, Hewlett-Packard Co. announced that its new chief executive, Meg Whitman, would receive a salary of $1 and about $16.1 million in stock options, which are valuable if the stock does well. How would you feel about this compensation package if you were a shareholder? What are the implications for moral hazard, efficiency, and risk sharing? (*Hint*: See Solved Problem 19.1.)

3. Trade-Off Between Efficiency in Production and in Risk Bearing

3.1 Traditionally, doctors were paid on a fee-for-service basis. Now doctors' pay is on a capitated basis: They are paid for treating a patient for a year, regardless of how much treatment is required. In this arrangement, doctors form a group and sign a capitation contract whereby they take turns seeing a given patient. What are the implications of this change in compensation for moral hazards and for risk bearing?

3.2 Padma has the rights to any treasure on the sunken ship the *Golden Calf*. Aaron is a diver who specializes in marine salvage. If Padma is risk averse and Aaron is risk neutral, does paying Aaron a fixed fee result in efficiency in risk bearing and production? Does your answer turn on how predictable the value of the sunken treasure is? Would another compensation scheme be more efficient? (*Hint*: See Solved Problem 19.3.)

3.3 Fourteen states have laws that limit whether a franchisor (such as McDonald's) can terminate a franchise agreement. Franchisees (such as firms that run individual McDonald's outlets) typically pay the franchisor a fixed fee or a share of revenues. What effects do such laws have on production efficiency and risk bearing? (*Hint*: See Solved Problem 19.3.)

3.4 Louisa is an avid cyclist who is currently working on her business degree. She normally rides an $800 bike to class. If Louisa locks her bike carefully—locks both wheels—the chance of theft for the term is 5%, but this careful locking procedure is time consuming. If she is less careful—just quickly locks the frame to a bike rack—the chance of theft is 20%. Louisa is risk averse and is considering buying theft insurance for her bike. She can buy two types of insurance. With full insurance, Louisa pays the premium and gets the full $800 value of the bike if it is stolen. Alternatively, with partial insurance, Louisa receives only 75% of the bike's value, $600, if the bike is stolen. Which contract is more likely to induce moral hazard problems? To break even on consumers like Louisa, what price would the risk-neutral insurance company have to charge for full insurance? If we observe Louisa buying partial insurance, what can we say about the trade-off between moral hazard and efficient risk bearing.

3.5 Suppose now that the publisher in Exercise 2.7 faces a downward-sloping demand curve. The revenue is $R(Q)$, and the publisher's cost of printing and distributing the book is $C(Q)$. Compare the equilibria for the following compensation methods in which the author receives the same total compensation from each method:

a. The author is paid a lump sum, $\mathcal{L}$.

b. The author is paid a share of the revenue.

c. The author receives a lump-sum payment and a share of the revenue.

Why do you think that authors are usually paid a share of the revenue? (*Hint*: See Solved Problems 19.2 and 19.3.) **M**

3.6 A health insurance company tries to prevent the moral hazard of "excessive" dentist visits by limiting the number of compensated visits that a patient can make in a year. How does such a restriction affect moral hazard and risk bearing? Show in a graph. (*Hint*: See Solved Problem 19.4.)

4. Monitoring to Reduce Moral Hazard

4.1 Many law firms consist of partners who share profits. On being made a partner, a lawyer must post a bond, a large payment to the firm that will be forfeited on bad behavior. Why?

*4.2 In Solved Problem 19.5 a firm calculates the optimal level of monitoring to prevent stealing. If $G = \$500$ and $\theta = 20\%$, what is the minimum bond that deters stealing? **M**

4.3 In Exercise 4.2, suppose that, for each extra $1,000 of bonding the firm requires a worker to post, the firm must pay that worker $10 more per period to get the worker to work for the firm. What is the minimum bond that deters stealing? (*Hint*: See Solved Problem 19.5.) **M**

4.4 Starting in 2008, Medicare would not cover the cost of a surgeon leaving an instrument in a patient, giving a patient transfusions of the wrong blood type, certain types of hospital-acquired infections, or other "preventable" mistakes (Liz Marlantes, "Medicare Won't Cover Hospital Mistakes: New Rules Aimed at Promoting Better Hospital Care and Safety," ABC News, August 19, 2007). Hospitals will have to cover these costs and cannot bill the patient. These changes are designed to provide hospitals with a stronger incentive to prevent those mistakes, particularly infections. The Centers for Disease Control and Prevention estimates that 2 million patients are annually infected in hospitals, costing society more than $27 billion. Nearly 100,000 of those infections are fatal. Many of these infections are preventable if hospitals more rigorously follow basic infection control procedures, including having doctors and nurses wash their hands between every patient treatment. Is Medicare's policy designed to deal with adverse selection or moral hazard? Is it likely to help? Explain.

4.5 Used cars receive lower prices if they were rental cars than if they were owned by individuals. Does this price difference reflect adverse selection or moral hazard? Could car rental companies reduce this problem by carefully inspecting rental cars for damage when renters return such cars? Why do car companies normally do only a cursory inspection?

4.6 Many substandard condo developments have been built by small corporations that declare bankruptcy or go out of business when legal actions are started against them by condo buyers. What legal remedies might reduce this moral hazard problem? If you were considering buying a condo in a new building, what characteristics of the builder would make you more likely to buy? Explain. (*Hint*: See the Application "Capping Oil and Gas Bankruptcies.")

4.7 In 2018, Amazon received a pair of patents for a wristband that can locate warehouse employees and track their hand movements in real time and an inventory management system using trackers and receivers to monitor workers' movements and breaks. Can Amazon use these innovations to address moral hazard problems? How do they help?

5. Contract Choice

5.1 List some necessary conditions for a firm to be able to sort potential employees by providing them with a choice of contracts.

6. Checks on Principals

6.1 In the Application "Layoffs Versus Pay Cuts," the firm uses either a pay cut or layoffs. Can you derive a superior approach that benefits both the firm and the workers? (*Hint*: Suppose that the firm's profit or some other variable is observable.)

7. Challenge

7.1 In the Challenge Solution, show that shareholders' expected earnings are higher with the new compensation scheme than with the original one.

7.2 Adrienne, a manager of a large firm, must decide whether to launch a new product or make a minor change to an existing product. The new product has a 30% chance of being a big success and generating profits of $20 million, a 40% chance of being fairly successful and generating profits of $5 million, and a 30% chance of being a costly failure and losing $10 million. Making minor changes in the old product would generate profits of $10 million for sure. Adrienne's contract gives her a bonus of 10% of any profits above $8 million arising from this decision. If Adrienne is risk neutral and cares only about her own income, what is her decision? Should shareholders be happy with this compensation contract? Describe a contract that would be better for both Adrienne and the shareholders (if any is possible). **M**

7.3 Curtis manages an electronics store in Wichita, Kansas. He considers carrying either cameras from Nikon Americas that come with a U.S. warranty or *gray market* Nikon cameras from a European supplier, which are the same cameras but their warranties are only good in Europe. The gray market cameras have a lower wholesale price. Curtis earns 10% of the store's profit (and no wage). If the store loses money, he leaves with nothing. He believes that if he sells the Nikon Americas cameras, the store's profit will be $400,000. The profit on the gray market cameras is more uncertain—will locals be willing to buy a less expensive camera without a warranty? If he sells the gray market camera, he believes that he has a 50% chance that the store's profit will be $1,000,000 and a 50% probability that the store will lose $300,000. Curtis and the store's owner are both risk neutral. Which camera does Curtis choose to sell? What choice would the owner prefer (if she were fully informed)? Construct an alternative compensation plan involving a salary such that Curtis will earn as much from selling Nikon Americas cameras and that will dissuade him from selling gray market cameras if doing so lowers the owner's expected earnings. **M**

7.4 Many firms pay bonuses or make contributions to an employee's pension fund on an annual basis but require a *vesting period*—often eight to ten years—during which the employee must stay with the company to obtain ownership of these assets. An employee who leaves the company before the vesting period loses any claim to the assets. How does *vesting* reduce moral hazard in employment relationships?

Calculus Appendix

In mathematics you don't understand things. You just get used to them.
—John von Neumann

This appendix reviews the basic tools from calculus and mathematics that we use throughout this book.[1] It emphasizes unconstrained and constrained maximization.

A.1 Functions

A *function* associates each member of a set with a single member of another set. In this section, we first examine *functions of a single variable* and then discuss *functions of several variables*.

Functions of a Single Variable

Suppose that we are interested in a variable x that is a member or an element of a set X. For example, the set X may be the nonnegative real numbers. A function f associates elements of the set X with elements of a set Y, which may be the same set as X. The function f is a *mapping* from X to Y, which we denote by $f: X \rightarrow Y$. The set X is the *domain* of the function f, while Y is the *range* of the function. In applying the mapping from an element of X to Y, we write $y = f(x)$.

We concentrate on real-number functions. Frequently, these functions map from the set of real numbers ($X = \mathbb{R}$) into the same set of real numbers ($Y = \mathbb{R}$). However, sometimes we consider functions with a domain that is an *interval* within the real numbers. For example, we might study a function that maps the numbers between zero and one. Such intervals are written as [0, 1] if the interval includes zero and one, or as (0, 1) if the endpoints of the interval are not included in the set. One can also use a parenthesis and a bracket, writing (0, 1] for the interval of real numbers that are strictly greater than zero but less than or equal to one. By writing that $x \in (0, 1]$, we mean that the variable x can take on only a value that is greater than zero and less than or equal to one.

Some examples of functions of a single variable include the

- *Identity function*: $f(x) = x$ for all $x \in X$.
- *Zero function*: $f(x) = 0$ for all $x \in X$.
- *Square root function*: $f(x) = \sqrt{x}$ for all $x \geq 0$.
- *Hyperbolic function*: $f(x) = 1/x$, which is not defined when $x = 0$.

---

[1]Ethan Ligon is the co-author of this appendix.

These examples are called *explicit* functions because we can write them in the form $y = f(x)$. Some functions are *implicit* mappings between X and Y and are written in the form $g(x, y) = 0$. For example, $x^2 + y^2 - 1 = 0$ implicitly defines y in terms of x. We can always express an explicit function f in implicit form by defining $g(x, y) = y - f(x)$. However, it is not possible to express every implicit function explicitly. For example, the implicit function $g(x, y) = ay^5 + by^4 + cy^3 + dy^2 + ey + x = 0$ cannot generally be rewritten so that y is a closed-form expression of the variable x and the parameters a, b, c, d, and e.

Functions of Several Variables

A function may depend on more than one variable. An example of such a function is $y = f(x_1, x_2)$, where $x \in X_1$ and $x_2 \in X_2$. Then the domain of the function is written as $X = X_1 \times X_2$, where the symbol $\times$ when applied to sets means to take all possible combinations of elements of the two sets. For example, the set $X = [0, 1] \times [0, 1]$ contains all the pairs of real numbers between zero and one, inclusive. The function f associates elements of the domain, the set $X = X_1 \times X_2$, with elements of the range, the set Y. That is, f is a mapping from X to Y, which may be denoted either by $f: X \to Y$ or by $f: X_1 \times X_2 \to Y$.

An example of mapping from a pair of variables to a single variable is the well-known measure of physical fitness, the *body mass index* (BMI), which is a function of weight (in kilograms) and height (in meters):

$$\text{BMI} = \frac{\text{weight}}{(\text{height})^2}.$$

If we let the variable z measure the BMI, w reflect the weight, and h denote the height, we can write this function more compactly as

$$z = f(w, h) = \frac{w}{h^2}.$$

Other examples of functions of two or more variables are the

- *Cobb-Douglas function with two variables:* $y = f(K, L) = 3L^{0.33}K^{0.66}$.
- *Cobb-Douglas function with two variables and two parameters:* $y = f(K, L) = AL^{\alpha}K^{1-\alpha}$, where A and α are parameters rather than variables—they represent unknown numbers rather than quantities that can change. The previous example is a special case, where $A = 3$ and $\alpha = \frac{1}{3}$.
- *Cobb-Douglas function with n variables:* $y = f(x_1, x_2, x_3, \ldots, x_n) = Ax_1^{\alpha_1}x_2^{\alpha_2} \ldots x_n^{\alpha_n}$.

A.2   Properties of Functions

We make extensive use of several key properties that functions may possess. In this section, we start by discussing the main properties that we use, which are *monotonicity* (the graph of a function always goes up or always goes down), *continuity* (there are no breaks in the graph of the function), *concavity* and *convexity* (the function consistently curves upward or downward), and *homogeneity* (the function "scales" up or down consistently). After reviewing these properties, we list three properties of the logarithmic function that we use repeatedly.

Monotonicity

A monotonic function is one that is either always *increasing* or always *decreasing*. For example, the identity function, $f(x) = x$, is monotonically increasing. That is, as x increases, so does the value of the function $f(x)$. Some functions are monotonic only under certain conditions. For example, the function $f(x) = 1/x$ is monotonically decreasing when x is positive. The function $f(x) = x^2$ isn't monotonic; it is decreasing when x is negative and increasing when x is positive.

Continuity

A function exhibits the property of *continuity* if a graph of the function has no jumps or breaks. A function can be continuous *at a point* if there are no jumps or breaks very near the point; if the function is continuous at all points, we say that the function is continuous. A sufficient condition for a function to be continuous at a point a is

$$\lim_{x \to a} f(x) = f(a),$$

which indicates that the limit of the function $f(x)$ as x approaches a is $f(a)$.[2]

Concavity and Convexity

Economists make extensive use of the properties of concavity and convexity. We say that the function f is *concave* over a region A if the graph of the function $f(x)$ never goes below the line drawn between *any* pair of points in A. For example, in panel a of Figure A.1, we evaluate a function f with a domain X. Within this domain, we choose a subset A, and we evaluate f at two points x and x' within this subset A. This procedure gives us two points in the range of f, $f(x)$ and $f(x')$. The line connecting the points $(x, f(x))$ and $(x', f(x'))$ is below $f(x)$ for all x between x and x'.

This "never below the line" test reflects the intuition of concavity for functions of a single variable. But for functions of multiple variables and for testing the concavity of a function that we cannot easily draw, we have a better test. To illustrate this approach, we examine the concavity of a function of a pair of variables (x, y) that maps $f: X \times Y \to Z$. Again, let A be a subset of the domain of f, $X \times Y$, and choose two points from the domain, (x, y) and (x', y'). The function f is concave over A if, for any value of θ such that $0 < \theta < 1$ and for any pair (x, y) and (x', y') in A,

$$f(\theta x + [1 - \theta]x', \theta y + [1 - \theta]y') \geq \theta f(x, y) + [1 - \theta]f(x', y'). \quad (A.1)$$

Equation A.1 is an extension of our "never below the line" test. If we let θ vary between zero and one, we can trace out all the values of the function f evaluated at points in A on the left-hand side of the inequality, while varying θ on the right-hand side of the expression traces out a line segment connecting the function f evaluated at (x, y) and at (x', y'). Thus, this expression says that the function lies above the connecting line.

---

[2]If an infinite sequence tends toward some particular value as we progress through that sequence, that value is the limit of the sequence. For example, in the sequence $\{1, \frac{1}{2}, \frac{1}{3}, \frac{1}{4}, \dots \}$ the nth element in the sequence equals $1/n$, where n is a positive whole number. As n gets larger, the value of $1/n$ tends to zero, so the limit of this sequence is zero (even though zero is not an element of the sequence).

Figure A.1 Concave and Convex Functions

Some functions are convex, some concave, and some neither. (a) This function is convex because a straight line drawn between any two points never goes above the curve. (b) This function is concave because a straight line drawn between two points never goes below the curve. (c) This function violates both of these conditions and thus is neither convex nor concave.

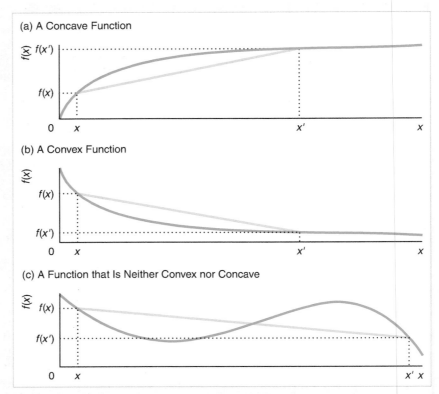

(a) A Concave Function

(b) A Convex Function

(c) A Function that Is Neither Convex nor Concave

Sometimes a distinction is drawn between a function that is *weakly concave* or *strictly concave*. A *weakly concave* function f satisfies the requirement in Equation A.1, while a *strictly concave* function satisfies a replacement condition:

$$f(\theta x + [1 - \theta]x', \theta y + [1 - \theta]y') > \theta f(x, y) + [1 - \theta]f(x', y').$$

A function is *convex* over a region A if the opposite of the concavity condition holds. That is, the function never goes *above* a line connecting points on the function, as panel b of Figure A.1 illustrates. The mathematical requirement is the same as the requirement for concavity with the inequality reversed: The function f is *weakly convex* over A if, for any value of θ such that $0 < \theta < 1$ and for any (x, y) and (x', y') in A,

$$f(\theta x + [1 - \theta]x', \theta y + [1 - \theta]y') \leq \theta f(x, y) + [1 - \theta]f(x', y').$$

The function is *strictly convex* if this expression holds with a strict inequality.

The function $f(x) = x^2$ is strictly convex. To demonstrate this convexity, we pick any two points on the real line x and x', and check that

$$f(\theta x + [1 - \theta]x') < \theta f(x) + [1 - \theta]f(x')$$

holds for this function. We substitute the actual function into this expression:

$$(\theta x + [1 - \theta]x')^2 < \theta x^2 + [1 - \theta](x')^2.$$

Rearranging terms,

$$\theta^2 x^2 + [1 - \theta]^2(x')^2 + 2\theta[1 - \theta]xx' < \theta x^2 + [1 - \theta](x')^2,$$

$$\theta[1 - \theta]x^2 + \theta[1 - \theta](x')^2 - 2\theta[1 - \theta]xx' > 0,$$

$$x^2 + (x')^2 - 2xx' = (x - x')^2 > 0.$$

Thus, this function is strictly convex.

In panel c of Figure A.1, the function x^3 is not concave or convex over the domain of real numbers: It is concave over the negative real numbers and convex over the positive real numbers. Finally, the Cobb-Douglas function $f(K, L) = AL^\alpha K^\beta$, where L and K are nonnegative real numbers, is concave if $\alpha + \beta \leq 1$.

Homogeneous Functions

A function $f(x_1, x_2, \ldots, x_n)$ is said to be *homogeneous* of degree γ if

$$f(ax_1, ax_2, \ldots, ax_n) = a^\gamma f(x_1, x_2, \ldots, x_n)$$

for any constant $a > 0$. For example, suppose that f is a production function and the set $\{x_i\}$ consists of inputs to production. Given a particular set of inputs $(x_1, x_2, \ldots, x_n)$, the production function tells us how much output, $q = f(x_1, x_2, \ldots, x_n)$, the firm can produce. What happens to q if we double all the inputs so that $a = 2$? If for any set of inputs, output always doubles, then the production function is homogeneous of degree one. If output does not change at all, then it is homogeneous of degree zero. If it always quadruples, it is homogeneous of degree two, and so on. Some other examples are

- The function $f(x) = 1$ is homogeneous of degree zero because doubling x leaves $f(x)$ unchanged.
- The square root function $f(x_1, x_2) = \sqrt{x_1 + x_2}$ is homogeneous of degree one-half because doubling x_1 and x_2 causes the function to change to $\sqrt{2x_1 + 2x_2} = \sqrt{2}\sqrt{x_1 + x_2} = 2^{0.5}\sqrt{x_1 + x_2}$.
- The function $f(x_1, x_2) = \sqrt{x_1 x_2}$ is homogeneous of degree one because $\sqrt{(2x_1)(2x_2)} = 2\sqrt{x_1 x_2}$.
- The Cobb-Douglas function $f(L, K) = AL^\alpha K^\beta$ is homogeneous of degree $\alpha + \beta$ because $A(2L)^\alpha(2K)^\beta = 2^{\alpha+\beta}AL^\alpha K^\beta$.
- The functions $f(x) = x + 1$ and $f(x_1, x_2) = x_1 + \sqrt{x_2}$ are not homogeneous of any degree.

Special Properties of Logarithmic Functions

Logarithms are wonderful, logarithms are fine.
Once you learn the rules of logs, you'll think they are sublime.

We use the logarithmic function repeatedly in this textbook because it has a number of desirable properties. For example, we can convert some multiplication problems into addition problems by using the logarithmic function. We always use the natural logarithm (or natural log) function of x, which we write as $\ln(x)$, where $x = e^{\ln(x)}$ for $x > 0$.

The key properties of logarithms that we use are

- The log of a product is equal to a sum of logs: $\ln(xz) = \ln(x) + \ln(z)$.
- The log of a number to a power is equal to the power times the log of the number: $\ln(x^b) = b \ln(x)$.
- It follows from this previous rule that the log of the reciprocal of x equals the negative of the log of x: $\ln(1/x) = \ln(x^{-1}) = -\ln(x)$.

A.3 Derivatives

We want a way to summarize how a function changes as its argument changes. One such measure is the slope. However, we generally use an alternative measure, the *derivative*, which is essentially the slope at a particular point. We illustrate the distinction between these two measures using a function of a single variable, $f: \mathbb{R} \to \mathbb{R}$.

The usual definition of a *slope* is "rise over run"—that is, the change in the value of a function when moving from point x_1 to another point x_2:

$$\text{Slope} = \frac{\text{rise}}{\text{run}} = \frac{f(x_2) - f(x_1)}{x_2 - x_1}.$$

This definition of a slope depends on comparing the function at *two* different points, x_1 and x_2. However, typically we want the slope of f at a point.

To determine the slope at a point, we first implicitly define the difference, h, between these points as $x_2 = x_1 + h$. Substituting this expression into our formula for the slope gives us

$$\frac{f(x_2) - f(x_1)}{x_2 - x_1} = \frac{f(x_1 + h) - f + (x_1)}{h}.$$

The derivative of a real-value function $f: \mathbb{R} \to \mathbb{R}$ at a point x in $\mathbb{R}$ is

$$\frac{df(x)}{dx} = \lim_{h \to 0} \frac{f(x + h) - f(x)}{h}. \tag{A.2}$$

In the text of this book, we use two different notational conventions to denote the derivative of a function. Here and in most places in the text, we write the derivative using the notation $df(x)/dx$. Sometimes for notational simplicity, we omit explicit reference to the argument of f, writing the derivative of f at x as df/dx where no ambiguity results.

The derivative has a graphical interpretation. The slope of a function between two points is equal to the slope of a straight line connecting those two points. The slope of such a straight line can be computed using the rise-over-run formula. In Figure A.2,

Figure A.2 Derivative and Slope

The slope of a function between x_1 and x_2 is equal to the slope (= rise over run) of a straight line connecting the two points $b = (x_1, f(x_1))$ and $(x_2, f(x_2))$. If we fix one of the points, b, and move the other point closer, then the run ($h = x_2 - x_1$) grows smaller and smaller. If the derivative exists, the rise, $f(x_2) - f(x_1) = f(x_1 + h) - f(x_1)$, will eventually get smaller as well, but typically at a different rate than the run. The limiting value of this slope is the derivative, which equals the slope of a line tangent to the function at b.

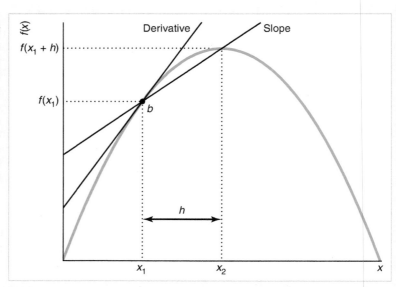

the slope of a function between x_1 and x_2 is equal to the slope of a straight line connecting the two points $b = (x_1, f(x_1))$ and $(x_2, f(x_2))$. Now fix one of the points, b, and move the other point ever closer so that the run ($h = x_2 - x_1$) gets smaller and smaller. If the derivative exists, the rise, $f(x_2) - f(x_1) = f(x_1 + h) - f(x_1)$, will eventually get smaller and smaller as well, but typically at a different rate than the run. The limiting value of the ratio of the rise to the run will be the slope of an infinitesimally short line—the slope of the function at a point. The limiting value of this slope is the derivative, which equals the slope of a line tangent to the function at b.

If $df(x)/dx$ is positive, the function is *increasing* at x. That is, as x increases slightly, the function evaluated at x also increases. Similarly, if $df(x)/dx$ is negative, the function is *decreasing* at x.

One problem with using derivatives instead of slopes is that in some circumstances, the derivative of a function may not be defined because the limit given in Equation A.2 does not exist. Discontinuous functions do not have derivatives at any point of discontinuity. For example, the derivative of the function $1/x$ does not exist at $x = 0$. The derivative also fails to exist for a continuous function at a kink, such as at $x = 0$ for the function $|x|$.

Rules for Calculating Derivatives

This book repeatedly uses a few rules for calculating the derivatives of functions.

- *The addition rule*: If a function $f: \mathbb{R} \to \mathbb{R}$ can be written as the sum of two other functions, so that $f(x) = g(x) + h(x)$, then

$$\frac{df(x)}{dx} = \frac{dg(x)}{dx} + \frac{dh(x)}{dx}.$$

  In words, this expression says that the derivative of the sum is equal to the sum of the derivatives.

- *The product rule*: If a function $f: \mathbb{R} \to \mathbb{R}$ can be written as the product of two other functions, so that $f(x) = g(x)h(x)$ where g and h are both differentiable at x, then

$$\frac{df(x)}{dx} = \frac{dg(x)}{dx}h(x) + g(x)\frac{dh(x)}{dx}.$$

  An important special case occurs when $g(x)$ is a constant, say, b. Then $dg(x)/dx = 0$, so the product rule yields the result that $dbh(x)/dx = bdh(x)/dx$.

- *The power rule*: If $f(x) = ax^b$, then the derivative of f at x, provided that the derivative exists, is

$$\frac{df(x)}{dx} = abx^{b-1}.$$

  For example, using the power rule, we can show that $d(bx^2)/dx = 2bx$. Applying this result and the product rule, we can determine the derivative $d(bx^3)/dx$:

$$\frac{dbx^3}{dx} = x\frac{dbx^2}{dx} + \frac{dx}{dx}bx^2 = x(2bx) + bx^2 = 3bx^2.$$

  Continuing in this vein using the product rule repeatedly, we learn that in general, $dbx^n/dx = nbx^{n-1}$.

- *The polynomial rule*: A polynomial function is a function that takes the form

$$f(x) = b_0 + b_1x + b_2x^2 + \dots + b_nx^n,$$

where n is a nonnegative whole number. The *order* of the polynomial is the largest exponent, n. Using the power rule repeatedly (as we just showed), the derivative of the polynomial $f(x)$ is

$$\frac{df(x)}{dx} = b_1 + 2b_2x + \ \cdots \ + nb_nx^{n-1}.$$

- *The reciprocal rule*: Using the power rule and the product rule, we can show that the derivative of the reciprocal of a function, $1/f(x)$, is

$$\frac{d[1/f(x)]}{dx} = -\frac{\dfrac{df(x)}{dx}}{[f(x)]^2}.$$

- *The quotient rule*: Using the reciprocal rule and the product rule, we can show that if $f(x) = g(x)/h(x)$, then

$$\frac{d[g(x)/h(x)]}{dx} = \frac{h(x)\dfrac{dg(x)}{dx} - g(x)\dfrac{dh(x)}{dx}}{[h(x)]^2}.$$

- *The chain rule*: We can compute the derivatives of functions such as $f(x) = g(h(x))$ by using all the previous rules,

$$\frac{df(x)}{dx} = \frac{dg(h(x))}{dx} = \frac{dg(h(x))}{dh(x)}\frac{dh(x)}{dx},$$

provided that h is differentiable at x and that g is differentiable at $h(x)$. As an example, let $h(x) = x^2$, and $g(z) = 2 + z^2$ so that $f(x) = g(h(x)) = 2 + x^4$. By direct differentiation, we know that $df(x)/dx = 4x^3$. We can derive the same result using the chain rule. First, we use the power rule to show that $dg(z)/dz = 2z$ and that $dh(x)/dx = 2x$. Second, we substitute $h(x)$ for z in the expression for $dg(z)/dz$, which gives us $dg(h(x))/dh(x)$, and apply the chain rule to obtain

$$\frac{dg(h(x))}{dx} = \frac{d[2 + h(x)]}{dh(x)}\frac{dh(x)}{dx} = (2x^2) \times (2x) = 4x^3.$$

- *The exponential rule*: For any differentiable function $g(x)$,

$$\frac{de^{g(x)}}{dx} = \frac{dg(x)}{dx}e^{g(x)}.$$

An important special case of this rule is that

$$\frac{dae^{bx}}{dx} = abe^{bx}.$$

- *The exponent rule*: An exponential function is one that can be written in the form $f(x) = a^x$, where a number a is raised to the power x. One can use the properties of logarithms together with the exponential rule and the chain rule to show that

$$\frac{da^x}{dx} = \frac{de^{\ln(a)x}}{dx} = \ln(a)a^x.$$

- *The logarithm rule*: The derivative of the function $\ln(x)$ is

$$\frac{d\ \ln(x)}{dx} = \frac{1}{x}.$$

Higher-Order Derivatives

If the derivative exists everywhere in the domain, we say that the function is *continuously differentiable*. For example, the function $f(x) = 1/x$ on the domain $(0, 1]$ is a continuously differentiable function. We can use the power rule to show that the ordinary derivative is

$$\frac{d[1/x]}{dx} = \frac{d[x^{-1}]}{dx} = -\frac{1}{x^2}.$$

This derivative is itself continuously differentiable on $(0, 1]$. Accordingly, we can use the power rule to differentiate this derivative a second time:

$$\frac{d[-1/x^2]}{dx} = \frac{d[-x^{-2}]}{dx} = \frac{2}{x^3}.$$

Rather than referring to this result as the "derivative of the derivative of $f(x)$," we call it the *second derivative of $f(x)$*, which we write as $d^2f(x)/dx^2$.

Higher-order derivatives are defined similarly. The derivative of the derivative of the derivative of $f(x)$, called the third derivative of $f(x)$, is written $d^3f(x)/dx^3$. In general, the *n*th order derivative of $f(x)$ is $d^nf(x)/dx^n$.

Partial Derivatives

When using a function of more than one variable, we want to know how the value of the function varies as we change one variable while holding the others constant. Consider a function of two real variables, $f: \mathbb{R}^2 \to \mathbb{R}$. The slope of this function at a point is a little more complicated to define than the slope of a function with a single argument, because the slope of the function at a point now depends on direction. For example, let

$$f(N, E) = N^2 - E^2 + 1.$$

The variable names are chosen to evoke a map, where N reflects the latitude and E denotes the longitude. The value of the function f evaluated at a point on this map can then be thought of as corresponding to the altitude (height). Figure A.3 shows the surface and contour lines of this function.

This function takes the value of zero at the origin but changes in quite different ways as one moves away from the origin, depending on the direction of the move. If one were to move directly to the northeast, then N and E would increase at the same rate (hence their squares do, too). Thus, if one moves directly to the northeast (or southwest), the altitude does not change. In the figure, the curves in the (N, E) plane are contour lines of the surface above the plane. The curves show that if E increases at the same rate as N, the elevation remains constant.

However, if one begins at the origin and heads directly north, then N increases while E remains fixed. One's altitude increases in this direction. If, on the other hand, one heads directly east, E increases while N remains fixed, and one heads downhill (after traveling E units, one attains an altitude of $1 - E^2$).

Going *just* north or *just* east gets at the idea behind the *partial derivative*: The idea is to vary the value of one variable while holding all the other variables fixed. This procedure also gives us an easy algorithm for computing the partial derivative of f with respect to, say, N: Just pretend that E is a constant, and compute the *ordinary* derivative. Thus, we have the partial derivative of f with respect to N,

$$\frac{\partial f(N, E)}{\partial N} = \frac{\partial (N^2 - E^2)}{\partial N} = \frac{\partial N^2}{\partial N} = 2N,$$

Figure A.3 Illustration of Partial Derivatives

The figure shows the surface and contour lines of the function $f(N, E) = N^2 - E^2 + 1$. If we move only in the N direction, the elevation rises at an increasing rate, whereas if we move only in the E direction, the elevation falls at the same increasing rate. The curves in the (N, E) plane are contour lines of the surface above the plane. The curves show that if E increases at the same rate as N, the elevation remains constant.

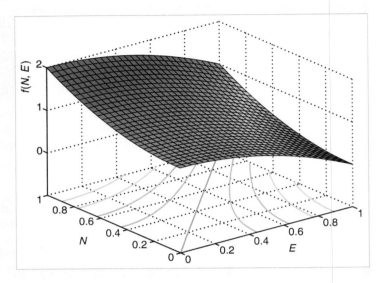

and the partial derivative of f with respect to E,

$$\frac{\partial f(N, E)}{\partial E} = \frac{\partial(N^2 - E^2)}{\partial E} = -\frac{\partial E^2}{\partial E} = -2E.$$

In the special case in which f is a function of only a single variable, the partial derivative is exactly the same as the ordinary derivative:

$$\frac{\partial f(x)}{\partial x} = \frac{df(x)}{dx}.$$

In the general case in which the function $f: \mathbb{R}^n \to \mathbb{R}$ depends on several variables, one can think of the partial derivative of f with respect to, say, the first variable as measuring the *direct* effect of a change in the first variable on the value of the function, while neglecting the effects that a change in this variable might have on *other* variables that might influence the value of $f(x)$. Just as the ordinary derivative of an ordinary derivative is called a second (ordinary) derivative, there are also higher-order partial derivatives. For example, the partial derivative of $g(x_1, x_2)$ with respect to x_1 is written as $\partial g(x_1, x_2)/\partial x_1$; the *second* partial derivative of $g(x_1, x_2)$ with respect to x_1 is written as $\partial^2 g(x_1, x_2)/\partial x_1^2$, while the second partial derivative of $g(x_1, x_2)$ with respect to x_2 is written as $\partial^2 g(x_1, x_2)/\partial x_2^2$.

We can derive second-order (or higher-order) derivatives that involve the repeated differentiation of the function with respect to more than one variable. For example, if we differentiate the partial derivative of our function $g(x_1, x_2)$ with respect to x_1, $\partial g(x_1, x_2)/\partial x_1$, with respect to x_2, we obtain the cross-partial derivative, $\partial^2 g(x_1, x_2)/(\partial x_1 \partial x_2)$. The order of differentiation doesn't matter for the functions we usually study. According to Young's Theorem, $\partial^2 f/(\partial x_1 \partial x_2) = \partial^2 f/(\partial x_2 \partial x_1)$ if the cross-partial derivatives $\partial^2 f/(\partial x_1 \partial x_2)$ and $\partial^2 f/(\partial x_2 \partial x_1)$ exist and are continuous. Similarly, $\partial^5 g(x_1, x_2)/\partial x_1^2 \partial x_2^3$ indicates partial differentiation of g with respect to x_1 twice and with respect to x_2 thrice, thus yielding a fifth-order partial derivative.

Euler's Homogeneous Function Theorem

A function $f: \mathbb{R}^n \to \mathbb{R}$ is *homogeneous* of degree γ if

$$f(tx_1, tx_2, \ldots, tx_n) = t^\gamma f(x_1, \ldots, x_n)$$

holds for all possible values of x_1, x_2, ... , x_n and constant scalar t. That is, multiplying each of the arguments of the function by t increases the value of the function by t^γ. The degree need not be an integer. For example, the Cobb-Douglas function $Ax_1^{\alpha_1}x_2^{\alpha_2} \dots x_n^{\alpha_n}$ is homogeneous of degree $\alpha_1 + \alpha_2 + \dots + \alpha_n$, where each α_i may be a fraction. Such a function satisfies Euler's homogeneous function theorem

$$\sum_{i=1}^{n} x_i \frac{\partial f(x_1, \dots, x_n)}{\partial x_i} = \gamma f(x_1, \dots, x_n).$$

A.4 Maximum and Minimum

Most microeconomic analysis concerns finding the maximum or minimum of a function. For example, a consumer chooses a bundle of goods to maximize utility, or a firm chooses inputs to minimize cost.

The problems of finding a maximum and finding a minimum may sound as though they are very different, but they are similar mathematically. We think of the problems of finding either *maxima* or *minima* as special cases of the more general problem of finding *extrema*.

Local Extrema

Mathematicians and economists are sometimes interested in the *local* properties of a function, or, equivalently, the properties of a function within the *neighborhood* of a point x. A local property is one that holds within a neighborhood of x—that is, within some positive (but possibly very small) distance $\varepsilon > 0$ from the point x. For example, a function has a local maximum at x^* if there exists an $\varepsilon > 0$ such that $f(x^*) \geq f(x)$ for all $x \in (x^* - \varepsilon, x^* + \varepsilon)$ —that is, in the neighborhood of x^*.

A *local* extremum of a function $f(x)$ is either a local minimum or a local maximum of the function f. If we move from the local extremum at x by an amount less than ε, the value of the function becomes less extreme. Figure A.4 graphs the function $f(x) = x \sin(6\pi x)$, which has many peaks and troughs. All the local extrema are indicated with bullets. Points a, b, and c are local maxima, while points d, e, and f are local minima. All these local maxima and local minima together compose the set of local extrema. Point a is a local maximum because if we either increase or decrease x just a little, the value of $f(x)$ decreases. Similarly, d is a local minimum because if we either increase or decrease x slightly, the value of $f(x)$ increases.

Global Extrema

The *global maximum* (usually called the *maximum*) is the largest local maximum, and the *global minimum* (or *minimum*) is the smallest local minimum. In Figure A.4, the global maximum is point c and the global minimum is point f. If there are two local maxima that are both equally large and larger than all other points, we would say that there are *two* global maxima.

Existence of Extrema

In economics, we often want to know if a function has a maximum or a minimum in the relevant domain. For example, we might examine whether there is a minimum for a function $f: [0, 1] \rightarrow \mathbb{R}$; that is, f takes values from the interval between zero and one (inclusive) and maps them into the real line.

Not all such functions have a maximum or a minimum. Continuity of a function is a *sufficient* condition for the existence of both a maximum and a minimum. This result is a consequence of the *Extreme Value Theorem*: If the function f is continuous and defined on the closed interval $[a, b]$, there is at least one c in $[a, b]$ such that $f(c) \geq f(x)$ for all x in $[a, b]$, and there is at least one d in $[a, b]$ such that $f(d) \leq f(x)$ for all x in $[a, b]$. Functions that are not continuous *might* have minima and maxima—but there's no guarantee.

Figure A.5 illustrates several possibilities. Panel a shows a continuous function, $y = f(x) = 24x - 75x^2 + 50x^3$, with a single minimum and a single (local and global) maximum in $[0, 1]$. In panel b, the continuous function $y = f(x) = 1$ has an infinite number of maxima and minima in $[0, 1]$. In panel c, the discontinuity in the function

$$y = \begin{cases} 24x - 75x^2 + 50x^3, & x < 0.8 \\ 24x - 75x^2 + 50x^3, & x > 0.8 \end{cases}$$

is shown as a hollow circle. Because of this missing point, there is a unique maximum, but there isn't a global minimum within $[0, 1]$. Finally, the discontinuous function plotted in panel d,

$$y = \begin{cases} 0, & x < 0.8 \\ 1, & x \geq 0.8, \end{cases}$$

has an infinite number of maxima and minima in $[0, 1]$.

Uniqueness of Extrema

As panels b and d of Figure A.5. illustrate, even when a function has global maxima or global minima, there may be more than one maximum or minimum. We want to determine when the function will have a unique solution. There is a unique global maximum if the function f is strictly concave, and a unique global minimum if f is strictly convex. For example, in panel a of Figure A.5, when x is less than about 0.46, where the curve hits the horizontal axis, the function is concave, so there is a single global maximum. However, to the right of this point, the function is convex and has a single global minimum.

Figure A.4 Illustration of Local and Global Extrema

The bullets indicate the local extrema. Point c is the global maximum, and point f is the global minimum.

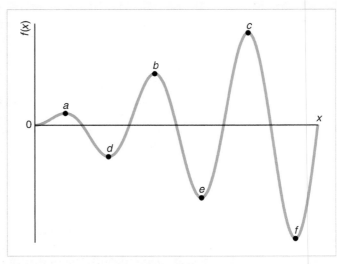

Figure A.5 Illustration of the Extreme Value Theorem

According to the Extreme Value Theorem, if a function is continuous and defined on the closed interval, it contains at least one minimum and at least one maximum. (a) This continuous function has a maximum at point a and a minimum at point b. (b) This continuous function has an infinite number of maxima and minima that equal one. (c) This function is discontinuous at the point marked with a hollow point, so the theorem cannot be used to draw inferences about the existence of minima and maxima. For the domain $(0, 1]$, the function has a maximum, but no minimum. (d) This discontinuous function has infinite maxima and minima.

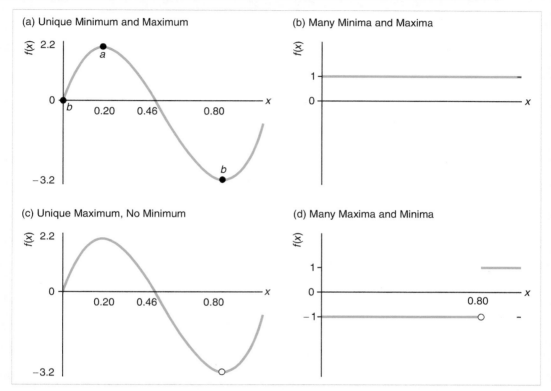

Interior Extrema

Often in the text, we care whether the maximum or minimum is located in the interior of the range of x or at one of the end points. To illustrate this distinction, we consider the function $f(x) = -(x - \frac{1}{2})^2/2$, where x lies within $[0, 1]$, as panel a of Figure A.6 shows. This function has a maximum at point a where $x^* = 0.5$, which we call an *interior* maximum because $x^* \in (0, 1)$ and it is not on the edge of the domain $[0, 1]$. That is, x^* is not zero or one. In contrast, in panel b, because the maximum of the function $g(x) = -x^2/2$ is zero at point a, which is on the edge or *corner* of the domain $[0, 1]$, the maximum of this function is *not* interior.

A.5 Finding the Extrema of a Function

Because it is not always practical to plot functions and look for extrema, we use calculus to find local extrema. The key insight is that for functions that are continuously differentiable, the *slope* of the function at any interior minimum or maximum

Figure A.6 Interior Extrema

In panel a, the maximum, point *a*, occurs at $x = 0.5$, which lies in the interior of the interval [0, 1]. In panel b, the maximum at *a* is at the corner—not in the interior of the domain.

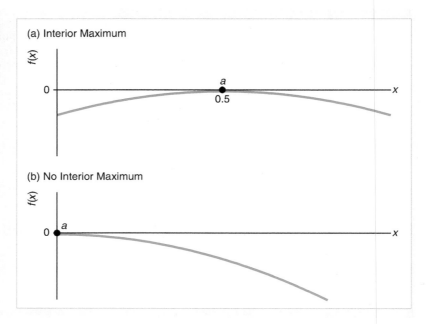

is zero. Figure A.7 illustrates that the slope of the graph at every interior local minimum or maximum is zero.

Because derivatives can be thought of as the slope of a function, one way to find all the interior local extrema of a continuously differentiable function is to find where the partial derivatives of the function equal zero. Let's begin with a problem that has only a single independent variable and $f: [0, 1] \rightarrow \mathbb{R}$, where f is assumed to be continuously differentiable and strictly concave. What is the importance of these assumptions?

There are two important consequences of our assumption that f is continuously differentiable. First, because f is continuously differentiable, it must also be continuous, so we know that it has a maximum. Second, because it is continuously differentiable, we know that its derivative exists, and hence we can use this derivative to determine the local extrema.

Because f is assumed to be strictly concave, we know that it has a unique global maximum. Thus, if we find a point x where $df(x)/dx = 0$, it follows that this point x is the unique global maximum of the function f over the interval [0, 1].

The usual way to write the problem of finding a maximum of a function $f(x)$ is

$$\max_x \ f(x),$$

where *max* is called the *max operator*, the variable x that appears below the max operator is the *choice variable*, and f is the function to be maximized and is called the *objective function*.

Any x^* in [0, 1] that solves $df(x^*)/dx = 0$ is a point at which the function $f(x)$ has a local maximum. The equation $df(x)/dx = 0$, in which we set the first-order derivative equal to zero, is called the *first-order condition*. The x^* that solves this equation, $df(x^*)/dx$, is called a *critical value*. Given our assumptions that f is continuously differentiable and concave, we know that x^* is a unique global maximum.

So far, we've assumed that f is concave, as in panel a of Figure A.7. In practice, we need to check whether the function is concave. For example, if we falsely assume

Figure A.7 Extrema and the First-Order Condition (F.O.C.)

If a function is continuously differentiable and concave, it must have a unique maximum. Further, if the F.O.C. has a solution (that is, the function has a point where its slope is zero), the F.O.C. characterizes the unique maximum. (a) This function is continuously differentiable and concave, so the F.O.C. identifies a unique maximum (at point a). (b) The function is continuously differentiable, so it has at least one maximum, but the function is not concave, so the maximum may not be unique (indeed, there are two maxima at the end points). The function is convex, so the F.O.C. characterizes a minimum. (c) The function is continuously differentiable, so it possesses a maximum in the interval [0, 1]. However, at point a where the F.O.C. holds, the function is neither concave nor convex, so a is neither a minimum nor a maximum—it is a saddle point. (d) The function is concave, so this maximum will be unique. However, the F.O.C. does not have a solution in the interval [0, 1]—there is no place where the function has a slope equal to zero—so the unique maximum is not characterized by the F.O.C.

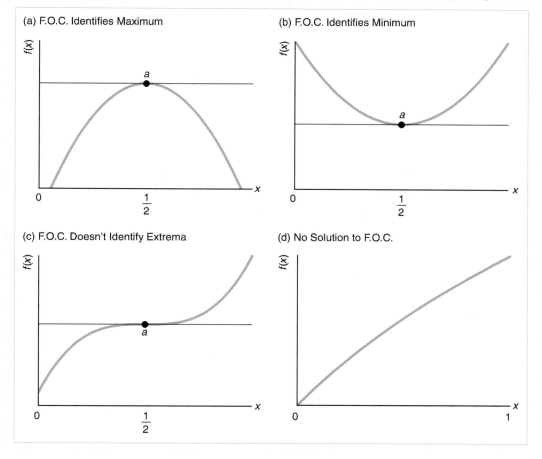

that the function is concave and it is convex, we may find a minimum rather than a maximum, as in panel b.

If $f(x^*)$ is at least twice-differentiable in a neighborhood of x^*, we can use the *second-order condition* to determine whether the function is concave in that neighborhood. The second-order condition for concavity is that the second derivative of $f(x^*)$ is negative, $d^2 f(x^*)/dx^2 < 0$. If this condition holds, we know that the x^* that the first-order condition identified is a unique maximum in this neighborhood of x^*. In contrast, if the second derivative is positive, we know that the function is convex in this neighborhood and that we have found a minimum.

Examples

We can illustrate this approach using several examples where f: $[0, 1] \to \mathbb{R}$. Our first maximization problem is

$$\max_x -\tfrac{1}{2}(x - \tfrac{1}{2})^2.$$

The first-order condition is $df(x)/dx = \tfrac{1}{2} - x = 0$, so $x^* = \tfrac{1}{2}$, as panel a of Figure A.7 shows. The second-order condition is $d^2f(x^*)/dx^2 = -1 < 0$, so $\tfrac{1}{2}$ is a maximum. One can demonstrate that this function f is continuously differentiable and concave throughout the domain, so $f(\tfrac{1}{2}) = 0$, point a, is the global maximum of this function.

Now consider the maximization problem

$$\max_x \tfrac{1}{2}(x - \tfrac{1}{2})^2.$$

The first-order condition is $df(x)/dx = x - \tfrac{1}{2} = 0$, so this problem has the same critical value, $x = \tfrac{1}{2}$, as in the previous example. Because f is continuously differentiable, we know that it has a maximum and a minimum on $[0, 1]$. The second-order condition is $d^2f(\tfrac{1}{2})/dx^2 = 1 > 0$ so $x^* = \tfrac{1}{2}$ is a minimum, as panel b of Figure A.7 shows. There are two global maxima, which are not interior, at $x = 0$ and $x = 1$.

The maximization problem

$$\max_x \tfrac{1}{3}(x - \tfrac{1}{2})^3$$

has a first-order condition $df(x)/dx = (x - \tfrac{1}{2})^2 = 0$, so the critical value is again at $x = \tfrac{1}{2}$. Because f is continuously differentiable, we know it has a maximum on $[0, 1]$, but as in the previous example, the maximum is not interior; instead, it occurs at $x = 1$. This function is neither concave nor convex at $x = \tfrac{1}{2}$, so $x^* = \tfrac{1}{2}$ is neither a minimum nor a maximum of f, as panel c of Figure A.7 illustrates. It is called a *saddle point*. We have a saddle point when the second-order condition is zero, as in this case: $d^2f(\tfrac{1}{2})/dx^2 = 2(x - \tfrac{1}{2}) = 2(\tfrac{1}{2} - \tfrac{1}{2}) = 0$. The sign of the second derivative changes from one side to the other of the saddle point.

Finally, the maximization problem

$$\max_x \ln(x + 1)$$

yields the first-order condition $1/(x + 1) = 0$. Here, f is continuously differentiable and strictly concave, so we know that a unique global maximum exists. However, there is no value of x in the $[0, 1]$ interval that solves the first-order condition. Consequently, we know that the unique global maximum is *not* interior (in this case, it occurs at the end point where $x = 1$), as panel d of Figure A.7 illustrates.

More generally, we may want to find the maximum of a function of several variables, and hence several choice variables appear under the max operator. To use calculus to solve such a maximization problem, we compute the partial derivatives of the objective function with respect to each of the choice variables and then set these equal to zero. These equations, in which the first-order partial derivatives are set equal to zero, are called the *first-order conditions*.

For example, let g: $[0, 1] \times [0, 1] \to \mathbb{R}$ and assume that g is continuously differentiable and strictly concave. Then we know, as we did for f, that g has a unique global maximum. Accordingly, we can write the problem as

$$\max_{x_1, x_2} g(x_1, x_2),$$

which yields the pair of first-order conditions

$$\frac{\partial g(x_1, x_2)}{\partial x_1} = 0, \tag{A.3}$$

$$\frac{\partial g(x_1, x_2)}{\partial x_2} = 0. \tag{A.4}$$

The solution to Equations A.3 and A.4 determines where the global maximum of g is located, if a solution exists. If a solution to these equations does not exist, then the maximum must lie on the boundary of the choice set $[0, 1] \times [0, 1]$, so either x_1 or x_2 (or both) must be equal to either zero or one at the maximum.

Indirect Objective Functions and the Envelope Theorem

Economic problems generally involve choice variables that are under the control of a person or a firm, such as how much of a good to buy or produce. Economic problems may also depend on *exogenous* parameters that influence the decision maker's behavior but are not under the decision maker's direct control, such as the price at which the good can be bought or sold. We can add these exogenous parameters to the formulation of a maximization problem.

To illustrate this approach, we examine a function $g: [0, 1] \times [0, 1] \times \mathbb{R} \to \mathbb{R}$. We write this function and its arguments as $g(x_1, x_2, z)$, where the variables x_1 and x_2 are choice variables and z is an exogenous parameter. We assume that g is continuously differentiable in all three of its arguments and is strictly concave in the first two (the choice variables). Consequently, g has a unique global maximum (even if g is not concave in the exogenous parameters).

The decision maker's problem of choosing x_1 and x_2 to maximize g given z is written as

$$\max_{x_1, x_2} g(x_1, x_2, z).$$

The first-order conditions are

$$\frac{\partial g(x_1, x_2, z)}{\partial x_1} = 0 \quad \text{and} \quad \frac{\partial g(x_1, x_2, z)}{\partial x_2} = 0,$$

so the optimal choice of x_1 and x_2 typically depends on the value of z. Accordingly, the values of x_1 and x_2 that solve the optimization problem for a given z may be written as $x_1^*(z)$ and $x_2^*(z)$.

Given a solution to the maximization problem, the value of g at the maximum is $g(x_1^*(z), x_2^*(z), z)$. Given some value z, the act of maximization determines the optimal values of x_1^* and x_2^*. Accordingly, we may sometimes write the maximum as

$$V(z) = g(x_1^*(z), x_2^*(z), z) = \max_{x_1, x_2} g(x_1, x_2, z).$$

The function $V(z)$ is called the *value function* because it tells us what the value of z is to the decision maker. It is also called the *indirect objective function*, in contrast to $g(x_1, x_2, z)$, which is the *direct objective function*.

A natural question to ask is how the value function changes when z changes. At first glance, this problem is very complicated because (as we have seen) a change in z has a direct effect on the value of $g(x_1, x_2, z)$ and it *also* causes the decision maker to change x_1 and x_2 in ways that may be complicated. However, at least for *small* changes in z, an important shortcut to solving this problem exists. The *Envelope Theorem* tells us that the direct effect of small changes in z matter but that the indirect effects do not. That is, according to the Envelope Theorem, the solution to our particular problem is

$$\frac{\partial V(z)}{\partial z} = \frac{\partial g(x_1, x_2, z)}{\partial z}. \tag{A.5}$$

We offer another, more general statement of this theorem below when we discuss the solutions to constrained maximization problems, and offer a constructive proof.

Comparative Statics

Not only do we want to know how a change in the exogenous parameter affects the value function, but we also want to know how this change in the exogenous parameter, z, affects the choice variables, x_1 and x_2. We can use our first-order conditions to answer this question because the first-order conditions show how the optimal choice of x_1 and x_2 depends on z. In our example, the first-order conditions are

$$\frac{\partial g\,(x_1^*(z),\, x_2^*(z),\, z)}{\partial x_1(z)} = 0 \quad \text{and} \quad \frac{\partial g(x_1^*(z),\, x_2^*(z),\, z)}{\partial x_2(z)} = 0.$$

Provided that the function g is twice continuously differentiable, we can then compute the derivatives of each of these first-order conditions with respect to the exogenous parameter:

$$\frac{\partial^2 g}{\partial x_1^2}\frac{dx_1^*(z)}{dz} + \frac{\partial^2 g}{\partial x_1 \partial x_2}\frac{dx_2^*(z)}{dz} + \frac{\partial g}{\partial z} = 0, \tag{A.6}$$

$$\frac{\partial^2 g}{\partial x_1 \partial x_2}\frac{dx_1^*(x)}{dz} + \frac{\partial^2 g}{\partial x_2^2}\frac{dx_2^*(z)}{dz} + \frac{\partial g}{\partial z} = 0, \tag{A.7}$$

where we omit the arguments to the function g for notational simplicity.

By treating the derivatives $dx_1^*(z)/dz$ and $dx_2^*(z)/dz$ as variables in the pair of linear Equations A.6 and A.7 and the partial derivatives of g as coefficients, we can solve this system of equations to determine how the maximizing choice of x_1 and x_2 changes for small changes in z. That is, we can solve for $dx_1^*(z)/dz$ and $dx_2^*(z)/dz$.

A.6 Maximizing with Equality Constraints

Most questions in microeconomics involve maximizing or minimizing an objective function subject to one or more *constraints*. For example, consumers maximize their well-being subject to a budget constraint. A firm chooses the cost-minimizing bundle of inputs subject to a feasibility constraint that summarizes which combinations of inputs can produce a given amount of output.

There are two commonly used approaches to solving problems with equality constraints mathematically: the substitution method and Lagrange's method. To illustrate these two approaches, we consider the problem of maximizing the function $g(x_1, x_2)$ subject to the constraint that $h(x_1, x_2) = z$, where z is an exogenous parameter. We write the constraint in implicit function form as $z - h(x_1, x_2) = 0$. This *constrained* maximization problem is written

$$\max_{x_1,\, x_2} g(x_1,\, x_2)$$

$$\text{s.t. } z - h(x_1,\, x_2) = 0. \tag{A.8}$$

Conceptually, we need to find the set of all those x_1 and x_2 that satisfy the constraint $z - h(x_1, x_2) = 0$, and from only this set, we need to choose those values of x_1 and x_2 that maximize $g(x_1, x_2)$.

Substitution Method

Sometimes we can solve a constrained maximization problem by substituting the constraint into the objective so that the problem becomes an unconstrained problem. We can rewrite the constraint as $x_1 = r(x_2, z)$. Because this solution for x_1 as a function of x_2 contains the information in the constraint, we can substitute it into our objective function and rewrite the problem as an unconstrained maximum:

$$\max_{x_2} g(r(x_2, z), x_2).$$

Because we wrote x_1 as a function of x_2, the unconstrained maximization problem has only one choice variable, x_2.

As with any unconstrained maximum problem, we use the first-order condition,

$$\frac{\partial g(r(x_2, z), x_2)}{\partial x_1} \frac{\partial r(x_2, z)}{\partial x_2} + \frac{\partial g(r(x_2, z), x_2)}{\partial x_2} = 0, \tag{A.9}$$

to find the critical value of the choice variable x_2. We solve the first-order equation, Equation A.9, for x_2^*, substitute this solution for x_2 into $x_1 = r(x_2, z)$ to obtain $x_1^* = r(x_2^*, z)$, and then substitute x_1^* and x_2^* into the objective function to determine the maximum.

The following example illustrates this approach, where the objective function is $g(x_1, x_2) = x_1 x_2$ and the constraint is $z - h(x_1, x_2) = z - x_1 - x_2$, so the constrained maximization problem is

$$\max_{x_1, x_2} \ln(x_1 x_2)$$
$$\text{s.t. } z - x_1 - x_2 = 0. \tag{A.10}$$

Using the constraint to solve for x_1 in terms of x_2, we find that $x_1 = r(x_2, z) = z - x_2$. Substituting this function into the objective function, we obtain the corresponding unconstrained maximization problem:

$$\max_{x_2} \ln((z - x_2)x_2) = \ln(z - x_2) + \ln(x_2).$$

Because the first-order condition is $-1/(z - x_2) + 1/x_2 = 0$, the solution of the first-order condition is $x_2^* = 0.5z$. Substituting this expression into the formula for x_1, we find that $x_1^* = z - 0.5z = 0.5z$. Evaluating the objective function at the maximizing values x_1^* and x_2^*, we find that $g(x_1^*, x_2^*) = \ln(0.25z^2)$.

The problem with using this method is that writing x_1 as a function of x_2 and z may be very difficult. If we have many constraints, this approach will usually be infeasible or impractical.

Lagrange's Method

Joseph Louis Lagrange developed an alternative method to solving a constrained maximization problem that works for a wider variety of problems than the substitution method does. As with the substitution method, Lagrange's method (or the Lagrangian method) converts a constrained maximization problem into an unconstrained maximization problem.

Solving a General Problem. The first step of Lagrange's method is to write the *Lagrangian function*, which is the sum of the original objective function, $g(x_1, x_2)$, and the left-hand side of the constraint, $z - h(x_1, x_2) = 0$, multiplied by a constant, λ, called the Lagrangian *multiplier*:

$$\mathcal{L}(x_1, x_2, \lambda; z) = g(x_1, x_2) + \lambda[z - h(x_1, x_2)]. \tag{A.11}$$

If $\lambda = 0$ or the constraint holds, the Lagrangian function is identical to the original objective function.

The second step is to find the critical values of the (unconstrained) Lagrangian function, Equation A.11, where the choice variables are the original ones and λ:

$$\mathcal{L}(x_1,\, x_2,\, \lambda;\, z) = g(x_1,\, x_2) + \lambda[z - h(x_1,\, x_2)]. \tag{A.12}$$

To do so, we use the first-order conditions:

$$\frac{\partial \mathcal{L}(x_1,\, x_2,\, \lambda;\, z)}{\partial x_1} = \frac{\partial g(x_1,\, x_2)}{\partial x_1} - \lambda\frac{\partial h(x_1,\, x_2)}{\partial x_1} = 0, \tag{A.13}$$

$$\frac{\partial \mathcal{L}(x_1,\, x_2,\, \lambda;\, z)}{\partial x_2} = \frac{\partial g(x_1,\, x_2)}{\partial x_2} - \lambda\frac{\partial h(x_1,\, x_2)}{\partial x_2} = 0, \tag{A.14}$$

$$\frac{\partial \mathcal{L}(x_1,\, x_2,\, \lambda;\, z)}{\lambda} = z - h(x_1,\, x_2) = 0. \tag{A.15}$$

We simultaneously solve the first-order conditions, Equations A.13, A.14, and A.15, for the critical values of $x_1^*(z)$, $x_2^*(z)$ and $\lambda^*(z)$. Then, we substitute $x_1^*(z)$ and $x_2^*(z)$ into the original objective function to determine the maximum value, $g(x_1^*(z),\, x_2^*(z))$.

The key result of Lagrange's method is that the solution to this unconstrained problem, Equation A.12, also satisfies the original constrained problem, Equation A.8. Lagrange's method can be generalized to handle problems with more choice variables and more constraints. For each constraint, we need an additional Lagrange multiplier.

An Example. To illustrate this method, we return to the problem A.10, where $g(x_1,\, x_2) = \ln(x_1 x_2)$ and the constraint is $z - h(x_1,\, x_2) = z - x_1 - x_2$. The Lagrangian is

$$\mathcal{L}(x_1,\, x_2,\, z,\, \lambda) = \ln(x_1 x_2) + \lambda(z - x_1 - x_2).$$

The first-order conditions are

$$1/x_2 = \lambda,\ 1/x_1 = \lambda \quad \text{and} \quad z - x_1 - x_2 = 0.$$

Solving these first-order conditions simultaneously, we find that

$$x_1^*(z) = 0.5z, \qquad x_2^*(z) = 0.5z, \qquad \text{and} \qquad \lambda^*(z) = 2/z.$$

Because this solution is the same as the one we obtained using the substitution method, the maximum value of our original objective function is also the same: $g(x_1^*(z),\, x_2^*(z)) = \ln(0.25z^2)$.

Interpreting the Lagrange Multiplier. The Lagrange multiplier not only helps us convert a constrained maximization problem to an unconstrained problem but also provides additional information that is often valuable in economic problems. The value of λ that solves the first-order conditions can be interpreted as the (marginal) cost of the constraint.

The change in the original objective function with respect to a change in z is

$$\frac{dg(x_1^*,\, x_2^*)}{dz} = \frac{\partial g}{\partial x_1}\frac{dx_1^*}{dz} + \frac{\partial g}{\partial x_2}\frac{dx_2^*}{dz}.$$

By substituting the first-order conditions for the original choice variables, Equations A.13 and A.14, into this expression, we obtain

$$\frac{dg(x_1^*,\, x_2^*)}{dz} = \lambda^*\frac{\partial h}{\partial x_1}\frac{dx_1^*}{dz} + \lambda^*\frac{\partial h}{\partial x_2}\frac{dx_2^*}{dz}. \tag{A.16}$$

Differentiating the first-order condition for the Lagrange multiplier, Equation A.15, we have the additional result that

$$\frac{\partial h}{\partial x_1}\frac{dx_1^*}{dz} + \frac{\partial h}{\partial x_2}\frac{sx_2^*}{dz} = 1. \tag{A.17}$$

Substituting Equation A.17 into Equation A.16, we find that

$$\frac{dg(x_1^*, x_2^*)}{dz} = \lambda^*. \tag{A.18}$$

Equation A.18 shows that the critical value of the Lagrange multiplier reflects the sensitivity of the original objective function to a change in the exogenous parameter, z. In our last example, a small increase in z changes the value of the objective function by a factor of $\lambda = 2/z$. The Lagrange multiplier shows the value of relaxing the constraint slightly.

A.7 Maximizing with Inequality Constraints

The method of solving constrained extremum problems devised by Lagrange is appropriate if the constraints hold with strict equality. This method works even when the constraint need not hold with equality in general, as long as we know that it *will* hold with equality at the solution to the problem. For example, even if Lisa, who would always like to consume more goods, doesn't *have* to spend all of her money, we know that she will. However, if we do not know whether a constraint will be satisfied with equality, we need new tools.

Figure A.8 illustrates the distinction between an unconstrained maximum and a maximum for a concave objective function $f(x)$ subject to an inequality constraint. The unconstrained function reaches a maximum at its peak, point a, where a line tangent to the curve is horizontal. That is, the first-order condition requires that $df(x)/dx = 0$.

Figure A.8 Constrained and Unconstrained Maxima

In the absence of constraints, the maximum occurs at point a. However, if the choice variable, x, is constrained to be less than or equal to z (that is, it lies to the left of the constraint line), the constrained maximum is point b, where the line tangent to the curve at the constrained maximum is upward sloping.

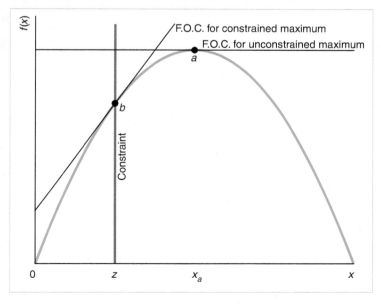

If x is constrained to be less than or equal to z, $x \leq z$, then point b in the figure is the constrained maximum. It occurs where the vertical constraint line at z intersects the function. There the line tangent to the function, or first-order condition, is upward sloping, so $df(x)/dx > 0$.

An inequality constraint need not bind. If z is so large that it exceeds the x corresponding to point a, x_a, then the inequality constraint does not bind and the maximum remains at a, where the unconstrained-maximum first-order condition holds. We can solve these types of problems mathematically by using the Kuhn-Tucker method, named after its inventors, Harold Kuhn and Albert Tucker. We start by applying the method to a specific example and then use it on a general problem.

An Illustration of the Kuhn-Tucker Method

The Kuhn-Tucker approach closely resembles the Lagrange approach except that it permits the use of inequality ("greater-than-or-equal-to") constraints as well as equality constraints. To illustrate this method, we consider the problem of trying to maximize an objective function $a \ln(x_1 + 1) + b \ln(x_2)$, where a and b are positive, subject to the inequality constraints that $z - p_1 x_1 - p_2 x_2 \geq 0$ *and* $x_1 \geq 0$, where p_1, p_2, and z are all positive. It is possible that these constraints could hold with equality. For example, it is possible that the solution to this problem involves setting x_1 equal to zero. We write this problem as

$$\max_{x_1, x_2} a \ln(x_1 + 1) + b \ln(x_2)$$

$$\text{s.t. } z - p_1 x_1 - p_2 x_2 \geq 0, \qquad x_1 \geq 0. \tag{A.19}$$

The collection of all the constraints on choice variables implicitly defines a set of "feasible" values for the choice variables. In the present example, the set of feasible values is defined by $\{(x_1, x_2) \mid z - p_1 x_1 - p_2 x_2 \geq 0 \text{ and } x_1 \geq 0\}$, called the *constraint set*.

We now formulate the Lagrangian function (the function is still named after Lagrange rather than after Kuhn and Tucker) by choosing some additional variables to multiply times the left-hand side of the constraints, and then adding these to the objective function,

$$\mathcal{L}(x_1, x_2; \lambda, \mu) = a \ln(x_1 + 1) + b \ln(x_2) + \lambda(z - p_1 x_1 - p_2 x_2) + \mu x_1,$$

where λ and μ are called the *Kuhn-Tucker multipliers* (or often simply *multipliers*).

Kuhn and Tucker showed that we can characterize the solution to problem A.19 using four conditions (two sets of two conditions each). The first two equations are the first-order conditions that are obtained by setting the partial derivatives of the Lagrangian function with respect to the original choice variables, x_1 and x_2, equal to zero:

$$\frac{\partial \mathcal{L}}{\partial x_1} = \frac{a}{x_1 + 1} - p_1 \lambda + \mu = 0, \tag{A.20}$$

$$\frac{\partial \mathcal{L}}{\partial x_2} = \frac{b}{x_2} - p_2 \lambda = 0. \tag{A.21}$$

The next two conditions, called *complementary slackness conditions*, state that the product of each multiplier and the left-hand side of the corresponding constraint equals zero:

$$\lambda(z - p_1 x_1 - p_2 x_2) = 0, \tag{A.22}$$

$$\mu x_1 = 0. \tag{A.23}$$

That is, either the constraint holds with equality or the multiplier is zero.

To find the solution to the problem A.19, we solve Equations A.20–A.23 in several steps. Combining the first-order conditions in Equations A.20 and A.21 with the complementary slackness conditions in Equations A.22 and A.23 gives us a system of equations that characterize any local extrema for the problem, provided that both objective function and constraints are all continuously differentiable in the choice variables.

Rearranging Equation A.21, we find that $\lambda = b/(p_2 x_2)$, so because b and p_2 are positive, λ is strictly positive: $\lambda > 0$. Combining this result with the first-order condition for x_1, Equation A.22, we find that the first constraint holds with equality: $z - p_1 x_1 - p_2 x_2 = 0$. Moreover, by substituting this expression for λ into the first-order condition for x_2, Equation A.21, we obtain

$$\frac{a}{x_1 + 1} + \mu = b\frac{p_1}{p_2 x_2}.$$

Multiplying both sides of this expression by $(x_1 + 1)$ yields

$$a + \mu x_1 + \mu = b(x_1 + 1)\frac{p_1}{p_2 x_2}.$$

However, $\mu x_1 = 0$ from Equation A.23, so we know that

$$(a + \mu)p_2 x_2 = b p_1 (x_1 + 1). \tag{A.24}$$

Now we have two cases to consider. Either x_1 or μ must be zero if Equation A.23 is to be satisfied. If $\mu = 0$ and we substitute that value into Equation A.24, we find that

$$x_2 = \frac{p_1}{p_2}\frac{b}{a}(x_1 + 1).$$

Substituting this expression into the complementary slackness condition for the first constraint, Equation A.22, and remembering that $\lambda > 0$, we find that

$$x_2 = \frac{b}{a + b}\frac{z}{p_2} \quad \text{and} \quad x_1 = \frac{a}{a + b}\frac{z}{p_1} - 1. \tag{A.25}$$

Now instead suppose that $x_1 = 0$, so Equation A.24 becomes

$$x_2 = \frac{p_1}{p_2}\frac{b}{a + \mu}.$$

Remembering that $\lambda > 0$ and substituting this expression into the complementary slackness condition for the first constraint, Equation A.22, we find that $\mu = p_1(b/z) - a$ and $x_2 = z/p_2$.

Thus we have two possible solutions. Either

$$x_1 = \frac{a}{a + b}\frac{z}{p_1} - 1, \quad x_2 = \frac{b}{a + b}\frac{z}{p_2}, \quad \text{and} \quad \mu = 0; \quad \text{or} \tag{A.26}$$

$$x_1 = 0, \quad x_2 = \frac{z}{p_2}, \quad \text{and} \quad \mu = p_1\frac{b}{z} - a. \tag{A.27}$$

This multiplicity of possible solutions, Equations A.26 and A.27, does *not* mean that both solve the maximization problem. Only one of these possible answers solves the maximization problem, and which one is the solution depends on the values of the parameters a, b, p_1, p_2, and z. There are several ways to check which is correct, conditional on these values. One way in this example is to substitute the actual values of a, b, z, and p_1 into the expression for x_1 in Equation A.25 and check whether it is positive. If not, $x_1 = 0$.

Conditions for Existence and Uniqueness. Although the Kuhn-Tucker method gives us a general means of *formulating* problems of finding constrained extrema, there is no guarantee that a solution to the Kuhn-Tucker formulation exists. Even if a solution does exist, there is no guarantee that it is unique.

In Section A.4, we summarized the sufficient conditions that guarantee the existence and uniqueness of solutions to *unconstrained* extrema problems. Now we would like some simple conditions guaranteeing both the existence and the uniqueness of a solution to the Kuhn-Tucker formulation of a *constrained* extremum problem.

We want to specify these conditions for a general Kuhn-Tucker problem with n choice variables x_1, x_2, ... , x_n, where we want to maximize an objective function $f: \mathbb{R}^n \to \mathbb{R}$ subject to m constraints, $g_j (x_1, x_2, \ldots, x_n) \geq 0$, for $j = 1, 2, \ldots, m$:

$$\max_{x_1, x_2, \ldots, x_n} f(x_1, x_2, \ldots, x_n)$$

$$\text{s.t. } g_j (x_1, x_2, \ldots, x_n) \geq 0, \quad \text{for} \quad j = 1, 2, \ldots, m. \qquad (A.28)$$

The *Slater condition* guarantees the existence of a solution to problem A.28. The Slater condition requires that the solution to the maximization problem is not determined entirely by the constraints for any of the choice variables: There exists a point $(x_1, x_2, \ldots, x_n)$ such that $g_j (x_1, x_2, \ldots, x_n) > 0$ for all $j = 1, 2, \ldots, m$. Because this condition holds with a strict inequality, the constraint set has a non-empty interior.

A local maximum exists if the objective function and constraints are continuously differentiable and if the Slater condition is satisfied. If $(x_1^*, \ldots, x_n^*)$ is a local maximum of the problem A.28, it is also global maximum if f is weakly concave and if g_j is weakly convex for all $j = 1, \ldots, m$. However, there could be more than one global maximum.

Sufficient conditions for a local maximum $(x_1^*, \ldots, x_n^*)$ to the problem A.28 to be a unique global maximum are that f is weakly concave; g_j is weakly convex for all $j = 1, 2, \ldots, m$; and one of two alternative conditions holds:

1. The objective function f is strictly concave; or
2. At least one of the constraints $g_j (x_1^*, \ldots, x_n^*) = 0$ and is strictly convex at $g_j (x_1^*, \ldots, x_n^*)$.

The Envelope Theorem. We can state and prove a version of the Envelope Theorem that holds for constrained extremum problems. To facilitate this discussion, we use our previous formulation of the Kuhn-Tucker problem, but we explicitly add an exogenous parameter z so that z can have a direct effect on the objective function as well as a direct effect on any of the constraints g_j,[3]

$$V(z) = \max_{x_1, x_2, \ldots, x_n} f(x_1, x_2, \ldots, x_n, z)$$

$$\text{s.t. } g_j(x_1, x_2, \ldots, x_n, z) \geq 0, \quad \text{for} \quad j = 1, 2, \ldots, m, \qquad (A.29)$$

---

[3]We could have added any finite number of such exogenous parameters; however, one is enough for our purposes.

where $V(z)$ is the maximized value of the objective function. The equivalent Lagrangian problem is

$$V(z) = \max_{x_1, x_2, \ldots, x_n} f(x_1, x_2, \ldots, x_n, z) + \sum_{j=1}^{m} \lambda_j g_j(x_1, x_2, \ldots, x_n, z), \quad (A.30)$$

where $\lambda_1, \lambda_2, \ldots, \lambda_m$ are the Kuhn-Tucker multipliers.

The first-order conditions are

$$\frac{\partial f}{\partial x_i} + \sum_{j=1}^{m} \lambda_j \frac{\partial g_j}{\partial x_i} = 0, \quad \text{for} \quad i = 1, \ldots, n \quad \text{and} \quad j = 1, \ldots, m, \quad (A.31)$$

and the complementary slackness conditions are

$$\lambda_j g (x_1, \ldots, x_n, z) = 0, \quad \text{for} \quad j = 1, \ldots, m. \quad (A.32)$$

The *Envelope Theorem* states that, if the constraints $g_j(x_1, x_2, \ldots, x_n, z)$ satisfy the Slater condition and if $x_i(z)$, $i = 1, 2, \ldots, n$, solve the first-order conditions, Equation A.31, and complementary slackness conditions, Equation A.32, then

$$\frac{\partial V(z)}{\partial z} = \frac{\partial f(x_1, \ldots, x_n, z)}{\partial z} + \sum_{j=1}^{m} \lambda_j \frac{\partial g_j}{\partial z}.$$

Proof. The value function $V(z) = f(x_1(z), \ldots, x_n(z), z) + \sum_{j=1}^{m} \lambda_j g_j(x_1, \ldots, x_n, z)$. Differentiating this expression with respect to z yields

$$\frac{\partial V(z)}{\partial z} = \frac{\partial f(x_1, \ldots, x_n, z)}{\partial z} + \sum_{i=1}^{n} \left[\frac{\partial f(x_1, \ldots, x_n, z)}{\partial x_i} \frac{\partial x_i(z)}{\partial z} \right.$$

$$+ \sum_{j=1}^{m} \lambda_j \frac{\partial g_j(x_1, \ldots, x_n, z)}{\partial x_i} \frac{\partial x_i(z)}{\partial z} \Bigg]$$

$$+ \sum_{j=1}^{m} \left[\frac{\partial \lambda_j(z)}{\partial z} g_j(x_1, \ldots, x_n, z) + \lambda_j(z) \frac{\partial g_j(x_1, \ldots, x_n, z)}{\partial z} \right].$$

Collecting terms, we can rewrite this equation as

$$\frac{\partial V(z)}{\partial z} = \frac{\partial f(x_1, \ldots, x_n, z)}{\partial z}$$

$$+ \sum_{j=1}^{m} \left[\frac{\partial \lambda_j(z)}{\partial z} g_j (x_1, \ldots, x_n, z) + \lambda_j(z) \frac{\partial g_j(x_1, \ldots, x_n, z)}{\partial z} \right]$$

$$+ \sum_{i=1}^{n} \left[\frac{\partial f(x_1, \ldots, x_n, z)}{\partial x_i} \frac{\partial x_i(z)}{\partial z} + \sum_{j=1}^{m} \lambda_j \frac{\partial g_j(x_1, \ldots, x_n, z)}{\partial x_i} \right] \frac{\partial x_i(z)}{\partial z}. \quad (A.33)$$

Using Equation A.31, the last bracketed expression in Equation A.33 equals zero. If we can show that the $\sum (\partial \lambda_j / \partial z) g_j$ expression in the other bracketed term is zero, we have proved the theorem. We know by the complementary slackness conditions that $\lambda_j g_j(x_1, x_2, \ldots, x_n, z) = 0$. If $g_j(x_1, x_2, \ldots, x_n, z) = 0$, then $(\partial \lambda_j / \partial z)$ $g_j(x_1, x_2, \ldots, x_m) = 0$. Alternatively, if $g_j(x_1, x_2, \ldots, x_n, z) > 0$, so that $\lambda_j = 0$, the Slater condition implies that $\partial \lambda_j(z) / \partial z = 0$, thus proving the theorem.

Comparative Statics. We can use the method of comparative statics when solving a problem with inequality constraints, but we need to keep track of which inequality constraints are binding. Let's return to our earlier problem A.19, where the Lagrangian function is $\mathscr{L} = a \ln(x_1 + 1) + b \ln(x_2) + \lambda(z - p_1 x_1 - p_2 x_2) + \mu x_1$ and has first-order conditions

$$\frac{a}{x_1 + 1} - \lambda p_1 + \mu = 0 \qquad \text{and} \qquad \frac{b}{x_2} - \lambda p_2 = 0,$$

and associated complementary slackness conditions

$$\lambda(z - p_1 x_1 - p_2 x_2) = 0, \tag{A.34}$$

$$\mu x_1 = 0. \tag{A.35}$$

These complementary slackness conditions complicate the comparative statics analysis. If a constraint is clearly binding, we don't have a problem, because we know how it affects the solution. Unfortunately, we do not always know if a constraint binds.

In this example, we may be confident that the first constraint binds, so we know that $\lambda > 0$. Consequently, we can divide both sides of Equation A.34 by λ to eliminate it from the complementary slackness conditions. However, we do not know whether the constraint $x_1 \geq 0$ binds without knowing the actual parameters.

In one approach, we initially assume that all the constraints *are* binding, and then use this assumption to substitute the constraints into the first-order conditions and solve them. Here we assume that the constraint, Equation A.35, holds, $x_1 = 0$. Using Equation A.27, $x_2 = z/p_2$. Substituting these solutions into the first-order conditions, we know that

$$a - \lambda p_1 + \mu = 0 \qquad \text{and} \qquad \frac{b}{z} - \lambda = 0,$$

or solving for μ and λ,

$$\mu = \frac{b}{z} p_1 - a \qquad \text{and} \qquad \lambda = b/z.$$

Consequently, we've potentially solved the entire system, with proposed solutions for x_1, x_2, and both the multipliers. However, our initial assumption that $x_1 = 0$ implies that $\mu > 0$ or that $(b/z)p_1 > a$. This last inequality is exactly what we need to check. If it's satisfied, then we have the correct solution that we're at a *corner*. If it's not, then the maximum is in the interior and not at a corner, and the constraint $x_1 \geq 0$ does not bind. If it's not binding, then $\mu = 0$. Now, we can go back and plug this condition into the first-order conditions, and solve. Given either set of these solutions, we can examine the effect of a change in a parameter.

Recipe for Finding the Constrained Extrema of a Function

The following is a step-by-step set of practical instructions for solving a constrained extrema problem. The focus of this section is very much on the mechanics of *how* rather than on the issues of *why*.

1. *Make the problem a maximization problem.* If the problem is to minimize $f(x_1, x_2, \ldots, x_n)$ subject to constraints, we can convert it into a maximization problem by maximizing *minus* the function subject to the same constraints.

2. *Rewrite any constraints so that they take the form of "greater than or equal to zero."* Here's a brief field guide to constraints and how to deal with them:

   a. *Greater than or equal to*: If the constraint is initially stated in the form of $g(x_1, x_2) \geq f(x_1, x_2)$, subtract the term $f(x_1, x_2)$ from both sides to obtain $g(x_1, x_2) - f(x_1, x_2) \geq 0$.

   b. *Less than or equal to*: Given an initial constraint of $g(x_1, x_2) \leq f(x_1, x_2)$, multiply both sides by -1, making it a greater-than-or-equal-to problem, and use the method in (a): $f(x_1, x_2) - g(x_1, x_2) \geq 0$.

   c. *Strictly greater than or strictly less than*: If your constraint is $g(x_1, x_2) > f(x_1, x_2)$ or $g(x_1, x_2) < f(x_1, x_2)$, you're in trouble! If this constraint has any effect on the problem, it will be to make it so that no solution exists. (Consider the problem of minimizing x such that $x > 0$ to see why this is a problem.) You have to reformulate your problem.

   d. *Equal to*: If it seems that the constraint truly has to hold with equality, put yourself in the shoes of the firm's manager, who is doing the maximizing. If the firm could somehow challenge the natural order of things and violate the constraint, would the firm prefer a "less-than-or-equal-to" constraint or a "greater-than-or-equal-to" constraint? For example, a firm facing a constraint that required output q to be equal to a function $f(x)$ of inputs x would, if the firm could violate the laws of nature, prefer that output was greater than production, or that $q \geq f(x)$. Let's give the firm the opposite of what it would want, imposing the constraint $q \leq f(x)$. Multiply both sides by -1 and then move the terms on the right-hand side to the left to get a "greater-than-or-equal-to-zero" constraint: $f(x) - q \geq 0$. Think again about whether the constraint *really* has to be an equality constraint—in this case, could the firm throw some output away? If the answer is yes, then you're done. Otherwise, add *another* "greater-than-or-equal-to" constraint but with the opposite sign. So, in the example of our firm, we would have both constraints:

$$f(x) - q \geq 0, \tag{A.36}$$

$$q - f(x) \geq 0. \tag{A.37}$$

   You can verify that these two inequality constraints imply a single equality constraint.

   Now you've got all your constraints formulated in the "greater-than-or-equal-to" form. Take a moment to be sure you haven't neglected any. Are there some choice variables that can't be negative? If so, add a nonnegativity constraint requiring them to be greater than or equal to zero.

3. *Construct the Lagrangian function.* Assign a multiplier to each of your constraints (it's traditional to use Greek letters for these multipliers), which you multiply times the left-hand side of the corresponding constraint, and add the products to the objective function you formulated in the first step.

4. *Partially differentiate the Lagrangian function.* Beginning with the first of your choice variables, partially differentiate the Lagrangian function with respect to this variable. Repeat for each of the remaining choice variables. Set each of these expressions equal to zero, yielding a collection of first-order conditions.

5. *List the complementary slackness conditions.* Take each of the products of the "greater-than-or-equal-to" constraints with their corresponding multipliers and set them equal to zero, yielding the complementary slackness conditions.

6. *Solve the system of equations.* Simultaneously solve the collection of first-order conditions and the complementary slackness conditions to find the critical values. The set of values of the choice variables that satisfy this system solve the constrained maximization problem.[4]

A.8   Duality

There's a close connection between constrained maxima and minima called *duality*. The following proposition makes this connection: Let λ be a scalar greater than zero. If there exists a solution $x^*(z)$ to the *primal* problem

$$V(z) = \max_x f(x, z) + \lambda(C(z) - g(x, z)), \tag{A.38}$$

then $x^*(z)$ also solves the *dual* problem

$$C(z) = \min_x g(x, z) + \frac{1}{\lambda}(V(z) - f(x, z)). \tag{A.39}$$

Proof. We need to show that the maximization problem A.38 is equivalent to the minimization problem A.39 when $\lambda > 0$. Because a solution $x^*(z)$ exists, the function $V(z)$ exists. Subtracting $V(z)$ from both sides of Equation A.38 yields

$$0 = \max_x[f(x, z) - V(z)] + \lambda(C(z) - g(x, z)).$$

Then subtracting $\lambda C(z)$ from both sides gives us

$$-\lambda C(z) = \max_x[f(x, z) - V(z)] - \lambda g(x, z).$$

Multiplying both sides by -1 transforms the max operator into the min operator,

$$\lambda C(z) = \min_x[V(z) - f(x, z)] + \lambda g(x, z),$$

and dividing both sides by the positive constant λ yields the result in Equation A.39.

This result implies that when we solve a primal constrained maximization problem *and the constraint binds*, then a dual representation of the problem also exists. To see why, consider the constrained problem

$$\max_x f(x, z)$$
$$\text{s.t.}\ \ g(x, z) \leq C(z).$$

For example, a firm could face this problem when it is maximizing output $f(x, z)$ subject to keeping its cost $g(x, z)$ below some critical level $C(z)$. The Lagrangian function corresponding to this problem is $\mathcal{L}(x, z) = f(x, z) + \lambda(C(z) - g(x, z))$. The result implies that if the maximizing choice of x given z (which in our example maximizes output subject to keeping cost below some limit) makes the constraint bind, then this same choice also solves the *dual* problem of minimizing $g(x, z)$ subject to satisfying the constraint $f(x, z) \geq V(z)$ [or, in our example, minimizing costs subject to keeping output above $V(z)$]. Further, the value of the multiplier in the dual problem will be the reciprocal of the value of the multiplier in the primal problem.

This result does not rely on the differentiability or shape of the functions f and g, only on the existence of a solution to the primal maximization problem. However, if the solution to the primal problem satisfies its associated first-order conditions and the constraint is binding, then the same first-order conditions will characterize the dual problem.

---

[4]We sometimes may be unable to find an explicit solution to these sets of equations, even if a solution exists. In such cases, we can use numerical techniques to find solutions, or we can employ the method of comparative statics to try to understand the character of the solution.

Regression Appendix

Economists use a *regression* to estimate economic relationships such as demand curves and supply curves. A regression analysis allows us to answer three questions:

1. How can we best fit an economic relationship to actual data?
2. How confident are we in our results?
3. How can we determine the effect of a change in one variable on another if many other variables are changing at the same time?

Estimating Economic Relations

We use a demand curve example to illustrate how regressions can answer these questions. The points in Figure B.1 show eight years of data on Nancy's annual purchases of candy bars, q, and the prices, p, she paid.[1] For example, in the year when candy bars cost 20¢, Nancy bought q_2 candy bars.

Because we assume that Nancy's tastes and income did not change during this period, we write her demand for candy bars as a function of the price of candy bars and unobservable random effects. We believe that her demand curve is linear and want to estimate the demand function:

$$q = a + bp + e,$$

where a and b are the coefficients we want to determine and e is an error term. This *error term* captures random effects that are not otherwise reflected in our function. For instance, in one year, Nancy took an economics course that raised her anxiety level, causing her to eat more candy bars than usual, resulting in a relatively large positive error term for that year.

The data points in the figure exhibit a generally downward-sloping relationship between quantity and price, but the points do not lie strictly on a line because of the error terms. There are many possible ways in which we could draw a line through these data points.

The way we fit the line in the figure is to use the standard criterion that our estimates *minimize the sum of squared residuals*, where a residual, $e = q - \hat{q}$, is the difference between an actual quantity, q, and the fitted or predicted quantity on the

---

[1] We use a lowercase q for the quantity demanded for an individual instead of the uppercase Q that we use for a market. Notice that we violated the rule economists usually follow of putting quantity on the horizontal axis and price on the vertical axis. We are now looking at this relationship as statisticians who put the independent or explanatory variable, price, on the horizontal axis and the dependent variable, quantity, on the vertical axis.

Figure B.1

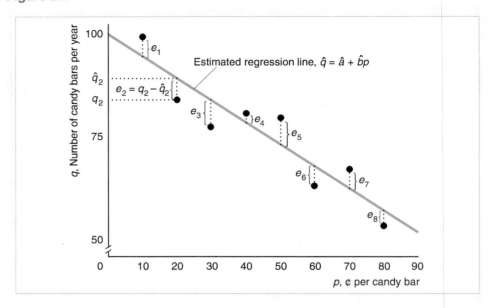

estimated line, $\hat{q}$. That is, we choose estimated coefficients $\hat{a}$ and $\hat{b}$ so that the estimated quantities from the regression line,

$$\hat{q} = \hat{a} + \hat{b}p,$$

make the sum of the squared residuals, $e_1^2 + e_2^2 + \ldots + e_8^2$, as small as possible. By summing the square of the residuals instead of the residuals themselves, we treat the effects of a positive or negative error symmetrically and give greater weight to large errors than to small ones.[2] In the figure, the regression line is

$$\hat{q} = 99.4 - 0.49p,$$

where $\hat{a} = 99.4$ is the intercept of the estimated line and $\hat{b} = -0.49$ is the slope of the line.

Confidence in Our Estimates

Because the data reflect random errors, so do the estimated coefficients. Our estimate of Nancy's demand curve depends on the *sample* of data we use. If we were to use data from a different set of years, our estimates, $\hat{a}$ and $\hat{b}$ of the true coefficients, a and b, would differ.

   If we had many estimates of the true parameter based on many samples, the estimates would be distributed around the true coefficient. These estimates are *unbiased* in the sense that the average of the estimates would equal the true coefficients.

---

[2]Using calculus, we can derive the $\hat{a}$ and $\hat{b}$ that minimize the sum of squared residuals. The estimate of the slope coefficient is a weighted average of the observed quantities, $\hat{b} = \sum_i w_i q_i$, where $w_i = (p_i - \bar{p})/\sum_i (p_i - \bar{p})^2$, $\bar{p}$ is the average of the observed prices, and $\sum_i$ indicates the sum over each observation i. The estimate of the intercept, $\hat{a}$, is the average of the observed quantities.

Computer programs that calculate regression lines report a *standard error* for each coefficient, which is an estimate of the dispersion of the estimated coefficients around the true coefficient. In our example, a computer program reports

$$\hat{q} = 99.4 - 0.49p,$$
$$(3.99) \ (0.08)$$

where below each estimated coefficient is its estimated standard error between parentheses.

The smaller the estimated standard error, the more precise the estimate, and the more likely it is to be close to the true value. As a rough rule of thumb, there is a 95% probability that the interval that is within two standard errors of the estimated coefficient contains the true coefficient.[3] Using this rule, the *confidence interval* for the slope coefficient, $\hat{b}$, ranges from $-0.49 - (2 \times 0.08) = -0.65$ to $-0.49 + (2 \times 0.08) = -0.33$. If zero were to lie within the confidence interval for $\hat{b}$, we would conclude that we cannot reject the hypothesis that the price has no effect on the quantity demanded. In our case, however, the entire confidence interval contains negative values, so we are reasonably sure that the higher the price, the less Nancy demands.

Multiple Regression

We can also estimate relationships involving more than one explanatory variable using a *multiple regression*. For example, Moschini and Meilke (1992) estimate a pork demand function in which the quantity demanded is a function of income, Y, and the prices of pork, p, beef, p_b, and chicken, p_c:

$$Q = 171 - 20p + 20p_b + 3p_c + 2Y.$$

The multiple regression is able to separate the effects of the various explanatory variables. The coefficient 20 on the p variable indicates that an increase in the price of pork by $1 per kg lowers the quantity demanded by 20 million kg per year, holding the effects of the other prices and income constant.

---

[3]The confidence interval is the coefficient plus or minus 1.96 times its standard error for large samples (at least hundreds of observations) in which the coefficients are normally distributed. For smaller samples, the confidence interval tends to be larger.

Answers to Selected Exercises

*I know the answer! The answer lies within the heart of all mankind! The answer is twelve?
I think I'm in the wrong building.*—**Charles Schultz**

Chapter 2

1.1 The demand curve for pork is $Q = 186 - 20p$.

1.2 The change in the demand for pork as income changes is $\partial Q/\partial Y = 2$. A \$100 increase in income causes the quantity demanded to increase by 0.2 million kg per year.

1.4 Both of these demand curves hit the price axis at 120. Thus, to derive the total demand, we add the two demand functions: $Q = Q_1 + Q_2 = (120 - p) + (60 - \frac{1}{2}p) = 180 - 1.5p$.

2.4 In the figure, the no-quota total supply curve, S in panel c, is the horizontal sum of the U.S. domestic supply curve, S^d, and the no-quota foreign supply curve, S^f. At prices less than $\bar{p}$, foreign suppliers want to supply quantities less than the quota, $\bar{Q}$. As a result, the foreign supply curve under the quota, $\bar{S}^f$, is

the same as the no-quota foreign supply curve, S^f, for prices less than $\bar{p}$. At prices above $\bar{p}$, foreign suppliers want to supply more but are limited to $\bar{Q}$. Thus, the foreign supply curve with a quota, $\bar{S}^f$, is vertical at $\bar{Q}$ for prices above $\bar{p}$. The total supply curve with the quota, $\bar{S}$, is the horizontal sum of S^d and $\bar{S}^f$. At any price above $\bar{p}$, the total supply equals the quota plus the domestic supply. For example, at p^*, the domestic supply is Q_d^* and the foreign supply is $\bar{Q}_f$, so the total supply is $Q_d^* + \bar{Q}_f$. Above $\bar{p}$, $\bar{S}$ is the domestic supply curve shifted $\bar{Q}$ units to the right. As a result, the portion of $\bar{S}$ above $\bar{p}$ has the same slope as S^d. At prices less than or equal to $\bar{p}$ the same quantity is supplied with and without the quota, so $\bar{S}$ is the same as S. At prices above $\bar{p}$, less is supplied with the quota than without one, so $\bar{S}$ is steeper than S, indicating that a given increase in price raises the quantity supplied by less with a quota than without one.

For Chapter 2, Exercise 2.3

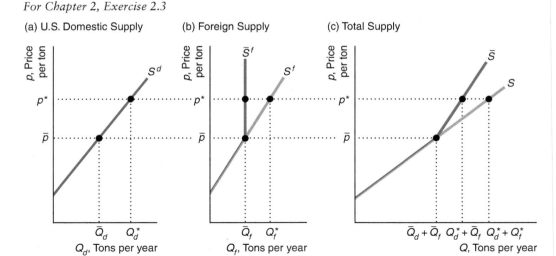

(a) U.S. Domestic Supply (b) Foreign Supply (c) Total Supply

3.1 The statement "Talk is cheap because supply exceeds demand" makes sense if we interpret it to mean that the *quantity* of talk *supplied* exceeds the *quantity demanded* at a price of zero. Imagine a downward-sloping demand curve that hits the horizontal, quantity axis to the left of where the upward-sloping supply curve hits the axis. (The correct aphorism is "Talk is cheap until you hire a lawyer.")

3.3 Equating the right-hand sides of the tomato supply and demand functions and using algebra, we find that $\ln p = 3.2 + 0.2 \ln p_t$. We then set $p_t = 110$, solve for $\ln p$, and exponentiate $\ln p$ to obtain the equilibrium price, $p \approx \$62.80$ per ton. Substituting p into the supply curve and exponentiating, we determine the equilibrium quantity, $Q \approx 11.91$ million short tons per year.

4.1 The supply shock is unusually good luck or an unexpected increase in the number of lobsters in the sea. This supply shock causes the supply curve to shift to the right and does not affect the demand curve. Thus, the equilibrium moves along the demand curve. The equilibrium price falls and the equilibrium quantity increases.

4.4 To determine the equilibrium price, we equate the right-hand sides of the supply function, $Q = 20 + 3p - 20r$, and the demand function, $Q = 220 - 2p$, to obtain $20 + 3p - 20r = 220 - 2p$. Using algebra, we can rewrite the equilibrium price equation as $p = 40 + 4r$. Substituting this expression into the demand function, we learn that the equilibrium quantity is $Q = 220 - 2(40 + 4r)$, or $Q = 140 - 8r$. By differentiating our two equilibrium conditions with respect to r, we obtain our comparative statics results: $dp/dr = 4$ and $dQ/dr = -8$.

4.7 The graph reproduces the no-quota total American supply curve of steel, S, and the total supply curve under the quota, $\bar{S}$, which we derived in the answer to Exercise 2.3. At a price below $\bar{p}$, the two supply curves are identical because the quota is not binding: It is greater than the quantity foreign firms want to supply. Above $\bar{p}$, $\bar{S}$ lies to the left of S. Suppose that the American demand is relatively *low* at any given price so that the demand curve, D^l, intersects both the supply curves at a price below $\bar{p}$. The equilibria both before and after the quota is imposed are at e_1, where the equilibrium price, p_1, is less than $\bar{p}$. Thus, if the demand curve lies near enough to the origin that the quota is not binding, the quota has no effect on the equilibrium. With a relatively *high* demand curve, D^h, the quota affects the equilibrium. The no-quota equilibrium is e_2, where D^h intersects the no-quota total supply curve, S. After the quota is imposed, the equilibrium is e_3, where D^h intersects the total supply curve with the quota, $\bar{S}$. The quota raises the price of steel in the United States from p_2 to p_3 and reduces the quantity from Q_2 to Q_3.

For Chapter 2, Exercise 4.7

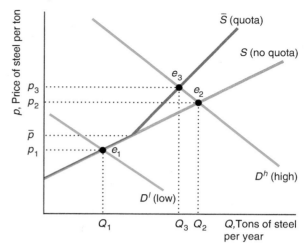

5.8 The elasticity of demand is $(dQ/dp)(p/Q) = (-9.5$ thousand metric tons per year per cent) $\times (45¢/1{,}275$ thousand metric tons per year$) \approx -0.34$. That is, for every 1% fall in the price, a third of a percent more coconut oil is demanded. The cross-price elasticity of demand for coconut oil with respect to the price of palm oil is $(dQ/dp_p)(p_p/Q) = 16.2 \times (31/1{,}275) \approx 0.39$.

6.4 We showed that, in a competitive market, the effect of a specific tax is the same whether it is placed on suppliers or demanders. Thus, if the market for milk is competitive, consumers will pay the same price in equilibrium regardless of whether the government taxes consumers or stores.

6.8 Differentiating quantity, $Q(p(t))$, with respect to t, we learn that the change in quantity as the tax changes is $(dQ/dp)(dp/dt)$. Multiplying and dividing this expression by p/Q, we find that the change in quantity as the tax changes is $\varepsilon(Q/p)(dp/dt)$. Thus, the closer ε is to zero, the less the quantity falls, all else the same.

Because $R = p(t)Q(p(t))$, an increase in the tax rate changes revenues by

$$\frac{dR}{dt} = \frac{dp}{dt}Q + p\frac{dQ}{dp}\frac{dp}{dt},$$

using the chain rule. Using algebra, we can rewrite this expression as

$$\frac{dR}{dt} = \frac{dp}{dt}\left(Q + p\frac{dQ}{dp}\right) = \frac{dp}{dt}Q\left(1 + \frac{dQ}{dp}\frac{p}{Q}\right) = \frac{dp}{dt}Q(1 + \varepsilon).$$

Thus, the effect of a change in t on R depends on the elasticity of demand, ε. Revenue rises with the tax if demand is inelastic ($-1 < \varepsilon < 0$) and falls if demand is elastic ($\varepsilon < -1$).

7.3 A usury law is a price ceiling, which causes the quantity that firms want to supply to fall.

7.4 We can determine how the total wage payment, $W = wL(w)$, varies with respect to w by differentiating. We then use algebra to express this result in terms of an elasticity:

$$\frac{dW}{dw} = L + w\frac{dL}{dw} = L\left(1 + \frac{dL}{dw}\frac{w}{L}\right) = L(1 + \varepsilon),$$

where ε is the elasticity of demand of labor. The sign of dW/dw is the same as that of $1 + \varepsilon$. Thus, total labor payment decreases as the minimum wage forces up the wage if labor demand is elastic, $\varepsilon < -1$, and increases if labor demand is inelastic, $\varepsilon > -1$.

9.2 Shifts of both the U.S. supply and U.S. demand curves affected the U.S. equilibrium. U.S. beef consumers' fear of mad cow disease caused their demand curve in the figure to shift slightly to the left from D^1 to D^2. In the short run, total U.S. production was essentially unchanged. Because of the ban on exports, beef that would have been sold in Japan and elsewhere was sold in the United States, causing the U.S. supply curve to shift to the right from S^1 to S^2. As a result, the U.S. equilibrium changed from e_1 (where S^1 intersects D^1) to e_2 (where S^2 intersects D^2). The U.S. price fell 15% from p_1 to $p_2 = 0.85p_1$, while the quantity rose 43% from Q_1 to $Q_2 = 1.43Q_1$. *Comment:* Depending on exactly how the U.S. supply and demand curves had shifted, it would have been possible for the U.S. price and quantity to have both fallen. For example, if D^2 had shifted far enough left, it could have intersected S^2 to the left of Q_1, and the equilibrium quantity would have fallen.

For Chapter 2, Exercise 9.2

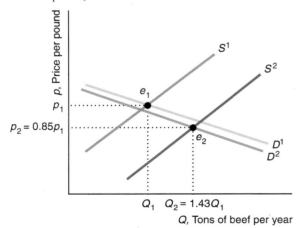

Q, Tons of beef per year

Chapter 3

1.5 If the neutral product is on the vertical axis, the indifference curves are parallel vertical lines.

2.2 Sofia's indifference curves are right angles (as in panel b of Figure 3.5). Her utility function is $U = \min(H, W)$, where *min* means the minimum of the two arguments, H is the number of units of hot dogs, and W is the number of units of whipped cream.

2.4 If we apply the trans (formation function $F(x) = x^\rho$ to the original utility function, we obtain the new utility function $V(q_1, q_2) = F(U(q_1, q_2)) = [(q_1^\rho + q_2^\rho)^{1/\rho}]^\rho = q_1^\rho + q_2^\rho$, which has the same preference properties as does the original function.

2.5 Given the original utility function, U, the consumer's marginal rate of substitution is $-U_1/U_2$. If $V(q_1, q_2) = F(U(q_1, q_2))$, the new marginal rate of substitution is $-V_1/V_2 = -[(dF/dU)U_1]/[(dF/dU)U_2] = -U_1/U_2$, which is the same as originally.

2.6 By differentiating we know that

$$U_1 = a(aq_1^\rho + [1 - a]q_2^\rho)^{(1-\rho)/\rho}\, q_1^{\rho-1} \text{ and}$$

$$U_2 = [1 - a](aq_1^\rho + [1 - a]q_2^\rho)^{(1-\rho)/\rho}\, q_2^{\rho-1}.$$

Thus, $MRS = -U_1/U_2 = -[(1 - a)/a](q_1/q_2)^{\rho-1}$.

3.1 Suppose that Dale purchases two goods at prices p_1 and p_2. If her original income is Y, the intercept of the budget line on the Good 1 axis (where the consumer buys only Good 1) is Y/p_1. Similarly, the intercept is Y/p_2 on the Good 2 axis. A 50% income tax lowers income to half its original level, $Y/2$. As a result, the budget line shifts inward toward the origin. The intercepts on the Good 1 and Good 2 axes are $Y/(2p_1)$ and $Y/(2p_2)$, respectively. The opportunity set shrinks by the area between the original budget line and the new line.

3.3 In the figure on the next page, the consumer can afford to buy up to 12 thousand gallons of water a week if not constrained. The opportunity set, area A and B, is bounded by the axes and the budget line. A vertical line at 10 thousand on the water axis indicates the quota. The new opportunity set, area A, is bounded by the axes, the budget line, and the quota line. Because of the rationing, the consumer loses part of the original opportunity set: the triangle B to the right of the 10-thousand-gallons quota line. The consumer has fewer opportunities because of rationing.

For Chapter 3, Exercise 3.3

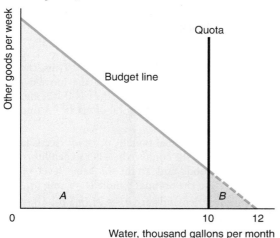

4.3 Andy's marginal utility of apples divided by the price of apples is $3/2 = 1.5$. The marginal utility for kumquats is $5/4 = 1.2$. That is, a dollar spent on apples gives him more extra utils than a dollar spent on kumquats. Thus, Andy maximizes his utility by spending all his money on apples and buying $40/2 = 20$ pounds of apples.

4.14 David's marginal utility of q_1 is 1 and his marginal utility of q_2 is 2. The slope of David's indifference curve is $-U_1/U_2 = -\frac{1}{2}$. Because the marginal utility from one extra unit of $q_2 = 2$ is twice that from one extra unit of q_1, if the price of q_2 is less than twice that of q_1, David buys only $q_2 = Y/p_2$, where Y is his income and p_2 is the price. If the price of q_2 is more than twice that of q_1, David buys only q_1. If the price of q_2 is exactly twice as much as that of q_1, he is indifferent between buying any bundle along his budget line.

4.15 Vasco determines his optimal bundle by equating the ratios of each good's marginal utility to its price.
   a. At the original prices, this condition is $U_1/10 = 2q_1q_2 = 2q_1^2 = U_2/5$. Thus, by dividing both sides of the middle equality by $2q_1$, we know that his optimal bundle has the property that $q_1 = q_2$. His budget constraint is $90 = 10q_1 + 5q_2$. Substituting q_2 for q_1, we find that $15q_2 = 90$, or $q_2 = 6 = q_1$.
   b. At the new price, the optimum condition requires that $U_1/10 = 2q_1q_2 = 2q_1^2 = U_2/10$, or $2q_2 = q_1$. By substituting this condition into his budget constraint, $90 = 10q_1 + 10q_2$, and solving, we learn that $q_2 = 3$ and $q_1 = 6$. Thus, as the price of chickens doubles, he cuts his consumption of chicken in half but does not change how many slabs of ribs he eats.

5.2 Consumers do not always notice taxes that are added at the register, so including the tax in the list price may discourage sales. This effect is less likely to be important for people buying a car because they are more likely to keep the tax in mind.

6.2 After West Virginia imposed a food tax, it was less expensive to buy food across the border for those people who lived close to the border. After the tax rose, people who live farther from the border started going to other states to buy their food. You can illustrate this effect using a diagram similar to that in the Challenge Solution.

Chapter 4

1.7 The figure shows that the price-consumption curve is horizontal. The demand for CDs depends only on income and the own price, $q_1 = 0.6Y/p_1$.

For Chapter 4, Exercise 1.7

(a) Indifference Curves and Budget Constraints

(b) CD Demand Curve

2.2 Guerdon's utility function is $U(q_1, q_2) = \min(0.5q_1, q_2)$. To maximize his utility, he always picks a bundle at the corner of his right-angle indifference curves. That is, he chooses only combinations of the two goods such that $0.5q_1 = q_2$. Using that expression to substitute for q_2 in his budget constraint, we find that

$$Y = p_1q_1 + p_2q_2 = p_1q_1 + p_2q_1/2 = (p_1 + 0.5p_2)q_1.$$

Thus, his demand curve for bananas is $q_1 = Y/(p_1 + 0.5p_2)$. The graph of this demand curve is downward sloping and convex to the origin (similar to the Cobb-Douglas demand curve in panel a of Figure 4.1).

2.4 The demand for CDs is $q_1 = 0.6Y/p_1$. Consequently, the Engel curve is a straight line with a slope of $dq_1/dY = 0.6/p_1$.

3.2 An opera performance must be a normal good for Don because he views the only other good he buys as an inferior good. To show this result in a graph, draw a figure similar to Figure 4.4, but relabel the vertical "Housing" axis as "Opera performances." Don's equilibrium will be in the upper-left quadrant at a point like *a* in Figure 4.4.

3.6 On a graph show L^f, the budget line at the factory store, and L^o, the budget constraint at the outlet store. At the factory store, the consumer maximum occurs at e_f on indifference curve I^f. Suppose that we increase the income of a consumer who shops at the outlet store to Y^* so that the resulting budget line L^* is tangent to the indifference curve I^f. The consumer would buy Bundle e^*. That is, the pure substitution effect (the movement from e_f to e^*) causes the consumer to buy relatively more firsts. The total effect (the movement from e_f to e_o) reflects both the substitution effect (firsts are now relatively less expensive) and the income effect (the consumer is worse off after paying for shipping). The income effect is small if (as seems reasonable) the budget share of plates is small. An ad valorem tax has qualitatively the same effect as a specific tax because both taxes raise the relative price of firsts to seconds.

3.8 We can determine the optimal bundle, e_1, at the original prices $p_1 = p_2 = 1$ by using the demand equation from Table 4.1: $q_1 = 4(p_2/p_1)^2 = 4$ and $q_2 = Y/p_2 - 4(p_2/p_1) = 10 - 4 = 6$. This optimal bundle is on an indifference curve where $U = 4(4)^{0.5} + 6 = 14$.

At the new bundle, e_2, where $p_1 = 2$ and $p_2 = 1$, $q_1 = 4(\frac{1}{2})^2 = 1$, and $q_2 = 10 - 4(1) = 8$. This optimal bundle is on an indifference curve where $U = 4(1)^{0.5} + 8 = 12$.

To determine e^*, we want to stay on the original indifference curve. We know that the tangency condition will give the same q_1 as at e_2 because q_1 depends on only the relative prices, so $q_1 = 1$. The question is what Y will compensate Siggi for the higher price so that he can stay on the original indifference curve. Because $q_2 = Y - 4(\frac{1}{2}) = Y - 4$, the utility is $U = 1 + (Y - 4) = Y - 3$. So the Y that results in $U = 14$ is $Y = 17$. Thus, the substitution effect is -3 (based on the movement from e_1 to e^*) and the income effect is 0 (the movement from e^* to e_2), so the total effect is -3 (movement from e_1 to e_2).

3.10 At Sylvia's optimal bundle, $q_1 = jq_2$ (see Chapter 3). Otherwise, she could reduce her expenditure on one of the goods and attain the same level of utility. Because at the optimal bundle $\overline{U} = \min(q_1, jq_2)$, the Hicksian demands are $q_1 = H_1(p_1, p_2, \overline{U}) = \overline{U}$ and $q_2 = H_2(p_1, p_2, \overline{U}) = \overline{U}/j$. The expenditure function is $E = p_1q_1 + p_2q_2 = p_1\overline{U} + p_2\overline{U}/j = (p_1 + p_2/j)\overline{U}$.

4.1 The CPI accurately reflects the true cost of living because Alix does not substitute between the goods as the relative prices change.

4.7 For example, if people do not substitute, the CPI (Laspeyres) index is correct and an index that averages the Laspeyres and the Paasche indexes underestimates the rate of inflation.

Chapter 5

1.2 At a price of 30, the quantity demanded is 30, so the consumer surplus is $\frac{1}{2}(30 \times 30) = 450$, because the demand curve is linear.

1.5 Hong and Wolak (2008) estimate that Area A is \$215 million and area B is \$118 (= 333 − 215) million (as you should have shown in your figure in the answer to Exercise 1.4).
  a. Given that the demand function is $Q = Xp^{-1.6}$, the revenue function is $R(p) = pQ = Xp^{-0.6}$. Thus, the change in revenue, −\$215 million, equals $R(39) - R(37) = X(39)^{-0.6} - X(37)^{-0.6} \approx -0.00356X$. Solving $-0.00356X = -215$, we find that $X \approx 60,353$.
  b. We follow the process in Solved Problem 5.1:

$$\Delta CS = -\int_{37}^{39} 60,353p^{-1.6}dp_1 = \frac{60,353}{0.6}p^{-0.6}\Big|_{37}^{39}$$

$$\approx 100,588(39^{-0.6} - 37^{-0.6})$$
$$\approx 100,588 \times (-0.00356) \approx -358.$$

This total consumer surplus loss is larger than the one estimated by Hong and Wolak (2008) because they used a different demand function. Given this total consumer surplus loss, area B is \$146(= 358 − 215) million.

1.7 The two demand curves cross at e_1 in the diagram. The price elasticity of demand, $\varepsilon = (dQ/dp)(p/Q)$, equals 1 over the slope of the demand curve, dp/dQ, times the ratio of the price to the quantity. Thus, at e_1 where both demand curves have the same price, p_1, and the same quantity, Q_1, the steeper the demand curve, the lower the elasticity of demand. If the price rises from p_1 to p_2, the consumer surplus falls from $A + C$ to A with the relatively elastic demand curve (a loss of C) and from $A + B + C + D$ to $A + B$ (a loss of $C + D$) with the relatively inelastic demand curve.

For Chapter 5, Exercise 1.7

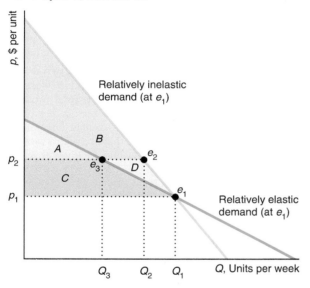

2.3 Because the good is inferior, the compensated demand curves cut the uncompensated demand curve, D, from below as the figure shows. Consequently, $|CV| = A$, $|\Delta CS| = A + B$, $|EV| = A + B + C$. $|CV| < |\Delta CS| < |EV|$.

For Chapter 5, Exercise 2.2

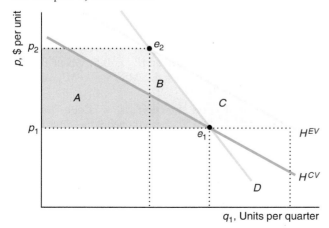

4.7 Under a progressive income tax system, the marginal tax rate increases with income, and the marginal tax rate is greater than the average tax rate. Suppose that the marginal tax rate is 20% on the first \$10,000 earned and 30% on the second \$10,000. Someone who earns \$20,000 pays a tax of \$2,000 ($= 0.2 \times \$10,000$) on the first \$10,000 of earnings and \$3,000 on the next \$10,000. That taxpayer's average tax rate is 25% ($= [\$2,000 + \$3,000]/\$20,000$).

4.8 The proposed tax system exempts an individual's first \$10,000 of income. Suppose that a flat 10% rate is charged on the remaining income. Someone who earns \$20,000 has an average tax rate of 5%, whereas someone who earns \$40,000 has an average tax rate of 7.5%, so this tax system is progressive.

4.10 As the marginal tax rate on income increases, people substitute away from work due to the pure substitution effect. However, the income effect can be either positive or negative, so the net effect of a tax increase is ambiguous. Also, because wage rates differ across countries, the initial level of income differs, again adding to the theoretical ambiguity. If we know that people work less as the marginal tax rate increases, we can infer that the substitution effect and the income effect go in the same direction or that the substitution effect is larger. However, Prescott's (2004) evidence alone about hours worked and marginal tax rates does not allow us to draw such an inference because U.S. and European workers may have different tastes and face different wages.

4.11 The figure shows Julia's original consumer equilibrium: Originally, Julia's budget constraint was a straight line, L^1 with a slope of $-w$, which was tangent to her indifference curve I^1 at e_1, so she worked 12 hours a day and consumed $Y_1 = 12w$ goods. The maximum-hours restriction creates a kink in Julia's new budget constraint, L^2. This constraint is the same as L^1 up to eight hours of work, and is horizontal at $Y = 8w$ for more hours of work. The highest indifference curve that touches this constraint is I^2. Because of the restriction on the hours she can work, Julia chooses to work eight hours a day and to consume $Y_2 = 8w$ goods, at e_2. (She will not choose to work fewer than eight hours. For her to do so, her indifference curve I^2 would have to be tangent to the downward-sloping section of the new budget constraint. However, such an indifference curve would have to cross the original indifference curve, I^1, which is impossible: see Chapter 3.) Thus, forcing Julia to restrict her hours lowers her utility: I^2 must be below I^1.

Comment: When I was in college, I was offered a summer job in California. My employer said,

"You're lucky you're a male." He claimed that, to protect women (and children) from overwork, an archaic law required him to pay women, but not men, double overtime after eight hours of work. As a result, he offered overtime work only to his male employees. Such clearly discriminatory rules and behavior are now prohibited. Today, however, both females and males must be paid higher overtime wages—typically 1.5 times as much as the usual wage. Consequently, many employers do not let employees work overtime.

For Chapter 5, Problem 4.11

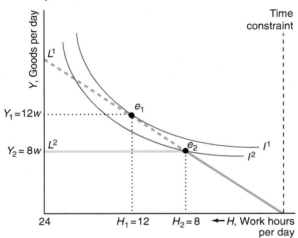

4.18 The government's tax revenue is $T = tH(w - t) = T = tH(\omega)$, where $\omega = w - t$, is the worker's after tax wage. If the government changes t, then the change in the tax revenue is

$$\frac{dT}{dt} = H(\omega) + t\frac{dH}{d\omega}\frac{d\omega}{dt} = H(\omega) - t\frac{dH}{d\omega}.$$

For lowering t to raise tax revenue (or raising t to lower tax revenue), we need $dT/d\omega < 0$, so that $H(\omega) < t(dH/d\omega)$. Rearranging this expression, we learn that $1/t < (dH/d\omega)/H(\omega)$. Multiplying both sides by ω, we find that the necessary condition is $\omega/t < (dH/d\omega)(\omega/H(\omega)) = \eta$, where η is the elasticity of supply of work hours with respect to the after-tax wage, ω.

5.2 Parents who do not receive subsidies prefer that poor parents receive lump-sum payments rather than a subsidized hourly rate for childcare. If the supply curve for childcare services is upward sloping, by shifting the demand curve farther to the right, the price subsidy raises the price of childcare for these other parents.

5.3 The government could give a smaller lump-sum subsidy that shifts the L^{LS} curve down so that it is parallel to the original curve but tangent to indifference curve I^2. This tangency point is to the left of e_2, so the parents would use fewer hours of childcare than with the original lump-sum payment.

Chapter 6

2.3 No, it is not possible for $q = 10$, $L = 3$, and $K = 6$ to be a point on this production function. Holding output and other inputs fixed, a production function shows the minimum amount needed of a given factor. As only 5 units of capital are needed to produce 10 units of output given that 3 units of labor are used, using 6 units of capital would imply excess capital.

3.1 One worker produces one unit of output, two workers produce two units of output, and n workers produce n units of output. Thus, the total product of labor equals the number of workers: $q = L$. The total product of labor curve is a straight line with a slope of 1. Because we are told that each extra worker produces one more unit of output, we know that the marginal product of labor, dq/dL, is 1. By dividing both sides of the production function, $q = L$, by L, we find that the average product of labor, q/L, is 1.

3.4 (a) Given that the production function is $q = L^{0.75}K^{0.25}$, the average product of labor, holding capital fixed at $\overline{K}$, is $AP_L = q/L = L^{-0.25}\overline{K}^{0.25} = (\overline{K}/L)^{0.25}$. (b) The marginal product of labor is $MP_L = dq/dL = \frac{3}{4}(\overline{K}/L)^{0.25}$. (c) At $\overline{K} = 16$, $AP_L = 2L^{0.25}$ and $MP_L = 1.5L^{0.25}$.

4.4 The isoquant looks like the right-angle ones in panel b of Figure 6.3 because the firm cannot substitute between paper and a press but must use them in equal proportions: one unit of paper and eight minutes of printing press services.

4.7 Using Equation 6.8, we know that the marginal rate of technical substitution is $MRTS = -MP_L/MP_K = -\frac{2}{3}$.

4.8 The isoquant for $q = 10$ is a straight line that hits the B axis at 10 and the G axis at 20. The marginal product of B is $MP_B = \partial q/\partial B = 1$ everywhere along the isoquant. Similarly, $MP_G = 0.5$. Given that B is on the horizontal axis, $MRTS = -MP_B/MP_G = -1/0.5 = -2$.

5.4 This production function is a Cobb-Douglas: $Q = L^{0.23}K^{0.10}M^{0.66}$. Even though it has three inputs instead of two, the same logic applies. We can calculate the returns to scale as the sum of the exponents: $\gamma = 0.23 + 0.10 + 0.66 = 0.99$. Thus, it has (nearly) constant returns to scale.

6.4 The marginal product of labor of Firm 1 is only 90% of the marginal product of labor of Firm 2 for a particular level of inputs. Using calculus, we find that the MP_L of Firm 1 is $\partial q_1/\partial L = 0.9\partial f(L, K)/\partial L = 0.9\partial q_2/\partial L$.

7.2 We do not have enough information to answer this question. If we assume that Japanese and American firms have identical production functions and produce using the same ratio of factors during good times, Japanese firms will have a lower average product of labor during recessions because they are less likely to lay off workers. However, it is not clear how Japanese and American firms expand output during good times: Do they hire the same number of extra workers? As a result, we cannot predict which country has the higher average product of labor.

Chapter 7

1.3 Because the firm can sell its pipes for $9 each, its opportunity cost of using a pipe is $9, and the sunk cost is $1 per pipe.

2.1 The amount Nicolas pays per month is a sunk cost during that month. His friend is correct that listening to more songs lowers his average (fixed) cost. However, doing so doesn't lower the cost that matters to him—the monthly service fee.

2.5 The total cost of building a 1-cubic-foot crate is $6. It costs four times as much to build an 8-cubic-foot crate, $24. In general, as the height of a cube increases, the total cost of building it rises with the square of the height, but the volume increases with the cube of the height. Thus, the cost per unit of volume falls.

2.13 Because the franchise tax is a lump-sum tax that does not vary with output, the more the firm produces, the less tax it pays per unit, $\mathcal{L}/q$. The firm's after-tax average cost, AC^a, is the sum of its before-tax average cost, AC^b, and its average tax payment per unit, $\mathcal{L}/q$. Because the franchise tax does not vary with output, it does not affect the marginal cost curve. The marginal cost curve crosses both average cost curves from below at their minimum points. The quantity q_a, at which the after-tax average cost curve reaches its minimum, is larger than the quantity q_b, at which the before-tax average cost curve achieves a minimum.

For Chapter 7, Exercise 2.12

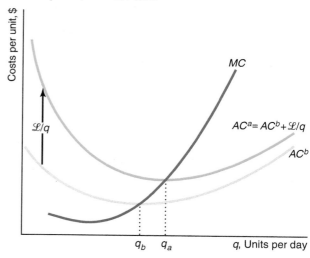

3.1 Let w be the cost of a unit of L and r be the cost of a unit of K. Because the two inputs are perfect substitutes in the production process, the firm uses only the less expensive of the two inputs. Therefore, the long-run cost function is $C(q) = wq$ if $w \leq r$; otherwise, it is $C(q) = rq$.

3.2 According to Equation 7.11, if the firm were minimizing its cost, the extra output it gets from the last dollar spent on labor, $MP_L/w = 50/200 = 0.25$, should equal the extra output it derives from the last dollar spent on capital, $MP_K/r = 200/1,000 = 0.2$. Thus, the firm is not minimizing its costs. It would save money if it used relatively less capital and more labor, from which it gets more extra output from the last dollar spent.

3.3 You produce your output, exam points, using as inputs the time spent on Question 1, t_1, and the time spent on Question 2, t_2. If you have diminishing marginal returns to extra time on each problem, your isoquants have the usual shapes: They curve away from the origin. You face a constraint that you may spend no more than 60 minutes on the two questions: $60 = t_1 + t_2$. The slope of the 60-minute isocost curve is -1: For every extra minute you spend on Question 1, you have one less minute to spend on Question 2. To maximize your test score, given that you can spend no more than 60 minutes on the exam, you want to pick the highest isoquant that is tangent to your 60-minute isocost curve. At the tangency, the slope of your isocost curve, -1, equals the slope of your isoquant, $-MP_1/MP_2$. That is, your score on the exam is maximized when $MP_1 = MP_2$, where the last minute spent on Question 1 would increase your score by as much as spending it on Question 2 would. Therefore, you've allocated your time on the exam wisely if you are indifferent as to which question to work on during the last minute of the exam.

3.5 From the information given and assuming that there are no economies of scale in shipping baseballs, it appears that balls are produced using a constant returns to scale, fixed-proportion production function. The corresponding cost function is $C(q) = (w + s + m)q$, where w is the wage for the time period it takes to stitch one ball, s is the cost of shipping one ball, and m is the price of all material to produce one ball. Because the cost of all inputs other than labor and transportation are the same everywhere, the cost difference between Georgia and Costa Rica depends on $w + s$ in both locations. As firms choose to produce in Costa Rica, the extra shipping cost must be less than the labor savings in Costa Rica.

4.2 The average cost of producing one unit is α (regardless of the value of β). If $\beta = 0$, the average cost does not change with volume. If learning by doing increases with volume, $\beta < 0$, so the average cost falls with volume. Here, the average cost falls exponentially (a smooth curve that asymptotically approaches the quantity axis).

4.3 a. If $r = 0$, the average cost (AC) of producing one unit is $a + b$ (regardless of the value of N). This case doesn't have any learning by doing.

b. If $r > 0$, then average cost falls as N rises, so learning by doing occurs.

c. As N gets very large, AC approaches a. Therefore, a is the lower limit for average cost—no matter how much learning is done, AC can never fall below a.

5.2 This firm has significant economies of scope, as producing gasoline and heating oil separately would cost approximately twice as much as producing them together. In this case, the measure of economies of scope, SC, is a positive number.

6.1 If $-w/r$ is the same as the slope of the line segment connecting the wafer-handling stepper and the stepper technologies, then the isocost will lie on that line segment, and the firm will be indifferent between using either of the two technologies (or any combination of the two). In all the isocost lines in the figure, the cost of capital is the same, and the wage varies. The wage such that the firm is indifferent lies between the relatively high wage on the C^2 isocost line and the lower wage on the C^3 isocost line.

6.3 The firm chooses its optimal labor-capital ratio using Equation 7.11: $MP_L/w = MP_K/r$. That is, $\frac{1}{2}q/(wL) = \frac{1}{2}q/(rK)$, or $L/K = r/w$. In the United States, where $w = r = 10$, the optimal $L/K = 1$, or $L = K$. The firm produces where $q = 100 = L^{0.5}K^{0.5} = K^{0.5}K^{0.5} = K$ Thus, $q = K = L = 100$. The cost is $C = wL + rK = 10 \times 100 + 10 \times 100 = 2,000$. At its Japanese plant, the optimal input ratio is $L^*/K^* = 1.1r/(w/1.1) = 11/(10/1.1) = 1.21$. That is, $L^* = 1.21K^*$. Thus, $q = (1.21K^*)^{0.5}(K^*)^{0.5} = 1.1K^*$. So $K^* = 100/1.1$ and $L^* = 110$. The cost is $C^* = [(10/1.1) \times 110] + [11 \times (100/1.1)] = 2,000$. That is, the firm will use a different factor ratio in Japan, but the cost will be the same. If the firm could not substitute toward the less expensive input, its cost in Japan would be $C^{**} = [(10/1.1) \times 100] + [11 \times 100] = 2,009.09$.

Chapter 8

2.3 How much the firm produces and whether it shuts down in the short run depend only on the firm's variable costs. (The firm picks its output level so that its marginal cost—which depends only on variable costs—equals the market price, and it shuts down only if market price is less than its minimum average variable cost.) Learning that the amount spent on the plant was greater than previously believed should not change the output level that the manager chooses. The change in the bookkeeper's valuation of the historical amount spent on the plant may affect the firm's short-run business profit but does not affect the firm's true economic profit. The economic profit is based on opportunity costs—the amount for which the firm could rent the plant to someone else—and not on historical payments.

2.6 The first-order condition to maximize profit is the derivative of the profit function with respect to q set equal to zero: $120 - 40 - 20q = 0$. Thus, profit is maximized where $q = 4$, so that $R(4) = 120 \times 4 = 480$, $VC(4) = (40 \times 4) + (10 \times 16) = 320$, $\pi(4) = R(4) - VC(4) - F = 480 - 320 - 200 = -40$. The firm should operate in the short run because its revenue exceeds its variable cost: $480 > 320$.

3.1 Suppose that a U-shaped marginal cost curve cuts a competitive firm's demand curve (price line) from above at q_1 and from below at q_2. By increasing output to $q_1 + 1$, the firm earns extra profit because the last unit sells for price p, which is greater than the marginal cost of that last unit. Indeed, the price exceeds the marginal cost of all units between q_1 and q_2, so it is more profitable to produce q_2 than q_1. Thus, the firm should either produce q_2 or shut down (if it is making a loss at q_2). We can also derive this result using calculus. For a competitive firm, the marginal revenue curve has zero slope, so the second-order condition, Equation 8.8, requires that marginal cost cut the demand line from below at q^*, the profit-maximizing quantity: $dMC(q^*)/dq > 0$.

3.9 Some lobstermen stayed in port because the price was below their average variable cost. Others had lower average variable costs or expected the price to rise before they landed their harvest, so they continued to fish.

3.11 The competitive firm's marginal cost function is found by differentiating its cost function with respect to quantity: $MC(q) = dC(q)dq = b + 2cq + 3dq^2$. The firm's necessary profit-maximizing condition is $p = MC = b + 2cq + 3dq^2$. We can use the quadratic formula to solve this equation for q for a specific price to determine its profit-maximizing output.

3.13 Suppose that a U-shaped marginal cost curve cuts a competitive firm's demand curve (price line) from above at q_1 and from below at q_2. By increasing output to $q_1 + 1$, the firm earns extra profit because the last unit sells for price p, which is greater than the marginal cost of that last unit. Indeed, the price exceeds the marginal cost of all units between q_1 and q_2, so it is more profitable to produce q_2 than q_1. Thus, the firm should either produce q_2 or shut down (if it is making a loss at q_2). We can derive this result using calculus. The second-order condition for a competitive firm requires that marginal cost cut the demand line from below at q^*, the profit-maximizing quantity: $dMC(q^*)/dq > 0$.

4.2 The shutdown notice reduces the firm's flexibility, which matters in an uncertain market. If conditions suddenly change, the firm may have to operate at a loss for six months before it can shut down. This potential extra expense of shutting down may discourage some firms from entering the market initially.

4.6 To derive the expression for the elasticity of the residual or excess supply curve in Equation 8.17, we differentiate the residual supply curve, Equation 8.16, $S^r(p) = S(p) - D^o(p)$, with respect to p to obtain

$$\frac{dS^r}{dp} = \frac{dS}{dp} - \frac{dD^o}{dp}.$$

Let $Q_r = S^r(p)$, $Q = S(p)$, and $Q_o = D(p)$. We multiply both sides of the differentiated expression by p/Q_r, and for convenience, we also multiply the second term by $Q/Q = 1$ and the last term by $Q_o/Q_o = 1$:

$$\frac{dS^r}{dp}\frac{p}{Q_r} = \frac{dS}{dp}\frac{p}{Q_r}\frac{Q}{Q} - \frac{dD^o}{dp}\frac{p}{Q_r}\frac{Q_o}{Q_o}.$$

We can rewrite this expression as Equation 8.17 by noting that $\eta_r = (dS^r/dp)(p/Q_r)$ is the residual supply elasticity, $\eta = (dS/dp)(p/Q)$ is the market supply elasticity, $\varepsilon_o = (dD^o/dp)(p/Q_o)$ is the demand elasticity of the other countries, and $\theta = Q/Q$ is the residual country's share of the world's output (hence $1 - \theta = Q_o/Q$ is the share of the rest of the world). If there are n countries with equal outputs, then $1/\theta = n$, so this equation can be rewritten as $\eta_r = n\eta - (n - 1)\varepsilon_o$.

4.7 a. The incidence of the federal specific tax is shared equally between consumers and firms, whereas firms bear virtually none of the incidence of the state tax (they pass the tax on to consumers).

    b. From Chapter 2, we know that the incidence of a tax that falls on consumers in a competitive market is approximately $\eta/(\eta - \varepsilon)$. Although the national elasticity of supply may be a relatively small number, the residual supply elasticity facing a particular state is very large. Using the analysis about residual supply curves, we can infer that the supply curve to a particular state is likely to be nearly horizontal—nearly perfectly elastic. For example, if the price in Maine rises even slightly relative to the price in Vermont, suppliers in Vermont will be willing to shift their entire supply to Maine. Thus, we expect the nearly full incidence to fall on consumers from a state tax but less from a federal tax, consistent with the empirical evidence.

    c. If all 50 states were identical, we could write the residual elasticity of supply, Equation 8.17, as $\eta_r = 50\eta - 49\varepsilon_o$. Given this equation, the residual supply elasticity to one state is at least 50 times larger than the national elasticity of supply, $\eta_r \geq 50\eta$, because $\varepsilon_o < 0$, so the $-49\varepsilon_o$ term is positive and increases the residual supply elasticity.

5.5 Because the clinics are operating at minimum average cost, a lump-sum tax that causes the minimum average cost to rise by 10% would cause the market price of abortions to rise by 10%. Based on the estimated price elasticity of between -0.70 and -0.99, the number of abortions would fall to between 7% and 10%. A lump-sum tax shifts upward the average cost curve but does not affect the marginal cost curve. Consequently, the market supply curve, which is horizontal and the minimum of the average cost curve, shifts up in parallel.

5.6 Each competitive firm wants to choose its output q to maximize its after-tax profit: $\pi = pq - C(q) - \mathcal{L}$. Its necessary condition to maximize profit is that price equals marginal cost: $p - dC(q)/dq = 0$. Industry supply is determined by entry, which occurs until profits are driven to zero (we ignore the problem of fractional firms and treat the number of firms, n, as a continuous variable): $pq - [C(q) + \mathcal{L}] = 0$. In equilibrium, each firm produces the same output, q, so market output is $Q = nq$, and the market inverse demand function is $p = p(Q) = p(nq)$. By substituting the market inverse demand function into the necessary and sufficient condition, we determine the market equilibrium (n^*, q^*) by the two conditions:

$$p(n^*q^*) - dC(q^*)/dq = 0,$$

$$p(n^*q^*)q^* - [C(q^*) + \mathcal{L}] = 0,$$

For notational simplicity, we henceforth leave off the asterisks. To determine how the equilibrium is affected by an increase in the lump-sum tax, we evaluate the comparative statics at $\mathcal{L} = 0$. We totally differentiate our two equilibrium equations with respect to the two endogenous variables, n and q, and the exogenous variable, $\mathcal{L}$:

$$dq(n[dp(nq)/dQ] - d^2C(q)/dq^2) + dn(q[dp(nq)/dQ]) + d\mathcal{L}(0) = 0,$$

$$dq(n[qdp(nq)/dQ] + p(nq) - dC/dq) + dn(q^2[dp(nq)/dQ]) - d\mathcal{L} = 0$$

We can write these equations in matrix form (noting that $p - dC/dq = 0$ from the necessary condition) as

$$\begin{vmatrix} n\dfrac{dp}{dQ} - \dfrac{d^2C}{dq^2} & q\dfrac{dp}{dQ} \\ nq\dfrac{dp}{dQ} & q^2\dfrac{dp}{dQ} \end{vmatrix} \begin{bmatrix} dq \\ dn \end{bmatrix} = \begin{bmatrix} 0 \\ 1 \end{bmatrix} d\mathcal{L}.$$

There are several ways to solve these equations. One is to use Cramer's rule. Define

$$D = \begin{vmatrix} n\dfrac{dp}{dQ} - \dfrac{d^2C}{dq^2} & q\dfrac{dp}{dQ} \\ nq\dfrac{dp}{dQ} & q^2\dfrac{dp}{dQ} \end{vmatrix}$$

$$= \left(n\dfrac{dp}{dQ} - \dfrac{d^2C}{dq^2} \right)q^2\dfrac{dp}{dQ} - q\dfrac{dp}{dQ}\left(nq\dfrac{dp}{dQ} \right)$$

$$= -\dfrac{d^2C}{dq^2}q^2\dfrac{dp}{dQ} > 0,$$

where the inequality follows from each firm's sufficient condition. Using Cramer's rule:

$$\dfrac{dq}{d\mathcal{L}} = \dfrac{\begin{vmatrix} 0 & q\dfrac{dp}{dQ} \\ 1 & q^2\dfrac{dp}{dQ} \end{vmatrix}}{D} = \dfrac{-q\dfrac{dp}{dQ}}{D} > 0,$$

$$\dfrac{dn}{d\mathcal{L}} = \dfrac{\begin{vmatrix} n\dfrac{dp}{dQ} - \dfrac{d^2C}{dq^2} & 0 \\ nq\dfrac{dp}{dQ} & 1 \end{vmatrix}}{D} = \dfrac{n\dfrac{dp}{dQ} - \dfrac{d^2C}{dq^2}}{D} < 0.$$

The change in price is

$$\dfrac{dp(nq)}{d\mathcal{L}} = \dfrac{dp}{dQ}\left[q\dfrac{dn}{d\mathcal{L}} + n\dfrac{dq}{d\mathcal{L}} \right].$$

$$= \dfrac{dp}{dQ}\left[\dfrac{\left(n\dfrac{dp}{dQ} - \dfrac{d^2C}{dq^2} \right)q}{D} - \dfrac{nq\dfrac{dp}{dQ}}{D} \right]$$

$$= \dfrac{dp}{dQ}\left(\dfrac{-\dfrac{d^2C}{dq^2}q}{D} \right) > 0.$$

Chapter 9

5.5 The specific subsidy shifts the supply curve, S in the figure, down by $s = 11¢$, to the curve labeled $S - 11¢$. Consequently, the equilibrium shifts from e_1 to e_2, so the quantity sold increases (from 1.25 to 1.34 billion rose stems per year), the price that consumers pay falls (from 30¢ to 28¢ per stem), and the amount that suppliers receive, including the subsidy, rises (from 30¢ to 39¢), so that the differential between what the consumers pay and what the producers receive is 11¢. Consumers and producers of roses are delighted to be subsidized by other members of society. Because the price to customers drops, consumer surplus rises from $A + B$ to $A + B + D + E$. Because firms receive more per stem after the subsidy, producer surplus rises from $D + G$ to $B + C + D + G$ (the area under the price they receive and above the original supply curve). Because the government pays a subsidy of 11¢ per stem for each stem sold, the government's expenditures go from zero to the rectangle $B + C + D + E + F$. Thus, the new welfare is the sum of the new consumer surplus and producer surplus minus the government's expenses. Welfare

For Chapter 9, Problem 5.5

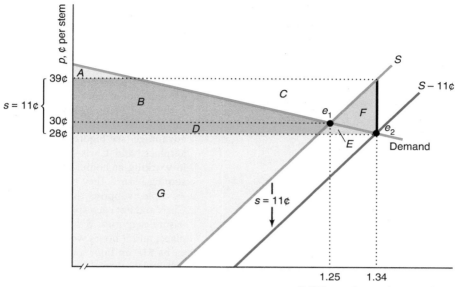

falls from $A + B + D + G$ to $A + B + D + G - F$. The deadweight loss, this drop in welfare $\Delta W = -F$, results from producing too much: The marginal cost to producers of the last stem, 39¢, exceeds the marginal benefit to consumers, 28¢.

5.8 If the tax is based on *economic* profit, the tax has no long-run effect because the firms make zero economic profit. If the tax is based on *business* profit and business profit is greater than economic profit, the profit tax raises firms' after-tax costs and results in fewer firms in the market. The exact effect of the tax depends on why business profit is less than economic profit. For example, if the government ignores opportunity labor cost but includes all capital cost in computing profit, firms will substitute toward labor and away from capital.

5.9 The Challenge Solution in Chapter 8 shows the long-run effect of a lump-sum tax in a competitive market. Consumer surplus falls by more than tax revenue increases, and producer surplus remains zero, so welfare falls.

5.11 a. The initial equilibrium is determined by equating the quantity demanded to the quantity supplied: $100 - 10p = 10p$. That is, the equilibrium is $p = 5$ and $Q = 50$. At the support price, the quantity supplied is $Q_s = 60$. The market clearing price was $p = 4$. The deficiency payment was $D = (p - p)Q_s = (6 - 4)60 = 120$.

b. Consumer surplus rises from $CS_1 = \frac{1}{2}(10 - 5)50 = 125$ to $CS_2 = \frac{1}{2}(10 - 4)60 = 180$. Producer surplus rises from $PS_1 = \frac{1}{2}(5 - 0)50 = 125$ to $PS_2 = \frac{1}{2} \times (6 - 0)60 = 180$. Welfare falls from $CS_1 + PS_1 = 125 + 125 = 250$ to $CS_2 + PS_2 - D = 180 + 180 - 120 = 240$. Thus, the deadweight loss is 10.

6.5 Without the tariff, the U.S. supply curve of oil is horizontal at a price of \$60 (S^1 in Figure 9.8), and the equilibrium is determined by the intersection of this horizontal supply curve with the demand curve. With a new, small tariff of t, the U.S. supply curve is horizontal at \$60 + t, and the new equilibrium quantity is determined by substituting $p = 60 + t$ into the demand function: $Q = 48.71(60 + t)p^{-0.37}$. Evaluated at $t = 0$, the equilibrium quantity remains at 17.5. The deadweight loss is the area to the right of the domestic supply curve and to the left of the demand curve between \$60 and \$60 + t (area $C + D + E$ in Figure 9.8) minus the tariff revenues (area D):

$$DWL = \int_{60}^{60+t} [D(p) - S(p)]\mathrm{d}p - t[D(p + t) - S(p + t)]$$

$$= \int_{60}^{60+t} [48.71p^{-0.25} - 3.45p^{0.25}]\mathrm{d}p$$

$$- t[48.71(p + t)^{-0.25} - 3.45(p + t)^{0.25}].$$

To see how a change in t affects welfare, we differentiate DWL with respect to t:

$$\frac{dDWL}{dt} = \frac{d}{dt}\left\{\int_{60}^{60+t}[D(p) - S(p)]dp\right.$$

$$\left. - t[D(60 + t) - S(60 + t)]\right\}$$

$$= [D(60 + t) - S(60 + t)] - [D(60 + t)$$

$$- S(60 + t)]$$

$$-t\left[\frac{dD(60 + t)}{dt} - \frac{dS(60 + t)}{dt}\right]$$

$$= -t\left[\frac{dD(60 + t)}{dt} - \frac{dS(60 + t)}{dt}\right].$$

If we evaluate this expression at $t = 0$, we find that $dDWL/dt = 0$. In short, applying a small tariff to the free-trade equilibrium has a negligible effect on quantity and deadweight loss. Only if the tariff is larger—as in Figure 9.8—do we see a measurable effect.

Chapter 10

1.6 A subsidy is a negative tax. Thus, we can use the same analysis that we used in Solved Problem 10.1 to answer this question by reversing the signs of the effects.

4.1 If you draw the convex production possibility frontier on Figure 10.5, you will see that it lies strictly inside the concave production possibility frontier. Thus, more output can be obtained if Jane and Denise use the concave frontier. That is, each should specialize in producing the good for which she has a comparative advantage.

4.2 As Chapter 4 shows, the slope of the budget constraint facing an individual equals the negative of that person's wage. Panel a of the figure illustrates that Pat's budget constraint is steeper than Chris's because Pat's wage is larger than Chris's. Panel b shows their combined budget constraint after they marry. Before they marry, each spends some time in the marketplace earning money and other time at home cooking, cleaning, and consuming leisure. After they marry, one of them can specialize in earning money and the other at working at home. If they are both equally skilled at household work (or if Chris is better), then Pat has a comparative advantage (see Figure 10.5) in working in the marketplace, and Chris has a comparative advantage in working at home. Of course, if both enjoy consuming leisure, they may not fully specialize. As an example, suppose that, before they got married, Chris and Pat each spent 10 hours a day in sleep and leisure activities, 5 hours working in the marketplace, and 9 hours working at home. Because Chris earns $10 an hour and Pat earns $20 an hour, they collectively earned $150 a day and worked 18 hours a day at home. After they marry, they can benefit from specialization. If Chris works entirely at home and Pat works 10 hours in the marketplace and the rest at home, they collectively earn $200 a day (a one-third increase) and still have 18 hours of work at home. If they do not need to spend as much time working at home because of economies of scale, one or both could work more hours in the marketplace, and they will have even greater disposable income.

Chapter 11

1.5 For a general linear inverse demand function, $p(Q) = a - bQ$, $dQ/dp = -1/b$, so the elasticity is $\varepsilon = -p/(bQ)$. The demand curve hits the horizontal (quantity) axis at a/b. At half that quantity (the

For Chapter 10, Exercise 4.2

(a) Unmarried

(b) Married

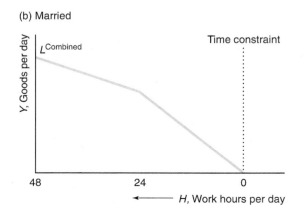

midpoint of the demand curve), the quantity is $a/(2b)$, and the price is $a/2$. Thus, the elasticity of demand is $\varepsilon = -p/(bQ) = -(a/2)/[ab/(2b)] = -1$ at the midpoint of any linear demand curve. As the chapter shows, a monopoly will not operate in the inelastic section of its demand curve, so a monopoly will not operate in the right half of its linear demand curve.

2.2 Gilead Sciences' Lerner Index is $(p - MC)/p = (84{,}000 - 136)/84{,}000 \approx 0.998$. Using Equation 11.11, we know that $(p - MC)/p \approx 0.998 = -1/\varepsilon$, so $\varepsilon \approx -1.002$.

2.4 Given that Apple's marginal cost was constant, its average variable cost equaled its marginal cost, $200. Its average fixed cost was its fixed cost divided by the quantity produced, $736/Q$. Thus, its average cost was $AC = 200 + 736/Q$. Because the inverse demand function was $p = 600 - 25Q$, Apple's revenue function was $R = 600Q - 25Q^2$, so $MR = dR/dQ = 600 - 50Q$. Apple maximized its profit where $MR = 600 - 50Q = 200 = MC$. Solving this equation for the profit-maximizing output, we find that $Q = 8$ million units. By substituting this quantity into the inverse demand equation, we determine that the profit-maximizing price was p = $400 per unit, as the figure shows. The firm's profit was $\pi = (p - AC)Q = [400 - (200 + 736/8)8 = \$864]$ million. Apple's Lerner Index was $(p - MC)/p = [400 - 200]/400 = \frac{1}{2}$. According to Equation 11.11, a profit-maximizing monopoly operates where $(p - MC)/p = -1/\varepsilon$. Combining that equation with the Lerner Index from the previous step, we learn that $\frac{1}{2} = -1/\varepsilon$, or $\varepsilon = -2$.

3.4 A tax on economic profit (of less than 100%) has no effect on a firm's profit-maximizing behavior. Suppose the government's share of the profit is β. Then the firm wants to maximize its after-tax profit, which is $(1 - \gamma)\pi$. However, whatever choice of Q (or p) maximizes π will also maximize $(1 - \gamma)\pi$. Consequently, the tribe's behavior is unaffected by a change in the share that the government receives. We can also answer this problem using calculus. The before-tax profit is $\pi_B = R(Q) - C(Q)$, and the after-tax profit is $\pi_A = (1 - \gamma)[R(Q) - C(Q)]$. For both, the first-order condition is marginal revenue equals marginal cost: $dR(Q)/dQ = dC(Q)/dQ$.

4.1 Yes. The demand curve could cut the average cost curve only in its downward-sloping section. Consequently, the average cost is strictly downward sloping in the relevant region.

6.1 Given the demand curve is $p = 10 - Q$, its marginal revenue curve is $MR = 10 - 2Q$. Thus, the output that maximizes the monopoly's profit is determined by $MR = 10 - 2Q = 2 = MC$, or $Q^* = 4$. At

that output level, its price is $p^* = 6$ and its profit is $\pi^* = 16$. If the monopoly chooses to sell 8 units in the first period (it has no incentive to sell more), its price is $2 and it makes no profit. Given that the firm sells 8 units in the first period, its demand curve in the second period is $p = 10 - Q/\beta$, so its marginal revenue function is $MR = 10 - 2Q/\beta$. The output that leads to its maximum profit is determined by $MR = 10 - 2Q/\beta = 2 = MC$, or its output is 4β. Thus, its price is $6 and its profit is 16β. It pays for the firm to set a low price in the first period if the lost profit, 16, is less than the extra profit in the second period, which is $16(\beta - 1)$. Thus, it pays to set a low price in the first period if $16 < 16(\beta - 1)$, or $2 < \beta$.

7.6 If a firm has a monopoly in the output market and is a monopsony in the labor market, its profit is $\pi = p(Q(L))Q(L) - w(L)L$ where $Q(L)$ is the production function, $p(Q)Q$ is its revenue, and $w(L)L$ —the wage times the number of workers—is its cost of production. The firm maximizes its profit by setting the derivative of profit with respect to labor equal to zero (if the second-order condition holds):

$$\left(p + Q(L)\frac{dp}{dQ} \right)\frac{dQ}{dL} - w(L) - \frac{dw}{dL}L = 0.$$

Rearranging terms in the first-order condition, we find that the maximization condition is that the marginal revenue product of labor,

$$MRP_L = MR \times MPL = \left(p + Q(L)\frac{dp}{dQ} \right)\frac{dQ}{dL}$$

$$= p\left(1 + \frac{1}{\varepsilon} \right)\frac{dQ}{dL},$$

equals the marginal expenditure,

$$ME = w(L) + \frac{dw}{dL}L = w(L)\left(1 + \frac{L}{w}\frac{dw}{dL} \right)$$

$$= w(L)\left(1 + \frac{1}{\eta} \right),$$

where ε is the elasticity of demand in the output market and η is the supply elasticity of labor.

Chapter 12

1.3 This policy allows the firm to maximize its profit by price discriminating if people who put a lower value on their time (so are willing to drive to the store and transport their purchases themselves) have a higher elasticity of demand than people who want to order by phone and have the goods delivered.

1.4 The colleges may be providing scholarships as a form of charity, or they may be price discriminating by lowering the final price for less wealthy families (who presumably have higher elasticities of demand).

3.6 See MyLab Economics Chapter Resources, Chapter 12, "Aibo," for more details. The two marginal revenue curves are $MR_J = 3,500 - Q_J$ and $MR_A = 4,500 - 2Q_A$. Equating the marginal revenues with the marginal cost of $500, we find that $Q_J = 3,000$ and $Q_A = 2,000$. Substituting these quantities into the inverse demand curves, we learn that $p_J = \$2,000$ and $p_A = \$2,500$. As the chapter shows, the elasticities of demand are $\varepsilon_J = p/(MC - p) = 2,000/(500 - 2,000) = -\frac{4}{3}$ and $\varepsilon_A = 2,500/(500 - 2,500) = -\frac{5}{4}$. Using Equation 12.9, we find that

$$\frac{p_J}{p_A} = \frac{2,000}{2,500} = 0.8 = \frac{1 + 1/(-\frac{5}{4})}{1 + 1/(-\frac{4}{3})} = \frac{1 + 1/\varepsilon_A}{1 + 1/\varepsilon_J}.$$

The profit in Japan is $(p_J - m)Q_J = (\$2,000 - \$500) \times 3,000 = \$4.5$ million, and the U.S. profit is \$4 million. The deadweight loss is greater in Japan, \$2.25 million $(= \frac{1}{2} \times \$1,500 \times 3,000)$, than in the United States, \$2 million $(= \frac{1}{2} \times \$2,000 \times 2,000)$.

3.7 By differentiating, we find that the American marginal revenue function is $MR_A = 100 - 2Q_A$, and the Japanese one is $MR_J = 80 - 4Q_J$. To determine how many units to sell in the United States, the monopoly sets its American marginal revenue equal to its marginal cost, $MR_A = 100 - 2Q_A = 20$, and solves for the optimal quantity, $Q_A = 40$ units. Similarly, because $MR_J = 80 - 4Q_J = 20$, the optimal quantity is $Q_J = 15$ units in Japan. Substituting $Q_A = 40$ into the American demand function, we find that $p_A = 100 - 40 = \$60$. Similarly, substituting $Q_J = 15$ units into the Japanese demand function, we learn that $p_J = 80 - (2 \times 15) = \$50$. Thus, the price-discriminating monopoly charges 20% more in the United States than in Japan. We can also show this result using elasticities. Because $dQ_A/dp_A = -1$, the elasticity of demand is $\varepsilon_A = -p_A/Q_A$ in the United States and $\varepsilon_J = -\frac{1}{2}p_J/Q_J$ in Japan. In the equilibrium, $\varepsilon_A = -60/40 = -3/2$ and $\varepsilon_J = -50/(2 \times 15) = -5/3$. As Equation 12.9 shows, the ratio of the prices depends on the relative elasticities of demand: $p_A/p_J = 60/50 = (1 + 1/\varepsilon_J)/(1 + 1/\varepsilon_A) = (1 - 3/5)/(1 - 2/3) = 6/5$.

3.10 From the problem, we know that the profit-maximizing Chinese price is $p = 3$ and that the quantity is $Q = 0.1$ (million). The marginal cost is $m = 1$. Using Equation 11.11, $(p_C - m)/p_C = (3 - 1)/3 = -1/\varepsilon_C$, so $\varepsilon_C = -3/2$. If the Chinese inverse demand curve is $p = a - bQ$, then the corresponding marginal revenue curve is $MR = a - 2bQ$. Warner maximizes its profit where $MR = a - 2bQ = m = 1$, so its optimal

$Q = (a - 1)/(2b)$. Substituting this expression into the inverse demand curve, we find that its optimal $p = (a + 1)/2 = 3$, or $a = 5$. Substituting that result into the output equation, we have $Q = (5 - 1)/(2b) = 0.1$ (million). Thus, $b = 20$, the inverse demand function is $p = 5 - 20Q$, and the marginal revenue function is $MR = 5 - 40Q$. Using this information, you can draw a figure similar to Figure 12.3.

3.13 If a monopoly manufacturer can price discriminate, its price is $p_i = m/(1 + 1/\varepsilon_i)$ in Country i, $i = 1, 2$. If the monopoly cannot price discriminate, it charges everyone the same price. Its total demand is $Q = Q_1 + Q_2 = n_1 p^{\varepsilon_1} + n_2 p^{\varepsilon_2}$. Differentiating with respect to p, we obtain $dQ/dp = \varepsilon_1 Q_1/p + \varepsilon_2 Q_2/p$. Multiplying through by p/Q, we learn that the weighted sum of the two groups' elasticities is $\varepsilon = s_1\varepsilon_1 + s_2\varepsilon_2$, where $s_i = Q_i/Q$. Thus, a profit-maximizing, single-price monopoly charges $\underline{p} = m/(1 + 1/\varepsilon)$.

Chapter 13

1.1 The payoff matrix in this prisoners' dilemma game is

		Duncan	
		Squeal	*Silent*
Larry	*Squeal*	-2 / -2	-5 / 0
	Silent	0 / -5	-1 / -1

If Duncan stays silent, Larry gets 0 if he squeals and -1 (a year in jail) if he stays silent. If Duncan confesses, Larry gets -2 if he squeals and -5 if he does not. Thus, Larry is better off squealing in either case, so squealing is his dominant strategy. By the same reasoning, squealing is also Duncan's dominant strategy. As a result, the Nash equilibrium is for both to confess.

1.3 No strategies are dominant, so we use the best-response approach to determine the pure-strategy Nash equilibria. First, identify each firm's best responses given each of the other firms' strategies (as we did in Solved Problem 13.1). This game has two Nash equilibria: (a) Firm 1 medium and Firm 2 low, and (b) Firm 1 low and Firm 2 medium.

1.7 Let the probability that a firm sets a low price be θ_1 for Firm 1 and θ_2 for Firm 2. If the firms choose their prices independently, then $\theta_1\theta_2$ is the probability that both set a low price, $(1 - \theta_1)(1 - \theta_2)$ is the probability that both set a high price, $\theta_1(1 - \theta_2)$ is the probability that Firm 1 prices low and Firm 2 prices high, and $(1 - \theta_1)\theta_2$ is the probability that Firm 1 prices high and Firm 2 prices low. Firm 2's expected payoff is $E(\pi_2) = 2\theta_1\theta_2 + (0)\theta_1 (1 - \theta_2) + (1 - \theta_1)\theta_2 + 6(1 - \theta_1)(1 - \theta_2) = (6 - 6\theta_1) - (5 - 7\theta_1)\theta_2$. Similarly, Firm 1's expected payoff is $E(\pi_1) = (0)\theta_1\theta_2 + 7\theta_1(1 - \theta_2) + 2(1 - \theta_1)\theta_2 + 6(1 - \theta_1)(1 - \theta_2) = (6 - 4\theta_2) - (1 - 3\theta_2)\theta_1$. Each firm forms a belief about its rival's behavior. For example, suppose that Firm 1 believes that Firm 2 will choose a low price with a probability $\hat{\theta}_2$. If $\hat{\theta}_2$ is less than $\frac{1}{3}$ (Firm 2 is relatively unlikely to choose a low price), it pays for Firm 1 to choose the low price because the second term in $E(\pi_1)$, $(1 - 3\hat{\theta}_2)\theta_1$, is positive, so as θ_1 increases, $E(\pi_1)$ increases. Because the highest possible θ_1 is 1, Firm 1 chooses the low price with certainty. Similarly, if Firm 1 believes $\hat{\theta}_2$ is greater than $\frac{1}{3}$, it sets a high price with certainty ($\theta_1 = 0$). If Firm 2 believes that Firm 1 thinks $\hat{\theta}_2$ is slightly below $\frac{1}{3}$, Firm 2 believes that Firm 1 will choose a low price with certainty, and hence Firm 2 will also choose a low price. That outcome, $\theta_2 = 1$, however, is not consistent with Firm 1's expectation that $\hat{\theta}_2$ is a fraction. Indeed, it is only rational for Firm 2 to believe that Firm 1 believes Firm 2 will use a mixed strategy if Firm 1's belief about Firm 2 makes Firm 1 unpredictable. That is, Firm 1 uses a mixed strategy only if it is *indifferent* between setting a high or a low price. It is indifferent only if it believes $\hat{\theta}_2$ is exactly $\frac{1}{3}$. By similar reasoning, Firm 2 will use a mixed strategy only if its belief is that Firm 1 chooses a low price with probability $\hat{\theta}_1 = \frac{5}{7}$. Thus, the only possible Nash equilibrium is $\theta_2 = \frac{5}{7}$ and $\theta_2 = \frac{1}{3}$.

1.8 We start by checking for dominant strategies. Given the payoff matrix, Toyota always does at least as well by entering the market. If GM enters, Toyota earns 10 by entering and 0 by staying out of the market. If GM does not enter, Toyota earns 250 if it enters and 0 otherwise. Thus, entering is Toyota's dominant strategy. GM does not have a dominant strategy. It wants to enter if Toyota does not enter (earning 200 rather than 0), and it wants to stay out if Toyota enters (earning 0 rather than −40). Because GM knows that Toyota will enter (entering is Toyota's dominant strategy), GM stays out. Toyota's entering and GM's not entering is a Nash equilibrium. Given the other firm's strategy, neither firm wants to change its strategy. Next, we examine how the subsidy affects the payoff matrix and dominant strategies. The subsidy does not affect Toyota's payoff, so Toyota still has a dominant strategy: It enters the market. With the subsidy, GM's payoff if it enters increases by 50: GM earns 10 if both enter and 250 if it enters and Toyota does not. With the subsidy, entering is a dominant strategy for GM. Thus, both firms' entering is a Nash equilibrium.

2.2 If the airline game is known to end in five periods, the equilibrium is the same as the one-period equilibrium. If the game is played indefinitely but one or both firms care only about current profit, then the equilibrium is the one-period one because future punishments and rewards are irrelevant to it.

3.9 The game tree illustrates why the incumbent may install the robotic arms to discourage entry even though its total cost rises. If the incumbent fears that a rival is poised to enter, it invests to discourage entry. The incumbent can invest in equipment that lowers its marginal cost. With the lowered marginal cost, it is credible that the incumbent will produce larger quantities of output, which discourages entry. The incumbent's monopoly (no-entry) profit drops from $900 to $500 if it makes the investment because the investment raises its total cost. If the incumbent doesn't buy the robotic arms, the rival enters because it makes $300 by entering and nothing if it stays out of the market. With entry, the incumbent's profit is $400. With the investment, the rival loses $36 if it enters, so it stays out of the

For Chapter 13, Exercise 3.9

For *Chapter 13, Exercise 3.10*

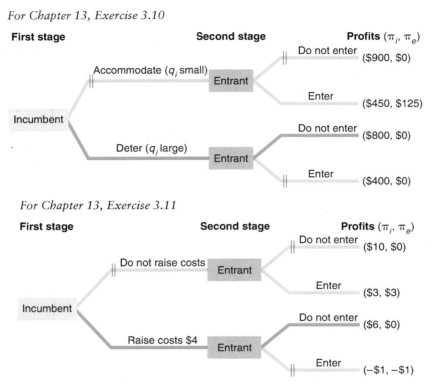

For *Chapter 13, Exercise 3.11*

market, losing nothing. (If the rival were to enter, the incumbent would earn $132.) Because of the investment, the incumbent earns $500. Nonetheless, earning $500 is better than earning $400, so the incumbent invests.

3.10 The incumbent firm has a *first-mover advantage*, as the game tree illustrates. Moving first allows the incumbent or leader firm to *commit* to producing a relatively large quantity. If the incumbent does not make a commitment before its rival enters, entry occurs and the incumbent earns a relatively low profit. By committing to produce such a large output level that the potential entrant decides not to enter because it cannot make a positive profit, the incumbent's commitment discourages entry. Moving backward in time (moving to the left in the diagram), we examine the incumbent's choice. If the incumbent commits to the small quantity, its rival enters and the incumbent earns $450. If the incumbent commits to the larger quantity, its rival does not enter and the incumbent earns $800. Clearly, the incumbent should commit to the larger quantity because it earns a larger profit and the potential entrant chooses to stay out of the market. Their chosen paths are identified by the darker blue in the figure.

2.11 It is worth more to the monopoly to keep the potential entrant out than it is worth to the potential

entrant to enter, as the figure shows. Before the pollution-control device requirement, the entrant would pay up to $3 to enter, whereas the incumbent would pay up to $\pi_i - \pi_d = \$7$ to exclude the potential entrant. The incumbent's profit is $6 if entry does not occur, and its loss is $1 if entry occurs. Because the new firm would lose $1 if it enters, it does not enter. Thus, the incumbent has an incentive to raise costs by $4 to both firms. The incumbent's profit is $6 if it raises costs rather than $3 if it does not.

Chapter 14

2.2 The profit-maximizing cartel output is the monopoly output. Setting $MR = MC$ yields $100 - 4Q = 20$, so $Q = 20$. Each of the four firms firm produces $q = 20/4 = 5$.

3.1 The inverse demand curve is $p = 1 - 0.001Q$. The first firm's profit is $\pi_1 = [1 - 0.001(q_1 + q_2)]q_1 - 0.28q_1$. Its first-order condition is $d\pi_1/dq_1 = 1 - 0.001(2q_1 + q_2) - 0.28 = 0$. If we rearrange the terms, the first firm's best-response function is $q_1 = 360 - \frac{1}{2}q_2$. Similarly, the second firm's best-response function is $q_2 = 360 - \frac{1}{2}q_1$. By substituting one of these best-response functions into the other, we learn that the Nash-Cournot equilibrium occurs at $q_1 = q_2 = 240$, so the equilibrium price is 52¢.

3.5 Given that the firm's after-tax marginal cost is $m + t$, the Nash-Cournot equilibrium price is $p = (a + n[m + t])/(n + 1)$, using Equation 14.17. Thus, the consumer incidence of the tax is $dp/dt = n/(n + 1) < 1(=100\%)$.

3.6 The monopoly will make more profit than the duopoly will, so the monopoly is willing to pay the college more rent. Although granting monopoly rights may be attractive to the college in terms of higher rent, students will suffer (lose consumer surplus) because of the higher textbook prices.

3.11 One approach is to show that a rise in marginal cost or a fall in the number of firms tends to cause the price to rise. The Challenge Solution shows the effect of a decrease in marginal cost due to a subsidy (the opposite effect). The section titled "The Cournot Model with Many Firms" shows that a decrease in the number of firms causes market power (the markup of price over marginal cost) to increase. The two effects reinforce each other. Suppose that the market demand curve has a constant elasticity of ε. We can rewrite Equation 14.10 as $p = m/[1 + 1(n\varepsilon)] = m\mu$, where $\mu = 1/[1 + 1(n\varepsilon)]$ is the markup factor. Suppose that marginal cost increases to $(1 + a)m$ and that the drop in the number of firms causes the markup factor to rise to $(1 + b)\mu$; then the change in price is $[(1 + a)m \times (1 + b)\mu] - m\mu = (a + b + ab)m\mu$. That is, price increases by the fractional increase in the marginal cost, a, plus the fractional increase in the markup factor, b, plus the interaction of the two, ab.

3.12 By differentiating its product, a firm makes the residual demand curve it faces less elastic everywhere. For example, no consumer will buy from that firm if its rival charges less and the goods are homogeneous. In contrast, some consumers who prefer this firm's product to that of its rival will still buy from this firm even if its rival charges less. As the chapter shows, a firm sets a higher price the lower the elasticity of demand at the equilibrium.

3.17 You can solve this problem using calculus or the formulas in Solved Problem 14.1.
  a. Using Equations 14.21 and 14.22 for the duopoly, $q_1 = (15 - 1 + 1)/3 = 5$, $q_2 = (15 - 1 - 2)/3 = 4$, $p_d = 6$, $\pi_1 = (6 - 1)5 = 25$, $\pi_2 = (6 - 2)4 = 16$. Total output is $Q_d = 5 + 4 = 9$. Total profit is $\pi_d = 25 + 16 = 41$. Consumer surplus

is $CS_d = \frac{1}{2}(15 - 6)9 = 81/2 = 40.5$. At the efficient price (equal to marginal cost of 1), the output is 14. The deadweight loss is $DWL_d = \frac{1}{2}(6 - 1)(14 - 9) = 25/2 = 12.5$.
  b. The monopoly equates its marginal revenue and (its lowest) marginal cost: $MR = 15 - 2Q_m = 1 = MC$. Thus, $Q_m = 7$, $p_m = 8$, $\pi_m = (8 - 1)7 = 49$. Consumer surplus is $CS_m = \frac{1}{2}(15 - 8)7 = 49/2 = 24.5$. The deadweight loss is $DWL_m = \frac{1}{2}(8 - 1)(14 - 7) = 49/2 = 24.5$.
  c. The average cost of production for the duopoly is $[(5 \times 1) + (4 \times 2)]/(5 + 4) = 1.44$, whereas the average cost of production for the monopoly is 1. The increase in market power effect swamps the efficiency gain, so consumer surplus falls while deadweight loss nearly doubles.

3.19 a. The Nash-Cournot equilibrium in the absence of government intervention is $q_1 = 30$, $q_2 = 40$, $p = 50$, $\pi_1 = 900$, and $\pi_2 = 1,600$.
  b. The Nash-Cournot equilibrium is now $q_1 = 33.3$, $q_2 = 33.3$, $p = 53.3$, $\pi_1 = 1,108.9$, and $\pi_2 = 1,108.9$.
  c. Because Firm 2's profit was 1,600 in part a, a fixed cost slightly greater than 1,600 will prevent entry.

4.1 a. Using Equation 14.16, the Nash-Cournot equilibrium quantity is $q_i = (a - m)/(nb) = (150 - 60)/3 = 30$, so $Q = 60$, and $p = 90$.
  b. In the Stackelberg equilibrium (Equations 14.31 and 14.32) if Firm 1 moves first, then $q_1 = (a - m)/(2b) = (150 - 60)/2 = 45$, $q_2 = (a - m)/(4b) = (150 - 60)/4 = 22.5$, $Q = 67.5$, and $p = 82.5$.

5.2 Given that the duopolies produce identical goods, the equilibrium price is lower if the duopolies set price rather than quantity. If the goods are heterogeneous, we cannot answer this question definitively.

5.3 Firm 1 wants to maximize its profit: $\pi_1 = (p_1 - 10)q_1 = (p_1 - 10)(100 - 2p_1 + p_2)$. Its first-order condition is $d\pi_1/dp_1 = 100 - 4p_1 + p_2 + 20 = 0$, so its best-response function is $p_1 = 30 + \frac{1}{4}p_2$. Similarly, Firm 2's best-response function is $p_2 = 30 + \frac{1}{4}p_1$. Solving, the Nash-Bertrand equilibrium prices are $p_1 = p_2 = 40$. Each firm produces 60 units.

6.5 In the long-run equilibrium, a monopolistically competitive firm operates where its downward-sloping demand curve is tangent to its average cost curve, as Figure 14.9 illustrates. Because its demand curve is downward sloping, its average cost curve must also be downward sloping in the equilibrium. Thus, the firm chooses to operate at less than full capacity in equilibrium.

Chapter 15

1.2 Before the tax, the competitive firm's labor demand was $p \times MP_L$. After the tax, the firm's effective price is $(1 - \alpha)p$, so its labor demand becomes $(1 - \alpha)p \times MP_L$.

1.8 The competitive firm's marginal revenue of labor is $MRP_L = pMP_L = p(L^\rho + K^\rho)^{1/\rho - 1}L^{\rho - 1}$.

2.1 An individual with a zero discount rate views current and future consumption as equally attractive. An individual with an infinite discount rate cares only about current consumption and puts no value on future consumption.

2.7 Because the first contract is paid immediately, its present value equals the contract payment of $1 million. Our pro can use Equation 15.15 and a calculator to determine the present value of the second contract (or hire you to do the job for him). The present value of a $2 million payment 10 years from now is $2,000,000/(1.05)^{10} \approx \$1,227,827$ at 5% and $2,000,000/(1.2)^{10} \approx \$323,011$ at 20%. Consequently, the present values are as shown in the table.

Payment	Present Value at 5%	Present Value at 20%
$500,000 today	$50,000	$500,000
$2 million in 10 years	$1,227,827	$323,011
Total	$1,727,827	$823,011

Thus, at 5%, he should accept Contract B, with a present value of $1,727,827, which is much greater than the present value of Contract A, $1 million. At 20%, he should sign Contract A.

2.12 Solving for *irr*, we find that *irr* equals 1 or 9. This approach fails to give us a unique solution, so we should use the *NPV* approach instead. The $NPV = 1 - 12/1.07 + 20/1.07^2 \approx 7.254$, which is positive, so that the firm should invest.

2.16 Currently, you are buying 600 gallons of gas at a cost of $1,200 per year. With a more gas-efficient car, you would spend only $600 per year, saving $600 per year in gas payments. If we assume that these payments are made at the end of each year, the present value of these savings for five years is $2,580 at a 5% annual interest rate and $2,280 at 10%. The present value of the amount you must spend to buy the car in five years is $6,240 at 5% and $4,960 at 10%. Thus, the present value of the additional cost of buying now rather than later is $1,760 (= $8,000 − $6,240) at 5% and $3,040 at 10%. The benefit from buying now is the present value of the reduced gas payments. The cost is the present value of the additional cost of buying the car sooner rather than later. At 5%, the benefit is $2,580 and the cost is $1,760, so you should buy now. However, at 10%, the benefit, $2,280, is less than the cost, $3,040, so you should buy later.

Chapter 16

1.2 Assuming that the painting is not insured against fire, its expected value is

$$(0.2 \times \$1,000) + (0.1 \times \$0) + (0.7 \times \$500) = \$550.$$

1.3 The expected value of the stock is $(0.25 \times 400) + (0.75 \times 200) = 250$. The variance is $(0.25 \times [400 - 250]^2) + (0.75 \times [200 - 250]^2) = 7,500$.

1.6 The expected punishment for violating traffic laws is θV, where θ is the probability of being caught and fined and V is the fine. If people care only about the expected punishment (that is, there's no additional psychological pain from the experience), increasing the expected punishment by increasing θ or V works equally well in discouraging bad behavior. The government prefers to increase the fine, V, which is costless, rather than to raise θ, which is costly because doing so requires extra police, district attorneys, and courts.

2.3 The expected value for Stock A, $(0.5 \times 100) + (0.5 \times 200) = 150$, is the same as for Stock B, $(0.5 \times 50) + (0.5 \times 250) = 150$. However, the variance of Stock A, $(0.5 \times [100 - 150]^2) + (0.5 \times [200 - 150]^2) = 2,500$, is less than that of Stock B, $(0.5 \times [50 - 150]^2) + (0.5 \times [250 - 150]^2) = 10,000$. Consequently, Jen's expected utility from Stock A, $(0.5 \times 100^{0.5}) + (0.5 \times 200^{0.5}) \approx 12.07$, is greater than from Stock B, $(0.5 \times 50^{0.5}) + (0.5 \times 250^{0.5}) \approx 11.44$, so she prefers Stock A.

2.5 As Figure 16.2 shows, Irma's expected utility of 133 at point *f* (where her expected wealth is $64) is the same as her utility from a certain wealth of Y.

2.7 Hugo's expected wealth is $EW = (\frac{2}{3} \times 144) + (\frac{1}{3} \times 225) = 96 + 75 = 171$ His expected utility is

$$EU = \left[\frac{2}{3} \times U(144)\right] + \left[\frac{1}{3} \times U(225)\right]$$
$$= \left[\frac{2}{3} \times \sqrt{144}\right] + \left[\frac{1}{3} \times \sqrt{225}\right]$$
$$= \left[\frac{2}{3} \times 12\right] + \left[\frac{1}{3} \times 15\right] = 13.$$

He would pay up to an amount P to avoid bearing the risk, where $U(EW - P)$ equals his expected utility from the risky stock, EU. That is, $U(EW - P) = U(171 - p) = \sqrt{171 - p} = 13 = EU$. Squaring both sides, we find that $171 - P = 169$, or $P = 2$. That is, Hugo would accept an offer for his stock today of $169 (or more), which reflects a risk premium of $2.

4.1 If they were married, Andy would receive half the potential earnings whether they stayed married or not. As a result, Andy will receive $12,000 in present-value terms from Kim's additional earnings. Because the returns to the investment exceed the cost, Andy will make this investment (unless a better investment is available). However, if they stay unmarried and split, Andy's expected return on the investment is the probability of their staying together, 1/2, times Kim's half of the returns if they stay together, $12,000. Thus, Andy's expected return on the investment, $6,000, is less than the cost of the education, so Andy is unwilling to make that investment (regardless of other investment opportunities).

Chapter 17

3.5 As Figure 17.3 shows, a specific tax of $84 per ton of output or per unit of emissions (gunk) leads to the social optimum.

3.8 a. Setting the inverse demand function, $p = 200 - Q$, equal to the private marginal cost, $MC^p = 80 + Q$, we find that the unregulated equilibrium quantity is $Q_p = (200 - 80)/2 = 60$. The equilibrium price is $p_p = 200 - 60 = 140$.

   b. Setting the inverse demand function, $p = 200 - Q$, equal to the new social marginal cost, $MC^s = 80 + 2Q$, we find that the socially optimal quantity is $Q_s = (200 - 80)/(1 + 2) = 40$. The socially optimal price is $p_s = 200 - 40 = 1$.

   c. Adding a specific tax t, the private marginal cost becomes $MC^p = 80 + (1 + t)Q$, so the equilibrium quantity is $Q = (200 - 80)/(2 + t)$. Setting that equal to $Q_s = 40$ and solving, we find that $t = 1$.

3.11 As the figure shows, the government uses its expected marginal benefit curve to set a standard at S or a fee at f. If the true marginal benefit curve is MB^1, the optimal standard is S_1 and the optimal fee is f_1. The deadweight loss from setting either the fee or the standard too high is the same, DWL_1. Similarly, if the true marginal benefit curve is MB^2, both the fee and the standard are set too low, but both have the same deadweight loss, DWL_2. Thus, the deadweight loss from a mistaken belief about the marginal benefit does not depend on whether the government uses a fee or a standard. When the government sets an emissions fee or standard, the amount of gunk

actually produced depends only on the marginal cost of abatement and not on the marginal benefit. Because the fee and standard lead to the same level of abatement at e, they cause the same deadweight loss.

For Chapter 17, Exercise 3.11

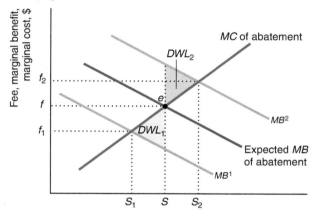

6.9 No. The marginal benefit of advertising exceeds the marginal cost.

7.1 There are several ways to demonstrate that welfare can go up despite the pollution. For example, one could redraw panel b with flatter supply curves so that area C became smaller than A (area A remains unchanged). Similarly, if the marginal pollution harm is very small, then we are very close to the no-distortion case, so that welfare will increase.

7.2 See Figure 9.7 (which corresponds to panel a). Going from no trade to free trade, consumers gain areas B and C, while domestic firms lose B. Thus, if consumers give firms an amount between B and $B + C$, both groups will be better off than with no trade.

Chapter 18

1.7 Because buyers are risk neutral, if they believe that the probability of getting a lemon is θ, the most they are willing to pay for a car of unknown quality is $p = p_1(1 - \theta) + p_2\theta$. If p is greater than both v_1 and v_2, all cars are sold. If $v_1 > p > v_2$, only lemons are sold. If p is less than both v_1 and v_2, no cars are sold. However, we know that $v_2 < p_2$ and that $p_2 < p$, so owners of lemons are certainly willing to sell them. (If sellers bear a transaction cost of c and $p < v_2 + c$, no cars are sold.)

2.2 Because insurance costs do not vary with soil type, buying insurance is unattractive for houses on good soil and relatively attractive for houses on bad soil. These incentives create a moral hazard problem: Relatively more homeowners with houses on poor soil buy insurance, so the state insurance agency will face disproportionately many bad outcomes in the next earthquake.

2.3 Brand names allow consumers to identify a particular company's product in the future. If a mushroom company expects to remain in business over time, it would be foolish for it to brand its product if its mushrooms are of inferior quality. (Just ask Babar's grandfather.) Thus, all else the same, we would expect branded mushrooms to be of higher quality than unbranded ones.

4.1 If almost all consumers know the true prices, and all but one firm charges the full-information competitive price, then it does not pay for a firm to set a high price. It gains a little from charging ignorant consumers the high price, but it sells to no informed customer. Thus, the full-information competitive price is charged in this market.

Chapter 19

1.2 By making this commitment, a company may be trying to assure customers who cannot judge how quickly a product will deteriorate that the product is durable enough to maintain at least a certain value in the future. The firm is trying to eliminate asymmetric information to increase the demand for its product.

2.1 This agreement led to very long conversations. Whichever of them was enjoying the call more apparently figured that he or she would get the full marginal benefit of one more minute of talking while having to pay only half the marginal cost. From this experience, I learned not to open our phone bill so as to avoid being shocked by the amount due (back in an era when long-distance phone calls were expensive).

2.2 A partner who works an extra hour bears the full opportunity cost of this extra hour but gets only half the marginal benefit from the extra business profit. The opportunity cost of extra time spent at the store is the partner's best alternative use of time. A partner could earn money working for someone else or use the time to have fun. Because a partner bears the full marginal cost but gets only half the marginal benefit (the extra business profit) from an extra hour of work, each partner works only up to the point at which the marginal cost equals half the marginal benefit. Thus, each has an incentive to put in less effort than the level that maximizes their joint profit, where the marginal cost equals the marginal benefit.

2.4 If Paula pays Arthur a fixed-fee salary of $168, Arthur has no incentive to buy any carvings for resale, given that the $12 per carving cost comes out of his pocket. Thus, Arthur sells no carvings if he receives a fixed salary and can sell as many or as few carvings as he wants. The contract is not incentive compatible. For Arthur to behave efficiently, this fixed-fee contract must be modified. For example, the contract could specify that Arthur gets a salary of $168 and that he must obtain and sell 12 carvings. Paula must monitor his behavior. (Paula's residual profit is the joint profit minus $168, so she gets the marginal profit from each additional sale and wants to sell the joint-profit-maximizing number of carvings.) Arthur makes $24 = $168 − $144, so he is willing to participate. Joint profit is maximized at $72, and Paula gets the maximum possible residual profit of $48.

2.5 Presumably, the promoter collects a percentage of the revenue of each restaurant. If customers can pay cash, the restaurants may not report the total amount of food they sell. The scrip makes such opportunistic behavior difficult.

4.2 The minimum bond that deters stealing is $2,500.

Definitions

I hate definitions. —Benjamin Disraeli

adverse selection: occurs when one party to a transaction possesses information about a hidden characteristic that is unknown to other parties and takes economic advantage of this information. (18)

agency problem (principal-agent problem): moral hazard in a principal-agent relationship. (19)

allocative efficiency: the situation in which every good or service is produced up to the point where no consumer is willing to pay more for it than the price at which someone else is willing to supply it. (9)

asymmetric information: the situation in which one party to a transaction has relevant information that another party lacks. (18)

auction: a sale in which a good or service is sold to the highest bidder. (13)

average cost (*AC*): the total cost divided by the units of output produced: $AC = C/q$. (7)

average fixed cost (*AFC*): the fixed cost divided by the units of output produced: $AFC = F/q$. (7)

average product of labor (AP_L): the ratio of output, q, to the number of workers, L, used to produce that output: $AP_L = q/L$. (6)

average variable cost (*AVC*): the variable cost divided by the units of output produced: $AVC = VC/q$. (7)

backward induction: a process in which we first determine the best response by the last player to move, next determine the best response for the player who made the next-to-last move, and then repeat the process until we reach the first move of the game. (13)

bad: something for which less is preferred to more, such as pollution. (3)

bandwagon effect: the situation in which a person places greater value on a good as more and more people possess it. (11)

barrier to entry: an explicit restriction or a cost that applies only to potential new firms—existing firms are not subject to the restriction or do not bear the cost. (9)

behavioral economics: adds insights from psychology and empirical research on human cognition and emotional biases to the rational economic model to better predict economic decision making. (3)

Bertrand equilibrium (*Nash-Bertrand equilibrium* or *Nash-in-prices equilibrium*): a set of prices such that no firm can obtain a higher profit by choosing a different price if the other firms continue to charge these prices. (14)

best response: the strategy that maximizes a player's payoff given its beliefs about its rivals' strategies. (13)

bounded rationality: a person's limited capacity to anticipate, solve complex problems, and enumerate all options. (3)

budget line (*budget constraint*): the bundles of goods that can be bought if a consumer's entire budget is spent on those goods at given prices. (3)

bundling (*package tie-in sale*): a type of tie-in sale in which two goods are combined so that customers cannot buy either good separately. (12)

cartel: a group of firms that explicitly agree (collude) to coordinate their activities. (14)

certainty equivalent: the amount of certain wealth that would yield the same utility as a risky prospect. (16)

certification: a report that a particular product meets or exceeds a given standard. (18)

cheap talk: unsubstantiated claims or statements. (18)

club good: a commodity that is nonrival but is subject to exclusion. (17)

collude: coordinate actions such as setting prices or quantities among firms. (14)

common knowledge: a piece of information known by all players, and it is known by all players to be known by all players, and it is known to be known to be known, and so forth. (13)

comparative advantage: the ability to produce a good at a lower opportunity cost than someone else. (10)

comparative statics: the method economists use to analyze how variables controlled by consumers and firms react to a change in *environmental variables* (also called *exogenous variables*) that they do not control. (2)

compensating variation (*CV*): the amount of money one would have to give a consumer to offset completely the harm from a price increase. (5)

complement: a good or service that is jointly consumed with another good or service. (2)

complete information: the situation where the strategies and payoff function are common knowledge among all players. (13)

constant returns to scale (*CRS*): the property of a production function whereby when all inputs are increased by a certain percentage, output increases by that same percentage. (6)

consumer surplus (*CS*): the monetary difference between the maximum amount that a consumer is willing to pay for the quantity of the good purchased and what the good actually costs. (5)

contingent fee: a payment to a lawyer that is a share of the award in a court case (usually after legal expenses are deducted) if the client wins and nothing if the client loses. (19)

contract curve: the set of all Pareto-efficient bundles. (10)

cost (*total cost, C*): the sum of a firm's variable cost and fixed cost: $C = VC + F$. (7)

cost efficient: minimizing the cost of producing a specified amount of output. (7)

Cournot equilibrium (*Nash-Cournot equilibrium* or *Nash-in-quantities equilibrium*): a set of quantities chosen by firms such that, holding the quantities of all other firms constant, no firm can obtain a higher profit by choosing a different quantity. (14)

credible threat: an announcement that a firm will use a strategy harmful to its rivals that the rivals believe is rational in the sense that it is in the firm's best interest to use it. (13)

cross-price elasticity of demand: the percentage change in the quantity demanded in response to a given percentage change in the price of another good. (2)

deadweight loss (*DWL*): the net reduction in welfare from a loss of surplus by one group that is not offset by a gain to another group. (9)

decreasing returns to scale (*DRS*): the property of a production function whereby output rises less than in proportion to an equal percentage increase in all inputs. (6)

demand curve: a plot of the demand function that shows the quantity demanded at each possible price, holding constant the other factors that influence purchases. (2)

demand function: the correspondence between the quantity demanded, price, and other factors that influence purchases. (2)

discount rate: a rate reflecting the relative value an individual places on future consumption compared to current consumption. (15)

diseconomies of scale: the property of a cost function whereby the average cost of production rises when output increases. (7)

dominant strategy: a strategy that produces a higher payoff than any other strategy the player can use for every possible combination of its rivals' strategies. (13)

duopoly: an oligopoly with two (*duo*) firms. (14)

durable good: a product that provides services for a long period, typically for many years. (7)

dynamic game: a game in which players move either sequentially or repeatedly. (13)

economic cost (*opportunity cost*): the value of the best alternative use of a resource. (7)

economic profit: revenue minus opportunity (economic) cost. (8)

economies of scale: the property of a cost function whereby the average cost of production falls as output expands. (7)

economies of scope: a situation in which it is less expensive to produce goods jointly than separately. (7)

efficiency in production: a situation in which the principal's and the agent's combined value (profits, payoffs) is maximized. (19)

efficiency in risk bearing: a situation in which risk sharing is optimal in that the person who least minds facing risk—the risk-neutral or less-risk-averse person—bears more of the risk. (19)

efficiency wage: an unusually high wage that a firm pays workers as an incentive to avoid shirking. (19)

efficient contract: an agreement with provisions that ensure that no party can be made better off without harming the other party. (19)

elasticity: the percentage change in one variable in response to a given percentage change in another variable, holding other relevant variables constant. (2)

elasticity of substitution (σ): the percentage change in the capital-labor ratio divided by the percentage change in the *MRTS*. (6)

endowment: an initial allocation of goods. (10)

endowment effect: the condition that occurs when people place a higher value on a good if they own it than they do if they are considering buying it. (3)

Engel curve: the relationship between the quantity demanded of a single good and income, holding prices constant. (4)

equilibrium: a situation in which no participant wants to change its behavior. (2)

equivalent variation (*EV*): the amount of money one would have to take from a consumer to harm the consumer by as much as the price increase. (5)

essential facility: a scarce resource that rivals must use to survive. (11)

excess demand: the amount by which the quantity demanded exceeds the quantity supplied at a specified price. (2)

excess supply: the amount by which the quantity supplied is greater than the quantity demanded at a specified price. (2)

exclusion: an owner of a good can prevent others from consuming it. (17)

exhaustible resources: nonrenewable natural assets that cannot be increased, only depleted. (15)

expansion path: the cost-minimizing combination of labor and capital for each output level. (7)

expected value: the weighted average of the values of each possible outcome, where the weights are the probability of each outcome. (16)

expenditure function: the relationship showing the minimal expenditures necessary to achieve a specific utility level for a given set of prices. (3)

extensive form: a representation of a game that specifies the *n* players, the sequence in which they make their moves, the actions they can take at each move, the information that each player has about players' previous moves, and the payoff function over all possible strategies. (13)

externality: the change in a person's well-being or a firm's production capability directly caused by the actions of other consumers or firms rather than indirectly through changes in prices. (17)

fair bet: a wager with an expected value of zero. (16)

fair insurance: a contract between an insurer and a policyholder in which the value of the contract to the policyholder is zero. (16)

firm: an organization that converts *inputs* such as labor, materials, and capital into *outputs*, the goods and services that it sells. (6)

fixed cost (*F*): a production expense that does not vary with the level of output. (7)

fixed input: a factor of production that cannot be varied practically in the short run. (6)

flow: a quantity or value that is measured per unit of time. (15)

free riding: benefiting from the actions of others without paying. (17)

game: a competition between players (such as individuals or firms) in which players use strategies. (13)

game theory: a set of tools that economists and others use to analyze players' strategic decision making. (13)

general-equilibrium analysis: the study of how equilibrium is determined in all markets simultaneously. (10)

Giffen good: a commodity for which a decrease in its price causes the quantity demanded to fall. (4)

good: a commodity for which more is preferred to less, at least at some levels of consumption. (3)

group price discrimination (*third-degree price discrimination*): a situation in which a firm charges different groups of customers different prices but charges a given customer the same price for every unit sold. (12)

hidden action: an attribute of a person or thing that is known to one party but unknown to others. (18)

hidden characteristic: an attribute of a person or thing that is known to one party but unknown to others. (18)

incentive compatible: a condition in which a contract provides inducements such that the agent wants to perform the assigned task rather than engage in opportunistic behavior. (19)

incidence of a tax on consumers: the share of the tax that consumers pay. (2)

income effect: the change in the quantity of a good a consumer demands because of a change in income, holding prices constant. (4)

income elasticity of demand (*income elasticity*): the percentage change in the quantity demanded in response to a given percentage change in income. (2)

increasing returns to scale (*IRS*): the property of a production function whereby output rises more than in proportion to an equal increase in all inputs. (6)

indifference curve: the set of all bundles of goods that a consumer views as being equally desirable. (3)

indifference map (*preference map*): a complete set of indifference curves that summarize a consumer's tastes. (3)

inferior good: a commodity of which less is demanded as income rises. (4)

interest rate: the percentage more that must be repaid to borrow money for a fixed period. (15)

internal rate of return (*irr*): the discount rate such that the net present value of an investment is zero. (15)

internalize the externality: to bear the cost of the harm that one inflicts on others (or to capture the benefit that one provides to others). (17)

isocost line: a plot of all the combinations of inputs that require the same (*iso*) total expenditure (*cost*). (7)

isoquant: a curve that shows the efficient combinations of labor and capital that can produce a single (*iso*) level of output (*quant*ity). (6)

Law of Demand: consumers demand more of a good the lower its price, holding constant tastes, the prices of other goods, and other factors that influence the amount they consume. (2)

learning by doing: the productive skills and knowledge of better ways to produce that workers and managers gain from experience. (7)

learning curve: the relationship between average costs and cumulative output. (7)

Lerner Index (*price markup*): the ratio of the difference between price and marginal cost to the price: $(p - MC)/p$. (11)

limit price: a price (or, equivalently, an output) that a firm sets so that another firm cannot enter the market profitably. (12)

limited liability: a condition whereby the personal assets of corporate owners cannot be taken to pay a corporation's debts even if it goes into bankruptcy. (6)

long run: a long enough period of time that all inputs can be varied. (6)

marginal cost (*MC*): the amount by which a firm's cost changes if it produces one more unit of output: $MC = \Delta C/\Delta q$. (7)

marginal product of labor (MP_L): the change in total output resulting from using an extra unit of labor, holding other factors (capital) constant. (6)

marginal profit: the change in the profit a firm gets from selling one more unit of output. (8)

marginal rate of substitution (*MRS*): the maximum amount of one good that a consumer will sacrifice (trade) to obtain one more unit of another good. (3)

marginal rate of technical substitution (*MRTS*): how many units of capital a firm can replace with an extra unit of labor while holding output constant. (6)

marginal rate of transformation (*MRT*): the trade-off the market imposes on the consumer in terms of the amount of one good the consumer must give up to obtain more of the other good. (3)

marginal revenue (*MR*): the change in revenue a firm gets from selling one more unit of output. (8)

marginal revenue product of labor (MRP_L): the additional revenue from the last unit of labor. (15)

marginal utility: the extra utility that a consumer gets from consuming the last unit of a good. (3)

market: an exchange mechanism that allows buyers to trade with sellers. (1)

market failure: cost inefficiency or allocative inefficiency. (9)

market power: the ability of a firm to charge a price above marginal cost and earn a positive profit. (11)

market structure: the number of firms in the market, the ease with which firms can enter and leave the market, and the ability of firms to differentiate their products from those of their rivals. (8)

microeconomics: the study of how individuals and firms make themselves as well off as possible in a world of scarcity, and the consequences of those individual decisions for markets and the entire economy. (1)

minimum efficient scale (*full capacity*): the smallest quantity at which the average cost curve reaches its minimum. (14)

mixed strategy: a strategy in which the player chooses among possible actions according to probabilities the player assigns. (13)

model: a description of the relationship between two or more economic variables. (1)

monopolistic competition: a market structure in which firms have market power but no additional firm can enter and earn a positive profit. (14)

monopoly: the only supplier of a good that has no close substitute. (11)

monopsony: the only buyer of a good in a market. (11)

moral hazard: opportunism characterized by an informed person's taking advantage of a less-informed person through an *unobserved action*. (18)

Nash equilibrium: a set of strategies such that, when all other players use these strategies, no player can obtain a higher payoff by choosing a different strategy. (13)

Nash-Bertrand equilibrium (*Bertrand equilibrium* or *Nash-in-prices equilibrium*): a set of prices chosen by firms such that no firm can obtain a higher profit by choosing a different price if the other firms continue to charge these prices. (14)

Nash-Cournot equilibrium (*Cournot equilibrium* or *Nash-in-quantities equilibrium*): a set of quantities chosen by firms such that, holding the quantities of all other firms constant, no firm can obtain a higher profit by choosing a different quantity. (14)

natural monopoly: a situation in which one firm can produce the total output of the market at lower cost than several firms could. (11)

network: an interconnected group of people or things. (11)

network externality: the situation where one person's demand for a good depends on the consumption of the good by others. (11)

nonlinear price discrimination (*second-degree price discrimination*): the situation in which a firm charges a different price for large quantities than for small quantities, but all customers who buy a given quantity pay the same price. (12)

nonuniform pricing: the practice of charging consumers different prices for the same product or charging a single customer a price that depends on the number of units purchased. (12)

normal form: a representation of a static game of complete information, which specifies the players in the game, their possible strategies, and the payoff function that specifies the players' payoffs for each combination of strategies. (13)

normal good: a commodity of which more is demanded as income rises. (4)

normative statement: a conclusion as to whether something is good or bad. (1)

oligopoly: a small group of firms in a market with substantial barriers to entry. (14)

open-access common property: unregulated resources to which everyone has free access and an equal right to exploit. (17)

opportunistic behavior: taking economic advantage of someone when circumstances permit. (18)

opportunity cost (*economic cost*): the value of the best alternative use of a resource. (7)

opportunity set: all the bundles a consumer can buy, including all the bundles inside the budget constraint and on the budget constraint. (3)

Pareto efficient: describing an allocation of goods and services such that any possible reallocation would harm at least one person. (10)

Pareto improvement: a change, such as a reallocation, that helps at least one person without harming anyone else. (10)

Pareto principle: the belief that society should favor a change that benefits some people without harming anyone else. (10)

partial-equilibrium analysis: an examination of equilibrium and changes in equilibrium in one market in isolation. (10)

patent: an exclusive right granted to the inventor to sell a new and useful product, process, substance, or design for a fixed time. (11)

payoffs (of a game): players' valuations of the outcome of the game, such as profits for firms, or incomes or utilities for individuals. (13)

perfect competition: a market structure in which buyers and sellers are price takers. (8)

perfect complements: goods that a consumer is interested in consuming only in fixed proportions. (3)

perfect price discrimination (*first-degree price discrimination*): the situation in which a firm sells each unit at the maximum amount each customer is willing to pay, so prices differ across customers, and a given customer may pay more for some units than for others. (12)

perfect substitutes: goods that a consumer is completely indifferent as to which to consume. (3)

pooling equilibrium: an equilibrium in which dissimilar people are treated (paid) alike or behave alike. (18)

positive statement: a testable hypothesis about cause and effect. (1)

price discrimination: charging consumers different prices for the same good based on individual characteristics of consumers, on membership in an identifiable subgroup of consumers, or on the quantity purchased by the consumers. (12)

price elasticity of demand (*demand elasticity* or *elasticity of demand*): the percentage change in the quantity demanded in response to a given percentage change in the price at a particular point on the demand curve. (2)

price elasticity of supply (*supply elasticity*): the percentage change in the quantity supplied in response to a given percentage change in the price. (2)

principal-agent relationship: a principal contracts with an agent to take an action on behalf of the principal. (19)

principal-agent problem (*agency problem*): moral hazard in a principal-agent relationship. (19)

prisoners' dilemma: a game in which all players have dominant strategies that lead to a profit (or another payoff) that is inferior to what they could achieve if they cooperated and pursued alternative strategies. (13)

private cost: the cost of production only, not including externalities. (17)

producer surplus: the excess of the revenue from selling a good and the minimum amount necessary for the seller to be willing to produce the good. (9)

production efficiency (*technological efficiency*): a situation in which the current level of output cannot be produced with fewer inputs, given existing knowledge about technology and how to organize production. (6)

production function: the relationship between the quantities of inputs used and the *maximum* quantity of output that can be produced, given current knowledge about technology and organization. (6)

production possibility frontier: a graph that shows the maximum amount of one good that can be produced for any quantity of the other good, using the available inputs and technology. (7)

profit (π): the difference between a firm's revenue, R, which is what it earns from selling a good, and its cost, C, which is what it pays for labor, materials, and other inputs: $\pi = R - C$. (6)

property right: ownership that gives exclusive control of a good. (17)

public good: a commodity or service whose consumption by one person does not preclude others from also consuming it. (17)

pure strategy: strategy in which each player chooses a single action. (13)

quantity demanded: the amount of a good that consumers are willing to buy at a given price during a specified period (such as a day or a year), holding constant the other factors that influence purchases. (2)

quantity supplied: the amount of a good that firms *want* to sell during a given time period at a given price, holding constant other factors that influence firms' supply decisions, such as costs and government actions. (2)

quota: a limit that a government sets on the quantity of a foreign-produced good that may be imported. (2)

rent: a payment to the owner of an input beyond the minimum necessary for the factor to be supplied. (9)

rent seeking: efforts and expenditures to gain a rent or a profit from government actions. (9)

requirement tie-in sale: a type of nonuniform pricing in which customers who buy one product from a firm are required to make all their purchases of another product from that firm. (12)

reservation price: the maximum amount a person is willing to pay for a unit of output. (12)

residual demand curve: the market demand that is not met by other sellers at any given price. (8)

residual supply curve: the quantity that the market supplies that is not consumed by other demanders at any given price. (8)

risk: the situation in which the likelihood of each possible outcome is known or can be estimated, and no single possible outcome is certain to occur. (16)

risk averse: unwilling to make a fair bet. (16)

risk neutral: indifferent about making a fair bet. (16)

risk preferring: willing to make a fair bet. (16)

risk premium: the amount that a risk-averse person would pay to avoid taking a risk. (16)

rival: a situation in which only one person can consume a good. (17)

rules of the game: regulations that determine the timing of players' moves (such as whether one player moves first), the various actions that are possible at a particular point in the game, and possibly other specific aspects of how the game is played. (13)

screening: an action taken by an uninformed person to determine the information possessed by informed people. (18)

separating equilibrium: an equilibrium in which one type of people takes actions (such as sending a signal) that allows them to be differentiated from other types of people. (18)

shirk: a moral hazard in which agents do not provide all the services they are paid to provide. (19)

short run: a period of time so brief that at least one factor of production cannot be varied practically. (6)

shortage: a persistent excess demand. (2)

signaling: an action taken by an informed person to send information to a less-informed person. (18)

snob effect: the situation in which a person places greater value on a good as fewer and fewer people possess it. (11)

social cost: the private cost plus the cost of the harms from externalities. (17)

standard: a metric or scale for evaluating the quality of a particular product. (18)

static game: a game in which each player acts only once and the players act simultaneously (or, at least, each player acts without knowing rivals' actions). (13)

stock: a quantity or value that is measured independently of time. (15)

strategy: a battle plan that specifies the actions or moves that a player will make conditional on the information available at each move and for any possible contingency. (13)

subgame: all the subsequent decisions that players may make given the actions already taken. (13)

subgame perfect Nash equilibrium: the situation in which players' strategies are a Nash equilibrium in every subgame. (13)

substitute: a good or service that may be consumed instead of another good or service. (2)

substitution effect: the change in the quantity of a good that a consumer demands when the good's price rises, holding other prices and the consumer's utility constant. (4)

sunk cost: a past expenditure that cannot be recovered. (7)

supply curve: the quantity supplied at each possible price, holding constant the other factors that influence firms' supply decisions. (2)

supply function: the correspondence between the quantity supplied, price, and other factors that influence the number of units offered for sale. (2)

tariff (*duty*)**:** a tax only on imported goods. (9)

technical progress: an advance in knowledge that allows more output to be produced with the same level of inputs. (6)

technological efficiency (*efficient production*)**:** property of a production function such that the current level of output cannot be produced with fewer inputs, given existing knowledge about technology and how to organize production. (6)

tie-in sale: a type of nonuniform pricing in which customers can buy one product or service only if they agree to purchase another as well. (12)

total cost (*C*)**:** the sum of a firm's variable cost and fixed cost: $C = VC + F$. (7)

total product of labor: the amount of output (or *total product*) that a given amount of labor can produce holding the quantity of other inputs fixed. (6)

transaction costs: the expenses, over and above the price of the product, of finding a trading partner and making a trade for the product. (2)

two-part pricing: a pricing system in which the firm charges each consumer a lump-sum *access fee* (or price) for the right to buy as many units of the good as the consumer wants at a per-unit *price*. (12)

two-sided market (two-sided network): an economic platform that has two or more user groups that provide each other with network externalities. (11)

uniform pricing: charging the same price for every unit sold of a particular good. (12)

utility: a set of numerical values that reflect the relative rankings of various bundles of goods. (3)

utility function: the relationship between utility measures and every possible bundle of goods. (3)

variable cost (*VC*)**:** a production expense that changes with the quantity of output produced. (7)

variable input: a factor of production whose quantity the firm can change readily during the relevant period. (6)

winner's curse: auction winner's bid exceeds the common-value item's value. (13)

References

Abelson, Peter, "The High Cost of Taxi Regulation, with Special Reference to Sydney," *Agenda*, 17(2), 2010: 41–70.

Adelaja, Adesoji O., "Price Changes, Supply Elasticities, Industry Organization, and Dairy Output Distribution," *American Journal of Agricultural Economics*, 73(1), February 1991: 89–102.

Aguiar, Mark, Mark Bils, Kerwin Kofi Charles, and Erik Hurst, "Leisure Luxuries and the Labor Supply of Young Men," National Bureau of Economic Research Working Paper, 2017.

Aigner, Dennis J., and Glen G. Cain, "Statistical Theories of Discrimination in Labor Markets," *Industrial and Labor Relations Review*, 30(2), January 1977: 175–187.

Akerlof, George A., "The Market for 'Lemons': Quality Uncertainty and the Market Mechanism," *Quarterly Journal of Economics*, 84(3), August 1970: 488–500.

Akerlof, George A., "Labor Contacts as Partial Gift Exchanges," *Quarterly Journal of Economics*, 97(4), November 1982: 543–569.

Alexander, Donald L., "Major League Baseball," *Journal of Sports Economics*, 2(4), November 2001: 341–355.

Altonji, Joseph G., and Ernesto Villanueva, "The Marginal Propensity to Spend on Adult Children," *B.E. Journal of Economic Analysis & Policy*, Advances, 7(1), 2007, Article 14.

Alyakoob, Mohammed, and Mohammed Rahman, "Shared Prosperity (or Lack Thereof) in the Sharing Economy," Working Paper, 2018.

Anderson, Michael, and Maximilian Auffhammer, "Pounds That Kill: The External Costs of Vehicle Weight," *Review of Economics Studies*, 81(2), April 2014: 535–571.

Arrow, Kenneth, *Social Choice and Individual Values*. New York: Wiley, 1951.

Association of Certified Fraud Examiners, *Report to the Nations*, 2018.

Ayres, Ian, and Joel Waldfogel, "A Market Test for Race Discrimination in Bail Setting," *Stanford Law Review*, 46(5), May 1994: 987–1047.

Backus, Matthew, Tom Blake, and Steven Tadelis, "Cheap Talk, Round Numbers, and the Economics of Negotiation," *Journal of Political Economy*, forthcoming.

Baggio, Michele, Alberto Chong, and Sungoh Kwon, "Helping Settle the Marijuana and Alcohol Debate: Evidence from Scanner Data," SSRN Working Paper, 2017.

Balafoutas, Loukas, Rudolf Kerschbamer, and Matthias Sutter, "Second-Degree Moral Hazard in a Real-World Credence Goods Market," *Economic Journal*, 127(599), February 2017: 1–18.

Baldwin, John R., and Paul K. Gorecki, *The Role of Scale in Canada/U.S. Productivity Differences in the Manufacturing Sector, 1970–1979*. Toronto: University of Toronto Press, 1986.

Balistreri, Edward J., Christine A. McDaniel, and Eina Vivian Wong, "An Estimation of US Industry-Level Capital-Labor Substitution Elasticities: Support for Cobb-Douglas," *North American Journal of Economics and Finance*, 14(3), December 2003: 343–356.

Barrett, Sean D., "Regulatory Capture, Property Rights and Taxi Deregulation: A Case Study," *Economic Affairs*, 23(4), 2003: 34–40.

Basker, Emek, "Raising the Barcode Scanner: Technology and Productivity in the Retail Sector," *American Economic Journal: Applied Economics*, 4(3), July 2012: 1–27.

Battalio, Raymond, John H. Kagel, and Carl Kogut, "Experimental Confirmation of the Existence of a Giffen Good," *American Economic Review*, 81(3), September 1991: 961–970.

Bauer, Thomas K., and Christoph M. Schmidt "WTP vs. WTA: Christmas Presents and the Endowment Effect," Institute for the Study of Labor Working Paper, 2008.

Baugh, Brian, Itzhak Ben-David, and Hoonsuk Park, "The 'Amazon Tax': Empirical Evidence from Amazon and Main Street Retailers," Ohio State University Working Paper, 2015.

Baumeister, Christiane, and Gert Peersman, "The Role of Time-Varying Price Elasticities in Accounting for Volatility Changes in the Crude Oil Market," *Journal of Applied Econometrics*, 28(7), November/December 2013: 1087–1109.

Beatty, T. K., and C. J. Tuttle, "Expenditure Response to Increases in In-Kind Transfers: Evidence from the Supplemental Nutrition Assistance Program," *American Journal of Agricultural Economics*, 97(2), March 2015: 390–402.

Becker, Gary S., *The Economics of Discrimination*, 2nd ed. Chicago: University of Chicago Press, 1971.

Benjamin, Daniel K., William R. Dougan, and David Buschena, *Journal of Risk and Uncertainty*, 22(1), January 2001: 35–57.

Berck, Peter, and Michael Roberts, "Natural Resource Prices: Will They Ever Turn Up?" *Journal of Environmental Economics and Management*, 31(1), July 1996: 65–78.

Bezman, Trisha L., and Craig A. Depken II, "Influences on Software Piracy: Evidence from the Various United States," *Economic Letters*, 90(3), March 2006: 356–361.

Bielen, David A., Richard G. Newell, and William A. Pizer, "Who Did the Ethanol Tax Credit Benefit? An Event Analysis of Subsidy Incidence," *Journal of Public Economics*, 161, May 2018: 1–14.

Bils, Mark, "Do Higher Prices for New Goods Reflect Quality Growth or Inflation?" *Quarterly Journal of Economics*, 124(2), May 2009: 637–675.

Blanciforti, Laura Ann, "The Almost Ideal Demand System Incorporating Habits: An Analysis of Expenditures on Food and Aggregate Commodity Groups," Ph.D. thesis, U.C. Davis, 1982.

Blau, David, and Edral Tekin, "The Determinants and Consequence of Child Care Subsidy Receipt by Low-Income Families," in Bruce Mery and Greg Duncan, *The Incentives of Government Programs and the Well-Being of Families*, Joint Center for Poverty Research, 2001.

Blundell, Richard, Joel L. Horowitz, and Matthias Parey, "Measuring the Price Responsiveness of Gasoline Demand: Economic Shape Restrictions and Nonparametric Demand Estimation," *Quantitative Economics*, 3(1), March 2012: 29–51.

Boomhower, Judson, "Drilling Like There's No Tomorrow: Bankruptcy, Insurance, and Environmental Risk," *American Economic Review*, forthcoming.

Borenstein, Severin, "ANWR Oil and the Price of Gasoline," U.C. Energy Institute, *Energy Notes*, 3(2), June 2005.

Borenstein, Severin, "The Private Net Benefits of Residential Solar PV: And Who Gets Them," Energy Institute at Haas Working Paper, May 2015.

Borenstein, Severin, and Nancy L. Rose, "Competition and Price Dispersion in the U.S. Airline Industry," *Journal of Political Economy*, 102(4), August 1994: 653–683.

Borjas, George J., "The Labor Demand Curve Is Downward Sloping: Reexamining the Impact of Immigration on the Labor Market," *Quarterly Journal of Economics*, 118(4), November 2003: 1335–1374.

Boroski, John W., and Gerard C. S. Mildner, "An Economic Analysis of Taxicab Regulation in Portland, Oregon," Cascade Policy Institute, www.cascadepolicy.org, 1998.

Boskin, Michael J., Ellen R. Dulberger, Robert J. Gordon, Zvi Griliches, and Dale W. Jorgenson, "The CPI Commission: Findings and Recommendations," *American Economic Review*, 87(2), May 1997: 78–93.

Boskin, Michael J., and Dale W. Jorgenson, "Implications of Overstating Inflation for Indexing Government Programs and Understanding Economic Progress," *American Economic Review*, 87(2), May 1997: 89–93.

Boulier, Bryan L., Tejwant S. Datta, and Robert S. Goldfarb, "Vaccination Externalities," *The B.E. Journal of Economic Analysis & Policy*, 7(1, Contributions), 2007: Article 23.

Bradbury, Hinton, and Karen Ross, "The Effects of Novelty and Choice Materials on the Intransitivity of Preferences of Children and Adults," *Annals of Operations Research*, 23(1–4), June 1990: 141–159.

Brander, James A., and M. Scott Taylor, "The Simple Economics of Easter Island: A Ricardo-Malthus Model of Renewable Resource Use," *American Economic Review*, 88(1), March 1998: 119–138.

Brander, James A., and Anming Zhang, "Market Conduct in the Airline Industry: An Empirical Investigation," *Rand Journal of Economics*, 21(4), Winter 1990: 567–583.

Bricker, Jesse, et al., "Changes in U.S. Family Finances from 2013 to 2016: Evidence from the Survey of Consumer Finances," *Federal Reserve Bulletin*, 103(2), September 2017: 1–41.

Brown, Jennifer, and John Morgan, "Reputation in Online Auctions: The Market for Trust," *California Management Review*, 49(1), Fall 2006: 61–81.

Brown, Jennifer, and John Morgan, "How Much Is a Dollar Worth? Tipping versus Equilibrium Coexistence on Competing Online Auction Sites," *Journal of Political Economy*, 117(4), August 2010: 668–700.

Brown, Stephen P. A., and Daniel Wolk, "Natural Resource Scarcity and Technological Change," *Economic and Financial Review* (Federal Reserve Bank of Dallas), First Quarter 2000: 2–13.

Brownlee, Oswald, and George Perry, "The Effects of the 1965 Federal Excise Tax Reductions on Prices," *National Tax Journal*, 20(3), September 1967: 235–249.

Bruich, Gregory A., "The Effect of SNAP Benefits on Expenditures: New Evidence from Scanner Data and the November 2013 Benefit Cuts," Harvard Working Paper, 2014.

Brunk, Gregory G., "A Test of the Friedman-Savage Gambling Model," *Quarterly Journal of Economics*, 96(2), May 1981: 341–348.

Brynjolfsson, Erik, Felix Eggers, and Avinash Gannamaneni, "Using Massive Online Choice Experiments to Measure Changes in Well-Being," NBER Working Paper, 2018.

Bucks, Brian K., Arthur B. Kennickell, Traci L. Mach, and Kevin B. Moore, "Changes in U.S. Family Finances from 2004 to 2007: Evidence from the Survey of Consumer Finances," *Federal Reserve Bulletin*, 2009, www.federalreserve.gov/pubs/bulletin/2009/pdf/scf09.pdf.

Buschena, David E., and Jeffrey M. Perloff, "The Creation of Dominant Firm Market Power in the Coconut Oil Export Market," *American Journal of Agricultural Economics*, 73(4), November 1991: 1000–1008.

Caliendo, Marco, Michel Clement, Domink Papies, and Sabine Scheel-Kopeinig, "The Cost Impact of Spam Filters: Measuring the Effect of Information System Technologies in Organizations," *Information Systems Research*, 23(3), September 2012: 1068–1080.

Camerer, Colin F., *Behavioral Game Theory: Experiments in Strategic Interaction*. New York: Russell Sage Foundation, 2003.

Camerer, Colin F., George Loewenstein, and Matthew Rabin, eds., *Advances in Behavioral Economics*. New York: Russell Sage Foundation, 2004.

Capehart, Kevin, and Elena C. Berg, "Fine Water: A Blind Taste Test," *Journal of Wine Economics*, 13(1), 2018: 20–40.

Card, David, and Alan B. Krueger, *Myth and Measurement: The New Economics of the Minimum Wage*. Princeton, NJ: Princeton University Press, 1995.

Carlton, Dennis W., and Jeffrey M. Perloff, *Modern Industrial Organization*, 4th ed. Reading, MA: Addison Wesley Longman, 2005.

Carlton, Dennis W., et al., "Are Legacy Airline Mergers Pro- or Anti-competitive? Evidence from Recent U.S. Airline Mergers," *International Journal of Industrial Organization*, forthcoming.

Carman, Hoy F., "Offsetting Price Impacts from Imports with Generic Advertising and Promotion Programs: The Hass Avocado Promotion and Research Order," *Review of Agricultural Economics*, 28(4), September 2006: 463–481.

Carpenter, Christopher, and Carlos Dobkin, "The Effect of Alcohol Consumption on Mortality: Regression Discontinuity Evidence from the Minimum Drinking Age," *American Economic Journal: Applied Economics*, 1(1), January 2009: 165–182.

Cascio, Elizabeth U., and Ayushi Narayan, "Who Needs a Fracking Education? The Educational Response to Low-Skill Biased Technological Change," NBER Working Paper, 2017.

Chandra, Ambarish, and Matthew Weinberg, "How Does Advertising Depend on Competition? Evidence from U.S. Brewing," University of Toronto manuscript, 2015.

Chandrasekaran, Deepa, Raji Srinivasan, and Debika Sihi, "Effects of Offline ad Content on Online Brand Search: Insights from Super Bowl Advertising," *Journal of the Academy of Marketing Science* 46(3), 2018: 403–430.

Chetty, Raj, Adam Looney, and Kory Kroft, "Salience and Taxation: Theory and Evidence," *American Economic Review*, 99(4), September 2009: 1145–1177.

Chirinko, Robert S., and Debdulal Mallick, "The Substitution Elasticity, Factor Shares, Long-Run Growth, and the Low-Frequency Panel Model," CESifo Working Paper, 2014.

Cho, Daegon, Ferreira, Pedro, and Telang, Rahul. "The Impact of Mobile Number Portability on Price, Competition and Consumer Welfare." (September 29, 2016). Available at SSRN: https://ssrn.com/abstract=2265104 or http://dx.doi.org/10.2139/ssrn.2265104.

Chouinard, Hayley, and Jeffrey M. Perloff, "Incidence of Federal and State Gasoline Taxes," *Economic Letters*, 83(1), April 2004: 55–60.

Chouinard, Hayley H., David Davis, Jeffrey T. LaFrance, and Jeffrey M. Perloff, "Fat Taxes: Big Money for Small Change," *Forum for Health Economics & Policy*, 10(2, 2), June 2007.

Clemens, Jeffrey, and Joshua D. Gottlieb, "Do Physicians' Financial Incentives Affect Medical Treatment and Patient Health?" *American Economic Review*, 104(4), April 2014: 1320–1349.

Coady, David, et al., "How Large Are Global Energy Subsidies?" *World Development*, 91, March 2017: 11–27.

Coase, Ronald H., "The Problem of Social Cost," *Journal of Law and Economics*, 3, October 1960: 1–44.

Cohen, Peter, et al., "Using Big Data to Estimate Consumer Surplus: The Case of Uber," NBER Working Paper, 2016.

Cohen, Peter, et al., "Using Big Data to Estimate Consumer Surplus: The Case of Uber," NBER Working Paper, 2016.

Cohen, Wesley M., Richard R. Nelson, and John P. Walsh, "Protecting Their Intellectual Assets: Appropriability Conditions and Why U.S. Manufacturing Firms Patent (or Not)," NBER Working Paper, 2000.

Cookson, J. Anthony, "Anticipated Entry and Entry Deterrence: Evidence from the American Casino Industry," *Management Science*, 64(5), May 2018: 2325–2344.

Crawford, David, John Del Roccili, and Richard Voith, "Comments on Proposed Tax Reforms," Econsult Corporation, June 9, 2004.

Crost, Benjamin, and Santiago Guerrero, The Effect of Alcohol Availability on Marijuana Use: Evidence from the Minimum Legal Drinking Age," *Journal of Health Economics*, 31(1), January 2012: 112–121.

Currie, Janet, and Firouz Gahvari, "Transfers in Cash and In-Kind: Theory Meets the Data," *Journal of Economic Literature*, 46(2), June 2008: 333–383.

Cutler, David M., Edward L. Glaeser, and Jesse M. Shapiro, "Why Have Americans Become More Obese?" *Journal of Economic Perspectives*, 17(3), Summer 2003: 93–118.

David, Guy, and Sara Markowitz, "Side Effects of Competition: The Role of Advertising and Promotion in Pharmaceutical Markets," NBER Working Paper, 2011.

Davies, James B., Susanna Sandström, Anthony Shorrocks, and Edward N. Wolff, "Estimating the Level and Distribution of Global Household Wealth," World Institute for Development Economic Research Working Paper, 2007.

Davis, Lucas, "Goin' for Broke in Texas . . . Protecting the Environment without Slowing Economic Growth," energyathaas.wordpress.com/2014/12/01/goin-for-broke-in-texas-protecting-the-environment-without-slowing-economic-growth, 2014.

Davis, Lucas W., "The Environmental Cost of Global Fuel Subsidies," *The Energy Journal*, 38, 2017: 7–27.

Davis, Lucas W., and Alex Chun, "A Deeper Look into the Fragmented Residential Solar Market," energyathaas .wordpress.com/2015/06/08/a-deeper-look-into-the-fragmented-residential-solar-market/, June 8, 2015.

Davis, Lucas W., and Lutz Kilian, "The Allocative Cost of Price Ceilings in the U.S. Residential Market for Natural Gas," *Journal of Political Economics*, 119(2), April 2011: 212–241.

Davis, Lucas W., and Erich Muehlegger, "Do Americans Consume Too Little Natural Gas? An Empirical Test of Marginal Cost Pricing," *Rand Journal of Economics*, 41(4), Winter 2010: 791–810.

De Loechker, Jan, and Jan Eeckhout, "Global Market Power," NBER Working Paper, 2018.

Deacon, Robert T., and Jon Sonstelie, "The Welfare Costs of Rationing by Waiting," *Economic Inquiry*, 27(2), April 1989: 179–196.

Dean, David, et al., *The Internet Economy in the G-20*, Boston Consulting Group, 2012, energyathaas.wordpress .com/2014/12/01/goin-for-broke-in-texas-protecting-the-environment-without-slowing-economic-growth/.

DeCicca, Philip, Donald S. Kenkel, and Feng Liu, "Reservation Prices: An Economic Analysis of Cigarette Purchases on Indian Reservations," National Bureau of Economic Research, 2014.

DeCicca, Philip, and Donald S. Kenkel, "Synthesizing Econometric Evidence: The Case of Demand Elasticity Estimates," National Bureau of Economic Research, 2015.

Delipalla, Sophia, and Michael Keen, "The Comparison Between Ad Valorem and Specific Taxation Under Imperfect Competition," *Journal of Public Economics*, 49(3), December 1992: 351–367.

DellaVigna, Stefano, "Psychology and Economics: Evidence from the Field," *Journal of Economic Literature*, 47(2), June 2009: 315–372.

de Mello, Joao, Daniel Mejia, and Lucia Suarez, "The Pharmacological Channel Revisited: Alcohol Sales Restrictions and Crime in Bogotá," Documento CEDE No. 2013-20, 2013.

Devine, Hilary, Tinh Doan, and Philip Stevens, "Explaining Productivity Distribution in New Zealand Industries: The Effects of Input Quality on Firm Productivity Differences," New Zealand Ministry of Economic Development, 2012.

Diewert, W. Edwin, and Alice O. Nakamura, eds., *Essays in Index Number Theory*, Vol. 1. New York: North Holland, 1993.

Dixit, Avinash K., and Robert S. Pindyck, *Investment Under Uncertainty*. Princeton, NJ: Princeton University Press, 1994.

Duan, Ying, Edith S. Hotchkiss, and Yawen Jiao, "Corporate Pensions and Financial Distress," SSRN Working Paper, January 2015.

Dunham, Wayne R., "Moral Hazard and the Market for Used Automobiles," *Review of Industrial Organization*, 23(1), August 2003: 65–83.

Dunne, Timothy, Shawn D. Klimek, Mark J. Roberts, and Daniel Yi Xu, "Entry, Exit, and the Determinants of Market Structure," *Rand Journal of Economics*, 44(3), Fall 2013: 462–487.

Eastwood, David B., and John A. Craven, "Food Demand and Savings in a Complete, Extended, Linear Expenditure System," *American Journal of Agricultural Economics*, 63(3), August 1981: 544–549.

Eckel, Catherine C., and Philip J. Grossman, "Altruism in Anonymous Dictator Games," *Games and Economic Behavior*, 16, 1996: 181–191.

Economides, Nicholas, "The Economics of Networks," *International Journal of Industrial Organization*, 14(6), October 1996: 673–699.

Econsult Corporation, *Choosing the Best Mix of Taxes for Philadelphia: An Econometric Analysis of the Impacts of Tax Rates on Tax Bases, Tax Revenue, and the Private Economy*, Report to the Philadelphia Tax Reform Commission, 2003.

Edelman, Benjamin, "Adverse Selection in Online 'Trust' Certifications and Search Results," *Electronic Commerce Research and Applications*, 10(1), January–February 2011: 17–25.

Edlin, Aaron S., and Pinar Karaca-Mandic, "The Accident Externality from Driving," *Journal of Political Economy*, 114(5), October 2006: 931–955.

Einav, Liran, Dan Knoepfle, Jonathan D. Levin, and Neel Sundaresan, "Sales Taxes and Internet Commerce," NBER Working Paper, 2012.

Ellsberg, Daniel, "Risk, Ambiguity, and the Savage Axioms," *Quarterly Journal of Economics*, 75(4), November 1961: 643–669.

Elshurafa, Amro M., et al., "Estimating the Learning Curve of Solar PV Balance–of–system for over 20 Countries: Implications and Policy Recommendations," *Journal of Cleaner Production*, 2018: forthcoming.

Engström, Per, and Eskil Forsell, "Demand Effects of Consumers' Stated and Revealed Preferences," Uppsala University Working Paper, 2013.

Environmental Protection Agency, *The Benefits and Costs of the Clean Air Act from 1990 to 2020*, www.epa.gov/clean-air-act-overview/benefits-and-costs-clean-air-act-1990-2020-report-documents-and-graphics, 2011.

Epple, Dennis, et al., "Market Power and Price Discrimination in the US Market for Higher Education," NBER Working Paper, 2017.

Epstein, Andrew J., "Do Cardiac Surgery Report Cards Reduce Mortality? Assessing the Evidence," *Medical Care Research and Review*, 63(4), August 2006: 403–426.

Evers, Michiel, Ruud De Mooij, and Daniel Van Vuuren, "The Wage Elasticity of Labour Supply: A Synthesis of Empirical Estimates," *De Economist*, 156(1), March 2008: 25–43.

Fan, Victoria Y., Dean T. Jamison, Lawrence H. Summers, "The Inclusive Cost of Pandemic Influenza Risk," NBER Working Paper, 2016.

Farrell, Joseph, and Matthew Rabin, "Cheap Talk," *Journal of Economic Perspectives*, 10(3), Summer 1996: 103–118.

Feng, Cong, Scott Fay, and K. Sivakumar, "Overbidding in Electronic Auctions: Factors Influencing the Propensity to Overbid and the Magnitude of Overbidding," *Journal of the Academy of Marketing Science*, 44(2), March 2016: 241–260.

Fisher, Franklin M., "The Social Cost of Monopoly and Regulation: Posner Reconsidered," *Journal of Political Economy*, 93(2), April 1985: 410–416.

Flath, David, "Industrial Concentration, Price-Cost Margins, and Innovation," *Japan and the World Economy*, 23(2), March 2011: 129–139.

Foulon, Jerome, Paul Lanoie, and Benoit Laplante, "Incentives for Pollution Control: Regulation or Information?" *Journal of Environmental Economics and Management*, 44(1), July 2002: 169–187.

Fowlie, Meredith, et al., "Default Effects and Follow-On Behavior: Evidence from an Electricity Pricing Program," Energy Institute at Haas, 2017.

Fox, Jeremy T., and Valerie Smeets, "Does Input Quality Drive Measured Differences in Firm Productivity?" *International Economic Review*, 52(4), November 2011: 961–989.

Friedman, Milton, and Leonard J. Savage, "The Utility Analysis of Choices Involving Risk," *Journal of Political Economy*, 56(4), August 1948: 279–304.

Fu, Chao, and Jesse Gregory, "Estimation of an Equilibrium Model with Externalities: Post-Disaster Neighborhood Rebuilding," *Econometrica*, forthcoming.

Furnham, Adrian, "Understanding the Meaning of Tax: Young Peoples' Knowledge of the Principles of Taxation," *Journal of Socio-Economics*, 34(5), October 2005: 703–713.

Garratt, Rod, Mark Walker, and John Wooders, "Behavior in Second-Price Auctions by Highly Experienced eBay Buyers and Sellers," *Experimental Economics*, 15(1), March 2012: 44–57.

Garrett, Thomas A., "An International Comparison and Analysis of Lotteries and the Distribution of Lottery Expenditures," *International Review of Applied Economics*, 15(20), April 2001: 213–227.

Gasmi, Farid, Jean-Jacques Laffont, and Quang H. Vuong, "Econometric Analysis of Collusive Behavior in a Soft-Drink Market," *Journal of Economics and Management Strategy*, 1(2), Summer 1992: 277–311.

Gere, Judith, and Ulrich Schimmack, "Benefits of Income: Associations with Life Satisfaction Among Earners and Homemakers," *Personality and Individual Differences*, 119, December 2017: 92–95.

Ghose, Anindya, and Sang Pil Han, "Estimating Demand for Mobile Applications in the New Economy," *Management Science*, 60(6), June 2014: 1470–1488.

Goldfarb, Avi, "What Is Different About Online Advertising?" *Review of Industrial Organization*, 44(2), March 2014: 115–129.

Goldfarb, Avi, and Catherine E. Tucker, "Search Engine Advertising: Channel Substitution when Pricing Ads to Context," *Management Science*, 57(3), March 2011: 458–470.

Golec, Joseph, and Maurry Tamarkin, "Do Bettors Prefer Long Shots Because They Are Risk Lovers, or Are They Just Overconfident?" *Journal of Risk and Uncertainty*, 11(1), July 1995: 51–64.

Gollin, Douglas, Casper Worm Hansen, and Asger Wingender, "Two Blades of Grass: The Impact of the Green Revolution," NBER Working Paper, 2018.

Grabowski, David C., and Michael A. Morrisey, "Do Higher Gasoline Taxes Save Lives?" *Economics Letters*, 90(1), January 2006: 51–55.

Grafton, R. Quentin, and Michael B. Ward, "Prices Versus Rationing: Marshallian Surplus and Mandatory Water Restrictions," *Economic Record*, 84(S1), September 2008: S57–S65.

Green, Richard, Richard Howitt, and Carlo Russo, "Estimation of Supply and Demand Elasticities of California Commodities," manuscript, May 2005.

Gruber, Jonathan H., and Sendhil Mullainathan, "Do Cigarette Taxes Make Smokers Happier," *Advances in Economic Analysis & Policy*, 5(1), 2005: Article 4.

Gruber, Jonathan, Anihdya Sen, and Mark Stabile, "Estimating Price Elasticities When There Is Smuggling: The Sensitivity of Smoking to Price in Canada," *Journal of Health Economics*, 22(5), September 2003: 821–842.

Guinnane, Timothy W., "The Historical Fertility Transition: A Guide for Economists," *Journal of Economic Literature*, 49(3), September 2011: 589–614.

Guner, Nezih, Remzi Kaygusuz, and Gustavo Ventura, "The Impact of Child-Related Transfers on Labour Supply, Welfare, and the Wider U.S. Economy," voxeu.org/article/child-related-transfers-labour-supply-and-welfare, 2017.

Hall, Robert E., "New Evidence on the Markup of Prices Over Marginal Costs and the Role of Mega-Firms in the US Economy," NBER Working Paper, 2018.

Hall, Robert E., and David M. Lilien, "Efficient Wage Bargains Under Uncertain Supply and Demand," *American Economic Review*, 69(5), December 1979: 868–879.

Hamilton, Stephen F., "The Comparative Efficiency of Ad Valorem and Specific Taxes Under Monopoly and Monopsony," *Economics Letters*, 63(2), May 1999: 235–238.

Hanson, Andrew, and Ryan Sullivan, "The Incidence of Tobacco Taxation: Evidence from Geographic Micro-Level Data," *National Tax Journal*, 62(4), December 2009: 677–698.

Harkness, Joseph, and Sandra Newman, "The Interactive Effects of Housing Assistance and Food Stamps on Food Spending," *Journal of Housing Economics*, 12(3), September 2003: 224–249.

Harrell, et al., "Expectancies for Cigarettes, E-Cigarettes, and Nicotine Replacement Therapies Among E-Cigarette Users (aka Vapers)," *Nicotine & Tobacco Research*, 17(2), February 2015: 193–200.

Hartmann, Wesley R., and Daniel Klapper, "Super Bowl Ads," *Marketing Science* 37(1), 2017: 78–96.

Haskel, Jonathan, and Raffaella Sadun, "Regulation and UK Retailing Productivity: Evidence from Micro Data," *Economica*, 79, July 2012: 425–448.

Hasker, Kevin, Bibo Jiang, and Robin C. Sickles, "Estimating Consumer Surplus in eBay Computer Monitor Auctions," in R. C. Sickles and W. C. Horrace, eds., *Festschrift in Honor of Peter Schmidt: Econometric Methods and Applications*. New York: Springer, 2014, Chapter 4: 83–102.

Hausman, Catherine, and Ryan Kellogg, "Welfare and Distributional Implications of Shale Gas," *Brookings Papers on Economic Activity*, 50(1), Spring 2015: 71–139.

Hendel, Igal, and Aviv Nevo, "Intertemporal Price Discrimination in Storable Goods Markets," *American Economic Review*, 103(7), December 2013: 2722–2751.

Henderson, Jason, "FAQs About Mad Cow Disease and Its Impacts," *The Main Street Economist*, December 2003.

Herod, Roger, "Analyzing the Metrics of Global Mobility Programs," *International HR Journal*, Summer 2008: 9–15.

Highhouse, Scott, Michael J. Zickar, and Maya Yankelevich, "Would You Work If You Won the Lottery? Tracking Changes in the American Work Ethic," *Journal of Applied Psychology*, 95(2), March 2010: 349–357.

Hill, Jason, S. Polasky, E. Nelson, D. Tilman, H. Huo, L. Ludwig, J. Neumann, H. Zheng, and D. Bonta, "Climate Change and Health Costs of Air Emissions from Biofuels and Gasoline," *Proceedings of the National Academy of Sciences*, 106(6), February 2009: 2077–2082.

Ho, Jason Y. C., Tirtha Dhar, and Charles B. Weinberg, "Playoff Payoff: Super Bowl Advertising for Movies," *International Journal of Research in Marketing*, 26(3), September 2009: 168–179.

Holt, Matthew, "A Multimarket Bounded Price Variation Model Under Rational Expectations: Corn and Soybeans in the United States," *American Journal of Agricultural Economics*, 74(1), February 1992: 10–20.

Hong, Seung-Hyun, and Frank A. Wolak, "Relative Prices and Electronic Substitution: Changes in Household-Level Demand for Postal Delivery Services from 1986 to 2004," *Journal of Econometrics*, 145(1–2), July 2008: 226–242.

Hossain, Md. Moyazzem, Tapati Basak, and Ajit Kumar Majumder, "An Application of Non-Linear Cobb-Douglas Production Function to Selected Manufacturing Industries in Bangladesh," *Open Journal of Statistics*, 2, October 2012: 460–468.

Hotelling, Harold, "The Economics of Exhaustible Resources," *Journal of Political Economy*, 39(2), April 1931: 137–175.

Howard, David H., Guy David, and Jason Hockenberry, "Selective Hearing: Physician-Ownership and Physicians' Response to New Evidence," *Journal of Economics & Management Strategy*, 26(1), Spring 2017: 152–168.

Hoynes, Hilary W., and Diane Whitmore Schanzenbach, "Consumption Responses to In-Kind Transfers: Evidence from the Introduction of the Food Stamp Program," *American Economic Journal: Applied Economics*, 1(4), October 2009: 109–139.

Hsieh, Wen-Jen, "Test of Variable Output and Scale Elasticities for 20 U.S. Manufacturing Industries," *Applied Economics Letters*, 2(8), August 1995: 284–287.

Irwin, Douglas A., "The Welfare Cost of Autarky: Evidence from the Jeffersonian Trade Embargo, 1807–09," *Review of International Economics*, 13(4), September 2005: 631–645.

Irwin, Douglas A., and Nina Pavcnik, "Airbus versus Boeing Revisited: International Competition in the Aircraft Market," *Journal of International Economics*, 64(2), December 2004: 223–245.

Ito, Harumi, and Darin Lee, "Assessing the Impact of the September 11 Terrorist Attacks on U.S. Airline Demand," *Journal of Economics and Business*, 57(1), January–February 2005: 75–95.

Jacobson, Michael F., and Kelly D. Brownell, "Small Taxes on Soft Drinks and Snack Foods to Promote Health," *American Journal of Public Health*, 90(6), June 2000: 854–857.

Jensen, Robert T., and Nolan H. Miller, "Giffen Behavior and Subsistence Consumption," *American Economic Review*, 98(4), September 2008: 1553–1577.

Jetter, Karen M., James A. Chalfant, and David A. Sumner, "Does 5-a-Day Pay?" *AIC Issues Brief*, No. 27, August 2004.

Jha, Prabhat, and Frank J. Chaloupka, "The Economics of Global Tobacco Control," *BMJ*, www.bmj.com/, 321, August 2000: 358–361.

Jhamb, Jordan, Dhaval Dave, and Gregory Colman, "The Patient Protection and Affordable Care Act and the Utilization of Health Care Services Among Young Adults," *International Journal of Health and Economic Development*, 1(1), January 2015: 8–25.

Johnson, Ronald N., and Charles J. Romeo, "The Impact of Self-Service Bans in the Retail Gasoline Market," *Review of Economics and Statistics*, 82(4), November 2000: 625–633.

Jordà, Òscar, et al., "The Rate of Return on Everything, 1870–2015," NBER Working Paper, 2017.

Kahneman, Daniel, Jack L. Knetsch, and Richard H. Thaler, "Experimental Tests of the Endowment Effect and the Coase Theorem," *Journal of Political Economy*, 98(6), December 1990: 1325–1348.

Kahneman, Daniel, and Amos Tversky, "Prospect Theory: An Analysis of Decision Under Risk," *Econometrica*, 47(2), March 1979: 313–327.

Kaiser, Ulrich, and Julian Wright, "Price Structure in Two-Sided Markets: Evidence from the Magazine Industry," *International Journal of Industrial Organization*, 24(1), January 2006: 1–28.

Kamiya, Shinichi, et al., "What Is the Impact of Successful Cyberattacks on Target Firms?" NBER Working Paper, 2018.

Kan, Kamhon, "Cigarette Smoking and Self-Control, *Journal of Health Economics*, 26(1), January 2007: 61–81.

Karp, Larry, "Global Warming and Hyperbolic Discounting," *Journal of Public Economics*, 89(2–3), February 2005: 261–282.

Katz, Michael L., and Carl Shapiro, "Systems Competition and Network Effects," *Journal of Economic Perspectives*, 8(2), 1994: 93–115.

Keane, Michael P., "Labor Supply and Taxes: A Survey," *Journal of Economic Literature*, 49(4), December 2011: 961–1075.

Keeler, Theodore E., Teh-Wei Hu, Paul G. Barnett, and Willard G. Manning, "Taxation, Regulation, and Addiction: A Demand Function for Cigarettes Based on Time-Series Evidence," *Journal of Health Economics*, 12(1), April 1993: 1–18.

Keeler, Theodore E., Teh-Wei Hu, Michael Ong, and Hai-Yen Sung, "The U.S. National Tobacco Settlement: The Effects of Advertising and Price Changes on Cigarette Consumption," *Applied Economics*, 36(15), August 2004: 1623–1629.

Kennickell, Arthur B., "Ponds and Streams: Wealth and Income in the U.S., 1989 to 2007," Federal Reserve Board, 2009.

Kennickell, Arthur B., "Tossed and Turned: Wealth Dynamics of U.S. Households 2007–2009," Federal Reserve Board, 2011.

Kim, DaeHwan, and J. Paul Leigh, "Are Meals at Full-Service and Fast-Food Restaurants Normal or Inferior?" *Population Health Management*, 14(6), December 2011: 307–315.

Kim, Jin-Woo, *When Are Super Bowl Advertisings Super?* University of Texas at Arlington Ph.D. dissertation, 2011.

Kim, Jin-Woo, Traci H. Freling, and Douglas B. Grisaffe, "The Secret Sauce for Superbowl Advertising," *Journal of Advertising Research*, 53(2), June 2013: 134–149.

Klemperer, Paul, *Auctions: Theory and Practice*. Princeton, NJ: Princeton University Press, 2004.

Knetsch, Jack L., "Preferences and Nonreversibility of Indifference Curves," *Journal of Economic Behavior and Organization*, 1992, 17(1): 131–139.

Knittel, Christopher R., and Victor Stango, "Celebrity Endorsements, Firm Value and Reputation Risk: Evidence from the Tiger Woods Scandal," *Management Science*, 60(1), January 2014: 21–37.

Kotchen, Matthew J., and Nicholas E. Burger, "Should We Drill in the Arctic National Wildlife Refuge? An Economic Perspective," NBER Working Paper, 2007.

Kowalski, Amanda E., "Extrapolation Using Selection and Moral Hazard Heterogeneity from Within the Oregon Health Insurance Experiment," NBER Working Paper, 2018.

Kreps, David M., and Jose A. Scheinkman, "Quantity Precommitment and Bertrand Competition Yield Cournot Outcomes," *Bell Journal of Economics*, 14(2), Autumn 1983: 326–337.

Kridel, Donald L., "Residential Demand for Wireless Telephony," in James Alleman, Áine Marie Patricia Ní-Shúilleabháin, and Paul N. Rappoport, eds., *The Economics of Information, Communication, and Entertainment*. New York: Springer, 2014: 171–182.

Krueger, Alan B., "Where Have All the Workers Gone? An Inquiry into the Decline of the U.S. Labor Force Participation Rate," *Brookings Paper on Economic Activity*, Fall 2017: 1–59.

Krueger, Alan B., and Orley Ashenfelter, "Theory and Evidence on Employer Collusion in the Franchise Sector," Princeton University Working Paper, 2017.

Kuroda, Sachiko, and Isamu Yamamoto, "Estimating Frisch Labor Supply Elasticity in Japan," *Journal of Japanese International Economies*, 22(4), December 2008: 566–585.

Lazear, Edward P., Kathryn L. Shaw, and Christopher T. Stanton, "Making Do with Less: Working Harder During Recessions," *Journal of Labor Economics*, 34(S1), January 2016: S333–S360.

Lazear, Edward P., Kathryn L. Shaw, and Christopher T. Stanton, "The Value of Bosses," *Journal of Labor Economics*, 33(4), October 2015: 823–861.

Lee, Young Han, and Ulrike Malmendier, "The Bidder's Curse," *American Economic Review*, 101(2), April 2011: 749–787.

Lelieveld, J., et al., "The Contribution of Outdoor Air Pollution Sources to Premature Mortality on a Global Scale," *Nature*, 525, September 2015: 367–371.

Levin, Richard C., Alvin K. Klevorick, Richard R. Nelson, and Sidney G. Winter, "Appropriating the Returns from Industrial Research and Development," *Brookings Papers on Economic Activity*, 3 (Special Issue on Microeconomics), 1987: 783–820.

Levitt, Steven D., and Jack Porter, "How Dangerous Are Drinking Drivers," *Journal of Political Economy*, 109(5), December 2001: 1198–1237.

Levy, Douglas E., and Ellen Meara, "The Effect of the 1998 Master Settlement Agreement on Prenatal Smoking," *Journal of Health Economics*, 25(2), March 2006: 276–294.

Li, Shanjun, Roger von Haefen, and Christopher Timmins, "How Do Gasoline Prices Affect Fleet Fuel Economy?" *American Economic Journal: Economic Policy*, 1(2), August 2009: 113–137.

Liddle, Brantley, "The Systemic, Long-Run Relation among Gasoline Demand, Gasoline Price, Income, and Vehicle Ownership In OECD Countries: Evidence from Panel Cointegration and Causality Modeling," *Transportation Research Part D: Transport and Environment*, 17(4), June 2012: 237–331.

Liebenstein, Harvey, "Bandwagon, Snob, and Veblen Effects in the Theory of Consumers' Demand," *Quarterly Journal of Economics*, 64(2), May 1950: 183–207.

Lindqvist, Erik, Robert Östling, and David Cesarini, "Long-Run Effects of Lottery Wealth on Psychological Well-Being, NBER Working Paper, 2018.

Lipsey, R. G., and Kelvin Lancaster, "The General Theory of Second Best," *Review of Economic Studies*, 24(1), October 1956: 11–32.

List, John A., "Does Market Experience Eliminate Market Anomalies?" *Quarterly Journal of Economics*, 118(1), February 2003: 41–71.

Lopez, Rigoberto A., and Emilio Pagoulatos, "Rent Seeking and the Welfare Cost of Trade Barriers," *Public Choice*, 79(1–2), April 1994: 149–160.

Luchansky, Matthew S., and James Monks, "Supply and Demand Elasticities in the U.S. Ethanol Fuel Market," *Energy Economics*, 31(3), May 2009: 403–410.

Lusk, Jayson L., and Amanda Weaver, "An Experiment on Cash and In-Kind Transfers with Application to Food Assistance Programs," *Food Policy*, 68, April 2017: 186–192.

MacAvoy, Paul W., "Tacit Collusion Under Regulation in the Pricing of Interstate Long-Distance Services," *Journal of Economics and Management Strategy*, 4(2), Summer 1995: 147–185.

MacAvoy, Paul W., *The Natural Gas Market*, New Haven: Yale University Press, 2000.

MacCrimmon, Kenneth R., and M. Toda, "The Experimental Determination of Indifference Curves," *Review of Economic Studies*, 56(3), July 1969: 433–451.

Machina, Mark, "Dynamic Consistency and Non-Expected Utility Models of Choice Under Uncertainty," *Journal of Economic Literature*, 27(4), December 1989: 1622–1668.

MacKie-Mason, Jeffrey K., and Robert S. Pindyck, "Cartel Theory and Cartel Experience in International Minerals Markets," in R. L. Gordon, H. D. Jacoby, and M. B. Zimmerman, eds., *Energy: Markets and Regulation: Essays in Honor of M. A. Adelman*. Cambridge, MA: MIT Press, 1986.

Madden, Janice F., *The Economics of Sex Discrimination*. Lexington, MA: Heath, 1973.

Markowitz, Sara, et al., "Estimating the Relationship Between Alcohol Policies and Criminal Violence and Victimization," NBER Working Paper, 2012.

Marks, Steven V., "A Reassessment of Empirical Evidence on the U.S. Sugar Program," in S. V. Marks and K. Maskus, eds., *The Economics and Politics of World Sugar Policy*. Ann Arbor, MI: University of Michigan Press, 1993.

McPhail, Lihong Lu, and Bruce A. Babcock, "Impact of US Biofuel Policy on US Corn and Gasoline Price Variability," *Energy*, 37(1), February 2012: 505–513.

Medoff, Marshall H., "A Pooled Time-Series Analysis of Abortion Demand," *Population Research and Policy Review*, 16(6), December 1997: 597–605.

Monteiro, Tiago, Marco Vasconcelos, and Alex Kacelnik, "Starlings Uphold Principles of Economic Rationality for Delay and Probability of Reward," *Proceedings of the Royal Society B*, 280(1756), April 2013: 1–6.

Moschini, Giancarlo, and Karl D. Meilke, "Production Subsidy and Countervailing Duties in Vertically Related Markets: The Hog-Pork Case Between Canada and the United States," *American Journal of Agricultural Economics*, 74(4), November 1992: 951–961.

Nash, John F., "Equilibrium Points in *n*-Person Games," *Proceedings of the National Academy of Sciences*, 36, 1950: 48–49.

Nash, John F., "Non-Cooperative Games," *Annals of Mathematics*, 54(2), July 1951: 286–295.

Neto, João Quariguasi Frota, Jacqueline Bloemhof, and Charles Corbett, "Market Prices of Remanufactured, Used and New Items: Evidence from eBay," *International Journal of Production Economics*, 171(3), 2016: 371–380.

Neumark, David, J. M. Ian Salas, and William Wascher, "Revisiting the Minimum Wage-Employment Debate: Throwing Out the Baby with the Bathwater?" *Industrial Labor Relations Review*, 67(3 supplement), May 2014: 608–648.

O'Donoghue, Ted, and Matthew Rabin, "Doing It Now or Later," *American Economic Review*, 89(1), March 1999: 103–124.

OECD (Organization for Economic Cooperation and Development), *Agricultural Policies in OECD Countries*, 2009.

Oliver, Matthew E., and Charles F. Mason, "Natural Gas Pipeline Regulation in the United States: Past, Present, and Future," *Foundations and Trends in Microeconomics*, 11(4), 2018: 227–288.

Oxfam, *Dumping Without Borders*, Oxfam Briefing Paper 50, 2003.

Paltsev, Sergey, et al., "Assessment of U.S. Cap-and-Trade Proposals," NBER Working Paper, 2007.

Panzar, John C., and Robert D. Willig, "Economies of Scale in Multi-Output Production," *Quarterly Journal of Economics*, 91(3), August 1977: 481–493.

Panzar, John C., and Robert D. Willig, "Economies of Scope," *American Economic Review*, 71(2), May 1981: 268–272.

Parry, Ian W. H., Margaret Walls, and Winston Harrington, "Automobile Externalities and Policies," *Journal of Economic Literature*, 45(2), June 2007: 373–399.

Perloff, Jeffrey M., and Ximing Wu, "Tax Incidence Varies Across the Price Distribution," *Economic Letters*, 96(1), July 2007: 116–119.

Perry, Martin K., "Forward Integration by Alcoa: 1888–1930," *Journal of Industrial Economics*, 29(1), September 1980: 37–53.

Pesko, Michael, and Casey Warman, "The Effect of Prices on Youth Cigarette and E-Cigarette Use: Economic Substitutes or Complements?" SSRN Working Paper, 2017.

Plott, Charles R., and Kathryn Zeiler, "The Willingness to Pay—Willingness to Accept Gap, the 'Endowment Effect,' Subject Misconceptions, and Experimental Procedures for Eliciting Values," *American Economic Review*, 95(3), June 2005: 530–545.

Pollak, Robert A., *The Theory of the Cost-of-Living Index*. New York: Oxford University Press, 1989.

Posner, Richard A., "The Social Cost of Monopoly and Regulation," *Journal of Political Economy*, 83(4), August 1975: 807–827.

Pratt, John W., "Risk Aversion in the Small and in the Large," *Econometrica*, 32(1–2), January/April 1964: 122–136.

Prescott, Edward C., "Why Do Americans Work So Much More Than Europeans?" *Federal Reserve Bank of Minneapolis Quarterly Review*, 28(1), July 2004: 2–13.

Prince, Jeffrey T., "Repeat Purchase amid Rapid Quality Improvement: Structural Estimation of Demand for Personal Computers," *Journal of Economics & Management Strategy*, 17(1), Spring 2008: 1–33.

Rabin, Matthew, "Psychology and Economics," *Journal of Economic Literature*, 36(1), March 1998: 11–46.

Rao, Justin M., and David H. Reiley, "The Economics of Spam," *Journal of Economic Perspectives*, 26(3), Summer 2012: 87–110.

Rawls, John, *A Theory of Justice*. New York: Oxford University Press, 1971.

Regan, Tracy L., "Generic Entry, Price Competition, and Market Segmentation in the Prescription Drug Market," *International Journal of Industrial Organization*, 26(4), July 2008: 930–948.

Richards, Timothy J., and Luis Padilla, "Promotion and Fast Food Demand," *American Journal of Agricultural Economics*, 91(1), February 2009: 168–183.

Roberts, Mark J., and Larry Samuelson, "An Empirical Analysis of Dynamic Nonprice Competition in an Oligopolistic Industry," *Rand Journal of Economics*, 19(2), Summer 1988: 200–220.

Roberts, Michael J., and Wolfram Schlenker, "Identifying Supply and Demand Elasticities of Agricultural Commodities: Implications for the US Ethanol Mandate," *American Economic Review*, 103(6), October 2013: 2265–2295.

Robidoux, Benoît, and John Lester, "Econometric Estimates of Scale Economies in Canadian Manufacturing," Working Paper No. 88–4, Canadian Department of Finance, 1988.

Robidoux, Benoît, and John Lester, "Econometric Estimates of Scale Economies in Canadian Manufacturing," *Applied Economics*, 24(1), January 1992: 113–122.

Rohlfs, Jeffrey H., "A Theory of Interdependent Demand for a Communications Service," *Bell Journal of Economics and Management Science*, 5(1), Spring 1974: 16–37.

Rohlfs, Jeffrey H., *Bandwagon Effects in High-Technology Industries*. Cambridge, MA: MIT Press, 2001.

Rossi, Robert J., and Terry Armstrong, *Studies of Intercollegiate Athletics*. Palo Alto, CA: Center for the Study of Athletics, American Institutes for Research, 1989.

Rousseas, S. W., and A. G. Hart, "Experimental Verification of a Composite Indifference Map," *Journal of Political Economy*, 59(4), August 1951: 288–318.

Ruffin, R. J., "Cournot Oligopoly and Competitive Behavior," *Review of Economic Studies*, 38(116), October 1971: 493–502.

Salgado, Hugo, "A Dynamic Firm Conduct and Market Power: The Computer Processing Market Under Learning-by-Doing," U.C. Berkeley Ph.D. dissertation, Chapter 2, 2008.

Salop, Joanne, and Steven C. Salop, "Self-Selection and Turnover in the Labor Market," *Quarterly Journal of Economics*, 90(4), November 1976: 619–627.

Salop, Steven C., "The Noisy Monopolist: Imperfect Information, Price Dispersion, and Price Discrimination," *Review of Economic Studies*, 44(3), October 1977: 393–406.

Salop, Steven C., "Practices That (Credibly) Facilitate Oligopoly Coordination," in Joseph E. Stiglitz and G. Frank Mathewson, eds., *New Developments in the Analysis of Market Structure*. Cambridge, MA: MIT Press, 1986.

Salvo, Alberto, and Cristian Huse, "Build It, But Will They Come? Evidence from Consumer Choice Between Gasoline and Sugarcane Ethanol," *Journal of Environmental Economics and Management*, 66(2), September 2013: 251–279.

Samuelson, Paul A., *Foundations of Economic Analysis*. Cambridge, MA: Harvard University Press, 1947.

Sappington, David E. M., and Dennis L. Weisman, "Price Cap Regulation: What Have We Learned from 25 Years of Experience in the Telecommunications Industry?" *Journal of Regulatory Economics*, 38(3), 2010: 227–257.

Scherer, F. M., "An Early Application of the Average Total Cost Concept," *Journal of Economic Literature*, 39(3), September 2001: 897–901.

Schmalensee, Richard, Paul L. Joskow, A. Denny Ellerman, Juan Pablo Montero, and Elizabeth M. Bailey, "An Interim Evaluation of Sulfur Dioxide Emissions Trading," *Journal of Economic Perspectives*, 12(3), Summer 1998: 53–68.

Schmitz, Hendrik, "More Health Care Utilization with More Insurance Coverage? Evidence from a Latent Class Model with German Data," *Applied Economics*, 44(34), December 2012: 4455–4468.

Schoemaker, Paul J. H., "The Expected Utility Model: Its Variants, Purposes, Evidence and Limitation," *Journal of Economic Literature*, 20(2), June 1982: 529–563.

Shapiro, Bradley T., "Positive Spillovers and Free Riding in Advertising of Prescription Pharmaceuticals: The Case of Antidepressants," *Journal of Political Economy*, 126(1), February 2018: 381–437.

Shapiro, Carl, and Joseph E. Stiglitz, "Equilibrium Unemployment as a Worker Discipline Device," *American Economic Review*, 74(3), June 1984: 434–444.

Shapiro, Carl, and Hal R. Varian, *Information Rules: A Strategic Guide to the Network Economy*. Boston: Harvard Business School Press, 1999.

Shapiro, Jesse M., "Is There a Daily Discount Rate? Evidence from the Food Stamp Nutrition Cycle," *Journal of Public Economics*, 89(2–3), February 2004: 303–325.

Shapiro, Joseph S., and Reed Walker, "Why Is Pollution from U.S. Manufacturing Declining? The Roles of Trade, Regulation, Productivity, and Preferences," NBER Working Paper, 2015.

Shearer, Bruce, "Piece Rates, Fixed Wages and Incentives: Evidence from a Field Experiment," *Review of Economic Studies*, 71(2), April 2004: 513–534.

Sheehan-Connor, Damien, "Environmental Policy and Vehicle Safety: The Impact of Gasoline Taxes," *Economic Inquiry*, 53(3), July 2015: 1606–1629.

Shelton, Cameron A., and Nathan Falk, "Policy Uncertainty and Manufacturing Investment: Evidence from U.S. State Elections," *American Economic Journal: Economic Policy*, November 2018: 135–152.

Shiller, Ben, and Joel Waldfogel, "Music for a Song: An Empirical Look at Uniform Song Pricing and Its Alternatives," *The Journal of Industrial Economics*, 59(4), December 2011: 630–660.

Simon, Kosali, Aparna Soni, and John Cawley, "The Impact of Health Insurance on Preventive Care and Health Behaviors: Evidence from the First Two Years of the ACA Medicaid Expansions," *Journal of Policy Analysis and Management*, 36(2), Spring 2017: 390–417.

Skeath, Susan E., and Gregory A. Trandel, "A Pareto Comparison of Ad Valorem and Unit Taxes in Noncompetitive Environments," *Journal of Public Economics*, 53(1), January 1994: 53–71.

Sood, Neeraj, Abby Alpert, and Jay Bhattacharya, "Technology, Monopoly, and the Decline of the Viatical Settlements Industry," NBER Working Paper 11164, March 2005, www.nber.org/papers/w11164.

Spence, A. Michael, *Market Signaling*. Cambridge, MA: Harvard University Press, 1974.

Spencer, Barbara J., and James A. Brander, "International R&D Rivalry and Industrial Strategy," *Review of Economic Studies*, 50(4), October 1983: 707–722.

Starr, Evan, J. J. Prescott, and Norma Bishara, "Noncompetes in the U.S. Labor Force," University of Michigan Law & Economics Research Paper, 2018.

Stephens-Davidowitz, Seth, Hal Varian, and Michael D. Smith, "Super Returns to Super Bowl Ads?" *Quantitative Marketing and Economics* 15(1), 2017: 1–28.

Stevenson, Betsey, and Justin Wolfers, "Subjective Well-Being and Income: Is There Any Evidence of Satiation?" *American Economic Review*, 103(3), May 2013: 598–604.

Stiglitz, Joseph E., "The Theory of 'Screening,' Education, and the Distribution of Income," *American Economic Review*, 65(3), June 1975: 283–300.

Stiglitz, Joseph E., "Equilibrium in Product Markets with Imperfect Information," *American Economic Review*, 69(2), May 1979: 339–345.

Stiglitz, Joseph E., "The Causes and Consequences of the Dependence of Quality on Price," *Journal of Economic Literature*, 25(1), March 1987: 1–48.

Subramanian, Ravi, and Ramanath Subramanyam, "Key Factors in the Market for Remanufactured Products," *Manufacturing & Service Operations Management*, 14(2), Spring 2012: 315–326.

Swinton, John R., and Christopher R. Thomas, "Using Empirical Point Elasticities to Teach Tax Incidence," *Journal of Economic Education*, 32(4), Fall 2001: 356–368.

Syverson, Chad, "Product Substitutability and Productivity Dispersion," *Review of Economics and Statistics*, 86(2), May 2004: 534–550.

Teillant, Aude, and Ramanan Laxminarayan, "Economics of Antibiotic Use in U.S. Swine and Poultry Production," *Choices*, 30(1), 1st Quarter 2015: 1–11.

Tekin, Erdal, "Single Mothers Working at Night: Standard Work and Child Care Subsidies," *Economic Inquiry*, 45(2), April 2007: 233–250.

Tian, Weiming, and Guang Hua Wan, "Technical Efficiency and Its Determinants in China's Grain Production," *Journal of Productivity Analysis*, 13(2), 2000: 159–174.

Tideman, T. Nicholaus, and Gordon Tullock, "A New and Superior Process for Making Social Choices," *Journal of Political Economy*, 84(6), December 1976: 1145–1159.

Tosun, Mehmet S., and Mark L. Skidmore, "Cross-Border Shopping and the Sales Tax: An Examination of Food Purchases in West Virginia," *The B.E. Journal of Economic Analysis & Policy*, 7(1), 2007: Article 63.

Trabandt, Mathias, and Harald Uhlig, "The Laffer Curve Revisited," *Journal of Monetary Economics*, 58(4), May 2011: 305–327.

Trabandt, Mathias, and Harald Uhlig, "How Do Laffer Curves Differ across Countries?" in A. Alesina and F. Giavazzi, eds., *Fiscal Policy After the Financial Crisis*, National Bureau of Economic Research, University of Chicago Press, 2013: 211–249.

Tullock, G., "The Welfare Cost of Tariffs, Monopolies, and Theft," *Western Economic Journal*, 5(3), June 1967: 224–232.

Tversky, Amos, and Daniel Kahneman, "The Framing of Decisions and the Psychology of Choice," *Science*, 211(4481), January 1981: 453–458.

Tyler, John H., Richard J. Murnane, and John B. Willett, "Estimating the Labor Market Signaling Value of the GED," *Quarterly Journal of Economics*, 115(2), May 2000: 431–468.

Urban, Glen L., Theresa Carter, and Steven Gaskin, "Market Share Rewards to Pioneering Brands: An Empirical Analysis and Strategic Implications," *Management Science*, 32(6), June 1986: 645–659.

Varian, Hal R., "Measuring the Deadweight Cost of DUP and Rent-Seeking Activities," *Economics and Politics*, 1(1), Spring 1989: 81–95.

Veracierto, Marcelo, "Firing Costs and Business Cycle Fluctuations," *International Economic Review*, 49(1), February 2008: 1–39.

Villegas, Daniel J., "The Impact of Usury Ceilings on Consumer Credit," *Southern Economic Journal*, 56(1), July 1989: 126–141.

Viscusi, W. Kip, *Employment Hazards*. Cambridge, MA: Harvard University Press, 1979.

von Neumann, John, and Oskar Morgenstern, *Theory of Games and Economic Behavior*. Princeton, NJ: Princeton University Press, 1944.

Waldfogel, Joel, "The Deadweight Loss of Christmas," *American Economic Review*, 83(5), December 1993: 1328–1336.

Waldfogel, Joel, "Does Consumer Irrationality Trump Consumer Sovereignty?" *Review of Economics and Statistics*, 87(4), November 2005: 691–696.

Waldfogel, Joel, *Scroogenomics*. Princeton, NJ: Princeton University Press, 2009.

Waldfogel, Joel, "Copyright Research in the Digital Age: Moving from Piracy to the Supply of New Products," *American Economic Review*, 102(3), May 2012: 337–342.

Warner, John T., and Saul Pleeter, "The Personal Discount Rate: Evidence from Military Downsizing Programs," *American Economic Review*, 91(1), March 2001: 33–53.

Watts, Tyler W., Greg J. Duncan, and Haonan Quan, "Revisiting the Marshmallow Test: A Conceptual Replication Investigating Links Between Early Delay of Gratification and Later Outcomes," *Psychological Science*, 29(7), 2018: 1159–1177.

Weinstein, Arnold A., "Transitivity of Preferences: A Comparison Among Age Groups," *Journal of Political Economy*, 76(2), March/April 1968: 307–311.

Weitzman, Martin L., "Prices vs. Quantities," *Review of Economic Studies*, 41(4), October 1974: 477–491.

Wellington, Donald C., "The Mark of the Plague," *Rivista Internazionale di Scienze Economiche e Commerciali*, 37(8), August 1990: 673–684.

Whitmore, Diane, "What Are Food Stamps Worth?" Princeton University Working Paper #468, July 2002, dataspace .princeton.edu/jspui/handle/88435/dsp01z603qx42c.

Williamson, Oliver E., "Credible Commitments: Using Hostages to Support Exchange," *American Economic Review*, 73(4), September 1983: 519–540.

Willig, Robert D., "Consumer's Surplus Without Apology," *American Economic Review*, 66(4), September 1976: 589–597.

Yellen, Janet L., "Efficiency Wage Models of Unemployment," *American Economic Review*, 74(2), May 1984: 200–205.

Zhang, Liang-Cheng, and Andrew C. Worthington, "Scale and Scope Economies of Distance Education in Australian Universities," *Studies in Higher Education*, 42(9), 2017: 1785–1799.

Zhang, Rui Kai Sun, Michael S. Delgado, and Subal C. Kumbhakar, "Productivity in China's High Technology Industry," *Technology Forecasting and Social Change*, 79(1), 2012: 127–141.

Sources for Applications and Challenges

Chapter 1

Applications Twinkie Tax: Jacobson and Brownell (2000). Bruce Bartlett, "The Big Food Tax," *National Review Online*, April 3, 2002. Chouinard et al. (2007). www.nytimes.com/2014/07/30/opinion/mark-bittman-introducing-the-national-soda-tax.html. "The Public's Views of Tax Reform and other Domestic Issues," Harvard T.H. Chan School of Public Health, September 2017.

Income Threshold Model and China: "Next in Line: Chinese Consumers," *Economist*, 326 (7795), January 23, 1993: 66–67. Jeff Pelline, "U.S. Businesses Pour into China," *San Francisco Chronicle*, May 17, 1994: B1–B2. *China Statistical Yearbook* (Beijing: China Statistical Publishing House, 2000). www.uschina.org/info/forecast/2007/foreign-investment .html. Jiang Wei, "FDI Doubles Despite Tax Concerns," *China Daily*, February 19, 2008. Keith Bradsher, "With First Car, a New Life in China," *New York Times*, April 24, 2008. www.worldometers.info/cars (viewed on May 6, 2012). "China January FDI Grows at Strongest Pace in Four Years," Reuters, February 15, 2015, CAAM. Production of Cars in China from 2008 to 2018 (in 1,000 units). www.statista.com/ statistics/281133/car-production-in-china/ (accessed March 26, 2018). www.acea.be/statistics/article/top-10-car-producing-countries-worldwide-and-eu (viewed on September 8, 2018).

Chapter 2

Challenge Quantities and Prices of Genetically Modified Foods: David Cronin, "Advantage GM in Europe," May 18, 2010, www.ipsnews.net/news.asp?idnews=51472. www .redgreenandblue.org/2011/03/23/is-europes-ban-on-monsantos-gmo-crops-illegal. www.guardian.co.uk/environment/2012/ feb/08/industry-claims-rise-gm-crops. GMO-Compass, www .gmo-compass.org/eng/agri_biotechnology/gmo_planting/257 .global_gm_planting_2013.html. *ISAAA Brief 49-2014: Executive Summary*, March 25, 2014, www.isaaa.org/resources/publi-cations/briefs/49/executivesummary/default.asp.

Cary Funk and Lee Rainie, "Public and Scientists' Views on Science and Society," www.pewinternet.org/2015/01/29/ public-and-scientists-views-on-science-and-society. www .justlabelit.org/right-to-know-center/labeling-around-the-world (viewed on April 30, 2018). Analysis and Gary Langer, "Poll: Skepticism of Genetically Modified Foods," ABC News, abcnews.go.com/Technology/story?id=97567&page=1, June 19, 2017. supportprecisionagriculture.org/nobel-laureate-gmo-letter_rjr.html (viewed on June 1, 2018). U.S Food and Drug Administration, "Labeling of Foods Derived from Genetically Engineered Plants," www .fda.gov/Food/IngredientsPackagingLabeling/GEPlants/ ucm346858.htm, March 1, 2018.

Applications Aggregating Corn Demand Curves: McPhail and Babcock (2012). www.ncga.com/worldofcorn.

The Opioid Epidemic's Labor Market Effects: Krueger (2017). www.drugabuse.gov/drugs-abuse/opioids. www.drugabuse.gov/drugs-abuse/opioids/opioid-crisis. www.bls.gov/webapps/legacy/cpsatab1.htm.

The Demand Elasticities for Google Play and Apple Apps: Ghose and Han (2014). www.statista.com/statistics/276623/ number-of-apps-available-in-leading-app-stores/ (viewed on June 1, 2018).

Oil Drilling in the Arctic National Wildlife Refuge: United States Geological Survey, "Arctic National Wildlife Ref-uge, 1002 Area, Petroleum Assessment, 1998, Including Economic Analysis," www.pubs.usgs.gov/fs/fs-0028-01/ fs-0028-01.pdf, April 2001. Energy Information Adminis-tration, "The Effects of Alaska Oil and Natural Gas Provisions of H.R. 4 and S. 1776 on U.S. Energy Markets," February 2002. Borenstein (2005). Phil Taylor, "GOP Governors Urge Expanded Offshore Drilling, Opening ANWR," *E&E News PM*, August 22, 2012. www .tonto.eia.doe.gov (viewed on May 11, 2013). Baumeister and Peersman (2013). Pamela King, "Interior Launches ANWR Leasing Review," www.eenews.net/greenwire/ 2018/04/19/stories/1060079573, April 19, 2018. www .eia.gov/outlooks/steo/report/global_oil.php (viewed on June 1, 2018).

Subsidizing Ethanol: "Ethanol Subsidies Are $82 per Bar-rel of Replaced Gasoline, Says Incendiary Baker Institute Report," www.biofuelsdigest.com/blog2/2010/01/07/ethanol-subsidies-are-82-per-barrel-of-replaced-gasoline-says-incendiary-baker-institute-report, July 1, 2010. Robert Pear, "After Three Decades, Tax Credit for Ethanol Expires," *New York Times*, January 1, 2012. McPhail and Babcock (2012). www.ers.usda.gov/topics/crops/corn/policy.aspx (viewed on April 12, 2015). Bielen, Newell, and Pizer (2018).

Venezuelan Price Ceilings and Shortages: William Neuman, "With Venezuelan Food Shortages, Some Blame Price Controls," *New York Times*, April 20, 2012 (source of the quote). William Neuman, "Protests Swell in Venezuela as Places to Rally Disappear," *New York Times*, February 20, 2014. Linette Lopez, "This Is a Food Line in Venezuela," *Business Insider*, February 28, 2014, www.businessinsider.com. Francisco Toro, "How Venezuela Turns Butter Vendors into Currency Manipulators," *New Republic*, March 4, 2014. S. B., "The Dividing Line, *Economist*, March 10, 2014. Rafael Romo, "Fistfights Amid Long Bread Lines in Venezuela," May 2014, www.cnn.com, www.customstoday.com.pk/smugglers-turn-venezuelan-crisis-into-colombian-cash-out-2 (viewed on March 31, 2015). Rafael Romo, "$755 for a Box of Condoms? No Protection from Shortages in Venezuela," February 6, 2015, www.cnn.com. Joshua Keating, "Venezuela Is Running Out of Toilet Paper," February 25, 2015, www.slate.com. Reuters, "Venezuelans Are Starving Amid Economic Crisis, Food Shortages," *New York Post*, February 22, 2018. Emma Graham-Harrison and Mariana Zuniga, "Over Half of Young Venezuelans Want to Flee as Economy Collapses, Poll Finds," *The Guardian*, March 6, 2018.

Chapter 3

Challenge Why Americans Buy E-Books and Germans Do Not: Biba, "Publishing Business Conference: International Trends in Ebook Consumption," March 20, 2012, www.teleread.com. Aaron Wiener, "We Read Best on Paper, Cultural Resistance Hobbles German E-Book Market," April 13, 2012, www.spiegel.de. Caroline Winter, "The Story Behind Germany's Scant E-Book Sales," *Bloomberg Businessweek*, April 19, 2012. Rüdiger Wischenbart et al., *The Global ebook Market*, O'Reilly: 2014. authorearnings.com/report/dbw2017/. Michael Koslowski, "The State of the European eBook Market, *GoodEReader*, March 16, 2017. goodereader.com/blog/e-book-news/the-state-of-the-european-ebook-market. www.vatlive.com/vat-rates/european-vat-rates/ (viewed on June 6, 2018). www.statista.com/statistics/707142/attitude-books-e-books/ and www.statista.com/statistics/778781/e-book-opinions-germany/ (viewed on June 6, 2018).

Applications You Can't Have Too Much Money: *Businessweek*, February 28, 2005, p. 13. Stevenson and Wolfers (2013). www.digitaljournal.com. Emily Alpert, "Happiness Tops in Denmark, Lowest in Togo, Study Says," *Los Angeles Times*, April 2, 2012. World Happiness Report 2018, worldhappiness.report/ed/2018/. Stevenson and Wolfers (2013). Gere and Schimmack (2017).

MRS Between Recorded Tracks and Live Music: The Cobb-Douglas utility function estimated using budget share information from *The Student Experience Report 2007*, National Union of Students. Budget allocations between live and recorded music are from the *Music Experience and Behaviour in Young People*, 2008 Survey, produced by the British Music Rights and the University of Hertfordshire.

Indifference Curves Between Food and Clothing: Eastwood and Craven (1981).

Utility Maximization for Recorded Tracks and Live Music: See sources for "*MRS* Between Recorded Tracks and Live Music" above.

How You Ask a Question Matters: Fowlie et al. (2017).

Chapter 4

Challenge Paying Employees to Relocate: Herod (2008). www.mthink.com/commitment-to-global-mobility-remains-strong, April 8, 2013. Mercer, "Global Mobility: The New Business Imperative," www.imercer.com/content/IGM-v3n1-intl-assignments-tackling-compensation.aspx, 2013. Expatistan, 2015, www.expatistan.com/cost-of-living/comparison/seattle/london (viewed on April 22, 2015). www.atlasvanlines.com/AtlasVanLines/media/Corporate-Relo-Survey/PDFs/2018survey-charts.pdf (viewed on June 8, 2018).

Applications Cigarettes Versus E-Cigarettes: Pesko and Warman (2017). www.cancer.org/healthy/stay-away-from-tobacco/e-cigarette-position-statement.html (viewed on June 6, 2018). www.cdc.gov/chronicdisease/resources/publications/aag/tobacco-use.htm (viewed on June 9, 2018).

Fast-Food Engel Curve: Kim and Leigh (2011).

Substituting Marijuana for Alcohol: Crost and Guerrero (2012). Baggio, Chong, and Kwon (2017).

Reducing the CPI Substitution Bias: Hausman (1997). Boskin et al. (1997). Boskin and Jorgenson (1997). Stephen B. Reed and Darren A. Rippy, "Consumer Price Index Data Quality: How Accurate Is the U.S. CPI?" www.DigitalCommons@ILR, 2012. Jeffrey Kling, "Using the Chained CPI to Index Social Security, Other Federal Programs, and the Tax Code for Inflation," testimony before the Subcommittee on Social Security, Committee on Ways and Means, U.S. House of Representatives, 2013. www.bls.gov/cpi/home.htm. www.bls.gov/ooh/Office-and-Administrative-Support/Postal-service-workers.htm (viewed on June 10, 2018).

Chapter 5

Challenge Per-Hour Versus Lump-Sum Childcare Subsidies: Blau and Tekin (2001). Elena Cherney, "Giving Day-Care Cash to Stay-at-Home Parents Sounds Like Politics to Some Canadians," *Wall Street Journal*, July 3, 2006: A2. Tekin (2007). Currie and Gahvari (2008). Guner, Kaygusuz, and Ventura (2017). www.acf.hhs.gov/opre/resource/child-care-subsidies-ccdf-program-overview-policy-differences-across-states-territories-october-1-2016, February 27, 2018. www.acf.hhs.gov/occ/resource/fiscal-year-2018-federal-child-care-and-related-appropriations, May 30, 2018. www.oecd.org/els/soc/PF3_1_Public_spending_on_childcare_and_early_education.pdf (viewed on June 12, 2018).

Applications Willingness to Pay and Consumer Surplus on eBay: Hasker, Jiang, and Sickles (2014). www.eBay.com, 2018.

Compensating Variation and Equivalent Variation for the Internet: David Dean et al., *The Internet Economy in the G-20*, Boston Consulting Group, 2012, www.bcgperspectives.com/Images/Internet_Economy_G20_tcm80-100409.pdf. Sarah Kidner, "What Would You Give Up for the Net?", conversation.which.co.uk/technology/what-would-you-give-up-for-internet-chocolate-coffee-sex, March 22, 2012. Wolfgang Bock et al., *The Growth of the Global Mobile Internet Economy*, Boston Consulting Group, 2015, www.transactives.com/Portals/24/docs/GPSS%202015/Growth_of_the_Global_Mobile_Internet_Economy_Feb_2015_tcm80-181599.pdf. Brynjolfsson, Eggers, and Gannamaneni (2018).

Food Stamps Versus Cash: Whitmore (2002). "U.S. Converting Food Stamps into Debit-Card Benefits," *Chattanooga Times Free Press*, June 23, 2004. U.S. Department of Agriculture, *Characteristics of Food Stamp Households: Fiscal Year 2007*, September 2008. Hoynes and Schanzenbach (2009). Margaret Andrews and David Smallwood, "What's Behind the Rise in SNAP Participation?", *Amber Waves*, March 2012. Bruich (2014). Beatty and Tuttle (2015). Lusk and Weaver (2017). www.fns.usda.gov/sites/default/files/pd/ SNAPsummary.pdf (viewed on June 21, 2018).

Fracking Causes Students to Drop Out: Cascio and Narayan (2017).

Chapter 6

Challenge Labor Productivity During Downturns: Flath (2011). Data files underlying Susan Fleck et al., "The Compensation-Productivity Gap: A Visual Essay," *Monthly Labor Review*, January 2011. Lazear, Shaw, and Stanton (2016). www.bls.gov/opub/btn/volume-6/below-trend-the-us-productivity-slowdown-since-the-great-recession.htm (viewed on June 18, 2018).

Applications Chinese State-Owned Enterprises: Gao Xu, "State-Owned Enterprises in China: How Big Are They?", January 19, 2010, www.blogs.worldbank.org/eastasiapacific/ state-owned-enterprises-in-china-how-big-are-they. National Bureau of Statistics of China, *China Statistical Yearbook*, various years. Chang-Tai Hsieh and Zheng (Michael) Song, "Grasp the Large, Let Go of the Small: The Transformation of the State Sector in China," NBER Working Paper, 2015. www.export.gov/article?id=China-State-Owned-Enterprises, July 25, 2017. chinadashboard.asiasociety.org/winter-2018/ page/state-owned-enterprise.

Malthus and the Green Revolution: Norman Borlaug, "Nobel Lecture," www.nobelprize.org, December 11, 1970. Gregg Easterbrook, "Forgotten Benefactor of Humanity," *Atlantic Monthly*, February 1997. Brander and Taylor (1998). Alan Barkema, "Ag Biotech," *The Main Street Economist*, October 2000. "Biotechnology and the Green Revolution: Interview with Norman Borlaug," www.actionBioscience.org, November 2002. United Nations, *Millennium Development Goals Report*, New York, 2008. www.ers.usda.gov/Data/AgProductivity, May 16, 2012. www.fao.org/NEWS/2000/000704-e.htm (viewed on May 17, 2012). Food and Agriculture Organization of the United Nations, *The State of Food Insecurity in the World*, 2017. ourworldindata.org/world-population-growth (viewed on June 24, 2018). reliefweb.int/report/world/global-report-food-crises-2018 (viewed on June 24, 2018). Gollin, Worm Hansen, and Wingender (2018).

Self-Driving Trucks: David H. Freedman, "Self-Driving Trucks," *MIT Technology Review*, March/April 2017. Conor Dougherty, "Self-Driving Trucks May Be Closer Than They Appear," *New York Times*, November 13, 2017. Alex Davies, "Self-Driving Trucks Are Now Delivering Refrigerators," wired.com, November 13, 2017. Aarian Marshall, "What Does Tesla's Automated Truck Mean for Truckers?" wired.com, November 17, 2017. Alexis C. Madrigal, "Could Self-Driving Trucks Be Good for Truckers?" *The Atlantic*, February 1, 2018.

Returns to Scale in Various Industries: Hsieh (1995). Flath (2011). Fox and Smeets (2011). Devine, Doan, and Stevens (2012). Hossain, Basak, and Majumder (2012). Zhang, Delgado, and Kumbhakar (2012).

Robots and the Food You Eat: Ken Teh, "Robot Waiters in China Never Lose Patience," Associated Press, December 22, 2010, www.washingtontimes.com. Ilan Brat, "Robots Step into New Planting, Harvesting Roles," *Wall Street Journal*, April 23, 2015. Aviva Rutkin, "Harvey, the Robot Farmer Fixing the US Labour Shortage," *New Scientist*, June 18, 2014, www .newscientist.com. Jesse McKinley, "With Farm Robotics, the Cows Decide When It's Milking Time," *New York Times*, April 22, 2014. Dyllan Furness, "Hate Ordering Fried Chicken from Human Beings? KFC's New Restaurant Has You Covered," www.digitaltrends.com/cool-tech/kfc-ai-robot-restaurant/, May 16, 2016. Chuck Thompson and Elaine Yu, "New Order? China Restaurant Debuts Robot Waiters," www.cnn .com/2016/04/19/travel/china-robot-waiters/, April 20, 2016. Peter Holley, "The Boston Restaurant Where Robots Have Replaced the Chefs," *Washington Post*, May 17, 2018.

A Good Boss Raises Productivity: Lazear, Shaw, and Stanton (2015).

Chapter 7

Challenge Technology Choice at Home Versus Abroad: James Hookaway, Patrick Barta, and Dana Mattioli, "China's Wage Hikes Ripple Across Asia," *Wall Street Journal*, March 13, 2012. www.semiconductors.org/industry_ statistics/historical_billing_reports (viewed on June 27, 2018). tradingeconomics.com/china/minimum-wages (viewed on June 27, 2018).

Applications The Opportunity Cost of an MBA: Peter Edmonston, "In Tough Times, M.B.A. Applications May Be an Economic Indicator," *New York Times*, October 7, 2008. www.gmac.com, various years (most recently, June 27, 2018).

The Sharing Economy and the Short Run: James R. Hagerty, "Startup Matches Heavy Equipment Owners and Renters," *Wall Street Journal*, May 28, 2015. www.gminsights.com/ industry-analysis/construction-equipment-rental-market (viewed on June 27, 2018).

Short-Run Cost Curves for a Japanese Beer Manufacturer: Flath (2011).

3D Printing: "Print Me a Stradivarius," www.economist .com/node/18114327, February 10, 2011. Lucas Mearian, "3D Printing Moves from Prototypes to Production," *Computerworld*, April 30, 2014. Lucas Mearian, "Is Apple Planning a 3D Printer?" *Computerworld*, May 21, 2015. Brian Deagon "3D Printers Gaining Traction with Nike, Boeing, HP Inc." *Investor's Business Daily*, March 24, 2016. phys .org/news/2016-06-airbus-3d-printed-mini-aircraft.html. Lucas Mearian, "Boeing Turns to 3D-Printed Parts to Save Millions on Its 787 Dreamliner," *Computerworld*, April 11, 2017. ultimaker.com/en/knowledge/2-3d-printed-car-components-for-time-and-cost-savings (viewed on June 29, 2018).

A Beer Manufacturer's Long-Run Cost Curves: Flath (2011).

Choosing an Inkjet or Laser Printer: www.dell.com. www .amazon.com.

Solar Power Learning Curves: Elshurafa et al. (2018).

Chapter 8

Challenge The Rising Cost of Keeping On Truckin':
"About Interstate Trucking Authority," www.ehow
.com/about_4739672_interstate-trucking-authority.html
(viewed on June 2012). www.fmcsa.dot.gov/rules-regulations/
rules-regulations.htm (viewed on June 2012). www
.dotauthority.com/ucr.htm?gclid=CKma5tebnqQCFSFZ
iAodN2bunA (viewed in June 2012). James L Gattuso,
"Truckers Don't Need Mandated Recorders," *Freemont
Tribune*, May 29, 2012. James Jaillet, "Logging Device
Mandate Could Come in 2016, Outlines Hardware Spec's,
Harassment Provisions," *Overdrive*, March 13, 2014.
William Cassidy, "US Regulators Add Some Flexibility to
Trucker ELD Work Rules," *Journal of Commerce*, May
31, 2018. www.fmcsa.dot.gov/regulations/title49/b/5/3
(viewed on June 30, 2018).

Applications Fracking and Shutdowns: Agis Salpukas,
"Low Prices Have Sapped Little Oil Producers," *New York
Times*, April 3, 1999: B1, B4. Robert Collier, "Oil's Dirty
Future," *San Francisco Chronicle*, May 22, 2005: A1, A14,
A15. Jon Birger, "Oil Shale May Finally Have Its Moment,"
Fortune, November 1, 2007. Judith Kohler, "Energy Firms
Cautious on Oil Shale," *OCRegister*, November 3, 2007.
Steve Austin, "Falling Oil Prices Slows US Fracking," www
.Oil-price.net, December 8, 2014. Shaw Tully, "The Shale
Oil Revolution Is in Danger," www.fortune.com, January
9, 2015. Reuters, "All Drill, No Pump: Oil Producers Are
Leaving Thousands of U.S. Wells Unfinished," *Fortune*,
March 24, 2017. Bradley Olson, "Frackers Could Make
More Money Than Ever in 2018, If They Don't Blow It,"
Wall Street Journal, January, 22, 2018. www.macrotrends
.net/2516/wti-crude-oil-prices-10-year-daily-chart (viewed on
July 11, 2018).

The Size of Ethanol Processing Plants: www.futures
.tradingcharts.com/chart/AC (viewed on June 18, 2012).
www.tradingeconomics.com/commodity/ethanol (viewed on
June 18, 2018). www.eia.gov/petroleum/ethanolcapacity/
(viewed on June 18, 2018). www.ethanolrfa.org/resources/
industry/statistics/ (viewed on June 20, 2018).

Industries with High Entry and Exit Rates: www
.choicesmagazine.org/choices-magazine/theme-articles/
theme-overview-addressing-the-challenges-of-entry-into-
farming/theme-overview-addressing-the-challenges-of-
entry-into-farming, 2016. www.ers.usda.gov/amber-waves/
2016-september/for-beginning-farmers,-business-survival-
rates-increase-with-scale-and-with-direct-sales-to-consumers
.aspx#.V_2jaPkrKUk. Katchova and Ahearn (2017). www
.census.gov/ces/dataproducts/bds/data.html/ (viewed on July 1,
2018). www.seia.org/state-solar-policy/california-solar
(viewed on July 5, 2018).

Upward-Sloping Long-Run Supply Curve for Cotton: International Cotton Advisory Committee, *Survey of the Cost
of Production of Raw Cotton*, September 1992: 5. *Cotton:
World Statistics*, April 1993: 4–5. The figure shows the supply of the major producing countries for which we have cost
information. The only large producers for whom cost data
are missing are India and China.

Reformulated Gasoline Supply Curves: Borenstein et al.
(2004). David R. Baker, "Rules Fuel Patchwork Quilt of

Gas Blends Nationwide," *San Francisco Chronicle*, June
19, 2005: B1, B3. Brown et al. (2008). Ronald D. White,
"Refinery Work Boosts Gasoline Prices in California," *Los
Angeles Times*, September 9, 2009. David R. Baker, "Why
Californians Are Paying Even More for Gas," *San Francisco
Chronicle*, September 23, 2009, p. A1. Auffhammer and Kel-
logg (2011). www.eia.gov/dnav/pet/pet_pri_gnd_a_epmrr_
pte_dpgal_w.htm (viewed on July 11, 2018).

Chapter 9

Challenge Liquor Licenses: Jim Saksa, "Rum Deal, Counting Up All the Ways America's Booze Laws Are Terrible,"
www.slate.com/articles/business/moneybox/2014/06/
america_s_booze_laws_worse_than_you_thought.html, June
12, 2014. Various state licensing websites: www.fundera
.com/blog/liquor-license (viewed on July 21, 2018).

Applications What's a Name Worth? www.forbes.com/
(viewed on July 21, 2018). www.cia.gov (viewed on July 21,
2018).

The Deadweight Loss of Christmas Presents: Waldfo-
gel (1993, 2005, 2009). Bauer and Schmidt (2008). Eve
Mitchell, "Cashing In," *Oakland Tribune*, June 12, 2011,
C1. Barbara Farfan, "2011 U.S. Christmas Holiday Retail
Data, Statistics, Results, Numbers Roundup Complete
U.S. Retail Industry Christmas Holiday Shopping Year-
Over-Year Results," December 29, 2011. Miguel Helft,
"Meet the Anti-Groupon," www.CNNMoney.com, April
30, 2012. www.tech.fortune.cnn.com/2012/04/30/wrapp/.
Matt Brownell, "Gift Cards," *Forbes*, December 12, 2012.
Jason Russell, "Christmas Gift Fraud Costs Billions,"
Washington Examiner, December 26, 2014. wallethub
.com/edu/gift-card-market-size/25590/ (viewed on July 22,
2018).

The Deadweight Loss from Gas Taxes: Blundell, Horowitz,
and Parey (2012).

Welfare Effects of Allowing Fracking: Hausman and Kellogg
(2015).

How Big Are Farm Subsidies and Who Gets Them?: www
.ewg.org/agmag/2017/11/federal-lawmakers-harvest-15-
million-farm-subsidies#.W2oIrdWpEkJ, December 7, 2017.
Organization for Economic Cooperation and Development,
www.oecd-ilibrary.org/agriculture-and-food/agricultural-
policy-monitoring-and-evaluation-2018_agr_pol-2018-en
and www.oecd.org/tad/agricultural-policies/producerandcon-
sumersupportestimatesdatabase.htm (viewed on August 7,
2018).

The Social Cost of a Natural Gas Price Ceiling: MacAvoy
(2000). Davis and Kilian (2011).

Russian Food Ban: "Russia to Ban All Agriculture Imports
from US: Report," www.nypost.com, August 6, 2014. "Inflation Soars Above 8% as Food Bans and Ruble Bite," *The
Moscow Times*, November 5, 2014. www.nbcnews.com/
storyline/ukraine-crisis/russias-sanctions-war-against-west-
explained-n412416, August 22, 2015. www.usnews.com/
news/best-countries/articles/2017-08-18/3-years-of-sanctions-
changes-russias-food-market, August 18, 2017. sputniknews.
com/world/201808071067013027-food-russia-embargo-eu-
losses, August 8, 2018.

Chapter 10

Challenge Anti-Price Gouging Laws: Davis (2008). Carden (2008). Michael Giberson, "Predictable Consequences of Anti-Price Gouging Laws," www.knowledgeproblem.com/2009/06/01/predictable-consequences-of-anti-price-gouging-laws, June 1, 2009. "Bill Allows Gas Price Increase in Emergency," www.ajc.com, March 22, 2010; "Price Gouging Law Goes into Effect Following State of Emergency Declaration," www.neworleans.com, April 29, 2010. Keith Goble, "Rhode Island Imposes Price-Gouging Protections," landlinemag.com, June 25, 2012. www.ag.ny.gov/press-release/ag-schneiderman-cracks-down-gas-stations-engaged-hurricane-sandy-price-gouging, May 2, 2013. "Virginia's Anti-Price Gouging Law Now in Effect," *Fairfax News*, February 12, 2014. "State Anti-Gouging Law in Effect Amid Winter Storm," wvgazette.com, March 5, 2015. Jack Brammer, "Beshear Issues Storm-Related Orders to Protect Against Price Gouging," www.Kentucky.com, February 17, 2015. www.pressdemocrat.com/news/8222032-181/governor-extends-protections-against-post-wildfire?sba=AAS, April 13, 2018. www.abc10.com/article/news/local/8-things-to-know-about-price-gouging-in-california/103-579151311, July 31, 2018.

Applications Partial-Equilibrium Versus Multimarket-Equilibrium Analysis in Corn and Soybean Markets: Holt (1992).
Urban Flight: Econsult (2003). Crawford, Del Roccili, and Voith (2004). beta.phila.gov/services/payments-assistance-taxes/business-taxes/wage-tax-employers/ (viewed on August 7, 2018).
Extremely Unequal Wealth: Sylvia Nasar, "The Rich Get Richer, but Never the Same Way Twice," *New York Times*, August 16, 1992: 3. Davies et al. (2007). Bucks et al. (2009). Kennickell (2009, 2011). Credit Suisse, *Global Wealth Databook 2017*, 2018. www.eml.berkeley.edu/~saez/TabFig2014prel.xls (viewed on July 10, 2015). Bricker et al. (2017). Collins, Chuck, and Josh Hoxie, *Billionaire Bonanza*, Institute for Policy Studies, November, 2017. www.oxfam.org/en/pressroom/pressreleases/2017-01-16/just-8-men-own-same-wealth-half-world. publications.credit-suisse.com/index.cfm/publikationen-shop/research-institute/global-wealth-databook-2017-en/, Table 6-5, 2018. publications.credit-suisse.com/index.cfm/publikationen-shop/research-institute/global-wealth-report-2017-en/, Table 1, 2018. www.oxfam.org/en/pressroom/pressreleases/2018-01-22/richest-1-percent-bagged-82-percent-wealth-created-last-year, January 22, 2018. www.forbes.com/billionaires/#58ce52ef251c, March 6, 2018.

Chapter 11

Challenge Brand-Name and Generic Drugs: www.fiercepharma.com/special-reports/top-10-patent-expirations-2015, December 17, 2014. Trefis Team, "Why Are Generic Drug Prices Shooting Up?", *Forbes*, February 27, 2015. "Pricey Hep C Successor Overtakes Solvadi," *Health News Florida*, July 13, 2015. www.drugs.com/article/patent-expirations.html (July 18, 2015). www.imshealth.com (July 18, 2015).

Applications Amazon Prime Revenue: Greg Bensinger, "Amazon Raises Prime Subscription Price to $99 a Year," *Wall Street Journal*, March 13, 2014. Jaclyn Cosgrove and Abha Bhattarai, "Amazon Prime's Price Is Jumping to $119 a Year—But There Are Ways Around Paying That Much," *Los Angeles Times*, April 27, 2018.
Apple's iPad: Chloe Albanesius, "iSuppli: iPad Could Produce Profits for Apple," www.pcmag.com, February 10, 2010. Don Reisinger, "IDC: Apple iPad Secures 87 Percent Market Share," www.cnet.com, January 18, 2011. Don Reisinger, "Study: iPad Tallies 89 Percent of Table Traffic," www.cnet.com, January 24, 2011. Jenna Wortham, "So Far Rivals Can't Beat iPad's Price," *New York Times*, March 6, 2011. www.abiresearch.com/press/3919-iPad+Remains+Dominant+in+1Q%E2%80%992012+While+Kindle+Fire+Fizzles, June 4, 2012. "Apple iPad Shipments Down 23% as Tablet Market Continues to Lose Steam," *Forbes*, April 30, 2015. www.statista.com/statistics/268711/global-market-share-of-the-apple-ipad-since-2010/ (viewed on August 10, 2018). The marginal cost estimate (slightly rounded) is from iSuppli. I assumed that the company's gross profit margin for 2010 of about 40% (www.forbes.com) held for the iPad and used that to calculate the fixed cost. I derived the linear demand curve by assuming Apple maximizes short-run profit using the information on price, marginal cost, and quantity.
Taylor Swift Concert Pricing: Randy Lewis, "Taylor Swift's '1989' Is 2015's Highest Grossing Concert Tour by Far," *Los Angeles Times*, December 30, 2015.

Anne Steele, "Why Empty Seats at Taylor Swift's Concerts Are Good for Business," *Wall Street Journal*, May 15, 2018.
The Botox Patent Monopoly: Mike Weiss, "For S.F. Doctor, Drug Botox Becomes a Real Eye-Opener," *San Francisco Chronicle*, April 14, 2002: A1, A19. Reed Abelson, "F.D.A. Approves Allergan Drug for Fighting Wrinkles," *New York Times*, April 16, 2002. Joseph Walker, "Botox Itself Aims Not to Age," *Wall Street Journal*, May 18, 2014. Ryan Sachetta and Cynthia Koons, "Worried About Wrinkles, Guys? Allergan Bets You'll Want 'Brotox,'" www.Bloomberg.com, June 17, 2015. www.statista.com/statistics/737477/global-sales-of-allergan-s-botox/ (viewed on August 10, 2018).
Natural Gas Regulation: Davis and Muehlegger (2009).
Movie Studios Attacked by 3D Printers!: Erich Schwartzel, "Hollywood's Other Piracy Problem: 3-D Printers," *Wall Street Journal*, July 20, 2015. Amazon.com for latest movie figurines (viewed on August 10, 2018).
Critical Mass and eBay: Ina Steiner, "Yahoo Closes Australian Auction Site," www.auctionbytes.com, August 7, 2003. Brown and Morgan (2006, 2010). John Barrett, "MySpace Is a Natural Monopoly," www.ecommercetimes.com, January 17, 2007. Carol Xiaojuan Ou and Robert M. Davison, "Why eBay Lost to TaoBao in China: The Global Advantage," *Communications of the ACM*, 52(1), January 2009: 145–148.

Chapter 12

Challenge Sale Price: Perloff and Wu (2007). Karen Datko, "My Ketchup Taste Test: It's an Upset!" www.msn.com, January 14, 2011. Rebecca Smithers, "Heinz Left Playing Tomato Catch-Up After Ketchup Tasting Trouncing," *The Guardian*, May 25, 2011. Andrew Adam Newman, "Ketchup

Moves Upmarket, with a Balsamic Tinge," *New York Times*, October 25, 2011. Whitney Filloon, "Heinz and French's Are Embroiled in a Ketchup and Mustard War," www.eater.com, April 23, 2015. www.wikinvest.com/stock/H.J._Heinz_Company_(HNZ) (viewed on August 1, 2015). www.heinz.com/our-company/press-room/trivia.aspx (viewed on August 1, 2015). news.kraftheinzcompany.com/press-release/financial/kraft-heinz-reports-fourth-quarter-and-full-year-2017-results (viewed on July 16, 2018). www.mordorintelligence.com/industry-reports/ketchup-market (viewed on July 19, 2018). www.statista.com/statistics/278061/us-households-most-used-brands-of-catsup--ketchup/ (viewed on July 19, 2018). www.wmcactionnews5.com/story/37938800/ketchup-global-industry-2018-sales-supply-and-consumption-forecasts-to-2021 (viewed on July 19. 2018).

Applications Disneyland Pricing: "Couple Tries for Year of Daily Disneyland Visits," *San Francisco Chronicle*, July 3, 2012. www.disneyland.com (viewed on August 2, 2015). Joseph Pimentel, "Disney Announces Discounted Tickets for SoCal Residents," www.ocregister.com, January 23, 2015.

Preventing Resale of Designer Bags: Eric Wilson, "Retailers Limit Purchases of Designer Handbags," *New York Times*, January 10, 2008. www.prada.com, www.gucci.com, www.saksfifthavenue.com (viewed on August 2, 2015).

Botox and Price Discrimination: See the sources for the Chapter 11 Application "Botox Patent Monopoly."

Google Uses Bidding for Ads to Price Discriminate: Goldfarb and Tucker (2008). Executive Office of the President of the United States, *Big Data and Differential Pricing*, February 2015.

Tesla Price Discrimination: www.inverse.com/article/31597-tesla-secret-profit, June 1, 2017. The source of the price information for the Tesla Model S D100 is www.tesla.com. Prices vary somewhat across European countries. We are using the price for the Netherlands. We are not including government subsidies or taxes. The shipping cost to Europe is sufficiently low that including it would not change our calculations. The 2017 quantity data (rounded) come from europe.autonews.com/article/20180220/ANE/180219831/tesla-model-s-outsells-german-luxury-flagships-in-europe (viewed on July 6, 2018). We estimated the linear demand curves using these data based on the assumption that Tesla is maximizing its profit.

Age Discrimination: Luis Gomez, "Why a California judge swiped left on Tinder's 30-or-older fees," *San Diego Union Tribune*, January 30, 2018.

Buying Discounts: Borenstein and Rose (1994). Jenna Wortham, "Coupons You Don't Clip, Sent to Your Cellphone," *New York Times*, August 29, 2009. "Up Front," *Consumer Reports*, September 2009: 7. Carmen Musick, "Computer Technology Fueling Coupon Trend," *Times News*, October 31, 2009, e-edition.timesnews.net/article/9018027/computer-technology-fueling-coupon-trend. "Up Front," *Consumer Reports*, September 2009: 7. www.forbes.com/sites/bryanpearson/2017/03/15/research-reveals-how-retailers-can-maximize-the-power-of-coupons/#74c3fe882f01. www.statista.com/statistics/630086/total-number-of-coupons-distributed-in-the-us/ (viewed on July 25, 2018). www.statista.com/statistics/630123/total-number-of-coupons-redeemed-in-the-us/ (viewed on July 25, 2018). *NCH Mid-Year 2018 Coupon Facts*, www.nchmarketing.com/couponindustrytrends.aspx, viewed August 19, 2018.

Pricing iTunes: Shiller and Waldfogel (2011).

Ties That Bind: www.hp.com (viewed on August 3, 2015). www.mlmlaw.com/library/guides/ftc/warranties/undermag.htm (viewed on August 3, 2015). hp.com (viewed on August 19, 2018).

Super Bowl Commercials: Ho, Dhar, and Weinberg (2009). Kim (2011). Kim, Freling, and Grisaffe (2013). Stephens-Davidowitz, Varian, and Smith (2017). Hartmann and Klapper (2017). Chandrasekaran, Srinivasan, and Sihi (2018), www.si.com/nfl/2018/01/11/super-bowl-lii-ad-cost (viewed on July 12, 2018).

Chapter 13

Challenge Intel and AMD's Advertising Strategies: Salgado (2008). www.cpubenchmark.net/market_share.html (viewed on August 20, 2019).

www.jonpeddie.com/store/market-watch (viewed on August 20, 2019).

Applications Strategic Advertising: "50 Years Ago . . . ," *Consumer Reports*, January 1986. Roberts and Samuelson (1988). Gasmi, Laffont, and Vuong (1992). Stuart Elliott, "Advertising," *New York Times*, April 28, 1994: C7. Salgado (2008). Richards and Padilla (2009). Davis and Markowitz (2011). Chandra and Weinberg (2015). prcouncil.net/wp-content/uploads/2018/01/Marketing-Fact-Pack-2018.pdf. adage.com/article/datacenter/200-leading-national-advertisers-2018-index/313794/. Shapiro (2018).

Boomerang Millenials: Richard Fry, "It's Becoming More Common for Young Adults to Live at Home—and for Longer Stretches." *Pew Research Center*, May 2017. www.pewresearch.org/fact-tank/2017/05/05/its-becoming-more-common-for-young-adults-to-live-at-home-and-for-longer-stretches/ (viewed on August 20, 2018). ec.europa.eu/eurostat/data/database (viewed on August 20, 2018).

Keeping Out Casinos: Cookson (2015).

Bidder's Curse: Lee and Malmendier (2011). Garratt, Walker, and Wooders (2012). Feng, Fay, and Sivakumar (2016).

GM's Ultimatum: Robert Schoenberger, "GM Sends Ultimatums to All Its 6000 US Dealers," *Cleveland Plain Dealer*, June 2, 2009. "GM Dealers Sue to Keep Doors Open," *Toronto Star*, November 27, 2009. Janet Kurnovich, "GM Canada Sued for $750 Million by Former Dealers," www.insurance-car.co, May 17, 2011. Greg Keenan, "Judge Dismisses Class Action by GM Canada Dealers, Upholds Claim Against Law Firm," *The Globe and Mail*, July 9, 2015. Jackson Hayes, "Trillium's $750M-class action against GM will not proceed to Supreme Court of Canada," *Canadian Autoworld*, January 24, 2018.

Chapter 14

Challenge Government Aircraft Subsidies: Irwin and Pavcnik (2004). John Heilpin, "WTO: Boeing Got $5B In Illegal Subsidies," March 12, 2012. www.247wallst.com/

aerospace-defense/2015/02/24/wto-to-examine-boeing-777x-subsidies.
www.reuters.com/article/2015/06/16/us-airshow-france-boeing-airbus-idUSKBN0OW0VM20150616. Robert Wall and Emre Peker, "WTO Ruling Advances U.S. and Boeing in Case Against Airbus," *Wall Street Journal*, July 13, 2018. www.opensecrets.org/orgs/summary.php?id=d000000100 (viewed on August 12, 2018).

Applications **Employer "No-Poaching" Cartels:** Mark Ames, "The Techtopus: How Silicon Valley's Most Celebrated CEOs Conspired to Drive Down 100,000 Tech Engineers' Wages," www.pando.com, January 23, 2014. Mark Ames, "Revealed: Apple and Google's Wage-Fixing Cartel Involved Dozens More Companies, Over One Million Employees," www.pando.com, March 22, 2014. Michael Liedtke, "Apple, Google, Other Tech Firms to Pay $415M in Wage Case," www.seattletimes.com, January 15, 2015. Ted Johnson, "Animation Workers Reach $100 Million Settlement with Disney in Wage-Fixing Suit," variety.com/2017/biz/news/disney-settlement-wage-fixing-anti-poaching-animation-1201975084/, January 17, 2017. Krueger and Ashenfelter (2017). Jackie Wattles, "7 Fast Food Chains Agree to End 'No-poach' Rules," money.cnn.com/2018/07/12/news/companies/no-poach-fast-food-industry-wages-attorneys-general/index.html, July12, 2018. Rachel Abrams, "7 Fast-Food Chains to End 'No Poach' Deals That Lock Down Low-Wage Workers," *New York Times*, July 12, 2018. Starr, Prescott, and Bishara (2018).

Cheating on the Maple Syrup Cartel: Ian Austen, "The Maple Syrup Mavericks," *New York Times*, August 23, 2015. www.siropderable.ca/home.aspx (viewed on August 24, 2015). Marie-Ève Dumont, "Trois autos de la SQ pour saisir leur sirop d'érable," *Le Journal de Montréal* (in French) (viewed on February 2, 2018). Giuseppe Valiante, "Quebec's Maple Syrup Industry Losing Ground as U.S. Imports Rise: Report, *The Star*, March 8, 2018. Jake Edminston and Graeme Hamilton, "The Last Days of Quebec's Maple Syrup Rebellion," *National Post*, April 6, 2018.

Airline Mergers: Carlton et al. (2018).

Mobile Number Portability: Cho, Ferreira, and Telang (2016).

How Do Costs, Price Markups, and Profits Vary Across Airlines?: Scott McCartney, "How Much of Your $355 Ticket Is Profit for Airlines?" *Wall Street Journal*, February 14, 2018. Tom Stalnaker, et al., *Oliver Wyman Airline Economic Analysis*, 2017–2018 Edition, www.oliverwyman.com/content/dam/oliver-wyman/v2/publications/2018/January/Airline_Economic_Analysis_AEA_2017-18_web.pdf.

Differentiating Bottled Water Through Marketing: David Lazarus, "How Water Bottlers Tap into All Sorts of Sources," *San Francisco Chronicle*, January 19, 2007. Vinnee Tong, "What's in That Bottle?" www.suntimes.com, July 28, 2007. Kevin Cowherd, "Bottled-Water Labeling: A Source of Irritation," *Baltimore Sun*, August 1, 2007. Venessa Wong, "Coca-Cola Wants to Buy the World a Milk," *Businessweek*, December 1, 2014. Dan Nosowitz, "Coca-Cola to Sell Sexy Lactose-Free Milk Product of Some Kind," www.modernfarmer.com, December 2, 2014. Khushbu Shah, "Coca-Cola's New 'Super Milk' Fairlife Is Super Weird," *Eater*, February 16, 2015. www.prnewswire.com/news-releases/us-bottled-water-market-will-net-us-222-bn-revenues-by-end-of-2024—persistence-market-research-report-616324704.html (viewed on July 12, 2018). www.statista.com/outlook/20010000/109/bottled-water/united-states#marketStudy (viewed on July 28, 2018). Capehart and Berg (2018).

Rising Market Power: Hall (2018). De Loecker and Eeckhout (2018).

Monopolistically Competitive Food Truck Market: Andrew S. Ross, "San Francisco Food Truck Empire Expanding," *San Francisco Chronicle*, February 18, 2011. www.mobilefoodnews.com, viewed on June 17, 2012. offthegridsf.com/about-3, viewed on March 29, 2013. offthegridsf.com/vendors#food (viewed on November 8, 2015). offthegrid.com/ (viewed on August 21, 2018)

Subsidizing the Entry Cost of Dentists: Dunne et al. (2013).

Chapter 15

Challenge **Does Going to College Pay?:** pdkpoll.org/results/the-value-of-a-degree-is-a-college-degree-worth-the-cost (viewed on August 30, 2018). trends.collegeboard.org/student-aid/figures-tables/undergraduate-enrollment-and-percentage-receiving-pell-grants-over-time (viewed on August 30, 2018). trends.collegeboard.org/college-pricing/figures-tables/average-published-undergraduate-charges-sector-2017-18. www.census.gov/data/tables/time-series/demo/educational-attainment/cps-historical-time-series.html (viewed on August 30, 2018). nces.ed.gov/programs/digest/current_tables.asp (viewed on August 30, 2018). trends.collegeboard.org/education-pays/figures-tables/lifetime-earnings-education-level (viewed on August 30, 2018). www.payscale.com/college-roi (August 30, 2018). The statistical analysis is based on annual earnings (wages of workers who are not self-employed and earn $10,000 or more per year) data from the 2017 U.S. Current Population Survey March Supplement ("NBER CPS Supplements," NBER, University of Chicago Press, www.nber.org/data/current-population-survey-data.html).

Applications **Black Death Raises Wages:** Wellington (1990). www.history-magazine.com/black.html. www.historylearningsite.co.uk/black_death_of_1348-to-1350.htm. www.bric.postech.ac.kr/science/97now/00_11now/001127a.html.

Saving for Retirement: Author's calculations.

Durability of Telephone Poles: Jonathan Marshall, "PG&E Cultivates Its Forest," *San Francisco Chronicle*, May 5, 1995: D1.

Falling Discount Rates and Self-Control: Shapiro (2004). Kan (2007). Gruber and Mullainathan (2005). Jeff Zeleny, "Occasional Smoker, 47, Signs Tobacco Bill," *New York Times*, June 23, 2009. www.gallup.com/poll/1717/Tobacco-Smoking.aspx (viewed on July 22, 2012). www.aspire2025.org.nz/2012/05/22/article-support-for-a-tobacco-endgame, May 22, 2012. www.gallup.com/poll/163763/smokers-quit-tried-multiple-times.aspx, July 31, 2013. www.gallup.com/poll/173990/smokers-say-higher-cigarette-taxes-unjust.aspx, July 18, 2014. www.globaltimes.cn/content/931484.shtml (viewed on September 3, 2015). news.gallup.com/poll/1717/tobacco-smoking.aspx (viewed on August 30, 2018).

Redwood Trees: Peter Berck and William R. Bentley, "Hotelling's Theory, Enhancement, and the Taking of the Redwood National Park," *American Journal of Agricultural Economics,* 79(2), May 1997: 287–298. Peter Berck, personal communications.

Chapter 16

Challenge BP and Limited Liability: Mark Long and Angel Gonzalez, "Transocean Seeks Limit on Liability," *Wall Street Journal,* May 13, 2010. David Leonhardt, "Spillonomics: Underestimating Risk," *New York Times,* May 21, 2010. Jef Feeley and Allen Johnson Jr., "BP Wins Final Approval of Guilty Plea Over Gulf Oil Spill," Bloomberg News, January 29, 2013, www.bloomberg.com/news/2013-01-29/bp-wins-final-approval-of-guilty-plea-over-gulf-oil-spill.html. Daniel Gilbert and Sarah Kent, "BP Agrees to Pay $18.7 Billion to Settle Deepwater Horizon Oil Spill Claims," *Wall Street Journal,* July 2, 2015. Ron Rousso, "BP Deepwater Horizon Costs Balloon to $65 Billion" Reuters, January 15, 2018.

Applications Risk of a Cyberattack: Kamiya et al. (2018).

Stocks' Risk Premium: "The Cost of Looking," *Economist,* 328(7828), September 11, 1993: 74. Leslie Eaton, "Assessing a Fund's Risk Is Part Math, Part Art," *New York Times,* April 2, 1995. www.standardandpoors.com (viewed on June 25, 2012). Jordà et al. (2017). pages.stern.nyu .edu/~adamodar/New_Home_Page/datafile/histretSP.html (viewed on September 1, 2018).

Gambling: Friedman and Savage (1948). Brunk (1981). Meghan Cox Gurdon, "British Accuse Their Lottery of Robbing the Poor to Give to the Rich," *San Francisco Chronicle,* November 25, 1995. Mark Maremont and Alexandra Berzon, "How Often Do Gamblers Really Win?" *Wall Street Journal,* October 11, 2013. newzoo.com/insights/articles/global-games-market-reaches-137-9-billion-in-2018-mobile-games-take-half/ (viewed on August 1, 2018). Quentin Fottrell, "Americans Lost $107B Legally Gambling Last Year," *New York Post,* May 2018. nypost.com/2018/05/16/americans-lost-107b-legally-gambling-last-year/ (viewed on August 1, 2018).

Failure to Diversify: Paul J. Lim, "Don't Paint Nest Eggs in Company Colors," *New York Times,* March 30, 2008. Duan, Hotchkiss, and Jiao (2015). Ron Lieber, "A Scary Movie: Filling Your 401(k) with Company Stock," *New York Times,* March 21, 2015. Robert Steyer, "Company Stock Option Fading from 401(k) Plans," www.pionline .com, February 23, 2015. www.icifactbook.org/ch8/18_fb_ch8 (viewed on August 30, 2018).

Flight Insurance: www.buy.travelguard.com (viewed on September 5, 2015). www.ntsb.gov/investigations/data/Pages/paxfatal.aspx (viewed on August 5, 2018). www.bts.gov/content/annual-passengers-all-us-scheduled-airline-flights-domestic-international-and-foreign-1 (viewed on August 5, 2018).

Flooded by Insurance Claims: Joseph B. Treaster, "Insurer Plans to Curb Sales Along Coasts," *New York Times,* October 10, 1996. Philip Bump, "Want to Be Mad About Government Insurance?" *Washington Post,* August 28, 2017. www.nytimes.com/2018/01/04/climate/losses-natural-disasters-insurance.html. Hiroko Tabuchi, "2017 Set a Record for Losses From Natural Disasters. It Could Get Worse," *New York Times,* January 2018. www.fema.gov/

national-flood-insurance-program/national-flood-insurance-program-reauthorization-guidance (viewed on August 10, 2018). www.fema.gov/national-flood-insurance-program/national-flood-insurance-program-reauthorization-guidance (viewed on August 30, 2018).

Biased Estimates: Benjamin, Dougan, and Buschena (2001). Arthur Hu, "Death Spectrum," www.arthurhu.com/index/health/death.htm#deathrank (viewed on August 14, 2015). www.cdc.gov/nchs/fastats/homicide.htm (viewed on September 5, 2015). www.medicinenet.com/are_poinsettia_plants_poisonous_fact_or_fiction/views.htm (viewed on September 5, 2015). www.floridamuseum.ufl.edu/shark-attacks/trends/location/usa/ (viewed on August 5, 2018). www.forbes.com/sites/duncanmadden/2018/04/06/the-annual-worldwide-shark-attack-summary-is-out/ (viewed on August 5, 2018).

Chapter 17

Challenge Trade and Pollution: Tideman and Tullock (1976). Lelieveld et al. (2015). www.wto.org (viewed on September 10, 2015). www.trade.gov (viewed on September 10, 2015). www.trade.gov/mas/ian/build/groups/public/@tg_ian/documents/webcontent/tg_ian_003368.pdf (viewed on September 2, 2018). data.oecd.org/trade/trade-in-goods-and-services.htm#indicator-chart (viewed on September 2, 2018). data.worldbank.org/indicator/NE.TRD.GNFS.ZS (viewed on September 2, 2018).

Applications Disney's Positive Externality: Lou Mongello, "Walt Disney World History 101—'How to Buy 27,000 Acres of Land and Have No One Notice,'" www.wdwradio .com/2005/02/wdw-history-101-how-to-buy-27000-acres-of-land-and-no-one-noticeq/, February 11, 2005. "The Secret Florida Land Deal That Became Walt Disney World," www .miamiherald.com/news/state/florida/article150733437.html, May 16, 2017.

Spam: A Negative Externality: Caliendo et al. (2012). Rao and Reiley (2012). www.spamlaws.com/spam-stats.html (viewed on September 6, 2018). www.propellercrm.com/blog/email-spam-statistics (viewed on September 6, 2018).

Why Tax Drivers: Levitt and Porter (2001). Grabowski and Morrisey (2006), Edlin and Karaca-Mandic (2006), Parry, Walls, and Harrington (2007), Anderson (2008). Hill et al. (2009). Anderson and Auffhammer (2014). Sheehan-Connor (2015). Lucas Davis, "Raise the Gas Tax," www.energyathaas .wordpress.com/2015/01/05/raise-the-gas-tax.

Buying a Town: Katharine Q. Seelye, "Utility Buys Town It Choked, Lock, Stock and Blue Plume," *New York Times,* May 13, 2002. cheshireohio.com/the-story/ (viewed on August 2, 2018). worldpopulationreview.com/us-cities/cheshire-oh-population/ (viewed on August 2, 2018).

Acid Rain Program: Dallas Burtraw, "Trading Emissions to Clean the Air: Exchanges Few but Savings Many," *Resources,* 122, Winter 1996: 3–6. Peter Passell, "For Utilities, New Clean-Air Plan," *New York Times,* November 18, 1994: C1, C6. Peter Passell, "Economic Scene," *New York Times,* January 4, 1996: C2. Boyce Rensberger, "Clean Air Sale," *Washington Post,* August 8, 1999: W7. Schmalensee et al. (1998). EPA (2011). www.epa.gov/airmarkets/so2-allowance-auctions (viewed on September 10, 2018). www.epa.gov/air-trends/sulfur-dioxide-trends (viewed on September 10, 2018).

Road Congestion: inrix.com/scorecard/key-findings-us/ (viewed on July 21, 2016). inrix.com/press-releases/scorecard-2017/ (viewed on September 4, 2018).

Microsoft Word Piracy: Business Software Alliance, *Software Management: Security Imperative, Business Opportunity— BSA Global Software Survey*, June 2018.

Free Riding on Measles Vaccinations: Jo Craven McGinty, "How Anti-Vaccination Trends Vex Herd Immunity: Measles Outbreak Underscores Vulnerabilities Posed by Subpar Inoculation Rates," *Wall Street Journal*, February 6, 2015. Walter A. Orenstein, Mark J. Papania, and Melinda E. Wharton, "Measles Elimination in the United States," *Journal of Infectious Diseases*, 189(Supplement 1), 2004: S1–S3. www.cdc.gov/mmwr/volumes/66/wr/mm6640a3.htm, October 13, 2017. www.cdc.gov/measles/cases-outbreaks.html (viewed on September 3, 2018). www.sacbee.com/entertainment/living/health-fitness/article216933070.html (viewed on September 3, 2018).

What's Their Beef?: Gina Holland, "Top Court Considers Challenge to Beef Ads," *San Francisco Chronicle,* December 9, 2004: C1, C4. www.extension.iastate.edu/agdm/articles/mceowen/McEowJuly05.htm. www.beefboard.org/promotion/checpromotion.asp (viewed on December 2009, August 2012, September 2015, July 2016, September 2018).

Chapter 18

Challenge **Dying to Work:** Viscusi (1979). Dick Meister, "Safety First!"

www.truth-out.org/safety-first61799, July 28, 2010. Kris Alingod, "Massey to Resume Operations in West Virginia Mine Despite Deaths," www.allheadlinenews.com, July 29, 2010. Tracie Mauriello and Len Boselovic, "Historic Fine Issued for Mine Disaster," *Pittsburgh Post-Gazette*, December 7, 2011. Kris Maher, "Agency Blames Massey for Fatal Mine Disaster," *Wall Street Journal*, June 29, 2011. Lateef Mungin and Farid Ahmed, "Report: 8 Arrested after Deadly Bangladesh Building Collapse," www.cnn.com, April 27, 2013. www.world.time.com/2013/06/10/bangladesh-factory-collapse-uncertain-future-for-rana-plaza-survivors, June 10, 2013. Ceylan Yeginsu, "Anger and Grief Simmer in Turkey a Year After Soma Mine Disaster," *New York Times*, June 2, 2015. Andrew Jones, "In Tianjin Blasts, a Heavy Toll for Unsuspecting Firefighters," *New York Times*, August 17, 2015. www.bls.gov/iif/oshcfoi1.htm (viewed on September 12, 2015). www.thehindu.com/news/national/other-states/boiler-explodes-in-ntpc-unchahar-plant/article19961812.ece, November 3, 2017. www.osha.gov/oshstats/commonstats.html (viewed July 30, 2018). www.bls.gov/news.release/cfoi.t04.htm (viewed on July 30, 2018).

www.ilo.org/global/topics/safety-and-health-at-work/lang--de/index.htm (viewed on July 30, 2018).

Applications **Discounts for Data:** Tara Siegel Bernard, "Giving Out Private Data for Discount in Insurance," *New York Times*, April 8, 2015. rootsrated.media/blog/these-health-insurance-companies-will-pay-you-to-exercise/, August 9, 2017.

Reducing Consumers' Information: Vince Dixon, "What Brands Are Actually Behind Trader Joe's Snacks?" eater.com,

August 9, 2017. www.nielsen.com/ca/en/insights/news/2018/private-label-brands-are-hungry-for-more-of-the-global-food-pie.html (viewed on August 17, 2018). Nielsen Company, *The Rise and Rise Again of Private Label*, 2018. www.forbes.com/sites/pamdanziger/2018/05/06/how-amazon-plans-to-dominate-the-private-label-market/ (viewed on September 6, 2018). money.cnn.com/2018/04/23/news/companies/sears-ceo-offers-buy-kenmore/index.html.

Adverse Selection and Remanufactured Goods: Subramanian and Subramanyam (2012). Neto (2016).

Cheap Talk in eBay's Best Offer Market: Backus, Blake, and Tadelis (forthcoming).

Chapter 19

Challenge **Clawing Back Bonuses:** Matthew Goldstein, "Why Merrill Lynch Got Burned," *Businessweek*, October 25, 2007. Elizabeth G. Olson, "Executive Pay Clawbacks: Just a Shareholder Pacifier?" www.management.fortune.cnn.com/2012/08/16/executive-pay-clawbacks. "Morgan Stanley Defers Bonuses for High-Earners," *Chicago Tribune*, January 15, 2013. www.execcomp.org/News/NewsStories/nearly-90-pct-of-fortune-100-companies-now-disclose-claw-back-policies-according-to-equilar-survey, October 25, 2013. Andrew Ackerman, "SEC Proposes Broadened Corporate Clawback Rules," *Wall Street Journal*, July 1, 2015. www.realtytrac.com (viewed on September 16, 2015). Michael Corkery, "Wells Fargo Fined $185 Million for Fraudulently Opening Accounts," *New York Times*, September 8, 2016. Gretchen Morgenson, "Executive Pay Clawbacks Are Gratifying, but Not Particularly Effective," *New York Times*, September 30, 2016. violationtracker.goodjobsfirst.org/parent/wells-fargo (viewed on September 7, 2018). www.shearman.com/perspectives/2018/04/embracing-the-quasi-clawback.

Applications **Honest Cabbie?:** Balafoutas, Kerschbamer, and Sutter (2017).

Sing for Your Supper: Personal communications.

Health Insurance and Moral Hazard: www.cnn.com/2015/03/16/politics/obamacare-numbers-16-million-insured-rate. Jhamb, Dave, and Coleman (2015). Simon, Soni, and Cawley (2017). Kowalski (2018). www.kff.org/uninsured/fact-sheet/key-facts-about-the-uninsured-population/ (viewed on September 7, 2018). www.nbcnews.com/politics/white-house/3-2-million-more-americans-were-uninsured-2017-n837986 (viewed on September 7, 2018). www.cbsnews.com/news/more-americans-are-going-without-health-insurance/ (viewed on September 7, 2018).

Capping Oil and Gas Bankruptcies: Davis (2014). Boomhower (forthcoming).

Walmart's Efficiency Wage: Neil Irwin, "How Did Walmart Get Cleaner Stores and Higher Sales? It Paid Its People More," *New York Times*, October 15, 2016. www.indeed.com/salaries/Cleaner-Salaries-at-Walmart (viewed on September 7, 2018).

Layoffs Versus Pay Cuts: Hall and Lilien (1979). Steven Greenhouse, "More Workers Face Pay Cuts, Not Furloughs," *New York Times*, August 3, 2010. www.bls.gov (September 7, 2018).

Index

Numbers

3D printers, competing with movie firm monopolies, 397

A

Abundance, prices of exhaustible resources and, 567
AC. See Average costs (*AC*)
ACA (Affordable Care Act), 689
Access fees, in two-part pricing, 433
Acid Rain Program, 628
Actions, game
  overview of, 453
  static games, 454
Ad valorem tariffs, 316
Ad valorem taxes
  having similar market effects as specific taxes, 47–48
  overview of, 42
  welfare effects on monopolies, 385–386
Advanced Micro Devices (AMD)
  applying Cournot model to nonidentical firms, 511–512
  Comparing Intel and AMD advertising strategies, 482–483
Adverse selection
  equalizing information to prevent, 652–655
  exercises, 669–671
  in insurance markets, 647–648
  moral hazard and, 696
  overview of, 647
  problems related to opportunism, 646–647
  with products of unknown quality, 648–651
  with products of variable quality, 651
  remanufactured goods and, 654–655
  summary, 668–669
Advertising
  comparing Intel and AMD strategies, 452, 482–483
  deciding how much to advertise, 443–444
  deciding whether to advertise, 442–443
  exercises, 451
  Google example, 423
  overview of, 441–442
  pricing and, 660
  prisoners' dilemma or joint profit maximization, 459–460

  spurious product differentiation, 510–511
  strategic, 460–461
  summary, 447
  Super Bowl commercials, 445
AFC (average fixed costs), 215–216
Affordable Care Act (ACA), 689
After-the-fact monitoring, reducing moral hazard, 695–696
Agents, in contracts
  efficiency of contracts, 676–677
  overview of, 673–674
  principal-agent problem, 674–675
  production efficiency and, 679
Agricultural price support
  farm subsidies, 310
  welfare effects of price floors, 307–310
Airlines
  antitrust laws, 497
  cost, price, markups, and profits, 510
  Cournot oligopoly model, 507–508
  duopoly equilibria, 520
  graphical solution to Stackelberg model, 514
  group price discrimination in airline tickets, 429
  maintaining cartels, 499
  mergers and, 500
  monopolistic competition, 530
  profit maximization (American Airlines example), 502
  subsidies, 490, 516–518, 531–533
Allais (certainty) effect, violations of expected utility theory, 602
Allocation of goods. *See also* Bundle of goods (market basket)
  applying Pareto principle to, 351
  efficiency vs. equity and, 357–358
  efficient allocation using competition, 341, 343–344
  mutually beneficial trades and, 337–339
  voting on, 354–356
Allocation of scarce resources, 1–2
Alternative price support, 308–309
Amazon, as disruptive technology, 402
AMD (Advanced Micro Devices)
  applying Cournot model to nonidentical firms, 511–512
  Comparing Intel and AMD advertising strategies, 482–483

Credits

p. 5, epigraph: Blores Razor, bloresrazor.com.

p. 5, cartoon, top: Pearson Education, Inc.

p. 5, cartoon, bottom: Dave Coverly/SPEEDBUMP

p. 10, photo: age fotostock/Superstock.

p. 10, epigraph: John L. Manson, "Let Go of Whatever Makes You Stop," Insight International, Inc., 1994.

p. 13, photo: Lev/Fotolia.

p. 16, cartoon: Pearson Education, Inc.

p. 24, cartoon: Pearson Education, Inc.

p. 32, photo: lurin/123RF.

p. 39, photo: Kyle T Perry/Shutterstock.

p. 49, photo: U.S. Government Printing Office.

p. 62, photo: Jeffrey M. Perloff.

p. 62, epigraph: Harry Rolnick, "The Complete Book of Coffee," Melitta, the University of California, 1982, p. 204.

p. 65, cartoon: Pearson Education, Inc.

p. 65, epigraph: 2012 poll, CouponCabin.com.

p. 73, cartoon: Pearson Education, Inc.

p. 75, photo: Kohlhuber Media Art/Shutterstock.

p. 84, excerpt: Donald N. Smith, president of Burger King from John L. Hess, "A Sizzling Battle in the Burger Business," New York Times, 13 Mar. 1997.

p. 105, photo: John Foxx/Stockbyte/Getty Images.

p. 116, photo: Elena Shashkina/Shutterstock.

p. 122, photo: Lukas Gojda/Shutterstock.

p. 129, epigraph: Kathleen Norris from Henry S. Kramer, "Game, Set, Match: Winning the Negotiations Game," ALM Publishing, 2001, p. 360.

p. 142, photo: Carla Mestas/Pearson Education Inc.

p. 146, photo: Jeffrey M. Perloff.

p. 159, photo: U.S. Department of Agriculture Inc.

p. 159, epigraph: Department of Social Services, Greenville, South Carolina, The Life Awareness Center.

p. 160, cartoon: Pearson Education, Inc.

p. 168, all photos: Library of Congress.

p. 177, photo: vario images GmbH/Alamy Stock Photo.

p. 188, photo, top: Pearson Education, Inc.

p. 188, photo, bottom: Micheline Pelletier Decaux/Sygma/Getty Images.

p. 198, cartoon: Pearson Education, Inc.

p. 202, cartoon: Pearson Education, Inc.

p. 203, photo: Wang Jianwei/Newscom.

p. 209, photo: Christian Delbert/Shutterstock.

p. 215, cartoon: Pearson Education, Inc.

p. 215, photo: Dmitry Kalinovsky/Shutterstock.

p. 240, photo: elenathewise/123RF.

p. 248, photo: Nomad Soul/Fotolia.

p. 265, diagram: jaddingt/Fotolia.

p. 271, epigraph: I. Bernard Cohen, "Howard Aiken: Portrait of a Computer Pioneer," Massachusetts Institute of Technology Press, 2000, p. 329.

p. 274, photo: Brocreative/Shutterstock.

p. 290, photo: Monkey Business/Fotolia.

p. 293, photo: Jeffrey M. Perloff.

p. 297, excerpt: Adam Smith, "An Inquiry into the Nature and Causes of the Wealth of Nations, Volume 2." G. Bell, 1887.

p. 301, cartoon: Pearson Education, Inc.

p. 302, photo: Jeffrey M. Perloff.

p. 315, photo: JackF/Fotolia.

p. 327, photo: National Oceanic and Atmospheric Administration (NOAA).

p. 352, photo (George Washington): National Gallery of Art, Washington, DC.

p. 352, photo (Abraham Lincoln): Library of Congress.

p. 353, all photos: Library of Congress.

p. 365, photo: Jeffrey M. Perloff.

p. 373, photo image from Simon Gribkov/EyeEm/Getty Images.

p. 380, cartoon: Pearson Education, Inc.

p. 390, photo: TanyaLovus/Shutterstock.